EDUCATIONAL PSYCHOLOGY

Developing Learners

EDUCATIONAL PSYCHOLOGY
Developing Learners

FOURTH EDITION

Jeanne Ellis Ormrod

University of Northern Colorado (Emerita)

University of New Hampshire

Merrill
Prentice Hall

Upper Saddle River, New Jersey
Columbus, Ohio

Library of Congress Cataloging-in-Publication Data

Ormrod, Jeanne Ellis.
    Educational psychology : developing learners / Jeanne Ellis Ormrod.—4th ed.
      p. cm.
    Includes bibliographical references (p.) and indexes.
    ISBN 0-13-088704-8
      1. Educational psychology. 2. Teaching. 3. Learning. 4. Classroom management. I.
Title.

LB1051 .066 2003
370 15—dc21

2002069330

Vice President and Publisher: Jeffery W. Johnston
Executive Editor: Kevin M. Davis
Development Editor: Julie Peters
Editorial Assistant: Autumn Crisp
Production Editor: Mary Harlan
Copy Editor: Sue Snyder Kopp
Design Coordinator: Diane C. Lorenzo
Cover Design: Ali Mohrman
Cover Image: Corbis Stock Market
Text Design: Carlisle Publishers Services
Photo Coordinator: Valerie Schultz
Illustrations: Rolin Graphics
Production Manager: Laura Messerly
Director of Marketing: Ann Castel Davis
Marketing Manager: Amy June
Marketing Coordinator: Tyra Cooper

This book was set in Berkeley by Carlisle Communications, Ltd. It was printed and bound by R. R. Donnelley & Sons Company. The cover was printed by Phoenix Color Corp.

Photo Credits: Bill Bachman/Photo Researchers: p. 115; Billy Barnes/PhotoEdit: p. 515; John Brooks/Getty Images: p. 261; David Buffington/Getty Images: p. 263; Susan Burger Photography: pp. 323, 500; Susan Burger Stock: pp. 83, 149, 172, 217, 277, 304, 312, 394, 512; Myrleen Ferguson Cate/PhotoEdit: p. 36; CNRI Science Photo Library/PhotoResearchers: p. 191; Paul Conklin/PhotoEdit: p. 426; Corbis: p. 258; Elizabeth Crews Photography: p. 444; Scott Cunningham/Merrill: pp. 3, 60, 64, 85, 144, 194, 221, 244, 335, 356, 370, 416, 421, 469, 485, 489, 491, 528, 566, 573, 586; Bob Daemmrich/The Image Works: p. 231; Bob Daemmrich/StockBoston: p. 226; Robert E. Daemmrich/Getty Images: p. 283; Mary Kate Denny/Getty Images: p. 113; Mary Kate Denny/PhotoEdit: pp. 410, 498, 540; Laura Dwight Photography: p. 298; Tony Freeman/PhotoEdit: pp. 232, 556; Catrina Genovese/Omni: p. 525; Getty Images: pp. 179, 241; Jeff Greenberg/Omni Photo Communications: p. 229; Jeff Greenberg/PhotoEdit: pp. 21, 346; Charles Gupton/Stock Boston: p. 378; Will Hart/PhotoEdit: facing p. 1, pp. 13, 189, 366, 458, 481, 552, 580; Richard Hutchings/PhotoEdit: pp. 169, 430, 478; Frank Johnston/Getty Images: p. 267; Bonnie Kamin/PhotoEdit: pp. 397, 510; Vicky Kasala/Getty Images: p. 235; Courtesy of The Learning Company: p. 451 (left); Mark Lewis/Getty Images: p. 214; Richard Lord/The Image Works: p. 25 (right); Anthony Magnacca/Merrill: pp. 25 (left), 49, 162, 495, 535, 561; Will McIntyre/Photo Researchers: p. 138; Will and Demi McIntyre/Photo Researchers: p. 381; Lawrence Migdale/Photo Researchers: p. 372; Michael Newman/PhotoEdit: pp. 18, 122, 438, 520, 571; Michael Provest/Silver Burdett Ginn: p. 302; Mark Richards/PhotoEdit: p. 46; Elena Rooraid/PhotoEdit: p. 359; Andy Sacks/Getty Images: p. 130; Ellen Senisi/The Image Works: p. 142; James L. Shaffer: p. 164; Frank Siteman/Index Stock Imagery: p. 306; Elliot Smith/International Stock Photo: p. 154; © 1999, Telegraph Colour Library/FPG International Corp.: p. 418; Courtesy of Vanderbilt University: p. 289; Rudi Von Briel/PhotoEdit: p. 392; Tom Watson/Merrill: pp. 7, 291, 319; Dana White/PhotoEdit: p. 310; James D. Wilson/Getty Images: p. 250; and David Young-Wolff/PhotoEdit: pp. 33, 102, 106, 186, 332, 348, 384, 388, 405, 434, 447, 464.

Pearson Education Ltd.
Pearson Education Australia Pty. Limited
Pearson Education Singapore Pte. Ltd.
Pearson Education North Asia Ltd.
Pearson Education Canada, Ltd.
Pearson Educación de Mexico, S.A. de C.V.
Pearson Education—Japan
Pearson Education Malaysia Pte. Ltd.
Pearson Education, *Upper Saddle River, New Jersey*

Merrill
Prentice Hall

10 9 8 7 6 5 4 3 2
ISBN: 0-13-088704-8

Preface

Each time I walk through the front door of a school building, I am reminded of how exciting and energizing it can be to interact and work daily with children and adolescents. Soon after I wrote the first edition of *Educational Psychology*, I had the good fortune to return to a middle school classroom teaching geography to two sections of sixth, seventh, and eighth graders. After writing the third edition of the book, I spent a year in middle schools in another capacity: as supervisor of teacher interns getting their feet wet in fifth- through eighth-grade classrooms. Both experiences confirmed what I have always known—that the principles of educational psychology have clear relevance to the decisions a classroom teacher must make on an ongoing basis. How children and adolescents learn and think, how they change as they grow and develop, why they do the things they do, how they are often very different from one another—our understanding of all these things has innumerable implications for classroom practice and, ultimately, for the lives of the next generation.

I have been teaching educational psychology since 1974, and I've loved every minute of it. I have written this textbook in much the same way that I teach my college classes. Because I want the field of educational psychology to captivate you the way it has captivated me, I have tried to make the book interesting, meaningful, and thought-provoking as well as informative. I have a definite philosophy about how future teachers can best learn and apply educational psychology—a philosophy that has guided me as I have written all four editions of the book. More specifically, I believe that you can construct a more accurate and useful understanding of the principles of educational psychology when you:

- Truly understand the nature of learning
- Focus on core principles of the discipline
- Relate the principles to your own learning and behavior
- Use the principles to understand the learning and behavior of children and adolescents
- Consistently apply the principles to classroom practice

I have incorporated numerous features into the book that will encourage you to do all of these things. I hope that you will learn a great deal from what educational psychology has to offer, not only about the students you will be teaching but also about yourself—a human being who continues to learn and develop even as an adult. The following pages describe the features of the book.

A DEEPER, MORE APPLIED APPROACH TO THE UNDERSTANDING OF EDUCATIONAL PSYCHOLOGY

Brief Contents

Chapter 16:
➤ Key Questions
Multiple Choice
Essay
Glossary
Web Destinations
Learning in the
    Content Areas
Student Artifact
    Library
Instructor
    Resources
Message Board
Chat
Other Options:
Help
Your Profile
Feedback
Site Search
➤ Syllabus

Understanding the Nature of Learning

One of the fundamental differences between this book and other introductory educational psychology texts is its greater coverage of learning. Other books have three or four chapters; this one has six—five in the book itself plus a sixth chapter on content-area learning in the *Study Guide and Reader* and on the accompanying Companion Website.

As I've written the book, I haven't just talked about the nature of learning; I've also applied what I know about learning to make your job as a learner much easier as you read the book. For instance, I've continually applied two principles that, in my mind, are central to effective learning. First is the principle of **meaningful learning**: Students learn and remember information more effectively when they relate it to what they already know. Second is the principle of **elaboration**: Students learn and remember information more effectively, and are also more likely to use it in new situations, when they spontaneously go *beyond* what they read, perhaps by drawing inferences, thinking of new examples, or speculating about possible applications.

So as you read the book, you will find that I often ask you to relate new concepts to your own knowledge and experiences. In addition, many of the comments and questions in the margins will encourage you to recall ideas we've discussed in previous chapters, think of new examples, or speculate about applications.

Focusing on Core Principles

Rather than superficially explore every aspect of educational psychology, I have chosen to offer in-depth treatment of fundamental concepts and principles that have broad applicability to classroom practice. If I myself couldn't imagine how a concept or principle could possibly be of use to a teacher, I left it out. I have often highlighted key principles in the *Principles/Assumptions* tables that appear throughout the book. I also pull together concepts in *Compare/Contrast* tables and in "The Big Picture" section at the end of each chapter. Each table includes educational implications and concrete examples.

TABLE 6.1   **PRINCIPLES/ASSUMPTIONS**

Basic Assumptions of Cognitive Psychology and Their Educational Implications

ASSUMPTION	EDUCATIONAL IMPLICATION	EXAMPLE
Influence of cognitive processes	Encourage students to think about class material in ways that will help them remember it.	When introducing the concept *mammal*, ask students to identify numerous examples.
Selectivity about what is learned	Help students identify the most important things for them to learn. Also help them understand why these things are important.	Give students questions that they should try to answer as they read their textbooks. Include questions that ask them to apply what they read to their own lives.
Construction of meaning	Provide experiences that will help students make sense of the topics they are studying.	When studying Nathaniel Hawthorne's *The Scarlet Letter*, ask students to get together in small groups to discuss possible reasons why Reverend Arthur Dimmesdale refuses to acknowledge that he is the father of Hester Prynne's baby.
Role of prior knowledge and beliefs	Relate new ideas to what students already know and believe about the world.	When introducing the vocabulary word *debut* to Mexican American students, relate it to *quinceañera*, a "coming-out" party that many Mexican American families hold for their fifteen-year-old daughters.
Active involvement in learning	Plan classroom activities that get students actively thinking about and using classroom subject matter.	To help students understand latitude and longitude, ask them to track the path of a hurricane using a series of latitude-longitude coordinates obtained on the Internet.

■ *People are selective about what they process and learn. People are constantly bombarded*

(Ausubel, 1978; Bransford & Johnson, 1972; Mayer, 199_) illustrations of the effectiveness of meaningful learning, try the following two exercises.

EXPERIENCING FIRSTHAND   *Two Letter Strings, Two Pictures*

1. Study each of the following strings of letters until you can remember them perfectly:

    AIIRODFMLAWRS   FAMILIARWORDS

2. Study each of the two pictures below until you can reproduce them accurately from memory.

Figures are from "Comprehension and Memory for Pictures" by G. H. Bower, M. B. Karlin, and A. Dueck, 1975, *Memory and Cognition, 3*, p. 217. Reprinted by permission of Psychonomic Society, Inc.

No doubt the second letter string was easier for you to learn because you could relate it

Relating Principles to Your Own Learning and Behavior

A central goal of this text is to help you discover more about yourself as a thinker and learner. If you can understand how you *yourself* learn, you will be in a better position to understand how your students learn and, as a result, to help them learn more effectively. Throughout the book, I've provided many exercises to help you discover important points firsthand and thereby construct a more complete, meaningful understanding of psychological principles of learning, development, motivation, and behavior. Appearing as *Experiencing Firsthand* features (see, for example, pages 127, 209, and 240), these exercises are in some ways similar to the "hands-on" activities that I often recommend for helping students learn in elementary and secondary classrooms. But because I often ask you to use your mind rather than your hands, you might more accurately think of them as "head-on" experiences. In addition, you will discover other features, including reflective margin notes and embedded scenarios, that will help you to understand your own learning.

REAL EDUCATIONAL APPLICATIONS AMONG REAL STUDENTS

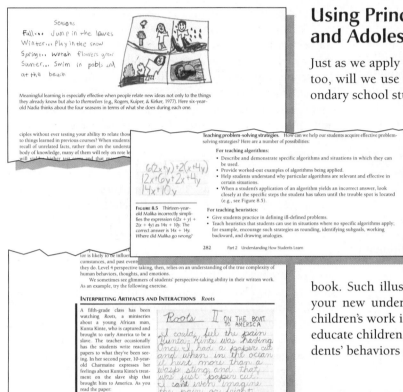

Using Principles to Understand Children and Adolescents

Just as we apply principles to an understanding of how *you* learn, so, too, will we use them to better understand how elementary and secondary school students learn and make sense of what they do and say in classrooms. Many of the *Case Studies* you will see in the book show how principles of learning, development, and motivation may be reflected in children's behaviors. Furthermore, you will continually encounter *Interpreting Artifacts and Interactions* features in which you will use concepts and principles you have been studying to analyze actual student artifacts (e.g., short stories, essays, problem solutions) and interviews. Additional artifacts that illustrate key ideas appear as figures throughout the book. Such illustrations provide you with the opportunity to apply your new understanding in an authentic context. Interpreting real children's work is a core assessment task of those who work with and educate children, and so you will have ongoing practice assessing students' behaviors and products.

Applying Principles to Classroom Practice

Throughout the text, I consistently apply psychological concepts and principles to classroom practice. Many of these applications appear as bulleted italicized statements within the text; others are summarized and illustrated in *Into the Classroom* features and *Students in Inclusive Settings* tables. Furthermore, you will find that the *Case Studies* at the end of each chapter focus on teachers and teaching; they will help you apply ideas you have encountered in the chapter and make instructional decisions based on what you have learned.

NEW AND EXPANDED CONTENT

Content Changes in the Fourth Edition

Much of the content from the third edition remains in the fourth edition. Two apparent "deletions" are not deletions at all. The content of the third edition's Chapter 9, "Learning in the Content Areas," has been updated and moved to the *Study Guide and Reader*. Some of the content of the third edition's Chapter 14, "Promoting Learning Through Student Interactions," has been moved to Chapter 7, where it appears in sections on "Knowledge Construction as a Social Process" and "Creating a Community of Learners"; the sections on class discussions, reciprocal teaching, cooperative learning, and peer tutoring now appear in Chapter 13. Such changes provided room to expand my coverage of two subjects—motivation and assessment—to two chapters each, as well as to increase coverage of the social aspects of learning and address additional topics of growing concern to educators.

Motivation. Research in motivation has grown by leaps and bounds in the last few years, and a single chapter is no longer sufficient to address it. Chapter 11, "Motivation and Affect," includes sections on the nature of motivation, social needs, and the role of affect from the third edition, but adds two new sections: an exploration of various theoretical perspectives of motivation and a consideration of basic human needs (especially self-worth and relatedness). Chapter 12, "Cognitive Factors in Motivation," includes my previous discussions of self-efficacy, self-determination, attributions, and group differences but also includes expanded discussions of goals and teacher expectations (the latter topic formerly appeared in Chapter 4) and new sections on expectancy/value theory and interest.

Assessment. The single chapter on assessment in the third edition was bursting at the seams, and it was clear that dividing the topic into two chapters was a necessary step for the fourth edition. Chapter 15 includes my earlier sections on forms of assessment and RSVP characteristics, expands the sections on diversity and the various purposes of assessment, and has new sections on standardized tests, types of test scores, high-stakes testing and accountability, and confidentiality and communication. Chapter 16 focuses on classroom assessment strategies; while it includes the third edition's sections on informal assessment, paper-pencil assessment, performance assessment, and summarizing achievement, it now includes more guidelines for constructing, administering, and scoring formal assessments (writing good paper-pencil items, developing rubrics, scoring performances analytically or holistically, etc.) and has new sections on self-assessment, risk taking, and item analysis.

Social Aspects of Learning. The fourth edition puts greater emphasis on the role that social interaction plays in development, learning, and motivation. Examples of this emphasis appear in the discussions of peer relationships and social cognition in Chapter 3, group meaning making in Chapter 7, collective self-efficacy in Chapter 10, the need for relatedness in Chapter 11, social goals in Chapter 12, and technology-based discussions in Chapter 13.

Other New and Expanded Topics. In addition to the increased coverage of motivation, assessment, and social aspects of learning, the book includes many other changes to reflect new perspectives in the field; as examples, see the sections "Importance of Ongoing Assessment in Classroom Decision Making" (Chapter 1), "Determinants of Moral Behaviors" (Chapter 3), "Navigating Different Cultures at Home and at School" and "World Views" (Chapter 4), "The Role of Dispositions in Higher-Level Thinking" (Chapter 8), "Functional Analysis and Positive Behavioral Support" (Chapter 9), and "Online Research" (Chapter 13).

Supplementary Materials

Numerous supplements to the textbook are available to enhance your learning and development as a teacher. In the continuing tradition of this text's innovation in teaching educational psychology using technology and media, four new ancillaries will be available to those using this text: a new simulation on assessment, an observation video, a Student Artifact Library containing examples of student work, and a collaborative Web site between Merrill and ASCD containing a wealth of resources for learning about teaching.

Study Guide and Reader. This resource provides many support mechanisms to help you learn and study more effectively, including focus questions to consider as you read the text, a chapter glossary, application exercises to give you practice in applying concepts and principles of educational psychology to classroom settings, answers to selected margin notes, sample test questions, and several supplementary readings.

Simulations in Educational Psychology and Research (Compact Disk). A compact disk accompanies the fourth edition of the textbook. This CD contains five activities that resemble actual research studies in educational psychology: "The Pendulum Experiment" (to be used with Chapter 2), "Assessing Moral Reasoning" (to be used with Chapter 3), "Bartlett's Ghosts" (to be used with Chapter 7), "Intuitive Physics" (to be used with Chapter 7 or 8), and "Assessment in the Balance" (to be used with Chapter 8 or 16). As you use the CD, you will find yourself "participating" in activities as either learners or teachers; the CD will ask you to respond to various situations and then give you feedback about your responses. The CD will also help you connect each activity with educational practice.

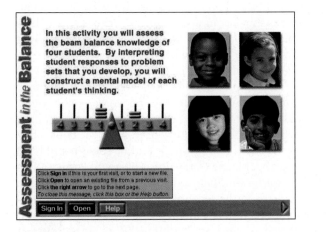

Companion Website. You can find the Website for *Educational Psychology: Developing Learners* at **www.prenhall.com/ormrod.** For each chapter of the book, the Website presents Key Questions that identify the chapter's central issues, a chapter glossary, key concepts linked to Internet destinations, and quick self-tests (multiple-choice and essay questions that let you self-assess what you've learned). The Website also provides a syllabus manager that your instructor may use to post and occasionally update the course syllabus, as well as an interactive "Message Board" through which you and your classmates can engage in discussions about chapter content.

Videotapes and Multimedia Guide. Videos are a highly effective means of visually demonstrating concepts and principles in educational psychology. The nine videotapes that accompany this textbook portray a wide variety of teachers, students, and classrooms in action. Seven videos present numerous case studies in many content domains and at a variety of grade levels; these include a new video, *Observing Children and Adolescents in Classroom Settings.* Two additional videos are: *A Private Universe* (which examines learner misconceptions in science) and Constance Kamii's *Double-Column Addition: A Teacher Uses Piaget's Theory* (which depicts a constructivist approach to teaching mathematics). Opportunities to react to these videos in class discussions will further enhance your ability to think analytically and identify good teaching practices. Your instructor will have a *Multimedia Guide* to help guide and enrich your interpretation and understanding of what you see in the videos.

Student Artifact Library. Available on both the Companion Website and PowerPoint Slides CD is a large collection of artifacts from actual preschool, elementary, middle, and secondary school classrooms. Many of these artifacts are examples of students' work: short stories, essays, problem solutions, drawings, and so on. Others are assignments, classroom activities, scoring rubrics, letters to parents, and the like, which teachers have developed. You and your instructor can apply concepts and principles of educational psychology to analyze and interpret these artifacts.

Joint Web Site with ASCD. A partnership between the Association for Supervision and Curriculum Development (ASCD) and Merrill Education has led to the development of www.EducatorLearningCenter.com—a Web site that includes articles from the journal *Educational Leadership,* lesson plans and strategies, excerpts from Merrill texts, videos, case studies, listservs where pre-service and in-service teachers can exchange ideas, and other resources to assist both novice and experienced teachers. A four-month subscription to this

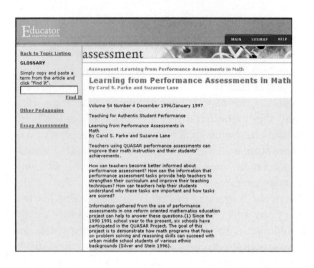

virtual "library" of resources is available to anyone who purchases a Merrill Education textbook.

Instructor's Manual. Available to your instructor are suggestions for learning activities, additional "head-on" exercises, supplementary lectures, case study analyses, discussion topics, group activities, and additional media resources. These have been carefully selected to provide opportunities to support, enrich, and expand on what you read in the textbook.

Transparencies. More than 100 acetate transparencies for in-class use include summative outlines and graphic organizers of essential concepts. These transparencies are designed to help you understand, organize, and remember the concepts and principles you are studying.

PowerPoint Slides and Supplementary Lectures and Activities. This CD-ROM for instructors includes PowerPoint versions of the transparencies, supplementary lectures, and activities that appear in the *Instructor's Manual,* as well as handouts from the *Multimedia Guide.*

Test Bank. Many instructors use the test questions that accompany this textbook. Some items (lower-level questions) will simply ask you to identify or explain concepts and principles you have learned. But many others (higher-level questions) will ask you to apply those same concepts and principles to specific classroom situations—that is, to actual student behaviors and teaching strategies. The lower-level questions assess your basic knowledge of educational psychology. But ultimately, it is the higher-level questions that will assess your ability to use principles of educational psychology in your own teaching practice.

Acknowledgments

Although I am listed as the sole author of this textbook, I have been fortunate to have had a great deal of assistance in writing it. First and foremost, I must thank my editor, Kevin Davis, whose ideas, insights, and unwavering commitment to the field of educational psychology have provided much of the driving force behind my writing and productivity. Kevin is a task master, make no mistake about it, and he in-

sists that I stretch my talents further with each new edition of the book. He has limitless ideas on how we can continue to make *Educational Psychology* and its ancillary materials ever more meaningful, user-friendly, and supportive to students and instructors alike, and he provides the guidance (scaffolding) I need to accomplish tasks that initially seem so impossible. After spending countless hours working with Kevin over the past ten years, I can say that he is not only my editor but also a very good friend.

I am equally indebted to Julie Peters, development editor for the fourth edition. Julie has been there day in and day out to answer questions about the many "little" things that need doing in such a massive undertaking, as well as to keep me focused on the big picture: how we can best help students and instructors in their efforts to understand, communicate about, and apply principles of educational psychology. Not only has she kept me on task, but she has also brightened many a day with encouraging words and a great sense of humor.

I must not forget two previous development editors who, while not working with me on this edition, have been instrumental in shaping the book's evolution over previous editions. Linda Montgomery brought creative ideas, a commitment to excellence, and extensive experience as both an elementary school teacher and an editor to the third edition. And Linda Peterson, who saw me through the first and second editions, helped define much of the pedagogy of the book and, with her continuing insistence on *application, application, application,* kept my focus on the things that future teachers really need to know.

Others at Merrill/Prentice Hall have also contributed in important ways. As production editor, Mary Harlan has coordinated and overseen the very complex process of transforming a manuscript into a book, simultaneously keeping track of a million little things that needed to be done yet always graciously accommodating my requests for last-minute changes. Copy editor Sue Kopp has looked closely at every word, finding places where I've been unclear or inconsistent, and often suggested better ways of communicating my ideas. Photo editor Valerie Schultz has found many photographs that have given life to the words on the page.

In addition to the folks at Merrill/Prentice Hall, numerous colleagues across the country have given the book a balance of perspectives that no single author could possibly do on her own. Drs. Margie Garanzini-Daiber and Peggy Cohen provided ideas for the *Students in Inclusive Settings* tables that were introduced in the second edition. Dr. Ann Turnbull offered helpful suggestions for enhancing my discussion of students with special needs in the third edition. For the current edition, Dr. Lynley Hicks Anderman has developed a Companion Website for the book that will support my readers in their efforts to assess their own learning, communicate with one another, and expand their knowledge of various topics in the book by visiting relevant sites on the World Wide Web.

Many other colleagues have strengthened the final product considerably by reviewing one or more versions of the book. Reviewers for the first, second, and third editions were: Joyce Alexander, Indiana University; Margaret D. Anderson, SUNY–Cortland; J. C. Barton, Tennessee Technical University; Timothy A. Bender, Southwest Missouri State University; Phyllis Blumenfeld, University of Michigan; Randy L. Brown, University of Central Oklahoma; Stephen L. Benton, Kansas State University; Karen L. Block, University of Pittsburgh; Kathryn J. Biacindo, California State University–Fresno; Barbara Bishop, Eastern New Mexico University; Robert Braswell, Winthrop College; Kay S. Bull, Oklahoma State University; Margaret W. Cohen, University of Missouri–St. Louis; Roberta Corrigan, University of Wisconsin–Milwaukee; Richard D. Craig, Towson State University; José Cruz, Jr., The Ohio State University; Peggy Dettmer, Kansas State University; Joan Dixon, Gonzaga University; Leland K. Doebler, University of Montevallo; Joanne B. Engel, Oregon State University; Kathy Farber, Bowling Green State University; William R. Fisk, Clemson University; Victoria Fleming, Miami University of Ohio; M. Arthur Garmon, Western Michigan University; Roberta J. Garza, Pan American University–Brownsville; Cheryl Greenberg, University of North Carolina–Greensboro; Richard Hamilton, University of Houston; Jennifer Mistretta Hampston, Youngstown State University; Arthur Hernandez, University of Texas–San Antonio; Frederick C. Howe, Buffalo State College; Dinah Jackson, University of Northern Colorado; Janina M. Jolley, Clarion University of Pennsylvania; Caroline Kaczala, Cleveland State University; CarolAnne M. Kardash, University of Missouri–Columbia; Nancy F. Knapp, University of Georgia; Mary Lou Koran, University of Florida; Randy Lennon, University of Northern Colorado; Pamela Manners, Troy State University; Hermine H. Marshall, San Francisco State University; Teresa McDevitt, University of Northern Colorado; Sharon McNeely, Northeastern Illinois University; Michael Meloth, University of Colorado–Boulder; Bruce P. Mortenson, Louisiana State University; Janet Moursund, University of Oregon; Gary A. Negin, California State University; Joe Olmi, The University of Southern Mississippi; Helen Osana, University of Missouri, Columbia; Judy Pierce, Western Kentucky University; James R. Pullen, Central Missouri State University; Gary F. Render, University of Wyoming; Robert S. Ristow, Western Illinois University; Gregg Schraw, University of Nebraska–Lincoln; Dale H. Schunk, Purdue University; Mark Seng, University of Texas; Glenn E. Snelbecker, Temple University; Johnna Shapiro, University of California–Davis; Harry L. Steger, Boise State University; Bruce Torff, Hofstra University; Ann Turnbull, University of Kansas; Julianne C. Turner, University of Notre Dame; Alice A. Walker, SUNY–Cortland; Mary Wellman, Rhode Island College; Jane A. Wolfle, Bowling Green State University; and Karen Zabrucky, Georgia State University.

Coming on board for the fourth edition were these reviewers: Joyce Alexander, Indiana University; Eric Anderman, University of Kentucky; Theodore Coladarci, University of Maine; Catherine Emihovich, SUNY–Buffalo; Pamela Manners, Troy State University; Helen Osana, Concordia University; Dale Schunk, University of North Carolina–Greensboro; and Enedina Vazquez, New Mexico State University.

On the home front, Ann Shump has joined me on a part-time basis to help gather artifacts and permissions for the book and Artifact Library. Ann knows everyone in town, or at least it seems so, and her gentle yet persistent ways have encouraged many teachers and children to contribute their work to help me elucidate important principles and strategies. Furthermore, some of my own students and teacher interns—especially Kathryn Broadhead, Ryan Francoeur, Gerry Holly, Michele Minichiello, Shelly Lamb, Melissa Tillman, Nick Valente, and Brian Zottoli—have agreed to let me use their interviews and experiences as examples and *Interpreting Artifacts and Interactions* features. Teachers and administrators in New Hampshire's Oyster River School District have allowed me to share their strategies with my readers; I especially thank Liz Birnam, Berneen Bratt, Tom Carroll, Barbara Dee, Jackie Filion, Sarah Gagnon, Sheila Johnson, Don Lafferty, Linda Mengers, Mark Nichols, Ann Reilly, and Gwen Ross.

Many young people, too, deserve thanks for letting me use their work. In particular, I want to acknowledge the contributions of Andrew and Katie Belcher; Noah and Shea Davis; Zachary Derr; Ben and Darcy Geraud; Dana Gogolin; Colin Hedges; Erin Islo; Laura Linton; Frederik Meissner; Meghan Milligan; Patrick Paddock; Alex, Jeff, and Tina Ormrod; Isabelle Peters; Ian Rhoades; Corey Ross; Ashton and Haley Russo; Connor Sheehan; Matt and Melinda Shump; and Grace Tober.

Last but certainly not least, I must thank my husband and children, who have been ever so patient as I have spent countless hours either buried in my books and journals or else glued to my computer. Without their continuing support and patience, this book would never have seen the light of day.

J. E. O.

Brief Contents

Contents

EDUCATIONAL PSYCHOLOGY
Developing Learners

1

Educational Psychology and Teacher Decision Making

*A*t some point in your life, you have undoubtedly tried to teach something to someone else. Perhaps you have already had some formal teaching experience in a public or private school. Perhaps you have given an oral presentation in one of your college classes or have helped a friend learn how to use a computer. Perhaps you have taught a small child how to tie shoelaces or ride a bicycle.

Reflect for a moment on the kinds of teaching experiences you've had. What strategies did you use in your attempts to help others learn? For instance, did you provide verbal explanations, demonstrate certain actions, ask your "students" to practice what you taught them, or give them feedback about their performance? And what assumptions about how people learn influenced the way that you chose to teach? For instance, did you assume that your students could learn something from listening to you describe it, or did you believe that demonstrating an action would be more effective? Did you think that "practice makes perfect"? Did you assume that feedback was essential for learning and motivation?

Helping others learn—and, in the process, helping them become more productive members of society—is what teaching is all about. As teachers, we find ourselves taking on a variety of roles, including subject matter experts, tutors, consultants, motivators, behavior managers, confidantes, and evaluators. Above all, we are *decision makers:* We must continually choose among many possible strategies for helping students learn, develop, and achieve. In fact, some researchers (C. M. Clark & Peterson, 1986) have estimated that classroom teachers must make a nontrivial instructional decision approximately once every two minutes!

Yet wise educational decisions are not made in a vacuum; they are based on a genuine understanding of how students learn and develop and on solid data about which classroom techniques are effective and which are not. We find considerable guidance in the field of **educational psychology**, which encompasses principles and theories related to human learning and motivation, child and adolescent development, individual and group differences, and psychological assessment, particularly as such topics relate to classroom practice.

In this first chapter we will get a taste of educational psychology by sampling research findings in development, learning, motivation, instruction, and classroom assessment practices. We will also address the following questions:

- How much can common sense guide us in our efforts to help students learn and develop?
- What kinds of conclusions can we draw from psychological and educational research studies?
- How can psychological principles and theories assist us as we make decisions about how best to help students learn and achieve? How can our ongoing assessment of students' work and behaviors help us as well?
- How can we continue to improve throughout our professional teaching careers?

Later in the chapter, we will have an overview of the book and discuss strategies for studying and learning educational psychology effectively.

CASE STUDY: *More Than Meets the Eye*

Rosa is a personable, outgoing 12-year-old. Born in South America, she has lived in this country for only three years, but she seems to have adjusted well to her new home. She now converses in English with just the slightest hint of an accent. She has made many friends and has an active after-school social life. She has blossomed into a talented athlete, seemingly a natural in almost any sport she tries, and is becoming especially proficient in volleyball and basketball. She also does well in art class and in the school choir, although she sometimes has trouble learning the lyrics.

But after three years in her new homeland, Rosa is still having difficulty in language arts, social studies, science, and mathematics. She often seems distracted in class and sometimes has trouble answering even the simplest questions her teachers ask her. Her test scores are inconsistent—sometimes quite high, but more frequently near the bottom of the class.

Rosa's teachers see occasional indicators that she is a bright and talented girl. For example, she is a skillful peacemaker who frequently steps in to help resolve interpersonal conflicts among her classmates. Her short stories, although often filled with grammatical and spelling errors, are imaginative and well developed. And of course there are the occasional high test scores. Rosa's teachers are convinced that Rosa is capable of achieving at a much higher level, but they are puzzled about just how to help her be more successful in her classroom activities.

■ What are some possible explanations for Rosa's poor academic performance? Could the source of difficulty lie in her limited experience with English? in her cultural background? in her motivation? in her study skills? in the ways that her knowledge is assessed? or perhaps in some combination of these things?

OOPS—A Pretest

You probably have several hypotheses about why Rosa might be having difficulty. You've been a student for many years now, and in the process you've certainly learned a great deal about how students learn and develop and about how teachers can best help them achieve. But exactly how much *do* you know? To help you find out, I've developed a short pretest, Ormrod's Own Psychological Survey (OOPS).

EXPERIENCING FIRSTHAND   *Ormrod's Own Psychological Survey (OOPS)*

Decide whether each of the following statements is *true* or *false.*

True/False

_____ 1. Most children 5 years of age and older are natural learners; they know the best way to learn something without having to be taught how to learn it.

_____ 2. When we compare boys and girls, we find that both groups are, on average, very similar in their mathematical and verbal aptitudes.

_____ 3. The best way to learn and remember a new fact is to repeat it over and over again.

_____ 4. Although students initially have many misconceptions about the world, they quickly revise their thinking once their teacher presents information that contradicts what they believe.

_____ 5. Students often misjudge how much they know about a topic.

_____ 6. Taking notes during a lecture usually interferes with learning more than it helps.

_____ 7. When a teacher rewards one student for appropriate behavior, the behavior of other students may also improve.

_____ 8. Anxiety sometimes helps students learn and perform more successfully in the classroom.

_____ 9. When we have children tutor their classmates in academic subject matter, we help only the students being tutored; the students doing the tutoring gain very little from the interaction.

_____ 10. The ways in which teachers assess students' learning influence what and how the students actually learn.

Now let's see how well you did on the OOPS. The answers, along with an explanation for each one, are as follows:

1. *Most children 5 years of age and older are natural learners; they know the best way to learn something without having to be taught how to learn it.* FALSE—Many students of all ages are relatively naive about how they can best learn something, and they often use inefficient strategies when they study. For example, most elementary students and a substantial number of high school students don't engage in **elaboration** as they study classroom material; that is, they don't analyze, interpret, or otherwise add their own ideas to the things they need to learn. (To illustrate, many students are likely to take the information presented in a history textbook strictly at face value; they rarely take time to consider why historical figures made the decisions they did or how some events may have led inevitably to others.) Yet elaboration is one of the most effective ways of learning new information: Students learn the information more quickly and remember it better. We will look at developmental trends in elaboration as we discuss cognitive development in Chapter 2. We'll also explore the very important role that elaboration plays in long-term memory as we discuss cognitive processes in Chapter 6.

How often do you elaborate when you read your textbooks?

2. *When we compare boys and girls, we find that both groups are, on average, very similar in their mathematical and verbal aptitudes.* TRUE—Despite commonly held beliefs to the contrary, boys and girls tend to be similar in their ability to perform both mathematical and verbal academic tasks. Any differences in the average performance of boys and girls in these areas are usually too small for teachers to worry about. We will explore gender differences—and similarities as well—in Chapter 4.

3. *The best way to learn and remember a new fact is to repeat it over and over again.* FALSE—Although repeating information over and over again is better than doing nothing at all, repetition is a relatively *ineffective* way to learn. Students learn information more easily and remember it longer when they connect it with the things they already know and when they elaborate on it. Chapter 6 describes several cognitive processes that promote students' long-term retention of school subject matter.

4. *Although students initially have many misconceptions about the world, they quickly revise their thinking once their teacher presents information that contradicts what they believe.* FALSE—As you will discover in Chapter 7, students typically have many misconceptions about the world (e.g., they may believe that rivers always run south rather than north or that the earth is round only in the sense that a pancake is round). They often hold strongly to these misconceptions even in the face of contradictory evidence or instruction. As teachers, one of our biggest challenges is to help students discard their erroneous beliefs in favor of more accurate and useful perspectives; some strategies for promoting such *conceptual change* appear in Chapter 7.

5. *Students often misjudge how much they know about a topic.* TRUE—Contrary to popular opinion, students are usually *not* the best judges of what they do and do not know. For example, many students think that if they've spent a long time studying a textbook chapter, they must know its content very well. Yet if they have spent most of their study time inefficiently (perhaps by "reading" without paying attention to meaning or by mindlessly copying definitions), they may know far less than they think they do. We will consider this *illusion of knowing* further in Chapter 8.

As teachers, we will continually be making decisions about how best to help students learn, develop, and achieve.

6. *Taking notes during a lecture usually interferes with learning more than it helps.* FALSE—In general, students who take notes learn more material from a lecture than students who don't take notes. Note taking appears to facilitate learning in at least two ways: It helps students put, or *store,* information into memory more effectively, and it allows them to review that information at a later time. Chapter 8 presents research concerning the effectiveness of note taking and other study strategies.

7. *When a teacher rewards one student for appropriate behavior, the behavior of other students may also improve.* TRUE—When teachers reward one student for behaving in a particular way, other students who have observed that student being rewarded sometimes begin to behave in a similar way. We will identify numerous roles that observation plays in learning as we explore social cognitive theory in Chapter 10.

8. *Anxiety sometimes helps students learn and perform more successfully in the classroom.* TRUE—Many people think that anxiety is always a bad thing. Yet for some classroom tasks, and especially for relatively easy tasks, a moderate level of anxiety actually *improves* students' learning and performance. We will consider the effects of anxiety on learning and performance in more detail in Chapter 11.

9. *When we have children tutor their classmates in academic subject matter, we help only the students being tutored; the students doing the tutoring gain very little from the interaction.* FALSE—When students teach one another, the tutors often benefit as much as the students being tutored. For instance, in one research study, fourth graders who were doing relatively poorly in mathematics served as arithmetic tutors for first and second graders; the tutors themselves showed a substantial improvement in arithmetic skills (Inglis & Biemiller, 1997). We will look more closely at the effects of peer tutoring in Chapter 13.

10. *The ways in which teachers assess students' learning influence what and how the students actually learn.* TRUE—What and how students learn depend, in part, on how they expect their learning to be assessed. For example, students typically spend more time studying the things they think will be on a test than the things they think the test won't cover. And they are more likely to organize and integrate class material as they study if they expect assessment activities to require such organization and integration. Chapter 15 describes the effects of classroom assessment practices on students' learning.

Keep an open mind as you read this book. When you encounter ideas that first seem incorrect, try to think of personal experiences and observations that support those ideas.

How many of the OOPS items did you answer correctly? Did some of the false items seem convincing enough that you marked them true? Did some of the true items contradict certain beliefs you had? If either of these was the case, you are hardly alone. College students often agree with statements that seem obvious but are, in fact, completely wrong (Gage, 1991; Lennon, Ormrod, Burger, & Warren, 1990). Furthermore, many students in teacher education classes reject research findings when those findings appear to contradict their own personal beliefs and experiences (Borko & Putnam, 1996; Holt-Reynolds, 1992; Wideen, Mayer-Smith, & Moon, 1998).

Drawing Conclusions from Psychological and Educational Research

It's easy to be persuaded by "common sense" and become convinced that what seems logical must be reality. Yet common sense and logic do not always tell us the true story about how people actually learn and develop, nor do they always give us accurate information about how best to help students succeed in the classroom. Educational psychologists believe that knowledge about teaching and learning should come from a more objective source of information—that is, from psychological and educational research.

Most of the ideas presented in this book are based either directly or indirectly on the results of research studies. Let's take a look at three major types of research—descriptive, correlational, and experimental—and at the kinds of conclusions we can draw from each one.

Descriptive Studies

A **descriptive study** does exactly what its name implies: It *describes* a situation. Descriptive studies might give us information about the characteristics of students, teachers, or schools; they might also provide information about the frequency with which certain events or behaviors occur. Descriptive studies allow us to draw conclusions about the way things are—the current state of affairs. The left column of Table 1.1 lists some examples of questions we could answer with descriptive studies.

Correlational Studies

Correlations are often described numerically with a statistic known as a *correlation coefficient.* Correlation coefficients are described in Appendix A.

A **correlational study** explores relationships among different things. For instance, it might tell us how closely two human characteristics are associated with one another, or it might give us information about the consistency with which certain human behaviors occur in conjunction with certain environmental conditions. In general, correlational studies enable us to draw conclusions about **correlation**—that is, about the extent to which two variables are interrelated.

TABLE 1.1   COMPARE/CONTRAST

Questions We Might Answer with Descriptive, Correlational, and Experimental Studies

DESCRIPTIVE STUDIES	CORRELATIONAL STUDIES	EXPERIMENTAL STUDIES
What percentage of high school students can think abstractly?	Are older students more capable of abstract thought than younger students?	Can abstract thinking skills be improved through specially designed educational programs?
What kinds of aggressive behaviors do we see in our schools, and with what frequencies do we see them?	Are students more likely to be aggressive at school if their parents are physically violent at home?	Which method is most effective in reducing aggressive behavior—reinforcing appropriate behavior, punishing aggressive behavior, or a combination of both?
How pervasive are gender stereotypes in books commonly used to teach reading in the elementary grades?	Are better readers also better spellers?	Which of two reading programs produces greater gains in reading comprehension?
How well have our nation's students performed on a recent standardized achievement test?	Do students who get the highest scores on multiple-choice tests also get the highest scores on essays dealing with the same material?	Do different kinds of tests (e.g., multiple choice vs. essay tests) encourage students to study in different ways and therefore affect what students actually learn?

The middle column of Table 1.1 lists some examples of questions we might answer with correlational studies. Notice how each of these questions asks about a relationship between two variables—between age and abstract thought, between student aggression and parental violence, between reading and spelling, or between multiple-choice test and essay performance.

Correlations between two variables allow us to make *predictions* about one variable if we know the status of the other. For example, if we find that older students are more capable of abstract thought than younger students, we can predict that tenth graders will benefit more from an abstract discussion of democratic government than fourth graders. If we find a correlation between multiple-choice test and essay scores, we can predict that those students who have done well on essays in a biology class will probably also do well on a national test covering the same topics in a multiple-choice format.

Experimental Studies

Descriptive and correlational studies describe things as they exist naturally in the environment. In contrast, an **experimental study**, or **experiment**, is a study in which the researcher somehow changes, or *manipulates*, one or more aspects of the environment (often called *independent variables*) and then measures the effects of such changes on something else. In educational research the "something else" being affected (often called the *dependent variable*) is usually some aspect of student behavior—perhaps an increase in achievement test scores, skill in executing a complex physical movement, persistence in trying to solve difficult mathematics problems, or ability to interact appropriately with classmates. When carefully designed, experimental studies enable us to draw conclusions about *causation*—about *why* behaviors occur.

The right column of Table 1.1 lists examples of questions that might be answered through experimental studies. Notice how each question addresses a cause-effect relationship—the effect of educational programs on abstract thinking, the effect of reinforcement and punishment on aggressive behavior, the effect of a reading program on the development of reading comprehension, or the effect of test questions on students' learning.

Can you think of other questions that each type of research might address?

As you can see from the examples in the table, the difference between correlational and experimental research is an important one: Whereas correlational studies let us draw conclusions about relationships, only experimental studies enable us to draw conclusions about cause and effect. The following section describes how one phenomenon in particular—visual-spatial thinking—has been studied with both correlational and experimental research studies and considers the conclusions we can draw from each type of study.

An Example: Research on Visual-Spatial Thinking

Visual-spatial thinking is the ability to imagine and mentally manipulate two- and three-dimensional figures. The exercise that follows provides three examples.

EXPERIENCING FIRSTHAND   *Three Examples of Visual-Spatial Thinking*

1. The figure on the left is a flag. Which one or more of the three figures on the right represent(s) the *same* side of the flag? Which one or more of them represent(s) the *flip* side?

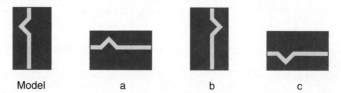

Model   a   b   c

2. When the figure on the left is folded along the dotted lines, it becomes a three-dimensional object. Which one or more of the four figures on the right represent(s) how this object might appear from different perspectives?

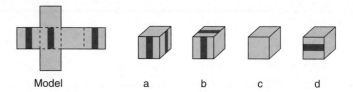

Model   a   b   c   d

3. When the object on the left is rotated in three-dimensional space, it can look like one or more of the objects on the right. Which one(s)?

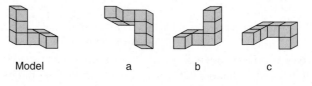

Model   a   b   c

Answer key: (1) Flags *a* and *b* are the flip side; flag *c* is the same side. (2) Depending on the perspective, the object might look like either *a* or *d*. (3) The object can be rotated to look like either *a* or *c*.

Three tasks modeled, respectively, after Thurstone & Jeffrey, 1956; Bennett, Seashore, & Wesman, 1982; and Shepard & Metzler, 1971.

Visual-spatial thinking appears to be related to mathematics achievement, although the nature of this relationship is not totally clear (Friedman, 1995; Hegarty & Kozhevnikov, 1999; Threadgill-Sowder, 1985). Many correlational studies have found a relationship between gender and visual-spatial thinking: On average, boys have slightly better visual-spatial thinking skills than girls (N. S. Anderson, 1987; Halpern & LaMay, 2000; Law, Pellegrino, & Hunt, 1993). Are males genetically more capable of visual-spatial thought? Do parents encourage their sons to think in "visual-spatial" ways more frequently than they encourage their daughters? Do the typical childhood experiences of boys promote greater development of visual-spatial thinking ability? Unfortunately, correlational studies, although they demonstrate that a relationship exists, do not tell us *why* it exists; they don't tell us whether genetics, parental encouragement, childhood experiences, or perhaps something else is the cause of the difference we see.

An experimental study by Sprafkin, Serbin, Denier, and Connor (1983) points to one probable cause of the gender difference in visual-spatial thinking. These researchers hypothesized that typical "male" toys (e.g., wooden blocks, Legos, trucks) provide greater opportunities for children to explore visual-spatial relationships than do typical "female" toys (e.g., dolls, board games). To test their hypothesis, they randomly selected half of the boys and girls enrolled in a preschool to be members of an experimental group, or **treatment group**, leaving the remaining children as an untrained **control group**. Children in both groups took a test of visual-spatial thinking, revealing that the treatment and control groups were equal (on average) in visual-spatial ability. During the next six weeks, the experimental group participated

Do you think you have good visual-spatial skills? If so, how did you develop them?

in twelve sessions involving instruction and structured play opportunities with blocks, building toys, puzzles, dominoes, and various other materials requiring visual-spatial thought. At the end of the six-week period, these specially trained children obtained higher average scores on a test of visual-spatial thinking than the untrained, control group children.

From this study with preschool children, we can draw a conclusion about a cause-effect relationship: We can say that structured exposure to certain types of toys promotes increased visual-spatial thinking ability. Other characteristics of the two groups of children were the same; for example, both groups began with equivalent visual-spatial thinking ability, and all the children attended the same preschool. Furthermore, because the children were randomly assigned to the training and nontraining conditions, we can assume that both groups were approximately the same (on average) in terms of such other factors as general intelligence, prior exposure to different types of toys, and home environment. Because the researchers eliminated other possible explanations for the differences they observed in the two groups of preschoolers, they could reasonably draw a conclusion about a cause-effect relationship: Increased exposure to certain types of toys fosters the development of visual-spatial thinking skills.

Here the researchers separated the possible variables affecting visual-spatial thinking and kept all but one of them constant. Chapter 2 describes this process of *separating and controlling variables.*

A Cautionary Note

To draw conclusions about causal relationships, we must eliminate other possible explanations for the outcomes we observe. As an example, imagine that the Hometown School District wants to find out which of two reading programs, *Reading Is Great* (RIG) or *Reading and You* (RAY), leads to better reading in third grade. The district asks each of its third-grade teachers to choose one of these two reading programs and use it throughout a particular school year. The district then compares the end-of-year achievement test scores of students in the RIG and RAY classrooms and finds that RIG students have gotten substantially higher reading comprehension scores than RAY students. We might quickly jump to the conclusion that RIG promotes better reading comprehension than RAY—in other words, that a cause-effect relationship exists between instructional method and reading comprehension. But is this really so?

Early exposure to certain types of toys encourages greater visual-spatial thinking ability for both boys and girls.

The fact is, the school district hasn't eliminated all other possible explanations for the difference in students' reading comprehension scores. Remember, the third-grade teachers selected the instructional program they used. Why did some teachers choose RIG and others choose RAY? Were the teachers who chose RIG different in some way from the teachers who chose RAY? Had RIG teachers taken more graduate courses in reading instruction, did they have higher expectations for their students, or did they devote more class time to reading instruction? If the RIG and RAY teachers were different from each other in any of these ways—or perhaps different in some other way we might not happen to think of—then the district hasn't eliminated an alternative explanation for why the RIG students have developed better reading skills than the RAY students. A better way to study the causal influence of reading program on reading comprehension would be to randomly assign teachers to the RIG and RAY programs, thereby making the two groups of teachers roughly equivalent in areas such as amount of education, expectations for students, and class time devoted to reading instruction.

Be careful that you don't jump too quickly to conclusions about what factors are affecting students' learning, development, and behavior in particular situations. Scrutinize descriptions of research carefully, always with this question in mind: *Have the researchers ruled out other possible explanations for their results?* Only when the answer to this question is an undeniable *yes* should you draw a conclusion about a cause-effect relationship.

Using Principles and Theories in Classroom Decision Making

When similar research studies yield similar results time after time, even under widely varying circumstances and with very different kinds of learners, educational psychologists derive general psychological **principles** describing specific factors that influence students' learning, development, and behavior. Oftentimes, educational psychologists also speculate about why these principles are true; in other words, they develop **theories** that describe possible underlying, unobservable mechanisms regulating human learning, development, and behavior. Psychological theories typically incorporate many principles and encompass a multitude of interrelationships. In essence, principles describe the *whats* of human behavior—they describe what things happen under what conditions—whereas theories describe *why* those things happen.

Throughout the book we will be examining innumerable principles and theories related to student learning and classroom practice. As you read about and study them, keep in mind that they are not necessarily set in stone; they simply represent our best guesses at the present time. As future research yields new information, our conceptions of human learning, development, and behavior will continue to evolve into more complete and accurate explanations.

Yet, incomplete and tentative as current principles and theories in educational psychology may be, they provide numerous ideas and insights about how best to help our students achieve academic and social success. To illustrate, picture yourself standing in front of thirty students. You are trying to teach them something; perhaps you are describing the difference between nouns and pronouns, or explaining how an automobile engine works, or encouraging them to project their voices as they rehearse a medley from *Phantom of the Opera.* Those thirty students are staring back at you with blank faces, and you're certain that they haven't learned a thing.

Why aren't your students learning? Following are just three of the many possible explanations:

■ *They don't believe they can learn what you are trying to teach them:* One well-established principle of motivation is that people are more likely to try to learn something if they believe they are capable of learning and mastering it. Such a belief—called *self-efficacy* by some theorists and *sense of competence* by others—plays a significant role in social cognitive theory (see Chapter 10) and may be particularly important for intrinsic (i.e., self-generated) motivation (see Chapter 12).

■ *They are having trouble comprehending something in the abstract manner you have explained it.* In an early theory of cognitive development, Jean Piaget proposed that children progress through four stages of increasingly complex and sophisticated thought and do not think abstractly until they reach the final stage, typically around age 11 or 12. Recent researchers have found partial support for Piaget's theory: Children show some evidence of abstract thought well before age 11, but they engage in it more frequently once they reach adolescence. (We will consider Piaget's theory and the development of abstract thinking in Chapter 2.)

■ *They don't have enough background knowledge to understand the material you are presenting.* A basic principle of learning and cognitive development is that a learner's prior knowledge affects the learner's ability to acquire new information and skills. In general, the more students already know about a topic, the more quickly and easily they learn additional things about that topic. (We will consider this principle, as well as possible theoretical explanations for it, in Chapters 2, 6, and 7.)

Each of these explanations leads to different instructional strategies for your class of thirty students. For instance, if your students don't believe they are capable of learning the knowledge or skills in question (i.e., if they have low self-efficacy), you might begin with fairly easy subject matter—something they can readily master—and gradually increase the difficulty level over time. If they have limited ability to think abstractly, you might make the material more concrete, perhaps by providing pictures, familiar examples, hands-on experiences, or opportunities to practice certain behaviors. If your students have insufficient background knowledge, you might find out what they do and don't know about the topic and build instruction on their current knowledge.

So which strategy or strategies do you try? Psychological principles and theories alone do not provide the answer. Ongoing assessment of students' achievement and progress is equally critical for teacher decision making.

Importance of Ongoing Assessment in Classroom Decision Making

Most teachers schedule regular assessments of what their students have learned, perhaps in the form of quizzes, compositions, projects, or presentations. But effective teachers don't limit themselves to such formal, planned evaluations. They continually observe their students in a variety of contexts—in the classroom, in the cafeteria, on the playground, on field trips, during extracurricular activities, with family members at parent-teacher conferences and school open houses—for clues about what the students might be thinking, feeling, and learning. Students' comments, questions, facial expressions, body language, work habits, and interactions with friends and classmates can provide valuable insights into their learning, development, and behavior. For instance, an informal "reading" of that hypothetical class of thirty students described earlier might give you some idea of whether they lack confidence in their ability to learn, are confused by the abstract presentation, or have insufficient knowledge about the topic.

We will explore the topic of assessment in depth in Chapters 15 and 16, yet you will find implications for assessment in every chapter. Throughout the book, *Interpreting Artifacts and Interactions* features will invite you to look below the surface of what children produce, say, and do and to form hypotheses about their knowledge, abilities, thoughts, and feelings. To get your feet wet in the process of assessment, try the following exercise.

INTERPRETING ARTIFACTS AND INTERACTIONS   *The Pet Who Came to Dinner*

Seven-year-old Justin wrote the story shown here. As you read it, consider what you might conclude about

- Justin's progress in writing
- Justin's family
- The nature of Justin's home life

Clearly, Justin has learned how to spell some words but has not yet learned many others; for example, he spells *once* as "owans" or "ouns," *drink* as "brick," *water* as "wodr," *rushed* as "rust," and *started* as "stor did." Overall, he knows which letters of the alphabet represent which sounds in speech. However, he sometimes reverses the letter *d* so that it looks like a *b*, and he occasionally leaves out a sound when he spells a word (notice how his spelling of *drink* begins with *b* and omits the *n* sound). He has learned some common English spelling patterns; for instance, his misspelling of *snoring* ("soreing") includes a silent *e* (which is present in the word *snore*) and a correct spelling of the *-ing* ending. He has learned appropriate uses for periods and apostrophes, but he does not always know when one sentence should end and another should begin. He has learned to tell a simple story, but he does so merely by listing a series of seemingly unrelated events, and he has not yet learned that the title of a story should appear in a line by itself, centered at the top of the page.

Justin's story tells us a few things about his family and home life as well. For instance, it appears that he lives with both his mother and father. The family gives at least some attention to nutrition (it serves "melk" at dinner) and has sufficient financial resources to provide dessert ("dasrt") after the main course. Justin also talks about the pet reading the newspaper ("nuwspapr"), suggesting that reading is a familiar activity in the home.

Are the conclusions about Justin accurate? Not necessarily. The conclusions we reach about our students, like the principles and theories that researchers have derived, can be only best guesses based on the evidence at hand. As such, we must think of them as *hypotheses* to be tested further rather than as *facts* set in stone. Nevertheless, they do give us guidance in the decisions we must continually make to help students learn, grow, and thrive.

Developing as a Teacher

As a beginning teacher, you may initially find your role a bit overwhelming. After all, you may have twenty-five to thirty-five students in your classroom at any one time, and they are all likely to have different backgrounds, ability levels, and needs. In such a situation, your role as decision maker will be a challenging one indeed. So in the first few weeks or months, you may need to rely heavily on the standard lessons that curriculum development specialists provide (Berliner, 1988). But as you gain experience, you will eventually be able to make decisions about routine situations and problems quickly and efficiently, giving you the time and energy to think creatively and flexibly about how best to teach your students (Borko & Putnam, 1996; Sternberg, 1996a).

The chapters that follow describe many ways you can help your students learn and develop. But it is equally important that *you* learn and develop as well, especially in your role as a teacher. Here are several strategies for doing so:

- *Continue to take courses in teacher education.* Additional coursework in teaching is one surefire way of keeping up to date on the latest theoretical perspectives and research results related to classroom practice. In general, teacher education definitely *does* enhance teaching effectiveness (Darling-Hammond, 1995).

- *Learn as much as you can about the subject matter you teach.* When we look at effective teachers—for example, those who are flexible in their approaches to instruction, help their students develop a thorough understanding of classroom subject matter, and convey obvious enthusiasm for whatever they are teaching—we typically find teachers who know their subject matter extremely well (Borko & Putnam, 1996; Brophy, 1991; Cochran & Jones, 1998; Phillip, Flores, Sowder, & Schappelle, 1994).

- *Learn as much as you can about specific strategies for teaching your particular subject matter.* In addition to knowing general teaching strategies, it is also helpful to develop strategies specific to the topic you are teaching; a repertoire of such strategies is known as **pedagogical content knowledge.** Effective teachers typically have a large number of strategies for teaching various topics and skills (Borko & Putnam, 1996; Brophy, 1991; Cochran & Jones, 1998; L. S. Shulman, 1986). Furthermore, they can usually anticipate—and so can also address—the difficulties students will have, as well as the kinds of errors students will make, in the process of mastering a skill or body of knowledge (Borko & Putnam, 1996; D. C. Smith & Neale, 1991). Some teachers keep journals or other records of the strategies they develop and use in particular situations; they then draw on some of the same strategies again when similar situations arise (Berliner, 1988).

- *Learn as much as you can about the culture(s) of the community in which you are working.* Throughout the book we will be identifying numerous ways in which students from diverse cultural backgrounds may think and behave differently than the ways *you* thought and behaved as a child. Yet a textbook can give only a sample of the many possible differences. You can more effectively become aware of the beliefs and practices of your own students' cultural groups if you participate in local community activities and converse regularly with community members (McCarty & Watahomigie, 1998; H. L. Smith, 1998).

- *Conduct your own research.* The research literature on learning, motivation, development, and instructional practice grows by leaps and bounds every year. Nevertheless, teachers sometimes encounter problems in the classroom that existing research findings don't address. In such circumstances, we have an alternative: We can conduct our own research. When we conduct systematic studies of issues and problems in our own schools, with the goal of seeking more effective interventions in the lives of our students, we are conducting **action research.**

Action research is becoming an increasingly popular endeavor among teachers, educational administrators, and other educational professionals. It takes a variety of forms; for example, it might involve assessing the effectiveness of a new teaching technique, gathering information about students' opinions on a schoolwide issue, or conducting an in-depth case study of a particular student (Cochran-Smith & Lytle, 1993; Mills, 2000). Many colleges and

INTO THE CLASSROOM: *Becoming a More Effective Teacher*

Use some of the standard lessons that curriculum development specialists provide, especially in your first few weeks or months in the classroom.

A science teacher consults the teaching manual that accompanies her class textbook for ideas about how to make science come alive for her students.

As you gain experience and confidence as a teacher, begin to adapt standard lessons and develop your own lessons.

When a high school social studies teacher begins using a new geography textbook, he peruses the teacher's manual that accompanies the book. He notices that the manual's lesson plans focus almost exclusively on meaningless memorization of geographic concepts and principles. Rather than use these lessons, he develops classroom activities of his own that will encourage his students to apply geography to real-life situations.

Keep a journal of the instructional strategies you use and their relative effectiveness.

As a way of winding down at bedtime, a new teacher reflects on his day in the classroom. He picks up the notebook and pen on his bedside table and jots down notes about the strategies that did and did not work well in class that day.

Seek the advice and suggestions of your more experienced colleagues.

A fourth-grade teacher is teaching her students long division, but after a week they still don't understand what they are supposed to do. In the teacher's lounge she consults with two of her fellow teachers for ideas about how she might approach the topic differently.

Continue your education, both formally and informally.

A middle school science teacher takes advantage of a tour package to Costa Rica designed specifically for teachers. There she will study the plants, animals, and ecology of the rain forest.

Conduct your own research to answer questions about your students and about the effectiveness of your teaching practices.

Over the course of the school year, a second-grade school teacher alternates among three different approaches to teaching the weekly spelling words. At the end of the school year, he compares his students' spelling quiz scores for each of the three methods and sees that one approach led to noticeably higher scores than the other two.

Remember that teaching, like any other complex skill, takes time and practice to master.

A teacher continues to try new instructional techniques that he sees described in professional journals. As he does so, he adds to his repertoire of effective teaching strategies and becomes increasingly able to adjust his methods to the diverse population of students in his classroom.

---

universities now offer courses in action research; two other good sources of information are Geoffrey Mills's *Action Research* (2000) and the online journal *Action Research International* (http://www.scu.edu.au/schools/gcm/ar/ari/arihome.html).

■ *Believe that you can become an effective teacher.* Earlier in the chapter I mentioned that students are more likely to try to learn something if they believe that they *can* learn it—in other words, if they have high self-efficacy. You, too, must have high self-efficacy. Believing that you can be a good teacher will help you persist in the face of occasional setbacks and ultimately be effective in the classroom (Ashton, 1985). Students who achieve at the highest levels are most likely to be those whose teachers have confidence in what they *themselves* can do for their students (Ashton, 1985; J. A. Langer, 2000; Tschannen-Moran, Woolfolk Hoy, & Hoy, 1998).

Teaching, like any other complex skill, takes time and practice to master. And you, like any other learner, will inevitably make a few mistakes, especially at the beginning. But you *will* improve over time. If you base classroom decisions on documented principles and sound educational practice, you can undoubtedly make a difference in the lives of your students (e.g., see Figure 1.1).

Looking Ahead to the Following Chapters

As teachers, we are decision makers. And we are most likely to make wise decisions when, in the process, we consider questions such as these:

- What characteristics do our students bring to the classroom?
- What do we know about how students learn?
- How can we convert our knowledge about development, diversity, and learning into effective teaching practice?

I know a great teacher and his name is Mr. Shipley. Mr. Shipley was my 6th grade teacher for Science, Social Studies, and Flex (or Study hall). This man is my favorite teacher for many reasons.

I had Science during first period and since, I don't think that it is the most interesting subject, I would often get bored and lose interest in what he was saying. But every so often Mr. Shipley would do something crazy and funny to kind-of snap me out of my daze and put me back into class. I thank him for that!

Mr. Shipley was always understanding and he seemed to have a special bond with kids. I was in his study hall and during that period, 6th period, the 7th graders had lunch. That is a free time to do whatever you want, so the 7th graders would wander down to talk to him. (Of course they'd ask for a Jolly Rancher from his famous stash in his desk!) I admire and was amazed to see how he continued to bring students from years past, down to him.

Not only was Mr. Shipley funny, understanding, and just a great, all around great teacher, he believed in me. Mr. Shipley had faith in me and that is something I knew my other teachers had, but rarely expressed. I always got an A or A+ in his classes and Language Arts, but Math was a struggle for me. I always ended up with a B+ in that class. But I tried harder and harder to get that B+ up to an A, but I just couldn't. So each time grade card time rolled around, I'd wind up with all A's and A+'s except for Math, a B+. I worked so hard all year for a 4.0 (straight A's) but wound up with an average of 3.899. Mr. Shipley always told me that I'd "get 'em next time." And I did! I am now in 7th grade with a 4.0, straight A's! Even in Math. I also made the tennis team, 1st doubles, Mr. Shipley believed in me All The Way! So, I owe a lot to him.

Mr. Shipley - the funny man, the understander, the believer: My favorite teacher!

Let's look briefly at how each part of the book addresses these questions. As we do so, let's also identify places where we might find possible strategies for helping Rosa, the student in our opening case study.

■ *What characteristics do our students bring to the classroom?* Part 1 of the book, "Understanding Student Development and Diversity," focuses on how our students are likely to be different from one another. Chapters 2 and 3 look at developmental changes in thinking, language, self-perceptions, social skills, and morality as students progress through the elementary and secondary school years. Chapters 4 and 5 describe common sources of diversity among students at the same grade, including intelligence, creativity, ethnicity, gender, socioeconomic background, and disabilities. For instance, when you read about Rosa, you may have wondered how her language and ethnic background influence her classroom performance. We'll identify strategies for addressing linguistic and ethnic differences in Chapters 2 and 4, respectively.

Although we will focus on development and diversity in Part 1, these two topics will frequently pop up in Parts 2 and 3 as well. For instance, we will consider developmental trends in our discussions of study strategies, reinforcement, self-efficacy, motivation, instruction, and assessment. Furthermore, every chapter includes a section on accommodating the student diversity we are likely to find in any classroom.

All students are unique individuals who bring different strengths and weaknesses to the classroom. In many cases, we will be able to accommodate our students' unique needs within the context of general classroom practices and activities. Yet some students have characteristics that require specially adapted instructional materials or practices. Now, more than ever before, many of these **students with special needs** are in general education classrooms—a practice called **inclusion**. Accordingly, every chapter includes a *Students in Inclusive Settings* table that provides instructional strategies for students within five general categories of special needs. These categories are described and illustrated in Table 1.2. Keep in mind, however, that categorizing students with special needs in *any* way is a controversial issue (more about this point in Chapter 5). Ultimately we must remember that all of our students, including those with special needs, can benefit from having instruction tailored to their unique characteristics.

■ *What do we know about how students learn?* Like many students, Rosa learns in some areas of the curriculum more successfully than in others. Part 2 of the book, "Understanding How Students Learn," explores the nature of human learning, thinking, behavior, and motivation. Chapters 6 through 8 focus on cognition—that is, on the mental processes involved in

TABLE 1.2   STUDENTS IN INCLUSIVE SETTINGS

Categories of Students with Special Educational Needs

GENERAL CATEGORY	DESCRIPTION	SPECIFIC CATEGORY(IES) INCLUDED	EXAMPLE
Students with specific cognitive or academic difficulties	These students exhibit an uneven pattern of academic performance; they may have unusual difficulty with certain kinds of tasks yet perform quite successfully on other tasks.	• Learning disabilities • Attention-deficit hyperactivity disorder • Speech and communication disorders	James has exceptional difficulty learning to read but seems to grasp ideas in science and mathematics quite easily.
Students with social or behavioral problems	These students exhibit social, emotional, or behavioral difficulties serious enough to interfere significantly with their academic performance.	• Emotional and behavioral disorders • Autism	Amy has frequent aggressive outbursts during which she hits or kicks whomever happens to be near her. She rarely interacts with either her teacher or her classmates in a socially acceptable manner.
Students with general delays in cognitive and social functioning	These students exhibit low achievement in virtually all academic areas, and they have social skills typical of much younger children.	• Mental retardation	Although Margaret is 11 years old, her academic skills are similar to those of a 7-year-old, and she often blurts out whatever is on her mind without considering how other people might react to her comments.
Students with physical and sensory challenges	These students have disabilities caused by diagnosed physical or medical problems.	• Physical and health impairments • Visual impairments • Hearing loss • Severe and multiple disabilities	After sustaining a brain injury in a car accident, Jonathan tires easily, and he has trouble remembering some of the things that he studies in class.
Students with advanced cognitive development	These students have unusually high ability in one or more areas.	• Giftedness	Mike shows exceptional skill and creativity in writing; for instance, he has won several district and statewide writing contests.

learning, remembering, studying, and problem solving. Chapters 9 and 10 consider how students' behaviors are influenced by environmental events, especially in the early years, and how students can become increasingly self-regulating over time. Chapters 11 and 12 examine a variety of factors that influence students' motivation to learn and achieve in classroom settings. (In the *Study Guide and Reader* that accompanies this book, you can find an additional chapter, "Learning in the Content Areas," which addresses learning processes and teaching strategies related to reading, writing, mathematics, science, and social studies.)

When reading about Rosa, you may have noticed that many of her strengths—her ability to interact with other people, her skill in volleyball and basketball, and her ability to perform in the school choir—are things she can learn through watching and modeling the behaviors of others; such *modeling* is a topic of Chapter 10. Rosa's *need for affiliation*—her desire for friendly relationships with others—is described in Chapter 11.

These students are engaged in discovery learning within the context of a cooperative learning activity. Discovery learning and cooperative learning are just two of the many instructional strategies we'll consider in Chapter 13.

■ *How can we convert our knowledge about development, diversity, and learning into effective teaching practice?* Part 3, "Understanding Instructional Processes," applies principles of student development, diversity, learning, and motivation to classroom practice. Chapter 13 identifies instructional strategies that are suitable for different situations and different students; for instance, when you read this chapter, you will discover that Rosa would probably learn quite effectively through cooperative learning activities. Chapter 14 presents strategies for maintaining a productive learning environment

UNDERSTANDING STUDENT DEVELOPMENT AND DIVERSITY

- What characteristics do our students bring to the classroom?

Chapter 2.   Cognitive and Linguistic Development
- How does logical thinking change with age?
- To what extent do students at different grade levels learn differently?
- How do students' language skills develop during the elementary and secondary school years?

Chapter 3.   Personal, Social, and Moral Development
- What can we do to promote students' self-esteem?
- What roles do students' friends and classmates play in development?
- How do we help students develop a "conscience" about right and wrong?

Chapter 4.   Individual and Group Differences
- What are intelligence and creativity?
- How do students' cultural backgrounds influence their classroom performance?
- How are boys and girls similar and different?

Chapter 5.   Students with Special Educational Needs
- Why are students with disabilities often educated in general education classrooms?
- In what ways are students with special needs different from their peers?
- What instructional strategies are effective for students with special needs?

UNDERSTANDING HOW STUDENTS LEARN

- What do we know about how students learn?

Chapter 6.   Learning and Cognitive Processes
- What is learning?
- What thinking processes help students learn classroom subject matter effectively?
- Why do students sometimes forget what they've learned?

Chapter 7.   Knowledge Construction
- Why do different students often learn different things from the same lesson?
- How can we help students learn new concepts?
- What effects do students' misconceptions about classroom topics have on learning?

Chapter 8.   Higher-Level Thinking Skills
- How can we help students learn to study effectively?
- How can we help students apply the things they learn to real-world situations?
- How can we facilitate problem solving and critical thinking skills?

Chapter 9.   Behaviorist Views of Learning
- What role does reinforcement play in learning?
- How can we encourage productive classroom behaviors?
- Should we ever use punishment and, if so, under what circumstances?

Chapter 10.   Social Cognitive Views of Learning
- What can students learn from watching others?
- How can we enhance students' self-confidence about performing classroom tasks?
- How can we help students regulate their own behavior and learning?

Chapter 11.   Motivation and Affect
- How does motivation affect learning and behavior?
- What social needs are students likely to have?
- How do anxiety and other emotions affect learning?

Chapter 12.   Cognitive Factors in Motivation
- How can we foster intrinsic motivation to learn?
- Why do some students have trouble accepting responsibility for their own actions?
- How might our expectations for students lead to a self-fulfilling prophecy?

UNDERSTANDING INSTRUCTIONAL PROCESSES

- How can we convert our knowledge about development, diversity, and learning into effective teaching practice?

Chapter 13.   Instructional Strategies
- Under what circumstances are verbal explanations (e.g., lectures) apt to be effective?
- In what situations might it be better to let students discover ideas for themselves?
- How do class discussions enhance students' learning?

Chapter 14.   Creating and Maintaining a Productive Classroom Environment
- How can we get the school year off to a good start?
- How can we keep discipline problems to a minimum?
- How can we collaborate with parents to maximize students' classroom performance?

Chapter 15.   Basic Concepts and Issues in Assessment
- How do classroom assessment practices affect students' learning?
- How do we know when the results of our assessments are accurate?
- What purposes can standardized tests serve?

Chapter 16.   Classroom Assessment Strategies
- What classroom assessment tools can best determine whether students are achieving instructional objectives?
- What guidelines can help us develop good paper-pencil tests and performance tasks?
- On what criteria should we base final grades?

Figure 1.2   Overview of the book: Examples of questions addressed in each chapter

in which students are actively engaged in achieving instructional objectives for much of the school day. Chapters 15 and 16 describe principles of effective assessment; at that point, we will identify several issues to consider when we see low test scores in students such as Rosa.

Figure 1.2 provides a graphic overview of the book, with examples of questions that each chapter addresses. Take a moment to think about specific topics you hope the book will cover and identify the chapters in which you are most likely to find them.

Studying Educational Psychology More Effectively

As you read the book, you will gain insights about how you can help your students more effectively learn the things you want to teach them. At the same time, I hope you will also gain insights about how *you yourself* can learn course material. But rather than wait until we get to our discussion of learning in Part 2, let's look briefly at three general principles of effective learning that you can apply as you read and study this book:

■ *Students learn more effectively when they relate new information to the things they already know.* Try to connect the ideas you read in the book with things you are already familiar with—for example, with your own past experiences, with your previous course work, with things you have observed in schools, or with your general knowledge about the world.

■ *Students learn more effectively when they elaborate on new information.* As you learned earlier, elaboration is a process of adding one's own ideas to new information. In most situations, elaboration enables us to learn information with greater understanding, remember it better, and apply it more readily when we need it. So try to think *beyond* the information you read. Generate new examples of concepts. Draw inferences from the research findings presented. Identify educational applications of various principles and theories.

■ *Students learn more effectively when they periodically check to make sure they have learned.* There are times when even the best of us don't concentrate on what we're reading—when we are actually thinking about something else as our eyes go down the page. So stop once in a while (perhaps once every two or three pages) to make sure you have really learned and understood the things you've been reading. Try to summarize the material. Ask yourself questions about it. Make sure everything makes logical sense to you. Don't become a victim of that *illusion of knowing* I mentioned earlier.

> How frequently do you apply these principles when you study?

Perhaps you are a student who has been following these principles for years. But in case you are someone for whom such learning strategies are relatively new, I've provided margin notes (designated by a *green bar*) to help you learn and study throughout the book. These notes will give you some suggestions for how you might think about the material in nearby paragraphs. With practice, the strategies I recommend will eventually become second nature to you as you read and study in all your classes.

Furthermore, the case studies in each chapter can help you relate chapter content to concrete classroom situations. An opening case study introduces you to a variety of concepts and principles and is frequently referred to throughout the chapter. The case study at the end of each chapter focuses on teachers and teaching and is followed by questions that ask you to apply concepts and principles you have just learned. You will find my own analyses of the ending cases in Appendix B.

The Big Picture

An additional feature of every chapter is a "Big Picture" section that synthesizes chapter content and summarizes key ideas. In this first "Big Picture" section, we identify the most important points of Chapter 1 to take with you into the classroom.

Importance of Research for Teachers

As the OOPS test may have shown you, you (like everyone) almost certainly have a few misconceptions about how students typically learn and develop and about how teachers can most effectively promote students' classroom success. Psychological and educational research provides a reality check for such misconceptions and may yield insights that fly in the face of many common-sense, seemingly logical ideas about instructional practice.

Some research studies are *descriptive* in nature, in that they describe existing characteristics of students, teachers, or instructional practices. Other studies are *correlational,* in that they provide information about relationships among variables—perhaps relationships among two or more student characteristics, or perhaps relationships between students' behaviors and the kinds of environments in which students live. Still other studies are *experimental*: The researcher manipulates one or more aspects of the environment and measures the effects of that manipulation on some aspect of student behavior. Correlational studies allow us to predict one characteristic when we have information about another, related characteristic, but only experimental studies allow us to draw conclusions about cause-effect relationships.

Principles, Theories, and Assessment in Decision Making

When research studies yield similar results time after time, educational psychologists derive principles and theories that describe and explain people's learning, development, and behavior. Although such principles and theories provide a starting point for classroom decision making, we can ultimately identify the most effective classroom strategies for our own classrooms only when we assess students' knowledge, interpretations, and progress using both planned assignments and informal observations on an ongoing basis.

Developing as a Teacher

Researchers continually add to our knowledge about how children and adolescents think and learn. As teachers, then, we must keep ourselves abreast of research results, theoretical developments, and educational innovations. In your first few months as a classroom teacher, you may initially find your classroom a bit overwhelming, but with experience and continuing education, you can almost certainly become an expert in the teaching profession.

Reading About and Studying Educational Psychology

As we explore the many ways that children and adolescents think and learn in the chapters that follow, you will undoubtedly discover many new strategies that can help you in your *own* learning. For the time being, however, keep these three strategies in mind as you read and study the book: (1) Relate new information to what you already know, (2) elaborate on that information, and (3) occasionally stop to test yourself on the content you've studied. As an example of the last strategy—self-assessment—read and analyze the following case study, "More Harm Than Good?"

PRAXIS Turn to Appendix C, "Matching Book and Ancillary Content to the PRAXIS™ Principles of Learning and Teaching Tests," to discover sections of this chapter that may be especially applicable to the PRAXIS™ tests.

Now go to our Companion Website at http://www.prenhall.com/ormrod to assess your understanding of chapter content with "Multiple-Choice Questions," apply comprehension in "Essay Questions," broaden your knowledge of educational psychology with related "Web Links," gain greater insight about classroom learning in "Learning in the Content Areas," and analyze and assess classroom work in the "Student Artifact Library."

CASE STUDY: More Harm Than Good?

Mr. Gualtieri, a high school mathematics teacher, begins his class one Monday with an important announcement. "I've just obtained some new instructional software programs for the school's computer laboratory. These programs will give you practice in solving mathematical word problems. I strongly encourage you to stay after school once or twice a week to get extra practice on the computer whenever you're having trouble with the homework assignments I give you."

Mr. Gualtieri is firmly convinced that the new instructional software will help his students perform better in mathematics. To test his hypothesis, he keeps a record of which students report to the computer lab after school and which students do not. He then looks at how well the two groups of students perform on his next classroom test. Much to his surprise, he discovers that, on average, the students who have stayed after school to use the computer software have gotten *lower* scores than those who did not stay after school. "How can this be?" he puzzles. "Is the computer software actually doing more harm than good?"

- Is the computer software somehow making mathematics more difficult for students? Or is there another possible explanation for the students' lower scores?
- Which kind of study has Mr. Gualtieri conducted: descriptive, correlational, or experimental?
- Did Mr. Gualtieri make a good or a bad decision in advising his students to use the computer software? Is there any way to answer this question from the information he has obtained?

Once you have answered these questions, compare your responses with those presented in Appendix B.

Key Concepts

educational psychology (p. 1)

elaboration (p. 3)

descriptive study (p. 4)

correlational study (p.4)

correlation (p. 4)

experimental study (experiment) (p. 5)

visual-spatial thinking (p. 6)

treatment group (p. 6)

control group (p. 6)

principle (p. 7)

theory (p. 7)

pedagogical content knowledge (p. 10)

action research (p. 10)

students with special needs (p. 12)

inclusion (p. 12)

2

Cognitive and Linguistic Development

*W*hat differences have you noticed in the nature of instruction at various grade levels? For instance, what things do first-grade teachers, sixth-grade teachers, and high school teachers do differently as they teach classroom subject matter? And how often have you seen teachers take differences among students at any *single* grade level into account? For instance, have you seen teachers tailor their instruction and assignments to students' unique talents and needs?

Such issues are the subject of Part 1 of the book, "Understanding Student Development and Diversity." Chapters 2 and 3 describe how children and adolescents change and develop as they grow older, with an emphasis on cognitive and linguistic development (Chapter 2) and personal, social, and moral development (Chapter 3). Chapters 4 and 5 describe common sources of diversity at any single grade level, looking especially at differences related to intelligence, creativity, ethnic background, gender, and socioeconomic status (Chapter 4) and at characteristics associated with various kinds of disabilities and other exceptionalities (Chapter 5). Once you have finished reading Part 1, you will have learned a wide variety of strategies for adapting instruction to the developmental levels and individual characteristics of the students you are likely to have in your classroom.

As we look at cognitive and linguistic development in this chapter, we will address several questions:

- What general principles characterize human development?
- What principles and theories can guide us in our efforts to adapt instruction to students' cognitive abilities and to promote their further cognitive development?
- How do students' language abilities change with age, and what implications do such changes have for classroom practice?
- How might our students differ from one another in their cognitive and linguistic development, and how can we accommodate such differences?

CASE STUDY: *Economic Activities*

The students in Mr. Sand's advanced high school geography course are struggling with their reading assignments, and they readily share their frustration with their teacher.

"The textbook is really *hard*. I can't understand it at all!" Lucy whines.

"Same here!" Mike shouts out. "I'm really trying, Mr. Sand, but most of the time I have no idea what I'm reading." Many other students nod their heads in agreement.

"Okay," Mr. Sand responds. "Let's see if we can figure out why you might be having trouble. Look at the section called 'Economic Activity' on page 55, which was part of last night's reading."

The class peruses this excerpt from the book:

> Economic activities are those in which human beings engage to acquire food and satisfy other wants. They are the most basic of all activities and are found wherever there are people. Economic activity is divided into four sections. *Primary activity* involves the direct harvesting of the earth's resources. Fishing off the coast of Peru, pumping oil from wells in Libya, extracting iron ore from mines in Minnesota, harvesting trees for lumber in Chile, and growing wheat in China are all examples of primary production. The commodities that result from those activities acquire value from the effort required in production and from consumer demand.

The processing of commodities is classified as a *secondary activity.* In this sector items are increased in value by having their forms changed to enhance their usefulness. Thus, a primary commodity such as cotton might be processed into fabric, and that fabric might be cut and assembled as apparel. Textile manufacturing and apparel manufacturing are both secondary activities.

An economic activity in which a service is performed is classified as a *tertiary activity.* Wholesaling and retailing are tertiary activities by which primary and secondary projects are made available to consumers. Other tertiary activities include governmental, banking, educational, medical, and legal services, as well as journalism and the arts.

The service economy of the technologically most developed countries has become so large and complex that a fourth sector of *quaternary activity* is sometimes included. Institutions and corporations that provide information are in the quaternary sector. (Clawson & Fisher, 1998, p. 55)

"Tell me the kinds of problems you had when you read this passage," Mr. Sand suggests. "Then maybe I can help you understand it better."

The students eagerly describe their difficulties.

"I never heard of some of the words. What's *tertiary* mean? What's *quaternary?*"

"Yeah. And what are *commodities?*"

"There's too much to learn. Do you expect us to memorize *all* of this stuff?"

"Okay, okay, I see your point," Mr. Sand responds. "I guess this stuff can be pretty abstract. No, I don't want you to memorize it all. What's most important is that you get the main idea, which in this case is that different levels of economic activity build on one another. Here, let me show you what I mean. We start out with primary activities, which involve direct use of natural resources." Mr. Sand writes "Primary activity—using natural resources" on the chalkboard. "Who can give me some examples of natural resources we use right here in Pennsylvania?"

"Coal," Sam suggests.

"Milk," Kristen adds.

"And vegetables," Nikki says.

"Excellent examples!" Mr. Sand exclaims. "Now in secondary activities, people change those items into other things that can be used." Mr. Sand writes "Secondary activity—changing natural resources into other products" on the board. "Let's identify some possible examples for this one. . . ."

- Why are the students having trouble reading their textbook? What characteristics of the text seem to be interfering with their understanding?
- What strategies does Mr. Sand use to help the students understand the passage about economic activities?

Basic Principles of Human Development

The college-level textbook Mr. Sand has chosen for his advanced geography class is very difficult for his high school students. As he points out, the book's content is quite abstract—it is almost completely removed from the concrete, everyday world that his students regularly encounter. The book also uses words—*tertiary, quaternary, commodities,* and so on—that are not part of the students' existing vocabularies. Without further information it is difficult to know whether Mr. Sand's choice of textbooks is developmentally appropriate, both cognitively or linguistically, for the students in his class. But Mr. Sand does do a couple of things that probably *are* appropriate for his students' developmental levels. First, he describes what his students need to do as they read and think about chapter content; in particular, he tells them to find the main ideas in what they are reading. Second, he shows them two things they can do to help them as they study: write down key concepts and generate new examples.

As we study various theories of cognitive and linguistic development in the pages ahead, we will gain additional insights about the case. But before we look at specific developmental theories, let's consider several principles that seem to hold true regardless of the aspect of development that we're talking about. Following are four important ones to keep in mind as you read Chapters 2 and 3:

■ *Development proceeds in a somewhat orderly and predictable pattern.* Human development is often characterized by **developmental milestones** that occur in a predictable sequence. For example, children typically learn to walk only after they have already learned to sit up and crawl. They learn the stereotypical behaviors of males and females—for example, that men are more likely to become doctors and women more likely to become nurses—only after they have learned to distinguish between men and women. They begin to think logically about abstract ideas only after they have learned to think logically about concrete objects and observable events. To some extent, then, we see **universals** in development: We see similar patterns in how children change over time regardless of the specific environment in which they are being raised.

■ *Different children develop at different rates.* Descriptive research in child and adolescent development tells us the average ages at which various developmental milestones are reached. For example, the average child can hop several times on one foot at age 3, starts using repetition as a way of learning information at age 7, and begins puberty at age 10 (for girls) or 11½ (for boys) (Berk, 2000; Kail, 1990; G. R. Levin, 1983). But not all children reach developmental milestones at the average age; some reach them earlier, some later.

You can find more information about physical development in the section "Physical Development Across Childhood and Adolescence" in the *Study Guide and Reader.*

Determining the approximate ages at which children can perform certain behaviors and think in certain ways allows us to form general expectations about the capabilities of children at a particular age level and to design our educational curriculum and instructional strategies around these expectations. At the same time, we should never jump to conclusions about what any individual student can and cannot do on the basis of age alone.

■ *Periods of relatively rapid growth (spurts) may appear between periods of slower growth (plateaus).* Development does not always proceed at a constant rate. For example, during the early elementary school years, children gain an average of two or three inches in height per year; during their adolescent growth spurt, they may grow as much as five inches per year (Berk, 2000; A. C. Harris, 1986). Toddlers may speak with a limited vocabulary and one-word "sentences" for several months, yet sometime around their second birthday a virtual explosion in language development occurs, with vocabulary expanding rapidly and sentences becoming longer and longer within just a few weeks.

Descriptive research of child development tells us the *average* age at which various developmental milestones are reached. But we must remember that individual children develop at different rates.

Some theorists use such patterns of uneven growth and change as evidence for distinct, qualitatively different periods in development. In a **stage theory**, development is characterized as progressing through a predictable sequence of stages, with earlier stages providing the foundation for, and so being prerequisite to, later ones. We will encounter stage theories in our discussions of both cognitive and moral development.

■ *Development is continually affected by both nature (heredity) and nurture (environment).* Virtually all aspects of development are affected either directly or indirectly by a child's genetic makeup. Not all inherited characteristics appear at birth; heredity continues to control a child's growth through the process of **maturation**, an unfolding of genetically controlled changes as the child develops. For example, motor skills such as walking, running, and jumping develop primarily as a result of neurological development, increased strength, and increased muscular control—changes that are largely determined by heredity. Furthermore, children are genetically endowed with particular ways of responding to their physical and social environments, and such **temperaments** influence their tendency to be calm or irritable, outgoing or shy, adventuresome or cautious, cheerful or fearful (Kagan, 1998; Rothbart & Bates, 1998).

This question of *nature vs. nurture* continues to be a source of controversy among developmental theorists. In your own opinion, how much are human characteristics influenced by heredity? by environment?

Yet the environment plays an equally critical role in most aspects of development. For example, although children's heights and body builds are primarily inherited characteristics, the nutritional value of the food they eat also makes a difference. Children's experiences with success and failure affect the development of their self-esteem and motivation. And the families and cultures in which children are raised significantly influence the cognitive abilities, moral values, and social skills they acquire.

Heredity and environment typically interact in their effects, such that we may never be able to disentangle the unique influences of nature and nurture on development (Collins, Maccoby, Steinberg, Hetherington, & Bornstein, 2000; Gottlieb, 2000; Turkheimer, 2000). In some situations, heredity predetermines a **sensitive period**, an age range during which a growing child can be especially influenced by environmental conditions. For instance, as we will discover later in the chapter, some theorists have found evidence that children learn a language more easily when they are exposed to it in their early years rather than in adolescence or adulthood. Others speculate about a possible sensitive period in cognitive development, as we shall see now.

Role of the Brain in Cognitive Development

At birth the human brain is equipped to sustain a young infant's life by enabling such behaviors as breathing, sucking, crying, sleeping, and learning simple associations. The brain continues to develop its capabilities throughout childhood and adolescence, and apparently in early adulthood as well (Giedd, Blumenthal, Jeffries, Castellanos, et al., 1999; Giedd, Blumenthal, Jeffries, Rajapakse, 1999; Sowell & Jernigan, 1998; Sowell, Thompson, Holmes, Jernigan, & Toga, 1999). In childhood and the years that follow, much of the brain's development occurs in the **cortex**, a region that lies at the front and top of the brain and controls many advanced cognitive processes that are distinctly human: interpreting, reasoning, planning, decision making, talking, and so on.

The brain does its work primarily through **neurons**, brain cells that specialize in receiving and transmitting information. Most psychologists believe that the interconnections between neurons, or **synapses**, provide the primary means through which people think, learn, and remember (Byrnes & Fox, 1998). In adults a single neuron may form more than a thousand synapses with other neurons, enabling it to communicate and coordinate with many other parts of the brain (R. F. Thompson, 1985).

The great majority of synapses form within the first ten years of life; in fact, people have more synapses at age 10 than at any other time (Bruer, 1997). Synapses that are used frequently remain intact; those that are not used at all eventually disappear (Bruer, 1999). Some well-meaning educators have proposed that the proliferation of synapses in the preschool and elementary years points to a sensitive period in brain development and urge us to maximize children's educational experiences specifically during this time period.

But before you, too, jump to this conclusion, consider this: Although adequate nutrition and everyday forms of stimulation are critical for normal neurological development, there is no evidence that intensive, "enriching" experiences in the early years enhance brain power over the long run (Bruer, 1999; R. A. Thompson & Nelson, 2001). In fact, many psychologists question the relevance of current neurological research for educational practice (R. D. Brown & Bjorklund, 1998; Bruer, 1999; Byrnes & Fox, 1998; Gardner, 2000; Mayer, 1998; Stanovich, 1998). They point out that new synapses continue to develop throughout life as a result of experience and that even adults can learn a great deal in areas they have never previously studied (R. D. Brown & Bjorklund, 1998; Fischer & Rose, 1996; O'Boyle & Gill, 1998). They further point out that, to date, we have no evidence to indicate that sensitive periods exist for traditional academic subjects such as reading, writing, or mathematics (Bruer, 1999; Geary, 1998; Greenough, Black, & Wallace, 1987).

It is imperative that we remain optimistic about the cognitive abilities that students can develop *throughout* the elementary and secondary grade levels (R. D. Brown & Bjorklund, 1998; Bruer, 1999; Byrnes & Fox, 1998). The enriching experiences we provide for our students *will* make a difference in their lives. Yet we should keep in mind that such experiences can bring about change only when students' maturational levels also allow such change to occur. The importance of both environment and maturation has been incorporated into a number of developmental theories. Jean Piaget's theory of cognitive development is a case in point.

Piaget's Theory of Cognitive Development

EXPERIENCING FIRSTHAND   *Beads, Beings, and Basketballs*

Take a moment to solve these three problems:

1. Here are ten wooden beads. Eight are brown and two are white.

   Are there more brown beads or more wooden beads?
2. If all children are human beings,
   And if all human beings are living creatures,
   Then must all children be living creatures?
3. If all children are basketballs,
   And if all basketballs are jellybeans,
   Then must all children be jellybeans?

You undoubtedly found the first problem ridiculously easy; there are, of course, more wooden beads than brown beads. You may have found the second problem a little more difficult but were probably able to conclude fairly quickly that, yes, all children must be living creatures. The third problem is a bit tricky: It follows the same line of reasoning as the second but the conclusion it leads to—all children must be jellybeans—contradicts what is true in reality.

In the early 1920s, the Swiss biologist Jean Piaget began studying children's responses to problems similar to these. He found, for instance, that 4-year-olds often have difficulty with the "beads" problem—they are likely to say that there are more *brown* beads than wooden beads—but that 7-year-olds almost always answer the question correctly. He found, too, that 10-year-olds have an easier time with logic problems that involve real-world phenomena (problems like the "human beings" problem) than with problems that involve hypothetical and contrary-to-fact ideas (problems like the "basketballs" problem); only adolescents can effectively deal with the latter kinds of problems.

Piaget was particularly curious about the origins of knowledge, a branch of philosophy known as *epistemology*. To discover where knowledge comes from and the forms that it takes as it develops, Piaget and his colleagues conducted a series of studies that provide many unique insights about how children think and learn about the world around them (e.g., Inhelder & Piaget, 1958; Piaget, 1928, 1952b, 1959, 1970, 1980). Let's explore basic assumptions underlying Piaget's theory and look at the four stages of logical thinking that he proposed.

Have you encountered Piaget's theory in other courses? What do you already know about his theory?

Piaget's Basic Assumptions

Piaget introduced a number of ideas and concepts to describe and explain the changes in logical thinking that he observed in children and adolescents:

■ *Children are active and motivated learners.* Piaget believed that children are not just passive receivers of environmental stimulation; instead, they are naturally curious about their world and actively seek out information to help them understand and make sense of it. They continually experiment with the objects they encounter, manipulating things and observing the effects of their actions. For example, when my son Alex was a child, he was always fiddling with and manipulating *something.* Some of his "experiments"—such as setting up and maintaining a terrarium in which two lizards could survive and grow—made his mother proud. Others—such as sitting on a kitchen barstool and seeing how far he could lean back on two legs without falling over—drove me absolutely crazy.

■ *Children construct knowledge from their experiences.* Children's knowledge is not limited to a collection of isolated pieces of information. Instead, children use the information they accumulate to construct an overall view of how the world operates. For example, through his experiences with lizards and a terrarium, Alex developed an understanding of how aspects of the environment such as food, water, and climate interact to sustain life. Through his experiences on the kitchen barstool, he learned a basic principle of physics: the law of gravity. Because Piaget proposed that children construct their own body of knowledge from their experiences, his theory is sometimes called a **constructivist** theory.

In Piaget's terminology the things that children learn and can do are organized as **schemes**—groups of similar thoughts or actions. To illustrate, an infant may have a scheme for putting things in her mouth; she calls on this scheme when dealing with a variety of objects, including her thumb, her toys, and her blanket. A 7-year-old may have a scheme for identifying snakes that includes their long, thin bodies, their lack of legs, and their slithery nature. A 13-year-old may have a scheme for what constitutes *fashion,* allowing her to classify her peers as being either "totally awesome" or "complete dorks."

Over time, children's schemes are modified with experience and become increasingly better integrated with one another. For instance, children begin to recognize the hierarchical interrelationships of some schemes: They learn that poodles and cocker spaniels are both dogs, that dogs and cats are both animals, and so on. Children's progressively more organized body of knowledge and thought processes allows them to think in increasingly sophisticated and logical ways.

■ *Children learn through the two complementary processes of assimilation and accommodation.* Although children's schemes change over time, the processes by which children develop them remain the same. Piaget proposed that learning and cognitive development occur as the result of two complementary processes: assimilation and accommodation. **Assimilation** is a process of dealing with an object or event in a way that is consistent with an existing scheme. For example, the infant may assimilate a new teddy bear into her putting-things-in-the-mouth scheme. The 7-year-old may quickly identify a new slithery object in the backyard as another snake. The 13-year-old may readily label a new classmate as being either awesome or dorkish.

But sometimes children cannot easily relate to a new object or event with their existing schemes. In these situations, one of two forms of **accommodation** will occur: They will either modify an existing scheme to account for the new object or event or form an entirely new scheme to deal with it. For example, the infant may have to open her mouth wider than usual to accommodate a teddy bear's fat paw. The 13-year-old may have to revise her existing scheme of fashion according to changes in what's hot and what's not. The 7-year-old may find a long, thin, slithery thing that can't possibly be a snake because it has four legs. After some research, the child develops a new scheme—*salamander*—for this creature.

Assimilation and accommodation typically work hand in hand as children develop their knowledge and understanding of the world. Children interpret each new event within the context of their existing knowledge (assimilation) but at the same time may modify their knowledge as a result of the new event (accommodation). Accommodation rarely happens without assimilation: Our students can benefit from (accommodate to) new experiences only when they can relate those experiences to their current knowledge and beliefs.

■ *Interaction with one's physical and social environments is essential for cognitive development.* New experiences are essential for learning and cognitive development to occur. For this reason, Piaget stressed the importance of allowing children to interact with their physical environment. By manipulating the environment—for example, by playing with sand and water, measuring things, practicing with footballs and basketballs, or experimenting in a science lab—children can develop an understanding of cause-effect relationships, the nature of physical characteristics such as weight and volume, and so on.

Social interaction is equally critical for cognitive development. Through interaction with other people, children begin to realize that different individuals see things differently and that their own view of the world is not necessarily a completely accurate or logical one. To illustrate, a preschool child may have difficulty seeing the world from anyone's perspective but his own. Through social interactions, both pleasant (e.g., a conversation) and unpleasant (e.g., an argument), he begins to realize that his own perspective is a unique one not shared by others. Similarly, an elementary school child may recognize the logical inconsistencies in what she says and does only after someone else points them out. And through discussions with classmates or adults about social and political issues, a high school student may modify some initially abstract and idealistic notions about how the world *should* be to reflect the constraints that the real world imposes.

■ *The process of equilibration promotes progression toward more complex levels of thought.* According to Piaget, when children can comfortably explain new events with existing schemes, they are in a state of **equilibrium**. But this equilibrium doesn't continue indefinitely. As chil-

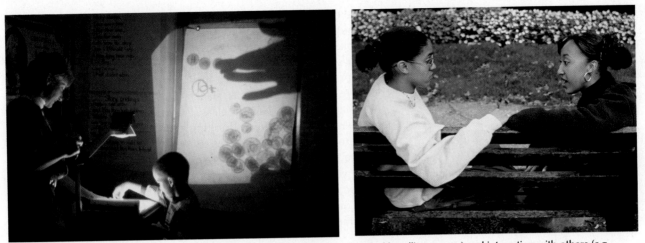

From Piaget's perspective, both interaction with concrete objects (e.g., counting and handling money) and interaction with others (e.g., sharing perspectives about a topic or problem) are essential for cognitive development.

dren grow, they often encounter events they cannot adequately explain given their current understanding of the world. Such inexplicable events create **disequilibrium**, a sort of mental discomfort. Only through replacing, reorganizing, or better integrating their schemes (in other words, through accommodation) do children become able to understand and explain those previously puzzling events. The movement from equilibrium to disequilibrium and back to equilibrium again is a process known as **equilibration**. Equilibration and children's need to achieve equilibrium promote the development of more complex levels of thought and knowledge.

To illustrate equilibration, let's return to the "beads" problem I gave you earlier. Imagine that we show the ten wooden beads (eight brown and two white) to 4-year-old Abby and ask her, "Are there more brown beads or more wooden beads?" Abby tells us that there are more brown beads and seems quite comfortable with this response; in other words, she is in equilibrium. Apparently Abby is having trouble thinking of the brown beads as belonging to two categories (*brown* and *wooden*) at the same time and so is actually comparing the brown beads to the beads left over (the white ones). So we ask her to count the brown beads (she counts eight of them) and then to count the wooden beads (she counts ten). "So then, Abby," we say, "there are *eight* brown beads and *ten* wooden beads. Are there more brown beads or more wooden beads?" If Abby can recognize the inconsistency in her reasoning—that eight cannot possibly be more than ten—she will experience disequilibrium. At this point, she may reorganize her thinking to accommodate the idea that some beads are both brown and wooden and so should be simultaneously included in both categories.

■ *Cognitive development can proceed only after certain genetically controlled neurological changes occur.* Piaget speculated that cognitive development depends to some degree on maturation of the brain. Piaget believed that because of their neurological immaturity, elementary school children cannot think as adults do, no matter what parents or teachers might do to encourage adultlike thinking. Preschoolers are even less neurologically mature and so are further limited in their cognitive abilities. Piaget hypothesized that major physiological changes take place when children are about 2 years old, again when they are 6 or 7, and again around puberty, and that these changes allow the development of increasingly complex thought. We should note that psychologists disagree about whether neurological advancements are truly responsible for the developmental changes that Piaget described (H. Epstein, 1978; R. W. Marsh, 1985; Rosser, 1994).

Piaget's Stages of Cognitive Development

A major feature of Piaget's theory is his description of four stages of logical reasoning capabilities:

1. Sensorimotor stage (birth until 2 years)
2. Preoperational stage (2 years until 6 or 7 years)
3. Concrete operations stage (6 or 7 years until 11 or 12 years)
4. Formal operations stage (11 or 12 years through adulthood)

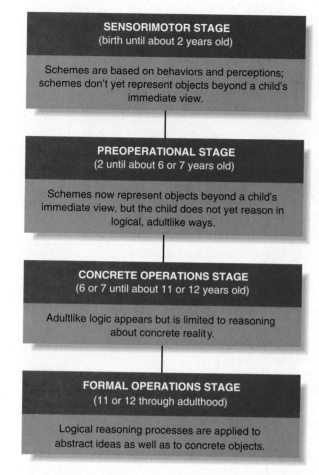

SENSORIMOTOR STAGE
(birth until about 2 years old)

Schemes are based on behaviors and perceptions; schemes don't yet represent objects beyond a child's immediate view.

PREOPERATIONAL STAGE
(2 until about 6 or 7 years old)

Schemes now represent objects beyond a child's immediate view, but the child does not yet reason in logical, adultlike ways.

CONCRETE OPERATIONS STAGE
(6 or 7 until about 11 or 12 years old)

Adultlike logic appears but is limited to reasoning about concrete reality.

FORMAL OPERATIONS STAGE
(11 or 12 through adulthood)

Logical reasoning processes are applied to abstract ideas as well as to concrete objects.

FIGURE 2.1 Piaget's stages of cognitive development

These stages are briefly summarized in Figure 2.1. Each stage has its own unique characteristics and capabilities, and each builds upon the accomplishments of former stages, so children must progress through the four stages in the same, invariant sequence.

For reasons described later, many psychologists question whether cognitive development is as stagelike as Piaget proposed (Flavell, 1994; Siegler, 1998). Nevertheless, Piaget's stages do provide insights into the nature of children's thinking at different age levels, and so it is helpful to examine the characteristics of each stage. Note that the ages given for each stage are *averages;* some children may reach a stage at a slightly younger age than average, and others may reach it at an older age. Also, some children may be *transitional* from one stage to the next and so may display characteristics of two adjacent stages during the same time period.

Sensorimotor Stage (birth until 2 years)

Imagine that we show a colorful stuffed clown to 6-month-old Karen. Karen reaches for it in much the same way that she reaches for her teddy bear and her stacking blocks; in other words, she has a reaching-and-grasping scheme into which she assimilates this new object. Karen then drops the clown and watches it fall to the floor, applying her letting-go and visually-following-a-moving-object schemes in the process. Now imagine that we put Karen's clown inside a box so that she can no longer see it. Karen seems to forget the clown and turns to play with something else, acting as if she cannot think about a clown she cannot actually see.

Piaget proposed that children in the **sensorimotor stage** develop schemes based primarily on behaviors and perceptions. They are not yet capable of *mental* schemes that enable them to think about objects beyond their immediate view, partly because they have few if any words they can use to mentally represent the things they cannot see.

Nevertheless, important cognitive capabilities emerge during the sensorimotor stage, especially as children begin to experiment with their environments through trial and error. For example, during the latter part of the stage, children develop **object permanence**, the realization that objects continue to exist even when they are removed from view. After repeatedly observing that certain actions lead to certain consequences, they also begin to develop an understanding of *cause-effect relationships*. Object permanence, cause and effect, and other ideas that develop during the sensorimotor stage are basic building blocks on which later cognitive development depends.

Preoperational Stage (2 years until 6 or 7 years)

Children in the **preoperational stage** can form schemes that are relatively independent of immediate perceptions and behaviors. For example, as Karen reaches this stage, she will be able to think about a clown without having one directly in front of her. This ability to represent external objects and events in one's mind (**symbolic thinking**) marks the beginning of true thought as Piaget defined it.

Language skills virtually explode during the early part of the preoperational stage. Children's rapidly increasing vocabularies provide labels for newly developed schemes and enable children to think about objects and events even when such things are not directly in sight. Language also provides the basis for a new form of social interaction—verbal communication. Children can now express their thoughts and receive information from other people in a way that previously was not possible.

At the same time, preoperational thinking has some definite limitations, especially as we compare it with concrete operational thinking (see Table 2.1). For example, children in this stage exhibit **preoperational egocentrism**, an inability to view situations from another person's perspective. They may have trouble understanding why they must share school supplies with a classmate or why they must be careful not to hurt someone else's feelings. They may play games together without ever checking to be sure they are all playing by the same rules.

TABLE 2.1   COMPARE/CONTRAST

Preoperational Versus Concrete Operational Thought

PREOPERATIONAL THOUGHT	CONCRETE OPERATIONAL THOUGHT
Preoperational Egocentrism Students do not see things from someone else's perspective; they think their own perspective is the only one possible. *Example:* A student tells a story without considering what prior knowledge the listener is likely to have.	**Differentiation of One's Own Perspective from the Perspectives of Others** Students recognize that others see things differently than they do; they realize that their own perspective may be incorrect. *Example:* A student asks for validation of his own thoughts (e.g., "Did I get that right?").
Lack of Conservation Students believe that amount (e.g., number, mass) changes when a substance is reshaped or rearranged, even though nothing has been added or taken away. *Example:* A student asserts that two rows of five pennies similarly spaced have equal amounts; but when one row is spread out so that it is longer than the other, she says that it has more pennies.	**Conservation** Students recognize that amount stays the same if nothing has been added or taken away, even if the substance is reshaped or rearranged. *Example:* A student asserts that two rows of five pennies have the same number of pennies regardless of their spacing.
Irreversibility Students don't recognize that certain processes can be undone, or reversed. *Example:* A student doesn't realize that a row of five pennies made longer can be shortened back to its original length; the student also treats addition and subtraction as two unrelated processes (e.g., Baroody, 1999).	**Reversibility** Students understand that certain processes can be reversed. *Example:* A student moves the five pennies in the longer row close together again to demonstrate that both rows have the same amount; she also recognizes that subtraction is the reverse of addition.
Inability to Reason About Transformations Students focus on static situations; they have difficulty thinking about change processes. *Example:* A student refuses to believe that a caterpillar can turn into a butterfly, instead insisting that the caterpillar crawls away and the butterfly comes to replace it (K. R. Harris, 1986).	**Ability to Reason About Transformations** Students can reason about change and its effects. *Example:* A student understands that a caterpillar becomes a butterfly through the process of metamorphosis.
Single Classification Students are able to classify objects in only one way at any given time. *Example:* A student denies that a mother can also be a doctor.	**Multiple Classification** Students recognize that objects may belong to several categories simultaneously. *Example:* A student acknowledges that a mother can also be a doctor, a spouse, and an artist.
Transductive Reasoning Students reason by combining unrelated facts; for instance, they infer a cause-effect relationship simply because two events occur close together in time and space. *Example:* A student believes that clouds make the moon grow (Piaget, 1928).	**Deductive Reasoning** Students can draw a logical inference from two or more pieces of information. *Example:* A student deduces that if all children are human beings and if all human beings are living things, then all children must be living things.

Children may also exhibit egocentrism through **egocentric speech**, saying things without really considering the perspective of the listener; for example, they may leave out critical details of a story, giving a fragmented version their listener cannot possibly understand.

Preoperational thinking is also illogical (at least from an adult's point of view), especially during the preschool years. You may recall 4-year-old Abby's insistence that there were more brown beads than wooden beads in a collection of ten wooden beads; this inability to think of objects as belonging to two categories simultaneously (e.g., recognizing that beads can be both brown and wooden at the same time) is known as **single classification**. Children in the preoperational stage may also exhibit **transductive reasoning**, drawing erroneous causal inferences about two events that occur close together in time and space; for example, a 6-year-old might say that it is cold in winter "because there is snow" (Piaget, 1929, p. 323). And consider the following situation:

We show 5-year-old Nathan the three glasses in Figure 2.2. Glasses A and B are identical in size and shape and contain an equal amount of water. We ask Nathan whether the

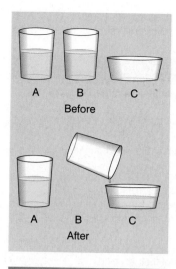

FIGURE 2.2 Conservation of liquid: Do Glasses A and C contain the same amount of water?

two glasses of water contain the same amount, and he replies confidently that they do. We then pour the water from Glass B into Glass C. We ask him whether the two glasses of water (A and C) have the same amount. Nathan replies, "No, that glass [pointing to Glass A] has more because it's taller."

Nathan's response illustrates lack of **conservation:** He does not realize that because no water has been added or taken away, the amount of water in the two glasses must be equivalent. Young children such as Nathan often confuse changes in appearance with changes in amount.

As children approach the later part of the preoperational stage, perhaps at around 4 or 5 years of age, they show early signs of being logical. For example, they sometimes draw correct conclusions about conservation problems (e.g., the water glasses problem) or about problems that require simultaneously classifying objects in two ways (e.g., the wooden beads problem). They cannot yet explain *why* their conclusions are correct, however; they base their conclusions on hunches and intuition rather than on any conscious awareness of underlying logical principles. When children move into the concrete operations stage, they become increasingly able both to make logical inferences and to explain the reasoning behind their conclusions.

Concrete Operations Stage (6 or 7 years until 11 or 12 years)

Piaget proposed that children's thought processes gradually become organized and integrated with one another into larger systems of mental processes. These systems, which he called **operations,** allow children to pull their thoughts together in ways that make sense and, therefore, to think more logically. Such integrated and coordinated thought emerges at the beginning of the **concrete operations stage.**

Concrete operational thought differs from preoperational thought in a number of ways (see Table 2.1). Children now realize that their own thoughts and feelings are not necessarily shared by others and may reflect personal opinions rather than reality. As a result, they know that they can sometimes be wrong and begin to seek out external validation for their ideas. They also show conservation: They readily understand that amount stays the same, despite changes in shape or arrangement, if nothing is added or taken away. In addition, they are capable of **multiple classification:** They can readily classify objects into two categories simultaneously. And they demonstrate **deductive reasoning:** They can draw logical inferences from the facts they are given.

Children continue to develop their newly acquired logical thinking capabilities during the elementary school years. For instance, they become capable of dealing with increasingly complex conservation tasks. Some forms of conservation, such as conservation of liquid and conservation of number (illustrated by the "pennies" problem in Table 2.1), appear at 6 or 7 years of age, but other forms may not appear until several years later. Consider the task involving conservation of weight in Figure 2.3. Using a balance scale, an adult shows a child that two balls of clay have the same weight. One ball is removed from the scale and smashed into a pancake shape. Does the pancake weigh the same as the unsmashed ball, or do the two pieces of clay weigh different amounts? Children typically do not achieve conservation of weight—that is, they do not realize that the flattened pancake weighs the same as the round ball it was earlier—until sometime between age 9 and 12 (Sund, 1976).

FIGURE 2.3 Conservation of weight: Ball A and Ball B initially weigh the same amount. When Ball B is flattened into a pancake shape, how does its weight now compare with that of Ball A?

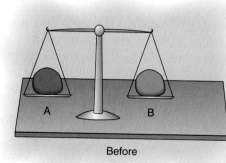

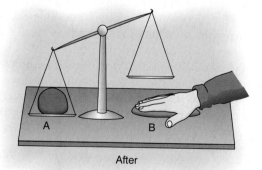

Concrete Operational Versus Formal Operational Thought

CONCRETE OPERATIONAL THOUGHT	FORMAL OPERATIONAL THOUGHT
Dependence on Concrete Reality Students can reason logically about concrete objects they can observe; they are unable to reason about abstract, hypothetical, or contrary-to-fact ideas. *Example:* A student has difficulty with the concept of negative numbers, wondering how something can possibly be less than zero.	**Ability to Reason About Abstract, Hypothetical, and Contrary-to-Fact Ideas** Students can reason about things that are not tied directly to concrete, observable reality. *Example:* A student understands negative numbers and is able to use them effectively in mathematical procedures.
Inability to Formulate and Test Multiple Hypotheses When seeking an explanation for a scientific phenomenon, students identify and test only one hypothesis. *Example:* When asked what makes a pendulum swing faster or more slowly, a student says that the weight of the pendulum is the determining factor.	**Formulation and Testing of Multiple Hypotheses** Students seeking an explanation for a scientific phenomenon formulate and test several hypotheses about possible cause-effect relationships. *Example:* When asked what makes a pendulum swing faster or more slowly, a student says that weight, length, and strength of the initial push are all possible explanations.
Inability to Separate and Control Variables When attempting to confirm or disconfirm a particular hypothesis about cause-effect relationships, students test (and thereby confound) more than one variable simultaneously. *Example:* In testing possible factors influencing the oscillation rate of a pendulum, a student adds more weight to the pendulum while at the same time also shortening the length of the pendulum.	**Separation and Control of Variables** When attempting to confirm or disconfirm a particular hypothesis, students test one variable at a time while holding all other variables constant. *Example:* In testing factors that influence a pendulum's oscillation rate, a student tests the effect of weight while keeping length and strength of push constant; the student then tests the effect of length while keeping weight and push constant.
Lack of Proportional Reasoning Students do not understand the nature of proportions. *Example:* A student does not understand the relationship between fractions and decimals.	**Proportional Reasoning** Students understand proportions and can use them effectively in mathematical problem solving. *Example:* A student works easily with proportions, fractions, decimals, and ratios.

Although students displaying concrete operational thought show many signs of logical thinking, their cognitive development is not yet complete (see Table 2.2). For instance, they have trouble understanding and reasoning about abstract and contrary-to-fact ideas, and they have difficulty handling problems that require them to consider many hypotheses or variables simultaneously. Such capabilities emerge in the final stage, formal operations.

Formal Operations Stage (11 or 12 years through adulthood)

Consider the following situation:

Julie and Joséfa are working together on an assignment on World War II for their high school history class. Julie is puzzled as she reads the assignment: *Given what you know about the strengths and weaknesses of the Allied forces and the Axis countries in 1941, how might the war have ended if the Japanese had not bombed Pearl Harbor?*

"I don't get it," Julie says.

"What don't you get?" Joséfa asks her.

"I don't understand what we're supposed to do."

"Well, we're supposed to speculate on what would have happened if Pearl Harbor hadn't been bombed. For example, maybe the United States wouldn't have joined the Allied forces. Maybe the Axis powers would have won the war. Maybe all of Europe would be Fascist right now."

Julie just shakes her head. "I still don't understand this assignment. After all, the Japanese did bomb Pearl Harbor. And because of that action, the United States joined the Allied forces. How can we pretend these things didn't happen?"

In adolescence, students become increasingly able to envision—and reason logically about—alternatives to reality. As an example, 12-year-old friends Zach and Fred have written a series of comic books featuring "nose" people as the main characters. Here, two pages from one of Zach's books depict an army of "noses" (led by Napoleon Nose), a time warp trap, and villain Dark Fang's evil new weapon.

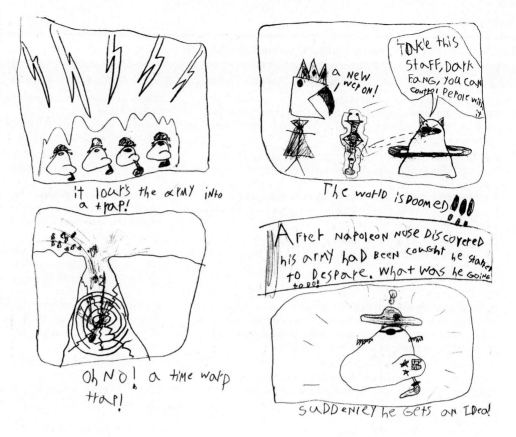

Julie's thinking is concrete operational: She is unable to speculate about what might have happened if the Japanese had not bombed Pearl Harbor, when in fact the Japanese *did* bomb Pearl Harbor. Yet Joséfa has no difficulty with the same task. Like Joséfa, students who show evidence of the **formal operations stage** can think about concepts that have little or no basis in concrete reality—concepts that are abstract, hypothetical, or contrary-to-fact. Furthermore, they recognize that what is logically valid is different from what is true in the real world; for example, if all children are basketballs, and if all basketballs are jellybeans, then all children must be jellybeans, even though, in the real world, children *aren't* jellybeans. Several abilities essential for sophisticated scientific and mathematical reasoning—formulating and testing multiple hypotheses, separating and controlling variables, and proportional reasoning—also emerge in the formal operations stage (see Table 2.2).

Let's consider how, from Piaget's perspective, students' capabilities in mathematics are likely to improve once formal operational thinking develops. Abstract problems, such as mathematical word problems, should become easier to solve. Students should become capable of understanding such concepts as *negative number, pi* (π), and *infinity;* for instance, they should now comprehend how temperature can be below zero and how two parallel lines will never touch even if they go on forever. And because they can now use proportions in their reasoning, they can study and understand fractions, ratios, and decimals, and they can use such proportions to solve problems.

Try the following exercise as an illustration of proportional reasoning.

EXPERIENCING FIRSTHAND   *Thinking About Proportions*

Mr. Little and Mr. Big are two men from the planet Xeron. People on Xeron don't use centimeters or inches to measure things; instead, they use a unit of measurement called a "greenie." Mr. Little is 4 greenies tall. Mr. Big is 7 greenies tall.

One day the two men travel to the planet Phylus. Phylus has a different unit of measurement—the "reddie." Mr. Little is 10 reddies tall. Figure out how tall Mr. Big is in reddies. (adapted from Ormrod & Carter, 1985).

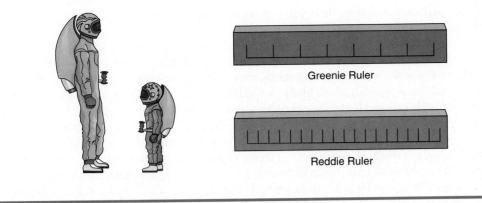

Greenie Ruler

Reddie Ruler

The proportions of the two men's heights in greenies and in reddies should be the same. If we think of Mr. Big's height as *x*, then:

$$\frac{4 \text{ greenies (Mr. Little)}}{7 \text{ greenies (Mr. Big)}} = \frac{10 \text{ reddies (Mr. Little)}}{x \text{ reddies (Mr. Big)}}$$

Solving for *x*, we find that Mr. Big is 17½ reddies tall. Six-year-olds can understand such simple fractions as ½, ⅓, and ¼ if they can relate these proportions to their everyday experiences (Empson, 1999). But complex proportional reasoning typically does not appear until students are 11 or 12 at the earliest (Schliemann & Carraher, 1993; Tourniaire & Pulos, 1985).

Scientific reasoning is also likely to improve once students are capable of formal operational thought. Three formal operational abilities—reasoning logically about hypothetical ideas, formulating and testing hypotheses, and separating and controlling variables—together allow formal operations individuals to use a *scientific method,* in which several possible explanations for an observed phenomenon are proposed and tested in a systematic manner. As an example, consider the pendulum problem in the exercise that follows.

EXPERIENCING FIRSTHAND *Pendulum Problem*

In the absence of other forces, an object suspended by a rope or string—a pendulum—swings at a constant rate (a playground swing and the pendulum of a grandfather clock are two everyday examples). Some pendulums swing back and forth rather slowly, whereas others swing more quickly. What characteristics of a pendulum determine how fast it swings? Write down at least three hypotheses as to what variable or variables might affect a pendulum's rate of swing (i.e., its oscillation rate).

Now gather several small, heavy objects (an eraser, a bolt, and a fishing sinker are three possibilities) and a piece of string. Tie one of the objects to one end of the string and set your pendulum in motion. Conduct one or more experiments to test each of your hypotheses.

What can you conclude? What variable or variables affect the rate with which a pendulum swings?

See "The Pendulum Experiment" in *Simulations in Educational Psychology and Research.*

What hypotheses did you generate? Four possible variables you might have considered are the weight of the object, the length of the string, the force with which the pendulum is pushed, and the height from which the object is released; you may have formed additional hypotheses as well.

Did you then test each hypothesis in a systematic fashion? A student capable of formal operational thinking *separates and controls variables,* testing one at a time while holding all others constant. For example, if you were testing the hypothesis that weight makes a difference, you might have tried objects of different weights while keeping constant the length of the string, the force with which you pushed each object (if you pushed it at all), and the height from which you released or pushed it. Similarly, if you hypothesized that the length of the string was a critical factor, you might have varied the length while continuing to use the same object and starting the pendulum in motion in the same manner. If you carefully separated

Recall our earlier discussion of the importance of separating and controlling variables in experimental research (Chapter 1).

and controlled each variable, then you would have come to the correct conclusion: Only length affects a pendulum's oscillation rate.

Because students capable of formal operational reasoning can deal with hypothetical and contrary-to-fact ideas, they can envision how the world might be different from—and possibly better than—the way it actually is. As a result, they may exhibit some idealism about social, political, ethical, or religious issues. Many secondary school students begin to show concern about world problems and to devote energy to worthy causes such as the environment or world hunger. Their devotion may be evident more in their talk than in their actions, however (Elkind, 1984), and they may offer recommendations for change that seem logical but aren't practical in today's world. For example, a teenager might argue that racism would disappear overnight if people would just begin to love one another, or suggest that a nation should eliminate its armed forces and weaponry as a way of moving toward world peace. Piaget proposed that adolescent idealism reflects **formal operational egocentrism**, an inability to separate one's own logical abstractions from the perspectives of others and from practical considerations. Only through experience do adolescents eventually begin to temper their optimism with some realism about what is possible in a given time frame and with limited resources.

> In your own words, can you summarize the characteristics of each of Piaget's four stages?

Current Perspectives on Piaget's Theory

Piaget's theory has sparked a great deal of research about children's cognitive development. In general, this research supports Piaget's proposed *sequence* in which different abilities emerge (Flavell, 1996; Siegler & Richards, 1982). For example, the ability to reason about abstract ideas emerges only after children are already capable of reasoning about concrete objects and events. The order in which various conservation tasks are mastered is much as Piaget described, too. Researchers are now questioning the *ages* at which various abilities actually appear, however. They are also finding that students' logical reasoning capabilities may vary considerably depending on their previous knowledge and experiences related to the topic at hand.

Capabilities of Infants and Preschool Children

Infants and preschoolers are apparently more competent than Piaget's descriptions of the sensorimotor and preoperational stages suggest. For instance, infants show preliminary signs of object permanence as early as 4 months of age (Baillargeon, 1987, 1993). And 3- and 4-year-olds are less egocentric than Piaget would have us believe. In many situations, preschoolers *can* take another individual's point of view; for example, if we ask them to show us their artwork, they hold it so that we (rather than they) can see it, and they can often identify such emotions as sadness or anger in other people (Lennon, Eisenberg, & Carroll, 1983; Newcombe & Huttenlocher, 1992; Siegler, 1998). Preschoolers can also draw logical deductions; for example, they frequently make inferences when they listen to stories (Donaldson, 1978; Gelman & Baillargeon, 1983). Children as young as 4 sometimes show conservation; for example, they are more likely to answer a conservation problem correctly if the transformation occurs out of sight so that they are not misled by appearances (Donaldson, 1978; Rosser, 1994; Siegel & Hodkin, 1982). Furthermore, many supposedly preoperational children can correctly solve multiple classification problems if words are used to draw attention to the entire group; for example, many 4- and 5-year-olds realize that in a *forest* of eight pine trees and two oak trees, there must of course be more trees than pine trees (Gelman & Baillargeon, 1983; L. B. Resnick, 1989; Rosser, 1994).

Erin Poetry Class 5th Grade

Dear God, Help Us

The black of war
Darkens the day,
There is no point;
I say.
Why do all these poor men die
Fighting those
Who could be friends.
Gun shots sound through the air
Only to bring sadness and despair.
Why do leaders sit around,
While innocent men
Fall to the ground.
When the grass is painted red,
you know
Some man has lost his head.
When you're in a war
you're guaranteed to come out sore.
While you are lying in pain,
slowly,
You'll become insane
The men you kill shouldn't die,
Their soul's shouldn't float in the sky.
As a solider gasps
One more time,
He should know
His honor is
Divine.

As students become increasingly able to reason about abstract, hypothetical, and contrary-to-fact ideas, they also become increasingly idealistic about how the world should be. Here 11-year-old Erin laments the pointlessness of war.

Capabilities of Elementary School Children

Piaget may also have underestimated the capabilities of elementary school students. For example, many elementary students occasionally show evidence of abstract and hypothetical thought (S. Carey, 1985; Metz, 1995). Consider this hypothetical (and therefore formal operational) situation:

All of Joan's friends are going to the museum today.

Pat is a friend of Joan.

Children as young as 9 can correctly deduce that "Pat is going to the museum today" even though the situation involves people they don't know and so has no basis in their own concrete reality (Roberge, 1970). Also, some older elementary school children are able to separate and control variables, especially when they are given hints about the importance of controlling all variables except the one they are testing (Danner & Day, 1977; Metz, 1995).

Capabilities of Adolescents

Consider again our opening case study in which Mr. Sand's high school geography students had trouble understanding an abstract college textbook. For most students, formal operational thought processes probably appear later and more gradually than Piaget originally proposed. High school and college students often have difficulty with tasks involving formal operational thinking (Byrnes, 1988; Karplus, Pulos, & Stage, 1983; Kuhn, Garcia-Mila, Zohar, & Andersen, 1995; Pascarella & Terenzini, 1991). Furthermore, students may demonstrate formal operational thought in one content domain while thinking more concretely in another. Evidence of formal operations typically emerges in the physical sciences earlier than in such subjects as history and geography; students often have difficulty thinking about abstract and hypothetical ideas in history and geography until well into the high school years (Lovell, 1979; Tamburrini, 1982).

Contemporary researchers have found that Piaget probably underestimated the capabilities of children in the elementary grades; for instance, elementary school children sometimes exhibit abstract thinking. Nevertheless, concrete experiences—such as observing chicks hatching in an incubator—provide the foundation of knowledge from which abstract ideas will eventually emerge.

Effects of Prior Knowledge and Experience

It is becoming increasingly apparent that the ability to think logically about a situation or topic depends greatly on a student's knowledge and background experiences. Preschoolers are less likely to exhibit transductive reasoning when they have accurate information about cause-effect relationships (S. Carey, 1985). Four-year-olds begin to show conservation after having experience with conservation tasks, especially if they can actively manipulate the task materials and discuss their reasoning with someone who already exhibits conservation (Field, 1987; Mayer, 1992; F. B. Murray, 1978). Nine- to 11-year-olds become increasingly able to separate and control variables when they have numerous experiences that require them to do so (Schauble, 1990). Ten-year-olds can learn to solve logical problems involving hypothetical ideas if they are taught relevant problem-solving strategies (S. Lee, 1985). Junior high and high school students, and adults as well, often apply formal operational thought to topics about which they have a great deal of knowledge and yet think concretely about topics with which they are unfamiliar (Girotto & Light, 1993; M. C. Linn, Clement, Pulos, & Sullivan, 1989; Schliemann & Carraher, 1993).

As an illustration of how knowledge affects formal operational thinking, consider the fishing pond in Figure 2.4. In a study by Pulos and Linn (1981), 13-year-old students were shown a similar picture and told, "These four children go fishing every week, and one child, Herb, always catches the most fish. The other children wonder why." If you look at the picture, it is obvious that Herb differs from the other children in several ways, including the kind of bait he uses, the length of his fishing rod, and his position by the pond. Students who were avid fishermen more effectively separated and controlled variables for this situation than they did for the pendulum problem described earlier, whereas the reverse was true for nonfishermen (Pulos & Linn, 1981).

Piaget Reconsidered

Can cognitive development truly be characterized as a series of stages? Some contemporary theorists have proposed stage theories that may more adequately account for current findings about children's logical thinking (e.g., Case & Okamoto, 1996; Fischer & Bidell, 1991). But many others now believe that cognitive development can better be described in terms of gradual *trends* rather than specific, discrete stages; they also believe that the nature of cognitive development may be somewhat specific to different contexts and content areas (Flavell, 1994;

FIGURE 2.4 What are some possible reasons that Herb is catching more fish than the others?
Based on Pulos & Linn, 1981.

Rosser, 1994; Siegler, 1998). Later in the chapter, when we consider information processing theory, we will identify several general developmental trends in children's ability to think and learn in the classroom.

Yet many of Piaget's basic assumptions—for instance, his beliefs that children construct their own understandings of the world, that they must relate new experiences to what they already know, and that they can most effectively learn when they interact with their physical and social environments—are ideas that have stood the test of time. And the many tasks that Piaget developed to study children's reasoning abilities (tasks dealing with conservation, classification, separation and control of variables, etc.) can give us valuable insights about the "logic" our students use when they think about their world. As a simple example, try the following exercise.

INTERPRETING ARTIFACTS AND INTERACTIONS *Poppies and Bluebells*

A 5-year-old girl in Piaget's laboratory (we'll call her Eva) is shown a drawing of a field that has 20 poppies and 3 bluebells. When an adult probes her reasoning about the flowers, the following conversation ensues. As you read the conversation, consider the following:

- The kind of reasoning that Eva exhibits
- The Piagetian stage with which such reasoning is associated
- The strategies the adult uses to assess Eva's reasoning and understanding

Adult:	Look, are there a lot of flowers or a few in this field?
Eva:	A lot.
Adult:	What colour are they?
Eva:	They're red and blue.
Adult:	The red ones are poppies and the blue ones are bluebells.
Eva:	Yes.
Adult:	I want to make a very big bunch. Must I pick the flowers or the poppies?
Eva:	The poppies.
Adult:	Show me the poppies.

[Eva points to the poppies.]

| Adult: | Show me the flowers. |

[Eva makes a circular motion to indicate the entire picture.]

| Adult: | Then will the bunch be bigger if I pick the flowers or the poppies? |

Eva:	If you pick the poppies.
Adult:	If I pick the poppies, what will be left?
Eva:	The bluebells.
Adult:	And if I pick the bluebells, what will be left?
Eva:	The poppies.
Adult:	And if I pick the flowers, what will be left?
Eva:	(Reflection.) Nothing at all.
Adult:	Then which will be bigger, the bunch of flowers or the bunch of poppies?
Eva:	I've told you already.
Adult:	Think.

[Adult repeats the question, "Will the bunch be bigger if I pick the flowers or the poppies?"]

Eva:	The bunch of poppies will be bigger.
Adult:	And what about the bunch of flowers?
Eva:	It won't be the same.
Adult:	Will it be bigger or smaller?
Eva:	Smaller.
Adult:	Why?
Eva:	Because you've made a big bunch of poppies. (dialogue from Piaget, 1952a, p. 167; format adapted)

In concluding that the bunch of poppies would be bigger than the bunch of flowers, Eva is showing reasoning similar to Abby's reasoning about the brown and white wooden beads: Although Eva knows the poppies are flowers, she seems unable to consider them as members of both the *poppy* and *flower* categories simultaneously when she makes the comparison. Hence, she is exhibiting single classification, a characteristic of Piaget's preoperational stage. Notice how the adult checks to be sure Eva knows which flowers are poppies and which are bluebells, and also that Eva knows that "picking the flowers" means none will be left in the field. Such follow-up questioning increases our confidence that Eva's conclusion reflects an error in her reasoning, not a misinterpretation of what the adult has asked her to do.

INTO THE CLASSROOM: *Applying Piaget's Theory*

Provide hands-on experiences with physical objects, especially when working with elementary school students. Allow and encourage students to explore and manipulate things.

A kindergarten teacher and his students work with small objects (e.g., blocks, buttons, pennies) to explore such basic elements of arithmetic as conservation of number and the reversibility of addition and subtraction.

Ask students to explain their reasoning, and challenge illogical explanations.

When learning about pendulums, students in a ninth-grade science class experiment with three variables (weight, length, and height from which the pendulum is first dropped) to see which variables determine the rate at which a pendulum swings. When a student asserts that weight affects oscillation rate, his teacher points out that he has simultaneously varied both weight and length in his experiment.

When students show signs of egocentric thought, express confusion or explain that others think differently.

A first grader asks, "What's this?" about an object that is out of the teacher's view. The teacher responds, "What's *what*? I can't see the thing you're looking at."

Be sure students have certain capabilities for mathematical and scientific reasoning (e.g., conservation of number, reversibility, proportional reasoning, separation and control of variables) before requiring them to perform complex tasks that depend on these capabilities.

In a unit on fractions in a seventh-grade math class, students express confusion about why $\frac{2}{3}$, $\frac{4}{6}$, and $\frac{8}{12}$ are all equivalent. Before beginning a lesson about how to add and subtract fractions with different denominators—processes that require an understanding of such equivalencies—their teacher uses concrete objects (e.g., sliced pizza pies, plastic rods that can be broken into small segments) to help students understand how two different fractions can be equal.

Relate abstract and hypothetical ideas to concrete objects and observable events.

To illustrate the idea that heavy and light objects fall at the same speed, an eighth-grade science teacher has students drop objects of various weights from a second-story window.

In the 1920s and 1930s, while Piaget was working in Switzerland, Russian psychologist Lev Vygotsky was also conducting research in an attempt to describe and explain children's cognitive development. Vygotsky's theory is quite different from Piaget's, and yet it, too, provides many valuable insights about how children's thinking skills develop over time.

Vygotsky's Theory of Cognitive Development

Vygotsky conducted numerous studies of children's thinking from the 1920s until his premature death from tuberculosis in 1934. Many Western psychologists did not fully appreciate the value and usefulness of his work until several decades later, when his major writings were translated into English (e.g., Vygotsky, 1962, 1978, 1987, 1997). Although Vygotsky never had the chance to develop his theory fully, his ideas are clearly evident in our views of learning and instruction today.

Vygotsky's Basic Assumptions

As you should recall, Piaget proposed that through assimilation and accommodation, children develop increasingly advanced and integrated schemes over time. In Piaget's view, cognitive development is largely an individual enterprise; growing children, it seems, do most of the mental work themselves.

In contrast, Vygotsky believed that the adults in a society foster children's cognitive development in an intentional and somewhat systematic manner. They continually engage children in meaningful and challenging activities and help them perform those activities successfully. Because Vygotsky emphasized the importance of society and culture for promoting cognitive growth, his theory is sometimes referred to as the **sociocultural perspective**. The following major assumptions provide a summary of this perspective:

■ *Complex mental processes begin as social activities; as children develop, they gradually internalize these processes and begin to use them independently.* Vygotsky believed that many thinking processes have their roots in social interactions. Children first talk about objects and events with adults and other knowledgeable individuals; in the process, they discover how the people around them think about those objects and events. As an example, consider our opening case study, "Economic Activities." When Mr. Sand discovers that his students are having difficulty understanding their geography text, he engages the class in a discussion of how new concepts relate to things they already know—a strategy that should help the students read difficult text more effectively in the future. (Unfortunately, he does so fairly late in the game, after his students have experienced considerable frustration with the assignment.)

After looking closely at this cricket, the children voice varying opinions about whether to keep it and, if so, how best to care for it. According to Vygotsky, the process of considering various points of view first occurs at a social level. Gradually children internalize the "arguing" process and become capable of looking at a situation from multiple perspectives by themselves.

In Vygotsky's view, dialogue with others is an essential condition for promoting cognitive development. Gradually, children incorporate the ways that adults and others talk about and interpret the world into their own ways of thinking. The process through which social activities evolve into internal mental activities is called **internalization**.

Not all mental processes emerge as children interact with adults, however; some also develop as they interact with their peers. As an example, children frequently argue with one another about a variety of matters—how best to carry out an activity, what games to play, who did what to whom, and so on. According to Vygotsky, childhood arguments help children discover that there are often several ways to view the same situation. Eventually, children can, in essence, internalize the "arguing" process, developing the ability to look at a situation from several different angles *on their own*.

■ *Thought and language become increasingly interdependent in the first few years of life.* For us as adults, thought and language are closely interconnected. We often think using the specific words that our language provides; for example, when we think about household pets, our thoughts contain words such as *dog* and *cat*. In addition, we usually express our thoughts when we converse with others; as we sometimes put it, we "speak our minds."

But Vygotsky proposed that thought and language are separate functions for infants and young toddlers. In these early years, thinking occurs independently of language, and when language appears, it is first used primarily as a means of communication rather than as a mechanism of thought. Sometime around age 2, thought and language become intertwined: Children begin to express their thoughts when they speak, and they begin to think in words.

When thought and language merge, we begin to see **self-talk** (also known as *private speech*), whereby children talk to themselves out loud. Recall Piaget's notion of *egocentric speech*, based on his observation that young children often say things without taking into account the listener's perspective. Vygotsky proposed that such speech is better understood as talking to *oneself* than as talking to someone else. Self-talk eventually evolves into **inner speech**: Children "talk" to themselves mentally rather than aloud. They continue to direct themselves verbally through tasks and activities, but others can no longer see and hear them do it. According to Vygotsky, both self-talk and inner speech have a similar purpose: By talking to themselves, children learn to guide and direct their own behaviors through difficult tasks and complex maneuvers in much the same way that adults have previously guided them (also see Berk, 1994; Schimmoeller, 1998). Self-talk and inner speech, then, are examples of the internalization process: Children gradually internalize the directions that they have initially received from those around them, so that they are eventually giving *themselves* directions.

Think about the situations in which you talk to yourself. Is it sometimes easier to perform a difficult task by talking your way through it?

■ *Through both informal conversations and formal schooling, adults convey to children the ways in which their culture interprets the world.* Let's return again to Mr. Sand's classroom. The textbook passage he discusses describes four kinds of economic activities: primary, secondary, tertiary, and quaternary. By presenting these four concepts, it shows the students how geographers conceptualize and categorize (i.e., how they think about) economic activities. More generally, adults share with children the language of their culture, including the specific concepts and terminology used in various academic disciplines (Vygotsky, 1962). Although Vygotsky, like Piaget, saw value in allowing children to make some discoveries themselves, he also saw value in having adults describe the discoveries of previous generations, both in informal conversations and through formal education.

To the extent that specific cultures pass along unique concepts, ideas, and beliefs, children of different cultural backgrounds will develop somewhat different knowledge, skills, and ways of thinking. Thus, Vygotsky's theory leads us to expect greater diversity among children, at least in cognitive development, than Piaget's theory does. For example, some cultures use a wide variety of maps (road maps, maps of subway systems, shopping mall layouts) and expose children to them early and frequently, whereas other cultures rarely if ever use maps (Trawick-Smith, 2000; Whiting & Edwards, 1988).

■ *Children can perform more challenging tasks when assisted by more advanced and competent individuals.* Vygotsky distinguished between two kinds of abilities that children are likely to have at any particular point in their development. A child's **actual developmental level** is the upper limit of tasks that he or she can perform independently, without help from anyone else. A child's **level of potential development** is the upper limit of tasks that he or she can perform with the assistance of a more competent individual. To get a true sense of children's cognitive development, Vygotsky suggested, we should assess their capabilities both when performing alone and when performing with assistance.

Children can typically do more difficult things in collaboration with adults than they can do on their own. For example, children just learning how to hit a baseball are often more successful when adults guide their swing. They can play more difficult piano pieces when adults help them locate some of the notes on the keyboard or provide suggestions about what fingers to use where. In the following instance, notice how a student who cannot independently solve division problems with remainders begins to learn the correct procedure through an interaction with her teacher:

These excerpts from 5-year-old Luisa's "Caterpillar Number Book" show how kindergartners might practice writing and using various numbers. Such an activity reflects elements of both Vygotsky's theory (number concepts are a part of the cultural heritage that adults pass along to children) and Piaget's theory (young children learn more effectively through concrete, hands-on experiences).

Teacher:	[writes 6)44 on the board] 44 divided by 6. What number times 6 is close to 44?
Child:	6.
Teacher:	What's 6 times 6? [writes 6]
Child:	36.
Teacher:	36. Can you get one that's any closer? [erasing the 6]

Child:	8.
Teacher:	What's 6 times 8?
Child:	64 . . . 48.
Teacher:	48. Too big. Can you think of something . . .
Child:	6 times 7 is 42. (A. L. Pettito, 1985, p. 251)

■ *Challenging tasks promote maximum cognitive growth.* The range of tasks that children cannot yet perform independently but *can* perform with the help and guidance of others is, in Vygotsky's terminology, the **zone of proximal development (ZPD)**. A child's zone of proximal development includes learning and problem-solving abilities that are just beginning to develop—abilities that are in an immature, "embryonic" form. Naturally, any child's ZPD will change over time; as some tasks are mastered, other, more complex ones appear on the horizon to take their place.

Vygotsky proposed that children learn very little from performing tasks they can already do independently. Instead, they develop primarily by attempting tasks they can accomplish only in collaboration with a more competent individual—that is, when they attempt tasks within their zone of proximal development. In a nutshell, it is the challenges in life—not the easy successes—that promote cognitive development.

As teachers, then, we should assign some tasks that our students can perform successfully only with help from others. In some cases, such assistance must come from more skilled individuals, such as adults or older students. In other situations, however, students of equal ability can work together on difficult assignments, thereby jointly accomplishing tasks that none of them might be able to accomplish on their own. Students with different zones of proximal development may sometimes need different tasks and assignments—a strong case for providing as much individualized instruction as possible.

Current Perspectives on Vygotsky's Theory

Vygotsky focused more on the processes through which children develop than on the characteristics that children of particular ages are likely to exhibit. Furthermore, his descriptions of such processes were often imprecise and lacking in detail (Haenan, 1996; E. Hunt, 1997; Wertsch, 1984). For these reasons, Vygotsky's theory has been more difficult for researchers to test and either verify or disprove than has Piaget's theory.

Nevertheless, many contemporary theorists and practitioners have made considerable use of Vygotsky's ideas. For instance, they describe the value of teaching students how to give themselves instructions (i.e., how to self-talk) as they complete challenging tasks; we will consider such *self-instructions* in Chapter 10. They also encourage us to use *guided participation, scaffolding, apprenticeships,* and *peer interaction* in promoting learning and cognitive development. Let's look briefly at each of these strategies.

Guided Participation

When you were a young child, did you sometimes help your mother, father, or an older sibling bake things in the kitchen? Did the "cook" let you pour, measure, and mix ingredients when you were old enough to do so? Did the cook also give you some guidance as you performed these tasks?

Older family members often allow young children to perform household tasks (cooking, cleaning, painting, and so on) while providing guidance about how to do these tasks appropriately. Teachers, too, often introduce students to adult tasks within a structured and supportive context. For instance, they might ask students to conduct laboratory experiments, write letters to government officials, or search the Internet for specific information, while always providing the support the students need to accomplish such tasks successfully.

When we assist our students as they perform adultlike activities, we engage them in **guided participation** in the world of adults (Radziszewska & Rogoff, 1991; Rogoff, 1990, 1991). As we guide them, we should also use some of the language that adults frequently use in such contexts; for example, when students conduct scientific experiments, we should use words such as *hypothesis, evidence,* and *theory* as we help them evaluate their procedures and results (Perkins, 1992).

Scaffolding

Theorists have given considerable thought to the kinds of assistance that can help children complete challenging tasks. The term **scaffolding** is often used here: Adults and other more competent individuals provide some form of guidance or structure that enables children to perform tasks in their zone of proximal development. To understand this concept, let's first think about how scaffolding is used in the construction of a new building. The *scaffold* is an external structure that provides support for the workers (e.g., a place where they can stand) until the building itself is strong enough to support them. As the building gains stability, the scaffold becomes less necessary and so is gradually removed.

In much the same way, an adult guiding a child through a new task may provide an initial scaffold to support the child's early efforts. In the teacher-student dialogue about division presented earlier, the teacher provided clues about how to proceed, such as searching for the multiple of 6 closest to, but still less than, 44. Similarly, a beginning piano book might help a student locate different musical notes (see Figure 2.5). As teachers, we can provide a variety of support mechanisms to help students master tasks within their zone of proximal development; here are some examples:

What task have you recently performed that was in your zone of proximal development? Who scaffolded your efforts so that you could successfully complete it?

- Work with students to develop a plan for dealing with a new task.
- Demonstrate the proper performance of the task in a way that students can easily imitate.
- Divide a complex task into several smaller, simpler tasks.
- Provide structure or guidelines about how the task should be accomplished.
- Provide a calculator, computer software (word processing programs, spreadsheets, etc.), or other technology that makes some aspects of the task easier.
- Ask questions that get students thinking in appropriate ways about the task.
- Keep students' attention focused on the relevant aspects of the task.
- Keep students motivated to complete the task.
- Remind students what their goal is in performing the task (e.g., what a problem solution should look like).
- Give frequent feedback about how students are progressing. (Gallimore & Tharp, 1990; Good, McCaslin, & Reys, 1992; Lajoie & Derry, 1993; P. F. Merrill et al., 1996; Rogoff, 1990; Rosenshine & Meister, 1992; D. Wood, Bruner, & Ross, 1976)

As students develop increasing competence, we can gradually withdraw some of these support mechanisms, eventually allowing students to perform the task independently. In a manner of speaking, when we remove such scaffolding, we allow and encourage students to stand on their own two feet.

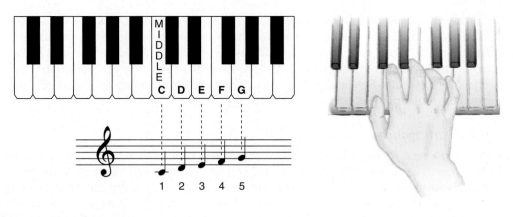

FIGURE 2.5 When children first begin piano lessons, diagrams, pictures of hand positions, numbered notes, and other aids provide scaffolding to help them remember which fingers go where.

Brother John

Are you sleep-ing, are you sleep-ing, Broth-er John, Broth-er John?

Apprenticeships

In an **apprenticeship** a learner works intensively with an expert to accomplish complex tasks that he or she cannot do independently. The expert provides considerable structure and guidance throughout the process, gradually removing scaffolding and giving the learner more responsibility as competence increases (Rogoff, 1990, 1991). Many cultures use apprenticeships to introduce children to the practices of the adult community, including such skills as weaving, tailoring, or midwifery (Lave & Wenger, 1991; Rogoff, 1990). We also see apprenticeships frequently in music instruction—for instance, in teaching a student how to play a musical instrument (D. J. Elliott, 1995).

Through an apprenticeship a student often learns not only how to perform a task but also how to *think about* a task; such a situation is sometimes called a **cognitive apprenticeship** (J. S. Brown, Collins, & Duguid, 1989; John-Steiner, 1997; Rogoff, 1990; W. Roth & Bowen, 1995). For instance, a student and a teacher might work together to accomplish a challenging task or solve a difficult problem (perhaps collecting data samples in biology fieldwork, solving a mathematical brainteaser, or translating a difficult passage from German to English). In the process of talking about various aspects of the task or problem, the teacher and student together analyze the situation and develop the best approach to take, and the teacher models effective ways of thinking about and mentally processing the situation.

Although apprenticeships can differ widely from one context to another, they typically have some or all of these features (A. Collins, Brown, & Newman, 1989):

- *Modeling.* The teacher carries out the task, simultaneously thinking aloud about the process, while the student observes and listens.
- *Coaching.* As the student performs the task, the teacher gives frequent suggestions, hints, and feedback.
- *Scaffolding.* The teacher provides various forms of support for the student, perhaps by simplifying the task, breaking it into smaller and more manageable components, or providing less complicated equipment.
- *Articulation.* The student explains what he or she is doing and why, allowing the teacher to examine the student's knowledge, reasoning, and problem-solving strategies.
- *Reflection.* The teacher asks the student to compare his or her performance with that of experts, or perhaps with an ideal model of how the task should be done.
- *Increasing complexity and diversity of tasks.* As the student gains greater proficiency, the teacher presents more complex, challenging, and varied tasks to complete.
- *Exploration.* The teacher encourages the student to frame questions and problems on his or her own and thereby to expand and refine acquired skills.

INTO THE CLASSROOM: *Applying Vygotsky's Theory*

Encourage students to talk themselves through difficult tasks.

As his students work on complex mathematical equations such as this one,

$$x = \frac{2(4 \times 9)^2}{6} + 3$$

a junior high school mathematics teacher gives students a mnemonic ("*Please excuse my dear Aunt Sally*") that they might repeat to themselves to help them remember the order in which they should perform various operations (*p*arentheses, *e*xponents, *m*ultiplication and *d*ivision, *a*ddition and *s*ubtraction).

Demonstrate and encourage adultlike ways of thinking about situations.

A high school chemistry teacher places two equal-size inflated balloons into two beakers of water, one heated to 25°C and the other heated to 50°C. The students all agree that the balloon placed in the warmer water expands more. "Now *how much more* did the 50-degree balloon expand?" the teacher asks. "Let's use Charles's Law to figure it out."

Present some tasks that students can perform successfully only with assistance.

A fifth-grade teacher assigns students their first research paper, knowing that he will have to give them a great deal of guidance as they work on it.

Provide sufficient support (scaffolding) to enable students to perform challenging tasks successfully; gradually withdraw the support as they become more proficient.

An elementary physical education teacher begins a lesson on tumbling by demonstrating forward and backward rolls in slow motion and physically guiding her students through the correct movements. As the students become more skillful, she stands back from the mat and gives verbal feedback about how to improve.

Have students work in small groups to accomplish complex tasks.

A middle school art teacher asks his students to work in groups of four or five to design large murals that depict various ecosystems—rain forest, desert, grassland, tundra, and so on—and the kinds of species of plants and animals that live in each one. The groups then paint their murals on the walls in the school corridors.

Apprenticeships are clearly labor-intensive; as such, their use in the classroom is not always practical or logistically feasible (e.g., De Corte, Greer, & Verschaffel, 1996). At the same time, we can certainly use elements of an apprenticeship model to help our students develop more complex skills. For example, we might use prompts like these to help students think about writing tasks in the same ways that expert writers do (Scardamalia and Bereiter, 1985):

- "My main point . . ."
- "An example of this . . ."
- "The reason I think so . . ."
- "To liven this up, I'll . . ."
- "I can tie this together by . . ."

Such prompts provide the same sort of guidance that an experienced writer might provide, and they help students develop more sophisticated writing strategies (Scardamalia & Bereiter, 1985).

Apprenticeships frequently take place in natural settings—for example, in a studio, workshop, or place of employment—and involve real-life tasks. Many theorists believe that such *authentic activities* are essential to effective instruction. We'll look at authentic activities more closely in Chapters 7 and 13.

Peer Interaction

As noted earlier, students can often accomplish more difficult tasks when they work together rather than alone; in such situations, students are essentially providing scaffolding for one another's efforts. In recent years, researchers and practitioners alike have become increasingly convinced that interactive approaches to instruction, in which students work collaboratively rather than in isolation, can be highly effective in promoting both cognitive development and classroom achievement. In Chapter 7 we'll consider the advantages and effects of peer interaction for classroom learning and achievement, and in Chapter 13 we'll examine instructional strategies that promote such interaction.

Vygotsky described several mechanisms (internalization, self-talk, and so on) through which children gradually acquire adultlike ways of thinking about the world. More recently, other researchers have likewise studied mechanisms that promote cognitive development, and they have done so with greater precision than Vygotsky did. Recent researchers have also tried to characterize the nature of thinking processes at various ages, but rather than focus on reasoning and logic (as Piaget did), they have looked at the development of cognition more generally. The perspective that many of these researchers have taken—information processing theory—is our next topic of discussion.

An Information Processing View of Cognitive Development

Stop for a moment to consider what you yourself have observed about children of different ages. Do you think children become better at paying attention as they grow older? Do you think older children remember more than younger children, or vice versa? In what ways do high school students learn and study differently from elementary students?

Such questions reflect information processing theory, an approach to cognitive development that has evolved largely within the last three or four decades. Information processing theory is actually a collection of theories that emphasize the development of **cognitive processes**—the processes through which children acquire, interpret, remember, manipulate, and make use of information.

Most information processing theorists reject Piaget's notion of discrete developmental stages. Instead, they believe that children's cognitive processes and abilities develop through more steady and gradual *trends;* for example, they propose that children learn faster, remember more, and can think about increasingly complex tasks as they grow. In the next few pages, we examine developmental trends in children's attention, learning strategies, knowledge, and metacognition.

Attention

Two trends in cognitive development relate to children's attention and its impact on learning:

■ *Children become less distractible over time.* Young children's attention often moves quickly from one thing to another, and it is easily drawn to objects and events unrelated to the task at hand. But as children grow older, they become better able to focus their attention on a particular task and keep it there, and they are less likely to be distracted by irrelevant occurrences (Dempster & Corkill, 1999; Lane & Pearson, 1982; Ruff & Lawson, 1990). For example, in one experiment (Higgins & Turnure, 1984), children at several grade levels were given a difficult learning task. Some children worked on the task in a quiet room, others worked in a room with a little background noise, and still others worked with a great deal of background noise. Preschool and second-grade children learned most quickly under the quiet conditions and most slowly under the very noisy conditions. But the sixth graders were able to learn just as easily in the noisy room as in the quiet room. Apparently, the older children could ignore the noise, whereas the younger children could not.

■ *How and what children learn depends increasingly on what they actually intend to learn.* Try the following exercise before you read further.

EXPERIENCING FIRSTHAND   *Six Cards*

Look at the six cards below. Try to remember the *colors* of the cards and the order in which each color appears. Study them for about 30 seconds and then cover them with your hand.

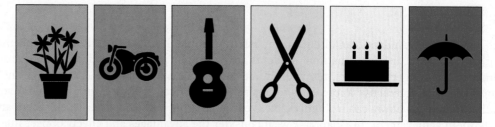

Now that you have covered the six cards, answer these questions:

■ In which spot is the yellow card? the green card? the blue card? the pink card?
■ Where is the cake? the flowers? the guitar? the pair of scissors?

Modeled after a task used by Maccoby & Hagen, 1965.

How accurately did you remember the colors of the cards? How accurately did you remember the objects pictured on the cards? If you are like most adults, you had better success remembering what you intended to learn (the colors) than what you did *not* intend to learn (the objects).

Perhaps because of their distractibility, younger children often remember many things unrelated to what they are supposed to be doing or learning (DeMarie-Dreblow & Miller, 1988; Hagen & Stanovich, 1977). For example, when students in grades 1 through 7 were asked to perform a series of tasks similar to the "Six Cards" exercise, older students remembered the background colors more accurately than younger students. Yet the older students were no better than the younger ones at remembering the objects pictured on the cards; in fact, the oldest group in the study remembered the *fewest* number of objects (Maccoby & Hagen, 1965). Older children, then, are better at learning and remembering the things they *intend* to learn; they are not necessarily better at learning irrelevant information.

Learning Strategies

Preschoolers often recognize the need to remember something but seem to have little idea of how to go about learning it, apart from looking or pointing at it (Kail, 1990; Wellman, 1988). As children grow older, however, they develop a number of **learning strategies**—specific methods of learning information—that help them learn and remember things. Following are four commonly observed trends in the development of learning strategies:

■ *Rehearsal increases during the elementary school years.* What do you do if you need to remember a telephone number for a few minutes? Do you repeat it to yourself over and over again as a way of keeping it in your memory until you dial it? This process of **rehearsal** is rare in kindergarten children but increases in frequency and effectiveness throughout the elementary school years (Bjorklund & Coyle, 1995; Gathercole & Hitch, 1993; Kail, 1990).

■ *Organization improves throughout the elementary and secondary grades.* Before you read further, try the following short learning exercise.

EXPERIENCING FIRSTHAND   *Mental Maneuver*

Read the twelve words below *one time only.* Then cover up the page and write the words down in the order they come to mind.

daisy	apple	dandelion
hammer	pear	wrench
tulip	pliers	peach
banana	rose	screwdriver

In what order did you remember the words? Did you recall them in their original order, or did you rearrange them somehow? If you are like most people, you grouped the words into three categories—flowers, tools, and fruit—and remembered one category at a time. In other words, you imposed **organization** on the information.

Research consistently shows that organized information is learned more easily and remembered more completely than unorganized information (see Chapter 6). As children grow older, they more frequently and effectively organize the information they receive. This tendency to organize begins in early childhood and continues to develop well into the high school years (Bjorklund, Schneider, Cassel, & Ashley, 1994; M. Carr, Kurtz, Schneider, Turner, & Borkowski, 1989; DeLoache & Todd, 1988; Hacker, 1998a; Plumert, 1994).

■ *Elaboration emerges around puberty and increases throughout adolescence.* If I tell you that I lived in Colorado for many years, you will probably conclude that I lived in or near the Rocky Mountains. You might also infer that perhaps I did a lot of skiing, hiking, or camping. In this situation, you are learning more than the information I actually gave you; you are also learning some information that you yourself are supplying. This process of using what you already know to expand on new information is called **elaboration**. In our "Economic Activities" case study, Mr. Sand encourages his students to elaborate by generating their own examples of economic concepts.

Elaboration clearly helps students learn and remember classroom material more effectively than they would otherwise (more about this in Chapter 6). Children begin to elaborate on their experiences as early as the preschool years (Fivush, Haden, & Adam, 1995). Yet as a strategy that children *intentionally* use to help them learn and make sense of new information, elaboration appears relatively late in development (usually around puberty) and gradually increases throughout the teenage years (Flavell, Miller, & Miller, 1993; Schneider & Pressley, 1989). Even in high school, it is primarily high-achieving students who use their existing knowledge to help themselves learn (Pressley, 1982). Low-achieving high school students often depend on more superficial, less "thoughtful" strategies (such as rehearsal) in their attempts to remember what they are studying.

We will examine rehearsal, organization, and elaboration in greater depth in Chapter 6.

Earlier we encountered the process of *construction* in our discussion of Piaget's basic assumptions. Both organization and elaboration are constructive in nature: You take new information, rearrange it or add to it based on what you already know, and so construct an understanding that is uniquely your own.

■ *Learning strategies become increasingly efficient and effective.* When children first acquire new learning strategies, they use them infrequently, effortfully, and often ineffectively. But with time and practice, they become increasingly adept at applying their strategies quickly, efficiently, and flexibly as they tackle challenging classroom learning tasks. As they gain competence and confidence with more sophisticated strategies, they gradually leave their less efficient ones behind (P. A. Alexander, Graham, & Harris, 1998; Flavell et al., 1993; Siegler, 1998).

Often, by looking closely at what students say and write, we can get a sense of the kinds of strategies they are and aren't using. As an example, try the following exercise.

INTERPRETING ARTIFACTS AND INTERACTIONS   *Dutch Cheese*

Ten-year-old Scott has written this research report about Dutch cheese. At the bottom of the report, he has pasted (1) a picture of Edam cheese, (2) a map of the Netherlands (with dairy regions circled in purple felt-tip pen), and (3) a photocopied picture of a Dutch cheese market; the numbers in his paper are intended to direct the reader to these three items. As you read Scott's report, speculate about

■ Strategies he used when reading about his topic and writing his paper
■ Strategies he did *not* use that might have made the report better and enhanced his learning

Scott has taken a somewhat superficial approach to reading and writing about Dutch cheese. It appears that he has simply taken a few facts he has read (perhaps paraphrasing them, perhaps reproducing them verbatim) without organizing or elaborating on them in any way that might help him remember them better. One exception to this pattern is his circling of dairy regions in the map of the Netherlands, indicating an effort to integrate (organize) a little bit of what he has learned. Middle school students often write reports in such a superficial manner, listing facts rather than pulling them together in a cohesive, organized, and elaborated fashion (Bereiter & Scardamalia, 1987; McCutchen, 1996).

Knowledge

Children's knowledge of specific topics and of the world in general—their **knowledge base**—changes in at least two ways as they develop:

■ *The amount of knowledge that children have increases over time.* There is no question that children acquire more and more information as they grow older. This increasing knowledge base is one reason why adults and older children learn new things more easily: They have more existing knowledge to help them understand and elaborate on new ideas and events (Flavell et al., 1993; Halford, 1989; Kail, 1990). As an example, consider the case of an Inuit (Eskimo) man named Tor.

EXPERIENCING FIRSTHAND *Tor of the Targa*

Tor, a young man of the Targa tribe, was out hunting in the ancient hunting territory of his people. He had been away from his village for many days. The weather was bad and he had not yet managed to locate his prey. Because of the extreme temperature he knew he must soon return but it was a matter of honor among his people to track and kill the prey single-handed. Only when this was achieved could a boy be considered a man. Those who failed were made to eat and keep company with the old men and the women until they could accomplish this task.

Suddenly, in the distance, Tor could make out the outline of a possible prey. It was alone and not too much bigger than Tor, who could take him single-handed. But as he drew nearer, a hunter from a neighboring tribe came into view, also stalking the prey. The intruder was older than Tor and had around his neck evidence of his past success at the hunt. "Yes," thought Tor, "he is truly a man." Tor was undecided. Should he challenge the intruder or return home empty handed? To return would mean bitter defeat. The other young men of the tribe would laugh at his failure. He decided to creep up on the intruder and wait his chance. (A. L. Brown, Smiley, Day, Townsend, & Lawton, 1977, p. 1460)

■ On what kind of terrain was Tor hunting?
■ What was the weather like?
■ What kind of prey might Tor have been stalking?

You probably used your knowledge about Inuits (Eskimos) to speculate that Tor was hunting polar bears or seals on snow and ice, possibly in freezing temperatures or a bad blizzard. But notice that the story itself didn't tell you any of these things; you had to *infer* them. Like you, older children often know a great deal about how Inuit people live and can use that information to help them to elaborate on, and so better understand and remember, this very ambiguous story about Tor. Younger children are less likely to make connections between a new situation and what they already know (A. L. Brown et al., 1977).

The more knowledge children already have, the more easily they can remember new information. In cases where children have more knowledge than adults, then children are often the more effective learners (Chi, 1978; Rabinowitz & Glaser, 1985). For example, when my son Alex and I used to read books about lizards together, Alex always remembered more than I did, because he was a self-proclaimed "lizard expert," and I myself knew very little about reptiles of any sort.

Might you see better performance in "low ability" students if you encourage them to work with a topic they know a lot about?

■ *Children's knowledge base becomes increasingly integrated.* Remember, older children are more likely to organize information as they learn it. They are also more likely to make connections between new information and the things they already know. Not surprisingly, then, children's knowledge becomes increasingly integrated as they grow older. The knowledge base of older children includes many associations and interrelationships among concepts and ideas; that of younger children is more likely to consist of separate, isolated facts (Bjorklund, 1987; Flavell et al., 1993). The more integrated knowledge base of older children is probably one reason why, as Piaget discovered, they can think more logically and draw inferences more readily.

As children grow older, they become increasingly able to draw inferences from what they see, in part because they have a larger and better integrated knowledge base to help them interpret their experiences.

Metacognition

As an adult with many years of formal education behind you, you have probably learned a great deal about how you think and learn. For example, you may have learned that you cannot absorb everything in a textbook the first time you read it, or that you remember information better when you elaborate on it, rather than when you simply repeat it over and over meaninglessly.

The term **metacognition** refers both to the knowledge people have about their own cognitive processes and to their intentional use of certain cognitive processes to facilitate learning and memory. As children develop, their metacognitive knowledge and skills improve in the following ways:

■ *Children become more aware of the limitations of their memories.* Young children tend to be overly optimistic about how much they can remember. As they grow older and encounter a greater variety of learning tasks, they discover that some things are more difficult to learn than others (Bjorklund & Green, 1992; Flavell et al., 1993). They also begin to realize that their memories are not perfect—that they cannot possibly remember everything they see or hear.

Let's consider an experiment with elementary school children (Flavell, Friedrichs, & Hoyt, 1970) as an example. Children in four age-groups (ranging from preschool to fourth grade) were shown strips of paper with pictures of one to ten objects. The children were asked to predict how many of the objects they could remember over a short period of time. The average predictions of each age-group and the average number of objects the different groups actually *did* remember were as follows:

Age-Group	Predicted Number	Actual Number
Preschool	7.2	3.5
Kindergarten	8.0	3.6
Grade 2	6.0	4.4
Grade 4	6.1	5.5

Notice how all four age-groups predicted that they would remember more objects than they actually could. But the older children were more realistic about the limitations of their memories than the younger ones. The kindergartners predicted they would remember eight objects, but they actually remembered fewer than four!

■ *Children become better able to identify the things they do and do not know.* Young children (e.g., those in the early elementary grades) often think they know or understand something before they actually do. As a result, they don't study classroom material as much as they should, and they often don't ask questions when they receive incomplete or confusing information (Markman, 1977; McDevitt, Spivey, Sheehan, Lennon, & Story, 1990).

Even high school and college students sometimes have difficulty assessing their own knowledge accurately. For example, they often think they can spell words they actually cannot spell (P. A. Adams & Adams, 1960; Ormrod & Wagner, 1987). And they often overestimate how well they will perform on an exam (Hacker, Bol, Horgan, & Rakow, 2000). My own students occasionally come to me expressing frustration about doing poorly on an exam. "I knew the material so well!" they tell me. But when we sit down and begin to talk about the exam material, it usually becomes clear that in fact they have only a very vague understanding of some ideas and an incorrect understanding of others.

■ *Children become more knowledgeable about effective learning strategies.* As mentioned earlier, children show greater use of such learning strategies as rehearsal, organization, and elaboration as they grow older. With experience they also become increasingly aware of which strategies are effective in different situations (Lovett & Flavell, 1990; Short, Schatschneider, & Friebert, 1993; Wellman, 1985). For example, consider the simple idea that when you don't learn something the first time you try, you need to study it again. This is a strategy that 8-year-olds use but 6-year-olds do not (Masur, McIntyre, & Flavell, 1973). In a similar way, tenth

INTO THE CLASSROOM: *Applying Information Processing Theory*

Minimize distractions, especially when working with young children.

As his class begins a writing assignment, a first-grade teacher asks his students to put all objects except pencil and paper inside their desks.

Base instruction on what students already know.

A music teacher introduces a new topic by saying, "We've already learned the scale in C major. Today we're going to study the scale in C minor and see how it is both similar to and different from C major."

Encourage learning strategies appropriate for the age-group.

A third-grade teacher encourages her students to study their spelling words by repeating the letters of each word over and over to themselves and by writing each word several times. Meanwhile, a high school history teacher asks her students to think about why certain historical events may have happened as they did; for example, she encourages them to speculate about the personal motives, economic circumstances, and political and social issues that may have influenced people's decision making at the time.

Identify situations in which various learning strategies are likely to be useful.

A sixth-grade teacher says to his class, "We've studied several features of the nine planets in our solar system—size, color, composition, distance from the sun, and duration of revolution around the sun. This sounds like a situation where a two-dimensional chart might help us organize the information."

Give students many opportunities to assess their own learning efforts and thereby to find out what they do and don't know.

A junior high school health teacher has students read a textbook chapter at home and then gives them a non-graded quiz to help them identify parts of the chapter that they may need to read again.

---

graders are more aware than eighth graders of the advantages of using elaboration to learn new information (Waters, 1982). Even so, many students of all ages (college students included) seem relatively uninformed about which learning strategies work most effectively in different situations (Ormrod & Jenkins, 1989; J. W. Thomas, 1993b; Waters, 1982). Consider one high-achieving high school student's reflections in the following exercise.

INTERPRETING ARTIFACTS AND INTERACTIONS   *What Do You Do . . . ?*

In recent years I have sometimes asked students in my educational psychology classes to interview elementary or high school students about study strategies. One of my students, Kathryn Broadhead, reported the following conversation with a high-achieving 16-year-old sophomore (I'll call him Mike) who was taking several challenging high school classes. As you read the conversation, consider

- The kinds of strategies Mike uses and the learning tasks for which he uses each one
- Mike's awareness of what he does (mentally) when he studies and learns

Kathryn: What do you do when you need to remember something?

Mike: I guess just repetition. "Repetition is the master of all teachers." I forgot who said that.

Kathryn: How do you study for a test? What kinds of things do you do in your head when you study?

Mike: I study differently for each subject. I don't study for math . . . never have, never will. It comes easily. Once I learn it the first time, I know it. English [literature] is more of asking questions. The more questions I have, the better I understand. Writing just comes naturally. History, well, that's mostly repetition. That's mainly where it [repetition] comes in . . . history, foreign languages [Latin and Spanish], and science.

Mike claims that he uses only repetition (i.e., rehearsal) when he studies, but it appears he is using this strategy primarily for history, foreign languages, and science. For English literature he says he asks questions; we can reasonably guess that his questions reflect his attempt to better understand (i.e., elaborate on) what he is reading. Mike has little awareness of how he approaches math ("it comes easily") or writing (it "just comes naturally"). The facility he has with math and writing suggests a well-integrated knowledge base in these areas, such that he can easily understand and elaborate on new material and so can readily recall the ideas and skills he may need for mathematical problems and writing tasks.

As teachers, we must remember that our students are likely to be less efficient learners than we are. A variety of factors that affect their ability to learn—attention, intention to learn, prior knowledge, awareness and use of effective learning strategies, and so on—develop gradually throughout the school years. We cannot expect that our students will always learn as quickly, or even in the same way, as we do.

Learning strategies make such a difference in students' classroom achievement that we shouldn't leave the development of these strategies to chance. As we ask our students to study and learn classroom subject matter, we should also give them suggestions about *how* they might study and learn it. Such an approach is consistent not only with information processing theory but also with Vygotsky's proposal that adults can better promote children's cognitive development by talking about how they themselves think about challenging tasks. Chapter 8 explores the nature of metacognitive knowledge and skills in more detail and provides suggestions for promoting students' metacognitive development.

No matter which theoretical perspective we take—whether it be Piaget's theory, Vygotsky's theory, or information processing theory—we find that children's language capabilities play a key role in their cognitive development. Piaget suggested that words help children mentally represent and think about external objects and events and that language in general is critical for the social interactions that enable children to think less egocentrically and more logically. In Vygotsky's view, verbal interaction and self-talk provide the means through which children gradually internalize and adopt the social processes and ways of thinking of the people around them. From an information processing point of view, much of the knowledge that children acquire about their world comes to them through conversations, explanations, books, and other verbal formats; furthermore, many of their learning strategies (e.g., rehearsal, organization, elaboration) are predominantly verbal in nature. We can better understand cognitive development, then, when we also know something about linguistic development.

Linguistic Development

What kinds of knowledge and skills are essential for effective communication with others? For instance, how important is a large vocabulary? What kinds of rules must we follow to combine words into meaningful sentences? What must we know about how to produce the various sounds of speech? And what courtesies must we show others when we converse with them?

Using human language is a very complex endeavor. Indeed, we must have a working knowledge of thousands of words, and we must be able to put these words together in particular ways. We must be able to articulate such vowel sounds as "ay" and "ee" and such consonants and consonant blends as "buh," "duh," and "struh." To be truly effective communicators, we also must follow certain social conventions as we speak; for instance, we should respond to someone else's greeting (e.g., "How are you?") with a greeting of our own (e.g., "Fine, thanks, and how about you?"), and we should let a person with whom we are conversing finish a sentence before we speak.

As teachers, we need to know what linguistic knowledge and skills students of different ages are likely to have so that we can form realistic expectations for their performance. In the pages that follow, we will briefly examine theoretical perspectives on language development and then look more closely at how various aspects of language are likely to change over time. We will also consider research findings related to second-language learning and bilingualism. Much of our focus will be on spoken language; you can learn more about the development of written language (reading and writing) in the chapter "Learning in the Content Areas" in the *Study Guide and Reader* that accompanies this book.

Theoretical Perspectives on Language Development

Many theorists believe that human beings are born with a predisposition to learn language—that, to some degree, our knowledge of language is "built in" (N. Chomsky, 1972; Gopnik, 1997; Karmiloff-Smith, 1993; Lenneberg, 1967). Although we almost certainly are not born knowing any *particular* language, we apparently inherit some constraints regarding the form our language must take. Theorists describe several sources of evidence to support such a contention. First, most languages seem to share certain characteristics, such as similar rules for forming negatives and asking questions (N. Chomsky, 1965). Second, all members of a particular society acquire what is more or less the *same* language, despite widely differing early childhood experiences and a general lack of systematic instruction in appropriate language use (Crain, 1993; Cromer, 1993). And third, there may be *sensitive periods* in some aspects of language development: In general, children benefit more from exposure to a particular language when they are young. For instance, children have an easier time mastering a language's various verb tenses and learning how to pronounce words flawlessly when they are immersed in the language within the first five to ten years of life (Bialystok, 1994a; Bruer, 1999; Newport, 1993).

But environment, too, must obviously play a role in language development. Children can learn a language only if the people around them converse in that language. It may be that children acquire language, at least in part, because it enables them to accomplish certain goals—perhaps to influence another person's behavior, obtain a desired object, and so on (E. Bates & MacWhinney, 1987; Budwig, 1995). Yet it is clear that children do not directly "absorb" the language spoken around them; instead, it appears that they use what they hear to *construct* their own understanding of the language, including knowledge about what words mean, rules governing how words can be combined into meaningful sentences, and so on (Cairns, 1996; Cromer, 1993; Karmiloff-Smith, 1993).

To communicate effectively, children must master many aspects of language; for instance, they must know the meanings of thousands of words, learn the complex rules that govern how words are put together, and acquire social conventions for interacting in culturally appropriate ways with adults and peers. Such knowledge and skills continue to develop throughout the school years, often with the guidance of teachers.

Trends in Language Development

Children begin using recognizable words sometime around their first birthday and are putting these words together by their second birthday. During the preschool years, they become capable of forming longer and more complex sentences. By the time they begin school at age 5 or 6, they use language that seems adultlike in many respects. Yet students' language capabilities continue to develop and mature throughout the school years. Numerous changes occur in both **receptive language**—the ability to understand what is heard and read—and **expressive language**—the ability to communicate effectively through speaking and writing. Let's examine several aspects of linguistic development—vocabulary, syntax, listening comprehension, oral communication, and metalinguistic awareness—and their implications for teachers.

Development of Vocabulary

One obvious change in students' language during the school years is the increase in their vocabulary. It has been estimated that the average first grader knows the meanings of 8,000 to 14,000 words, whereas the average high school graduate knows the meanings of at least 80,000 words (S. Carey, 1978; Nippold, 1988). Children learn some words through direct vocabulary instruction at school, but they probably learn many more by inferring meaning from the contexts in which they hear or read the words (Nippold, 1988; Owens, 1996; Pinker, 1987).

Students' knowledge of word meanings, known as **semantics**, is not always an all-or-none thing. In many cases, their early understanding of a word's meaning is somewhat vague and "fuzzy"; they have a general idea of what the word means but define it imprecisely and sometimes use it incorrectly. Through repeated encounters with words in different contexts and through direct feedback when they use words incorrectly, students continue to refine their understandings of what various words mean.

Can you think of words whose meanings are still unclear to you?

One common error that students make in their understanding of words is **undergeneralization**: The meaning they attach to a word is too restricted, leaving out some situations to which the word applies. For example, I once asked my son Jeff, then 6 years old, to tell me what an *animal* is. He gave me this definition:

It has a head, tail, feet, paws, eyes, noses, ears, lots of hair.

Like Jeff, young elementary school children often restrict their meaning of *animal* primarily to mammals, such as dogs and horses, and insist that fish, birds, and insects are *not* animals (S. Carey, 1985; Saltz, 1971).

Another frequent error is **overgeneralization**: The meaning students attach to a word is too broad, and so they use it in situations where it's not appropriate. For example, when I asked Jeff to give me some examples of *insects,* he included black widow spiders in his list. Jeff overgeneralized: All insects have six legs, so eight-legged spiders do not qualify.

Sometimes even common words have subtleties that children don't master until the upper elementary grades or later. For example, 9-year-old children sometimes confuse situations in which they should use the articles *a* and *the* (Reich, 1986). Children in the upper elementary and junior high grades have trouble with many connectives, such as the words *but, although, yet, however,* and *unless* (Nippold, 1988; Owens, 1996). As an illustration, do the following exercise.

EXPERIENCING FIRSTHAND *Using Connectives*

In each of the following pairs of sentences, identify the one that makes more sense:

Jimmie went to school, but he felt sick.

Jimmie went to school, but he felt fine.

The meal was good, although the pie was bad.

The meal was good, although the pie was good.

Even 12-year-olds have trouble identifying the correct sentence in pairs like these, reflecting only a vague understanding of the connectives *but* and *although* (Katz & Brent, 1968). (The first sentence is the correct one in both cases.)

Words such as *but* and *although* may be particularly difficult for elementary school children because their meanings are fairly abstract. As you should recall from our discussion of cognitive development, abstract thinking emerges slowly (in Piaget's view, not until early adolescence). Young children in particular are apt to define words in terms of the obvious, concrete aspects of their world (Anglin, 1977; Ausubel et al., 1978). For example, when Jeff was 4, he defined *summer* as the time of year when school is out and it's hot outside. But when he was in middle school, after he had developed a capacity for abstract reasoning and had studied the seasons in his science class, he was able to define summer in terms of the earth's tilt relative to the sun—a far more abstract notion.

To some extent, we must obviously tailor our lessons and reading materials to our students' vocabulary, yet we must not restrict instruction only to words that students already know. One way to promote students' semantic development is to teach vocabulary words and definitions directly, for instance, by having students define new vocabulary in their own words and use this vocabulary in a variety of contexts. We should also correct any misconceptions (e.g., under- or overgeneralizations) that reveal themselves in students' speech. And we must encourage our students to *read, read, read:* Children and adolescents learn many new words through their reading activities (Stanovich, 2000; Swanborn & de Glopper, 1999). The discussion of concept learning in Chapter 7 presents additional ways of teaching word meanings.

Development of Syntax

EXPERIENCING FIRSTHAND *Four Sentences*

Which of the following sentences are grammatically correct?

The flowers in the garden have grown up straight and tall.

I in garden the pick weeds nasty dare don't.

Why they not does they homework when suppose?

Why aren't you doing your homework?

You undoubtedly recognized that the first and last sentences are grammatically correct and that the two middle ones are not. But *how* were you able to tell the difference? Can you describe the specific grammatical rules you used to make your decisions? The rules that we use to put words together into grammatically correct sentences—rules of **syntax**—are incredibly complex, and to a great extent we aren't consciously aware of the nature of these rules (N. Chomsky, 1972; N. C. Ellis, 1994).

By the time children begin school, they have already acquired many syntactic rules; nevertheless, their knowledge of correct syntax continues to develop throughout the elementary years (Owens, 1996; Reich, 1986). For instance, children in the early elementary grades often make an error known as **overregularization**: They apply syntactical rules in situations in which such rules don't apply (Bryant, Nunes, & Aidinis, 1999; Cazden, 1968; G. F. Marcus, 1996). To illustrate, young children might add *-ed* to indicate past tense or *-s* to indicate plural when such suffixes are inappropriate (e.g., "I *goed* to the store," "I have two *feets*"). This overregularization gradually disappears as children learn the words they should actually use (e.g., past tenses of irregular verbs) in such situations.

We see further evidence of incomplete syntactic development in children's responses to the complex sentences they hear. For example, children in one study (C. S. Chomsky, 1969) were shown a doll with a blindfold over its eyes and asked, "Is this doll easy to see or hard to see?" Children as old as 8 had trouble interpreting the question. The following conversation with 6-year-old Lisa provides an illustration:

Experimenter:	Is this doll easy to see or hard to see?
Lisa:	Hard to see.
Experimenter:	Will you make her easy to see.
Lisa:	If I can get this untied.
Experimenter:	Will you explain why she was hard to see.
Lisa:	(To doll) Because you had a blindfold over your eyes.
Experimenter:	And what did you do?
Lisa:	I took it off. (C. S. Chomsky, 1969, p. 30)

Children in the early elementary grades may also have difficulty interpreting passive sentences and sentences with two or more clauses (Karmiloff-Smith, 1979; O'Grady, 1997; Owens, 1996; Sheldon, 1974). Often they seem to rely on word order when interpreting such sentences. For instance, if first graders were to hear the sentence "Grandma was visited by her friends," they might conclude that Grandma did the visiting (O'Grady, 1997). If they heard the sentence "The horse kicked the pig after he jumped over the fence," many would say that the horse kicked the pig *before* it jumped over the fence, even though the word *after* clearly communicates the opposite sequence (E. V. Clark, 1971).

Students' knowledge of syntax and grammar continues to develop even at the secondary level (e.g., Perera, 1986). At this point, most syntactical development probably occurs as the result of formal language instruction—perhaps courses in language arts, English composition, and foreign language (Maratsos, 1998). Therefore, we should continue instruction and practice in grammar and composition throughout the high school years. Our students are more likely to improve their speech and writing when they have ample opportunities to express their ideas orally and on paper and when they receive direct feedback about ambiguities and grammatical errors in their speech and writing.

Development of Listening Comprehension

Our students' ability to comprehend what they hear will obviously be influenced by their knowledge of vocabulary and syntax. But other factors contribute to students' listening comprehension as well. For instance, children's conceptions of what listening comprehension *is* seem to change during the elementary school years. Children in the early elementary grades believe they are good listeners if they simply sit quietly without interrupting the teacher. Older children (e.g., 11-year-olds) are more likely to recognize that good listening also requires an *understanding* of what is being said (McDevitt et al., 1990). Elementary school children also differ in their beliefs about what to do when they don't understand something the teacher says. Many children, younger ones especially, apparently believe that it is inappropriate to ask for clarification, perhaps because they have previously been discouraged from asking questions at school or at home (McDevitt, 1990; McDevitt et al., 1990). For example, children growing up in certain cultures, including those in many Asian and Mexican American communities, may have learned that initiating a conversation with an adult is disrespectful (Delgado-Gaitan, 1994; Trawick-Smith, 2000).

Furthermore, young children's comprehension of what they hear is influenced by the context in which they hear it. Using various nonverbal contextual clues, they recognize that what

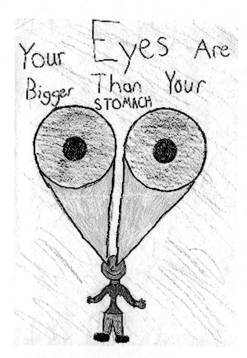

is said in a situation is sometimes different from what is actually meant. For example, they may interpret a statement such as "Goodness, this class is noisy today!" to mean "Be quiet" (Flavell, 1985). They may also realize that by asking "Whose jacket is this lying on the floor?" their teacher is actually requesting the jacket's owner to pick it up and put it where it belongs. But unfortunately, younger children are sometimes so dependent on the context for determining the meaning of language that they don't listen carefully enough to understand a spoken message accurately. They may "hear" what they *think* we mean, based on their beliefs about our intentions, rather than hearing what we really do mean (Donaldson, 1978). It is important, then, not only to ask students whether they understand what they hear but also to check for that understanding by asking them to rephrase a message in their own words.

As children get older, they become less dependent on context to understand what others say to them. They also become increasingly able to look beyond the literal meanings of messages (Owens, 1996; Winner, 1988). Children in the early elementary grades take the words they hear at face value; for instance, when we describe someone as being "tied up" or "hitting the roof," they are likely to take us literally (see Figure 2.6). And they have little success drawing generalizations from such proverbs as "Look before you leap" or "Don't put the cart before the horse." Students' ability to interpret proverbs in a generalized, abstract fashion continues to develop even in the high school years (Owens, 1996).

FIGURE 2.6 Adults typically use the expression "Your eyes are bigger than your stomach" figuratively, perhaps to describe a situation in which someone has ordered more food than can possibly be eaten. Here, however, 8-year-old Jeff interprets the expression quite literally.

Development of Oral Communication Skills

To speak effectively, children must know how to pronounce words correctly. During the preschool and early elementary years, many children have difficulty pronouncing some sounds in the English language; for instance, they may struggle with *r, th, dr, sl,* and *str* (Owens, 1996). Most students have mastered the sounds of English by age 8 or 9; if pronunciation difficulties continue after that time, we may want to consult with the school's speech pathologist about remediation strategies.

To communicate their ideas effectively, children also need to consider the characteristics (e.g., age, prior knowledge, perspective) of the person receiving their message. As noted earlier, young children sometimes say things without really considering the listener's perspective (Piaget called this *egocentric speech*). Even 4-year-olds adapt their speech somewhat to the age of their listeners; for example, they use simpler language with 2-year-olds than they do with their peers (McDevitt & Ford, 1987; Shatz & Gelman, 1973). Yet throughout elementary school, children have some difficulty taking other characteristics of their listeners into account; for example, they don't always consider what prior information their listeners are likely to have (Glucksberg & Krauss, 1967; McDevitt & Ford, 1987). As teachers, we must let our students know exactly when we don't understand them. For instance, we can ask them to explain who or what they are talking about when they refer to people or things with which we are unfamiliar, and we can express our confusion when they describe events and ideas ambiguously.

Another component of effective oral communication is **pragmatics**, the social conventions governing appropriate verbal interactions with others. Pragmatics include not only rules of etiquette—taking turns speaking when conversing with others, saying goodbye when leaving, and so on—but also strategies for beginning and ending conversations, changing the subject, telling stories, and arguing effectively. Children continue to refine their knowledge of pragmatics throughout the elementary grades (Owens, 1996); my own observation has been that this process continues into the middle and high school years (often even longer). When students haven't mastered certain social conventions—for instance, when they interrupt frequently or change the subject without warning—others may find their behavior irritating or strange; a lack of pragmatic skills, then, can seriously interfere with students' relationships with their peers. It is important to observe students' pragmatic skills as they interact both with us and with their classmates and to give students guided practice in any skills they may be lacking.

Development of Metalinguistic Awareness

Throughout the school years, students exhibit a tendency to "play" with language by creating rhymes, chants, jokes, puns, and so forth (Christie & Johnsen, 1983; Owens, 1996). Such wordplay is almost certainly beneficial; for instance, rhymes help students discover the relationships between sounds and letters, and jokes and puns may help students come to realize that words and phrases often have more than one meaning (L. Bradley & Bryant, 1991; Cazden, 1976). In the latter case, students are developing their **metalinguistic awareness**—the ability to think about the nature of language itself.

Metalinguistic awareness seems to emerge relatively late in the game. During the elementary years, students gradually become capable of determining when sentences are grammatically acceptable and when they are not (Bowey, 1986). As they move into the upper elementary and middle school grades, they begin to consider the various functions of words in a sentence (nouns, verbs, adjectives, etc.); such growth is almost certainly due, at least in part, to the formal instruction they receive about parts of speech. High school students enhance their metalinguistic awareness still further as they consider the figurative nature of words—the nonliteral meanings of proverbs, the symbolism in poems and literature, and so on. Studying a second language also promotes metalinguistic awareness, as we shall see now.

Learning a Second Language

As the adult workplace becomes increasingly international in scope, the need is greater than ever for children to learn one or more languages in addition to their native tongue. As noted earlier, there may be a sensitive period for learning language, thus making exposure to a language in the first few years of life ideal. Yet research evidence regarding the best time to learn a *second* language is mixed and often tainted by serious methodological problems (Bialystok, 1994a; Hakuta & McLaughlin, 1996; Long, 1995; Newport, 1993). In general, early instruction in a second language is important for mastering correct pronunciations, especially if the language is very different from a student's native tongue, and perhaps also for mastering complex grammatical constructions (Bialystok, 1994a, 1994b; Bruer, 1999; Johnson & Newport, 1989). Aside from such possible limitations, children and adolescents can acquire fluency in a second language regardless of when they begin instruction.

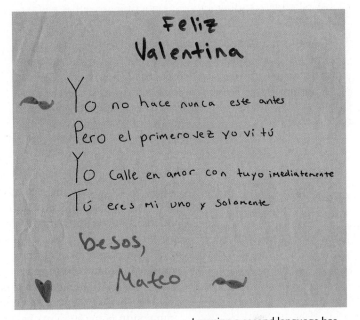

Learning a second language has both cognitive and social benefits. Here Matt, an eighth grader, uses his rudimentary knowledge of Spanish to create a Valentine's Day card.

Although there may be no hard-and-fast sensitive period for learning a second language, beginning second-language instruction in the early years has definite advantages. For one thing, it appears that learning a second language facilitates achievement in such other academic areas as reading, vocabulary, and grammar (Diaz, 1983; Reich, 1986). Instruction in a foreign language also sensitizes young children to the international and multicultural nature of the world. Students who learn a second language during the elementary school years express more positive attitudes toward people who speak that language and are more likely to enroll in foreign language classes in high school (Reich, 1986).

Bilingualism

A *bilingual* student speaks two languages fluently. Some bilingual children have been raised in families in which two languages are spoken regularly. Others have lived for a time in a community where one language is spoken and then moved to a community where a different language is spoken. Still others live in a bilingual society—for example, in Canada (where both English and French are spoken), Wales (where both English and Welsh are spoken), and certain ethnic communities in the United States (where a language such as Spanish or Chinese is spoken along with English).

Research reveals some advantages to being bilingual. For example, bilingual children, when they are truly fluent in both languages, tend to perform better on tasks requiring complex cognitive functioning (e.g., on intelligence tests or on tasks requiring creativity). They also appear to have greater metalinguistic awareness—a better understanding of the nature of language itself (Bialystok, 2001; Diaz & Klingler, 1991; Garcia, 1994; C. E. Moran & Hakuta, 1995).

Promoting bilingualism. In some situations, learning a second language is critical; this is the case for non-English-speaking students whose families intend to become long-term or permanent residents of an English-speaking country. In other situations, learning a second language, though not

INTO THE CLASSROOM: *Facilitating Language Development*

Teach vocabulary related to topics being studied. Look for and correct students' misconceptions of word meanings.

A science teacher explains and illustrates the concepts *speed* and *acceleration* and corrects students who erroneously use one term in place of the other.

Teach conventions of word usage and syntax.

A high school English teacher describes the situations in which it is appropriate to use *who* and *whom* and then gives her students practice using both words correctly.

Help students understand that being good listeners involves understanding and remembering as well as paying attention.

A fourth-grade teacher invites a police officer to speak to her class about bicycle safety. Following the officer's departure, she asks her students to summarize the important things to remember when riding a bicycle.

Give students lots of practice presenting their ideas orally to others. Provide specific and constructive feedback about how well they are communicating.

A high school history teacher has each student give an oral report on a topic related to early American history. After each report he speaks with the student individually, identifying parts of the report that were especially effective and providing suggestions for giving a better report the next time.

Spend time looking at the nature of language itself.

A sixth-grade teacher asks, "Has anyone ever heard the expression 'A stitch in time saves nine'? What does that expression mean? Is it only about sewing?"

Encourage all students to learn a second language.

A second-grade teacher spends a few minutes each day teaching her students some simple French vocabulary and phrases. She also encourages them to use their French during lunch and on the playground.

essential, is highly desirable; this is the case for English-speaking students who may wish eventually to study or work in societies where a different language is spoken. But bilingualism also has immediate social benefits in the classroom: In cases where different students speak only one of two different languages (perhaps some speaking only English and others speaking only Spanish), teaching students one another's languages increases student interaction (A. Doyle, 1982).

How can we help children become fluent in a second language? It appears that the best approach depends on the circumstances. For English-speaking students learning a second language while still living in their native country, total **immersion** in the second language—hearing and speaking it almost exclusively within the classroom—is the method of choice. Total immersion helps students become proficient in a second language relatively quickly, and any adverse effects of such immersion on students' achievement in other areas of the curriculum appear to be short-lived (Collier, 1992; Cunningham & Graham, 2000; Krashen, 1996; W. P. Thomas, Collier, & Abbott, 1993).

In contrast, for non-English-speaking students who have recently immigrated to this country, total immersion in English may actually be detrimental to their academic progress. For these students, **bilingual education**—wherein instruction in academic subject areas is given in students' native language while they are simultaneously taught to speak and write in English—leads to higher academic achievement (e.g., in reading, mathematics, and social studies), greater self-esteem, and a better attitude toward school (Moll & Diaz, 1985; C. E. Snow, 1990; Willig, 1985; S. C. Wright & Taylor, 1995).

Why does immersion work better for some students while bilingual education is more effective for others? As discussed earlier, language is critical for children's cognitive development, promoting social interaction and providing a symbolic means through which they can mentally represent and think about their world. We therefore need a method of teaching a second language without losing the first language in the process. In this country, English-speaking students immersed in a second language at school still have many opportunities—at home, with their friends, and in the local community and culture—to continue using and developing their English. But recent immigrants to this country often have little opportunity outside their immediate families to use their native language. If these students are taught exclusively in English, they may very well lose proficiency in one language (their native tongue) before developing proficiency in another (Pérez, 1998; Willig, 1985; S. C. Wright, Taylor, & Macarthur, 2000).

Given the many advantages of second-language learning and bilingualism, we should think seriously about promoting bilingualism in *all* students (Navarro, 1985; NCSS Task Force on Ethnic Studies Curriculum Guidelines, 1992). Doing so would not only promote our students' cognitive and linguistic development but also enhance communication, interaction, and interpersonal understanding among students with diverse linguistic and cultural backgrounds (Minami & Ovando, 1995).

Considering Diversity in Cognitive and Linguistic Development

As previously noted, the *order* in which children acquire specific cognitive and linguistic capabilities is often similar from one child to the next, but the *rate* at which they acquire these abilities may differ considerably (e.g., see Figure 2.7). So for any particular age-group, we are likely to find considerable diversity in the developmental levels of our students. From the perspective of Piaget's theory, we may see signs of both preoperational and concrete operational thinking in the primary grades; for example, some students may demonstrate conservation while others do not conserve. Similarly, we may find evidence of both concrete and formal operational thinking at the middle school and high school levels; for example, some students will think more abstractly than others, and students will differ in such abilities as hypothetical reasoning, separation and control of variables, and proportional thought. From Vygotsky's point of view, we will inevitably have students with different zones of proximal development: The cognitive challenges necessary for optimal cognitive development will vary from one student to the next. And from an information processing perspective, we will find diversity in the learning strategies that our students use, as well as in the background knowledge and experiences from which they can draw as they try to understand and elaborate on new information.

Children's cognitive development may also differ depending on the cultures in which they've been raised. For instance, some of the logical reasoning abilities that Piaget described (e.g., conservation, separation and control of variables) and some of the learning strategies (e.g., rehearsal) that information processing theorists have identified appear earlier in children raised in Western countries than in children raised in developing countries, presumably because such cognitive processes are more highly valued and more systematically promoted in Western culture (Berk, 2000; N. S. Cole, 1990; Trawick-Smith, 2000). When we consider cognitive abilities that other cultures value more than we do (e.g., the ability to judge the right amount of clay to use in making a pot, or the ability to locate food in a barren desert), children in our society fall short (Kearins, 1981; Price-Williams, Gordon, & Ramirez, 1969; Rogoff & Waddell, 1982).

We will find diversity in students' language capabilities as well. For example, our students will vary considerably in the size of their vocabulary and in their knowledge of complex syntactical structures. Some students may express themselves using a **dialect**—a form of English characteristic of a particular ethnic group or region of the country—different from the one that we ourselves use (more about dialects in Chapter 4). Other students may have **limited English proficiency (LEP)**—they will be fluent in their native language but not in English—and so have difficulties both in communicating their ideas and in understanding others. Finally, our students are likely to have acquired varying social conventions when conversing with others—varying pragmatic skills—depending on the families and cultures in which they've been raised. We will identify strategies for accommodating some of these differences in our discussion of ethnicity in Chapter 4.

As teachers, we must continually be aware of the specific cognitive and linguistic abilities and weaknesses that individual students possess and then tailor instruction accordingly. For example, our students will display more advanced reasoning skills when we ask them to deal with topics with which they are familiar. And as we have seen, students with limited English proficiency will achieve at higher levels in a bilingual education program.

FIGURE 2.7 Students exhibit considerable diversity in the age at which they acquire formal operational capabilities. Here 10-year-old Laura shows some ability to envision alternatives to reality. In Piaget's theory such an ability appears, on average, at age 11 or 12.

Accommodating Students with Special Needs

We are especially likely to see differences in cognitive and linguistic development in our students with special needs. For example, we may have a few students who show especially advanced

TABLE 2.3

STUDENTS IN INCLUSIVE SETTINGS

Promoting Cognitive and Linguistic Development in Students with Special Educational Needs

CATEGORY	CHARACTERISTICS YOU MIGHT OBSERVE	SUGGESTED CLASSROOM STRATEGIES
Students with specific cognitive or academic difficulties	• Distractibility, difficulty paying and maintaining attention • Few effective learning strategies • Possible difficulties with abstract reasoning • Difficulties in listening comprehension • Difficulties in expressive language (e.g., in syntax)	• Make sure you have students' attention before giving instructions or presenting information. • Keep distracting stimuli to a minimum. • Teach learning strategies within the context of classroom lessons. • Encourage students to use self-talk to help themselves deal with challenging situations. • Seek assistance from a speech pathologist when students have unusual difficulties with listening comprehension or spoken language.
Students with social or behavioral problems	• Lack of attention, as reflected in restlessness, daydreaming, etc. • Delayed language development (some students with autism) • Uneven performance on cognitive tasks (some students with autism)	• Capture students' attention by gearing instruction toward their personal interests. • Provide intensive instruction and practice for any delayed cognitive or linguistic skills. (Also use strategies presented above for students with specific cognitive or academic difficulties.)
Students with general delays in cognitive and social functioning	• Reasoning abilities characteristic of younger children (e.g., preoperational thought in the upper elementary grades, inability to think abstractly in the secondary grades) • Lack of learning strategies such as rehearsal and organization • Less developed knowledge base to which new information can be related • Delayed language development (e.g., in vocabulary, listening comprehension)	• Present new information in a concrete, hands-on fashion. • Teach simple learning strategies (e.g., rehearsal) within the context of classroom lessons. • Give instructions in concrete and specific terms.
Students with physical or sensory challenges	• Less developed knowledge base to which new information can be related, due to limited experiences in the outside world • Possible cognitive and/or language deficiencies (if brain damage is present) • Delayed language development (if students have long-term hearing loss) • Difficulties with articulation (if students have limited muscular control or are congenitally deaf)	• Provide the basic life experiences that students may have missed because of their disabilities. • Identify any specific cognitive and/or language deficiencies, and adjust instruction and assessment practices accordingly. • Provide intensive instruction in the cognitive and/or language skills that students are lacking.
Students with advanced cognitive development	• Appearance of formal operational thinking (e.g., abstract thought) at an earlier age • Tendency for many regular classroom tasks to be below students' zone of proximal development • Greater knowledge base to which new information can be related • Advanced vocabulary • More sophisticated expressive language	• Provide opportunities through which students can explore classroom topics in greater depth or complexity. • Provide opportunities for students to proceed through the curriculum at a more rapid pace.

Sources: Beirne-Smith, Ittenbach, & Patton, 2002; Butterfield & Ferretti, 1987; Carter & Ormrod, 1982; Cone, Wilson, Bradley, & Reese, 1985; Diaz & Berk, 1995; A. W. Gottfried, Gottfried, Bathurst, & Guerin, 1994; M. Harris, 1992; Mastropieri, Scruggs, & Butcher, 1997; Mercer, 1997; Morgan & Jenson, 1988; Piirto, 1999; Pressley, 1995; Turnbull, Turnbull, Shank, & Leal, 1999; Winner, 1997.

cognitive development (e.g., students who are gifted); we may also have one or two who have not yet acquired the cognitive abilities typical of their age-group (e.g., students with mental retardation). We may have students with exceptional difficulties in specific aspects of cognition despite otherwise normal cognitive development (e.g., students with learning disabilities or attention-deficit hyperactivity disorder). Finally, we may have students who display impairments in speech that significantly interfere with their classroom performance (e.g., students with speech and communication disorders). Chapter 5 looks more closely at all of these students with special needs.

Table 2.3 presents specific characteristics related to cognitive and linguistic development that we may see in students with a variety of special educational needs. It also presents numerous strategies for helping such students achieve academic success.

In this chapter we have considered several theoretical perspectives of, as well as developmental trends in, cognitive and linguistic development. Let's now summarize some of the key points and identify common themes that have run throughout our discussion.

Developmental Principles in the Classroom

Children develop skills and abilities in a somewhat predictable sequence, although not always at the same rate, and their development depends on environment as well as heredity. As teachers, we need to monitor the growth and development of our students and be sure they acquire the skills necessary for future learning. We must also remember that what we do in the classroom will likely impact our students' development over the long run.

Cognitive Development

Piaget's four stages give us a rough idea of when various logical thinking capabilities will emerge, and Piagetian tasks (e.g., conservation problems) can provide valuable insights about how our students are reasoning. Regardless of developmental stage, all learners benefit from building on prior knowledge, discovering relationships among concepts and ideas, and encountering perplexing events and tasks that encourage them to think in more sophisticated ways.

Vygotsky's theory encourages us to share with growing children the ways that we, as adults, think about and interpret the events around us. It also encourages us to help students develop by challenging them and stretching the limits of what they know and can do. As we do so, we must give them the guidance and support (the scaffolding) they need to perform difficult tasks successfully.

Information processing theorists believe that cognitive capabilities improve over time, but not necessarily in the discrete stages that Piaget proposed. We must remember that our students will often be less efficient learners than we are; for example, they will have shorter attention spans, less knowledge to which they can relate school subject matter, less sophisticated learning strategies, and less awareness of their own thought processes.

Linguistic Development

We see continuing development in language—for instance, in vocabulary, syntax, listening comprehension, oral communication, and metalinguistic awareness—throughout the school years. Whether we have English-speaking students, bilingual students, or nonnative speakers of English, we need to be aware of the ways in which language can foster or hinder classroom performance. We must adapt our instruction and instructional materials to our students' existing linguistic knowledge and skills. At the same time, we can do many things to promote students' language development; for instance, we can explicitly teach vocabulary and grammar, give students many opportunities to practice oral communication skills, and teach them one or more foreign languages.

General Themes in Cognitive and Linguistic Development

At first glance, the three views of cognitive development described in this chapter seem very different from one another. Piaget's theory portrays cognitive development as a sequence of relatively discrete stages, each with its own set of abilities and limitations. In contrast, information processing theorists describe cognitive development in terms of gradual changes in cognitive processes and metacognitive awareness. And Vygotsky's approach looks more at the social factors that foster cognitive development than at specific changes in children's thinking. Furthermore, our discussion of language development has focused not on thinking and reasoning processes or the environmental conditions that promote them, but instead on the development of specific language skills and abilities.

Despite the varying directions in which this chapter has gone, several themes have appeared repeatedly. These themes, summarized in Table 2.4, are the following:

■ *Children tend to think in qualitatively different ways at different ages.* Qualitative changes in children's thinking processes are elements of both Piaget's theory and information processing theory. Piaget portrayed these changes as reflecting four distinct stages of thought and reasoning capabilities. Information processing theorists have instead proposed that young children lack many learning strategies (e.g., organization, elaboration) and the metacognitive sophistication (e.g., knowing *when* they know something) that adolescents possess. Some trends in language development reflect qualitative changes in cognition as well; for example, children's ability to correctly interpret figurative language (e.g., "Your eyes are bigger than your stomach") rests squarely on their ability to reason about abstract ideas. In general, children become capable of increasingly complex and abstract thought processes, learning strategies, and language as they grow older.

■ *Children actively construct their knowledge.* All three perspectives of cognitive development portray children not as passive receptacles for incoming information, but as active, constructive *builders* of knowledge. Piaget described cognitive development as a process of constructing one's own understanding of the world. Vygotsky believed that children actively talk themselves through difficult tasks and that children and adults often work collaboratively to develop a viable approach to a task. And information processing theorists have proposed that children use such constructive learning processes as organization and elaboration to help them learn and remember classroom subject matter. Constructive processes are presumed to occur in language development—for instance, in acquiring word meanings and syntactical rules—as well. Chapter 7 explores the process of knowledge construction in greater depth.

■ *Development builds upon prior acquisitions.* Children rarely learn new knowledge and skills in isolation from the things they have already learned; instead, they use what they know to help them acquire more complex understandings and processes. For instance, Piaget proposed that children adapt to their world through the two processes of assimilation and accommodation, both of which involve relating new experiences to previously learned information. Information processing theorists also stress the importance of prior knowledge: The more children already know about the world, the greater their ability to understand, elaborate on, and remember new information.

■ *Challenging situations and tasks promote development.* We saw the importance of challenge most clearly in Vygotsky's concept of the zone of proximal development. Yet challenge plays a role in

TABLE 2.4

PRINCIPLES/ASSUMPTIONS

General Themes Characterizing Cognitive and Linguistic Development

THEME	EDUCATIONAL IMPLICATION	EXAMPLE
Children tend to think in different ways at different ages.	Ask students to describe how they are thinking about classroom subject matter and to explain the logic they are using when drawing conclusions.	Ask high school students what they do and how they think when they study for tests. If some of them depend primarily on rehearsal to learn classroom material, teach them how they might also organize and elaborate on the ideas they are studying.
Children actively construct their knowledge.	Give students many opportunities to experience new events, manipulate unfamiliar objects, and experiment with various ways of solving problems.	Before beginning instruction on multiplication and division, ask third graders to work in small groups to figure out how many days' worth of carrots Bugs Bunny has if he has 75 carrots and eats 5 carrots each day. After all groups have arrived at an answer, ask students to explain their procedures and reasoning to the class (Hiebert et al., 1997).
Development builds upon prior acquisitions.	Ensure that students have prior knowledge and experiences to which they can relate new material. Use their background knowledge to help them understand new ideas.	When describing the representative nature of a democratic government, show middle school students how the federal legislature is similar to the student government system at their own school.
Challenging situations and tasks promote development.	Present tasks and problems that encourage students to use their existing knowledge and skills in new ways or that require them to develop new knowledge and skills.	Ask students in a high school history class to develop a computer-based presentation about a particular topic that their classmates can use to learn more about the topic. Teach the students how to incorporate text, images, and sound into their presentations (Lehrer, 1993).
Social interaction is critical for development.	Give students opportunities to share their ideas, perspectives, and beliefs.	Ask first graders to describe how their families celebrate holidays. Through such discussions, the students can discover that not everyone views the world as they do—in this case, that different cultures, and even different families within a particular culture, have widely varying holiday traditions.

other perspectives as well. From Piaget's view, children modify their schemes and develop new ones only when they cannot easily interpret new events using their existing schemes—that is, when they experience disequilibrium. From an information processing view, children develop more sophisticated learning strategies only when their present ones are not sufficiently effective. And children are likely to develop more sophisticated receptive and expressive language capabilities only if specific tasks require them to do so.

■ *Social interaction is critical for development.* Social interaction is a key element in both Vygotsky's and Piaget's theories. Vygotsky stressed the importance of dialogue between children and

adults as a means of helping children acquire more mature ways of thinking about and interpreting objects and events. And both Piaget and Vygotsky pointed out that when children disagree and argue with one another, they begin to appreciate that any single situation often may be viewed from multiple perspectives. Language development, too, depends heavily on social interaction: Children can learn to understand and produce language only if they encounter the language of others. In fact, a child's social world has ramifications far beyond cognitive and linguistic development; it also has ramifications for personal, social, and moral development, as you will discover in Chapter 3.

CASE STUDY: *In the Eye of the Beholder*

Ms. Kontos is teaching a unit on vision to her fifth-grade class. She shows her students a diagram of the various parts of the human eye: lens, cornea, retina, and so on. She then explains that people can see objects because light from the sun or another light source bounces off those objects and into the eye. To illustrate this idea, she shows them this picture:

"Do you all understand how our eyes work?" she asks. Her students nod that they do.

The next day, Ms. Kontos gives her students this picture:

She asks them to draw how light travels so that the child can see the tree. More than half of the students draw lines something like this:

Obviously, most of Ms. Kontos' students have not really learned what she thought she had taught them.

- What went wrong? Can you explain the students' inability to learn within the context of Piaget's theory of cognitive development? Can you explain it using some of Vygotsky's ideas? Can you explain it from an information processing perspective?
- In what ways might students' language capabilities have been insufficient to enable them to understand?
- What things might Ms. Kontos have done differently?

Once you have answered these questions, compare your responses with those presented in Appendix B.

PRAXIS Turn to Appendix C, "Matching Book and Ancillary Content to the PRAXIS™ Principles of Learning and Teaching Tests," to discover sections of this chapter that may be especially applicable to the PRAXIS™ tests.

Now go to our Companion Website at http://www.prenhall. com/ormrod to assess your understanding of chapter content with "Multiple-Choice Questions," apply comprehension in "Essay Questions," broaden your knowledge of educational psychology with related "Web Links," gain greater insight about classroom learning in "Learning in the Content Areas," and analyze and assess classroom work in the "Student Artifact Library."

Key Concepts

developmental milestone (p. 21)
universals (in development) (p. 21)
stage theory (p. 21)
maturation (p. 21)
temperament (p. 21)
sensitive period (p. 22)
cortex (p. 22)
neuron (p. 22)
synapse (p. 22)
constructivism (p. 24)
scheme (p. 24)
assimilation (p. 24)
accommodation (p. 24)
equilibrium (p. 24)
disequilibrium (p. 25)
equilibration (p. 25)
sensorimotor stage (p. 26)
object permanence (p. 26)
preoperational stage (p. 26)
symbolic thinking (p. 26)
preoperational egocentrism (p. 26)
irreversibility (p. 27)

egocentric speech (p. 27)
reversibility (p. 27)
single classification (p. 27)
transductive reasoning (p. 27)
conservation (p. 28)
operations (p. 28)
concrete operations stage (p. 28)
multiple classification (p. 28)
deductive reasoning (p. 28)
separation and control of variables (p. 29)
proportional reasoning (p. 29)
formal operations stage (p. 30)
formal operational egocentrism (p. 32)
sociocultural perspective (p. 36)
internalization (p. 36)
self-talk (private speech) (p. 37)
inner speech (p. 37)
actual developmental level (p. 37)
level of potential development (p. 37)
zone of proximal development (ZPD) (p. 38)
guided participation (p. 39)
scaffolding (p. 39)

apprenticeship (p. 40)
cognitive apprenticeship (p. 40)
cognitive processes (p. 42)
learning strategy (p. 43)
rehearsal (p. 43)
organization (p. 43)
elaboration (p. 43)
knowledge base (p. 45)
metacognition (p. 46)
receptive language (p. 49)
expressive language (p. 49)
semantics (p. 49)
undergeneralization (p. 49)
overgeneralization (p. 49)
syntax (p. 50)
overregularization (p. 51)
pragmatics (p. 52)
metalinguistic awareness (p. 53)
immersion (p. 54)
bilingual education (p. 54)
dialect (p. 55)
limited English proficiency (LEP) (p. 55)

3

Personal, Social, and Moral Development

*W*hat people in your life have had a significant impact on the kind of person you are today? How have parents or other family members influenced the ways that you think about yourself, the manner in which you interact with others, or the moral values that guide your decisions? Can you think of teachers who've had a major effect on your self-confidence, your interpersonal skills, or your moral values? In what ways have your friends and classmates also played a role in the development of these characteristics?

School is not just a place where students learn reading, writing, and arithmetic. It is also a place where they develop beliefs about their own abilities, acquire strategies for getting along with other people, and explore various perspectives on right and wrong. In other words, school is a place where students grow personally, socially, and morally as well as academically.

In this chapter we will consider children's personal development (their personalities and self-perceptions), social development (their ability to interact effectively with other people), and moral development (their understanding of right and wrong behavior). In our discussion we will address questions such as these:

- How do heredity and environment influence students' personal, social, and moral development?
- How do students' self-concepts and self-esteem affect their classroom performance and academic achievement? How can we help students think positively about themselves and their abilities?
- How do peer relationships change with age? What cognitive abilities enhance such relationships?
- How can we help students learn effective ways of interacting with their peers? What strategies are likely to promote productive relationships and friendships among diverse groups of students?
- In what ways do students' moral reasoning and behavior change over time, and how can we promote their moral and prosocial development?

CASE STUDY: *The Bad Apple*

Adam seems to cause problems wherever he goes. In the classroom he is rude and defiant. On a typical school day he comes to class late, slouches in his seat, rests his feet on his desk, yells obscenities at classmates and his teacher, and stubbornly refuses to participate in classroom activities.

Away from his teacher's watchful eye, Adam's behavior is even worse. He shoves and pushes students in the hall, steals lunches from smaller boys in the cafeteria, and frequently initiates physical fights on the school grounds.

For obvious reasons, no one at school likes Adam very much. His classmates say that he's a bully, and their parents describe him as a "bad apple," rotten to the core. Even his teacher, who tries to find the best in all of her students, has seen few redeeming qualities in Adam and is beginning to write him off as a lost cause.

Adam doesn't seem to be bothered by the hostile feelings he generates. He's counting the days until he can legally drop out of school.

- Why does Adam behave the way he does? What possible factors in his environment—perhaps at home, at school, or among his peers—might have contributed to his aggressiveness, impulsiveness, and apparent self-centeredness?
- How might a teacher help Adam develop more appropriate and productive behavior?

Influence of Heredity and Environment on Personal, Social, and Moral Development

You may have formed several hypotheses about why Adam behaves as he does. Perhaps a parent encourages aggressive behavior, or at least does nothing to *discourage* it. Perhaps Adam lives in a high-crime neighborhood in which violence is commonplace and aggression is the best means of self-defense. Perhaps Adam's family can't afford to provide breakfast at home or lunch at school, or perhaps family members never taught Adam that stealing infringes on the rights of others. At school, perhaps previous teachers have tolerated Adam's obscene language. Perhaps classmates have learned to stay away from him because of his inappropriate social skills, and he now finds that pushing, shoving, and picking fights are the only ways he can get their attention.

The hypotheses just listed identify several environmental factors that may have led Adam to behave as he does. Yet hereditary factors may play a role as well: Environmental conditions often interact with genetic predispositions to determine the personalities and interpersonal skills that students exhibit. Let's look briefly at one genetic factor—temperament—and three environmental factors—parents, culture, and peers—that appear to influence personal, social, and moral development.

Temperamental Differences

Children seem to have certain personalities almost from birth. For instance, some are cheerful and easy to care for; others are fussy and demanding. Such differences reflect **temperament,** a genetic predisposition to respond in particular ways to one's physical and social environments. Researchers have identified many characteristics that emerge early in life and appear to have genetic origins, including general activity level, adventurousness, shyness, irritability, and distractibility (Bouchard, Lykken, McGue, Segal, & Tellegen, 1990; Kagan, Snidman, & Arcus, 1992; Lanthier & Bates, 1997; Plomin, 1989).

Keep in mind, however, that genetic differences in temperament are only *predispositions* to behave in certain ways, and environmental factors may point different children with the same predisposition in somewhat different directions (R. A. Thompson, 1998). For example, temperamentally shy children are more likely to feel comfortable around other children if they have attended preschool before beginning kindergarten or first grade. Similarly, distractible children are more likely to keep their attention focused on classroom tasks if they can work at their own desk, rather than at a table with other students (Pfiffner & Barkley, 1998).

Effects of Parenting

The behaviors of parents and other caregivers influence children's personalities from the very beginning of life. For example, when parents and their infants form a strong, affectionate bond (a process called **attachment**), the infants are likely to develop into amiable, independent, self-confident, and cooperative children who adjust easily to the classroom environment and establish productive relationships with teachers and peers. In contrast, those who do not become closely attached to a parent or some other individual early in life can be immature, dependent, unpopular, and prone to disruptive and aggressive behaviors later on (Hartup, 1989; Jacobson & Wille, 1986; S. Shulman, Elicker, & Sroufe, 1994; Sroufe, 1983; Sroufe, Carlson, & Schulman, 1993).

For more information about various parenting styles, see the chapter "Parenting Styles and Children's Behavior" in the *Study Guide and Reader* that accompanies this book.

General patterns of childrearing—*parenting styles*—also appear to play a role in children's personal, social, and moral development. For most children, the ideal situation appears to be **authoritative parenting,** in which parents provide a loving and supportive home, hold high expectations and standards for performance, explain why some behaviors are acceptable and others are not, and enforce household rules consistently. Children from authoritative homes are happy, energetic, self-confident, and likeable; they make friends easily and show self-control and concern for the rights and needs of others (Baumrind, 1989; W. A. Collins et al., 2000; Lamborn, Mounts, Steinberg, & Dornbusch, 1991; Maccoby & Martin, 1983; Rohner, 1998; L. Steinberg, Elmen, & Mounts, 1989). In contrast, children from very controlling homes tend to be unhappy, anxious, and lacking in social skills; those from very permissive homes tend to be selfish, unmotivated, impulsive, and disobedient (Baumrind, 1989; Maccoby & Martin, 1983). Children whose parents use harsh disciplinary methods can be defiant, explosive, and unpredictable; those from exceptionally abusive homes tend to have emotional difficulties and low self-esteem and can be oppositional and aggressive (Nix et al., 1999; R. A. Thompson & Wyatt, 1999). Thinking back to the opening case study, we might wonder whether Adam's impulsiveness, self-centeredness, and aggressiveness are, at least in part, a result of ineffective parenting.

Keep in mind, however, that research on parenting is typically *correlational* in nature: It shows relationships between parenting styles and children's characteristics but does not necessarily indicate that certain parenting behaviors *cause* certain characteristics in children. Many children do well despite unhappy conditions at home (Masten & Coatsworth, 1998; R. A. Thompson & Wyatt, 1999). In some cases, parents' behaviors are probably the result of how *their children* treat *them* (Clarke-Stewart, 1988; J. R. Harris, 1998; Maccoby & Martin, 1983; Stice & Barrera, 1995). Recall our earlier discussion of temperament: Some children are naturally quieter and more easygoing, whereas others are more lively or irritable. When children are quick to comply with their parents' wishes, parents may have no reason to be overly controlling. When children are hot-tempered, parents may have to impose more restrictions on behavior and administer consequences for misbehaviors more frequently. We must be careful that we don't always place total credit or blame on parents for their parenting styles.

As teachers, we can serve as valuable resources to parents about possible strategies for promoting their children's development. With newsletters, parent-teacher conferences, and parent discussion groups, we can share ways of helping children develop age-appropriate behaviors. The important thing is to communicate information *without* pointing fingers or being judgmental about parenting behaviors.

Effects of Culture

Beginning early in their lives, most children learn that there are certain things that they can or should do and other things that they definitely should *not* do. For example, many parents teach their toddlers not to hit other children, first-grade teachers ask their students to sit quietly rather than interrupt when someone else is speaking, and high school teachers expect their students to turn in homework assignments on time.

To some degree, different cultural groups encourage different behaviors. For example, in China, many children are raised to be shy, whereas in Zambia, smiling and sociability are apt to be the norm (X. Chen, Rubin, & Sun, 1992; Hale-Benson, 1986; D. Y. F. Ho, 1986, 1994). European-American families often encourage assertiveness and self-reliance, but families from many other countries (e.g., Mexico, China, Japan, India) encourage restraint, obedience, and deference to elders (Chao, 1994; Goodnow, 1992; Joshi & MacLean, 1994; Rothbaum, Weisz, Pott, Miyake, & Morelli, 2000; Trawick-Smith, 2000).

The process of molding behavior so that children fit in with a particular cultural group is called **socialization**. Through socialization children learn the culture's **norms**, the rules determining acceptable and unacceptable behavior. They also learn the specific **roles** that different people occupy within their society—the patterns of behavior acceptable for people having various functions within the group. For example, children usually learn that different behaviors are considered appropriate for the teachers and students in a classroom. Many children also develop the notion that boys and girls should behave differently and that men and women should do likewise. Each culture has its own norms regarding acceptable behavior and defines the roles of various individuals (e.g., teachers vs. students, males vs. females) in a somewhat unique fashion.

In Chapter 4 we will look more closely at how boys and girls, as well as children from various ethnic groups, are often socialized quite differently.

Children typically learn their earliest lessons about society's expectations from parents and other family members, who teach them personal hygiene, table manners, rudimentary interpersonal skills (e.g., saying "please" and "thank you"), and so on. Yet teachers become equally important socialization agents once children reach school age. For example, in our society, teachers typically expect and encourage behaviors such as the following (Helton & Oakland, 1977; R. D. Hess & Holloway, 1984):

- Obeying school rules
- Behaving in an orderly fashion
- Showing respect for authority figures
- Controlling impulses
- Following instructions
- Working independently

Children may experience some culture shock when they first enter school, especially if behaviors expected at school are very different from those expected at home.

- Completing assigned tasks
- Helping and cooperating with classmates
- Striving for academic excellence
- Delaying satisfaction of immediate needs and desires in order to attain long-term goals

When behaviors expected of students at school differ from those expected at home, children may become confused, nonproductive, sometimes even resistant (R. D. Hess & Holloway, 1984). In other words, they may experience some **culture shock** when they first enter school.

As teachers, we must especially encourage our students to exhibit those behaviors essential for long-term school success—behaviors such as obeying school rules, following instructions, and working independently. For example, when we expect students to work independently, even those students who have not had this expectation placed on them at home show improved work habits (J. L. Epstein, 1983). At the same time, students will need our guidance, support, and patience when our expectations differ from those of their family or cultural group.

Peer Influences

Parents, teachers, and other adults in one's culture are hardly the only people to have a say in students' personal, social, and moral development. Peers, too, influence such development, and they do so in a myriad of ways—for instance by serving as examples of how one "should" behave, providing direct feedback and more subtle cues about students' social competence and likability, offering comfort and support in times of stress or uncertainty, creating interpersonal conflicts that encourage students to learn skills in negotiation and compromise, and presenting multiple perspectives on moral issues. The effects of friends, classmates, and other peers will be a key focus throughout the chapter.

Development of a Sense of Self

EXPERIENCING FIRSTHAND   *Describing Yourself*

On a sheet of paper, list ten adjectives or phrases that describe the kind of person you think you are.

How did you describe yourself? Are you a good student? Are you physically attractive? Are you friendly? likable? moody? intelligent? test-anxious? strong? uncoordinated? Your answers to these questions tell you something about your **self-concept**—your beliefs about yourself, your personality, your strengths and weaknesses. They may also tell you something about your **self-esteem**—your judgments and feelings about your own value and worth.

Students tend to have an overall, general feeling of self-worth: They believe either that they are good, capable individuals or that they are somehow inept or unworthy (Harter, 1990; H. W. Marsh & Craven, 1997). At the same time, they are usually aware that they have both strengths and weaknesses, that they do some things well and other things poorly (Harter, 1982; H. W. Marsh & Craven, 1997; H. W. Marsh & Yeung, 1997, 1998). For example, students may have somewhat different views about themselves in these areas (Harter, 1982):

- *Cognitive competence.* Students have general beliefs about their academic ability and performance. For example, they may describe themselves as being smart and performing academic tasks successfully, or perhaps instead as being stupid and doing poorly in school.
- *Social competence.* Students have general beliefs about their ability to relate to other people, especially their peers. For example, they may describe themselves as having many friends and being liked, or instead as having trouble making friends and being unpopular.

- *Physical competence.* Students have general beliefs about their ability to engage in physical activities such as sports and outdoor games. For example, they may describe themselves as being athletic and often selected for team sports, or instead as being uncoordinated and frequently excluded from team sports.

In which of these three areas do you perceive yourself to be strongest?

Students typically make still finer distinctions when judging themselves, especially as they get older (D. Hart, 1988; Harter, Whitesell, & Junkin, 1998; H. W. Marsh, 1990b; Schell, Klein, & Babey, 1996). For example, students may define themselves as poor readers but good in mathematics. They also are likely to see a difference between at least two aspects of their physical selves—their athletic capabilities and their physical attractiveness to others. Thus, self-concept appears to have several levels of specificity, as Figure 3.1 illustrates.

Students may even have differing beliefs about themselves regarding specific tasks and situations within a particular domain. For instance, although I don't think of myself as being a very good athlete—I'm not very strong, and I have little endurance—I know that I'm a fairly decent water-skier and racquetball player. And although I'm generally shy around people I've never met, I can be quite friendly once I've gotten to know them. When we talk about people's self-beliefs in such specific areas, we are talking about their **self-efficacy**—their beliefs about whether they are capable of achieving certain goals or outcomes (e.g., Bandura, 1982, 1997). We will look at self-efficacy more closely in Chapter 10.

Students tend to behave in ways that mirror their beliefs about themselves, and those who have positive self-views are more likely to succeed academically, socially, and physically (Assor & Connell, 1992; Ma & Kishor, 1997; Pintrich & Garcia, 1994; Yu, Elder, & Urdan, 1995). Those who see themselves as "good students" are more likely to pay attention, follow directions in class, use effective learning strategies, work independently and persistently to solve difficult problems, and enroll in challenging courses. In contrast, those who believe they are "poor students" are likely to misbehave in class, study infrequently or not at all, neglect to turn in homework assignments, and avoid taking difficult subjects. Along a similar vein, students who see themselves as friendly and likable are apt to seek the company of their classmates and perhaps run for student council, whereas those who believe they are disliked by classmates may keep to themselves or act with hostility and aggression toward their peers. Students with a high sense of physical competence will go out for extracurricular athletics, whereas those who see themselves as total klutzes probably will not.

Before you read ahead, can you predict what some of the factors affecting self-concept might be?

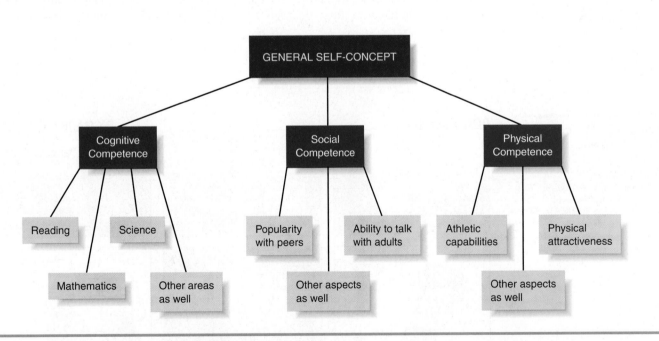

FIGURE 3.1 Self-concept is multifaceted and hierarchical in nature.

Factors Influencing the Development of Self-Views

Simply telling students that they are "good" or "smart" or "popular" is unlikely to make much of a dent in low self-esteem (Damon, 1991; L. Katz, 1993; H. W. Marsh & Craven, 1997). Furthermore, vague, abstract statements such as "You're special" have little meaning in the concrete realities of young children (McMillan, Singh, & Simonetta, 1994). However, two factors definitely *do* influence whether students form positive or negative self-concepts: students' own prior behaviors and performance, and the behaviors of other individuals. Each one offers insights as to how, as teachers, we can enhance our students' sense of self.

Students' Prior Behaviors and Performance

As we have seen, students' self-concepts influence the ways in which they behave. Yet the reverse is true as well: Students' self-assessments depend on how successfully they have behaved in the past (Damon, 1991; H. W. Marsh, 1990a). Students are more likely to believe that they have an aptitude for mathematics if they have been successful in previous math classes, to believe that they are likable individuals if they have been able to make and keep friends, or to believe that they are capable athletes if they have been victorious in athletic competitions.

The interplay between self-perceptions and behavior can create a vicious cycle: A poor self-concept leads to less productive behavior, which leads to fewer successes, which perpetuates the poor self-concept. (This might be the case for Adam in our opening case study.) To break the cycle, we must make sure that our students have numerous opportunities to succeed at academic, social, and physical tasks (Damon, 1991; L. Katz, 1993; Leary, 1999; H. W. Marsh & Craven, 1997). For example, we can gear assignments to their developmental levels and cognitive capabilities. We can make sure they have mastered the necessary prerequisite knowledge and skills *before* we assign new tasks. But we must remember that success in very *easy* activities is unlikely to have much of an impact, as Figure 3.2 humorously illustrates. Instead, we should assign challenging tasks, giving students the structure and support (the scaffolding) they need to accomplish those tasks successfully.

Behaviors of Others

Other people's behaviors influence students' self-perceptions in at least two ways. First, how students evaluate their own performance depends to some extent on how it compares to the performance of those around them, and especially to that of their peers (Guay, Boivin, & Hodges, 1999; H. W. Marsh, Chessor, Craven, & Roche, 1995; Nicholls, 1984). Older students in particular are likely to judge themselves in comparison with classmates: Those who see

FIGURE 3.2 We are unlikely to boost students' self-esteem by rewarding easy accomplishments.
DOONESBURY © G. B. Trudeau. Reprinted with permission of UNIVERSAL PRESS SYNDICATE. All rights reserved.

themselves performing better than others are likely to develop more positive self-perceptions than those who consistently find themselves falling short. To help our students develop positive self-concepts, then, we probably want to minimize competition and other situations in which students might compare themselves unfavorably with others.

Second, students' self-perceptions are affected by how others behave *toward* them (Harter, 1988, 1996; Hartup, 1989; Ryan & Lynch, 1989). Through their behaviors, adults and peers communicate their evaluations of a student and their beliefs about his or her worth as a person. For example, parents who accept their children as they are and who treat their children's interests and problems as important are likely to have children with positive self-concepts and high self-esteem. Parents who punish their children for the things they cannot do, without also praising for things done well, are likely to have children with low self-esteem (Griffore, 1981; Harter, 1983b). When parents and teachers have high expectations and offer support and encouragement for the attainment of challenging goals, students tend to have more positive self-concepts and greater confidence in their own academic capabilities (Eccles, Jacobs, Harold-Goldsmith, Jayaratne, & Yee, 1989; Eccles [Parsons], 1983; M. J. Harris & Rosenthal, 1985). Meanwhile, peers communicate information about students' social competence—perhaps by seeking out a student's companionship, ridiculing a student in front of others, and so on.

Obviously we can't always control how other people treat our students. But we can make sure that *we* respond to students in ways that will boost rather than lower self-esteem. Students who misbehave usually capture our attention more readily than those who behave appropriately, so it is often easier to criticize undesirable behavior than to praise desirable behavior. As teachers, we must make a concerted effort to catch students in the act of doing something well and praise them accordingly. We must be specific about what we are praising, because we will usually be more successful in improving particular aspects of our students' self-concepts than in improving their overall sense of self-worth (H. W. Marsh, 1990b). More generally, we must treat our students with respect—for example, by asking them about their personal views and opinions about academic subject matter, seeking their input in important classroom decisions, and communicating a genuine interest in their well-being (e.g., L. Katz, 1993).

We do not necessarily want to convince students that they are more capable than they really are, however. If their beliefs about themselves and their abilities are unrealistically high, they may lash out when people or circumstances provide evidence that threatens their inflated self-esteem (R. F. Baumeister, Smart, & Boden, 1996). Furthermore, our students can improve in areas of academic weakness and acquire more productive classroom behaviors only if we let them know when they are doing something ineffective or inappropriate. It is inevitable, then, that we occasionally give negative feedback. The trick is to give that negative feedback while also communicating respect and affection for our students as human beings. For example, when students make mistakes in their academic work, we can point out that errors are a natural part of the learning process and can provide valuable information about how to improve in knowledge and skills (Clifford, 1990). When students behave inappropriately in the classroom, we can communicate that although we like them, we disapprove of their present actions—for example, by saying something such as, "You're generally a very kind person, Gail, but you hurt Jenny's feelings just now by making fun of her new outfit."

Have you ever heard a student say something that threatens a classmate's self-esteem? How might a teacher intervene in such a situation?

Developmental Changes in Students' Self-Views

One early theorist, Erik Erikson, proposed that people's views of both themselves and others change in significant ways throughout the lifespan. His theory of eight psychosocial stages, presented in Figure 3.3, was a prominent and influential perspective of personal development in the 1960s and 1970s. Since then, developmental theorists have taken issue with several of Erikson's stages (see the footnotes in Figure 3.3). Although Erikson's theory provides a general idea of the ages at which various issues in personal development are likely to emerge, considerable flexibility and diversity exist in these time lines.

Let's look now at what more recent researchers have found about developmental changes during childhood and adolescence.

FIGURE 3.3 Erikson's eight stages of psychosocial development

Erik Erikson (1963, 1972) described a series of eight "psychosocial" stages through which people proceed over the course of development. Each stage presents a unique developmental task, and the way in which an individual deals with each task has a particular impact on that individual's personal development.

Trust versus mistrust (infancy). According to Erikson, the major developmental task of infants is to learn whether or not other people can be trusted to satisfy basic needs. A child's parents and other primary caretakers play a key role here. When caretakers can be depended on to feed a hungry stomach, change an uncomfortable diaper, and provide physical affection at regular intervals, an infant learns *trust*—that others are consistently dependable and reliable. When caretakers ignore the infant's needs, are inconsistent in attending to them, or are even abusive, the infant may instead learn *mistrust*—that the world is an undependable, unpredictable, and possibly dangerous place.

Autonomy versus shame and doubt (toddler years). With the increased muscular coordination that results from physiological maturation and the increased mobility that accompanies learning to crawl and walk, toddlers become capable of satisfying some of their own needs. They are learning to feed themselves, wash and dress themselves, and use the bathroom. When parents and other caretakers encourage self-sufficient behavior, toddlers develop a sense of *autonomy*—a sense of being able to handle many problems on their own. But when caretakers demand too much too soon, refuse to let children perform tasks of which they are capable, or ridicule early attempts at self-sufficiency, children may instead develop *shame and doubt* about their ability to handle the problems that the environment presents.

Initiative versus guilt (preschool years). During the preschool years, children become increasingly capable of accomplishing tasks on their own, rather than depending on adults to do those tasks for them. With this growing independence, they begin to make their own decisions about the activities they want to pursue. Sometimes they initiate projects that they can readily accomplish, but at other times they undertake projects that are beyond their limited capabilities or that interfere with the plans and activities of others. When parents and preschool teachers encourage and support their efforts, while also helping them make realistic choices that do not conflict with the needs of others, children develop *initiative*—independence in planning and undertaking activities.[a] When adults instead discourage the pursuit of independent activities or dismiss them as silly and bothersome, then children may develop *guilt* about their needs and desires.

Industry versus inferiority (elementary school years). Erikson proposed that the elementary school years are critical for the development of self-confidence. Ideally, elementary school provides

[a]Erikson did not address the very important role that culture plays in personal and emotional development. For example, many cultures intentionally discourage autonomy, initiative, and self-assertiveness in young children, sometimes as a way of protecting them from the very real dangers of their environments (X. Chen et al., 1992; Harwood, Miller, & Irizarry, 1995; and G. J. Powell, 1983).

Tina drew this self-portrait in second grade. Young children think largely of observable characteristics and behaviors when they define themselves.

Childhood

During the preschool and elementary school years, children tend to define themselves in terms of concrete, easily observable characteristics and behaviors (D. Hart, 1988; Harter, 1983a). As an example, when my son Alex was 9, he described himself this way:

I have brown hair, brown eyes. I like wearing short-sleeved shirts. My hair is curly. I was adopted. I was born in Denver. I like all sorts of critters. The major sport I like is baseball. I do fairly well in school. I have a lizard, and I'm going to get a second one.

Most preschoolers have positive self-concepts and high self-esteem; in fact, they often believe they are more capable than they actually are (Flavell et al., 1993). One reason for this overconfidence may be that they have few opportunities to compare their own performance to that of their age-mates. Instead, their self-assessments are probably based primarily on the progress they continue to make in accomplishing "big boy" and "big girl" tasks.

Children's self-esteem often drops soon after they begin elementary school (Harter, 1990; Stipek, 1981), perhaps because of the many new challenges—both academic and social—that school presents. As children have more and more opportunities to compare themselves with their classmates during the elementary grades, their self-assessments become increasingly realistic (Chapman, Tunmer, & Prochnow, 2000; Paris & Cunningham, 1996; Pintrich & Schunk, 2002).

FIGURE 3.3 continued

many opportunities for children to achieve the recognition of teachers, parents, and peers by producing things (*industry*)—for example, by drawing pictures, solving addition problems, and writing sentences. When children are encouraged to make and do things and are then praised for their accomplishments, they begin to demonstrate industry by being diligent, persevering at tasks until they complete them, and putting work before pleasure. If children are instead ridiculed or punished for their efforts or if they find that they are incapable of meeting their teachers' and parents' expectations, they may develop feelings of *inferiority* and inadequacy about their own capabilities.

Identity versus role confusion (adolescence). As they make the transition from childhood to adulthood, adolescents ponder the roles they will play in the adult world. Initially, they are likely to experience some *role confusion*—mixed ideas and feelings about the specific ways in which they will fit into society—and may experiment with a variety of behaviors and activities (e.g., tinkering with cars, baby-sitting for neighbors, engaging in extracurricular activities at school, affiliating with particular political or religious groups). Eventually, Erikson proposed, most adolescents achieve a sense of *identity* regarding who they are and where their lives are headed.[b]

Intimacy versus isolation (young adulthood). Once people have established their identities, they are ready to make commitments to one or more other individuals. They become capable of forming *intimate,* reciprocal relationships with others (e.g., through marriage or close friendships) and willingly make the sacrifices and compromises that such relationships require.[c] When people cannot form these intimate relationships (perhaps because of their reluctance or inability to forego the satisfaction of their own needs), then a sense of *isolation* may result.

Generativity versus stagnation (middle age). During middle age, the primary developmental task is one of contributing to society and helping to guide future generations. When an individual makes a contribution during this period, perhaps by raising a family or by working toward the betterment of society, a sense of *generativity*—a sense of productivity and accomplishment—results. In contrast, an individual who is self-centered and unable or unwilling to help society move forward develops a feeling of *stagnation*—a dissatisfaction with the relative lack of productivity.

Integrity versus despair (retirement years). According to Erikson, the final developmental task is retrospection. Individuals look back on their lives and accomplishments. They develop feelings of contentment and *integrity* if they believe that they have led a happy, productive life. They may instead develop a sense of *despair* if they look back on a life of disappointments and unachieved goals.

[b]Most people probably do not achieve a sense of identity as early or as easily as Erikson suggested (see the section "Late Adolescence" on pp. 70–72).

[c]Erikson based his stages on his work with men; for many women, a focus on intimacy occurs simultaneously with, and in some cases may even precede, a focus on identity (Josselson, 1988).

Early Adolescence

As children reach adolescence and gain an increasing capability for abstract thought, they begin to think of themselves in terms of general traits, such as "smart," "athletic," or "friendly" (Harter, 1988; Rosenberg, 1986). Consider my daughter Tina's self-description when she was in sixth grade:

> I'm cool. I'm awesome. I'm way cool. I'm twelve. I'm boy crazy. I go to Brentwood Middle School. I'm popular with my fans. I play viola. My best friend is Lindsay. I have a gerbil named Taj. I'm adopted. I'm beautiful.

Although Tina listed several concrete features about herself (her school, her best friend, her gerbil), she had clearly developed a fairly abstract self-perception that included such traits as "cool," "awesome," "boy crazy," "popular," and "beautiful." Tina's focus on coolness, popularity, and beauty, rather than on intelligence or academic achievement (or, I might add, modesty), is fairly typical: Social acceptance and physical appearance are far more important to most young adolescents than academic competence (D. Hart, 1988; Harter, 1990; Harter et al., 1998).

Students' self-concepts and self-esteem often drop as they make the transition from elementary school to junior high school, with the drop being more pronounced for girls (Eccles & Midgley, 1989; H. W. Marsh, 1990b; Sadker & Sadker, 1994; Wigfield & Eccles, 1994). The physiological changes that occur with puberty may be a factor: Although students' self-concepts depend increasingly on their beliefs about their appearance and popularity, boys and girls alike tend to think of themselves as being somewhat less attractive once they reach adolescence (Bender, 1997; Cornell et al., 1990; Harter, 1990). The changing school environment probably also has a negative impact. Traditional junior high schools often differ from elementary schools in

Many school districts now have *middle schools* designed to ease this transition. We'll look at the nature of middle schools in Chapter 11.

Musical ♪ ♫ ♩

Equestrian ∪

Lovable ♥ ♥ ♥ ♥

Imaginative

Noble

Dancer

Animal-lover

As students get older, they increasingly include abstract qualities in their self-descriptions. In this self-description, 12-year-old Melinda identifies several abstract characteristics: musical, lovable, imaginative, noble, and animal-lover.

several ways (Eccles & Midgley, 1989). For one thing, students don't have the opportunity to form the close-knit, supportive relationships with teachers that many of them had in elementary school. Students may also discover that their school grades are based more on competitive criteria—that is, on how well they perform in comparison with their classmates. Furthermore, at a time when they probably have an increased need for close friendships, students may find themselves in classes with many people they don't know. With all of these unsettling changes occurring simultaneously, it is not surprising that we see a temporary drop in young adolescents' self-esteem.

Two additional phenomena characterize the self-perceptions of young adolescents. First, these students often believe that, in any social situation, everyone else's attention is focused squarely on them—a phenomenon known as the **imaginary audience** (Elkind, 1981; Lapsley, 1993; R. M. Ryan & Kuczkowski, 1994). Because they believe themselves to be the center of attention, young teenagers (girls especially) are often preoccupied with their physical appearance and are quite critical of themselves, assuming that everyone else is equally observant and critical. Extreme sensitivity to embarrassment, when coupled with inadequate social skills, can lead some adolescents to respond with undue violence when their peers insult or verbally attack them (Lowry, Sleet, Duncan, Powell, & Kolbe, 1995).

A second noteworthy phenomenon in early adolescence is the **personal fable**: Young teenagers often believe themselves to be completely unlike anyone else (Elkind, 1981; Lapsley, 1993). For instance, they often think that their own feelings are completely unique—that those around them have never experienced such emotions. Hence, they may insist that no one else, least of all parents and teachers, could possibly know how they feel. Furthermore, they may have a sense of invulnerability and immortality, believing that they are immune to the normal dangers of life. Thus, many adolescents take seemingly foolish risks, such as experimenting with drugs and alcohol, having unprotected sexual intercourse, or driving at high speeds (Arnett, 1995; DeRidder, 1993; Packard, 1983; S. P. Thomas, Groër, & Droppleman, 1993).

The development of both the imaginary audience and personal fable may, to some extent, reflect students' changing cognitive abilities during the adolescent years. Some theorists have proposed that both the imaginary audience and the personal fable are symptoms of the *adolescent egocentrism* that Piaget described (Elkind, 1981). Others suggest that the two phenomena result from adolescents' increasing ability to look at the world from other people's perspectives and their growing concern about what others think of them (Lapsley, 1993; R. M. Ryan & Kuczkowski, 1994). Still others believe that adolescents' risk-taking behaviors may be partly the result of developmental changes in the brain (Spear, 2000). Whatever the origins of these phenomena, they appear to peak in early adolescence and then slowly decline (Lapsley, 1993).

Late Adolescence

By late adolescence, most students have sufficiently recovered from the "double whammy" of puberty and a changing school environment that they enjoy positive self-concepts and general

Such an excessive concern about appearance illustrates a phenomenon known as the *imaginary audience*: Elizabeth believes that she is the focus of everyone else's attention.
© Lynn Johnston Productions, Inc./Dist. by United Feature Syndicate, Inc.

FOR BETTER OR FOR WORSE / Lynn Johnston

Promote success on classroom tasks.

A teacher provides a list of questions that students should try to answer as they study for an upcoming quiz.

Hold reasonably high expectations for students' performance.

A junior high school swimming coach encourages students to come out for the swim team regardless of past experience. She works as closely with newcomers as with experienced swimmers, so that all team members can improve.

Give positive feedback for students' accomplishments. Provide negative feedback within the context of overall positive regard.

The same swimming coach tells a student, "Your crawl stroke has really improved. Your timing on the butterfly is a bit off; let's work on that today."

Communicate a genuine interest in students' well-being.

When a new seventh-grade student is visibly teary-eyed during class, her teacher invites her to take a walk with him during lunchtime. The student describes the trouble she is having making friends at her new school, and together they develop some strategies to address the problem.

Give students opportunities to examine and try out a variety of adultlike roles.

A third-grade teacher develops a list of classroom chores, such as getting a hot lunch count, delivering messages to the main office, and feeding the class goldfish and rabbit. He assigns these chores to students on a rotating basis.

mental health (Nottelmann, 1987; S. I. Powers, Hauser, & Kilner, 1989; Wigfield & Eccles, 1994). As they reach the high school years, their self-concepts begin to include a sense of **identity**: a self-constructed definition of who they are, what things they find important, and what goals they want to accomplish in life. Memberships in various groups—perhaps informal cliques at school, organized clubs or teams, or ethnic neighborhoods or communities—often play a key role in adolescents' identities (Phinney, 1989; Trawick-Smith, 2000; Wigfield, Eccles, & Pintrich, 1996). Not only do such groups help students define who they are, but they also endorse values and goals that students may adopt for themselves. Furthermore, a strong sense of ethnic or racial identity and pride can often help students from minority groups deal with the racist behaviors that they sometimes face (McAdoo, 1985; Spencer & Markstrom-Adams, 1990). Consider this statement by Eva, an African American high school student, as an example:

> I'm proud to be black and everything. But, um, I'm aware of, you know, racist acts and racist things that are happening in the world, but I use that as no excuse, you know. I feel as though I can succeed. . . . I just know that I'm not gonna let [racism] stop me. . . . Being black is good. I'm proud to be black but you also gotta face reality. And what's going on, you know, black people are not really getting anywhere in life, but I know I will and I don't know—I just know I will. (Way, 1998, p. 257)

In their ongoing search for identity, adolescents may adopt temporary "identities," aligning themselves strongly with a particular peer group, adhering rigidly to a single brand of clothing, or insisting on a certain hairstyle. For example, as a 15-year-old, my son Alex described himself as a "skater"—someone for whom skateboarding becomes a way of life as well as a form of transportation—and insisted on wearing the oversized shirts and hip-hugging, baggy pants (revealing at least six inches' worth of boxer shorts!) that came with the territory.

Erik Erikson proposed that most people achieve a sense of identity by the end of adolescence (see Figure 3.3). But more recent evidence indicates that, even by the high school years, only a small minority of students have begun to think seriously about the eventual role they will play in society and to identify lifelong goals (Archer, 1982; Durkin, 1995; Marcia, 1980, 1988). Most adolescents need considerable time to explore various options for themselves—options related to careers, political beliefs, religious affiliations, and so on—before they achieve a true sense of their adult identity. Marcia (1980) has observed four distinct patterns of behavior that may characterize the status of an adolescent's search for identity:

- *Identity diffusion.* The adolescent has made no commitment to a particular career path or ideological belief system. Some haphazard experimentation with particular roles or beliefs may have taken place, but the individual has not yet embarked on a serious exploration of issues related to self-definition.

- *Foreclosure.* The adolescent has made a firm commitment to an occupation, a particular set of beliefs, or both. The choices have been based largely on what others (especially parents) have prescribed, without an earnest exploration of other possibilities.
- *Moratorium.* The adolescent has no strong commitment to a particular career or set of beliefs but is actively exploring and considering a variety of professions and ideologies. In essence, the individual is undergoing an identity crisis.
- *Identity achievement.* The adolescent has previously gone through a period of moratorium and emerged with a commitment to particular political or religious beliefs, a clear choice of occupation, or both.

The ideal situation is to proceed through a period of moratorium—a period of searching and experimentation that may continue into early adulthood—before finally settling on a clear identity (Berzonsky, 1988; Marcia, 1988). Foreclosure—identity choice *without* prior exploration—rules out potentially more productive alternatives, and identity diffusion leaves young people without a clear sense of direction in life.

As teachers, we must be continually aware of our students' progress in assessing themselves and their capabilities, because such self-assessments may have a significant impact on students' academic success and social adjustment. In the following exercise, see what you can learn about one middle school student.

INTERPRETING ARTIFACTS AND INTERACTIONS   *Which Is Easier—Being a Girl or a Boy?*

In her language arts class, 13-year-old Trish wrote a response to the statement "It's easier to be a girl than boy." As you read her composition, look for evidence regarding

- Her feelings about being female
- Her general self-esteem
- An imaginary audience

Obviously, we can only speculate about Trish's self-concept and self-esteem from a single writing sample. However, despite her concern that girls go through more changes than boys (male readers would almost certainly disagree!), Trish appears to have generally positive feelings about being female, as well as about herself more generally: She looks favorably on the increasing independence that women have achieved over the years and has had "a pretty good time being a girl." Evidence for the imaginary audience phenomenon can be seen in Trish's remark that, at soccer games, her teammates are concerned more about their appearance than about the game. Such perceptiveness shows *perspective taking,* an important ingredient for successful interactions with peers. We learn more about perspective taking and peer relationships as we turn our attention to social development.

Social Development

Let's return to the case study presented at the beginning of the chapter. Adam engages in several socially inappropriate behaviors: He pushes other students in the corridor, picks fights in the schoolyard, and yells obscenities in class. As a result, his peers want little to do with him, and his teacher has just about given up on him.

As our students grow older, they should be acquiring more effective strategies for getting along with their classmates. They should also be growing more perceptive about how those around them are likely to think, act, and react—that is, more adept in *social cognition*. In the next few pages, we will learn more about peer relationships and social cognition. We will then identify strategies for fostering students' social skills and promoting interaction across diverse groups.

Peer Relationships

The classroom is very much a "social" place: Students interact regularly with one another, and most of them actively seek out friendly relationships with classmates. In fact, for many students, socializing with and gaining the acceptance of peers are more important than classroom learning and achievement (B. B. Brown, 1993; Dowson & McInerney, 2001; W. Doyle, 1986a). Peer relationships, especially friendships, serve several functions in children's and adolescents' personal and social development:

■ *Peer interactions provide an arena for learning and practicing social skills.* A child's relationships with parents and teachers are usually lopsided, unequal ones, such that the adults have the upper hand and control the nature of interactions. But in most relationships with peers, each individual is an equal partner. This equality provides a situation in which a child can begin to develop skills in negotiation, persuasion, cooperation, compromise, emotional control, and conflict resolution (Asher & Parker, 1989; Erwin, 1993; Maxmell, Jarrett, & Dickerson, 1998; Sutton-Smith, 1979).

■ *Peers offer social and emotional support.* Young children see their age-mates primarily as sources of recreation (Youniss & Volpe, 1978). As they grow older, they find that friendships provide comfort and safety—a group with whom to eat lunch, a "safe haven" from playground bullies, and so on—as well (Eckert, 1989; Pellegrini & Bartini, 2000). Once children reach puberty, they rely increasingly on their peers for emotional support, especially in times of trouble or confusion (Levitt, Guacci-Franco, & Levitt, 1993; R. M. Ryan, Stiller, & Lynch, 1994). Although some students adjust quite successfully on their own, as a general rule those students who have the acceptance and support of their peers have higher self-esteem, fewer emotional problems (e.g., depression), and higher school achievement (Buhrmester, 1992; Guay et al., 1999; Levitt et al., 1999; R. M. Ryan et al., 1994; Wentzel, 1999).

Many adolescents (particularly girls) may reveal their innermost thoughts to their friends (Basinger, Gibbs, & Fuller, 1995; Levitt et al., 1993). Friends often understand a teenager's perspective—the preoccupation with physical appearance, the concerns about the opposite sex, and so on—when no one else seems to. By sharing their thoughts and feelings with one another, students may discover that they aren't as unique as they once thought and gradually abandon the personal fable I spoke of earlier (Elkind, 1981).

■ *Peers are influential socialization agents.* Children and adolescents socialize one another in several ways (Erwin, 1993; Ginsburg, Gottman, & Parker, 1986; J. R. Harris, 1998; A. M. Ryan, 2000). They define options for leisure time, perhaps getting together in a study group or smoking cigarettes on the corner. They offer new ideas and perspectives, perhaps demonstrating how to do an "Ollie" on a skateboard or presenting arguments for becoming a vegetarian. They serve as role models and provide standards for acceptable behavior, showing what is possible, what is admirable, what is cool. They reinforce one another for acting in ways deemed appropriate for their age, gender, or ethnic group. And they sanction one another for stepping beyond acceptable bounds, perhaps through ridicule, gossip, or ostracism. Such **peer pressure** has its greatest effects during the junior high school years, and teenagers who have

Young adolescents often strive to look cool in the eyes of their peers, as this drawing by 11-year-old Marci illustrates.

weak emotional bonds to their families seem to be especially vulnerable (Berndt, Laychak, & Park, 1990; Erwin, 1993; Ryan & Lynch, 1989; Urdan & Maehr, 1995).

Most students want to be accepted by their classmates. As they reach puberty, their heightened concern for how others might evaluate them (recall our discussion of the *imaginary audience*) can lead them to be quite conforming—that is, to rigidly imitate their peers' choices in dress, music, slang, and behavior. By looking and sounding like others, they may feel that they better fit in with their classmates (Hartup, 1983; Owens, 1996).

Many peers encourage such desirable qualities as truthfulness, fairness, cooperation, and abstinence from drugs and alcohol (Berndt & Keefe, 1996; Damon, 1988; McCallum & Bracken, 1993). Others, however, encourage violence, criminal activity, and other antisocial behaviors (Berndt, Hawkins, & Jiao, 1999; Dishion, Spracklen, Andrews, & Patterson, 1996; Gottfredson, 2001; Lowry et al., 1995). Some peers encourage academic achievement, yet others convey the message that academic achievement is undesirable, perhaps by making fun of "brainy" students or by encouraging such behaviors as cheating on homework, cutting class, and skipping school (Berndt, 1992; B. B. Brown, 1993; Knapp & Woolverton, 1995). In fact, in some ethnic minority groups, a student who achieves good grades is "acting White"—a label some students want to avoid at all costs (B. B. Brown, 1993; Ogbu, 1992). Consider what happened to the professional basketball player Kareem Abdul-Jabbar when, as a 9-year-old African American student, he enrolled in a new school:

> I got there and immediately found I could read better than anyone in the school. . . . When the nuns found this out they paid me a lot of attention, once even asking me, a fourth grader, to read to the seventh grade. When the kids found this out I became a target. . . . I got all A's and was hated for it; I spoke correctly and was called a punk. I had to learn a new language simply to be able to deal with the threats. I had good manners and was a good little boy and paid for it with my hide. (Abdul-Jabbar & Knobles, 1983, p. 16)

Keep in mind that, while peer pressure certainly exists, its effects on children's behaviors have probably been overrated (Berndt & Keefe, 1996). Most children and adolescents acquire a strong set of values and behavioral standards from their families, and they do not necessarily discard these values and standards once they enter the school building (B. B. Brown, 1990; W. A. Collins et al., 2000; Hartup, 1983). Furthermore, students tend to choose friends who are similar to them in motives, styles of behavior, academic achievement, and leisure-time activities (W. A. Collins et al., 2000; Kindermann, McCollam, & Gibson, 1996; A. M. Ryan, 2000). They also actively think about and evaluate what their peers ask them to do; they rarely accept anyone's suggestions without question (B. B. Brown, 1990). In some cases, students lead "double lives" that enable them to attain academic success while maintaining peer acceptance; for example, although they attend class and do their homework faithfully, they may feign disinterest in scholarly activities, disrupt class with jokes or goofy behaviors, and express surprise at receiving high grades (B. B. Brown, 1993; Covington, 1992). We can help these students maintain their "image" by sometimes allowing them to demonstrate their achievements to us privately—through written assignments or in one-on-one conversations—instead of in front of their classmates.

Some peers are, of course, more influential than others. Here we will look at three types of peer relationships: friendships, larger social groups, and romantic relationships. We will then consider the nature and effects of popularity and social isolation.

Friendships

Close friends tend to be similar in age and are usually of the same sex, although some older children and adolescents have close friends of the opposite sex as well (Gottman, 1986; Hartup, 1992; Kovacs, Parker, & Hoffman, 1996). Friends also tend to be of the same race; cross-race friendships are more common when the number of available peers is relatively small—for instance, in small classes or rural communities (Hallinan & Teixeria, 1987; Roopnarine, Lasker, Sacks, & Stores, 1998).

Friends find activities that are mutually meaningful and enjoyable, and over time they acquire a common set of experiences that enable them to share certain perspectives on life (Gottman, 1986; Suttles, 1970). Friends care for and help one another, and ultimately how they *feel* about one another is more important than what they *do* with one another (J. L. Epstein, 1986; Rubin, Bukowski, & Parker, 1998). Because friends have an emotional investment in their relationship, they work hard to look at a situation from one another's point of view and to resolve any disputes that threaten to separate them; as a result, they develop increased perspective-taking and conflict-resolution skills (Basinger et al., 1995; DeVries, 1997; Newcomb & Bagwell, 1995). Close friendships foster self-esteem and, especially at the secondary school level, provide a sense of identity for students—a sense that they "belong" to a particular group (Berndt, 1992; Knapp & Woolverton, 1995).

Larger Social Groups

Most children and adolescents interact regularly with, and clearly enjoy the company of, many peers besides their close friends. Over time, many form larger social groups that regularly associate and socialize (Eisenberg, Martin, & Fabes, 1996; Gottman & Mettetal, 1986). Initially, such groups are usually comprised of a single sex, but in adolescence they often include both boys and girls (Gottman & Mettetal, 1986; J. R. Harris, 1995).

Once children or adolescents gel as a group, they prefer other group members over nonmembers, and they develop feelings of loyalty to individuals within the group. In some cases, they also develop feelings of hostility and rivalry toward members of other groups (J. R. Harris, 1995, 1998; Sherif, Harvey, White, Hood, & Sherif, 1961). If you look back on your own adolescent years, you may recall that you and your friends attached names to members of different groups—perhaps "brains," "jocks," "druggies," or "geeks" (Eckert, 1989; J. R. Harris, 1995; Pipher, 1994).

Larger groups become a particularly prominent feature of students' social worlds once they reach puberty. Researchers have described at least three distinct types of groups during the adolescent years: cliques, subcultures, and gangs. **Cliques** are moderately stable friendship groups of perhaps three to ten individuals, and such groups provide the setting for most voluntary social interactions (Crockett, Losoff, & Peterson, 1984; J. L. Epstein, 1986; Kindermann et al., 1996). Clique boundaries tend to be fairly rigid and exclusive (some people are "in," others are "out"), and memberships in various cliques often affect students' social status (Wigfield et al., 1996).

Some teenagers also affiliate with a well-defined **subculture**, a group that resists a powerful dominant culture by adopting a significantly different way of life (J. S. Epstein, 1998). Such a group may be considerably larger than a clique and may not have the tight-knit cohesiveness and carefully drawn boundaries of a clique. Instead, it is defined by common values, beliefs, and behavior patterns. Some subcultures are relatively benign; for example, the baggy-pants skaters with whom my son Alex affiliated spent much of their free time riding their skateboards and addressing almost everyone as "dude." Other subcultures are more worrisome, such as those that endorse racist and anti-Semitic behaviors (e.g., "skinheads") and those that practice Satanic worship and rituals (C. C. Clark, 1992). Adolescents are more likely to affiliate with subcultures when they feel alienated from the dominant culture (perhaps that of their school or that of society more generally) and want to distinguish themselves from it in some way (C. C. Clark, 1992; J. R. Harris, 1998).

A **gang** is a cohesive social group characterized by initiation rites, distinctive colors and symbols, ownership of a specific "territory," and feuds with one or more rival groups (A. Campbell, 1984). Typically, gangs are governed by strict rules for behavior, with stiff penalties for rule violations. Adolescents (and sometimes children as well) affiliate with gangs for a variety of reasons (A. Campbell, 1984; C. C. Clark, 1992; Parks, 1995; Simons, Whitbeck, Conger, & Conger, 1991). Some do so as a way of demonstrating their loyalty to their family, friends, or neighborhood. Some seek the status and prestige that gang membership brings. Some have poor academic records and perceive the gang as an alternative arena in which they might gain recognition for their accomplishments. Many members of gangs have had troubled relationships with their families, or they have been consistently rejected by peers, and so they

As children get older, and especially as they reach adolescence, they increasingly think of friends as people who can be trusted and relied upon. Yet to some degree, even first graders realize that friends provide more than recreation, as this description by 6-year-old Katie (who depicts herself and friend Meghan playing with dolls) illustrates.

Were you part of a social group in adolescence? If so, how would you characterize it?

turn to gangs to get the emotional support they can find nowhere else. As teachers, we can definitely make a difference in the lives of any gang members who might be in our classes (S. G. Freedman, 1990; Parks, 1995). We must, first and foremost, show these students that we truly care about them and their well-being—for instance, by being willing listeners in times of trouble and by providing the support they need to achieve both academic and social success. We must also have some awareness of students' backgrounds—their cultural values, economic circumstances, and so on—so that we can better understand the issues with which they may be dealing.

In the latter years of high school, a greater capacity for abstract thought may allow students to think of other people more as unique individuals and less as members of specific categories. Many older adolescents gain new awareness of the characteristics they share with people from diverse backgrounds. Perhaps as a result, ties to specific peer groups tend to dissipate, hostilities between groups soften, and young people become more flexible about the people with whom they associate (B. B. Brown, Eicher, & Petrie, 1986; Gavin & Fuhrman, 1989; Larkin, 1979; Shrum & Cheek, 1987).

Romantic Relationships

Once students reach puberty, romance may often be on their minds and distract them from their schoolwork.

As students move through the middle school and high school grades, the biological changes of puberty are accompanied by new, often unsettling, feelings and sexual desires (Larson, Clore, & Wood, 1999). Not surprisingly, then, romance is often on adolescents' minds and is a frequent topic of conversation at school (B. B. Brown, Feiring, & Furman, 1999). From a developmental standpoint, romantic relationships have definite benefits: They can address students' needs for companionship, affection, and security, and they provide an opportunity to experiment with new social skills and interpersonal behaviors (Furman & Simon, 1999; B. C. Miller & Benson, 1999). At the same time, romance can wreak havoc with adolescents' emotions (Larson et al., 1999). Adolescents have more extreme mood swings than younger children or adults, and for many, this instability may be due, in part, to the excitement and frustrations of being romantically involved (or *not* involved) (Arnett, 1999; Larson et al., 1999).

Initially, "romances" often exist more in students' minds than in reality (Gottman & Mettetal, 1986). For example, consider Sandy's recollection of her first foray into couplehood:

> In about fifth and sixth grade, all our little group that we had . . . was like, "OK," you know, "we're getting ready for junior high," you know, "it's time we all have to get a boyfriend." So I remember, it was funny, Carol, like, there were two guys who were just the heartthrobs of our class, you know . . . so, um, I guess it was Carol and Cindy really, they were, like, sort of the leaders of our group, you know, they were the, yeah, they were just the leaders, and they got Tim and Joe, each of those you know. Carol had Tim and Cindy had Joe. And then, you know, everyone else, then it kind of went down the line, everyone else found someone. I remember thinking, "Well, who am I gonna get? I don't even like anybody," you know. I remember, you know, all sitting around, we were saying, "OK, who can we find for Sandy?" you know, looking, so finally we decided, you know, we were trying to decide between Al and Dave and so finally I took Dave, you know. (Eckert, 1989, p. 84)

Middle school students' romantic thoughts may also involve crushes on people who are out of reach—perhaps favorite teachers, movie idols, or rock stars (B. B. Brown, 1999; Miller & Benson, 1999).

Eventually, however, many students begin to date, especially if their friends are also dating. Students' early choices in dating partners are often based on physical attractiveness or social status, and their dates involve only limited and superficial interaction (B. B. Brown, 1999; Collins & Sroufe, 1999; Downey, Bonica, & Rincón, 1999). As students move into the high school grades, some form more intense, affectionate, and long-term relationships with members of the opposite sex, and these relationships often (but by no means always) lead to some degree of sexual intimacy (B. B. Brown, 1999; J. Connolly & Goldberg, 1999). The age of first sexual intercourse has decreased steadily over the last few decades, perhaps in part because the media often communicate the message that sexual activity is appropriate (Brooks-Gunn & Paikoff, 1993; Larson et al., 1999). In the United States the average age of first sexual intercourse is now around age 16, and the majority of adolescents are sexually active by 18, but the age varies considerably as a function of gender (boys begin earlier) and ethnic background (Hofferth, 1990; Katchadourian, 1990; Moore & Erickson, 1985).

As they reach high school (perhaps even earlier), some students find themselves attracted to their own sex either instead of or in addition to the opposite sex. Adolescence is a particularly confusing time for homosexual and bisexual students. Some students actively try to ignore or stifle what they perceive to be deviant urges. Others accept their sexual yearnings yet struggle to form an identity while feeling different and isolated from peers (Morrow, 1997; C. J. Patterson, 1995). Many gay, lesbian, and bisexual students describe feelings of anger and depression, some entertain thoughts of suicide, and a higher than average proportion drop out of school (Elia, 1994; Patterson, 1995).

Teenagers often have mixed feelings about their early sexual experiences (Alapack, 1991), and those around them—parents, teachers, peers—are often uncertain about how to handle the topic (Katchadourian, 1990). When parents and teachers do broach the topic of sexuality, they often raise it in conjunction with *problems*, such as irresponsible behavior, substance abuse, disease, and unwanted pregnancy. They rarely raise the topic of homosexuality except within the context of acquired immune deficiency syndrome (AIDS) and other risks (M. B. Harris, 1997).

As teachers, the extent to which we talk about sexuality with our students must, in part, be dictated by the policies of the school and the values of the community in which we work. At the same time, especially if we are teaching at the middle school or high school level, we must be aware that romantic and sexual relationships, whether real or imagined, are a considerable source of excitement, frustration, confusion, and distraction for our students, and we must lend a sympathetic and open-minded ear to those students who seek our counsel and support.

Popularity and Social Isolation

When my daughter Tina was in junior high school, she sometimes told me, "No one likes the popular kids." Her remark was, of course, self-contradictory, and I usually told her so, but in fact it was consistent with research findings. When middle school students are asked to identify the most popular members of the student body, they identify students who have dominant social status at school (perhaps those who belong to a prestigious social group) but in many cases are aggressive or stuck-up (Parkhurst & Hopmeyer, 1998). Truly **popular students**—those whom many peers choose as people they would like to do things with—may or may not hold high-status positions, but they are kind and trustworthy (Parkhurst & Hopmeyer, 1998). Students who are popular in this way typically have good social skills; for instance, they know how to initiate and sustain conversations, are sensitive to the subtle social cues that others give them, and adjust their behavior to changing circumstances. They also tend to show genuine concern for their peers; for instance, they are more likely to help, share, cooperate, and empathize with others (Caprara, Barbaranelli, Pastorelli, Bandura, & Zimbardo, 2000; Crick & Dodge, 1994; Wentzel & Asher, 1995).

What were your perceptions of the "popular" students at your school?

In addition to asking students whom they would most like to do something with, researchers often ask them to identify classmates whom they would *least* like to do something with. Those who are frequently selected are known as **rejected students**. Students from minority groups often find themselves the targets of derogatory remarks and other forms of racism and discrimination, as do students from low-income families (Nieto, 1995; Olneck, 1995; Pang, 1995; Phelan, Yu, & Davidson, 1994). And students with few social skills—for example, those who are impulsive and disruptive, and those who continually try to draw attention to themselves (remember Adam in the opening case)—typically experience peer rejection (Asher & Renshaw, 1981; Pellegrini et al., 1999; Putallaz & Heflin, 1986).

Researchers have identified a third category as well. **Neglected students** are those whom classmates rarely choose as someone they would either most like or least like to do something with (Asher & Renshaw, 1981). Neglected students tend to be quiet and keep to themselves. Some prefer to be alone, others may simply not know how to go about making friends, and still others may be quite content with the one or two close friends that they have (Guay et al., 1999; Rubin & Krasnor, 1986). "Neglected" status is often only temporary; those whom researchers categorize as neglected at one time are not always the ones so categorized in follow-up assessments.

Teachers can help offset the hard feelings that peer rejection or neglect may engender by being particularly warm and attentive to socially isolated students (Wentzel, 1999). Yet because of their social isolation, rejected and neglected students have fewer opportunities to develop the social skills that many of them desperately need (Coie & Cillessen, 1993).

When they do interact with their classmates, their behaviors may be counterproductive, leaving them more isolated than ever. Consider the plight of a seventh-grader named Michelle:

Think back to our discussion of self-concept. What do Michelle's behaviors tell us about her self-perceptions of social competence?

> Michelle is an extremely bright student, and her academic accomplishments have earned her much teacher praise over the years. But despite her many scholastic successes, Michelle has few friends. To draw attention to herself, she talks incessantly about her academic achievements. Her classmates interpret such bragging as a sign of undeserved arrogance, and so they insult her frequently as a way of knocking her down a peg or two. In self-defense, Michelle begins hurling insults at her classmates as soon as she sees them—beating them to the punch, so to speak.

When students routinely offend or alienate others, their peers seldom give them the kind of constructive feedback that allows them to improve their behavior on future occasions, and so it may be up to us, as teachers, to give them that guidance. But the strategies we use should take into account how accurately students assess the thoughts and feelings of those around them. We turn to the topic of social cognition now.

Social Cognition

In our discussion of cognitive development in Chapter 2, we considered how students become increasingly able to understand and think logically about the physical world and academic subject matter. Yet children and adolescents also grow more adept at recognizing and understanding the perspectives and behaviors of other people. When our students consider how the people around them are likely to think, act, and react, they are engaging in **social cognition**.

As you might guess from what you have learned about cognitive development, students in the early elementary grades tend to think of other people in a fairly concrete fashion and focus on observable characteristics and behaviors. However, they do have some awareness of people's underlying psychological characteristics; for instance, they realize that people often have certain goals or intentions in mind when they behave in particular ways, and they can accurately identify various emotions reflected in people's facial expressions (Astington, 1991;

TABLE 3.1   COMPARE/CONTRAST

Selman's Five Levels of Perspective Taking

LEVEL	AGE RANGE	DESCRIPTION
Level 0: Egocentric perspective taking	Most preschool and a few early elementary students	Students are incapable of taking anybody else's perspective. They don't realize that others have thoughts and feelings different from their own.
Level 1: Subjective perspective taking	Most early and middle elementary students	Students realize that others have thoughts and feelings different from their own but perceive these in a simplistic, one-dimensional fashion.
Level 2: Second-person, reciprocal perspective taking	Many upper elementary school students	Students realize that others may have mixed and possibly contradictory feelings about a situation. They also understand that people's actions may not reflect their feelings and that people sometimes do things they didn't intend to do.
Level 3: Third-person, mutual perspective taking	Many middle school and junior high school students	Students not only see things from their own and another's perspective but also can take an "outside" perspective of the two-person relationship. They appreciate the need to satisfy both oneself and another simultaneously and therefore understand the advantages of cooperation, compromise, and trust.
Level 4: Societal, symbolic perspective taking	Some junior high and many high school students	Students recognize that people are a product of their environment—that past events and present circumstances contribute to personality and behavior. They begin to develop an understanding of the *unconscious*—the idea that people are not always aware of why they act as they do.

Sources: Selman, 1980; Selman & Schultz, 1990.

Dunn, Bretherton, & Munn, 1987). As they get older, they think increasingly about the thoughts, emotions, personality traits, and other psychological characteristics of other people (Barenboim, 1981; Livesley & Bromley, 1973).

Within any particular grade level, however, children and adolescents vary considerably in their interest in and awareness of other people's thoughts and feelings. Those who *do* consider such matters are more socially skillful, make friends more easily, and have better self-understanding (Bosacki, 2000; Izard et al., 2001). Here we look at two aspects of social cognition that influence students' ability to get along with peers: perspective taking and social information processing.

Perspective Taking

To truly understand and get along with other people, being aware of others' physical and psychological characteristics is not enough. Students must also be able to step into other people's shoes—that is, to look at the world from other viewpoints. Consider the following situation as an example.

EXPERIENCING FIRSTHAND   *Holly's Dilemma*

Holly is an 8-year-old girl who likes to climb trees. She is the best tree climber in the neighborhood. One day while climbing down from a tall tree she falls off the bottom branch but does not hurt herself. Her father sees her fall. He is upset and asks her to promise not to climb the trees any more. Holly promises.

Later that day, Holly and her friends meet Sean. Sean's kitten is caught up in a tree and cannot get down. Something has to be done right away or the kitten may fall. Holly is the only one who climbs trees well enough to reach the kitten and get it down, but she remembers her promise to her father. . . .

Does Holly know how Sean feels about the kitten?

Does Sean know why Holly cannot decide whether or not to climb the tree? . . .

What does Holly think her father will think of her if he finds out?

Does Holly think her father will understand why she climbed the tree? (Selman & Byrne, 1974, p. 805)

To answer these questions, you must look at the situation from the perspectives of three individuals: Sean, Holly, and Holly's father. Such **perspective taking** helps people make sense of actions that might otherwise be puzzling and choose responses that are most likely to achieve desired results and maintain positive interpersonal relationships.

As you should recall from Chapter 2, Jean Piaget proposed that, with age, children become better able to look at the world from other people's viewpoints. By presenting situations like the "Holly" story and asking children to view them from various perspectives, Robert Selman (1980; Selman & Schultz, 1990) has characterized the development of perspective taking as consisting of five levels (see Table 3.1).

According to Selman, most preschoolers are incapable of taking anyone else's perspective (they are at Level "0").[1] But by the time children reach the primary grades, most have begun to realize that people have different thoughts and feelings as well as different physical features (Level 1). They view someone else's perspective as a relatively simplistic, one-dimensional entity, however; for example, another person is simply happy, sad, or angry. Furthermore, they tend to equate behavior with feelings: A happy person will smile, a sad person will pout or cry, and so on. Their interpretations of someone else's actions are also overly simplistic, as the following scenario illustrates:

Donald is a new student in a second-grade classroom. A group of boys in the class openly ridicule his unusual hairstyle and shun him at lunch and on the playground. After school one of the boys makes a cruel remark about Donald's hair, and Donald responds by punching him. The boys decide that Donald is a "mean kid."

How is Selman's Level 0 similar to Piaget's preoperational stage of cognitive development?

---

[1]Selman may have underestimated preschoolers' perspective-taking ability. When young children communicate, they listen to what other people say, respond appropriately, and take into account how their listeners might be thinking and feeling (Garvey & Horgan, 1973; Mueller, 1972; Rubin & Pepler, 1995).

The boys at Donald's new school are interpreting his behavior in a simplistic, Level 1 fashion. They do not yet appreciate the many feelings that Donald may be experiencing: anxiety about a new school and community, shame about a hairstyle that was popular at his previous school, and frustration about his inability to make new friends.

As they approach the upper elementary grades, children are likely to show signs of Level 2 perspective taking. They now know that other people can have mixed, conflicting feelings about a situation. They also realize that people may feel differently from what their behaviors indicate—that they may try to hide their true feelings. At this point, too, children understand that people may do things that they didn't really want or intend to do. For example, Level 2 children would be more likely to appreciate Donald's predicament and to understand that his aggressive behavior might reflect something other than a mean streak. They might also recognize that Donald's punch was an unintended reaction to a thoughtless insult.

In middle and secondary school, most individuals are at Selman's two highest levels of perspective taking, in which they are able to take an "outsider's" perspective of interpersonal relationships. Children and adolescents at Levels 3 and 4 appreciate the need to satisfy both oneself and another simultaneously and therefore understand the advantages of cooperation, compromise, and trust. Not surprisingly, then, friendships often become relationships of mutual sharing and support in the middle and junior high school grades. Additional aspects of perspective taking emerge at Level 4: Teenagers begin to recognize that an individual's behavior is likely to be influenced by many factors—including one's thoughts, feelings, present circumstances, and past events—and that other people are not always aware of why they act as they do. Level 4 perspective taking, then, relies on an understanding of the true complexity of human behaviors, thoughts, and emotions.

We sometimes see glimmers of students' perspective-taking ability in their written work. As an example, try the following exercise.

INTERPRETING ARTIFACTS AND INTERACTIONS   *Roots*

A fifth-grade class has been watching *Roots*, a miniseries about a young African man, Kunta Kinte, who is captured and brought to early America to be a slave. The teacher occasionally has the students write reaction papers to what they've been seeing. In her second paper, 10-year-old Charmaine expresses her feelings about Kunta Kinte's treatment on the slave ship that brought him to America. As you read the paper:

■ Look for evidence of perspective taking
■ Speculate about Charmaine's development of perspective-taking ability in terms of Selman's levels

Roots II ON THE BOAT TO AMERICA

I could feel the pain Kunta-Kinte was having. Once I had a paper cut and when in the ocean it hurt more than a wasp sting, and that was just paper cut! I can't even imagine the pain or fright that Kunta-Kinte had being taken from his family and home. Or his parents hurt finding out that their first son was being taken to be a slave, their son that had just become a man. I also am horrified about how they treated women. Belly-warmers! The makes angre!

Charmaine certainly shows some perspective-taking ability: She talks about Kunta Kinte's "pain" and "fright" and about his parents' "hurt" at losing their firstborn son. She acknowledges that she cannot fully grasp Kunta Kinte's physical pain, as her own experience with pain has been limited to having a paper cut in salt water. (Charmaine makes an excellent point here: Students' ability to take the perspective of another may be limited by the extent to which they have had similar experiences.) Although Charmaine may, in fact, be capable of more advanced perspective taking, we see no evidence of her awareness of mixed and complex emotions or of people's behaviors contradicting their feelings. Hence, the paper reflects Selman's Level 1.

How can we promote greater perspective taking in our students? One strategy is to present perspectives one level above that of our students (using Piaget's terminology, such an approach might create *disequilibrium*). For example, with preschoolers, we can continually point out how their classmates' feelings differ from their own (Level 1). In the early and middle elementary grades, we can begin to discuss situations in which students may have mixed feelings or want to hide their feelings—situations such as going to a new school, trying a difficult but enjoyable sport for the first time, or celebrating a holiday without a beloved family member present (Level 2). At the middle and secondary school grades, we can explore aspects of psychology, so that students begin to understand the many ways in which people really are a product of their environment (Level 4).

A second strategy is to create opportunities for students to encounter multiple, and often equally legitimate, perspectives and beliefs. For example, at the upper elementary grades, we can provide opportunities for students to work more closely with one another on school projects so that they begin to discover the advantages of cooperation, compromise, and trust (Level 3). And students at all grade levels benefit from hearing a variety of perspectives, including those of different genders, races, cultures, religions, and political belief systems.

Social Information Processing

In Chapter 2 we considered information processing theory, which focuses on the specific cognitive processes involved in thinking about and interpreting situations, experiences, and classroom subject matter. For example, learning partially depends on what people pay *attention* to, and students often attach particular meanings to information and events through the process of *elaboration*. Information processing theory has relevance to people's understanding of social situations as well as academic topics (Crick & Dodge, 1996; Dodge, 1986). For instance, when students interact with their peers, they pay attention to one or more particular behaviors (e.g., facial expressions, verbal remarks, bodily movements) and try to make sense of (interpret) those behaviors. They then combine their interpretations with their previous knowledge and experiences to identify one or more possible responses and choose what is, in their eyes, the most appropriate course of action.

Chapter 6 looks at information processing theory in greater depth.

Aggression and Social Cognition

In the opening case study, we saw a student who exhibited a variety of aggressive behaviors—pushing and shoving, yelling obscenities, starting fights, and so on. More generally, **aggressive behavior** is an action intentionally taken to hurt another person either physically (perhaps by hitting, shoving, or fighting) or psychologically (perhaps by embarrassing, insulting, or ostracizing). Aggression among children and adolescents occurs more frequently at school, especially in areas where adult supervision is minimal (e.g., hallways, parking lots), than at any other location (Astor, Meyer, & Behre, 1999; Finkelhor & Ormrod, 2000).

Researchers have identified two distinct groups of aggressive students (Crick & Dodge, 1996; Poulin & Boivin, 1999; Vitaro, Gendreau, Tremblay, & Oligny, 1998). Those who engage in **proactive aggression** deliberately aggress against someone else as a means of obtaining desired goals. Those who engage in **reactive aggression** act aggressively primarily in response to frustration or provocation. Of the two groups, students who exhibit proactive aggression are more likely to have difficulty maintaining friendships with others (Poulin & Boivin, 1999). They may also direct considerable aggression toward particular children; those who do so are often known as *bullies* (G. R. Patterson, Littman, & Bricker, 1967; Pellegrini et al., 1999; D. Schwartz, Dodge, Pettit, & Bates, 1997). Their hapless victims often are children who are immature, anxious, friendless, and lacking in self-confidence—some also have disabilities—and so are relatively defenseless (Hodges, Malone, & Perry, 1997; Juvonen, Nishina,

& Graham, 2000; Little, 2002; H. W. Marsh, Parada, Yeung, & Healey, 2001; D. Schwartz, Mc-Fadyen-Ketchum, Dodge, Pettit, & Bates, 1999).

Some children and adolescents are genetically more predisposed to aggression than their peers, and others may exhibit heightened aggression as a result of neurological damage (Raine & Scerbo, 1991; D. C. Rowe, Almeida, & Jacobson, 1999). Yet cognitive and motivational factors play a key role in aggressive behavior as well, and several of these factors relate to our preceding discussion of social cognition.

Poor perspective-taking ability.   Students who are highly aggressive tend to have limited ability to look at situations from other people's perspectives or to empathize with their victims (Coie & Dodge, 1998; Damon & Hart, 1988; R. F. Marcus, 1980).

Misinterpretation of social cues.   Aggressive students tend to perceive hostile intent in others' behaviors, especially when such behaviors have ambiguous meanings (Graham & Hudley, 1994; Lochman & Dodge, 1994). This **hostile attributional bias** is especially prevalent in children who are prone to *reactive* aggression (Crick & Dodge, 1996).

Poor social problem-solving skills.   Aggressive students often have limited ability to generate effective solutions to social dilemmas; for instance, they are apt to think that hitting, shoving, or barging into the middle of a game are suitable behaviors (Lochman & Dodge, 1994; Neel et al., 1990; D. Schwartz et al., 1998; Shure & Spivack, 1980).

Prevalence of self-serving goals.   For most students, establishing and maintaining interpersonal relationships is a high priority. For aggressive students, however, more self-serving goals—perhaps maintaining an inflated self-image, seeking revenge, or gaining power and dominance—often take precedence (Baumeister et al., 1996; Crick & Dodge, 1996; Erdley & Asher, 1996; Lochman, Wayland, & White, 1993; Pellegrini et al., 1999).

Beliefs about the appropriateness and effectiveness of aggression.   Many aggressive students believe that violence and other forms of aggression are perfectly acceptable ways of resolving conflicts and retaliating for others' misdeeds; for instance, they may believe that they need to teach someone a "lesson" (Astor, 1994; Boldizar, Perry, & Perry, 1989; E. Staub, 1995; Zelli, Dodge, Lochman, & Laird, 1999). Those who display high rates of *proactive* aggression are also apt to believe that aggressive action will yield positive results—for instance, that it will enhance their social status (Dodge, Lochman, Harnish, Bates, & Pettit, 1997; C. H. Hart, Ladd, & Burleson, 1990; Pellegrini & Bartini, 2000).

Without intervention, many aggressive children (especially those who exhibit proactive aggression) show a continuing pattern of aggression and violence as they grow older (Eron, 1980; Kupersmidt & Coie, 1990; Vitaro et al., 1998). The specific strategies we use to help aggressive students become more prosocial must, of course, be tailored to the cognitions and motives that underlie their aggression (Crick & Dodge, 1996). Such strategies as encouraging perspective taking, helping students interpret social situations more accurately, and teaching effective social problem-solving skills are all potentially useful in reducing aggression and other disruptive behaviors (C. E. Cunningham & Cunningham, 1998; Guerra & Slaby, 1990; Hudley & Graham, 1993).

As teachers, we can draw on our understanding of social cognition (including perspective taking and social information processing) as we work to help all our students—including aggressive students—interact effectively and form friendships with their classmates. Let's apply what we have learned as we identify strategies for fostering the development of social skills.

Fostering Social Skills

Social skills are the things that we do to interact effectively with other people—showing courtesy, initiating conversations, negotiating, cooperating, and so on. Some social skills are aimed at benefiting someone else more than ourselves; such **prosocial behaviors** include sharing, helping, comforting, and showing empathy for another person's feelings. As you might expect, students who have better social skills tend to have more friends, and their friendships tend to be of higher quality (Fabes et al., 1999; A. J. Rose & Asher, 1999).

Schools and classrooms, because they present complex social situations, provide an ideal context in which social skills and prosocial behaviors can develop (Deutsch, 1993; S. N. Elliott & Busse, 1991). As teachers, we can do many things to help students acquire effective ways of interacting with others and forming productive interpersonal relationships. Following are several possibilities:

■ *Provide numerous opportunities for social interaction.* Students gain considerable information about which social behaviors are and are not effective simply by interacting with one another. For instance, students' play activities—whether they be the fantasy play of preschoolers and kindergartners or the rule-based games of older children and adolescents—can promote cooperation, sharing, perspective taking, and conflict resolution skills (Creasey, Jarvis, & Berk, 1998; Gottman, 1986; Rubin, 1982). Students are, of course, more likely to learn effective social skills when they have opportunities to interact with classmates who exhibit prosocial behaviors, rather than with those who are disruptive and aggressive (Dishion, McCord, & Poulin, 1999).

Peer relationships are critical for social and emotional development.

■ *Plan cooperative activities.* When students participate in cooperative games, rather than in competitive ones, their aggressive behaviors toward one another decrease (Bay-Hinitz, Peterson, & Quilitch, 1994). Further, when they engage in cooperative classroom assignments, they can learn and practice help-giving, help-seeking, and conflict-resolution skills, and they develop a better sense of justice and fairness regarding their peers (Damon, 1988; Lickona, 1991; N. M. Webb & Farivar, 1994). Chapter 13 offers several suggestions for conducting effective cooperative learning activities.

■ *Encourage perspective taking.* We've previously identified two ways to help students gain greater perspective-taking ability: (a) expose them to thinking that, from Selman's perspective, is one level up from their current thinking; and (b) ask them to offer their varied viewpoints on classroom events and academic subject matter. In addition, we can simply ask students to look at situations as particular people might see them. The following report from an elementary school teacher illustrates the long-term benefits that encouraging perspective taking can have:

> During gym lesson five of the boys misbehaved and were dismissed from class. They acted out their anger by insulting the gym teacher and the other staff greatly by answering back, shouting and even swearing, and throwing eggs at the school buildings. The gym teacher called me up and told me what had happened. He expected me to deal with the situation and said that the boys might be expelled from gym lessons for the rest of the school year if they did not change their behavior. When the boys came to my class they were very upset. I took a deep breath and thought to myself: Be calm . . . and think logically. . . . I was very calm and asked the boys what happened. As they all started talking at once, interrupted each other, and disagreed about the details, I told them I was not going to blame them at this point but I wanted them to write an essay at home about what had happened. I told them they were supposed to return the essays the next day with their parents' signature, which all of them did. They were written sincerely in the sense that they described clearly what they had done but to my surprise without any regret or tendency to see the staff members' point of view. Having read the essays I decided to discuss the event in class. . . . The children defined the problem and thought about the feelings of those involved. I spent a considerable time asking them to consider the staff members' feelings, whether they knew of somebody who worked in a place similar to the gym, which in fact they did, how that person felt, etc. Gradually, the boys' vehemence subsided. I never blamed them so that they wouldn't become defensive, because then I thought I might lose them. Instead, I tried to improve their understanding of the opinions and feelings of other people, which might differ from their own. After our discussion I contacted the gym teacher and told him how I had dealt with the situation. The boys improved their behavior in gym class, and this never happened again. (Adalbjarnardottir & Selman, 1997, pp. 423–424)[2]

■ *Help students interpret social situations in an accurate and productive way.* Students will interact more appropriately with their peers if they can accurately interpret their peers' behaviors and intentions (Graham, 1997; Guerra & Slaby, 1990). For example, in one research study involving third- through fifth-grade boys (Hudley & Graham, 1993), students attended a series of training sessions in which, through role playing, discussions of personal experiences, brainstorming, and similar activities, they practiced making inferences about other

---

[2]Reprinted from *Teaching and Teacher Education, 13,* S. Adalbjarnardottir and R. L. Selman, "'I Feel I Have Received a New Vision': An Analysis of Teachers' Professional Development as They Work with Students on Interpersonal Issues," pp. 409–428, copyright 1997, with permission from Elsevier Science.

people's intentions and identifying appropriate courses of action. They also learned several guidelines to remind them of how to behave in various situations; for example, they might think to themselves, "When I don't have the information to tell what he meant, I should act as if it were an accident" (p. 128). Following the training, the students were less likely to presume hostile intent or endorse aggressive retaliation in interpersonal situations, and their teachers rated them as less aggressive than control-group students.

- *Teach specific social skills, provide opportunities for students to practice them, and give feedback.* We can teach students appropriate ways of behaving both through explicit verbal instructions and through modeling desired behaviors. Such instruction is especially likely to be effective when we also ask students to practice their newly learned social skills (perhaps through role playing) and give them concrete feedback about how they are doing (S. N. Elliott & Busse, 1991; S. Vaughn, 1991; Zirpoli & Melloy, 2001).

- *Label and praise appropriate behaviors when they occur.* We should identify and praise the specific social skills that we see our students exhibit (Vorrath, 1985; Wittmer & Honig, 1994). For example, we might say, "Thank you for being so helpful," or, "I'm glad that you two were able to cooperate so well as you worked on your project."

- *Describe students as having desirable social behaviors.* We can openly describe our students as being helpful, courteous, or generous (Grusec & Redler, 1980; Wittmer & Honig, 1994). For example, 8-year-olds who are told, "You're the kind of person who likes to help others whenever you can," are more likely to share their belongings with others at a later date (Grusec & Redler, 1980).

- *Teach social problem-solving strategies.* Some students lack productive strategies for solving social problems; for example, they may barge into a game without asking or respond aggressively to any provocation (J. N. Hughes, 1988; Neel et al., 1990). One strategy we can teach them is to think carefully about a situation before responding and then talk themselves through the appropriate behaviors for dealing with it (J. N. Hughes, 1988). A second strategy, for our classroom as a whole, is *mediation training,* which teaches students how to mediate conflicts among classmates by asking the opposing sides to express their differing points of view and then work together to devise a reasonable resolution (Deutsch, 1993; Sanchez & Anderson, 1990; Stevahn, Johnson, Johnson, & Real, 1996). We will discuss both of these strategies in more depth when we consider self-regulation in Chapter 10.

- *Establish and enforce firm rules for acceptable classroom behavior.* In addition to encouraging appropriate social behaviors, we must actively *discourage* such inappropriate behaviors as inconsiderateness, aggression, and prejudicial remarks (Bierman, Miller, & Stabb, 1987; Braukmann, Kirigin, & Wolf, 1981; Schofield, 1995). We must have clear guidelines for classroom behavior and impose consequences when such guidelines are not followed (see Chapters 9 and 14). By establishing and enforcing firm rules about aggressive and other antisocial behaviors while simultaneously teaching appropriate social skills, we will often see noticeable improvements in behavior.

Even when our students are able to relate effectively with one another, we may find that many of them interact almost exclusively within a small, close-knit group or clique and that a few others remain socially isolated. Yet students have much of value to learn from their classmates, including those very different from themselves. So let's also consider how we can promote social interaction among diverse groups of students.

Promoting Social Interaction Among Diverse Groups

Simply putting students in the same school building is seldom sufficient to promote interaction among individual students or among groups of students. For example, students often divide themselves along ethnic lines when they eat lunch and interact in the schoolyard (Schofield, 1995). Immigrant students rarely interact with long-term residents, and newcomers to a school are often socially isolated (Olneck, 1995; Pérez, 1998). Many students with special needs are neglected or rejected by their classmates (Hymel, 1986; Juvonen & Hiner, 1991; Yuker, 1988).

As teachers, we often must take proactive steps to broaden the base of our students' social interactions. Some of the strategies just listed for fostering social skills can be effective for promoting social interaction among diverse groups; for example, activities that involve cooperation rather than competition often reduce hostile attitudes toward members of other groups (Devine, 1995; Oskamp, 2000). Following are several additional strategies:

■ *Set up situations in which students can form new friendships.* We can do many simple things to encourage students to get to know one another. We can arrange situations that compel them to work or play cooperatively with their classmates; for example, we can develop structured cooperative learning activities in which all group members must share equal responsibility, or we can provide play equipment that requires the participation of several students (Banks, 1994; Schofield, 1995). We can assign a partner to a student with special needs—a classmate who can provide assistance when needed, perhaps reading to a student with a visual impairment, tutoring a student with a learning disability, or taking notes for a student with a physical impairment. Finally, the very simple practice of giving students assigned seats in class and then occasionally changing those assignments increases the number of friends that they make (Schofield, 1995).

Assigning partners to students with special needs is one way we can encourage new friendships to develop.

■ *Minimize or eliminate barriers to social interaction.* Students are less likely to interact with their classmates when physical, linguistic, or social barriers keep them from doing so. For example, I am reminded of a junior high girl who could not negotiate the cafeteria steps with her wheelchair and so always ended up eating lunch alone. Obviously, we must campaign for the removal of any physical impediments to the mobility of students with special needs. We can also teach groups of students who speak different languages (including American Sign Language, with which many students with hearing loss communicate) some basic vocabulary and simple phrases in one another's native tongues. Social barriers may begin to crumble if we actively address the prejudices and tensions that sometimes separate diverse ethnic groups; we will identify specific strategies for doing so in our discussion of multicultural education in Chapter 4.

■ *Encourage and facilitate participation in extracurricular activities.* Extracurricular activities provide additional opportunities for students to interact and work cooperatively with a wide range of classmates (Genova & Walberg, 1984; Phelan et al., 1994; Schofield, 1995). We must be careful, however, that no single group of students dominates in membership or leadership in any particular activity (Sleeter & Grant, 1999). To ensure equal access to activities, schools may need to make arrangements for after-school transportation for some students (Schofield, 1995).

■ *Develop nondisabled students' understanding of students with special needs.* Nondisabled students sometimes feel resentment or anger about inappropriate behaviors that they believe a classmate with special needs should be able to control (Juvonen, 1991; Juvonen & Weiner, 1993). For example, they are less likely to be tolerant of students with cognitive difficulties or emotional and behavioral disorders than they are of students with obvious physical disabilities (Madden & Slavin, 1983; Ysseldyke & Algozzine, 1984). As teachers, we must help nondisabled students become aware of any difficulties that students with special needs may have as a result of a disability. At the same time, we must also show them—and, ideally, give them opportunities to discover on their own—the many ways in which such students are normal children with the same thoughts, feelings, and needs as anyone else their age (e.g., Peck, Donaldson, & Pezzoli, 1990).

Extracurricular activities not only provide a means through which students can interact with their classmates but also can be a source of success for students who struggle with academic tasks. Here 7-year-old Daniel, who has attention-deficit hyperactivity disorder (ADHD) and cognitive processing deficits that make reading and writing quite difficult, expresses his love of baseball.

■ *Help change the reputations of formerly antisocial students.* Unfortunately, students' bad reputations often live on long after their behavior has changed for the better. Even after students show dramatic improvements in behavior, their classmates may continue to dislike and reject them (Bierman et al., 1987; Juvonen & Hiner, 1991; Juvonen & Weiner, 1993). For example, in the case of formerly aggressive students, the perception of many classmates is "once a bully, always a bully." So when we work to improve the behaviors of antisocial students, we must work to improve their reputations as well—for example, by placing them in structured cooperative learning groups where they can use their newly developed social skills or by encouraging their

Give students numerous opportunities to interact with one another in pairs or small groups.

A middle school teacher has students work in groups of three on a complex library research project. She structures the assignment in such a way that each group member has a clearly defined role to perform.

When appropriate to do so, let students work out their own interpersonal difficulties.

When several second graders argue about whose turn it is to use the classroom computer, their teacher encourages them to work out a plan that will allow fair and equitable use of the computer each week.

Foster perspective taking.

A fourth-grade teacher prepares his class for the arrival of a new student, first by discussing the feelings of uncertainty, apprehension, and loneliness that the student is likely to have and then by helping the class identify steps it can take to make the student feel at home.

Help students learn to interpret others' behaviors and intentions accurately and to identify appropriate responses to a variety of social situations.

A special education teacher meets weekly with three boys who have a history of lashing out at others at the slightest provocation. Through a series of role-playing activities, she has the boys enact various scenarios in which one student inconveniences or causes harm to another, and she asks them to brainstorm possible motives behind the "aggressive" behaviors. The group also discusses and practices courses of action that productively resolve each situation and preserve positive peer relationships.

Promote social interaction among diverse groups.

A junior high school science teacher decides how students will be paired for weekly lab activities. She changes the pairings every month and frequently pairs students from different ethnic backgrounds.

Consistently model respect for diversity.

A high school English teacher listens patiently and attentively as a student with a speech impediment stumbles over his words. At one point, she gives a stern look to a classmate who is giggling at the student's plight.

---

active involvement in extracurricular activities. In one way or another, we must help them show their peers that they have changed and are worth getting to know better.

■ *Encourage a general feeling of respect for others.* Teachers who effectively cultivate friendships among diverse groups of students are often those who communicate a consistent message over and over again: We must all respect one another as human beings (Turnbull, Pereira, & Blue-Banning, 2000). Fernando Arias, a high school vocational education teacher, has put it this way:

> In our school, our philosophy is that we treat everybody the way we'd like to be treated. . . . Our school is a unique situation where we have pregnant young ladies who go to our school. We have special education children. We have the regular kids, and we have the drop-out recovery program . . . we're all equal. We all have an equal chance. And we have members of every gang at our school, and we hardly have any fights, and there are close to about 300 gangs in our city. We all get along. It's one big family unit it seems like. (Turnbull et al., 2000, p. 67)

Truly productive interpersonal relationships depend on students' ability to respect one another's rights and privileges, to see things from one another's perspective, and to support classmates who are going through hard times. Such capabilities are aspects of students' moral development, a topic we turn to now.

Moral and Prosocial Development

The domain of morality includes such traits as honesty, fairness, dependability, concern for the rights and welfare of others, and prosocial behavior—helping, sharing, comforting, and so on. The term *immoral behavior* typically refers to actions that are unfair, cause physical or emotional harm, or violate the rights of others (Smetana, 1983; Turiel, 1983). In our opening case study, Adam was engaging in a number of immoral behaviors: He was routinely stealing lunches in the cafeteria and, through his aggressive behaviors, trying to inflict harm on his classmates.

Students' beliefs about moral and immoral behavior—their beliefs about what's right and wrong—affect their actions at school and in the classroom. For example, we will see fewer in-

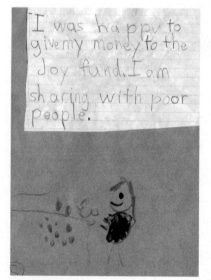

On a page in her "Happiness Book," 6-year-old Jaquita expresses her pleasure in behaving prosocially.

stances of theft or violence when students respect the property and safety of their classmates, and fewer cases of cheating when students believe that cheating is morally unacceptable. By acting morally and prosocially, students will gain greater support from their teachers and classmates and thereby achieve greater academic and social success over the long run (Caprara et al., 2000).

Students' beliefs about morality also affect how they think about and understand the topics they study in school. For instance, students' moral values are likely to influence their reactions when they read descriptions of the Holocaust during World War II or discuss recent acts of terrorism around the world.[3] Their sense of human dignity may enter in when they read the anti-Semitic statements that some characters in Shakespeare's *The Merchant of Venice* make about a Jewish money-lender. And the importance of fairness and respect for the rights of others certainly come into play in any discussions about good sportsmanship on the athletic field. Students simply cannot avoid moral issues in their school activities.

As teachers, we play a significant role in the moral and prosocial development of our students (Pollard, Kurtines, Carlo, Dancs, & Mayock, 1991; Rushton, 1980). Consider the teacher who prepares a class for the arrival of a new student, first by discussing the feelings of uncertainty, apprehension, and loneliness that the student is likely to have, and then by helping the class identify steps it can take to make the student feel at home. This teacher is facilitating perspective taking and setting the stage for students to behave prosocially toward the newcomer. Now consider the teacher who ignores incidents of selfishness and aggression in class and on the playground, perhaps using the rationale that students should always work things out among themselves. This teacher is doing little to promote students' social and moral growth and in fact may inadvertently be sending them the message that antisocial behavior is quite acceptable.

In the pages that follow, we explore the multidimensional nature of moral development. We will first consider moral reasoning, with a particular emphasis on the work of Lawrence Kohlberg and Carol Gilligan. Later, we will consider the role that emotions—guilt, shame, empathy, and sympathy—and other factors play in moral decision making and behavior. Finally, we will identify strategies for promoting moral and prosocial development in the classroom.

Development of Moral Reasoning: Kohlberg's Theory

EXPERIENCING FIRSTHAND *Heinz's Dilemma*

See "Assessing Moral Reasoning" in *Simulations in Educational Psychology and Research.*

In Europe, a woman was near death from a rare form of cancer. There was one drug that the doctors thought might save her, a form of radium that a druggist in the same town had recently discovered. The druggist was charging $2,000, ten times what the drug cost him to make. The sick woman's husband, Heinz, went to everyone he knew to borrow the money, but he could only get together about half of what the drug cost. He told the druggist that his wife was dying and asked him to sell it cheaper or let him pay later. But the druggist said no. So Heinz got desperate and broke into the man's store to steal the drug for his wife. (Kohlberg, 1984, p. 186)

■ Should Heinz have stolen the drug? What would *you* have done if you were Heinz? Which is worse, stealing something that belongs to someone else or letting another person die a preventable death? Why?

■ Do you think that people younger than yourself might answer the same questions differently? How do you think a typical fifth grader might respond? A typical high school student?

The story of Heinz and his dying wife illustrates a **moral dilemma**, a situation to which there is no clear-cut right or wrong response. Lawrence Kohlberg presented a number of moral dilemmas to people of various ages and asked them to propose solutions for each one. Here are three solutions to Heinz's dilemma proposed by elementary and secondary school students. I have given the students fictitious names so that we can refer to them again later.

---

[3] I am writing this chapter in September, 2001, soon after the attacks on the World Trade Center and Pentagon. Such terrorist acts remind us just how important it is for young people to develop compassion and caring for—as well as an appreciation for the dignity and value of—all human beings.

James (a fifth grader):

Maybe his wife is an important person and runs a store, and the man buys stuff from her and can't get it any other place. The police would blame the owner that he didn't save the wife. He didn't save an important person, and that's just like killing with a gun or a knife. You can get the electric chair for that. (Kohlberg, 1981, pp. 265–266)

Jesse (a high school student):

If he cares enough for her to steal for her, he should steal it. If not he should let her die. It's up to him. (Kohlberg, 1981, p. 132)

Jules (a high school student):

In that particular situation Heinz was right to do it. In the eyes of the law he would not be doing the right thing, but in the eyes of the moral law he would. If he had exhausted every other alternative I think it would be worth it to save a life. (Kohlberg, 1984, pp. 446–447)

Each student offers a different reason to justify why Heinz should steal the lifesaving drug. James bases his decision on the possible advantages and disadvantages of stealing or not stealing the drug for Heinz alone; he does not consider the perspective of the dying woman at all. Likewise, Jesse takes a very self-serving view, proposing that the decision to either steal or not steal the drug depends on how much Heinz loves his wife. Only Jules considers the value of human life in justifying why Heinz should break the law.

After obtaining hundreds of responses to moral dilemmas, Kohlberg proposed that the development of moral reasoning is characterized by a series of qualitatively distinct stages (e.g., Colby, Kohlberg, Gibbs, & Lieberman, 1983; Kohlberg, 1984). These stages, as in any stage theory, form an invariant sequence: An individual progresses through them in order, without skipping any. Each stage builds upon the foundation laid by earlier stages but reflects a more integrated and logically consistent set of moral beliefs than those before it. Kohlberg grouped his stages into three *levels* of morality: the preconventional, conventional, and postconventional levels. These three levels and the two stages within each one are described in Table 3.2.

Why is this level called *preconventional*?

As you can see, **preconventional morality** is the earliest and least mature form of morality, in that the individual has not yet adopted or internalized society's conventions regarding what is right or wrong. The preconventional individual's judgments about the morality of behavior are determined primarily by physical consequences: Behaviors that lead to rewards and pleasure are "right," and behaviors that lead to punishment are "wrong." James's response to the Heinz dilemma is a good example of preconventional (Stage 1) thinking: He considers the consequences of Heinz's actions only for Heinz himself. Kohlberg also classified Jesse's response as a preconventional (in particular, a Stage 2) response. Jesse is beginning to recognize the importance of saving someone else's life, but the decision to do so ultimately depends on whether or not Heinz loves his wife; in other words, it depends on *his* feelings alone.

Conventional morality is characterized by an acceptance of society's conventions concerning right and wrong: The individual obeys rules and follows society's norms even when there is no reward for obedience and no punishment for disobedience. Adherence to rules and conventions is somewhat rigid; a rule's appropriateness or fairness is seldom questioned. Conventional individuals believe in the Golden Rule ("Treat others as you would like them to treat you") and in the importance of keeping promises and commitments.

People who exhibit **postconventional morality** have developed their own set of abstract principles to define what actions are morally right and wrong—principles that typically include such basic human rights as life, liberty, and justice. They tend to obey rules consistent with their own abstract principles, and they may *disobey* rules inconsistent with those principles. Jules's response to the Heinz dilemma illustrates postconventional (Stage 5) reasoning: Jules proposed that the woman's well-being would be better served by breaking the law than by obeying it. Most people never reach postconventional reasoning (even in adulthood), and Kohlberg found Stage 6 reasoning to be extremely rare (Colby & Kohlberg, 1984, 1987; Reimer et al., 1983). We find an example of Stage 6 reasoning in Martin Luther King Jr.'s "Letter from a Birmingham Jail":

One may well ask, "How can you advocate breaking some laws and obeying others?" The answer lies in the fact that one has not only a legal but a moral responsibility to obey just laws. One has a moral responsibility to disobey unjust laws, though one must do so openly, lovingly

TABLE 3.2

COMPARE/CONTRAST

Kohlberg's Three Levels and Six Stages of Moral Reasoning

LEVEL	AGE RANGE	STAGE	NATURE OF MORAL REASONING
Level I: Preconventional morality	Seen in preschool children, most elementary school students, some junior high school students, and a few high school students	Stage 1: Punishment-avoidance and obedience	Individuals make decisions based on what is best for themselves, without regard for others' needs or feelings. They obey rules only if established by more powerful individuals; they disobey when they can do so without getting caught. The only "wrong" behaviors are ones that will be punished.
		Stage 2: Exchange of favors	Individuals begin to recognize that others also have needs. They may attempt to satisfy others' needs if their own needs are also met in the process ("you scratch my back, I'll scratch yours"). They continue to define right and wrong primarily in terms of consequences to themselves.
Level II: Conventional morality	Seen in a few older elementary school students, some junior high school students, and many high school students (Stage 4 typically does not appear until the high school years)	Stage 3: Good boy/good girl	Individuals make decisions based on what actions will please others, especially authority figures (e.g., parents, teachers, popular classmates). They are concerned about maintaining interpersonal relationships through sharing, trust, and loyalty, and they take other people's perspectives and intentions into account in their decision making.
		Stage 4: Law and order	Individuals look to society as a whole for guidelines concerning what is right or wrong. They know that rules are necessary for keeping society running smoothly and believe it is their "duty" to obey them. However, they perceive rules to be inflexible; they don't necessarily recognize that as society's needs change, rules should change as well.
Level III: Postconventional morality	Rarely seen before college (Stage 6 is extremely rare even in adults)	Stage 5: Social contract	Individuals recognize that rules represent an agreement among many people about appropriate behavior. They think of such rules as being useful mechanisms that maintain the general social order and protect individual human rights, rather than as absolute dictates that must be obeyed simply because they are "the law." They also recognize the flexibility of rules; rules that no longer serve society's best interests can and should be changed.
		Stage 6: Universal ethical principle	Individuals adhere to a few abstract, universal principles (e.g., equality of all people, respect for human dignity and rights, commitment to justice) that transcend specific norms and rules for behavior. They answer to a strong inner conscience and willingly disobey laws that violate their own ethical principles. Stage 6 is an "ideal" stage that few people ever reach.

Sources: Colby & Kohlberg, 1984; Colby et al., 1983; Kohlberg, 1976, 1984, 1986; Reimer, Paolitto, & Hersh, 1983; Snarey, 1995.

and with a willingness to accept the penalty. An individual who breaks a law that conscience tells him is unjust, and accepts the penalty to arouse the conscience of the community, is expressing in reality the highest respect for law. An unjust law is a human law not rooted in eternal law and natural law. A law that uplifts human personality is just; one which degrades human personality is unjust. (King, 1965, cited in Kohlberg, 1981, pp. 318–319)

Factors Affecting Progression Through Kohlberg's Stages

As you may have inferred from the age ranges given in Table 3.2, students at any particular grade level are not always reasoning at the same level and stage. We see the greatest variability in high school students, some of whom may show Stage 4 reasoning while others are still reasoning at Stage 1. Kohlberg drew on two aspects of Piaget's theory of cognitive development—the stages of logical reasoning and the concept of disequilibrium—to explain the progression to higher stages of moral reasoning.

Do you know anyone who is very intelligent yet reasons at a preconventional level?

First, Kohlberg proposed that advanced moral reasoning requires formal operational thought (Kohlberg, 1976). Postconventional reasoning is based on abstract principles, and even Stage 4 reasoning requires an abstract understanding of the purpose of laws and rules: to help society run smoothly. Hence, the latter stages of moral reasoning typically do not appear until adolescence. At the same time, progression to an advanced stage of cognitive development does not guarantee equivalent moral development; for example, it is quite possible to be formal operational in logical reasoning but preconventional in moral reasoning. In other words, Kohlberg maintained that cognitive development is a *necessary but insufficient* condition for moral development to occur.

Kohlberg suggested that individuals progress to a higher stage of moral development only when they experience *disequilibrium*—that is, when they realize that their beliefs about morality cannot adequately address the events and dilemmas they experience. By struggling with the various dilemmas and challenges they face, individuals gradually restructure their thoughts about morality and, as a result, move from one stage to the next. As teachers, we can best create disequilibrium by presenting a moral argument just one stage above the stage at which a student is currently reasoning—for instance, by presenting "law and order" logic (Stage 4) to a student who is concerned primarily with gaining the approval of others (Stage 3). If our moral argument is too much higher than the student's current stage, then the student is unlikely to understand and remember what we are saying (e.g., Narvaez, 1998) and so unlikely to experience disequilibrium.

What Research Tells Us About Kohlberg's Theory

A great deal of research on moral development has followed on the heels of Kohlberg's theory. Some research supports Kohlberg's sequence of stages: Generally speaking, people seem to progress through the stages in the order Kohlberg proposed (Colby & Kohlberg, 1984; Reimer et al., 1983; Snarey, 1995; Stewart & Pascual-Leone, 1992). At the same time, it appears that people are not always completely in one stage: Their moral thought usually reflects a particular stage, but they also show occasional instances of reasoning in the two surrounding stages. Furthermore, although the first four stages are found in a wide variety of cultural groups, postconventional moral reasoning is not seen in all cultures (Snarey, 1995).

Researchers have found, too, that young children are probably more advanced than Kohlberg suggested. Even preschoolers have some internal standards of right and wrong, regardless of what authority figures might tell them and regardless of what consequences certain behaviors may or may not bring (Laupa & Turiel, 1995; Smetana, 1981; Tisak, 1993). By the time they are 6 or 7, most children clearly recognize that certain behaviors that are harmful or unfair to others are inherently wrong, whereas behaviors that violate commonly accepted *social conventions* (e.g., burping in public, calling teachers by their first name) are less serious (P. Davidson, Turiel, & Black, 1983; Nucci & Nucci, 1982a, 1982b; Turiel, 1983).

The "fishing" study described in Chapter 2 illustrated how logical reasoning may be somewhat content-specific. Here we find that moral reasoning may be content-specific as well.

An additional problem is that, although Kohlberg's stages suggest that people's moral reasoning should be relatively consistent from one occasion to the next, in fact people's reasoning depends considerably on situational variables (Rest, Narvaez, Bebeau, & Thoma, 1999; Turiel, 1998). For example, students are more likely to think of lying as immoral if it causes someone else harm than if it has no adverse effect—that is, if it is just a "white lie" (Turiel, Smetana, & Killen, 1991). And moral reasoning influences students' decisions about using drugs only when they view drug use as potentially harmful to others (Berkowitz, Guerra, & Nucci, 1991).[4]

Finally, Kohlberg's theory has been criticized for focusing on moral *thinking* rather than on moral *behavior.* Some researchers have found that people at higher stages of moral reasoning do

---

[4]To account for such inconsistent, situation-specific reasoning, some theorists have proposed a *neo-Kohlbergian* theory: Over time, individuals acquire three distinct moral belief systems, or *schemas*: (1) a "personal interests" schema (reflecting preconventional thinking), (2) a "maintaining norms" schema (reflecting conventional thinking), and (3) a "postconventional" schema. The first emerges in childhood, the second and third in adolescence or adulthood. As people grow older, many begin to prefer the "maintaining norms" schema over the "personal interests" schema and, later, the "postconventional" schema over the other two. However, even morally advanced adults may show an occasional preference for their own personal interests (Rest et al., 1999).

tend to behave more morally as well (Bear & Richards, 1981; Blasi, 1980; Reimer et al., 1983). For example, students at the higher stages are less likely to cheat in the classroom, more likely to help people in need, more likely to disobey orders that would cause harm to another individual, and less likely to engage in criminal and other delinquent activities (Blasi, 1980; Chandler & Moran, 1990; Kohlberg, 1975; Kohlberg & Candee, 1984). Generally speaking, however, the relationship between moral reasoning and moral behavior is a weak one at best (Blasi, 1980; Eisenberg, 1987). Clearly, then, Kohlberg's theory does not give us the total picture of how morality develops.

Despite such weaknesses, Kohlberg's theory offers valuable insights into the nature and development of children's and adolescents' moral thinking. For example, it shows us that children's moral reasoning does not simply result from adults handing down particular moral values and preachings but instead emerges out of children's own, personally constructed beliefs (hence, Kohlberg's theory is very much a *constructivist* approach). Kohlberg's theory also highlights the importance of social interaction in creating disequilibrium and thereby nudging students toward more advanced and complex views of morality.

Possible Gender Differences in Moral Reasoning: Gilligan's Theory

Kohlberg developed his stages after studying how people solved moral dilemmas, but consider this quirk in his research: Subjects in his early studies were predominantly males. Carol Gilligan (1982, 1987) believes that Kohlberg's theory does not adequately describe female moral development. Kohlberg's stages emphasize issues of fairness and justice but omit other aspects of morality, especially compassion and caring for those in need, that Gilligan suggests are more characteristic of the moral reasoning and behavior of females. She argues that females are socialized to stress interpersonal relationships and to take responsibility for the well-being of others to a greater extent than males; therefore, females develop a morality that emphasizes a greater concern for others' welfare. The dilemma that follows illustrates a morality based on compassion.

EXPERIENCING FIRSTHAND *The Porcupine Dilemma*

A group of industrious, prudent moles have spent the summer digging a burrow where they will spend the winter. A lazy, improvident porcupine who has not prepared a winter shelter approaches the moles and pleads to share their burrow. The moles take pity on the porcupine and agree to let him in. Unfortunately, the moles did not anticipate the problem the porcupine's sharp quills would pose in close quarters. Once the porcupine has moved in, the moles are constantly being stabbed. The question is, what should the moles do? (Meyers, 1987, p. 141; adapted from Gilligan, 1985)

According to Gilligan, males are more likely to view the problem as that of someone's rights being violated. For example, they might point out that the burrow belongs to the moles, and so the moles can legitimately throw the porcupine out. If the porcupine refuses to leave, some may argue that the moles are well within their rights to kill him. In contrast, females are more likely to show compassion and caring when addressing the dilemma. For example, they may suggest that the moles simply cover the porcupine with a blanket; this way, his quills won't annoy anyone and everyone's needs will be met (Meyers, 1987).

Gilligan raises a good point: Males and females are often socialized quite differently, as you will discover in Chapter 4. Furthermore, by including compassion for other human beings as well as consideration for their rights, she broadens our conception of what morality *is* (L. J. Walker, 1995). But in fact, most research studies do *not* find major gender differences in moral reasoning (Eisenberg et al., 1996; Nunner-Winkler, 1984; L. J. Walker, 1991). And as Gilligan herself has acknowledged, males and females alike reveal concern for both justice and compassion in their moral reasoning (L. M. Brown, Tappan, & Gilligan, 1995; Gilligan & Attanucci, 1988; Turiel, 1998; L. J. Walker, 1995).

Both Kohlberg and Gilligan portray moral development largely in terms of logic and reasoning. Yet other developmentalists suggest that morality has an affective (emotional) component as well. Let's look at some of their findings.

**hopes
goals
dreams
happiness
   broken
   destroyed
   eliminated
   exterminated
no steps forward
no evolution
no prosperity
no hope
But
maybe
perhaps
except
if we
help
together
we stand
a chance.**

In this poem Matt, a middle school student, shows empathy for victims of the Holocaust.

In what ways is Eisenberg's Level 3 similar to Kohlberg's Stage 3?

Emotional Components of Moral Development

How do you feel when you inadvertently cause inconvenience for someone else? when you hurt someone else's feelings? when a friend suddenly and unexpectedly loses a close family member? Perhaps such feelings as shame, guilt, empathy, and sympathy come to mind. All of these emotions are associated with moral development.

By the time children reach the middle elementary grades, most of them occasionally feel **shame**: They feel embarrassed or humiliated when they fail to meet the standards for moral behavior that parents and teachers have set for them (Damon, 1988). Shortly thereafter, as they begin to develop their *own* standards for behavior, they sometimes experience **guilt**—a feeling of discomfort when they know that they have caused someone else pain or distress (Damon, 1988; Hoffman, 1991). Both shame and guilt, though unpleasant in nature, are good signs that students are developing a sense of right and wrong and that their future behaviors will improve.

Shame and guilt emerge when children believe they have done something wrong. In contrast, **empathy**—experiencing the same feelings as someone in unfortunate circumstances—motivates moral and prosocial behavior even in the absence of wrongdoing (Damon, 1988; Eisenberg, 1982; Hoffman, 1991). Empathy is especially likely to promote such behavior when it leads to **sympathy**, whereby children not only assume another person's feelings but also have concerns for the individual's well-being (Eisenberg & Fabes, 1991; Turiel, 1998).

Empathy continues to develop throughout the elementary school years and often during the high school years as well (Eisenberg, 1982). At the primary grade levels, students show empathy only to people they know, such as friends and classmates. But by the late elementary school years, students may also begin to feel empathy for people they *don't* know—perhaps for the poor, the homeless, or those in catastrophic circumstances (Damon, 1988; Hoffman, 1991).

Nancy Eisenberg and her colleagues (Eisenberg, 1982; Eisenberg, Carlo, Murphy, & Van Court, 1995; Eisenberg, Lennon, & Pasternack, 1986) have identified five levels of prosocial reasoning, reflecting different degrees of empathy and sympathy, that can help us predict how students of different ages are likely to behave in situations that call for altruism and other prosocial behaviors (see Table 3.3). These five levels are not true stages, in that children and adolescents do not necessarily progress through them in a sequential or universal fashion. Instead, children may reason at two or more different levels in any particular time period (Eisenberg, Miller, Shell, McNalley, & Shea, 1991). Generally speaking, however, children and adolescents show increasing use of the upper levels, and less frequent use of lower ones, as they grow older (Eisenberg et al., 1995).

As teachers, we are often in a position to foster empathy and prosocial behavior in our students. For instance, we can ask students to imagine how people must have felt during particularly traumatic and stressful events in history, or possibly even have them role-play such events (Brophy & Alleman, 1996; Brophy & VanSledright, 1997). We can encourage them to engage in such prosocial behaviors as cooperating and sharing with one another and comforting classmates whose feelings have been hurt, and we can acknowledge and reward such behaviors when we see them. Furthermore, as the curriculum provides an increasingly broader view of the country and world in which we all live, we can expose our students to situations in which other people's needs may be far greater than their own.

Determinants of Moral Behavior

Most children act more morally and prosocially as they grow older; for example, they become increasingly generous (Eisenberg, 1982; Rushton, 1980). Gains in moral reasoning, perspective taking, and empathy are, of course, partly responsible for this trend. Yet motivational factors come into play as well. Children and adolescents typically have many goals: Although they may want to do the right thing, they may also be concerned about whether others will approve of their actions and about what positive or negative consequences might result. Students are more likely to act in accordance with their moral standards if the benefits are high (e.g., they gain others' approval or respect) and the personal costs are low (e.g., an act of altruism involves little sacrifice; Batson & Thompson, 2001; Eisenberg, 1987; Narváez & Rest, 1995).

In adolescence some students begin to integrate a commitment to moral values into their overall sense of identity (Arnold, 2000; Blasi, 1995; Kurtines, Berman, Ittel, & Williamson,

TABLE 3.3　　　　　　　　　　　　　　　　　　　　　　　　　　　COMPARE/CONTRAST

Eisenberg's Five Levels of Prosocial Reasoning

LEVEL	AGE RANGE	DESCRIPTION
Level 1: Selfish and self-centered orientation	Most preschool and many early elementary students	Students show little interest in helping others apart from serving their own interests. They are most likely to behave prosocially toward another person when they like that person and believe they will probably get something in return.
Level 2: Superficial "needs of others" orientation	Some preschool and many elementary school students	Students show some concern for others' physical and emotional needs and may express willingness to help another person even at personal sacrifice to themselves. Yet their concern lacks true understanding of, or empathy for, the other person's perspective. For example, a student might say, "He's hungry," or "She needs this," without further explanation.
Level 3: Approval and stereotypic good boy/girl orientation	Some elementary and secondary school students	Students advocate prosocial behavior on the grounds that it's the "right" thing to do and that they will be liked or appreciated if they help. However, they hold stereotypical views of what "good" and "bad" people do. For example, a child may explain that "It's nice to help out" or "She'll be my friend if I help her."
Level 4: Empathic orientation	A few elementary and many secondary students	Students express true empathy for another person's situation and a willingness to help other people based on those empathic feelings. Furthermore, they seem genuinely concerned with the well-being of another person and are able to perceive a situation from that person's perspective. For instance, they might say, "I know just how she feels," or "I'd feel badly if I didn't help him because then he'd be in pain."
Level 5: Internalized values orientation	A few high school students	Students express internalized values about helping other people—values that reflect concern for equality, dignity, human rights, and the welfare of society as a whole. These individuals maintain their self-respect by behaving in accordance with such values. For instance, they might say, "I couldn't live with myself if I didn't help out," or "It's the responsibility of all of us to help one another whenever we can."

Sources: Eisenberg, 1982; Eisenberg et al., 1995; Eisenberg et al., 1986; Eisenberg, Lennon, & Roth, 1983.

1995; Youniss & Yates, 1999). They think of themselves as moral, caring individuals and place a high priority on demonstrating these values. Their acts of altruism and compassion are not limited to their friends and acquaintances, but extend to the community at large. For example, in one study (D. Hart & Fegley, 1995), researchers conducted in-depth interviews with fifteen inner-city Hispanic and African American teenagers who showed an exceptional commitment to helping others (by volunteering many hours at Special Olympics, a neighborhood political organization, a nursing home, etc.). These teens did not necessarily display more advanced moral reasoning (as defined by Kohlberg's stages) than their peers, but they were more likely to describe themselves in terms of moral traits and goals (e.g., helping others) and to mention certain ideals toward which they were striving.

In the "Describing Yourself" exercise earlier in the chapter, did you list any characteristics that might suggest a strong moral identity?

Promoting Moral Development in the Classroom

Some well-meaning individuals have suggested that society is in a sharp moral decline and urge parents and educators to impart desirable moral traits (honesty, integrity, loyalty, responsibility, etc.) through lectures at home and in school, as well as through firm control of children's behavior. In fact, there is no evidence to indicate that the present generation of young people is in any way less "moral" than previous generations (Turiel, 1998). Furthermore, lecturing students about morally appropriate behavior and imposing firm control on their actions do little to instill a particular set of moral values (Damon, 1988; Higgins, 1995; Turiel, 1998). Research suggests, however, that several other strategies *can* make a difference:

■ *Give reasons why some behaviors are unacceptable.* Although it is important to impose consequences for immoral or antisocial behaviors, punishment by itself often focuses children's attention primarily on their own hurt and distress (Hoffman, 1975). To promote moral development, we must instead focus students' attention on the hurt and distress their behaviors have caused *others*. Thus, we should give them reasons that certain behaviors are unacceptable—an approach known as **induction** (Hoffman, 1970, 1975). For example, we might describe how a behavior harms someone else either physically ("Having your hair pulled the way you just pulled Mai's can really be painful") or emotionally ("You probably hurt John's feelings when you call him names like that"). We might also show students how they have caused someone else inconvenience ("Because you ruined Marie's jacket, her parents are making her work around the house to earn the money for a new one"). Still another approach is to explain someone else's perspective, intention, or motive ("This science project you've just ridiculed may not be as fancy as yours, but I know that Michael spent many hours working on it and is quite proud of what he's done").

Induction is victim-centered: It helps students focus on the distress of others and recognize that they themselves have been the cause of it (Hoffman, 1970). The consistent use of induction in disciplining children, particularly when accompanied by *mild* punishment for misbehavior, appears to promote cooperation with rules and facilitate the development of such prosocial characteristics as empathy, compassion, and altruism (Baumrind, 1971; G. H. Brody & Shaffer, 1982; Hoffman, 1975; Maccoby & Martin, 1983; Rushton, 1980).

■ *Provide practice in recognizing others' emotional states.* We will have less need to explain someone else's feelings if our students are able to recognize those feelings on their own. Yet many students, young ones especially, are poor judges of the emotional states of others. With preschoolers, we can orally label a classmate's feelings as "sadness," "disappointment," or "anger" (Chalmers & Townsend, 1990; Wittmer & Honig, 1994). In later years, we might ask students to describe to one another exactly how they feel about particular misbehaviors directed toward them (Doescher & Sugawara, 1989). Or we might ask them how they themselves would feel in the same situation (Hoffman, 1991). As teachers, we also should describe our own emotional reactions to any inappropriate behaviors (Damon, 1988).

■ *Expose students to numerous models of moral behavior.* Children and adolescents are more likely to exhibit moral and prosocial behavior when they see others behaving in morally appropriate ways. For example, when adults or peers are generous and show concern for others, children tend to do likewise (Rushton, 1980; C. C. Wilson, Piazza, & Nagle, 1990). Yet by the same token, when children see their peers cheating, they themselves are more likely to cheat (Sherrill, Horowitz, Friedman, & Salisbury, 1970). Television, too, provides both prosocial and antisocial models for children. When children watch television shows that emphasize perspective taking and prosocial actions (e.g., *Sesame Street, Mister Rogers' Neighborhood, Barney & Friends*), they are more likely to exhibit such behaviors themselves; when they see violence on television, they, too, are more likely to be violent (Hearold, 1986; Rushton, 1980; Singer & Singer, 1994).

As teachers, we teach by what we do as well as by what we say. When we model compassion and consideration for the feelings of others, such behaviors may rub off on our students. When we are instead self-centered and place our own needs before those of others, our students may follow suit.

We will look at the effects of modeling in more detail in Chapter 10.

We can also present models of moral behavior found in literature (Ellenwood & Ryan, 1991). For example, in Harper Lee's *To Kill a Mockingbird*, set in the highly segregated and racially charged Alabama of the 1930s, a lawyer defends an obviously innocent African American man who is charged with murder; in doing so, he exemplifies a willingness to fight for high moral principles in the face of strong social pressure to let the man hang for the crime. In John Gunther's *Death Be Not Proud*, a young boy is generous and considerate despite his impending death from cancer.

■ *Encourage discussions about moral issues and dilemmas.* Kohlberg proposed that children develop morally when they are challenged by moral dilemmas they cannot adequately deal with at their current stage of moral reasoning. Research confirms his belief: Classroom discussions of controversial topics and moral issues appear to promote increased perspective taking and the transition to more advanced moral reasoning (De Lisi & Golbeck, 1999; DeVries & Zan, 1996; D. W. Johnson & Johnson, 1988; Power, Higgins, & Kohlberg, 1989; Schlaefli, Rest, & Thoma, 1985).

Social and moral issues often arise at school. Sometimes these issues relate to inappropriate student behaviors that occur in most classrooms at one time or another (e.g., cheating, plagiarism, theft, interpersonal conflicts). At other times they are intrinsic in course content. Consider the following questions that might emerge in discussions related to history, social studies, science, or literature:

- Is it appropriate to engage in armed conflict, and hence to kill others, when two groups of people disagree about political or religious issues?
- Is military retaliation for acts of terrorism justified even when it may involve killing innocent people?
- How can a capitalistic society encourage free enterprise while at the same time protecting the rights of citizens and the ecology of the environment?
- Should laboratory rats be used to study the effects of cancer-producing agents?
- Was Hamlet justified in killing Claudius to avenge the murder of his father?

Social and moral issues will not always have right or wrong answers. As teachers, we can encourage student discussions of such issues in a variety of ways (Reimer et al., 1983). First, we can provide a trusting and nonthreatening classroom atmosphere in which students feel free to express their ideas without censure or embarrassment. Second, we can help students identify all aspects of a dilemma, including the needs and perspectives of the various individuals involved. Third, we can help students explore their reasons for thinking as they do—that is, to clarify and examine the principles on which their moral judgments are based.

Chapter 13 offers additional suggestions for conducting effective classroom discussions.

■ *Engage students in community service.* As we have seen, adolescents are more likely to act in moral and prosocial ways when they have integrated a commitment to moral ideals into their overall sense of identity. Such integration is more probable when students become actively involved in service to others even before they reach puberty (Youniss & Yates, 1999). Through ongoing community service activities—food and clothing drives, visits to homes for the elderly, community cleanup efforts, and so on—elementary and secondary students alike learn that they have the skills and the responsibility for helping those less fortunate than themselves and in other ways making the world a better place in which to live. In the process, they also begin to think of themselves as concerned, compassionate, and moral citizens (Youniss & Yates, 1999).

INTO THE CLASSROOM: *Promoting Moral and Prosocial Development*

Encourage prosocial behavior, and acknowledge and reward it when it occurs.

A kindergarten teacher commends a student for consoling a classmate whose feelings have been hurt.

Talk about reasons why some behaviors are inappropriate, noting especially the harm or inconvenience that those behaviors have caused.

A second-grade teacher explains to Sarah that because she has thoughtlessly left her chewing gum on Margaret's chair, Margaret's mother must now pay to have Margaret's new pants professionally cleaned.

Model appropriate moral and prosocial behavior.

A junior high school teacher mentions that he will be working at a Habitat for Humanity project on Saturday and asks if any of his students would like to join him.

Incorporate moral issues and dilemmas into classroom discussions.

When discussing the Vietnam War, a high school history teacher mentions that many young men in the United States escaped the draft by going to Canada. She asks her students to decide whether they think such behavior was appropriate and to explain their reasoning.

Remember that standards for what is "moral" and "immoral" differ somewhat from one culture to another.

A teacher sees a student inadvertently knock a classmate's jacket off its hook. The teacher mentions the incident to the student, but he denies that he had anything to do with the fallen jacket. Remembering that in this student's culture, lying is an acceptable way of saving face, the teacher doesn't chastise the student; instead, she asks him to do her the "favor" of returning the jacket to its hook. A short time later, she engages her class in a conversation about the importance of being careful around other people's belongings.

Considering Diversity in Personal, Social, and Moral Development

These are not easy times in which to grow up, and many of our students will have experienced challenges that we ourselves may never have imagined as children. More than half of our students are likely to spend at least part of their childhood in a single-parent home; for example, some will have been raised by unmarried mothers, and many others will have lived through a divorce. Violence in schools and on the streets is widespread, especially in low-income areas (Finkelhor & Ormrod, 2000; Gorski & Pilotto, 1993; Lowry et al., 1995; Parks, 1995). Temptations to experiment with drugs and alcohol are everywhere (G. R. Adams, Gullotta, & Markstrom-Adams, 1994; S. P. Thomas et al., 1993). With students facing such challenges, we must be especially supportive, acting as willing listeners and communicating regularly how much we value each and every one of them (Ogden & Germinario, 1988; Parks, 1995).

Even when our students haven't experienced significant personal challenges, their personalities, social skills, and moral beliefs will vary considerably from one student to the next. To some extent, these differences will be a product of diverse parenting styles and cultural backgrounds. For instance, some ethnic groups encourage a strong sense of identity with one's family, and possibly with one's ethnic group as well (i.e., they encourage a strong **ethnic identity**); students from such backgrounds may take more pride in the accomplishments of their families or communities than in their own, individual achievements (Olneck, 1995; Pang, 1995; Phinney, 1989). We may find, too, that members of many minority groups, while often having high self-esteem in general, may have little faith in their ability to achieve academic success (Covington, 1992; Elrich, 1994; Graham, 1994; van Laar, 2000). For some students from minority backgrounds, we may need to make a special effort to foster positive self-perceptions. For example, we can help them explore their cultural backgrounds as a way of fostering an appreciation of their ethnic roots (Phinney, 1989; S. Wright & Taylor, 1995). And we must certainly provide whatever scaffolding they need to be successful on academic tasks.

We will see diversity in students' social development as well as their personal development. Some students may have had few opportunities to form friendships and, as a result, few opportunities to develop effective ways of interacting with their peers. For instance, children in some families are encouraged to stay close to home, perhaps to perform household chores, care for younger brothers and sisters, or play with older siblings (Trawick-Smith, 2000). Children who have recently immigrated from a non-English-speaking country may have only a limited ability to communicate with other children in their neighborhoods and classrooms (A. Doyle, 1982).

Conceptions of moral and immoral behavior are also likely to differ somewhat depending on students' backgrounds. Although lying is generally discouraged in our own society, it is a legitimate way of saving face in certain cultures (Triandis, 1995). Some ethnic groups (including many from Asia and South America) value loyalty and foster prosocial behavior more than others do (Greenfield, 1994; Markus & Kitayama, 1991; P. B. Smith & Bond, 1994; Triandis, 1995). Whereas some ethnic groups emphasize the importance of being considerate of other people (e.g., "Please be quiet so that your sister can study"), others emphasize the importance of tolerating inconsiderate behavior (e.g., "Please try not to let your brother's radio bother you when you study") (Grossman, 1994). Although virtually all cultures espouse the importance of both individual rights and responsibility for others, many cultural groups tend to place greater emphasis on one than the other (J. G. Miller & Bersoff, 1992; Shweder, Mahapatra, & Miller, 1987; Snarey, 1995; Turiel, 1998). As teachers, we must remember that our students' notions of moral behavior may sometimes be quite different from our own. At the same time, of course, we should never accept behavior that violates such basic principles as equality or respect for the rights and well-being of others.

Accommodating Students with Special Needs

Some of our students will undoubtedly have special educational needs related to their personal, social, or moral development (see Table 3.4). Many of our students with special needs will have lower self-esteem than their classmates (Brown-Mizuno, 1990; T. Bryan, 1991; H. W. Marsh

Promoting Personal, Social, and Moral Development in Students with Special Educational Needs

CATEGORY	CHARACTERISTICS YOU MIGHT OBSERVE	SUGGESTED CLASSROOM STRATEGIES
Students with specific cognitive or academic difficulties	• Low self-esteem related to areas of academic difficulty • Greater susceptibility to peer pressure (if students have learning disabilities or ADHD) • Difficulty in perspective taking or accurately interpreting social situations (for some students with learning disabilities or ADHD) • In some cases, poor social skills and few friendships; tendency to act without thinking through the consequences of one's actions (especially if students have ADHD)	• Promote academic success (e.g., by providing extra scaffolding for classroom tasks). • Give students the opportunity to "show off" the things they do well. • Use induction to promote perspective taking (e.g., focus students' attention on how their behaviors have caused harm or distress to others). • Teach any missing social skills.
Students with social or behavioral problems	• Rejection by peers; few friendships • Difficulty in perspective taking and recognizing others' emotional states • Deficits in ability to interpret social cues (e.g., perceiving hostile intent in innocent interactions) • Poor social skills and social problem-solving ability; limited awareness of how poor their social skills actually are • Poor impulse control; difficulty controlling emotions • Less empathy for others	• Explicitly teach social skills, provide opportunities to practice them, and give feedback. • Establish and enforce firm rules regarding acceptable classroom behavior. • Label and praise appropriate behaviors. • Teach social problem-solving strategies (e.g., through mediation training). • Provide opportunities for students to make new friends (e.g., through cooperative learning activities). • Help students recognize the outward signs of various emotions. • Use induction to promote empathy and perspective taking.
Students with general delays in cognitive and social functioning	• Generally low self-esteem • Social skills typical of younger children • Difficulty identifying and interpreting social cues • Concrete, often preconventional, ideas of right and wrong	• Scaffold academic success. • Teach social skills, provide opportunities to practice them, and give feedback. • Specify rules for classroom behavior in specific, concrete terms. • Label and praise appropriate behaviors.
Students with physical or sensory challenges	• Fewer friends and possible social isolation • Fewer opportunities to develop appropriate social skills	• Maximize opportunities for students to interact with their classmates. • Assign "buddies"—classmates who can assist students with tasks that they cannot perform themselves due to a disability. • Teach any missing social skills.
Students with advanced cognitive development	• Above-average social development and emotional adjustment (although some extremely gifted students may have difficulty because they are so *very* different from their peers) • High self-esteem with regard to academic tasks (more typical of males than females) • Conflicts (especially for females) between the need to develop and display abilities on the one hand and to gain peer acceptance on the other • For some students, more advanced moral reasoning • Concerns about moral and ethical issues at a younger age than peers • Greater perspective taking	• Be sensitive to students' concerns about how their exceptional abilities may affect their relationships with classmates. • Engage students in conversations about ethical issues and moral dilemmas. • Involve students in projects that address social problems at a community, national, or international level.

Sources: Barkley, 1998; Beirne-Smith et al., 2002; Bierman et al., 1987; Cartledge & Milburn, 1995; Coie & Cillessen, 1993; Dempster & Corkill, 1999; Flavell et al., 1993; Gresham & MacMillan, 1997; Grinberg & McLean-Heywood, 1999; Harter et al., 1998; Heward, 2000; Hughes, 1988; Juvonen & Weiner, 1993; B. K. Keogh & MacMillan, 1996; Lind, 1994; H. W. Marsh & Craven, 1997; Mercer, 1997; Milch-Reich et al., 1999; Neel et al., 1990; Piirto, 1999; Schonert-Reichl, 1993; Schumaker & Hazel, 1984; Turnbull et al., 1999; Winner, 1997; Zeaman & House, 1979; Zirpoli & Melloy, 2001.

& Craven, 1997). Students with mental retardation will typically have less understanding of how to behave in social situations than their nondisabled peers (Greenspan & Granfield, 1992). Students with emotional and behavioral disorders will frequently have poor perspective-taking and social problem-solving abilities and so may have few if any friends (Harter et al., 1998; Lind, 1994).

Students with certain disabilities (e.g., emotional and behavioral disorders, attention-deficit hyperactivity disorder, autism, mental retardation) may have particular difficulty drawing accurate inferences from others' behaviors and body language (C. Gray & Garaud, 1993; Leffert, Siperstein, & Millikan, 1999; Lochman & Dodge, 1994; Milch-Reich, Campbell, Pelham, Connelly, & Geva, 1999). For instance, as we have seen, those with a history of aggressive and violent behavior may perceive hostile intentions in the most innocent of their classmates' actions.

Additional characteristics that you may see in students with special needs, along with strategies for promoting the personal, social, and moral development of such students, are presented in Table 3.4.

The Big Picture

In this final section of the chapter, we recap what we have learned about personal, social, and moral development and summarize the characteristics we are likely to see in students of different ages. We then identify several general themes that have appeared repeatedly throughout our discussion.

Personal Development

Students' personal characteristics and behavior patterns are the result of many things, including biological predispositions, parental childrearing styles, cultural expectations, and peer influences. As students progress through childhood and adolescence, they form and continually modify perceptions of themselves; for instance, they acquire beliefs about their general characteristics and abilities (self-concept), develop opinions and feelings about their value and worth (self-esteem), learn the specific things they can and cannot do (self-efficacy), and begin to construct a definition of who they are as people, what things they find important, and what goals they hope to accomplish (identity). Students derive such self-perceptions not only from their prior experiences (e.g., their successes and failures) but also from the behaviors of others. As teachers, then, we must provide the support our students need to be successful and give them feedback that engenders optimism about future accomplishments.

Social Development

Productive peer relationships are critical for optimal social and emotional development. Peers provide a testing ground in which students can experiment with and practice their emerging social skills. They can offer support and comfort in times of trouble or uncertainty. And in general, they provide innumerable opportunities for students to develop an ability to consider situations from multiple perspectives, draw conclusions about others' motives and intentions, and identify effective solutions to interpersonal problems. Some peers endorse antisocial and other counterproductive behaviors, to be sure, but many others encourage the kinds of interpersonal skills—especially caring, cooperation, helping, and other prosocial behaviors—that are likely to promote students' long-term social growth.

For the great majority of children and adolescents, their hours at school are the most "social" part of each day. As teachers, then, we may sometimes need to monitor and guide interactions between classmates to ensure that such interactions are productive. For various reasons, some of our students are likely to be rejected or neglected by their classmates, and these students may be in particular need of our guidance and support. Furthermore, we should take steps to promote communication and interaction across diverse ethnic, socioeconomic, and linguistic groups, as well as between students with and without disabilities; by doing so, we help our students discover that all of their peers have legitimate perspectives and valuable qualities to offer.

Moral Development

As children move through the grade levels, most gradually acquire a definite sense of right and wrong, such that they follow internal standards for appropriate behavior rather than act solely out of self-interest. This developmental progression is the result of many things, including increasing capacities for abstract thought and empathy, an evolving appreciation for human rights and others' welfare, and ongoing encounters with moral dilemmas and problems. Even at the high school level, however, students do not always take the moral high road, as personal needs and self-interests almost invariably enter into their moral decision making. As teachers, we can help students develop more advanced moral reasoning and increasingly prosocial behavior by giving them reasons why certain behaviors are unacceptable, encouraging them to recognize how others feel in various situations, exposing them to models of moral behavior, challenging their thinking with moral issues, and providing opportunities for community service and other prosocial behavior.

Characteristics of Different Age-Groups

Pulling together what we have learned about students' sense of self, peer relationships, social cognition, and moral development, we can summarize students' characteristics in the elementary, middle school, and high school years as follows:

Elementary school years. In the elementary years, students encounter innumerable academic tasks and social situations and have many opportunities to compare their performance to that of their peers, and so they gain an increasing understanding of their strengths and weaknesses. As they mature physically and socially, their social circles increase, and friends become frequent companions and playmates. Most elementary school students can look at events from other people's perspectives, show some capacity for empathy, and understand that behaviors that cause harm or are unfair to others are fundamentally wrong. Nevertheless, they are often more concerned about the consequences of their behaviors for themselves than for other people, and their prosocial behaviors may be influenced by fairly stereotypical notions of what "good boys and girls" should do to help others.

Middle school years. In the middle school grades, students believe that they are unlike anyone else (the personal fable) and have a heightened awareness of what others think of them (the imaginary audience). Friendships become more important and supportive, and social groups become more rigid and exclusive. Increasingly, they can take an outsider's perspective of a two-person relationship and so appreciate the need for cooperation, compromise, and mutual trust. From Kohlberg's perspective, many young adolescents are in Stage 2 (defining acceptable behavior as "anything I can get away with") or Stage 3 (adhering to rules or group norms primarily to attain the approval of teachers, influential classmates, or other real or imagined authority figures). Yet, although some still act prosocially to gain the approval of those around them, others are now motivated by true feelings of empathy for a person in need.

High school years. By high school, many students are beginning to form an identity that encompasses who they are as people, what things they find important, and what goals they hope to achieve. They now see their peers more as complex individuals than as stereotypical members of a particular group, their social groups are less rigid and exclusive, and many form romantic bonds with others. Most high school students reason at Kohlberg's conventional level of development, having internalized society's views (or perhaps the views of a subgroup) of what is right and wrong. But they still see rules in a somewhat rigid manner—as absolute and inflexible entities, rather than as socially agreed on and therefore changeable mechanisms for protecting human rights and promoting the advancement of society. A few students in this age range (those at Eisenberg's Level 5) show a true commitment to preserving and enhancing the rights, equality, and dignity of all human beings.

General Themes in Personal, Social, and Moral Development

Although we have addressed a variety of topics in this chapter, several general themes have been evident throughout. These themes, summarized in Table 3.5, are as follows:

■ *Standards for acceptable behavior, along with reasons why these standards must be upheld, are essential for optimal development.* Well-adjusted children are often those who grow up in an authoritative environment in which rules are set for appropriate behavior, reasons for the rules are spelled out, and infractions of the rules are punished. Perspective taking and moral development are promoted when any punishment is accompanied by induction—by a description of how one's misbehavior has caused physical or emotional harm to someone else. As teachers,

---

TABLE 3.5

General Themes Characterizing Personal, Social, and Moral Development

THEME	EDUCATIONAL IMPLICATION	EXAMPLE
Standards for acceptable behavior, along with the reasons behind them, are essential for development.	Establish rules and expectations for classroom behavior that preserve all students' rights and welfare. When students do not adhere to such standards, administer appropriate consequences and help students understand how their actions have caused harm or inconvenience to someone else.	If a student maliciously ruins a classmate's work (e.g., a homework assignment or art project), point out that the classmate spent quite a bit of time completing the work and insist that the student make amends.
Interaction with peers provides the impetus for many advancements.	Include many opportunities to interact with peers in the daily schedule, both in and outside the classroom.	When teaching art in the lower elementary grades, provide one set of art supplies (e.g., crayons, scissors, glue) for each table, so that children sitting at the same table must share. Give the children some guidelines about how to share the materials fairly.
Development is best fostered in a warm, supportive environment.	Continually communicate the message that you like students and want them to succeed. Design lessons and activities in which students cooperate with and help one another, and assign projects to which every student has something valuable to contribute.	In a cooperative learning activity, have students work in groups of three to read and study a section of their textbook. Group members take one of three roles: (a) *reader* (who reads a paragraph), (b) *questioner* (who develops two or three thought-provoking questions about the material presented), and (c) *responder* (who answers the questions). The students rotate these three roles for succeeding paragraphs.
Personal, social, and moral understandings are self-constructed.	Encourage students to exchange views about social and moral issues. When students have difficulty getting along with their peers, help them reflect on their peers' perspectives and intentions.	Hold a classroom debate on the pros and cons of capital punishment, perhaps after first having students conduct library research to support their perspectives.

we must communicate clearly to students what behaviors are and are not acceptable at school and explain why certain behaviors will not be tolerated.

■ *Interaction with others, especially peers, provides the impetus for many personal, social, and moral advancements.* Social interaction is critical not only for children's cognitive and linguistic development (see Chapter 2) but also for personal, social, and moral development. For example, students learn a great deal about their own strengths and weaknesses by observing the behaviors of others. Relationships with peers provide an arena in which to practice existing social skills and experiment with new ones. Conversations about controversial topics and moral issues are critical for the development of perspective taking and moral reasoning. Classroom discussions and other opportunities for social interaction must therefore be an important and frequent component of classroom life.

■ *Development is best fostered within the context of a warm, supportive environment.* We first saw the importance of a loving yet firm environment in our discussion of authoritative parent-ing. We also discovered the very important role that positive feedback plays in the development of students' self-concepts and self-esteem. And we learned that students are more likely to express their ideas about moral issues in a classroom in which they feel free to express their ideas openly and honestly.

■ *Students' personal, social, and moral understandings are self-constructed.* Just as children and adolescents construct their own knowledge and beliefs about the physical world, so, too, do they construct their own beliefs about themselves (e.g., their self-concepts and identities), the nature of other people (e.g., their interpretations of peers' motives and intentions), and morality (e.g., their definitions of right and wrong behavior). As teachers, we cannot simply tell students what they should and shouldn't do and believe; rather, we must create opportunities for them to construct their own understandings of their personal, social, and moral worlds. The final case study illustrates how many students still have a long road to travel in their efforts to construct mature moral understandings.

CASE STUDY: *A Discussion of Runaway Slaves*

Mr. Dawson's eighth-grade American history class is learning about the large cotton plantations prevalent in the Southern states before the Civil War. Mr. Dawson explains that such plantations probably would not have been possible without the thousands of slaves who picked the cotton.

"Sometimes the slaves would run away," he says. "And when they did, White people who believed that slavery was wrong would hide them or help them escape to the North. But helping runaway slaves was against the law; a person could be put in jail for doing so. Was it right for these people to help the slaves? Would *you* have helped a slave run away?"

"I don't think I would," says Mark. "Some of the plantation owners might have been my friends, and I wouldn't want them to get angry at me."

"I don't think I would either," says Lacy. "After all, it was against the law. I'd get punished if I broke the law. I wouldn't want to end up in jail."

"I think I might do it," says Kevin, "but only if I was sure I wouldn't get caught."

"I agree with Kevin," says Pam. "Besides, if I were really nice to the slave, he might help me around the house or in my garden."

Mr. Dawson is appalled at what his students are telling him. Where is their sense of injustice about the enslavement of human beings? Isn't the very notion of slavery inconsistent with the idea that all people are created equal?

■ Are you as surprised as Mr. Dawson is? What stages of moral reasoning are evident in the opinions of these four students? Are these stages typical or atypical for eighth graders?

Once you have answered these questions, compare your responses with those presented in Appendix B.

Key Concepts

temperament (p. 62)

attachment (p. 62)

authoritative parenting (p. 62)

socialization (p. 63)

norms (p. 63)

roles (p. 63)

culture shock (p. 64)

self-concept (p. 64)

self-esteem (p. 64)

self-efficacy (p. 65)

imaginary audience (p. 70)

personal fable (p. 70)

identity (p. 71)

peer pressure (p. 73)

clique (p. 75)

subculture (p. 75)

gang (p. 75)

popular students (p. 77)

rejected students (p. 77)

neglected students (p. 77)

social cognition (p. 78)

perspective taking (p. 79)

aggressive behavior (p. 81)

proactive aggression (p. 81)

reactive aggression (p. 81)

hostile attributional bias (p. 82)

social skills (p. 82)

prosocial behavior (p. 82)

moral dilemma (p. 87)

preconventional morality (p. 88)

conventional morality (p. 88)

postconventional morality (p. 88)

shame (p. 92)

guilt (p. 92)

empathy (p. 92)

sympathy (p. 92)

induction (p. 94)

ethnic identity (p. 96)

4

Individual and Group Differences

As you discovered in Chapters 2 and 3, children change in many ways as they grow older, and so students at one age level are often quite different from those at another. What differences have you observed among students of the *same* age? For instance, have you noticed that some students seem to learn more quickly and easily than their classmates, or that some are more creative than others when they complete assigned tasks? When we talk about how students of the same age often differ from one another, perhaps in ways that reflect intelligence or creativity, we are talking about **individual differences.**

Sometimes we find consistent differences among various groups of students. For example, you may have noticed that people from particular ethnic groups or regions of the country have certain ways of saying things—perhaps using different words, pronunciations, and grammatical structures than you do—even though you and they both speak English. But have you also noticed that females tend to form closer, more intimate friendships than males, or that, on average, students from lower-income families have lower educational and career aspirations than their classmates from middle-income families? When we talk about how students of one group typically differ from those of another group, we are talking about **group differences.**

This chapter describes how we can adapt our classroom practices to accommodate individual and group differences. More specifically, we will address questions such as these:

- To what extent will knowledge about individual and group differences enable us to draw conclusions about particular students?
- What do we mean by the term *intelligence,* and how can we promote intelligent behavior in all of our students?
- How can we foster creativity in the classroom?
- In what ways are students from various cultural and ethnic groups apt to be alike and different from one another? What implications do their differences have for classroom practice?
- In what ways are males and females alike and different? What can we do to provide equitable educational opportunities for both boys and girls?
- How can we accommodate the unique needs of students from lower socioeconomic groups?
- What characteristics can help us identify students at risk for school failure, and how can we help these students achieve academic success?

CASE STUDY: *Hidden Treasure*

Six-year-old Lupita has just enrolled in Ms. Padilla's kindergarten classroom. The daughter of migrant workers, Lupita has been raised in Mexico by her grandmother, who has had limited financial resources and been able to provide very few playthings such as toys, puzzles, crayons, and scissors. Ms. Padilla rarely calls on Lupita in class because of her apparent lack of academic skills; she is afraid of embarrassing Lupita in front of her classmates. By midyear, Ms. Padilla is thinking about holding Lupita back for a second year of kindergarten.

Lupita is always quiet and well behaved in class; in fact, she's so quiet that Ms. Padilla sometimes forgets she's even there. Yet a researcher's video camera captures a different side to Lupita. On one occasion, Lupita is quick to finish her Spanish assignment and so begins to work on a puzzle during her free time. A classmate approaches, and he and Lupita begin playing with a box of toys. A teacher aide asks the boy whether he has finished his Spanish assignment, implying that he should return to complete it, but the boy does not understand the aide's subtle message. Lupita gently persuades the boy to go back and finish his work. She then returns to her puzzle and successfully fits most of it together. Two classmates having difficulty with their own puzzles request Lupita's assistance, and she competently and patiently shows them how to assemble puzzles and how to help each other.

Ms. Padilla is amazed when she views the videotape, which shows Lupita to be a competent girl with strong teaching and leadership skills. Ms. Padilla readily admits, "I had written her off . . . her and three others. They had met my expectations and I just wasn't looking for anything else." Ms. Padilla and her aides begin working closely with Lupita on academic skills, and they often allow her to take a leadership role in group activities. At the end of the school year, Lupita obtains achievement test scores indicating exceptional competence in language skills and mathematics, and she is promoted to first grade.

- Why might a teacher believe that Lupita has poor academic skills? Might Lupita's background be a reason? Might her classroom behavior be a reason?
- What might have happened to Lupita if her behavior with classmates had gone unnoticed? How might her academic life have been different?

Based on a case study in Carrasco, 1981.

Keeping Individual and Group Differences in Perspective

We will inevitably find that some students learn more easily than others. For example, Lupita finishes assignments and completes puzzles more quickly than some of her classmates. We will also find differences in how accurately our students remember information, how readily they connect ideas with one another, and how easily and creatively they apply their knowledge to new situations and problems.

Some of Lupita's behaviors may be partly due to either her Mexican heritage or her gender. For example, she is proficient in Spanish and displays the cooperative attitude encouraged in many Hispanic cultures. She is so quiet in class that her teacher often forgets she's there; as we will discover later, girls are, on average, less assertive in whole-class situations than boys.

In observing our students day after day, we are likely to draw inferences about their academic capabilities, just as Ms. Padilla did for Lupita. Yet we must be careful that such inferences are never set in stone—that we keep an open mind about how each student is likely to perform in future situations. For example, we will soon discover that creativity is domain-specific: Some students may be creative in science, whereas others are more creative in fine arts. We will find, too, that intelligence can change over time, especially during the early years, and that students often behave more intelligently in some contexts than in others.

When considering group differences, such as those among diverse ethnic groups and those between males and females, we need to keep in mind two very important points. First, *there is a great deal of individual variability within any group.* I will be describing how students of different groups behave *on average,* yet some students may be very different from that "average" description. Second, *there is almost always a great deal of overlap between two groups.* Consider gender differences in verbal ability as an example. Research studies often find that girls demonstrate slightly higher verbal performance than boys (Halpern & LaMay, 2000). This difference is sometimes statistically significant; in other words, we cannot explain it as something that happens just by chance in one particular study. Yet the average difference between girls and boys in verbal ability is quite small, with a great deal of overlap between the two groups. Figure 4.1 shows the typical overlap between boys and girls on measures of verbal ability: Notice how many of the boys are *better* than some of the girls despite the average advantage for girls.

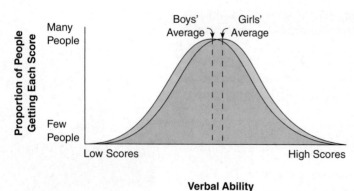

FIGURE 4.1 Typical "difference" between boys and girls on tests of verbal ability

TABLE 4.1

PRINCIPLES/ASSUMPTIONS

General Principles Regarding Student Diversity

GENERAL PRINCIPLE	EDUCATIONAL IMPLICATION	EXAMPLE
Differences among students are subject to change over time; they are not necessarily permanent differences.	Never make long-range predictions about students' future success or failure based on their present behaviors.	Although a student currently shows little creativity, believe that creative behavior is possible, and plan instructional activities that promote such creativity.
There is a great deal of variability among members of any single ethnic group, gender, or socioeconomic group.	Be careful not to draw conclusions about students' characteristics and abilities simply on the basis of their gender, ethnic background, or other group membership.	Have considerable optimism that, with reasonable support from you and your colleagues, many students from lower socioeconomic backgrounds can pursue college degrees.
When two groups differ *on average* in terms of a particular characteristic, considerable overlap usually exists between the two groups with respect to that characteristic.	Remember that average differences between groups don't necessarily apply to individual members of those groups.	Although boys have historically developed their athletic abilities more than girls (on average), nevertheless provide equal opportunities for both genders to achieve athletic success.
Students achieve at higher levels when instruction takes individual and group differences into account.	Consider students' unique backgrounds and abilities when planning instructional activities.	Use cooperative learning activities more frequently when students' cultural backgrounds emphasize the value of cooperation and group achievement.

As we shall discover in Chapter 12, teachers' preconceived notions about how students will behave may actually *increase* the differences among those students. At the same time, if we are to maximize the learning and development of all students, then we should be aware of individual and group differences that may influence students' classroom performance. Several general principles regarding student diversity are presented in Table 4.1.

This chapter identifies many differences that are likely to affect our students' academic achievement, as well as strategies for accommodating those differences. We should never ask ourselves whether particular students can learn and achieve in the classroom. We should instead ask how we, as teachers, can most effectively help *every* student master the knowledge and skills essential for school and lifelong success.

For more information on this point, see the section "Teacher Expectations and Attributions" in Chapter 12.

Intelligence

What kinds of behaviors lead you to believe that someone is "intelligent"? Do you think that intelligence is a general ability that contributes to success in many different areas? Or is it possible for an individual to be intelligent in one area yet not in another? What exactly *is* intelligence?

Unfortunately, psychologists have not yet reached consensus on the answers to these questions. But here are several components of what many theorists construe **intelligence** to be:

- It is *adaptive*. It involves modifying and adjusting one's behaviors to accomplish new tasks successfully.
- It is related to *learning ability*. Intelligent people learn information more quickly and easily than less intelligent people.
- It involves the *use of prior knowledge* to analyze and understand new situations effectively.
- It involves the complex interaction and coordination of *many different mental processes*.
- It may be seen in *different arenas*—for example, on academic tasks or in social situations.
- It is *culture-specific*. What is "intelligent" behavior in one culture is not necessarily intelligent behavior in another culture. (Laboratory of Human Cognition, 1982; Neisser et al., 1996; Sternberg, 1997; Sternberg & Detterman, 1986)

Think of someone you think is intelligent. Does that individual's behavior fit these criteria?

For most theorists, intelligence is somewhat distinct from what a person has actually learned (e.g., as reflected in school achievement). At the same time, intelligent thinking and intelligent behavior do depend on prior learning. The more students know about their environment and about the tasks they need to perform, the more intelligently they can

One component of intelligence is the ability to use prior knowledge to analyze new situations. These students are trying to calculate the volume of the large pyramid by applying geometric principles they've learned in their math class.

behave. Intelligence, then, is not necessarily a permanent, unchanging characteristic. As you will soon discover, it can be modified through experience and learning.

Measuring Intelligence

Curiously, although psychologists cannot pin down exactly what intelligence *is*, they have been trying to measure it for almost a century. In the early 1900s, school officials in France asked Alfred Binet to develop a method of identifying those students unlikely to benefit from regular school instruction and therefore in need of special educational services. To accomplish the task, Binet devised a test that measured general knowledge, vocabulary, perception, memory, and abstract thought. In doing so, he designed the earliest version of what we now call an **intelligence test**. To get a feel for what intelligence tests are like, try the following exercise.

EXPERIENCING FIRSTHAND   *A Mock Intelligence Test*

Answer each of these questions:

1. What does the word *quarrel* mean?
2. How are a goat and a beetle alike?
3. What should you do if you get separated from your family in a large department store?
4. Three kinds of people live on the planet Zircox: bims, gubs, and lops. All bims are lops. Some gubs are lops. Which one of the following must also be true?
   a. All bims are gubs.   c. Some gubs are bims.
   b. All lops are bims.   d. Some lops are bims.
5. Complete the following analogy: ⧖ is to ⧖ as ◖● is to?
   a. ●●   b. ◖○   c. ⬮   d. ▷◁

These test items are modeled after items on many modern-day intelligence tests. Think, for a moment, about the capabilities you needed to answer them successfully. Does general knowledge about the world play a role? Is knowledge of vocabulary important? Is abstract thought involved? The answer to all three questions is yes. Although intelligence tests have evolved considerably since Binet's time, they continue to measure many of the same abilities that Binet's original test did.

IQ Scores

Scores on intelligence tests were originally calculated by using a formula involving division; hence, they were called "intelligence quotient," or **IQ**, scores. Even though we still use the term IQ, intelligence test scores are no longer based on the old formula. Instead, they are determined by comparing a student's performance on the test with the performance of others in the same age-group. A score of 100 indicates average performance: Students with this score have performed better than half of their age-mates on the test and not as well as the other half. Scores below 100 indicate below-average performance on the test; scores above 100 indicate above-average performance.

Figure 4.2 shows the percentage of students getting scores at different points along the scale (e.g., 12.9% get scores between 100 and 105). Notice how the curve is high in the middle and low at both ends. This tells us that we have many more students obtaining scores close to 100 than we have students scoring very much higher or lower than 100. For example, if we add up the percentages in different parts of Figure 4.2, we find that approximately two-thirds (68%) of students score within 15 points of 100 (i.e., between 85 and 115). In contrast, only 2 percent of students score as low as 70, and only 2 percent score as high as 130. This symmetric and predictable distribution of scores happens by design rather than by chance; psychologists have created a method of scoring intelligence test performance that intentionally yields such a distribution. (You can find a more detailed explanation of IQ scores in the discussion of *standard scores* in Chapter 15.)

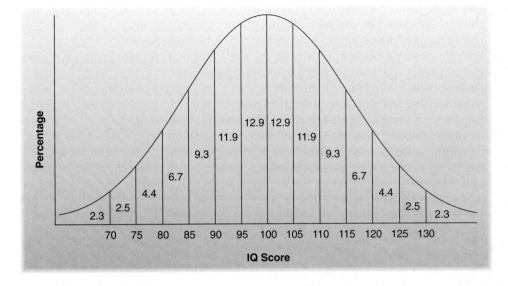

FIGURE 4.2 Percentage of IQ scores in different ranges

IQ and School Achievement

Modern intelligence tests have been designed with Binet's original purpose in mind: to predict how well individual students are likely to perform in the classroom and similar situations. Studies repeatedly show that performance on intelligence tests is correlated with school achievement (N. Brody, 1997; Gustafsson & Undheim, 1996; Sattler, 2001). On average, children with higher IQ scores do better on standardized achievement tests, have higher school grades, and complete more years of education. In other words, IQ scores often *do* predict school achievement, albeit imprecisely. As a result, intelligence tests are frequently used by school psychologists and other specialists to identify those students who may have special educational needs.

While recognizing the relationship between intelligence test scores and school achievement, we must also keep three points in mind about this relationship. First, intelligence does not necessarily *cause* achievement; it is simply correlated with it. Even though students with high IQs typically perform well in school, we cannot say conclusively that their high achievement is actually the result of their intelligence. Intelligence probably does play an important role in school achievement, but many other factors are also involved—factors such as motivation, quality of instruction, family economics, parental support, and peer group norms.

Second, the relationship between IQ scores and achievement is not a perfect one; there are exceptions to the rule. For a variety of reasons, some students with high IQ scores do not perform well in the classroom. And other students achieve at higher levels than we would predict from their IQ scores alone. Therefore, we should never base our expectations for students' achievement solely on intelligence test scores.

Third and most important, we must remember that IQ scores simply reflect a student's performance on a particular test at a particular time and that some change is to be expected over the years. In fact, the longer the time interval between two measures of intelligence, the greater the fluctuation in IQ we are likely to see, especially with young children (Hayslip, 1994; McCall, 1993; C. E. Sanders, 1997).

When might it be appropriate for a teacher to use intelligence test results? What potential dangers are there in relying solely on IQ scores as a measure of students' abilities?

Limitations of Intelligence Tests

As you can see, intelligence tests are hardly instruments that can determine a person's "true" intelligence (if, in fact, such a thing even exists). Yet on some occasions, we might find ourselves considering IQ scores along with other information as we make instructional decisions about some of our students—for example, as we meet with colleagues and parents to identify the most appropriate instructional program for a student with special educational needs. It is critical, then, to be aware of the following limitations of traditional intelligence tests:

- Different kinds of intelligence tests often yield somewhat different scores.
- A student's performance on any test is inevitably affected by many temporary factors present at the time the test is taken, including general health, mood, fatigue, time of day, and the number of distracting stimuli. (Such temporary factors affect a test's *reliability*—a concept we will consider in Chapter 15.)

- Test items focus on a limited set of skills that are important in mainstream Western culture, and particularly in school settings; they do not necessarily tap into skills that may be more highly valued in other contexts or other societies.
- Some students may be unfamiliar with the content or types of tasks involved in particular test items and perform poorly on those items as a result.
- Students with limited English proficiency (LEP) are at an obvious disadvantage when an intelligence test is administered in English.
- Some students (e.g., minority students who want to avoid "acting White") may not be motivated to perform at their best and so may obtain scores that underestimate their capabilities. (Dirks, 1982; Heath, 1989; Neisser et al., 1996; Ogbu, 1994; Perkins, 1995; Sternberg, 1996b; Zigler & Finn-Stevenson, 1992)

Are any of your prior beliefs about intelligence tests inconsistent with what you've just read? If so, can you resolve the inconsistencies?

Used within the context of other information, IQ scores can, in many cases, give a general idea of a student's current cognitive functioning. But as you can see from the limitations just listed, we should always maintain a healthy degree of skepticism about the accuracy of IQ scores, especially when students come from diverse cultural backgrounds or have acquired only limited proficiency in English.

How Theorists Conceptualize Intelligence

Up to this point, we have been talking about intelligence as it is represented by a single IQ score. Yet not all theorists believe that intelligence is a single entity that people "have" in varying degrees; some theorists instead propose that people may behave more or less intelligently in different situations and on different kinds of tasks. Here we will look at four very different perspectives on the nature of intelligence. We'll first consider the traditional idea that intelligence is a single, generalized trait—a concept often referred to as the g factor. We will then examine two theories, developed by Howard Gardner and Robert Sternberg, that portray intelligence as multidimensional and context-dependent. Finally, we will address the concept of "distributed" intelligence.

Spearman's Concept of g

Whenever we use an IQ score as an estimate of a person's cognitive ability, we are, to some extent, buying into the notion that intelligence is a single entity. Historically, considerable evidence has supported this idea (McGrew, Flanagan, Zeith, & Vanderwood, 1997; Neisser et al., 1996; Spearman, 1927). Although various intelligence tests yield somewhat different scores, people who score high on one test tend to score high on others as well. Charles Spearman (1904, 1927) called this single entity a *general factor*, or **g**.[1] Some contemporary information processing theorists believe that g is a reflection of the speed and efficiency with which people can process information, learning tasks, and problem situations (N. Brody, 1992; Dempster & Corkill, 1999; Vernon, 1993).

Gardner's Theory of Multiple Intelligences

In addition to a general factor in intelligence, many researchers have found evidence for more specific abilities as well, and measures of these abilities can sometimes predict performance on particular school tasks more accurately than general intelligence tests do (McGrew et al., 1997; Neisser et al., 1996; Thurstone, 1938). Howard Gardner (1983, 1998, 1999; Gardner & Hatch, 1990) suggests that there are at least eight different abilities, or *intelligences*, that are relatively independent of one another (see Table 4.2).[2] Gardner's perspective presents the possibility that most, and quite possibly all, of our students may be quite intelligent in one way

In which of Gardner's intelligences are you most "intelligent"?

---

[1]Spearman suggested that several more specific (s) factors come into play as well, with different factors having greater or lesser influence depending on the task.

[2]Gardner (1999) suggests that there may also be a ninth intelligence, *existential intelligence*, that involves the "capacity to locate oneself with respect to the furthest reaches of the cosmos—the infinite and the infinitesimal—and the related capacity to locate oneself with respect to such existential features of the human conditions as the significance of life, the meaning of death, the ultimate fate of the physical and the psychological worlds, and such profound experiences as love of another person or total immersion in a work of art" (Gardner, 1999, p. 60). Gardner acknowledges that the evidence for existential intelligence is somewhat weaker than that for the other eight intelligences, hence its exclusion from Table 4.2.

Gardner's Multiple Intelligences

TYPE OF INTELLIGENCE	EXAMPLES OF RELEVANT BEHAVIORS
Linguistic Intelligence The ability to use language effectively	• Making persuasive arguments • Writing poetry • Being sensitive to subtle nuances in word meanings
Logical-Mathematical Intelligence The ability to reason logically, especially in mathematics and science	• Solving mathematical problems quickly • Generating mathematical proofs • Formulating and testing hypotheses about observed phenomena[a]
Spatial Intelligence The ability to notice details of what one sees and to imagine and manipulate visual objects in one's mind	• Conjuring up images in one's mind • Drawing a visual likeness of an object • Making fine discriminations among very similar objects
Musical Intelligence The ability to create, comprehend, and appreciate music	• Playing a musical instrument • Composing a musical work • Having a keen awareness of the underlying structure of music
Bodily-Kinesthetic Intelligence The ability to use one's body skillfully	• Dancing • Playing basketball • Performing pantomime
Interpersonal Intelligence The ability to notice subtle aspects of other people's behaviors	• Reading another's mood • Detecting another's underlying intentions and desires • Using knowledge of others to influence their thoughts and behaviors
Intrapersonal Intelligence Awareness of one's own feelings, motives, and desires	• Discriminating among such similar emotions as sadness and regret • Identifying the motives guiding one's own behavior • Using self-knowledge to relate more effectively with others
Naturalist Intelligence The ability to recognize patterns in nature and differences among various life-forms and natural objects	• Identifying members of particular plant or animal species • Classifying natural forms (e.g., rocks, types of mountains) • Applying one's knowledge of nature in such activities as farming, landscaping, or animal training

[a]This example may remind you of Piaget's theory of cognitive development. Many of the stage-specific characteristics that Piaget described fall within the realm of logical-mathematical intelligence.

or another. Some students may show exceptional promise in language, others may be talented in music, and still others may be able to learn mathematics more easily than their classmates.

Gardner proposes that the various intelligences manifest themselves somewhat differently in different cultures. For example, in our culture, spatial intelligence might be reflected in painting, sculpture, or geometry. But among the Gikwe bushmen of the Kalahari Desert, it might be reflected in one's ability to recognize and remember many specific locations over a large area (perhaps over several hundred square miles), identifying each location by its rocks, bushes, and other landmarks (Gardner, 1983).

Gardner presents some evidence to support the existence of multiple intelligences. For example, he describes people who are quite skilled in one area (perhaps in composing music) and yet have seemingly average abilities in other areas. He also points out that people who suffer brain damage sometimes lose abilities that are restricted primarily to one intelligence; for instance, one person might show deficits primarily in language, whereas another might have difficulty with tasks that require spatial skills.

Among psychologists, reviews of Gardner's theory are mixed. Some theorists do not believe that Gardner's evidence is sufficiently compelling to support the notion of eight distinctly different abilities (Berk, 2000; N. Brody, 1992; Kail, 1998). Others disagree that abilities in specific domains, such as in music or bodily movement, are really "intelligence" per se (Bracken, McCallum, & Shaughnessy, 1999; Sattler, 2001). Many theorists are simply taking a wait-and-see attitude about Gardner's theory until more research is conducted.

Close attention to detail in 10-year-old Luther's drawing of a plant suggests some talent in what Gardner calls *naturalist* intelligence.

Despite such a lukewarm reception in psychological circles, many educators have whole-heartedly embraced Gardner's theory of multiple intelligences because of its optimistic view of human potential. This perspective encourages us to use many different teaching methods so that we may capitalize on students' diverse abilities (Armstrong, 1994; L. Campbell, Campbell, & Dickinson, 1998; Gardner, 1995, 2000). For example, when my son Jeff took high school biology, he had to write a short story that included at least four examples of living things (either plants or animals) changing energy from one form into another—an assignment in which both linguistic and logical-mathematical intelligence played substantial roles. Consider, too, how an eighth-grade teacher took advantage of two girls' musical intelligence to teach spelling:

> [B]oth [girls] enjoyed playing the piano. [I] asked the girls to label the piano keys with the letters of the alphabet, so that the girls could "play" the words on their keyboards. Later, on spelling tests, the students were asked to recall the tones and sounds of each word and write its corresponding letters. Not only did spelling scores improve, but the two pianists began thinking of other "sound" texts to set to music. Soon, they performed each classmate's name and transcribed entire sentences. (L. Campbell et al., 1998, p. 142)

Whether or not human beings have eight or more distinctly different intelligences, they certainly benefit when they are encouraged to think about a particular topic in several ways—perhaps with words, pictures, bodily movements, and so on (more about multiple forms of *encoding* in Chapter 6). The following exercise lets you apply Gardner's theory to an actual classroom assignment.

INTERPRETING ARTIFACTS AND INTERACTIONS   *Ur*

In a unit on ancient cultures of the Mideast, students in a sixth-grade class are having a fictional friend "visit" various civilizations and "send" picture postcards home to them. Eleven-year-old Shea has made the following postcard for her friend Sarah McBear's visit to ancient Ur. As you look at the postcard, speculate about

- Which of Gardner's eight intelligences came into play in making the postcard
- How much Shea learned about Ur and ziggurats from the activity

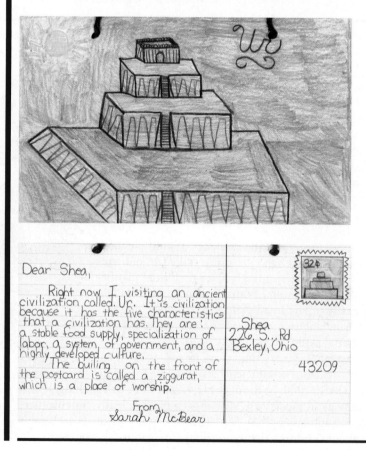

At a minimum, writing the note from Sarah involves linguistic intelligence, and drawing the picture of the ziggurat involves spatial intelligence. The postcard activity is a clever way of helping students think about ancient civilizations in greater depth than they might if they were simply reading about them in a textbook. At the same time, however, Shea appears to be parroting back what she has learned without giving it much thought. For instance, she says that Ur qualifies as a civilization because it has five characteristics, yet she lists only four and does not notice the discrepancy. Furthermore, she defines a ziggurat merely as a "place of worship." Hence, Shea is showing little or none of the *elaboration* that I spoke of in Chapter 2 (and will address further in Chapter 6).

Sternberg's Triarchic Theory

Whereas Gardner focuses on different kinds of intelligence, Robert Sternberg focuses more on the nature of intelligence itself. Sternberg (1984, 1985, 1998b) suggests that intelligent behavior involves an interplay of three factors, all of which may vary from one occasion to the next: (1) the environmental *context* in which the behavior occurs, (2) the way in which one's prior *experiences* are brought to bear on a particular task, and (3) the *cognitive processes* required by that task. These three dimensions are summarized in Figure 4.3. Let's look at each one in more detail.

Environmental Context
- Adapts behavior to fit the environment
- Adapts the environment to fit one's needs
- Selects an environment conducive to success

Prior Experience
- Deals with a new situation by drawing on past experience
- Deals with a familiar situation quickly and efficiently

Cognitive Processes
- Interprets new situations in useful ways
- Separates important information from irrelevant details
- Indentifies effective problem-solving strategies
- Finds relationships among seemingly different ideas
- Makes effective use of feedback
- Applies other cognitive processes

Role of environmental context. Earlier in the chapter, we noted that intelligence is both *adaptive* and *culture-specific*. Sternberg proposes that intelligent behavior involves adaptation: Individuals must adapt their behaviors to deal successfully with specific environmental conditions, modify the environment to better fit their own needs, or select an alternative environment more conducive to success. He also proposes that behavior may be more or less intelligent in different cultural contexts. For example, learning to read is an adaptive response in some cultures yet may be an irrelevant skill in others.

FIGURE 4.3 Sternberg's three dimensions of intelligence

Sternberg has identified three general skills that may be particularly adaptive in Western culture. One such skill is *practical problem-solving ability*—for example, one's ability to correctly identify the problem in a particular situation, to reason logically (both deductively and inductively), and to generate a multitude of possible problem solutions. A second skill is *verbal ability*—for example, one's ability to speak and write clearly, to develop and use a large vocabulary, and to understand and learn from what one reads. A third skill is *social competence*—for example, one's ability to relate effectively with other human beings, to be sensitive to others' needs and wishes, and to provide leadership.

Role of prior experiences. Sternberg proposes that intelligent behavior sometimes reflects one's ability to deal successfully with a brand new task or situation. On other occasions, it reflects one's ability to deal with more familiar tasks and situations in a rapid and efficient manner. In both cases, one's prior experiences play a critical role.

When dealing with a new task or situation, people must make some sort of new response. But to do so, they must draw on their past experiences, considering the kinds of responses that have been effective in similar situations. Try the following exercise as an illustration.

EXPERIENCING FIRSTHAND   *Finding the Bus Station*

You and two friends, Bonnie and Clyde, drive to a small city about two or three hours away to do some sight-seeing. Once there, Bonnie and Clyde decide to spend the night so that they can attend a concert scheduled for the following day. You, however, want to return home the same day. You've been traveling in Bonnie's car, and now the only way you can get back home is to take a bus. How might you find your way to the bus station? What strategies have you used in other situations that might help you in your efforts?

One strategy is to find a telephone book and look up *bus lines*. Another is to ask directions of a police officer, hotel clerk, or other seemingly knowledgeable person. Still another is to find the city's central business district and wander around; bus stations in most cities are located somewhere in the downtown area. Each of these strategies may be similar to an approach you've used in the past—perhaps to find a friend's house, a suitable place to eat, or a pharmacy open on Saturday nights.

When people deal with more familiar situations, intelligent behavior involves developing **automaticity**—an ability to respond quickly and efficiently—in either mentally processing or physically performing a task. As an example, try the following exercise.

EXPERIENCING FIRSTHAND *Solving for x*

How quickly can you solve for *x* in this problem?

$$\frac{4}{5} = \frac{x}{30}$$

If you were able to identify the correct answer (24) very quickly and without a great deal of thought and effort, then you show some automaticity (and hence some intelligence) in your ability to solve mathematical problems involving proportions. Automaticity results from experience—from performing certain tasks over and over again. (Chapter 6 discusses automaticity in more depth.)

Role of cognitive processes.   In addition to considering how context and prior experience affect behavior, we must also consider how an individual thinks about (mentally processes) a particular task. Sternberg proposes that many cognitive processes are involved in intelligent behavior: interpreting new situations in ways that promote successful adaptation, separating important and relevant information from unimportant and irrelevant details, identifying possible strategies for solving a problem, finding relationships among seemingly different ideas, making effective use of external feedback about one's performance, and so on. Different cognitive processes are likely to be more or less important in different situations, and an individual may behave more or less "intelligently" depending on the specific abilities needed at the time.

To date, research neither supports nor refutes Sternberg's belief that intelligence has this "triarchic" nature, and in fact Sternberg's theory is sufficiently vague that it is difficult to test empirically (Sattler, 2001; Siegler, 1998). At the same time, the theory reminds us that an individual's ability to behave "intelligently" may vary considerably depending on the particular context and on the specific knowledge, skills, and cognitive processes that a task requires. Some theorists believe that context makes all the difference in the world—a belief that is clearly evident in the concept of *distributed intelligence*.

Distributed Intelligence

Implicit in our discussion so far has been the assumption that intelligent behavior is something that people engage in with little if any help from the objects or people around them. But some theorists point out that people are far more likely to think and behave intelligently when they have the support of their physical and social environments (Pea, 1993; Perkins, 1992, 1995; Sternberg & Wagner, 1994). For example, it's easier for many people to solve for *x* in $\frac{4}{5} = \frac{x}{30}$ if they have pencil and paper, or perhaps even a calculator, with which to work the problem out. It should be easier to find the local bus station if one can debate the pros and cons of various strategies with a few friends. As noted in Chapter 2, virtually anyone can perform more difficult tasks when he or she has the support structure, or *scaffolding*, to do so.

This idea that intelligent behavior depends on people's physical and social support systems is sometimes referred to as **distributed intelligence**. People can "distribute" their thinking (and therefore think more intelligently) in at least three ways (Perkins, 1992, 1995). First, they can use physical objects, and especially technology (e.g., calculators, computers), to handle and manipulate large amounts of information. Second, they can work with other people to explore ideas and solve problems; after all, two heads are usually better than one. And third, they can represent and think about the situations they encounter using the various symbolic systems their culture provides—for instance, the words, diagrams, charts, mathematical equations, and

What implications does such environmental support have for the *development* of intelligence? Use Vygotsky's concept of *zone of proximal development* (see Chapter 2) in your answer.

so on that help them simplify or summarize complex topics and problems. As teachers, rather than asking the question, "How intelligent are our students?" we should instead be asking, "How can we help our students think as intelligently as possible? What tools, social networks, and symbolic systems can we provide?"

Heredity, Environment, and Group Differences

Three fairly consistent research findings are that, on average, African American families have lower incomes than European American families, students from lower-income families get lower IQ scores than students from upper- and middle-income families, and European American students get higher IQ scores than African American students (N. Brody, 1992; McLoyd, 1998; Neisser, 1998a). In *The Bell Curve*, Herrnstein and Murray proposed that these differences are due largely to heredity—in other words, that European Americans have a genetic advantage over African Americans. As you might guess, the book's proposal that there are racial differences in intelligence has generated considerable controversy and a great deal of outrage.

The concept of distributed intelligence suggests that students can often think more intelligently by using technology to manipulate large bodies of data, brainstorming possible problem solutions with classmates, and using symbolic systems (words, mathematical symbols, charts, diagrams, etc.) to simplify complex ideas and processes.

Scholars have poked so many holes in *The Bell Curve* that it doesn't seem to hold water (Jacoby & Glauberman, 1995; J. Marks, 1995; Montagu, 1999). For instance, they find numerous weaknesses in the research studies and statistical analyses that Herrnstein and Murray described; as one simple example, they remind us that we can ultimately never draw conclusions about causation by looking only at correlational studies. They argue that any innate intelligence differences between races have not had sufficient time to evolve, nor does it seem logical that some groups would evolve to be less adaptive (i.e., less intelligent) than others. They point out, too, that the very concept of *race*, though widely used to categorize people in our society, actually has no basis in biology: It is virtually impossible to identify a person's "race" by analyzing his or her DNA.

Research tells us that heredity probably does play some role in intelligence. For instance, identical twins tend to have more similar IQ scores than fraternal twins do, even when each is raised in a different home (Bouchard, 1997; Plomin, 1994). And in many respects, the cognitive abilities of adopted children more closely resemble those of their biological parents than those of their adoptive parents, particularly as the children grow older (Plomin, Fulker, Corley, & DeFries, 1997; McGue, Bouchard, Iacono, & Lykken, 1993).

Yet the environment clearly has an effect on IQ scores as well. For instance, poor nutrition in the early years of development (including the nine months before birth) leads to lower IQ scores, as does a mother's excessive use of alcohol during pregnancy (D'Amato, Chitooran, & Whitten, 1992; Neisser et al., 1996; Ricciuti, 1993). Attending school has a consistently positive effect on IQ scores (Ceci & Williams, 1997; Ramey, 1992). Changing a child's environment from an impoverished one to a more stimulating one (e.g., through adoption) can result in IQ gains of 15 points or more (Capron & Duyme, 1989; Scarr & Weinberg, 1976; Zigler & Seitz, 1982). Furthermore, researchers are finding that, worldwide, there is a slow but steady increase in people's IQ scores—a trend that is probably due to better nutrition, better schooling, an increased amount of daily stimulation (through increased access to television, reading materials, etc.), and other improvements in people's environments (Flynn, 1987; Neisser, 1998b).

Many psychologists believe that it may ultimately be impossible to separate the effects of heredity and environment—that the two interact to influence children's cognitive development and measured IQ in ways that cannot be disentangled (Bidell & Fischer, 1997; Petrill & Wilkerson, 2000; Simonton, 2001; Wahlsten & Gottlieb, 1997). Yet we have considerable evidence that IQ differences between African American and European American children are due largely to *differences in environment*—more specifically, to economic circumstances that affect the quality of prenatal and postnatal nutrition, availability of stimulating books and toys, access to educational opportunities, and so on (Brooks-Gunn, Klebanov, & Duncan, 1996; McLoyd, 1998). We find, too, that African American and European American children have, in recent years, become increasingly *similar*; this trend can be attributed only to more equitable environmental conditions for the two groups (Neisser et al., 1996). Furthermore, we must remember that IQ scores are definitely *not* perfect measures of intelligence. In general, then, we should assume that African American and European American children (and presumably other racial and ethnic groups as well) have equivalent potential to develop intelligence and various cognitive abilities.

Being Optimistic About Students' Potential

Contemporary views of intelligence give us reason to be optimistic about our students' abilities. If intelligence is as multifaceted as theorists such as Gardner and Sternberg believe, then scores from any single IQ test cannot possibly give a complete picture of students' "intelligence" (Neisser et al., 1996). In fact, we are likely to see intelligent behavior in many of our students—perhaps in *all* of them—in one way or another (Gardner, 1995). One student may show promise in mathematics, another may be an exceptionally gifted writer, a third may be skillful in interpersonal relationships, and a fourth may show talent in art, music, or physical education. Furthermore, as Sternberg's triarchic theory points out, intelligent behavior draws on a variety of cognitive processes that can clearly improve over time with experience and practice (Sternberg et al., 2000). And the notion of distributed intelligence suggests that intelligent behavior should be relatively commonplace when students have the right tools, social groups, and symbolic systems with which to work.

For optimal intellectual development, students need a variety of stimulating experiences throughout the childhood years, including age-appropriate toys and books, frequent verbal interactions with adults and other children, and numerous opportunities to practice important behavioral and cognitive skills (R. H. Bradley & Caldwell, 1984; Brooks-Gunn et al., 1996; Ericsson & Chalmers, 1994; R. D. Hess & Holloway, 1984; McGowan & Johnson, 1984). When parents and other caretakers cannot provide such experiences, most welcome the availability of enriching preschool and after-school programs. Regularly attending such programs can greatly enhance a student's cognitive development and potential to lead a productive life (F. A. Campbell & Ramey, 1994, 1995; Slaughter-Defoe, 2001).

We must remember, too, that to the extent that intelligence is culture-dependent, intelligent behavior is likely to take different forms in children from different ethnic backgrounds (Gardner, 1995; Neisser et al., 1996; Perkins, 1995; Sternberg, 1985). For example, in our case study of Lupita, we saw a kindergarten girl with an exceptional ability to work cooperatively with others; cooperation is a valued skill among many Mexican Americans. As another example, the intelligence of Navajo students may be reflected in their ability to help their family and tribal nation, to perform cultural rituals, or to demonstrate expert craftsmanship (Kirschenbaum, 1989). We must be careful not to limit our conception of intelligence only to students' ability to succeed at traditional academic tasks.

Finally, intelligence—no matter how we define it—can never be the only characteristic that affects our students' academic achievement. Learning strategies, motivation, and creativity also play important roles. It is to the last of these, creativity, that we turn now.

Creativity

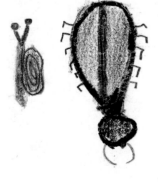

Bugs are big,

Bugs are small.

Bugs are black,

Bugs are all...

NEAT!

My critter-happy son Alex wrote and illustrated the poem on the left as a second grader. His teacher thought the poem reflected a certain degree of creativity; so did his not-so-objective mother. What do *you* think?

What exactly do we mean by the term **creativity?** Like intelligence, creativity is often defined differently by different people. But most definitions of creativity (Ripple, 1989; Runco & Chand, 1995) include two components:

- *New and original behavior:* Behavior not specifically learned from someone else
- *An appropriate and productive result:* A useful product or effective problem solution

Both criteria must be met before we identify behavior as creative.

To illustrate these two criteria, let's say that I am giving a lecture on creativity and want a creative way of keeping my students' attention. One possible solution would be to come to class stark naked. This solution certainly meets the first criterion for creativity: It is new and original behavior, and I did not learn it from any other teacher. It does not, however, meet the second criterion: It isn't appropriate or productive within the context of our culture. A second possible solution might be to give my students several challenging problems that require creative thinking. This approach is more likely to meet both criteria. Not only is it a relatively original way of teaching, but it is also appropriate and productive for students to learn about creativity by exploring the process firsthand.

Although a certain degree of intelligence is probably necessary for creative thinking, intelligence and creativity are somewhat independent abilities (Sternberg, 1985; I. A. Taylor,

1976; Torrance, 1976). In other words, highly intelligent students are not always the most creative ones. Many theorists believe that the cognitive processes involved in intelligence and creativity may be somewhat different (e.g., see Kogan, 1983). Tasks on intelligence tests often involve **convergent thinking**—pulling several pieces of information together to draw a conclusion or to solve a problem. In contrast, creativity often involves **divergent thinking**—starting with one idea and taking it in many different directions. To see the difference firsthand, try the following exercise.

EXPERIENCING FIRSTHAND *Convergent and Divergent Thinking*

On a sheet of paper, write your responses to each of the following:

- Why are houses more often built with bricks than with stones?
- What are some possible uses of a brick? Try to think of as many different and unusual uses as you can.
- Add improvements to the wagon drawing so that the object will be more fun to play with.

Modeled after Torrance, 1970.

To answer the first question, you must use convergent thinking to pull together the things you know about several different objects (bricks, stones, and houses). But the other two items require divergent thinking about a single object: You consider how a brick might be used in many different contexts and how a child's wagon might be embellished in a wide variety of ways.

Creativity is probably *not* a single entity that people either have or don't have (e.g., Hocevar & Bachelor, 1989). Rather, it is probably a combination of many specific characteristics, thinking processes, and behaviors. Among other things, creative individuals tend to

- Interpret problems and situations in a flexible manner
- Possess a great deal of information relevant to a task
- Combine existing information and ideas in new ways
- Evaluate their accomplishments in accordance with high standards
- Have a passion for—and therefore invest much time and effort in—what they are doing (Csikszentmihalyi, 1996; Glover, Ronning, & Reynolds, 1989; Runco & Chand, 1995; Russ, 1993; Simonton, 2000; Weisberg, 1993)

Furthermore, creativity is probably somewhat specific to different situations and different content areas (R. T. Brown, 1989; Feldhusen & Treffinger, 1980; Ripple, 1989). Students may show creativity in art, writing, or science, but they aren't necessarily creative in all those areas. As teachers, we must be careful not to label particular students as "creative" or "not creative." Instead we should keep our eyes and minds open for instances of creative thinking or behavior in many (perhaps *all*) of our students.

Fostering Creativity in the Classroom

Certain components of creative thinking may have a hereditary component, yet environmental factors play an equally important role in creativity's development (Esquivel, 1995; Ripple, 1989; Simonton, 2000; Torrance, 1976). Research studies suggest several strategies for promoting creativity in the classroom:

- *Show students that creativity is valued.* We are more likely to foster creativity when we show students that we value creative thoughts and behaviors. One way to do this is to encourage and reward unusual ideas and responses. For example, we can express excitement when students complete a project in a unique and unusual manner. As we grade assignments and test papers, we should acknowledge responses that, though not what we were expecting, are legitimately correct. Engaging in creative activities ourselves also shows that we value creativity (Feldhusen & Treffinger, 1980; Hennessey & Amabile, 1987; Parnes, 1967; Torrance & Myers, 1970).

Creativity is specific to different content domains. Some students may be creative artists, others creative writers, and still others creative scientists.

Here we are distinguishing
between *intrinsic* and *extrinsic*
motivation, concepts we will
explore in Chapters 11 and 12.

■ *Focus students' attention on internal rather than external rewards.* Students are more creative when they engage in activities because they enjoy them and take pride in what they have done; they are less creative when they work for external rewards such as grades (Hennessey, 1995; Lubart, 1994). Therefore, we can foster creativity by giving students opportunities to explore their own special interests—interests they will gladly pursue without having to be prodded. For example, we might encourage students to choose a topic about which they are genuinely curious when they are planning a project for the science fair. We can also foster creativity by downplaying the importance of grades, instead focusing students' attention on the internal satisfaction that their creative efforts bring (Hennessey, 1995; Hennessey & Amabile, 1987; Perkins, 1990). For example, we might tell students in an art class:

> Please don't worry too much about grades. As long as you use the materials appropriately and give each assignment your best shot, you will do well in this class. The important thing is to find an art form that you enjoy and through which you can express yourself.

■ *Promote mastery of a subject area.* Creativity in a particular subject area is more likely to occur when students have considerable mastery of the subject; it is unlikely to occur when students have little or no understanding of the topic (Simonton, 2000). One important way of fostering creativity, then, is to help students master course content (Amabile & Hennessey, 1992; Perkins, 1990; Sternberg, 1985). For example, if we want our students to apply scientific principles in a creative manner—perhaps as they conduct a science fair experiment or develop a solution to an environmental problem—we should make sure that they first have those principles down pat.

We will look at the nature of
higher-level thinking in greater
depth in Chapter 8 and at the
value of higher-level questions in
Chapter 13.

■ *Ask thought-provoking questions.* Students are more likely to think creatively when we ask them questions that require them to use previously learned information in a new way (these are frequently called **higher-level questions**). Questions that ask students to engage in divergent thinking may be particularly helpful (Feldhusen & Treffinger, 1980; Feldhusen, Treffinger, & Bahlke, 1970; Perkins, 1990; Torrance & Myers, 1970). For example, during a unit on the Pony Express, we might ask:

- What are all the ways mail might have been transported across the United States at that time?
- Can you think of some very unusual way that no one else has thought of to transport mail today? (Feldhusen & Treffinger, 1980, p. 36)

■ *Give students the freedom and security to take risks.* Creativity is more likely to appear when students feel comfortable taking risks; it is unlikely to appear when they are afraid of failing (Houtz, 1990). To encourage risk taking, we can allow students to engage in certain activities without evaluating their performance. We can also urge them to think of their mistakes and failures as an inevitable—but usually temporary—aspect of the creative process (Feldhusen & Treffinger, 1980; Hennessey & Amabile, 1987; Pruitt, 1989). For example, when students are writing a creative short story, we might give them several opportunities to get our feedback, and perhaps the feedback of their peers, before they turn in a final product.

■ *Provide the time that creativity requires.* Students need time to experiment with new materials and ideas, to think in divergent directions, and occasionally to make mistakes. A critical aspect of promoting creativity, then, is to give them that time (Feldhusen & Treffinger, 1980; Pruitt, 1989). For example, when teaching a foreign language, we might ask small groups of students to create and videotape a television commercial spoken entirely in that language. This is hardly a project that students can do in a day; they may need several weeks to brainstorm various ideas, write and revise a script, find or develop the props they need, and rehearse their lines. Creative ideas and projects seldom emerge overnight.

Using what you have learned about the nature of creativity and about strategies for promoting it, try the following exercise.

INTERPRETING ARTIFACTS AND INTERACTIONS   *What Can This Be?*

Ms. Simmons wants to encourage more creative thinking in her students, so she draws this figure on the board:

She asks her students to draw as many pictures as possible using this figure as a starting point. One student's ideas appear in the artifact that follows. As you examine the artifact, consider these questions:

- Does the activity require convergent or divergent thinking?
- Are activities like this likely to promote greater creativity on classroom tasks over the long run? Why or why not?

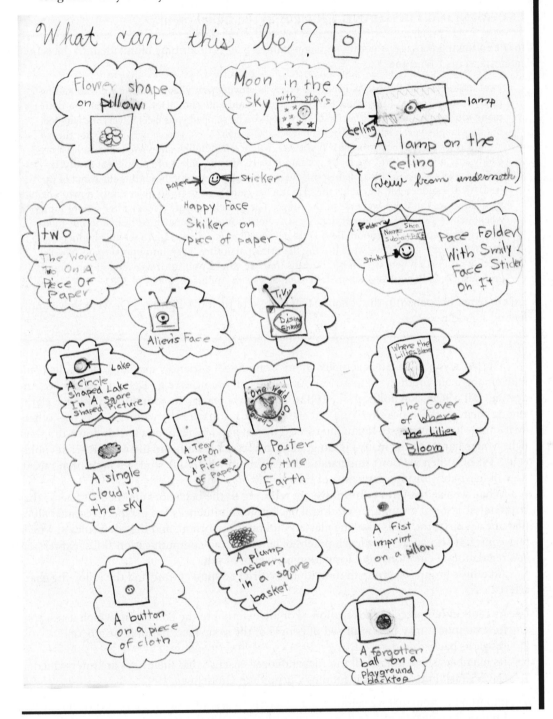

The activity requires divergent thinking, a key component of creative thinking. By assigning the activity, the teacher is showing her students that she values creative ideas. However, creativity is not a single entity that we can easily "train" with simple exercises such as this one. Instead, it may take different forms in different content areas, and students are more apt to be creative in a particular area when they have considerable mastery of that area. Thus, we can reasonably predict that the activity—though undoubtedly enjoyable for many of the students—may do little if anything to promote creativity over the long run.

Like intelligence, creativity often takes different forms in different cultures: What constitutes a work of art or "good music" might vary from one culture to another. As we shall see now, the diverse cultural and ethnic backgrounds among our students will manifest themselves in many other ways as well.

Cultural and Ethnic Differences

EXPERIENCING FIRSTHAND *Ruckus in the Lunchroom*

In the following passage, a young teenager named Sam is describing an incident in the school cafeteria to his friend Joe:

> I got in line behind Bubba. As usual the line was moving pretty slow and we were all getting pretty restless. For a little action Bubba turned around and said, "Hey Sam! What you doin' man? You so ugly that when the doctor delivered you he slapped your face!" Everyone laughed, but they laughed even harder when I shot back, "Oh yeah? Well, you so ugly the doctor turned around and slapped your momma!" It got even wilder when Bubba said, "Well man, at least my daddy ain't no girl scout!" We really got into it then. After a while more people got involved— 4, 5, then 6. It was a riot! People helping out anyone who seemed to be getting the worst of the deal. All of a sudden Mr. Reynolds the gym teacher came over to try to quiet things down. The next thing we knew we were all in the office. The principal made us stay after school for a week; he's so straight! On top of that, he sent word home that he wanted to talk to our folks in his office Monday afternoon. Boy! Did I get it when I got home. That's the third notice I've gotten this semester. As we were leaving the principal's office, I ran into Bubba again. We decided we'd finish where we left off, but this time we would wait until we were off the school grounds. (R. E. Reynolds, Taylor, Steffensen, Shirey, & Anderson, 1982, p. 358)

Exactly what happened in the school cafeteria? Were the boys fighting? Or were they simply having a good time?

The story you just read is actually about "sounding," a friendly exchange of insults common among male youth in some African American communities (e.g., DeLain, Pearson, & Anderson, 1985; R. E. Reynolds et al., 1982). Some boys engage in sounding to achieve status among their peers—those throwing out the greatest insults are the winners—whereas others do it simply for amusement. If you interpreted the cafeteria incident as a knock-down-drag-out fight, you're hardly alone; many eighth graders in a research study did likewise (R. E. Reynolds et al., 1982). When we don't understand the culture in which our students have been raised, we will inevitably misinterpret some of their behaviors.

When we use the term **culture**, we are referring to the behaviors and belief systems that characterize a social group. One's cultural background influences the perspectives and values that one acquires, the skills that one masters and finds important, and the adult roles to which one aspires. It also guides the development of language and communication skills, expression and regulation of emotions, and formation of a sense of self.

An **ethnic group** is a group of individuals with a common culture and the following characteristics:

- Its roots either precede the creation of or are external to the country in which it resides; for example, it may be comprised of people of the same race, national origin, or religious background.
- Its members share a sense of interdependence—a sense that their lives are intertwined. (NCSS Task Force on Ethnic Studies Curriculum Guidelines, 1992)

It is important to note that we cannot always determine a student's ethnicity strictly on the basis of physical characteristics (e.g., race) or birthplace (Wlodkowski & Ginsberg, 1995). For instance, my daughter Tina, although she was born in Colombia and has Hispanic and Native American ancestors, was raised by two European American parents; ethnically, Tina is probably more "White" than anything else.

It is becoming increasingly apparent that our schools are not adequately meeting the needs of the diverse cultural and ethnic groups they serve. Students from ethnic minorities (especially African American and Hispanic students) are often *at risk*: They achieve at levels far below their actual capabilities, and an alarming number never graduate from high school (D. Y. Ford, 1996; Losey, 1995; Roderick & Camburn, 1999).[3] Considerable research links such low achievement levels to the fact that a disproportionate number of minority students come from low socioeconomic backgrounds (McLoyd, 1998; Murdock, 2000); we will examine the particular challenges of such a background a bit later in the chapter. Oftentimes an additional challenge for minority students is that they must simultaneously navigate different cultures at home and at school, as we shall see now.

Navigating Different Cultures at Home and at School

You may recall from Chapter 3 that many children entering school for the first time experience some culture shock. This culture shock is more intense for some groups of students than for others (Casanova, 1987; Ramsey, 1987). Most schools in North America and western Europe are based largely on European-American, middle-class, "mainstream" culture, so students with this cultural background often adjust quickly to the classroom environment. But students who come from other cultural backgrounds, sometimes with very different norms regarding acceptable behavior, may initially find school a confusing and incomprehensible place. For example, recent immigrants may not know what to expect from others or what behaviors others expect of them (C. R. Harris, 1991; Igoa, 1995). Children raised in a society where gender roles are clearly differentiated—where males and females are expected to behave very differently—may have difficulty adjusting to a school in which similar expectations are held for boys and girls (Kirschenbaum; 1989; Vasquez, 1988). Any such **cultural mismatch** between home and school cultures can interfere with students' adjustment to the school setting, and ultimately with their academic achievement as well (García, 1995; C. D. Lee & Slaughter-Defoe, 1995; Ogbu, 1992; Phelan et al., 1994).

Cultural mismatch is compounded when teachers misinterpret the behaviors of students from ethnic minority groups. For example, we may misinterpret the nature of students' verbal exchanges, just as you might have misinterpreted Sam's behavior in the cafeteria. Certain Native American communities find it unnecessary to say hello or good-bye (Sisk, 1989), yet a teacher from another culture may misunderstand when he or she isn't greeted in the morning. In other Native American communities, people rarely express their feelings through facial expressions (Montgomery, 1989), giving some teachers the mistaken impression that students are bored or disinterested. When students' behaviors differ enough from our own and we misinterpret them as being inappropriate, unacceptable, or just plain "odd," we may jump to the conclusion that these students are unable or unwilling to be successful in the classroom (B. T. Bowman, 1989; Hilliard & Vaughn-Scott, 1982).

As students gain experience with the culture of their school, they become increasingly aware of their teacher's and peers' expectations for behavior and ways of thinking, and many eventually become adept at switching their cultural vantage point as they move from home to school and then back home again (Hong, Morris, Chiu, & Benet-Martínez, 2000; LaFromboise, Coleman, & Gerton, 1993; Phelan et al., 1994). One Mexican American student's recollection provides an example:

> At home with my parents and grandparents the only acceptable language was Spanish; actually that's all they really understood. Everything was really Mexican, but at the same time they wanted me to speak good English. . . . But at school, I felt really different because everyone was American, including me. Then I would go home in the afternoon and be Mexican again. (Padilla, 1994, p. 30)

Not all students make an easy adjustment, however. Some students actively resist adapting to the school culture, perhaps because they view it as being inconsistent with—even contradictory to—their own cultural background and identity (Ogbu, 1994, 1999; Phelan et al., 1994). Still others try desperately to fit in at school yet find inconsistencies between home and school

Can you think of ways in which your own school environment was mismatched with the culture in which you were raised?

---

[3]We find cause for optimism in the fact that the achievement gap between European Americans, on the one hand, and African American and Hispanic students, on the other, narrowed in the 1970s and 1980s (Neisser, 1998b). Significant differences among the groups continue, however.

difficult to resolve, as a teacher who worked with Muslim children from Pakistan and Afghanistan reports:

> During the days of preparation for Ramadan Feast, the children fasted with the adults. They were awakened by their parents before dawn. They had breakfast and then went back to sleep until it was time to get themselves ready for school. In school they refrained from food or drink—even a drop of water—until sunset. By noon, especially on warm days, they were a bit listless. I had observed that they refrained from praying in a public school even though prayer was a part of their cultural attitude. They spoke about their obligation to pray five times daily. In their writing they expressed the conflict within:
>
> > *I always think about my country. I think about going there one day, seeing it and practicing my religion with no problems. Here we don't have enough priests. We call them mullah. Here we have only the mosque. The mullah is important because we learn the Koran from him. I can't practice my religion. Before sunrise, I can pray with my family. But at school we can't say to my teacher, "Please, teacher, I need to pray."* (Igoa, 1995, p. 135)

As teachers, we will rarely, if ever, have a classroom in which all students share our own cultural heritage. Clearly, then, we must educate ourselves about the ways in which students from various ethnic backgrounds are likely to be different from one another and from ourselves.

Examples of Ethnic Diversity

Tremendous cultural variation exists within African American, Asian American, Hispanic, Native American, and European American groups. Thus, we must be careful not to form stereotypes about any group. At the same time, we must be aware of group differences that may exist so that we can better understand why our students sometimes behave as they do.

Researchers have identified a variety of ways in which the cultures of some ethnic minority students may be different from the culture of a typical North American classroom. In the next few pages, we will consider potential differences in the following areas:

Before you read further, can you predict what some of these cultural differences might be?

- Language and dialect
- Sociolinguistic conventions
- Cooperation versus competition
- Private versus public performance
- Eye contact
- Conceptions of time
- Types of questions
- Family relationships and expectations
- World views

Language and dialect.   An obvious cultural difference is in language. For example, in the United States, more than 6 million students speak a language other than English at home, and in some large city school systems, more than a hundred different languages are spoken (McKeon, 1994; National Association of Bilingual Education, 1993; U.S. Bureau of the Census, 1994). Children who have not encountered English before they begin school will naturally have difficulty with schoolwork in an English-based classroom.

Even when children speak English at home, they may use a form of English different from the **Standard English** that is typically considered acceptable in school. More specifically, they may speak in a different **dialect**—a form of English that includes some unique pronunciations and grammatical structures. For example, some African American children speak in an **African American dialect**, using sentences such as these:

He got ten dollar.

Momma she mad.

I be going to dance tonight.

Nobody don't never like me. (Owens, 1995, p. A-8)

At one time, researchers believed that an African American dialect represented an erroneous and less complex form of speech than Standard English and urged educators to teach students to speak "properly" as quickly as possible. But we now realize that African American dialects are, in fact, very complex language systems with their own predictable grammatical rules and their own unique idioms and proverbs. Furthermore, these dialects promote communication and complex thought as readily as Standard English (DeLain et al., 1985; Fairchild & Edwards-Evans, 1990; Owens, 1996).

For many students, their native language or dialect is part of their cultural identity (McAlpine, 1992; Torres-Guzmán, 1998; Ulichny, 1994). The following incident among rural Native American students at a boarding school in Alaska is an example:

> Many of the students at the school spoke English with a native dialect and seemed unable to utter certain essential sounds in the English language. A new group of speech teachers was sent in to correct the problem. The teachers worked consistently with the students in an attempt to improve speech patterns and intonation, but found that their efforts were in vain.
>
> One night, the boys in the dormitory were seeming to have too much fun, and peals of laughter were rolling out from under the door. An investigating counselor approached cautiously, and listened quietly outside the door to see if he could discover the source of the laughter. From behind the door he heard a voice, speaking in perfect English, giving instructions to the rest of the crowd. The others were finding the situation very amusing. When the counselor entered the room he found that one of the students was speaking. "Joseph," he said, "You've been cured! Your English is perfect." "No," said Joseph returning to his familiar dialect, "I was just doing an imitation of you." "But if you can speak in standard English, why don't you do it all of the time?" the counselor queried. "I can," responded Joseph, "but it sounds funny, and I feel dumb doing it." (Garrison, 1989, p. 121)

Most educators recommend that all students develop proficiency in Standard English because success in mainstream adult society will be difficult to achieve without it, and members of ethnic communities typically echo this view (Casanova, 1987; Craft, 1984; Ogbu, 1999). At the same time, we should recognize that other languages and dialects are very appropriate means of communication in many situations (Fairchild & Edwards-Evans, 1990; C. D. Lee & Slaughter-Defoe, 1995; Ulichny, 1994). For example, although we may wish to encourage Standard English in most written work or in formal oral presentations, we might find other dialects quite appropriate in creative writing or informal classroom discussions (Smitherman, 1994). Ideally, we should encourage students to be proficient in *both* Standard English and their local language or dialect, so that they can communicate effectively in a wide variety of contexts (Ogbu, 1999; A. R. Warren & McCloskey, 1993). One teacher of African American students explains to them that facility with two dialects is a form of bilingualism:

> I don't want them to be ashamed of what they know but I also want them to know and be comfortable with what school and the rest of the society requires. When I put it in the context of "translation" they get excited. They see it is possible to go from one to the other. It's not that they are not familiar with Standard English. . . . They hear Standard English all the time on TV. It's certainly what I use in the classroom. But there is rarely any connection made between the way they speak and Standard English. I think that when they can see the connections and know that they can make the shifts, they become better at both. They're bilingual! (Ladson-Billings, 1994a, p. 84)

Sociolinguistic conventions.   In our discussion of linguistic development in Chapter 2, I introduced the concept of *pragmatics*, general behavioral skills important for conversing effectively with others. Pragmatics include **sociolinguistic conventions**: specific language-related behaviors that appear in some cultures or ethnic groups but not in others. For example, in some Native American groups, silence is valued, and in some Hispanic and rural southern African American communities, children are expected to speak only when spoken to (Menyuk & Menyuk, 1988; Owens, 1996). Yet people from European American backgrounds may feel uncomfortable with silence and say things just to fill in gaps in a conversation (Irujo, 1988). And in many African American, Puerto Rican, and Jewish families, adults and children alike sometimes speak spontaneously and simultaneously; in such settings, waiting for one's turn may mean being excluded from the conversation altogether (Trawick-Smith, 2000).

We also see ethnic differences in the amount of time that individuals wait before they respond to other people's comments or questions. For instance, students from some Native American communities pause before answering a question as a way of showing respect, as this statement by a Northern Cheyenne illustrates:

> Even if I had a quick answer to your question, I would never answer immediately. That would be saying that your question was not worth thinking about. (Gilliland, 1988, p. 27)

Teachers frequently ask questions of their students and then wait for an answer. But exactly how long *do* they wait? Research indicates that most teachers wait a second or even less for students to reply. Research also indicates that when teachers wait for longer periods of time—for three seconds or even longer—students, especially those from ethnic minority groups, are more likely to answer teachers' questions and participate in class discussions (Mohatt & Erickson, 1981; Rowe, 1987; Tharp, 1989). Not only does such an extended **wait time** allow students to show respect, but it also gives students with limited English proficiency some mental "translation" time (Gilliland, 1988). (Chapter 6 identifies additional advantages of increasing wait time.)

Yet we should also be aware that some native Hawaiian students, rather than wanting time to think or show respect, may have a preference for **negative wait time:** They often interrupt teachers or classmates who haven't finished speaking. Such interruptions, which many might interpret as rude, are instead a sign of personal involvement in the community culture of those students (Tharp, 1994).

Cooperation versus competition.   School achievement in a traditional classroom is often a solitary, individual endeavor. Students receive praise, stickers, and good grades when they perform at a high level, regardless of how their classmates are performing. Sometimes, though, school achievement is quite competitive: A student's performance is evaluated in comparison with the performance of classmates. For example, some teachers may identify the "best" papers or drawings in the class; others may grade "on a curve," with some students doing very well and others inevitably failing.

Why do you think some teachers encourage competition among their students?

Yet in some cultures, it is neither individual achievement nor competitive achievement that is recognized, but rather *group* achievement: The success of the village or community is valued over individual success. Students from such cultures (e.g., many Native American, Mexican American, Southeast Asian, and Pacific Islander students) are more accustomed to working cooperatively than competitively, and for the benefit of the community rather than for themselves (Garcia, 1992; Lomawaima, 1995; Tharp, 1994). They may therefore resist when asked to compete against their classmates; 16-year-old Maria put it this way:

> I love sports, but not competitive sports. [My brother is] the same way. I think we learned that from our folks. They both try to set things up so that everyone wins in our family and no one is competing for anything. (Pipher, 1994, p. 280)

Students from cooperative cultures may also be confused when teachers scold them for helping one another on assignments or for "sharing" answers, and they may feel uncomfortable when their individual achievements are publicly acknowledged. Group work, with an emphasis on cooperation rather than competition, often facilitates the school achievement of these students (García, 1995; Losey, 1995; McAlpine & Taylor, 1993; L. S. Miller, 1995).

In some cultures, such as in many Mexican American and Native American communities, group achievement is valued over individual or competitive achievement. Children from such cultures are therefore more accustomed to working cooperatively.

Private versus public performance.   In many classrooms, learning is a very public enterprise. Individual students are often asked to answer questions or demonstrate skills in full view of their classmates, and they are encouraged to ask questions themselves when they don't understand. Such practices, which many teachers take for granted, may confuse or even alienate the students of some ethnic groups (Eriks-Brophy & Crago, 1994; Garcia, 1994; Lomawaima, 1995). For example, children raised in the Yup'ik culture of Alaska are expected to learn by close, quiet observation of adults; they rarely ask questions or otherwise interrupt what the adults are doing (Garcia, 1994). Children from some ethnic backgrounds, including many Puerto Ricans and Native Americans, have been taught that speaking directly and assertively to adults is rude (Hidalgo, Siu, Bright, Swap, & Epstein, 1995; Lomawaima, 1995). Many Native American children are also accustomed to practicing a skill privately at first, performing in front of a group only after they have attained a reasonable level of mastery (Garcia, 1994; S. Sanders, 1987; Suina & Smolkin, 1994). Native Hawaiian students may willingly respond as a group when their teacher asks a question yet remain silent when called on individually; apparently, these one-on-one interactions with adults remind many students of scoldings they have received from their parents (Au, 1980). As you might guess, then, many students from diverse ethnic backgrounds perform better when they can work one-on-one with the teacher or in a cooperative setting with a small group of classmates (Cazden & Leggett, 1981; Vasquez, 1990). They may also feel more comfortable practicing new skills in privacy until they have sufficiently mastered them (Fuller, 2001).

Eye contact.   For many of us, looking someone in the eye is a way of indicating that we are trying to communicate with that person or that we are listening intently to what the person is saying. But in many Native American, African American, Mexican American, and Puerto Rican communities, a child who looks an adult in the eye is showing disrespect. In these communities, children are taught to look down in the presence of adults (Gilliland, 1988; Irujo, 1988; Torres-Guzmán, 1998). The following anecdote shows how a teacher's recognition of this culturally learned behavior can make a difference:

> A teacher [described a Native American] student who would never say a word, nor even answer when she greeted him. Then one day when he came in she looked in the other direction and said, "Hello, Jimmy." He answered enthusiastically, "Why hello Miss Jacobs." She found that he would always talk if she looked at a book or at the wall, but when she looked at him, he appeared frightened. (Gilliland, 1988, p. 26)

Conceptions of time.   Many people regulate their lives by the clock: Being on time to appointments, social engagements, and the dinner table is important. This emphasis on punctuality is not characteristic of all cultures, however; for example, many Hispanic and Native American communities don't observe strict schedules and timelines (H. G. Burger, 1973; Garrison, 1989; Gilliland, 1988). Not surprisingly, children from these communities may be chronically late for school and have difficulty understanding the need to complete school tasks within a certain time frame.

To succeed in mainstream Western society, students eventually need to learn punctuality. At the same time, we must recognize that not all of our students will be especially concerned about clock time when they first enter our classrooms. Certainly we should expect students to arrive at class on time and to turn in assignments when they are due. But we must be patient and understanding when, for cultural reasons, students do not develop such habits immediately.

Types of questions.   Here are some typical questions that elementary school teachers ask beginning students:

- "What's this a picture of?"
- "What color is this?"
- "What's your sister's name?"

These questions seem simple enough to answer. But in fact, different cultures teach children to answer different kinds of questions. Parents from European American backgrounds frequently ask their children to identify objects and their characteristics. Yet in some other ethnic groups, parents rarely ask their children questions that they themselves know the answers to (Crago, Annahatak, & Ningiuruvik, 1993; Heath, 1980, 1989; Rogoff & Morelli, 1989). For example, parents in African American communities in parts of the southeastern United States are more likely to ask questions involving comparisons and analogies; rather than asking "What's that?" they may instead ask "What's that like?" (Heath, 1989). Furthermore, children in these same communities are specifically taught *not* to answer questions that strangers ask about personal and home life—questions such as "What's your name?" and "Where do you live?" The complaints of parents in these communities illustrate how much of a cultural mismatch there can be between the children and their European American teachers:

- "My kid, he too scared to talk, 'cause nobody play by the rules he know. At home I can't shut him up."
- "Miss Davis, she complain 'bout Ned not answerin' back. He says she asks dumb questions she already know about." (Heath, 1980, p. 107)

Teachers' comments about these children reflect their own lack of understanding about the culture from which the children come:

- "I would almost think some of them have a hearing problem; it is as though they don't hear me ask a question. I get blank stares to my questions. Yet when I am making statements or telling stories which interest them, they always seem to hear me."
- "The simplest questions are the ones they can't answer in the classroom; yet on the playground, they can explain a rule for a ballgame or describe a particular kind of bait with no problem. Therefore, I know they can't be as dumb as they seem in my class." (Heath, 1980, pp. 107–108)

Family relationships and expectations. In some ethnic groups—for example, in many Hispanic, Native American, and Asian communities—family bonds and relationships are especially important. Students raised in these cultures are likely to feel responsibility for their family's well-being and a strong sense of loyalty to other family members; they will also go to great efforts to please their parents (Abi-Nader, 1993; Banks & Banks, 1995; Fuligni, 1998).

In most cultures, school achievement is valued highly, and parents encourage their children to do well in school (Duran & Weffer, 1992; Fuligni, 1998; Hossler & Stage, 1992; A. H. Yee, 1992). But in a few cases, classroom achievement may be less valued than achievement in other areas. For example, in some very traditional Native American and Polynesian communities, children are expected to excel in art, dance, and other aspects of their culture rather than in more academic pursuits such as reading or mathematics (Kirschenbaum, 1989; Reid, 1989). We must certainly be sensitive to situations in which the achievements that *we* think are important are not those valued by students' families. Whenever possible, we must show our students how the school curriculum and classroom activities relate to their own cultural environment and their own life needs.

We must also maintain open lines of communication with our students' parents. Because some parents, especially parents of minority children, may be intimidated by school personnel, teachers often need to take the first step in establishing productive parent-teacher relationships. When teachers and parents realize that both groups want students to succeed in the classroom, they are more likely to work cooperatively to promote student achievement (Banks & Banks, 1995; Salend & Taylor, 1993; R. L. Warren, 1988). Chapter 14 identifies some specific strategies for working effectively with parents.

World views. The cultural and ethnic differences we've identified so far reveal themselves, in one way or another, in students' behaviors. Yet recall our earlier definition of culture: the behaviors and *belief systems* that characterize a social group. Our beliefs and assumptions about the world are often so integral to our everyday thinking that we take them for granted and are seldom consciously aware of them. Some beliefs that permeate the curriculum in traditional Western schools are not universally shared, however. Consider the following examples:

- After a major hurricane ripped through southern Florida in the summer of 1992, many fourth and fifth graders attributed the hurricane to natural causes, but some children from minority backgrounds, because of explanations heard from family members, neighbors, or church groups, believed that people's actions or supernatural forces also played a role in the hurricane's origins and destructiveness (O. Lee, 1999).
- When American high school students talk about American history, European Americans are likely to depict historical events as leading up to increasing freedom, equality, and democracy for its citizens. African Americans are more likely to depict historical events as contributing to or maintaining racist and oppressive attitudes and practices (T. Epstein, 2000).
- Whereas most students of European descent think of "progress" as comprising technological advancements and a higher standard of living, Navajo students are more likely to think of progress as comprising spiritual advancement (Nelson-Barber & Estrin, 1995).

Such beliefs and perspectives will invariably color how our students interpret what they learn in history, science, and other subject areas, for reasons you'll discover in Chapters 6 and 7.

Creating a More Multicultural Classroom Environment

Clearly, we must be sensitive to the ways in which students of various ethnic groups are likely to act and think differently from one another. But it is just as important that we help our students develop the same sensitivity: As adults, they will inevitably have to work cooperatively with people from a wide variety of backgrounds. It is in our students' best interests, then, that we promote awareness and understanding of numerous cultures in our classrooms. We can do so through strategies such as the following:

- Incorporating the values, beliefs, and traditions of many cultures into the curriculum
- Working to break down ethnic stereotypes
- Promoting positive social interactions among students from various ethnic groups
- Fostering democratic ideals

Incorporating the Values, Beliefs, and Traditions of Many Cultures into the Curriculum

Multicultural education should not be limited to cooking ethnic foods, celebrating Cinco de Mayo, or studying famous African Americans during Black History Month. Rather, effective **multicultural education** integrates the perspectives and experiences of numerous cultural groups throughout the curriculum and gives all students reason for pride in their own cultural heritage (Banks, 1995; García, 1995; Hollins, 1996; NCSS Task Force on Ethnic Studies Curriculum Guidelines, 1992).

As teachers, we can incorporate content from different ethnic groups into many aspects of the school curriculum. Here are some examples:

- In literature, read the work of minority authors and poets.
- In art, consider the creations and techniques of artists from around the world.
- In physical education, learn games or folk dances from other countries and cultures.
- In mathematics, use mathematical principles to address multicultural tasks and problems (e.g., using graph paper to design a Navajo rug).
- In history, look at wars and other major events from diverse perspectives (e.g., the Spanish perspective of the Spanish-American War, the Japanese perspective of World War II, the Native American perspective of the pioneers' westward migration in North America).
- In social studies, look at different religious beliefs and their effects on people's behaviors (e.g., see Figure 4.4).
- In current events, consider such issues as discrimination and oppression. (Boutte & McCormick, 1992; Casanova, 1987; Cottrol, 1990; K. Freedman, 1996; NCSS Task Force on Ethnic Studies Curriculum Guidelines, 1992; Nelson-Barber & Estrin, 1995; Pang, 1995; Sleeter & Grant, 1999; Ulichny, 1994)

As we explore various cultures, we should look for commonalities as well as differences. For example, we might study how various cultural groups celebrate the beginning of a new

In his high school Spanish class, Ben created this burlap-and-yarn eagle inspired by Mexican designs. A culture's art should be just one focus of a multicultural education that also looks at the culture's beliefs, values, and world views.

Figure 4.4 Thirteen-year-old Melinda wrote about the Shinto religion of Japan for her language arts and social studies classes. Students were required to go beyond the facts to draw their own conclusions and relate what they had learned to their personal lives. The excerpts from Melinda's paper that appear here show her efforts to do so.

Shinto has some neat mythology. In the 700's A.D. many myths and legends were written. Mythology says Japan and Japanese people were created by deities. The creator god was said to have created the world and established customs and laws. The legend of how the Japanese islands were created is told like this: Two gods, Izanagi and Izanami, looked down from the "bridge of heaven," and wondered what was below. Izanagi took a jeweled spear and lowered the point. As Izanagi moved it around it splashed into the ocean. Izanagi raised the jeweled spear and the salt water dried into "pearly drops." The pearly drops fell off into the ocean and formed the islands of Japan. Izanagi and Izanami decided to live on the islands. After many years they had three children. One was the sun goddess, whose grandson was the first emperor of Japan. Her two brothers were the moon god and the wind god.

Shinto gods are called Kami. It is believed that these spirits are found in the basic forces of fire, wind, and water. Most influence agriculture and this of course was how the earliest people survived. They relied on what they grew to live. So the gods had to help them grow their crops or they died. It seems natural for people to worship things that will help them survive, and worshiping forces that affect what you grow was the common practice in early history. These basic forces even affect the survival of modern people. We all still need agriculture to live and forces of nature really determine whether crops grow or not.

Shintoists never developed strong doctrines, such as the belief in life after death that many other religions have. However they have developed some moral standards such as devotion, sincerity, and purity. . . .

All Shintoists have a very good and simple set of rules or practice. They want to be honorable, have feelings for others, support the government, and keep their families safe and healthy. I think these are good principles for all people, whether they practice a religion or not. . . .

year, discovering that "out with the old and in with the new" is a common theme among many such celebrations (Ramsey, 1987). At the secondary level, it can be beneficial to explore issues that adolescents of all cultures face: gaining the respect of elders, forming trusting relationships with peers, and finding a meaningful place in society (Ulichny, 1994). One important goal of multicultural education should be to communicate that, underneath it all, people are more alike than different.

Breaking Down Ethnic Stereotypes

EXPERIENCING FIRSTHAND   *Picture This #1*

Form a picture in your mind of someone from each of the following three places. Focus on the *first* image that comes to mind in each case.

> The Netherlands (Holland)
>
> Mexico
>
> Hawaii

Now answer yes or no to each of these questions:

- Was the person from the Netherlands wearing wooden shoes?
- Was the person from Mexico wearing a sombrero?
- Was the person from Hawaii wearing a hula skirt or flowered lei?

If you answered yes to any of the three questions, then one or more of your images reflected an ethnic stereotype. Most people in the Netherlands, Mexico, and Hawaii do *not* routinely wear wooden shoes, sombreros, or hula skirts and leis.

Although we and our students should certainly be aware of true differences among various ethnic groups, it is counterproductive to hold a **stereotype**—a rigid, simplistic, and inevitably erroneous caricature—of any particular group. As teachers, we must make a concerted effort to develop and select curriculum materials that represent all cultural groups in a positive and competent light; for example, we should choose textbooks, works of fiction, and videotapes that portray people of diverse ethnic backgrounds as legitimate participants in mainstream society, rather than as exotic "curiosities" who live in a separate world. And we must definitely avoid or modify curriculum materials that portray members of minority groups in an overly simplistic, romanticized, exaggerated, or otherwise stereotypical fashion (Banks, 1994; Boutte & McCormick, 1992; Ladson-Billings, 1994b; Pang, 1995).

Stereotypes don't exist only in curriculum materials; they exist in society at large as well. We can help break down ethnic stereotypes in several simple yet effective ways. For one thing, we can arrange opportunities for students to meet and talk with successful minority models. We can also explore the historical roots of cultural differences with our students—for example, by explaining that such differences sometimes reflect the various economic and social circumstances in which particular ethnic groups have historically found themselves. And finally, we must emphasize that individual members of any single ethnic group will often be very different from one another (Garcia, 1994; Lee & Slaughter-Defoe, 1995; McAlpine & Taylor, 1993; Spencer & Markstrom-Adams, 1990; Trueba, 1988).

Promoting Positive Social Interactions Among Students from Various Cultural Groups

When students from various cultural groups interact regularly, and particularly when they come together as equals, work toward a common goal, and see themselves as members of the same "team," they are more likely to accept one another's differences—and perhaps even *value* them (Dovidio & Gaertner, 1999; Oskamp, 2000; Ramsey, 1995). Such interactions can sometimes occur within the context of planned classroom activities; for example, we can hold classroom discussions in which our students describe the traditions, conventions, and perceptions of their own ethnic or racial groups (K. Schultz, Buck, & Niesz, 2000). We can also promote friendships among students of diverse ethnic backgrounds by using some of the strategies identified in Chapter 3—for instance, by using cooperative learning activities, teaching the rudiments of other students' native languages, and encouraging schoolwide participation in extracurricular activities. By learning to appreciate the multicultural differences within a single

INTO THE CLASSROOM: *Accommodating Cultural and Ethnic Differences*

Build on students' background experiences.

A language arts teacher asks a classroom of inner-city African American students to vote on their favorite rap song. She puts the words to the song on an overhead transparency and asks students to translate each line for her. In doing so, she shows students how their local dialect and Standard English are interrelated, and she gives them a sense of pride in being bilingual (Ladson-Billings, 1994a).

Use curriculum materials that represent all ethnic groups in a positive and competent light.

A history teacher peruses a history textbook to make sure that it portrays members of all ethnic groups in a nonstereotypical manner. He supplements the text with readings that highlight the important roles that members of various ethnic groups have played in history.

Expose students to successful models from various ethnic backgrounds.

A teacher invites several successful professionals from minority groups to speak with her class about their ca-

reers. When some students seem especially interested in one or more of these careers, she arranges for the students to spend time with the professionals in their workplaces.

Provide opportunities for students of different backgrounds to get to know one another better.

For a cooperative learning activity, a teacher forms groups that integrate students from various neighborhoods and ethnic groups.

Educate yourself about the cultures in which students have been raised.

A teacher accepts an invitation to have dinner with several of his students and their families, all of whom are dining together one evening at one family's home on the Navajo Nation in western New Mexico. During his visit, the teacher discovers why his students are always interrupting one another and completing one another's sentences: Their parents converse with one another in a similar manner (Jackson & Ormrod, 1998).

---

classroom, our students take an important first step toward appreciating the multicultural nature of the world at large (Casanova, 1987; Craft, 1984; Pettigrew & Pajonas, 1973).

Unfortunately, not all schools have a culturally diverse population. In such homogeneous schools, we may have to take our students, either physically or vicariously, beyond school boundaries. For example, we can engage our students in community action projects that provide services to particular ethnic groups—perhaps in preschools, nursing homes, or city cultural centers. Or we can initiate a "Sister Schools Program" in which students from two ethnically different communities regularly communicate through the mail or the Internet, possibly exchanging news, stories, photographs, art projects, and various artifacts from the local environment (Koeppel & Mulrooney, 1992).

Fostering Democratic Ideals

Ultimately, any multicultural education program must include such democratic ideals as human dignity, equality, justice, and appreciation of diverse viewpoints (Cottrol, 1990; NCSS Task Force on Ethnic Studies Curriculum Guidelines, 1992; Sleeter & Grant, 1999). We better prepare our students to function effectively in a democratic society when we help them understand that virtually any nation includes a diversity of cultures and that such diversity provides a richness of ideas and perspectives that will inevitably yield a more creative, productive society overall. The following passage that 16-year-old Randy wrote for his American history class illustrates:

To me, diversity is not only a fact of life, but it is life. To be different and unique is what allows people to live a fulfilling life. To learn and admire other people's differences is perhaps one of the keys to life and without that key, there will be too many doors that will be locked, keeping you out and not allowing you to succeed. To learn that a majority of one kind in one place may be a minority of another kind in another place can help to initiate an outlook on life that promotes perspective and reason of any situation.

Teaching respect for diverse perspectives does not necessarily mean that we accept all beliefs as equally acceptable; for instance, we should certainly not embrace a culture that blatantly violates some people's basic human rights. It does mean, however, that we and our students should try to understand another cultural group's behaviors within the context of that culture's beliefs and assumptions.

A democracy involves **equity**—freedom from bias or favoritism—as well as equality. To help students achieve maximal classroom success, we must be equitable in our treatment of them; in other words, we must tailor instruction to meet the unique characteristics of each and every one. The notion of equitable treatment applies not only to students of diverse ethnic backgrounds but also to both boys and girls. Let's consider how boys and girls are likely to be different and how we can help students of both genders achieve academic success.

Gender Differences

What differences between boys and girls did you notice when you were in elementary school? when you were in high school? What differences do you see now that you are taking college classes?

In their academic abilities, boys and girls are probably more similar than you think. But in other respects, they may be more different than you realize. Researchers have investigated possible differences between males and females in numerous areas; general trends in their findings, along with educational implications, are presented in Table 4.3.

As Table 4.3 shows, girls and boys are similar in general intellectual ability; any differences in aptitudes for specific academic areas are small, with a great deal of overlap between the two groups (e.g., refer back to the gender differences in verbal ability depicted in Figure 4.1). Girls are generally more concerned about doing well in school, yet boys have greater confidence in their *ability* to succeed. Boys and girls alike tend to be more motivated to achieve in gender-stereotypical areas, and they have greater self-confidence about their chances for success in these areas. As teachers, we should expect our male and female students to have similar academic aptitudes for different subject areas; furthermore, we should encourage both groups to achieve in all areas of the curriculum.

Origins of Gender Differences

Obviously, heredity determines the differences in physical characteristics we see in males and females both at birth and when they reach puberty. Because of heredity, girls reach puberty earlier than boys, and after puberty, boys are taller and have more muscle tissue than girls. Courtesy of male hormones, adolescent males are better than their female age-mates at tasks involving strength and have a greater inclination toward aggression (Collaer & Hines, 1995; J. R. Thomas & French, 1985). Both hormonal differences and subtle differences in brain structure may be partly to blame for the small gender differences in verbal and visual-spatial abilities (Halpern & LaMay, 2000; O'Boyle & Gill, 1998).

Despite such physical differences, many theorists believe that biology plays a relatively minor role in the development of gender differences (Harway & Moss, 1983; Huston, 1983; R. Rosenthal & Rubin, 1982; Ruble, 1988). One likely explanation for many differences is socialization: Boys and girls are taught that some behaviors are more appropriate for males and that others are more appropriate for females. To see what I mean, try the following exercise.

EXPERIENCING FIRSTHAND *Picture This #2*

Form a picture in your mind of each of the following individuals. Focus on the *first* image that comes to mind in each case.

Bank president	Scientist
Kindergarten teacher	Building contractor
Fashion model	Secretary

Now answer this question: Which individuals did you picture as male, and which did you picture as female?

If you are like most people, your bank president, scientist, and building contractor were males, and your kindergarten teacher, fashion model, and secretary were females. Gender stereotypes—rigid ideas about how males and females "typically" behave—persist throughout our society, and even preschool children are aware of them (Bornholt et al., 1994; Eisenberg et al., 1996).

Are the findings in Table 4.3 consistent with your own observations of males' and females' behaviors? If not, can you resolve the discrepancies?

In what ways is the environment different for boys and girls? Can you generate some hypotheses before you read further?

TABLE 4.3

Gender Differences and Their Educational Implications

CHARACTERISTIC	SIMILARITIES AND DIFFERENCES	EDUCATIONAL IMPLICATION
Scholastic abilities	Boys and girls have similar general intellectual ability (e.g., IQ scores). Girls are often slightly better at verbal (language-based) tasks. Especially after puberty, boys may be somewhat better at visual-spatial tasks and mathematical problem solving (although girls often do better in computation). In recent years, boys and girls have become increasingly *similar* in their academic performance.	Expect boys and girls to have similar aptitudes for all academic subject areas.
Physical and motor skills	Boys are temperamentally disposed to be more active than girls. Before puberty, boys and girls have similar physiological capability, but boys tend to develop their physical and motor skills more than girls. After puberty, boys have the advantage in height and muscular strength. Girls have better fine motor skills.	Assume that both genders have similar potential for developing physical and motor skills, especially during the elementary school years.
Motivation for school tasks	Girls are generally more concerned about doing well in school. They tend to work harder on school assignments, earn higher grades, and are more likely to graduate from high school. Boys exert more effort in stereotypically masculine areas (e.g., mathematics, science, mechanical skills); girls work harder in stereotypically feminine areas (e.g., reading, literature, art). Boys are more active in both positive ways (e.g., they talk and ask questions more in class) and negative ways (e.g., they exhibit more behavior problems).	Encourage both boys and girls to achieve in all areas of the curriculum.
Self-esteem	Boys are more likely to have self-confidence in their ability to control the world and solve problems; girls are more likely to see themselves as competent in interpersonal relationships. Boys and girls also tend to have greater self-confidence in areas consistent with their own stereotypes about what males and females should do. In general, boys tend to rate their performance on tasks more positively than girls do, even when actual performance is the same for both genders.	Show students that they can be successful in counterstereotypical subject areas. For example, show girls that they can have just as much success in learning mathematics and science as boys do.
Explanations for success and failure	Especially in stereotypically masculine domains (e.g., math), boys and girls interpret success and failure differently. Boys tend to attribute successes to enduring ability (e.g., intelligence, natural talent) and failures to a lack of effort. In contrast, girls attribute successes to effort (working hard) and failures to a lack of ability. Boys' beliefs in greater natural ability make them more optimistic about their chances for future success.	Convince girls that their past and present successes indicate an ability to succeed and that they can avoid or overcome failure with sufficient effort.
Expectations and career aspirations	Although girls are more likely to see themselves as college-bound, boys have higher long-term expectations for themselves, especially in stereotypically masculine areas. Career aspirations tend to be consistent with gender stereotypes; furthermore, girls (but not boys) tend to choose careers that won't interfere with their future roles as spouses and parents.	Expose students to successful male and female models in a variety of roles and professions. Also, provide examples of people successfully juggling careers with marriage and parenthood.
Interpersonal relationships	Boys exhibit more physical aggression, although girls can be just as aggressive as boys in more subtle and less physical ways (e.g., by tattling, gossiping, or snubbing peers). Girls are more affiliative: They form closer and more intimate interpersonal relationships, seem to be more aware of others' feelings and intentions, and are more concerned about maintaining group harmony. Boys feel more comfortable than girls in competitive situations; girls prefer cooperative environments that offer social support.	Teach both genders less aggressive and more prosocial ways of interacting with one another. To accommodate girls' more affiliative nature, provide opportunities for cooperative group work and frequent interaction with classmates.

Sources: Becker, 1986; Binns, Steinberg, Amorosi, & Cuevas, 1997; Block, 1983; Bornholt, Goodnow, & Cooney, 1994; Bosacki, 2000; D. A. Cole, Martin, Peeke, Seroczynski, & Fier, 1999; Collaer & Hines, 1995; Crick & Grotpeter, 1995; Deaux, 1984; Durkin, 1987; W. O. Eaton & Enns, 1986; Eccles, 1989; Eccles, Wigfield, & Schiefele, 1998; Eccles [Parsons], 1984; Eisenberg et al., 1996; Fennema, 1987; Gustafsson & Undheim, 1996; Halpern, 1997b; Halpern & LaMay, 2000; Hedges & Nowell, 1995; Hegarty & Kozhevnikov, 1999; Hyde, Fennema, & Lamon, 1990; Hyde & Linn, 1988; Inglehart, Brown, & Vida, 1994; Jacklin, 1989; G. P. Jones & Dembo, 1989; Jovanovic & King, 1998; A. Kelly & Smail, 1986; M. C. Linn & Hyde, 1989; M. C. Linn & Petersen, 1985; Loeber & Stouthamer-Loeber, 1998; H. M. Marks, 2000; McCall, 1994; McCallum & Bracken, 1993; J. D. Nichols, Ludwin, & Iadicola, 1999; Pajares & Valiante, 1999; Paulson & Johnson, 1983; E. Rowe, 1999; J. Smith & Russell, 1984; Stipek, 1984; J. R. Thomas & French, 1985; Vermeer, Boekaerts, & Seegers, 2000.

We must convince girls that they have just as much potential for learning such subjects as mathematics and science as boys do.

Many aspects of society conspire to teach growing children to conform to gender stereotypes. For example, parents are more likely to encourage their sons to be independent, athletic, and aggressive, and they tend to have higher career expectations for their sons than for their daughters, especially in stereotypically male professions (Block, 1983; Fagot, Hagan, Leinbach, & Kronsberg, 1985; Parsons, Adler, & Kaczala, 1982; Ruble, 1988; J. R. Thomas & French, 1985). In addition, girls and boys are given different toys and play different games (Block, 1983; P. A. Campbell, 1986; Etaugh, 1983). Girls get dolls and stuffed animals, and they play "house" and board games—toys and activities that foster the development of verbal and social skills. Boys get blocks, model airplanes, and science equipment, and they play football, basketball, and video games—toys and activities that foster greater development of visual-spatial skills (Frost, Shin, & Jacobs, 1998; Liss, 1983; Sprafkin et al., 1983). Although gender-stereotypical expectations for males and females are evident in virtually any society, they are more pronounced in some cultures than in others (Fuller, 2001).

The media promote gender-stereotypical behavior as well. Movies, television programs, and books (including many elementary reading primers) often portray males and females in gender-stereotypical ways: Males are aggressive leaders and successful problem solvers, whereas females are domestic, demure, and obedient followers (Durkin, 1987; Huston et al., 1992; Ruble & Ruble, 1982; Sadker & Sadker, 1994). Furthermore, males appear much more prominently in history and science textbooks than females do (Eisenberg et al., 1996; Sadker, Sadker, & Klein, 1991). As teachers, we must make a concerted effort to develop and select curriculum materials that represent both genders in a positive and competent light; nonsexist materials reduce gender stereotypes when students are exposed to them on a continual and consistent basis (Fennema, 1987; Horgan, 1995; Sadker & Miller, 1982).

As noted in Chapter 3, schools are important socialization agents for children, and such socialization often includes further encouragement of gender-stereotypical behaviors. Let's look at how the behaviors of two particularly influential groups of people—peers and teachers—promote the development of gender differences.

Peer Behaviors

Playmates and classmates often encourage adherence to traditional gender stereotypes. They tend to respond more positively to children who play in "gender appropriate" ways and more negatively to those who do not (Eisenberg et al., 1996; Fagot & Leinbach, 1983; Huston, 1983). They may also ridicule or avoid students who enroll and excel in "gender inappropriate" subjects, such as high school girls who excel in science and mathematics (Casserly, 1980; Sadker & Sadker, 1994; Schubert, 1986). As a result, many students will engage in counterstereotypical activities only when their successes in such activities can be hidden from peers (Eccles, 1989; Huston, 1983; Ruble, 1988). As teachers, we can do a great deal to keep student achievement out of the public eye—for example, by keeping grades confidential[4] and perhaps by allowing students to demonstrate their achievement through written assignments rather than through oral responses to in-class questions.

Remember how quiet and passive Lupita was in our opening case study? Boys often take a more active role in class than girls, especially when the two are asked to work together; for example, when paired in a science lab, boys handle the equipment and perform experiments while girls watch or take notes (Eccles, 1989; Jovanovic & King, 1998; Kahle & Lakes, 1983). For this reason, it may sometimes be beneficial to group girls with girls, and boys with boys, to ensure that girls participate more actively in classroom activities (Kahle & Lakes, 1983; MacLean, Sasse, Keating, Stewart, & Miller, 1995). Girls are also more likely to assume the role of leader in same-sex groups and, in the process, to develop valuable leadership skills (Fennema, 1987).

---

[4]In the United States there are legal as well as pedagogical reasons for keeping grades confidential. The Family Educational Rights and Privacy Act (1974) mandates that a student's records, including grades, be shared only with the student, his or her parents or legal guardians, and school personnel directly involved in the student's education and well-being. (See Chapter 15 for more details.)

INTO THE CLASSROOM: *Promoting Gender Equity*

Use your knowledge of typical gender differences to create greater equity for males and females, *not* to form expectations about how successful males and females are likely to be in various activities.

A physical education teacher realizes that most of the girls in her class have probably not had as much experience throwing overhand as the boys have, so she gives them basic instruction and extra practice in the overhand throw.

Be on the lookout for gender stereotypes in classroom materials, and use some materials that portray both genders in a counterstereotypical fashion.

An English teacher assigns Harper Lee's *To Kill a Mockingbird,* in which an attorney named Atticus Finch is portrayed as a gentle, affectionate, and compassionate man, and his daughter Scout is portrayed as a courageous and adventuresome 8-year-old. The teacher also assigns Zora Neale Hurston's *Their Eyes Were Watching God,* in which an African American woman grows from a teenager dependent entirely on others to meet her needs into a self-sufficient woman who can easily fend for herself.

Occasionally ask students to work together in single-sex pairs or groups.

A science teacher has students work in groups of three boys or three girls to conduct an assigned laboratory activity.

Monitor yourself to see if you are unintentionally treating boys and girls differently.

A French teacher decides to count the number of times that he calls on boys and girls during class. He finds that he calls on boys more than three times as often as he calls on girls, partly because the boys raise their hands more frequently. To combat his bad habit, he institutes a new procedure: He alternates between boys and girls when he calls on students, and he sometimes calls on students who are not raising their hands.

Teacher Behaviors

During the past twenty years, schools have shown increasing efforts to treat boys and girls similarly (Eccles, 1989). For example, girls' sports are enjoying more publicity and financial support than ever before. Nevertheless, differences in the treatment of boys and girls continue. For instance, teachers tend to give more attention to boys—partly because, on average, boys ask more questions and present more discipline problems (Altermatt, Jovanovic, & Perry, 1998; Sadker & Sadker, 1994; L. C. Wilkinson & Marrett, 1985). When girls cannot answer a question, their teachers tend to tell them the correct answer; but when boys have equal difficulty, their teachers usually help them think through the correct answer on their own (Sadker & Sadker, 1985). Boys are told to try harder when they fail; girls are simply praised for trying (P. A. Campbell, 1986; Eccles & Jacobs, 1986; L. H. Fox, 1981).

In most cases, teachers are probably unaware that they discriminate between boys and girls the way they do. The first step toward ensuring more equitable treatment of males and females is to become aware of existing inequities. Then we can try to correct those inequities—for example, by interacting frequently with *all* of our students, helping them think through correct answers, encouraging them to persist when they experience difficulty, and holding high expectations for everyone.

In the last few pages, we have considered numerous strategies for treating male and female students, as well as students from diverse ethnic backgrounds, in an equitable fashion. Yet equity must be extended to students of different socioeconomic circumstances as well. Let's look at some characteristics that students from lower-income families, including those growing up in true poverty, are likely to have, as well as at some strategies for helping these students achieve classroom success.

Socioeconomic Differences

The concept of **socioeconomic status** (often abbreviated as **SES**) encompasses a number of variables, including family income, parents' occupations, and parents' levels of education. Students' school performance is correlated with socioeconomic status: Higher-SES students tend to have higher academic achievement, and lower-SES students tend to be at greater risk for dropping out of school (McLoyd, 1998; L. S. Miller, 1995; Portes, 1996; Stevenson, Chen, & Uttal, 1990). As students from lower-SES families move through the grade levels, they fall further and further behind their higher-SES peers (Jimerson, Egeland, & Teo, 1999).

Factors Interfering with School Success

Several factors, described in the following paragraphs, probably contribute to the generally lower school achievement of low-SES students. Students who face only one or two of the challenges listed here often do quite well in school, but those who face most or all of them are at high risk for academic failure (Grissmer, Williamson, Kirby, & Berends, 1998).

Poor nutrition. Some lower-income families cannot afford nutritional meals for their children. As noted earlier, poor nutrition in the early developmental years is associated with lower IQ scores; it is also associated with poorer attention and memory, impaired learning ability, and lower school achievement (D'Amato et al., 1992; L. S. Miller, 1995). Poor nutrition can influence school achievement both directly—for instance, by hampering early brain development—and indirectly—for instance, by leaving children listless and inattentive in class (Sigman & Whaley, 1998; R. A. Thompson & Nelson, 2001). As teachers, we must take any necessary steps to ensure that our students are adequately fed; for instance, we can make sure that all eligible children have access to the free and reduced-cost meal programs that the school district offers.

Emotional stress. Students function less effectively when they are under stress, and many low-SES families live in chronically stressful conditions (McLoyd, 1998). Perhaps as a result, students from lower-income families show higher-than-average rates of depression and other emotional problems (Caspi, Taylor, Moffitt, & Plomin, 2000; Seaton et al., 1999). Obviously, the economic problems of the poor family are a source of anxiety; children may wonder where their next meal is coming from or how long it will be before their landlord evicts them for not paying the rent. The preponderance of single-parent homes among low-SES families is another source of stress; a single parent may be overwhelmed with worries about supporting the family (Scott-Jones, 1984). We must continually be on the lookout for signs that our students are undergoing unusual stress at home and provide whatever support we can for these students. In some instances, such support may involve nothing more than being a willing listener; in other cases, we may want to consult with a school district social worker about possible support systems and agencies in the local community.

Fewer early experiences that foster school readiness. Many students from low-SES families lack some of the basic knowledge and skills (e.g., familiarity with letters and numbers) on which successful school learning so often depends (Case & Okamoto, 1996; McLoyd, 1998; Portes, 1996). Access to early educational opportunities that might develop such skills—books, educational toys, trips to zoos and museums, and so on—is always somewhat dependent on a family's financial resources. Low-income parents may often be so preoccupied with providing basic necessities such as food and warm clothing that they also have little time or energy to consider how they might promote their children's cognitive development. Furthermore, many low-SES parents have poor reading skills and so can provide few reading experiences to lay a foundation for reading instruction in the early elementary years (Hess & Holloway, 1984; Laosa, 1982). As teachers, it is essential that we identify and teach any missing basic skills; when we do so, we are likely to see significant improvements in our students' classroom performance (S. A. Griffin, Case, & Capodilupo, 1995; McLoyd, 1998).

Lower quality schools. Unfortunately, students who are in most need of a good education are those least likely to have access to it. On average, schools that serve low-income neighborhoods offer lower-quality instruction, less challenging coursework, and fewer opportunities to develop advanced thinking skills than schools in wealthier neighborhoods (Duke, 2000; Eccles et al., 1998; R. Ferguson, 1998).

Peer rejection. Students from lower-income families are often rejected by their more economically fortunate classmates; as a result, they may have fewer opportunities to become actively involved in school activities (Knapp & Woolverton, 1995). The strategies described in Chapter 3 in the sections "Fostering Social Skills" and "Promoting Social Interaction Among Diverse Groups" should prove useful in helping these students forge new friendships.

Lower aspirations. Students from low-SES backgrounds, especially girls, typically have lower aspirations for educational and career achievement (Knapp & Woolverton, 1995; S. M.

You can learn more about the effects of early literacy experiences in the chapter "Learning in the Content Areas" in the *Study Guide and Reader.*

Taylor, 1994). Teachers, too—even those who teach kindergarten and first grade—often have lower expectations for students from lower-income families (McLoyd, 1998; Portes, 1996). Certainly we must encourage *all* of our students to aim high in their educational and professional goals. We must also provide the extra support they need to achieve such goals; offering help sessions for challenging classroom material, finding low-cost academic enrichment programs available during the summer, and helping students fill out applications for college scholarships are just a few of the forms that such support might take.

Less parental involvement in children's education. The great majority of parents at all income levels want their children to get a good education (Stevenson et al., 1990). Some parents in lower-SES households are actively involved in their children's learning and education, and their children achieve at higher levels as a result (Jimerson et al., 1999). But many others have had little education themselves, so they may not be capable of helping their children with assigned schoolwork (Finders & Lewis, 1994). Furthermore, economic factors may prevent some parents from becoming actively involved in their children's schooling; lower-income parents often have difficulty getting off work, finding suitable child care, and arranging transportation to visit school and meet with teachers (Finders & Lewis, 1994; Heymann & Earle, 2000; Salend & Taylor, 1993). In addition, some parents may have had bad experiences when they themselves were students and so feel uncomfortable in a school setting (Finders & Lewis, 1994). As teachers, we should be especially flexible about when and where we meet with the parents of lower-income students; we should also be especially conscientious about establishing comfortable, trusting relationships with them (Finders & Lewis, 1994; Salend & Taylor, 1993).

Working with Homeless Students

Children of homeless families typically face far greater challenges than other low-SES students. Many will have health problems, low self-esteem, a short attention span, poor language skills, and inappropriate behaviors (Coe, Salamon, & Molnar, 1991; McLoyd, 1998; Pawlas, 1994). Some may be reluctant to come to school because they lack bathing facilities and appropriate clothing (Gollnick & Chinn, 1994). And some may have moved so frequently from one school to another that there are large gaps in their academic skills (Pawlas, 1994).

As teachers, we, too, will face unusual challenges when teaching students who live in homeless shelters. Following are several suggestions for giving them the extra support they may need to achieve both academic and social success at school (Pawlas, 1994):

- Pair new students with classmates who can "show them the ropes"—for example, by explaining school procedures and making introductions to other students.
- Provide a notebook, clipboard, or other portable "desk" on which students can do their homework at the shelter.
- Find adult or teenage volunteers to serve as tutors at the shelter.
- Enlist the help of civic organizations to collect clothing and school supplies for the students.
- Meet with parents at the shelter rather than at school.
- Share copies of homework assignments, school calendars, and newsletters with shelter officials.

Fostering Resilience

Fortunately, many students of low-income families succeed in school despite exceptional hardships (Humphreys, 1992; Nieto, 1995; B. Williams & Newcombe, 1994). Some seem to be **resilient students:** They develop characteristics and coping skills that help them rise above their adverse circumstances. As a group, resilient students have likable personalities, positive self-concepts, strong motivation to succeed, and high yet realistic goals. They believe that success comes with hard work, and their bad experiences serve as constant reminders of the importance of getting a good education (Masten & Coatsworth, 1998; McMillan & Reed, 1994; Werner, 1995).

Resilient students usually have one or more individuals in their lives whom they trust and can turn to in difficult times (Masten, 2001; McLoyd, 1998; Werner, 1995). Such individuals may be family members, neighbors, or school personnel; for example, resilient students often mention teachers who have taken a personal interest in them and been instrumental in their school success (McMillan & Reed, 1994; Paris & Cunningham, 1996). As teachers, we are most likely to promote resilience in low-SES students when we show them that we like and respect them, are available and willing to listen to their views and concerns, hold high expectations for their performance, and provide the encouragement and support they need to succeed both inside and outside of the classroom (Masten & Coatsworth, 1998; McMillan & Reed, 1994; Werner, 1995).

Building on Students' Strengths

Although many students from lower-SES backgrounds may lag behind their classmates in such basic academic skills as reading, writing, and computation, they bring other strengths to the classroom. For example, they are often more clever at improvising with everyday objects (Torrance, 1995). If they work part-time to help their families make ends meet, they may have a good understanding of the working world. If they are children of single, working parents, they may know far more than their classmates about cooking, cleaning house, and taking care of younger siblings. If financial resources have been particularly scarce, they may know firsthand what it is like to be hungry for days at a time or to live in an unheated apartment in the winter; they may therefore have a special appreciation for basic human needs and true empathy for victims of war or famine around the world. As teachers, then, we must remember that students who have grown up in poverty may, in some respects, have more knowledge and skills than their more economically advantaged peers. Such knowledge and skills can often provide a basis for teaching classroom subject matter. Furthermore, students who are willing to talk about the challenges they've faced can sensitize their classmates to the serious inequities that currently exist in our society.

Students at Risk

Do you remember classmates in elementary school who never seemed to complete assignments or get their homework done? Do you remember classmates in high school who did poorly in most of their classes and rarely participated in extracurricular activities? How many of those students eventually graduated from high school? What are they doing now?

Students at risk are students with a high probability of failing to acquire the minimum academic skills necessary for success in the adult world. Many of them drop out before high school graduation; many others graduate without basic skills in reading or mathematics (National Assessment of Educational Progress, 1985; Slavin, 1989). Such individuals are often ill equipped to make productive contributions to their families, communities, or society at large.

Characteristics of Students at Risk

Some students at risk are those with identified special educational needs; for example, they may have learning disabilities or emotional and behavioral problems that interfere with learning and achievement. Others may be students whose cultural backgrounds don't mesh easily with the dominant culture at school. Still others may be students from home environments in which academic success is neither supported nor encouraged.

Students at risk come from all socioeconomic levels, but children of poor, single-parent families are especially likely to leave school before high school graduation. Boys are more likely to drop out than girls. African Americans, Hispanics, and Native Americans are more likely to drop out than European American and Asian American students. Students in large cities and rural areas are more likely to drop out than students in the suburbs. Students at greatest risk for dropping out are those whose families speak little or no English and whose own knowledge of English is also quite limited (García, 1995; Hardre & Reeve, 2001; L. S. Miller, 1995; Nieto, 1995; Portes, 1996; Raber, 1990; Roderick & Camburn, 1999; Rumberger, 1995; L. Steinberg, Blinde, & Chan, 1984; U.S. Department of Education, 1997).

In addition, students at risk, especially those who eventually drop out of school, typically have some or all of the following characteristics:

- *A history of academic failure.* High school dropouts often have a history of poor academic achievement going back as far as third grade (Garnier, Stein, & Jacobs, 1997; Lloyd, 1978). On the average, they have less effective study skills, earn lower grades, obtain lower achievement test scores, and are more likely to have repeated a grade level than their classmates who graduate (Battin-Pearson et al., 2000; Jozefowicz, Arbreton, Eccles, Barber, & Colarossi, 1994; Raber, 1990; Steinberg et al., 1984; L. D. Wilkinson & Frazer, 1990).

- *Older age in comparison with classmates.* Because low achievers are more likely to have repeated a grade, they are often older than their classmates (Raber, 1990; L. D. Wilkinson & Frazer, 1990). Some (though not all) research studies find that students who are overage in comparison with classmates are those most likely to drop out of school (D. C. Gottfredson, Fink, & Graham, 1994; Roderick, 1994; Rumberger, 1995).

- *Emotional and behavioral problems.* Potential dropouts tend to have lower self-esteem than their more successful classmates. They also are more likely to exhibit disruptive behavior, create discipline problems, use drugs, and engage in criminal activities (Finn, 1991; Garnier et al., 1997; Jozefowicz et al., 1994; Rumberger, 1995; U.S. Dept. of Education, 1992).

- *Lack of psychological attachment to school.* Students who are at risk for academic failure are less likely to identify with their school or to perceive themselves as a vital part of the school community; for example, they engage in fewer extracurricular activities and are more likely to express dissatisfaction with school in general (Finn, 1989; Hymel, Comfort, Schonert-Reichl, & McDougall, 1996; Rumberger, 1995).

What are possible reasons why some students don't participate in their school's extracurricular activities?

- *Increasing disinvolvement with school.* Dropping out is not necessarily an all-or-none thing. In fact, many high school dropouts show lesser forms of "dropping out" many years before they officially leave school. For example, future dropouts are absent from school more frequently than their peers, even in the early elementary grades (Finn, 1989; G. A. Hess, Lyons, & Corsino, 1990; Jozefowicz et al., 1994). They are more likely to have been suspended from school, and they are more likely to show a long-term pattern of dropping out, returning to school, and dropping out again (Raber, 1990). Over time, then, we see decreasing involvement—physical, academic, and social—in school activities.

The characteristics just listed are by no means sure-fire indicators of which students will drop out, however. For instance, many dropouts are from two-parent, middle-income homes, and many are involved in school activities (Hymel et al., 1996; Janosz, Le Blanc, Boulerice, & Tremblay, 2000).

Why Students Drop Out

Students drop out for a variety of reasons. A few have little family support or encouragement for school success. Others have extenuating life circumstances; for example, they may have medical problems, take an outside job to help support the family, or become pregnant. Many simply become dissatisfied with school: They don't do well in their classes, have trouble getting along with their classmates, find the school environment too dangerous or restrictive, or perceive the curriculum to be boring and irrelevant to their needs (Hardre & Reeve, 2001; Portes, 1996; Raber, 1990; Rumberger, 1995; Steinberg et al., 1984). Sadly, teacher behaviors sometimes enter into the picture as well, as the following dialogue between an interviewer (Ron) and two at-risk high school students (George and Rasheed) reveals:

Ron:	Why do you think someone drops out of school?
George:	I think people drop out of school cuz of the pressure that school brings them. Like, sometimes the teacher might get on the back of a student so much that the student doesn't want to do the work. . . . And then that passes and he says, "I'm gonna start doing good. . . ." Then he's not doing as good as he's supposed to and when he sees his grade, he's, "you mean I'm doin' all that for nothin'? I'd rather not come to school."
Ron:	Okay, all right.
Rasheed:	I think kids drop out of school because they gettin' too old to be in high school. And I think they got, like, they think it's time to get a responsibility and to get a job and stuff. And, like George says, sometimes the teachers, you know, tell you to drop out, knowing that you might not graduate anyway.
Ron:	How does a teacher tell you to drop out?

Rasheed:	No, they recommend you take the GED program sometimes.[5] Like, some kids just say, "Why don't you just take the GED. Just get it over with." Then, job or something.
Ron:	You talked about a kid being too old. Why is a kid too old?
Rasheed:	Cuz he got left back too many times. (Farrell, 1990, p. 91)

Helping Students at Risk Stay in School

Students who are at risk for academic failure are a diverse group of individuals with a diverse set of needs, and there is probably no single strategy that can keep every student in school until high school graduation (Finn, 1991; Janosz et al., 2000). Nevertheless, we can do several things to help many students at risk succeed and stay in school:

■ *Identify students at risk as early as possible.* We begin to see indicators of "dropping out," such as low school achievement and high absenteeism, as early as elementary school. And such other signs as low self-esteem, disruptive behavior, and lack of involvement in school activities often appear years before students officially withdraw from school. So it is quite possible to identify at-risk students early in their school careers and to take steps to prevent or remediate academic difficulties before they become insurmountable. Research indicates clearly that for students at risk, prevention and early intervention are more effective than later intervention efforts (Ramey & Ramey, 1998; Slavin, Madden, & Karweit, 1989).

■ *Create a warm, supportive school and classroom atmosphere.* Schools that have high success rates with students at risk for academic failure tend to be schools that communicate a sense of caring, concern, and high regard for students (L. W. Anderson & Pellicer, 1998). Chapter 14 presents several strategies for creating a warm and supportive atmosphere in its section "Creating an Effective Classroom Climate."

■ *Make the curriculum relevant to students' lives and needs.* Students are more likely to stay in school, and also more likely to learn and achieve at high levels, if they find the curriculum relevant to their own cultural values, life experiences, and personal needs (Knapp et al., 1990; Lee-Pearce, Plowman, & Touchstone, 1998; Ramey & Ramey, 1998). To increase the relevance of school for students at risk, we should place academic skills within the context of real-world tasks, and particularly within the context of students' local environments. As an example, a mathematics teacher at an inner-city middle school consistently encouraged her students to identify problems in their community and work to solve them (Tate, 1995). One of her classes expressed concern about the thirteen liquor stores located within 1,000 feet of their school, in part because of the inebriated customers and drug dealers that the stores attracted. The students used yardsticks and maps to calculate the distance of each store from the school, gathered information about zoning restrictions and other city government regulations, identified potential violations, met with a local newspaper editor (who published an editorial describing the situation), and eventually met with state legislators and the city council. As a result of their efforts, city police monitored the liquor stores more closely, major violations were identified (leading to the closing of two stores), and the city council made it illegal to consume alcohol within 600 feet of the school (Tate, 1995).

Such a project might enhance students' *collective self-efficacy*— the belief that, working together, they can make a difference (see Chapter 10).

■ *Communicate high expectations for academic success.* Although many students at risk have a history of academic failure, under *no* circumstances should we write these students off. On the contrary, we should communicate to them that school success is both possible and expected and, furthermore, that they are capable of achieving at high levels (L. W. Anderson & Pellicer, 1998; Garcia, 1994; Garibaldi, 1993; Ladson-Billings, 1994a). We can acknowledge past learning problems but let students know that there are ways to overcome those problems and that we will help them acquire the knowledge and skills they need for classroom success (Alderman, 1990).

---

[5]Rasheed is referring to a general equivalency diploma, obtained by taking a series of achievement tests rather than completing the requirements for high school graduation.

INTO THE CLASSROOM: *Helping Students at Risk for Academic Failure and Dropping Out*

Identify at-risk students as early as possible.

A second-grade teacher speaks with the principal and school counselor about possible ways to help a student who is frequently absent from school and seems to have little interest in her schoolwork.

Use students' strengths to promote high self-esteem.

A school forms a singing group (the "Jazz Cats") for which students in a low-income, inner-city elementary school must try out. The group performs at a variety of community events, and the students enjoy considerable visibility for their talent. Group members exhibit increased self-esteem, improvement in other school subjects, and greater teamwork and leadership skills (Jenlink, 1994).

Communicate high expectations for students' performance.

A mathematics teacher tells a group of junior high school students, "Yes, I know that you're finding fractions difficult right now. But I also know that you can learn fractions if you try hard and practice using them. Why don't we try a different approach to learning them today—one that might work a little better for us?"

Provide extra support for academic success.

A high school English teacher meets with a small group of low-reading-level students to read and discuss print materials in their areas of interest.

Show students that they are personally responsible for their successes.

A teacher says to a student, "Your essay about recent hate crimes in the city is very powerful. You've given the topic considerable thought, and you've clearly mastered some of the techniques of persuasive writing that we've talked about this semester. I'd like you to think seriously about submitting your essay to the local paper for its editorial page. Can we spend some time during lunch tomorrow fine-tuning the grammar and spelling?"

Help students to identify with their school.

A teacher encourages a student with a strong throwing arm to go out for the school baseball team and introduces the student to the baseball coach. The coach, in turn, expresses his enthusiasm for having the student join the team and asks several current team members to help him feel at home during team practices.

■ *Provide extra academic support.* Because students at risk often have a history of academic failure and may have little support for academic achievement at home, these students may need more than the usual amount of assistance from teachers and other school personnel to succeed. Here are some specific ways to facilitate their academic success:

- Help them develop more effective reading and learning strategies.
- Adapt instruction to their current skills and knowledge.
- Give them relatively structured tasks and tell them exactly what is expected.
- Develop mastery of one skill before moving to a more difficult one.
- Assess their progress frequently and give them specific criteria for measuring their own success.
- Increase one-on-one teacher-student interactions.
- Deliver as much instruction as possible within the context of general education; make any necessary instruction in self-contained settings as brief as possible.
- Solicit parent and community cooperation with the school program. (Alderman, 1990; Covington & Beery, 1976; Garibaldi, 1993; Slavin, Karweit, & Madden, 1989)

As you may have noticed, these recommendations would be helpful for *any* student. Research indicates that the most effective programs for students at risk are those that incorporate common, educationally sound teaching practices (Slavin et al., 1989).

■ *Show students that they are the ones who have made success possible.* When we help students at risk improve academically, we must help them recognize that *they themselves* are responsible for their success (Alderman, 1990). For example, we might give messages such as these:

- "Wow, look how much you've improved! That extra practice really helped."
- "You really deserved this A. You are writing in complete sentences now, and you are checking your work for spelling and punctuation errors."

With such messages we increase students' *self-efficacy* through the *attributions* we give for their success. We will discuss these concepts in Chapters 10 and 12.

■ *Encourage and facilitate identification with school.* Students at risk may need extra encouragement to become involved in academic and social activities at school. To help them become more involved in, and feel more psychologically attached to, the school community, we can do the following:

- Establish close working relationships with students.
- Include instructional techniques that promote active class involvement (e.g., class discussions, cooperative learning).
- Encourage participation in athletic programs, extracurricular activities, and student government. (This is especially important when students are having academic difficulties, because it provides an alternative way of experiencing school success.)
- Involve students in school policy and management decisions.
- Give students positions of responsibility in managing school activities.
- Provide rewards (e.g., trips to a local amusement park) for good attendance records. (Finn, 1989; Garibaldi, 1992; Newmann, 1981; M. G. Sanders, 1996)

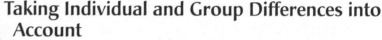

Students are far more likely to stay in school and try to succeed in school activities when they feel as if they truly belong there.

Students are more likely to stay in school when they feel as if they truly belong there.

Taking Individual and Group Differences into Account

As you have seen, it is often quite helpful to know how individual differences (e.g., intelligence or creativity) and group differences (e.g., those associated with a particular ethnic group, gender, or socioeconomic level) potentially affect the beliefs and behaviors that different students bring with them to the classroom. At the same time, *we must never form expectations for individual students on the basis of specific abilities or group differences alone.* As you will discover when you read Chapter 12, low teacher expectations for student performance, and the teaching behaviors that result from such expectations, often lead to lower achievement than we might see otherwise.

Accommodating Students with Special Needs

We will sometimes see the individual and group differences discussed in this chapter reflected in the characteristics of our students with special needs. For instance, students from lower socioeconomic backgrounds are more likely to be identified as having either cognitive or behavioral difficulties that require special educational services (U.S. Dept. of Education, 1996). Some cultures discourage females, even those with high IQ scores and considerable academic promise, from pursuing advanced educational opportunities; as a result, some female students are reluctant to make the most of their advanced cognitive abilities (M. L. Nichols & Ganschow, 1992). Other gender differences exist as well; for example, we will more often see specific cognitive or academic difficulties (e.g., learning disabilities) among boys than girls, and we are likely to observe different kinds of problems in boys and girls with emotional and behavioral disorders (Caseau, Luckasson, & Kroth, 1994; Halpern, 1997b; U.S. Dept. of Education, 1992). Table 4.4 presents numerous instances of individual and group differences among students with special needs, along with classroom strategies specifically related to such differences.

All students have strengths and talents that we can foster, and *all* students have the potential to develop new skills and abilities. Furthermore, the unique background and qualities that each student brings to class—for example, the realization by many girls that career aspirations must ultimately be balanced against dedication to family, the preference of students from some ethnic backgrounds for cooperative rather than competitive endeavors, and the firsthand awareness of some students from low-income homes regarding such social issues as poverty and homelessness—together create a situation in which we and our students have much to learn from one another.

TABLE 4.4

Considering Individual and Group Differences in Students with Special Educational Needs

CATEGORY	CHARACTERISTICS YOU MIGHT OBSERVE	SUGGESTED CLASSROOM STRATEGIES
Students with specific cognitive or academic difficulties	• In most cases, average or above-average scores on traditional intelligence tests • Greater frequency in males than females (for learning disabilities and attention-deficit hyperactivity disorder) • Higher than average dropout rate (students with learning disabilities)	• Remember that students with difficulties in one area (e.g., those with specific learning disabilities) may nevertheless be capable of average or above-average performance in other areas.
Students with social or behavioral problems	• Gender differences in the specific problems exhibited, with males more likely to exhibit overt misbehaviors (e.g., aggression, antisocial behavior) and females more likely to exhibit internalized problems (e.g., depression, social withdrawal, excessive anxiety) • Greater frequency in lower-SES students • Higher dropout rate than for any other category of special needs (for students with emotional or behavioral disorders)	• Be on the lookout for possible emotional problems when students (especially girls) are exceptionally quiet or withdrawn. • Take steps to decrease the likelihood of students dropping out (e.g., make the curriculum relevant, provide extra support for academic success).
Students with general delays in cognitive and social functioning	• Low scores on traditional intelligence tests • Gender differences and socioeconomic differences, with delays (e.g., mental retardation) being more common in males and in students from lower-SES backgrounds • Higher than average dropout rate	• Look for and nurture individual students' strengths in the various intelligences identified by Gardner. • Remember that the great majority of students from low-SES backgrounds have average or above-average intelligence.
Students with physical or sensory challenges	• Average intelligence in most cases • Chronic illness more common in students from lower-income families	• Assume an average ability to learn classroom subject matter unless there is compelling evidence to the contrary.
Students with advanced cognitive development	• High scores on traditional intelligence tests (less true for students from culturally diverse backgrounds) • Often, exceptional talents only in specific domains (e.g., language, math, music) • Divergent thinking (e.g., asking unusual questions, giving novel responses) • Giftedness possibly manifested in different ways in different cultures (e.g., richness of oral language among African American students, exceptional sensitivity to others' perspectives among Native American students) • More self-doubt about own abilities among females than males • In some cultures, discouragement of females from acting too "intelligently" or pursuing advanced education • Little exposure to female and minority high-ability role models	• Recognize that giftedness may reveal itself differently in students from diverse backgrounds. • Accept and encourage divergent thinking, including responses that you haven't anticipated. • Help students accurately appraise their own abilities. • Encourage females as well as males to achieve at high levels, while also identifying avenues whereby students can demonstrate their talents in ways that their families and local cultures value. • Expose students to talented female and minority role models.

Sources: Alderman, 1990; American Psychiatric Association, 1994; Barga, 1996; Barkley, 1998; Beirne-Smith et al., 2002; Davis & Rimm, 1998; Eisenberg et al., 1996; Finn, 1989; Garibaldi, 1993; Halpern, 1997b; Heward, 2000; Knapp et al., 1990; Maker & Schiever, 1989; McLoyd, 1998; M. L. Nichols & Ganschow, 1992; Nolen-Hoeksema, 2001; Piirto, 1999; Pressley, 1995; Sadker & Sadker, 1994; Torrance, 1989; Turnbull et al., 1999; U.S. Dept. of Education, 1992, 1997.

The Big Picture

As we have seen, students in any single classroom will be diverse in terms of both individual differences (e.g., those based on intelligence or creativity) and group differences (e.g., those based on ethnicity, gender, or SES). Yet we must repeatedly remind ourselves that there is *considerable individual variability within any group* and a *great deal of overlap between any two groups.* Thus, we must never jump to conclusions about individual students based solely on IQ scores, data about creative potential, or group membership. Table 4.5 reviews some of the individual and group differences described in this chapter and provides several ideas about how to accommodate such differences without letting them bias our judgments.

TABLE 4.5   PRINCIPLES/ASSUMPTIONS

Taking Individual and Group Differences into Account

GENERAL PRINCIPLES	EDUCATIONAL IMPLICATION	EXAMPLE
Intelligence is partly a function of environment and can change over time. In addition, different students are likely to be intelligent in different ways.	Never jump to conclusions about what students will or will not be able to do, and do not assume that a student having difficulty in one area will necessarily have difficulty in another.	Never use IQ scores as the sole indicator of students' potential for academic success. Factors such as quality of instruction, student motivation, parental support, and peer group norms will also have a significant effect.
Students tend to be creative in specific content domains rather than show creativity across all subject areas. Furthermore, students' level of creativity is influenced by environmental conditions.	Foster students' creativity in a particular area by valuing creative products, encouraging students to take risks, and giving them the time they need to generate new ideas.	Form small, cooperative groups that work together over several days or weeks to develop a play, short story, scientific invention, or new team sport.
Each ethnic group has its own norms for appropriate behavior. People from one culture sometimes misinterpret the behaviors of those from a different culture.	Be careful not to interpret students' actions according to your own cultural standards for behavior.	When students share answers, don't assume they are intentionally cheating; their culture may value group achievement over individual achievement. Provide opportunities for both group and individual accomplishments, and make it clear when each is expected.
On average, male and female students have similar or equal abilities in all academic areas; however, most have greater self-confidence in areas consistent with traditional gender stereotypes.	Encourage girls and boys equally in all areas of the curriculum—in science, mathematics, language arts, art, music, physical education, and so on—and in extracurricular activities.	Expose students to successful individuals in different professions, making sure they see both men and women in these roles.
Low-income parents sometimes have difficulty giving their children the resources, experiences, and support on which successful school learning often builds.	When necessary, provide additional support and experiences at school (e.g., needed school supplies, one-on-one homework assistance, numerous field trips) to help students achieve academic success. At the same time, remember that students from low-SES backgrounds have probably had valuable experiences that their wealthier classmates have not.	Incorporate enriching outside experiences into the curriculum; for example, take students to museums, the zoo, and the city library.

Before we look at the chapter's final case study, let's briefly identify key points about individual differences, group differences, and students at risk.

Individual Differences

Intelligence and creativity, although somewhat influenced by genetic factors, are also the product of environmental conditions. For example, students are more apt to behave intelligently when they have physical and social support systems (e.g., computers, cooperative groups) to help them in their efforts—in other words, when intelligence is *distributed*. They are more apt to think creatively when they are encouraged to take risks and focus their attention on internal rather than external rewards. And both intelligence and creativity are bolstered by a rich body of knowledge, skills, and experiences on which to draw.

Group Differences

Students' knowledge, beliefs, priorities, motives, preferences, and interpretations are likely to vary somewhat for different cultural and ethnic groups, genders, and socioeconomic backgrounds. Although biology may occasionally contribute to these differences (e.g., hormonal differences make teenage boys stronger than teenage girls, and a few students who live in poverty may suffer from severe dietary deficiencies), the vast majority of group differences are the result of socialization, living conditions, diverse educational experiences, and other environmental factors. As teachers, we should hold high expectations for all of our students while also providing the guidance and support they may need to meet those expectations.

Students at Risk

Some students fail to acquire the minimum academic skills necessary for success in the adult world; for instance, they may graduate from high school without having learned to read or write, or they may drop out before graduation. Whenever we can, we should tailor our curricular materials and instructional methods to the unique strengths and needs of every student, but doing so may be especially crucial for the students at risk for academic failure.

Ms. Stewart has noticed that only a few students actively participate in her junior high school science classes. When she asks a question, especially one that requires students to draw inferences from information presented in class, the same hands always shoot up. She gives the matter some thought and realizes that all of the active participants are White and that most of them are boys.

She sees the same pattern in students' involvement in lab activities. When she forms small groups for particular lab assignments, the same students (notably the White males) always take charge. The females and minority males take more passive roles, either providing assistance to the group "leaders" or else just sitting back and watching.

Ms. Stewart is a firm believer that students learn much more about science when they participate in class and when they engage in hands-on activities. She is concerned about the lack of involvement of many of her students. She wonders whether they really even care about science.

- What are some possible reasons why the girls and minority students are not participating in classroom activities? What strategies might Ms. Stewart use to increase their participation?

Once you have answered these questions, compare your responses with those presented in Appendix B.

PRAXIS Turn to Appendix C, "Matching Book and Ancillary Content to the PRAXIS™ Principles of Learning and Teaching Tests," to discover sections of this chapter that may be especially applicable to the PRAXIS™ tests.

 Now go to our Companion Website at http://www.prenhall.com/ormrod to assess your understanding of chapter content with "Multiple-Choice Questions," apply comprehension in "Essay Questions," broaden your knowledge of educational psychology with related "Web Links," gain greater insight about classroom learning in "Learning in the Content Areas," and analyze and assess classroom work in the "Student Artifact Library."

Key Concepts

individual differences (p. 103)
group differences (p. 103)
intelligence (p. 105)
intelligence test (p. 106)
IQ score (p. 106)
g (general factor in intelligence) (p. 108)
automaticity (p. 112)
distributed intelligence (p. 112)
creativity (p. 114)

convergent thinking (p. 115)
divergent thinking (p. 115)
higher-level question (p. 116)
culture (p. 118)
ethnic group (p. 118)
cultural mismatch (p. 119)
Standard English (p. 120)
dialect (p. 120)
African American dialect (p. 120)

sociolinguistic conventions (p. 121)
wait time (p. 122)
negative wait time (p. 122)
multicultural education (p. 125)
stereotype (p. 126)
equity (in instruction) (p. 128)
socioeconomic status (SES) (p. 131)
resilient students (p. 133)
students at risk (p. 134)

5

Students with Special Educational Needs

*W*hat weaknesses do you have in comparison with your fellow students? Perhaps you sometimes have more difficulty remembering course material, or perhaps you are so shy that you rarely talk to your classmates. Yet at the same time, can you think of ways in which you surpass most of your peers? Perhaps you are someone for whom learning a foreign language comes easily, or perhaps you are an exceptional softball player or long-distance runner.

All students are unique individuals, with different patterns of strengths and weaknesses. They differ considerably in cognitive abilities; for instance, some learn complex classroom material quickly and easily, while others struggle just to master basic concepts and skills. They also show a wide variety of social and emotional characteristics; for example, some may be friendlier and more outgoing than others, and some may appear more self-confident than their classmates are. And students have varying physical capabilities—varying degrees of physical strength, muscular coordination, eyesight, and hearing ability. Most of the time we can accommodate students' individual differences within general education practices and activities. But once in a while students have characteristics that require specially adapted instructional materials or practices; in other words, they are **students with special needs**.

In the United States, federal legislation protects the civil rights of students with special educational needs. This legislation supports inclusive education, whereby most students with exceptionalities spend part or all of the school day in general education classrooms. In this chapter we will focus on the things that regular classroom teachers need to know to meet the unique educational needs of these students. In particular, we will consider questions such as these:

- Why are most students with special needs educated in general education classrooms rather than in "special" classes or schools?
- What laws protect the rights of students with disabilities?
- How do educators typically categorize various kinds of special needs, and what characteristics are associated with each category?
- How can we help students with cognitive deficits, behavioral problems, and physical disabilities be successful in general education classrooms?
- What can we do to maximize the growth of students who show exceptional gifts and talents?
- What general principles can guide us in our efforts to provide maximally beneficial classroom experiences for *all* students with special needs?

CASE STUDY: *Four Students*

Jonathan is a boy with many strengths: He is friendly and outgoing, enjoys playing the trumpet, and is the star pitcher on his Little League baseball team. Academically, Jonathan does average work in mathematics but has unusual difficulty with any subject that involves a lot of reading. A recent score on a standardized reading achievement test indicates that Jonathan's reading ability is well below that of other students at his grade level.

Andrea is a very aggressive student. When she speaks to other girls, it is usually to insult them, and she frequently starts fights for no apparent reason. Not surprisingly, Andrea has no real friends among her classmates. Furthermore, she has trouble relating with her teachers: She refuses to participate in classroom discussions, doesn't complete assignments, and resists all efforts to help her.

Midori shows great promise in art; her clay sculptures and pen-and-ink drawings often bring awards at local art shows. But Midori has difficulty with language. She must look closely at people's faces when they speak to her and yet still does not always understand their meaning correctly. When she speaks, her voice has a strange monotone and hollow sound to it.

Angelo has an unusually rich vocabulary for a boy his age, using words such as *inordinate* and *commensurate* in his everyday speech. And he seems to know more than most adults about certain subjects; for example, he reads every book about astronomy and space travel that he can get his hands on. But Angelo is getting poor grades in school because he doesn't complete his classroom assignments; he'd much rather read Carl Sagan's *Cosmos* than do his math homework. Angelo insists that schoolwork is too "boring" to bother with.

- Each of these students is exceptional in one way or another. Can you guess what the "special need" of each student might be?

Educating Students with Special Needs in General Education Classrooms

Despite normal intelligence (e.g., as evidenced in his average performance in mathematics and his strengths in social skills, music, and baseball), Jonathan has a *learning disability* that hinders his progress in learning to read. Andrea, who has difficulty relating effectively with others, has an *emotional or behavioral disorder.* Midori has trouble understanding and producing spoken language because she is *deaf.* And Angelo finds typical classroom activities boring because he long ago mastered many of the skills now being taught in his classroom; he is intellectually *gifted.*

In the United States, more than two-thirds of students with special educational needs are in general education classrooms for part or all of the school day (U.S. Dept. of Education, 1996). In fact, federal legislation mandates a practice known as **inclusion:** School districts must educate students with special needs, including those with severe and multiple disabilities, in regular classrooms in their neighborhood schools to the greatest extent possible. Let's look briefly at the history of the inclusion movement in the United States and at federal legislation that lends its support to this movement.

Historical Overview of the Inclusion Movement

Until the late 1960s, children with significant disabilities—for example, those who were blind, used a wheelchair, or had mental retardation—were educated in almost complete isolation from their nondisabled peers (if, in fact, they were educated at all). During the 1800s, the most common approach was to place such students in separate, specialized institutions. In the first half of the twentieth century, students with disabilities began to be educated in public schools, but usually within special classrooms designed for their particular needs. Such **self-contained classes** were smaller than regular classes, were taught by specially trained teachers, and had a curriculum adapted to specific disabilities. It was widely believed that such classes could better promote the educational achievement of students with special needs.

But beginning in the late 1960s, many parents and educators began to question the removal of students with special needs from general education classrooms. In an era of increasing concern for human rights and the equal treatment of people from all racial and ethnic groups, students from ethnic minority groups were nevertheless being placed in special classes (and therefore taken *out* of the typical classroom environment) in greater proportions than nonminorities. Further-

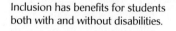

Inclusion has benefits for students both with and without disabilities.

more, researchers frequently found that students did not benefit from special classroom placement: Their academic and social development was no better, and in fact was sometimes worse, than that of similar students who remained in regular classrooms (e.g., Madden & Slavin, 1983).

What additional concerns might people have had about self-contained classes?

Laws passed within the past three decades have mandated the increasing integration of students with special needs into classrooms with their nondisabled peers. Initially, such integration often took the form of **mainstreaming**: having students with special needs join general education classes only when their abilities enabled them to participate in normally scheduled activities as successfully as other students. Under such conditions, some students remained in regular classrooms for a good part of the school day but went to "resource rooms" or "learning centers" for specialized instruction in areas of particular difficulty (e.g., for reading or mathematics). Other students were nothing more than occasional visitors in regular classes, joining their peers primarily for such specialized activities as art, music, and physical education.

Many people were concerned—in fact, some were outraged—that such practices gave students a fragmented, inconsistent educational experience and interfered with students' ability to develop normal peer relationships and social skills (e.g., Hahn, 1989; Will, 1986). Others argued that *all* students, including those with severe and multiple disabilities, have the right to be educated in general education classrooms and in neighborhood schools with their nondisabled peers (e.g., Kunc, 1984; S. Stainback & Stainback, 1985, 1990). They proposed that students with special needs should be able to participate in all aspects of regular school life; in addition to receiving academic instruction with nondisabled classmates, they should be able to join their peers on the playground, in the cafeteria, and in extracurricular activities. This practice of integrating all students with special needs into the overall community and "life" of the neighborhood school embodies the spirit of the inclusion movement.

Public Law 94-142: The Individuals with Disabilities Education Act (IDEA)

Supporting the inclusion movement, at least in the United States, is key federal legislation that mandates including all students in general education classrooms to the greatest extent possible. In 1975 the U.S. Congress passed Public Law 94-142, which is now known as the **Individuals with Disabilities Education Act (IDEA)**. IDEA has been amended several times, in 1983 (PL 98-199), 1986 (PL 99-457), and 1990 (PL 101-476), and it was reauthorized in 1997 (PL 105-17). IDEA now grants educational rights to people with cognitive, emotional, or physical disabilities from birth until age 21, and it guarantees several rights for students with disabilities:

- A free and appropriate education
- Fair and nondiscriminatory evaluation
- Education in the least restrictive environment
- An individualized education program
- Due process

These are summarized in Table 5.1. Let's look at each one more closely.

A Free and Appropriate Education

All students with disabilities are entitled to a free educational program designed specifically to meet their unique educational needs. For example, a student with a learning disability who has unusual difficulty with reading is entitled to a special educational program designed to promote greater development of reading skills. This program might involve additional instructional time in reading, a different instructional approach, or tailor-made reading materials. A student who uses a wheelchair may not be able to participate physically in the school's traditional unit on basketball, but she can possibly benefit from some aspects of the unit (for example, practice in dribbling or shooting baskets) and from certain modifications of the sport (e.g., playing in district-wide wheelchair basketball games).

Underlying the guarantee of a free and appropriate education is the concept of *zero reject*: A school district must enroll all students regardless of their disabilities and provide appropriate educational services no matter how severe the disabilities might be. Furthermore, a school district cannot expel students whose inappropriate behavior is the result of their disabilities.

Five Premises on Which the Individuals with Disabilities Education Act (IDEA) Is Based

ASSUMPTION	EXPLANATION	EDUCATIONAL IMPLICATION
A free and appropriate education	Students with disabilities are entitled, free of cost, to an educational program designed to meet their unique educational needs.	Students must be given instruction and materials adapted to their abilities and disabilities. For example, a student who is blind may have reading material in Braille. A student with mental retardation may be given intensive instruction in basic arithmetic and considerable practice working with money.
Fair and nondiscriminatory evaluation	School personnel must use evaluation methods that give a complete, accurate, and meaningful indication of each student's specific educational needs.	Students must be assessed in all areas related to potential disabilities. Evaluation methods must take the student's native language, cultural background, and any suspected physical or communication difficulties into account.
Education in the least restrictive environment	Students with disabilities are entitled to the most typical and standard educational environment that can reasonably meet their specific needs. They must also be given sufficient supplementary aids and support services to make success in that environment possible.	Many students with disabilities attend a general education classroom for most or all of the school day, although some of their instruction, materials, and assignments may be adapted to meet their unique educational abilities and needs.
An individualized education program (IEP)	An instructional program for each student must be identified and described in written form. Several things must be specified, including short- and long-term educational goals, the methods used to accomplish these goals, appropriate educational placements, any specialized services that the school will provide, and the procedures used to evaluate the student's progress.	After identifying a particular student's educational needs, a team comprised of teachers, appropriate specialists, and the student's parents (and sometimes the student) collaborate to develop an IEP that addresses how the school district will address those needs. Members of the team touch base regularly to ensure that the student is making reasonable progress. They modify the IEP at least once a year, but more frequently if new needs or issues arise.
Due process	Students' rights, as well as those of parents acting on behalf of their children, must be preserved throughout the decision-making process.	Parents (as well as any student who has reached the age of 18) can give or withhold permission to have a student evaluated for special services, and they have the right to see all school records concerning a student. Furthermore, any disagreements between parents and the school district about the most appropriate educational program for a student should be addressed through mediation, a formal hearing, or both.

Fair and Nondiscriminatory Evaluation

When determining whether a student has a particular disability that requires special services, a team of individuals is formed to conduct an evaluation of that student's specific needs. This multidisciplinary team typically consists of the student's parents or guardians, at least one general education teacher, at least one special education teacher, and often one or more specialists who can appropriately administer evaluation instruments and interpret the results that they yield. If the student is at least 18 years old, he or she is also a member of the evaluation team; in some instances, students younger than 18 participate in team decision making as well. The exact makeup of each team depends on the needs of the student and varies somewhat from state to state.

Why is it important for parents to be included in the multidisciplinary team?

To avoid a biased assessment, school personnel use tests and other evaluation tools that can provide an accurate, meaningful, and complete indication of the specific disabling conditions. Evaluation instruments must be administered by individuals trained in their use, and evaluation procedures must take students' backgrounds and any suspected physical or communication difficulties into account. Tests must be administered in students' primary language; for example, if a student is learning English but has been raised in a Spanish-speaking home, tests are given in Spanish. Students must be assessed in all areas related to their potential disability and so may be assessed with regard to any one or more of the following characteristics:

general intelligence, specific academic aptitude, social and emotional status, communication skills, vision, hearing, health, and motor skills. As a final safeguard, students must be evaluated on the basis of multiple assessment methods, *never* on the basis of a single test score.

Education in the Least Restrictive Environment

The **least restrictive environment** is the most typical and standard educational environment that can reasonably meet a student's needs. Students with disabilities should not be segregated from their classmates; instead, they should be included in the same academic environment, extracurricular activities, and social interactions as their nondisabled peers. The general rule here is that educators must begin by assuming that a student *will* be educated within a regular classroom context and given sufficient supplementary aids and support services to make success in that context possible. Exclusion from general education is warranted only when teachers or other students are clearly jeopardized (e.g., as would be the case when a student with an emotional or behavioral disorder is extremely violent) or when, even with proper support and assistance, the student cannot make appreciable progress in meeting educational goals in a general education classroom (Turnbull et al., 1999).

Individualized Education Program (IEP)

An instructional program tailored to the student's strengths and weaknesses, called an **individualized education program (IEP)**, must be developed and described in written form for each student identified as having a special educational need. The IEP is typically developed by the same multidisciplinary team that has evaluated the student. All team members agree to and sign the IEP and then continue to review and (if appropriate) revise it at least once a year—more frequently if conditions warrant doing so or if a parent or teacher requests a review.

An IEP typically has the following components:

- A description of the student's current educational performance
- Short-term objectives and long-term instructional goals for the student
- The methods to be used in accomplishing the instructional objectives, including the services of any specialists that may be required and any curricular and instructional supports that the school will provide
- Criteria and procedures to be used in evaluating the success of the prescribed methods

If applicable, the team must also describe the extent to which the student will receive some educational programming outside the context of the regular classroom and justify why such placement is in the student's best interests. Figure 5.1 presents a more detailed description of the components of an IEP. We will look at excerpts from a particular student's IEP a bit later in the chapter.

Due Process

Implicit in IDEA is the assumption that a student with disabilities has the same rights as any other U.S. citizen. IDEA mandates several practices that ensure that the student's rights, as well as those of the parents acting on behalf of their child, are preserved throughout the decision-making process:

- Parents must be notified in writing before the school takes any action (e.g., testing, change in educational placement) that may change their child's educational program.
- Parents can give or withhold permission to have their child evaluated for special education services.
- At their request, parents can see all school records about their child.
- If parents and the school system disagree on the most appropriate placement for a child, mediation or a hearing before an impartial individual (someone who is not an employee of the school district) can be used in an attempt to resolve the differences.

Is Inclusion in the Best Interest of Students?

Despite the clear mandates of IDEA, inclusion continues to be a controversial and hotly debated practice among both theorists and practitioners (Brantlinger, 1997; B. K. Keogh & MacMillan, 1996; W. Stainback & Stainback, 1992). Some experts worry that when students with special needs are in a regular classroom for the entire school day, they cannot possibly

FIGURE 5.1 Typical components of an IEP.

The IEP is a written statement for a student, age 3 to 21, who has been identified as having a special educational need. Any IEP that is developed or revised should contain the following:

- The student's present levels of educational performance, including:
  - How the student's disability affects his or her involvement and progress in the general curriculum (for students 6–21 years old), *or*
  - How the child's disability affects his or her participation in appropriate activities (for children 3–5 years old)
- Measurable annual goals, including "benchmarks" or short-term objectives, related to:
  - Meeting needs resulting from the disability, to ensure that the student is involved in and can progress through the general curriculum
  - Meeting each of the student's other disability-related needs
- The special education, related services, supplementary aids, program modifications, and supports that will be provided so that the student can:
  - Advance appropriately toward attaining the annual goals
  - Be involved in and progress through the general curriculum
  - Participate in extracurricular and other nonacademic activities
  - Be educated and participate in general education with other students with disabilities and with students who do not have disabilities
- The extent, if any, to which the student will *not* participate with nondisabled students in general education classes and in extracurricular and other nonacademic activities of the general curriculum, as well as justifications for such exclusion
- How the student's progress toward annual goals will be assessed and how the student's parents will be regularly informed of the student's progress toward those goals
- The projected date for beginning services and program modifications and the anticipated frequency, location, and duration of each
- Any individual modifications in the administration of state or district-wide assessments of student achievement, so that the student can participate in those assessments; moreover, if the IEP determines that the student will not participate in a particular state or district-wide assessment or any part of an assessment, why that assessment is not appropriate for the student and how the student will be alternatively assessed
- Transition plans, including:
  - Beginning at age 14 and each year thereafter, a statement of the student's needs that are related to transition services, including those that focus on the student's courses of study (e.g., the student's participation in advanced-placement courses or in a vocational education program)
  - Beginning at age 16 (or sooner, if the IEP team decides it is appropriate), a statement of needed transition services, including, when appropriate, a statement of the interagency responsibilities or any other needed linkages
  - Beginning at least one year before the student reaches the age of majority under state law (usually at age 18), a statement that the student has been informed of those rights under IDEA that will transfer to the student from the parents when the student becomes of age

Note: Adapted from EXCEPTIONAL LIVES 2/E by Turnbull et al. © 1999. Adapted by permission of Pearson Education, Inc., Upper Saddle River, NJ.

get the intense specialized instruction that many need to achieve essential basic skills in reading, mathematics, and so on (Manset & Semmel, 1997; Zigmond et al., 1995). Others voice the concern that the trend to educate all students in general education classrooms is based more on philosophical grounds than on research results (Lieberman, 1992).

In fact, many research studies indicate that placement in general education classrooms can have benefits such as these:

Why do you think students placed in regular classrooms often have more appropriate classroom behavior? Why do you think they may have better self-concepts and more positive attitudes about school?

- Academic achievement equivalent to (and sometimes higher than) what it would be in a self-contained classroom
- More positive self-concept and greater self-esteem
- More frequent interaction with nondisabled peers
- Better social skills
- More appropriate classroom behavior

We are especially likely to see such benefits when regular classroom materials and instruction are tailored to students' specific educational needs and academic levels (Halvorsen & Sailor, 1990; P. Hunt & Goetz, 1997; Scruggs & Mastropieri, 1994; Slavin, 1987; S. Stainback &

Stainback, 1992). It is important to note, however, that many studies comparing the effectiveness of regular class versus special class placement are correlational rather than experimental studies, making it difficult to draw firm conclusions about causal relationships (Madden & Slavin, 1983; D. M. Murphy, 1996). Furthermore, research has focused more on students with mild disabilities than severe disabilities and more on students in the elementary grades rather than secondary grades (B. K. Keogh & MacMillan, 1996).

Students with special needs are probably not the only ones who benefit from inclusive practices. Nondisabled students often benefit as well: They develop an increasing awareness of the very heterogeneous nature of the human race and discover that individuals with special needs, apart from some obvious disabilities, are in many respects very much like themselves (P. Hunt & Goetz, 1997; D. Staub, 1998). As an example, I think of my son Jeff's friendship with classmate Evan during their third-grade year:

> Evan was a 10-year-old boy with severe physical and cognitive disabilities. Wheelchair-bound, he had only minimal use of his arms and legs. He was fed by means of a tube inserted into his throat, and a teacher aide was by his side throughout the school day to tend to his health needs. The only recognizable word in Evan's oral vocabulary was *hi;* more often, he simply communicated by making the sound "aaaahhh."
>
> Early in the school year, the teacher asked Jeff to be a "special friend" to Evan. Jeff sat with Evan in class and at lunch and would talk to him whenever the schedule allowed time for conversation. Jeff would also give Evan things to feel and manipulate; Evan especially liked feeling and playing with the pieces of Velcro on Jeff's winter gloves. The boys' teacher marveled at how Jeff could convince Evan to perform assigned tasks when no one else could.
>
> As Jeff's mother, I saw an additional benefit of Jeff's friendship with Evan. Normally a very shy child, Jeff became increasingly self-confident that he was, indeed, a genuinely likable person. When the two boys passed in the hallway, Evan always made it clear through his gestures and facial expressions that he was delighted to see his friend. And on one occasion, when Evan was given the opportunity to invite a friend to accompany him on his weekly trip to the swimming pool, he chose Jeff—an invitation that Jeff considered to be the greatest of compliments.
>
> Several years later, Jeff's reflections on his friendship were these: "It made me realize that Evan was a person too. It made me realize that I could have a friendship with a boy with disabilities. Doing things that made Evan happy made me happy as well. I knew that *Evan* knew that we were friends."

The Current Conception of Inclusion

In the early years of IDEA—in particular, in the late 1970s and throughout the 1980s—many classroom teachers continued to use their regular curriculum and methods for their nondisabled students and adapted the curriculum and methods as necessary to accommodate students with special needs. In such a situation, one or more special education teachers would visit the classroom periodically to give guidance and support or perhaps to provide individualized instruction to students with special needs. But within the past decade or so, two notable changes have occurred (Turnbull et al., 1999). First, truly inclusive practices require individualization of instruction for *all* students, not just those with identified needs. Such individualization must necessarily entail a major overhaul of traditional curriculum materials and instructional practices, rather than just occasional "add-ons" and modifications. Second, effective teaching is seen as involving an equal, collaborative partnership between regular classroom teachers and special educators; thus, we are likely to see a great deal of **cooperative teaching**, in which at least two teachers teach all students—both those with disabilities and those without—throughout the school day (e.g., Thousand, Villa, & Nevin, 1994).

Students with special needs are more successful in the general education classroom when instruction and materials are adapted to meet their individual needs.

Before identifying the specific kinds of curricular materials and instructional practices that are likely to be most effective for students with special educational needs, it may help us to consider how various disabilities are categorized in special education.

General Categories of Students with Special Needs

Why do you think it is so difficult to define some categories of special needs?

The practice of classifying students with special needs has some inherent difficulties. For one thing, experts often disagree about how to define categories of special needs; categories that cannot be described in terms of a readily observable physical condition (e.g., learning disabilities, emotional and behavioral problems, giftedness) are especially difficult to pin down with precise definitions. Experts also disagree about the best ways of identifying members of those categories, yet different methods of identification sometimes lead to different conclusions as to which students have special needs. Even when experts do agree on such issues, any category of students with special needs includes students who are often as different as they are similar, so these students often require different types of support and services (Adelman, 1996; MacMillan & Meyers, 1979). A final concern is that labels such as "mental retardation" or "learning disability" may unintentionally communicate the message that students with special needs are somehow inferior; thus, these labels may adversely affect self-esteem. It is important to note, however, that some students with special needs develop low self-esteem as a result of their disabilities (perhaps because they consistently experience failure or because other people treat them as "different") before any label is ever applied to them at school (M. C. Reynolds, 1984).

Despite such disadvantages, most educators continue to classify students with special needs because of the advantages in doing so. Although members of the same category are in some respects very different from one another, they also tend to have characteristics in common; these similarities allow educators to make certain generalizations about how to foster the academic and social development of students in any given category. In addition, special needs categories provide a rallying point around which social and political forces can promote the interests of these students. For example, over the years such organizations as the American Association on Mental Retardation and the Autism Society of America, and such journals as the *Journal of Learning Disabilities* and *Gifted Child Quarterly*, have emerged to support these students. Special interest groups are often instrumental in collecting information, supporting and publishing research, and facilitating federal and state legislation to help

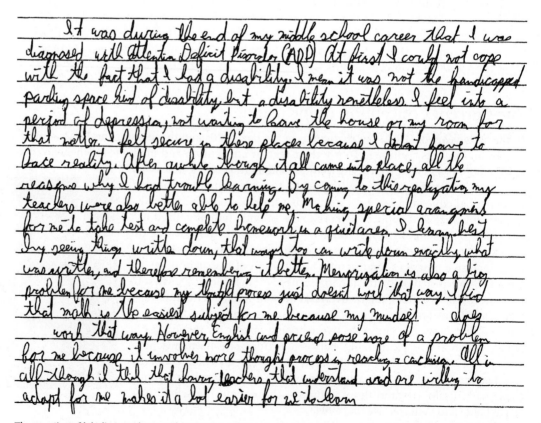

The practice of labeling students with special needs has both advantages and disadvantages, as this reflection by 17-year-old Colin illustrates.

students with special needs (Hobbs, 1980).[1] But probably the most influential factor affecting educators' use of categories and labels, at least in the United States, is that federal funds, available to support special educational services for up to 12 percent of the student population, are provided only when students have been formally identified as having a particular disabling condition.

Using People-First Language

EXPERIENCING FIRSTHAND   *The Importance of Being Fatheaded*

The person who sold you this book told me that you have an unusually large head. I consulted with your professor and a few of your classmates, who confirmed the report: You do indeed have a big head.

So, you fatheaded person, continue reading. As a fathead, you will undoubtedly learn a great deal about students with special needs in the pages that follow. You will not, however, learn anything about fatheaded people, because little research has been conducted on fatheads, and there is no evidence to indicate that fatheads require special educational services.

At the same time, you may want to seek out other fatheads who attend the same institution that you do. You will undoubtedly find that you have a great deal in common with them; for instance, all of you cast big shadows and have very strong neck muscles. Furthermore, you can consult with the other fatheads about places to shop for extra-large hats and giant-size bottles of shampoo.

Did I offend you just now? If so, why? Look back at the passage and try to identify what I might have said to rub you the wrong way. But at the same time, assume that my assessment is accurate—that you do, indeed, have a large head.

One thing that may have offended you is the fact that once I determined that you were a fathead, that label dominated everything I said about you. In reality, even though you are fatheaded, you have many other traits as well, including, almost certainly, some very admirable ones. Perhaps you are intelligent, likable, considerate, and honest, with a good sense of humor and high moral standards. The label *fatheaded* dominated my characterization of you, to the exclusion of your many other qualities.

Special educators worry that attaching certain labels to students may have this kind of effect—that it may focus our attention on a particular disabling condition rather than on the many ways in which students are in other respects just ordinary human beings. To minimize such an effect, special educators urge us all to use **people-first language** whenever we refer to students with disabilities—in other words, to mention the person *before* the disability. For instance, we might say *students with mental retardation* rather than *mentally retarded student* or *student who is blind* rather than *blind student*. Placing the person before the disability when we speak and write can help us remind both ourselves and others that a disability is only one of many characteristics that a particular student has.

An Overall Organizational Scheme

I have organized our discussion of students with various special needs using the five general categories that appear in the "Inclusion" tables throughout the book. Table 5.2 lists the specific kinds of special needs that fall within each category. Note that one of the special needs listed in the table—giftedness—is not specifically covered by IDEA.[2] In the United States, the

---

[1]Many of these organizations have home pages on the World Wide Web. As examples, you may want to log on to www.aamr.org (American Association on Mental Retardation), www.asha.org (American Speech-Language-Hearing Association), www.autism-society.org (Autism Society of America), www.ccbd.net (Council for Children with Behavioral Disorders), www.cec.sped.org (Council for Exceptional Children), www.ldanatl.org (Learning Disabilities Association of America), or www.nagc.org (National Association for Gifted Children).

[2]IDEA does not specifically identify attention-deficit hyperactivity disorder as a qualifying condition, but students with ADHD are typically eligible for services under the category "other health impaired" (Barkley, 1998).

TABLE 5.2

STUDENTS IN INCLUSIVE SETTINGS

General and Specific Categories of Students with Special Needs

GENERAL CATEGORY	SPECIFIC CATEGORIES	DESCRIPTION
Students with specific cognitive or academic difficulties	Learning disabilities	Difficulties in specific cognitive processes (e.g., in perception, language, memory, or metacognition) that cannot be attributed to such other disabilities as mental retardation, emotional or behavioral disorders, or sensory impairments
	Attention-deficit hyperactivity disorder (ADHD)	Disorder marked by either or both of these characteristics: (a) difficulty focusing and maintaining attention and (b) frequent hyperactive and impulsive behavior
	Speech and communication disorders	Impairments in spoken language (e.g., mispronunciations of certain sounds, stuttering, or abnormal syntactical patterns) or language comprehension that significantly interfere with classroom performance
Students with social or behavioral problems	Emotional or behavioral disorders	Emotional states or behaviors that are present over a substantial period of time and significantly disrupt academic learning and performance
	Autism	Condition marked by varying degrees of impaired social interaction and communication, repetitive behaviors, and restricted interests; a strong need for a predictable environment also commonly observed
Students with general delays in cognitive and social functioning	Mental retardation	Condition marked by significantly below-average general intelligence and deficits in adaptive behavior (i.e., in practical and social intelligence)
Students with physical or sensory challenges	Physical and health impairments	Physical or medical conditions (usually long-term) marked by one or more of these three characteristics: limited energy and strength, reduced mental alertness, or little muscle control
	Visual impairments	Malfunctions of the eyes or optic nerves that prevent normal vision even with corrective lenses
	Hearing loss	Malfunctions of the ear or associated nerves that interfere with the perception of sounds within the frequency range of normal speech
	Severe and multiple disabilities	Presence of two or more disabilities, the combination of which requires significant adaptations and highly specialized educational services
Students with advanced cognitive development	Giftedness	Unusually high ability or aptitude in one or more of these areas: general intellectual ability, aptitude in a specific academic field, creativity, visual or performing arts, or leadership

Jacob K. Javits Gifted and Talented Student Education Act (PL 103-382, reauthorized in 1994 by PL 103-382, XIV) encourages, but does not necessarily mandate, special educational services for students who are gifted. In addition, many state governments either encourage or mandate such services (Council for Exceptional Children, 1995). Most students with exceptional gifts and talents are unlikely to reach their full potential within the context of regular classroom assignments and activities; for this reason, many school districts *do* provide special programs for these students.

Students with Specific Cognitive or Academic Difficulties

Some students with special educational needs may show few if any outward signs of physical disability yet have cognitive difficulties that interfere with their ability to learn academic material or perform typical classroom tasks. This section describes three categories of special needs that involve specific cognitive or academic difficulties: learning disabilities, attention-deficit hyperactivity disorder, and speech and communication disorders.

Learning Disabilities

Remember Jonathan, the first student in the case study at the beginning of the chapter? Jonathan exhibits average performance in mathematics and has notable strengths in social skills, music, and baseball. Yet Jonathan's reading skills are well below grade level. Despite his ability to handle many aspects of his life, Jonathan has a learning disability that hinders his progress in learning to read.

Students with **learning disabilities** comprise the largest single category of students with special needs (U.S. Dept. of Education, 1996). Educators have not reached complete agreement about how best to define this category. Nevertheless, most apply the following criteria when classifying a student as having a learning disability (Mercer, Jordan, Allsopp, & Mercer, 1996; National Joint Committee on Learning Disabilities, 1994):

- *The student has significant difficulties in one or more specific cognitive processes.* For instance, the student may have difficulties in perception, language, memory, or metacognition. Such difficulties are typically present throughout the individual's life and are assumed to result from a specific, possibly inherited dysfunction of the central nervous system (J. G. Light & Defries, 1995; Manis, 1996). Figure 5.2 lists some forms that a student's learning disability may take.
- *The student's difficulties cannot be attributed to other disabilities, such as mental retardation, an emotional or behavioral disorder, hearing loss, or a visual impairment.* Many students with learning disabilities have average or above-average intelligence. For example, they may obtain average scores on an intelligence test, or at least on some of its subtests.
- *The student's difficulties interfere with academic achievement to such a degree that special educational services are warranted.* Students with learning disabilities invariably show poor performance in one or more specific areas of the academic curriculum. At the same time, they may exhibit average or above-average achievement in other subjects. Consider once again Jonathan's average performance in math but below-average performance in reading. This uneven pattern in Jonathan's achievement is typical of students with learning disabilities.

FIGURE 5.2 Examples of cognitive processing deficiencies in students with learning disabilities.

Perceptual difficulty. Students may have difficulty understanding or remembering the information they receive through a particular sensory modality. For example, they may have trouble perceiving subtle differences between similar sounds in speech (a difficulty in auditory discrimination), retaining a clear image of letters they have seen (a difficulty in visual-spatial perception), or remembering the correct order of letters in a word (a difficulty in memory for a visual sequence).

Memory difficulty. Students may have less capacity for remembering the information they receive, over either the short or long run; more specifically, they may have problems with either *working memory* or *long-term memory* (see Chapter 6).

Metacognitive difficulty. Students may have difficulty using effective learning strategies, monitoring their progress toward learning goals, and in other ways directing their own learning.

Difficulty processing oral language. Students may have trouble understanding spoken language or remembering what they have been told.

Reading difficulty. Students may have trouble recognizing printed words or comprehending what they read. An extreme form of this condition is known as *dyslexia.*

Written language difficulty. Students may have problems in handwriting, spelling, or expressing themselves coherently on paper. An extreme form of this condition is known as *dysgraphia.*

Mathematical difficulty. Students may have trouble thinking about or remembering information involving numbers. For example, they may have a poor sense of time or direction or they may have difficulty learning basic number facts. An extreme form of this condition is known as *dyscalculia.*

Difficulty with social perception. Students may have trouble interpreting the social cues and signals that others give them (e.g., they may have difficulty perceiving another person's feelings or reactions to a situation) and therefore may respond inappropriately in social situations.

Sources: Conte, 1991; Eden, Stein, & Wood, 1995; Landau & McAninch, 1993; Lerner, 1985; H. L. Swanson, 1993; H. L. Swanson, Cooney, & O'Shaughnessy, 1998; Turnbull et al., 1999; Wong, 1991a, 1991b.

Common Characteristics

Students identified as having a learning disability are a particularly heterogeneous group: They are probably far more different than they are similar (Bassett et al., 1996; Chalfant, 1989; National Joint Committee on Learning Disabilities, 1994). Students with learning disabilities typically have many strengths; however, they may face such challenges as these:

- Difficulty sustaining attention when confronted with competing stimuli
- Poor reading skills
- Ineffective learning and memory strategies
- Difficulty with tasks involving abstract reasoning
- Poor self-concept and low motivation for academic tasks (especially if they receive no remedial assistance in their areas of difficulty)
- Poor motor skills
- Poor social skills
  (Chapman, 1988; Gresham & MacMillan, 1997; Mastropieri & Scruggs, 2000; Mercer, 1997; H. L. Swanson, 1993; Wong, 1991b.)

Students with learning disabilities often have less effective learning and memory skills, lower self-esteem, and less motivation to succeed at academic tasks.

It is important to remember that the characteristics just listed are typical of many students with learning disabilities, but they certainly do not describe *all* of these students. For instance, some students with learning disabilities are attentive in class and work diligently on assignments, and some (like Jonathan) are socially skillful and popular with their peers (Heward, 2000).

Learning disabilities may also manifest themselves somewhat differently in elementary and secondary school students (Lerner, 1985). At the elementary level, students with learning disabilities are likely to exhibit poor attention and motor skills and often have trouble acquiring one or more basic skills. As these students reach the upper elementary grades, they may also begin to show emotional problems, due at least partly to frustration about their repeated academic failures.

At the secondary school level, difficulties with attention and motor skills may diminish. But at this level, students with learning disabilities may be particularly susceptible to emotional problems. On top of dealing with the usual emotional issues of adolescence (e.g., dating, peer pressure), they must also deal with the more stringent demands of the junior high and high school curriculum. Learning in secondary schools is highly dependent on reading and learning from relatively sophisticated textbooks, yet the average high school student with a learning disability reads at a third- to fifth-grade level and has acquired few if any effective study strategies (Alley & Deshler, 1979; E. S. Ellis & Friend, 1991). To get a sense of how these students may feel under such circumstances, try the following exercise.

EXPERIENCING FIRSTHAND   *A Reading Assignment*

Read the following passage carefully. I will be testing you on its contents later in the chapter.

> Personality research needs to refocus on global traits because such traits are an important part of everyday social discourse, because they embody a good deal of folk wisdom and common sense, because understanding and evaluating trait judgments can provide an important route toward the improvement of social judgment, and because global traits offer legitimate, if necessarily incomplete, explanations of behavior. A substantial body of evidence supporting the existence of global traits includes personality correlates of behavior, interjudge agreement in personality ratings, and the longitudinal stability of personality over time. Future research should clarify the origins of global traits, the dynamic mechanisms through which they influence behavior, and the behavioral cues through which they can most accurately be judged. (Funder, 1991, p. 31)

How well do you think you are likely to perform on the upcoming test over the passage?

You probably found the passage more challenging to read than the rest of the chapter. In fact, this passage is a fairly typical one from *Psychological Science,* a professional journal written for highly educated people; many of its readers hold doctoral degrees. Essentially, I was asking you to read something that was written well above your usual reading level. (If it's any consolation, I won't *really* be testing you on its contents.)

I hope that, during the exercise, you experienced just a little bit of the frustration that high school students with learning disabilities probably experience each day. Yet secondary school teachers rarely teach reading or study skills as a part of their course content (Lerner, 1985). For many students with learning disabilities, school success may constantly feel like an uphill battle. Perhaps for this reason, students with learning disabilities are among those most at risk for dropping out of school (Barga, 1996).

Adapting Instruction

As we have seen, students with learning disabilities comprise a very heterogeneous group, and instructional strategies must be tailored to their specific strengths and weaknesses. Nevertheless, there are several strategies that should benefit a broad range of students:

■ *Minimize potentially distracting stimuli.* Because many students with learning disabilities are easily distracted, we should minimize the presence of other stimuli likely to compete for their attention. For example, we might make sure that the classroom is fairly quiet during seatwork time. Or we might pull down window shades when students in other classes are playing in the schoolyard.

■ *Use multiple modalities to present information.* Some students with learning disabilities have difficulty learning information through a particular modality—for example, through seeing or listening. We therefore need to be flexible in the modalities we use to communicate information to these students. In different situations, we might want to use visual, auditory, tactile (touch), or even kinesthetic (movement) approaches (J. W. Wood, 1998). For example, when teaching a student how to read and spell a particular word, we might write the word for the student (visual input), say its letters aloud (auditory input), have the student feel the word spelled with letters cut out of sandpaper (tactile input), have the student trace or write the word (kinesthetic), and have the student repeat the word's letters (both kinesthetic and auditory). In our lectures to secondary students, we may want to incorporate videos, graphics, and other visual materials; we might also encourage students to audiotape the lectures (J. W. Wood & Rosbe, 1985).

■ *Analyze students' errors for clues about their processing difficulties.* Like anyone else, students with learning disabilities are likely to make errors in responding to questions, problems, and other academic tasks. Rather than thinking of certain responses simply as being wrong, we can look closely at errors for clues about the specific difficulties students are having (Lerner, 1985). For example, a student who solves a subtraction problem this way:

$$\begin{array}{r} 85 \\ -\ 29 \\ \hline 64 \end{array}$$

I trust a policeman.

The errors in 7-year-old Daniel's writing give clues about his processing difficulties. Because he has trouble identifying each sound he hears in speech, he omits some sounds and misrepresents others. His teacher has written what he intended to say: "I trust a policeman."

may be applying an inappropriate rule (*always subtract the smaller number from the larger one*) to subtraction. A student who reads the sentence

I drove the car.

as "I drove the *cat*" may be having trouble using context clues in reading words and sentences. A student who reads the same sentence as "I drove the *cab*" may be overly dependent on context and not attending closely enough to the actual words on the page. Analyzing a student's errors, then, is an important step in identifying the knowledge and skills that may require remediation.

■ *Teach learning and memory strategies.* Many students with learning disabilities benefit from being taught specific strategies for performing tasks and remembering classroom subject matter. For example, we might teach students to give themselves mental "instructions" that help them follow the appropriate steps of a task (Turnbull et al., 1999). We might teach them to identify the underlying themes of stories by asking themselves such questions as "What was the main character's problem?" and "Was what happened good or bad? Why?" (Wilder & Williams, 2001). We might teach them how to take notes and then periodically monitor their notes for accuracy and completeness (J. W. Wood & Rosbe, 1985). We might also teach them certain **mnemonics**, or memory tricks, to help them remember particular facts (Mastropieri & Scruggs, 1992). As an example, Figure 5.3 presents one very simple mnemonic—a way of

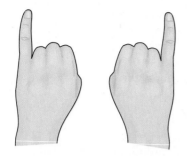

The lower case letters *b* and *d* are frequently confused by young students with learning disabilities. Clenched fists, with the palms facing away from the student and the little fingers pointing upward, form rough representations of these two letters. By "reading" their hands in the normal left-to-right fashion, students can more easily remember the difference between *b* and *d*—*b* comes first in both the alphabet and the fists.

FIGURE 5.3 A mnemonic for remembering the letters *b* and *d*

helping students remember the difference between the letters *b* and *d*. Additional strategies that are likely to help students who have learning disabilities study and learn more effectively are described in Chapters 6 and 8.

■ *Provide study aids.* In addition to teaching more effective study strategies, we can also provide scaffolding to support the sometimes overwhelming task of studying classroom material. For instance, we can provide study guides that help students identify important ideas (Mastropieri & Scruggs, 1992). We can show how material is organized, perhaps with outlines that enumerate major and subordinate ideas or with graphics that show how key concepts are interrelated (Brigham & Scruggs, 1995; J. W. Wood & Rosbe, 1985). We can let students copy (or receive a duplicate of) the notes of a classmate who is a particularly good note taker (Turnbull et al., 1999).

These teaching strategies don't necessarily apply only to students with learning disabilities. Many of them should also be helpful when working with students with attention-deficit hyperactivity disorder, a category of special needs that we turn to now.

Attention-Deficit Hyperactivity Disorder (ADHD)

Almost all children can be inattentive, hyperactive, and impulsive at one time or another. But students with **attention-deficit hyperactivity disorder (ADHD)** typically have marked deficits in these areas, as follows (American Psychiatric Association, 1994; Barkley, 1998):

- *Inattention.* Students may have considerable difficulty focusing and maintaining attention on assigned tasks. For instance, they often have trouble listening to and following directions, make frequent and careless mistakes, are easily distracted by highly appealing alternatives, and may fail to persist at tasks that require sustained mental effort.
- *Hyperactivity.* Students may seem to have an excess amount of energy. For instance, they are likely to be fidgety, move around the classroom at inappropriate times, talk excessively, have difficulty working or playing quietly, and perhaps act as if they are "driven by a motor."
- *Impulsivity.* Students almost invariably have difficulty inhibiting behaviors that are inappropriate for the situation at hand. For instance, they may blurt out answers, interrupt others, begin an assignment without waiting for instructions, have trouble waiting for their turn, or engage in risky or destructive behavior without thinking about the potential consequences.

Students with ADHD do not always show all three of these characteristics. For instance, some are inattentive without also being hyperactive. But all students with ADHD appear to have one characteristic in common: an *inability to inhibit inappropriate responses* (Barkley, 1998).

ADHD is assumed to have a biological and possibly genetic origin; it seems to run in families and is far more common in boys than in girls (Barkley, 1998; Faraone et al., 1995; Landau & McAninch, 1993). But once identified as having ADHD, many students can be helped through medication (e.g., Ritalin), often in combination with behavioral strategies (see Chapter 9), to control the symptoms (DuPaul, Barkley, & Connor, 1998).

I am just done with book. I really like this book that I chose and it was a good chose. She dose not go back to Sac Fransico and find her peo pals she stay io the Artic. . I would be saved too and cold. Mya X has survied there. About done.

Like many students with ADHD, 10-year-old Joshua has specific cognitive processing difficulties. Although he has the math skills of a typical fifth grader, the book report shown here reflects his delayed reading comprehension and writing skills. Josh can more easily express his thoughts orally.

Common Characteristics

In addition to inattentiveness, hyperactivity, and impulsivity, students identified as having ADHD may have characteristics such as these:

- Cognitive processing difficulties
- Poor school achievement
- Exceptional imagination and creativity

- Classroom behavior problems (e.g., disruptiveness, noncompliance with classroom rules)
- Difficulty interpreting and reasoning about social situations
- Greater emotional reactivity (e.g., excitability, hostility) in interactions with peers
- Few friendships; in some instances, outright rejection by peers
  (Barkley, 1998; Gresham & MacMillan, 1997; Grodzinsky & Diamond, 1992; Hallowell, 1996; Lahey & Carlson, 1991; Landau & McAninch, 1993; E. P. Lorch et al., 1999; Milch-Reich et al., 1999)

Some students with ADHD may also be identified as having a learning disability or an emotional or behavior disorder, while others may be gifted (Barkley, 1998; Conte, 1991; R. E. Reeve, 1990). The symptoms associated with ADHD may diminish somewhat in adolescence, but to some degree they persist throughout the school years, making it difficult for students to handle the increasing demands for independence and responsible behavior that come in high school (Barkley, 1998; Claude & Firestone, 1995; E. L. Hart, Lahey, Loeber, Applegate, & Frick, 1995). Accordingly, students with ADHD are at greater risk than normal for dropping out of school (Barkley, 1998).

Adapting Instruction

Researchers and practitioners have offered several suggestions for helping students with ADHD:

■ *Modify students' schedules and work environments.* The symptoms of ADHD tend to get progressively worse as the day goes on; ideally, then, students should have most academic subjects and challenging tasks in the morning rather than in the afternoon. Furthermore, students with ADHD often are distracted by what they see and hear in the classroom and have difficulty working in group situations. Moving their desks away from distractions (e.g., away from the door and window, not too close to classmates) and close to the teacher (where both independent and group work can be monitored) can enhance their attention and achievement (Barkley, 1998).

■ *Teach attention-maintaining strategies.* As is true for students with learning disabilities, we can certainly remove stimuli that are likely to compete for students' attention. But in addition, we can teach students concrete strategies for keeping their attention on an assigned task (Buchoff, 1990). For instance, we can ask them to keep their eyes on us when we're giving directions or providing new information. We can also tell them what specifically to listen for; for instance, we might say, "Listen carefully while I explain the things you should include in your essay." And we can encourage them to move to a new location if the current one presents too many distracting sights or sounds.

INTO THE CLASSROOM: *Helping Students with Specific Cognitive or Academic Difficulties*

Give students the extra structure they may need to succeed on academic tasks.

A teacher provides a particular format (scaffolding) for writing an expository paragraph: one sentence expressing the main idea, followed by three sentences that support the idea and a concluding sentence.

Help students pay attention.

A teacher has a student with attention-deficit hyperactivity disorder sit near her desk, away from distractions that classmates may provide; she also encourages the student to keep his desk clear of all objects and materials except those with which he is presently working (Buchoff, 1990).

When reading difficulties are evident, minimize dependence on reading materials or provide materials written at a lower level.

For two high school students reading well below grade level, a teacher finds some supplementary reading materials related to the topics the class is studying; although written for adults, these materials use simpler language than the class textbook. The teacher also meets with the students once a week for verbal explanations of class material and a hands-on exploration of scientific principles.

Look at students' errors for clues about possible processing difficulties.

When a student spells *refrigerator* as "refegter" and *hippopotamus* as "hepopoms," her teacher hypothesizes that she has difficulty relating written words to the phonetic sounds they represent.

■ *Provide outlets for excess energy.* To help students control excess energy, we should intersperse quiet academic work with frequent opportunities for physical exercise (Pfiffner & Barkley, 1998). We might also give them a "settling-in" time after recess or lunch before we ask them to engage in any activity that involves quiet concentration (Pellegrini & Horvat, 1995); for instance, many elementary teachers begin the afternoon by reading a chapter from a high-interest storybook.

■ *Help students organize and use their time effectively.* Because of their inattentiveness and hyperactivity, students with ADHD often have difficulty completing their daily classroom tasks. Several strategies can help these students organize themselves and use class time more effectively. We can show them how to establish a daily routine (including times to sharpen pencils, gather work materials together, etc.) and post that routine on their desks (Buchoff, 1990). We can break large tasks into smaller ones and set a short time limit for each subtask (Pfiffner & Barkley, 1998). We can provide daily or weekly "to-do" lists on which students check off completed assignments (Buchoff, 1990; J. W. Wood & Rosbe, 1985). And we can provide a folder in which students can transport their homework assignments to and from school (Buchoff, 1990).

■ *Teach and encourage appropriate classroom behaviors.* A structured environment with clear expectations for behavior and definite consequences for appropriate and inappropriate actions is often effective for students with ADHD (Buchoff, 1990; Landau & McAninch, 1993; N. Nussbaum & Bigler, 1990; Pfiffner & Barkley, 1998). Our discussion of behaviorist techniques in Chapter 9 will provide many useful strategies for creating such an environment.

Speech and Communication Disorders

If you have studied a foreign language, think back to your early attempts to speak the language. Did you feel awkward, knowing that your pronunciation and grammar were almost certainly flawed? Did you sometimes worry that your imperfect speech might make you look foolish to your teacher or classmates? If you had such feelings, then you perhaps have an inkling of how many students with speech and communication disorders feel when they are asked to speak in class.

Speech and communication disorders are impairments in spoken language or in language comprehension that significantly interfere with students' classroom performance. Examples include persistent articulation problems (mispronunciations of certain sounds and words), stuttering, abnormal syntactical patterns, and difficulty understanding the speech of others. Speech and communication disorders are also suspected when students fail to demonstrate age-appropriate language (e.g., a kindergartner who communicates only by pointing and gesturing, or a third grader who says, "Him go," instead of, "He's gone"). In many cases, the exact causes of these disorders are unknown (Wang & Baron, 1997).

The great majority of students with speech and communication disorders are in general education classrooms for most or all of the school day (U.S. Dept. of Education, 1996). Some of these students may have other disabilities as well, such as hearing loss or mental retardation (Turnbull et al., 1999). But many others are, in all other respects, just typical students.

Common Characteristics

Several characteristics are sometimes, although not always, observed in students with speech and communication disorders:

- Reluctance to speak
- Embarrassment and self-consciousness when speaking
- Difficulties in reading and writing
  (Fey, Catts, & Larrivee, 1995; LaBlance, Steckol, & Smith, 1994; Rice, Hadley, & Alexander, 1993)

Adapting Instruction

Typically, a trained specialist will work with students to help them improve or overcome their speech and communication difficulties—perhaps within the regular classroom context or perhaps in a separate setting. Nevertheless, general education teachers can assist in several ways:

We clied (climbed) up the pley gonds (playground) hist (highest) prot (part) of it and we wavd anr (waved our) roms (arms) the ick (ice) crem trok (cream truck) did not stop. Boom! iTooio thundr (Thunder) said Mac.

We saw a big bolt rit (right) in frot of (front) us. Connor shoted (shouted) lats (let's) get oof of (out) here! So we got oof cyce (out quick). We Whent (went) in the ick (ice) creme shop (cream) apsted (instead) we bot (bought)

ick creme (Ice cream). They get us (gave) a Free mape (map) we stred to (started) go back. We went oll (all) ofer tone (over town). but ven (then) fond ot (found out) connors hoes (house) was ocenst the stert (across street).

Seven-year-old Isaac receives speech therapy at school to address his consistent mispronunciation of certain sounds (e.g., he says "th" as "v"). In his writing, he sometimes spells words as he says them rather than as he hears them (e.g., he writes "ven" for *then*).

■ *Encourage regular oral communication.* Because students with speech and communication disorders need as much practice in classroom-based "public" speaking as their classmates, we can encourage them to talk in class, provided that doing so does not create exceptional stress for them (Patton, Blackbourn, & Fad, 1996).

■ *Listen patiently.* When students have difficulty expressing themselves, we may be tempted to assist them—for example, by finishing their sentences. But we better help students with speech and communication disorders when we allow them to complete their own thoughts, no matter how long it takes them to do so. We must learn to listen attentively and politely to students with speech problems without criticizing or ridiculing them, and we must encourage other students to do likewise (Lewis & Doorlag, 1991; Patton et al., 1996).

■ *Ask for clarification when the message is unclear.* On occasions when we haven't understood what students are saying, we should explain the things we *did* understand and ask them to clarify the rest. Honest feedback helps students learn how well they are communicating (Patton et al., 1996).

General Recommendations for Students with Specific Cognitive or Academic Difficulties

In addition to the instructional strategies described in the preceding pages, there are several more general strategies we can use to help students with specific cognitive or academic difficulties:

■ *Promote success on academic tasks.* Many of the students just described, especially those with learning disabilities or attention-deficit hyperactivity disorder, perform poorly on academic tasks and assignments. They may lack some of the basic concepts and skills that their nondisabled peers have already acquired and so need individualized instruction and practice to fill in the gaps. Many theorists suggest that one or another form of *direct instruction*, whereby students are specifically taught the things they need to learn, is the most effective approach to take here (E. S. Ellis & Friend, 1991; Tarver, 1992; Turnbull et al., 1999). Other theorists recommend that we also teach students specific ways of *thinking* about classroom tasks. For example, when we teach students how to write stories or essays, we should give them extensive instruction and practice in each phase of the writing process: planning, drafting, editing, and revising (Hallenbeck, 1996).

See Chapter 13 for more details about direct instruction.

■ *Clearly describe expectations for academic performance.* Students will have an easier time performing classroom tasks successfully when they know exactly what we expect them to do. We may sometimes need to explain in very concrete and precise terms what an assigned task entails. For instance, before students begin a science lab activity, we may want to remind them about how they should carefully follow the steps described on the lab sheet, what safety precautions they should take while using the equipment, and what components they should be sure to include in their lab reports.

■ *Consider students' reading skills when assigning reading materials.* Many students with specific cognitive or academic difficulties have poor reading skills. We may therefore need to consider methods of presenting academic content other than using standard grade-level textbooks. As alternatives, we might reduce the amount of reading required of these students, substitute materials written at a simpler (yet not "babyish") level, or present information through some medium other than written text (E. S. Ellis & Friend, 1991; Lewis & Doorlag, 1991; Turnbull et al., 1999).

Chapters 10 and 12 describe the nature of self-confidence (more specifically, *self-efficacy*) and its role in motivation.

■ *Take steps to enhance self-confidence and motivation.* Because students with specific cognitive or academic difficulties have typically had a history of failure at certain kinds of tasks—including many tasks that seem to come easily to their classmates—they are likely to have little self-confidence and little motivation to perform those tasks. It may be especially important, then, that we help students recognize that they are making progress and that they do some things very well (Buchoff, 1990). For example, we can set daily goals for them that we know they can attain. We can have them keep journals in which they describe the successes they have achieved each day. And we can give them opportunities to do tasks that they enjoy and usually perform successfully (Buchoff, 1990).

Our focus so far has been on cognitive and academic difficulties. For some students, however, social and behavioral problems predominate over academic concerns. It is to such students that we turn now.

Students with Social or Behavioral Problems

Many students have minor social, emotional, or behavioral difficulties at one time or another, particularly during times of unusual stress or major life changes. Such difficulties are often temporary, especially when students have the support of caring adults. Yet a few students show a pattern of behavioral problems that seriously interfere with their academic learning and performance, to the point where they require special educational services. This section looks at two groups of students who fall into this category: those with emotional and behavioral disorders and those with autism.

Emotional and Behavioral Disorders

Can you recall former classmates who had emotional or behavioral problems severe enough to interfere with their academic achievement?

Our opening case introduced Andrea, an aggressive student who has difficulty relating effectively with others and refuses to become involved in classroom activities. Students with an **emotional or behavioral disorder** become identified as students with special needs—and therefore as students who qualify for special educational services—when their problems have a substantial negative impact on classroom success and achievement. As is true for students with learning disabilities, students with emotional and behavioral disorders exhibit a wide variety of problems and are often more different from one another than they are similar. Examples of such problems include an inability to establish and maintain satisfactory interpersonal relationships with adults and peers, excessive and long-term depression or anxiety, exaggerated mood swings, and exceptionally aggressive or antisocial behavior.

The symptoms of emotional and behavioral disorders are often divided into two broad categories. **Externalizing behaviors** have direct or indirect effects on other people; examples are aggression, defiance, disobedience, lying, stealing, and lack of self-control. **Internalizing behaviors** primarily affect the student with the disorder; examples are anxiety, depression, withdrawal from social interaction, eating disorders, and suicidal tendencies. Although students with externalizing behaviors are those that teachers are more likely to refer for evaluation and possible special services (M. M. Kerr & Nelson, 1989), students with internalizing behaviors are often at just as much risk for school failure.

Some emotional and behavioral disorders are believed to result from environmental factors, such as child abuse, inconsistent parenting practices, stressful living conditions, exposure to violence, and family drug or alcohol abuse (H. C. Johnson & Friesen, 1993; G. R. Patterson, DeBaryshe, & Ramsey, 1989; Shaffer, 1988). At the same time, biological causes, such as inherited predispositions, chemical imbalances, brain injuries, and illnesses, may also contribute to emotional and behavioral problems (Hallowell, 1996; H. C. Johnson & Friesen, 1993). Some students with a genetic predisposition for an emotional or behavioral disorder exhibit few if any signs of a problem until adolescence; consider the case of Kirk:

As a high school freshman, Kirk was a well-behaved, likable student who was getting As and Bs in his classes and showed particular promise in science and mathematics. During his sophomore year, however, his grades began to slip, and he occasionally exhibited mildly hostile or defiant behaviors. Concerned, Kirk's parents and teachers imposed stricter limits on his behavior, but Kirk increasingly resisted such attempts to keep him in line. By the end of his junior year, Kirk was hanging out regularly with high school dropouts who engaged in minor criminal activities, and his grades had fallen to Cs and Ds.

When Kirk failed three classes during the fall of his senior year, thereby jeopardizing his chances of graduating with his class, the school principal called him, his parents, and his faculty advisor to a meeting to determine how to help Kirk get back on track. At the meeting, the principal described several occasions on which Kirk had acted disoriented, belligerent, and seemingly "high" on marijuana or some other illegal substance. At this point, an appropriate and constructive response on Kirk's part would have been to appear contrite and willing to change his behavior so that he could graduate—an essential goal given his strong desire to attend college the following year. Instead, Kirk sat at the meeting smirking (seemingly gleeful about the anger he had instilled in others) and focusing his attention on picking the peanuts out of a bowl of trail mix on the conference room table. By the end of the meeting, the principal was so infuriated by his behavior that she expelled him from school.

A few days after his expulsion, Kirk was arrested for carrying an illegal weapon (a knife) on school property. Over the next two weeks, as he waited in the juvenile detention facility for his court hearing, his mental condition deteriorated rapidly, and a judge ordered his hospitalization in the state mental institution.

Kirk was eventually diagnosed with *bipolar disorder*, a condition (usually inherited) characterized by excessive mood swings (hence, the disorder is sometimes called manic depression) and in some cases (including Kirk's) by distorted thought processes. Bipolar disorder often does not appear until adolescence, even though its biological underpinnings have been present since birth (Griswold & Pessar, 2000).

Factors at school may exacerbate the challenges that students with emotional and behavioral problems already face. Their inappropriate behaviors not only interfere with academic achievement but also incur rejection by their classmates, thus leading to social as well as academic failure. Many students, especially those with externalizing behaviors, may eventually seek the companionship of the few peers who *will* accept them—peers who typically behave in similarly inappropriate ways. Antisocial students often provide mutual support for one another's antisocial behavior and may introduce one another to drugs, alcohol, or criminal activity (Dishion et al., 1999; G. R. Patterson et al., 1989). Such difficulties undoubtedly contribute to the high dropout rate of students with emotional and behavioral disorders: Fewer than 50 percent of these students graduate from high school (Bassett et al., 1996; Koyanagi & Gaines, 1993).

Why are these students so often disliked by their classmates?

Common Characteristics

Although students with emotional and behavioral disorders are a very heterogeneous group indeed, many of them exhibit the following characteristics:

- Difficulty interacting with others in socially acceptable ways
- Difficulty establishing and maintaining satisfactory interpersonal relationships
- Poor self-concept
- Frequent absences from school
- Deteriorating academic performance with increasing age
- Lack of awareness of the severity of their problems
  (DuPaul & Eckert, 1994; Grinberg & McLean-Heywood, 1999; Leiter & Johnsen, 1997;

McGlynn, 1998; Morgan & Jenson, 1988; Richards, Symons, Greene, & Szuszkiewicz, 1995; Turnbull et al., 1999)

Some students with emotional or behavioral disorders have other special needs as well, including learning disabilities, mental retardation, or giftedness (Fessler, Rosenberg, & Rosenberg, 1991; Turnbull et al., 1999).

Adapting Instruction

Effective educational programs for students with emotional and behavioral disorders are usually individualized and tailored to the unique needs of each student. Nevertheless, several strategies may benefit many of these students:

■ *Show an interest in students' well-being.* Many students with emotional and behavioral disorders have few positive and productive relationships with individuals outside school; we can often help these students simply by showing them that we care about their welfare (Diamond, 1991). For example, we can greet them warmly when we see them in the hallway. We can express concern when they seem upset, worried, or overly stressed. We can lend a ready and supportive ear when they want to share their ideas, opinions, feelings, or frustrations. And we can let them know that such sharing is welcome by revealing aspects of our own personal lives (Diamond, 1991).

■ *Make classroom activities relevant to students' interests.* Students with emotional and behavioral disorders are more likely to get involved in their schoolwork when teachers take their personal interests into account (Clarke et al., 1995; McWhiter & Bloom, 1994). Chapter 12 identifies several ways we can meet important instructional objectives while also addressing students' interests.

To create "win-win" situations with students who misbehave frequently, teach them strategies for controlling their own behavior and give them choices when appropriate.

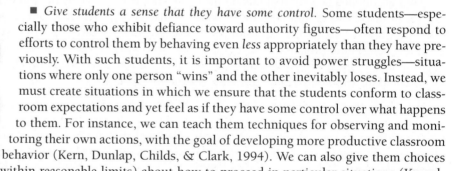

■ *Give students a sense that they have some control.* Some students—especially those who exhibit defiance toward authority figures—often respond to efforts to control them by behaving even *less* appropriately than they have previously. With such students, it is important to avoid power struggles—situations where only one person "wins" and the other inevitably loses. Instead, we must create situations in which we ensure that the students conform to classroom expectations and yet feel as if they have some control over what happens to them. For instance, we can teach them techniques for observing and monitoring their own actions, with the goal of developing more productive classroom behavior (Kern, Dunlap, Childs, & Clark, 1994). We can also give them choices (within reasonable limits) about how to proceed in particular situations (Knowlton, 1995). We will examine such approaches in more depth in our discussions of *self-regulation* in Chapter 10 and *self-determination* in Chapter 12.

■ *Be alert for signs of possible child abuse or neglect.* Possible indicators of abuse or neglect are frequent or serious physical injuries (e.g., bruises, burns, broken bones), untreated medical needs, obvious hunger, lack of warm clothing in cold weather, and exceptional knowledge about sexual matters (Turnbull et al., 1999). As teachers, we are both morally and legally obligated to report any cases of suspected child abuse to the proper authorities. You should consult with your principal about the specific policy in your own school district.

■ *Be alert for signs that a student may be contemplating suicide.* Seriously depressed students often exhibit behaviors indicating that they may be thinking about taking their own lives. Warning signs include

- Sudden withdrawal from social relationships
- Disregard for personal appearance
- A dramatic personality change
- A sudden elevation in mood
- A preoccupation with death and morbid themes
- Overt or veiled threats (e.g., "I won't be around much longer")
- Actions that indicate "putting one's affairs in order" (e.g., giving away prized possessions) (Kerns & Lieberman, 1993)

As teachers, we must take any of these warning signs seriously. We must show potentially suicidal students that we care very much about what happens to them, and we should seek trained help, such as the school psychologist or counselor, immediately (McCoy, 1994).

It is also essential that we help students with emotional and behavioral disorders acquire more appropriate behaviors—both those important for interacting effectively with others and those essential for maintaining a classroom environment conducive to learning. Strategies to improve behavior are likely to help students with autism as well; accordingly, I will describe such strategies after we discuss autism in the section that follows.

Autism

Autism is a condition that is almost certainly caused by a brain abnormality (Gillberg & Coleman, 1996). Perhaps the most central characteristic of this disability is a marked impairment in social interaction: Many students with autism form weak if any emotional attachments to other people and prefer to be alone (Denkla, 1986; Schreibman, 1988). Several other characteristics are also frequently seen in individuals with this condition: communication impairments (e.g., absent or delayed speech), repetitive behaviors (e.g., continually rocking or waving fingers in front of one's face), narrowly focused and odd interests (e.g., an unusual fascination with watches), aggression toward self or others, and a strong need for a predictable environment (American Psychiatric Association, 1994; E. G. Carr et al., 1994; Dalrymple, 1995; Turnbull et al., 1999). Some theorists have speculated that underlying autism may be either an undersensitivity or oversensitivity to sensory stimulation and that the abnormal behaviors so commonly observed reflect various attempts to make the environment more tolerable (R. C. Sullivan, 1994; D. Williams, 1996). Temple Grandin, a woman who has gained international prominence as a designer of livestock facilities, recalls what it was like to be a child with autism:

> From as far back as I can remember, I always hated to be hugged. I wanted to experience the good feeling of being hugged, but it was just too overwhelming. It was like a great, all-engulfing tidal wave of stimulation, and I reacted like a wild animal. . . .
>
> When I was little, loud noises were also a problem, often feeling like a dentist's drill hitting a nerve. They actually caused pain. I was scared to death of balloons popping, because the sound was like an explosion in my ear. Minor noises that most people can tune out drove me to distraction. (Grandin, 1995, pp. 63, 67)

Although the majority of students with autism are educated in self-contained classrooms or special schools, approximately one-fifth of them are enrolled in general education classrooms for part or all of the school day (U.S. Department of Education, 1996).[3]

Common Characteristics

In addition to the traits just listed, students with autism often have these characteristics:

- A lack of basic social skills (e.g., making eye contact, seeking comfort from others when hurt or upset)
- Impaired social cognition (e.g., interpreting social situations, inferring others' thoughts and intentions)
- Echolalia (i.e., continually repeating a portion of what someone has just said)
- Strong attachments to certain inanimate objects
- Abnormal movements (e.g., an awkward gait, repetitive gestures)
- Strong visual-spatial thinking skills
  (Denkla, 1986; Grandin, 1995; Gray & Garaud, 1993; Koegel, 1995; Leary & Hill, 1996; Leslie, 1991; Schreibman, 1988; D. Williams, 1996)

Although some students with autism have average or above-average intelligence, others have varying degrees of mental retardation (Ritvo & Freeman, 1978). Individuals with autism often show great variability in their specific abilities. In a few instances, students with autism

---

[3]For children with *Asperger syndrome,* a condition that shares some features with autism, the proportion enrolled in general education classes is considerably higher (Little, 2002). Students with Asperger syndrome exhibit major difficulties in social cognition and social functioning despite average or above-average intelligence.

Have you seen the movie *Rain Man?* Dustin Hoffman plays a man with autism and mental retardation who is especially adept at calculating probabilities.

may exhibit **savant syndrome**, in that they possess an extraordinary ability (such as exceptional musical talent) that is quite remarkable in contrast to other aspects of their mental functioning (Cheatham, Smith, Rucker, Polloway, & Lewis, 1995; Winner, 2000b).

Adapting Instruction

Just as is true for all students, a high priority for our students with autism is that they master academic content and skills commensurate with their ability. Many of the strategies I describe for helping students with learning disabilities, ADHD, and mental retardation learn academic subject matter may help students with autism as well. In addition, the following three strategies may be useful:

■ *Change the arrangement of the classroom as infrequently as possible.* Many students with autism apparently find security in the predictability of their environment (Dalrymple, 1995) and so may become excessively upset when objects or pieces of furniture in a familiar environment are rearranged. If we will have a student with autism in class, we should identify a physical layout for the classroom that will be serviceable throughout the school year and change it later only if absolutely necessary.

■ *Follow a regular daily or weekly schedule.* To the extent possible, we should schedule certain activities at the same time each day or on a particular day of each week. When the schedule changes (perhaps because of a fire drill or school assembly), we should prepare the student well in advance of the change and indicate when the schedule will be back to normal again (Dalrymple, 1995).

■ *Use visual approaches to instruction.* Because students with autism often have strong visual-spatial skills but deficits in oral communication, a heavy emphasis on visual materials can be beneficial (Hogdon, 1995; Quill, 1995). For instance, we might use objects, pictures, and photographs to convey ideas about academic topics. We might also provide a visual depiction of a student's daily schedule and give some sort of visual cue to indicate the start of a new activity.

General Recommendations for Students with Social or Behavioral Problems

Although the causes of emotional and behavioral disorders and those of autism are probably quite different, both groups of students may nevertheless benefit from some of the same teaching strategies. Certainly we want to promote success on academic tasks, perhaps by using some of the instructional strategies recommended earlier for students with specific cognitive or academic difficulties. In addition, students with social or behavioral problems may need extra assistance in learning appropriate and productive classroom behaviors:

Students with emotional and behavioral disorders may need considerable guidance on how to interact appropriately with their peers.

■ *Teach interpersonal skills.* Many students with social or behavioral problems have never really learned appropriate ways of relating to other people and have trouble interpreting the nonverbal social cues (e.g., the body language) that guide effective social interaction. Some students lack even the most basic social skills, and many others have difficulty cooperating, communicating, or resolving interpersonal conflicts. Directly teaching these students how to interact effectively with others is one obvious approach (see the section "Fostering Social Skills" in Chapter 3). Frequent opportunities to interact with both peers and adults, such as through structured cooperative learning activities in the classroom or through "partner" programs with young adults in the community, may also be valuable (Slavin, 1990; Turnbull et al., 1999). In addition, many research studies have shown that behaviorist techniques (described in Chapter 9) can be quite powerful in bringing about behavior change in students with social or behavioral problems (E. G. Carr et al., 1994; Koegel, Koegel, & Dunlap, 1996; Landau & McAninch, 1993; Morgan & Jenson, 1988; Turnbull et al., 1999).

■ *Communicate clear expectations for behavior.* When students exhibit serious behavior problems, it is especially important to specify exactly which behaviors are acceptable and unacceptable in precise and concrete language. For example, we can provide specific guidelines about when students can speak in class and when they are free to move about the classroom. Students are more likely to behave appropriately in the classroom when they are given reasonable limits for their behavior.

■ *Try to anticipate problems and then nip them in the bud.* After we have gotten to know our students fairly well, we can in some cases predict the circumstances that are likely to precede and possibly trigger undesirable behaviors. For instance, I think of Ben, a 9-year-old boy who, although usually mild-mannered, had occasional unpredictable temper tantrums that would disrupt the entire class. Eventually his teacher discovered that Ben's ears always turned red just before an outburst; this discovery allowed her to divert Ben's tantrums to a punching bag, where he could unleash his feelings with only minimal distraction to the rest of the class (Jackson & Ormrod, 1998). As another example, consider the case of Samantha:

> Samantha was a 9-year-old third grader who had been identified as having autism and moderate speech disabilities. She frequently ran out of the classroom, damaging school property and other students' belongings in her flight. When the teacher aide or another adult tried to intervene, she would fight back by biting, scratching, hitting, kicking, and pulling hair.
>
> The multidisciplinary team working with Samantha eventually discovered that Samantha's destructive and aggressive behaviors were more likely to occur when she was given a difficult academic assignment or had reason to anticipate such an assignment. Departures from the routine schedule or the absences of favorite teachers further increased the probability of such responses. (DeVault, Krug, & Fake, 1996)

Once Samantha's team had determined the circumstances likely to provoke her inappropriate behaviors, her teachers were in a better position to deal with those behaviors. We will find out just what the team did to help Samantha in our discussion of *positive behavioral support* in Chapter 9.

■ *Specify and follow through on consequences.* When working with students with social or behavioral problems, it is especially important that we describe the consequences—either reinforcing or punishing—to which various behaviors will lead; it is equally critical that we follow through with those consequences (Knowlton, 1995; Pfiffner & Barkley, 1998). At the

---

INTO THE CLASSROOM: *Helping Students with Social or Behavioral Problems*

Make expectations for classroom behavior clear and specific.

A teacher reminds a student, "You cannot borrow Mary's bottle of glue without asking. Check with Mary first to make sure it's all right for you to use her things. If Mary says no, ask another student."

Give feedback about specific behaviors rather than general areas of performance.

A teacher tells a student, "You did a good job in study hall today. You focused your attention on your homework, and you didn't retaliate when Jerome accidentally brushed past you on his way to my desk."

Specify and follow through on consequences for appropriate and inappropriate behaviors.

A teacher tells a student, "Sam, you know that certain four-letter words, such as the two that you just used, are unacceptable in this classroom. You also know the consequence for such behavior, so please go to the time-out corner for ten minutes."

Teach interpersonal skills.

When a student's only comments to classmates are derogatory remarks, her teacher meets with her after school to demonstrate more appropriate ways of initiating interaction. Together, they practice the new strategies through various role-playing situations.

Show an interest in students' well-being.

A teacher who sees a girl weeping quietly every day in class takes her aside when the other students have gone to lunch. As the student describes the nasty divorce proceedings in which her parents are involved, the teacher empathizes, explaining that his own parents divorced in an equally unpleasant fashion. He also connects her with a weekly support group that the school psychologist has formed for students whose parents are going through divorce.

Expect gradual improvement rather than immediate perfection.

A teacher is pleased that a student who once refused to participate in classroom activities now gets involved in activities two or three days a week, even though that student still has some days when little is accomplished.

same time, we should also give students explicit feedback about their behavior. When praising desirable behavior, rather than saying "Well done" or "Nice job," we should describe exactly what behaviors we are praising. When imposing punishment for inappropriate behavior, we should tell students exactly what they have done wrong. For example, we might say, "You borrowed Austin's book without asking him first. You know that taking other students' possessions without their permission is against class rules."

You should be aware that the job of helping students with social or behavioral problems is often a challenging one. Many of these students will at first resist any efforts to help them. It may only be when they themselves can observe the natural consequences of their changing behavior—for example, when they start to make new friends or when they get along better with their teachers—that they begin to recognize the value of the assistance you are giving them.

Students with General Delays in Cognitive and Social Functioning

One of the categories in the "Students in Inclusive Settings" tables located throughout the book is *students with general delays in cognitive and social functioning.* I intentionally used this term so that it might include any student who had a pattern of developmental delays in all areas, whether the student was specifically identified as having a disability or not. For instance, educators sometimes use the term *slow learner* to describe a student who obtains intelligence test scores in the 70s and has difficulties with virtually all aspects of the academic curriculum yet does not qualify for special educational services. A student with more pronounced developmental delays may be specifically identified as having *mental retardation*—a diagnosis that, in the United States, falls under the auspices of IDEA.

Mental Retardation

Students with **mental retardation** show developmental delays in most aspects of their academic and social functioning. Students must exhibit *both* significantly below-average general intelligence and deficits in adaptive behavior before they are identified as having mental retardation (American Association on Mental Retardation, 1992):

- *Significantly below-average general intelligence.* Intelligence test scores of students with mental retardation are quite low—usually no higher than 65 or 70, reflecting performance in the bottom 2 percent of their age-group (B. K. Keogh & MacMillan, 1996; Turnbull et al., 1999). These students show other signs of below-average intelligence as well; for instance, they learn slowly and perform quite poorly on school tasks in comparison with their age-mates. And they show consistently poor achievement across virtually all academic subject areas.

Have you ever interacted with individuals who have mental retardation? In what ways did their social skills seem immature? What particular strengths did these people have?

- *Deficits in adaptive behavior.* Low intelligence test scores and poor academic performance are insufficient evidence to classify students as having mental retardation. An additional criterion is a deficit in **adaptive behavior:** These students show limitations in *practical intelligence*—managing the ordinary activities of daily living—and *social intelligence*—conducting themselves appropriately in social situations. In these respects, students with mental retardation often exhibit behaviors typical of children much younger than themselves. Figure 5.4 lists the kinds of adaptive skills with which students may have difficulty.

Mental retardation is often caused by genetic conditions; for example, most children with Down syndrome have delayed cognitive development. Other cases are due to biological but noninherited causes, such as severe malnutrition during the mother's pregnancy or oxygen deprivation associated with a difficult birth (B. K. Keogh & MacMillan, 1996). In still other situations, environmental factors, such as parental neglect or an extremely impoverished and unstimulating home environment, may be at fault; accordingly, children from poor, inner-city neighborhoods are overrepresented in the students who are identified as having mental retardation (Batshaw & Shapiro, 1997; A. A. Baumeister, 1989; M. Wagner, 1995).

Although usually a long-term condition, mental retardation is not necessarily a lifelong disability, especially when the presumed cause is environmental rather than genetic (Landesman & Ramey, 1989). As an example, I think of 12-year-old Steven:

FIGURE 5.4 Adaptive skills used in identifying students with mental retardation.

Communication: Skills related to understanding and expressing ideas through spoken and written language and through body language

Self-care: Skills related to hygiene, eating, dressing, and grooming

Home-living: Skills related to general functioning at home, including housekeeping, laundry, food preparation, budgeting, and home safety

Social: Skills related to social interaction, including adhering to social conventions for interaction, helping others, recognizing feelings, forming friendships, controlling impulses, and abiding by rules

Community use: Skills related to using community resources effectively, including shopping, using local transportation and facilities, and obtaining services

Self-direction: Skills related to making choices, following a schedule, initiating activities appropriate to the context, completing required tasks, seeking needed assistance, and solving problems

Health and safety: Skills related to personal health maintenance, basic first aid, physical fitness, basic safety, and sexuality

Functional academics: Skills acquired in the academic curriculum that have direct application to independent living, such as reading, writing, and basic arithmetic

Leisure: Skills related to initiating self-chosen leisure and recreational activities based on personal interests, playing socially with others, and abiding by age and cultural norms for activities undertaken

Work: Skills related to holding a job, including specific job skills, appropriate social behavior, completion of tasks, awareness of schedules, and money management

Derived from the ten adaptive skills described by the American Association on Mental Retardation, 1992.

Steven had no known genetic or other organic problems but had been officially labeled as having mental retardation based on his low scores on a series of intelligence tests. His prior schooling had been limited to just part of one year in a first-grade classroom in inner-city Chicago. His mother had pulled him out after a bullet grazed his leg while he was walking to school one morning; fearing for her son's safety, she would not let him outside the apartment after that, not even to play, and certainly not to walk the six blocks to school.

When a truant officer finally appeared at the door one evening in May five years later, Steven and his mother quickly packed their bags and moved to a small town in northern Colorado. They found residence with Steven's aunt, who persuaded Steven to go back to school. After considering Steven's intelligence and achievement test scores, the school psychologist recommended that he attend a summer school class for students with special needs.

Steven's summer school teacher soon began to suspect that Steven's main problem might simply be a lack of the background experiences necessary for academic success. One incident in particular stands out in her mind. The class had been studying nutrition, and so she had asked her students to bring in some fresh vegetables to make a large salad for their morning snack. Steven brought in a can of green beans. When a classmate objected that the beans weren't fresh, Steven replied, "The hell they ain't! Me and Momma got them off the shelf this morning!"

If Steven didn't know what *fresh* meant, the teacher reasoned, then he might also be lacking many of the other facts and skills on which any academic curriculum is invariably based. She and the teachers who followed her worked hard to help Steven make up for all those years in Chicago when he had experienced and learned so little. By the time Steven reached high school, he was enrolling in regular classes and maintaining a 3.5 grade-point-average. (based on Jackson & Ormrod, 1998, pp. 63–66)

Based on this information, does Steven meet the two criteria for mental retardation presented earlier?

Common Characteristics

Although most students with mental retardation are educated in self-contained classrooms or at separate schools or other facilities, a small proportion of them attend general education classes for part or all of the school day (U.S. Dept. of Education, 1996). Students with mental retardation are likely to display many or all of the following characteristics:

- A desire to "belong" and fit in at school
- Less general knowledge about the world
- Poor reading and language skills

- Lack of metacognitive awareness and few, if any, effective learning and memory strategies
- Difficulty with abstract ideas
- Difficulty generalizing something learned in one situation to a new situation
- Difficulty filling in details when instructions are incomplete or ambiguous
- Poor motor skills
- Immature play behaviors and interpersonal skills
- Excessive dependence on others in decision making
  (Beirne-Smith et al., 2002; Butterfield & Ferretti, 1987; DuPaul & Eckert, 1994; Gresham & MacMillan, 1997; F. P. Hughes, 1998; Kail, 1990; Patton et al., 1996; Turnbull et al., 1999.)

Adapting Instruction

Many of the strategies I've previously described in this chapter are likely to be useful for helping students with mental retardation. Here are some additional strategies to keep in mind:

■ *Pace instruction slowly enough to ensure a high rate of success.* When working with a student who has mental retardation, we should move through topics and assign new tasks slowly enough that the student experiences a high degree of success. Students with mental retardation typically have a long history of failure at academic tasks; hence they need frequent success experiences to learn that they *can* succeed in school.

■ *Explain tasks concretely, specifically, and completely.* As noted earlier, students with mental retardation have difficulty filling in details correctly when instructions are ambiguous or incomplete. If we tell a student only to "Take this absentee sheet to the principal's office," it may not occur to the student to return to the classroom after completing the errand. Instead, we should provide concrete, specific, and complete instructions; for example, we might say, "John, go to the principal's office, give Mrs. Smith the absentee sheet, and come back here" (Patton et al., 1996, p. 105).

■ *Provide considerable scaffolding to facilitate effective cognitive processing.* Students with mental retardation often have little awareness of how to direct and regulate their own learning. So it is often helpful to provide extra guidance to assist in cognitive processing. For instance, we can help students focus their attention by using such phrases as "get ready," "look," or "listen" (Turnbull et al., 1999). We can teach them a few simple, concrete memory strategies, such as repeating instructions to themselves or physically rearranging a group of items they need to remember (Fletcher & Bray, 1995; Turnbull, 1974). We can also provide simple,

---

INTO THE CLASSROOM: *Helping Students with General Delays in Cognitive and Social Functioning*

Introduce new material at a slower pace, and provide many opportunities for practice.

A teacher gives a student only two new addition facts a week because any more than two seem to overwhelm him. Every day, the teacher has the student practice writing the new facts and review addition facts learned in previous weeks.

Explain tasks concretely and in very specific language.

An art teacher gives a student explicit training in the steps he needs to take at the end of each painting session: (1) Rinse the paintbrush out at the sink, (2) put the brush and watercolor paints on the shelf in the back room, and (3) put the painting on the counter by the window to dry. Initially the teacher needs to remind the student of every step in the process; however, with time

and practice, the student eventually carries out the process independently.

Give students explicit guidance about how to study.

A teacher tells a student, "When you study a new spelling word, it helps if you repeat the letters out loud while you practice writing the word. Let's try it with *house,* the word you are learning this morning. Watch how I repeat the letters—H . . . O . . . U . . . S . . . E—as I write the word. Now you try doing what I just did."

Encourage independence.

A high school teacher teaches a student how to use her calculator to figure out what she needs to pay for lunch every day. The teacher also gives the student considerable practice in identifying the correct bills and coins to use when paying various amounts.

---

structured study guides that quite specifically tell students what to focus on when they study (Mastropieri & Scruggs, 1992).

■ *Include vocational and general life skills in the curriculum.* After high school, most students with mental retardation join the adult work force rather than go on to higher education. Accordingly, an important part of any high school curriculum for students with mental retardation is training in general life and work skills. Because of students' limited ability to generalize what they have learned from one situation to another, it is especially important to teach life and work skills in realistic settings that closely resemble those in which students will find themselves once they leave school (Turnbull et al., 1999).

At this point, we turn our attention to a very different group of students—those with physical and sensory challenges. Yet as you will soon discover, some (but by no means all) of these students may also have some of the cognitive or social difficulties that characterize other students with special needs.

When instruction is appropriately paced and provides sufficient scaffolding, students with mental retardation can succeed in a wide variety of domains.

Students with Physical and Sensory Challenges

Some of our students with special needs will have obvious physical or sensory disabilities caused by medically detectable physiological conditions. In this section we will look at four kinds of physical or sensory disabilities: physical and health impairments, visual impairments, hearing loss, and severe and multiple disabilities.

Physical and Health Impairments

Physical and health impairments are general physical or medical conditions (usually long-term) that interfere with school performance to such an extent that special instruction, curricular materials, equipment, or facilities are necessary. Students in this category may have limited energy and strength, reduced mental alertness, or little muscle control. Examples of specific conditions that may qualify students for special services include traumatic brain injury, spinal cord injury, cerebral palsy, muscular dystrophy, epilepsy, cystic fibrosis, asthma, heart problems, arthritis, cancer, and AIDS. The majority of students with physical and health impairments attend general education classrooms for part or all of the school day (U.S. Dept. of Education, 1996).

Common Characteristics

It is difficult to generalize about students with physical and health impairments because their conditions are so very different from one another. Nevertheless, several noteworthy characteristics are common to many of these students:

- Learning ability similar to that of nondisabled students
- Fewer opportunities to experience and interact with the outside world in educationally important ways (e.g., less use of public transportation, fewer visits to museums and zoos, fewer family trips)
- Low stamina and a tendency to tire easily
- Possible low self-esteem, insecurity, embarrassment, or overdependence (depending partly on how parents and others have responded to their impairments) (Patton et al., 1996; J. W. Wood, 1998)

Adapting Instruction

To get a glimpse of the kinds of challenges that many students with physical disabilities face each day, try the following exercise.

EXPERIENCING FIRSTHAND *Stiffen Up*

Stand up, and then make your arms and legs totally straight and stiff. Also stiffen your wrists, fingers, and neck. While keeping all of these body parts totally stiff, try the following activities:

■ Skip around the room.
■ Bend over and touch your toes.

- Find a tissue or handkerchief and blow your nose.
- Go back to your chair and sit down.
- Take a piece of scrap paper and use it to mark this page. Turn back to the beginning of the chapter (p. 143) and read the first paragraph, then return to this page.
- While continuing to keep your elbows, wrists, and fingers completely stiff, try "cutting" an imaginary sheet of paper using an imaginary pair of scissors. Then "glue" two pieces of paper together using an imaginary bottle of rubber cement. Remember to "unscrew" the top off the bottle before you use it.

Now return your body to its usual, more relaxed state.

What kinds of difficulties did you encounter in your stiffness? You were probably able to skip around the room, although not as quickly and gracefully as you would otherwise. You may have been able to touch your toes as well, but did you find that your stiff neck made the task more difficult? And how did you blow your nose? I myself found that I couldn't do it in any way that would be presentable in a public place.

You may have experienced varying degrees of difficulty with the last three activities as well. Can you think of special equipment that might help you perform these activities more successfully? Would a different kind of chair be more comfortable? Would a metal book holder help you keep the textbook open while you read it? Might specially shaped scissors better fit your stiff fingers?

Although we will not always need to modify the class curriculum for students with physical and health impairments, we will definitely want to make other accommodations:

- *Be sensitive to specific needs and disabilities, and accommodate them flexibly.* Despite normal learning capabilities, students with physical and health impairments may not be able to perform certain tasks as easily as their classmates. For example, one student may require extra time with a writing assignment and perhaps should not be held to the same standards of neatness and legibility. Another may need to respond to test questions orally rather than on paper. Still another may tire easily and need to take frequent breaks from school tasks. In your previously "stiffened" condition, you may have needed all of these accommodations. Consider the case of Wesley as another example:

> During his junior year in high school, Wesley sustained a serious head injury in a motorcycle accident. Although he had previously been an excellent student, he returned to school his senior year with special educational needs. It took him much longer to read and process information than was true before the accident. Wesley tended to forget things that weren't written down for him. And he grew tired after only an hour or two of class.
>
> Wesley's teachers did several things to accommodate his needs that year. They let him finish in-class assignments at home. They allowed him to take tests by himself in a room near the main office and gave him as much time as he needed to respond to test items. They wrote instructions on the chalkboard where he could see and copy them, and they alerted him to crucial course content by saying, "This is important, so put it in your notes." Furthermore, the school counselor scheduled no classes during the third and fourth class periods so that Wesley could take a nap in the nurse's office. (based on Jackson & Ormrod, 1998, pp. 91–93)

- *Know what to do in emergency situations.* Some students have conditions that may result in occasional, potentially health-threatening situations. For example, a student with diabetes may go into insulin shock, a student with asthma may have trouble breathing, or a student with epilepsy may have a *grand mal* seizure. We should consult with school medical personnel to learn ahead of time exactly how to respond to such emergencies.

- *If the student and parents give their permission, educate classmates about the nature of the disability.* Although many classmates are apt to treat a student with a physical or health impairment with kindness and respect, others may be less considerate and tolerant. In some situations, such mistreatment may be due to ignorance about the nature of the disability, and accurate information must be made available. In one widely publicized case, Ryan White, a student with AIDS, was initially barred from his neighborhood school because of classmates' and parents' unwarranted fear that other children would be infected (R. White & Cunningham,

1991). Ryan returned to school only after the public was convinced that AIDS was not a condition that could be contracted through breathing or normal bodily contact. Even so, his reception was hardly a warm one. According to Ryan, some students behaved very badly indeed:

> [K]ids backed up against their lockers when they saw me coming, or they threw themselves against the hallway walls, shouting, "Watch out! Watch out! There he is!" (R. White & Cunningham, 1991, p. 118)

Only when his family moved to a different school district—one that went to great lengths to inform parents and students about the true nature of AIDS—did Ryan find teachers and peers who were happy to have him in their school building and classrooms.

Visual Impairments

Students with **visual impairments** have malfunctions of their eyes or optic nerves that prevent them from seeing normally even with corrective lenses, to the point where their classroom performance is affected. Some students are totally blind; others have limited sensitivity to light, perhaps seeing fuzzy patterns of light and dark. Still others have a restricted visual field (sometimes called *tunnel vision*), whereby they can see only a very small area at a given time. Visual impairments are caused by congenital abnormalities in, or later damage to, either the eye or the visual pathway to the brain.

Common Characteristics

Students with visual impairments are likely to have many or all of these characteristics:

- Normal functioning of other senses (hearing, touch, etc.)
- General learning ability similar to that of nondisabled students
- Fewer opportunities to experience and interact with the outside world in educationally important ways (for example, less exposure to maps, films, and other visual material); as a result, a more limited vocabulary and less general knowledge about the world
- Reduced capability to imitate the behaviors of others
- Inability to observe the body language and other nonverbal cues often present in human interactions, leading to occasional misperceptions of intended meanings
- Occasional confusion, particularly in chaotic situations such as on the playground or in the lunchroom
- A general feeling of uncertainty and anxiety as a result of having no visual knowledge of the events happening within the classroom
- In the primary grades, less knowledge about the conventions of written language (direction of print, punctuation, etc.)
  (M. Harris, 1992; Patton et al., 1996; M. C. Reynolds & Birch, 1988; Tompkins & McGee, 1986; Turnbull et al., 1999; Tuttle & Tuttle, 1996)

Adapting Instruction

Specialists will typically give students who are blind or have limited vision the training they need in Braille, orientation and mobility, and specially adapted computer technology. Apart from such additions to the curriculum, regular classroom content and objectives are usually appropriate for these students.

At the same time, we can help students with visual impairments learn and achieve more successfully with strategies such as the following:

■ *Orient students ahead of time to the physical layout of the classroom.* Students with serious visual impairments should be given a chance to explore the classroom before other students have arrived—ideally, well before the first day of class. We can help students locate various objects in the classroom (wastebasket, pencil sharpener, etc.) and can point out special sounds (such as the buzzing of a clock on the wall) so students can get their bearings (J. W. Wood, 1998).

■ *Use visual materials with sharp contrast for students with partial sight.* Students with visual impairments will obviously have limited success in learning from ordinary printed materials such as textbooks, posters, charts, and maps. Some students can benefit from visual materials provided that the various features of those materials are easily distinguishable from one another. For example, some students with partial sight may be able to read large print books (available at most public libraries). Students' eyes will tend to tire quickly, however, so we should limit the use of visual materials to short periods of time (Patton et al., 1996).

■ *Find ways of transmitting information through other modalities.* For students who are blind, we must find viable alternatives for presenting classroom material. We can obtain Braille copies of required books and assignments or audiotapes of novels and other literature. We can engage students in hands-on activities involving objects they can feel and manipulate. Plastic relief maps that portray mountains, valleys, and coastlines three-dimensionally can be embellished by making pin pricks along borders or placing small dabs of nail polish on major cities. When exclusively visual material must be used for large-group instruction, this material should be described in detail to students with visual impairments—perhaps by their teacher, an aide, or a fellow student.

■ *Allow extra time for learning and performance.* Learning by hearing often takes more time than learning by seeing: When students *look* at something, they can perceive a great deal of information all at once, but when they *listen* to it, they receive it just one piece at a time. Hence we may often need to give students with visual impairments extra time to learn classroom material and complete assignments (M. B. Rowe, 1978).

Hearing Loss

Our opening case study profiled Midori, a girl with exceptional talent in art. Midori has trouble understanding what others say to her, and her own voice has a monotonous and hollow sound to it. Midori has never actually heard the sound of human language because she has been deaf since birth.

Students with **hearing loss** have a malfunction of the ear or associated nerves that interferes with the perception of sounds within the frequency range of normal human speech. Students who are completely *deaf* have insufficient sensation to understand any spoken language, even with the help of a hearing aid. Students who are *hard of hearing* understand some speech but experience exceptional difficulty in doing so. Approximately half of the students identified as having hearing loss are in general education classrooms for part or all of the school day (U.S. Dept. of Education, 1995).

Think about struggling to hear conversation at a noisy party. Might the frustration you feel be similar to how a student with hearing loss feels?

Common Characteristics

Most students with hearing loss have normal intellectual abilities (Braden, 1992; Schirmer, 1994). However, they may have characteristics such as the following:

- Delayed language development, especially if the hearing impairment was present at birth or occurred early in life, because of reduced exposure to spoken language
- Less oral language than hearing classmates
- Some ability to read lips (*speechreading*)
- Proficiency in sign language, such as American Sign Language (ASL) or finger spelling (a manual alphabet through which words can be spelled)[4]

- Less developed reading skills, especially if other aspects of language development have been delayed
- Less general knowledge about the world than their peers, due to reduced exposure to verbal information
- In some cases, social isolation and more limited social skills due to the reduced ability to communicate with others (Bassett et al, 1996; Chall, 1996; Gearheart, Weishahn, & Gearheart, 1992; M. C. Reynolds & Birch, 1988; M. B. Rowe, 1978; Turnbull et al., 1999)

Adapting Instruction

Specialists typically provide training in such communication skills as American Sign Language, finger spelling, and speechreading. Aside from

Many students with hearing loss have proficiency in American Sign Language. ASL is not a word-for-word representation of English; it has its own unique vocabulary and syntax.

[4]When children who are deaf are exposed to sign language beginning in the first few months of life, their development in sign language progresses at a rate similar to the development of spoken language skills in hearing children (M. Harris, 1992; L. A. Pettito, 1997).

the addition of these topics, the regular school curriculum is appropriate for most students with hearing loss. Teachers can do a number of things to help these students learn and achieve successfully:

■ *Minimize irrelevant noise.* Even when students with hearing loss wear hearing aids, what they hear is apt to be somewhat distorted or diminished. For students who have some ability to hear sounds, then, it is helpful to minimize any irrelevant and potentially distracting noises in the classroom. For instance, carpet on the floor and multiple bulletin boards on the walls can absorb some of the extraneous noises that will inevitably be present. And students may be better able to focus on important auditory messages if such noisy devices as pencil sharpeners and fans are as far away as possible (Turnbull et al., 1999).

■ *Supplement auditory presentations with visual information and hands-on experiences.* For obvious reasons, we should supplement any auditory presentations (such as directions, lectures, or classroom discussions) with information provided through other (especially visual) modalities. For example, we can write important points on the chalkboard. We can illustrate key ideas with pictures and other graphics. We can offer reading materials that duplicate lectures. We can ask a classroom aide or student volunteer to take notes on in-class discussions. And we can use concrete activities (e.g., role playing, experiments, field trips) to make potentially abstract ideas come alive.

■ *Take steps to maximize students' hearing capabilities and ability to speechread.* Students who are hard-of-hearing are most likely to understand words spoken in a normal tone of voice (not overly loud) and with a distinct but otherwise normal pronunciation of words (Gearheart et al., 1992; J. W. Wood, 1998). They should sit in places where they can clearly see the speaker's face. Furthermore, we should speak only while facing students, and never while sitting in a dark corner or standing in front of a window or bright light (Patton et al., 1996; Turnbull et al., 1999).

■ *Occasionally check for understanding by asking students to repeat what you've said.* Even the most skillful speechreaders won't always get our messages exactly as we've transmitted them. To make sure students correctly understand what we are telling them, we can occasionally ask them to repeat what we've said. By doing so, we can identify and correct misunderstandings (Gearheart et al., 1992; Patton et al., 1996).

■ *Address deficiencies in reading and other language skills.* We must be sure to address any language and reading deficiencies that students may have (Bassett et al., 1996). In some cases, a special educator or other specialist can give us guidance and assistance in this regard. Many of the strategies in Chapter 2 (see the section on language development) and the chapter "Learning in the Content Areas" in the *Study Guide and Reader* (see the sections on reading and writing) may also be helpful.

■ *Teach elements of American Sign Language and finger spelling to other class members.* Some students with hearing loss, because of their reduced ability to communicate, may feel relatively isolated from their peers and teachers. One effective way of opening the lines of communication is for other class members, ourselves included, to gain some competence in American Sign Language and finger spelling. For instance, I once taught at a school where *every* student—those with hearing loss and those without—received some instruction in signing. One girl in my class was totally deaf yet was quite popular with her classmates; I often observed her and her friends communicating freely and easily both before and after (and, unfortunately, sometimes at inappropriate times *during*) class.

Severe and Multiple Disabilities

Students with **severe and multiple disabilities** have two or more of the disabilities already described and require significant adaptations and highly specialized services in their educational program. These disabilities are almost always due to organic causes, such as genetic abnormalities or serious complications before or during birth. Despite their extensive need for special services, some students with severe and multiple disabilities (such as my son Jeff's friend Evan, whom I described earlier in the chapter) may be in general education classrooms for part of the school day.

Common Characteristics

Students who have severe and multiple disabilities often have these characteristics:

- Varying degrees of intellectual functioning (some students may have average intelligence that is hidden beneath a limited ability to communicate)
- Limited awareness of surrounding stimuli and events; periods of alertness and responsiveness in some cases
- Limited communication skills (often consisting of gestures, facial expressions, or other nonverbal means), which can sometimes be facilitated by technology
- Limited adaptive behaviors (e.g., social skills, self-care skills)
- Significant delays in motor development
- Mild or severe sensory impairments
- Extensive medical needs (e.g., medications, intravenous tubes)
  (Guess, Roberts, Siegel-Causey, & Rues, 1995; Turnbull et al., 1999)

Adapting Instruction

Should we have students with severe and multiple disabilities in our classrooms, we will almost certainly work with one or more specialists or teacher aides that assist us in their education. Yet we must keep in mind that, despite extensive disabilities, these students are full-fledged members of the class and should participate in all curricular activities to the extent that they can do so. In addition to using the many strategies described earlier in the chapter, we can accommodate students with severe and multiple disabilities in ways such as these:

■ *Identify and teach those behaviors and skills most essential for a student's general welfare and successful inclusion in the classroom.* Almost any student with special needs, no matter how serious his or her disabilities, has some capacity to adapt to a new environment. We should therefore identify those behaviors that will enhance the student's learning and performance for the time that we will have them—behaviors that may include more effective ways of communicating, rudimentary word recognition or arithmetic skills, or the use of new technologies specially designed for certain disabling conditions. In teaching a basic skill, we may find it useful to guide the student slowly through the skill one step at a time, verbally or manually scaffolding his or her actions, and then gradually removing such assistance as the student develops increasing competence, self-confidence, and independence.

■ *Pair students with and without disabilities in the same activity, having different objectives for different students.* It may sometimes be appropriate to pair a nondisabled student with a student who has disabilities and have the two work cooperatively on a classroom task. In some cases, they might be working to achieve different objectives within the same content area; for example, when two students conduct a science experiment, one might be learning methods of scientific experimentation while the other is mastering basic scientific concepts. In other cases, the pair might be working to achieve objectives in two completely different areas; for example, while one is learning experimentation techniques, the other may be practicing communication skills (Giangreco, 1997).

■ *Keep the mind-set that all students can and should participate in regular classroom activities to the fullest extent possible.* As we have moved toward greater inclusion of students with disabilities in recent years, many educators have found that when they keep open minds about what their students can accomplish, and especially when they think creatively and collaboratively about how they can adapt regular classroom activities to accommodate students with special needs, almost all students can participate in some meaningful way in virtually all classroom activities (Logan, Alberto, Kana, & Waylor-Bowen, 1994; Salisbury, Evans, & Palombaro, 1997).

General Recommendations for Students with Physical and Sensory Challenges

Like other students with special needs, students with physical and sensory challenges should have as normal an education as we can reasonably provide for them. We have identified a number of specific ways to help students in the various disability categories adjust successfully to the classroom environment. Several more general strategies can also facilitate the classroom success of students with physical and sensory challenges:

■ *Provide access to the same educational opportunities that other students have.* Partly as a result of federal legislation, individuals with physical and sensory challenges now have greater access to educational opportunities than they did twenty or thirty years ago; for example, the now commonplace wheelchair ramps leading into schools and other public buildings were virtually nonexistent when I was a child. Nevertheless, we must consider how the physical conditions within our own classrooms may possibly interfere with students' access to important educational facilities and materials, and we may have to make a concerted effort to ensure equal access. For example, to accommodate children in wheelchairs, we may need to widen the aisles between classroom desks and place items taped to walls or posted on bulletin boards at eye level (Stephens, Blackhurst, & Magliocca, 1988). We may also need to make special arrangements that allow students with disabilities to accompany our classes on field trips.

■ *Treat students in the same way that you treat their classmates without disabilities.* Students with physical and sensory challenges adjust to their circumstances more successfully when other individuals treat them normally—for example, by expecting them to perform the same tasks as other students when they are capable of doing so and by avoiding behaviors that reflect pity or patronization. As one simple example, we should speak to students directly, rather than asking a third person (such as a parent or therapist), "How is Johnny doing today?"

■ *Provide assistance only when students really need it.* In their eagerness to help students with physical or sensory challenges, many adults inadvertently perform tasks and solve problems that these students are perfectly capable of handling on their own. Yet one of our goals for these students is to promote their independence, not their dependence on others. So when we see that students are having difficulty with a task, we should ask them if they need assistance before we try to help them.

■ *Use technological innovations to facilitate student learning and performance.* There has been a virtual explosion of technological aids to help students with physical and sensory challenges in their daily school activities. For example, many computers have been adapted for the visually impaired: Some calculators "talk" as buttons are pushed and answers are displayed, some computers "tell" a student what appears on the computer screen, and some computer printers print in Braille. Specially adapted joysticks or voice recognition systems can help students with limited muscle control use a classroom computer. Machines known as augmentative communication devices can provide synthesized speech to facilitate the communication of individuals incapable of normal speech (Stephens et al., 1988; Turnbull et al., 1999).

Now that you've learned about various disabilities, try the following assessment exercise.

INTERPRETING ARTIFACTS AND INTERACTIONS   *Looking at an IEP*

Eight-year-old Harry (a pseudonym) has been identified as having special educational needs, and a team consisting of Harry's classroom teacher, the school's resource room teacher, the school psychologist, the school counselor, and Harry's father has developed an individualized education program (IEP) for Harry. As you read the following excerpts from Harry's IEP, think about

- The particular disability that Harry may have
- The extent to which the IEP is likely to guide instruction

Strengths: Intelligent, creative, good visual memory, enjoys working on the computer, likes structured activities, persists at difficult tasks when motivated

Needs: To follow classroom expectations, to be productive, to be more socially appropriate and less anxious in social situations, to be less impulsive

Strategies

- Establish eye contact before giving directions.
- Encourage Harry to repeat directions to make sure he understands.
- Provide structure to help Harry meet written expectations and organize himself.
- Use one-on-one coaching to ward off potential outbursts and encourage Harry to be productive.
- Use behavioral techniques to help Harry control excess verbiage, begin tasks on time, and meet classroom expectations.
- Break tasks down into smaller units that Harry can follow sequentially.
- Encourage Harry to increase his positive self-talk.
- Provide positive reinforcement when Harry takes responsibility for his own work.
- Give advance notice about transitions and the end of activities.
- Communicate frequently with home to share positive accomplishments.

Accommodations

- Support in the areas of written language, behavior management, productivity, and meeting classroom expectations.
- Counseling to support emotional control, appropriate and courteous language, and social skills.
- Accommodations for the length of assignments and amount of written work.

Instructional Objectives

Written Language
- Harry will sustain his independent writing for a specified period of time, writing first and then drawing.
- Harry will commit basic sight, phonetic, and content area words to memory for spelling with 80 percent accuracy on weekly tests.
- Harry will be able to identify and apply correct punctuation to the end of a sentence.

Study/Organizational/Behavioral Skills
- Harry will follow his teacher's directions and begin a task within a given amount of time.
- Harry will complete a task within a given amount of time.
- Given advance warning, Harry will make successful transitions to new activities.
- With teacher guidance, Harry will work cooperatively in a small group and contribute positively.

Social/Emotional Functioning
- Harry will increase his awareness of the emotions of others, as demonstrated by their facial expressions.
- Harry will increase his understanding that others may have a legitimate point of view.
- Harry will increase his understanding that his behaviors may upset other people (i.e., when he talks too loudly or behaves disrespectfully).

To what category of special needs do you think Harry belongs? As you read the IEP, you may have formed several hypotheses: perhaps a learning disability, attention-deficit hyperactivity disorder, or an emotional or behavioral disorder. In reality, school personnel have identified Harry as having an *emotional handicap,* the school district's terminology for what we have been calling an emotional or behavioral disorder. As you can see, categorizing students as having particular disabilities is not always a clearcut process, especially when, like Harry, a student has deficits in several areas. Ultimately, the most important goal is not so much to give

Harry a specific "diagnosis" as it is to modify instructional materials and practices to best meet his individual needs and help him develop both academically and socially. How helpful will this IEP be in guiding instruction? Certainly the strategies identified provide some useful ideas for working with Harry, and the instructional objectives listed provide some goals to shoot for. But several critical things are missing from the excerpts presented here. For instance, what is Harry's *present level of performance* in each of these areas? How will Harry's progress on each goal be *objectively measured*? Which team members (e.g., classroom teacher, resource room teacher, counselor) are responsible for which objectives, and in which settings? Ideally, an IEP should include such information (see Figure 5.1). (Harry's complete IEP addresses some but not all of these issues.)

We have considered many ways of helping students with a variety of disabilities adapt successfully to a general education environment. Yet an additional group of students—those who show exceptional ability in one or more areas—may also have special educational needs. The next section addresses the specific needs of these students.

Students with Advanced Cognitive Development

Think back, for a moment, to your own childhood. Did you show a strong aptitude for reading or mathematics? exceptional creativity in art? an unusual flair for music, dance, or drama? Might you have benefited from an instructional program that nurtured your talents? Were you frustrated that your talents were *not* nurtured as much as they might have been?

Many of our students are likely to have advanced abilities, either in specific subject areas or across the board, that warrant our attention and encouragement. As you examine the Inclusive Settings tables that appear throughout this book, you should think of *students with advanced cognitive development* as being on a continuum of abilities rather than being a distinct category separate from their classmates. In fact, we will want to nurture the specific gifts and talents that *all* of our students are likely to bring to the classroom (Council for Exceptional Children, 1995).

Yet some students are so far above the norm that special educational services are advisable. Let's look more closely at the nature of such *giftedness*.

Giftedness

Giftedness is unusually high ability or aptitude in one or more areas, to the point where special educational services are necessary to help a student meet his or her full potential. Students who are gifted (sometimes called *gifted and talented*) show exceptional achievement or promise in one or more of the following areas:

- General intellectual ability
- Aptitude in a specific academic field
- Creativity
- Visual or performing arts
- Leadership
  (Jacob K. Javits Gifted and Talented Students Education Act of 1988 [PL 100-297, IV(B); PL 103-382, XIV]; U.S. Dept. of Education, 1993)

When we try to pin down giftedness more precisely, we find considerable disagreement about how to do so (Carter, 1991; B. K. Keogh & MacMillan, 1996). Although many school districts identify gifted students primarily on the basis of general IQ scores, often using 125 or 130 as a cutoff point (B. K. Keogh & MacMillan, 1996; J. Webb, Meckstroth, & Tolan, 1982), some experts argue that multiple criteria should be applied when determining students' eligibility for special services (Renzulli, 1978; Renzulli & Reis, 1986; Sternberg & Zhang, 1995). For instance, one theorist has argued that we should consider creativity and task commitment as well as IQ scores (Renzulli, 1978). Furthermore, scores on general intelligence tests may be largely irrelevant when identifying students who show exceptional promise in specific academic fields, creativity, the arts, or leadership.

Whatever its nature, giftedness is probably the result of both genetic predispositions and environmental nurturance (Simonton, 2001; Winner, 2000b). Furthermore, it is apt to take different forms in different cultures (recall Chapter 4's discussion of the culture-dependent nature of intelligence). For example, among African American students, giftedness may be reflected in oral language, such as in colorful speech, creative storytelling, or humor (Torrance, 1989). Among Native Americans, giftedness may be reflected in interpersonal skills, such as in sensitivity to the feelings of others or skill at effectively mediating disagreements (Maker & Schiever, 1989). Although some minority students are identified as gifted through traditional intelligence testing, the tendency to rely heavily on such testing is probably a key reason that many minority populations are underrepresented among students classified as gifted (C. R. Harris, 1991; Maker & Schiever, 1989; U.S. Dept. of Education, Office of Civil Rights, 1993).

We must note, too, that gifted students often hide their talents to some degree, making their identification even more difficult. Many students fear that peers will ridicule them for their high academic abilities and enthusiasm for academic topics, especially at the secondary school level (Covington, 1992; DeLisle, 1984). Girls in particular are likely to hide their talents, especially if they have been raised in cultures that do not value high achievement in females (Covington, 1992; Davis & Rimm, 1998). Gifted Asian Americans, because of cultural traditions of obedience, conformity, and respect for authority, may be reluctant to engage in creative activities and may willingly comply when asked to perform unchallenging assignments (Maker & Schiever, 1989).

Common Characteristics

Students who are gifted tend to be quite different from one another in their unique strengths and talents, and students who show exceptional talent in one area may show only average ability in another (Winner, 2000b). Yet many students who are gifted have characteristics such as these:

- More advanced vocabulary, language, and reading skills
- Ability to learn more quickly, easily, and independently than their age-mates
- More advanced and effective cognitive processing and metacognitive skills
- Greater flexibility in ideas and approaches to tasks
- Appearance of formal operational thought processes (e.g., abstract thinking) at an earlier age
- High standards regarding their performance (in a few cases, to the point of unhealthy perfectionism)
- High motivation to achieve on challenging tasks; feelings of boredom about easy tasks
- Positive self-concept, especially with regard to academic endeavors
- Above-average social development and emotional adjustment (although a few extremely gifted students may have difficulties because they are so *very* different from their peers) (Candler-Lotven, Tallent-Runnels, Olivárez, & Hildreth, 1994; Carter & Ormrod, 1982; B. Clark, 1997; Cornell et al., 1990; A. W. Gottfried et al., 1994; Hoge & Renzulli, 1993; Janos & Robinson, 1985; Lupart, 1995; Parker, 1997; Rabinowitz & Glaser, 1985; Winner, 2000a, 2000b)

Angelo, whom we met in the opening case study, exhibits several of these characteristics, including a rich vocabulary, ability to learn independently, and boredom with easy tasks.

We should note here that a student can be gifted and also have a disability. For example, some gifted students have learning disabilities, ADHD, emotional or behavioral disorders, or physical or sensory challenges (Brown-Mizuno, 1990; Hettinger & Knapp, 2001). In such situations, we must address the students' disabilities as well as their unique gifts when we plan instruction.

Adapting Instruction

Why else might some individuals oppose special services for students who are gifted? What is your opinion of such programs?

Why do students who are gifted need special services? Critics of gifted education argue that students with high abilities can certainly achieve normal school objectives without assistance. They also propose that special services for these students foster a certain degree of "elitism," conveying the message that some students are somehow more privileged than others. But consider this statement from someone who was gifted:

> People like me are aware of their so-called genius at ten, eight, nine. . . . I always wondered, "Why has nobody discovered me? In school, didn't they see that I'm more clever than anybody in this school? That the teachers are stupid, too? That all they had was information that I didn't need?" It was obvious to me. Why didn't they put me in art school? Why didn't they train me? I was different, I was always different. Why didn't anybody notice me? (cited in Gardner, 1983, p. 115)

This individual was a well-known public figure in the 1960s and 1970s. Can you guess who he was?

Many students with special gifts and talents become frustrated when their school experiences don't provide tasks and assignments that challenge them and help them develop their unique abilities. Recalling Lev Vygotsky's view of cognitive development from Chapter 2, we could say that gifted students are unlikely to be working within their zone of proximal development if we limit them to the tasks we assign to other students; thus, they are unlikely to develop new cognitive skills. Furthermore, many of these students are bored by typical classroom activities: Instruction seems too slow and often deals with what they already know (Feldhusen, Van Winkel, & Ehle, 1996; Winner, 2000b). As a result, they may lose interest in school tasks and put in only minimal effort (Feldhusen, 1989). In fact, gifted students are among our schools' greatest underachievers; when required to progress at the same rate as their nongifted peers, they achieve at levels far short of their capabilities (Carter, 1991; Gallagher, 1991; Reis, 1989). (By the way, the gifted individual I quoted earlier was John Lennon of the Beatles.)

We can foster the special abilities and talents of gifted students in numerous ways. Following are several strategies that theorists and practitioners recommend:

■ *Provide individualized tasks and assignments.* Even though students who are gifted are a very heterogeneous group, many schools provide the same curriculum and materials for all students whom they've identified as being gifted. In fact, no single program can meet the specific needs of each and every student. Different students may need special services in very different areas—for example, in mathematics, creative writing, or studio art. Some students who are gifted—especially those with limited English background—may even need training in certain basic skills (C. R. Harris, 1991; Udall, 1989).

■ *Form study groups of students with similar interests and abilities.* In any school building, there are likely to be several students who have common interests and abilities, and it may sometimes be helpful to pull them together into study groups where they can cooperatively pursue a particular topic or task (Fiedler, Lange, & Winebrenner, 1993; Stanley, 1980). Forming homogeneous study groups has several advantages. First, a single teacher can meet the needs of several students simultaneously. Second, students appear to benefit both academically and socially from increased contact with other students who have similar interests (J. A. Kulik & Kulik, 1997; McGinn, Viernstein, & Hogan, 1980). And third, students are less likely to try to hide their talent and enthusiasm for the subject matter when they work with classmates who share similar ability and motivation (Feldhusen, 1989).

In some cases, a study group may explore a topic with greater depth and more sophisticated analysis than other students do (an *enrichment* approach). For example, in a geometry class, those students who show high ability might be asked to work together on an exceptionally challenging geometric proof. In other cases, a study group may simply move through the standard school curriculum at a more rapid pace (an *acceleration* approach). For example, students reading well above the level of their classmates might be assigned books not ordinarily encountered until more advanced grade levels.

■ *Teach complex cognitive skills within the context of specific subject areas.* Some programs for the gifted have tried to teach complex thought processes like creativity and problem solving as skills totally separate from school subject matter. But this approach tends to have minimal impact on students' cognitive development; in fact, it often focuses on skills that many students have already acquired. Instead, we are better advised to teach complex thinking skills within the context of specific topics—for example, reasoning and problem solving skills in science, or creativity in writing (M. C. Linn et al., 1989; Moon, Feldhusen, & Dillon, 1994; Pulos & Linn, 1981; Stanley, 1980).

■ *Provide opportunities for independent study.* Many students who are gifted have advanced learning and metacognitive skills and a strong motivation to learn academic subject matter (Candler-Lotven et al., 1994; Lupart, 1995). Accordingly, independent study in topics of interest may be especially appropriate for these students. When we provide opportunities for independent study, however, we should teach students the study habits and research skills they will need to use their time and resources effectively.

■ *Encourage students to set high goals for themselves.* Just as gifted students are capable of higher performance in specific areas, so they should also be setting higher goals for themselves

Students who are identified as gifted show exceptional achievement or promise in general intellectual ability, aptitude in a specific academic field, creativity, leadership, or visual and performing arts.

in those areas. We should encourage students to aim high, while at the same time not asking them to expect perfection for themselves (Patton et al., 1996; Parker, 1997; Sanborn, 1979). For instance, some students may have given little or no thought to attending college, perhaps because their families have never expected them to pursue higher education; under such circumstances, we might give them the opportunity to visit a college campus and explore possible means of funding a college education (Spicker, 1992).

■ *Seek outside resources.* A single school is likely to have students with exceptional potential in so many different areas that no single adult—not even a specialist in gifted education—can reasonably meet all of their needs (L. H. Fox, 1979; Stanley, 1980). It might sometimes be appropriate to identify suitable *mentors*—individuals with expertise in a particular area who help students develop their own talent in that area. In other circumstances, outside agencies—for example, laboratories, government offices, private businesses, volunteer community groups, theater groups, and art and videotaping studios—may provide an arena in which students can develop their unique talents (Ambrose, Allen, & Huntley, 1994; Piirto, 1999; Seeley, 1989).

Considering Diversity When Identifying and Addressing Special Needs

Sadly, a disproportionately large number of students identified as having disabilities are from ethnic minority groups and low-income neighborhoods (McLoyd, 1998; U.S. Dept. of Education, 1996, 1997). At the same time, relatively few students from some minority groups, especially African Americans and Hispanic Americans, are enrolled in programs for the gifted (U.S. Dept. of Education, Office of Civil Rights, 1993).

Most theorists believe that differences in environment account for the disproportionate numbers of students from certain ethnic backgrounds found in special education programs (McLoyd, 1998; H. W. Stevenson et al., 1990). Students from some ethnic minority groups are more likely than their classmates to grow up in lower-income neighborhoods, where lack of adequate medical care, poor prenatal and infant nutrition, maternal drug and alcohol abuse, increased exposure to lead paint (which, if ingested, can cause brain damage), more stressful and violent living conditions, and less access to early educational resources can contribute to lower intellectual functioning and more serious behavior problems (Conlon, 1992; McLoyd, 1998).

The inequitable representation of particular groups in various categories of disabilities poses a dilemma for educators. On the one hand, we don't want to use categories such as *mental retardation* or *emotional or behavioral disorder* for students whose classroom performance and behavior may be due primarily to the adverse environmental conditions in which they have been raised. On the other hand, we also don't want to deprive these students of special educational services that might very well help them learn and achieve more successfully over the long run. In such situations, we need to conduct fair and nondiscriminatory evaluations of students' needs and, if students qualify under a special needs category, create individualized education programs (IEPs) to meet those needs. We should consider these categories of special needs as *temporary* classifications—ones that may no longer be applicable as students' classroom performance improves. The case of Steven, the boy with the "fresh" can of green beans described earlier in the chapter, is a classic example of this approach: Although Steven was initially identified as having mental retardation (which qualified him for special services), he eventually acquired the background knowledge and skills of which he had been deprived during his early years, and by high school he was attending classes as a student with no disability classification whatsoever. It's important to remember that students are identified under a special education category because they need specialized services; all students, with and without disability classifications, have changing needs that evolve over time.

We have already noted some possible reasons for the underrepresentation of some ethnic minority groups in gifted programs. As teachers, it is important to remember that many students from minority groups may not be identified as gifted when traditional intelligence tests and other standardized measures are used. It is critical that we be on the lookout for students who show other signs of special abilities and talents and so are likely to benefit from enriched educational experiences. Here are some examples of traits that may indicate giftedness in students from diverse cultural backgrounds:

- Ability to learn quickly from one's experiences
- Exceptional communication skills (e.g., articulateness, richness of language)
- Originality and resourcefulness in thinking and problem solving
- Ability to generalize what one has learned to other, seemingly unrelated, tasks and ideas
- Unusual sensitivity to the needs and feelings of others
  (Frasier, 1989; Maker & Schiever, 1989; Torrance, 1989)

For the growth of our society over the long run, it is imperative that we nurture the many gifted and talented students that we find in *all* cultural and ethnic groups.

The Big Picture

Let's summarize what we've learned so far about inclusion and categories of special needs. We will then identify a number of strategies that may be equally applicable for most—and in some cases all—students who have special educational needs.

Inclusion

Increasingly, students with special needs are being educated in general education classrooms for part or all of the school day, and such *inclusion* is often beneficial for students' academic, personal, and social development. In the United States, inclusive practices are encouraged by the *Individuals with Disabilities Education Act* (IDEA), which mandates that public schools offer the most typical classroom experience that can reasonably meet the needs of a student with a disability.

Categories of Students with Special Needs

In this chapter we have organized the various kinds of special educational needs into the five general categories used in the Inclusive Settings tables throughout the book. More specific categories are as follows:

Specific Cognitive or Academic Difficulties

- *Learning disabilities:* Difficulties in one or more specific cognitive processing skills, accompanied by average or above-average abilities in other areas
- *Attention-deficit hyperactivity disorder (ADHD):* Disorder characterized by inattention, hyperactivity, and impulsiveness—behaviors that may reflect a more general inability to inhibit inappropriate responses
- *Speech and communication disorders:* Significant impairments in speech or language comprehension

Social and Behavioral Problems

- *Emotional and behavioral disorders:* Disorders characterized by either externalizing behaviors (directed toward others) or internalizing behaviors (directed toward oneself) that significantly interfere with academic performance and, often, with effective interpersonal relationships
- *Autism:* Condition characterized by a marked impairment in social interaction and communication, repetitive behaviors, and narrowly focused interests; may be due to an abnormal sensitivity to environmental stimuli

General Delays in Cognitive and Social Functioning

- *Mental retardation:* Condition characterized by low intellectual functioning across the board, as well as by deficits in adaptive behavior

Physical and Sensory Challenges

- *Physical and health impairments:* Physical conditions that result in reduced energy, alertness, or muscle control
- *Visual impairments:* Malfunction of the eyes or optic nerves that prevents normal sight even with corrective lenses
- *Hearing loss:* Malfunction of the ear or associated nerves that interferes with the perception of sounds within the frequency range of normal human speech
- *Severe and multiple disabilities:* Two or more disabilities that, in combination, require significant adaptations and highly specialized services

Advanced Cognitive Development

- *Giftedness:* Unusually high ability or aptitude in one or more areas

While such categories often give us ideas about how best to serve students with special needs, we must always remember that students in any single category are apt to be more different than they are similar. Accordingly, we must tailor every student's educational program to his or her unique strengths and needs.

Strategies for Helping All Students with Special Needs

Despite the great diversity we are likely to see among our students with special needs, the following recommendations should apply to all of our students with disabilities. Many of them are applicable to our students with advanced cognitive abilities as well.

■ *Obtain as much information as possible about each student.* We must remember that students identified as having a particular special educational need are *individuals* first, each with a unique set of strengths and weaknesses. The more we know about students' specific needs—whether academic, social, behavioral, or medical—the better our position to help each and every student succeed at classroom tasks and activities (e.g., B. A. Keogh & Becker, 1973; Stephens et al., 1988).

■ *Consult and collaborate with specialists.* To help students with special needs, school districts usually employ a variety of educational specialists, including special educators, counselors, school psychologists, nurses, speech pathologists, and physical and occupational therapists. Although some students leave the classroom for part of the day to work with these specialists, the movement toward greater inclusion means that more and more special services are now being provided within the regular classroom context. As classroom teachers, we need to work closely and collaboratively with educational specialists to develop and deliver an appropriate program for each student (B. L. Driver, 1996; Scruggs & Mastropieri, 1994).

■ *Communicate regularly with parents.* In accordance with IDEA, parents are part of the multidisciplinary team that determines the most appropriate program for a student with special needs. A student's parents can provide invaluable information for helping us identify and carry out strategies that are likely to promote the student's academic and social growth. Parents can often tell us what works and what does not, and they can alert us to certain conditions or events at home that may trigger problem behaviors in class. Furthermore, we can more effectively bring about

desired behavioral changes if we have the same expectations for behavior both at school and at home. We should keep in mind, however, that some parents, especially those from certain cultural backgrounds, may believe that educational decisions are better left in the hands of "experts" and that as parents they have little to contribute (DeGangi, Wietlisbach, Poisson, Stein, & Royeen, 1994; Harry, Allen, & McLaughlin, 1995). In some situations, then, we may need to make an extra effort to actively involve parents in planning for their child's educational success. In cultures in which extended families play a key role in children's lives, we may want to get other family members (perhaps grandparents, aunts, or uncles) involved as well.

■ *When reasonable, hold the same expectations for students with disabilities as for other students.* Sometimes disabilities make it difficult or even impossible for students to accomplish particular school tasks. Aside from such tasks, we should generally hold the same expectations for our students with special needs as we hold for other students. Rather than thinking of reasons why a student *cannot* do a particular task, we should instead be thinking about how we can help that student *do* it. In fact, if we think about it, we can identify many people who've achieved great success despite major disabilities. Here are just a few examples (Armstrong, 1994):

- Albert Einstein had a learning disability (dyslexia).
- Vincent Van Gogh and Edgar Allan Poe had emotional problems.
- In the latter part of his career, Ludwig von Beethoven was completely deaf.
- Helen Keller was both deaf and blind.
- Franklin Delano Roosevelt had polio, which left him dependent on a wheelchair.
- Stephen Hawking, the world-renowed astrophysicist, has amyotrophic lateral sclerosis (Lou Gehrig's disease), a progressive neuromuscular disorder that has left him unable to walk, talk, or use pencil and paper.

■ *Identify prerequisite knowledge and skills a student may not have acquired.* Some students lack knowledge and skills essential for their school success, perhaps because of inexperience or perhaps as a direct result of a disability. Students from impoverished home environments may have had little or no exposure to things that many of us take for granted; for instance, if they have never been to a zoo or a farm and if they have never looked at picture books with their parents, then they may have no idea what a lion, elephant, cow, or horse is. Students with reduced physical mobility have probably not had as many opportunities to manipulate objects in their environment. Students with visual impairments have not been able to observe many of the cause-effect relationships that form a foundation for learning science—for instance, the changes in wood's appearance when it is burned (M. B. Rowe, 1978). And students who have had few opportunities to interact with other children may have poorly developed interpersonal skills.

■ *Be flexible in approaches to instruction.* Some instructional methods may work better than others for teaching students with special needs, and we cannot always predict which methods will be most effective for individual students. For example, special educators often try a variety of strategies for helping students with learning disabilities practice and learn their spelling (e.g., having students spell the word aloud, trace the letters with their fingers, type each word on a keyboard). If we don't succeed with a particular approach, we should try again. But each time, we might want to try *differently*.

■ *Include students in planning and decision making.* So far, we have been working on the assumption that we, as teachers, will decide what strategies to use with students who have special educational needs. Although gifted programs often give students a fair amount of autonomy to choose topics and methods of study, educational programs for students with other special needs are often highly structured, to the point where students have little say regarding what and how they learn (Wehmeyer, 1996). But increasingly, special educators are recognizing the importance of letting students with special needs make some choices about academic goals and curriculum (Sands & Wehmeyer, 1996). Student decision making can ultimately promote greater *self-regulation*—increasing independence from, and less need for, the guidance of other people. It can also lead to a greater feeling of *self-determination*—a sense of being able to set one's own life course, which many theorists believe is essential for intrinsic motivation (see Chapters 10 and 12).

By simply talking with students, we can often get a better idea about how best to meet their unique needs. As an example, try the following exercise.

INTERPRETING ARTIFACTS AND INTERACTIONS
The Trouble with School

A researcher asks a junior high school student who is gifted what she believes to be the most serious problem in today's schools. As you read the student's response, consider

- What she most wants to do at school
- What instructional strategies might be most appropriate for her

> They won't let us learn. . . . What I mean is, they seem to think they have to keep us all together all the time. That means in the subjects I'm good at I can't learn more because I'm always waiting for others to catch up. I guess if I get too far ahead I'll be doing the next year's work, but I can't understand what's wrong with that if that's what I'm ready for. (Feldhusen et al., 1996, p. 48)

Clearly, this student wants to learn new things—she wants to be challenged—in her classes, and she is frustrated that she spends much of the school day rehashing material she's already mastered. Her desire to do "next year's work" suggests an acceleration approach, perhaps in a small group or through independent study.

■ *Promote interaction between students with special needs and their nondisabled classmates.* One feature often found in classrooms where students with special needs thrive is frequent interaction between these students and their nondisabled classmates (Scruggs & Mastropieri, 1994). Such interaction is likely to enhance the social skills of our nondisabled students as well as those with special needs.

Yet positive social interaction does not necessarily happen on its own (Hymel, 1986; Juvonen & Hiner, 1991; Yuker, 1988). Some students with special needs are readily welcomed by their nondisabled peers. Others are poorly accepted, sometimes even rejected or victimized, by their classmates (Cook & Semmel, 1999; Morrison, Furlong, & Smith, 1994; Yuker, 1988). For a variety of reasons, some students with disabilities may not know how, or may be less able, to develop and maintain friendly relationships. And nondisabled classmates may feel resentment or anger about inappropriate behaviors that they believe a classmate should be able to control (Juvonen, 1991; Juvonen & Hiner, 1991). Thus, nondisabled students are often willing to accept students with obvious physical or sensory disabilities (such as cerebral palsy or deafness) but may reject students who behave differently without an obvious physical reason for doing so (Madden & Slavin, 1983; Semmel, Gottlieb, & Robinson, 1979; Ysseldyke & Algozzine, 1984).

To pave the way for a smooth integration of students with special needs into our classrooms, we must take steps to promote appropriate social interactions between these students and their nondisabled peers. Following are several strategies:

1. *Teach effective social skills.* Some students may need explicit instruction in how to share, how to cooperate in work and play, how to initiate a conversation, or how to respond appropriately to the statements and questions of others (Bassett et al., 1996; S. Vaughn, 1991).

2. *Provide examples of effective interaction.* It is often helpful to illustrate effective social interaction taking place. For instance, we can use books, plays, or puppet shows to show people with and without disabilities forming friendships, working cooperatively, or being mutually helpful (Aiello, 1988).

3. *Ask students with and without disabilities to assist their classmates.* We might ask a hearing student to take notes for a student with hearing loss or a physical disability, or we might ask a student who is blind to help a nondisabled classmate identify the sounds of particular instruments in a musical score. In addition to promoting greater social interaction, such "giving," prosocial behaviors also help build a *community of learners,* an idea we will consider in Chapter 7.

4. *Provide opportunities for cooperation on academic tasks and in recreation.* We can encourage interaction through such instructional strategies as cooperative learning and peer tutoring (both strategies are described in Chapter 13). We can also provide toys and games that require the participation of several students (DuPaul, Ervin, Hook, & McGoey, 1998; Madden & Slavin, 1983; Martin, Brady, & Williams, 1991).

5. *Encourage students with special needs to participate in extracurricular activities and community events.* Activities outside the classroom provide an additional arena in which friendships between students with and without disabilities can form (Turnbull, Pereira, & Blue-Banning, 2000). For instance, I think of Gabe, a student with Down syndrome and mild mental retardation who attended school in my hometown when I lived in Colorado. Gabe was an avid sportsman, participating in his school's swimming and football teams. I remember once seeing him at a swim meet; although he was clearly in last place in his event, Gabe's teammates cheered him on throughout the race and, after he finished, congratulated him and gave him "high fives" for his performance.

6. *Develop nondisabled students' understanding of students with special needs.* Many of our nondisabled students may need to be educated not only about students' disabilities but also about the *strengths* that these students have. We must communicate the message that, in many ways, students with special needs are normal children with the same thoughts, feelings, and needs as other children their age. As an example, consider the messages that one teacher, Mr. Fields, conveyed about Danny, a boy with mental retardation. Mr. Fields often publicly described Danny as someone who had better manners than many of his classmates and was, in general, "hard not to like." When he asked Danny questions about classroom subject matter, Mr. Fields would discourage other students from providing the answers for Danny by saying something such as, "No, no, no, I'm asking him. I want to know what *he's* thinking" (Turnbull et al., 2000).

■ *Look for gradual improvement rather than overnight success.* Because many students with disabilities are likely to improve slowly and gradually, we should look for small, day-to-day improvements rather than expect immediate perfection. By focusing on small improvements, we and our students alike can be encouraged by the changes we do see rather than being discouraged by any problems that persist (Gearheart et al., 1992; Patton et al., 1996).

■ *Individualize instruction for all students.* Students with special needs blend in better with their classmates when instruction is individualized for everyone. This way, they are not singled out by virtue of any special attention or help they receive. Thus, to the extent that our time and resources allow us to do so, we should try to individualize instruction for *all* students (T. Bryan, 1991; Madden & Slavin, 1983; M. C. Reynolds & Birch, 1988). When instruction is individually tailored to each and every student's unique needs, everyone benefits.

■ *Keep your eyes open for students who may qualify for special services.* When students have physical challenges (e.g., when they have a chronic illness or sensory impairment), their disability is typically identified outside of school, in many cases long before they ever set foot in a classroom. But students' nonphysical needs—those in the cognitive, social, and behavioral domains—often go unidentified for months, perhaps even years, after children begin their formal schooling.

As we gain experience as teachers, we become increasingly aware of what abilities and behaviors are typical for a particular age-group, and so we are often in an excellent position to identify children who are *atypical* in one way or another. While we will need to depend on some of our more specialized colleagues (school psychologists, counselors, etc.) to conduct the in-depth assessments necessary to identify a particular disability or area of giftedness, the job of referring our students for such assessments—and thereby gaining them access to the special services they may need—will ultimately be up to us. The final case study illustrates this very important role.

PRAXIS Turn to Appendix C, "Matching Book and Ancillary Content to the PRAXIS™ Principles of Learning and Teaching Tests," to discover sections of this chapter that may be especially applicable to the PRAXIS™ tests.

Now go to our Companion Website at http://www.prenhall.com/ormrod to assess your understanding of chapter content with "Multiple-Choice Questions," apply comprehension in "Essay Questions," broaden your knowledge of educational psychology with related "Web Links," gain greater insight about classroom learning in "Learning in the Content Areas," and analyze and assess classroom work in the "Student Artifact Library."

CASE STUDY: Quiet Amy

Mr. Mahoney has been teaching kindergarten for fifteen years, and he has learned through experience that many kindergartners have some temporary difficulty adjusting to the school environment, especially if they haven't previously attended daycare or preschool. But Amy is giving him cause for concern; after being in his class for almost two months, her behavior has changed very little from what it was on the first day of school. Amy never speaks, either to him or to the other children, even when she is directly spoken to; on the infrequent occasions when she wants to communicate—perhaps to express her desire for a particular object or her distress about a classroom event—she does so primarily by looking and pointing at something or someone in the room. She has trouble following even the simplest directions, almost as if she hasn't heard what she's been instructed to do. And she appears distracted during the daily storybook readings and science lessons. The only activities that seem to give her pleasure are arts and crafts; she enjoys working with construction paper, crayons, scissors, and glue, and her creations are often among the most inventive in the class.

To see if he can identify the root of Amy's difficulties, Mr. Mahoney visits her mother, a single woman raising five other children in addition to Amy. "Amy doesn't talk at home, either," the mother admits. "I work two jobs to make ends meet, and I haven't been able to spend as much time with her as I'd like. Her brothers and sisters take good care of her, though. They always seem to know what she wants, and they make sure that she has it."

"My conversation with Mom didn't give me any ideas about how to help Amy," Mr. Mahoney thinks as he drives home after his visit. "It does seem, though, that Amy's primary caretakers are her brothers and sisters, who probably mean well by always responding to her nonverbal behaviors but are doing nothing to encourage her to speak. When I get to school tomorrow morning, my first order of business will be to refer Amy for an in-depth evaluation."

■ Mr. Mahoney suspects that Amy may qualify for special educational services. If she does, in what category of special needs might she fall? Can you develop at least three *different* hypotheses as to where her difficulties may lie?

■ Amy's evaluation will undoubtedly take several weeks to complete. In the meantime, what strategies might Mr. Mahoney try to improve Amy's classroom performance?

Once you have answered these questions, compare your responses with those presented in Appendix B.

Key Concepts

students with special needs (p. 143)

inclusion (p. 144)

self-contained class (p. 144)

mainstreaming (p. 145)

Individuals with Disabilities Education Act (IDEA) (p. 145)

least restrictive environment (p. 147)

individualized education program (IEP) (p. 147)

cooperative teaching (p. 149)

people-first language (p. 151)

learning disabilities (p. 153)

mnemonic (p. 155)

attention-deficit hyperactivity disorder (ADHD) (p. 156)

speech and communication disorders (p. 158)

emotional and behavioral disorders (p. 160)

externalizing behavior (p. 160)

internalizing behavior (p. 160)

autism (p. 163)

savant syndrome (p. 164)

mental retardation (p. 166)

adaptive behavior (p. 166)

physical and health impairments (p. 169)

visual impairments (p. 171)

hearing loss (p. 172)

severe and multiple disabilities (p. 173)

giftedness (p. 177)

6

Learning and Cognitive Processes

*W*hat do you mean when you say that you have *learned* something? Do you think differently about some aspect of the world than you did previously? Has your behavior improved or otherwise changed in some way? What specific changes have actually taken place as a result of your learning?

We are always learning new things. As children, we learn a variety of motor skills, such as eating with a fork, holding a pencil, and writing the letters of the alphabet. We also learn innumerable pieces of information, such as the spelling of the word *cat*, the meaning of *atom*, and the location of the Panama Canal. Furthermore, we learn patterns and relationships among pieces of information, such as the "at" pattern found in words like *cat* and *sat*, the relationship between atoms and molecules, and the role that the Panama Canal plays in world trade. And we learn that certain situations call for certain behaviors; for instance, we raise our hands when we wish to speak in class, turn in an assignment on the day it is due, and apologize when we have hurt someone else's feelings.

Human learning—a complex, multifaceted process that often involves changes in both thinking and behavior—is the topic of Part 2 of the book, "Understanding How Students Learn." The first three chapters examine the cognitive processes involved in learning, focusing on basic principles of cognition (Chapters 6 and 7) and complex thinking skills (Chapter 8). Chapters 9 and 10 look at the ways in which behavior often changes as people learn and at the environmental conditions that bring about such changes. Finally, Chapters 11 and 12 describe the numerous effects of motivation on cognition, behavior, and learning.

This chapter addresses the following questions:

- What is *learning*, and what general theoretical perspectives can we use to describe and explain it?
- What basic assumptions and concepts are central to cognitive psychologists' beliefs about learning?
- What is the nature of human memory?
- What cognitive processes are involved in learning (*storing*) something new, and how can teachers best help students use these processes?
- What factors influence students' ability to remember (*retrieve*) information over the long run, and why do students sometimes forget what they've previously learned?
- What are the advantages of giving students time to process classroom material?

To learn about the specific forms that thinking and learning may take in reading, writing, mathematics, science, and social studies, read the chapter "Learning in the Content Areas" in the *Study Guide and Reader* that accompanies this book.

CASE STUDY: *Darren's Day at School*

At the dinner table one night, Darren's mother asks him, "How was your day at school?"

Darren shrugs, thinks for a moment, and says, "OK, I guess."

"What did you learn?" his father asks.

"Nothing much," Darren replies.

Nothing much, indeed! Let's look at several slices of Darren's school day and see how much he actually *did* learn.

During his daily math lesson, Darren is studying the multiplication tables for the number 9. He finds that some multiplication facts are easy to learn because he can relate them to things he already knows; for example, $9 \times 2 = 18$ is like adding 9 plus 9, and $9 \times 5 = 45$ can be derived from counting by fives. Others, such as $9 \times 4 = 36$ and $9 \times 8 = 72$, are more difficult because he can't connect them to any number facts he has learned before. When Ms. Caffarella finds Darren and a few of his classmates struggling, she teaches the class two tricks for learning the nines multiplication table:

1. The first digit in the product is 1 less than the number by which 9 is being multiplied. For 9×6, the first digit in the product must be $6 - 1$, or 5.
2. The two digits of the product, when added together, equal nine. Because 5 plus 4 equal 9, the product of 9×6 must be 54.

With these two tricks, Darren discovers a pattern in the nines table that helps him recite the table correctly.

During a geography lesson, Ms. Caffarella describes the trip she took to Greece last summer. She holds up a picture postcard of the Parthenon and explains that the building is constructed entirely of marble. Darren is sitting near the back of the room and can't see the picture very clearly; he envisions a building made entirely of marbles and silently wonders how the ancient Greeks managed to glue them all together.

In physical education, Darren's class has begun a unit on soccer. Darren has never played soccer before, and his first attempts to move and control the ball with his feet are clumsy and inept. His teacher watches his footwork closely, praising him when he moves his feet appropriately, and eventually Darren is dribbling and passing the ball successfully to his classmates.

In the afternoon's art lesson, Darren's class is making papier-mâché masks. His friend Carla gives her mask a very large nose by adding a crumpled wad of paper below the eye holes and then covering and shaping the wad with several pieces of glued paper. Darren watches her closely throughout the process and then makes a nose for his mask in a similar way.

- What has Darren learned during his math, geography, physical education, and art lessons? Can you identify one or more principles of learning that might describe what has happened in each situation?

Looking at Learning from Different Perspectives

Despite his apparent amnesia at the dinner table, Darren has clearly learned a number of things at school that day, including the nines table in multiplication, the "fact" that the Parthenon was made with marbles, some rudimentary techniques for moving a soccer ball, and a strategy for sculpting with papier-mâché.

But exactly what do we mean by the word **learning?** Theorists disagree about how to define the term. Some propose a definition such as this one:

Definition 1:

Learning is a relatively permanent change in behavior due to experience.

Others propose a definition along these lines:

Definition 2:

Learning is a relatively permanent change in mental associations due to experience.

How are these two definitions similar? How are they different?

You may notice two ways in which the definitions are similar. First, both describe learning as a *relatively permanent change*—something that lasts for a period of time. Second, the change is *due to experience*. It results from specific experiences that students have had—perhaps a lesson in multiplication, a teacher's description of the Parthenon, soccer instruction, or the opportunity to watch a classmate work with papier-mâché.

But now look at how our two definitions differ. The first one describes learning as a change in *behavior,* the second one as a change in *mental associations.* In Darren's day at school, we see several examples of learning as a change in behavior: Darren recites the nines tables correctly for the first time, shows improvement in his ability to dribble a soccer ball, and tries a new way of shaping papier-mâché. We also see several examples of learning as a change in

Not all changes reflect learning; some are short-lived and unrelated to specific experiences. For example, feelings of fatigue, stomachaches, and eye blinks are temporary, and students soon return to their original alert, healthy, and open-eyed states.

mental associations: Darren relates $9 \times 2 = 18$ to $9 + 9 = 18$, relates the marble in the Parthenon to the marbles he has at home, and remembers the steps that his friend Carla used to make a nose.

Some learning theories focus on how people's behaviors change over time and on the environmental conditions that bring such changes about. Other theories focus more on internal mental processes—on thinking—than on observable behaviors. Let's look briefly at each of these approaches.

From a teacher's perspective, what are the potential advantages of defining learning as a change in behavior? as a change in mental associations?

Learning as a Change in Behavior

A problem we encounter when we study "thinking" is that we can never actually *see* thought processes such as "remembering," "paying attention," or "studying." All we can really observe is behavior: what people do and say. For example, we can't really observe Karl "remember"; we can only hear him say, "Oh, yes, now I remember . . . the capital of Spain is Madrid." We cannot truly determine whether Karen is "paying attention"; we can only see whether she is directing her eyes toward the teacher. Nor do we know that Keith is "studying" simply because we see him looking at his textbook.

Before the turn of the century, many psychologists attempted to study thinking and learning by asking people to "look" inside their own minds and describe what they were thinking (i.e., to engage in *introspection*). But beginning in the early 1900s, some psychologists began to criticize this approach for its subjectivity and lack of scientific rigor. They proposed that to study learning in an objective, scientific manner, theorists must focus on two things that can be observed: people's behaviors (**responses**) and the environmental events (**stimuli**) that precede and follow those responses. Since then, many psychologists have attempted to describe and understand learning and behavior primarily through an analysis of stimulus-response relationships. Such psychologists are called *behaviorists*, and their theories of learning are collectively known as **behaviorism.**

We see an example of the behaviorist perspective in action in Darren's physical education class. The teacher watches Darren's *footwork* (his responses) and gives him *praise* (a stimulus) when he makes the right moves. Rather than worry about what Darren might be thinking about soccer, the teacher focuses exclusively on Darren's behavior and provides a desirable consequence when it shows improvement. The teacher is applying a simple behaviorist principle: *A response that is followed by a desired (reinforcing) stimulus is more likely to occur again.*

Learning as a Change in Mental Associations

During the first half of the twentieth century, many psychologists adhered to the behaviorist perspective, especially in North America. As the years went by, however, it became increasingly clear that behaviorism alone could not give us a complete picture of learning. For example, early behaviorists believed that learning can occur only when learners actually behave in some way—perhaps when they make a response and experience the consequences of that response. But in the 1940s, some psychologists proposed that people can also learn a new behavior simply by watching and imitating what *other* people do (N. E. Miller & Dollard, 1941). This idea of *modeling* provided the impetus for an alternative perspective that considers how people learn from observing those around them. Originally called *social learning theory,* this perspective has increasingly incorporated cognitive processes into its explanations of learning; it is now more commonly called **social cognitive theory.**

We find an example of modeling in Darren's experience with the papier-mâché masks. Darren watches Carla as she makes a nose for her mask; after she finishes, he follows the same steps. Notice that Darren imitates what Carla has done only after she has already completed her nose; hence, he makes his nose by using his *memory* of what he has previously observed Carla do. According to social cognitive theorists, learning itself occurs at the time that observation takes place; a behavior change as a result of that learning may or may not occur. For example, Darren might possibly watch Carla and remember what she has done, yet choose *not* to make his nose in the same way.

Social cognitive theory proposes that people can learn a new behavior simply by watching and imitating what other people do.

By the 1960s, many learning theorists were beginning to realize that they could not completely understand learning unless they considered thinking as well as behavior, and they began to conceptualize learning as a mental rather than a behavioral change. These psychologists shifted their attention away from a detailed analysis of stimulus-response relationships

FIGURE 6.1   The evolution of
learning theories

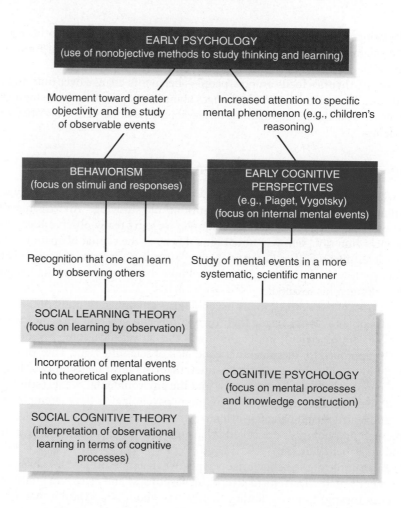

and focused more on the thought processes involved in learning new knowledge and skills. A perspective known as **cognitive psychology**—one that addressed such mental phenomena as memory, attention, concept learning, problem solving, and reasoning—soon emerged (e.g., Neisser, 1967). Some cognitive psychologists have incorporated the ideas of such early theorists as Jean Piaget and Lev Vygotsky into their explanations of how people learn. (My description of the evolution of learning theories is depicted graphically in Figure 6.1.)

What about behaviorists' concern that thinking cannot be studied objectively? Cognitive and social cognitive theorists propose that by observing people's responses to various stimuli, it is possible to draw *inferences*—to make educated guesses—about the internal mental events that probably underlie those responses. As an example of how we might learn about thought processes by observing people's behaviors, turn back to "Mental Maneuver," the Experiencing Firsthand exercise in Chapter 2. If you have not already done the exercise, do it now.

Did you write the words down in the order in which you read them? Probably not. If you are like most people, then you recalled the words by category—perhaps flowers first, then tools, then fruit. From the order in which you wrote the words (from your *behavior*), we can draw an inference about an internal cognitive process that occurred as you learned the words: You mentally *organized* them into categories.

Researchers are certainly not the only ones who can draw inferences about cognitive processes from observable behaviors; we, as teachers, can do likewise. By observing what our students say and write, by asking them to explain their reasoning, by looking closely at their mistakes, and so on, we can make some educated guesses about what and how they are thinking about classroom topics.

Can you think of examples of how scientists in other disciplines have drawn inferences about unobservable phenomena?

Learning and the Brain

Regardless of the perspective we take to understand learning, we can reasonably assume that learning has a biological basis in the brain. The neuropsychology of learning is a very young science and, to date, gives us only the most general picture of how and where learning occurs. For example, we know from animal studies that learning results in an increase in both the size and number of the interconnections (**synapses**) between brain cells (**neurons**) (R. D. Hawkins & Bower, 1989; A. M. Turner & Greenough, 1985). We know, too, that most of the mental "action" during learning and memory tasks takes place in the upper, caplike part of the brain known as the **cortex** (e.g., Kimberg, D'Esposito, & Farah, 1997; Nadel & Jacobs, 1998; E. E. Smith, 2000). As you may recall from Chapter 2, the cortex is also the part of the brain that changes most during the school years.

I occasionally hear educators talking about applying "brain research" in the classroom. When I listen closely to what they are saying, they are typically talking about what we have learned from studies of *behavior* rather than from studies of brain anatomy and physiology. Although studies of the brain may some day give us some ideas about how best to help children and adolescents learn, for the time being we must turn to psychology rather than biology for guidance about effective teaching strategies (e.g., see Bruer, 1997).

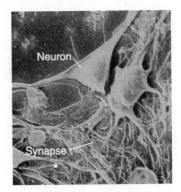

Learning is, at least in part, a process of forming new connections (synapses), as well as modifying existing ones, among brain cells (neurons). This photo shows neurons in the cortex of the human brain.

Keeping an Open Mind About Theories of Learning

The three psychological perspectives of learning we will consider in this book—behaviorism, social cognitive theory, and cognitive psychology—encompass different views of several fundamental issues. As a result, each perspective will take us in a somewhat different direction as we explore the nature of human learning. Yet keep in mind that no single theoretical orientation gives a complete picture of how people learn. All three perspectives offer valuable lessons for helping our students achieve in the classroom.

In terms of the number of articles published in professional journals and the number of presentations given at professional conferences, cognitive psychology's view of learning is the one most in vogue at present (e.g., Robins, Gosling, & Craik, 1999). Hence, this is the perspective we will take as we begin our exploration of how we can help our students learn effectively in classroom settings, and we will rely on it almost exclusively in Chapters 6 through 8. When we shift our attention to behaviorism in Chapter 9, we will find that we can help students learn more appropriate and productive behaviors if we identify environmental stimuli that promote such behaviors. I have saved social cognitive theory for Chapter 10 because it integrates elements of both cognitive psychology and behaviorism; at that point, we will consider several topics that have implications for classroom practice, including modeling, self-efficacy, and self-regulation. As we discuss motivation in Chapters 11 and 12, we will find that all three perspectives provide useful strategies for helping our students *want* to learn.

Basic Assumptions of Cognitive Psychology

Underlying cognitive psychology are several basic assumptions about how people learn. These assumptions, summarized in Table 6.1, are as follows:

What concepts and principles can you recall from the discussion of information processing theory in Chapter 2?

■ *Cognitive processes influence the nature of what is learned.* As noted earlier, cognitive psychologists view learning as an internal mental phenomenon, not an external behavior change. Furthermore, how people think about and interpret their experiences affects what they learn from those experiences. Cognitive psychologists have offered numerous explanations for how people mentally process information; many of these theories are collectively known as **information processing theory**.

As an illustration of the role that cognitive processes play, consider how Darren relates $9 \times 2 = 18$ to $9 + 9 = 18$ and relates $9 \times 5 = 45$ to counting by fives. Consider, too, how the teacher's description of a pattern in the nines table helps Darren remember more difficult facts such as $9 \times 8 = 72$. These two examples illustrate two principles from cognitive psychology: (1) *People learn new information more easily when they can relate it to something they already know*, and (2) *People learn several pieces of new information more easily when they can relate them to an overall organizational structure.*

This focus on the nature of cognitive processes can be extremely helpful to us as teachers. We must consider not only *what* we want our students to learn but also *how* they can most effectively learn it.

TABLE 6.1

PRINCIPLES/ASSUMPTIONS

Basic Assumptions of Cognitive Psychology and Their Educational Implications

ASSUMPTION	EDUCATIONAL IMPLICATION	EXAMPLE
Influence of cognitive processes	Encourage students to think about class material in ways that will help them remember it.	When introducing the concept *mammal*, ask students to identify numerous examples.
Selectivity about what is learned	Help students identify the most important things for them to learn. Also help them understand why these things are important.	Give students questions that they should try to answer as they read their textbooks. Include questions that ask them to apply what they read to their own lives.
Construction of meaning	Provide experiences that will help students make sense of the topics they are studying.	When studying Nathaniel Hawthorne's *The Scarlet Letter*, ask students to get together in small groups to discuss possible reasons why Reverend Arthur Dimmesdale refuses to acknowledge that he is the father of Hester Prynne's baby.
Role of prior knowledge and beliefs	Relate new ideas to what students already know and believe about the world.	When introducing the vocabulary word *debut* to Mexican American students, relate it to *quinceañera*, a "coming-out" party that many Mexican American families hold for their 15-year-old daughters.
Active involvement in learning	Plan classroom activities that get students actively thinking about and using classroom subject matter.	To help students understand latitude and longitude, ask them to track the path of a hurricane using a series of latitude-longitude coordinates obtained on the Internet.

It is useful to distinguish between *sensation*—one's ability to sense stimuli in the environment—and *perception*—one's interpretation of stimuli. What the body senses is not always perceived (interpreted).

■ *People are selective about what they process and learn.* People are constantly bombarded with information. For example, consider the various stimuli you are encountering at this very moment. How many separate stimuli appear on these two open pages of your textbook? How many objects do you see right now *in addition to* your textbook? How many sounds are reaching your ears? How many objects—on your fingertips, on your toes, at your back, around your waist—do you feel? I suspect that you had been ignoring most of these stimuli until just now; you were not processing them until I asked you to do so. People can handle only so much information at a given time, and so they must be selective: They focus on what they think is important and ignore everything else.

As an analogy, consider the hundreds of items that a typical household receives in the mail each year, including all the packages, letters, bills, brochures, catalogs, fliers, advertisements, requests for donations, and sweepstakes announcements. Do you open, examine, and respond to every piece of mail? Probably not. If you're like me, then you "process" only a few key items (e.g., packages, letters, bills, and some miscellaneous things that catch your eye). You may inspect other items long enough to know that you don't need them; you may even discard some items without opening them at all.

In much the same way, our students will encounter a great deal of new information every day—information delivered by way of teacher instruction, textbooks, bulletin boards, classmates' behaviors, and so on. They will inevitably make choices as to which pieces of information are most important. They will select a few stimuli to examine and respond to in depth, give other stimuli just a cursory glance, and ignore other stimuli altogether. As teachers, we must help our students make wise decisions about the pieces of information they choose to attend to, process, and save.

■ *Meaning is constructed by the learner, rather than being derived directly from the environment.* The process of **construction** lies at the core of many cognitive theories of learning: Peo-

FIGURE 6.2 Can you construct a person from each of these pictures?

From "Age in the Development of Closure Ability in Children" by C. M. Mooney, 1957, *Canadian Journal of Psychology*, 11, p. 220. Copyright 1957. Canadian Psychological Association. Reprinted with permission.

ple take many separate pieces of information and use them to create an understanding or interpretation of the world around them (e.g., Bransford & Franks, 1971; Hegland & Andre, 1992; Marshall, 1992; Neisser, 1967). To experience the process of construction firsthand, try the following exercise.

EXPERIENCING FIRSTHAND   *Three Faces*

Figure 6.2 contains three pictures. What do you see in each one? Most people perceive the picture on the left as being that of a woman, even though many of her features are missing. Enough features are visible—an eye, parts of the nose, mouth, chin, and hair—that you can construct a meaningful perception from them. Is enough information available in the other two figures for you to construct two more faces? Construction of a face from the figure on the right may take you a while, but it can be done.

Objectively speaking, the three groups of black splotches in Figure 6.2, and especially the two on the right, leave a lot to the imagination. For example, the woman in the middle is missing half of her face, and the man on the right is missing the top of his head. Yet knowing how human faces typically appear was probably enough to enable you to add the missing features (mentally) and perceive a complete picture. Curiously, once you have constructed faces from the figures, they then seem obvious. If you were to close this book now and not pick it up again for a week or more, you would probably see the faces almost immediately, even if you had had considerable difficulty perceiving them originally.

We see the process of construction in our case study as well. When Ms. Caffarella describes the Parthenon's marble construction, Darren envisions a building made of marbles similar to the ones he has at home (such a misconception has been described by Sosniak & Stodolsky, 1994). He combines new information with what he already knows to construct meaning.

Some cognitive theories focus primarily on the ways that learners construct knowledge; many of these theories are collectively known as **constructivism**. We first encountered the constructivist perspective in Chapter 2: As early as the 1920s, Jean Piaget proposed that children construct their own understandings of the world based on their experiences with their physical and social environments.

As teachers, we must remember that our students won't necessarily learn information exactly as we present it to them; in fact, they will each interpret classroom subject matter in their own, idiosyncratic ways. In some cases our students, like Darren, may even learn *mis*information. Accordingly, we should frequently monitor students' understanding by asking questions, encouraging dialogue, and listening carefully to students' ideas and explanations.

■ *Prior knowledge and beliefs play a major role in the meanings that people construct.* Perhaps the major reason that different students in the same classroom learn different things is that they have different bodies of knowledge and beliefs from which to draw as

This student might have more prior knowledge about shellfish and other sea creatures because of her recent trip to Florida.

they interpret new information and events. Students all have their own personal histories, and they are likely to come from a wide variety of neighborhoods and cultural backgrounds. Most cognitive psychologists believe that existing understandings of the world have a major influence on what and how effectively people can learn from their experiences. We will repeatedly see the effects of prior knowledge and beliefs in this and the next two chapters.

■ *People are actively involved in their own learning.* As should be clear by now, cognitive psychologists do not believe that people simply "absorb" knowledge from their surroundings. Instead, people are, and in fact *must be,* active participants in their own learning. Cognitive processing and knowledge construction require a certain amount of mental "work." In our discussion of memory in the pages ahead, we will begin to find out what this work involves—in other words, what our students must do (mentally) to learn effectively.

Basic Terminology in Cognitive Psychology

Four concepts—memory, storage, encoding, and retrieval—will be important in our upcoming discussions of the cognitive processes involved in learning.

Memory. The term **memory** refers to learners' ability to "save" things (mentally) that they have previously learned. In some instances, we will use the term to refer to the actual process of saving learned knowledge or skills over a period of time. In other instances, it will refer to a "location"—perhaps *working memory* or *long-term memory*—where learners "put" what they learn.

Storage. The term **storage** refers to the acquisition of new knowledge—the process of putting what is learned into memory in the first place. For example, you have, I hope, been *storing* the ideas that you have been reading in this chapter. And each time you go to class, you undoubtedly store some of the ideas presented in the lecture or class discussion. You may store other information from class as well—perhaps the name of the person sitting next to you (George), the shape and size of the classroom (rectangular, about 15 by 30 meters), or the pattern of the instructor's shirt (orange and purple horizontal stripes).

Encoding. We don't always store information exactly as we receive it. We usually modify it in some way; that is, we **encode** it. For example, when you listen to a story, you may picture some of the story's events in your mind. When you see that orange and purple striped shirt, you may think, "Hmmm, this instructor has really bad taste."

People frequently store information in a different way from how it was presented to them. For example, they may change information from auditory to visual form, as when they form a mental picture of a story they are listening to. Or they may change information from visual to auditory form, as when they read aloud a passage from a textbook. Furthermore, encoding often involves assigning specific *meanings* and *interpretations* to stimuli and events. As an illustration, try this exercise.

EXPERIENCING FIRSTHAND   *The Old Sea Dog at the Admiral Benbow Inn*

Read the following passage *one time only:*

> He was a very silent man by custom. All day he hung round the cove, or upon the cliffs, with a brass telescope; all evening he sat in a corner of the parlour next the fire, and drank rum and water very strong. Mostly he would not speak when spoken to; only look up sudden and fierce, and blow through his nose like a fog-horn; and we and the people who came about our house soon learned to let him be. Every day, when he came back from his stroll, he would ask if any seafaring men had gone by along the road. At first we thought it was the want of company of his own kind that made him ask this question; but at last we began to see he was desirous to avoid them. When a seaman put up at the "Admiral Benbow" (as now and then some did, making by the coast road for Bristol), he would look in at him through the curtained door before he entered the parlour; and he was always sure to be as silent as a mouse when any such was present. For me, at least, there was no secret about the matter; for I was, in a way, a sharer in his alarms. He had taken me aside one day, and promised me a silver fourpenny on the first of

every month if I would only keep my "weather-eye open for a seafaring man with one leg," and let him know the moment he appeared. Often enough, when the first of the month came round, and I applied to him for my wage, he would only blow through his nose at me, and stare me down; but before the week was out he was sure to think better of it, bring me my fourpenny piece, and repeat his orders to look out for "the seafaring man with one leg." (from Robert Louis Stevenson's *Treasure Island*)

Now that you have finished the passage, take a few minutes to write down as much of the passage as you can remember.

As you reflected on the passage you had just read, you probably remembered that the man was afraid of a one-legged seafarer. You may also have recalled that the man paid the story's narrator some money to keep an eye out for such an individual. But could you remember *each and every detail* about the events that took place? Could you recall the *exact words* that the author used to describe the man's behavior? If you are like most people, you stored the gist of the passage (its general meaning) without necessarily storing the specific words. This tendency to encode gist rather than verbatim information increases as children get older (Brainerd, Reyna, Howe, & Kingma, 1990).

Retrieval.   Once you have stored information in your memory, you may later discover that you need to use the information. The process of remembering previously stored information—that is, "finding" the information in memory—is called **retrieval**. The following exercise illustrates this process.

Think of an exam you have taken recently. Which student would have done better on that exam: one who had encoded course information verbatim or one who had encoded its meanings?

EXPERIENCING FIRSTHAND   *Retrieval Practice*

See how quickly you can answer each of the following questions:

1. What is your name?
2. In what year did World War II end?
3. What is the capital of Spain?
4. What did you have for dinner three years ago today?
5. When talking about serving appetizers at a party, we sometimes use a French term instead of the word *appetizer*. What is that French term, and how is it spelled?

As you probably just noticed when you tried to answer these questions, retrieving information from memory is sometimes an easy, effortless process; for example, you undoubtedly had little difficulty remembering your name. But other things stored in memory can be retrieved only after some thought and effort; for example, it may have taken you some time to remember that World War II ended in 1945 and that the capital of Spain is Madrid. Still other things, even though they may have been stored in memory at one time, may never be retrieved at all; perhaps a dinner menu three years ago and the correct spelling of *hors d'oeuvre* fall into this category.

How is information stored and encoded in memory? And what factors influence the ease with which we can retrieve it later? Let's take a look at a model of how human memory might work.

A Model of Human Memory

Cognitive psychologists do not agree about the exact nature of human memory. But many of them believe that memory may have three components: a sensory register, a working (short-term) memory, and a long-term memory.[1] A three-component model of human

---

[1]Some models of memory also include a *central executive*, which oversees the flow of information throughout the memory system. However, theorists have yet to pin down its exact nature, and its functions seem to overlap with those of working memory (Kimberg et al., 1997). For simplicity, I have left a central executive out of the model presented here.

FIGURE 6.3 A model of the human memory system

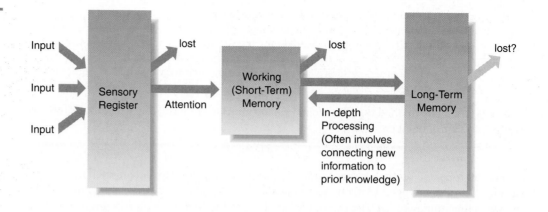

memory, based loosely on one proposed by Atkinson and Shiffrin in 1968 but modified to reflect more recent research findings, is presented in Figure 6.3. Please note that in referring to three components of memory, I am *not* necessarily referring to three separate parts of the brain. The model of memory that I describe has been derived from studies of human behavior, not from studies of the brain. In the pages that follow, we will look at the characteristics of each component of memory and at how information is moved from one component to the next.

The Nature of the Sensory Register

If you have ever played with a lighted sparkler at night, then you've undoubtedly noticed the tail of light that follows a sparkler as you wave it about. If you have ever daydreamed in class, then you may have noticed that when you tune back in to the lecture, you can still "hear" three or four words spoken just *before* you started paying attention to your instructor again. The sparkler's tail and the words that linger after they have already been spoken are not "out there" in the environment—they are recorded in your sensory register.

The **sensory register** is the component of memory that holds the information you receive—*input*—in more or less its original, *unencoded* form. Probably everything that your body is capable of seeing, hearing, and otherwise sensing is stored in the sensory register. In other words, the sensory register has a *large capacity;* it can hold a great deal of information at one time.

That's the good news. The bad news is that information stored in the sensory register doesn't last very long (Cowan, 1995; Wingfield & Byrnes, 1981). Visual information—what you *see*—probably lasts for less than a second. As a child, I never could spell out my entire first name (Jeanne) with a sparkler; the *J* had always faded before I got to the first *N*, no matter how quickly I wrote. Auditory information—what you *hear*—probably lasts slightly longer, perhaps for two or three seconds. To keep information for any time at all, then, we need to move it to *working memory*. Whatever information isn't moved is probably lost, or forgotten.

Moving Information to Working Memory: The Role of Attention

Sensory information, such as the light cast by a sparkler, doesn't last very long no matter what we do. But we can preserve a memory of it by encoding it in some minimal way—for instance, by perceiving the letters *Jea* written in the sparkler's curlicue tail. The first step in this process is **attention:** *Whatever people pay attention to (mentally) moves into working memory.* Anything in the sensory register that does not get a person's attention disappears from the memory system. For example, imagine yourself reading a textbook for one of your classes. Your eyes are moving down each page, but meanwhile you are thinking about something altogether different—a recent fight with a friend, a high-paying job advertised in the newspaper, or your growling stomach. What have you learned from the textbook? Absolutely nothing. Even though your eyes were focused on the words in your book, you weren't really paying attention to those words. Now imagine yourself in class the following day. Your mind is not on the class discussion, but on something else—a fly on the wall, the instructor's orange and purple shirt, or (again) your growling stomach. As a result, you will remember nothing about that class discussion.

Unfortunately, people can attend to only a very small amount of information at any one time. In other words, attention has a *limited capacity*. For example, if you are in a room where several conversations are occurring at once, you can usually attend to—and therefore can learn from—only one of those conversations; this phenomenon is sometimes called the *cocktail party phenomenon* (Cherry, 1953; Norman, 1969). If you are sitting in front of the television with your textbook open in your lap, you can attend to the *I Love Lucy* rerun *or* to your book, but not to both simultaneously. If you are preoccupied in class with your instructor's ghastly taste in clothing, you are unlikely to be paying attention to the content of the lecture.

Exactly *how* limited is the limited capacity of human attention? People can often perform two or three well-learned, automatic tasks at once; for example, you can walk and chew gum simultaneously, and you can probably drive a car and drink a Coke at the same time. But when a stimulus or event is detailed and complex (as is true for both textbooks and *I Love Lucy* reruns) or when a task requires considerable thought (understanding a lecture and driving a car on an icy mountain road are examples of tasks requiring one's utmost concentration), then people can usually attend to only *one* thing at a time (J. R. Anderson, 1990; Reisberg, 1997).

Because of the limited capacity of human attention, only a very small amount of information stored in one's sensory register ever moves on to working memory. The vast majority of information that the body initially receives is quickly lost from the memory system, much as we might quickly discard all that junk mail we receive every day.

Attention in the Classroom

Obviously, it is critical that our students pay attention to the things that we want them to learn. To some extent, we can tell which students are paying attention by their overt behaviors (Grabe, 1986; Piontkowski & Calfee, 1979). But appearances can be deceiving. For example, you can probably think of times when, as a student, you looked at a teacher without really hearing anything the teacher said. You can probably also think of times when you looked at a textbook without a single word on the page sinking in. Attention is not just a behavior, it is also a mental process. It is not enough that students' eyes and ears are directed toward their classroom material. Their minds must be directed toward it as well.

How can we be sure our students are really paying attention? For one thing, we can ask questions in class that test students' understanding of the ideas we are presenting; our students are more likely to keep their minds on a lecture or assignment if they know that they will be immediately accountable for it (Grabe, 1986; Piontkowski & Calfee, 1979). We can also ask students to put classroom material to use—for example, by having them draw an inference or solve a problem using new information. A third strategy is to encourage students to take notes; research tells us that note taking usually helps students learn information, partly because it makes them pay attention to what they are hearing or reading (Di Vesta & Gray, 1972; Kiewra, 1989).

Every classroom has students who have difficulty keeping their minds on school subject matter. Such students are more likely to pay attention when they are seated near their teacher (Pfiffner & Barkley, 1998; Schwebel & Cherlin, 1972). We can also help these students by providing a stimulating classroom environment in which everyone *wants* to pay attention. Our students are more likely to be attentive when they find exciting new things to learn every day, when we use a variety of methods to present classroom material, and when we are lively and enthusiastic about a topic. They are less likely to keep their minds on their work when they study the same topics and follow the same routine day after day, and when, as teachers, we seem to be as bored with the subject matter as they are (Berlyne, 1960; Good & Brophy, 1994; Zirin, 1974).

Of course, students cannot keep their minds on any particular topic forever. They need occasional breaks from intensive mental activity (Pellegrini & Bjorklund, 1997). Some breaks are built into the daily school schedule in such forms as recess, passing periods, and lunch. But we may want to give students additional mental breathers as well—perhaps by asking them to perform a physical task related to the topic at hand or perhaps, after an intensive work session, by giving them a chance to take a one-minute stretch.

The discussion of motivation in Chapters 11 and 12 offers additional ideas for capturing and keeping students' attention.

The Nature of Working (Short-Term) Memory

Working memory, sometimes known as **short-term memory,** is the component of memory where new information stays while it is mentally processed; we might think of it as a temporary

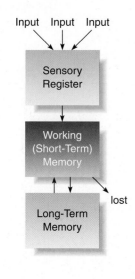

Input Input Input

Sensory
Register

Working
(Short-Term)
Memory

lost

Long-Term
Memory

Do you see why this process is
called *maintenance* rehearsal?

Did you have this misconception
about short-term memory before
you read this section?

holding bin for new information.[2] Working memory is also where much of our thinking, or cognitive processing, occurs. It is where we try to make sense of a lecture, understand a textbook passage, or solve a problem.

Generally speaking, working memory is the component that probably does most of the work of the memory system. It has two characteristics that are particularly worth noting: a short duration and a limited capacity.

Short Duration

Imagine that you need to call a friend, so you look up the friend's telephone number in the phone book. Once you have the number in your head, you discover that someone else is using the phone. You have no paper and pencil handy. What do you do to remember the number until the phone is available?

Because you've paid attention to the number, it is presumably in your working memory. But working memory, as its alternative name "short-term memory" implies, is *short*. Unless you do something further with the telephone number, it will probably last only five to twenty seconds at the most (e.g., L. R. Peterson & Peterson, 1959). To keep it in your head until the phone is available, you might simply repeat it to yourself over and over again. This process, known as **maintenance rehearsal**, keeps information in working memory for as long as you're willing to continue talking to yourself. But once you stop, the number quickly disappears (e.g., Landauer, 1962; Sperling, 1967).

I sometimes hear students talking about putting class material in "short-term memory" so that they can do well on an upcoming exam. Such a statement reflects the common misconception that this component of memory lasts for several days, weeks, or even months. Now you know otherwise: Information stored in working memory lasts less than half a minute unless it is processed further. Working memory is obviously *not* the "place" to leave information that you need for an exam later in the week, or even for information that you'll need for a class later today.

Limited Capacity

Let's put your working memory to work for a moment.

EXPERIENCING FIRSTHAND   *A Divisive Situation*

Try computing the answer to this division problem in your head:

$$59\sqrt{49{,}383}$$

Did you find yourself having trouble remembering some parts of the problem while you were dealing with other parts? Did you ever arrive at the correct answer of 837? Most people cannot solve a division problem with this many digits unless they can write the problem on paper. The fact is, working memory just doesn't have room to hold all that information at once—it has a *limited capacity* (G. A. Miller, 1956; Simon, 1974).

Just like other human beings, our students will have limited space in their working memories, so they can learn only so much so fast. We must keep this in mind as we plan classroom lessons and activities. A mistake that many new teachers make is to present too much information too quickly, and their students' working memories simply can't keep up. Instead, we should present new information in such a way that students have time to process it all. In addition to slowing our pace, we might repeat the same idea several times (perhaps rewording it each time), stop to write important points on the chalkboard, and provide numerous examples and illustrations.

Even when the pace of instruction is appropriate, our students can probably never learn *everything* presented to them in class or in a textbook. Most teachers and textbooks present much more information than students can possibly store (Calfee, 1981). For example, one psychologist (E. D. Gagné, 1985) has estimated that students are likely to learn only about

---

[2]Research indicates that working memory probably has several components for different kinds of information—for example, for visual versus auditory information (e.g., Baddeley, 1986; E. E. Smith, 2000)—but descriptions of them are beyond the scope of this discussion.

one to six new ideas from each minute of a lecture—a small fraction of the ideas typically presented during that time! Although they must continually make choices about what to learn and what *not* to learn, students aren't always the best judges of what is important (Garner, Alexander, Gillingham, Kulikowich, & Brown, 1991; Mayer, 1984; R. E. Reynolds & Shirey, 1988). We can help them make the right choices, however, if we tell them what information is most important, give them guidelines on how and what to study, and omit unnecessary details from our lessons.

Moving Information to Long-Term Memory: Connecting New Information with Prior Knowledge

In the memory model depicted in Figure 6.3, you will notice that the arrows between working memory and long-term memory go in both directions. The process of storing new information in long-term memory usually involves drawing on "old" information already stored there; in other words, it necessitates using prior knowledge. Here are three examples:

> When Patrick reads about the feuding between the Montagues and the Capulets in *Romeo and Juliet,* he thinks, "Hmmm . . . sounds a lot like the relationship my family has with our next-door neighbors."

> Paolo discovers that the initial letters of each of the five Great Lakes—Huron, Ontario, Michigan, Erie, and Superior—spell the word *HOMES.*

> Like many young children, Priscilla believes that the world is flat. When her teacher tells her that the world is round, Priscilla pictures a flat, circular disk (which is, of course, round *and* flat).

Each student is connecting new information with something that he or she already knows or believes. Patrick finds a similarity between *Romeo and Juliet* and his own neighborhood. Paolo connects the five Great Lakes with a common, everyday word. And Priscilla relates the idea that the world is round to her previous conception of a flat world and to the many flat, circular objects (e.g., coins, pizzas) she has encountered over the years.

Later in the chapter we will look more specifically at the processes through which information is stored in long-term memory. But before we do so, let's examine the characteristics of long-term memory and the nature of the "old" information stored within it.

The Nature of Long-Term Memory

Long-term memory is the final component of the human memory system. This component holds information for a relatively long time—perhaps a day, a week, a month, a year, or one's entire lifetime. Your own long-term memory is where you've stored such pieces of information as your name, a few frequently used telephone numbers, your general knowledge about the world, and the things you've learned in school (perhaps the year in which World War II ended, the capital of Spain, or the correct spelling of *hors d'oeuvre*). It is also where you've stored your knowledge about how to perform various behaviors, such as how to ride a bicycle, swing a baseball bat, or write a cursive letter *J*.

Long-term memory has three characteristics especially worth noting: a long duration, an essentially unlimited capacity, and a rich network of interconnections.

(Indefinitely) Long Duration

As you might guess, information stored in long-term memory lasts much longer than information stored in working memory. But exactly *how* long is long-term memory? As you well know, people often forget things that they have known for a day, a week, or even longer. Some psychologists believe that information may slowly "weaken" and possibly disappear from long-term memory, especially if it is not used regularly (J. R. Anderson, 1990; Reisberg, 1997;

THE FAR SIDE® BY GARY LARSON

© 1986 FarWorks, Inc. All Rights Reserved/Dist. by Creators Syndicate

"Mr. Osborne, may I be excused? My brain is full."

Working memory is a bottleneck in the human memory system, in that it has a very limited capacity. In contrast, long-term memory probably has as much room as we would ever need.

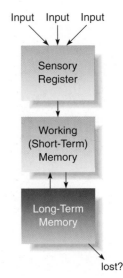

D. L. Schacter, 1999). Others instead believe that once information is stored in long-term memory, it remains there permanently but may in some cases be extremely difficult to retrieve (Loftus & Loftus, 1980). The exact duration of long-term memory has not been determined and perhaps never can be (Eysenck & Keane, 1990).

Unlimited Capacity

Long-term memory seems to be capable of holding as much information as a learner needs to store there—there is probably no such thing as a person "running out of room." In fact, for reasons you will discover shortly, the more information already stored in long-term memory, the easier it is to learn new things.

Interconnectedness

Theorists have discovered that the information stored in long-term memory is organized and interconnected to some extent. To see what I mean, try the following exercise.

EXPERIENCING FIRSTHAND   *Horse #1*

What is the first word that comes to your mind when you hear the word *horse*? And what word does that second word remind you of? And what does that third word remind you of? Beginning with the word *horse*, follow your train of thought, letting each word remind you of another one, for a sequence of at least eight words. Write down your sequence of words as each word comes to mind.

You probably found yourself easily following a train of thought from the word *horse*, perhaps something like the route I followed:

horse → cowboy → lasso → rope → knot → Girl Scouts → cookies → chocolate

Can you summarize the model of memory described in the last few pages?

The last word in your sequence might be one with little or no obvious relationship to horses. Yet you can probably see a logical connection between each pair of words in the sequence. Cognitive psychologists believe that related pieces of information in long-term memory are often connected with one another, perhaps in a network similar to the one depicted in Figure 6.4.

FIGURE 6.4
Interconnectedness in long-term memory

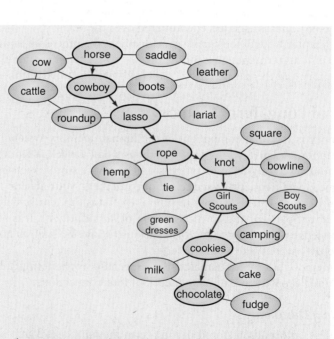

Long-term memory is organized, such that related pieces of information are often associated with one another. Here we can follow the author's train of thought from "horse" to "chocolate."

Critiquing the Three-Component Model

In the last few pages, we have considered the sensory register, working memory, and long-term memory. But are there really three separate components of human memory, and are they as distinctly different from one another as I have portrayed them? Not all cognitive psychologists agree that the three-component model is an accurate representation of how human memory works, and research yields mixed results as to whether the different components of memory can be neatly distinguished (Cowan, 1995; Crowder, 1993; Eysenck & Keane, 1990).

Some psychologists (J. R. Anderson, 1995; Cowan, 1995; Sadoski & Paivio, 2001) have proposed that working and long-term memory are not separate components but instead simply reflect different **activation** states of a single memory. According to this view, all information stored in memory is in either an active or inactive state. Active information, which may include both incoming information and information previously stored in memory, is what people are paying attention to and processing—information that I have previously described as being in working memory. As attention shifts, other pieces of information in memory become activated, and the previously activated information gradually becomes inactive. The bulk of information stored in memory is in an inactive state, so that we are not consciously aware of it; this is information that I have previously described as being in long-term memory.

The three-component model, though not perfect, is similar to how many cognitive psychologists conceptualize human memory. This model also emphasizes aspects of memory that are important for us to keep in mind as we teach. For example, it highlights the importance of *attention* in learning, the *limited capacity* of attention and working memory, the *interconnectedness* of the knowledge that learners acquire, and the importance of *relating* new information with things learned on previous occasions.

Regardless of whether there are three truly distinct components of memory, some aspects of memory are definitely "long-term." Certainly we remember many things for a considerable length of time, and in this sense, at least, these things are in long-term memory. Let's look more closely at the nature of long-term memory storage.

Long-Term Memory Storage

What forms does "knowledge" take in long-term memory? How do people think about and process new information and skills so they can remember them later? As teachers, what can we do to help our students engage in effective long-term memory storage processes? These are issues that we turn to now.

The Various Forms of Knowledge

Information is probably encoded in long-term memory in a number of different forms (e.g., J. R. Anderson, 1995; E. D. Gagné, 1985; Sadoski & Paivio, 2001). For example, some information is stored in a *verbal* form, perhaps as actual words. Things that you remember word for word—for example, your name, your address, the nursery rhyme "Jack and Jill," Hamlet's soliloquy—are all verbally encoded. Other information is encoded in the form of *imagery,* or how that information appears perceptually. For example, if, in your mind, you can "see" the face of a relative or "hear" that person's voice, then you are retrieving images. Finally, a great deal of information in long-term memory is encoded *semantically,* as underlying meanings. For example, when you listen to a lecture or read a textbook, you probably store the gist of the message more frequently than you store the words themselves. All of these examples are instances of **declarative knowledge**—knowledge that relates to the nature of *how things are.*

Yet people acquire **procedural knowledge** as well; in other words, they learn *how to do things* (e.g., J. R. Anderson, 1983; Phye, 1997; Tulving, 1983). For example, you probably know how to ride a bicycle, wrap a birthday present, and multiply a three-digit number by a two-digit number. To perform such actions successfully, you must adapt your behavior to changing conditions; for example, when you ride a bicycle, you must be able to turn left or right when an object blocks your path, and you must be able to come to a complete stop when

no two pieces of matter
cwh accupy the same
space at the same time.

ovrflod the BloIks

kup
the
BuBs
mene
so
por
we

tok up
all the
room

FIGURE 6.5 Students learn and remember information more effectively if they encode it in a variety of ways. Here 9-year-old Nicholas records his findings from a third-grade science experiment in both words and a picture. Nick has difficulties with written language skills that qualify him for special educational services. Notice how he misspells many words and writes up from the bottom of the page. (Translation: "We poured so many cubes [that] the cup overflowed. The blocks took up all the room.")

you reach your destination. Accordingly, procedural knowledge must include information about how to respond under different circumstances.

In many situations, information may be encoded in more than one form simultaneously. For example, stop and think about your last educational psychology class session. Can you recall some of the ideas (meanings) presented at that class? Can you recall what your instructor looked like that day (an image)? Can you recall specific words that were spoken or written on the chalkboard (verbal encoding)?

Research evidence indicates that information encoded in multiple ways is more easily retrieved from long-term memory than information encoded in just one way. For example, students more readily learn and remember information that they receive in both a verbal form (e.g., a lecture or textbook passage) and a graphic form (e.g., a picture, map, or diagram) (Kulhavy, Lee, & Caterino, 1985; Sadoski & Paivio, 2001; Winn, 1991). Thus, by presenting information to students in multiple modalities, or perhaps by explicitly asking them to represent it in at least two different ways (e.g., see Figure 6.5), we increase the likelihood that they will be able to remember it over the long run.

How Declarative Knowledge Is Learned

Consider this situation:

In biology class, Kanesha has been struggling to learn the names of all the bones in the human body from head (cranium) to toe (metatarsus). She has learned a few bones quickly and easily; for example, it makes sense that the *nasal bone* is near the nose, and she remembers the *humerus* (upper arm bone) by thinking of it as being just above one's funny (humorous?) bone. But she is still confused about a few bones; for example, the *tibia* and *fibula* have similar-sounding names and are located in the same place (the lower leg). And she keeps thinking that the *sternum* (at the front of the chest) is in back just like the stern of a boat. She has trouble remembering many of the other bones—the coccyx, ulna, sacrum, clavicle, patella—because she's never encountered these words before and can't relate them to anything she knows.

To prepare for her upcoming biology quiz, Kanesha looks at a diagram of the human skeleton and whispers the name of each bone to herself several times. She also writes each name on a sheet of paper. "These terms should certainly sink in if I repeat them enough times," she tells herself.

Kanesha scores only 70 percent on the biology quiz. As she looks over her incorrect answers, she sees that she confused the tibia and the fibula, labeled the ulna as "clavicle," put the sternum in the wrong place, and completely forgot to label the coccyx, sacrum, and patella.

Why are some of the bones easier for Kanesha to remember than others? Which of Kanesha's strategies for learning the bones are probably most effective?

Kanesha is thinking about different bones in different ways. She makes some kind of logical "sense" of the nasal bone and humerus; she also tries to make sense of the sternum, but her strategy backfires when she relates this bone to the stern of a boat. Kanesha gives little if any thought to why the other bones have the names they do. The extent to which Kanesha mentally processes the material she needs to learn and the *ways* in which she processes it affect her performance on the biology quiz.

The specific cognitive processes that a person uses when trying to learn new information affect the individual's ability to remember and use that information later. In the next few pages, we will consider five processes (summarized in Table 6.2) that people use in storing declarative information in long-term memory: rehearsal, meaningful learning, organization, elaboration, and visual imagery.

Rehearsal

Earlier I described how maintenance rehearsal—repeating something over and over again verbally—helps us keep information in working memory indefinitely. Early theorists (e.g., R. C. Atkinson & Shiffrin, 1968) believed that **rehearsal** is also a means through which in-

Five Possible Ways of Learning Declarative Knowledge

PROCESS	DEFINITION	EXAMPLE	EFFECTIVENESS	EDUCATIONAL IMPLICATION
Rehearsal	Repeating information verbatim, either mentally or aloud	Repeating a word-for-word definition of *inertia*	Relatively ineffective: Storage is slow, and later retrieval is difficult	Suggest that students use rehearsal as a last resort only.
Meaningful learning	Making connections between new information and prior knowledge	Putting a definition of *inertia* into one's own words or identifying examples of inertia in one's own life experiences	Effective if associations made with prior knowledge are appropriate ones	Help students connect new information to things they already know.
Organization	Making connections among various pieces of new information	Studying how one's lines in a play relate to the play's overall story line	Effective if organizational structure is legitimate and if it consists of more than just a "list" of separate facts	Present material in an organized way, and point out the organizational structure and interrelationships in the material.
Elaboration	Adding additional ideas to new information based on what one already knows	Thinking about possible reasons why historical figures behaved as they did	Effective if the ideas added are appropriate inferences	Encourage students to go beyond the information itself—for example, to draw inferences and speculate about possible implications.
Visual imagery	Forming a mental picture of information	Imagining how various characters and events in *Ivanhoe* might have looked	Individual differences in effectiveness; especially beneficial when used to supplement meaningful learning, organization, or elaboration	Illustrate verbal instruction with visual materials (e.g., pictures, maps, diagrams).

formation is stored in long-term memory. In other words, if we repeat something often enough, it might eventually sink in.

The main disadvantage in using rehearsal is that we make few if any connections between new information and the knowledge already in our long-term memory. Thus, we are engaging in **rote learning**: We are learning information verbatim, without attaching any meaning to it. Contrary to what many students think, rote (meaningless) learning is a slow and relatively ineffective way of storing information in long-term memory (J. R. Anderson, 1995; Ausubel, 1968; Craik & Watkins, 1973). Furthermore, for reasons you will discover later, information stored by rote learning is more difficult to retrieve later on.

If you have already read the discussion of cognitive development in Chapter 2, then you may remember that rehearsal is one of the first strategies that students develop (usually in the early elementary school years). Verbally rehearsing information is probably better than not processing it at all, and in cases where students have little if any prior knowledge to draw on to help them understand new material (as when Kanesha was trying to learn *tibia, fibula, coccyx, ulna*, etc.), rehearsal may be one of the few strategies that they can use (E. Wood, Willoughby, Reilley, Elliott, & DuCharme, 1994). But regardless of our students' age or experience, we should encourage them to use other, more effective methods—meaningful learning, organization, elaboration, and visual imagery—whenever possible.

Meaningful Learning

The process of **meaningful learning** involves recognizing a relationship between new information and something else already stored in long-term memory. When we use words like *comprehension* or *understanding,* we are talking about meaningful learning. Here are some examples:

> When Juan reads that World War II ended on August 10, 1945, he thinks, "Hey, August tenth is my birthday!"

> Students in a German class notice that the German word *Buch* is pronounced like its English equivalent, *book.*

> Jane encounters a new subtraction fact: $4 - 2 = 2$. "That makes sense," she thinks. "After all, two plus two are four, and this is just doing the same thing backward."

> When Julian reads J. D. Salinger's *Catcher in the Rye,* he sees similarities between Holden Caulfield's emotional struggles and his own adolescent concerns.

Meaningful learning is similar to Piaget's concept of *assimilation* (see Chapter 2).

Research clearly indicates that meaningful learning is more effective than rote learning (Ausubel et al., 1978; Bransford & Johnson, 1972; Mayer, 1996). As illustrations of the effectiveness of meaningful learning, try the following two exercises.

EXPERIENCING FIRSTHAND *Two Letter Strings, Two Pictures*

1. Study each of the following strings of letters until you can remember them perfectly:

   AIIRODFMLAWRS   FAMILIARWORDS

2. Study each of the two pictures below until you can reproduce them accurately from memory.

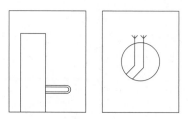

Figures are from "Comprehension and Memory for Pictures" by G. H. Bower, M. B. Karlin, and A. Dueck, 1975, *Memory and Cognition, 3,* p. 217. Reprinted by permission of Psychonomic Society, Inc.

No doubt the second letter string was easier for you to learn because you could relate it to something you already knew: "familiar words." How easily were you able to learn the two pictures? Do you think that you could draw them from memory a week from now? Do you think that you would be able to remember them more easily if they had meaningful titles such as "a midget playing a trombone in a telephone booth" and "an early bird who caught a very strong worm"? The answer to the latter question is a very definite yes (Bower et al., 1975).

Some students approach school assignments with meaningful learning in mind: They turn to what they already know to try to make sense of new information. These students are likely to be the high achievers in the classroom. Other students instead use rote learning strategies, such as repeating something over and over to themselves without really thinking about what they are saying. As you might guess, these students learn less successfully (Britton, Stimson, Stennett, & Gülgöz, 1998; Novak, 1998; Van Rossum & Schenk, 1984).

Yet we cannot always blame students when they take a relatively meaning*less* learning approach to their studies. Inadvertently, many teaching practices encourage students to learn school subjects by rote. Think back to your own experiences in school. How many times were you allowed to define a word by repeating a dictionary definition, rather than being expected to explain it in your own words? In fact, how many times were you *required* to learn something word for word? And how many times did an exam test your knowledge of facts or principles without ever testing your ability to relate those facts and principles to everyday life or to things learned in previous courses? When students expect an upcoming test to focus on the recall of unrelated facts, rather than on the understanding and application of an integrated

Seasons
Fall... Jump in the leaves
Winter... Play in the snow
Spring... watch flowers grow
Sumer... Swim in pobls and at the beach

Meaningful learning is especially effective when people relate new ideas not only to the things they already know but also to *themselves* (e.g., Rogers, Kuiper, & Kirker, 1977). Here 6-year-old Nadia thinks about the four seasons in terms of what she does during each one.

body of knowledge, many of them will rely on rote learning, believing that such an approach will yield a higher test score and that meaningful learning would be counterproductive (Crooks, 1988). It is little wonder that meaningful learning is the exception rather than the rule in many classrooms (Cooney, 1991; McCaslin & Good, 1996; Novak & Musonda, 1991; Schoenfeld, 1985).

Why do some students learn things meaningfully, whereas others persist in their attempts at rote memorization? At least three conditions probably facilitate meaningful learning (Ausubel et al., 1978):

■ *The student has a meaningful learning set.* When students approach a learning task believing that they can make sense of the information—that is, when they have a **meaningful learning set**—they are more likely to learn that information meaningfully. For example, students who recognize that chemical reactions occur in accordance with familiar mathematical principles are more likely to make sense of those reactions. Students who realize that historical events can often be explained in terms of human personality are more likely to understand why World War II occurred.

A *meaningful learning set* is an example of a *disposition*, a concept we will consider in Chapter 8.

My daughter Tina once came home from middle school with an assignment to learn twelve of the gods and goddesses of ancient Greece (e.g., Zeus was the king of gods; Athena, the goddess of the city and civilization; Apollo, the god of light; Aphrodite, the goddess of love). Unfortunately, there had been little discussion in school of the relevance of these gods and goddesses to anything else Tina knew—for example, to the city of Athens or to the Apollo space flights. And I was reluctant to introduce my daughter to the word *aphrodisiac* simply to help her remember Aphrodite. As a result, Tina had no meaningful learning set for the twelve gods and goddesses—no expectation of connecting them with their domains in any meaningful way. Refusing my motherly offers to help, yet determined to do well on an upcoming quiz, Tina confined herself to her room and rehearsed those gods and goddesses over and over until she could recite all twelve. A month later, I asked her how many she could still recall. She remembered only Zeus.

Do we present information merely as "something to be learned" or instead as something that can help students better understand their world? Do we ask students to define new terminology by using the exact definitions presented in the textbook or instead require them to define terms in their own words? When asking students to give examples of a concept, do we expect examples already presented in the textbook or instead request that students generate new ones? How we present a learning task clearly affects the likelihood of our students adopting a meaningful learning set (Ausubel et al., 1978). Ideally, we must communicate our belief that students *can* and *should* make sense of the things they study.

■ *The student has previous knowledge to which the new information can be related.* Meaningful learning can occur only when long-term memory contains a relevant **knowledge base**, information to which a new idea can be connected. Students will better understand scientific principles if they have already seen those principles in action, either in their own lives or in the laboratory. They will more easily learn the events of an important battle if they have visited the battlefield. They will better understand how large the dinosaurs really were

If meaningful learning relies on relevant prior knowledge, what are the implications for teaching students from diverse cultural backgrounds?

Calvin and Hobbes

by Bill Watterson

if they have seen life-size dinosaur skeletons at a museum of natural history. The more information a student has already stored in long-term memory, the easier it is for that student to learn new information, because there are more things with which that new information can be associated.

■ *The student is aware that previously learned information is related to new information.* Students often don't make the connection between new and prior information; as a result, they resort to rote learning strategies unnecessarily. Oftentimes we can promote meaningful learning by reminding students of things they know that bear directly on a topic of classroom study (Machiels-Bongaerts, Schmidt, & Boshuizen, 1991; L. B. Resnick, 1989; Spires & Donley, 1998). For example, we can relate works of literature to students' own thoughts, feelings, and experiences. We can point out instances when foreign language vocabulary is similar to words in English. We can tie science to students' day-to-day observations and experiences. And we can relate mathematics to such commonplace activities as cooking, building a treehouse, or throwing a ball.

The two storage processes discussed next—organization and elaboration—also involve relating new information to prior knowledge; hence, both of these processes incorporate meaningful learning. Yet each one has an additional twist as well.

Organization

Have you ever had an instructor who came to class and spoke aimlessly for an hour, flitting from one idea to another in an unpredictable sequence? Have you ever read a textbook that did the same thing, so that you never knew how ideas related to one another? In general, how easily can you learn in a situation where information is disorganized?

The fact is, we learn and remember a body of new information more easily when we organize it in some way (e.g., Bjorklund et al., 1994; Mandler & Pearlstone, 1966; Tulving, 1962). Such **organization** invariably involves making connections among various pieces of new information; it often involves making connections with existing knowledge as well. Consider these examples of how students might organize school learning tasks:

Giorgio is trying to remember a list of eleven events leading up to the American Revolution: the Navigation Acts, the Sugar Act, the Stamp Act, the Tea Act, the Boston Massacre, the Boston Tea Party, the attack of the *Gaspee,* the Battle of Lexington, the Battle of Concord, the Battle of Bunker Hill, and the signing of the Declaration of Independence. He puts them into three groups: British legislation, acts of colonial defiance, and pre-war battles.

Genevieve's ten spelling words end with a "long e" sound. She decides to group the words based on their endings (*y, ey,* or *ie*) like this:

body	key	movie
family	donkey	cookie
party	monkey	calorie
gravy		

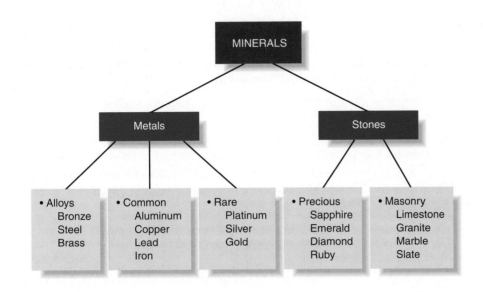

FIGURE 6.6 We remember information more easily when it is organized in some way.

Figure from "Hierarchical Retrieval Schemes in Recall of Categorized Word Lists" by G. H. Bower, M. C. Clark, A. M. Lesgold, and D. Winzenz in *Journal of Verbal Learning and Verbal Behavior,* Volume 8, 323–343, copyright 1969, Elsevier Science (USA), reproduced by permission of the publisher.

When Greg is trying to learn the components of the human memory system, he makes a chart indicating their capacity and duration, like the following:

	Sensory Register	Working Memory	Long-term Memory
Capacity	large	small	large
Duration	very short: <1 second—visual 2–3 sec.—auditory	5–20 seconds	indefinitely long

Learners are more likely to organize information if the material fits an organizational structure with which they are already familiar—for example, if the material can be placed into discrete categories or into a hierarchical arrangement (Bousfield, 1953; Bransford & Franks, 1971; DuBois, Kiewra, & Fraley, 1988; Gauntt, 1991). They are also more likely to organize new material if it has been presented to them with its organizational structure laid out. As an illustration, let's consider the results of a classic experiment (Bower, Clark, Lesgold, & Winzenz, 1969). College students were given four study trials in which to learn 112 words falling into four categories (e.g., minerals, plants). For some students, the words were arranged in an organized fashion (Figure 6.6 is an example). For other students, the words were arranged randomly. Look at the average number of words that each group remembered after one study period (about four minutes) and again after three additional study periods:

Number of Study Periods	Organized Words	Unorganized Words
1	73 (65%)	21 (19%)
4	112 (100%)	70 (63%)

Notice that, after studying the words one time, students with organized words remembered more than three times as many words as students who received them in mixed-up order. After four study periods, students with the organized words remembered the entire list of 112!

Unfortunately, many students tend to "organize" the things they study merely as a list of separate facts, rather than as a set of interrelated ideas (Kletzien, 1988; B. J. F. Meyer, Brandt, & Bluth, 1980). As teachers, how can we help our own students organize class material more effectively? Obviously, we should organize new material in a logical way before we present it. We can then draw students' attention to this organizational structure. For example, we might point out the categories in which facts can be grouped, the hierarchical nature of concepts, or the important interrelationships (e.g., cause-and-effect) among various ideas. We can also present related pieces of information close together in time; students are more likely to associate related ideas when they encounter those ideas together (Glanzer & Nolan, 1986; Hayes-Roth & Thorndyke, 1979).

Additional strategies are *concept mapping* (Chapter 8) and *advance organizers* (Chapter 13).

Elaboration

People sometimes use their prior knowledge to expand on a new idea, thereby storing *more* information than was actually presented. This process of adding to newly acquired information in some way is called **elaboration**. Following are some examples:

Maria learns that an allosaur had powerful jaws and sharp, pointed teeth. "Allosaurs must have been meat eaters," she deduces.

Marcus gets a note from a friend who writes, "Meat me by the bak door after skool." Marcus translates his friend's message as, "Meet me by the back door after school."

When I took a course in Mandarin Chinese in high school, I learned that the Chinese word *wǒmen* means "we." "Aha," I thought to myself, "the sign on the rest room that *we* girls use says *women.*"

In most cases, the more students elaborate on new material—the more they use what they already know to help them understand and interpret the material—the more effectively they will store it in long-term memory (J. R. Anderson, 1995). I remember very little of the Chinese I learned in high school, but the meaning of the word *wǒmen* remains indelibly stored in my long-term memory. Students who elaborate on the things they learn in school are usually better students than those who simply take information at face value (McDaniel & Einstein, 1989; Pressley, 1982; Waters, 1982).

As teachers, we will often want our students to go beyond the information actually presented to them. We can help them to elaborate in numerous ways. For example, we can ask frequent questions along these lines:

- Why do you think this happens?
- Can you think of some examples of this concept?
- How could we use this idea in our everyday lives?
- What things can you conclude from this information?

We can also encourage students to talk about a topic among themselves, ask them to explain an idea on paper, or simply give them time to think about new information. The following assessment activity illustrates yet another strategy.

INTERPRETING ARTIFACTS AND INTERACTIONS *Moving to Ohio*

In a unit on westward migration in the United States during the 1800s, a third-grade teacher asks her students to imagine traveling west with their families by covered wagon and to write several "journal entries" describing their trip. Following is an excerpt from one of 8-year-old Shea's entries. (It will help you to know that Noah and Drew are Shea's younger brother and sister; Kevin is her father.) As you read the excerpt, consider these questions:

- What long-term memory storage processes does the assignment promote?
- What things does Shea write that suggest that she is, in fact, engaging in these processes?

For a moment we all just looked at each other. I am scared. What will Ohio be like? My dad quietly took his and my mom's stuff and put it in the back of the wagon. Drew started to cry and my mom held her. It was 8 o'clock. With all of us dressed in our warmest things and holding our things Noah, Drew, and

I climbed into the back of the wagon. 3 beds made from the quilts and pillows off our bed were on the wagon floor. Right away Drew and Noah fell a sleep. I climbed to the back of the and looked at the firmilyar town. We soon would be leaving. Half an hour later we were out of North

Carolina. At 9 o'clock we'll be at the Appalachian Mountains," said my dad. "Thats where we'll stop for to night." "Oh, Kevin," said my mom. "Are you sure its safe? Maybe we should turn back?" "No," my dad said firmly "were not turning back."

By giving such an assignment, the teacher presumably wants her students to relate the westward migration to their own experiences traveling to unknown places (i.e., to learn meaningfully) and, in the process, to draw inferences about the thoughts and feelings that the people may have had about the trip (i.e., to elaborate). In the excerpt we see evidence of both meaningful learning and elaboration. For instance, from her own experience, Shea knows that leaving familiar ("firmilyar") territory can be unsettling and assumes that the travelers are afraid ("I'm scared") and uncertain ("are you sure it's safe?") yet also determined ("were [we're] not turning back"). At the same time, some of Shea's knowledge about modern-day travel is probably not applicable to travel in the 1800s. For instance, she thinks that leaving North Carolina would take only half an hour (unlikely unless the family lived right by the state line) and that the family can travel until 9:00 (which would mean traveling at dusk or after dark). As teachers, while we should continually encourage our students to relate new material to the things they already know, we must also monitor their thinking for any inappropriate connections.

Visual Imagery

Earlier in the chapter, I mentioned imagery as one possible way in which information might be encoded in long-term memory. Numerous research studies indicate that **visual imagery**— forming mental pictures of objects or ideas—can be a particularly effective method of storing information (Dewhurst & Conway, 1994; Johnson-Glenberg, 2000; Sadoski, Goetz, & Fritz, 1993; Sadoski & Paivio, 2001). To show you how effective visual imagery can be, let me teach you a few of the Mandarin Chinese words I studied in high school.

EXPERIENCING FIRSTHAND / Five Chinese Words

Try learning these five Chinese words by forming the visual images I describe (don't worry about learning the marks over the words):

Chinese Word	English Meaning	Image
fáng	house	Picture a *house* with *fangs* growing on its roof and walls.
mén	door	Picture a rest room *door* with the word *MEN* painted on it.
ké	guest	Picture someone giving someone else (the *guest*) a *key* to the house.
fàn	food	Picture a plate of *food* being cooled by a *fan*.
shū	book	Picture a *shoe* with a *book* sticking out of it.

At this point, find something else to do for a couple of minutes. Stand up and stretch, get a glass of water, or use the bathroom. But be sure to come back to your reading in just a minute or two. . . .

Now that you're back, cover the list of Chinese words, English meanings, and visual images. Try to remember what each word means:

ké   fàn   mén   fáng   shū

Did the Chinese words remind you of the visual images that you stored? Did the images help you remember the English meanings of the Chinese words?

You may have remembered all five words easily, or you may have remembered only one or two. People differ in their ability to use visual imagery: Some form visual images quickly and easily, whereas others form them only slowly and with difficulty (Behrmann, 2000; J. M. Clark & Paivio, 1991; Kosslyn, 1985). For those in the former category, imagery can be a powerful means of storing information in long-term memory.

As teachers, we can promote the use of visual imagery in several ways. We can ask students to imagine how certain events in literature or history might have looked (Sadoski & Paivio, 2001). We can provide visual materials (pictures, charts, graphs, etc.) that illustrate important, but possibly abstract, ideas (Atkinson et al., 1999; Verdi, Kulhavy, Stock, Rittschof, & Johnson, 1996). And we can ask students to draw their *own* illustrations or diagrams of the things they are learning (Edens & Potter, 2001; Van Meter, 2001); Figure 6.7 provides an example.

The last three storage processes—organization, elaboration, and visual imagery—are clearly *constructive* in nature: They all involve combining several pieces of information into a

INTO THE CLASSROOM: *Helping Students Learn New Information*

Let students know what information is most important to learn.

> When a history teacher prepares his students for an upcoming exam on World War I, he reminds them, "When you study for the test, you should try to understand how the specific events that we discussed contributed to the progress and eventual outcome of the war. Know when each event occurred in relation to other events, but don't try to learn each and every date."

Present the same ideas in more than one form.

> A biology teacher shows her class a diagram of the human heart. She traces the flow of blood with her finger as she describes how the heart pumps blood through the body.

Communicate the belief that students can and should make sense of the things they study.

> Students in a high school first-aid class have learned that when people suffer from traumatic shock, many normal bodily functions are depressed because insufficient blood is circulating through the body. The teacher asks, "Given what you have learned about traumatic shock, why do experts recommend that if we find a person in shock, we have them lie down and keep them warm but not hot?"

Show students how new material relates to things they already know.

> When describing the law of gravity, a teacher asks, "What happens when you let go of something? Which way does it fall? Have you ever seen anything fall *up*?"

Present information in an organized fashion.

> A teacher groups new spelling words by letter pattern. For example, she gives students a list of *uff* words (e.g., *buff, muff, stuff*) and *ough* words (e.g., *rough, tough, enough*).

Encourage students to elaborate on class material.

> A social studies teacher describes a general principle of geography: New settlements often spring up at the junctions of two or more major transportation routes. She then asks her class, "Why do you think that might be so?"

Encourage students to form visual images that capture the things they are studying.

> An elementary teacher is reading a short story to his class. After reading a description of the story's main character, he stops and asks his class to imagine the person just as the author has described her—a woman with tousled gray hair, twinkling brown eyes, and a warm, welcoming smile.

Begin at a level consistent with students' existing knowledge base.

> At the beginning of the school year, a mathematics teacher gives her students a pretest covering the mathematical concepts and operations they studied the year before. She finds that many students still have difficulty computing the perimeter and area of a rectangle. She reviews these procedures and gives students additional practice with them before beginning a unit on computing the volume of objects with rectangular sides.

FIGURE 6.7 8-year-old Ronald illustrates the role of a chrysalis in the life cycle of a butterfly; in his words, it "elaes [allows] a caterpillar to trn into a butterfly."

meaningful whole. When we organize information, we rearrange the specific items we need to learn so that they fit within a familiar framework (categories, a hierarchy, or the like). When we elaborate on new information, we use what we already know to help us make better sense of it. And when we use visual imagery, we construct mental pictures (perhaps a house with fangs, or a rest room door with *MEN* painted on it) based on how certain objects typically look. In Chapter 7 we will examine the constructive nature of long-term memory storage more closely.

How Procedural Knowledge Is Learned

Some of the procedures that people learn—for example, driving a stick shift, baking a cake, and serving a volleyball—consist primarily of overt behaviors. Many others—for instance, solving for *x* in an algebraic equation, making sense of difficult reading material, and surfing the Internet—are largely mental in nature. Most procedures obviously involve a combination of physical behaviors and mental activities.

Procedural knowledge ranges from relatively simple actions (e.g., holding a pencil correctly or using scissors) to far more complex ones. Complex procedures are usually not learned in one fell swoop. Instead, they are acquired slowly over time, often only with

Help students understand the logic behind the procedures they are learning.

> As a teacher demonstrates the correct way to swing a tennis racket, she asks her students, "Why is it important to have your feet apart rather than together? Why is it important to hold your arm straight as you swing?"

When skills are especially complex, break them into simpler tasks that students can practice one at a time.

> Knowing how overwhelming the task of driving a car can initially be, a driver education teacher begins behind-the-wheel instruction by having students practice steering and braking in an empty school parking lot. Only later, after students have mastered these skills, does he have them drive in traffic on city streets.

Provide mnemonics that can help students remember a sequence of steps.

> In a unit on basketball, a teacher coaches her students on an effective approach to making a free throw. "Just remember BEEF," she says. "*B*alance the ball, put your *e*lbows in, *e*levate your arms, and *f*ollow through."

Give students many opportunities to practice new skills, and provide the feedback they need to help them improve.

> A science teacher asks his students to write lab reports after each week's lab activity. Many of his students have had little or no previous experience in scientific writing, so when he grades the reports, he writes numerous comments as well. Some comments describe the strengths that he sees, and others provide suggestions for making the reports more objective, precise, or clear.

a great deal of practice (J. R. Anderson, 1983; Ericsson & Chalmers, 1994; Proctor & Dutta, 1995).

Researchers are just beginning to identify the cognitive processes involved in storing procedural knowledge. To some extent, of course, learners store procedures as actual behaviors. Yet many procedures, particularly complex ones, may begin largely as declarative knowledge—in other words, as *information* about how to execute a procedure rather than as the actual *ability* to execute it (J. R. Anderson, 1983, 1987). When learners use declarative knowledge to guide them as they carry out a new procedure, their performance is slow and laborious, the activity consumes a great deal of mental effort, and they often talk themselves through their actions. As they continue to perform the activity, however, their declarative knowledge gradually evolves into procedural knowledge. This knowledge becomes fine-tuned over time and eventually allows learners to perform an activity quickly, efficiently, and effortlessly (J. R. Anderson, 1983, 1987).

Theorists have suggested several teaching strategies that seem to help students learn and remember procedures more effectively. For instance, we can demonstrate a procedure or show pictures of its specific steps (R. M. Gagné, 1985). We can verbalize our thoughts, thereby demonstrating *mental* procedures, as we engage in a complex task (Schunk, 1981). We can encourage students to use verbal rehearsal as they learn a new skill—in other words, to repeat the required steps over and over to themselves (Weiss & Klint, 1987). And as you might guess, our students will be more likely to remember a procedure when we give them a chance to carry it out themselves and when we provide regular feedback about how they are doing (R. L. Cohen, 1989; Heindel & Kose, 1990; Proctor & Dutta, 1995). When procedures are fairly complicated, we may want to break them down into smaller tasks and have students practice each one separately at first (J. R. Anderson, Reder, & Simon, 1996). Chapter 8 describes additional strategies for facilitating the acquisition of procedural knowledge within the context of such complex cognitive processes as metacognition and problem solving.

Which of these strategies remind you of Vygotsky's theory of cognitive development (described in Chapter 2)?

Prior Knowledge and Working Memory in Long-Term Memory Storage

Occasionally, students' prior knowledge interferes with something they need to learn; as examples, consider Darren's confusion about the marble Parthenon, Kanesha's difficulty learning where the sternum is located, and Shea's assumption that people moving by covered wagon would travel after dark. But in general, a relevant knowledge base helps students store classroom subject matter much more effectively (P. A. Alexander, Kulikowich, & Schulze, 1994;

Hamman et al., 1995; Schneider, 1993). Students' prior knowledge contributes to their learning in several ways:

- It helps them determine what is most important to learn; thus, it helps them direct their *attention* appropriately.
- It enables them to understand something—that is, to engage in *meaningful learning*—instead of learning it by rote.
- It provides a framework for *organizing* new information.
- It helps them *elaborate* on information—for example, by filling in missing details, clarifying ambiguities, or drawing inferences. (Ausubel et al., 1978; Bjorklund, Muir-Broaddus, & Schneider, 1990; Carpenter & Just, 1986; Lindberg, 1991; Rumelhart & Ortony, 1977; West, Farmer, & Wolff, 1991; P. T. Wilson & Anderson, 1986)

Do you now see why Kanesha had such difficulty remembering the coccyx, ulna, sacrum, clavicle, and patella?

Yet as we noted in our discussion of meaningful learning, it is not enough that students have the knowledge they need to interpret new material; they must also be *aware* that the knowledge is relevant. They must then retrieve it from their long-term memories while thinking about the new material, such that they have both the "old" and the "new" in working memory simultaneously and can make the appropriate connections (Bellezza, 1986; Glanzer & Nolan, 1986).

As teachers, we should keep students' existing knowledge in mind and use it as a starting point whenever we introduce a new topic. For example, we might begin a first-grade unit on plants by asking students to describe what their parents do to keep flowers or vegetable gardens growing. Or, in a secondary English literature class, we might introduce Sir Walter Scott's *Ivanhoe* (in which Robin Hood is a major character) by asking students to tell the tale of Robin Hood as they know it. We should also remember that students from diverse cultural backgrounds are likely to have different knowledge bases and modify our starting points accordingly.

Using Mnemonics in the Absence of Relevant Prior Knowledge

When you were in elementary and secondary school, there were probably many times when you had difficulty making sense of classroom subject matter. Perhaps you had trouble learning the symbols for some of the chemical elements because those symbols seemed unrelated to the elements' names (Why is *Au* the symbol for gold?). Perhaps you couldn't remember words in a foreign language because those words were very different from their English equivalents. Or perhaps you couldn't remember lists of things (e.g., four things you should do when treating a victim of shock, eleven events leading up to the American Revolution) because they always contained several seemingly unrelated items, and one item didn't help you remember any of the others.

When students are likely to have trouble finding relationships between new material and their prior knowledge, or when a body of information has an organizational structure with no apparent logic behind it (e.g., as is true for many lists), special memory tricks known as **mnemonics** can help them learn classroom material more effectively. Three commonly used mnemonics are verbal mediation, the keyword method, and superimposed meaningful structures.

Verbal Mediation

A **verbal mediator** is a word or phrase that creates a logical connection, or "bridge," between two pieces of information. Verbal mediators can be used for such paired pieces of information as foreign language words and their English meanings, countries and their capitals, chemical elements and their symbols, and words and their spellings. Following are some examples:

Information to Be Learned	Verbal Mediator
Handschuh is German for "glove."	A glove is a *shoe* for the *hand*.
Quito is the capital of Ecuador.	Mos*quitos* at the equator.
Au is the symbol for gold.	'*Ay, you* stole my gold watch!
The word *principal* ends in *pal* (not *ple*).	The principal is my *pal*.

In our earlier case study, Kanesha uses a verbal mediator to help her remember one of the bones: She thinks of the humerus as being just above the funny (*humorous*) bone.

Keyword Method

Like verbal mediation, the **keyword method** aids memory by making a connection between two things. This technique is especially helpful when there is no logical verbal mediator to fill the gap—for example, when there is no obvious sentence or phrase to relate a foreign language word to its English meaning. The keyword method involves two steps, which I will illustrate using the Spanish word *amor* and its English meaning *love*:

1. Identify a concrete object to represent each piece of information. The object may be either a commonly used symbol (e.g., a heart to symbolize *love*) or a sound-alike word (e.g., a suit of armor to represent *amor*). Such objects are **keywords**.
2. Form a picture in your mind of the two objects together. To remember that *amor* means *love*, you might picture a knight in a suit of armor with a huge red heart painted on his chest.

You used the keyword method when you did the "Five Chinese Words" exercise earlier. Following are some additional examples:

Information to Be Learned	Visual Image
Das Pferd is German for "horse."	Picture a *horse* driving a *Ford*.
Augusta is the capital of the state of Maine.	Picture *a gust of* wind blowing through a horse's *mane*.
Tchaikovsky composed "Swan Lake."	Picture a *swan* swimming on a *lake*, wearing a *tie* and *coughing*.

Superimposed Meaningful Structure

A larger body of information (e.g., a list of items) can often be learned by superimposing a meaningful organization—a familiar shape, word, sentence, rhythm, poem, or story—on that information. Here are some examples of such **superimposed meaningful structures**:

Information to Be Learned	Superimposed Meaningful Structure
The shape of Italy	A "boot"
The shape of France	A "bearskin rug"
The Great Lakes (Huron, Ontario, Michigan, Erie, Superior)	HOMES
Lines on the treble clef (EGBDF)	Elvis' guitar broke down Friday, *or* every good boy does fine.
The distinction between stalagmites and stalactites	When the "mites" go up, the "tites" come down.
The number of days in each month	Thirty days has September . . .

Superimposed meaningful structures can be used to remember procedures as well as declarative information. Following are three examples that my students have shared with me:

Procedure to Be Learned	Superimposed Meaningful Structure
Turning a screw (clockwise to tighten it, counterclockwise to loosen it)	Righty, tighty. Lefty, loosey.
Throwing a free throw in basketball	BEEF: *b*alance the ball, *e*lbows in, *e*levate the arms, *f*ollow through.
Multiplying a mathematical expression of the form $(ax + b)(cx + d)$	FOIL: multiply the *f*irst terms within each set of parentheses, then the two *o*uter terms, then the two *i*nner terms, and finally the *l*ast terms.

Research consistently supports the effectiveness of mnemonics in student learning (Bower & Clark, 1969; Bulgren, Schumaker, & Deshler, 1994; M. S. Jones, Levin, Levin, & Beitzel, 2000; Pressley, Levin, & Delaney, 1982; Scruggs & Mastropieri, 1989). In addition to helping students store information and procedures in long-term memory, mnemonics also appear to help students retrieve what they stored at an earlier time. We turn to the topic of retrieval now.

Long-Term Memory Retrieval

As you learned earlier in the chapter, some information is easily retrieved from long-term memory. But it may take you considerable time to "find" some of the other information you have stored there. Try the following exercise as an example.

EXPERIENCING FIRSTHAND   *More Retrieval Practice*

The answer to each of the following questions has appeared earlier in this chapter. See how many answers you can retrieve from your long-term memory and how quickly you can retrieve each one.

1. What are the five Great Lakes?
2. What is the German word for "book"?
3. In what year did World War II end?
4. Who wrote *Catcher in the Rye*?
5. About how long does information remain in working memory before it disappears?
6. How do you spell the French term for "appetizer"?

Can you still remember what the Mandarin Chinese words *ké, fàn, mén, fáng,* and *shū* mean? Can you retrieve the visual images you stored to help you remember these words?

Did you find yourself unable to remember one or more of the answers even though you know you "processed" the information at the time you read it? If so, then you have just discovered firsthand that, in some cases, information is retrieved from long-term memory only with great difficulty, or perhaps not at all.

The Nature of Long-Term Memory Retrieval

Retrieving information from long-term memory appears to be a process of following a "pathway" of associations. One idea reminds us of another idea, which reminds us of still another, and so on, just as we saw in the "Horse #1" exercise earlier in the chapter. Retrieval is successful only when we eventually stumble on the information we are looking for. We are most likely to do so if we have connected the desired information to something else—presumably something logically related to it—in long-term memory.

To illustrate this idea, I return once again to all those letters, bills, advertisements, and so on that arrive in your mailbox throughout each year. Imagine that, on average, you receive five important items—things you really need to save—every day. At six postal deliveries a week and 52 weeks a year, you have been saving 1,560 pieces of mail every year. If you have been saving your mail for the last fifteen years, then you have 23,400 really important things stashed somewhere in your home.

One day you hear that stock in a clothing company (Mod Bod Jeans, Inc.) has tripled in value. You remember that your wealthy Aunt Agnes sent you some Mod Bod stock certificates for your birthday several years ago, and you presumably decided that they were important enough to save. But where in the world did you put them? How long will it take you to find them among all those important letters, bills, brochures, catalogs, fliers, and sweepstakes announcements?

How easily you find the certificates and, in fact, whether you find them at all depend on how you have been storing your mail as you've accumulated it over the years. If you've stored it in a logical, organized fashion—for example, by putting all paid bills on a closet shelf, all mail order catalogs on the floor under the window, and all items from relatives in a file cabinet (in alphabetical order by last name)—then you should quickly retrieve Aunt Agnes's gift. But if you simply tossed each day's mail randomly around the house, you will be searching your home for a long, long time, possibly without ever finding a trace of that Mod Bod stock.

Like a home with fifteen years' worth of mail, long-term memory contains a great deal of information. And like finding the Mod Bod certificates, the ease with which information is retrieved from long-term memory depends somewhat on whether that information is stored in a logical "place"—that is, whether it is connected with related pieces of information. By making those important connections with existing knowledge, we will know where to "find" the information when we need it later on. In contrast, learning something by rote is like throwing

If this student has been studying classroom subject matter by relating it to what he already knows about the world, then he should be able to retrieve it easily as he works on this writing assignment.

Aunt Agnes's gift randomly among thousands of pieces of unorganized mail: We may never retrieve it again.

Factors Affecting Retrieval

Even when we connect new information to our existing knowledge base, we can't always find it when we need it. At least four factors promote our ability to retrieve information from long-term memory:

- Making multiple connections with existing knowledge
- Learning information to mastery and beyond
- Using knowledge frequently
- Having a relevant retrieval cue

Making Multiple Connections with Existing Knowledge

If retrieving information from long-term memory is a process of following a pathway of associations, what happens if we take the wrong route and go in an inappropriate direction? In such a situation, we may never find what we are looking for.

We are more likely to retrieve information when we have many possible pathways to it—in other words, when we have associated the information with many other things in our existing knowledge base. Making multiple connections is like using cross-references in your mail storage system. You may have filed the Mod Bod stock in the "items from relatives" file drawer, but you've also written the stock's location on notes left in many other places—perhaps with your birth certificate (after all, you received the stock on your birthday), with your income tax receipts, or in your safe-deposit box. By looking in any one of these logical places, you will discover where to find your valuable stock.

As teachers, we can help students more effectively remember classroom subject matter over the long run if we help them connect it to numerous pieces of information in their existing knowledge base. For example, we can show them how new material relates to

- Concepts and ideas within the same subject area (e.g., showing them how multiplication is related to addition)
- Concepts and ideas in other subject areas (e.g., talking about how scientific discoveries have affected historical events)
- Students' general knowledge of the world (e.g., drawing parallels between the "Black Death" of the fourteenth century and the modern-day AIDS epidemic)
- Students' personal experiences (e.g., finding similarities between the family feud in *Romeo and Juliet* and students' own interpersonal conflicts)
- Students' current activities and needs outside of the classroom (e.g., showing how persuasive writing skills might be used to craft a personal essay for a college application)

The more interrelationships our students form among pieces of information in long-term memory, the more easily they can retrieve those pieces later on.

Learning Things to Mastery and Beyond

Is it enough for students to demonstrate mastery of information or skills—for example, to write all their spelling words correctly—on just one occasion? Probably not. Research tells us that people are far more likely to retrieve the material they have learned if they continue to study and practice it, ideally in a variety of contexts (Graham, Harris, & Fink, 2000; Semb & Ellis, 1994; L. A. Shepard, 2000; Underwood, 1954).

When students continue to practice information and skills they have already mastered, they eventually achieve **automaticity:** They can retrieve what they've learned quickly and effortlessly and can use it almost without thinking (J. R. Anderson, 1983; P. W. Cheng, 1985; Proctor & Dutta, 1995; Schneider & Shiffrin, 1977). As an example, think of a complicated skill—perhaps driving a car—that you can perform easily. Your first attempts at driving many years ago probably required a great deal of mental effort. But now you can drive without having to pay much attention to what you are doing—you execute the skill automatically.

If you have already read Chapter 4, then you may recall that automaticity plays a role in Robert Sternberg's theory of intelligence.

Remember, working memory has a limited capacity: It can only do so much at one time. When much of its capacity must be used for retrieving single facts or executing simple procedures, little room is left for understanding more complex situations or dealing with more difficult tasks. One key reason for learning some facts and procedures to automaticity, then, is to free up enough working memory capacity for students to tackle the complex tasks that require those facts and procedures (D. Jones & Christensen, 1999; Proctor & Dutta, 1995; L. B. Resnick, 1989; Stanovich, 2000). For example, second graders reading a story can better focus their efforts on understanding it if they don't have to sound out words like *before* and *after*. Fourth graders faced with the multiplication problem

87

× 59

can solve it more easily if they can quickly retrieve such basic facts as $9 \times 8 = 72$ and $5 \times 7 = 35$. High school chemistry students can more easily interpret Na_2CO_3 (sodium carbonate) if they don't have to stop to think about what the symbols *Na*, *C*, and *O* represent.

Unfortunately, automaticity is achieved in only one way: practice, practice, and more practice. This is not to say, however, that we must continually assign drill-and-practice exercises involving isolated facts and procedures. Quite the contrary, such activities are often boring and unlikely to convince students of the value of what they are learning. A more effective approach is to routinely incorporate basic knowledge and skills into a variety of meaningful and enjoyable activities, such as problem-solving tasks, group projects, games, brainteasers, and so on.

Using Knowledge Frequently

Frequently used knowledge is retrieved more easily than knowledge that is used rarely or not at all (Brown & McNeill, 1966; Yarmey, 1973). It is easier to remember your own birthday than the birthday of a friend or relative. It is easier to remember the current year than the year in which World War II ended. And it is definitely easier to remember the spelling of *information* than the spelling of *hors d'oeuvre*, even though both terms have the same number of letters.

As teachers, we should occasionally have classroom activities that require students to review what they have learned earlier in the year or in previous years. For example, we might have occasional refresher discussions of "old" material, or we might ask students to use the material to understand new topics or solve new problems. Research is clear on this point: Occasional review enhances students' memory for information over the long run, especially when review sessions are spaced out over several months or years (Bahrick, Bahrick, Bahrick, & Bahrick, 1993; Dempster, 1991; Di Vesta & Smith, 1979; McDaniel & Masson, 1985).

Having a Relevant Retrieval Cue

If you were educated in North America, then you probably learned the names of the five Great Lakes at one time or another. Yet you may have trouble retrieving all five names, even though they are all still stored in your long-term memory. Perhaps Lake Michigan doesn't come to mind when you retrieve the other four. The *HOMES* mnemonic provides a **retrieval cue**, or hint about where to "look" in long-term memory. The mnemonic tells you that one lake begins with the letter *M*, and so you search among the *M* words in your long-term memory until (we hope) you find "Michigan." Learners are more likely to retrieve information when relevant retrieval cues are present to start their search of long-term memory in the right direction (e.g., Tulving, 1983; Tulving & Thomson, 1973).

For another example of how retrieval cues can aid retrieval, try the following exercise.

EXPERIENCING FIRSTHAND *Recall Versus Recognition*

Earlier in the chapter, I described a process that keeps information in working memory for longer than the usual five to twenty seconds. Can you retrieve the name of that process from your long-term memory? See if you can before you read any further.

What kinds of assessment procedures are most likely to encourage automaticity? What kinds are least likely to encourage it?

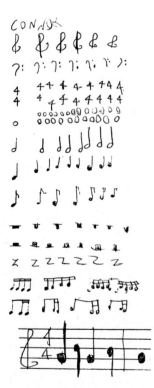

Developing automaticity does not necessarily require the drill and practice in which Connor engages in his sixth-grade music class. Automaticity can also develop when basic concepts and skills are repeatedly embedded in more meaningful activities.

If you can't remember the term to which I am referring, then try answering the same question posed in a multiple-choice format:

What do we call the process that keeps information in working memory for longer than the usual five to twenty seconds?

    a. facilitative construction
    b. internal organization
    c. short-term memorization
    d. maintenance rehearsal

Did you experience an "Aha, now I remember" feeling? The correct answer is *d*. Perhaps the multiple-choice format provided a retrieval cue for you, directing you to the correct answer you had stored in long-term memory. Generally, it is easier to remember something in a **recognition task** (in which you simply need to recognize correct information among irrelevant information or incorrect statements) than in a **recall task** (in which the correct information must be retrieved in its entirety from long-term memory) (Semb, Ellis, & Araujo, 1993). A recognition task is easier because it provides more retrieval cues to aid you in your search of long-term memory.

As teachers, we won't always want to help students retrieve information by putting that information right in front of them. Nevertheless, there will be occasions when providing hints is certainly appropriate. For example, when Sheri asks how the word *liquidation* is spelled, we might say, "*Liquidation* means to make something liquid. How do you spell *liquid*?" When Shawn wants to know what the symbol *Au* stands for, we might help him retrieve the answer with a hint like this one: "In class we talked about how *Au* comes from the Latin word *aurum*. Can you remember what aurum means?" Another example comes from one of my former teacher interns, Jess Jensen. A student in her eighth-grade history class had been writing about the Battle of New Orleans, which was a decisive victory for the United States in the War of 1812. The following exchange took place:

Student: Why was the Battle of New Orleans important?

Jess: Look at the map. Where is New Orleans?

(The student locates New Orleans.)

Jess: Why is it important?

Student: Oh! It's near the mouth of the Mississippi. It was important for controlling transportation up and down the river.

In the early grades, teachers typically provide many retrieval cues for their students: They remind students about the tasks they need to do and when they need to do them ("I hear the fire alarm. Remember, we all walk quietly during a fire drill"; or "It's time to go home. Do you all have the field trip permission slip to take to your parents?"). But as they grow older, students must develop greater independence, relying more on themselves and less on their teachers for the things they need to remember. At all grade levels, we can teach students ways of providing retrieval cues for *themselves*. For example, if we expect first graders to bring back those permission slips tomorrow, we might ask them to write a reminder on a piece of masking tape that they put on their jackets or lunch boxes. If we give junior high school students a

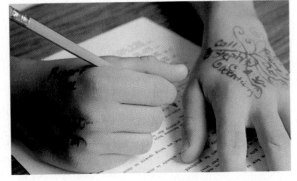

Ultimately, students must learn to develop their own retrieval cues. This student has written notes to himself on his hands.

major assignment due several weeks later, we might suggest that they help themselves remember the due date by taping a note to the bedside table or by making an entry on the kitchen calendar.

Now that you know something about retrieval and the factors that affect it, try the following assessment activity.

INTERPRETING ARTIFACTS AND INTERACTIONS   *Moving to Canada*

Another of my former teacher interns, Gerry Holly, was teaching a unit on Canada to his eighth-grade geography students. The class had already reviewed information about the topography (mountain ranges, rivers, etc.) and climate of various regions in the country. They had also studied social, political, and cultural issues (e.g., the separatist movement and use of French in Quebec). As you read the following classroom dialogue, consider

- How Gerry hoped his students would respond when he asked his question
- What the students' responses revealed about their ability to retrieve and use what they had learned
- What Gerry might do differently next time

Gerry:	Imagine that you're moving to Canada. Where would you go, and why? How would your life be different?
Student:	I'd go to Cambridge, Ontario, because I have relatives there.
Student:	Toronto, to see the Raptors [a basketball team] play!
Student:	I'd move to northern Quebec so I could swim in Hudson Bay.

Gerry was trying to help his students relate what they had learned about the physical and social environment of Canada to their own lives and needs. For instance, he hoped that they might retrieve what they had learned about the scenery, typical weather, or social milieu of various parts of Canada in making their decision. Unfortunately, the first two students retrieved none of that information in making their choices, and the third retrieved one piece of information (Hudson Bay) without retrieving another, equally important piece (Hudson Bay is *much* too cold for swimming). An excellent intern, Gerry learned very quickly that he would occasionally need to provide retrieval cues to get his students to use what they had learned. To do so, he might ask, "*Given what you now know about Canada's topography, climate, and social conditions,* where would you go, and why?"

Even so, a retrieval cue would not necessarily have enabled all of Gerry's students to recall what they had learned about Canada. And perhaps when you did the "Recall Versus Recognition" exercise a few minutes ago, you couldn't remember *maintenance rehearsal* even when it was staring you in the face. Let's now look at some of the reasons why people forget.

Why People Sometimes Forget

Fortunately, we don't need to remember everything. For example, we probably have no reason to remember the phone number of a florist we called yesterday, the plot of last week's *I Love Lucy* show, or the due date of an assignment we turned in last semester. Much of the information we encounter is—like our junk mail—not worth keeping, and forgetting enables us to get rid of that needless clutter (D. L. Schacter, 1999).

But as we have just seen, we sometimes have trouble recalling what we *do* need. Psychologists have numerous explanations for why people seem to forget. Here we consider five of them: failure to retrieve, reconstruction error, interference, decay, and failure to store.

Failure to Retrieve

A man at the supermarket looks familiar, but you can't remember who he is or when you met him. He smiles at you and says, "Hi there, nice to see you again." Gulp. You desperately search your long-term memory for his name, but you have clearly forgotten who this man is.

A few days later, you have a bowl of chili for dinner. The chili reminds you of the "Chili for Charity" supper at which you worked a few months back. Of course! You and the man at the supermarket had stood side by side serving chili to hundreds of people that night. Oh yes, you recall, his name is Melville Herman.

One reason we forget is an **inability to retrieve**: We can't locate information stored in long-term memory (e.g., Schacter, 1999). Sometimes we stumble on the information later, while "looking" for something else. But sometimes we never do retrieve the information, perhaps because we learned it by rote or because we don't have sufficient retrieval cues to adequately guide our search in long-term memory.

Reconstruction Error

Retrieval isn't necessarily an all-or-nothing phenomenon. Sometimes we retrieve part of the information we are seeking from long-term memory but cannot recall the rest. In such situations we may fill in the gaps using our general knowledge and assumptions about the world

(Kolodner, 1985; Roediger & McDermott, 2000; P. T. Wilson & Anderson, 1986). Even though the gaps are filled in "logically," they aren't always filled in correctly—a form of forgetting called **reconstruction error.** Chapter 7 looks at the reconstructive nature of retrieval in greater detail.

Interference

EXPERIENCING FIRSTHAND   *Six Chinese Words*

Here are six more Mandarin Chinese words and their English meanings (for simplicity, I've omitted the "tone" marks on the words). Read them two or three times and try to store them in your long-term memory. But don't do anything special to learn the words; for example, don't intentionally develop mnemonics to help you remember them.

Chinese	English
jung	middle
ting	listen
sung	deliver
peng	friend
ching	please
deng	wait

Now cover up the list of words and test yourself. What was the word for *friend? please? listen? wait?*

Did you find yourself getting confused, perhaps forgetting which English meaning went with each Chinese word? If you did, then you were the victim of **interference.** The various pieces of information that you stored in your long-term memory were interfering with one another; in a sense, the pieces were getting "mixed up." Notice that I told you *not* to use mnemonics to learn the Chinese words. Interference is especially likely to occur when pieces of information are similar to one another and when they are learned by rote (e.g., Dempster, 1985; Postman & Underwood, 1973; Underwood, 1948, 1957).

Recall the earlier case involving Kanesha. The similarity between *tibia* and *fibula* is one reason she confuses the names of the two bones.

Decay

As noted earlier, some psychologists believe that information remains in long-term memory forever. But others propose that information may weaken over time and perhaps disappear altogether, especially if it is not used frequently (J. R. Anderson, 1990; Reisberg, 1997; D. L. Schacter, 1999). Theorists sometimes use the word **decay** when describing this gradual fading process.

Failure to Store

Last on my list of reasons for forgetting is **failure to store:** Information never reached long-term memory to begin with. Perhaps a person receiving a piece of information didn't pay attention to it, so it never went beyond the sensory register. Or perhaps the learner, after attending to it, didn't process it any further, so it went no farther in the memory system than working memory. Obviously, failure to store is not an explanation of information loss; however, it is one possible reason why students who *think* they have learned something cannot recall it later on (D. L. Schacter, 1999).

When students informally test themselves as they learn and study, failure to store is less likely to be a problem. We will consider this process of *monitoring comprehension* in Chapter 8.

　　All five explanations for forgetting underscore the importance of instructional strategies we've identified earlier: For instance, we must make sure that our students are paying attention, help them relate new material to things they already know, and give them opportunities to review, practice, and apply that material frequently.

　　Yet even when we encourage effective storage processes, and even when we give students helpful retrieval cues, long-term memory storage and retrieval processes don't always happen instantaneously. For example, it may take time for students to relate new material to their existing knowledge and, at some later date, to retrieve all the "pieces" of what they have learned. What happens when teachers give students more time to process and retrieve information? The results can be quite dramatic, as we shall see now.

Where important information is concerned, never assume that once is enough.

A language arts teacher introduces the parts of speech (e.g., nouns, verbs, adjectives) early in the school year. Because these concepts will be important for students to know when they study a foreign language in later grades, he continues to review them throughout the year—for example, by frequently incorporating them into classroom activities.

When information must be retrieved rapidly, occasionally assign drill-and-practice exercises that enable students to learn it to automaticity.

An elementary school teacher gives frequent practice in the addition and subtraction facts until each student can add and subtract single digits quickly and accurately. To make such practice both motivating and informative, she has students time their performance each day and chart their continuing improvement on graph paper.

Teach students to develop their own retrieval cues for things they need to remember.

A teacher suggests that students tape a note to their jackets, reminding them to return their permission slips tomorrow.

When important details are difficult to fill in logically, make sure students learn them well.

A teacher gives students extra practice in troublesome spelling words, such as those that are spelled differently than they are pronounced (e.g., *people, February*).

Provide retrieval cues when appropriate.

When a student puzzles over how to compute the area of a circle, her teacher says, "We studied this last week. Do you remember the formula?" When the student shakes her head, the teacher continues, "Because the problem involves a circle, the formula probably includes *pi*, doesn't it?"

Giving Students Time to Process: Effects of Increasing Wait Time

Consider the following situation.

Mr. Smith likes to ask questions in his classroom. He also likes to keep class sessions going at a rapid pace. A typical day goes something like this:

Mr. Smith:	Why is it warmer in summer than in winter?
Amelia:	Because the sun is hotter.
Mr. Smith:	Well, yes, the sun *feels* hotter. What changes in the earth make it feel hotter?
Arnold:	The earth is closer to the sun in the summer.
Mr. Smith:	That's a possibility, Arnold. But there's something we need to consider here. When it's summer in the Northern Hemisphere, it's winter in the Southern Hemisphere. When North America is having its warmest days, Australia is having its coldest days. Can we use the earth's distance from the sun to explain that?
Arnold:	Uh . . . I guess not.
Mr. Smith:	So . . . why is it warmer in summer than in winter? (No one responds.) Do you know, Angela? (She shakes her head.) How about you, Andrew?
Andrew:	Nope.
Mr. Smith:	Can you think of anything we discussed yesterday that might help us with an explanation? (No one responds.) Remember, yesterday we talked about how the earth changes its tilt in relation to the sun throughout the year. This change in the earth's tilt explains why the days get longer throughout the winter and spring and why they get shorter during the summer and fall. (Mr. Smith continues with an explanation of how the angle of the sun's rays affects temperature on earth.)

Mr. Smith is hoping that his students will draw a connection between information they learned yesterday (changes in the earth's tilt relative to the sun) and today's topic (the seasons).

Unfortunately, Mr. Smith is moving too quickly from one question to the next and from one student to another. His students don't make the connection he expects because he simply doesn't give them enough time to do so.

The problem with Mr. Smith's lesson is one seen in many classrooms: too short a **wait time**. When teachers ask students a question, they typically wait one second or less for a response. If students don't respond in that short time interval, teachers tend to speak again—sometimes by asking different students the same question, sometimes by rephrasing the question, sometimes even by answering the question themselves (M. B. Rowe, 1974, 1987). Teachers are equally reluctant to let much time lapse after students answer questions or make comments in class; once again, they typically allow *one second or less* of silence before responding to a statement or asking another question (M. B. Rowe, 1987).

How much wait time do your own instructors exhibit? Is it long enough to promote good classroom discussions?

If we consider basic principles of cognitive psychology—for example, the importance of relating new information to prior knowledge and the difficulty often associated with retrieving information from long-term memory—then we realize that one second is a very short time indeed for students to develop their responses. When teachers instead allow at least *three seconds* to elapse after their own questions and after students' comments, dramatic changes can occur in both students' and teachers' behaviors:

Changes in students' behaviors:

- *More class participation.* More students participate in class; this is especially true for females and students from ethnic minority groups. Students are more likely to answer questions correctly and to contribute spontaneously to a class discussion, perhaps by asking their own questions, presenting their own perspectives, and responding to one another's comments.
- *Better quality of responses.* Students give a greater variety of responses to the same question, and their responses are longer and more sophisticated. They are more likely to support their reasoning with evidence or logic and more likely to speculate when they don't know an answer.
- *Better overall classroom performance.* Students are more likely to feel confident that they can master the material and more motivated to learn it. Academic achievement increases, and discipline problems decrease.

Changes in teachers' behaviors:

- *Different kinds of questions.* Teachers ask fewer "simple" questions (e.g., those requiring recall of facts) and a greater number of complex questions (e.g., those requiring students to elaborate or develop alternative explanations).
- *Increased flexibility in teaching.* Teachers modify the direction of discussion to accommodate students' comments and questions, and they allow their classes to pursue a topic in greater depth than they had originally anticipated.
- *Higher expectations.* Teachers' expectations for many students, especially previously low-achieving students, begin to improve. (Mohatt & Erickson, 1981; M. B. Rowe, 1974, 1987; Tharp, 1989; Tobin, 1987)

From the perspective of cognitive psychology, increasing wait time appears to have two benefits for student learning (Tobin, 1987). First, it allows students more time to process classroom subject matter. Second, it appears to change the very nature of teacher-student discussions; for example, teachers are more likely to ask challenging, thought-provoking questions. In fact, the nature of the questions that teachers ask is probably as important as—and perhaps even more important than—the amount of wait time per se (Giaconia, 1988).

When our objective is simple recall—when students need to retrieve classroom material very quickly, to "know it cold"—then wait time should be short. As we have seen, students may sometimes need rapid-fire drill and practice to learn information and skills to automaticity. But when our objectives include more complex processing of ideas and issues, longer wait time may provide both teachers and students the time that they need to think things through.

When teachers increase wait time to three seconds or longer, students participate more actively and give more complex responses to questions.

TABLE 6.3

STUDENTS IN INCLUSIVE SETTINGS

Facilitating Cognitive Processing in Students with Special Educational Needs

CATEGORY	CHARACTERISTICS YOU MIGHT OBSERVE	SUGGESTED CLASSROOM STRATEGIES
Students with specific cognitive or academic difficulties	• Deficiencies in one or more specific cognitive processes (e.g., perception, encoding) • Distractibility, inability to sustain attention (in some students) • Difficulty screening out irrelevant stimuli • Less working memory capacity, or less efficient use of working memory • Impulsivity in responding	• Analyze students' errors as a way of identifying possible processing difficulties. • Identify weaknesses in specific cognitive processes and provide instruction that enables students to compensate for these weaknesses. • Present information in an organized fashion and make frequent connections to students' prior knowledge as ways of promoting more effective long-term memory storage. • Teach mnemonics to aid long-term memory storage and retrieval. • Encourage greater reflection before responding—for instance, by reinforcing accuracy rather than speed, or by teaching self-instructions (see Chapter 10). • Intersperse activities that require sustained attention with opportunities for physical exercise.
Students with social or behavioral problems	• Lack of attention because of off-task thoughts and behaviors • Difficulty shifting attention quickly (for students with autism) • Possible difficulties in other cognitive processes (e.g., undiagnosed learning disabilities)	• Make sure you have students' attention before giving instructions or presenting information. • Refer students to a school psychologist for evaluation and diagnosis of possible learning disabilities.
Students with general delays in cognitive and social functioning	• Slower cognitive processing • Difficulty with attention to task-relevant information • Reduced working memory capacity, or less efficient use of working memory • Smaller knowledge base on which to build new learning	• Keep instructional materials simple, emphasizing relevant stimuli and minimizing irrelevant stimuli. • Provide clear instructions that focus students' attention on desired behaviors (e.g., "Listen," "Write," "Stop"). • Pace instruction to allow students enough time to think about and process information adequately (e.g., provide ample wait time after questions). • Assume little prior knowledge about new topics (i.e., "begin at the beginning").
Students with physical or sensory challenges	• Normal cognitive processing ability in most students • Less general knowledge due to limited experiences in the outside world	• Assume equal ability for learning and understanding new information and skills, but consider how students' physical and sensory challenges may interfere with some learning processes. • Expose students to life experiences they may have missed due to their disabilities.
Students with advanced cognitive development	• More rapid cognitive processing • Larger knowledge base (the nature of which will vary, depending on students' cultural backgrounds) • More interconnections among ideas in long-term memory • More rapid retrieval of information from long-term memory	• Proceed through topics more quickly or in greater depth. • Create interdisciplinary lessons to foster integration of material in long-term memory.

Sources: Barkley, 1998; Beirne-Smith et al., 2002; Bulgren et al., 1994; Butterfield & Ferretti, 1987; B. Clark, 1997; Courchesne et al., 1994; Heward, 2000; Landau & McAninch, 1993; Lorch et al., 1999; Mercer, 1997; Morgan & Jenson, 1988; Piirto, 1999; Pressley, 1995; Rabinowitz & Glaser, 1985; H. L. Swanson et al., 1998; Turnbull et al., 1999.

Accommodating Diversity in Cognitive Processes

As we've explored basic principles of cognitive psychology in this chapter, we've considered many factors—attention, working memory capacity, long-term memory storage processes, prior knowledge, retrieval, and so on—that influence what and how well our students are likely to learn and remember classroom material. Naturally, our students will differ considerably with regard to these factors; for example, they will have unique knowledge bases on which to draw, and they will elaborate differently on the ideas we present (e.g., Cothern, Konopak, & Willis, 1990; Grant & Gomez, 2001; R. E. Reynolds et al., 1982). They may also have had varying experiences with different kinds of memory tasks. For instance, students from traditional North American classrooms are likely to have had more experience learning lists of things, whereas students from some African countries may have an easier time remembering stories and students from some Australian cultures may have an easier time remembering the locations of objects (Flavell et al., 1993). Furthermore, as noted in Chapter 4, students from diverse backgrounds will especially benefit from extended wait time; for instance, some Native American students may wait several seconds before responding as a way of showing respect for an adult, and those with limited proficiency in English may require some "mental translation" time.

Facilitating Cognitive Processing in Students with Special Needs

Some of our students with special educational needs may have particular trouble attending to and processing classroom subject matter in an effective manner. This will certainly be true for students with learning disabilities (by definition, they have difficulty with certain cognitive processes), and it will often be true for students with ADHD as well (Barkley, 1998; Lorch et al., 1999; Mercer, 1997). Furthermore, students with mental retardation will typically process information more slowly than their classmates, and students with emotional and behavioral disorders may have trouble keeping their attention on the task at hand (Courchesne et al., 1994; Turnbull et al., 1999). In contrast, gifted students are likely to process new ideas more rapidly and in a more complex manner than many of their classmates (B. Clark, 1997; Heward, 2000). Table 6.3 identifies cognitive processing differences we are likely to see in students with special educational needs.

Virtually all of our students, including those without any identified special needs, will occasionally have difficulty learning or remembering class material. Accordingly, many of the instructional strategies in Table 6.3—getting students' attention, analyzing their errors, teaching them mnemonics, and so on—need not be limited to use with students with special needs. *All* of our students can benefit from help in processing information more effectively.

The Big Picture

As teachers, we must always consider not only what students are doing but also what they are *thinking*. The specific ways that students interpret and make sense of classroom material, and in fact the extent to which they interpret and make sense of it *at all*, influence how quickly and easily they learn it, how successfully they retrieve it, and (as we shall discover in Chapter 8) how likely they are to apply it to real-world situations and problems. Let's pull together what we have learned about effective cognitive processes and review key strategies for encouraging such processing in the classroom.

Effective Cognitive Processes

Long-term memory appears to have as much capacity as we could ever need; in fact, the more information we have already stored

there, the more easily we can learn new material. Yet attention and working memory have a limited capacity (we can attend to and think about only a small amount of information at any one time), creating a major bottleneck in the memory system.

To learn and remember something effectively, we must, first and foremost, give it our undivided attention; that is, we must mentally focus on it and, for at least a brief time, make it the psychological center of our cognitive universe. We must then actively try to make it more meaningful, organized, logical, and vivid for ourselves—for instance, by identifying ways in which it is similar to things we already know, finding interconnections among its various pieces, drawing inferences from it, or forming a visual image that helps us understand it better. To ensure that we master the flawless execution of certain procedures, and to ensure that we can recall basic knowledge and skills quickly and efficiently, we must practice some things over and over at regular intervals and in different contexts.

Encouraging Effective Cognitive Processes in the Classroom

Basic principles of effective cognitive processing apply not only to ourselves but also, of course, to the children and adolescents we will have in our classrooms. As teachers, we must continually emphasize the importance of *understanding* classroom subject matter—making sense of it, drawing inferences from it, seeing how it all ties together, and so on—rather than simply memorizing it in a relatively "thoughtless" manner. This emphasis must be reflected not only in our words, but also in our instructional activities, classroom assignments, and assessment practices. For instance, rather than just presenting important ideas in classroom lectures and asking students to take notes, we might also ask thought-provoking questions that require students to evaluate, synthesize, or apply what they are learning. As an alternative to asking students to memorize procedures for adding two two-digit numbers, we might ask them to suggest at least three *different* ways they might solve problems such as 15 + 45 or 29 + 68 and to justify their reasoning. Rather than assessing their knowledge of history by asking them to recite names, places, and dates, we might ask them to explain why certain historical events happened and how those events altered the course of subsequent history. Such approaches will not only make students' learning more meaningful and effective but will also enhance their belief that classroom topics are interesting, enjoyable, and in some way relevant to their own lives.

PRAXIS Turn to Appendix C, "Matching Book and Ancillary Content to the PRAXIS™ Principles of Learning and Teaching Tests," to discover sections of this chapter that may be especially applicable to the PRAXIS™ tests.

Now go to our Companion Website at http://www.prenhall.com/ormrod to assess your understanding of chapter content with "Multiple-Choice Questions," apply comprehension in "Essay Questions," broaden your knowledge of educational psychology with related "Web Links," gain greater insight about classroom learning in "Learning in the Content Areas," and analyze and assess classroom work in the "Student Artifact Library."

CASE STUDY: *How Time Flies*

Ms. Llewellyn is a first-year social studies teacher at an American high school; she recently completed her degree in United States history and knows her subject matter well. Her history classes begin in September with a study of early explorers of the Western Hemisphere. By early October, students are reading about the colonial settlements of the 1600s. By December, they have covered the French and Indian War, the Revolutionary War, and the Declaration of Independence. The winter months are spent studying the nineteenth century (e.g., the Industrial Revolution, the Civil War), and the spring is spent studying the twentieth century (including both world wars, the Korean War, the Vietnam War, the Persian Gulf crisis, and modern-day terrorism).

Ms. Llewellyn has high expectations for her students. In her daily class lectures, she describes historical events in detail, hoping to give her students a sense of how complex many of these events really were. In addition to having students read the usual high school textbook, she also assigns articles in the historical journals that she herself reads.

Occasionally, Ms. Llewellyn stops a lecture a few minutes before the bell rings to ask questions that check her students' recall of the day's topics. Although her students can usually remember the main gist of her lecture, they have difficulty with the details, either mixing them up or forgetting them altogether. A few students remember so little that she can hardly believe they were in class that day. Her students perform even more poorly on monthly essay exams; it's obvious from their written responses that they can remember little of what Ms. Llewellyn has taught them.

"I explained things so clearly to them," she tells herself. "Perhaps these kids just don't want to learn."

- Why might Ms. Llewellyn's students be having difficulty learning and remembering the things that she teaches them? Can you think of possible reasons related to the class curriculum? to Ms. Llewellyn's style of teaching? to Ms. Llewellyn's reading assignments?
- From the perspective of cognitive psychology, what would you do differently than Ms. Llewellyn?

Once you have answered these questions, compare your responses with those presented in Appendix B.

Key Concepts

7

Knowledge Construction

*T*hink back to a time when you tried to carry on a conversation with someone in a noisy room—maybe at a party, in a bar where a band was playing, or in a workshop with loud machinery operating nearby. You probably couldn't hear everything the other person was saying. But perhaps you were able to hear enough to get the gist of what the other person was trying to tell you. You combined what you *did* hear with things that you could see (e.g., gestures and facial expressions) and with things that you already knew about the topic under discussion. We often construct meanings from the stimuli around us—meanings that aren't necessarily obvious from the stimuli themselves, and meanings that may or may not be accurate.

As we discovered in the preceding chapter, many cognitive psychologists do not believe that learning is a simple process of absorbing information from the environment. Instead, learning involves constructing one's own knowledge from one's experiences. This chapter focuses on constructive processes in learning and memory. More specifically, we will address these questions:

- How are both storage and retrieval constructive in nature?
- How do people sometimes work together in their efforts to construct meaning?
- What forms might constructed knowledge take?
- Why do students sometimes acquire misconceptions about the world, and how do such beliefs affect later learning?
- What strategies can we use to help students construct accurate and useful knowledge about classroom topics?
- What strategies can we use to encourage students to correct their misconceptions about the world? In other words, how can we promote *conceptual change*?
- In what ways are constructive processes likely to be different in students with diverse backgrounds and needs?

CASE STUDY: *Pulling It All Together*

Rita is a fourth grader who attends school in Michigan. Her class has recently had a unit on Michigan's state history. Rita still knows little about U.S. history; she will study this subject as a fifth grader next year. Despite her limited background in history, Rita responds eagerly to an interviewer's questions about the New World.

Interviewer:	Our country is in the part of the world called America. At one time, America was called the New World. Do you know why it was called the New World?
Rita:	Yeah. We learned this in social studies.
Interviewer:	What did you learn?
Rita:	Because they used to live in England, the British, and they didn't know about . . . they wanted to get to China 'cause China had some things they wanted. They had some cups or whatever—no, they had furs. They had fur and stuff like that and they wanted to have a shorter way to get to China so they took it and they landed in Michigan, but it wasn't called Michigan. I think it was the British that landed in Michigan and they were there first and so they tried to claim that land, but it didn't work out for some reason so they took some furs and brought them

back to Britain and they sold them, but they mostly wanted it for the furs. So then the English landed there and they claimed the land and they wanted to make it a state, and so they got it signed by the government or whoever, the big boss, then they were just starting to make it a state so the British just went up to the Upper Peninsula and they thought they could stay there for a little while. Then they had to fight a war, then the farmers, they were just volunteers, so the farmers went right back and tried to get their family put back together again.

Interviewer: Did you learn all this in state history this year?
Rita: Um hum. (VanSledright & Brophy, 1992, p. 849)

- Which parts of Rita's response accurately describe the history of the New World? Which parts are clearly *inaccurate*?
- Can you identify at least two instances in which Rita has pulled together unrelated ideas in her constructed "knowledge" about history?

Constructive Processes in Learning and Memory

Rita has taken bits and pieces of information she has learned in school and pulled them into a scenario that makes sense to her. In the process, she has developed some unique interpretations of historical events. For example, she knows that the British wanted something that could be obtained in the Far East; she also knows that there was once a high demand for animal furs in England. Put them together and *voilà!*—the Chinese had the furs that the British wanted. (In reality, the Far East offered spices, not furs.) Notice, too, how Rita maintains that the British found a shorter way to get to China—one that apparently went right through Michigan. Although Rita's description of historical events has a few elements of truth, these elements have been combined to form an overall "knowledge" of history that could give any historian heart failure.

Rita may have constructed her unique view of history at the time she learned it—that is, during storage. But she also may have constructed it while the adult was interviewing her—in other words, while she was retrieving what she'd previously learned. Let's consider how construction can occur during both storage and retrieval.

Construction in Storage

EXPERIENCING FIRSTHAND   *Rocky*

Read the following passage *one time only:*

> Rocky slowly got up from the mat, planning his escape. He hesitated a moment and thought. Things were not going well. What bothered him most was being held, especially since the charge against him had been weak. He considered his present situation. The lock that held him was strong but he thought he could break it. He knew, however, that his timing would have to be perfect. Rocky was aware that it was because of his early roughness that he had been penalized so severely—much too severely from his point of view. The situation was becoming frustrating; the pressure had been grinding on him for too long. He was being ridden unmercifully. Rocky was getting angry now. He felt he was ready to make his move. He knew that his success or failure would depend on what he did in the next few seconds. (R. C. Anderson, Reynolds, Schallert, & Goetz, 1977, p. 372)

Now summarize what you've just read in two or three sentences.

Were you able to make sense of the passage? What did you think it was about? A prison escape? A wrestling match? Or perhaps something else altogether? The passage about Rocky includes a number of facts but leaves a lot unsaid; for example, it tells us nothing about where Rocky was, what kind of "lock" was holding him, or why timing was of the utmost importance. Yet you were probably able to use the information you were given to construct an overall understanding of Rocky's situation. Most people do find meaning of one sort or another in the passage (R. C. Anderson et al., 1977).

Different people often construct different meanings from the same stimuli, in part because they each bring their own unique prior experiences and knowledge bases to the same situation. For example, when the Rocky passage was used in an experiment with college students, physical education majors frequently interpreted it as a wrestling match, but music education majors (most of whom had little or no knowledge of wrestling) were more likely to think that it was about a prison break (R. C. Anderson et al., 1977).

Furthermore, people often interpret what they see and hear based on what they *expect* to see and hear. As an example, try the following exercise.

Even though these girls are working together on a science activity, their prior knowledge and beliefs may lead each one to derive a different understanding from the experience.

EXPERIENCING FIRSTHAND   *Nursery Rhymes*

Here are three well-known nursery rhymes. Read them *as quickly as you can,* and read them *one time only.*

1   **Hey Diddle Diddle**

2   Hey diddle diddle,
3   The cat and the fiddle.
4   The cow jumped over the moon.
5   The little dog laughed to see such sport,
6   And tha dish ran away with the spoon.

7   **This Little Piggy**

8   This little piggy want to market
9   This little piggy stayed home
10   This little piggy had roost beef
11   This little piggy had none
12   This little piggy went wee, wee, wee all the way home.

13   **Little Bo Peep**

14   Little Bo Peep
15   Has lost her sheep
16   And dosn't know where to find them.
17   Leave them alone
18   And they'll come home,
19   Waggng their tails behind them.

You may have noticed one or two typographical errors in the rhymes. But did you catch them all? Altogether, five words were misspelled: *the* (line 6), *went* (line 8), *roast* (line 10), *doesn't* (line 16), and *wagging* (line 19). If you didn't notice all the errors—and many people don't—then your perception of the nursery rhymes was influenced by what words you *expected* to see in them.

Prior knowledge and expectations are especially likely to influence learning when new information is ambiguous (e.g., Eysenck & Keane, 1990). To see what I mean, try another exercise.

EXPERIENCING FIRSTHAND   *A Pen-and-Ink Sketch*

Take a look at Figure 7.1. Look at the details carefully. Notice the shape of the head, the facial features, and the relative proportion of one part to another. But what exactly *do* you see?

FIGURE 7.1   What do you see in this picture?

From "The Role of Frequency in Developing Perceptual Sets" by B. R. Bugelski & D. A. Alampay, 1961, *Canadian Journal of Psychology, 15,* p. 206. Copyright 1961. Canadian Psychological Association. Reprinted with permission.

Did you see a picture of a rat or mouse, or did you see a bald-headed man? In fact, the drawing isn't a very good picture of *anything;* too many details have been left out. Despite the missing pieces, people can usually make sense of Figure 7.1. Whether they see a man or a rodent depends, in large part, on whether they expect to see a human being or a nonhuman creature (Bugelski & Alampay, 1961). People's interpretations of ambiguous information are

FIGURE 7.2 As you can see from her journal entries, 8-year-old Darcy initially interpreted a casual remark to the school nurse in a way very different from the teacher's intended meaning. Fortunately, the teacher corrected the misunderstanding a few days later.

October 22nd, 2001

I went to a new school today. My teacher's name is Mrs. Whaley. I accidentally cracked an egg on my head. Mrs. Whaley told the nurse that I was a showoff and a nuisance. I got really sad and wanted to run away from school, but I didn't leave.

• • •

October 27th, 2001

We presented our book reports today. I was the last one to present my book report. Whenever I did my book report, they laughed at me, but the teacher said they were laughing with me. I asked the teacher why she had called me a nuisance the first day. And she said, "Darcy, I didn't call you a nuisance. I was saying to Mrs. Larson that it was a nuisance to try to wash egg out of your hair." I was so happy. I decided to like Mrs. Whaley again.

particularly susceptible to biases and expectations because so much of the information necessary for an "accurate" perception (if such is possible) is simply not available.

As teachers, we will find our students constructing their own idiosyncratic meanings and interpretations in virtually every area of the classroom curriculum. For example, as the "Rocky" exercise illustrates, the activity of reading is often quite constructive in nature: Students combine the ideas that they read with their prior knowledge and then draw logical conclusions about what the text is trying to communicate (Dole, Duffy, Roehler, & Pearson, 1991; Otero & Kintsch, 1992). So, too, will we find constructive processes in such subject areas as mathematics, science, and social studies (R. Driver, Asoko, Leach, Mortimer, & Scott, 1994; L. B. Resnick, 1989; VanSledright & Brophy, 1992). When we want our students to interpret classroom subject matter in particular ways, we must be sure to communicate clearly and unambiguously, so that there is little room for misinterpretation. We must also leave little room for doubt in the messages we communicate about nonacademic matters, as Figure 7.2 illustrates.

> Skillful readers often skip some of the words on the page and yet understand what they read quite accurately. How is this possible?

Construction in Retrieval

Have you ever remembered an event very differently than someone else did? Were you and the other person both equally convinced of the accuracy of your memories? How might constructive processes explain this difference of opinion?

As noted in Chapter 6, retrieval isn't always an all-or-nothing phenomenon. Sometimes we retrieve only certain parts of whatever information we are looking for in long-term memory. In such situations, we may construct our "memory" of an event by combining the tidbits we can retrieve with our general knowledge and assumptions about the world (Kolodner, 1985; Loftus, 1991; Rumelhart & Ortony, 1977). As an example of how retrieval of a specific event or idea often involves drawing on our knowledge about other things as well, try the following exercise.

EXPERIENCING FIRSTHAND *Missing Letters*

Can you fill in the missing letters of these five words?

1. sep - rate
2. exist - nce
3. adole - - - nce
4. retr - - val
5. hors d'o - - - - -

Were you able to retrieve the missing letters from your long-term memory? If not, then you may have found yourself making reasonable guesses, using either your knowledge of how the words are pronounced or your knowledge of how words in the English language are typically spelled. For example, perhaps you used the "i before e except after c" rule for word 4; if so, then you reconstructed the correct spelling of *retrieval*. Perhaps you used your knowledge that *ance* is a common word ending. Unfortunately, if you used this knowledge for word 2, then you spelled *existence* incorrectly. Neither pronunciation nor typical English spelling patterns would have helped you with *hors d'oeuvre*, a term borrowed from the French. (The correct spellings for words 1 and 3 are *separate* and *adolescence*.)

When people fill in the gaps in what they've retrieved based on what seems "logical," they often make mistakes—a phenomenon known as **reconstruction error**. Rita's version of what she learned in history is a prime example: She retrieved certain facts from her history lessons (e.g., the British wanted furs; some of them eventually settled in what is now Michigan) and constructed a scenario that made sense to her. So, too, will our own students sometimes fall victim to reconstruction error, pulling together what they can recall in ways we may hardly recognize (Leichtman & Ceci, 1995; Roediger & McDermott, 2000). If important details are difficult to fill in logically, we must make sure our students learn them well enough to retrieve them directly from long-term memory.

> What implications does the notion of reconstruction error have for the credibility of eyewitness testimony?

Up to this point, we have been talking about construction as a process that occurs within a single learner. Theories that focus on how people, as individuals, construct meaning from events are collectively known as **individual constructivism**. Views about memory storage processes such as organization, elaboration, and visual imagery (see Chapter 6) have an element of individual constructivism, as do Piaget's theory of cognitive development and many explanations of language development (see Chapter 2). Yet sometimes people work *together* to construct meaning and knowledge, as we shall see now.

Knowledge Construction as a Social Process

Think about times when you've been confused about material in one of your high school or college classes. In such situations, did you ever work cooperatively with classmates (who were just as confused as you were) to make sense of the material *together*? Quite possibly, by sharing your various interpretations, you jointly constructed a better understanding of the subject matter than any of you could have constructed on your own. Unlike individually constructed knowledge, which may differ considerably from one individual to another, socially constructed knowledge is shared by two or more people simultaneously. A perspective known as **social constructivism** focuses on such collective efforts to impose meaning on the world.

Students who share their interpretations with one another often construct more complex understandings of the subject matter than they could have constructed on their own.

Sometimes meaning is constructed by a group of people at a single point in time. For example, this would be the case if, by working together in a study group, you and a few classmates made sense of puzzling course material. At other times, the social construction of meaning may take weeks, years, or even centuries, as is seen in the evolution of such academic disciplines as mathematics, science, history, psychology, and economics. Through these disciplines, people have developed concepts (e.g., *pi* [π], *molecule,* and *revolution*) and principles (e.g., *Pythagorean theorem, supply-and-demand,* and the *limited capacity of working memory*) to simplify, organize, and explain the very diverse nature of the world. Literature, music, and fine arts help us to impose meaning on the world as well—for example, by trying to portray the thoughts and feelings that characterize human experience. Here we see the very critical role that *culture* plays in knowledge construction: To the extent that different groups of people use different concepts and principles to explain their physical experiences, and to the extent that they have unique bodies of literature, music, and art to capture their psychological experiences, they will inevitably see the world in very diverse ways (Hong et al., 2000; O. Lee, 1999; Tomasello, 2000).

Benefits of Group Meaning-Making in the Classroom

Increasingly, theorists and practitioners are recognizing the value of having students work together to construct meaning about classroom subject matter—for instance, to explore, explain, discuss, and debate certain topics either in small groups or as an entire class. By having students share their ideas and perspectives with one another, we enhance their understanding of a particular topic in several ways:

- We encourage students to clarify and organize their ideas well enough to verbalize them to others.
- We provide opportunities for students to *elaborate* on what they have learned—for example, by drawing inferences, generating hypotheses, and asking questions.
- We expose students to the views of others—views that may reflect a more accurate understanding of the topics under discussion.
- We enable students to discover flaws and inconsistencies in their own thinking, thereby helping them identify gaps in their understanding.
- We help students discover how people from different cultural and ethnic backgrounds may interpret the world in different, yet perhaps equally valid, ways. (L. M. Anderson, 1993; Banks, 1991; Barnes, 1976; M. Carr & Biddlecomb, 1998; Fosnot, 1996; Hatano & Inagaki, 1993; E. H. Hiebert & Raphael, 1996; K. Hogan, Nastasi, & Pressley, 2000; A. King, 1999; Schwarz, Neuman, & Biezuner, 2000; N. M. Webb & Palincsar, 1996)

As a result, students who work as a group are likely to construct a more complex understanding of a topic than any single student could do alone. Some theorists (A. L. Brown et al., 1993; Hewitt & Scardamalia, 1998; Salomon, 1993a, 1993b) refer to such "group thinking" as **distributed cognition**, a concept that overlaps with *distributed intelligence* (Chapter 4).

Yet as we have seen in earlier chapters, and will continue to see in later chapters, the benefits of student interaction are not restricted to a better understanding of the particular topic under discussion. Consider these additional advantages:

When students must explain their thinking to someone else, they usually organize and elaborate on what they've learned. These processes help them develop a more integrated and thorough understanding of the material.

- Disagreements among peers are likely to promote progress to higher stages of cognitive and moral development (see the discussion of Piaget's and Kohlberg's theories in Chapters 2 and 3, respectively).
- By arguing about issues with one another, children eventually internalize the "arguing" process and so acquire the ability to look at a single issue from multiple perspectives (see the discussion of Vygotsky's theory in Chapter 2).
- Students can develop more effective interpersonal skills (see Chapter 3).
- Students can model effective ways of thinking about and studying academic subject matter for one another (see the discussion of *metacognition* in Chapter 8).
- In the process of debating controversial material, students may gain a more sophisticated view of the nature of knowledge and learning; for instance, they may recognize that acquiring "knowledge" involves acquiring an integrated set of ideas about a topic and that such knowledge is likely to evolve gradually over time (see the discussion of *epistemological beliefs* in Chapter 8).
- Students may develop greater self-confidence for performing a task when they see their peers accomplishing the same task successfully (see the discussion of *self-efficacy* in Chapter 10).
- Students may be more motivated to participate in learning activities in which they also can satisfy their social needs (see the discussion of *relatedness* in Chapter 11).

Clearly, then, students have a great deal to gain—not only cognitively, but also personally, socially, and motivationally—from conversing with one another regularly about classroom subject matter. Later in the chapter we will discuss several strategies for promoting the social construction of meaning. In the meantime, however, let's look at the forms that constructed knowledge—whether derived individually or socially—might take.

Organizing Knowledge

In the process of constructing knowledge, people also organize it in a variety of ways, thereby creating the interconnected long-term memory described in Chapter 6. This section introduces several ways in which people appear to organize the things they learn: *concepts, schemas, scripts,* and *personal theories.* Of these, we will spend the most time looking at concepts, not because they are the most important, but simply because researchers have been studying them for a longer time and so have a better understanding of them.

Concepts

A **concept** is a way of mentally grouping or categorizing objects or events. For instance, the concept *furniture* encompasses such objects as chairs, tables, beds, and desks. The concept *swim* encompasses a variety of actions—breast stroke, crawl, dog paddle—that all involve propelling oneself through water.

Students learn thousands of concepts during their school years. They learn some concepts quickly and easily. They acquire others more gradually and continue to modify them over time; in the meantime, they may have an "almost-but-not-quite" understanding of what the concepts are. Following are several examples of such partial understanding:

> Lonnigan thinks of an *animal* as something with four legs and fur. He is quite surprised when his teacher says that fish, birds, and insects are also animals.

> Lisa correctly defines a *rectangle* as a geometric figure composed of two sets of parallel lines that are joined by right angles; this definition appropriately includes squares as examples of rectangles. Yet when she is shown a variety of shapes and asked to pick out all the rectangles, she doesn't identify the squares as being rectangles (P. S. Wilson, 1988).

> Luis learns that a *noun* is "a person, place, or thing." Using this definition, he classifies words like *you* and *me* as nouns because they refer to people. Only later, when Luis learns about other parts of speech, does he realize that *you* and *me* are pronouns rather than nouns.

In some cases, students **undergeneralize** a concept: They have too narrow a view as to which objects or events are included. Lonnigan undergeneralizes when he excludes fish, birds, and insects from his concept of *animal*. And Lisa's current conception of a *rectangle* is an undergeneralization because she doesn't realize that squares are also rectangles. On other occasions, students may **overgeneralize** a concept: They may identify objects and events as examples of a concept when in fact they are nonexamples. For instance, Luis overgeneralizes when he identifies *you* and *me* as nouns. Students don't fully understand what a concept is until they can identify both examples (**positive instances**) and nonexamples (**negative instances**) of the concept with complete accuracy.

Theorists have differing opinions about what people actually learn when they acquire a new concept. Let's consider how a concept might be learned as a *feature list*, a *prototype*, or a set of *exemplars*; let's also consider how numerous concepts are often interconnected in long-term memory.

Concepts as Feature Lists

Some theorists propose that learning a concept involves learning the specific attributes, or *features*, that characterize positive instances of the concept. **Defining features** are characteristics present in *all* positive instances. For example, a *circle* must be round, a *square* must have four equal sides connected at 90° angles, and an *animal* must be a consumer of food (rather than produce its own food through photosynthesis).

The task of identifying a concept's defining features is not always an easy one. As an example, consider this situation:

> A father goes to work. On the way home from work in the evening he stops at a bar to have a drink. His friends there are drunkards and he becomes a drunkard too. Is he still a father? (Saltz, 1971, p. 28)

Most 8-year-old children deny that a drunkard can still be a father (Saltz, 1971). Their response reflects their ignorance of the defining features of the concept *father*. Rather than recognize that fatherhood is defined simply in terms of a biological or adoptive relationship, many young children believe that a defining feature of fatherhood is "goodness," so a "bad" drunkard is automatically disqualified. "Goodness" is a **correlational feature** of fatherhood—a feature present in many positive instances of the concept but not essential for concept membership.

A concept is most easily learned when its defining features are concrete and obvious—in other words, when they are **salient**—rather than when they are abstract or difficult to pin down.

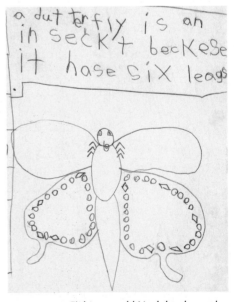

a dut terfly is an in seckt beckese it hase six leags

Eight-year-old Noah has learned one of the defining features of *insect*: six legs.

As an example, the concept *red* has a single defining feature—a particular range of light wavelengths—that is easily seen by anyone who isn't color-blind. But what about the defining feature of *plant*? The process of photosynthesis is not readily observable. Instead, we are more apt to notice other characteristics of plants (e.g., that they have leaves or that they grow in gardens) that are correlational rather than defining features.

When children first encounter concepts, they are sometimes led astray by correlational features, particularly if those features are more salient than the defining ones (Anglin, 1977; Keil, 1989; Mervis, 1987). Thus, we should not be surprised to find Lisa omitting squares from her concept of *rectangle*. Most of the rectangles that Lisa has seen have probably had noticeably different widths and lengths. Nor is it surprising that Lonnigan excludes fish and birds from his concept of *animal*. Two very obvious correlational features—fur and four legs—have undoubtedly characterized many of the critters that people in Lonnigan's life have specifically labeled as "animals" (S. Carey, 1985).

How do people learn a concept's defining features? The following exercise illustrates one possible mechanism.

EXPERIENCING FIRSTHAND   *Squerkles*

Figure 7.3 shows a bird's-eye view of some positive and negative instances of a lizardlike creature known as a *squerkle*. Before you read further, look at the figure and see whether you can determine what defines a squerkle.

While trying to learn what a squerkle is, you may have noticed yourself forming various hypotheses about its defining features. For example, when you saw four pointy-nosed squerkles and two round-nosed nonsquerkles on the top row, you may have thought that nose shape determines whether a critter is a squerkle. But then you would have found a pointy-nosed nonsquerkle and a round-nosed squerkle and so would have abandoned that hypothesis. Perhaps you thought that all squerkles had black eyes—until you reached the bottom row. I hope that you eventually discovered the defining feature of a squerkle: horizontal lines on either the body or the tail. Black eyes and pointy noses are correlational fea-

FIGURE 7.3 Learning the concept *squerkle*

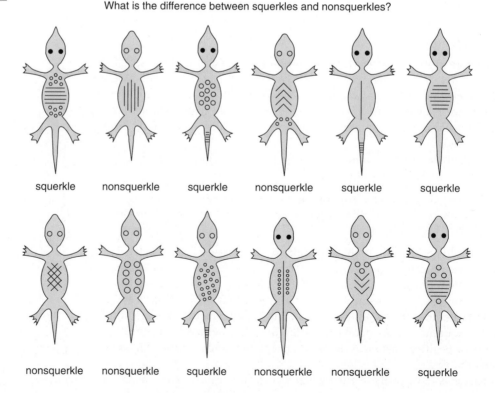

What is the difference between squerkles and nonsquerkles?

| squerkle | nonsquerkle | squerkle | nonsquerkle | squerkle | squerkle |

| nonsquerkle | nonsquerkle | squerkle | nonsquerkle | nonsquerkle | squerkle |

tures of squerkles: Most squerkles have them, and only a few nonsquerkles have them. Other characteristics, such as dots, tail length, and number of toes, are features that are totally irrelevant to squerkleness.

To some extent, learning a concept may be similar to the process you just went through: Learners form hypotheses about a concept's defining features and then test them against the positive and negative instances they encounter (Bruner, Goodnow, & Austin, 1956; M. Levine, 1966). As new examples disprove a particular hypothesis, learners continue to revise their idea of what the concept is. By providing a variety of positive and negative instances of concepts, and also by asking students to generate their *own* examples of concepts, we enable students to test and refine their hypotheses about—and hence to develop a more accurate understanding of—those concepts (H. C. Ellis & Hunt, 1983; M. D. Merrill & Tennyson, 1977; Tennyson & Cocchiarella, 1986).

We can often short-circuit the hypothesis-testing process by simply telling students what a concept's defining features are—in other words, by presenting a definition (R. M. Gagné, 1985; Tennyson & Cocchiarella, 1986). Definitions are especially effective when a concept's defining features are nonsalient or abstract. Children can usually learn what *red* means and what a *circle* is even without a definition because redness and roundness are fairly obvious characteristics. But the defining features of *father* and *plant* are far less salient; for concepts like these, a definition can be quite helpful.

Are definitions likely to be effective when students learn them by rote? Why or why not?

Concepts as Prototypes

EXPERIENCING FIRSTHAND   *Visual Images*

Close your eyes and picture a *bird*. Take a good look at the visual image you create.
Now close your eyes again and picture a *vehicle*. Once again, look closely at your image.

What came to mind when I asked you to picture a bird and a vehicle? If you are like most people, you probably visualized a relatively small bird, perhaps one about the size of a robin or sparrow, rather than a penguin or an ostrich. Likewise, your picture of a vehicle probably resembled a car or a truck, rather than a skateboard or an elevator.

For many concepts, learners seem to construct a mental **prototype**: an idea (perhaps a visual image) of a "typical" example (Rosch, 1973a, 1973b, 1977; Tennyson & Cocchiarella, 1986). Prototypes are usually based on the positive instances that learners encounter most frequently. For instance, people see small birds, cars, and trucks more frequently than they see large birds, skateboards, and elevators.

Once learners have formed a prototype for a particular concept, they compare new objects and events against the prototype. Objects or events similar to the prototype are easily identified as positive instances of the concept. Objects or events very different from the prototype are sometimes mistakenly identified as negative instances of the concept. As an illustration, let's say that your prototype of an *animal* looks something like a small dog, perhaps similar to Figure 7.4. How likely are you to recognize that the following critters are also animals?

Students continually encounter new concepts as they study classroom subject matter, and such concepts often help them make better sense of their physical and social worlds.

Horse	Whale
Grizzly bear	Earthworm
Frog	Sponge
Person	

The more different the critter is from your doglike prototype, the less likely you are to identify it as an animal.

In some cases, a single "best example" represents a concept fairly accurately. In such situations, it makes sense to present the example to students as a way of helping them construct a mental prototype for the concept. Yet we must make sure that our students also know the concept's defining features so that they can correctly recognize any positive instances that *don't* closely resemble the prototype—so that they can identify an ostrich as a bird, a square as a rectangle, and so on.

FIGURE 7.4 A possible prototype for the concept *animal*

Concepts as Exemplars

We probably cannot explain all concept learning strictly in terms of feature lists and proto-types. For one thing, how we categorize an object depends on the context in which we find it. For instance, if a cuplike object contains flowers, we might identify it as a *vase* rather than a *cup;* if it contains mashed potatoes, we might instead identify it as a *bowl* (Labov, 1973; B. Schwartz & Reisberg, 1991). Furthermore, not all concepts lend themselves readily to a spe-cific set of defining features or a single prototype (Eysenck & Keane, 1990; Hampton, 1981; McCloskey & Glucksberg, 1978). For instance, I myself have a difficult time identifying the defining features or a typical example of *music:* Classical, rock, jazz, country-western, rap, and Oriental music are all quite different from one another.

In some cases, knowledge of a concept may be based more on a variety of examples, or **exemplars,** than on a set of defining features or a single prototype (Reisberg, 1997; B. H. Ross & Spalding, 1994; Sadoski & Paivio, 2001). Exemplars can give learners an idea of the vari-ability they are likely to see in any category of objects or events. For instance, the concept *fruit* may bring to mind many different things: Apples, bananas, raspberries, pineapples, and co-conuts are all possibilities. If you encounter a new instance of fruit—a blackberry, let's say—you could compare it to the variety of exemplars you have already stored and find one (a raspberry, perhaps) that is relatively similar.

Students typically learn concepts more effectively when they are given many examples rather than only one or two. The examples we provide should illustrate the full range of the concept so that students do not undergeneralize; for example, we might illustrate the concept *mammal* with whales and platypuses as well as with cats and dogs (E. V. Clark, 1971; M. D. Merrill & Tennyson, 1978; Tennyson & Cocchiarella, 1986).

It is possible that prototypes or exemplars are used to identify positive instances in clear-cut situations, whereas defining features are used in other, more ambiguous ones—for in-stance, when deciding whether a sponge is an *animal* (Andre, 1986; Glass & Holyoak, 1975; Glass, Holyoak, & Santa, 1979). It may also be that children rely on prototypes or exemplars in the early years and then discover defining features later on. For example, as a preschooler, my son Jeff adamantly denied that the concept *animal* includes people, fish, and insects. When he began studying the animal kingdom in school, he learned a biology-based definition of *an-imal* that incorporates some of its major features: a form of life that derives its food from other organisms, responds immediately to its environment, and can move its body. At that point Jeff acknowledged that people, fish, and creepy-crawlies are legitimate animals. (Someday, how-ever, he may learn that biologists do not completely agree on a definition of *animal* and that true defining features of the concept are difficult to identify.)

Interconnectedness of Concepts

In addition to learning concepts, students also learn how concepts are interrelated. In many situations, concepts are nested within one another in a hierarchical fashion. For instance, as a student, you learned that *dogs* and *cats* are both *mammals,* that *mammals* and *birds* are both *vertebrates,* and that *vertebrates* and *invertebrates* are both *animals.* The more general, all-encompassing concepts (those near the top of the hierarchy) tend to be relatively ab-stract, whereas the more specific ones (those near the bottom of the hierarchy) tend to be fairly concrete (Flavell et al., 1993; Rosch, Mervis, Gray, Johnson, & Boyes-Braem, 1976). Given what we learned about cognitive development in Chapter 2, we can predict that in many instances, children are going to learn the specific (concrete) concepts earlier than they learn the more general (abstract) ones.

As you discovered in Chapter 2, Piaget described young children as being unable to view objects as belonging to two or more categories at the same time—a phenomenon known as *single classification.* As children reach the concrete operations stage, they become capable of *multiple classification.* From the perspective of contemporary cognitive psychology, however, multiple classification is not necessarily an ability that children either have or don't have. In-stead, children become able to categorize objects in two or more ways simultaneously when they learn how various concepts are interrelated—knowledge that is likely to evolve, at least in part, as a result of formal education (Flavell et al., 1993).

The Into the Classroom feature "Facilitating Concept Learning" offers suggestions for teaching concepts in a variety of academic disciplines. In the following exercise, you will find a strategy that one teacher has used.

A middle school mathematics teacher designed the following worksheet to teach her students the concept *quadrilateral*. As you examine it, think about

- The defining features of a quadrilateral
- The strategies the teacher is using to teach the concept
- Additional strategies the teacher might use to enhance students' understanding of the concept

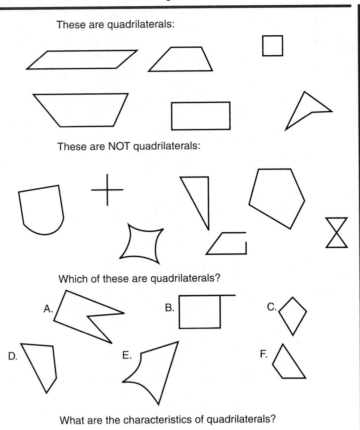

These are quadrilaterals:

These are NOT quadrilaterals:

Which of these are quadrilaterals?

A.   B.   C.

D.   E.   F.

What are the characteristics of quadrilaterals?

Worksheet courtesy of Dinah Jackson.

INTO THE CLASSROOM: *Facilitating Concept Learning*

Provide a definition of the concept.

A geometry teacher defines a *sphere* as "the set of points in three-dimensional space that are equidistant from a single point."

Make defining features concrete and salient.

A teacher illustrates the concept *insect* with a line drawing that emphasizes its defining features, such as three body parts and three pairs of legs, in bold black lines. At the same time, the drawing downplays other, irrelevant characteristics that students might see, such as the insect's color or the presence of wings.

Present a variety of positive instances.

A music teacher plays a *primary chord* in several keys.

Present a "best example," or prototype.

To illustrate the concept *democracy,* a social studies teacher describes a hypothetical, "ideal" government.

Present negative instances—especially "near misses"—to show what the concept is not.

When a teacher describes what a *mammal* is, he shows students frogs and lizards and explains why these animals are not mammals.

Ask students to identify positive and negative instances from among numerous possibilities.

A language arts teacher gives students a list of sentences and asks them to identify the sentences containing a *dangling participle.*

Ask students to generate their own positive instances of the concept.

A teacher asks students to think of examples of *adjectives* that they use frequently in their own conversations.

Show students how various concepts are related to one another.

A science teacher explains that the concepts *velocity* and *acceleration* have somewhat different meanings, even though they both involve speed.

If you could not recall what a quadrilateral was from your own schooling, the exercise probably enabled you to discover that a quadrilateral is a closed figure made up of four straight line segments that connect at their end points but do not otherwise intersect. To teach the concept, the teacher presents both positive and negative instances; in the process, she illustrates the variability that quadrilaterals can have and includes some almost-but-not-quite nonexamples ("near misses"). Furthermore, the teacher assesses students' understanding by asking them to identify new positive and negative instances and to identify a quadrilateral's defining features. One weakness of the activity is that it does not encourage students to relate the concept to real-world objects; for instance, the teacher might ask students to identify examples of quadrilaterals among two-dimensional items in the classroom. A second weakness is that the activity does not encourage students to relate the concept *quadrilateral* to other geometric figures; for instance, the teacher might ask students to list the kinds of shapes that quadrilaterals include (squares, rectangles, parallelograms, and rhombi are all possibilities). The forms of knowledge we consider next—schemas, scripts, and (later) personal theories—typically incorporate at least two, and often many, concepts, as well as some of the relationships among them.

Schemas and Scripts

EXPERIENCING FIRSTHAND   *Horse #2*

Take a moment to think about what you know about horses. For instance, what do they look like? How do they spend their time? Where are you most likely to see them? Write down as many things about a horse as you can think of.

Some theorists propose that much of the information stored in long-term memory is organized as **schemas**—organized bodies of knowledge about particular objects or phenomena (e.g., Rumelhart & Ortony, 1977). Schemas give us an idea of how things "typically" are. For example, you probably had little difficulty retrieving many different things about horses, perhaps including their elongated heads, tendency to graze in pastures, and frequent appearance at race tracks. The various things you know about horses are closely interrelated in your long-term memory in the form of a "horse" schema.

Not only do schemas provide a means for organizing information, but they also influence how we interpret new situations. As an example, try the following exercise.

EXPERIENCING FIRSTHAND   *John*

Read the following passage *one time only:*

> John was feeling bad today so he decided to go see the family doctor. He checked in with the doctor's receptionist, and then looked through several medical magazines that were on the table by his chair. Finally the nurse came and asked him to take off his clothes. The doctor was very nice to him. He eventually prescribed some pills for John. Then John left the doctor's office and headed home. (Bower, Black, & Turner, 1979, p. 190)

You probably had no trouble understanding the passage because you have been to a doctor's office yourself and have a schema for how those visits usually go. You can therefore fill in a number of details that the passage doesn't ever tell you. For example, you probably inferred that John must have *gone* to the doctor's office, although the story omits this essential step. Likewise, you probably concluded that John took his clothes off in the examination room, *not* in the waiting room, even though the story never makes it clear where John did his striptease. When a schema involves a predictable sequence of events related to a particular activity, as is the case in a visit to the doctor's office, it is sometimes called a **script**.

Students from diverse cultural backgrounds may sometimes come to school with different schemas and scripts and so may interpret the same classroom materials or activities differently (Lipson, 1983; R. E. Reynolds et al., 1982; Steffensen, Joag-Dev, & Anderson, 1979). As an illustration, try the next exercise.

What is a typical script for a trip to the grocery store? to the movies? to a fast-food restaurant?

Read the following story *one time only*:

> One night two young men from Egulac went down to the river to hunt seals, and while they were there it became foggy and calm. Then they heard war-cries, and they thought, "Maybe this is a war-party." They escaped to the shore, and hid behind a log. Now canoes came up, and they heard the noise of paddles, and saw one canoe coming up to them. There were five men in the canoe, and they said:
>
> "What do you think? We wish to take you along. We are going up the river to make war on the people."
>
> One of the young men said: "I have no arrows."
>
> "Arrows are in the canoe," they said.
>
> "I will not go along. I might be killed. My relatives do not know where I have gone. But you," he said, turning to the other, "may go with them."
>
> So one of the young men went, but the other returned home.
>
> And the warriors went on up the river to a town on the other side of Kalama. The people came down to the water, and they began to fight, and many were killed. But presently the young man heard one of the warriors say, "Quick, let us go home: that Indian has been hit." Now he thought: "Oh, they are ghosts." He did not feel sick, but they said he had been shot.
>
> So the canoes went back to Egulac, and the young man went ashore to his house, and made a fire. And he told everybody and said, "Behold I accompanied the ghosts, and we went to fight. Many of our fellows were killed, and many of those who attacked us were killed. They said I was hit, and I did not feel sick."
>
> He told it all, and then he became quiet. When the sun rose he fell down. Something black came out of his mouth. His face became contorted. The people jumped up and cried.
>
> He was dead. (Bartlett, 1932, p. 65)

Now cover the story and write down as much of it as you can remember.

See "Bartlett's Ghosts" in *Simulations in Educational Psychology.*

Compare your own rendition of the story with the original. What differences do you notice? Your version is almost certainly the shorter of the two, and you probably left out a number of details. But did you also find yourself distorting certain parts of the story so that it made more sense to you?

A Native American ghost story, "The War of the Ghosts" is probably not totally consistent with the schemas and scripts you've learned if you were raised in another culture. In an early study of long-term memory (Bartlett, 1932), students at England's Cambridge University were asked to read the story twice and then to recall it at various times later on. The students' recollections of the story often included additions and distortions that made the story more consistent with English culture. For example, people in England rarely go "to the river to hunt seals" because seals are saltwater animals. Students might therefore say that the men went to the river to *fish*. Similarly, the ghostly element of the story did not fit comfortably with the religious beliefs of most Cambridge students and so was often modified. For example, one student was asked to recall the story six months after he had read it; notice how the version he remembers leaves out many of the story's more puzzling aspects (puzzling, at least, from the perspective of the Cambridge students):

> Four men came down to the water. They were told to get into a boat and to take arms with them. They inquired, "What arms?" and were answered "Arms for battle." When they came to the battlefield they heard a great noise and shouting, and a voice said: "The black man is dead." And he was brought to the place where they were, and laid on the ground. And he foamed at the mouth. (Bartlett, 1932, pp. 71–72)

As teachers, we need to find out whether students have the appropriate schemas and scripts—the organized bodies of knowledge about specific topics and events—to understand the subject matter we are teaching. When our students *don't* have such knowledge, we may sometimes need to back up and help them develop it before we forge full-steam ahead with new material.

Personal Theories

EXPERIENCING FIRSTHAND   *Coffeepots and Raccoons*

Consider each of the following situations:

1. People took a coffeepot that looked like this:
   They removed the handle, sealed the top, took off the top knob, sealed the opening to the spout, and removed the spout. They also sliced off the base and attached a flat piece of metal. They attached a little stick, cut a window in it, and filled the metal container with birdseed. When they were done, it looked like this:

   After these changes, was this a coffeepot or a bird feeder?

2. Doctors took this raccoon:
   and shaved away some of its fur. They dyed what was left black. Then they bleached a single stripe all white down the center of the animal's back. Then, with surgery, they put in its body a sac of super smelly odor, just as a skunk has. After they were all done, the animal looked like this:

   After the operation, was this a skunk or a raccoon?

Both scenarios based on Keil, 1989, p. 184.

Chances are, you concluded that the coffeepot had been transformed into a bird feeder but that the raccoon was still a raccoon despite its cosmetic make-over and major surgery; even fourth graders come to these conclusions (Keil, 1986, 1989). Now how is it possible that the coffeepot could be made into something entirely different, whereas the raccoon could not?

Long before they start school, children begin to construct general belief systems—**personal theories**—about how the world operates (Keil, 1989, 1994; Wellman & Gelman, 1998). These theories include many concepts and the relationships (e.g., correlational and cause-effect relations) among them. For example, even children as young as 8 or 9 seem to make a basic distinction between human-made objects (e.g., coffeepots, bird feeders) and biological entities (e.g., raccoons, skunks). Furthermore, they seem to conceptualize the two categories in fundamentally different ways: Human-made objects are defined largely by the *functions* they serve (e.g., keeping coffee warm, feeding birds), whereas biological entities are defined primarily by their origins (e.g., the parents who brought them into being, their DNA). Thus, when a coffeepot begins to hold birdseed rather than coffee, it becomes a bird feeder because its function has changed. But when a raccoon is cosmetically and surgically altered to look and smell like a skunk, it still has raccoon parents and raccoon DNA and so cannot possibly *be* a skunk (Keil, 1987, 1989). Thinking along similar lines, even preschoolers will tell you that you can't change a yellow finch into a bluebird by giving it a coat of blue paint or dressing it in a "bluebird" costume (Keil, 1989).

Students' personal theories about the world seem to guide them as they identify potential defining features of the concepts they are learning (Keil, 1987). For example, if you were trying to learn what a *horse* is, knowing that it's an animal would lead you to conclude that its location (in a stable, a pasture, a shopping mall, or whatever) is irrelevant. In contrast, if you were trying to learn what the *equator* is, knowing that it's something on a map of the world should lead you to suspect that location is of the utmost importance.

By the time children reach school age, they have developed some preliminary theories and beliefs about the physical world, the biological world, and even the mental world—that is, the nature of thinking (Wellman & Gelman, 1998). These theories and beliefs have often evolved with little or no guidance from other, more knowledgeable individuals; as a result, they may include some erroneous beliefs, or **misconceptions**, about how the world operates. Let's look at the origins and effects of such misconceptions.

When Knowledge Construction Goes Awry: Origins and Effects of Misconceptions

When learners construct their own understandings, there is, of course, no guarantee that they will construct accurate ones. For example, recall how, in the opening case study, Rita thinks that the British went to China to get furs and that they traveled through Michigan along the way. And consider how 7-year-old Rob thinks mountains are formed:

Interviewer:	How were the mountains made?
Rob:	Some dirt was taken from outside and it was put on the mountain and then mountains were made with it.
Interviewer:	Who did that?
Rob:	It takes a lot of men to make mountains, there must have been at least four. They gave them the dirt and then they made themselves all alone.
Interviewer:	But if they wanted to make another mountain?
Rob:	They pull one mountain down and then they could make a prettier one. (dialogue from Piaget, 1929, p. 348)

Construction workers and professional landscapers apparently play a major role in Rob's personal theory about the physical world.

Research tells us that children and adolescents typically have many misconceptions about the world around them. One common one in the elementary grades is the assumption that living creatures and nonliving natural objects (rocks, mountains, etc.) exist for a particular purpose; for example, children might think that some rocks are pointy so that animals living nearby can scratch themselves when they get an itch (Kelemen, 1999). Figure 7.5 lists other common misconceptions; its emphasis on misconceptions in the sciences reflects the fact that the bulk of the research about children's misconceptions has been conducted by science educators.

Students' misconceptions probably have a variety of sources. Sometimes they result from how things *appear* to be (diSessa, 1996; Duit, 1991; Reiner, Slotta, Chi, & Resnick, 2000); for example, from our perspective on the earth's surface, the sun looks as if it moves around the earth, rather than vice versa. Sometimes misconceptions are encouraged by common expressions in language; for instance, we often talk about the sun "rising" and "setting" (Duit, 1991; Mintzes, Trowbridge, Arnaudin, & Wandersee, 1991). Sometimes learners infer incorrect cause-effect relationships between two events simply because those events often occur at the same time (Byrnes, 1996; Keil, 1991). Perhaps even fairy tales and television cartoon shows play a role in promoting misconceptions (Glynn, Yeany, & Britton, 1991); as an example, think of cartoon bad guys who run off a cliff and remain suspended in air until they realize that there's nothing holding them up. Unfortunately, students may also acquire erroneous ideas from other people, including, in some instances, teachers and textbook authors (Begg, Anas, & Farinacci, 1992; Duit, 1991). Yet often students' misconceptions simply arise out of their own well-intended efforts to make sense of what they see. Consider this teacher's anecdote about a young boy's interpretation of evaporating water:

> Wesley and I had become friends over a forlorn empty fish tank. It *did* contain big rocks and enough water to cover them. He had recounted to me that they had to put water in the tank almost every week, and I had asked him where he thought that water went. Wesley had answered, "Into the rocks." (F. P. L. Hawkins, 1997, p. 337)

Sometimes students' misconceptions arise out of their well-intended efforts to make sense of what they see.

Unfortunately, students' existing misconceptions can wreak havoc on new learning (Lipson, 1982; Reiner et al., 2000; K. J. Roth & Anderson, 1988). Thanks to the processes of meaningful learning and elaboration—processes that usually facilitate learning—students may

FIGURE 7.5 Common student misconceptions

ASTRONOMY

Fact: The earth revolves around the sun.
Misconception: The sun revolves around the earth. It "rises" in the morning and "sets" in the evening, at which point it "goes" to the other side of the earth.

Fact: The earth is shaped more or less like a sphere.
Misconception: The earth is shaped like a round, flat disk.

BIOLOGY

Fact: A living thing is something that carries on such life processes as metabolism, growth, and reproduction.
Misconception: A living thing is something that moves and/or grows. The sun, wind, clouds, and fire are living things.

Fact: A plant is a food producer.
Misconception: A plant grows in a garden and is relatively small. Carrots and cabbage are vegetables, not plants. Trees are plants only if they are small.

PHYSICS

Fact: An object remains in uniform motion until a force acts upon it; a force is needed only to *change* speed or direction.
Misconception: Any moving object has a force acting upon it. For example, a ball thrown in the air continues to be pushed upward by the force of the throw until it begins its descent.

Fact: Gravity is the force whereby any two masses are attracted together.
Misconception: Gravity is "glue" or "sticky stuff" that holds people to the earth.

GEOGRAPHY

Fact: The Great Lakes contain fresh water.
Misconception: The Great Lakes contain salt water.

Fact: Rivers run from higher elevation to lower elevation.
Misconception: Rivers run from north to south (going "down" on a map). For example, rivers can run from Canada into the United States, but not vice versa.

EDUCATIONAL PSYCHOLOGY

Fact: Meaningful learning is more effective than rote learning.
Misconception: Rote learning is more effective than meaningful learning.

Fact: Negative reinforcement is the removal of a stimulus (usually an aversive, or unpleasant, one). It increases the frequency of the behavior it follows. (We'll study negative reinforcement in Chapter 9.)
Misconception: Negative reinforcement is the presentation of an aversive stimulus (e.g., a scolding, a spanking). Its effect, if any, is to decrease the frequency of a behavior that it follows. Essentially, the term is just a nicer way of saying "punishment."

Sources: S. Carey, 1986; Kyle & Shymansky, 1989; Lennon et al., 1990; Maria, 1998; J. Nussbaum, 1985; Sneider & Pulos, 1983; Vosniadou, 1994; Vosniadou & Brewer, 1987; geography misconceptions courtesy of R. K. Ormrod.

Even college students have been known to ignore information presented in class when it is inconsistent with their prior beliefs (Holt-Reynolds, 1992).

change or distort new information to fit their existing misbeliefs. As a result, students can spend a great deal of time learning the wrong thing! Consider the case of Barry, an eleventh grader whose physics class was studying the idea that an object's mass and weight do *not* affect the speed at which it falls. Students were instructed to design and build a container for an egg that would keep the egg from breaking when they dropped it from a third-floor window. They were told that, on the day of the egg drop, they would also record the time it took for the eggs to reach the ground. Convinced that heavier objects fall faster, Barry added several nails to his egg's container. Yet when he dropped it, classmates timed its fall at 1.49 seconds, a time very similar to that for other students' lighter egg containers. He explained this result to his teacher (and presumably to himself as well) by rationalizing "[t]hat the people weren't timing real good" (Hynd, 1998a, p. 34).

As teachers, our job is twofold: Not only must we help students construct accurate understandings of the world around them, but we must also encourage them to discard any erroneous beliefs they have previously constructed. As we consider how to promote both knowledge construction and conceptual change in the next two sections, we will identify some strategies for accomplishing both of these goals.

Promoting Effective Knowledge Construction

Knowing that learning is a constructive process does not necessarily tell us how we can most effectively promote such learning (K. R. Harris & Alexander, 1998; Hirsch, 1996; Nuthall, 1996). In fact, cognitive psychologists believe there are many ways to help students construct a rich and sophisticated knowledge base. A few possibilities are

- Providing opportunities for experimentation
- Presenting the ideas of others
- Emphasizing conceptual understanding
- Using authentic activities
- Promoting dialogue
- Creating a community of learners

Providing Opportunities for Experimentation

By interacting and experimenting with the objects around them, students can discover many characteristics and principles of the world firsthand (e.g., Fosnot, 1996). As teachers, we can create numerous hands-on opportunities for students to touch, manipulate, modify, combine, and recombine concrete objects. For example, at the elementary school level, we might use beads or pennies to help students discover basic addition and subtraction facts, or we might use two balls of clay and a scale to promote the realization that an object's weight remains the same despite changes in its shape (Piaget's notion of *conservation*). At the secondary level, such activities as science labs, in-class demonstrations, and computer simulations should also help our students construct knowledge about the world around them.

Teachers often teach students clearly delineated, step-by-step procedures for accomplishing certain tasks. Yet on some occasions, it might be more helpful to let students develop such procedures *on their own* through experimentation. For example, when teaching cooking, it may sometimes be more productive to cast aside recipes and instead let students try different combinations and proportions of ingredients (Hatano & Inagaki, 1993). As another example, let's consider a study in which kindergarten students had one of two different experiences raising animals (Hatano & Inagaki, 1993). Some students had pet rabbits in their classrooms; they took turns feeding and taking care of the rabbits by using procedures their teacher had carefully prescribed for them. Other students were raising goldfish at home; these students had to make their own decisions about how best to care for their pets and, in doing so, could experiment with feeding schedules, water purity, and other variables that might affect the fish's welfare. The students who raised the goldfish appeared to develop a more accurate understanding of animals in general—for example, learning that baby animals grow bigger over time—and were able to apply what they learned from their own pets to other species. One goldfish owner, when asked whether one could keep a baby frog the same size forever, said, "No, we can't, because the frog will grow bigger as the goldfish grew bigger. My goldfish were small before, but now they are big" (Hatano & Inagaki, 1993, p. 121).

Unfortunately, the researchers didn't eliminate other possible explanations for their results. Besides teacher-prescribed versus self-chosen procedures, what other differences between the two groups might account for the study's results?

Presenting the Ideas of Others

As noted earlier, knowledge is constructed not only by people working independently but also by people working together over the course of years or centuries to make sense of complex phenomena. Although it may sometimes be beneficial to have our students discover basic principles for themselves (reinventing the wheel, so to speak), we must also provide opportunities for them to hear and read about the ideas of others—the concepts, principles, theories, and so on, that society has developed to explain both the physical and psychological aspects of human experience (R. Driver, 1995; Vygotsky, 1962). Our students are most likely to construct a productive view of the world when they have the benefit of experiencing the world firsthand *and* the benefit of learning how those before them have interpreted human experience.

We needn't present others' ideas in a didactic, this-is-how-it-is manner, however. For instance, we might apply Vygotsky's notion that, in informal discussions with children, we can help them impose meaning on the objects and events around them by attaching labels, identifying underlying principles, or imposing certain interpretations (Eacott, 1999; Feuerstein,

Klein, & Tannenbaum, 1991; John-Steiner & Mahn, 1996). Teacher Katherine Maria took this approach in a series of conversations with 6½-year-old Jennifer about the nature of gravity. Katherine had been trying to help Jennifer understand that people and objects in the southern hemisphere don't fall off the earth just because, from the standpoint of someone looking at a globe, they are located on the earth's "bottom" side. Katherine related the following discussion between herself (K) and Jennifer (J) to show the progress Jennifer was making in her understanding of gravity:

> I used [an] inflatable globe and a figure stuck to the lower part of South America to explain to Jennifer that I had visited this place and had not fallen off the earth. We then had [this] discussion . . . :

K: What would happen if there was a hole in the earth and this person (the figure stuck to South America) dropped a ball through it?

J: People might think that if you dropped a rock into the hole it might go back out.

K: Why would they think that?

J: Because it's at the bottom of the earth.

K: Uh huh.

J: They think that maybe the gravity did that.

K: But what does gravity pull you toward?

J: Down.

K: (sticking the figure on the top of the inflatable globe): If you're standing here, where is down?

Jennifer points her finger in a downward direction. I move the figure to the South Pole.

K: But suppose this was you. If you were here, where is down?

Jennifer points to a spot in the middle of the globe.

K: Yeah, so it's pulling toward the?

J: Middle.

K: Right. So where would the rock end up then?

J: In the middle. (Maria, 1998, p. 13)

Students can more effectively construct meaningful interpretations of events when they examine how others have interpreted similar events. For example, by reading classic works of literature, they view daily life from the perspectives of numerous authors.

Emphasizing Conceptual Understanding

Let's look again at our opening case study. Rita has acquired a few miscellaneous facts in her history lessons, but she clearly has no idea about how those facts are interconnected. Unfortunately, such learning of isolated facts, without any sense of how they fit together, is all too common at both the elementary and secondary grade levels (J. Hiebert & Lefevre, 1986; Hollon, Roth, & Anderson, 1991; McCaslin & Good, 1996; McRobbie & Tobin, 1995; Paxton, 1999).

Without a doubt, students benefit more from acquiring facts, concepts, and ideas in an integrated, interrelated, and meaningful fashion; in other words, they benefit from developing a **conceptual understanding** of academic subject matter (L. M. Anderson, 1993; Bédard & Chi, 1992; J. J. White & Rumsey, 1994). For example, rather than simply memorize basic mathematical computation procedures, students should learn how those procedures reflect underlying principles of mathematics. Rather than learn historical facts as a list of unrelated people, places, and dates, students should place those facts within the context of major social and religious trends, migration patterns, economic considerations, characteristics of human personality, and so on.

Following are several ways in which we might help students develop a conceptual understanding of classroom subject matter:

- Organize units around a few core ideas and themes, always relating specific content back to this core.
- Explore each topic in depth—for example, by considering many examples, examining cause-effect relationships, and discovering how specific details relate to more general principles.

- Explain how new ideas relate to students' own experiences and to things they have previously learned.
- Show students—through the things we say, the assignments we give, and the criteria we use to evaluate learning—that conceptual understanding of classroom subject matter is far more important than knowledge of isolated facts.
- Ask students to teach what they have learned to others—a task that encourages them to focus on main ideas and pull them together in a way that makes sense. (L. M. Anderson, 1993; Brophy & Alleman, 1992; Hatano & Inagaki, 1993; Prawat, 1993; VanSledright & Brophy, 1992; J. J. White & Rumsey, 1994)

Construction of an integrated understanding of any complex topic will inevitably take time. Accordingly, many educators advocate a *less is more* principle: *Less* material studied more thoroughly is learned *more* completely and with greater understanding (Brophy & Alleman, 1992; Kyle & Shymansky, 1989; Marshall, 1992; Sizer, 1992).

Using Authentic Activities

Many theorists suggest that students can construct a more useful, productive, and integrated knowledge base if they learn classroom subject matter within the context of **authentic activities**—activities similar to those encountered in the outside world. For example, rather than have students practice writing skills through short, artificial writing exercises, we might ask them to write stories or essays or to send letters to real people. Students' writing improves in both quality and quantity when they engage in such authentic writing tasks (E. H. Hiebert & Fisher, 1992). Likewise, rather than have students develop map interpretation skills (e.g., interpreting symbols, scale, and latitude and longitude) by answering a series of unrelated questions in a workbook, we might instead have them construct their own maps, asking them to choose appropriate symbols and scale and to integrate information about latitude and longitude. Although students may sometimes feel a bit overwhelmed by the complexity of such map-making activities, they are likely to gain a more complete understanding of how to use and interpret maps effectively than do students who simply engage in workbook exercises (Gregg & Leinhardt, 1994).

Authentic activities can relate to virtually any area of the curriculum. For example, we might ask students to

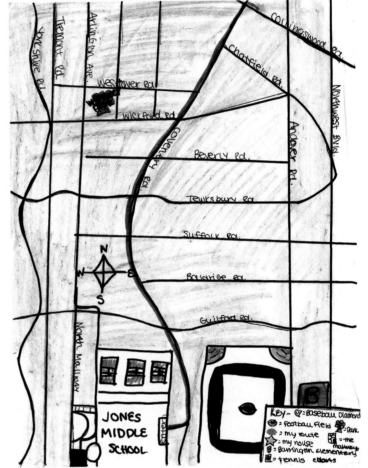

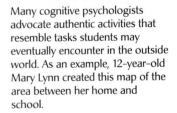

Many cognitive psychologists advocate authentic activities that resemble tasks students may eventually encounter in the outside world. As an example, 12-year-old Mary Lynn created this map of the area between her home and school.

Give an oral report	Play in an athletic event
Write an editorial	Complete an art project
Participate in a debate	Perform in a concert
Find information in the library	Tutor a classmate
Conduct an experiment	Make a videotape
Graph data	Perform a workplace routine
Construct a chart or model	Develop classroom Web pages to showcase
Create and distribute a class newsletter	special projects
Converse in a foreign language	

In many cases, these activities may require considerable support (scaffolding) to ensure that students carry them out successfully. As such, they may remind you of the *guided participation* that I described within the context of Vygotsky's theory in Chapter 2.

By placing classroom activities in real-world contexts, we help our students discover the reasons why they are learning academic subject matter. We also increase the likelihood that, later on, they will actually use the information and skills we have taught them (A. Collins, Brown, & Newman, 1989; De Corte, Greer, & Verschaffel, 1996). More specific benefits depend, of course, on the nature of the activity, as the following exercise reveals.

INTERPRETING ARTIFACTS AND INTERACTIONS   *Littering*

A class of fourth graders has written letters to the city council about the problem of littering in their hometown of Bexley. The artifact to the right is one example. As you read it, consider

- The "authenticity" of the assignment
- The knowledge, skills, or attitudes the assignment might foster

Dear Bexley City Council,

I suggest that a law should be passed that say littering is not allowed. The law would help keep Bexley looking nice.

Everyday when I go outside to walk to school or to a friend's house, I find at least two pieces of litter someone else put in our yard.

No one in my family ever litters. I think it is because we feel so strongly about protecting the environment. This why I am writing this letter.

I always see signs on the lamp posts saying, "Keep Bexley Beautiful," and I think this would be the first step to keep Bexley beautiful.

I know I am only a fourth grade student, but I would like you to consider my idea. Thank you for your time.

Sincerely,
Cindy M.

Letter-writing assignments are certainly authentic if, in fact, the letters are actually mailed. At a minimum, the assignment will enable students to practice their writing and editing skills (Cindy will, we hope, catch the error in the first paragraph: *say* should be *says*). It might also discourage them from littering on future occasions. The assignment might be even more effective if the teacher uses it as a springboard for other class activities—perhaps learning more about town ordinances (does Bexley already have a law against littering?), city governance (how does the town council reach its decisions?), or psychology (why do people litter in the first place?).

Educators are becoming increasingly convinced of the effectiveness of authentic activities for promoting learning. We will revisit their importance when we discuss *transfer* in Chapter 8, *values* in Chapter 12, and *instructional strategies* in Chapter 13, and we will consider a related topic, *authentic assessment,* in Chapters 15 and 16.

Promoting Dialogue

Chapter 13 describes strategies for promoting student dialogue through class discussion, reciprocal teaching, computer technology, and cooperative learning.

We have already identified numerous advantages to having students talk with one another about classroom topics. And in fact, students *do* seem to remember new ideas and experiences more effectively and accurately when they talk about these things with others (Hacker, 1998b; Schank & Abelson, 1995; Tessler & Nelson, 1994; Wasik, Karweit, Burns, & Brodsky, 1998). Accordingly, many theorists recommend that classroom dialogues be a regular feature of classroom instruction (J. Hiebert et al., 1997; Marshall, 1992; Paris & Cunningham, 1996; Sosniak & Stodolsky, 1994).

As an example of how students might work together to construct meaning, let's look in on Ms. Lombard's fourth-grade class, which has been studying fractions. Ms. Lombard has never taught her students how to divide a number by a fraction. Nevertheless, she gives them the following problem, which can be solved by dividing 20 by $\frac{3}{4}$:[1]

> Mom makes small apple tarts, using three-quarters of an apple for each small tart. She has 20 apples. How many small apple tarts can she make? (J. Hiebert et al., 1997, p. 118)

---

[1] In case your memory of how to divide by a fraction is rusty, you can approach the problem $20 \div 3/4$ by inverting the fraction and multiplying, like so: $20 \times 4/3 = 80/3 = 26\ 2/3$. Thus, Mom can make 26 tarts and have enough apple to make two-thirds of another tart. If she has two-thirds of the three-fourths of an apple she needs to make another whole tart, then she has half an apple left over ($2/3 \times 3/4 = 1/2$).

Ms. Lombard asks the students to work in small groups to figure out how they might solve the problem. One group of four girls—Jeanette, Liz, Kerri, and Nina—has been working on the problem for some time and so far has arrived at such answers as 15, 38, and 23. We join them midway through their discussion, when they've already agreed that they can use three-fourths of each apple to make a total of 20 tarts:

Jeanette: In each apple there is a quarter left. In each apple there is a quarter left, so you've used, you've made twenty tarts already and you've got a quarter of twenty see—

Liz: So you've got twenty quarters *left*.

Jeanette: Yes, . . . and twenty quarters is equal to five apples, . . . so five apples divided by—

Liz: Six, seven, eight.

Jeanette: But three-quarters equals three.

Kerri: But she can't make only three apple tarts!

Jeanette: No, you've still got twenty.

Liz: But you've got twenty quarters, if you've got twenty quarters you might be right.

Jeanette: I'll show you.

Liz: No, I've drawn them all here.

Kerri: How many quarters have you got? Twenty?

Liz: Yes, one quarter makes five apples and out of five apples she can make five tarts which will make that twenty-five tarts and then she will have, wait, one, two, three, four, five quarters, she'll have one, two, three, four, five quarters. . . .

Nina: I've got a better . . .

Kerri: Yes?

Liz: Twenty-six quarters and a remainder of one quarter left. (J. Hiebert et al., 1997, p. 121)

The discussion and occasional disagreements continue, and the girls eventually arrive at the correct answer: Mom can make 26 tarts and then will have half an apple left over.

As the preceding conversation illustrates, classroom dialogues can help students achieve a conceptual understanding of classroom subject matter—for instance, a conceptual understanding of what it means to divide by a fraction (J. Hiebert et al., 1997; Lampert, Rittenhouse, & Crumbaugh, 1996). Yet classroom dialogues have an important benefit for teachers as well: By carefully monitoring students' comments and questions, we can identify and address any misconceptions that might interfere with their ability to acquire further knowledge and skills (Presseisen & Beyer, 1994; Sosniak & Stodolsky, 1994).

INTO THE CLASSROOM: *Promoting Knowledge Construction*

Provide opportunities for experimentation.

A teacher has students experiment with clay and water to discover the principle that a certain quantity of a solid displaces the same amount of water regardless of the shape that the solid takes.

Expose students to others' interpretations of the world.

A teacher has students read poetry from a variety of countries and cultures.

Focus on an in-depth understanding of a few key ideas instead of covering many topics superficially.

A teacher tells his class, "As we study the geography of South America, we aren't going to worry about memorizing a lot of place names. Instead, we will look at how topography and climate have influenced the economic and cultural development of different regions of the continent."

Include authentic activities in the curriculum.

A teacher has students develop and cook a menu that includes all the basic food groups.

Create opportunities for small-group or whole-class discussions in which students can freely exchange their views.

A teacher asks students to speculate on how the Japanese people must have felt after the atomic bomb was dropped over Hiroshima.

Have students work in groups to research certain topics and then teach one another what they have learned.

In a unit on zoology, different groups of students "major" in different classes of vertebrates (e.g., mollusks, segmented worms, sponges) and then prepare illustrated "textbooks" that they share with their classmates in other groups.

Creating a Community of Learners

With the benefits of dialogue and other forms of student interaction in mind, and with the goal of promoting the social construction of meaning, some psychologists and educators suggest that we create a **community of learners**—a classroom in which we and students consistently work to help one another learn (A. L. Brown & Campione, 1994; Prawat, 1992; Rogoff, Matusov, & White, 1996). A classroom that operates as a community of learners is likely to have characteristics such as the following:

- All students are active participants in classroom activities.
- Discussion and collaboration among two or more students are common occurrences and play a key role in learning.
- Diversity in students' interests and rates of progress is expected and respected.
- Students and teacher coordinate their efforts at helping one another learn; no one has exclusive responsibility for teaching others.
- Everyone is a potential resource for the others; different individuals are likely to serve as resources on different occasions, depending on the topics and tasks at hand. (In some cases, students may "major" in a particular topic and thereby become local "experts" on that topic.)
- The teacher provides some guidance and direction for classroom activities, but students may also contribute to such guidance and direction.
- Students regularly critique one another's work.
- The process of learning is emphasized as much as, and sometimes more than, the finished product. (A. L. Brown & Campione, 1994, 1996; Campione, Shapiro, & Brown, 1995; Rogoff, 1994; Rogoff et al., 1996)

As one example of how a community of learners might be structured (Brown & Campione, 1994), students are divided into small groups to study different subtopics falling within a general theme; for instance, subtopics for the theme *changing populations* might be *extinct, endangered, artificial, assisted,* and *urbanized.* Each group conducts research and prepares teaching materials related to its subtopic. The class then reassembles into new groups that include at least one representative from each of the previous groups; within these groups, the students teach one another the things they have learned.

This approach illustrates the *jigsaw technique,* described in Chapter 13.

We can also use a computer network to promote a community of learners (Hewitt & Scardamalia, 1998). For instance, we might have all students store their classwork (short stories, essays, problem solutions, etc.) as computer files that their classmates can read and respond to. We also can create ongoing "chat rooms" in which students present questions or issues to which others respond. As an example, consider three students' online responses to another student's question, "How does heat affect solids?"; note that they use the headings "My theory" and "I need to understand" to structure their discussion:

This electronic dialogue illustrates the use of CSILE, an approach described in the section "Technology-Based Discussions" in Chapter 13.

JA: *My theory:* I think that heat makes solids burn or melt. I think that my prediction is right because I've seen solids melt and burn.

AR: *My theory:* I think that if a solid comes in contact with heat, it becomes hot. I also think it might change colour. Generally if any solid comes in contact with heat then it becomes hot. I think that the solid would become hot faster if it could conduct energy well. If an object didn't conduct energy well then it would heat up, but take a longer time than an object that conducts energy well. It might change colour because we think that if something is very hot it is white or red and sort of hot it is orange or yellow. There might be some truth to this.

AD: *My theory:* I think that it depends on how much heat there is. I also think that it depends on what sort of solid it is. For instance, the heat that might melt rubber might not melt metal. (This last sentence might be wrong, I'm just using it as an example.)

I need to understand: What makes wood burn instead of melt?

My theory: I think that it might have something to do with wood being organic, because I can't think of anything that is organic, and would melt. (dialogue from Hewitt & Scardamalia, 1998, p. 85)

Such online discussions may be especially valuable for students who are shy or for other reasons feel uncomfortable communicating with their classmates in a more public fashion (Hewitt & Scardamalia, 1998).

A community of learners incorporates several instructional strategies that we'll consider in more detail in Chapter 13, including discovery learning, class discussions, cooperative learning, and peer tutoring. It also is, in many respects, similar to the approach that scientists and other scholars take when they advance the frontiers of knowledge: They conduct individual and collaborative research, share ideas, build on one another's findings, and so on. Hence, this approach may help students acquire some rather sophisticated and adultlike knowledge-building skills (A. L. Brown & Campione, 1996; Hewitt & Scardamalia, 1998; Karpov & Haywood, 1998).

Researchers have not yet systematically compared the academic achievement of communities of learners to the achievement of more traditional classrooms. Case studies do indicate that classes structured as communities of learners have some positive effects, however. For one thing, these classes appear to promote fairly complex thinking processes for extended periods of time (A. L. Brown & Campione, 1994). They are also highly motivating for students; for instance, students often insist on going to school even when they are ill, and they are disappointed when summer vacation begins (Rogoff, 1994). To illustrate, one eighth-grade English teacher described her experiences with a community of learners this way:

> The classroom became . . . like a dining-room table, where people could converse easily about books and poems and ideas. I would watch my students leave the classroom carrying on animated conversations about which book was truly Robert Cormier's best, why sequels are often disappointing, which books they planned to reread or pack into their trunks for summer camp. Books became valuable currency, changing hands after careful negotiation: "Okay, you can borrow Adams's *So Long and Thanks for All the Fish* (Pocket), but you have to lend me the first two books in the Xanth series." The shelves neatly lined with class sets of books gradually gave way to a paperback library, stocked with books donated by students and their families, bonus copies from book clubs, and books I ordered with my budgeted allotment each year. (S. Moran, 1991, pp. 439)

Ultimately, a community of learners can help create a *sense of community* in the classroom—a sense that we and our students have shared goals, are mutually respectful and supportive of one another's efforts, and believe that everyone makes an important contribution to classroom learning. We will look at this idea more closely in Chapter 14.

At the same time, we should note a couple of potential weaknesses that communities of learners, and group discussions more generally, may have (A. L. Brown & Campione, 1994; Hynd, 1998b). For one thing, what students learn will inevitably be limited to the knowledge that they themselves acquire and share with one another. Second, students may occasionally pass on their own misconceptions to their classmates. Obviously, then, when we conduct classroom discussions or structure our classrooms as communities of learners, we must carefully monitor student interactions to make sure that students ultimately acquire thorough and accurate understandings of the subject matter they are studying. If they do not, we may need to take active steps to encourage conceptual change. We look at strategies for doing so now.

Promoting Conceptual Change

Teachers often present new information in class with the expectation that such information will replace any erroneous beliefs that students currently have. Yet research indicates that students of all ages often hold quite stubbornly to their misconceptions, even after considerable instruction that explicitly contradicts those misconceptions (Carey, 1986; Chambliss, 1994; Chinn & Brewer, 1993; Shuell, 1996). Consider the following situation described by J. F. Eaton, Anderson, & Smith (1984):

See "Intuitive Physics" in *Simulations in Educational Psychology and Research.*

This study is depicted in the case study "In the Eye of the Beholder" at the end of Chapter 2.

> A class of fifth graders was about to study a unit on light and vision. A pretest revealed that most students believed incorrectly that vision occurs simply as the result of light shining on an object and making it bright. During the unit, the teacher presented the correct explanation of human vision: Light must be reflected off an object *and then travel to the eye* before the object can be seen. Even though students both read and heard the correct explanation of how people see objects, most of them "learned" what they already believed: that an object can be seen as soon as light hits it. Posttest results indicated that only 24 percent of the class had learned the correct explanation.

Why are students' misconceptions often so resistant to change? Theorists have offered several possible explanations:

- As noted earlier, students' existing misconceptions may often color their understanding of new information. Learners are likely to interpret new information in ways that are consistent with what they already "know" about the world, to the point where they continue to believe what they have always believed.
- Students also tend to look for information that confirms their existing beliefs and to ignore or discredit any *disconfirming* evidence (Duit, 1991; Gunstone & White, 1981; Hynd, 1998b; Kuhn, Amsel, & O'Loughlin, 1988). (Recall Barry's insistence that his classmates "weren't timing real good"; Hynd, 1998a, p. 34.)
- Students' existing beliefs are often consistent with their everyday experiences; in contrast, more accurate explanations (perhaps commonly accepted scientific principles or theories) may be fairly abstract and difficult to relate to everyday reality (P. A. Alexander, 1997; R. Driver et al., 1994; M. C. Linn, Songer, & Eylon, 1996). For example, although the law of inertia tells us that force is needed to *start* an object in motion but not to *keep* it in motion, we know from experience that if we want to move a heavy object across the floor, we have to continue pushing it until we get it where we want it (R. Driver et al., 1994).

Students often have erroneous beliefs about how the earth, sun, and moon move in relation to one another. These students are trying to get a better understanding of the solar system through computer simulations and a multimedia presentation.

- Some erroneous beliefs are integrated into cohesive personal theories, with many interrelationships existing among various ideas; in such a situation, changing misconceptions involves changing an entire organized body of knowledge rather than a single belief (Chambliss, 1994; Derry, 1996; C. L. Smith, Maclin, Grosslight, & Davis, 1997). For example, the belief that the sun revolves around the earth may be part of a more general "earth-centered" view of things, perhaps one that includes the moon, stars, and various other heavenly bodies revolving around the earth. In reality, of course, the moon revolves around the earth, the earth revolves around the sun, and the other stars are not directly involved with the earth one way or the other. Yet the earth-centered view is a much easier one to understand and accept (on the surface, at least), and everything seemingly fits together quite nicely.
- In many situations, students learn new information without letting go of their prior beliefs, so that two inconsistent ideas are kept in memory simultaneously (Chambliss, 1994; Keil & Silberstein, 1996; Mintzes et al., 1991; Winer & Cottrell, 1996). Sometimes this happens because students learn the new information by rote, without relating it to what they already know and believe (Chambliss, 1994; Strike & Posner, 1992). In other cases, it may occur because existing misconceptions are not easily retrievable from long-term memory (Keil & Silberstein, 1996). In either situation, students will not realize that the new things they have learned contradict what they already believe.

When our students hold misconceptions about the world, we must help them revise their thinking, to undergo **conceptual change**. Table 7.1 identifies four principles regarding how conceptual change may come about. The following strategies are derived from these four principles:

■ *Identify existing misconceptions before instruction begins.* As teachers, we can more easily address students' misconceptions when we know what those misconceptions are (Kyle & Shymansky, 1989; Putnam, 1992; K. J. Roth & Anderson, 1988; Vosniadou & Brewer, 1987). Thus, we should probably begin any new topic by assessing students' current beliefs about the topic—perhaps simply by asking a few informal questions. The following conversation illustrates the kinds of misconceptions that questioning may reveal:

Adult:	What is rain?
Child:	It's water that falls out of a cloud when the clouds evaporate.
Adult:	What do you mean, "clouds evaporate"?
Child:	That means water goes up in the air and then it makes clouds and then, when it gets too heavy up there, then the water comes and they call it rain.
Adult:	Does the water stay in the sky?
Child:	Yes, and then it comes down when it rains. It gets too heavy.
Adult:	Why does it get too heavy?

TABLE 7.1   PRINCIPLES/ASSUMPTIONS

Principles for Promoting Conceptual Change

PRINCIPLE	EDUCATIONAL IMPLICATION	EXAMPLE
Conceptual change is more likely to occur when existing misconceptions are identified before instruction begins.	Probe students' understanding of a topic through a short pretest or a series of discussion questions.	When beginning a unit on gravity, ask, "If we were to drop a penny and a golf ball from a second-story window at exactly the same time, would one of them land sooner than the other, or would they both land at the same time?" If students predict that a golf ball would land sooner than a penny, have them conduct an experiment to test their prediction.
Students are most likely to revise their current beliefs about the world when they become convinced that these beliefs are incorrect.	Show students how new information contradicts the things they currently believe.	If students believe that sweaters keep people warm by generating heat, leave a sweater outside during a cold night, then ask students whether it feels warm the following morning (Gardner, 2000).
Students must be motivated to learn correct explanations for the phenomena they observe.	Show students how correct explanations relate to their own personal interests.	Demonstrate how the laws of physics relate to auto mechanics and, indirectly, to auto repair.
Some misconceptions may persist despite instruction designed to contradict them.	Carefully scrutinize what students say and write, not only during a lesson but after the lesson as well, for signs of partial or total misunderstanding.	When a student says that a spider is an *insect*, respond: "A spider is actually an *arachnid*, not an insect. Think back to what we learned about insects. Why don't spiders fit in that category?"

Child:	'Cause there's too much water up there.
Adult:	Why does it rain?
Child:	'Cause the water gets too heavy and then it comes down.
Adult:	Why doesn't the whole thing come down?
Child:	Well, 'cause it comes down at little times like a salt shaker when you turn it upside down. It doesn't all come down at once 'cause there's little holes and it just comes out.
Adult:	What are the little holes in the sky?
Child:	Umm, holes in the clouds, letting the water out. (dialogue from Stepans, 1991, p. 94)

As you well know, this conception of a cloud as a "salt shaker" is hardly consistent with the scientifically accepted view of how and why rain comes about.

Informal pretesting will be particularly important in your first few years of teaching. As you gain experience teaching a particular topic year after year, you may eventually find that you can anticipate what your students' prior beliefs and misbeliefs about the topic are likely to be.

■ *Convince students that their existing beliefs are inadequate.* As teachers, we can more effectively promote conceptual change when we show our students how new information contradicts what they currently believe and when we demonstrate why their existing conceptions are inadequate. To accomplish these ends, we might use strategies such as these:

- Asking questions that challenge students' current beliefs
- Presenting phenomena that students cannot adequately explain within their existing perspectives, then asking them to explain why these phenomena might have occurred
- Engaging students in discussions of the pros and cons of various explanations
- Explicitly pointing out the differences between students' beliefs and "reality"
- Showing how the correct explanation of an event or phenomenon is more plausible (i.e., makes more sense) than students' existing explanations
(Chan, Burtis, & Bereiter, 1997; Hynd, 1998b; Pine & Messer, 2000; Posner, Strike, Hewson, & Gertzog, 1982; Prawat, 1989; K. J. Roth, 1990; Slusher & Anderson, 1996; Vosniadou & Brewer, 1987)

Students will notice inconsistencies between new information and their previously acquired beliefs only if they try to make connections between the "new" and the "old"—in other words, if they engage in meaningful learning (Chinn & Brewer, 1993; O. Lee & Anderson, 1993; Pintrich, Marx, & Boyle, 1993; Slusher & Anderson, 1996). In Chapter 6 we found that students who engage in meaningful rather than rote learning acquire new information more quickly and retrieve it more easily. Here we see an additional reason to encourage meaningful learning: It helps "undo" existing misconceptions.

■ *Motivate students to learn correct explanations.* Students are most likely to engage in meaningful learning and undergo conceptual change when they are motivated to do so (O. Lee & Anderson, 1993; Pintrich et al., 1993). For example, students should be interested in the subject matter they are studying, set their sights on mastering it, and believe that they are actually capable of mastering it (Pintrich et al., 1993). Chapter 12 identifies a variety of strategies for fostering such motives and beliefs.

■ *Monitor what students say and write for persistent misconceptions.* Because of students' natural tendency to reinterpret new information within the context of what they already know and believe, some misconceptions may be especially resistant to change despite our best efforts. These misconceptions are sometimes blatantly incorrect; at other times, they may be sort-of-but-not-quite correct. As an example of the latter situation, students sometimes define the concept *transparent* as "something you can see through" (K. J. Roth & Anderson, 1988). Although such a definition is consistent with how we ordinarily speak about transparency, it may nevertheless reflect the erroneous belief that sight originates with the eye and goes outward to and through the transparent object. The term is more accurately defined as "something light passes through."

Throughout each lesson we should continue to check students' beliefs about the topic at hand, looking for subtle signs that their understanding is not quite accurate and giving corrective feedback when necessary. As an example, consider the following classroom discussion about vision and opaque objects. Using an overhead projector, Ms. Ramsey is showing her fifth graders a picture of a girl standing in front of her house; there is an 8-foot wall between the girl and the family car.

Ms. Ramsey:	. . . Why can't the girl see around the wall?
Annie:	The girl can't see around the wall because the wall is opaque.
Ms. Ramsey:	What do you mean when you say the wall is opaque?
Annie:	*You can't see through it. It is solid.*
Brian:	(calling out) The rays are what can't go through the wall.
Ms. Ramsey:	I like that answer better. Why is it better?
Brian:	The rays of light bounce off the car and go to the wall. They can't go through the wall.
Ms. Ramsey:	Where are the light rays coming from originally?
Students:	The sun.
Annie:	*The girl can't see the car because she is not far enough out.*
Ms. Ramsey:	So you think her position is what is keeping her from seeing it. (She flips down the overlay with the answer.) Who was better?
Students:	Brian.
Ms. Ramsey:	(to Annie) Would she be able to see if she moved out beyond the wall?
Annie:	Yes.
Ms. Ramsey:	Why?
Annie:	*The wall is blocking her view.*
Ms. Ramsey:	Is it blocking her view? What is it blocking?
Student:	Light rays.
Ms. Ramsey:	Light rays that are doing what?
Annie:	If the girl moves out beyond the wall, then the light rays that bounce off the car are not being blocked. (K. J. Roth & Anderson, 1988, pp. 129–130)

Notice how Ms. Ramsey is not satisfied with Annie's original answer that the wall is opaque. With further questioning, it becomes clear that Annie's understanding of opaqueness is off target: She talks about the girl being unable to "see through" the wall, rather than about light's in-

INTO THE CLASSROOM: *Promoting Conceptual Change*

Check for prior misconceptions that may lead students to interpret new information incorrectly.

> When a fourth-grade teacher asks, "What is gravity?" one of his students replies that it's "a force that pulls you down." The teacher points to Australia on a globe and asks, "What do you think would happen if we traveled to Australia? Would gravity pull us off the earth and make us fall into space?"

Show how new information contradicts the things that students currently believe.

> When several students express their stereotypical beliefs that new immigrants to the country are "lazy," their teacher invites several recent immigrants to visit the class and describe their efforts and experiences in adapting to a new culture.

Ask questions that challenge students' misconceptions.

> A physics teacher has just begun a unit on inertia. Several students assert that when a baseball is thrown in the air, some force continues to act upon the ball, pushing it upward until it begins to drop. The teacher asks, "What force in the air could possibly be pushing that ball upward once it leaves the thrower's hand?"

Show students how your alternative explanation is more plausible and useful than their original misconception.

> The same physics teacher points out that the baseball continues to move upward even though no force pushes it in that direction. He explains the concept of *inertia* within this context: The ball needs a force only to get it *started* in a particular direction. Once the force has been exerted, other forces (gravity and air resistance) alter the ball's speed and direction.

Give students corrective feedback about responses that reflect misunderstanding.

> A psychology teacher says to a student, "Hmmm, you just told me that you could learn a foreign language by playing audiotapes while you sleep. But didn't we just discover last week that attention is essential for effective cognitive processing?"

When pointing out misconceptions that students have, do so in a way that maintains their self-esteem.

> When a student expresses an erroneous belief, her teacher says, "You know, many of my students come to class thinking exactly that. It's a very logical thing to think. But the truth of the matter is. . . ."

ability to pass through the wall. With Ms. Ramsey's continuing insistence on precise language, Annie eventually begins to bring light rays into her explanation (K. J. Roth & Anderson, 1988).

Assessment of students' comprehension is important *after* a lesson as well. We are more likely to detect and correct misconceptions when we ask students to *use* and *apply* what they have learned (as Ms. Ramsey does in the conversation just presented), rather than just to spit back memorized facts, definitions, and formulas (Pine & Messer, 2000; K. J. Roth, 1990; K. J. Roth & Anderson, 1988). For example, if we want students in a social studies class to understand that there are usually valid and compelling perspectives on both sides of any controversial issue, rather than to believe that controversy is always a matter of the "good guys" versus the "bad guys," we might ask them to engage in a debate in which they must convincingly present a perspective contrary to their own beliefs. If students in a creative writing class have previously learned that complete sentences are always essential in good writing and we want to convince them otherwise, we might ask them to find examples of how incomplete sentences are sometimes used quite effectively in short stories and novels.

Considering Diversity in Constructive Processes

As we have seen, our students will inevitably interpret classroom subject matter in unique, idiosyncratic ways. Different students will have different knowledge bases—different concepts, schemas, scripts, personal theories, and so on—that they will use to make sense of any new situation. For example, students of different cultural backgrounds may come to us with somewhat different concepts and, therefore, with somewhat different ways of categorizing and interpreting their experiences. To illustrate, when giving directions, natives of Hawaii rarely speak of north, south, east, and west; instead, they are more likely to talk about going toward the sea (*makai*) or toward the mountains (*mauka*). Some students may even have concepts that we ourselves don't have; for example, many Mexican Americans have different names for varieties of peppers that, for me, all fall into one category—hot peppers. Furthermore, some schemas and scripts are likely to be specific to particular cultures, and subject matter that incorporates those schemas and scripts will cause difficulty for students from other cultural backgrounds. This is a principle that you may have discovered firsthand when you did "The War of the Ghosts" exercise.

As we help our students construct a meaningful understanding of the world around them, we can increase their multicultural awareness by promoting *multiple constructions* of the same situation. For example, we might present the western migration across North America during the 1700s and 1800s from two different perspectives: that of the European settlers and that of the Native Americans already residing on the land. One simple way to do this is to point out that migrating peoples are referred to as *pioneers* or *settlers* in most United States history books but might instead have been called *foreigners* or *invaders* by Native Americans (Banks, 1991). Ultimately, we must help our students to understand the very complex nature of human "knowledge" and to appreciate the fact that there may be several, equally valid interpretations of any single event.

How might you introduce multiple perspectives into the subject matter you will be teaching?

A community of learners may be especially valuable when we have a diverse classroom of students (Garcia, 1994; Ladson-Billings, 1995). Such a community values the contributions of all students, using everyone's individual backgrounds, cultural perspectives, and unique abilities to enhance the overall performance of the class. It also provides a context in which students can form friendships across the lines of ethnicity, gender, socioeconomic status, and disability—friendships that, as noted in Chapters 3 and 4, are so critical for students' social development and multicultural understanding.

Accommodating Students with Special Needs

We will see evidence of diversity in constructive processes in our students with special educational needs. For example, students with learning disabilities may construct inappropriate meanings from stories that they hear (Pressley, 1995; J. P. Williams, 1991). Students with emo-

TABLE 7.2

STUDENTS IN INCLUSIVE SETTINGS

Promoting Knowledge Construction in Students with Special Educational Needs

CATEGORY	CHARACTERISTICS YOU MIGHT OBSERVE	SUGGESTED CLASSROOM STRATEGIES
Students with specific cognitive or academic difficulties	• Possible holes in students' knowledge base that may limit meaningful understanding of some classroom topics • Occasional unusual or inappropriate interpretations of prose • Occasional misinterpretations of social situations	• Determine students' prior knowledge about a new topic; remind them of what they *do* know about the topic. • Monitor students' comprehension of prose; correct misinterpretations. • Present alternative interpretations of others' behaviors.
Students with social or behavioral problems	• Frequent misinterpretations of social situations	• Present alternative interpretations of others' behaviors and identify suitable courses of action based on the most reasonable interpretation of a given situation.
Students with general delays in cognitive and social functioning	• Smaller knowledge base from which to draw • Difficulty constructing an accurate interpretation when information is ambiguous or incomplete	• Assume little if any prior knowledge about topics unless you have evidence to the contrary; remind students of what they *do* know about a topic. • Present information clearly and unambiguously.
Students with physical or sensory challenges	• Limited knowledge base to which students can relate new information, due to fewer opportunities to interact with the outside world	• Provide the background experiences (e.g., field trips) that students need to make sense of classroom subject matter.
Students with advanced cognitive development	• Larger knowledge base from which to draw • Rapid concept learning • Greater conceptual understanding of classroom material (e.g., greater understanding of cause-effect relationships) • Greater ability to draw inferences	• Assign challenging tasks that enable students to develop and use their advanced understanding of topics. • Ask thought-provoking questions that encourage inference drawing.

Sources: Butterfield & Ferretti, 1987; Graham & Hudley, 1994; Hughes, 1988; Lochman & Dodge, 1994; Patton et al., 1996; Piirto, 1999; Pressley, 1995; Schumaker & Hazel, 1984; Turnbull et al., 1999; J. P. Williams, 1991.

tional and behavioral disorders may construct counterproductive interpretations of social situations; for example, they might "see" an act of aggression in an innocent gesture or "hear" an insult when none was intended; recall our discussion of *hostile attributional bias* in Chapter 3. Table 7.2 identifies some patterns that researchers have found in the constructive processes of students with special needs; it also presents suggestions for helping these students acquire appropriate meanings from academic and social situations.

The Big Picture

Before we turn to our final case study, let's take a moment to recap some of the key points of the chapter. In particular, let's look once again at constructive processes, ways in which knowledge might be organized, and strategies for promoting knowledge construction and conceptual change.

Constructive Processes

Many cognitive psychologists believe that individuals *construct* knowledge from their experience, rather than simply absorb it in the form presented to them; their resulting "reality" is not necessarily identical to the reality of the external world. Constructive processes may occur both when information is being received (during storage) and when it is later recalled (during retrieval). Some theorists describe the processes by which people construct their own personal understandings of the world; this perspective is sometimes called *individual constructivism*. Other theorists focus more on people's collective efforts to impose meaning on the world around them; this perspective is frequently called *social constructivism*.

Regardless of whether our students acquire their understandings on their own or with the help of others, they will all construct somewhat unique interpretations of the ideas and events they encounter both in and outside of the classroom. Such constructions will affect their understandings not only of academic subject matter but also of themselves, their interpersonal relationships, and their views about morality (see Chapter 3). Many of their interpretations, though perhaps different from those of other people, may be equally valid and appropriate. But others—for example, beliefs that the earth is flat, that rote learning is more effective than meaningful learning, or that a classmate is trying to pick a fight—may interfere with their future success in the outside world. As teachers, we must help our students interpret the world around them in ways that are likely to be productive over the long run.

Organizing Knowledge

Children and adolescents, like all human beings, organize what they learn in a variety of ways. One of the most basic organizational structures is a *concept*, a mental grouping of objects or events. Concepts and other sources of information are often integrated still further into entities that theorists refer to as *schemas* (organized bodies of knowledge about particular objects or phenomena), *scripts* (schemas that involve a predictable sequence of events), and *personal theories* (general belief systems about the world). The more organized students' knowledge is, the more readily they can remember it later on (see Chapter 6), and the more easily they can apply what they know to new situations and problems (see Chapter 8). At the same time, tightly integrated bodies of information and beliefs—perhaps including deep-seated misconceptions—often become increasingly stable and resistant to change, even in the face of contradictory evidence.

Promoting Knowledge Construction and Conceptual Change

As teachers, we can help students construct accurate interpretations of the world around them and pull such interpretations into a well-integrated *conceptual understanding* of classroom topics. We can do so in a variety of ways—for instance, by having them experiment with physical objects and phenomena; carry out real-world, authentic activities; and interact with, question, and challenge their classmates about challenging tasks and controversial topics. Yet we must also be alert to the misconceptions that they may either bring with them to the classroom or acquire from instructional activities and make a pointed effort to convince and motivate them to change their beliefs. Furthermore, we can increase their multicultural awareness by promoting *multiple constructions* of the same situation—by encouraging them to look at events from the perspectives of different groups.

CASE STUDY: *Earth-Shaking Summaries*

Ms. Jewell spends the first half hour of her seventh-grade geography class describing how earthquakes occur. She introduces the theory of *plate tectonics*—the notion that the earth's crust is made up of many separate pieces (*plates*) that rest upon a layer of hot, molten rock (the *mantle*). She explains that plates occasionally shift and rub against each other, making the immediate area shake and leaving *faults* in the earth's surface.

Her students listen attentively throughout her explanation. When she finishes, she asks whether there are any questions. Finding that there are none, she says, "Great! I'm glad you all understand. What I'd like you to do now is to take out a piece of paper and write a paragraph answering this question: *Why do we have earthquakes?*" She has read in a professional journal that asking students to summarize what they've learned often helps them to remember it better later on, and she figures that the task she's just assigned is an excellent way to encourage summarization.

Ms. Jewell collects students' papers as they leave for their next class. As she glances quickly through the stack, she is distressed by what she sees. Some of her students have provided a relatively complete and accurate description of plate tectonics. But the responses of others are vague enough to make her uneasy about how thoroughly they understood her explanation; here are two examples:

Frank: The earth's crust shifts around and shakes us up.

Mitchell: Earthquakes happen when really big plates on the earth move around.

And three of her students clearly have made little sense of the lesson:

Adrienne: Scientists use technology to understand how earthquakes happen. They use computers and stuff.

Toni: When there are earthquakes, people's plates move around the house.

Jonathan: Earthquakes aren't anybody's fault. They just happen.

Ms. Jewell sighs, clearly discouraged by the feedback she's just gotten about her lesson. "I guess I still have a lot to learn about teaching this stuff," she concludes.

- Why is Ms. Jewell not convinced that Frank and Mitchell have mastered the material? What critical aspects of the lesson did each boy omit in his response?
- What pieces of information from the lesson did Adrienne, Toni, and Jonathan apparently use when answering Ms. Jewell's question? Can you explain their responses using the concept of knowledge construction?
- What instructional strategies might Ms. Jewell have used to help her students gain a better understanding of plate tectonics?

Once you have answered these questions, compare your responses with those presented in Appendix B.

PRAXIS Turn to Appendix C, "Matching Book and Ancillary Content to the PRAXIS™ Principles of Learning and Teaching Tests," to discover sections of this chapter that may be especially applicable to the PRAXIS™ tests.

Now go to our Companion Website at http://www.prenhall.com/ormrod to assess your understanding of chapter content with "Multiple-Choice Questions," apply comprehension in "Essay Questions," broaden your knowledge of educational psychology with related "Web Links," gain greater insight about classroom learning in "Learning in the Content Areas," and analyze and assess classroom work in the "Student Artifact Library."

Key Concepts

reconstruction error (p. 231)
individual constructivism (p. 231)
social constructivism (p. 231)
distributed cognition (p. 232)
concept (p. 233)
undergeneralization (p. 233)
overgeneralization (p. 233)
positive instance (p. 233)

negative instance (p. 233)
defining feature (p. 233)
correlational feature (p. 233)
salience (of features) (p. 233)
prototype (p. 235)
exemplar (p. 236)
schema (p. 238)
script (p. 238)

personal theory (p. 240)
misconception (p. 241)
conceptual understanding (p. 244)
authentic activity (p. 245)
community of learners (p. 248)
conceptual change (p. 250)

8

Higher–Level Thinking Skills

*T*ake a moment to reflect on your years as a college student. You've certainly spent a great many hours studying the information and skills that are central parts of your college curriculum, and you've undoubtedly learned a great deal. But how effectively do you *think about* the material you encounter in your college courses? After so many years of practice in learning academic subject matter, have you learned how to study effectively? Can you apply what you've learned to situations and problems in your own life? Do you evaluate new information and ideas with a critical eye, or do you simply take them at face value?

The preceding two chapters described how human beings learn and remember declarative and procedural knowledge. In this chapter we will focus on people's ability to understand and direct their own learning processes and on their ability to use and evaluate what they learn. In particular, we will address the following questions:

- What do we mean by the term *higher-level thinking*?
- How does *metacognition*—students' knowledge and beliefs about their own cognitive processes—influence their ability to learn successfully?
- What *study strategies* seem to facilitate academic achievement, and how can we help our students acquire these strategies?
- Under what circumstances are learners most likely to apply *(transfer)* what they've learned to new situations?
- What cognitive processes are involved in effective *problem solving,* and how can we help students solve problems more successfully?
- What is *critical thinking,* and how can we promote it in the classroom?
- How do *dispositions* enter into higher-level thinking processes?

As we address these questions, I hope that you, as a student yourself, will learn more effective ways of studying, applying, and evaluating the subject matter you encounter in your *own* college classes.

CASE STUDY: *A Question of Speed*

Mary is studying for tomorrow's exam in her physics class. As she looks over her class notes, she finds the following statement in her notebook:

Velocity equals acceleration times time.

She also finds a formula expressing the same idea:

$$v = a \times t$$

Mary dutifully memorizes the statement and formula until she knows both by heart. The following day, Mary encounters this problem on her physics exam:

An automotive engineer has designed a car that can reach a speed of 50 miles per hour within 5 seconds. What is the car's rate of acceleration?

She puzzles over the problem for several minutes. She thinks about a car reaching 50 miles per hour: Is this the car's acceleration, its velocity, or something else altogether?

She realizes that she doesn't know the difference between acceleration and velocity. She finally turns in her exam with this and several similar questions unanswered.

She later confides to a classmate, "I really blew that test today, but I don't know why. I mean, I really studied *hard!*"

- How does Mary study for her physics exam? What things does she *not* do as she studies—things that might have led to better performance?
- If you were Mary's physics teacher, how might you help Mary study more effectively for the next exam?

The Nature of Higher-Level Thinking

One critical mistake that Mary makes is to use only rote learning as she studies for her exam. Although she memorizes "velocity equals acceleration times time," she never really learns what velocity and acceleration *are*. (*Velocity* is the speed at which an object travels in a particular direction. *Acceleration* is the rate at which an object's velocity changes.) As a result, she is unable to apply her knowledge in any meaningful way.

From Chapters 6 and 7, you have already learned a great deal about learning. For example, from the discussion of long-term memory storage in Chapter 6, you've discovered that people store new information more effectively when they relate it to things they have previously learned—that is, when they engage in such cognitive processes as meaningful learning and elaboration. From the discussion of knowledge construction in Chapter 7, you've discovered that learning is often a process of creating one's own, idiosyncratic knowledge base by combining both new and old information into something that makes some sort of "sense." Let's now put to work some of the things that you know about learning. Let's see what you can learn about a new topic: the world's diminishing rain forests.

EXPERIENCING FIRSTHAND   *Rain Forests*

Read this passage, then answer the questions that follow.

Almost half of the world's plants and animals live in its rain forests. From tropical plants we get a variety of foods (e.g., fruits, nuts, coffee, chocolate) and ingredients for many household products (e.g., toothpaste, fabric dyes, pesticides). Furthermore, plants that grow only in rain forests produce substances used in treatments for Hodgkin's disease, multiple sclerosis, and Parkinson's disease. One researcher studying the rain forest of Costa Rica estimated that 15 percent of its plants had potential for treating cancer.

Valuable as they are, rain forests are diminishing at an alarming rate every year. Millions of people in developing countries rely on rain forest land for farming. They clear large areas to grow their crops, slashing and burning the existing vegetation. Within a few years, they deplete the soil of its nutrients, and so they must move farther into the rain forest to find new farmland. Oftentimes cattle ranchers occupy the land that peasant farmers have left behind, but soon the soil cannot even support grasses to feed cattle.

Each day we lose 75,000 acres of rain forest to such short-sighted practices—a rate that translates into about 27 million acres (an area the size of Austria) annually. (based on Hosmer, 1987, p. 6)

1. What are three illnesses that can be treated by using rain forest plants?
2. How does peasant farming change the nature of rain forest land?
3. Why do peasants continue to farm more and more rain forest land despite the environmental consequences of doing so?
4. What things might be done to halt the destruction of rain forests?
5. What are the most useful ideas to be gained from the passage?

Which of the five questions were the easiest ones to answer? Which questions were the most *important* ones to answer? You may have found questions 1 and 2 relatively easy because the answers were clearly stated in the passage. These two **lower-level questions** asked you to recall information that was specifically given to you. You may have found the last three questions more difficult because you couldn't find the answers in the passage itself. To answer question 3, you had to apply something that you know about people in general—the fact that people usually do whatever they must do in order to survive—to your understanding of the peasant farmers' plight. To answer question 4, you had to combine your prior knowledge with information in the passage to generate possible solutions to a difficult problem. And to answer question 5, you needed to make a judgment about what information was most likely to be useful to you at a later time. Such **higher-level questions**, which ask you to go *beyond* the information actually presented, are usually more difficult than lower-level questions. Yet these higher-level questions are often the most important ones for learners to address.

There is certainly value in having students master basic facts and skills. At the same time, students should also be able to apply, analyze, synthesize, evaluate, and in other ways mentally manipulate information; in other words, they should engage in **higher-level thinking** on a regular basis. Thus, the ideal school curriculum should address *both* lower-level and higher-level forms of thinking and learning (Bloom, Englehart, Furst, Hill, & Krathwohl, 1956; N. S. Cole, 1990; Onosko & Newmann, 1994; Paxton, 1999).

Metacognition, transfer, problem solving, and critical thinking are all examples of higher-level thinking. As we explore these topics, we will identify numerous strategies for helping students think about and use classroom subject matter in new, productive, and otherwise "intelligent" ways.

Metacognition and Study Strategies

What specific study strategies do you use? For example, do you take notes? Do you try to relate certain concepts and principles to your own life and experiences? Do you occasionally test yourself on class material to see how well you have learned it? What does your current grade point average tell you about the effectiveness of your study strategies?

Students vary considerably in the study strategies they use. Consider these three students:

Kate is studying for a biology exam that will include multiple-choice, short-answer, and essay questions. She moves her eyes down each of the assigned pages in the textbook, but all the while she is thinking about the upcoming school dance. Kate seems to think that as long as her eyes are looking at the page, the information printed on it will somehow sink in.

Ling is studying for the same exam. She spends most of her time memorizing terms and definitions in her textbook. Eventually, she can recite many of them word for word.

Sarah, too, is studying for the biology exam. She focuses her efforts on trying to understand basic biological principles and on generating new examples of those principles.

Which student is likely to do best on the biology exam? Considering what we now know about learning and memory, we can predict that Sarah will get the highest score of the three girls. Unfortunately, Ling has not yet discovered that she learns better when she relates new ideas to her prior knowledge than when she memorizes things at a rote level. And poor Kate knows even less about how to learn effectively: She's not even paying attention to what she thinks she is reading!

The concept **metacognition** includes learners' knowledge and beliefs regarding their own cognitive processes, as well as their attempts to regulate those cognitive processes to maximize learning and memory. For example, metacognition includes

- Knowing the limits of one's own learning and memory capabilities
- Knowing what learning tasks one can realistically accomplish within a certain amount of time
- Knowing which learning strategies are effective and which are not
- Planning an approach to a learning task that is likely to be successful
- Using effective learning strategies to process and learn new material
- Monitoring one's own knowledge and comprehension—in other words, knowing when information has been successfully learned and when it has not
- Using effective strategies for retrieval of previously stored information

Unfortunately, many school classrooms devote most of their time to lower-level tasks at the expense of higher-level ones (Blumenfeld, 1992; Freiberg, 1987; Tobin, 1987).

Higher-level thinking involves application, analysis, synthesis, evaluation, and other elaborative processes.

Metacognition takes somewhat different forms in different subject areas. For more details, see the chapter "Learning in the Content Areas" in the *Study Guide and Reader*.

To illustrate, you have undoubtedly learned by now that you can acquire only so much information so fast; you cannot possibly absorb the contents of an entire textbook in one hour. You have also learned that you can learn information more quickly and recall it more easily when you organize it logically. And perhaps you have discovered the advantage of checking yourself as you read a textbook, stopping every so often to make sure that you've understood what you've just read. In other words, you are metacognitively aware of some things that you need to do (mentally) to learn new information effectively.

The more students know about effective learning strategies—the greater their metacognitive awareness—the higher their classroom achievement is likely to be (Baker, 1989; Perkins, 1995; P. L. Peterson, 1988). Furthermore, students who use more sophisticated metacognitive strategies are more likely to undergo conceptual change when such change is warranted (Gunstone, 1994; Wittrock, 1994).

Did you have misconceptions about how best to study before you read this book?

Unfortunately, many students are unaware of how they can best learn and remember information. Younger children (those in the elementary grades) are especially naive about effective learning strategies (see the sections "Learning Strategies" and "Metacognition" in Chapter 2). But older students are also prone to misconceptions about how they can best learn and remember. For example, many students at all grade levels (even those in college) erroneously believe that rote learning is an effective way to study (Barnett, 2001; Pintrich & De Groot, 1990; Prawat, 1989; Schommer, 1994a).

With each transition to a higher educational level (from elementary to middle school, junior high to high school, or high school to college), teachers expect students to learn more material and think about it in a more sophisticated fashion. Thus, the simple learning strategies that students develop in grade school (e.g., rehearsal) become less and less effective with each passing year (e.g., Hacker, 1998a). Yet all too often, teachers teach academic content areas—history, biology, mathematics, and so on—without also teaching students how to *learn* in those content areas (Hamman, Berthelot, Saia, & Crowley, 2000; Pressley et al., 1990; E. Wood, Motz, & Willoughby, 1997). When left to their own devices, most students develop effective strategies very slowly (if at all) and so over the years encounter increasing difficulty in their attempts to master classroom subject matter. And when they *don't* master it, they may not know why they have failed, nor may they know how to improve their chances of succeeding the next time around (Hacker et al., 2000; Loranger, 1994; O'Sullivan & Joy, 1990).

In the upcoming sections we review research findings on a variety of study strategies. We then consider factors that influence students' use of such strategies, as well as ways in which we can help our own students study and learn more effectively.

Effective Study Strategies

Research studies point to a number of effective study strategies, including

- Identifying important information
- Taking notes
- Retrieving relevant prior knowledge
- Organizing
- Elaborating
- Summarizing
- Monitoring comprehension

As we examine these strategies in the pages that follow, you will undoubtedly find some that you yourself use as you study course material.

Identifying Important Information

What cues do you use to identify important ideas in your textbooks? Are you more likely to believe that something is important if it's printed in italics or boldface type? Do you look for important points in headings, introductions, concluding paragraphs, or summaries? Do you focus on definitions, formulas, or lists of items?

Students rarely learn everything they read in a textbook or remember everything they hear in the classroom. Obviously, then, they must be selective in studying course content. The things they choose to study—whether main ideas and critical pieces of information, or isolated facts and trivial details—inevitably affect their learning and school achievement (Dee-Lucas & Larkin, 1991; Dole et al., 1991; R. E. Reynolds & Shirey, 1988).

Students often have difficulty separating central and important information from the trivial and unimportant. Here are some features of books and classroom lectures on which students often focus:

- *The first sentence of a lesson or paragraph.* Many students erroneously believe that the main idea (and perhaps *only* idea) of a paragraph is always found in the first sentence (Mayer, 1984). (In writing instruction, students are often taught to put the main idea first; hence, it is not surprising that they expect to find the same pattern in the writings of others.)
- *Items that look different.* Definitions and formulas often stand out in a textbook, perhaps because they appear in *italics* or **boldface type** or perhaps because they are

set apart

from the rest of the text. As a result, students often focus on them to the exclusion of other, potentially more important information (Mayer, 1984). For example, when reading scientific proofs, students often focus their attention on specific equations, rather than on the verbal text that makes those equations meaningful (Dee-Lucas & Larkin, 1991).
- *Items presented in more than one way.* Students are more likely to view material as important when it is presented in several different ways. For example, they are more likely to pay attention to things that teachers describe verbally *and* write on the chalkboard (Kiewra, 1989).
- *Items that are intrinsically interesting.* Students at all levels attend more to interesting statements than to uninteresting ones even if the most interesting statements are relatively unimportant (P. A. Alexander & Jetton, 1996; Garner, Brown, Sanders, & Menke, 1992; Harp & Mayer, 1998).

Thus, when important ideas are presented within the middle of a lesson or paragraph, without any obvious cues to make them stand out, and especially when those ideas do not grab students' immediate interest, students often overlook them.

As teachers, we can help our students learn more effectively by letting them know what ideas are most important in lectures and reading materials. We could, of course, simply tell them exactly what to study. But we can also get the same message across through more subtle means:

- Provide a list of objectives for a lesson.
- Write key concepts and major ideas on the chalkboard.
- Ask questions that focus students' attention on important ideas.

Students often need help distinguishing important ideas from more trivial information, especially when they first begin to study a topic.

Students (especially low-achieving ones) are more likely to learn the important points of a lesson when such "prompts" are provided for them (Kiewra, 1989; R. E. Reynolds & Shirey, 1988; Schraw & Wade, 1991). As our students become better able to distinguish important from unimportant information on their own, we can gradually phase out our guidance.

Do such prompts remind you of the concept of *scaffolding?*

Taking Notes

No doubt you have at one time or another missed a class and therefore had to rely on a fellow student's notes from the class lecture. And no doubt you discovered that the classmate's notes were different (perhaps *very* different) from the notes that you yourself usually take. For twenty students in the same classroom, we will find twenty different sets of notes. Each student makes unique assumptions about what is important, what is useful, and what is likely to be on an upcoming exam, and these assumptions influence the amount and type of notes that the student takes.

In general, note taking is associated with more successful classroom learning; in fact, when students have *no* opportunity either to take or review notes, they may recall very little of what they hear in a lecture (Hale, 1983; Kiewra, 1989). The process of note taking seems to serve two very important functions (Barnett, Di Vesta, & Rogozinski, 1981; Di Vesta & Gray, 1972; Kiewra, 1989). First, it helps learners pay attention to and *encode* information, thus allowing for more effective storage in memory. Second, it provides a means of *external storage* for the information. Long-term memory is often unreliable (recall our discussion of forgetting in Chapter 6), whereas notebooks are fairly dependable and allow students to review the material on one or more later occasions.

Why is review important? (For the answer, see the section "Using Knowledge Frequently" in Chapter 6.)

The extent to which note taking helps students learn and achieve naturally depends on the quantity and quality of the notes taken, as the following exercise illustrates.

INTERPRETING ARTIFACTS AND INTERACTIONS   *King Midas*

To help her students learn how to take notes in class, a seventh-grade language arts teacher gives them a note-taking form to fill in during a unit on Greek mythology. At the end of the unit, the students can use their notes—but *only* their notes—as they take a test about the myths they have studied. Following are two students' notes on the story "King Midas and the Golden Touch." As you look at the notes, consider

- Which set of notes you'd rather have as you study for and take the test
- How much the form scaffolds students' note-taking efforts

Story Note taking Form (left)
Title: King Midas and the golden touch
Author:
I. Characters (write a few notes after each character's name to describe them, make a abbreviation after the character's name for further notes)
a. King Midas— King of Phrygia
b. Silenus - a demigod
c. Dionysus - god of whine
d. Daughter of King Midas
e.
f.
g.
h.
i.
II. Setting (write a few notes after the place to describe it, try to discover the time period)
a.
b.
c.
III. Events
a. Silenus was someone tearing up km's rosebushs
b. Silenus tutored dionysus, dionysus watches over silenus
c. silenus got a feast from km, silenus stayed for a while
d. Dionysus wants to pay km for being nice to silenus
Dionysus gives him a wish.
e. Km picks gold now everything he touches turns to gold
f. Km Turns daughter to gold km washes everything
In the Pactolus loses gold touch.
IV. Conflict (what is the problem, who is involved)
a.
b.
V. Solution (how did the problem work itself out, was there a lesson to learn)
a.
b.

Story Note taking Form (right)
Title: King midas and the golden touch
Author:
I. Characters (write a few notes after each character's name to describe them, make a abbreviation after the character's name for further notes)
a. King Midas
b. first guard
c. Second guard
d. Silenous
e. Dionysus
f. Daughter of the king
g.
h.
i.
II. Setting (write a few notes after the place to describe it, try to discover the time period)
a. Castle
b.
c.
III. Events
a. Sylinus destroys roses
b. King gets him
c.
d.
e.
f.
IV. Conflict (what is the problem, who is involved)
a. every thing he touches turns to gold
b.
V. Solution (how did the problem work itself out, was there a lesson to learn)
a.
b.

No doubt you preferred the notes on the left, which give a relatively complete synopsis of the King Midas story: Had you attended the class yourself, these notes might provide enough retrieval cues to help you remember the story fairly accurately. In contrast, the notes on the right are too brief and disjointed to make much sense. In general, quantity of notes is positively correlated with achievement: Students who take more notes do better (Kiewra, 1989). But the quality of notes is equally critical: Notes must reflect the main ideas of a lesson or reading assignment (A. L. Brown, Campione, & Day, 1981; Kiewra, 1985; B. M. Taylor, 1982). Good notes seem to be especially valuable for students who have little prior knowledge about the subject matter they are studying (Shrager & Mayer, 1989).

Particularly in the years when students are first starting to take notes in class (typically in the middle school or junior high grades), we will want to scaffold their efforts by giving them an idea about what things are most important to include (Pressley, Yokoi, van Meter, Van Etten, & Freebern, 1997; Yokoi, 1997). One approach is to provide a specific structure to use, much as this language arts teacher does. The two students whose notes are depicted here didn't follow the structure to the letter (one neglected to address the setting and conflict, and neither addressed the solution), but they at least had some guidance about the things they should have been thinking about as they listened in class. Another strategy to consider, especially if our students are novice note-takers, is to occasionally check their notebooks for accuracy and appropriate emphasis and then give constructive feedback.

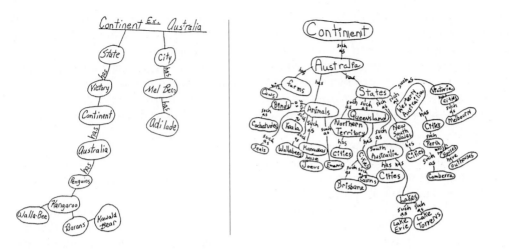

FIGURE 8.1 Concept maps constructed by two fifth-grade students after watching a slide lecture on Australia

From *Learning How to Learn* (pp. 100–101) by J. D. Novak and D. B. Gowin, 1984, Cambridge, England: Cambridge University Press. Copyright 1984 by Cambridge University Press. Reprinted with the permission of Cambridge University Press.

Retrieving Relevant Prior Knowledge

Students can engage in meaningful learning only to the extent that they have previous knowledge to which they can relate new information and are also *aware* of the potential relationship (Ausubel et al., 1978). How can we encourage students to think about the things they already know as they encounter new information? One approach is to model this strategy for our students. For example, we might read aloud a portion of a textbook, stopping occasionally to tie an idea in the text to something previously studied in class or to something in our own personal experiences. We can then encourage our students to do likewise, giving suggestions and guiding their efforts as they proceed (Spires, Donley, & Penrose, 1990). Especially when working in the elementary grades, we might want to provide specific questions that remind students to think about what they already know as they read and study:

- What do you already know about your topic?
- What do you hope to learn about your topic?
- Do you think what you learn by reading your books will change what you already know about your topic? (questions from H. Thompson & Carr, 1995, p. 9)

With time and practice, our students should eventually get in the habit of retrieving relevant prior knowledge with little or no assistance from us (Spires et al., 1990).

Does this approach also remind you of scaffolding?

Organizing

As we discovered in Chapter 6, organized information is stored and retrieved more easily than unorganized information. When students engage in activities that help them organize what they are studying, they learn more effectively (DuBois et al., 1988; M. A. McDaniel & Einstein, 1989; Mintzes, Wandersee, & Novak, 1997). For example, one useful way of organizing information is *outlining* the material—a strategy that may be especially helpful to low-achieving students (Baker, 1989; McDaniel & Einstein, 1989; Wade, 1992).

Another strategy that promotes organization is making a **concept map**, a diagram that depicts the concepts of a unit and their interrelationships (Novak, 1998; Novak & Gowin, 1984). Figure 8.1 shows concept maps constructed by two fifth graders after they watched a slide lecture on Australia. The concepts themselves are in circles; their interrelationships are designated by lines and phrases that link pairs of concepts. The map on the right shows many more interconnections among concepts than does the map on the left, and we can reasonably assume that the student who drew the right-hand map learned the subject matter more effectively.

As another example of concept mapping in action, try the following exercise.

EXPERIENCING FIRSTHAND   *Mapping Concepts About Concepts*

Quickly review the beginning of the "Concepts" section in Chapter 7 (pp. 233–234). These paragraphs contain numerous concepts concerning the topic of concept learning:

Undergeneralization   Defining features
Overgeneralization   Correlational features
Positive instances   Salient features
Negative instances

The text also talks about how these concepts are related to one another; for example, *overgeneralization* is a case of incorrectly identifying *negative instances* as examples of a concept, and a concept is easier to learn when its *defining features* are *salient*.

On a separate sheet of paper, make a concept map with the seven "concepts about concepts" just listed. Write the concepts down in an arrangement that makes sense to you, circle each one, and then add lines and phrases to describe the interrelationships between pairs of concepts.

There is certainly more than one "correct" way to map the seven concepts; Figure 8.3 (see p. 268) shows just one of many possibilities. I hope that the exercise helped you organize some of the things you learned about concepts in the preceding chapter. I hope that it also gave you a better understanding of the process of concept mapping itself.

Students benefit in numerous ways from constructing their own concept maps for classroom material. By focusing on how key concepts relate to one another, students organize material better. They are also more likely to notice how new concepts are related to concepts they already know; thus, they are more likely to learn the material meaningfully. Furthermore, when students construct a concept map from verbal material (e.g., from a lecture or a textbook), they can encode that material in long-term memory visually as well as verbally. And the very process of concept mapping may promote a more sophisticated perspective of what learning *is;* more specifically, students may begin to realize that learning is not just a process of "absorbing" information but instead involves actively making connections among ideas (Holley & Dansereau, 1984; Mintzes et al., 1997; Novak, 1998; Novak & Gowin, 1984).

Not only do concept maps help students, they can also help teachers. When we develop a concept map for a lesson, the organizational scheme of that lesson becomes clearer, and we have a better idea about how to sequence the presentation of ideas. And when we examine the concept maps that our students have constructed, students' understanding of a lesson becomes readily apparent, as do any misconceptions that students may have (Novak, 1998; Novak & Gowin, 1984; Novak & Musonda, 1991). For example, the two concept maps in Figure 8.1 reveal considerable differences in depth and organization of knowledge about Australia. Furthermore, the map on the left reveals a few misconceptions; for instance, Adelaide is *not* part of Melbourne; it is a different city altogether! If geographic knowledge about Australia is an instructional objective, then this student clearly needs further instruction to correct such misinformation.

Elaborating

Whether they are reading, taking notes in a lecture, or studying for an exam, students typically do better when they elaborate on course material—for example, when they draw inferences from it or consider its implications. To illustrate, imagine that Pai and Paulo are studying the same reading passage in history. Pai focuses on facts presented in the passage, trying to remember who did what and when. Paulo tries to go beyond the material he actually reads, speculating about possible reasons for people's actions, thinking about how a historical event has relevance to current events, and so on. Pai and Paulo may do equally well on simple, fact-based questions about the passage. But Paulo will do better on tasks that involve drawing inferences; he will also explain and integrate the material more effectively (Paxton, 1999; Van Rossum & Schenk, 1984).

How can we encourage our students to elaborate as they study class material? For one thing, when we model retrieval of relevant prior knowledge, we can model elaboration as well—for example, by stopping to identify our own examples of a concept we are reading about, to consider the implications of a new principle, and so on. We can also give students specific questions to consider as they listen to a lecture or read their textbook; for example:

Frog and and Toad are friends. Toad is very silly. One of silliest things that Toad does is when he sings songs to his seeds and reads poems to his seeds and plays music for his seeds. He also reads books to his seeds.

In this book report, 7-year-old Ashton shows some elaboration when he says that Toad's habit of singing and reading to his seeds is "very silly." However, most children don't *intentionally* elaborate as a way to learn and remember information until sometime around puberty (see Chapter 2).

- Explain why . . . .
- How would you use . . . to . . . ?

- What is a new example of . . . ?
- What do you think would happen if . . . ?
- What is the difference between . . . and . . . ? (questions from A. King, 1992, p. 309)

Yet another approach is to teach our students to develop and answer their *own* elaborative questions using a strategy known as **elaborative interrogation**[1] (Kahl & Woloshyn, 1994; A. King, 1992, 1994, 1999; Rosenshine, Meister, & Chapman, 1996; E. Wood et al., 1999). For example, let's say our students are studying this fact: The Gulf Stream warms the British Isles. We might encourage them to ask themselves, "*How does the Gulf Stream warm the British Isles?*" and then generate a reasonable answer to the question. Or if our students are studying two or more related concepts (e.g., series and parallel circuits; monarchies, theocracies, and democracies), we might encourage them to ask questions concerning the similarities and differences among the concepts.

In elaborative interrogation, students learn how to ask one another questions that encourage application, analysis, and other higher-level thinking skills.

Elaborative interrogation is often not an easy strategy for students to acquire; accordingly, they may sometimes use it more effectively, at least at first, when they work in pairs or small groups to develop and answer questions (A. King, 1994; Rosenshine et al., 1996; E. Wood et al., 1999). As an example, fifth graders Katie and Janelle are working together to study class material about tide pools. In the following dialogue, Katie's job is to ask Janelle questions that encourage elaboration:

Katie: How are the upper tide zone and the lower tide zone different?

Janelle: They have different animals in them. Animals in the upper tide zone and splash zone can handle being exposed—have to be able to use the rain and sand and wind and sun—and they don't need that much water and the lower tide animals do.

Katie: And they can be softer 'cause they don't have to get hit on the rocks.

Janelle: Also predators. In the spray zone it's because there's predators like us people and all different kinds of stuff that can kill the animals and they won't survive, but the lower tide zone has not as many predators.

Katie: But wait! Why do the animals in the splash zone have to survive? (A. King, 1999, p. 97)

Notice how the two girls are continually relating the animals' characteristics to survival in different tide zones, and eventually Katie asks why animals in the splash zone even *need* to survive. Such analyses are very sophisticated indeed for fifth graders. Imagine what high school students, with their increasing capacity for abstract thinking, might be able to do!

In Chapter 13 we will look at *reciprocal teaching,* another effective means of showing students how to elaborate as they read.

Summarizing

Another important study strategy is summarizing the material being studied (Dole et al., 1991; Hidi & Anderson, 1986; A. King, 1992). Effective summarizing usually entails at least three processes (Hidi & Anderson, 1986; Spivey, 1997):

- Separating important from unimportant information
- Condensing details into more general ideas
- Identifying important relationships among those general ideas

Many students have trouble summarizing material even at the high school level (V. Anderson & Hidi, 1988/1989). Probably the best way of helping students develop this strategy is to ask them to summarize what they hear and read on a regular basis (e.g., see Figure 8.2). For example, we might occasionally give homework assignments asking them to write a summary of a textbook chapter. Or we might ask them to work in cooperative groups to develop a brief oral presentation that condenses information they've learned about a particular topic. At first we should restrict summarizing assignments to short, simple, and well-organized passages involving material with which students are familiar; we can assign more challenging material as students become more proficient summarizers (V. Anderson & Hidi, 1988/1989).

> The weight of a glacier makes it move down the mountains toward the sea. Glaciers move so slowly that you cannot see them move. Sometimes they move ten feet in one day. They might move less then an inch in one day.

FIGURE 8.2 Eight-year-old Neville summarizes a lesson about glaciers.

---

[1]You may also see the term *guided peer questioning.*

In this map, connections are correctly interpreted by starting at the top and following the lines downward.

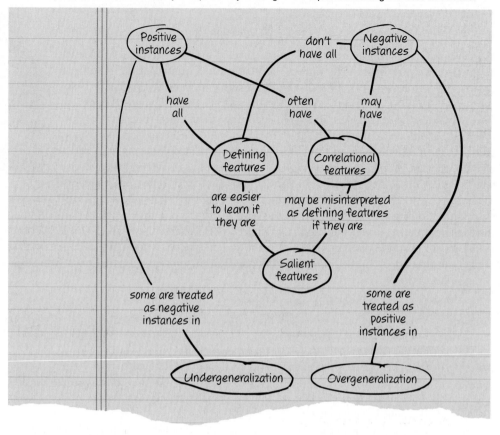

Monitoring Comprehension

EXPERIENCING FIRSTHAND   *Looking Back*

Stop for a minute and ask yourself this question:

> *What have I learned from the last five pages of this textbook?*

Write your answer on a piece of scrap paper.

Now go back and look at the five pages just before this one. Does your answer include all the major points covered in these pages? Is there something that you thought you understood but realize now that you didn't? Is there something that you never learned at all—perhaps something that you were "reading" when your mind was someplace altogether different?

Successful students engage in **comprehension monitoring**: They periodically check themselves to make sure they understand what they are reading or hearing. Furthermore, they take steps to correct the situation when they *don't* comprehend, perhaps by rereading a section of a textbook or asking a question in class (Hacker, 1998b; Haller, Child, & Walberg, 1988; Stone, 2000). In contrast, low achievers seldom check themselves or take appropriate action when they don't comprehend. Poor readers, for instance, rarely reread paragraphs that they haven't sufficiently understood the first time around (Baker & Brown, 1984).

Many students at all grade levels engage in little if any comprehension monitoring (Dole et al., 1991; Markman, 1979; J. W. Thomas, 1993a). When students don't monitor their own comprehension, they don't know what they know and what they don't know: They may think they have mastered something when they really haven't (D. L. Butler & Winne, 1995; Hacker, 1998b; Stone, 2000). This **illusion of knowing** is seen in students at all levels, even college students (Baker, 1989). Perhaps you have a friend who has difficulty on exams despite many hours of reading and studying the textbook. Perhaps you even find yourself in this predicament on occasion. If so, then your friend and you may not be adequately monitoring your comprehension—for example, by asking yourselves questions periodically to make certain you are learning the things you read. Our case study at the beginning of the chapter provides another example of the illusion of knowing: When Mary studies, she fails to realize that she doesn't understand the difference between *velocity* and *acceleration,* so she is later quite surprised to find herself doing poorly on her test.

To be successful learners—and more specifically, to *know what they know*—students should monitor their comprehension both *while* they study and *after* they study (Hacker et al., 2000; T. O. Nelson & Dunlosky, 1991; Spires, 1990). As teachers, we can promote better comprehension-monitoring skills by teaching students **self-questioning.** Not only might we provide questions that students can answer as they go along, but we can also encourage students to formulate and ask *themselves* questions; such questions might include both simple, fact-based questions and the elaborative questions described earlier. Furthermore, we can suggest that they test one another: Classmates may detect gaps or misconceptions in understanding that students themselves are unaware of (Hacker, 1998b). When students test themselves and one another over the material they are studying, they have a better sense of what they do and don't know, and as a result they ultimately learn the material more completely and meaningfully (Rosenshine et al., 1996; Wong, 1985). Because students are often better judges of what they have learned *after* they have studied, rather than during the study session itself (T. O. Nelson & Dunlosky, 1991; Weaver & Kelemen, 1997), we should also suggest that they follow up their studying with a self-test at a later time.

As you read a textbook, when is the information in working memory? in long-term memory? With your answers in mind, explain why students should monitor their comprehension both as they read and also at a later time.

EXPERIENCING FIRSTHAND *Self-Reflection*

Which study strategies do you use frequently? Which do you use seldom or not at all? Take a minute to fill in the empty boxes in Table 8.1.

Judging from the entries you have made in Table 8.1, do you think that you are using effective study strategies? Do you see areas for improvement? Study strategies are complex metacognitive skills that are not easily acquired; your own strategies will undoubtedly continue to improve over time as you study increasingly challenging material in your college courses.

Some of the study strategies just described, such as taking notes and making outlines, are behaviors we can actually see. Others, such as retrieving relevant prior knowledge and monitoring comprehension, are internal mental processes that we can't see. It is probably the latter set of strategies—internal mental processes—that ultimately affect students' learning (Kardash & Amlund, 1991). As we help students develop study strategies, we must remember that behavioral strategies (e.g., taking notes) will be most useful when they facilitate more effective cognitive processing.

TABLE 8.1

Which Study Strategies Do You Use, and When?

STUDY STRATEGY	IN WHICH CLASSES OR SUBJECTS DO YOU USE THIS STRATEGY FREQUENTLY?	IN WHICH CLASSES OR SUBJECTS MIGHT YOU USE THIS STRATEGY MORE OFTEN?	WHAT FACTORS AFFECT YOUR ABILITY TO USE THIS STRATEGY SUCCESSFULLY?
Identifying important information			
Taking notes			
Retrieving relevant prior knowledge			
Organizing			
Elaborating			
Summarizing			
Monitoring comprehension			

Factors Affecting Strategy Use

At least four factors appear to influence students' choice and use of strategies: knowledge base, previous comprehension monitoring, beliefs about the nature of knowledge and knowledge acquisition, and training in study strategies.

Knowledge base. Students are more likely to use effective strategies when they have a fair amount of prior knowledge about a topic (Greene, 1994; Schneider, 1993; E. Wood et al., 1994). Considering what you've learned about long-term memory storage processes, this principle should hardly surprise you. Such processes as meaningful learning, organization, and elaboration all involve making connections between new material and things already stored in long-term memory—connections that are more likely to be made when long-term memory contains information directly relevant to the topic at hand.

Previous comprehension monitoring. Students are likely to acquire and use new, more effective strategies only if they realize that their prior strategies have been *ineffective*. And they will come to such a conclusion only if they monitor their comprehension regularly and so are aware that they are not learning and understanding classroom subject matter as well as they would like (Kuhn et al., 1995; Lodico, Ghatala, Levin, Pressley, & Bell, 1983; Loranger, 1994). Comprehension monitoring, then, does not just affect students' understanding of classroom subject matter. It also plays a pivotal role in the development of *other* metacognitive strategies.

Beliefs about the nature of knowledge and knowledge acquisition. Students have differing views about the nature of knowledge and knowledge acquisition; in other words, they have differing **epistemological beliefs.** For example, I once had a conversation with my son Jeff, then an eleventh grader, about the Canadian Studies program that the local university had just added to its curriculum. Jeff's comments revealed a very simplistic view of what "history" is:

Jeff: The Canadians don't have as much history as we [Americans] do.
Me: Of course they do.
Jeff: No, they don't. They haven't had as many wars.
Me: History's more than wars.
Jeff: Yeah, but the rest of that stuff is really boring.

As I write this fourth edition of the book, Jeff is a college freshman and happily discovering that history is a lot more than wars and some other "stuff" that's "really boring." But it's frustrating that he had to wait so long to find this out.

You might think of epistemological beliefs as examples of the *personal theories* (in this case, theories about the nature of knowledge and learning) discussed in Chapter 7 (Hofer, 2001; Hofer & Pintrich, 1997).

Students' epistemological beliefs often influence how they study and learn (Hofer & Pintrich, 1997; Purdie, Hattie, & Douglas, 1996; Schommer, 1997). For example, many students believe that knowledge is black and white (ideas are indisputably either right or wrong) and that you either have that knowledge or you don't. But other students recognize that there may be different, equally valid viewpoints on the same topic that could all legitimately be called "knowledge" (Schommer, 1994b). The former students are more likely to believe that learning should be a relatively rapid process, and so they will give up quickly if they find themselves struggling to understand classroom material (Schommer, 1994b).

As another example, some students believe that when they read a textbook, they are passively absorbing information directly from the page; they may also believe that learning from a textbook means studying isolated facts. In contrast, other students believe that learning from reading requires them to construct their own meanings by actively organizing and applying the information presented in the textbook. It is those students who think of reading as a constructive process who are most likely to process what they read in a meaningful and effective fashion (Paxton, 1999; Purdie et al., 1996; Schommer, 1994b; Schommer-Aikins, in press).

As teachers, we must communicate to our students—in what we *say* as well as what we *do* (e.g., what activities we assign, how we assess students' learning)—what we ourselves have already learned about knowledge and knowledge acquisition (Hofer & Pintrich, 1997; Schommer, 1994b):

- Knowledge does not always mean having clear-cut answers to difficult, complex issues.
- Knowledge involves knowing the interrelationships among ideas, as well as the ideas themselves.

- Learning involves active construction of knowledge, rather than just a passive "reception" of it.
- Understanding a body of information and ideas sometimes requires persistence and hard work.

In doing so, we increase the likelihood that our students will apply effective study strategies, critically evaluate classroom subject matter, and undergo conceptual change when they encounter explanations that contradict their current beliefs (Hofer & Pintrich, 1997; Purdie et al., 1996; Schommer, 1994b; C. L. Smith, Maclin, Houghton, & Hennessey, 2000; Strike & Posner, 1992).

Study strategies training. Can students be taught to study more effectively? Research studies answer this question with a firm yes (see the reference list at the bottom of Table 8.2). Effective study skills training programs often include components such as these:

- Time management (e.g., planning when and how long to study)
- Effective learning and reading strategies
- Note-taking strategies
- Specific memory techniques (e.g., mnemonics)
- Comprehension-monitoring strategies
- Test-taking strategies

Graduates of successful study skills training programs are more confident about their ability to succeed in the classroom and, in fact, do achieve at higher levels (e.g., Paris, 1988; Pressley, El-Dinary, Marks, Brown, & Stein, 1992; J. E. Wilson, 1988).

How can we help students *learn how to learn?* Researchers have identified several principles that describe the conditions under which students are most likely to acquire and use effective study skills. Table 8.2 presents these principles, along with their implications for classroom practice.

As teachers, we should not only teach our students to learn and study more effectively but must also monitor how they typically *do* learn and study. Let's look at what one high school student does when she studies.

INTERPRETING ARTIFACTS AND INTERACTIONS   *Emily's Strategies*

For an assignment in my educational psychology class, Melissa Tillman interviewed an 18-year-old senior whom I'll call "Emily." In her early high school years, Emily was earning mostly Cs and Ds, but by the end of eleventh grade she had started to work more diligently on her schoolwork, and at the time of this interview, she was earning As and Bs. As you read the interview, consider

- What strategies Emily uses when she studies
- How effective these strategies are
- What Emily believes about the nature of learning and academic subject matter (i.e., her epistemological beliefs)

Melissa:	How did you learn to study for a test?
Emily:	I'm not really sure. I never learned the correct way to study for a test. I use my own methods, and they seem to be working because I'm now receiving the grades I want.
Melissa:	How did you go about studying for a test when you were younger?
Emily:	Honestly, I never really studied too hard. I never studied for math tests because I didn't know how to. For other subjects like history, I'd just skim over the text. Skimming the text never made the material stick in my head. I guess I never really had a strategy for studying.
Melissa:	Now that you're receiving good grades, how do you study for a test?
Emily:	Well, it's different for every subject. Now when I study for a math test, I do many practice problems. When I'm studying for a history or science test, I first review my notes. My favorite thing to do is make flash cards with the important facts. I then go through the flash cards many times and try to learn the facts on them.
Melissa:	What do you mean, "learn" the facts on them?

TABLE 8.2

PRINCIPLES/ASSUMPTIONS

Promoting More Effective Study Strategies

PRINCIPLE	EDUCATIONAL IMPLICATION	EXAMPLE
Study strategies are most effectively learned within the context of particular content domains.	When presenting academic content through lectures, reading assignments, and so on, simultaneously teach students how to study that content.	Give students specific questions to ask themselves (thereby facilitating comprehension monitoring) as they read their textbooks.
Group learning situations often promote the development of effective strategies, perhaps because students verbalize and model various ways to think about classroom subject matter.	Occasionally ask students to study instructional materials in pairs or small cooperative learning groups.	Have students work in pairs to develop and answer questions that require them to elaborate on textbook content.
Students are more likely to acquire sophisticated study strategies when their initial efforts are scaffolded to promote success.	Scaffold students' attempts to use new strategies—for instance, by modeling the strategies, giving clues about when to use them, and giving feedback on appropriate and inappropriate strategy use.	To encourage students to organize material in a particular way, provide an organizational chart that cooperative learning groups fill out.
Students learn more effectively when their study strategies are numerous and varied.	As opportunities arise, continue to introduce new strategies—note taking, elaboration, self-questioning, mnemonics, and so on—throughout the school year.	Suggest that students use such mnemonics as verbal mediation and the keyword method to learn the capitals of South American countries or the meanings of Japanese vocabulary words.
Students are more likely to use effective study strategies when they understand why those strategies are useful.	Explain the usefulness of various strategies in ways that students understand.	Show students how note taking helps them keep their minds from wandering during class and how comprehension monitoring enables them to identify gaps in their knowledge.
Students use strategies more effectively if they know when each one is most appropriate.	Point out occasions in which particular strategies are likely to be helpful.	Give students opportunities to elaborate on material—by drawing implications, generating new examples, and so on—when they must apply it to new situations.
Students are most likely to master effective strategies when they can practice them regularly across a wide variety of tasks.	Give students numerous and varied opportunities to apply metacognitive strategies.	Ask students' previous teachers what strategies they have taught and then explain how such strategies are applicable for current learning tasks as well.
Students are likely to use effective strategies only when they believe such strategies can ultimately help them learn more effectively.	When teaching study strategies, make sure each student is eventually able to apply them successfully. Also, expose students to peers who model effective use of the strategies.	After a lecture, place students in small groups where they look at the notes each group member has taken and then combine all notes into a single, comprehensive set.

Sources: P. A. Alexander et al., 1998; R. C. Anderson et al., 2001; Barnett et al., 1981; Borkowski, Carr, Rellinger, & Pressley, 1990; D. L. Butler & Winne, 1995; A. Collins et al., 1989; Hacker, 1998b; Hattie, Biggs, & Purdie, 1996; Kahl & Woloshyn, 1994; A. King, 1992, 1994; Kucan & Beck, 1997; Kuhn et al., 1995; Mayer & Wittrock, 1996; Meloth & Deering, 1994; Nist, Simpson, Olejnik, & Mealey, 1991; Palincsar & Brown, 1984; Paris, 1988; Paris & Winograd, 1990; Pintrich, Garcia, & De Groot, 1994; Pressley, Borkowski, & Schneider, 1987; Pressley, El-Dinary, et al., 1992; Pressley, Harris, & Marks, 1992; Rosenshine & Meister, 1992; Rosenshine et al., 1996; Starr & Lovett, 2000; J. W. Thomas, 1993a; Vygotsky, 1978; C. E. Weinstein, Goetz, & Alexander, 1988; West et al., 1991; Winne, 1995; E. Wood et al., 1994.

Emily:	I guess I try to memorize the facts. I'll go through the flash cards many times and say them over and over in my head until I remember them.
Melissa:	How do you know when a fact is memorized?
Emily:	I'll repeat a fact over and over in my head until I think I've memorized it. Then I'll leave and do something else, like get a snack. I know I've memorized something if I still remember it after taking my break.
Melissa:	Do you consider yourself a good textbook reader?
Emily:	Not really. Textbooks are pretty boring. I'll try to read everything in the textbook, but at times I find myself looking for boldface print. Phrases in bold print are important.

Melissa:	What are some good methods for studying for a test?
Emily:	I really like the flash card method because it helps me to memorize facts. I also like to re-read the text and my notes. Another good method is outlining the text, but this method takes too long so I rarely use it.

Emily uses several strategies: solving practice problems (for math), taking and reviewing notes, making flash cards and repeating what's on them, and (rarely) outlining a reading assignment. Although she makes some attempt to impose meaning on what she is studying (e.g., she identifies "important facts"), her heavy reliance on flash cards and rehearsal and her view that "phrases in bold print are important" indicate that she engages primarily in rote learning and reads her textbooks only superficially. (From what she says, we can't tell what she does when she works on the math problems.) One good sign is that she monitors her comprehension after a delay, but nevertheless she is concerned primarily about learning things verbatim ("I know I've memorized something if I still remember it after taking my break"). Apparently, Emily believes that, with the exception of math (which involves solving problems), most school subjects consist of isolated facts that must be committed to memory.

How students learn and study school subject matter has implications not only for how effectively they can remember it but also for how likely they are to *use* it on later occasions, as we shall see in our upcoming exploration of transfer.

Transfer

Consider these four students:

Elena is bilingual: She speaks both English and Spanish fluently. She begins a French course in high school and immediately recognizes many similarities between French and Spanish. "Aha," she thinks, "my knowledge of Spanish will help me learn French."

In his psychology class, Larry learns the principle of reinforcement: A response followed by a reinforcing stimulus is more likely to occur again. Later that day, he thinks about playing a video game before doing his homework. "Oh, no," he says to himself, "that would be backward. I need to do my homework *first*. Playing the video game can be my reinforcer."

In her history class, Stella discovers that she does better on exams when she takes more notes. She decides to take more notes in her geography class as well, and once again the strategy pays off.

Ted's mathematics class has been working with decimals for several weeks. His teacher asks, "Which number is larger, 4.4 or 4.14?" Ted recalls something that he knows about whole numbers: Numbers with three digits are larger than numbers with only two digits. "The larger number is 4.14," he mistakenly concludes.

People often use information and skills they have learned in one situation to help them in another situation. What students learn in school and at home can potentially help them later on—perhaps in more advanced classwork, in their personal lives, or in their later careers. But occasionally students (like Ted) learn something at one time that, rather than helping, actually *interferes* with something they must learn or do later.

When something students have previously learned affects how they learn or perform in another situation, **transfer** is occurring. Ideally, transfer of knowledge should be a major objective for classrooms at all grade levels. When people cannot use their basic arithmetic skills to compute correct change or balance a checkbook, when they cannot use their knowledge of English grammar in a job application or business report, and when they cannot apply their knowledge of science to an understanding of personal health or environmental problems, then we have to wonder whether the time spent learning the arithmetic, the grammar, and the science might have been better spent doing something else. As we explore the nature of transfer in this section, we will identify numerous ways to help students apply classroom subject matter to new situations, both in their future academic studies and in the outside world.

Basic Concepts in Transfer

We begin our discussion by distinguishing between various kinds of transfer—in particular, between positive and negative transfer, and between specific and general transfer.

Positive Versus Negative Transfer

Positive transfer occurs when something that a person has learned in one situation *helps* that person learn or perform in another situation. Positive transfer took place when Elena's Spanish helped her learn French, when Larry's knowledge of reinforcement influenced his decision to do his homework before playing a video game, and when Stella's experiences with note taking in history class improved her performance in geography.

In contrast, **negative transfer** occurs when prior knowledge *hinders* a person's learning or performance at a later time. This was the situation for poor Ted: He transferred a principle related to whole numbers (one number is always larger than another if it has more digits) to a situation where it didn't apply: the comparison of decimals. We also see negative transfer at work when students erroneously apply rules of pronunciation and grammar in their native language as they begin to study a different language (Littlewood, 1984). We see it, too, in some students' tendency to confuse the various wars they've studied in history, perhaps "recalling" that the American Revolution was a battle between the English and the French (as was true for the French and Indian War) or between the Northern and Southern states (as was true for the American Civil War) (McKeown & Beck, 1990).

In Chapter 7 we discovered that previously acquired misconceptions can have a negative impact on learning. Here we see that *correct* ideas and information sometimes have a negative impact as well, in that students may apply them inappropriately in new situations. A bit later, as we consider theoretical perspectives of transfer, we will identify a strategy for minimizing negative transfer.

Specific Versus General Transfer

Transfer from one situation to another often occurs when the two situations overlap in content. Consider Elena, the student fluent in Spanish who is now taking French. Elena should have an easy time learning to count in French because the numbers (*un, deux, trois, quatre, cinq*) are very similar to the Spanish she has already learned (*uno, dos, tres, cuatro, cinco*). When transfer occurs because the original learning task and the transfer task overlap in content, we have **specific transfer.**

Now consider Stella's strategy of taking more notes in geography because note taking was beneficial in her history class. History and geography don't necessarily overlap in content, but a strategy that she developed in one class has been effectively applied in the other. Here is an instance of **general transfer:** Learning in one situation affects learning and performance in a somewhat dissimilar situation.

Research tells us that specific transfer occurs far more frequently than general transfer (W. D. Gray & Orasanu, 1987). In fact, the question of whether general transfer occurs at all has been the subject of considerable debate. Many early educators believed that certain subjects (e.g., Latin, Greek, mathematics, logic) had great potential for general transfer: Because these subjects required considerable attention to precision and detail, they would "strengthen" students' minds and thereby enable students to tackle many other, unrelated tasks more easily. This **formal discipline** perspective of transfer persisted throughout the first several decades of the twentieth century. For example, when I was in high school in the mid-1960s, most college-bound students were encouraged to take both French and Latin, the only two languages that the school offered. Taking French made a great deal of sense: Growing up in Massachusetts, we were within a day's drive of French-speaking Quebec. "But why should I take Latin," I asked my guidance counselor. "I can only use it if I attend Catholic mass or run across phrases like 'caveat emptor' or 'in Deo speramus.' Hardly anyone speaks the language anymore." The counselor pursed her thin red lips and gave me a look that told me that she knew best. "Latin will discipline your mind," she told me. "It will help you learn better."

Research has generally discredited this "mind as muscle" notion of transfer (Perkins & Salomon, 1989; E. L. Thorndike 1924). For example, practice in memorizing poems does not necessarily make one a faster poem memorizer (James, 1890). And studying computer programming,

Can you think of a recent situation in which you exhibited positive transfer? negative transfer?

THE FAR SIDE® BY GARY LARSON

Right side! One two, one two, one two, left side! One two, one two, one two, one... C'mon! Keep those cerebellums up!... One two, one two...

Brain aerobics

The formal discipline view of transfer portrays the mind as a muscle that benefits from general mental exercise.

though often a worthwhile activity in its own right, does not necessarily help a person with dissimilar kinds of logical tasks (Mayer & Wittrock, 1996; Perkins & Salomon, 1989). Such results have led some theorists to suggest that general transfer is a rare animal indeed—that, in fact, knowledge and thinking skills acquired in specific contexts are unlikely to be used outside those contexts (Hirschfeld & Gelman, 1994; Lave & Wenger, 1991; P. Light & Butterworth, 1993; Singley & Anderson, 1989). This principle is often referred to as **situated cognition:** Knowledge and thinking skills are *situated* within the context in which they develop.

Does this discussion contradict what you previously believed about the value of general mental exercise? If so, have you undergone *conceptual change* regarding this issue?

If you have read the discussion of cognitive development in Chapter 2, then you have already seen examples of situated cognition. As you may recall, Piaget proposed that such thinking abilities as abstract thought, proportional reasoning, and separation and control of variables emerge at about 11 or 12 years of age (at the onset of the formal operations stage) and are then used in a wide variety of tasks. Yet we reviewed evidence in Chapter 2 to indicate that students do not acquire formal operational abilities in one fell swoop and then apply them equally across all subject domains. Instead, students are more likely to exhibit formal operational reasoning in some domains than in others, and they are especially likely to exhibit them in contexts where they have the most experience.

Within the past few years, theorists have increasingly come to realize that the knowledge and skills learned in school are *not* always limited to the specific contexts in which they have been acquired (J R. Anderson, Greeno, Reder, & Simon, 2000; J. R. Anderson, Reder, & Simon, 1996, 1997; Bereiter, 1997). For instance, we frequently see general transfer in metacognition: When students acquire effective learning strategies within the context of one academic discipline, those strategies often transfer positively to learning in a very different discipline (Brooks & Dansereau, 1987; Perkins, 1995; Pressley, Snyder, & Cariglia-Bull, 1987). In addition, many students apply some of the skills they learn in school, such as skills in reading and arithmetic, to a broad range of out-of-school tasks (J. R. Anderson et al., 1996).

Factors Affecting Transfer

Although both specific and general transfer do occur, students often *don't* transfer the knowledge and skills they learn in school on occasions when such knowledge and skills are clearly applicable (Mayer & Wittrock, 1996; Perkins, 1992; Renkl, Mandl, & Gruber, 1996). Research reveals that a number of factors influence the extent to which transfer occurs:

- Amount of instructional time
- Extent to which learning is meaningful rather than rote
- Extent to which principles rather than facts are learned
- Variety of examples and opportunities for practice
- Degree of similarity between two situations
- Length of time between the two situations
- Extent to which information is seen as context-free rather than context-bound

These factors are summarized as general principles in Table 8.3. Let's look briefly at each one.

Amount of instructional time. Instructional time is clearly an important variable affecting transfer: The more time students spend studying a particular topic, the more likely they are to transfer what they learn to a new situation (Gick & Holyoak, 1987; Schmidt & Bjork, 1992; Voss, 1987). Conversely, when students study a great many topics without learning very much about any one of them, they are unlikely to apply what they have learned at a later date. Here we see another instance of the *less is more* principle introduced in Chapter 7: Our students are more likely to transfer their school learning to new situations, including those beyond the classroom, when we have them study a few things in depth and learn them *well,* rather than study many topics superficially (Brophy, 1992b; Porter, 1989).

Extent to which learning is meaningful. In Chapter 6 we identified two advantages of meaningful learning over rote learning: Information is stored more quickly and is retrieved more easily. An additional advantage is that information learned in a meaningful fashion is more likely to be transferred or applied to a new situation (Bereiter, 1995; Brooks & Dansereau, 1987; Mayer & Wittrock, 1996).

Remember, meaningful learning involves connecting information with what one already knows. The more associations students make between new information and the various other

TABLE 8.3   PRINCIPLES/ASSUMPTIONS

Basic Principles of Transfer

PRINCIPLE	EDUCATIONAL IMPLICATION	EXAMPLE
As **instructional time** increases, the probability of transfer also increases.	To promote transfer, teach a few topics in depth, rather than many topics superficially.	When teaching a unit on the geography of South America, focus on environmental and cultural similarities and differences across the continent, instead of presenting a lengthy, encyclopedia-like list of facts about each country.
Meaningful learning leads to greater transfer than rote learning.	Encourage students to relate new material to the things they already know.	When introducing the concept *gravity* to third graders, ask them to think about what happens whenever they throw an object into the air (i.e., it comes back down).
Principles transfer more readily than facts.	Teach general principles (e.g., cause-effect relationships) related to each topic, along with general strategies based on those principles.	When teaching a unit on softball, basketball, soccer, or tennis, tell students, "Keep your eye on the ball," and explain why such vigilance is important.
Numerous and varied **examples** and **opportunities for practice** promote transfer.	Illustrate new concepts and principles with a variety of examples, and engage students in activities that let them practice new skills in different contexts.	After teaching students what a complete sentence is, have them practice writing complete sentences in essays, short stories, and class newsletter articles.
As the **similarity** between two situations increases, so does the probability of transfer from one situation to the other.	Make school tasks as similar as possible to the tasks that students are likely to encounter in the outside world.	When teaching students about the foods that make a balanced diet, have them prepare a healthful lunch with groceries from a local food store.
Transfer is more likely when only a **short amount of time** has elapsed after students have studied a topic.	Present topics as close in time as possible to the occasions when students may need to use those topics.	After having students learn and play the F Major scale in an instrumental music class, have them practice several musical pieces in the key of F Major.
Transfer is more likely when students perceive classroom material to be **context-free** rather than context-bound.	Relate topics in one discipline to topics in other disciplines and to tasks in the outside world.	When teaching students how to solve for *x* in algebra, give them word problems in which they must solve for an unknown in such contexts as physics, building construction, and sewing.

things in their long-term memories, the more likely it is that they will "find" (retrieve) that information at a time when it will be useful.

Extent to which principles rather than facts are learned.   People can transfer general (and perhaps somewhat abstract) principles more easily than specific, concrete facts (J. R. Anderson et al., 1996; Judd, 1932; Perkins & Salomon, 1987). The following exercise illustrates this idea.

EXPERIENCING FIRSTHAND   *Central Business Districts*

Consider these two ideas from geography:

- Boston's central business district is located near Boston Harbor.
- The central business districts of most older cities, which were settled before the development of modern transportation, are found in close proximity to a navigable body of water, such as an ocean or a river.

Which statement would be more helpful to you if you were trying to find your way around Liverpool, Toronto, or Pittsburgh?

No doubt the second would prove more useful to you. The first one is a fact about a particular city, whereas the second one reflects a general principle applicable to many different cities.

Specific facts have an important place in the classroom; for example, students should know what two plus three equal, what the Berlin Wall signified, and where to find Africa on a globe. Yet facts themselves have limited utility in new situations. The more we can instead emphasize general principles—for example, that two whole numbers added together always equal a larger number, that a country's citizens sometimes revolt when their government officials act unjustly, and that the cultures of various nations are influenced by their location and climate—the more we facilitate students' ability to transfer what they learn.

Think about the subject matter you will be teaching. What general principles are likely to have wide applicability for students?

Variety of examples and opportunities for practice. Students are more likely to apply something they learn if, within the course of instruction, they are given many examples and opportunities to practice in different situations (Cox, 1997; Reimann & Schult, 1996; J. A. Ross, 1988; Schmidt & Bjork, 1992). For example, students will be more apt to use their knowledge of fractions and ratios in the future if they practice using this knowledge in such activities as cooking, converting dollars to a foreign currency, and drawing objects to scale. By using knowledge in many contexts, students store that knowledge in association with all those contexts and so are more likely to retrieve the information on a future occasion (Perkins & Salomon, 1987; Voss, 1987).

Similarity of the two situations. Let's return to the problem that Mary encounters in our case study at the beginning of the chapter:

An automotive engineer has designed a car that can reach a speed of 50 miles per hour within 5 seconds. What is the car's rate of acceleration?

Imagine that Mary eventually learns how to solve this problem using the $v = a \times t$ principle. Because the velocity (v) is 50 miles per hour and the time (t) is 5 seconds, the rate of acceleration (a) must be 10 miles per hour per second.

Now Mary encounters two additional problems:

A car salesperson tells a customer that a particular model of car can reach a speed of 40 miles per hour within 8 seconds. What is the car's rate of acceleration?

A biologist reports that a cheetah she has been observing can attain a speed of 60 kilometers per hour within a 10-second period. How quickly can the cheetah increase its speed?

Children are more likely to transfer their knowledge of fractions and ratios to future situations if they practice using fractions and ratios in a variety of contexts.

Which problem do you think Mary will find easier to solve?

Transfer is more likely to occur when a new situation appears to be similar to a previous situation (Bassok, 1990; Blake & Clark, 1990; Di Vesta & Peverly, 1984). Mary will probably have an easier time solving the problem involving the car salesperson because it superficially resembles the problem about the automotive engineer: Both problems involve cars, and both use miles as the unit of measure. The cheetah problem, even though it can be solved using the same approach as the other two, involves a different domain (animals) and a different unit of measure (kilometers).

Here we see the value of *authentic activities* in the curriculum. Of the many examples and opportunities for practice that we give our students, at least some should be very similar to the situations that students are likely to encounter in future studies or in the outside world. The more that school tasks resemble students' later life experiences, the more likely it is that our students will put their school learning to use (Perkins, 1992).

Yet we should note that the similarity of two situations, while promoting positive transfer, may promote negative transfer as well. Try the following exercise as an example.

EXPERIENCING FIRSTHAND   *A Division Problem*

Consider this division problem:

$$20 \div 0.38$$

Is the answer larger or smaller than 20?

If you applied your knowledge of division by whole numbers here, you undoubtedly concluded that the answer is smaller than 20. In fact, the answer is approximately 52.63, a number *larger* than 20. Has this exercise reminded you of Ted's erroneous conclusion—4.14 is larger than 4.4—based on his knowledge of how whole numbers can be compared? Many students, even at the university level, show negative transfer of whole-number principles to situations involving decimals (Tirosh & Graeber, 1990). Working with decimals appears, on the surface, to be similar to working with whole numbers; the only difference—a very important one, as it turns out—is a tiny decimal point.

To prevent negative transfer, we, as teachers, must be sure to point out the differences between two superficially similar topics. For example, Ted's teacher could have identified some of the specific ways in which decimals are *not* like whole numbers. As another example, I find that my own students in educational psychology often have trouble using the term *maturation* correctly in our discussions of child development because the term has a different meaning in everyday conversation. Therefore, when I first introduce the concept of maturation, I take great pains to show students how psychology's meaning of the word (the unfolding of genetically controlled developmental changes) differs from the meaning they are familiar with (developmental changes in general).

Length of time between the two situations. People are most likely to apply new information soon after they have learned it. They are less likely to use that information as time goes on (Gick & Holyoak, 1987). Whenever possible, then, we should try to present topics to students at a time close to when students will need to use those topics.

To illustrate, consider again the physics principle that Mary learns in the opening case study: $v = a \times t$ (velocity equals acceleration times time). The formula tells Mary how to calculate velocity when she knows both the acceleration and the time. But let's say that she instead wants to calculate the rate of acceleration, as she needed to do for the "car" and "cheetah" problems. If Mary is studying algebra concurrently with her physics class, or else has studied it very recently, she is more likely to see the usefulness of algebra in rearranging the formula like so: $a = v/t$.

Perception of information as context-free rather than context-bound. In many cases, we would like our students to transfer their knowledge in one content domain to a different domain—for example, to transfer math to physics, grammar to creative writing, history to current events, and health to personal eating habits. Yet students tend to think of academic subject areas as being distinct, unrelated disciplines; they also tend to think of their school learning as being separate from real-world concerns (Perkins & Simmons, 1988; Rakow, 1984). When students see what they learn in school as being related only to a particular topic or discipline, or *context-bound,* they are unlikely to transfer it to situations outside that context (P. A. Alexander & Judy, 1988; J. R. Anderson et al., 1996; Bassok, 1996; diSessa, 1982; Renkl et al., 1996).

What implications does this idea have for classroom assessment practices?

When we teach material within a particular academic discipline, then, we should relate that material to other disciplines and to the outside world as often as possible (Blake & Clark, 1990; Perkins, 1992). For example, we might show students how human digestion provides a justification for categorizing food into several basic food groups or how economic issues affect tropical rain forests. We can also encourage students to brainstorm specific situations in which they could apply what they are learning in class (J. R. Anderson et al., 1996). Ideally, we should have students use what they learn in many different contexts, including a variety of authentic activities, so that eventually their knowledge and skills become *context-free* (A. Collins et al., 1989).

Importance of Retrieval in Transfer

See "Intuitive Physics" in *Simulations in Educational Psychology.*

The factors we've just examined point to a key principle in transfer: From a cognitive perspective, information learned in one situation helps in another situation only if the information is *retrieved* within the context of that second situation (Cormier, 1987; Gick & Holyoak, 1987; Halpern, 1998). Several factors—in-depth study, meaningful learning, focus on general principles, variety of examples and practice opportunities, and perception of a domain as context-free—are likely to encourage students to make numerous connections between class material and other aspects of their world, and such multiple connections will invariably enhance the likelihood of retrieving that material on occasions where it is potentially relevant. Students are *unlikely* to apply information they have not previously connected to other things (information they have learned by rote), partly because they probably won't retrieve it when they need it and partly because they won't see its relevance even if they *do* retrieve it.

Another factor—similarity between the learning situation and transfer situation—is related to retrieval as well. Students are more likely to transfer what they learn in one situation to a similar (rather than dissimilar) situation because a similar situation provides *retrieval cues* that remind students of specific, relevant things they have already learned (Gick & Holyoak, 1987; Perkins & Salomon, 1989; Sternberg & Frensch, 1993). Yet another factor—the time elapsed between initial learning and later transfer situation—probably affects retrieval indirectly. As we discovered in our discussion of forgetting in Chapter 6, information stored in long-term memory may weaken (decay) over time, particularly if it is not used regularly.

The factors that affect transfer also affect one very important form of transfer: solving problems. Cognitive psychologists have offered additional insights about problem solving as well, as you shall see now.

Problem Solving

EXPERIENCING FIRSTHAND *Four Problems*

How many of these problems can you solve?

1. You buy two apples for 25¢ each and one pear for 40¢. How much change will you get back from a dollar bill?
2. You are building a treehouse with the shape and dimensions illustrated in Figure 8.4. You need to buy planks for a slanted roof. How long must those planks be to reach from one side of the treehouse to the other?
3. You want to demonstrate that metal battleships float even though metal is denser (and so heavier) than water. You don't have any toy boats made of metal. What can you use instead to illustrate the principle that a metal object with a hollow interior can float on water?
4. Every day almost 75,000 acres of tropical rain forest disappear. What steps might be taken to curtail this alarming rate of deforestation?

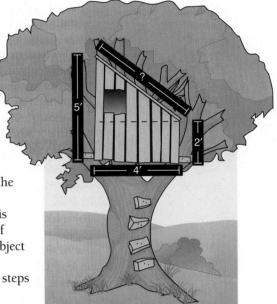

How long do the roof planks of this treehouse need to be?

FIGURE 8.4 Building a treehouse

Sometimes problems are straightforward and relatively easy to solve. For example, problem 1 requires only simple addition and subtraction procedures; you probably had little difficulty finding the correct solution, 10¢. Problem 2 (Figure 8.4) is more difficult, partly because you don't encounter such problems very often. But if you have studied geometry, then you undoubtedly learned the Pythagorean theorem: In any right triangle, the square of the hypotenuse equals the sum of the squares of the other two sides. Looking at the top part of the treehouse (from the dotted line upward) as a triangle, we can find the length for the roof planks (x) this way:

$$x^2 = (5 - 2)^2 + 4^2$$
$$x^2 = 9 + 16$$
$$x^2 = 25$$
$$x = 5$$

Yet problems don't always have a single correct solution. For example, if you are looking for a metal object with a hollow interior to float on water (problem 3), you might use a number of different objects to solve your problem—possibly a pie plate, a bucket, or a thimble. And you might identify several possible ways of addressing rain forest deforestation (problem 4), but you probably wouldn't know which of these (if any) are correct solutions (i.e., which ones would successfully help preserve tropical rain forests) until you actually implemented them.

This section of the chapter explores the multifaceted nature of human problem solving. After defining several basic concepts, we will examine cognitive factors that help or hinder successful problem solving; in the process, we will also identify strategies for helping students become more successful problem solvers. As we go along, you may find places where you can apply (*transfer!*) what you have previously learned about transfer.

Basic Concepts in Problem Solving

As the four problems you just tackled illustrate, the problems that people need to solve may differ widely in their content and scope; for example, one problem may relate to a backyard treehouse and another may relate to the devastation of tropical rain forests. The four problems also call for very different strategies to solve them; for example, one problem might be solved by using the Pythagorean theorem, whereas another might be solved only by a world summit conference. Yet virtually all problems can be considered to be either *well-defined* or *ill-defined* (or perhaps somewhere in between), and virtually all problem-solving strategies can be categorized as either *algorithms* or *heuristics*. Let's consider these two distinctions.

Well-Defined and Ill-Defined Problems

See "Assessment in the Balance" in *Simulations in Educational Psychology.*

The distinction between well-defined and ill-defined problems is better conceptualized as a continuum than an "either-or" situation.

Problems differ in the extent to which they are clearly specified and structured. A **well-defined problem** is one in which the goal is clearly stated, all information needed to solve the problem is present, and only one correct answer exists. Calculating the amount of change one gets from a dollar (problem 1) and determining the length of planks needed for a treehouse roof (problem 2) are examples of well-defined problems. In both cases, we know exactly what is required to solve the problem.

In contrast, an **ill-defined problem** is one in which the desired goal is unclear, information needed to solve the problem is missing, or several possible solutions to the problem exist. To some extent, finding a suitable substitute for a metal ship (problem 3) is an ill-defined problem: A number of objects might serve as a ship substitute, and some might work better than others. The rain forest deforestation problem (problem 4) is even less defined. First, the goal—curtailing deforestation—is ambiguous. Do we want to stop deforestation altogether or just slow it down a bit? If we just want to decrease the rate, what rate is acceptable? Second, we undoubtedly need more information to solve the problem. For example, it would be helpful to determine whether previously cleared and farmed lands can be reclaimed and rejuvenated, and to identify economically reasonable alternatives to slash-and-burn farming practices. Some of this needed information may require extensive research. Finally, there is no single "correct" solution for problem 4: Curtailing deforestation will undoubtedly require a number of steps taken more or less simultaneously. Ill-defined problems, then, are usually more difficult to solve than well-defined ones.

Most problems presented in school are well-defined: A question clearly specifies a goal, all needed information is present (no more, no less), and only one answer is correct. Consider this typical mathematics word problem as an example:

> Old MacDonald has planted potatoes in a field 100 yards long and 50 yards wide. If the field yields an average of 5 pounds of potatoes in each square yard, how many pounds of potatoes can MacDonald expect to harvest from his field?

In this problem, the goal is clear: Determine how many pounds of potatoes the field will yield. We also have all the information needed to solve the problem, with no irrelevant information to distract us. And there is only one correct answer, with no room for debate.

But the real world presents ill-defined problems far more often than well-defined ones, and students need practice in dealing with them (L. B. Resnick, 1988; Sternberg et al., 2000). Consider this problem as an example:

> Old MacDonald's son wants to go to a small, coeducational college 200 miles away. Mac-Donald does not know whether he can afford the college tuition; it all depends on how well his potato crop does this summer. What should MacDonald tell his son?

Notice how the problem has a rather vaguely stated goal: determining what MacDonald should say to his son. It does not identify the specific questions he needs to address before he gives an answer. Nor does it give us all the information we need to solve the problem, such as the size of MacDonald's potato field, the predicted size of his crop, the probable value of the potatoes, the family's day-to-day living expenses, or the cost of college tuition. Finally, there may be no single correct answer: Whether MacDonald encourages his son to go to college depends not only on finances but also on his beliefs about the value of a college education and on his need to have his son stay at home to help with farm chores.

Calvin and Hobbes

by Bill Watterson

Some problems can be solved by an algorithm, a set of step-by-step instructions that guarantees a correct solution.

One way of helping our students learn to solve problems is to teach them techniques for better defining ill-defined problems. For example, we can teach them how to break large problems into smaller, well-defined ones (e.g., determining the probable size of the potato crop, calculating the farmer's daily living expenses). We can also teach them to distinguish information they need (e.g., the size of the farmer's potato field) from information they may *not* need (e.g., the fact that the college is coeducational). And we can teach techniques for finding missing information (e.g., how to measure distance, how to use the library or Internet to find the market price of potatoes, how to obtain information about tuition rates at different colleges).

Problem-Solving Strategies: Algorithms and Heuristics

Some problems can be successfully solved by following specific, step-by-step instructions—that is, by using an **algorithm.** For example, we can put a new bicycle together by following the "Directions for Assembly" that come with it. We can calculate the length of a slanted roof by using the Pythagorean theorem. When we follow an algorithm faithfully, we invariably arrive at a correct solution.

Yet not all problems come equipped with directions for assembly. There are no rules we can follow to identify a substitute metal ship, no list of instructions to help us solve the deforestation problem. When there is no algorithm for solving a problem, people may instead use a **heuristic,** a general problem-solving strategy that may or may not yield a workable solution. For example, one heuristic that we might use in solving the deforestation problem is this: Identify a new behavior that adequately replaces the problem behavior (in particular, find something else that peasant farmers can do to meet their survival needs). As another example of a heuristic, consider the addition problem in the exercise that follows.

EXPERIENCING FIRSTHAND   *Grocery Shopping*

Solve this addition problem *as quickly as you possibly can:*

You are purchasing three items at the store, at these prices:

$19.95
$39.98
$29.97

About how much money are you spending? (Don't worry about a possible sales tax.)

The fastest way to solve the problem is to round off and approximate. The first item costs about $20, the second about $40, and the third about $30; therefore, you are spending about $90 on your shopping spree. Rounding is often an excellent heuristic for arriving quickly at approximate answers to mathematical problems.

Students in our schools get far more practice solving well-defined problems than ill-defined ones, and they are taught many more algorithms than heuristics. For example, they are likely to

Using the subject matter you will be teaching, develop two problems, one well-defined and one ill-defined. Do your problems require algorithms or heuristics to be solved?

spend more school time learning problem-solving strategies useful in determining the length of planks needed for a treehouse roof than strategies applicable to the problem of deforestation. And they are likely to spend more time using laws of physics to make predictions about when battleships will float on water than wrestling with ways of preventing the conflicts that require those battleships in the first place. Yet many real-world problems—problems that our students will encounter after graduation—probably cannot be solved with cut-and-dried algorithms. Furthermore, few true algorithms exist for solving problems outside the domains of mathematics and science.

Problem-solving strategies, algorithms and heuristics alike, are often specific to a particular content domain. But here are three general problem-solving heuristics that our students may find helpful in a variety of contexts:

- *Identify subgoals.* Break a problem into two or more subproblems that can be better defined and more easily solved.
  Example: Students wrestling with the problem of diminishing rain forests identify several smaller problems: poor economic circumstances of local residents, lack of good agricultural land, and lack of government regulation of deforestation practices. They then discuss possible ways to solve each problem.
- *Work backward.* Begin at the goal of the problem (i.e., the solution needed) and work backward, one step at a time, toward the initial problem statement.
  Example: A student is given this problem:

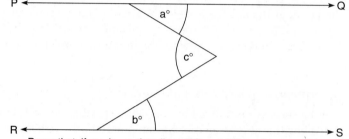

Prove that, if $a + b = c$, then lines PQ and RS must be parallel.

To prove this statement, the student decides to start with the idea that the two lines are, in fact, parallel and then work backward, step by step, to show that $a + b$ must equal c.
- *Draw an analogy.* Identify a situation analogous to the problem situation and derive potential problem solutions from that analogy.
  Example: A student attempting to calculate the volume of an irregularly shaped object recognizes that, just as she herself displaces water when she steps into the bathtub, the object will displace its volume when immersed in water. She places the object into a container filled to the brim with water, collects the water that sloshes out, and measures the amount.

Teaching problem-solving strategies. How can we help our students acquire effective problem-solving strategies? Here are a number of possibilities:

For teaching algorithms:

- Describe and demonstrate specific algorithms and situations in which they can be used.
- Provide worked-out examples of algorithms being applied.
- Help students understand why particular algorithms are relevant and effective in certain situations.
- When a student's application of an algorithm yields an incorrect answer, look closely at the specific steps the student has taken until the trouble spot is located (e.g., see Figure 8.5).

For teaching heuristics:

- Give students practice in defining ill-defined problems.
- Teach heuristics that students can use in situations where no specific algorithms apply; for example, encourage such strategies as rounding, identifying subgoals, working backward, and drawing analogies.

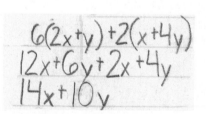

FIGURE 8.5 Thirteen-year-old Malika incorrectly simplifies the expression $6(2x + y) + 2(x + 4y)$ as $14x + 10y$. The correct answer is $14x + 14y$. Where did Malika go wrong?

For teaching both algorithms and heuristics:

- Teach problem-solving strategies within the context of specific subject areas (*not* as a topic separate from academic content).
- Provide scaffolding for difficult problems—for example, by breaking them into smaller and simpler problems, giving hints about possible strategies, or providing partial solutions.
- Ask students to explain what they are doing as they work through a problem.
- Have students solve problems in small groups, sharing ideas about problem-solving strategies, modeling various approaches for one another, and discussing the merits of each approach. (R. K. Atkinson, Derry, Renkl, & Wortham, 2000; Barron, 2000; Crowley & Siegler, 1999; Heller & Hungate, 1985; Mayer, 1985, 1992; Noddings, 1985; Reimann & Schult, 1996; L. B. Resnick, 1983)

As we have seen, well-defined problems are usually more easily solved than ill-defined ones, and problems that can be solved with algorithms are generally easier than those that require heuristics. But there are several other factors, all cognitive in nature, that affect problem-solving success as well.

Cognitive Factors Affecting Problem Solving

Cognitive psychologists have identified several factors that affect problem-solving success:

- Working memory capacity
- Encoding of the problem
- Depth and integration of one's knowledge relevant to the problem
- Retrieval of relevant information from long-term memory
- Metacognitive processes

As we consider each factor, we will identify additional ways to help our students become more effective problem solvers.

Before you read further, can you guess how each of these factors affects problem solving?

Working Memory Capacity

You may recall from an exercise in Chapter 6 just how difficult it is to solve a long division problem in your head. Remember, working memory has a limited capacity: It can hold only a few pieces of information and can accommodate only so much cognitive processing at any one time. If a problem requires an individual to deal with too much information at once or to manipulate that information in a very complex way, working memory capacity may be insufficient for effective problem processing. Once working memory capacity is exceeded, the problem cannot be solved (Johnstone & El-Banna, 1986; Perkins, 1995).

Our students can overcome the limits of their working memories in at least two ways. One obvious way is to create an external record of information relevant to the problem—for example, by writing that information on a piece of paper. (This is typically our strategy when we do long division problems, so that we don't have to hold all the numbers in working memory at once.) Another way to overcome working memory capacity is to learn some skills to a level of automaticity—in other words, to learn them to a point where they can be retrieved quickly, easily, and almost without conscious thought (N. Frederiksen, 1984a; Mayer & Wittrock, 1996; Rabinowitz & Glaser, 1985; Schneider & Shiffrin, 1977).

As an illustration of the role that automaticity plays in problem solving, try the following exercise.

Students who learn basic skills to automaticity have more working memory capacity to handle complex tasks that require such skills.

EXPERIENCING FIRSTHAND   *A Multiplication Problem*

See whether you can do this multiplication problem *in your head*. Look at it once, then close your eyes and try to solve it.

$$\begin{array}{r} 23 \\ \times\ 9 \\ \hline \end{array}$$

Were you able to remember the problem at the same time that you were calculating the answer? If so, it was probably because you could remember basic multiplication facts ($9 \times 2, 9 \times 3$) without having to think very hard about them. But imagine instead that once you had put the problem in your working memory, you had to stop and think about what 9×3 equals: "Hmm, let me see . . . 9 plus 9 is 18 . . . and I need to add 9 more, so that's 19, 20, 21, 22, 23, 24, 25, 26, 27 . . . and now what was the second top number again?" At this rate, you would never arrive at the correct answer of 207. When people must use a significant portion of working memory capacity for retrieving or reconstructing basic skills and information (e.g., for recalling multiplication facts, spelling, or the meaning of *deforestation*), they may not have enough capacity left to solve the problems (e.g., solving complex mathematical equations, writing a persuasive essay, or identifying methods of curtailing deforestation) that require such skills and information.

Encoding of the Problem

When we discussed cognitive processes in Chapter 6, we talked about *encoding,* changing the form of new information while storing it in memory. Encoding is clearly a factor that affects problem-solving ability. Sometimes students have trouble encoding a problem in any way that allows them to begin working to solve it. As an example, see whether you can solve the problem in the following exercise.

EXPERIENCING FIRSTHAND   *Pigs and Chickens*

Old MacDonald has a barnyard full of pigs and chickens. Altogether there are 21 heads and 60 legs in the barnyard (not counting MacDonald's own head and legs). How many pigs and how many chickens are running around the barnyard?

Can you figure out the answer? If you are having difficulty, try thinking about the problem this way:

Imagine that the pigs are standing in an upright position on only their two hind legs; their front two legs are raised over their heads. Therefore, all the animals—pigs and chickens alike—are standing on two legs. Can you now figure out how many legs are on the ground and how many must be in the air? From this, can you determine the number of pigs and chickens there must be?

In case you are still having difficulty with the problem, follow this logic:

- Obviously, because there are 21 heads, the number of pigs plus the number of chickens must equal 21.
- Because each animal has 2 legs on the ground and because there must be twice as many legs on the ground as there are number of heads, there are 42 (21×2) legs on the ground.
- Because there are 42 legs on the ground, there must be 18 ($60 - 42$) pigs' legs in the air.
- Because each pig has 2 front legs, there must be 9 ($18 \div 2$) pigs.
- Because there are 9 pigs, there must be 12 ($21 - 9$) chickens.

How could you use algebra to solve this problem?

Some ways of encoding a problem promote more successful problem solving than others.

If you initially had trouble solving the pigs-and-chickens problem, you may have been struggling to encode the problem in any way that allowed you to solve it. Students often have trouble solving mathematical word problems because they don't know how to translate those problems into procedures or operations with which they are familiar (Mayer, 1992; L. B. Resnick, 1989; Reusser, 1990).

At other times, students may encode a problem in a seemingly logical way that nevertheless fails to yield a correct problem solution. As an example, take a stab at the problem in the following exercise.

EXPERIENCING FIRSTHAND   *The Candle Problem*

You are in a room with a bulletin board firmly affixed to the wall about 4 feet above the floor. Your task is to *stand a candle upright* in front of the bulletin board. You do not want the candle touching the bulletin board, because the candle's flame must not singe the bulletin board. Instead, you need to place the candle about a centimeter away. How can you accomplish the task with the following materials?

Small candle

Metal knitting needle

Matches

Box of thumbtacks

12-inch plastic ruler

See whether you can solve the problem before you read further.

Based on Duncker, 1945.

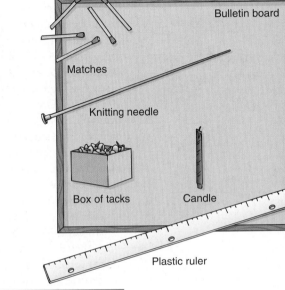

As it turns out, the ruler and knitting needle are useless in solving the candle problem (if you try to puncture the candle with the knitting needle, you will probably break the candle; if you try to balance the ruler on a few tacks, it will probably fall down). The easiest solution is to fasten the thumbtack box to the bulletin board with tacks and then attach the candle to the top of the box with either a tack or some melted wax. Many people don't consider this solution, however, because they encode the box only as a *container of tacks*, thereby overlooking its potential use as a candle stand. When we encode a problem in a way that excludes potential solutions, we are the victims of a **mental set.**

Mental sets in problem solving sometimes emerge when students practice solving a particular kind of problem (e.g., doing subtraction problems in math; or calculating velocity, given time and acceleration, in physics) without also practicing other kinds of problems at the same time (E. J. Langer, 2000; Luchins, 1942). Such repetitive practice can lead students to encode problems in a particular way without really thinking about the problems; that is, it can lead to automaticity in encoding. Although automaticity in the basic information and skills needed for problem solving is often an advantage (it frees up working memory capacity), automaticity in *encoding* problems may lead students to solve them incorrectly and so in many cases is a *dis*advantage (E. J. Langer, 2000).

Following are several strategies we can use to help students encode problems more effectively yet not fall victim to counterproductive mental sets:

- Present problems in a concrete way; for example, provide real objects that students can manipulate or an illustration of a problem's components (A. S. Luchins & Luchins, 1950; Mayer, 1992).
- Encourage students to make problems concrete *for themselves*; for example, encourage them to draw a picture or diagram of a problem (Anzai, 1991; Mayer, 1986; Prawat, 1989; K. Schultz & Lochhead, 1991).
- Point out any features of problems that students *can* solve, and when those features appear again in a different problem, indicate that the same information can be applied or the same approach to problem solution can be used (Prawat, 1989).

The candle problem illustrates a particular kind of mental set— *functional fixedness*—whereby an individual thinks of an object as having only one possible function and so overlooks another function that the object might serve.

- Give problems that look very different on the surface yet require the same or similar problem-solving procedures (Z. Chen, 1999).
- Mix up the kinds of problems that students tackle in any given practice session (E. J. Langer, 2000).
- Have students work in cooperative groups to identify different ways of representing a single problem—perhaps as a formula, a table, and a graph (Brenner et al., 1997; J. C. Turner, Meyer, et al., 1998).

Depth and Integration of Knowledge Relevant to the Problem

Let's return once again to Mary in our opening case study. Mary has learned a principle of physics (velocity equals acceleration multiplied by time) by rote, without really comprehending what she was studying. As a result, she is unable to use her knowledge to solve a problem about a car's rate of acceleration.

Research consistently indicates that when people have a thorough, conceptual understanding of a topic—when they have stored a great deal of information about it, with various pieces of information appropriately organized and interrelated in long-term memory—they can more easily use their knowledge to solve problems (P. A. Alexander & Judy, 1988; Heller & Hungate, 1985; Voss, Greene, Post, & Penner, 1983). For example, students are more likely to apply a principle of physics to a specific situation if they understand the concepts underlying that principle and the situations to which it relates. They are more likely to apply the Pythagorean theorem to the calculation of a diagonal roof if they have learned the theorem at a meaningful level and have associated it with such ideas as "diagonal" and "measurement." And when proposing possible solutions to the problem of rain forest destruction, they are more likely to draw from their knowledge of several disciplines (e.g., from ecology, economics, and psychology) if they have stored ideas from those disciplines in an interrelated, cross-disciplinary fashion.

In contrast, when students have limited knowledge about a certain topic, and particularly when they don't have a conceptual understanding of it, they are likely to encode problems related to that topic on the basis of superficial problem characteristics (Chi, Feltovich, & Glaser, 1981; Schoenfeld & Hermann, 1982). For example, when I was in elementary school, I recall that some of my classmates were having difficulty deciding how to attack word problems. I remember a teacher telling us that the word *left* in a problem indicates that subtraction is called for. Encoding a "left" problem as a subtraction problem works well in some instances, such as this one:

Tim has 7 apples. He gives 3 apples to Emily. How many apples does he have left?

But it is inappropriate in other instances, such as this one:

Ana went shopping. She spent $3.50 and then counted her money when she got home. She had $2.35 left. How much did Ana have when she started out? (L. B. Resnick, 1989, p. 165)

The latter problem requires addition, not subtraction. Obviously, words alone can be deceiving.

In what areas do you have the depth of knowledge necessary for solving problems successfully? In what areas has your relative lack of knowledge been a handicap?

The fact that conceptual understanding facilitates problem solving is yet another reason for teaching a few topics thoroughly, rather than many topics superficially (the *less is more* notion once again). It also suggests that, for any given procedure or principle, we should provide many and different examples and opportunities for practice. Students can study arithmetic operations by using such diverse examples as balancing a checkbook, calculating change, or predicting the possible profits and necessary supplies (number of cups, amount of lemonade mix, etc.) for a lemonade stand. They can learn basic principles of geography (e.g., that large cities are almost always located near major transportation junctions) by examining maps of different countries, as well as by exploring their own local geographic environment. Only by spending time with a certain topic and studying a variety of examples can students learn that topic in a meaningful fashion and make multiple connections with situations to which that subject matter applies. All too often, students don't have these critical opportunities (e.g., Porter, 1989).

We should note here that our students are also more likely to make connections between classroom material and its potential applications when they anticipate situations in which they might need to use the material to solve problems (J. R. Anderson et al., 1996). Not only should we focus more of our classroom instruction on the application of information, but we should focus more of our assessment procedures on application as well (Bransford, Franks, Vye, & Sherwood, 1989; Sternberg & Frensch, 1993). Following is an example of an assessment task in which students apply their knowledge of geographic principles to several related problems:

How many of your exams have tested your ability to remember information, but not *apply* information? Did such exams give you the message that knowing something was important but using it was not?

A map of a hypothetical country includes information about where bodies of water (e.g., river, lakes) and various forms of vegetation (grasslands, forests, etc.) are located. It also includes information about elevation, rainfall, and temperature ranges. A particular spot on the map is marked "X." Students are asked questions such as these:

- If people living at the point marked "X" on the map began to migrate *or* expand, where would they go and what direction might they take?
- What would be the distribution of population in country "X"; that is, where would many people live, few, and so on?
- Where would large cities develop in country "X"?
- How would you judge country "X"s economic potential; that is, what areas might be best for development, which worst, and so on? (questions from Massialas & Zevin, 1983, pp. 121, 127).

By incorporating the application of classroom material into our classroom assignments and tests, we indirectly teach students that this information can be used in a variety of contexts and furthermore *should* be used in these contexts. We will revisit the importance of assessing higher-level thinking skills in our discussion of classroom assessment in Chapters 15 and 16.

Retrieval of Relevant Information from Long-Term Memory

Obviously, students cannot solve a problem unless they retrieve from long-term memory the information necessary to solve it. But as we discovered in Chapter 6, long-term memory contains a great deal of information, and people cannot possibly retrieve it all in any given situation. Successful problem solving therefore requires that an individual search the right "places" in long-term memory at the right time.

The parts of long-term memory that a student searches depends on how the student encoded the problem in the first place. For example, if a student sees the word *left* in a word problem and thinks "subtraction," that student will retrieve rules of subtraction even when addition is required. If a student encodes a box only as a container for tacks, that student will not retrieve other characteristics of boxes (e.g., their flat surfaces, their relative sturdiness) that might be useful in solving the candle problem. When people have a mental set about a problem, they may unnecessarily restrict their search of long-term memory, overlooking stored information that is critical for problem solution.

INTO THE CLASSROOM: *Promoting Successful Transfer and Problem Solving*

Teach important topics in depth and be sure students learn them thoroughly.

A teacher of a second-year Spanish class teaches only two new verb tenses (preterit and imperfect) during fall semester, saving other tenses (e.g., near past, near future) for later instruction.

Tie class material to what students already know.

After teaching that water expands when it freezes, a science teacher explains that many of the bumps seen in country roads are frost heaves caused by freezing water.

Give students practice in dealing with ill-defined problems and show them how to make such problems more well-defined.

A teacher asks students in an interdisciplinary class to wrestle with the problem of diminishing rain forests. He starts them off by asking, "What should be the final goal of preservation efforts?" and "What are some of the biological, social, and political factors that you need to consider as you try to solve this problem?"

Teach the basic information and skills needed in problem solving to a level of automaticity.

An elementary school teacher makes sure that his students have thoroughly mastered the basic multiplication and division facts before teaching them long division.

Provide opportunities for students to apply what they have learned to new situations and problems.

A geography teacher asks students to apply their knowledge of human settlement patterns in explaining why the populations of various countries are distributed as they are.

Ask students to apply what they know in tests and other assessment activities.

A science teacher asks students to use principles of physics to describe how they might singlehandedly move a 500-pound object to a location twenty feet away.

Make school tasks similar to the tasks that students are likely to encounter in the outside world.

An English teacher teaches persuasive writing skills by having students write editorials for the school newspaper.

In some cases, our students may be the victims of situated cognition: They may associate a problem-solving strategy only with a particular context and so do not retrieve and apply it when they find themselves in a different context (Lave, 1993; Saljo & Wyndhamn, 1992; Schliemann & Carraher, 1993). As an illustration, let's consider a study with 15- and 16-year-old students (Saljo & Wyndhamn, 1992). The students were asked to figure out how much postage they should put on an envelope that weighed a particular amount, and they were given a table of postage rates with which to determine the correct amount. When students were given the task in a social studies class, most of them used the postage table to find the answer. But when students were given the task in a math class, most of them tried to *calculate* the postage, sometimes figuring it to several decimal places. Curiously, the students in the social studies class were more likely to solve the problem correctly; as a former social studies teacher myself, I suspect that the students were well accustomed to finding information in tables and charts in that particular class. In contrast, many of the students in the math class apparently never considered pulling the correct postage directly from the table. Instead, they tried to apply some of the mathematical strategies that served them so well in their daily assignments—strategies that were counterproductive in this situation.

Metacognitive Processes

Earlier in the chapter we discovered the importance of metacognition for effective learning and studying. Metacognitive processes play an important role in problem solving as well. For instance, effective problem solvers tend to

- Identify one or more goals that reflect problem solution
- Break a complex problem into two or more subproblems
- Plan a systematic, sequential approach to solving the problem and any subproblems
- Continually monitor and evaluate their progress toward their goal(s)
- Identify any obstacles that may be impeding their progress
- Change to a new strategy if the current one does not seem to be working
  (J. E. Davidson & Sternberg, 1998; Dominowski, 1998)

Such metacognitive processes enable students to use problem-solving strategies flexibly, to apply them to more complex problem situations, and to know when particular strategies are and are not appropriate (J. E. Davidson & Sternberg, 1998; Dominowski, 1998). In contrast, *in*effective problem solvers tend to apply problem-solving procedures mindlessly, without any real understanding of what they are doing or why they are doing it (M. Carr & Biddlecomb, 1998; J. E. Davidson & Sternberg, 1998).

To some extent, students' metacognitive problem-solving processes depend on their conceptual understanding of the subject matter they are dealing with (M. Carr & Biddlecomb, 1998; J. E. Davidson & Sternberg, 1998). Yet students can also be taught more effective metacognitive processes. For instance, we can enhance students' metacognitive awareness when we ask them to explain what they are doing, and why they are doing it, as they work on a problem (Dominowski, 1998; Johanning, D'Agostino, Steele, & Shumow, 1999). We can also give them questions they can ask *themselves* as they work on a problem—questions such as "What are we trying to do here?" "Are we getting closer to our goal?" "What didn't work?" (A. King, 1999, p. 101). Such approaches are especially effective when students work in pairs or small groups on challenging problems and must explain and defend their reasoning to one another (Johanning et al., 1999; A. King, 1999).

Using Computer Technology to Promote Effective Problem Solving

Throughout our discussion of problem solving, we have identified numerous strategies for enhancing students' problem-solving effectiveness. Most of these have relied on fairly traditional classroom resources and techniques, such as having students use pencil and paper to write down or diagram a problem or having them meet in small groups to explain and justify their problem-solving strategies. Yet we can often capitalize on computer technology to foster students' problem-solving capabilities as well. For instance, we can

- Use computer-based tutoring programs to promote mathematical and scientific reasoning and problem solving
- Show students how to use spreadsheets to analyze complex sets of data

Such instructional strategies are more likely to be helpful for average-ability rather than high-ability students (J. E. Davidson & Sternberg, 1998). Why might this be so?

- Use computer simulations that allow students to formulate hypotheses, design experiments to test those hypotheses, and interpret the virtual results
- Present complex real-world problems (i.e., authentic activities) that students must solve (Cognition and Technology Group at Vanderbilt, 1990, 1996; Vye et al., 1998)

We find an example of the last of these—presenting authentic activities—in the Adventures of Jasper Woodbury series,[2] in which middle school students encounter a number of real-life problem situations presented through videodisc technology. In one episode, "Journey to Cedar Creek," Jasper has just purchased an old boat that he is hoping to pilot home the same day. Because the boat has no running lights, he must figure out whether he can get home by sunset, and because he has spent all his cash and used his last check, he must figure out whether he has enough gas to make the trip. Throughout the video, all the information students need to answer these questions is embedded in authentic contexts (e.g., a marine radio announces time of sunset, and mileage markers are posted at various landmarks along the river), but students must sift through a lot of irrelevant information to find it. In another episode, "The Right Angle," teenager Paige Littlefield is searching for a cave in which her Native American grandfather left her a special gift before he died. The grandfather gave her directions to the cave that require knowledge and use of geometric principles (e.g., "From the easternmost point of Black Hawk Bluff, travel at a bearing of 25° until you are almost surrounded by rock towers. Go to Flat Top Tower. . . . You will know Flat Top Tower because at a distance of 250 feet from the northern side of its base, the angle of elevation of its top is 45°"). Using the grandfather's directions and a topographical map of Paige's ancestral home country, students must locate the cave. There are numerous ways to approach each Jasper problem, and students work in small groups to brainstorm and carry out possible problem solutions. Students of all ability levels find the Jasper series highly motivating, and they can transfer what they learn from one problem when solving similar problems (Cognition and Technology Group at Vanderbilt, 1990; Learning Technology Center, Vanderbilt University, 1996).

The Adventures of Jasper Woodbury series uses videodisc technology to present authentic problem-solving tasks. To assist Jasper in his decision making in "Journey to Cedar Creek," students must use information presented in real-world contexts to determine distance, speed, and gas mileage.

In the Jasper series we again see the value of authentic activities—in this case, authentic activities with a problem-solving component. When students use certain principles and skills to solve problems in authentic contexts, they will be more likely to retrieve those principles and skills later on when they encounter similar problems in the adult world. Authentic activities will be important not only in promoting effective problem solving but also in promoting critical thinking skills, as we will discover in the next section.

Before we leave the topic of problem solving, however, let's consider the effectiveness of one teacher's approach to teaching problem solving.

INTERPRETING ARTIFACTS AND INTERACTIONS   *Dogs, Cats, Hamsters, Penguins, and Ladybugs*

A third-grade teacher asks her students to write and then solve their own subtraction problems; 8-year-old Morris's problem appears to the right. As you look at Morris's work, consider

- What benefits this approach might have
- Whether this activity engages students in an authentic activity

> I had 4 Dogs, 3 Cats, 14 hamsters, 9 Panguens, And 1,000 ladybugs. I gave away 46 ladybugs, 1 Dog, 2 Cats, 3 hamsters, And 5 Panguns. how many anamials did I have left.
>
> $$\begin{array}{r} 9\;9\;8\;\cancel{10} \\ -5\;7 \\ \hline 9\;9\;7\;3 \end{array}$$

Undoubtedly the teacher hopes that the activity will encourage students to apply mathematics to their own lives and, perhaps, to look around for situations in which subtraction

---

[2]You can learn more about the Jasper series by visiting http://www.vanderbilt.edu/researchers.html. Once there, select either "Learning Technology Center" or "Learning Sciences Institute" (the center's name is changing as I write this) and then select "Products."

How might the teacher have modified the activity to increase its authentic nature?

might be appropriate and useful. As you can see, however, Morris writes a problem that seems highly artificial: The probability that he would have that many hamsters, penguins, and ladybugs is quite small. In essence, Morris writes a traditional mathematical word problem that has little relevance for his own life circumstances; thus, the activity is, at least for Morris, not a truly authentic one.

Critical Thinking

EXPERIENCING FIRSTHAND   *Happiness Is a Well-Behaved Classroom*

Here is a research finding presented at the annual conference of the American Educational Research Association in 1994:

> Teachers who feel happy when they teach are more likely to have well-behaved students (Emmer, 1994).

If you want to have well-behaved students, then, should you try to feel happy when you enter the classroom each morning?

If you answered yes to my question, then you made a mistake that I warned you about in Chapter 1: You drew a conclusion about a cause-effect relationship (i.e., teacher happiness causes good behavior in students) on the basis of a correlational research study. Although Dr. Emmer found that teacher happiness and student behavior are *associated* with one another, he did not necessarily find that teacher happiness *causes* good behavior (nor did he say that he did). In fact, there are other possible explanations for the correlation. For instance, perhaps good student behavior makes teachers feel happy (rather than vice versa), or perhaps teachers who use effective teaching techniques feel happy *and* keep students on task as the result of using those techniques (Emmer, 1994).

Evaluating the research findings you read about is an example of critical thinking. More generally, **critical thinking** involves evaluating the accuracy and worth of information or arguments (Beyer, 1985). Critical thinking may take a variety of forms, depending on the context. For instance, it may involve any one or more of the following (Halpern, 1997a, 1998):

- *Verbal reasoning:* Understanding and evaluating the persuasive techniques found in oral and written language (e.g., deductive and inductive logic). For example, consider this:

  > Aren't you tired of sniffles and runny noses all winter? Tired of always feeling less than your best? Get through a whole winter without colds. Take Eradicold Pills as directed. (R. J. Harris, 1977, p. 605)

  Do Eradicold Pills reduce cold symptoms? The passage provides no proof that they do. Instead, it simply includes the suggestion to "Take Eradicold Pills as directed" within the context of a discussion of undesirable symptoms—a common ploy in persuasive advertising.

- *Argument analysis:* Discriminating between reasons that do and do not support a particular conclusion. For example, imagine this situation:

  > You have a beat-up old car and have several thousand dollars to get the car in working order. You can sell the car in its present condition for $1,500, or you can invest a couple of thousand dollars on more repairs and then sell it for $3000. What should you do? (modeled after Halpern, 1998)

  Obviously, it makes more sense to sell the car now: If you sell the car for $3,000 after making $2,000 worth of repairs, you make $500 less than you would otherwise. Yet many people mistakenly believe that their *past* investments justify making additional ones, when in fact past investments are irrelevant to the present state of affairs (Halpern, 1998).

- *Probabilistic reasoning:* Determining the likelihood and uncertainties associated with various events. As an example, consider the following situation:

  > You have been rolling a typical six-sided die (i.e., one member of a pair of dice). You know for a fact that the die is not "loaded" (it's not heavier on one side than another),

and yet in the past 30 rolls you have not rolled a number 4 even once. What are the odds that you will get a 4 in the next roll?

Many people mistakenly believe that a roll of 4 is long overdue and so is more likely in the next roll than it would be otherwise.[3] In fact, on any roll of an unloaded (fair) die, the probability is 1 in 6 that its outcome will be a 4, *regardless* of the outcomes of any previous rolls.

- *Hypothesis testing:* Evaluating the value of data and research results in terms of the methods used to obtain them and their potential relevance to particular conclusions. When hypothesis testing includes critical thinking, it involves considering questions such as these:

> Was an appropriate method used to measure a particular outcome?
>
> Have other possible explanations or conclusions been eliminated?
>
> Can the results obtained in one situation be reasonably generalized to other situations?

The "happiness" exercise you did earlier illustrates this form of critical thinking.

- *Decision making:* Identifying several alternatives and selecting the best alternative. For example, when, as teachers, we choose a particular approach to teaching a topic by considering several possible strategies and weighing the pros and cons of each one, we are engaging in critical thinking.

The nature of critical thinking will obviously be different in different content domains. For instance, in writing, critical thinking may involve reading the first draft of a persuasive essay to look for errors in logical reasoning or for situations in which opinions have not been sufficiently justified. In science, critical thinking may involve revising present theories or beliefs to account for new evidence; in other words, it may involve conceptual change. In history, it may involve drawing inferences from various historical documents, attempting to determine whether things *definitely* happened a particular way or only *maybe* happened that way.

All too often, students at all grade levels (even college students) take the information they see in textbooks, advertisements, media reports, and elsewhere at face value; in other words, they engage in little or no critical thinking as they consider its accuracy and worth. Students are more likely to look analytically and critically at new information if they believe that even experts' understanding of any single topic continues to evolve as new evidence accumulates; they are less likely to engage in critical thinking if they believe that "knowledge" is an absolute, unchanging entity (Kardash & Scholes, 1996; Kuhn, 2001; Schommer-Aikins, in press). In other words, students' *epistemological beliefs* enter into the critical thinking process.

Critical thinking takes different forms in different content domains.

Perhaps because the term *critical thinking* encompasses such a variety of different skills, research about how to promote critical thinking skills in the classroom is sketchy at best. Nevertheless, theorists have offered a few suggestions:

- Teach fewer topics, but in greater depth—the *less is more* principle yet again (Onosko, 1989; Onosko & Newmann, 1994).
- Encourage some intellectual skepticism—for instance, by urging students to question and challenge the ideas that they read and hear—and communicate the message that our knowledge and understanding of any single topic will continue to change over time (Kardash & Scholes, 1996; Kuhn, 2001; Onosko, 1989).
- Model critical thinking—for instance, by thinking aloud while analyzing a persuasive argument or scientific report (Onosko & Newmann, 1994).
- Show students that critical thinking involves considerable mental effort, but that the benefits often make the effort worthwhile (Halpern, 1998).

---

[3]Such reasoning is sometimes called the *gambler's fallacy.*

- Give students many and varied opportunities to practice critical thinking—for instance, by identifying flaws in the logical arguments presented in persuasive essays and by evaluating the quality and usefulness of scientific findings (Halpern, 1998).
- Ask questions such as these to encourage critical thinking:

> What additional information do I need?
>
> What information is relevant to this situation? What information is irrelevant?
>
> What persuasive technique is the author using? Is it valid, or is it designed to mislead the reader?
>
> What reasons support the conclusion? What reasons do *not* support the conclusion?
>
> What actions might I take to improve the design of this study?
> (based on Halpern, 1998, p. 454)

Might such questions be useful in your own studying as well?

- Have students debate controversial issues from several perspectives, occasionally asking them to take a perspective quite different from their own (Reiter, 1994).
- Embed critical thinking skills within the context of authentic activities as a way of helping students retrieve those skills later on, both in the workplace and in other aspects of adult life (Derry, Levin, Osana, & Jones, 1998; Halpern, 1998).

As we've examined the nature of metacognition, transfer, problem solving, and critical thinking in this chapter, you have, I hope, discovered that all of these processes involve knowledge and strategies that most students can readily acquire with time, appropriate educational experiences, and practice. Yet even when students have the capability to engage in higher-level thinking processes, they do not always do so. One key reason may be their *dispositions,* a topic we turn to now.

The Role of Dispositions in Higher-Level Thinking

By **disposition,** I mean a general inclination to approach a task in a particular way—perhaps in a very thoughtful, analytical way, on the one hand, or in a very thought*less,* unquestioning way, on the other. For example, when I was once observing one of my teacher interns teach a unit on Canada, a boy in his class asked whether the province of Quebec was bigger than Texas. The map of Canada at the front of the room did not show Texas, but it did show Alaska, which was clearly smaller than Quebec. Another boy answered his classmate's question by reasoning: "If Alaska's the largest state, then Quebec *must* be bigger than Texas." His response

---

INTO THE CLASSROOM: *Fostering Critical Thinking*

Teach elements of critical thinking.

In a unit on persuasion and argumentation, a junior high school language arts teacher explains that a sound argument meets three criteria (Halpern, 1997a): (1) The evidence presented to justify the argument is accurate and consistent; (2) the evidence is relevant to, and provides sufficient support for, the conclusion; and (3) there is little or no missing information that, if present, would lead to a contradictory conclusion. The teacher then has students practice applying these criteria to a variety of persuasive and argumentative essays.

Foster epistemological beliefs that encourage critical thinking.

Rather than teach history as a collection of facts to be memorized, a high school history teacher portrays the discipline as an attempt by informed but inevitably biased scholars to interpret and make sense of historical events. On several occasions, he asks his students to read two or three different historians' accounts of the same incident and to look for evidence of personal bias in each one (Paxton, 1999).

Embed critical thinking skills within the context of authentic activities.

In a unit on statistical and scientific reasoning, an eighth-grade class studies concepts related to probability, correlation, and experimental control. Then, as part of a simulated "legislative hearing," the students work in small groups to develop arguments for or against a legislative bill concerning the marketing and use of vitamins and other dietary supplements. To find evidence to support their arguments, the students apply what they've learned about statistics and experimentation as they read and analyze journal articles and government reports about the possible benefits and drawbacks of nutritional supplements (Derry et al., 1998).

showed a disposition to reason logically from the information he had, rather than always to seek answers from an authority figure.

We have already encountered one example of a disposition: In Chapter 6 we learned that students are more likely to engage in meaningful learning—to try to make sense of what they are studying—when they have a *meaningful learning set*. Just as a meaningful learning set makes meaningful learning more probable, certain dispositions increase the likelihood that students will use their higher-level thinking skills. Following are just a few examples of dispositions that are apt to lead to higher-level thinking (Halpern, 1997a; Perkins, Tishman, Ritchhart, Donis, & Andrade, 2000):

- Curiosity about puzzling events
- Willingness to suspend judgment in the absence of compelling evidence
- Persistence in the face of obstacles
- Desire to check work for accuracy
- Willingness to acknowledge errors in reasoning and use them to make improvements in the future

As you can see, a disposition is as much an attitude as it is an ability, and it involves motivation as much as it involves cognition (Halpern, 1997a; Kuhn, 2001; Perkins et al., 2000).

Sadly, students often *don't* have the disposition to approach classroom tasks (or, for that matter, tasks in the real world) in a thoughtful, analytical manner. As an example, a sixth grader learning how to compute means, medians, modes, and ranges was practicing with a hypothetical set of test scores (79, 43, 85, 90, 90, 65, 71, 88, 0, 89). As you can see in Figure 8.6, the student calculated a mean (average) of 710, a number that cannot possibly be correct, yet she failed to notice her error or take steps to correct it.

Several factors may underlie many students' tendency *not* to engage in higher-level thinking on any regular basis. Sometimes, students are simply unaware that anything is lacking in their relatively thoughtless approach to tasks (Halpern, 1997a). At other times, they may be aware of more effective processes but believe that such processes involve too much time and trouble (Sitko, 1998). In some cases, *teachers* discourage the disposition to think analytically and critically about classroom material, as the following classroom exchange illustrates:

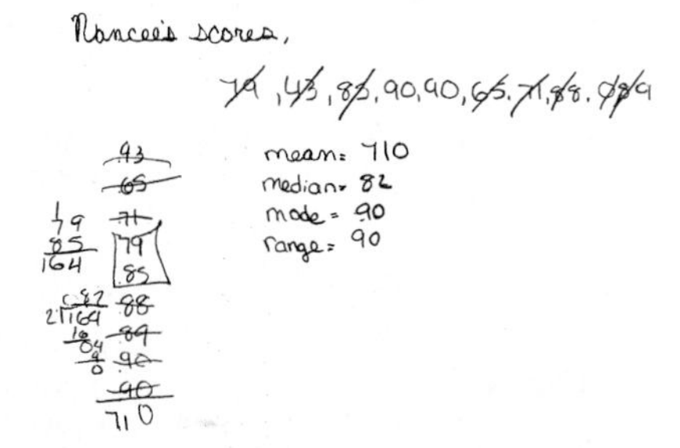

Teacher: Write this on your paper . . . it's simply memorizing this pattern. We have meters, centimeters, and millimeters. Let's say . . . write millimeters, centimeters, and meters. We want to make sure that our metric measurement is the same. If I gave you this decimal, let's say .234 m (yes, write that). In order to come up with .234 m in centimeters, the only thing that is necessary is that you move the decimal. How do we move the decimal? You move it to the right two places. (Jason, sit up please.) If I move it to the right two places, what should .234 m look like, Daniel, in centimeters? What does it look like, Ashley?

Ashley: 23.4 cm.

Teacher: Twenty-three point four. Simple stuff. In order to find meters, we're still moving that decimal to the right, but this time, boys and girls, we're only going to move it one place. So, if I move this decimal one place, what is my answer for millimeters? (dialogue from J. C. Turner, Meyer, et al., 1998, p. 741)

Undoubtedly, this teacher means well: She wants her students to understand how to convert from one unit of measurement to another. But notice the attitude she engenders: "Write this . . . it's simply memorizing this pattern."

As teachers, we must not only show our students *how* to engage in higher-level thinking skills—choosing effective study strategies, applying what they've learned to new situations and problems, critically evaluating what they hear and read, and so on—but we must also encourage them to *want* to use such skills with various classroom topics. We might do so by modeling such skills in our own approach to classroom subject matter, making them an important part of many classroom activities, and incorporating them into assignments, quizzes, and other forms of assessment.

Considering Diversity in Higher-Level Thinking Processes

We have noted the importance of a solid knowledge base for effective study strategies and successful problem solving. Students with different backgrounds will, of course, have different

FIGURE 8.6 Computing a mean (average) of 710 for a group of scores that range from 0 to 90, this sixth grader shows little disposition to check her work to make sure it makes sense. Can you identify the two errors in the student's calculations?

Courtesy of Dinah Jackson.

knowledge bases, and such diversity will naturally affect their ability to deal with higher-level thinking tasks. For instance, our students will use more effective study strategies when they read textbook materials consistent with their own cultural experiences (Pritchard, 1990).

Furthermore, students' previous experiences may have influenced the particular thinking skills they've developed. For example, thanks to the phenomenon of situated cognition, some students may have developed effective problem-solving strategies within the contexts of their own home and neighborhood environments (e.g., easily performing complex mathematical calculations while selling gum and candy on the street) yet have difficulty transferring what they've learned to more formal classroom tasks (Carraher, Carraher, & Schliemann, 1985; Gay & Cole, 1967). In some cultures, respect for one's elders may be highly valued, and so critical thinking and analysis of elders' beliefs may be strongly discouraged (Delgado-Gaitan, 1994). And students

TABLE 8.4 — STUDENTS IN INCLUSIVE SETTINGS

Promoting Higher-Level Thinking Skills in Students with Special Educational Needs

CATEGORY	CHARACTERISTICS YOU MIGHT OBSERVE	SUGGESTED CLASSROOM STRATEGIES
Students with specific cognitive or academic difficulties	• Less metacognitive awareness or control of learning • Use of few and relatively inefficient learning strategies • Increased strategy use after training • Difficulty in transferring learned information to new situations • Difficulties in problem solving, perhaps because of limited working memory capacity, inability to identify important aspects of a problem, inability to retrieve appropriate problem-solving strategies, or limited metacognitive problem-solving skills	• Teach more effective learning strategies (e.g., taking notes, using mnemonics, finding general themes in reading material) and identify occasions when each strategy is likely to be useful. • Scaffold students' use of new learning strategies (e.g., provide outlines to guide note taking, ask questions that encourage retrieval of prior knowledge). • Present simple problems at first, then gradually move to more difficult ones as students gain proficiency and self-confidence. • Teach techniques for minimizing the load on working memory during problem solving (e.g., writing the parts of a problem on paper, making a diagram of the problem situation).
Students with social or behavioral problems	• Limited metacognitive awareness of own processing difficulties (for some students) • Few effective learning strategies (for some students) • Deficiencies in social problem-solving skills	• Provide guidance in using effective learning and study strategies (e.g., give outlines that guide note taking and ask questions that encourage retrieval of prior knowledge). • Teach social problem-solving skills (see Chapter 10 for ideas).
Students with general delays in cognitive and social functioning	• Lack of metacognitive awareness or control of learning • Lack of learning strategies, especially in the absence of strategies training • Difficulty in transferring information and skills to new situations • Few effective problem-solving strategies	• Teach relatively simple learning strategies (e.g., rehearsal, specific mnemonics) and give students ample practice using them. • Teach new information and skills in the specific contexts and situations in which you want students to use them. • Present simple problems and guide students through each step of the solutions.
Students with physical or sensory challenges	• No consistent deficits in higher-level thinking processes; any deficits observed may be due to students' limited experiences with tasks that require higher-level thinking	• Address any deficits in higher-level thinking skills using strategies that you would use with nondisabled students, making appropriate accommodations for physical and sensory limitations.
Students with advanced cognitive development	• Use of relatively sophisticated learning strategies • Greater transfer of learning to new situations • Greater effectiveness in problem solving, more sophisticated problem-solving strategies, greater flexibility in strategy use, less susceptibility to mental sets	• Place greater emphasis on higher-level thinking skills (e.g., transfer, problem solving) within the curriculum. • Teach higher-level thinking skills within the context of specific classroom topics rather than in isolation from academic content.

Sources: Beirne-Smith et al., 2002; Brownell, Mellard, & Deshler, 1993; Candler-Lotven et al., 1994; Campione et al., 1985; B. Clark, 1997; DuPaul & Eckert, 1994; N. R. Ellis, 1979; Frasier, 1989; Grodzinsky & Diamond, 1992; K. R. Harris, 1982; Heward, 2000; M. C. Linn et al., 1989; Maker, 1993; Mastropieri & Scruggs, 2000; McGlynn, 1998; Meichenbaum, 1977; Mercer, 1997; Piirto, 1999; Porath, 1988; Pressley, 1995; Pulos & Linn, 1981; Scruggs & Mastropieri, 1992; Slife, Weiss, & Bell, 1985; Stanley, 1980; H. L. Swanson, 1993; Torrance, 1989; Turnbull et al., 1999; Wilder & Williams, 2001; Wong, 1991a.

whose previous educational experiences have focused on drills and rote memorization (e.g., as is true in some schools in Asia) may have little awareness of the value of such learning strategies as meaningful learning and elaboration (D. Y. F. Ho, 1994; Purdie & Hattie, 1996).

Accommodating Students with Special Needs

We are especially apt to find diversity in the higher-level thinking skills of our students with special needs. Table 8.4 presents characteristics common in these students.

Particularly noteworthy is the diversity in students' metacognitive awareness and use of study strategies. Many of our students with learning disabilities, and some with emotional and behavioral disorders as well, will demonstrate little knowledge or use of effective strategies (McGlynn, 1998; H. L. Swanson, 1993; Wong, 1991a). Students with mental retardation are likely to show even greater deficits in metacognitive skills; in addition, they will often have difficulty transferring any strategies they learn to new situations (Campione, Brown, & Bryant, 1985). In contrast, students who are gifted will typically have more sophisticated study strategies than their classmates (Candler-Lotven et al., 1994).

For many students with special needs, we may have to teach complex cognitive skills explicitly and with considerable **metacognitive scaffolding**—that is, with close guidance and assistance in the use of specific learning strategies. For example, we might provide partially filled-in outlines to guide students' note taking; Figure 8.7 presents an example of such an outline. We might also tell students when particular strategies (e.g., elaboration, comprehension monitoring) are appropriate and model the use of such strategies with specific classroom subject matter (E. S. Ellis & Friend, 1991). Finally, we must give students opportunities to practice their newly acquired strategies, along with feedback about how effectively they are using each one (E. S. Ellis & Friend, 1991).

MUSCLES

A. *Number of Muscles*

    1.   There are approximately _____ muscles in the human body.

B. *How Muscles Work*

    1.   Muscles work in two ways:

        a.   They _____, or shorten.

        b.   They _____, or lengthen.

C. *Kinds of Muscles*

    1.   _____ muscles are attached to the bones by _____.

        a.   These muscles are _____(voluntary/involuntary).

        b.   The purpose of these muscles is to _____

                _____.

    2.   _____ muscles line some of the body's _____.

        a.   These muscles are _____(voluntary/involuntary).

        b.   The purpose of these muscles is to _____

                _____.

    3.   The _____ muscle is the only one of its kind; it is also called the _____.

        a.   This muscle is _____ (voluntary/ involuntary).

             The purpose of this muscle is to _____

                _____.

FIGURE 8.7 An example of metacognitive scaffolding: A partially filled-in outline that can guide students' note taking

If you have already read the discussion of individual differences in Chapter 4, then you are familiar with Robert Sternberg's theory of intelligence. Sternberg proposes that specific cognitive processes are one critical aspect of human intelligence. To the extent that our students are able to process information in sophisticated ways—to separate important information from irrelevant details, find relationships among seemingly different ideas, apply what they have learned to new situations, identify effective problem-solving strategies, critically analyze and evaluate what they read, and so on—they all become more "intelligent" human beings.

If we focus classroom activities on the learning of isolated facts, and if we also use assessment techniques that emphasize students' knowledge of those facts, our students will naturally begin to believe that school learning is a process of absorbing information in a rote, meaningless fashion and then regurgitating it later on. In contrast, if we focus class time and activities on *doing things with* information—for instance, understanding, organizing, elaborating, applying, analyzing, and critically evaluating it—then our students should acquire the cognitive processes, skills, and dispositions that will serve them well in the world beyond the classroom.

General Strategies for Promoting Higher-Level Thinking Skills

Throughout the chapter we've identified numerous strategies for fostering effective study strategies, transfer, problem solving, and critical thinking. Let's briefly revisit those strategies that are likely to foster a wide variety of higher-level thinking skills:

■ *Emphasize meaningful learning and conceptual understanding over rote memorization.* Our students can better apply and critique classroom subject matter when they acquire an integrated, cohesive, and thorough understanding of that subject matter. Thus, we have repeatedly encountered the *less is more* principle: Teaching a few topics in depth is ultimately more effective than skimming over the surface of a great many.

■ *Teach higher-level thinking skills within the context of specific topics.* As teachers, we will occasionally run across packaged curricular programs designed to teach complex mental processes such as study strategies, problem solving, or critical thinking. But as a general rule, we are better advised to teach higher-level thinking skills within the context of specific topics—for example, teaching critical thinking and problem-solving skills as we study science or teaching creative thinking as we study writing (M. C. Linn et al., 1989; Porath, 1988; Pulos & Linn, 1981; Stanley, 1980).

■ *Communicate that much of what we "know" about the world is subject to change as new evidence comes in.* Learners' epistemological beliefs about a particular academic discipline, as well as about knowledge and learning more generally, have a significant impact on how learners study, what they learn, how readily they apply classroom subject matter, and how often they critically evaluate it. Some classroom topics are fairly certain, to be sure; 2 + 2 will always equal 4 (as long as we're working with a base-10 number system), mammals definitely have backbones (i.e., they are vertebrates), and Columbus's first trip across the Atlantic is well documented as having occurred in 1492. Yet many other things—how the brain works, why some historical figures behaved as they did, how best to curb deforestation, and so on—are still a source of considerable debate, and we should say so.

■ *Encourage higher-level thinking through group discussions and projects.* When students talk with one another, they must verbalize (and therefore become more metacognitively aware of) what and how they themselves are thinking. They also hear other (possibly better) interpretations, problem-solving strategies, and critical analyses. Invariably, too, they scaffold one another's attempts at higher-level tasks that might be too difficult for any of them to accomplish individually.

■ *Use authentic activities to promote transfer of thinking skills to real-life settings.* We do not necessarily want to make the school day just one authentic activity after another, as students may need the time and opportunity to practice certain things (basic math facts, grammatical rules, the symbols for various elements in chemistry, etc.) without too much distraction (J. R. Anderson et al., 1996). Yet unless authentic activities are a regular part of the school curriculum, students may find little relevance in the skills they are learning for their own lives.

■ *Foster dispositions as well as skills.* Students are more likely to apply higher-level thinking skills to classroom tasks—and to situations and problems in their outside lives as well—if they are in the *habit* of doing so. Undoubtedly the best place for this habit to develop is where students most frequently encounter new ideas, perspectives, and ways of doing things: at school.

■ *Incorporate higher-level thinking into assessment activities.* As you will discover in Chapter 16, it is fairly easy to construct assignments and tests that assess knowledge of basic facts and procedures. But it is ultimately more important that we assess what students can *do* with that knowledge. In Chapter 16 we will identify a variety of strategies for assessing higher-level thinking skills.

CASE STUDY: *Checks and Balances*

Mr. Chen has just finished a unit on the three branches of the United States government: executive, legislative, and judicial. He is appalled at some of his students' responses to an essay question he gives. Following are some examples of his students' responses to this question:

How do the three branches of government provide a system of "checks and balances"? Use an example to illustrate how one branch might serve as a check and balance for another branch. Do *not* use an example that was presented in class.

Debra: The judicial branch finds out if people are innocent or guilty. The executive branch executes the sentences that guilty people get.

Mark: The system of checks and balances is when one branch of government makes sure another branch doesn't do something wrong. I can't think of any examples.

Seth: I don't have anything about this in my notes. Checks and balances have something to do with the way the government spends money.

Karen: I did all the reading, honest I did! But now I can't remember anything about this.

- How thoroughly have these students learned the material that Mr. Chen was trying to teach them? Why are they apparently unable to identify new examples of checks and balances?
- What evidence do you see that Mr. Chen's students have poor study skills? If you were teaching Mr. Chen's class, what might you do to help the students study and learn more effectively?

Once you have answered these questions, compare your responses with those presented in Appendix B.

PRAXIS Turn to Appendix C, "Matching Book and Ancillary Content to the PRAXIS™ Principles of Learning and Teaching Tests," to discover sections of this chapter that may be especially applicable to the PRAXIS™ tests.

Now go to our Companion Website at http://www.prenhall.com/ormrod to assess your understanding of chapter content with "Multiple-Choice Questions," apply comprehension in "Essay Questions," broaden your knowledge of educational psychology with related "Web Links," gain greater insight about classroom learning in "Learning in the Content Areas," and analyze and assess classroom work in the "Student Artifact Library."

Key Concepts

lower-level question (p. 261)
higher-level question (p. 261)
higher-level thinking (p. 261)
metacognition (p. 261)
concept map (p. 265)
elaborative interrogation (p. 267)
comprehension monitoring (p. 268)
illusion of knowing (p. 268)
self-questioning (p. 269)

epistemological beliefs (p. 270)
transfer (p. 273)
positive transfer (p. 274)
negative transfer (p. 274)
specific transfer (p. 274)
general transfer (p. 274)
formal discipline (p. 274)
situated cognition (p. 275)
well-defined problem (p. 280)

ill-defined problem (p. 280)
algorithm (p. 281)
heuristic (p. 281)
mental set (p. 285)
critical thinking (p. 290)
disposition (p. 292)
metacognitive scaffolding (p. 295)

9

Behaviorist Views of Learning

As we grow from young infants into mature adults, we learn thousands of new behaviors. As toddlers, we learn to walk, feed ourselves, and ask for what we want. As preschoolers, we learn to brush our teeth, ride a tricycle, and use scissors. During the elementary school years, we begin to use a calculator, write in cursive letters, and play team sports. As adolescents, we may learn how to drive a car, ask someone for a date, or perform in an orchestra. In many cases, we develop such behaviors because our environment encourages us—perhaps even requires us—to do so.

Chapter 6 briefly introduced a theoretical perspective known as **behaviorism**, which focuses on how environmental stimuli bring about changes in people's behaviors. In this chapter we will look more closely at this perspective and use behaviorist theories to understand how, as teachers, we can help students acquire behaviors that are perhaps more complex, productive, or prosocial than the ones they exhibit when they first enter our classrooms. In particular, we will address these questions:

- What basic assumptions are central to behaviorists' beliefs about learning?
- How can we explain students' emotional responses to classroom events using the behaviorist notion of classical conditioning?
- What strategies can we use to encourage desirable behaviors in the classroom?
- What behaviorist principles can assist us in our efforts to reduce inappropriate classroom behaviors?
- How can we apply behaviorist principles systematically to address especially difficult classroom behaviors?

CASE STUDY: *The Attention Getter*

James is the sixth child in a family of nine children. He likes many things; for example, he likes rock music, comic books, basketball, and strawberry ice cream. But more than anything else, James likes attention.

James is a skillful attention getter. He gets his teacher's attention by blurting out answers in class, throwing paper clips and erasers in the teacher's direction, and refusing to turn in classroom assignments. He gets the attention of classmates by teasing them, poking them, or writing obscenities on the rest room walls. By the middle of the school year, James is getting an extra bonus as well: His antics send him to the main office often enough that he has the school principal's attention at least once a week.

It's true that the attention James gets is often in the form of a teacher's scolding, a classmate's angry retort, or the principal's admonishment that "We can't have any more of this behavior, young man." But after all—attention is attention.

- Why do you think James chooses such inappropriate behaviors (rather than more appropriate ones) as a way of getting the attention of others? Can you speculate on possible reasons?
- Exactly what has James learned? Can you derive a principle of learning from James's attention-getting behavior?

Basic Assumptions of Behaviorism

As you consider James's situation, think back to your own experiences as a student in elementary and secondary school. Which students received the most attention, those who behaved appropriately or those who behaved inappropriately? Chances are that it was the *misbehaving* students to whom your teachers and classmates paid the most attention (e.g., J. C. Taylor & Romanczyk, 1994). James has undoubtedly learned that if he wants to be noticed—if he wants to stand out in a crowd—then he must behave differently than other students.

Our case study illustrates a basic assumption of behaviorism: People's behaviors are largely the result of their experiences with environmental stimuli. This and other key assumptions that underlie behaviorist views of learning (summarized in Table 9.1) are as follows:

■ *People's behaviors are largely the result of their experiences with environmental stimuli.* Many behaviorists believe that, with the exception of a few simple reflexes, a person is born as a "blank slate" (sometimes referred to by the Latin term *tabula rasa*), with no inherited tendency to behave one way or another. Over the years, the environment "writes" on this slate, slowly molding, or **conditioning**, the individual into an adult who has unique characteristics and ways of behaving.

Is this "blank slate" assumption inconsistent with anything you've read in earlier chapters?

As teachers, we must keep in mind the very significant effect that students' past and present environments are likely to have on their behaviors. We can use this basic principle to our advantage: By changing the environmental events that our students experience, we may also be able to change the way they behave.

■ *Learning can be described in terms of relationships among observable events—that is, relationships among stimuli and responses.* As mentioned in Chapter 6, behaviorists have traditionally believed that phenomena occurring inside a person (thoughts, beliefs, feelings, etc.) cannot be observed and so cannot be studied scientifically. Some behaviorists describe a person as a "black box"—something that cannot be opened for inspection. Psychological inquiry should instead focus on things that can be observed and studied objectively, they say; more specifically, it should focus on the **responses** that learners make (symbolized as *R*s) and the environmental **stimuli** (*S*s) that bring those responses about (e.g., Kimble, 2000).

TABLE 9.1   **PRINCIPLES / ASSUMPTIONS**

Basic Assumptions of Behaviorism and Their Educational Implications

ASSUMPTION	EDUCATIONAL IMPLICATION	EXAMPLE
Influence of the environment	Develop a classroom environment that fosters desirable student behaviors.	When a student often has trouble working independently, inconspicuously praise her every time she completes an assignment without having to be prompted.
Focus on observable events (stimuli and responses)	Identify specific stimuli (including your own behaviors) that may be influencing the behaviors that students exhibit.	If a student frequently engages in disruptive classroom behavior, consider whether you might be encouraging such behavior by giving the student attention every time it occurs.
Learning as a behavior change	Don't assume that learning has occurred unless students exhibit a change in classroom performance.	Look for concrete evidence that learning has taken place rather than assume that students have learned simply because they say they understand what they are studying.
Contiguity of events	If you want students to associate two events (stimuli and/or responses) with each other, make sure those events occur close together in time.	Include enjoyable yet educational activities in each day's schedule as a way of helping students associate school subject matter with pleasurable feelings.
Similarity of learning principles across species	Remember that research with nonhuman species often has relevance for classroom practice.	Reinforce a hyperactive student for sitting quietly for successively longer periods of time—a *shaping* process based on early research studies with rats and pigeons.

Not all behaviorists hold firmly to the black box assumption, however. In recent years, many have begun to incorporate cognitive processes and other internal phenomena into their theoretical explanations (DeGrandpre, 2000; Forsyth & Eifert, 1998; Rachlin, 1991; Rescorla, 1988; B. Schwartz & Reisberg, 1991; A. R. Wagner, 1981). It is becoming increasingly evident, even to behaviorists, just how difficult it is to omit thinking from our explanations of learning and behavior. As you read the chapter, you will find that I occasionally allude to internal phenomena in my discussion of behaviorist principles; in doing so, I reveal my own biases as a cognitive psychologist, and "pure" behaviorists might object.

■ *Learning involves a behavior change.* From a behaviorist perspective, learning itself should be defined as something that can be observed and documented; in other words, it should be defined as a change in behavior. This definition can be especially useful for us as teachers. To illustrate, consider this scenario:

> Your students look at you attentively as you explain a difficult concept. When you finish, you ask, "Any questions?" You look around the room, and not a single hand is raised. "Good," you think, "they all understand."

But *do* your students understand? On the basis of what you've just observed, you really have no idea whether they do or not. Only observable behavior changes—perhaps an improvement in test scores, a greater frequency of independent reading, or a reduction in hitting and kicking—can ultimately tell us that learning has occurred. Accordingly, this idea will resurface as we begin our discussion of assessment in Chapter 15.

■ *Learning is most likely to take place when stimuli and responses occur close together in time.* For stimulus-response relationships to develop, certain events must occur in conjunction with other events. When two events occur at more or less the same time, we say that there is **contiguity** between them. The following two examples illustrate contiguity:

> One of your instructors scowls at you as she hands back the exam she has just corrected. You discover that you have gotten a D− on the exam, and you get an uncomfortable feeling in the pit of your stomach. The next time your instructor scowls at you, that same uncomfortable feeling returns.

> Another instructor smiles and calls on you every time you raise your hand. Although you are fairly quiet in your other classes, you find yourself raising your hand and speaking up more and more frequently in this one.

In the first situation, the instructor's scowl and the D− on your exam are presented more or less simultaneously; here we see contiguity between two stimuli. In the second situation, your response of raising your hand is followed immediately by the instructor's smile and his calling on you; in this case, we see contiguity between a response and two stimuli (although smiling and calling on you are responses that the instructor makes, they are *stimuli* for *you*). In both situations, your behavior has changed: You've learned to respond with an unpleasant feeling in your stomach every time a particular instructor scowls, and you've learned to raise your hand and speak up more frequently in another instructor's class.

■ *Many species of animals, including humans, learn in similar ways.* Behaviorists are well known for their experiments with such animals as rats and pigeons. They assume that many species share similar learning processes; hence, they apply the learning principles that they derive from observing one species to their understanding of how many other species (including humans) learn.

Students in my own educational psychology classes sometimes resent having their own learning compared to the learning of rats and pigeons. But the fact is that behaviorist theories developed from the study of nonhuman animals often *do* explain human behavior. In the pages that follow, we will focus on two behaviorist theories—classical conditioning and operant

"Stimulus, response! Stimulus, response! Don't you ever *think*?"

What animals have you observed learning something new? Can you think of any similarities in the ways that animals and people learn?

conditioning—that have been derived largely from animal research yet can help us understand many aspects of human learning and behavior.

Classical Conditioning

Consider this situation:

Classical conditioning often helps us understand students' feelings about various school activities. This boy's feelings about soccer will be influenced both by his success at the sport and by the quality of his interactions with teammates.

> Alan has always loved baseball. But in a game last year, he was badly hurt by a wild pitch while he was up at bat. Now, although he still plays baseball, he gets anxious whenever it is his turn at bat, to the point where his heart rate increases and he often backs away from the ball instead of swinging at it.

One possible explanation of Alan's learning is **classical conditioning**, a theory that explains how we sometimes learn new responses as a result of two stimuli (in this case, the sight of an oncoming baseball and the pain of the ball's impact) being present at approximately the same time. Alan's current responses to a pitched ball—his physiological feelings of anxiety and his backing away—are ones that he didn't exhibit before his painful experience with a baseball; thus, learning has occurred.

Classical conditioning was first described by Ivan Pavlov (e.g., 1927), a Russian physiologist who was conducting research about salivation. Pavlov often used dogs as his research subjects and presented meat to get them to salivate. He noticed that the dogs frequently began to salivate as soon as they heard the lab assistant coming down the hall, even though they could not yet smell the meat the assistant was carrying. Curious about this phenomenon, Pavlov conducted an experiment to examine more systematically how a dog learns to salivate to a new stimulus. His experiment went something like this:

1. Pavlov flashes a light. The dog does not salivate to the light stimulus. Using *S* for stimulus and *R* for response, we can symbolize Pavlov's first observation like so:

$$S \text{ (light)} \quad \rightarrow \quad R \text{ (none)}$$

2. Pavlov flashes the light again and presents meat immediately afterward. He repeats this procedure several times, and the dog salivates every time. The dog is demonstrating something that it already knows how to do—salivate to meat—so it has not yet learned anything new. We can symbolize Pavlov's second observation like so:

$$\left. \begin{array}{l} S \text{ (light)} \\ S \text{ (meat)} \end{array} \right\} \quad \rightarrow \quad R \text{ (salivation)}$$

3. Pavlov flashes the light once more, but this time without any meat. The dog salivates; in other words, it has learned a new response to the light stimulus. We can symbolize Pavlov's third observation this way:

$$S \text{ (light)} \quad \rightarrow \quad R \text{ (salivation)}$$

In more general terms, classical conditioning proceeds as follows:

1. It begins with a stimulus-response association that already exists—in other words, with an *unconditioned* stimulus-response association. For example, Pavlov's dog salivates automatically whenever it smells meat, and Alan becomes anxious and backs away whenever he encounters a painful stimulus; no learning is involved in either case. When a stimulus leads to a particular response without prior learning, we say that an **unconditioned stimulus (UCS)** *elicits* an **unconditioned response (UCR)**. The unconditioned response is typically an automatic, involuntary one—one over which the learner has little or no control.

2. Conditioning occurs when a **neutral stimulus**—one that doesn't elicit any particular response—is presented immediately before the unconditioned stimulus. For example, in the case of Pavlov's dog, a light is presented immediately before the meat; in the case of Alan, a baseball is pitched immediately before the painful hit. Conditioning is especially likely to occur when both stimuli are presented together on several occasions and when the neutral stimulus occurs *only* when the unconditioned stimulus is about to follow (R. R. Miller & Barnet, 1993; Rachlin, 1991; Rescorla, 1967).

The word *elicit,* meaning "draw forth or bring out," is frequently used in descriptions of classical conditioning.

3. Before long, the new stimulus also elicits a response, usually one very similar to the unconditioned response. The neutral stimulus has become a **conditioned stimulus (CS)** and the response to it a **conditioned response (CR)**. For example, Pavlov's dog acquires a conditioned response of salivation to a new, conditioned stimulus—the light. Likewise, Alan acquires conditioned responses of anxiety and backing away to a pitched baseball. Like the unconditioned response, the conditioned response is an involuntary one; it occurs automatically every time the conditioned stimulus is presented.

Classical Conditioning of Emotional Responses

EXPERIENCING FIRSTHAND   *"Classical" Music*

Some songs make people feel certain ways. For example, Handel's "Water Music" always elicits especially "happy" feelings in me, perhaps because it's the music that was played at my wedding. The theme from the old television show *Dragnet* still elicits tinges of anxiety in me because the show frightened me when I was a young child. Take a minute and think about particular songs you might listen to if you wanted to experience each of the following feelings:

Feeling	Song
Happiness	_____
Relaxation	_____
Anxiety	_____
Sadness	_____

Why do the songs bring out such feelings? Can you trace those feelings to significant occasions in your life when each song was playing?

In some cases, your emotional reactions to a song may be attributable simply to the mood that the song conveys. But in other cases, a song may make you feel the way you do because you associate it with particular events. Consider the case of Brenda:

> At the school dance, Brenda has one dance with Joe, a boy she has a tremendous crush on. They dance to "Michelle," an old Beatles song. Later, whenever Brenda hears "Michelle," she feels happy.

In this situation, Joe is initially the source of Brenda's good feelings. A second stimulus—"Michelle"—is associated with Joe, and so the song begins to elicit those same feelings. From a classical conditioning perspective, we can analyze the situation this way:

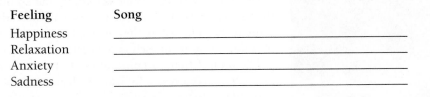

UCS: Joe   →   UCR: good feelings about Joe
CS: "Michelle"   →   CR: good feelings about "Michelle"

Following are some other examples of how emotional responses might be learned through classical conditioning. Notice that in every case, two stimuli are presented together. One stimulus already elicits a response, and as a result of the pairing, the second stimulus begins to elicit a similar response.

> Bernard falls into a swimming pool and almost drowns. A year later, when his mother takes him to the local recreation center for a swimming lesson, he cries hysterically as she tries to drag him to the side of the pool.

UCS: inability to breathe   →   UCR: fear of being unable to breathe
CS: swimming pool   →   CR: fear of the swimming pool

> Bobby misses a month of school because of illness. When he returns to school, he does not know how to do his long division assignments. After a number of frustrating experiences in which he cannot solve long division problems, he begins to feel anxious whenever he encounters a division task.

UCS: failure/frustration   →   UCR: anxiety about failure
CS: long division   →   CR: anxiety about long division

The best part of third grade was
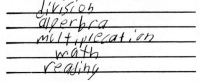
division
algebra
multiplication
math
reading

In a personal "yearbook," Ashton identifies math and reading as being the best part of his third-grade year. He clearly associates these subjects with pleasure rather than anxiety.

Do you remember the earlier example of learning to respond negatively to an instructor's scowl? Can you explain your learning from the perspective of classical conditioning?

Beth's teacher catches Beth writing a letter to one of her classmates during class. The teacher reads the note to the entire class, revealing some very personal and private information about Beth. Beth now feels embarrassed whenever she goes into that teacher's classroom.

UCS: humiliation   →   *UCR:* embarrassment in response to humiliation

CS: teacher/classroom   →   *CR:* embarrassment in response to teacher/classroom

Classical conditioning is frequently used to explain why people sometimes respond emotionally to what might otherwise be fairly "neutral" stimuli. When a particular stimulus is associated with something that makes us happy or relaxed, it may begin to elicit those same feelings of happiness or relaxation. When a stimulus is associated with something that makes us fearful or anxious, it, too, may begin to elicit feelings of fear and anxiety.

When students associate school with pleasant stimuli, they learn that school is a place where they want to be.

As teachers, we must maintain a classroom whose stimuli (including our own behaviors toward students) are those likely to elicit such responses as enjoyment or relaxation, *not* fear or anxiety. When students associate school with pleasant stimuli—positive feedback, enjoyable activities, and so on—they soon learn that school is a place where they want to be. But when they instead encounter unpleasant stimuli in school—negative comments, public humiliation, or constant frustration and failure—they may eventually learn to fear or dislike a particular activity, subject area, teacher, or (perhaps) school in general.

Generalization

When people learn a conditioned response to a new stimulus, they may also respond in the same way to similar stimuli—a phenomenon known as **generalization.** For example, a boy who learns to feel anxious about long division tasks may generalize that anxiety to other aspects of mathematics. And a girl who experiences humiliation in one classroom may generalize her embarrassment to other classrooms as well. In behaviorist theory, generalization is the primary means through which learners *transfer* what they have learned in one setting to new situations. Here we see one more reason why students should associate pleasant feelings with classroom subject matter. Students' reactions to school and class activities may generalize (transfer) to situations far beyond the classroom itself.

Extinction

Pavlov discovered that conditioned responses don't necessarily last forever. By pairing a light with meat, he conditioned a dog to salivate to the light alone. But later, when he flashed the light repeatedly without ever again following it with meat, the dog salivated less and less. Eventually, the dog no longer salivated when it saw the light flash. When a conditioned stim-

---

INTO THE CLASSROOM: *Applying Principles of Classical Conditioning*

Create a positive classroom environment.

A third-grade teacher plans many activities that make classroom learning enjoyable. He never ridicules students for mistakes they may make.

Be sure that students associate success with all areas of the curriculum.

A high school mathematics teacher takes a mastery approach to teaching algebra, making sure that her stu-

dents master each concept and procedure before moving to more advanced material.

When a particular subject or task arouses anxiety in students, present it slowly and gradually while they are happy and relaxed.

When teaching a water-phobic child to swim, a swimming instructor begins the first lesson by playing games in the baby pool, moving to deeper water very gradually as the child seems comfortable about doing so.

ulus occurs repeatedly *in the absence of* the unconditioned stimulus—for example, when a light is never again associated with meat, when mathematics is never again associated with failure, or when a teacher is never again associated with humiliation—the conditioned response may decrease and eventually disappear. In other words, **extinction** occurs.

Many conditioned responses fade over time. Unfortunately, many others do not; a person's fear of water or anxiety about mathematics may persist for years. One reason that fears and anxieties may continue over time is that people tend to avoid those situations that cause such emotional reactions. If they stay away from a stimulus that makes them fearful, they never have a chance to experience that stimulus in the absence of the unconditioned stimulus with which it was originally paired. As a result, they have no opportunity to learn *not* to be afraid—they have no opportunity for the response to undergo extinction.

As teachers, how can we reduce the counterproductive conditioned responses that our students may exhibit—for example, their fear of water or their mathematics anxiety? Psychologists have learned that one way to extinguish a negative emotional reaction to a particular conditioned stimulus is to introduce that stimulus *slowly and gradually* while the student is happy or relaxed (M. C. Jones, 1924; Wolpe, 1969). For example, if Bernard is afraid of water, we might begin his swimming lessons someplace where he feels at ease—perhaps on dry land or in the baby pool—and move to deeper water only as he begins to feel more comfortable. If Bobby gets overly anxious every time he attempts a mathematics problem, we might revert back to easier problems—those he can readily solve—and gradually increase the difficulty of his assignments only as he demonstrates greater competence and self-confidence.

There is nothing like success to help students feel good about being in the classroom. One thing we can do to promote student success is structure the classroom environment so that appropriate behaviors are reinforced and inappropriate behaviors are not. It is to the role that reinforcement plays in learning—to operant conditioning—that we turn now.

We will consider the nature and effects of anxiety in more detail in Chapter 11.

Operant Conditioning

Mark is a student in Ms. Ferguson's geography class. This is what happens to Mark during the first week in October:

Monday. Ms. Ferguson asks the class to locate Colombia on the globe. Mark knows where Colombia is, and he sits smiling, with his hands in his lap, hoping that Ms. Ferguson will call on him. Instead, Ms. Ferguson calls on another student.

Tuesday. Ms. Ferguson asks the class where Colombia got its name. Mark knows that Colombia is named after Christopher Columbus, so he raises his hand a few inches. Ms. Ferguson calls on another student.

Wednesday. Ms. Ferguson asks the class why people in Colombia speak Spanish rather than English or French. Mark knows that Colombians speak Spanish because the country's early European settlers came from Spain. He raises his hand high in the air. Ms. Ferguson calls on another student.

Thursday. Ms. Ferguson asks the class why Colombia grows coffee but Canada does not. Mark knows that coffee can be grown only in certain climates. He raises his hand high and waves it wildly back and forth. Ms. Ferguson calls on him.

Friday. Whenever Ms. Ferguson asks a question that Mark can answer, Mark raises his hand high and waves it wildly about.

Notice how several of Mark's behaviors in geography class, such as sitting quietly, smiling, and raising his hand politely, bring no results. But waving his hand wildly does bring Mark the result that he wants: his teacher's attention. The response that has attracted Ms. Ferguson's attention continues. Other responses disappear.

The change in Mark's behavior illustrates **operant conditioning**, a form of learning described by many behaviorists and most notably by B. F. Skinner (e.g., 1953, 1954, 1968). The basic principle of operant conditioning is a simple one:

A response that is followed by a reinforcing stimulus (a reinforcer) is more likely to occur again.

When behaviors are followed by desirable consequences, they tend to increase in frequency. When behaviors don't produce results, they typically decrease and may even disappear altogether.

Students often learn and demonstrate new behaviors for the consequences those behaviors bring. Following are some examples:

Sergio brings a fancy new bicycle to school and finds himself surrounded by classmates who want to ride it. Suddenly Sergio has several new "friends."

Samirah decreases the number of steps that she takes when she bowls. She now gets more strikes and spares than she used to.

Shawn studies hard for his French vocabulary quiz. He gets an A on the quiz.

Sharon copies her answers to the French quiz from Shawn's paper. She, too, gets an A on the quiz.

Many appropriate and productive behaviors—such as studying French or trying a new approach to bowling—are acquired because of the desirable consequences to which they lead. Many inappropriate and undesirable behaviors—such as cheating on a quiz or waving one's hand wildly about—may be acquired for the same reason.

Operant conditioning can occur only under two conditions. First, of course, the learner must make a response; that is, the learner must *do* something. Behaviorists believe that little is accomplished by having students sit quietly and listen passively to their teacher; instead, students are more likely to learn when they are making active, overt responses in the classroom (e.g., Drevno et al., 1994). Second, the reinforcer should be **contingent** on the learner's response; that is, it should occur when, and *only* when, the desired response has occurred. A teacher who praises students only when they behave appropriately is making reinforcement contingent on desired behavior. In contrast, the teacher who laughs at the antics of a chronically misbehaving student is providing reinforcement even when an acceptable response hasn't occurred, so the student's behavior is unlikely to improve.

As teachers, we should be sure to reinforce the behaviors we want our students to learn and acquire. If we want students to read frequently, volunteer in class, demonstrate good form in dribbling and passing a soccer ball, or work cooperatively with their classmates, we should reinforce such behaviors as they occur. At the same time, we should be careful *not* to reinforce any inappropriate and counterproductive behaviors that students exhibit. If we repeatedly allow Jane to turn in assignments late because she tells us that she forgot her homework and if we often let Jake get his way by bullying his classmates on the playground, then we are reinforcing (and hence increasing) Jane's excuse making and Jake's aggressiveness.

As teachers, we must consider how our own actions affect students' behavior. This teacher is reinforcing one student's diligence at the plant center with attention and affection.

How is the concept of *contingency* different from *contiguity*?

Contrasting Classical and Operant Conditioning

Like classical conditioning, operant conditioning involves both a stimulus and a response. But operant conditioning is different from classical conditioning in two important ways:

- *The way in which conditioning comes about.* Classical conditioning results from the *pairing of two stimuli,* one (the UCS) that initially elicits a response and another (the CS) that begins to elicit the same or a similar response. In contrast, operant conditioning occurs when *a response is followed by a reinforcer.*
- *The nature of the response.* In classical conditioning, the response is involuntary: When a particular (conditioned) stimulus is present, the response follows almost automatically. For example, Alan doesn't *choose* to be anxious about a baseball pitched in his direction; he simply *is* anxious. In operant conditioning, however, the response is usually a voluntary one: The learner can control whether or not it occurs. For example, when, in the opening case study, James blurts out answers, throws erasers across the room, or teases classmates, he is willingly behaving in these ways. No particular stimulus is forcing him to do so.

Reinforcement in the Classroom

EXPERIENCING FIRSTHAND   *What Would It Take?*

Imagine this scenario:

You are currently enrolled in my educational psychology class. As your instructor, I ask you to spend an hour after class tutoring two classmates who are having difficulty understanding the course material. You have no other commitments for that hour, but you'd really rather spend the time at a nearby coffee shop where you know several of your friends are having lunch. What would it take for you to spend the hour tutoring your classmates instead of joining your friends? Would you do it to gain my approval? Would you do it if I gave you a candy bar? Would you do it if I gave you five dollars? Would you do it simply because it made you feel good inside to be helping someone else? Write down a reward—perhaps one I have listed or perhaps a different one altogether—that would persuade you to help your classmates instead of meeting your friends.

Now imagine this second scenario:

A few weeks later, I ask you to spend the weekend (eight hours a day on both Saturday and Sunday) tutoring the same two struggling classmates. What would it take this time to convince you to do the job? Would my approval do the trick? Would a candy bar? five dollars? five *hundred* dollars? Or would your internal sense of satisfaction be enough? Once again, write down what it would take for you to agree to help your classmates.

Obviously, there are no right answers for the exercise you just completed. Different people would agree to tutor their classmates for different reasons. But you were probably able to identify at least one consequence in each situation that would entice you to give up your own personal time to help your classmates.

We often talk about giving students rewards for their academic achievements and for appropriate classroom behaviors. But as you may have noticed, I have not used the term *reward* in my description of operant conditioning, and for a very important reason. The word *reward* brings to mind things we would all agree are pleasant and desirable—things like candy, praise, money, trophies, or special privileges. But some individuals increase their behavior for consequences that others would not find so appealing. A **reinforcer** is *any consequence that increases the frequency of a particular behavior,* whether other people find that consequence pleasant or not. The act of following a particular response with a reinforcer is called **reinforcement.**

Let's return once again to our attention-getting student. James learned that he could get his teacher's attention by blurting out answers in class, throwing objects around the room, and refusing to turn in classroom assignments. We can assume that James's teacher is not smiling or praising him for such behavior. Probably the teacher is frowning, scolding, or even yelling. We don't usually think of frowning, scolding, and yelling as rewards. Yet those consequences are leading to an increase in James's misbehaviors, so they are apparently reinforcing for James.

Reinforcement comes in all shapes and sizes. In the next few pages we will look at two basic distinctions that operant conditioning theorists make—primary versus secondary reinforcers, and positive versus negative reinforcement—and in the process will identify a number of potentially effective reinforcers in classroom settings. We will then consider how both timing and motivation influence a reinforcer's effectiveness.

Recall that behaviorists focus on stimuli and responses. Which of these is reinforcement: a *stimulus* or a *response?*

Primary Versus Secondary Reinforcers

A **primary reinforcer** satisfies a basic physiological need; food, water, warmth, and oxygen are all examples. To some extent, physical affection and cuddling may address biological needs as well (Harlow & Zimmerman, 1959; Vollmer & Hackenberg, 2001). And for an adolescent addicted to an illegal substance, the next "fix" is also a primary reinforcer (Lejuez, Schaal, & O'Donnell, 1998).

In contrast, a **secondary reinforcer** does not satisfy any physiological need yet becomes reinforcing over time through its association with another reinforcer. For example, perhaps praise was once associated with a special candy treat from mother, or a good grade was associated with a hug from father. Through such associations, consequences such as praise, good grades, money, feelings of success, and perhaps even scolding become reinforcing in their own right: They become secondary reinforcers.

Secondary reinforcers are far more common in classrooms than primary reinforcers. But we must remember that secondary reinforcers are *learned* reinforcers, and not everyone has come to appreciate them. Although most of our students will probably respond positively to such consequences as praise or a good grade, a few students may not.

GARFIELD / Jim Davis

Positive Versus Negative Reinforcement

Up to this point, we have been speaking of reinforcement as the *presentation* of a particular reinforcing stimulus. But in some cases, we can also reinforce a behavior through the *removal* of a stimulus. Operant conditioning theorists distinguish between these two situations by using the terms *positive reinforcement* and *negative reinforcement*.

Positive reinforcement. Whenever a particular stimulus is *presented* after a behavior, and the behavior increases as a result, positive reinforcement has occurred. This is the case whether or not the presented stimulus is one that others would agree is pleasant and desirable. For instance, some students will make a response to get a teacher's praise, but others (like James in our case study) may behave to get themselves a scolding. Most students will work for As, but a few may actually prefer Cs or even Fs. Depending on the individual, any one of these stimuli—the praise, the scolding, the A, or the F—may be a positive reinforcer. Following are examples of the forms that positive reinforcement may take:

- A **concrete reinforcer** is an actual object—something that can be touched (e.g., a snack, a sticker, or a toy). Concrete reinforcers are especially likely to be effective with young children (e.g., Rimm & Masters, 1974).
- A **social reinforcer** is a gesture or sign (e.g., a smile, a hug, attention, praise, or "thank you") that one person gives another for a certain behavior. As teachers, we can often use simple social gestures—smiles, compliments, nods of approval, and expressions of appreciation—as classroom reinforcers (L. Katz, 1993; Piersel, 1987; Schepis, Reid, & Fitzgerald, 1987). We can also provide opportunities for students to reinforce one another for desirable academic and social behaviors (G. W. Evans & Oswalt, 1968; Northup et al., 1995).
- An **activity reinforcer** is an opportunity to engage in a favorite activity. Students will often do one thing, even something they don't like to do, if doing so enables them to do something they do enjoy; this phenomenon is sometimes called the **Premack principle** (Premack, 1959, 1963). For example, students are more likely to sit quietly if being quiet enables them to go to lunch. And students at risk for dropping out of school are more likely to come to school regularly if a good attendance record will earn them a trip to a local amusement park (M. G. Sanders, 1996).
- Sometimes the simple message that an answer is correct or that a task has been done well—**positive feedback**—is reinforcement enough. Positive feedback is most effective when it tells students in explicit terms what they are doing well and what they can do to improve their performance even further (Bangert-Drowns, Kulik, Kulik, & Morgan, 1991; D. L. Butler & Winne, 1995; Feltz, Chaase, Moritz, & Sullivan, 1999). As an example, see Figure 9.1.

The reinforcers just listed are **extrinsic reinforcers**, those provided by the external environment (often by other people). Yet positive reinforcers may also be **intrinsic reinforcers**, those supplied by learners themselves or inherent in the tasks being performed. Students engage in some activities simply because they enjoy those activities or because they like to feel competent and successful. When students perform certain behaviors in the absence of any observable reinforcers—when they read an entire book without putting it down, when they do extra classwork without being asked, when they practice on their electric guitars into the wee hours of the morning—they are probably working for the intrinsic reinforcement that such

---

Science Fiction Book Project

Name Matt

Title 20,000 Leagues under The Sea

Author Jules Verne

Type of project:
Comic strip

Presentation:
Very good summary and description of your project.   A

Project:
Excellent drawings, Matt! Captions in a strip should tell more of the story, though. You don't show how/why these places are connected.   A-

FIGURE 9.1 In commenting on Matt's book project, the teacher is explicit about what he can do to improve but vague about what he has done well. Knowing what *specific* things made his summary and project description "very good" would help Matt repeat these things in the future.

behaviors yield. Intrinsic reinforcers are *not* observable events; as such, they do not fit comfortably within traditional behaviorist theory. Yet people clearly do engage in some behaviors solely for the intrinsic satisfaction that those behaviors bring. We will talk more about such *intrinsic motivation* in Chapters 11 and 12.

From our perspective as teachers, positive feedback (an extrinsic reinforcer) and the feelings of pleasure and satisfaction that such feedback can bring (intrinsic reinforcers) are probably the most desirable forms of classroom reinforcement. Yet we must remember that the classroom successes that yield such forms of reinforcement can occur only when classroom instruction has been carefully tailored to individual skill levels and abilities, and only when students have learned to value academic achievement. When students are not motivated to achieve academic success (for whatever reasons), then social reinforcers, activity reinforcers, and (if necessary) even concrete reinforcers can be used to increase desired classroom behaviors.

How might you determine which reinforcers are most effective for your students?

EXPERIENCING FIRSTHAND   *Take Two on "What Would It Take?"*

In a preceding exercise, you considered what would entice you to spend time tutoring classmates when you'd really rather join your friends at the local coffee shop. For each one of these consequences of tutoring your classmates, determine the kind of reinforcer it reflects:

Consequence	Kind of Reinforcer
You gain my approval.	_____
You get a candy bar.	_____
You get five dollars.	_____
You feel good about helping somebody else.	_____

You can find the correct answers below—but no peeking until you've made your own decisions!

Answer key: My approval is a social reinforcer, the candy bar and the money are concrete reinforcers, and feeling good about what you have done is an intrinsic reinforcer. Of these, only the candy bar is a primary reinforcer; the other three are secondary reinforcers.

Negative reinforcement.   As we have just seen, positive reinforcement involves the presentation of a stimulus. In contrast, negative reinforcement brings about the increase of a behavior through the *removal* of a stimulus (typically an unpleasant one). The word *negative* here is not a value judgment; it simply refers to the act of taking away a stimulus.[1] When people make a response to get rid of something, they are being negatively reinforced. We saw an example of negative reinforcement in our opening case study. When James misbehaved, he was often sent to the principal's office; this negatively reinforced his behavior because it enabled him to *get out of class*, thereby removing a stimulus—the class environment—that may have been aversive for him. (If James liked spending time with the principal, then he was receiving positive reinforcement as well.)

Following are additional examples of negative reinforcement:

A rat is getting an electric shock through the floor of its cage. It learns to press a metal bar to terminate the shock.

What stimulus is removed in each case? What response is being reinforced as a result?

Rhonda must read *Ivanhoe* for her English literature class before the end of the month. She doesn't like having this assignment hanging over her head, so she finishes it early. When she's done, she no longer has to worry about it.

Reuben is in the same literature class. Whenever he sits down at home to read *Ivanhoe*, he finds the novel confusing and difficult to understand. He quickly ends his study sessions by finding other things that he "needs" to do instead—things like playing basketball with his friends, washing his hair, or folding his laundry.

Ms. Randolph yells at her rowdy seventh graders. They quiet down. By yelling, Ms. Randolph terminates a noisy and unpleasant situation, even if only temporarily.

---

[1] You might draw an analogy between positive and negative reinforcement and positive and negative numbers. Positive numbers and positive reinforcement both *add* something to a situation. Negative numbers and negative reinforcement both *subtract* something from a situation.

In the examples just presented, notice how negative reinforcement sometimes promotes desirable behaviors (such as completing an assignment early) and at other times promotes undesirable behaviors (such as procrastination). Notice, as well, how students are not the only ones who respond to reinforcement in the classroom. After all, teachers are human beings too!

As teachers, we will use negative reinforcement rarely if at all; ideally, we want to create a classroom environment in which there are few stimuli that students want to be rid of. Nevertheless, we should recognize that negative reinforcement *does* have an effect on behavior. Some students may finish an assignment more to "get it out of the way" than for any intrinsic satisfaction that the assignment brings. Others may engage in inappropriate classroom behavior as a way of avoiding the assignment altogether. When certain responses enable students to remove unpleasant stimuli—perhaps classroom assignments or perhaps even the classroom itself—those responses will increase in frequency.

Importance of Timing

In B. F. Skinner's original conception of operant conditioning, reinforcement is likely to be effective only if it occurs *immediately* after a desired response has occurred; in other words, the response and the reinforcing stimulus should occur in close contiguity. Considerable research indicates that timing does make a difference: The more closely a reinforcer follows a response, the more effective it is likely to be (J. A. Kulik & Kulik, 1988; Rachlin, 1991).

Yet as children get older, they become better able to **delay gratification**: They can forego small, immediate reinforcers for the larger reinforcers that their long-term efforts are likely to bring down the road (Green, Fry, & Myerson, 1994; Rotenberg & Mayer, 1990). Whereas a preschooler is likely to choose a small reinforcer she can have *now* over a larger and more attractive reinforcer she cannot get until tomorrow, an 8-year-old is more willing to wait a day or two for the more appealing item. Many adolescents can delay gratification for weeks at a time. For instance, as a 16-year-old, my son Jeff worked long hours stocking shelves at the local grocery store (hardly a rewarding activity!) to earn enough money to pay half the cost of a $400-a-night limousine for the junior prom.

Some children and adolescents are better able to delay gratification than others, and those who can are less likely to yield to temptation, more carefully plan their future actions, and achieve at higher levels in academic settings (Durkin, 1995; Shoda, Mischel, & Peake, 1990; Veroff, McClelland, & Ruhland, 1975). However, even 4- and 5-year olds can learn to delay gratification for a few hours if their teachers tell them that rewards for desired behaviors (such as sharing toys with other children) will be coming later in the day (Fowler & Baer, 1981). Teaching children effective "waiting" strategies—for example, encouraging them to focus their attention on something else during the duration, or teaching them such self-talk as "If I wait a little longer, I will get the bigger one"—enhances their ability to delay gratification as well (Binder, Dixon, & Ghezzi, 2000).

Role of Motivation

In the opening case study, James engages in a variety of inappropriate behaviors to gain the attention of his teacher, his classmates, and sometimes his principal. Students are far more likely to misbehave if they have very little social contact with others *unless* they misbehave (McGill, 1999). We might reasonably guess that James would prefer more appropriate interactions with adults and peers, yet for whatever reasons (perhaps because his academic performance rarely gains his teacher's praise, perhaps because his social skills are insufficient to make and maintain friendships) he seldom has such interactions.

We will look at motivation in more detail in Chapters 11 and 12, but for now we should note that motivation plays a significant role in determining the consequences that students find reinforcing (McGill, 1999; Michael, 2000). For example, some students (like James) may thrive on teacher scoldings even though others dislike them. Some students may respond well to praise, but others (perhaps those who don't want to be labeled "teacher's pet" by their peers) may view a teacher's praise as a fate worse than death (e.g., Pfiffner, Rosen, & O'Leary, 1985). Some students may work at academic tasks simply for the feelings of success and accomplishment that such activities bring, but others may work diligently at the same tasks only if doing so leads to social benefits—perhaps the respect of classmates or the opportunity to spend time with friends. Some students like get-

---

Did you previously think of negative reinforcement as something that leads to a *decrease* in behavior? If so, have you revised your understanding of this concept?

Can you use the concept of *working memory* (Chapter 6) to explain why immediate reinforcement might be better than delayed reinforcement?

Ideally, students should perceive class activities as interesting and enjoyable challenges rather than as boring, tedious tasks to complete as quickly as possible. In other words, positive reinforcement should be far more common than negative reinforcement.

ting As, but others (perhaps those afraid of being labeled a "nerd") may actually prefer Cs. An important principle of operant conditioning, then, is that *different stimuli are reinforcing for different individuals*. We must never make assumptions about what specific events are reinforcing for particular students.

At this point, let's stop for a moment to examine one teacher's use of reinforcement to encourage desired classroom behavior.

INTERPRETING ARTIFACTS AND INTERACTIONS   *Paper Trophy*

At the end of the school year, a kindergarten teacher awards paper "trophies" to each of her students. Five-year-old Katie receives the trophy depicted here. As you look at the trophy, consider

- What kind of reinforcement it represents
- How effective the reinforcement is likely to be

SPORTSMANSHIP TROPHY

EARNED BY
Katie
FOR EXCELLENT ATTITUDE

AWARDED BY
Mrs. Praul

The trophy is a secondary, positive reinforcer. If it were an *actual* trophy, it would be a concrete reinforcer, but in its paper version, it is probably better classified as positive feedback. Although the teacher's intentions are good, the trophy is likely to have limited impact on Katie's future behavior. For one thing, it is awarded at the end of the school year, so it is neither immediate nor contingent on a particular behavior. Second, because Katie is only 5 years old, she thinks about the world in a concrete rather than abstract fashion (see Chapter 2) and so may have difficulty understanding what an "excellent attitude" is or how it relates to her own behavior (McMillan et al., 1994).

Using Reinforcement Effectively

As teachers, we may often want to use reinforcement to help students behave more productively. Several strategies will increase the likelihood that our use of reinforcement is effective:

- *Specify the desired behavior at the beginning.* Behaviorists recommend that we describe, up front, the behavior we want students to learn and demonstrate. They further urge us to describe this end result—the **terminal behavior**—in specific, concrete, observable terms. Rather than talk about the need for students to "learn world history," we might instead talk about students being able to describe the antecedents and consequences of World War I. Rather than say that students should "learn responsibility," we might instead talk about their need to follow instructions, bring the necessary books and supplies to class every day, and turn in assignments by the due date. By specifying the terminal behavior at the very beginning, we give both ourselves and our students a target to shoot for (see the discussion of *instructional objectives* in Chapter 13), and we can better determine whether we are, in fact, making progress toward that target.

■ *Identify consequences that are truly reinforcing for each student.* The use of reinforcement is far more effective when reinforcers are tailored to individual students than when the same consequences are used for everyone (e.g., Pfiffner et al., 1985). How can we determine which reinforcers are likely to be effective with particular students? One approach is to ask students themselves (or perhaps their parents) about the consequences they find especially appealing. Another approach is to observe students' behaviors, keeping a lookout for consequences that students seem to appreciate. The one thing that we don't want to do is *guess* about the reinforcers we should use.

In some cases, we can let students choose their own reinforcers, and perhaps even choose different reinforcers on different occasions (L. G. Bowman, Piazza, Fisher, Hagopian, & Kogan, 1997; Fisher & Mazur, 1997). One mechanism through which we can do this is a **token economy**, whereby students who exhibit desired behaviors receive *tokens* (poker chips, specially marked pieces of colored paper, etc.) that they can later use to "purchase" a variety of **backup reinforcers**—perhaps small treats, free time in the reading center, or a prime position in the lunch line.

Whenever possible, however, we should stay away from concrete reinforcers such as toys and candy. Such reinforcers can be expensive, and they also distract students' attention away from the task at hand—their schoolwork. Fortunately, many nontangible reinforcers can be effective with school-age children and adolescents, including positive feedback, special privileges, favorite activities, and parental reinforcement at home for school behaviors (e.g., Feltz et al., 1999; Homme, deBaca, Devine, Steinhorst, & Rickert, 1963; Kelley & Carper, 1988).

Playing a team sport is an example of a behavior reinforced by a group contingency: The team wins together or loses together.

■ *When trying to encourage the same behavior in a group of students, consider using a group contingency.* Up to this point, we have been talking about reinforcing students for their own, individual behaviors. But positive reinforcement can also take the form of a **group contingency**: Students are reinforced only when *everyone* in a particular group (perhaps a cooperative learning group, perhaps an entire class) achieves at a certain level or behaves appropriately. Group contingencies are clearly effective in improving academic achievement and classroom behavior, provided that everyone in the group is capable of making the desired response (Barbetta, 1990; Lentz, 1988). Consider the following examples as evidence:

A class of 32 fourth graders was not doing very well on weekly spelling tests. On average, only 12 students (38%) had perfect spelling tests in any given week. Hoping for improvement, their teacher announced that any student with a perfect test score would get free time later in the week. The new reinforcement program had a noticeable effect: The average number of perfect spelling tests rose to 25 a week (80%). But then the teacher added a group contingency: Whenever the entire class achieved perfect spelling tests by Friday, the class could listen to the radio for 15 minutes. The group contingency produced an average of 30 perfect spelling tests (94%) a week (Lovitt, Guppy, & Blattner, 1969).

Another fourth-grade teacher was dealing with an unusually unruly class: In any given minute, chances were that one or more students would be talking out of turn or getting out of their seats. In a desperate move, the teacher divided the class into two teams that competed in a "good behavior game." Each time a student was observed talking out of turn or getting out of his or her seat, the student's team received a chalk mark on the chalkboard. The team that received fewer marks during a lesson won special privileges— for example, being first in the lunch line or having free time at the end of the day. When both teams had five marks or fewer, everyone won privileges. Misbehaviors in the class dropped almost immediately to less than 20 percent of their initial frequency (Barrish, Saunders, & Wolf, 1969).

Group contingencies are probably effective for at least two reasons. One reason may be peer pressure: Students encourage their classmates to achieve and behave appropriately, and they then reinforce those classmates for doing so (O'Leary & O'Leary, 1972). Furthermore, students begin to tutor one another in academic subjects, a practice that enhances achievement (e.g., Pigott, Fantuzzo, & Clement, 1986). Group contingencies play an important role in *cooperative learning,* an instructional strategy we will discuss in Chapter 13.

■ *Make response-consequence contingencies explicit.* Reinforcement is more likely to be effective when students know exactly what consequences will follow various behaviors. For example, kindergarten students are more likely to respond appropriately when they are told, "The quietest group will be first to get in line for lunch." High school students are more likely to complete their Spanish assignments if they know that by doing so they will be able to take a field trip to a local Cinco de Mayo festival.

One explicit way of communicating our expectations is through a **contingency contract.** To develop such a contract, the teacher meets with a student to discuss a problem behavior (e.g., perhaps the student has a tendency to talk to friends during independent seatwork or makes rude comments to classmates). The teacher and student then identify and agree on desired behaviors that the student will demonstrate (e.g., completing seatwork assignments within a certain time frame or speaking with classmates in a friendly and respectful manner). The two also agree on one or more reinforcers for those behaviors (e.g., a certain amount of free time or points earned toward a particular privilege or prize) that the student values. Together the teacher and the student write and sign a contract that describes both the behaviors that the student will perform and the reinforcers that will result. Contingency contracts have consistently been shown to be an effective strategy for improving a wide variety of academic and social behaviors (Brooke & Ruthren, 1984; D. L. Miller & Kelley, 1994; Rueger & Liberman, 1984; Welch, 1985).

■ *When giving reinforcement publicly, make sure that all students have an opportunity to earn it.* In our attempts to improve the behavior of some students, we may unintentionally slight other, equally deserving students. Furthermore, some students may be unable to exhibit particular behaviors through no fault of their own. Consider the case of Dung, a Vietnamese immigrant whose family circumstances were such that he was always late to school:

> [E]very week on Friday after school, the teacher would give little presents to kids that were good during the week. And if you were tardy, you wouldn't get a present. . . . I would never get one because I would always come to school late, and that hurt at first. I had a terrible time. I didn't look forward to going to school. (Igoa, 1995, p. 95)

Ultimately, school should be a place where *all* of our students can, in one way or another, earn reinforcement and in other ways be successful. Classrooms are busy places, however, and it may be all too easy to overlook a few students who desperately want and need our attention. In such cases, we can explicitly *teach* them appropriate ways of seeking out and getting reinforcement—for instance, by raising their hands or walking quietly to our desks at an appropriate time, asking questions (e.g., "How am I doing?" "What do I do next?"), and keeping us informed of their progress ("Look, I'm all finished!") (Craft, Alberg, & Heward, 1998; K. A. Meyer, 1999).

■ *Administer reinforcement consistently.* As you might guess, responses increase more quickly when they are reinforced each and every time they occur—that is, when they lead to **continuous reinforcement.** As teachers, we will see more rapid improvements in our students' behavior if we reinforce desired responses whenever we observe them. Continuous reinforcement, then, is most important when students are first *learning* a behavior. Once they have mastered it and exhibit it frequently, we may want to reinforce it less often (more about the advantages of such *intermittent reinforcement* later in the chapter).

■ *Monitor students' progress.* When we use reinforcement in the classroom, behaviorists urge us to determine, as objectively as possible, whether our efforts are bringing about the desired results. More specifically, they urge us to assess the frequency of the terminal behavior both before and during our attempts to increase it through operant conditioning. The frequency of a behavior *before* we intentionally begin reinforcement is called the **baseline** level of that behavior. Some behaviors occur frequently even when they are not being explicitly reinforced, whereas other behaviors occur rarely or not at all.

By comparing the baseline frequency of a response with its frequency after we begin reinforcing it, we can determine whether the reinforcer we are using is actually bringing about a behavior change. As an example, let's look once again at James in the opening case study. James rarely turns in classroom assignments; this is a behavior with a low baseline. An obvious reinforcer to use with James is attention, a consequence that, until now, has effectively reinforced such counterproductive behaviors as blurting out answers in class and throwing objects across the room. When we make our attention contingent on James's turning in assignments, rather than on his refusals to do so, we should see an almost immediate increase in the number of assignments we receive from James. If we see no significant change in James's behavior, we need to consider alternative reinforcers; in other words, we need to find out what it will take for James to work productively in the classroom.

But what if a desired behavior has a baseline level of *zero?* How can we encourage behaviors that students never exhibit at all? Operant conditioning theorists provide a solution to this problem: the process of shaping.

Shaping New Behaviors

Consider this situation:

> Donald seems very shy and withdrawn. He rarely interacts with other students, either in class or on the playground. When he is in a situation where he must interact with a classmate, he doesn't seem to know how to behave.

Donald has apparently not learned how to interact effectively with his classmates. How might we help Donald develop appropriate social behaviors when the baseline level for such behaviors is essentially zero?

When a desired behavior occurs rarely or not at all, we can use a procedure called **shaping**. Shaping is a process of reinforcing a series of responses that increasingly resemble the desired terminal behavior; that is, it involves reinforcing successively closer and closer approximations to that behavior. To shape a new response, we

1. First reinforce any response that in some way resembles the terminal behavior
2. Then reinforce a response that more closely approximates the terminal behavior (no longer reinforcing the previously reinforced response)
3. Then reinforce a response that resembles the terminal behavior even more closely
4. Continue reinforcing closer and closer approximations to the terminal behavior
5. Finally reinforce only the terminal behavior

Each response in the sequence is reinforced every time it occurs until we see it regularly. Only at that point do we begin reinforcing a behavior that more closely approaches the terminal behavior.

To illustrate this process, let's consider how we might shape Donald's social behavior. We might first reinforce him for something that he occasionally does, such as smiling at a classmate. After we begin to see him smiling frequently (perhaps after a few days or weeks), we might reinforce him only when he makes a verbal response to the comments or questions of a classmate. When that behavior occurs frequently, we might reinforce him only when he initiates a conversation. Later steps to take would be reinforcing Donald for approaching a group of peers, for suggesting a group activity, and so on (see Figure 9.2).

Donald is extremely shy and rarely interacts with his classmates. We can teach him social skills through a process of *shaping*—that is, by reinforcing a series of successively more social behaviors. For example, we can reinforce Donald for: (1) smiling at a classmate, (2) responding appropriately to a classmate's question, (3) initiating a conversation with a single classmate, then (4) initiating interaction with a larger group.

FIGURE 9.2 Shaping Donald's social behavior

As teachers, we must remember that it may often be unreasonable to expect students to make drastic changes in their behavior overnight. When we want them to exhibit responses radically different from the things they are doing now, we may need to shape their behavior by first reinforcing one small step in the right direction, then by reinforcing another small step, and then yet another, until eventually the desired terminal behavior is achieved. If we want rambunctious Bernadette to sit still for twenty-minute periods, we may first have to reinforce her for staying in her seat for just *two* minutes, gradually increasing the "sitting" time required for reinforcement as she makes progress. In much the same way, we can (and often do) use shaping to teach students to work independently on classroom assignments. We begin by giving first graders structured tasks that may take only five to ten minutes to complete. As students move through the elementary school years, we expect them to work independently for longer periods of time, and we also give them short assignments to do at home. By the time they reach high school, students have extended study halls (where, with luck, they study independently) and complete lengthy assignments at home. In the college years, student assignments require a great deal of independence and self-direction.

How might you use shaping to teach an 8-year-old to write in cursive? a 12-year-old to swing a baseball bat? an aggressive high school student to behave prosocially?

Effects of Antecedent Stimuli and Responses

On what occasions are you most likely to look up a word you don't know how to spell? On what occasions are you most likely to describe your personal beliefs about effective teaching? On what occasions are you *unlikely* to do these things? Take a moment to jot down some answers to these questions.

In our discussion of operant conditioning so far, we have focused on the *consequences* of desired behaviors. Yet you have undoubtedly learned that some behaviors are more likely to be reinforced in some situations than in others. For example, the behavior of looking up a word to find its correct spelling is more likely to be reinforced when you are writing a research paper than when you are writing a note to a friend; we could diagram the situation this way:

$$S_{Paper} \quad \rightarrow \quad R \quad \rightarrow \quad S_{Reinforcement}$$
$$S_{Note} \quad \rightarrow \quad R \quad \rightarrow \quad \text{(no consequence)}$$

Similarly, talking about effective teaching practices is more likely to be reinforced when you are sitting in your educational psychology class than when you are at a party or the movies.

You may also have noticed that you are more likely to make a particular response when you are already making similar kinds of responses. For example, you are more likely to look up an unknown word when you have just looked up a different word and so have the dictionary lying open in front of you. And you are more likely to volunteer your opinions about teaching practices when you have already made a few comments in class—when you are "on a roll," so to speak.

Researchers have found that the stimuli and responses that precede a particular desired response (i.e., the **antecedent stimuli** and **antecedent responses**) often influence the frequency of the response. Here we will look at four phenomena—cueing, setting events, generalization, and discrimination—that involve antecedent stimuli and one—behavioral momentum—that involves antecedent responses.

Cueing

Students are more likely to behave appropriately when they are given reminders (often called *cues* or *prompts*) that certain behaviors are expected of them (e.g., Northup et al., 1995; B. A. Taylor & Levin, 1998). Such **cueing** sometimes involves a nonverbal signal, such as turning the overhead lights on and off a few times to remind students to talk quietly rather than loudly. At other times, it involves a verbal reminder, either direct or indirect, about what students should be doing:

How are the concepts of *cueing* and *retrieval cue* (Chapter 6) similar? How are they different?

- "I hear the signal for a fire drill. *Everyone line up quietly and then walk in single file to the outside door.*"
- "Students who *have their desks clear* go to lunch first."

- "After you have all *read pages 14 through 19 in your textbooks,* I will hand out information about the school ski trip."
- "I see some *art supplies that still need to be put back on the shelves* before you can go home."

Setting Events

In cueing we use specific stimuli to prompt students to behave in particular ways. An alternative approach is to create an overall environment—a **setting event**—that is likely to foster the desired behaviors. For example, young children are more likely to interact with their classmates during free play time if they have a relatively small area in which to play and if the toys available to them (balls, puppets, toy housekeeping materials) encourage cooperation and group activity (W. H. Brown, Fox, & Brady, 1987; Frost et al., 1998; Martin et al., 1991). Similarly, the nature of the games children are asked to play influences the behaviors they exhibit: Cooperative games promote cooperative behavior, whereas competitive games promote aggressive behavior (Bay-Hinitz et al., 1994).

Generalization

Once people have learned that a response is likely to be reinforced in one set of circumstances (i.e., in the presence of one antecedent stimulus), they are likely to make the same response in a similar situation; in other words, they show **generalization**. For example, after Bernadette has learned to sit quietly and attentively in her kindergarten class, she may generalize that behavior to her first-grade class. After Donald has learned how to make friends at school, he may begin to apply the same skills in his out-of-school activities.

This process of generalization should remind you of the generalization that occurs in classical conditioning: In both cases, an individual learns a response to one stimulus and then responds in the same way to a similar stimulus. The major difference is one of learner control: Generalization involves an automatic, involuntary response in classical conditioning but a voluntary response in operant conditioning.

Discrimination

Sometimes people learn that responses are reinforced only when certain stimuli (certain environmental conditions) are present. For example, Bernadette might learn that she can get up and leave the classroom when, and only when, her teacher has given her permission to do so. Donald might discover that a classmate who smiles at him is more likely to reinforce his attempts at being friendly than a classmate who scowls. When people learn that responses are reinforced in the presence of one stimulus but not in the presence of another (perhaps very similar) stimulus, they have learned **discrimination** between the two stimuli.

Occasionally our students may overgeneralize, exhibiting responses they have learned in situations where such responses are unproductive or inappropriate. In such cases, we must teach them to discriminate between suitable and unsuitable stimulus conditions. For instance, we should describe in very concrete terms the circumstances in which certain behaviors are and are not productive and acceptable. We then must be sure that we reinforce students for exhibiting behaviors *only* in situations where those behaviors are appropriate.

Behavioral Momentum

In many cases, students are more likely to make desired responses if they are already making similar responses—a phenomenon known as **behavioral momentum** (Ardoin, Martens, & Wolfe, 1999; Belfiore, Lee, Vargas, & Skinner, 1997; Mace et al., 1988; Nevin, Mandell, & Atak, 1983). Consider this situation as an example:

> Two high school students, Allison and Roberta, have a history of refusing to do the academic tasks that their teachers assign. A researcher finds that the girls more willingly attempt difficult three-digit multiplication problems after they have first worked on a few simple one-digit problems (Belfiore et al., 1997).

Similarly, we might ask students to tidy up a messy classroom after they have already cleaned their own desktops, or to try a backward roll after they have already executed a forward roll successfully. In general, we can promote behavioral momentum by assigning relatively easy or enjoyable tasks that lead naturally into more complex and potentially frustrating ones.

Now that we have considered basic principles of operant conditioning, let's take a look at how one teacher applies these principles in her classroom.

INTERPRETING ARTIFACTS AND INTERACTIONS   *Auction*

How might we encourage students to read independently? One third-grade teacher's approach is described below. As you read about it, consider

- What behaviorist strategy it reflects
- What advantages and disadvantages it might have

> The teacher gives her students a token each time they read 25 pages in a chapter book appropriate for their reading level. She gives them two additional tokens when they finish a book and another one for writing a reaction to it. Once every couple of months, the teacher holds a class auction where the students can use their tokens to bid on and buy various inexpensive items she has purchased (cute pencils, erasers, combs, etc.). She arranges the process so that each student gets something in the first round of the auction; after that, children with more tokens have more purchasing power.

The teacher is using a token economy to reinforce reading behavior. By doing so, many students will probably read more than they would otherwise, and her use of tokens as reinforcers allows flexibility in how different students are reinforced: If the array of backup reinforcers is broad enough, presumably all students will be able to purchase something that they want. Potential downsides to this strategy are that (a) students might choose books based on brevity rather than intrinsic appeal (they get two extra tokens each time they finish a book) and (b) students might "read" so quickly that they don't really think about the content (recall our discussion of attention in Chapter 6). In essence, the students may become more interested in the extrinsic reinforcers they get for reading than in any intrinsic pleasure reading brings them (more about this point in Chapter 12). The teacher will need to monitor her students' independent reading activities—for instance, by occasionally asking them questions about what they are reading—to make sure that the benefits outweigh any possible drawbacks.

Reducing and Eliminating Undesirable Behaviors

Our focus up to this point has been on promoting desirable behaviors. Yet we will also need to address *undesirable* behaviors—those that interfere with students' own learning and achievement, and possibly with the learning and achievement of their classmates as well. How do we decrease, perhaps even eliminate, such behaviors? Behaviorists offer several possible strategies, including extinction, cueing inappropriate behaviors, reinforcing incompatible behaviors, and punishment.

Extinction

How is extinction similar in classical and operant conditioning? How is it different?

What happens when a response is no longer reinforced? As you might guess, a nonreinforced response decreases in frequency and usually returns to its baseline level. Like the decrease of a conditioned response in classical conditioning, the decrease of a nonreinforced response in operant conditioning also is known as **extinction**. For example, the class clown whose jokes are ignored may stop telling jokes. The aggressive child who never gets what she wants by hitting or shoving others may become less aggressive. One way of reducing the frequency of an inappropriate behavior, then, is simply to make sure it is never reinforced.

Unfortunately, teachers and other adults often inadvertently reinforce the very behaviors they want to eliminate. For example, a girl who copies her homework assignment word for word from a classmate and then receives a high grade for that assignment is reinforced for representing someone else's work as her own. A boy whose comments in class are so obnoxious that his teacher has no choice but to give him the attention he seeks is also being reinforced for inappropriate behavior. As teachers, we must look reflectively at our own behaviors in the classroom, being careful *not* to reinforce, either intentionally or unintentionally, those responses that are not likely to help our students over the long run.

There are several points to keep in mind about extinction, however. First of all, once reinforcement stops, a previously reinforced response doesn't always decrease immediately. Sometimes the behavior initially *increases* for a short time (Lerman & Iwata, 1995; McGill, 1999). To illustrate how this might occur, imagine that you have a cantankerous television set that gives you a clear picture only when you bang its side once or twice. Eventually, something changes in the inner workings of your set, so that banging is no longer an effective remedy. As you desperately try to get a clear picture, you may bang your television a number of times in succession (more times than you usually do) before giving up that response. In much the same way, the class clown who is now being ignored may tell more jokes at first and the aggressive child may act out more frequently before learning that such behaviors no longer produce the desired results.

Second, we may sometimes find situations in which a response doesn't decrease even when we remove a reinforcer. In such situations—when extinction doesn't occur—chances are that we haven't been able to remove *all* reinforcers of the response. Perhaps the behavior is leading to a naturally reinforcing consequence; for example, a class clown's peers may continue to snicker even when the teacher ignores his jokes. Or perhaps the response is intrinsically reinforcing; for example, a student's physically aggressive behavior may release pent-up energy (and so may "feel good") even if it doesn't otherwise get her what she wants. Only when all reinforcers are removed will extinction occur.

Finally, we must remember that extinction can occur with desirable behaviors as easily as with undesirable ones. The student who is never called on in class may stop raising his hand. The student who never passes a paper-pencil test no matter how hard she studies may eventually stop studying. As teachers, we must be very sure that, while counterproductive classroom behaviors are not being reinforced, productive responses *are* being reinforced, either through such extrinsic reinforcers as attention, praise, or favorite activities or through the intrinsic satisfaction that classroom accomplishments bring.

Cueing Inappropriate Behaviors

Just as we can use cueing to remind students about what they should be doing, we can also use this strategy to remind them about what they should *not* be doing. For example, we might use *body language*—perhaps making eye contact, raising an eyebrow, or frowning—to let students know that we disapprove of their behavior and would like it to cease (Emmer, 1987; Palardy & Mudrey, 1973; Shrigley, 1979; Woolfolk & Brooks, 1985). When body language doesn't get the attention of a misbehaving student, a more obvious cue is *physical proximity:* moving closer to the student and standing there until the problem behavior stops (Emmer, 1987; Woolfolk & Brooks, 1985). Particularly if we are walking around the room anyway during a classroom activity, this strategy can attract the attention of the guilty party without at the same time drawing undue attention from classmates.

Yet sometimes subtlety just doesn't work, and so we have to be more explicit. In such cases, a brief *verbal cue*—stating a student's name, reminding a student about correct behavior, or (if necessary) pointing out an inappropriate behavior—may be in order (Davis & Thomas, 1989; Emmer, 1987; Northup et al., 1995). For example, we might say something as simple as, "Please keep your eyes on your own work," or, "Lucy, put the magazine away."

Reinforcing Incompatible Behaviors

EXPERIENCING FIRSTHAND   *Asleep on Your Feet*

Have you ever tried to sleep while standing up? Horses can do it, but most of us humans really can't. In fact, there are many pairs of responses that we can't possibly perform simultaneously. Take a minute and identify something that you cannot possibly do when you perform each of these activities:

When you:	You cannot simultaneously:
Sit down	_____
Eat crackers	_____
Take a walk	_____

Simple body language is often an effective cue. While this teacher is temporarily preoccupied, her hand on a student's shoulder provides a subtle reminder about what he should and should not be doing.

Two behaviors are **incompatible** when they cannot be performed simultaneously. For example, sitting is incompatible with standing. Eating crackers is incompatible with singing, or at least with singing *well.* Taking a walk is incompatible with taking a nap. In each case, it is physically impossible to perform both activities at exactly the same time.

When our attempts at extinction or cueing are unsuccessful, another way to reduce an inappropriate behavior is to reinforce an incompatible (and presumably more desirable) one; the inappropriate response must inevitably decrease as the incompatible one increases (e.g., Krumboltz & Krumboltz, 1972; Zirpoli & Melloy, 2001). This is the approach we are taking when we reinforce a hyperactive student for sitting down: Sitting is incompatible with getting-out-of-seat and roaming-around-the-room behaviors. It is also an approach that we might use to deal with forgetfulness (we reinforce students when they remember to do what they were supposed to do), being off-task (we reinforce on-task behavior), and verbal abusiveness (we reinforce prosocial statements). And consider how we might deal with a chronic litterbug:

Walt is a junior high school student who consistently leaves garbage—banana peels, sunflower seed shells, and so on—on the lunchroom floor, in school corridors, and on the playground. When the school faculty establishes an "anti-litter" committee, it decides to put Walt on the committee. The committee eventually elects Walt as its chairman.

Under Walt's leadership, the committee institutes a massive anti-litter campaign, complete with posters and lunchroom monitors, and Walt receives considerable recognition for the campaign's success. Curiously (or perhaps not), school personnel no longer find Walt's garbage littering the school grounds. (Krumboltz & Krumboltz, 1972)

Punishment

Some misbehaviors require an immediate remedy—they interfere significantly with students' learning, and they may threaten students' physical safety or psychological well-being as well—and so we cannot simply wait for gradual improvements over time. Consider this student as an example:

> Bonnie doesn't handle frustration very well. Whenever she encounters a difficulty or obstacle that she cannot immediately overcome, she responds by hitting, kicking, or breaking something. Over the course of the school year, she has knocked over several pieces of furniture, smashed two windows, made several dents in the wall, and broken innumerable pencils. Not only is Bonnie's behavior hindering her academic progress, but it's also getting very expensive.

Bonnie's inappropriate behaviors are difficult to extinguish because they aren't really being reinforced to begin with (not extrinsically, at least). They are also behaviors with no obvious incompatible responses that we can reinforce. And we can reasonably assume that Bonnie's teacher has already cued her about her inappropriate behavior on many occasions. When other strategies are inapplicable or ineffective, punishment may be a useful alternative.

Earlier in the chapter, we defined a reinforcer as a consequence that increases the frequency of a particular behavior. **Punishment** can be defined as a consequence that *decreases* the frequency of the response it follows.

All punishing consequences fall into one of two groups. **Presentation punishment** involves presenting a new stimulus, presumably something that a student finds unpleasant and doesn't want. Spankings, scoldings, and teacher scowls, if they lead to a reduction in the behavior they follow, are all instances of presentation punishment. **Removal punishment** involves removing a previously existing stimulus, presumably one that a student finds desirable and doesn't want to lose. The loss of a privilege, a fine (involving the loss of money or points), and "grounding" (when certain pleasurable outside activities are missed) are all possible examples of removal punishment.

Can you describe positive reinforcement, negative reinforcement, presentation punishment, and removal punishment in your own words? Can you think of examples of each concept?

Over the years I have observed many occasions when people have used the term *negative reinforcement* when they were really talking about punishment. Remember, negative reinforcement increases a response, whereas punishment has the opposite effect. Table 9.2 should help you understand how negative reinforcement, presentation punishment, and removal punishment are all very different concepts.

Strictly speaking, punishment is not a part of operant conditioning. Many early behaviorists believed that punishment is a relatively *in*effective means of changing behavior—that it may temporarily suppress a response but can never eliminate it—and suggested that teachers focus their efforts on reinforcing desirable behaviors, rather than on punishing undesirable ones. More recently, however, behaviorists have found that some forms of punishment can be quite effective in reducing problem behaviors.

Effective Forms of Punishment

As a general rule, we will want to use relatively mild forms of punishment in the classroom; severe consequences may lead to such unwanted side effects as resentment, hostility, or truancy. Researchers and educators have identified several forms of mild punishment that can be effective in reducing classroom misbehaviors: reprimands, response cost, logical consequences, time-out, and in-school suspension.

Verbal reprimands (scolding). Although some students seem to thrive on teacher scolding because of the attention that it brings, most students, particularly if they are scolded relatively infrequently, find verbal reprimands to be unpleasant and punishing (Pfiffner & O'Leary, 1993; Van Houten, Nau, MacKenzie-Keating, Sameoto, & Colavecchia, 1982). In general, reprimands are more effective when they are immediate, brief, and unemotional; they also work better when they are given in a soft voice and in close proximity to the student, perhaps be-

Distinguishing Among Positive Reinforcement, Negative Reinforcement, and Punishment

CONSEQUENCE	EFFECT	EXAMPLES
Positive reinforcement	Response *increases* when a new stimulus (presumably one that the person finds desirable) is *presented.*	• A student *is praised* for writing an assignment in cursive. She begins to write other assignments in cursive as well. • A student *gets his lunch money* by bullying a girl into surrendering hers. He begins bullying his classmates more frequently.
Negative reinforcement	Response *increases* when a previously existing stimulus (presumably one that the person finds undesirable) is *removed.*	• A student *no longer has to worry* about a research paper he has completed several days before the due date. He begins to do his assignments ahead of time whenever possible. • A student *escapes the principal's wrath* by lying about her role in a recent incident of school vandalism. She begins lying to school faculty whenever she finds herself in an uncomfortable situation.
Presentation punishment	Response *decreases* when a new stimulus (presumably one that the person finds undesirable) is *presented.*	• A student *is scolded* for taunting other students. She taunts others less frequently after that. • A student *is ridiculed by classmates* for asking a "stupid" question during a lecture. He stops asking questions in class.
Removal punishment	Response *decreases* when a previously existing stimulus (presumably one that the person finds desirable) is *removed.*	• A student *is removed from the softball team for a week* for showing poor sportsmanship. She rarely shows poor sportsmanship in future games. • A student *loses points on a test* for answering a question in a creative but unusual way. He takes fewer risks on future tests.

cause they are less likely to be noticed and so less likely to draw the attention of classmates (O'Leary, Kaufman, Kass, & Drabman, 1970; Pfiffner & O'Leary, 1993). Reprimands should be given in private whenever possible: When scolded in front of their classmates, some students may relish the peer attention, but others (e.g., many Native American and Hispanic students) may feel totally humiliated (Fuller, 2001).

Response cost. Response cost involves the loss either of a previously earned reinforcer or of an opportunity to obtain reinforcement; thus, it is an instance of removal punishment. For example, teachers of students with chronic behavior problems sometimes incorporate response cost into a point system or token economy: They award points, check marks, plastic chips, or the like for good behavior (reinforcement) and take away these things for inappropriate behavior (response cost). Students who accumulate a sufficient number of points or tokens can use them to "buy" objects, privileges, or enjoyable activities that are otherwise not available. Response cost is especially effective when coupled with reinforcement of appropriate behavior (Iwata & Bailey, 1974; Lentz, 1988; Rapport, Murphy, & Bailey, 1982).

Logical consequences. A logical consequence is a consequence that follows naturally or logically from a student's misbehavior; in other words, the punishment fits the crime. For example, if a student destroys a classmate's possession, a reasonable consequence is for the student to replace it or pay for a new one. If two close friends talk so much that they aren't getting their assignments done, a reasonable consequence is for them to be separated. If a student intentionally makes a mess in the cafeteria, a reasonable consequence is to clean it up. The use of logical consequences makes "logical" sense, and numerous research studies and case studies vouch for its effectiveness (Dreikurs, 1998; Lyon, 1984; Schloss & Smith, 1994; L. S. Wright, 1982).

Time-out. In time-out, a misbehaving student is placed in a dull, boring (but not scary) situation—perhaps a separate room designed especially for time-outs, a little-used office, or a remote corner of the classroom. A student undergoing time-out has no opportunity to interact with classmates and no opportunity to obtain reinforcement. The length of the time-out

Can you explain how *release* from a time-out situation is *negative reinforcement*?

is often quite short (perhaps two to ten minutes, depending on the age of the student), but the student is not released from the time-out situation until inappropriate behavior (e.g., screaming, kicking) has stopped. Time-outs have been used successfully to reduce a variety of noncompliant, disruptive, and aggressive behaviors (e.g., Pfiffner & Barkley, 1998; Rortvedt & Miltenberger, 1994; A. G. White & Bailey, 1990). Although some theorists argue that time-out is not really punishment, most students find the boredom of a time-out to be somewhat unpleasant.

In-school suspension. In-school suspension is similar to time-out in that the student is placed in a quiet, boring room within the school building; however, it often lasts one or more school days and involves close adult supervision. Students receiving in-school suspension spend the day working on the same assignments that their nonsuspended peers do and so are able to keep up with their schoolwork. But they have no opportunity for interaction with classmates and friends—an aspect of school that is reinforcing to most students. Although in-school suspension programs have not been systematically investigated through controlled research studies, practitioners report that these programs are often effective in reducing chronic misbehaviors, particularly when part of the suspension session is devoted to teaching appropriate behaviors and tutoring academic skills and when the supervising teacher acts as a supportive resource rather than as a punisher (Gootman, 1998; Huff, 1988; Pfiffner & Barkley, 1998; J. S. Sullivan, 1989).

Just as we must use different reinforcers for different students, we must also individualize our use of punishment. For example, some students enjoy the attention that verbal reprimands bring (remember James in the opening case study). A few may even appreciate the peace and quiet of an occasional time-out (Pfiffner & Barkley, 1998; Solnick, Rincover, & Peterson, 1977). If we find that a particular form of punishment produces no substantial decrease in a student's behavior, we should conclude that it isn't really a punishing consequence for that student and that a different form of punishment is called for in the future.

Ineffective Forms of Punishment

Several forms of punishment are typically *not* recommended: physical punishment, psychological punishment, extra classwork, and out-of-school suspension.

Physical punishment. Physical punishment is generally not advised for school-age children (W. Doyle, 1990; Zirpoli & Melloy, 2001); furthermore, its use in the classroom is *illegal* in many places. Even mild physical punishment, such as a spank or slap with a ruler, can lead to such undesirable behaviors as resentment of the teacher, inattention to school tasks, lying, aggression, vandalism, avoidance of school tasks, and truancy. When carried to extreme lengths, physical punishment constitutes child abuse and may cause long-term or possibly even permanent physical damage.

Psychological punishment. Psychological punishment—any consequence that seriously threatens a student's self-esteem—is also not recommended (Davis & Thomas, 1989; J. E. Walker & Shea, 1995). Embarrassing remarks and public humiliation can lead to some of the same side effects as physical punishment (e.g., resentment of the teacher, inattention to school tasks, truancy from school) and have the potential to inflict long-term psychological harm. By deflating students' self-perceptions, it may also lower students' expectations for future performance and their motivation to learn and achieve (more on this point in the discussion of *self-efficacy* in Chapters 10 and 12).

Extra classwork. Asking a student to complete make-up work for time missed in school is a reasonable and justifiable request. But assigning extra classwork or homework beyond that required for other students is inappropriate if it is assigned simply to punish a student's wrongdoing (Cooper, 1989; Corno, 1996). In this case, we have a very different side effect: We inadvertently communicate the message that "schoolwork is unpleasant."

Out-of-school suspension. Teachers and administrators are negatively reinforced when they suspend a problem student. After all, they get rid of something they don't want—a problem! But out-of-school suspension is usually *not* an effective means of changing a student's behavior (Moles, 1990; J. D. Nichols, Ludwin, & Iadicola, 1999; Pfiffner & Barkley, 1998). In the first place, being suspended from school may be exactly what the student wants, in which case inappropriate behaviors are being reinforced rather than punished. Second, because many students with chronic behavior problems also tend to do poorly in their schoolwork, suspension involves a loss of valuable instructional time and interferes with any psychological "attachment" to school, thereby decreasing even further the students' chances for academic and social success (J. D. Nichols et al., 1999; Skiba & Raison, 1990).

An additional form of punishment—missing recess—gets mixed reviews regarding its effectiveness. In some situations, missing recess may be a logical consequence for students who fail to complete their schoolwork during regular class time due to off-task behavior. Yet research tells us that, at least at the elementary level, students can more effectively concentrate on school tasks when they have occasional breaks from academic activities (Maxmell et al., 1998; Pellegrini, Huberty, & Jones, 1995). Perhaps the best piece of advice here is to withdraw recess privileges infrequently, if at all, and to monitor the effectiveness of such a consequence on students' classroom behavior over the long run.

Suspension from school may actually reinforce inappropriate school behavior rather than punish it.

Using Punishment Humanely

A frequent criticism of using punishment is that it is "inhumane," or somehow cruel and barbaric. Indeed, certain forms of punishment, such as physical abuse or public humiliation, do constitute inhumane treatment. We must be *extremely careful* in our use of punishment in the classroom. When administered judiciously, however, some forms of mild punishment can lead to a rapid reduction in misbehavior without causing physical or psychological harm. And when we can decrease counterproductive classroom behaviors quickly and effectively—especially when those behaviors are harmful to self or others—then punishment may, in fact, be one of the most humane approaches we can take. Following are several guidelines for using punishment effectively and humanely:

■ *Inform students ahead of time that certain behaviors will be punished, and explain how those behaviors will be punished.* When students are informed of response-punishment contingencies ahead of time, they are less likely to engage in the forbidden behaviors; they are also less likely to be surprised or resentful if punishment must be administered (G. D. Gottfredson & Gottfredson, 1985; Moles, 1990). Ultimately, students should learn that their behaviors influence the consequences that they experience—that they have some control over what happens to them. We will consider this idea of control more closely when we look at *attribution theory* in Chapter 12.

■ *Follow through with specified consequences.* One mistake that some teachers make is to continually threaten punishment without ever following through. One warning is desirable, but repeated warnings are not. The teacher who says, "If you bring that rubber snake to class one more time, Tommy, I'm going to take it away," but never does take the snake away, is giving the message that no response-punishment contingency really exists.

■ *Administer punishment privately.* By administering punishment in private, we protect our students from public embarrassment or humiliation. We also eliminate the possibility that the punishment will draw the attention of classmates—a potential reinforcer for the very behavior we are trying to eliminate.

■ *Explain why the punished behavior is unacceptable.* We must explain exactly why a certain behavior cannot be tolerated in the classroom (perhaps because it interferes with learning, threatens the safety or self-esteem of other students, or damages school property). Punishment is far more effective when accompanied by one or more reasons why the punished behavior is unacceptable (Cheyne & Walters, 1970; Parke, 1974; D. G. Perry & Perry, 1983). (Recall our discussion of *induction* in Chapter 3.)

■ *Emphasize that it is the behavior that is undesirable, not the student.* As teachers, we must emphasize to students that certain behaviors interfere with their success in learning—that they are preventing themselves from becoming the very best that they can be.

■ *Simultaneously teach and reinforce desirable alternative behaviors.* Punishment of misbehavior is almost always more effective when appropriate behaviors are being reinforced at the same time (Pfiffner & Barkley, 1998; Ruef, Higgins, Glaeser, & Patnode, 1998; Walters &

Don't inadvertently reinforce undesirable behaviors.

A teacher realizes that a particular "problem" student, a girl who makes frequent inappropriate remarks in class, seems to thrive on any kind of attention. He also realizes that the girl's behavior has gotten worse instead of better. Rather than continue to reinforce the girl by scolding her publicly, he meets with her after school and together they develop a contingency contract designed to improve her behavior.

Cue students when you see them behaving inappropriately.

As she describes the morning's assignment, a teacher notices that two boys on the other side of the classroom are whispering, giggling, and obviously not paying attention. While continuing her description of the assignment, she walks slowly across the room and stands next to the boys.

Reinforce behaviors that are incompatible with undesirable behaviors.

A student is out of her seat so frequently that she gets little of her own work done and often distracts her classmates from doing theirs. Her teacher discusses the problem behavior with her, and together they decide that she will earn points for staying in her seat and keeping on task; she may use the points to "buy" time with her friends at the end of the day.

When a misbehavior must be suppressed quickly, choose a mild punishment, yet one that is likely to deter the behavior in the future.

When members of the school soccer team have an unexcused absence from team practice, they are not allowed to play in that week's soccer game.

Describe both appropriate and inappropriate behaviors, as well as their consequences, in concrete and explicit terms.

The soccer coach reminds students that students who miss practice will sit out at the next game and all students who *do* make practice will play at least part of the game.

When misbehaviors continue despite all reasonable efforts to correct them, seek the advice of experts.

A teacher consults with the school psychologist about three students who are often physically aggressive in their interactions with classmates. Together they develop a strategy to help these students.

Grusec, 1977). Furthermore, by reinforcing desirable responses as well as punishing undesirable ones, we give students the positive, optimistic message that, yes, behavior can and will improve. Ultimately, the overall classroom atmosphere we create must be a positive one that highlights the good things that students do and deemphasizes the "bad" (e.g., R. E. Smith & Smoll, 1997).

Maintaining Desirable Behaviors over the Long Run

As noted in our discussion of extinction, responses that are no longer reinforced decrease in frequency and often return to their baseline level; in some cases, the responses disappear altogether. Yet we cannot continue to reinforce every student each time that he or she engages in appropriate behavior. And we won't be able to reinforce our students at all after they leave our classrooms at the end of the school year. So how can we ensure that our students will continue to behave in productive ways over the long run? Two viable strategies are promoting intrinsic reinforcement and using intermittent reinforcement.

Promoting Intrinsic Reinforcement

The advantage of intrinsic reinforcers is that they come from students themselves, rather than from some outside source. Students will often engage in activities that are enjoyable or satisfy their curiosity. They will also exhibit behaviors that lead to success and to feelings of mastery, accomplishment, and pride. Ideally, it is such internal consequences that are most effective in sustaining productive behaviors both in the classroom and in the outside world.

Yet success is not always achieved easily and effortlessly. Many of the tasks that our students will tackle in school—reading, writing, solving mathematical problems, reasoning scientifically, understanding historical and social events, participating skillfully in team sports, learning to play a musical instrument—are complex, challenging, and often frustrating, especially at first. When students struggle with a challenging task and encounter frequent failure, we should probably provide extrinsic reinforcement for the little improvements they make. And when we find that we must break down a complex task into smaller pieces that, though easier to accomplish, are less fulfilling in their own right (e.g., when we assign drill-and-practice exercises to foster basic reading or math skills), we will probably need to reinforce students' many seemingly "meaningless" successes. Once our students have mastered tasks and skills to a level that brings them frequent successes and feelings of mastery, however, extrinsic reinforcers should no longer be necessary (Covington, 1992; Lepper, 1981). In fact, for reasons that you will discover in Chapter 12, it may actually be counterproductive to provide extrinsic reinforcers when students are already finding intrinsic reinforcement in the things they are doing.

One statement in this paragraph is based on the concept of *shaping*. Another reflects the concept of *scaffolding* (Chapter 2). Can you identify each of these statements?

Using Intermittent Reinforcement

Earlier in the chapter, I mentioned that desired responses increase more quickly when they are reinforced every time they occur. Yet once those responses are occurring regularly, such *continuous reinforcement* may not be optimal. We may instead want to switch to **intermittent reinforcement**, reinforcing desired behavior on some occasions and not doing so on others.

To show you what I mean, let's consider Molly and Maria, two students with low baseline levels for volunteering in class. Their teacher, Mr. Oliver, decides to reinforce the girls for raising their hands. Every time Molly raises her hand, Mr. Oliver calls on her and praises her response; she is receiving continuous reinforcement. But when Maria raises her hand, Mr. Oliver doesn't always notice her. He calls on Maria whenever he sees her hand in the air, but he doesn't often look in her direction; she is therefore receiving intermittent reinforcement. As you've already learned, Molly's volunteering behavior should increase more rapidly than Maria's.

But let's move ahead in time a few months. Thanks to Mr. Oliver's attentiveness to Molly and Maria, both girls are now volunteering frequently in class. Mr. Oliver turns his attention to several other students who have been failing to participate. Foolishly, he no longer reinforces either Molly or Maria for raising her hand. As you might expect, the girls begin to participate less; in other words, we see signs of extinction. But for which girl will class participation extinguish more rapidly?

If you predicted that Molly's volunteering will decrease more rapidly than Maria's, you are correct. Responses that have previously been reinforced continuously tend to extinguish relatively quickly once reinforcement stops. But because Maria has been receiving intermittent reinforcement, she is accustomed to being occasionally ignored. It may take her longer to realize that she is no longer going to be called on when she raises her hand. Behaviors that have previously been reinforced intermittently decrease slowly (if at all) once reinforcement stops; in other words, they are more *resistant to extinction* (e.g., Freeland & Noell, 1999).

Once students have acquired a desired terminal behavior, we should continue to reinforce that behavior intermittently, especially if it does not otherwise lead to intrinsic reinforcement. Mr. Oliver doesn't need to call on Molly and Maria every time they raise their hands, but he should certainly call on them once in a while. In a similar manner, we might occasionally reinforce diligent study habits, completed homework assignments, prosocial behaviors, and so on, even for the best of students, as a way of encouraging such responses to continue.

Which form of reinforcement, continuous or intermittent, would you use to teach your students to persist at difficult tasks?

Addressing Especially Difficult Classroom Behaviors

Educators and other practitioners sometimes apply behaviorism in a very systematic way, especially when they want to address difficult and chronic behavior problems. Here we consider three systematic approaches for modifying especially challenging behaviors: applied behavior analysis, functional analysis, and positive behavioral support.

Applied Behavior Analysis

A group of procedures that systematically apply traditional behaviorist principles are collectively known as **applied behavior analysis** (also called *behavior modification, behavior therapy, or contingency management*). Applied behavior analysis, or **ABA**, is based on the assumptions that behavior problems result from past and present environmental circumstances and that modifying a student's present environment will promote more productive responses. When teachers and therapists use ABA to help a student acquire more appropriate classroom behavior, they typically use strategies such as these:

- Describe both the present behaviors and the desired terminal behaviors in observable, measurable terms.

- Identify one or more effective reinforcers.
- Develop a specific intervention or treatment plan—one that may involve reinforcement of desired behaviors, shaping, extinction, reinforcement of incompatible behaviors, punishment, or some combination of these.
- Measure the frequency of desired and/or undesirable behaviors both before treatment (i.e., at baseline level) and during treatment.
- Monitor the treatment program for effectiveness by observing how various behaviors change over time, and modify the program if necessary.
- Take steps to promote generalization of newly acquired behaviors (e.g., by having the student practice the behaviors in a variety of realistic situations).
- Gradually phase out the treatment (e.g., through intermittent reinforcement) after the desired behaviors are acquired.

Hundreds of research studies tell us that the systematic use of behaviorist principles can lead to significant improvements in academic performance and classroom behavior. For example, when we reinforce students for successful achievement, we find improvements in such subjects as mathematics, reading, spelling, and creative writing (Piersel, 1987). When we reinforce appropriate classroom behaviors, such as paying attention and interacting cooperatively and prosocially with classmates, misbehaviors decrease (S. N. Elliott & Busse, 1991; E. McNamara, 1987; Ormrod, 1999). In many situations, ABA is effective when other approaches have not been (Emmer & Evertson, 1981; O'Leary & O'Leary, 1972; Piersel, 1987).

One probable reason that ABA often works so well is that students know exactly what is expected of them. Consistent use of reinforcement for appropriate responses gives a clear message about which behaviors are acceptable and which are not. Another likely reason is that, through the gradual process of *shaping*, students begin to learn new behaviors only when they are truly ready to acquire them, and so their probability of achieving both success and reinforcement is very high.

Can you think of other possible reasons for the success of behaviorist techniques?

Functional Analysis and Positive Behavioral Support

Traditional ABA focuses on changing response-reinforcement contingencies to bring about more appropriate behavior. More recently, some theorists have suggested that we also consider the purposes, or *functions,* that students' inappropriate behaviors may serve. In particular, they recommend identifying the specific conditions (i.e., antecedent stimuli) present when students tend to misbehave and also the consequences (i.e., reinforcers and/or punishments) that typically follow such misbehaviors, like so:

$$\text{Antecedent} \rightarrow \text{Behavior} \rightarrow \text{Consequence}$$

Such an approach is known as **functional analysis.** For example, we have speculated that James, in our opening case study, misbehaves to get the attention he apparently cannot get in any other way. Functional analyses have shown that students with chronic classroom behavior problems often misbehave when they are asked to do difficult or unpleasant tasks (this is the *antecedent*) and that their misbehavior either (a) allows them to avoid having to do such tasks or (b) gains the attention of their teacher or peers (these are possible *consequences*) (K. M. Jones, Drew, & Weber, 2000; K. A. Meyer, 1999; Van Camp et al., 2000).

Another approach takes the process a step further: After identifying the purposes that a student's inappropriate behaviors may serve, the teacher also identifies more productive behaviors to serve the same purposes and designs an environment to encourage those productive behaviors. This approach, sometimes known as **positive behavioral support,** involves strategies such as these (Koegel et al., 1996; Ruef et al., 1998):

- Teach desirable behaviors that can serve the same purpose as—and can therefore replace—the inappropriate behaviors.
- Consistently reinforce desired behaviors in ways that the student truly appreciates.
- Modify the classroom environment to minimize conditions that might trigger inappropriate behaviors.
- Establish a predictable daily routine as a way of minimizing anxiety and making the student feel more comfortable and secure.
- Give the student frequent opportunities to make choices; in this way, the student can often gain desired outcomes without having to resort to inappropriate behaviors.

- Make adaptations in the curriculum, instruction, or both to maximize the likelihood of academic success (e.g., by building on the student's interests and preferred activities, presenting material at a slower pace, or interspersing challenging tasks among easier and more enjoyable ones).

I'll illustrate the use of positive behavioral support with Samantha, a student that I first described in Chapter 5:

> Samantha was a 9-year-old third grader who had been identified as having autism and moderate speech disabilities. She frequently ran out of the classroom, damaging school property and other students' belongings in her flight. When a teacher or other adult tried to intervene, she would fight back by biting, scratching, hitting, kicking, and pulling hair. On such occasions, school personnel would often call her parents and ask that they come to take her home.
>
> The multidisciplinary team working with Samantha eventually discovered that her destructive and aggressive behaviors were more likely to occur when she was given a difficult academic assignment or had reason to anticipate such an assignment. Departures from the routine schedule or the absences of favorite teachers further increased the probability of such responses.
>
> The team hypothesized that Samantha's undesirable behaviors served two purposes: They helped her avoid unpleasant academic tasks and enabled her to gain the attention of valued adults. The team suspected, too, that Samantha felt as if she had little or no control over classroom activities and that she yearned for social interaction with her teachers and classmates. (DeVault et al., 1996)

The team took several steps to address the roots of Samantha's inappropriate behaviors and help her acquire more productive ones (DeVault et al., 1996):

- Samantha was given a consistent and predictable daily schedule that included frequent breaks from potentially challenging academic tasks and numerous opportunities to interact with others.
- When Samantha felt that she needed a break from her academic work, she could ask to spend some time in the "relaxation room," a quiet and private space where she could sit in a beanbag chair and listen to soothing audiotapes.
- When a teacher observed behaviors that might escalate into aggression or flight from the classroom, he or she would remind Samantha that she could best deal with frustration and stress by spending some time in the relaxation room.
- On occasions when Samantha attempted to leave the classroom, an adult would place her immediately in the relaxation room, where she could calm down without a great deal of adult attention.
- Samantha was given "goal sheets" from which she could choose the academic tasks she would work on, the length of time she would work on them, and the specific reinforcer she would receive for achieving any particular goal.
- Samantha was taught how to ask for assistance when she needed it—a strategy that she could use instead of fleeing from the classroom when she encountered a challenging task.
- Samantha was given explicit instruction in how to interact appropriately with her classmates. Initially, she earned points for appropriate social behaviors, and she could trade these points for weekend family trips to Dairy Queen or a video store. Eventually, however, the behaviors themselves led to natural consequences—friendly interactions with her peers—that made such concrete reinforcers unnecessary.

Samantha's behavior changed dramatically within the course of a few months. By the time she was 12 years old and in sixth grade, her grades consistently earned her a place on the honor roll, and she had a group of friends with whom she participated in several extracurricular activities. Her teachers described her as sociable, inquisitive, and creative; her principal called her a "model student" (DeVault et al., 1996).

Positive behavioral support clearly has elements of behaviorist theory, including its focus on structuring an environment that reinforces desired behaviors and extinguishes undesirable ones. At the same time, it also incorporates contemporary theories of motivation, as reflected in its attempts to minimize anxiety, provide opportunities for choice making, and promote mastery of classroom tasks. The importance of doing all of these things will become clearer when we discuss motivation in Chapters 11 and 12.

Considering Diversity in Student Behaviors

When we take a behaviorist perspective, we realize that our students bring their own unique set of prior experiences to the classroom; such diversity in previous environments is undoubtedly one of the reasons for the different behaviors we see in the classroom. For one thing, our students will have been reinforced and punished—by their parents, siblings, previous teachers, peers, and so on—for different kinds of behaviors. Some students may have been reinforced for completing tasks in a careful and thorough manner, whereas others may have been reinforced for completing tasks quickly but sloppily. Some students may have been reinforced for initiating interactions with age-mates; others may have been punished (perhaps in the form of peer rejection) for similar outgoing behavior. Some diversity in students' classroom responses will also be due to the different behaviors that varying cultures encourage (reinforce) and discourage (punish) in their children.

Furthermore, we will see differences in the secondary reinforcers to which students respond. Remember, secondary reinforcers are those that become reinforcing over time through their association with other reinforcing stimuli; thus, the relative effectiveness of such reinforcers as praise and positive feedback will depend on the extent to which such associations have been made. For example, some Native American students may feel uncomfortable when praised for their work as individuals yet feel quite proud when they receive praise for group success (Fuller, 2001). Such preference for group praise is consistent with the cooperative spirit in which these students have been raised (see the discussion of ethnic differences in Chapter 4).

Finally, our students will have had varying experiences with the specific stimuli and general activities they will encounter at school. For example, when they throw a softball for the first time at school, some may be able to generalize from previous experiences throwing a baseball, whereas others may have to start from scratch in developing the skill. When they find themselves in an argument with a classmate, some may try to resolve the conflict through negotiation and compromise, whereas others may engage in a knock-down-drag-out fight.

With such diversity in mind, we will inevitably need to tailor our strategies to the particular students with whom we are working. Effective reinforcers, baseline rates of desired behaviors, and responses to particular stimuli will all be different for each student.

Accommodating Students with Special Needs

A behaviorist approach allows us to consider characteristics of students with special needs from a somewhat different angle than we have in previous chapters. Table 9.3 illustrates how responses, reinforcement, generalization, and discrimination may be somewhat different in some of our students with special needs.

Strengths and Potential Limitations of Behavioral Approaches

Behaviorist techniques are especially helpful when we need to address chronic classroom behavior problems. Although such approaches as applied behavior analysis, functional analysis, and positive behavioral support can be quite time-consuming (J. N. Hughes, 1988), they are often effective when other approaches have not been.

Psychologists have had mixed feelings about the value of behaviorist techniques in addressing *academic* problems, however. Although reinforcement and other behaviorist strategies often lead to improved academic performance, we should note the following drawbacks:

■ *Attempts at changing behaviors ignore cognitive factors that may be interfering with learning.* When students are capable of learning a new skill but are not motivated to do so, the use of reinforcement may be all that is needed to bring about the desired behavior change. But when cognitive deficiencies interfere with the acquisition of a new skill (e.g., perhaps a student has little background knowledge or ineffective study strategies), reinforcement alone may be insufficient. In the latter situation, we may need to employ teaching techniques based more on the cognitive theories we examined in Chapters 6 through 8.

In a number of places throughout the chapter, I have sneaked unobservable phenomena (thoughts, feelings, etc.) into my description of behaviorist principles. Can you find some places where I have done so?

Encouraging Appropriate Behaviors in Students with Special Educational Needs

CATEGORY	CHARACTERISTICS YOU MIGHT OBSERVE	POSSIBLE CLASSROOM STRATEGIES
Students with specific cognitive or academic difficulties	• Inappropriate classroom behaviors (in some students) • Difficulty discriminating among similar stimuli, especially when perceptual deficits exist • Difficulty generalizing responses from one situation to another	• Be explicit about, and consistently reinforce, desired classroom behaviors. • Emphasize differences among similar stimuli (e.g., the letters *b, d, p,* and *q*) and provide opportunities to practice making subtle discriminations. • Promote generalization of new responses (e.g., by pointing out similarities among different situations and by teaching skills in real-world contexts).
Students with social or behavioral problems	• Inappropriate responses, especially in social situations; difficulty determining when and where particular responses are appropriate • A history of inappropriate behaviors being reinforced (e.g., intrinsically or by teacher attention) • Responsiveness to teacher praise if given in private (for students with emotional and behavioral disorders) • Difficulty generalizing appropriate responses to new situations	• Describe desired behaviors clearly. • Give precise feedback regarding students' behavior. • Reinforce desired behaviors using teacher attention, private praise, activity reinforcers, group contingencies (for students with emotional and behavioral disorders). • Reinforce accomplishments immediately using concrete reinforcers, activity reinforcers, or praise (especially for students with autism). • Shape desired behaviors over time; expect gradual improvement rather than immediate perfection. • Punish inappropriate behaviors (e.g., using time-out or response cost); consider ABA, functional analysis, or positive behavioral support for persistently challenging behaviors. • Promote generalization of new responses to appropriate situations (e.g., by teaching skills in real-world contexts and providing opportunities to role-play new responses).
Students with general delays in cognitive and social functioning	• High reinforcing value of extrinsic reinforcers • Behaviors more likely to increase when reinforcement is immediate rather than delayed • Inappropriate responses in social situations • Difficulty discriminating between important and unimportant stimuli • Difficulty generalizing responses from one situation to another	• Cue students regarding appropriate behaviors. • Reinforce accomplishments immediately (e.g., using concrete reinforcers, activity reinforcers, praise). • Use continuous reinforcement during the acquisition of new responses. • Shape desired behaviors over time; expect gradual improvement rather than immediate perfection. • Reprimand minor misbehaviors; use time-out or response cost for more serious and chronic misbehaviors. • Emphasize the stimuli to which you want students to attend. • Promote generalization of new responses (e.g., by teaching skills in real-world contexts and by reinforcing generalization).
Students with physical or sensory challenges	• Loss of some previously learned behaviors if students have had a traumatic brain injury	• Shape desired behaviors over time; expect gradual improvement rather than immediate perfection.
Students with advanced cognitive development	• Unusual and sometimes creative responses to classroom tasks	• Keep an open mind regarding acceptable responses to classroom assignments. • Encourage and reinforce creative responses.

Sources: Barbetta, 1990; Barbetta, Heward, Bradley, & Miller, 1994; Beirne-Smith et al., 2002; Buchoff, 1990; E. S. Ellis & Friend, 1991; Gearheart et al., 1992; Heward, 2000; Landau & McAninch, 1993; Mercer, 1997; Morgan & Jenson, 1988; Patton et al., 1996; Pfiffner & Barkley, 1998; Piirto, 1999; Pressley, 1995; Turnbull et al., 1999.

■ *Reinforcement for accomplishing academic tasks may encourage students to do those tasks quickly rather than thoroughly.* Students receiving extrinsic reinforcers for their academic work sometimes show less interest in *non*reinforced school activities, less desire to perform beyond minimal standards of performance, and less risk taking and creativity in assignments (Brophy, 1986; Clifford, 1990; Lepper & Hodell, 1989).

■ *Extrinsic reinforcement of a behavior already motivated by intrinsic reinforcement may undermine the intrinsically reinforcing value of that behavior.* Students often engage in activities because of the intrinsic reinforcers—for example, for pleasure or feelings of success—that those activities bring. Some research studies indicate that enjoyable activities can be increased by extrinsic reinforcers but will then *decrease* to a below-baseline frequency once the extrinsic reinforcers are removed (J. A. Bates, 1979; Lepper & Greene, 1978; Lepper & Hodell, 1989). (We will identify a possible reason for this puzzling finding in our discussion of *self-determination* in Chapter 12.) Before using extrinsic reinforcers to increase certain behaviors, then, we should be sure that such reinforcers are truly necessary—that students show no intrinsic motivation to develop the academic skills essential for their school success.

The Big Picture

Clearly, we can understand a great deal about human learning and behavior by looking at stimulus-response principles. Conditions already present in a learner's environment—antecedent stimuli—tend to evoke certain kinds of responses either involuntarily (in classical conditioning) or voluntarily (in operant conditioning). Those responses, in turn, may lead to changes in the learner's environment; for instance, they may lead to reinforcement or punishment. If we think of reinforcing and punishing consequences as *stimuli* (because indeed they are), then we see a continuing interaction between the learner and his or her environment, like so:

$$S \rightarrow R \rightarrow S \rightarrow R \rightarrow S \rightarrow R \rightarrow \ldots$$

By changing any part of this chain of events—whether by altering the classroom environment (the stimulus conditions) or by teaching students a more effective way of responding to that environment—we can help students acquire more productive classroom behaviors. For instance, we can increase students' on-task behavior and simultaneously decrease their off-task behavior by

giving them attention (reinforcement) only when they are on task. And we can help them gain the attention (reinforcement) of their peers by teaching and shaping increasingly effective social skills.

Helpful as they may be, however, stimulus-response principles alone do not give us a complete picture of human learning. For example, although reinforcement may increase the amount of time that students study, it does not necessarily increase the effectiveness of that study time; cognitive psychology provides more guidance as to how we can help students learn information more effectively, remember it longer, and apply it to new situations more readily. Furthermore, it appears that people learn not only the behaviors that they themselves are reinforced for but also the behaviors they see reinforced for *others*; social cognitive theory, which we consider in the next chapter, provides more guidance on helping students learn through their observations of others. In addition, motivational factors play a key role in determining what consequences are likely to be reinforcing at any given time; we will explore the nature of motivation in Chapters 11 and 12.

PRAXIS Turn to Appendix C, "Matching Book and Ancillary Content to the PRAXIS™ Principles of Learning and Teaching Tests," to discover sections of this chapter that may be especially applicable to the PRAXIS™ tests.

Now go to our Companion Website at http://www.prenhall. com/ormrod to assess your understanding of chapter content with "Multiple-Choice Questions," apply comprehension in "Essay Questions," broaden your knowledge of educational psychology with related "Web Links," gain greater insight about classroom learning in "Learning in the Content Areas," and analyze and assess classroom work in the "Student Artifact Library."

CASE STUDY: *Hostile Helen*

Mr. Washington has a close-knit group of friends in one of his high school vocational education classes. He is concerned about one particular student in this group, a girl named Helen. Helen uses obscene language in class. She is rude and disrespectful to Mr. Washington. She taunts and insults classmates outside her own circle of friends. And she is physically aggressive toward school property—she defaces furniture, kicks equipment, punches walls, and so on.

At first, Mr. Washington tries to ignore Helen's hostile and aggressive behaviors, but this strategy doesn't lead to any improvement in her behavior. He then tries praising Helen on those rare occasions when she does behave appropriately, but this strategy doesn't seem to work either.

- In behaviorist terminology, what is Mr. Washington trying to do when he ignores Helen's inappropriate behavior? What are some possible reasons this approach isn't working?
- In behaviorist terminology, what is Mr. Washington trying to do when he praises Helen's appropriate behavior? What are some possible reasons this approach isn't working either?
- How might *you* use behaviorist learning principles to bring about a behavior change in Helen?

Once you have answered these questions, compare your responses with those presented in Appendix B.

Key Concepts

behaviorism (p. 299)
conditioning (p. 300)
response (R) (p. 300)
stimulus (S) (p. 300)
contiguity (p. 301)
classical conditioning (p. 302)
unconditioned stimulus (UCS) (p. 302)
unconditioned response (UCR) (p. 302)
neutral stimulus (p. 302)
conditioned stimulus (CS) (p. 303)
conditioned response (CR) (p. 303)
generalization in classical conditioning (p. 304)
extinction in classical conditioning (p. 305)
operant conditioning (p. 305)
contingency (p. 306)
reinforcer (p. 307)
reinforcement (p. 307)
primary reinforcer (p. 307)
secondary reinforcer (p. 307)
positive reinforcement (p. 308)

concrete reinforcer (p. 308)
social reinforcer (p. 308)
activity reinforcer (p. 308)
Premack principle (p. 308)
positive feedback (p. 308)
extrinsic reinforcer (p. 308)
intrinsic reinforcer (p. 308)
negative reinforcement (p. 309)
delay of gratification (p. 310)
terminal behavior (p. 311)
token economy (p. 312)
backup reinforcer (p. 312)
group contingency (p. 312)
contingency contract (p. 313)
continuous reinforcement (p. 313)
baseline (p. 313)
shaping (p. 314)
antecedent stimulus (p. 315)
antecedent response (p. 315)
cueing (p. 315)

setting event (p. 316)
generalization in operant conditioning (p. 316)
discrimination (p. 317)
behavioral momentum (p. 317)
extinction in operant conditioning (p. 318)
incompatible behaviors (p. 319)
punishment (p. 320)
presentation punishment (p. 320)
removal punishment (p. 320)
verbal reprimand (p. 320)
response cost (p. 321)
logical consequence (p. 321)
time-out (p. 321)
in-school suspension (p. 322)
psychological punishment (p. 322)
intermittent reinforcement (p. 325)
applied behavior analysis (ABA) (p. 325)
functional analysis (p. 326)
positive behavioral support (p. 326)

10

Social Cognitive Views of Learning

*W*hat behaviors have you learned by observing other people do them first? Can you think of any academic skills you've learned by watching or listening to someone else? Perhaps you learned a mathematical procedure or the correct conjugation of *estudiar*. What about social skills? Perhaps you observed how to answer the telephone or how to apologize to someone whose feelings you've hurt. And what about psychomotor skills? Perhaps you discovered how to swing a softball bat or write letters in cursive. We learn a wide variety of behaviors by observing our parents, our teachers, our peers, people we see in the media, and the many other individuals we encounter in our daily lives. We also learn which behaviors are likely to get us ahead—and which behaviors are not—by seeing their consequences for ourselves and others. Eventually we develop a sense of what we ourselves are capable of doing, and we begin to direct our behavior toward goals that we value and think we can achieve.

In this chapter we will explore **social cognitive theory** (also called *social learning theory*), a perspective that can help us understand what, when, and how people learn by observing others, and how people ultimately begin to assume some control over their own behavior. In the process, we will address questions such as these:

- What basic assumptions are central to the social cognitive perspective of learning?
- How do cognitive processes influence the effects that reinforcement and punishment have on behavior?
- How can we effectively use modeling to facilitate students' learning?
- What role does *self-efficacy* play in learning, and how can we enhance it in our students?
- How can we help students take control of their own behavior and learning? In other words, how can we promote *self-regulation*?

CASE STUDY: *Parlez-vous français?*

Nathan isn't taking French because he wants to; he has enrolled in French I only because his mother insisted. Although he does well in his other high school courses, he's convinced that he will be a failure in French. After all, three friends who took French last year got mostly Ds and Fs on quizzes and homework, and two of them dropped the class after the first semester.

On the first day of French class, Nathan notices that most of his classmates are girls; the few boys in the class are students he doesn't know very well. He sits sullenly in the back row, convinced that he will do no better in French than his friends did. "I do OK in math and science, but I'm just no good at learning languages," he tells himself. "Besides, learning French is a 'girl' thing."

Although Nathan comes to class every day, his mind usually wanders to other topics as his teacher explains simple syntactical structures and demonstrates the correct pronunciation of new vocabulary words. He makes feeble attempts at homework assignments but quickly puts them aside whenever he encounters anything he doesn't immediately understand.

Sure enough, Nathan is right: He can't do French. He gets a D− on his first exam.

- What has Nathan learned about French by observing other people?
- Why do Nathan's beliefs lead to a self-fulfilling prophecy?

Basic Assumptions of Social Cognitive Theory

You might initially think that Nathan has learned nothing from observing others because he has apparently not benefited from his teacher's explanations and demonstrations. Yet at second glance, you might realize that Nathan *has* learned something through observation after all: He has seen what happened to his three friends and concluded that *he* probably won't succeed in French class either. As we proceed through the chapter, you will discover some reasons why Nathan has apparently learned more from his friends than he has from his teacher.

Social cognitive theory has its roots in behaviorism, but over the past few decades it has increasingly incorporated cognitive processes into its explanations of learning; it now provides a nice blend of ideas from behaviorism and cognitive psychology. Yet it addresses *motivation* to a greater degree than either the cognitive or behaviorist perspective; accordingly, it provides a good transition to our discussion of motivation in Chapters 11 and 12. Social cognitive theory has developed in large part through the research efforts of Albert Bandura at Stanford University. You will find references to Bandura and others who build on his ideas (e.g., Dale Schunk, Barry Zimmerman) throughout the chapter.

As you read the chapter, look for references to motivation in the sections on modeling, self-efficacy, and self-regulation.

In our case study of Nathan, we can see one basic assumption underlying social cognitive theory: People can learn from observing others. This and several other assumptions are summarized in Table 10.1. Let's look at them more closely:

- *People can learn by observing others.* In our discussion of operant conditioning in the preceding chapter, we found that learning is sometimes a process of trial and error: People try many different responses, increasing the ones that bring about desirable consequences and eliminating the unproductive ones. Social cognitive theorists contend that people don't always have to "experiment" in this way; instead, they can acquire many new responses simply by observing the behaviors of people around them. For example, a student might learn how to solve a long division problem, spell the word *synonym* correctly, or mouth off at the teacher simply by watching someone else do these things first.

TABLE 10.1   **PRINCIPLES / ASSUMPTIONS**

Basic Assumptions of Social Cognitive Theory and Their Educational Implications

ASSUMPTION	EDUCATIONAL IMPLICATION	EXAMPLE
Learning by observation	Help students acquire new behaviors more quickly by demonstrating those behaviors yourself.	Demonstrate appropriate ways to deal with and resolve interpersonal conflicts. Then ask students to role-play conflict resolution in small groups, and commend those who use prosocial strategies.
Learning as an internal process that may or may not be reflected in behavior	Remember that learning does not always appear immediately, but may instead be reflected in students' later behaviors.	When one student engages in disruptive classroom behavior, take appropriate steps to discourage it. Otherwise, classmates who have witnessed the misbehavior may be similarly disruptive in the future.
Goal-directed behavior	Encourage students to set goals for themselves, especially goals that are challenging yet achievable.	When teaching American Sign Language to students to help them communicate with a classmate who is deaf, ask them to predict how many new words and phrases they can learn each week.
Self-regulation of behavior	Teach students strategies for helping themselves learn effectively and behave appropriately.	Give students some concrete suggestions about how they can remind themselves to bring needed supplies to school each day.
Indirect effects of reinforcement and punishment	Ensure that the consequences of students' behaviors communicate the right messages about which actions are and are not acceptable in the classroom.	To encourage students to speak in German, respond to questions only if students make a reasonable attempt to ask the questions in German.

■ *Learning is an internal process that may or may not result in a behavior change.* Some of the things people learn appear in their behavior immediately, other things affect their behavior at a later time, and still others may never influence their behavior at all. For example, you might attempt to swing a tennis racket as soon as you learn the correct form. But you probably won't demonstrate that you've learned how to apologize tactfully until a time when an apology is necessary. And you might *never* walk barefoot over hot coals, no matter how many times you see someone else do it. Social cognitive theory, like cognitive psychology, defines learning as an internal mental process that may or may not be reflected in the learner's behavior.

Social cognitive theorists propose that people can sometimes learn more quickly and easily by watching how others behave and noticing which behaviors lead to reinforcement and which lead to punishment.

■ *Behavior is directed toward particular goals.* Because you are reading this book, you probably want to become a teacher or enter some related profession, and you are taking an educational psychology class to help you attain that goal. Social cognitive theorists propose that people often set goals for themselves and direct their behavior accordingly; in essence, they are *motivated* to accomplish their goals. Students are likely to have a variety of goals—perhaps a high grade point average, a college scholarship, popularity with classmates, athletic prowess, or a reputation as the class clown. Throughout the chapter we will see the relevance of such goals for learning and behavior.

■ *Behavior eventually becomes self-regulated.* From a behaviorist perspective, people's behaviors are governed largely by the things that happen *to* them—the stimuli they encounter, the reinforcers that follow their behaviors, and so on. In contrast, social cognitive theorists believe that people eventually begin to regulate their *own* learning and behavior. As an example, let's consider Shih-tai, a third grader who is learning to write in cursive. A traditional behaviorist might tell us that Shih-tai can best learn cursive if her teacher reinforces her for increasingly more appropriate responses, thereby shaping skillful penmanship over a period of several weeks or months. But a social cognitive theorist might suggest that Shih-tai can learn to write cursive letters more effectively by looking carefully at the examples her teacher has written on the chalkboard, copying those letters as closely as possible, and then comparing the letters she has written with those on the board. If she is happy with her work, she will give herself a mental pat on the back; if she is not, she may continue to practice until her letters are comparable with those of the teacher. From the social cognitive perspective, people often set their own standards for acceptable and unacceptable behavior and then strive to behave in accordance with those standards.

Do you think your own behaviors are regulated more by the environment or by your own standards for what is acceptable and what is not?

■ *Reinforcement and punishment have several indirect effects (rather than a direct effect) on learning and behavior.* Operant conditioning theorists believe that reinforcement is necessary for learning, in that responses increase only when they are reinforced. Some behaviorists have also argued that punishment is an effective counterpart to reinforcement, decreasing the frequency of a behavior it follows. Implied in the behaviorist perspective is the idea that reinforcement and punishment are directly responsible for the behavior changes we see.

Reinforcement and punishment are less critical in social cognitive theory, but they have several indirect effects on learning and behavior. In the section that follows, we will find out exactly how reinforcement and punishment fit into the social cognitive perspective.

The Social Cognitive View of Reinforcement and Punishment

According to social cognitive theorists (e.g., Bandura, 1977, 1986; T. L. Rosenthal & Zimmerman, 1978), both reinforcement and punishment influence learning and behavior in several ways:

- People form *expectations* about the likely consequences of future responses based on how current responses are reinforced or punished.
- People's expectations are also influenced by their observations of the consequences that follow other people's behaviors—in other words, by *vicarious experiences*.
- Expectations about probable future consequences affect how people *cognitively process* new information.
- Expectations also affect how people *choose to behave*.

- The *nonoccurrence of an expected consequence* may have a reinforcing or punishing effect in and of itself.

Let's see how each of these factors plays out in social cognitive theory.

Expectations

Perhaps you have taken a course in which all the exam questions were based on the textbook, without a single question coming from class lectures. After the first exam, did you find yourself studying the textbook very carefully but skipping class frequently? On the other hand, perhaps you have taken a course in which exams were based almost *entirely* on class lectures and activities. In that situation, did you go to class regularly but seldom bother to open your textbook?

According to social cognitive theory, people form expectations about the consequences likely to result from various behaviors. When we find that a particular response is reinforced every time we make it, we typically expect to be reinforced for behaving that way in future situations. When we discover that a response frequently leads to punishment, we expect that response to be punished on later occasions as well. For example, you use your own experiences with classroom tests to form expectations as to what specific behaviors (e.g., reading your textbook, going to class) are likely to be reinforced on future tests.

Can you think of an occasion when you chose not to do something because of the ridicule you thought it might bring you?

Students sometimes form expectations about what things will be reinforced and punished on the basis of very little hard data. For example, one student might believe (perhaps erroneously) that by bragging about his high test scores, he will gain the admiration of his classmates (a reinforcer). Another student might believe that her classmates will ridicule and reject (i.e., punish) her for being smart, regardless of whether they would actually do so.

From the social cognitive perspective, reinforcement increases the frequency of a behavior only when students think or know that the behavior is being reinforced—that is, when they are *aware* of a response-reinforcement contingency (Bandura, 1986). As teachers, then, we should be very clear about what we are reinforcing, so that our students know the real response-reinforcement contingencies operating in the classroom. For example, if Sam gets an A on an essay but we don't let him know *why* he earned that grade, he won't necessarily know how to get an A the next time. To improve Sam's performance, we might tell him that the essay earned an A because he supported his opinion with a logical train of thought. Similarly, if we praise Sandra for her "good game" at the basketball tournament even though she scored only one basket, she may understandably be a bit confused. We might instead tell her that we were pleased with her high energy level and cooperation with other team members throughout the game.

Vicarious Experiences

When I was in third grade, I entered a Halloween costume contest dressed as "Happy Tooth," a character in several toothpaste commercials at the time. I didn't win the contest; a "witch" won first prize. So the following year, I entered the same contest dressed as a witch, figuring that I was a shoo-in for first place. Our expectations about the consequences of certain responses come not only from making those responses ourselves but also from observing what happens when others make them. In other words, we sometimes experience reinforcement and punishment *vicariously*.

People who observe someone else getting reinforced for a particular behavior tend to exhibit that behavior more frequently themselves—a phenomenon known as **vicarious reinforcement**. For example, by watching the consequences that their classmates experience, students might learn that studying hard leads to good grades, that being elected to class office brings status and popularity, or that neatness counts.

Conversely, when we see someone else get punished for a certain behavior, we are *less* likely to behave that way ourselves—a phenomenon known as **vicarious punishment**. For example, when a coach benches a football player for poor sportsmanlike conduct, other players will be less likely to mimic such behavior. But unfortunately, vicarious punishment may suppress desirable behaviors as well. For example, when a teacher belittles a student for asking a "silly" question, other students may be reluctant to ask questions of their own.

As teachers, we must be extremely careful that we don't vicariously reinforce undesirable behaviors or vicariously punish desirable ones. If we give too much attention to a misbehaving student, others who want our attention may misbehave as well. If we ridicule a student who unwittingly volunteers an incorrect answer or erroneous belief, classmates will hardly be eager to respond to our questions or express their ideas and opinions.

Cognitive Processing

EXPERIENCING FIRSTHAND *Planning Ahead*

Quickly skim the contents of Chapter 11 and get a general sense of the topics it includes. Once you have done so, imagine yourself in each of these situations:

1. Your educational psychology instructor announces, "Chapter 11 won't be on your test, but please read it anyway." How thoroughly and carefully will you read the chapter? Jot down a brief answer to this question.
2. The following day, your educational psychology instructor announces, "I gave you some incorrect information yesterday. In reality, half of next week's test will be based on the ideas presented in Chapter 11." *Now* how thoroughly and carefully will you read the chapter? Once again, jot down a brief answer.

If you don't expect to be reinforced for reading Chapter 11, you may very well *not* read it too carefully (perhaps you'll read it later, you think to yourself, but you have many other things to do right now). If, instead, you discover that getting an A in your educational psychology course depends on your knowing the material in Chapter 11 like the back of your hand, you are apt to read it slowly and carefully, possibly trying to learn and remember each and every detail.

When we believe that we will be reinforced for learning something, we are more likely to pay attention to it and mentally process it in an effective fashion. When we *don't* expect to be reinforced for learning it, we are far less likely to think about or process it in any significant way. As an example of the latter situation, let's return to Nathan in our opening case study. Already convinced that he can't learn French, Nathan pays little attention to what his teacher says in class, and he makes only half-hearted efforts to complete his homework assignments.

Choice of Behavior

People learn many things that they never demonstrate because there is no reinforcement for doing so. To see what I mean, try the following exercise.

EXPERIENCING FIRSTHAND *Dr. X*

How many of the following questions can you answer about your educational psychology instructor? For lack of a better name, I'm going to call your instructor "Dr. X."

1. Is Dr. X right-handed or left-handed?
2. Is Dr. X a flashy dresser or a more conservative one?
3. What kind of shoes does Dr. X wear to class?
4. Does Dr. X wear a wedding ring?
5. Does Dr. X bring a briefcase to class each day?

If you've been going to class regularly, you probably know the answers to at least two of the questions, and possibly you can answer all five, even though you never thought you'd have a reason to know such information. Every time I teach educational psychology, I take a minute sometime during the semester to hide my feet behind the podium; I then ask my students to tell me what my shoes look like. My students first look at me as if I have two heads; information about my shoes is something that many of them have learned, but until now they have had absolutely no reason to demonstrate their knowledge. After a few seconds of awkward silence, at least a half dozen students (usually those sitting in the first two rows) begin to describe my shoes, right down to the rippled soles, scuffed leather, and beige stitching.

Students learn many things in the classroom. They learn facts and figures, they learn ways of getting their teacher's attention, and they may even learn such tiny details as which classmate stores Twinkies in his desk and what kind of shoes the teacher wears to school. Of all the things they learn, students will be most likely to demonstrate the ones they think will bring them reinforcement. The things they think will *not* be reinforced may remain hidden forever.

When students work diligently for a reinforcer that they hope to obtain in the future, they are working for an **incentive**. Incentives are never guaranteed: Students never know that they are going to get an A on a test when they study for it or that they are going to win a Halloween costume contest when they enter it. An incentive is an expected or hoped-for consequence, one that may or may not actually occur.

Students don't work for incentives they don't believe they can achieve. For example, in a classroom of thirty seventh graders, a classroom competition in which one prize will be awarded for the highest test score provides an incentive to just a handful of top achievers. An incentive is effective only if it is obtainable and a student perceives it as such. Therefore, when we provide incentives for student achievement, we should make sure our students believe they have some chance of achieving those incentives.

Nonoccurrence of Expected Consequences

When I entered the Halloween costume contest as a witch, I lost once again. (First prize went to a girl with a metal colander over her head. She was dressed as *Sputnik*, the first satellite launched into space by what was then the Soviet Union.) That was the last time I entered a Halloween contest. I had expected reinforcement and felt cheated when I didn't get it. Social cognitive theorists propose that the nonoccurrence of expected reinforcement is a form of punishment (e.g., Bandura, 1986). When people think that a certain response is going to be reinforced, yet the response is *not* reinforced, they are less likely to exhibit that behavior in the future.

Can you recall an occasion when, as a student, you did not receive the reinforcement you expected? How did you feel and behave when that happened?

Perhaps you can think of a time when you broke a rule, expecting to be punished, but got away with your crime. Or perhaps you can remember seeing someone else break a rule without being caught. When nothing bad happens after a forbidden behavior, people may actually feel as if they have been reinforced for that behavior. Just as the nonoccurrence of reinforcement is a form of punishment, the nonoccurrence of punishment is a form of reinforcement (Bandura, 1986).

When students work hard to achieve a desired end result—perhaps a compliment, high grade, or special privilege—and the anticipated result doesn't materialize, they will be unlikely to work as hard the next time. And when students break school rules yet are not punished for doing so, they are more likely to break those rules again. As teachers, it is important that we follow through with promised reinforcements for desirable student behaviors. It is equally important that we impose the consequences students have come to expect for undesirable behaviors.

As we have seen, students learn many behaviors from observing those around them. But they don't necessarily model everything they see someone else do. When do students imitate the behaviors they see? And what kinds of people are they most likely to imitate? It is to such questions about *modeling* that we turn now.

Modeling

Consider these research findings:

- In one experiment, young children were taught not to speak to strangers through one of two techniques. One group of children heard a lecture about the dangers of following strangers and about the things they should do if a stranger tried to entice them; nevertheless, very few of these children tried to resist a friendly stranger who later appeared on the playground. A second group of children actually observed another child demonstrate techniques for resisting strangers; most of these children resisted the stranger's advances (Poche, Yoder, & Miltenberger, 1988).
- When children see aggressive models—whether those models are people the children know, people on television, or cartoon characters—they are more likely to be aggressive themselves. Boys in particular are likely to model the aggressive behaviors they observe (Bandura, Ross, & Ross, 1961, 1963; Bushman & Anderson, 2001; Eron, 1980; Lowry et al., 1995; Steuer, Applefield, & Smith, 1971).

INTO THE CLASSROOM: *Administering Consequences from a Social Cognitive Perspective*

Describe the specific behaviors you are reinforcing, so that students are aware of the response-reinforcement contingencies operating in the classroom.

A teacher tells his class, "Because everyone got at least 80 percent of the math problems correct this morning, we will have ten minutes of free time at the end of the day."

Make sure students believe that they can achieve the incentives offered in the classroom.

A teacher realizes that if she were to grade her students' science projects on a curve, only a few students could possibly get As. Instead, she gives her students a checklist of the specific criteria she will use to grade the science projects; she tells her class that any project meeting all the criteria will get an A.

Tell students what behaviors are unacceptable in the classroom and describe the consequences that will result when those behaviors occur.

A teacher reminds students that anyone seen pushing in the lunch line will go to the end of the line.

Follow through with the reinforcements you have promised for desirable student behaviors; also follow through with the adverse consequences students expect for undesirable behaviors.

When announcing tryouts for an upcoming holiday play, a teacher tells students that only those who sign up ahead of time may try out. Although she later regrets making this statement—some of the most talented students don't sign up in time—she sticks to her word during tryout sessions and turns away anyone whose name does not appear on her sign-up sheet.

Remember that the consequences you administer for a particular student's behavior have a potential effect on any students who observe those consequences.

The student council president, even though she is well liked and highly respected by both students and teachers, is nevertheless punished in accordance with school rules when she is caught cheating on an exam.

- After watching adults demonstrate such behaviors as cooperation, sympathy, sharing, and generosity, children are more likely to demonstrate similar prosocial behaviors (R. Elliott & Vasta, 1970; Friedrich & Stein, 1973; Radke-Yarrow, Zahn-Waxler, & Chapman, 1983; Rushton, 1980).
- When a model preaches one set of moral values and practices another, observers are more likely to do what the model *does* than what the model *says* (J. H. Bryan, 1975).

We learn many different things through modeling. We learn such motor skills as holding a pencil, whittling a piece of wood, and dribbling a basketball by seeing how other people do these things. We also acquire skills in such academic areas as arithmetic, reading, and art more readily by observing others. And we develop interpersonal skills and moral values, at least in part, by watching and imitating the people around us.

Most of the models from which we learn are **live models**—real people that we actually see doing something. In a classroom setting, students may learn something by watching their teacher solve an algebraic equation, observing a visiting police officer demonstrate important rules of bicycle safety, or seeing a classmate perform a flawless hook shot on the basketball court. But we are also influenced by **symbolic models**—real or fictional characters portrayed in books, in films, on television, and through various other media. For example, students can learn valuable lessons from studying the behaviors of important figures in history or reading stories about people who accomplish great things in the face of adversity.

Think of specific people who might serve as positive role models (either real or symbolic) for your own students.

How Modeling Affects Behavior

Social cognitive theorists (e.g., Bandura, 1977, 1986; T. L. Rosenthal & Zimmerman, 1978) propose that modeling has several possible effects on human behavior: observational learning, response facilitation, response inhibition, and response disinhibition.

Observational learning effect. The observational learning effect occurs when *the observer acquires a new behavior demonstrated by the model.* By seeing and hearing models, students learn how to dissect an earthworm, swim the elementary back stroke, and pronounce *¿Estudia usted español?* correctly. They may also acquire the political and religious beliefs that they hear their parents advocate. And they may adopt the attitudes of their

teachers—perhaps enthusiasm about baseball, fear of mathematics, or disdain for the study of history (e.g., Rushton, 1980).

Response facilitation effect. The response facilitation effect occurs when *the observer displays a previously learned behavior more frequently after seeing a model being reinforced for that behavior* (i.e., after receiving vicarious reinforcement). As an example, consider this situation:

> Billy returns to school in September to discover that his expensive new jeans are no longer in style. All his classmates are now wearing old, well-worn jeans; those with holes in the knees are especially fashionable. When he arrives home after his first day of school, Billy digs through his dresser drawers and the family rag bag, looking for old jeans. The next day, much to his parents' dismay, Billy goes to school wearing a pair of jeans with one large hole in the left knee and a three-inch rip running up the right thigh. The brand new jeans that Billy's mother has purchased for him are relegated to the top shelf of his closet, where they remain for the rest of the school year.

Our students are more likely to wear ragged old jeans if their classmates appear to be winning popularity with this attire. Similarly, they are more likely to complete their reading assignments on time and to work cooperatively rather than competitively with classmates—behaviors they may have learned long ago—if they see others being reinforced for doing so.

Response inhibition effect. The response inhibition effect occurs when *the observer displays a previously learned behavior less frequently after seeing a model being punished for that behavior* (i.e., after receiving vicarious punishment). Students tend to inhibit (*not* engage in) behaviors that result in adverse consequences for those around them. For example, students are less likely to be aggressive on the playground if they see their friends being punished for aggression. They are less likely to cheat on assignments if their peers are caught in the act. And they are less likely to volunteer to answer questions in class when the incorrect answers of their classmates are ridiculed.

Response disinhibition effect. The response disinhibition effect occurs when *the observer displays a previously forbidden or punished behavior more frequently after seeing a model exhibit the behavior without adverse consequences.* Although students will inhibit behaviors leading to punishment, they may begin to engage in behaviors they have previously inhibited if they observe those behaviors going unpunished for other people. For example, students are more likely to chew gum, copy homework from classmates, or fight in the corridors if they see other students getting away with such behaviors. Remember, the nonoccurrence of expected punishment is reinforcing, so naturally any forbidden activities that seem to have no adverse effects for others may easily increase.

Yet students don't always model the people around them. What factors determine when students are most likely to imitate the behaviors they see? A look at characteristics of effective models will help us with the answer.

Characteristics of Effective Models

EXPERIENCING FIRSTHAND   *Five People*

Write down the names of five people whose behaviors you would like to imitate in some way. Then, beside each name, write down one or more of the reasons *why* you admire these individuals.

Social cognitive theorists have found some consistency in the types of models that others are most likely to imitate (Bandura, 1986; T. L. Rosenthal & Bandura, 1978). Effective models typically exhibit one or more of the following characteristics—characteristics that you probably see reflected in the list you just created.

Why is this called the disinhibition effect?

How are the response facilitation and response disinhibition effects similar? How are they different?

FIGURE 10.1 Students in Barbara Dee's seventh-grade language arts class chose these examples of effective figurative writing from the books they were reading. Such examples can serve as models for students' own writing efforts.

"The blackness of the night came in, like snakes around the ankles."
—Caroline Cooney's *Wanted*, p. 176

"Flirtatious waves made passes at the primly pebbled beach."
—Lilian Jackson Braun's *The Cat Who Saw Stars*, p. 120

"Water boiled up white and frothy, like a milkshake."
—Lurlene McDaniel's *For Better, for Worse, Forever*, p. 60

"Solid rocket boosters suddenly belched forty-four million horsepower."
—Ben Mikaelsen's *Countdown*, p. 148

"I try to swallow the snowball in my throat."
—Laurie Halse Anderson's *Speak*, p. 72

Competence.   Students will typically try to imitate people who do something well, not those who do it poorly. They will try to imitate the basketball skills of a professional basketball player, rather than those of the class klutz. They will copy the fashions of a popular classmate, rather than those of a student who is socially isolated. They will adopt the mathematical problem-solving procedures of teachers who clearly know what they are doing, rather than the procedures of teachers who make frequent mistakes at the chalkboard. Figure 10.1 illustrates how one teacher effectively uses competent models to teach creative writing.

Prestige and power.   Children and adolescents often imitate people who are famous or powerful. Some effective models—a world leader, a renowned athlete, a popular rock star—are famous at a national or international level. The prestige and power of other models—a head cheerleader, the captain of the high school hockey team, a gang leader—may be limited to a more local environment.

In addition to modeling desired behaviors ourselves, we can expose our students to a variety of models that they are likely to view as prestigious and powerful. For example, we might invite respected professionals (e.g., police officer, nurse, newspaper reporter) to visit our classroom and talk with students about topics within their areas of expertise. We might also have students read and learn about appropriate models through such media as books and films; for example, students might read Helen Keller's autobiography or watch news clips of Martin Luther King, Jr.

"Gender appropriate" behavior.   Remember Nathan's belief that French is a "girl" thing? Students are most likely to model behaviors they believe are appropriate for their gender (with different students inevitably defining *gender appropriate* somewhat differently). For example, many girls and boys limit their academic choices and career aspirations to the subjects and professions they believe are "for women" and "for men," respectively. Some girls may shy away from careers in mathematics as being too "masculine." Some boys may not take typing because they perceive it to be a secretarial skill, and most secretaries are women. Yet mathematics and keyboarding are useful skills for both genders. Exposure to numerous examples of people in so-called nontraditional careers—female mathematicians and engineers, male secretaries and nurses—can help broaden students' perceptions as to what behaviors are gender appropriate. In the process, such models can also broaden students' academic choices and possibly enhance their career aspirations.

Behavior relevant to the learner's own situation.   Students are most likely to model the behaviors they believe will help them in their own circumstances. A boy may wear the torn jeans that his popular classmates wear if he thinks he can become popular with such attire; however, he will have less reason to dress this way if he thinks that his thick glasses and adolescent acne will prevent him from ever being popular regardless of his clothing. A teenage girl may be tempted to join her friends in drinking beer if she thinks that doing so will help her to be accepted by them; she is less likely to indulge if she is the "designated driver" and knows that her friends are depending on her to stay sober.

In the classroom we are likely to model a variety of behaviors throughout the day. But our students will adopt these behaviors only if they believe that such responses will truly be useful and productive for them. Therefore, we must show them how the problem-solving methods we teach, the writing skills we demonstrate, and the physical fitness regimen we advocate are all applicable to their own situations.

Our students are less likely to perceive the relevance of modeled behaviors when the model is different from them in some obvious way. For example, students from cultures other than our own may think that some of the things we try to teach them don't apply to their own cultural circumstances. Similarly, students with disabilities may believe that they are incapable of accomplishing the things a nondisabled teacher demonstrates. So it is important that we include individuals from minority cultures and individuals with disabilities in the models we present to our students. Minority students benefit from observing successful minority adults, and students with disabilities become more optimistic about their own futures when they meet adults successfully coping with and overcoming their own disabilities (Pang, 1995; L. E. Powers, Sowers, & Stevens, 1995).

You can probably think of teachers you admired and wanted to be like. Most teachers have one or more characteristics of an effective model; for example, students typically view their teachers as being competent and having power, at least within the school environment. So as teachers, we "teach" not only by what we say but also by what we do. It is critical that we model appropriate behaviors and *not* model inappropriate ones. Do we model fairness to all students, or favoritism to a small few? Do we model enthusiasm and excitement about the subject matter being taught, or merely tolerance for a dreary topic that the class must muddle through as best it can? Do we expound on the virtues of innovation and creativity yet use the same curriculum materials year after year? Our actions often speak louder than our words.

Yet even when models are competent and prestigious and even when they exhibit behaviors that students think are appropriate for themselves as well, successful modeling does not necessarily occur. What must students do to learn modeled behavior effectively? Let's find out.

**IN THE BLEACHERS
by Steve Moore**

"Don't cry, Megan. Remember, it's not whether Daddy wins the brawl in the stands that's important. It's how you played the game."

When we work with children, our actions will often speak louder than our words.

Helping Students Learn from Models

According to social cognitive theorists (e.g., Bandura, 1986), four conditions are necessary before a student can successfully model someone else's behavior: attention, retention, motor reproduction, and motivation.

Attention. In the opening case study, Nathan paid little attention to his French teacher. Yet to learn effectively, *the learner must pay attention to the model*. Before imitation is possible, our students must observe carefully as we show proper procedures in the science lab, watch closely as we demonstrate the elementary backstroke, or listen attentively as we pronounce *Comment allez-vous?*

Retention. After paying attention, *the learner must remember what the model does*. If you have already read the discussion of cognitive processes in Chapter 6, then you know that students are more likely to remember information they have encoded in memory in more than one way—perhaps both as a visual image and as a verbal representation. As teachers, then, we may often want to describe what we are doing as we demonstrate behaviors. For example, we should explain what we are doing as we model the process of long division, perhaps like so:

> First I have to decide what number to divide 4 into. I take 276, start on the left and move toward the right until I have a number the same as or larger than 4. Is 2 larger than 4? No. Is 27 larger than 4? Yes. So my first division will be 4 into 27. Now I need to multiply 4 by a number that will give an answer the same as or slightly smaller than 27. How about 5? 5 × 4 = 20. No, too small. Let's try 6. 6 × 4 = 24. Maybe. Let's try 7. 7 × 4 = 28. No, too large. So 6 is correct. (Schunk, 1998, p. 146)

"Chicken"   "Airplane"   "Soldier"

FIGURE 10.2 Students can often more easily remember a complex behavior, such as the arm movements for the elementary backstroke, when those behaviors have verbal labels.

We may also want to give descriptive labels to complex behaviors that might otherwise be difficult to remember (Gerst, 1971; T. L. Rosenthal, Alford, & Rasp, 1972). To illustrate, when teaching swimming, an easy way to help students remember the sequence of arm positions in the elementary backstroke is to teach them "chicken" (arms bent with hands tucked under armpits), "airplane" (arms straight out to the side), and "soldier" (arms straight and held close to the torso; see Figure 10.2). It may be especially helpful for students to repeat such labels aloud as they copy a model's actions (R. L. Cohen, 1989; Mace, Belfiore, & Shea, 1989; Schunk, 1989c). As an example, consider the following set of self-instructions taught to students who are first learning a basic tennis stroke:

1. Say *ball* to remind yourself to look at the ball.
2. Say *bounce* to remind yourself to follow the ball with your eyes as it approaches you.
3. Say *hit* to remind yourself to focus on contacting the ball with the racket.
4. Say *ready* to get yourself into position for the next ball to come your way. (Ziegler, 1987)

Tennis students taught to give themselves these simple instructions—*ball, bounce, hit,* and *ready*—improve the accuracy of their returns more quickly than students not taught to do so (Ziegler, 1987).

Motor reproduction.   In addition to attending and remembering, *the learner must be physically capable of reproducing the modeled behavior.* When a student lacks the ability to reproduce an observed behavior, motor reproduction obviously cannot occur. For example, first graders who watch a high school student throw a softball do not possess the muscular coordination to mimic that throw. Secondary school students who haven't yet learned to roll their *R*s will have trouble repeating the Spanish teacher's tongue twister:

Erre con erre cigarro, erre con erre barril.

Rápido corren los carros del ferrocarril.

It will often be useful to have students imitate a desired behavior immediately after they watch us demonstrate it. When they do so, we can give them the feedback they need to improve their performance. Modeling accompanied by verbal guidance and frequent feedback—a technique sometimes known as *coaching*—is often more effective than modeling alone (S. N. Elliott & Busse, 1991; Kitsantis, Zimmerman, & Cleary, 2000; Schunk & Swartz, 1993; Zirpoli & Melloy, 2001). At the same time, we must keep in mind a point made in Chapter 4: Students from some ethnic groups (e.g., many Native Americans) may prefer to practice new behaviors in private at first, showing us what they have learned only after they have achieved sufficient mastery.

Motivation.   Finally, *the learner must be motivated to demonstrate the modeled behavior.* Some students may be eager to show what they have observed and remembered; for example, they may have seen the model reinforced for a certain behavior and so have already been vicariously reinforced. But other students may not have any motivation to demonstrate something they have seen a model do, perhaps because the model was punished or perhaps because they don't see the model's actions as being appropriate for themselves. In Chapters 11 and 12, we will identify numerous strategies for increasing students' motivation to exhibit desired behaviors.

When all four factors—attention, retention, motor reproduction, and motivation—are present, modeling can be an extremely powerful teaching technique (e.g., Kitsantis et al., 2000; Schloss & Smith, 1994; Schunk & Hanson, 1985). As an example, consider the following lesson.

INTERPRETING ARTIFACTS AND INTERACTIONS   *Fielding a Ground Ball*

In a recent educational psychology class, I asked my students to apply one or more principles of learning to teach a topic or skill to an elementary or high school student. One student, Ryan Francoeur, then a starting player on the university's baseball team, taught his 8-year-old cousin Collin how to field a ground ball (i.e., one traveling low to the ground) in baseball. As you read the following excerpts from Ryan's report, think about

- Principles of social cognitive theory that Ryan put into practice
- Principles of other theories that Ryan applied

I began by setting up a tripod and a video camera and videotaping Collin fielding a series of ground balls hit by me. This was done before Collin had any instruction from me, but Collin's baseball skills are already very good for his age, and his fundamentals are very strong. . . . I videotaped an episode of "Baseball Tonight," which is on every night during the major league baseball season. I then edited the video and showed Collin parts of the video that I felt were good examples of how to properly field a ground ball. This seemed to do the trick, and it was fun to watch Collin watching the tape, because he is a very attentive child and gave the videotape and me his complete focus.

Next I modeled the steps to Collin on how to form the correct base for fielding the ground ball and the steps on receiving the hit ball. I slowly explained each and every step to Collin, and had him do each one for me and tell me why he was doing it after he did it. Collin did very well at this, and I think [his] telling me why he was doing each step helped him remember the steps. . . .

I found that my next step . . . worked very well with Collin, and definitely increased his performance. He also liked this technique because I was presenting him with harder tasks, and he too felt that he was accomplishing something by me making each task harder. . . . First I allowed Collin to use his baseball glove while fielding the ball, and Collin had very little difficulty. Next, I told Collin to take away his glove and just use his bare hands for fielding the ball. Not only did Collin do well at this step, but also I watched him as he fielded the ball with soft hands like he was catching an egg; this was encouraging because this is one of the steps I had explained to him earlier. The final task was for Collin to field the ball with a flat wooden board attached to his hand; this is extremely difficult even for good players since you cannot squeeze a glove or hand around the ball. Collin had some difficulty in getting used to this step, but with more practice he continued to improve. After doing all of these tasks, I then videotaped Collin taking another series of ground balls.

I finished my lesson by showing Collin three videotapes. First was the original videotape of Collin fielding ground balls, followed by the videotape of him fielding the balls after the lesson. We were both amazed at his improvement, and his smiling let me know that he was happy with his advancement. The final video I showed Collin was the video of "Baseball Tonight," which was the same one he had watched earlier. I pointed out to Collin the similarities in techniques between himself and the pro players, and he thought that this was very neat. I made sure that Collin also understood that he still had things he needed to work on, and that he could only improve with lots of practice. . . .

Overall I would say his response was very positive, and that he enjoyed the lesson. I think he really liked it when I gave him analogies that he could relate to. He really liked the analogies of thinking of his arms, hands, and fingers as the jaw, mouth, and teeth of an alligator, and he demonstrated it perfectly. I was very surprised to see how much this analogy worked for him. Also he liked the analogy of thinking of his belly button as a vacuum cleaner sucking up the ball and glove; he laughed a lot when I demonstrated that for him. The only thing that I think bothered him during the lesson was when he didn't do something quite right, and he began getting frustrated. . . . I tried to explain to him that even the best make mistakes, and that he just had to continue working on what he was having trouble with. Collin also responded better than I had hoped to the videotapes. He especially liked it when I was comparing what he was doing with the pros; you could tell by his giggling that he thought it was pretty cool.

As you may have noticed, Ryan used competent and prestigious models (one live model—himself—and several symbolic models on the videotapes) to teach Collin how to field a ground ball. Furthermore, he made sure that all four conditions for successful modeling were met. First, he engaged Collin's *attention* with videotapes and one-on-one instruction on how to field a ground ball. Second, he helped Collin *retain* what he was learning by using vivid analogies (soft egg, alligator jaws, vacuum cleaner) and asking Collin to explain why he was doing each step. Third, Ryan encouraged *motor reproduction* by adapting his requests to Ryan's current ability level and then gradually asking him to perform increasingly difficult tasks (eventually asking him to field a ball using a wooden board). Fourth, Ryan *motivated* Collin by making the lesson enjoyable and showing him how his skills were becoming more like those of professional players.

In teaching his lesson, Ryan borrowed from other theoretical perspectives as well. He borrowed from Vygotsky and other cognitive developmentalists when he gave Collin a challenging task (a task presumably within Collin's zone of proximal development) and gradually increased its difficulty as Collin became more proficient. He borrowed from cognitive psychology when he asked Collin to relate certain actions to things Collin already knew—for instance, "thinking of his belly button as a vacuum cleaner sucking up the ball and glove." And he borrowed from behaviorism when he gave Collin positive feedback—for instance, by showing Collin how much he had improved and by pointing out the ways in which his technique had become similar to that of the pros. As teachers, we are more likely to be effective when we apply a variety of theoretical perspectives in the classroom (recall our discussion about "Keeping an Open Mind" in Chapter 6).

As Ryan's lesson so aptly demonstrates, modeling doesn't just enhance students' performance. It can also boost their self-confidence that they can accomplish the things they observe skilled models accomplishing. For example, when a student from an impoverished neighborhood meets someone from the same neighborhood who has succeeded at becoming a physician, and when a student with a physical disability meets an individual with cerebral palsy who is a top executive at the local bank, these students may begin to believe that they, too, are capable of such achievements. Students who believe in their own abilities have developed *self-efficacy*, a topic we turn to now.

Self-Efficacy

EXPERIENCING FIRSTHAND *Self-Appraisal*

Take a moment to answer the following questions:

1. Do you believe that you'll be able to understand educational psychology by reading this textbook and thinking carefully about its content? Or do you believe that you're going to have trouble with the material regardless of how much you study?
2. Do you think you could learn to execute a reasonable swan dive from a high diving board if you were shown how to do it and given time to practice? Or do you believe you're such a klutz that no amount of training and practice would help?
3. Do you think you could walk barefoot over hot coals unscathed? Or do you think the soles of your feet would be burned to a crisp?

People are more likely to engage in certain behaviors when they believe they are capable of executing those behaviors successfully—that is, when they have high **self-efficacy** (e.g., Bandura, 1997). For example, I hope you believe that, with careful thought about what you read, you will be able to understand the ideas in this textbook; in other words, I hope you have high self-efficacy for learning educational psychology. You may or may not believe that, with instruction and practice, you will eventually be able to perform a passable swan dive; in other words, you may have high or low self-efficacy about learning to dive. You are probably quite

skeptical that you could ever walk barefoot over hot coals, so my guess is that you have low self-efficacy regarding this activity.

The concept of self-efficacy is similar to the concept of *self-concept*, but with an important difference. Self-concept is conceptualized as pervading a wide variety of activities; for instance, we tend to describe people as having a generally positive or negative self-concept. Self-efficacy is more situation-specific; for example, people may have high self-efficacy about understanding an educational psychology textbook but not about understanding a book about neurosurgery. They may have high self-efficacy about learning to perform a swan dive but not about swimming the entire length of a swimming pool underwater.

How do students' feelings of self-efficacy affect their behavior? And how do feelings of high or low self-efficacy develop? In the next few pages, we will identify several answers to these two questions.

A student must believe that she has the ability to make friends before she will actually try to make them.

How Self-Efficacy Affects Behavior

According to social cognitive theorists, people's sense of self-efficacy affects their choice of activities, their effort and persistence, and their learning and achievement (Bandura, 1982, 2000; Schunk, 1989c; Zimmerman, Bandura, & Martinez-Pons, 1992):

Choice of activities.   Imagine yourself on registration day, perusing the hundreds of courses in the semester schedule. You fill most of your schedule with required courses, but you have room for an elective. Only two courses are offered at the time slot you have open. Do you sign up for Advanced Psychoceramics, a challenging seminar taught by the famous Dr. Josiah S. Carberry? Or do you sign up for an English literature course known across campus as being an "easy A"? Perhaps you find the term *psychoceramics* a bit intimidating, and you think that you can't possibly pass such a course, especially if Dr. Carberry is as grouchy a man as everybody claims. So you settle for the literature course, knowing it is one in which you can succeed.

People tend to choose tasks and activities at which they believe they can succeed and to avoid those at which they think they will fail. Students who believe that they can succeed at mathematics are more likely to take math courses than students who believe that they are mathematically incompetent. Students who believe that they can win a role in the school musical are more likely to try out than students with little faith in their acting or singing ability.

Such effort and persistence reflect the *intrinsic motivation* of students with high self-efficacy (more about this concept in Chapters 11 and 12).

Effort and persistence.   Think back once again to our case study of Nathan. As you may recall, Nathan was convinced that he couldn't learn French. Because of his low self-efficacy, he gave up quickly on French homework assignments whenever he encountered something he didn't understand.

Students with a high sense of self-efficacy are more likely to exert effort in attempting to accomplish a task. They are also more likely to persist (to "try, try again") when faced with obstacles to their success. In contrast, students with low self-efficacy about a particular task will put in little effort and will give up quickly when they encounter obstacles.

Learning and achievement.   Students with high self-efficacy tend to *learn and achieve more* than students with low self-efficacy even when actual ability levels are the same (Bandura, 1986; Eccles, Wigfield, et al., 1989). In other words, among students of equal ability, those students who *believe* they can do a task are more likely to accomplish it successfully than those who believe they are incapable of success. Students with high self-efficacy may achieve at superior levels partly because they engage in cognitive processes that promote learning—paying attention, organizing, elaborating, and so on (Pintrich & Schunk, 2002). As teachers, then, we should do whatever we can to enhance our students' beliefs that they can be successful at school tasks.

Factors in the Development of Self-Efficacy

Perceptions of self-efficacy are usually fairly accurate: Students typically have a good sense of what they can and cannot do (Bandura, 1986). Ideally, it is probably best that they slightly *over*rate their competence; by doing so, they are more likely to try challenging tasks that help them develop new skills and abilities (Assor & Connell, 1992; Bandura, 1997). But sometimes students (girls especially) *under*estimate their chances of success, perhaps because of a few bad experiences (D. A. Cole et al., 1999; D. Phillips & Zimmerman, 1990). For example, a girl who gets a C in science from a teacher with exceptionally strict grading criteria may erroneously believe that she is "no good" in science. A new boy at school whose attempts at being friendly are rejected by two or three thoughtless classmates may erroneously believe that no one likes him. Students who underestimate their capabilities try less hard and are less persistent at challenging school tasks (D. Phillips & Zimmerman, 1990).

According to social cognitive theorists (e.g., Bandura, 1986, 1989, 1997; Schunk, 1989a; Schunk, Hanson, & Cox, 1987), several factors affect the development of self-efficacy:

What factors in Nathan's situation may have contributed to his low self-efficacy for learning French?

- One's own previous successes and failures
- Messages from others
- Successes and failures of others
- Successes and failures of the group as a whole

One's Own Successes and Failures

Students feel more confident that they can succeed at a task when they have succeeded at that task or at similar ones in the past (Bandura, 1986). For example, Edward is more likely to believe that he can learn to divide fractions if he has already mastered the process of multiplying fractions. Elena will be more confident about her ability to play field hockey if she has already developed skills in soccer. One important strategy for promoting our students' self-efficacy, then, is to help them be successful in various academic disciplines—for instance, by teaching important basic skills to mastery and by providing the necessary instructional support that enables students to make noticeable progress on difficult and complex tasks.

We find developmental differences in *how far back* students look when they consider their prior successes and failures. Perhaps because of more limited cognitive abilities, children in the early elementary grades typically recall only their most recent experiences when judging their competence to perform a particular activity; in contrast, older children and adolescents are likely to consider a long-term pattern of successes and failures (Eccles et al., 1998). We can help students of all ages develop high self-efficacy by showing them in a concrete way—for instance, by comparing earlier work samples with their current efforts—just how much they've improved over time (R. Butler, 1998a). We can also show them how their successes are the result of their own hard work and so are hardly a fluke (Pintrich & Schunk, 2002).

Once students have developed a high sense of self-efficacy, an occasional failure is unlikely to dampen their optimism. In fact, when these students encounter small setbacks on the way to achieving success, they learn that sustained effort and perseverance are key ingredients of that success; in other words, they develop **resilient self-efficacy** (Bandura, 1989). When students *consistently* fail at an activity, however, they tend to have little confidence about their ability to succeed at that activity in the future. For instance, students with learning disabilities—students who typically have encountered failure after failure in classroom activities—often have low self-efficacy for mastering school subject matter (Schunk, 1989c).

Messages from Others

We can sometimes enhance students' self-efficacy by assuring them that they can, in fact, be successful (e.g., Zeldin & Pajares, 2000). Statements such as "You can do this problem if you work at it" or "I bet Judy will play with you if you just ask her" do give students a slight boost in self-confidence. But this boost will be short-lived unless students' efforts at a task ultimately meet with success (Schunk, 1989a).

Sometimes the messages we give students are implied rather than directly stated, yet such messages can have just as much of an effect on self-efficacy. For example, by giving constructive criticism about how to improve a poorly written research paper—criticism that indirectly communicates the message that "I know that you can do better, and here are some suggestions how"—we can enhance students' self-confidence about writing such research papers (Parsons, Kaczala, & Meece, 1982; Pintrich & Schunk, 2002). In some cases, we communicate our beliefs about students' competence through our actions rather than our words. For example, if we give struggling students more assistance than they really need, we may inadvertently communicate the message that "I don't think you can do this on your own" (Schunk, 1989b).

Successes and Failures of Others

We often form opinions about our own self-efficacy by observing the successes and failures of other people, especially those similar to ourselves (Eccles et al., 1998; Zeldin & Pajares, 2000). For example, you are more likely to enroll in Dr. Carberry's Advanced Psychoceramics class if several of your friends have done well in the course. After all, if they can do it, so can you. But if your friends in the course have been dropping like flies, then (like Nathan) you may suspect that your own chances of succeeding are pretty slim.

In much the same way, students often consider the successes and failures of their classmates, especially those of similar ability, when appraising their own chances of success. So we can enhance students' self-efficacy, and ultimately their willingness to try to master classroom subject matter, by pointing out that others like themselves have mastered that material (Schunk, 1983b, 1989c). For example, a class of chemistry students horrified about the number of chemical symbols they must learn can perhaps be reassured with a statement such as this: "I know it seems like a lot to learn in such a short amount of time. My students last year thought so too, but they found that they could learn the symbols within three weeks if they studied a few new symbols each day."

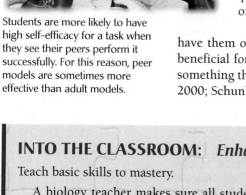

Students are more likely to have high self-efficacy for a task when they see their peers perform it successfully. For this reason, peer models are sometimes more effective than adult models.

When students actually *see* others of similar age and ability successfully reaching a goal, they are especially likely to believe that they, too, can achieve that goal. Hence, students sometimes develop greater self-efficacy when they see a fellow student model a behavior than when they see their teacher model that same behavior. For example, in one study (Schunk & Hanson, 1985), elementary school children having trouble with subtraction were given 25 subtraction problems to complete. Children who had seen another student successfully complete the problems got an average of 19 correct, whereas those who saw a teacher complete the problems got only 13 correct, and those who saw no model at all solved only 8!

So another way to enhance our students' self-efficacy for academic tasks is to have them observe their peers successfully accomplishing those tasks. It may be especially beneficial for students to see one or more peers struggling with a task or problem at first— something they themselves are likely to do—and then eventually mastering it (Kitsantis et al., 2000; Schunk et al., 1987; Schunk & Zimmerman, 1997).

INTO THE CLASSROOM: *Enhancing Self-Efficacy*

Teach basic skills to mastery.

A biology teacher makes sure all students clearly understand the basic structure of DNA before moving to mitosis and meiosis, two topics that require a knowledge of DNA's structure.

Help students make noticeable progress on difficult tasks.

In November a creative writing teacher shows students samples of their work from September and points out ways in which each student has improved over the two-month period.

Present some tasks that are challenging but achievable so that students succeed at them only with effort and perseverance.

A physical education teacher tells her students, "Today we've seen how far each of you can go in the broad jump. We will continue to practice the broad jump a little bit every week. Let's see if each one of you can jump at least two inches farther when I test you again at the end of the month."

Assure students that they can be successful and remind them that others like themselves have succeeded before them.

Students in beginning band express frustration about learning to play their instruments. Their teacher reminds them that students in last year's beginning band—like themselves—started out with little knowledge but eventually mastered their instruments.

Have students see successful peer models.

The students in beginning band class hear the school's advanced band (last year's beginning band class) play a medley from the Broadway musical *Cats*.

Provide opportunities to work in small groups on especially challenging tasks.

A fifth-grade teacher has students work in groups of three or four to write research papers about early colonial life in North America. The teacher makes sure that the students in each group collectively have the skills in library research, writing, word processing, and art necessary to complete the task. She also makes sure that every student has some unique skills to contribute to the group effort.

Successes and Failures of the Group as a Whole

In Chapter 4 we noted that students can often think more "intelligently" when they work together rather than alone (recall our discussion of distributed intelligence), and in Chapter 7 we noted that students who participate in group discussions often gain a more complex understanding of a topic (recall our discussion of group meaning-making). Here we find yet another benefit of co-operation and collaboration: Students may have greater self-efficacy when they work in a group than when they work alone. Such **collective self-efficacy** depends not only on students' perceptions of their own and others' capabilities but also on their perceptions of how effectively they can work together and coordinate their roles and responsibilities (Bandura, 1997, 2000).

The concept of collective self-efficacy is fairly new, and research to date has focused primarily on adults (Bandura, 1997; Goddard, 2001; Tschannen-Moran et al., 1998). Yet we can reasonably assume that students are likely to have higher self-efficacy when they work in groups, provided that those groups are functioning smoothly and effectively. We will consider strategies for fostering effective group work in our discussion of cooperative learning in Chapter 13.

We should note here that teachers, too, can have collective self-efficacy. If the teachers at a school believe that, as a group, they can make a significant difference in the lives of their students, their students achieve at higher levels and have higher self-efficacy themselves (Goddard, 2001; Goddard, Hoy, & Woolfolk Hoy, 2000; Tschannen-Moran et al., 1998).

When students have high self-efficacy about accomplishing classroom tasks and mastering academic subject matter, they have a critical prerequisite for directing and regulating their own learning. We turn to this process of *self-regulation* now.

Self-Regulation

EXPERIENCING FIRSTHAND *Self-Reflection About Self-Regulation*

In each of the following situations, choose the alternative that most accurately describes your own attitudes and behavior as a college student. No one will see your answers except you, so be honest!

1. In terms of my final course grades, I am trying very hard to:
   a. Earn all As.
   b. Earn all As and Bs.
   c. Earn at least a C in every class.
   d. Keep my overall grade point average above the minimally acceptable level for the program I am in.

2. As I am reading or studying a textbook:
   a. I often notice when my attention is wandering, and I immediately get my mind back on my work.
   b. I sometimes notice when my attention is wandering, but not always.
   c. I often get so lost in my daydreams that I waste a lot of time.

3. Whenever I finish a study session:
   a. I write down how much time I have spent on my schoolwork.
   b. I make a mental note of how much time I have spent on my schoolwork.
   c. I don't really think much about the time I have spent.

4. When I turn in an assignment:
   a. I usually have a very good idea of the grade I will get on it.
   b. I have a rough idea of the grade I will get; I can usually tell when it will be either very good or very bad.
   c. I am often surprised by the grade I get.
   d. I don't really think much about the quality of what I have done.

5. When I do exceptionally well on an assignment:
   a. I feel good about my performance and often treat myself in some way (e.g., by going out with friends).
   b. I feel good about my performance but don't do anything special for myself afterward.
   c. I don't feel any differently than I had before I received my grade.

The standards we set for ourselves, the ways in which we monitor and evaluate our own cognitive processes and behaviors, and the consequences we impose on ourselves for our successes and failures are all aspects of **self-regulation**. If our thoughts and actions are under our *own* control, rather than being controlled by the people and circumstances around us, we are self-regulating individuals (Zimmerman, 1998).

Ideally, our students should become increasingly self-regulated as they grow older, and in fact many of them do (Bronson, 2000; Eccles et al., 1998; van Kraayenoord & Paris, 1997). Once they reach adulthood and leave the relatively structured and protective environments of home and school, they will make most of their own decisions about what they should accomplish and how they should behave. Ultimately, we want them to make wise choices that enable them to achieve their goals and make productive contributions to society.

In the pages that follow, we will identify some of the things that learners do when they engage in *self-regulated behavior*. We will then use what we have learned to consider how we might promote *self-regulated learning* and *self-regulated problem solving*.

Self-Regulated Behavior

By observing how our environment reacts when we behave in particular ways—by discovering that some behaviors are reinforced and others are punished or in some other way discouraged—we begin to distinguish between appropriate and inappropriate responses. As we develop an understanding about which responses are appropriate (for ourselves, at least) and which are not, we begin to control and monitor our own behavior (Bandura, 1986). Five aspects of such **self-regulated behavior** are summarized in Figure 10.3. Let's look at the nature and potential implications of each one.

Self-Determined Goals and Standards

As human beings, we tend to identify certain goals for ourselves and then engage in the kinds of behaviors that can help us achieve those goals. We also set standards for our own behavior; in other words, we determine criteria for evaluating our own performance.

Different students will inevitably adopt different goals and standards for themselves. For example, Robert may be striving for a report card with straight As, whereas Richard is content with Cs. Rebecca may be seeking out many friends of both sexes, whereas Rachel believes that a single, steady boyfriend is the best companion. To some extent, the goals and standards that students set for themselves are modeled after those that they see other people adopt (Bandura, 1986; Locke & Latham, 1990). For example, at the high school I attended, many students wanted to go to the best college or university they possibly could; in such an environment, others began to share the same academic aspirations. But at a different high school, getting a job after graduation (or perhaps even *instead* of graduation) might be the aspiration more commonly modeled by a student's classmates.

Students from low-income families typically set low goals for themselves in terms of career aspirations (Durkin, 1995). Can you explain this fact in light of the discussion here?

FIGURE 10.3 Components of self-regulated behavior

Before the response:	During the response:	After the response:
• *Self-Determined Goals and Standards:* Students determine goals to be achieved and standards for acceptable behavior.	• *Self-Monitoring:* Students observe and monitor their own performance. • *Self-Instructions:* Students give themselves instructions (either aloud or silently) to help them guide their actions.	• *Self-Evaluation:* Students judge the quality of their performance. • *Self-Imposed Contingencies:* Students impose their own consequences for success or failure.

Students are more likely to be motivated to work toward goals—and thus more likely to accomplish them—when they have set those goals for themselves, rather than when others have imposed goals on them (M. E. Ford, 1992; Spaulding, 1992). So one way we can help students develop self-regulation is to provide situations in which they set their own goals. For example, we might ask them to decide how many addition facts they are going to learn by Friday, determine the topic they wish to study for a research project, or identify the particular gymnastic skills they wish to master.

Ideally, we should encourage our students to establish goals and standards that are challenging yet realistic. When students have goals and standards that are too low—for instance, when intelligent students are content getting Cs on classroom assignments—then they will not achieve at maximal levels. In contrast, when students' standards are too high—for example, when they are satisfied only if every grade is 100 percent—then they are doomed to frequent failure and equally frequent self-recrimination. Such students may become excessively anxious or depressed when they can't achieve the impossible goals they have set for themselves (Bandura, 1986; Covington, 1992).

To facilitate appropriate goal setting, we can show our students that challenging goals are attainable, perhaps by describing individuals of similar ability who have attained them with reasonable effort. In some situations, we might even want to provide incentives that encourage students to set and achieve challenging goals (Stipek, 1996). At the same time, we must help any overly ambitious students understand and accept the fact that no one is perfect and that an occasional failure is nothing to be ashamed of.

Self-selected goals promote a greater sense of *self-determination*, a topic we will consider in Chapter 12.

Self-Monitoring

An important part of self-regulation is to observe oneself in action—a process known as **self-monitoring** (also known as *self-observation*). To make progress toward important goals, we must be aware of how well we are doing presently; we must know which aspects of our performance are working well and which need improvement. Furthermore, when we see ourselves making progress toward our goals, we are more likely to continue with our efforts (Schunk & Zimmerman, 1997).

Yet students aren't necessarily accurate observers of their own behavior; they aren't always aware of how frequently they do something wrong or how *in*frequently they do something right. To help students attend to the things that they do and don't do, we can have them observe and record their own behavior. If Raymond is speaking out of turn too frequently, we can bring the seriousness of the problem to his attention by asking him to make a check mark on a piece of paper every time he catches himself speaking out of turn. If Olivia has trouble staying on task during assigned activities, we can ask her to stop and reflect on her behavior every few minutes (perhaps with the aid of an egg timer), determining whether she was staying on task during each interval. Figure 10.4 provides an example of the type of form we might give Olivia to record her observations.

Research indicates clearly that such self-focused observation and recording can bring about changes (sometimes dramatic ones) in student behavior. For example, self-observation can be used to increase students' attention to their work (their *time on task*) and the number of assignments they are likely to complete. It is also effective in reducing aggressive responses and such disruptive classroom behaviors as talking out of turn and getting out of one's seat (Allen, 1998; Belfiore & Hornyak, 1998; K. R. Harris, 1986; Mace & Kratochwill, 1988; Webber, Scheuermann, McCall, & Coleman, 1993).

Self-Observation Record for *Olivia*

Every ten minutes, put a mark to show how well you have been staying on task.

+ means you were almost always on task
1/2 means you were on task about half the time
− means you were hardly ever on task

9:00-9:10	9:10-9:20	9:20-9:30	9:30-9:40	9:40-9:50	9:50-10:00
+	+	−	+	1/2	−
10:00-10:10	10:10-10:20	10:20-10:30	10:30-10:40	10:40-10:50	10:50-11:00
1/2	−	*recess*		+	1/2
11:00-11:10	11:10-11:20	11:20-11:30	11:30-11:40	11:40-11:50	11:50-12:00

FIGURE 10.4 Example of a self-observation sheet for staying on task

Self-Instructions

Consider the formerly "forgetful" student who, before leaving the house each morning, now asks herself, "Do I have everything I need for my classes? I have my math homework for period 1, my history book for period 2, my change of clothes for gym during period 3. . . ." And consider the once impulsive student who now pauses before beginning a new assignment and says to himself, "OK, what am I supposed to do? Let's see . . . I need to read the directions first. What do the directions tell me to do?" And consider as well the formerly aggressive student who has learned to count to ten every time she gets angry—an action that gives her a chance to cool off.

Sometimes students simply need a reminder about how to respond in particular situations. By teaching students how to talk themselves through these situations using **self-instructions**, we provide them with a means through which *they remind themselves* about appropriate actions, thereby helping them to control their own behavior. Such a strategy is often effective in working with students who otherwise seem to behave without thinking (Casey & Burton, 1982; Meichenbaum, 1985).

One effective way of teaching students to give themselves instructions involves five steps (Meichenbaum, 1977):

1. The teacher models self-instruction by repeating instructions aloud while simultaneously performing the activity.
2. The teacher repeats the instructions aloud while the student performs the activity.
3. The student repeats the instructions aloud while performing the activity.
4. The student whispers the instructions while performing the activity.
5. The student simply "thinks" the instructions while performing the activity.

Can you relate steps 3, 4, and 5 to Vygotsky's notions of *self-talk* and *inner speech* (Chapter 2)?

Through these five steps, impulsive elementary school children can effectively learn to slow themselves down and think through what they are doing (Meichenbaum & Goodman, 1971). For example, notice how one formerly impulsive student was able to talk his way through a matching task in which he needed to find two identical pictures among several very similar ones:

> I have to remember to go slowly to get it right. Look carefully at this one, now look at these carefully. Is this one different? Yes, it has an extra leaf. Good, I can eliminate this one. Now, let's look at this one. I think it's this one, but let me first check the others. Good, I'm going slow and carefully. Okay, I think it's this one. (Meichenbaum & Goodman, 1971, p. 121)

Self-Evaluation

Both at home and in school, students' behaviors are frequently judged by others—their parents, teachers, classmates, and so on. But eventually our students should also begin to judge their *own* behavior; in other words, they should engage in **self-evaluation**. Their ability to evaluate themselves with some degree of objectivity and accuracy will be critical for their long-term success in the adult world (Vye et al., 1998).

Once our students have developed appropriate goals and standards, and once they have developed some objective techniques for observing their own behavior, there are many ways in which we can allow and encourage them to evaluate their own performance. For example, we can have them

Chapter 16 describes *portfolios* in greater depth.

- Assemble portfolios of what they think is their best work, with self-evaluations of each entry
- Write in daily or weekly journals, in which they address the strengths and weaknesses of their performance
- Participate in peer conferences, in which several students discuss their reactions to one another's work
 (Paris & Ayres, 1994; Paris & Paris, 2001)

We might also have students complete self-assessment instruments that show them what to look for as they judge their work (Paris & Ayres, 1994). For example, to evaluate a project they have just completed, students might respond to questions such as these:

- What did you like about this project?
- What would have made this project better?
- What grade do you feel you earned on this project? Justify your response. (based on Paris & Ayres, 1994, p. 78)

FIGURE 10.5 After a cooperative group activity with three other girls, Rochelle and her teacher independently evaluate Rochelle's performance and that of the entire group using various criteria. With the two evaluations side by side, Rochelle can learn to assess her own performance more accurately.

May Project

Name __Melinda__

Partners __Britta   Emily   Misa__

Project description __Travel Guide__

Evaluate with a 1 for weak, a 2 for fair, a 3 for good, a 4 for very good, and a 5 for excellent.

Student	Teacher	
4	4	1. The task was a major amount of work in keeping with a whole month of effort.
5	4	2. We used class time quite well.
4	5	3. The workload was quite evenly divided. I did a fair proportion.
4	5	4. I showed commitment to the group and to a quality project.
5	4	5. My report went into depth; it didn't just give the obvious, commonly known information.
5	5	6. The project made a point: a reader (or viewer) could figure out how all of the details fitted together to help form a conclusion.
5	5	7. The project was neat, attractive, well assembled. I was proud of the outcome.
4	5	8. We kept our work organized; we made copies; we didn't lose things or end up having to redo work that was lost.
5	4	9. The work had a lot of original thinking or other creative work.
4	4	10. The project demonstrated mastery of basic language skills—composition, planning, oral communication, writing.
45	45	Total

Comments:

46 group average   (A)^G   (A)^I

Students who hold different standards for themselves will naturally judge the same behavior in different ways. For example, if Robert and Richard both get all Bs on their report cards, Robert (with the straight-A standard) will judge his performance to be unacceptable, whereas Richard (with acceptability defined as C) will go home and celebrate. It is essential, then, that we help our students use appropriate criteria for evaluating their performance (Yell, Robinson, & Drasgow, 2001; Zuckerman, 1994). For example, when asking them to analyze the quality of a summary they have just written, we might ask them to agree or disagree with statements such as these:

- I included a clear main idea statement.
- I included important ideas that support the main idea.
- My summary shows that I understand the relationships between important concepts.
- I used my own words rather than words copied from the text. (Paris & Ayres, 1994, p. 75)

Or, when asking students to evaluate their on-task behavior in class on a scale of 1 to 5, we might reinforce them when their own self-assessments closely match the ones we ourselves give them (D. J. Smith, Young, West, Morgan, & Rhode, 1988). Figure 10.5 shows a form that one teacher has used to help students learn to evaluate their work using a variety of criteria.

How effectively students learn to evaluate their own performance will depend partly on what we ask them to look for when they scrutinize their work, as the following exercise illustrates.

An eighth-grade mathematics teacher asks his students to keep track of how well they do on their homework assignments and quizzes. Thirteen-year-old Lea's "math grade log" appears below. As you look at her log, consider

■ What aspects of performance it focuses Lea's attention on
■ What aspects of performance it allows Lea to ignore

First Quarter

Math Grade Log		Name Lea Demers		Total
				(as needed)
Assignment		Due Date	Points/Points Possible	
1 Anagram Name		8-27	5/5	5/5
2 1-1 #2-42 even		8/26	5/5	10/10
3 Your Life in Math		8/27	5/5	15/15
4 1-2 #2-52 evens		8/30	5/5	20/20
5 1-3 #2-46 even		8/31	5/5	25/25
6 1-5 #1-36		9/1	5/5	30/30
7 Quiz 1-1 to 1-3		9/2	20/25	50/55
8 4-4's Problem		9/1	6/5	56/60
9 TI Programming A		9/3	5/5	61/65
10 Quiz 1-5 to 1-8		9/10	23/25	84/90
11 1-7 #1-48		9/7	5/5	89/95

Lea's log can certainly help her keep track of the assignment and quiz scores she is getting in her math class. Notice, however, that the log focuses her attention entirely on the number of problems she is getting right. Nowhere does she have a place to record the types of problems she is getting wrong, the kinds of errors she is making, or any other information that might help her improve her performance. Our students can evaluate themselves effectively, and thereby improve their performance over the long run, only if they use qualitative as well as quantitative criteria.

Self-Imposed Contingencies

How do you feel when you accomplish a difficult task—for example, when you earn an A in a challenging course, get elected president of an organization, or make a three-point basket in a basketball game? How do you feel when you fail in your endeavors—for example, when you get a D on an exam because you forgot to study, thoughtlessly hurt a friend's feelings, or miss an easy goal in a soccer game?

When you accomplish something you've set out to do, especially if the task is complex and challenging, you probably feel quite proud of yourself and give yourself a mental pat on the back. In contrast, when you fail to accomplish that task, you are probably unhappy with your performance; you may also feel guilty, regretful, or ashamed. Likewise, as our students become increasingly self-regulated, they will begin to reinforce themselves (perhaps by feeling proud or telling themselves they did a good job) when they accomplish their goals. And they will also begin to punish themselves (perhaps by feeling sorry, guilty, or ashamed) when they do something that does not meet their own performance standards. As an example, see Figure 10.6.

Yet such **self-imposed contingencies** are not necessarily confined to people's emotional reactions to their own behaviors. Many self-regulating individuals reinforce themselves in far more concrete ways when they accomplish something successfully. For example, I have a colleague who goes shopping every time she completes a research article or report (she has one of the best wardrobes in town). I myself am more frugal: When I finish each major section of a chapter, I either help myself to whatever sweets I can find in the kitchen, or I take a half hour to watch one of my favorite quiz shows (I am a little chubbier than my colleague, but I have a wealth of knowledge of game-show trivia and would almost certainly beat her in a game of Trivial Pursuit).

Thus, an additional way to help students become more self-regulating is to teach them self-reinforcement. When students begin to reinforce themselves for appropriate responses—perhaps by giving themselves some free time, allowing themselves to engage in a favorite activity, or simply praising themselves—their classroom behavior often improves significantly (K. R. Harris, 1986; S. C. Hayes et al., 1985). For example, in one research study, students who were perform-

Do you reinforce yourself in some tangible way for your accomplishments? If so, how?

FIGURE 10.6 Sixteen-year-old Melinda expresses guilt and pride—two examples of self-imposed contingencies—in this piece about horseback riding.

"Sit up,
    shoulders back,
        drop your right shoulder."
Now I feel guilty because I'm making the horse work harder.
"Heels down,
    elbows at your sides,
        lower leg back,
            drop your right shoulder down and back."
Now I feel like I have no talent and like I'm hurting the horse.
"More impulsion from the left hind leg!
    Send him into the rein more!"
Now I'm thinking, "This is so complicated!"
"Good job!
    Walk when you're ready and give him the rein.
        Did you feel that?"
"Yeah!"
"Good! That was really good!
    You've accomplished so much with him and your position."
Now I feel warm inside and proud. All this time has paid off and I realize that's why I love horseback
    riding so much!

ing poorly in arithmetic were taught to give themselves points when they did well on their assignments; they could later use these points to "buy" a variety of items and privileges. Within a few weeks, these students were doing as well as their classmates on both in-class assignments and homework (H. C. Stevenson & Fantuzzo, 1986). In some instances, self-reinforcement is just as effective as reinforcement administered by a teacher (Bandura, 1977).

EXPERIENCING FIRSTHAND   *More Self-Reflection*

Return to the exercise "Self-Reflection About Self-Regulation" at the beginning of this section. Consider what you have just learned about effective self-regulation to evaluate your responses to each question.

Self-Regulated Learning

Social learning theorists and cognitive psychologists alike are beginning to realize that to be truly effective learners, students must engage in some of the self-regulating activities just described. In fact, not only must students regulate their own behaviors, but they must also regulate their own cognitive processes. In particular, **self-regulated learning** includes the following processes, many of which are *metacognitive*:

- *Goal-setting.* Self-regulated learners know what they want to accomplish when they read or study. For instance, they may want to learn specific facts, get an overall understanding of the ideas being presented, or simply acquire enough knowledge to do well on a classroom exam (Nolen, 1996; Winne & Hadwin, 1998; Wolters, 1998; Zimmerman, 1998).
- *Planning.* Self-regulated learners determine ahead of time how best to use the time and resources they have available for a learning task (Zimmerman, 1998; Zimmerman & Risemberg, 1997).
- *Attention control.* Self-regulated learners try to focus their attention on the subject matter at hand and to clear their minds of potentially distracting thoughts and emotions (Corno, 1993; Harnishfeger, 1995; Kuhl, 1985; Schutz & Davis, 2000; Winne, 1995).
- *Application of learning strategies.* Self-regulated learners choose different learning strategies depending on the specific goal they hope to accomplish. For example, the way they read a magazine article depends on whether they are reading it for entertainment or studying for an exam (Linderholm, Gustafson, van den Broek, & Lorch, 1997; Winne, 1995).
- *Self-motivational strategies.* Self-regulated learners keep themselves on task with a variety of strategies, such as competing against their own prior performance, finding ways to

Self-regulated learners seek assistance when they need it and are especially likely to ask for help with skills that will make them more independent.

make a boring activity more interesting or challenging, imagining themselves completing an activity successfully, or varying the procedures they use for successive tasks or problems (Corno, 1993; Kuhl, 1987; Sansone, Weir, Harpster, & Morgan, 1992).

- *Solicitation of outside help when needed.* Truly self-regulated learners don't necessarily try to do everything on their own. On the contrary, they recognize when they need other people's help and seek out such assistance; they are especially likely to ask for the kind of help that will enable them to work more independently in the future (R. Butler, 1998b; A. M. Ryan, Pintrich, & Midgley, 2001).
- *Self-monitoring.* Self-regulated learners continually monitor their progress toward their goals, and they change their learning strategies or modify their goals if necessary (D. L. Butler & Winne, 1995; Carver & Scheier, 1990; Zimmerman & Risemberg, 1997). *Comprehension monitoring* (described in Chapter 8) is an example of such self-monitoring.
- *Self-evaluation.* Self-regulated learners determine whether what they have learned fulfills the goals they have set for themselves (D. L. Butler & Winne, 1995; Schraw & Moshman, 1995; Zimmerman & Risemberg, 1997). Ideally, they also use their self-evaluations to modify their selection and use of various learning strategies on future occasions (Winne & Hadwin, 1998).

In addition to such activities, self-regulated learning requires **intrinsic motivation**—motivation that comes from within the individual, rather than from such outside influences as extrinsic reinforcers (Bronson, 2000; Zimmerman & Risemberg, 1997). One important factor in intrinsic motivation is high self-efficacy: Students must believe that they have the ability to accomplish the learning task successfully (more about this point in Chapter 12).

Now that we've considered the general nature of self-regulated learning, let's look at how it might be reflected in a particular student's approach to studying.

INTERPRETING ARTIFACTS AND INTERACTIONS   *Different Ways of Learning*

As an assignment for my educational psychology class, one of my students, Shelly Lamb, interviewed her 17-year-old sister Becky about study habits. As you read the conversation, think about

- The specific metacognitive and self-regulatory strategies that Becky uses
- Becky's metacognitive awareness of what she does as she studies

Shelly: What are the different ways that you learn?

Becky: By doing it myself, not just watching. I can pick up random facts by reading, they are easy to make sense of. When I read a textbook, I have to stop and think about it, then I get the concept. I learn some from lectures, but it is harder to stop and think about the material, so I learn less. When a teacher does an example out on the board, I have to do it myself to get it and see where it comes from.

Shelly: When you have a test, how do you study for it and when?

Becky: I don't usually study; I just look over the notes. If I have to memorize something, I repeat it over and over or write it down, which is like repeating it. I sometimes use [word association], patterns and oversimplification to remember. I will also look it over at night and then again in the morning. I derive math formulas, those I don't memorize. . . .

Shelly: In your own words, what is thinking?

Becky: Having a conversation with myself, an inner dialogue. . . .

Shelly: What types of study skills do you practice on a regular basis?

Becky: Organize homework. I rewrite my assignments. I do smaller tasks first, then put the bigger ones in a pile. I do the easier ones first then writing and studying I do last. Long-term projects I do last, or first if I want to force myself to do them. . . .

Shelly: If you have a lot of work for one subject and a few things in other subjects, in what kind of order do you attack the tasks?

Becky: I do the little ones first and then leave the big task till the end. I get more of a sense of accomplishment that way.

Shelly: At what time of day do you learn best? [At what time do you best] study on your own?

Becky: I learn better early in the day. I am in a better mood and I am not sick of school yet. At the end of the day, my brain is full. I study best in the morning, that's when I edit my essays from the night before. . . .

Now that you've read Becky's description of how she studies and learns, it may not surprise you to learn that she is a high-achieving high school senior. Becky uses a wide variety of strategies to regulate her learning and studying: She prioritizes her assignments and plans the best times for doing each one (e.g., "I do the easier ones first then writing and studying I do last"), chooses certain strategies that have proven to be effective for her (e.g., "I will . . . look it over at night and then again in the morning"), motivates herself to take on challenges (e.g., "Long-term projects I do last, or first if I want to force myself to do them"), and knows how to reinforce herself when she completes her work (e.g., "I get more of a sense of accomplishment that way"). Becky describes exactly what she does *behaviorally* as she studies, and she sometimes knows what she is doing *cognitively* as well—for example, using "patterns" (reflecting organization) and deriving formulas (reflecting elaboration). Yet she is not always totally aware of her mental processes: A great deal is undoubtedly going on inside her head when she has "to stop and think" or when she "just look[s] over the notes."

When students are self-regulated learners, they set more ambitious academic goals for themselves, learn more effectively, and achieve at higher levels in the classroom (D. L. Butler & Winne, 1995; Zimmerman & Risemberg, 1997). Furthermore, a great deal of adolescent and adult learning—doing homework, reading, surfing the Internet, and so on—occurs in isolation from other people and so requires considerable self-regulation (Winne, 1995). Unfortunately, however, few students develop a high level of self-regulated learning, perhaps in part because traditional instructional practices do little to encourage it (Paris & Ayres, 1994; Zimmerman & Risemberg, 1997).

To promote self-regulated learning, we must, of course, teach students the kinds of cognitive processes that facilitate learning and memory (see the discussion of metacognition in Chapter 8). In addition, theorists have suggested the following strategies:

- Encourage students to set some of their own goals for learning and then to monitor their progress toward those goals.
- Give students opportunities to learn and achieve without teacher direction or assistance, including both independent learning activities in which students study by themselves (e.g., seatwork assignments, homework) and group activities in which students help one another learn (e.g., peer tutoring, cooperative learning).
- Occasionally assign activities (e.g., research papers, creative projects) in which students have considerable leeway regarding goals, use of time, and so on.
- Provide scaffolding as needed to help students acquire self-regulating strategies (e.g., show them how to use checklists to identify what they need to do each day and to determine when they have completed all assigned work).
- Model self-regulating cognitive processes by "thinking aloud" about such processes, and then give students constructive feedback as they engage in similar processes.
- Consistently ask students to evaluate their own performance, and have them compare their self-assessments to teacher assessments. (Belfiore & Hornyak, 1998; Bronson, 2000; A. King, 1997; McCaslin & Good, 1996; Paris & Paris, 2001; N. E. Perry, 1998; Schunk & Zimmerman, 1997; J. W. Thomas, 1993b; Winne & Hadwin, 1998; Zimmerman & Risemberg, 1997)

Self-Regulated Problem Solving

We can sometimes use self-regulation techniques (especially self-instructions) to help students develop more effective problem-solving skills. For example, to promote greater creativity in their solutions to academic problems, we might encourage them to give themselves instructions such as these:

I want to think of something no one else will think of, something unique. Be freewheeling, no hangups. I don't care what anyone thinks; just suspend judgment. I'm not sure what I'll come up with; it will be a surprise. The ideas can just flow through me. . . . (Meichenbaum, 1977, p. 62)

What theoretical perspective does Becky's comment about "having a conversation with myself, an inner dialogue" remind you of?

Help students set challenging yet realistic goals and standards.

A teacher encourages a pregnant student to stay in school until she graduates. Together they discuss strategies for juggling motherhood and schoolwork.

Have students observe and record their own behavior.

A student with attention-deficit hyperactivity disorder frequently tips his chair back to the point where he is likely to topple over. Concerned for the student's safety, his teacher asks him to record each instance of such behavior on a sheet of graph paper. Both student and teacher notice how quickly the behavior disappears once the student has become aware of his bad habit.

Teach students instructions they can give themselves to remind them of what they need to do.

To help a student control her impulsive behavior on multiple-choice tests, her teacher has her mentally say this to herself as she reads each question: "Read the entire question. Then look at each answer carefully and decide whether it is correct or incorrect. Then choose the answer that seems most correct of all."

Encourage students to evaluate their own performance.

A science teacher gives students a list of criteria to evaluate the lab reports they have written. In assigning grades, she considers how accurately students have evaluated their own reports.

Teach students to reinforce themselves for appropriate behavior.

A teacher helps students develop more regular study habits by encouraging them to make a favorite activity—for example, shooting baskets, watching television, or calling a friend on the telephone—contingent on completing their homework first.

Give students opportunities to practice learning with little or no help from their teacher.

A middle school social studies teacher distributes various magazine articles related to current events in the Middle East, making sure that each student receives an article appropriate for his or her reading level. He asks students to read their articles over the weekend and prepare a one-paragraph summary to share with other class members. He also provides guidelines about what information students should include in their summaries.

Provide strategies that students can use to solve interpersonal problems.

A teacher teaches her students a sequence to follow when they find themselves in a conflict with a classmate: *identify* the source of the conflict, *listen* to each other's perspectives, *verbalize* each other's perspectives, and *develop* a solution that provides a reasonable compromise.

To help students deal more effectively with social conflicts and other interpersonal problems, we might ask them to take steps such as these:

1. Define the problem.
2. Identify several possible solutions.
3. Predict the likely consequences of each solution.
4. Choose the best solution.
5. Identify the steps required to carry out the solution.
6. Carry the steps out.
7. Evaluate the results. (S. N. Elliott & Busse, 1991; Meichenbaum, 1977; Weissburg, 1985; Yell et al., 2001)

Such **self-regulated problem-solving strategies** often help students who have difficulty interacting appropriately with their peers (e.g., students who are either socially withdrawn or overly aggressive) to develop more effective interpersonal skills (K. R. Harris, 1982; Meichenbaum, 1977; Yell et al., 2001).

Another approach is **mediation training**, a strategy for helping students *help one another* solve interpersonal problems. More specifically, we teach students how to mediate conflicts among classmates by asking the opposing sides to express their differing points of view and then working together to devise a reasonable resolution (Deutsch, 1993; D. W. Johnson & Johnson, 1996, 2001; Stevahn, Oberle, Johnson, & Johnson, 2001). For example, in a study involving several classrooms at the second through fifth grade levels (D. W. Johnson, Johnson, Dudley, Ward, & Magnuson, 1995), students were trained to help their peers resolve interpersonal conflicts by asking the opposing sides to do the following:

1. Define the conflict (the problem)
2. Explain their own perspectives and needs
3. Explain the *other* person's perspectives and needs

4. Identify at least three possible solutions to the conflict
5. Reach an agreement that addressed the needs of both parties

The students took turns serving as mediator for their classmates, such that everyone had experience resolving the conflicts of others. In comparison to students in an untrained control group, students who completed the training more frequently resolved their *own* interpersonal conflicts in ways that addressed the needs of both parties, and they were less likely to ask for adult intervention. Similarly, in a case study involving adolescent gang members (Sanchez & Anderson, 1990), students were given mediation training and asked to be responsible for mediating gang-related disputes. After only one month of training, rival gang members were exchanging friendly greetings in the corridors, giving one another the "high five" sign, and interacting at lunch; meanwhile, gang-related fights virtually disappeared from the scene.

Teachers sometimes intervene when students have an interpersonal conflict. But *mediation training*, whereby students learn how to help one another resolve their differences, is more likely to promote self-regulation.

As we consider how best to help our students become self-regulated learners and problem solvers, we should keep in mind a point that Lev Vygotsky made many years ago: Many complex cognitive processes have their roots in social interactions, including interactions with teachers and classmates. Over time, the things that students may initially do on a social level—setting group goals, identifying effective ways to approach a particular learning task or solve a particular problem, discussing appropriate evaluation criteria, guiding others' learning and behavior, and so on—eventually become internalized in the form of mental processes that students can use to guide their *own* learning and behavior (Biemiller, Shany, Inglis, & Meichenbaum, 1998; Zimmerman, 1998).

When students set challenging goals for themselves and achieve those self-chosen goals through their own efforts, their self-efficacy is enhanced and their motivation to undertake new challenges increases (Bandura, 1989; Bandura & Schunk, 1981). And when students have a high sense of self-efficacy and engage in self-regulating activities, they are more likely to believe that they control their environment, rather than that their environment controls them. In fact, social cognitive theorists assert that people, their behaviors, and the environment all have a somewhat "controlling" influence on one another, as we shall see now.

Reciprocal Causation

Throughout the chapter we've discussed aspects of learners' environments and the behaviors that result from various environmental conditions. We have also talked about such personal variables as expectations and self-efficacy that learners bring with them to a task. Now which one of these three factors—environment, behavior, or person—lays the foundation for learning? According to social cognitive theorists, all three are essential ingredients, and each one influences the other two. This interdependence among environment, behavior, and person is known as **reciprocal causation** (Bandura, 1989). Some examples of how each factor affects the other two are listed in Table 10.2.

As a concrete illustration of how environment, behavior, and personal factors can mutually influence one another, let's consider "Scene One" in the case of Lorraine:

Scene One

Lorraine, a student in Mr. Broderick's seventh-grade social studies class, often comes to class late and ill-prepared for the day's activities. In class she spends more time interacting with her friends (e.g., whispering, passing notes) than getting involved in classroom activities. Lorraine's performance on most exams and assignments (when she turns the latter in at all) is unsatisfactory.

One day in mid-October, Mr. Broderick takes Lorraine aside to express his concern about her lack of classroom effort. He suggests that Lorraine could do better if she paid more attention in class; he also offers to work with her twice a week after school to help her understand class material. Lorraine is less optimistic, describing herself as "not smart enough to learn this stuff."

For a week or so after her meeting with Mr. Broderick, Lorraine seems to buckle down and exert more effort, but she never does stay after school for extra help. And before long, Lorraine is back to her old habits. Mr. Broderick eventually concludes that she is a lost cause and decides to devote his time and effort to helping more motivated students.

TABLE 10.2

COMPARE/CONTRAST

Mutual Influences (Reciprocal Causation) Among Environment, Behavior, and Person

		A GENERAL EXAMPLE	AN EXAMPLE IN LORRAINE'S CASE (SCENE ONE)	AN EXAMPLE IN LORRAINE'S CASE (SCENE TWO)
Effect of Environment	On Behavior	Reinforcement and punishment affect future behavior.	Teacher's ignoring Lorraine leads to future classroom failure.	New instructional methods lead to improved academic performance.
	On Person	Feedback from others affects sense of self-efficacy.	Teacher's ignoring Lorraine perpetuates low self-efficacy.	New instructional methods capture Lorraine's interest and attention.
Effect of Behavior	On Environment	Specific behaviors affect the amount of reinforcement and punishment received.	Poor classroom performance leads to the teacher meeting privately with Lorraine, then eventually ignoring her.	Better academic performance leads to more reinforcement from the teacher.
	On Person	Success and failure affect expectations for future performance.	Poor classroom performance leads to low self-efficacy.	Better academic performance leads to higher self-efficacy.
Effect of Person	On Environment	Self-efficacy affects choices of activities and therefore the specific environment encountered.	Attention to classmates rather than classroom activities affects environment experienced.	Attention to classroom activities leads to greater influence of teacher's instruction.
	On Behavior	Attention, retention, motor reproduction, and motivation affect degree to which one imitates modeled behavior.	Attention to classmates rather than classroom activities leads to academic failure.	Greater self-efficacy and increased motivation lead to more persistent study habits.

Lorraine's low self-efficacy (a *person* factor) is probably one reason that she spends so much class time engaged in task-irrelevant activities (*behaviors*). The fact that she devotes her attention (another *person* factor) to her classmates, rather than to her teacher, affects the particular stimuli that she experiences (her *environment*). Lorraine's poor performance on assignments and exams (*behaviors*) affects both her self-efficacy (*person*) and Mr. Broderick's treatment of her (*environment*). By eventually concluding that Lorraine is a lost cause, Mr. Broderick begins to ignore Lorraine (*environment*), contributing to her further failure (*behavior*) and even lower self-efficacy (*person*). (See Table 10.2 for examples of such interactive effects under the column marked "Scene One.") Clearly, Lorraine is showing signs of being at risk for long-term academic failure.

Can you think of occasions when you, like Lorraine, might have doomed yourself to failure through your own behaviors?

But now imagine that, after reading several research articles about how to work with students at risk, Mr. Broderick develops greater optimism that he can break the vicious cycle of environment/behavior/person for students such as Lorraine. Midway through the school year, he makes the following changes in his classroom:

- He communicates clearly and consistently that he expects all students to succeed in his classroom.
- He incorporates students' personal experiences and interests into the study of social studies.
- He identifies specific, concrete tasks that students will accomplish each week.
- He provides guidance and structure for how each task should be accomplished.
- After consulting with the school's reading specialist and school psychologist, he helps students develop more effective reading and learning strategies.
- He gives a quiz every Friday so that students can assess their own progress.
- When students perform well on these quizzes, he reminds them that they themselves are responsible for their performance.

Let's see what happens next, as we consider "Scene Two":

Scene Two

By incorporating students' personal experiences and interests into his daily lesson plans, Mr. Broderick begins to capture Lorraine's interest and attention. She begins to realize that social studies has implications for her own life and becomes more involved in classroom activities. With the more structured assignments, better guidance about how to study class material, and frequent quizzes, Lorraine finds herself succeeding in a subject at which she has previously experienced only failure. Mr. Broderick is equally pleased with her performance, something he tells her frequently through his facial expressions, his verbal feedback, and his willingness to provide help whenever she needs it.

By the end of the school year, Lorraine is studying course material more effectively and completing her assignments regularly. She is eagerly looking forward to next year's social studies class, confident that she will continue to do well.

Once again, we see the interplay among environment, behavior, and person. Mr. Broderick's new instructional methods (*environment*) engage Lorraine's attention (*person*) and facilitate her academic performance (*behavior*). Lorraine's improved academic performance, in turn, influences Mr. Broderick's treatment of her (*environment*) and her own self-efficacy (*person*). And her improved self-efficacy, her greater attention to classroom activities, and her increased motivation to succeed (all *person* variables) affect her ability to benefit from Mr. Broderick's instruction (*environment*) and her classroom success (*behavior*). (See the column marked "Scene Two" in Table 10.2 for examples of such interactive effects.)

As you can see, then, the things we do in the classroom—the *environment* we create—affect both the behaviors that students exhibit and the personal factors that influence their learning. Students' behaviors and personal factors, in turn, influence the future classroom environment that they experience. As teachers, we must create and maintain a classroom environment that helps students develop the behaviors (e.g., academic and social skills) and personal characteristics (e.g., high self-efficacy and the expectation that their efforts will be rewarded) that are likely to bring them academic and personal success.

Can you explain reciprocal causation in your own words? Can you provide an example from your own experience?

Considering Diversity from a Social Cognitive Perspective

Social cognitive theory provides several insights into how we can adapt our classroom practices to serve students with diverse backgrounds, characteristics, and needs. The concepts of *modeling, self-efficacy,* and *self-regulation* can be especially useful in this context.

Using Diverse Models to Promote Success and Self-Efficacy

Two principles identified earlier in the chapter are particularly pertinent when discussing diversity in the classroom:

- Students are most likely to model the behaviors they believe are relevant to their own situation.
- Students develop greater self-efficacy for a task when they see others like themselves performing the task successfully.

Both principles lead to the same conclusion: *Students need models who are similar to themselves in race, cultural background, socioeconomic status, gender, and (if applicable) disability.* As teachers, we cannot possibly be all things to all students. We must therefore expose our students to as wide a variety of successful models—child and adolescent models as well as adults—as we possibly can. In some cases, we may be able to find such models within the school building itself. In other cases, we may be able to invite people from the local community or region to visit the classroom. Occasionally, as Ryan discovered when he taught his cousin Collin how to field a ground ball (see "Fielding a Ground Ball" on pp. 344–345), we may even find it effective to videotape students performing desired behaviors and then have them watch *themselves* being successful (Kehle, Clark, & Jenson, 1996).

Symbolic models—like the professional ball players Collin watched on videotape—can teach students a great deal as well. For example, we might ask our students to read biographies or autobiographies about such successful individuals as Maya Angelou (who, as an African American growing up in Arkansas in the 1930s, was raised in an environment of poverty and racial intolerance), Franklin D. Roosevelt (who had polio and was wheelchair-bound), and Stephen Hawking (who has a degenerative nerve disorder and can communicate only through computer technology). Or we might have students watch the video *Stand and Deliver,* the story of eighteen Mexican American high school students from a lower-income neighborhood in East Los Angeles who, through hard work and perseverance, earned college credit by passing the National Advanced Placement Calculus Exam.

TABLE 10.3

Promoting Social Learning in Students with Special Educational Needs

CATEGORY	CHARACTERISTICS YOU MIGHT OBSERVE	SUGGESTED CLASSROOM STRATEGIES
Students with specific cognitive or academic difficulties	• Difficulty predicting the consequences of specific behaviors • Low self-efficacy for academic tasks in areas where there has been a history of failure • Less self-regulation of learning and behavior	• Help students form more realistic expectations about the consequences of their behaviors. • Scaffold students' efforts on academic tasks to increase the probability of success. • Identify students' areas of strength and provide opportunities to tutor other students in those areas. • Promote self-regulation (e.g., by teaching self-observation, self-instructions, self-reinforcement).
Students with social or behavioral problems	• Unusual difficulty in learning from the social environment (for students with autism) • Difficulties predicting the consequences of specific behaviors • Friendships with peers who are poor models of effective social skills or prosocial behavior (for students with emotional and behavioral disorders) • Little self-regulation of behavior • Deficits in social problem solving	• Help students recognize and interpret social cues and nonverbal language. • Discuss possible consequences of various courses of action in social conflict situations (for students with emotional and behavioral disorders). • Model appropriate classroom behaviors; for students with autism, combine modeling with explicit verbal instruction, and use visual aids to communicate desired behaviors. • Provide opportunities for students to interact with peers who model effective social and prosocial behaviors. • Videotape students exhibiting appropriate behaviors and then have them view themselves as models for such behavior. • Teach self-regulation (e.g., self-observation, self-instructions, self-regulated problem-solving strategies).
Students with general delays in cognitive and social functioning	• Low self-efficacy for academic tasks • Tendency to watch others for guidance about how to behave • Low goals for achievement (possibly as a way of avoiding failure) • Little if any self-regulation of learning and behavior	• Scaffold students' efforts on academic tasks to increase the probability of success. • Model desired behaviors; identify peers who can also serve as appropriate models. • Encourage students to set high yet realistic goals for their own achievement. • Promote self-regulation (e.g., by teaching self-observation, self-instructions, self-reinforcement).
Students with physical or sensory challenges	• Few opportunities to develop self-regulation skills due to health limitations, a tightly controlled environment, or both	• Teach skills that promote self-sufficiency and independence. • Teach students to make positive self-statements (e.g., "I can do it!") to enhance their self-efficacy for acting independently.
Students with advanced cognitive development	• High self-efficacy for academic tasks • High goals for performance • More effective self-regulated learning • For some students, a history of easy successes and, hence, little experience dealing with failure effectively	• Provide the academic support that students need to reach their goals. • Provide opportunities for independent study. • Provide challenging tasks at which students may sometimes fail; teach constructive strategies for dealing with failure (e.g., persistence, using errors to guide future practice efforts).

Sources: Balla & Zigler, 1979; Bandura, 1989; Beirne-Smith et al., 2002; Biemiller et al., 1998; C. E. Cunningham & Cunningham, 1998; E. S. Ellis & Friend, 1991; J. N. Hughes, 1988; Kehle, Clark, Jenson, & Wampold, 1986; Lupart, 1995; Mercer, 1997; Morgan & Jenson, 1988; J. R. Nelson, Smith, Young, & Dodd, 1991; Piirto, 1999; Sands & Wehmeyer, 1996; Schumaker & Hazel, 1984; Schunk et al., 1987; Turnbull et al., 1999; Yell et al., 2001.

Although we may differ from our students in many ways, we are likely to be powerful models for them nonetheless. Regardless of our own heritage, we must *always* model acceptance and respect for people with diverse backgrounds and characteristics.

Promoting Self-Regulation in Students with Special Needs

Most of our students will undoubtedly stand to gain from teaching strategies that promote greater self-regulation. But students with special educational needs will often be among those in greatest need of becoming more self-regulated (Sands & Wehmeyer, 1996). Such students are especially likely to benefit when we encourage them to set and strive for their own goals, particularly when those goals are concrete, specific, and accomplishable within a short period of time. Students with special needs will also be well served when we teach them self-observation, self-reinforcement techniques, and self-regulated problem-solving skills (Abery & Zajac, 1996; C. E. Cunningham & Cunningham, 1998; E. S. Ellis & Friend, 1991; L. E. Powers et al., 1996; Schunk, 1991; Yell et al., 2001).

Table 10.3 presents a social cognitive perspective of characteristics commonly seen in students with special needs; it also presents a number of strategies for promoting the academic and social success of these students. As you will undoubtedly notice, the concepts *modeling*, *self-efficacy*, and *self-regulation* appear repeatedly throughout the table.

The Big Picture

As you read about social cognitive theory in this chapter, perhaps you noticed that certain ideas kept popping up over and over again. Let's look at some of the central concepts that tie social cognitive theory together. After that, we'll consider how the social cognitive perspective compares to the theories of learning we've considered in previous chapters.

Unifying Ideas in Social Cognitive Theory

As I look back at our preceding discussions of underlying assumptions, reinforcement and punishment, modeling, self-efficacy, or self-regulation, I find three general ideas permeating much of social cognitive theory:

The power of observation. As noted early on, social cognitive theory focuses on how people learn by watching others. The process of learning new behaviors from models is the most obvious example, but observation has other effects as well. For instance, people learn what behaviors are most likely to lead to reinforcement and punishment by watching what happens to other people (i.e., through vicarious experiences). They develop beliefs about what tasks they are and are not capable of doing (i.e., they develop high or low self-efficacy) in part by watching their peers either succeed or fail at those tasks. As they become increasingly self-regulating, the standards that they set for their own behavior are often modeled after those that they see others adopt.

The role of control. The environment, personal variables, and behavior all influence one another (this is the idea of *reciprocal causation*). Yet much of social cognitive theory focuses on how people can clearly be masters of their environments. For instance, they can often choose the activities in which they participate, thereby controlling the particular experiences they have. When they observe models demonstrating certain behaviors, they control what and if they learn by paying attention (or not) and by encoding what they see (or not) in particular ways. When they self-regulate, they take charge of their own behavior and learning—for instance, by setting their own goals, monitoring their own progress, and evaluating their own performance. And their self-efficacy for various tasks encompasses their beliefs about *how well* they can master and control their environment.

The importance of motivation. As we examined the assumptions that underlie social cognitive theory, we noted that people's behavior is very often goal-directed. Furthermore, people form expectations about the probable future consequences of various behaviors by observing what happens to themselves and to others for exhibiting those behaviors, and they are likely to exhibit the behaviors that others model only if they think that doing so is likely to benefit them. To be truly motivated—to consciously choose certain activities, work hard at them, and persist in the face of failure—people must have high self-efficacy and believe that they will ultimately achieve success. Ultimately, people take charge of their own motivation—for instance, by imposing their own response-reinforcement contingencies and by using a variety of strategies for staying on task during self-regulated learning activities.

Comparing the Three Perspectives of Learning

If you have been reading the chapters of Part 2 in sequence, then you have now examined three different theoretical perspectives of learning: cognitive psychology, behaviorism, and social cognitive theory. At the beginning of Chapter 6, I briefly identified some ways in which these perspectives differ from one another. Now that you have studied each perspective in depth, it might be helpful to make additional comparisons. Table 10.4 identifies some of the major ways in which the three theories are similar and different.

It is important to reiterate a point made in Chapter 6: *No single theoretical orientation can give us a complete picture of how people learn.* All three perspectives provide valuable lessons about how to help students achievement in the classroom. For example, principles from cognitive psychology give us ideas about how we can help students remember information and apply it to new situations and problems. Principles from behaviorism yield strategies for helping students develop and maintain more productive classroom behaviors. Principles from social cognitive theory show us how we can effectively model the skills we want students to acquire and how we can promote greater self-regulation. And principles from all three perspectives are useful for motivating students to succeed in the classroom, as you will discover in the next two chapters.

TABLE 10.4 COMPARE/CONTRAST

Comparing the Three Perspectives of Learning

ISSUE	COGNITIVE PSYCHOLOGY	BEHAVIORISM	SOCIAL COGNITIVE THEORY
Learning is defined as . . .	an internal mental phenomenon that may or may not be reflected in behavior.	a behavior change.	an internal mental phenomenon that may or may not be reflected in behavior.
The focus of investigation is on . . .	cognitive processes.	stimuli and responses that can be readily observed.	both behavior and cognitive processes.
Principles of learning describe how . . .	people mentally process the information they receive and construct knowledge from their experiences.	people's behaviors are affected by environmental stimuli.	people's observations of those around them affect behavior and cognitive processes.
Consequences of behavior . . .	are not a major focus of consideration.	must be experienced directly if they are to affect learning.	can be experienced either directly or vicariously.
Learning and behavior are controlled . . .	primarily by cognitive processes within the individual.	primarily by environmental circumstances.	partly by the environment and partly by cognitive processes; people become increasingly self-regulated (and therefore less controlled by the environment) over time.
Educational implications focus on how we can help students . . .	process information in effective ways and construct accurate and complete knowledge about classroom topics.	acquire more productive classroom behaviors.	learn effectively by observing others.

CASE STUDY: *Teacher's Lament*

"Sometimes a teacher just can't win," complains Mr. Adams, a sixth-grade teacher. "At the beginning of the year, I told my students that homework assignments would count for 20 percent of their grades. Yet some students hardly ever turned in any homework, even though I continually reminded them about their assignments. After reconsidering the situation, I decided that I probably shouldn't use homework as a criterion for grading. After all, in this poor, inner-city neighborhood, many kids don't have a quiet place to study at home.

"So in November, I told my class that I wouldn't be counting homework assignments when I calculated grades for the first report card. Naturally, some students—the ones who hadn't been doing their homework—seemed relieved. But the students who *had* been doing it were absolutely furious! And now hardly anyone seems to turn in homework anymore."

- Why were the students who had been doing their homework regularly so upset? Can you explain their reaction using social cognitive theory?
- From a social cognitive perspective, Mr. Adams inadvertently punished some students and reinforced others. Which students in the class were reinforced, and how? Which students were punished, and how?
- What might Mr. Adams do to encourage and help all students to complete homework assignments?

Once you have answered these questions, compare your responses with those presented in Appendix B.

PRAXIS Turn to Appendix C, "Matching Book and Ancillary Content to the PRAXIS™ Principles of Learning and Teaching Tests," to discover sections of this chapter that may be especially applicable to the PRAXIS™ tests.

Now go to our Companion Website at http://www.prenhall.com/ormrod to assess your understanding of chapter content with "Multiple-Choice Questions," apply comprehension in "Essay Questions," broaden your knowledge of educational psychology with related "Web Links," gain greater insight about classroom learning in "Learning in the Content Areas," and analyze and assess classroom work in the "Student Artifact Library."

Key Concepts

11

Motivation and Affect

*W*hat motivated you to open your textbook and start reading this chapter today? Perhaps you have an upcoming quiz or exam on the topic of motivation. Perhaps you want to show that you've done the assigned reading when your instructor calls on you in class. Or perhaps you are simply curious about the nature of human motivation and want to learn some strategies for motivating your own students when you become a teacher.

We have already touched on the topic of motivation in previous chapters. For instance, in our discussion of knowledge construction in Chapter 7, we found that students are more likely to revise their incorrect beliefs about a topic—that is, to undergo conceptual change—when they are motivated to do so. In our discussion of complex cognitive processes in Chapter 8, we learned that students are more apt to engage in effective learning strategies, apply what they've learned to new situations and problems, and think critically when they have the *disposition* to do so. In our exploration of behaviorism in Chapter 9, we discovered that certain consequences are likely to be reinforcing to some students yet not others, presumably because different students have different motives. And motivational issues pervaded much of our discussion of social cognitive theory—modeling, self-efficacy, self-regulation, and so on—in Chapter 10.

In this chapter we will begin to look at motivation in greater depth. We will examine various theoretical perspectives of motivation, consider some of the basic needs that people may have, and find out how emotion (or *affect*) enters into the motivational equation. We will also look at some of the ways in which schools and teachers influence students' motivation and affect. As we proceed through the chapter, we will address questions such as these:

- What is the nature of motivation, and how does it affect learning?
- What theoretical approaches have psychologists used to study and explain motivation?
- What basic needs are our students likely to have, and how can we help them satisfy these needs?
- What roles do emotions (*affect*) play in learning? How can we keep students' anxiety about classroom tasks at a productive level?
- To what extent are students likely to have diverse needs and motives, and how can we address this diversity?

We will continue our exploration of motivation in Chapter 12, where our focus will be on the cognitive factors that influence students' motivation to study, learn, and achieve in the classroom.

CASE STUDY: *Quick Draw*

Unlike her more socially oriented classmates, Anya is a quiet student who usually prefers to be alone. Whenever she has free time in class, she grabs a pencil and a piece of paper and begins to sketch. Her love of drawing appears at other times as well. For example, she decorates her notebooks with elaborate doodles. She embellishes stories and essays with illustrations. She even draws pictures of the words on each week's spelling list.

Not surprisingly, Anya looks forward to her art class, paying particularly close attention on those days when her art teacher describes or demonstrates a new drawing technique. She buries herself in every drawing assignment, seemingly oblivious to the classroom around her. Anya's art teacher notes with pride how much Anya's skill at drawing has improved over the course of the school year.

Anya makes no bones about her interest. "When I grow up, I want to be a professional artist," she states emphatically. "In the meantime, I'm going to practice, practice, practice."

■ Which of Anya's behaviors reflect her interest in art? Are these behaviors likely to enhance her performance in art class? If so, how?

The Nature of Motivation

When it comes to art, Anya is highly motivated. We can reasonably draw this conclusion based on her close attention in class, her eagerness to draw whenever she can, and her career goal. **Motivation** is something that energizes, directs, and sustains behavior; it gets students moving, points them in a particular direction, and keeps them going. We often see students' motivation reflected in *personal investment* and *cognitive engagement* in an activity (Maehr & Meyer, 1997; Paris & Paris, 2001; L. Steinberg, 1996).

Virtually all students are motivated in one way or another. One student may be keenly interested in classroom subject matter and so may seek out challenging coursework, participate actively in class discussions, and earn high marks on assigned projects. Another student may be more concerned with the social side of school, interacting with classmates frequently, attending extracurricular activities almost every day, and perhaps even running for a student government office. Still another may be focused on athletics, excelling in physical education classes, playing or watching sports most afternoons and weekends, and faithfully following a physical fitness regimen. And yet another student, perhaps because of an undetected learning disability, poor social skills, or a seemingly uncoordinated body, may be interested primarily in *avoiding* academics, social situations, or athletic activities.

Anya brings her strong interest in art with her when she enters the classroom. Yet motivation is not always something that people "carry around" inside of them; it can also be influenced by environmental conditions. When we talk about how the environment can enhance a person's motivation to learn particular things or behave in particular ways, we are talking about **situated motivation** (Paris & Turner, 1994; Rueda & Moll, 1994). As we proceed through this chapter and the next, we will find that, as teachers, we can do many things to create a classroom environment that motivates students to learn and behave in ways that will promote their long-term success.

How is *situated motivation* similar to *situated cognition,* a concept discussed in Chapter 8?

How Motivation Affects Learning and Behavior

Motivation has several effects on students' learning and behavior, which I've summarized in Figure 11.1:

■ *It directs behavior toward particular goals.* As we discovered in Chapter 10, social cognitive theorists propose that individuals set goals for themselves and direct their behavior toward those goals. Motivation determines the specific goals toward which people strive (Maehr & Meyer, 1997; Pintrich et al., 1993). Thus, it affects the choices that students make—whether to enroll in trigonometry or studio art, whether to watch the Superbowl game or write an assigned research paper, whether to try out for the lead in the school play or simply sit in the audience and watch the performance.

■ *It leads to increased effort and energy.* Motivation increases the amount of effort and energy that students expend in activities directly related to their needs and goals (Csikszentmihalyi & Nakamura, 1989; Maehr, 1984; Pintrich et al., 1993). It determines whether students pursue a task enthusiastically and wholeheartedly on the one hand, or apathetically and lackadaisically on the other.

FIGURE 11.1 How motivation affects learning and behavior

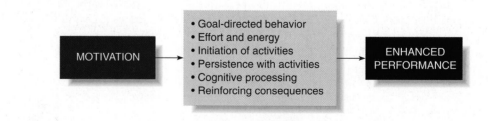

■ *It increases initiation of, and persistence in, activities.* Students are more likely to begin a task that they actually *want* to do. They are also more likely to continue that task until they've completed it, even when they are occasionally interrupted or frustrated in their efforts to do so (Larson, 2000; Maehr, 1984; Wigfield, 1994).

■ *It enhances cognitive processing.* Motivation affects what and how information is processed (Eccles & Wigfield, 1985; Pintrich & Schunk, 2002; Voss & Schauble, 1992). For one thing, motivated students are more likely to pay attention, and as we have seen, attention is critical for getting information into both working memory and long-term memory. They also try to understand material—to learn it meaningfully—rather than simply "go through the motions" of learning in a superficial, rote fashion.

■ *It determines what consequences are reinforcing.* The more students are motivated to achieve academic success, the more proud they will be of an A and the more upset they will be by an F or perhaps even by a B (remember our discussion of self-imposed contingencies in Chapter 10). The more students want to be accepted and respected by their peers, the more meaningful membership in the "in group" will be, and the more painful the ridicule of classmates will seem. To a student uninterested in athletics, making the school football team is no big deal, but to a student whose life revolves around football, making or not making the team may be a consequence of monumental importance.

■ *It leads to improved performance.* Because of these other effects—goal-directed behavior, energy and effort, initiation and persistence, cognitive processing, and reinforcement—motivation often leads to improved performance. As you might guess, then, our students who are most motivated to learn and excel in classroom activities will also tend to be our highest achievers (A. E. Gottfried, 1990; Schiefele, Krapp, & Winteler, 1992; Walberg & Uguroglu, 1980). Conversely, students who are least motivated are at high risk for dropping out before they graduate from high school (Hardre & Reeve, 2001; Hymel et al., 1996; Vallerand, Fortier, & Guay, 1997).

Can you find each of these effects in the case study of Anya?

Intrinsic Versus Extrinsic Motivation

Consider these two students in a trigonometry class:

Sheryl detests mathematics and is taking the class for only one reason: Earning a C or better in trigonometry is a requirement for a scholarship at State University, where she desperately wants to go to college.

Shannon has always liked math. Trigonometry will help her get a scholarship at State University, but in addition, Shannon truly wants to understand how to use trigonometry. She sees its usefulness for her future profession as an architect. Besides, she's discovering that trigonometry is actually a lot of fun.

Sheryl exhibits **extrinsic motivation**: She is motivated by factors external to herself and unrelated to the task she is performing. Students who are extrinsically motivated may want the good grades, money, or recognition that particular activities and accomplishments bring. Essentially, they are motivated to perform a task as a means to an end, not as an end in and of itself. In contrast, Shannon exhibits **intrinsic motivation**: She is motivated by factors within herself and inherent in the task she is performing. Students who are intrinsically motivated may engage in an activity because it gives them pleasure, helps them develop a skill they think is important, or is the ethically and morally right thing to do. Students with a high level of intrinsic motivation sometimes become so focused on and absorbed in an activity that they lose track of time and completely ignore other tasks (Csikszentmihalyi, 1990, 1996).

Students are most likely to show the beneficial effects of motivation when they are *intrinsically* motivated to engage in classroom activities. Intrinsically motivated students tackle assigned tasks willingly and are eager to learn classroom material, are more likely to process information in effective ways (e.g., by engaging in meaningful learning, elaboration, and visual imagery), and more likely to achieve at high levels. In contrast, extrinsically motivated students may have to be enticed or prodded, may process information only superficially, and are often interested in performing only easy tasks and meeting minimal classroom requirements (A. E. Gottfried, Fleming, & Gottfried, 2001; Larson, 2000; Schiefele, 1991; Spaulding, 1992; Tobias, 1994; Voss & Schauble, 1992).

Some researchers believe that our schools foster extrinsic motivation far more often than intrinsic motivation (R. M. Ryan, Connell, & Grolnick, 1992; Spaulding, 1992). Has this been true in your own experience?

Students learn more and are more likely to engage in meaningful learning and elaboration when they are genuinely interested in what they are learning.

Many researchers have found that students' intrinsic motivation for learning school subject matter declines during the school years. In the early elementary grades, children are often eager and excited to learn new things at school. But sometime between grades 3 and 9, children become less intrinsically motivated, and more *extrinsically* motivated, to learn and master school subject matter (Covington & Müeller, 2001; Harter, 1992; J. M. T. Walker, 2001). Their intrinsic motivation may be especially low when they make the often anxiety-arousing transition from elementary to secondary school (more about this transition later in the chapter).

This decline in intrinsic motivation for academic subject matter is probably the result of several factors. As students move through the grade levels, they are increasingly reminded of the importance of good grades (extrinsic motivators) for promotion, graduation, and college admission, and many begin to realize that they are not necessarily "at the top of the heap" in comparison with their peers (Covington & Müeller, 2001; Harter, 1992). Furthermore, they become more cognitively able to set and strive for long-term goals, and they begin to evaluate school subjects in terms of their relevance to such goals, rather than in terms of any intrinsic appeal. And they may grow increasingly impatient with the overly structured, repetitive, and boring activities that they too often find at school (Battistich, Solomon, Kim, Watson, & Schaps, 1995; Larson, 2000).

This is not to say, however, that extrinsic motivation is necessarily a bad thing. Oftentimes students are motivated by both intrinsic and extrinsic factors simultaneously (Bronson, 2000; Covington, 2000; Hidi & Harackiewicz, 2000). For example, although Shannon enjoys studying trigonometry, she also knows that a good grade in her trigonometry course will help her get a scholarship at State U. Furthermore, good grades and other external rewards for her achievements may confirm that she is, in fact, mastering the subject matter she is studying. And as we noted in Chapter 10, extrinsic motivation, perhaps in the form of extrinsic reinforcers for academic achievement or productive behavior, may be essential for getting some students on the road to successful classroom learning and productivity. Yet intrinsic motivation is ultimately what will sustain our students over the long run: It will encourage them to make sense of and apply the things they are studying, and it will increase the odds that they continue to read and learn about science, history, and other academic subject matter long after they have graduated and ventured out into the adult world.

The origins of both extrinsic and intrinsic motivation have been the source of considerable debate for many years. Let's look at how various researchers have studied and tried to explain the nature of motivation and how it emerges.

Theoretical Perspectives of Motivation

Researchers and theorists have approached the study of motivation from four major angles: the trait, behaviorist, social cognitive, and cognitive perspectives.

The Trait Perspective

Trait theorists propose that motivation takes the form of relatively enduring personality characteristics that people have to a greater or lesser extent. For example, children and adolescents differ in their tendency to forge friendly relationships with others and in their desire to gain other people's regard and respect (more about such needs for *affiliation* and *approval* shortly). They may also differ in the extent to which they seek out new, exciting, and possibly dangerous experiences—that is, in the extent to which they are *sensation seekers* (Snow, Corno, & Jackson, 1996).

Of the various needs that people might have, the majority of research has focused on the need for achievement, more often called **achievement motivation**. Achievement motivation is the need for excellence for its own sake, without regard for any external rewards that one's accomplishments might bring (e.g., J. W. Atkinson & Feather, 1966; McClelland, Atkinson, Clark, & Lowell, 1953; Veroff et al., 1975). Children with high achievement motivation seek out challenging tasks that they know they can accomplish with effort and persistence. They rarely rest on their laurels; instead, they set increasingly higher standards for excellence as their current standards are met (Eccles et al., 1998; Veroff et al., 1975).

In its earliest conceptualization, achievement motivation was thought to be a general characteristic that students exhibit consistently in a variety of tasks across many domains.

More recently, however, many theorists have proposed that this need may instead be somewhat specific to particular tasks and occasions (e.g., Dweck & Elliott, 1983; Stipek, 1996; Wigfield, 1997). Theorists are also beginning to explain achievement motivation in terms of specific cognitive factors that influence the choices students make and the tasks they pursue. Thus, explanations of achievement motivation have shifted away from a "trait" approach to a more cognitive approach. In Chapter 12 we will examine several cognitive factors that contribute to students' motivation to achieve in the classroom.

Although the trait approach to motivation is losing prominence in contemporary theory and research, personality characteristics clearly *do* influence the motives that students exhibit in the classroom. As an example, try the following exercise.

INTERPRETING ARTIFACTS AND INTERACTIONS   *There's Nothing to Do in Greeley*

When my daughter Tina was in ninth grade, she took part in a districtwide writing assessment. For the assessment, she was asked to write an essay in response to the statement "There is nothing to do in Greeley" (her hometown). As you read her essay, speculate about

- What traits guided Tina's choices for leisure-time activity
- What Tina most enjoyed about school

There is nothing to do in Greeley! I know every parent has heard that line before!

I am going to disagree with this quote. I think that it depends on who the person is who's saying this. The person who is proposing this is really remarking that they do not choose to do anything, not that there is little or nothing to do.

From my experiences with nothing to do, I have always been successful with curing that awful plague of boredom. When caught with this disease I usually call my friends who may also be suffering. Our phone conversations typically consist of at least two remedies and finally a cure. I myself often suggest a few good ideas to our problem, but if the case is really nasty my cronies and I work together to find the solution. Anybody can find entertainment if they really choose to.

Greeley isn't half as bad as people see it to be. I guess we Greeley folk are lucky we aren't living somewhere like Ordway, Colorado. Or better yet, how about Black Pebble, North Dakota? I'll bet you have never even heard of Black Pebble! Probably not, since it is in the middle of nothing. I heard about it from a book I have called Places Never Even Dreamed of in the U.S. The person who wrote that book must have been homesick with boredom.

Luckily, if you are ever caught in an uninviting situation one can find many thrills. For example, if you are forced to go see a movie (with the gang) that you have already seen five times, then why not bring a needle and thread? While everyone else is engulfed in the movie you can be busily sewing their sleeves together! See what I mean? If not, read on. If two people are sitting next to each other, there is a little bit of space between them because of the arm slot. Simply grasp the clothing you can get without them noticing and go at it! That will probably take up part of the show. The other half will go by quickly as you try to refrain from blowing up with laughter. If this isn't your fancy, then try to think of something else. You can do it!

All in all, remember, there is always something to do no matter what the situation is if you have a creative mind that's ready to run wild!

Tina's essay is as informative in what it *doesn't* say as in what it does say. Notice how her solution to finding something to do rests entirely on other people; she doesn't mention reading a good book, sewing a new outfit, or finding some other means of solitary entertainment. From the time she was a toddler, Tina was happy only when she was with others, and by the time she was 10, those "others" had to be her peers. Thus, Tina had a high need for affiliation—a need that made hanging out with friends her highest priority both in and outside of school. Furthermore, her thoughts about provoking others (e.g., by sewing their clothes together) suggest that she was a bit of a sensation seeker; as her mother, I can tell you that she sought enough thrills in her adolescent years that I was quite relieved (and a bit surprised) that she lived to see her high school graduation.

The Behaviorist Perspective

From a behaviorist perspective, people behave primarily to obtain reinforcing outcomes (or perhaps to avoid punishing ones), and many of the behaviors they exhibit are those responses that have been reinforced in the past. For instance, students might study hard if their teacher praises them for their efforts, and they might misbehave in class if doing so gains them the attention of their teacher and classmates.

Early behaviorists proposed that specific consequences are reinforcing only if they address a particular **drive,** an internal state in which something necessary for optimal functioning (food, water, warmth, etc.) is missing. For example, a hungry person finds food reinforcing, a thirsty person enjoys water, a cold person enjoys a fire and warm blanket, and so on. In recent years, however, motivation theorists have largely left drive reduction theory by the wayside (Bolles, 1975; Graham & Weiner, 1996). For one thing, learning sometimes occurs without satisfying, or reducing, any apparent drive (e.g., Sheffield, Wulff, & Backer, 1951). And a great deal of human behavior seems to be aimed at accomplishing long-term goals rather than fulfilling short-term needs (Pintrich & Schunk, 2002). Furthermore, people sometimes behave in ways that actually *increase* drive (Rachlin, 1991), perhaps by going to scary movies, riding roller coasters, or (like Tina) sewing unsuspecting people's clothes together.

Rather than focusing on physiological needs and drives, many behaviorists now look more generally at the purposes that particular behaviors may serve for people (see the discussion of *functional analysis* in Chapter 9). Other theorists, whether or not they take a behaviorist approach to learning and motivation, nevertheless recognize that the consequences of behaviors can certainly affect students' motivation to exhibit those behaviors. For instance, psychologists of a variety of theoretical persuasions have studied the circumstances under which *feedback* is likely to be effective. In general, feedback is most effective when it provides information that students cannot get on their own, identifies specific strengths that students have and specific weaknesses that can be addressed, and maintains students' self-efficacy and self-esteem (Kluger & DeNisi, 1998; T. D. Little, Oettingen, Stetsenko, & Baltes, 1995; Pintrich & Schunk, 2002).

The Social Cognitive Perspective

As we noted in Chapter 10, social cognitive theory has contributed in several important ways to our understanding of motivation. For instance, this perspective places heavy emphasis on the *goals* that people are striving for, as reflected in the choices they make and the behaviors they exhibit. It also acknowledges that the reinforcement and punishment that follow various behaviors affect people's *expectations* for the consequences of their future behaviors. And it points out that people's beliefs about their own capability to perform a particular activity (their *self-efficacy*) is a key factor in their decision to engage in and persist at that activity. All three of these concepts—goals, expectations, and self-efficacy—have emerged as important cognitive factors in motivation, and so we will revisit them in Chapter 12.

The Cognitive Perspective

As you might guess, cognitive psychologists focus on how mental processes affect motivation. They propose that human beings are naturally inclined to make sense of their world, that their curiosity is often piqued by new and puzzling events, and that they are especially motivated by perceived discrepancies between new information and their existing beliefs (e.g., recall Piaget's concept of *disequilibrium,* described in Chapter 2). People try to make sense of the things that happen to them as well—for instance, by identifying possible causes of (*attributions* for) their successes and failures ("I got an A on my report because I'm smart," "I didn't get to start in Saturday's game because the coach doesn't like me," etc.). This need to make sense of one's environment and experiences is undoubtedly a primary source of intrinsic motivation, but it is probably not the only source. For instance, some cognitive theorists propose that two other conditions are essential for intrinsic motivation: (1) People must have some sense of mastery over their world (i.e., they must have a *sense of competence* or *self-efficacy*), and (2) they must believe that they have some control over the direction their lives are taking (i.e., they must have a *sense of self-determination*).

Within the last two or three decades, the cognitive and social cognitive perspectives have dominated theory and research in motivation (A. M. Ryan, 2000; Winne & Marx, 1989), and so you will see their influence throughout this chapter and the next. Yet we must keep in mind that no single theory gives us a complete picture of human motivation. Each of the perspectives just summarized provides pieces of the motivation "puzzle," and so each offers useful ideas about how we can motivate students in classroom settings. Table 11.1 contrasts the four perspectives and describes the general educational implications of each one.

To motivate students in the classroom, a cognitive psychologist might propose capitalizing on their natural curiosity by presenting new and puzzling situations.

TABLE 11.1

Comparing Theoretical Perspectives of Motivation

ISSUE	TRAIT THEORIES	BEHAVIORISM	SOCIAL COGNITIVE THEORY	COGNITIVE PSYCHOLOGY
Sources of motivation are . . .	relatively stable characteristics and personality traits.	the consequences of various behaviors.	personal goals, beliefs about one's own ability to perform tasks successfully, and expectations regarding the likely outcomes of future efforts.	inconsistencies between current beliefs and new experiences, interpretations of past successes and failures, and perceptions of personal competence and control.
Examples of motivational concepts are . . .	achievement motivation, need for affiliation, need for approval.	drive, reinforcement, punishment, functional analysis, feedback.	goals, self-efficacy, expectations.	curiosity, interest, disequilibrium, attributions, sense of competence, sense of self-determination.
Educational implications focus on . . .	identifying motivational traits and using instructional strategies that address students' individual needs.	administering consequences that increase desirable behaviors and decrease nonproductive ones.	encouraging efforts toward self-chosen goals and facilitating success through instruction, modeling, and ongoing guidance and support.	pointing out how new information contradicts students' existing beliefs, showing students how their successes and failures are due to factors within their control (e.g., effort, learning strategies), and providing opportunities for choice and self-direction.

What Basic Needs Do People Have?

As I described the four perspectives of motivation in the preceding section, I occasionally talked about *needs*; for instance, I mentioned the needs for affiliation and approval, the need for achievement, and the need to make sense of the world. Over the years, psychologists have speculated that people have a wide variety of needs, some of which are essential for physical survival and others of which are important for psychological well-being.

As an example, one early theorist, Abraham Maslow (e.g., 1973, 1987), proposed that people have five basic needs that they try to satisfy:

1. *Physiological*: Needs related to physical survival (needs for food, water, oxygen, warmth, etc.)
2. *Safety*: The need to feel safe and secure in one's environment
3. *Love and belonging*: The need to have affectionate relationships with others and to be accepted as part of a group
4. *Esteem*: The need to feel good about oneself and to believe that others also perceive oneself favorably
5. *Self-actualization*: The need to reach one's full potential—to become all that one is capable of becoming

You can learn more about Maslow's theory in the chapter "Maslow's Hierarchy of Needs" in the *Study Guide and Reader* that accompanies this book.

Maslow further proposed that these needs form a hierarchy, such that people satisfy the most basic ones before addressing the others. More specifically, they will try to satisfy their physiological needs first, then their need for safety, and still later their needs for love, belonging, and esteem. Only when such needs have been met do they strive for self-actualization, whereby they explore areas of interest, learn for the sake of learning, and so on. Unfortunately, Maslow's hierarchy of needs was based on very little hard evidence, and so many theorists continue to regard his theory as being more conjecture than fact. Nevertheless, it provides a helpful reminder for us as teachers: Our students are unlikely to pursue classroom tasks with much interest or energy until their more basic needs (e.g., an adequate diet, a safe classroom environment, the positive regard of their teacher and classmates) have been addressed.

It goes without saying that people must place high priority on their physiological and safety needs: Satisfying such needs is essential not only for personal survival but also for the long-term survival of the species. But what other needs do human beings almost invariably have? Here we look at two needs that have considerable empirical support and have definite implications for teachers: the need for self-worth and the need for relatedness.

Self-Worth

One early theorist proposed that people have an intrinsic need to feel *competent*—to believe that they can deal effectively with their environment (R. White, 1959). To achieve this sense of competence, children spend a great deal of time engaged in exploring and attempting to master the world. The need for competence may have evolutionary significance: It pushes people to develop ways of dealing more effectively with environmental conditions and thus increases their chances of survival.

More recently, Martin Covington (1992) has proposed that *protecting* one's sense of competence—something he calls **self-worth**—is one of people's highest priorities. Obviously, achieving success on a regular basis is one way of maintaining, perhaps even enhancing, this self-worth. But consistent success isn't always possible, especially when people face challenging tasks. In such instances, students may protect their sense of self-worth by making excuses that seemingly justify their poor performance, or they may refuse to engage in the tasks at all (Covington, 1992). Furthermore, some may do things that actually *undermine* their chances of success—a phenomenon known as **self-handicapping**. Self-handicapping takes a variety of forms, including these:

- *Setting unattainably high goals*: Working toward goals that even the most able individuals couldn't achieve
- *Procrastinating*: Putting a task off until success is virtually impossible
- *Reducing effort*: Putting forth an obviously insufficient amount of effort to succeed
- *Using alcohol or drugs*: Taking substances that will inevitably reduce performance (Covington, 1992; M. E. Ford, 1996; E. E. Jones & Berglas, 1978; Riggs, 1992; Urdan & Midgley, 2001)

It might seem paradoxical that students who want to be successful would engage in such behaviors. But if they believe they are unlikely to succeed at a particular task, they increase their chances of *justifying* their failure (and therefore maintaining self-worth) by acknowledging that, under the circumstances, success wasn't very likely to begin with (Covington, 1992; E. E. Jones & Berglas, 1978; Riggs, 1992).

Students who have a strong sense of self-worth rarely engage in self-handicapping and so, as you might guess, achieve at higher levels than those who consistently self-handicap (Urdan & Midgley, 2001). Curiously, students are *less* likely to engage in self-handicapping when their chances of success are slim; in such situations, failure does not indicate low ability and so does not threaten their sense of self-worth (Covington, 1992).

Ideally, students' sense of self-worth should be based on a reasonably accurate appraisal of what they can and cannot accomplish. Students who underestimate their abilities will set unnecessarily low goals for themselves and give up easily after only minor setbacks. Those who overestimate their abilities (perhaps because they have been lavished with praise by parents or teachers, or perhaps because school assignments have been consistently easy and nonchallenging) may set themselves up for failure by forming unrealistically high expectations for themselves or by not exerting a sufficient amount of effort to succeed (Paris & Cunningham, 1996; D. Phillips & Zimmerman, 1990; Pintrich & Schunk, 2002; H. W. Stevenson et al., 1990). The strategies we've previously identified for enhancing students' self-concept, self-esteem, and self-efficacy in Chapters 3 and 10—for instance, scaffolding their efforts at challenging tasks—can also help them maintain a healthy sense of self-worth.

Relatedness

How much time do you spend with other people? Do you enjoy being with others for a good part of each day? Or, like Anya, do you prefer to spend much of your time alone? How much do you care about what other people think of you? Do you continually worry about how others might judge your words and actions? Or do you have such confidence in your convictions that you do what you think is best regardless of any social repercussions?

To some extent, we are all social creatures: We live, work, and play with our fellow human beings. Some theorists have proposed that people of all ages have a fundamental need to feel socially connected and to secure the love and respect of others; in other words, they have a **need for relatedness** (Connell, 1990; Connell & Wellborn, 1991). As is true for the need for competence, the need for relatedness may be important from an evolutionary standpoint, in

FIGURE 11.2 In this personal narrative, 11-year-old Ben describes a school field trip to a Civil War battlefield. In the last paragraph he reveals what was, from his perspective, the *most* valuable part of the trip: the chance to be with his friends for the entire day.

My Trip to Gettysburg

"Honk!" sounded the bus. We had just left for one of the best times of my life. My friends, mom, teachers, and I were all going.

Last spring was my trip to Gettysburg. We had to wake up at 5:00 a.m. When we got there, I said "Hi!" to everyone in my group. We were at Gettysburg on time even though the bus was late.

When we got there, we went to the tour center and watched an informational video about Gettysburg. Now we were ready for a tour of the real battlefield the union and confederate soldiers fought on. Our guide tried to convince us that Lee was a great general. He told us the book and movie were a lie based on Longstreet's autobiography.

Then we went to the Wax Museum. It was cool! They looked so real. I liked the battlefield scene most.

We went to the Stonehenge for dinner. After that we went to the Jennie Wade house. While we where [sic] there we had a wax person talk to us. Finally we left. We watched three movies on the way home.

There were a lot of cool things I did at Gettysburg, but most of all I got closer to my friends because we spent all 18 hours together. We ate together, sat with each other on the bus, and went to every activity together. That's why I call it the best time of my life!!

that people who live in cohesive, cooperative social groups are more likely to survive than people who go it alone (R. Wright, 1994).

Students' need for relatedness may manifest itself in a wide variety of behaviors. Many children and adolescents place high priority on interacting with friends, often at the expense of getting their schoolwork done (Dowson & McInerney, 2001; W. Doyle, 1986a; Wigfield, Eccles, Mac Iver, Reuman, & Midgley, 1991). They may also be concerned about projecting a favorable public image—that is, by looking smart, popular, athletic, or cool to others (Juvonen, 2000). And some may exhibit their need for relatedness by showing concern for other people's welfare or helping peers who are struggling with classroom assignments (Dowson & McInerney, 2001; M. E. Ford, 1996). The need for relatedness seems to be especially high in the middle school years (B. B. Brown et al., 1986; Juvonen, 2000; A. M. Ryan & Patrick, 2001). (For example, see Figure 11.2.) Young adolescents tend to be overly concerned about what others think, prefer to hang out in tight-knit groups, and are especially susceptible to peer influence (see the discussions of the *imaginary audience, cliques,* and *peer pressure* in Chapter 3).

As teachers, we must remember that social relationships will be among our students' highest priorities (Dowson & McInerney, 2001; Geary, 1998). Our students are more likely to be academically successful—and more likely to stay in school rather than drop out—when they believe that their teachers and peers like and respect them and when they feel that they belong to the classroom community (Goodenow, 1993; Hymel et al., 1996; Ladd, 1990; A. M. Ryan & Patrick, 2001). In our discussions of *classroom climate* and *sense of community* in Chapter 14, we will consider how we can foster such beliefs and feelings.

Individual Differences in the Need for Relatedness

Although the need for relatedness may be universal, some children and adolescents seem to have a greater need for interpersonal relationships than others (Kupersmidt, Buchele, Voegler, & Sedikides, 1996). Let's briefly take a "trait" approach to motivation as we consider research related to needs for affiliation and approval.

Need for affiliation. Students differ in the extent to which they desire and actively seek out friendly relationships with others; in other words, they differ in their **need for affiliation**. For example, as I mentioned earlier, my daughter Tina has always been a very social creature; the thought of spending more than a couple of hours alone horrifies her. In contrast, my son Jeff, although he enjoys the companionship of others, is often quite content to spend an afternoon creating a Bart Simpson cartoon on the computer or designing the "executive mansion" in which, so he tells me, he intends to live some day.

Students' needs for affiliation will be reflected in the choices they make at school (Boyatzis, 1973; French, 1956; Wigfield et al., 1996). For example, students with a low need for affiliation may prefer to work alone, whereas students with a high need for affiliation more often prefer to work in small groups. When choosing work partners, students with a low affiliation need are apt to choose classmates whom they believe to be competent at the task to be performed; students with a high affiliation need are apt to choose their friends even if these friends are relatively incompetent. In high school, students with a low need for affiliation are likely to choose a class schedule that meets their own interests and ambitions, whereas students with a high need for affiliation are more likely to choose one that enables them to be with their friends. As you can see, then, a high need for affiliation often interferes with maximal classroom learning and achievement (Urdan & Maehr, 1995; Wentzel & Wigfield, 1998).

As teachers, we cannot ignore the high need for affiliation that many students bring to the classroom. On the contrary, as we plan our daily lessons and classroom activities, we must provide opportunities for students to interact with one another. Ideally, we should find ways to help students learn academic subject matter *and* meet their affiliation needs simultaneously (Wentzel & Wigfield, 1998). Although some classroom objectives may be best accomplished when students work independently, others can be accomplished just as easily (perhaps even more so) when students work together. Group-based activities, such as discussions, debates, role playing, cooperative learning tasks, and competitions among two or more teams of equal ability, all provide the means through which students can satisfy their need for affiliation while simultaneously acquiring new knowledge and skills (Brophy, 1987; Urdan & Maehr, 1995).

We must remember, too, that many of our students will want to affiliate not only with their classmates but with teachers as well. Therefore, we should show our students that we like them, enjoy being with them, and are concerned about their well-being (McKeachie, Lin, Milholland, & Isaacson, 1966; Stipek, 1996). We can communicate our fondness for students in numerous ways—for example, by expressing an interest in their outside activities and accomplishments, providing extra help or support when it is needed, or lending a sympathetic ear. These "caring" messages may be especially important for students from culturally different backgrounds: Such students are more likely to succeed in our classroom if we show interest in their lives and concern for their individual needs (Phelan, Davidson, & Cao, 1991).

Need for approval. Another need in which we see individual differences is the **need for approval**, a desire to gain the acceptance and positive judgments of other people (Igoe & Sullivan, 1991; Juvonen & Weiner, 1993; Urdan & Maehr, 1995). Students with a high need for approval are overly concerned with pleasing others and tend to give in easily to peer pressure, for fear that they might otherwise be rejected (Crowne & Marlowe, 1964; Wentzel & Wigfield, 1998). Whereas other students might engage in a school task for the pleasure that success at the task brings, students with a high need for approval are likely to engage in the task primarily to please their teacher and will persist at it only as long as their teacher praises them for doing so (Harter, 1975; S. C. Rose & Thornburg, 1984).

In the early years, children are most apt to seek the approval of adults, such as parents and teachers. As they get older, and especially as they move into adolescence, they are usually more interested in gaining the approval of their peers (Juvonen & Weiner, 1993; Urdan & Maehr, 1995). Cultural background may also influence whether children and adolescents prefer adult or peer approval; for instance, many teenagers from Asian cultures highly value the approval of adult authority figures (e.g., Dien, 1998).

When students have a high need for approval, we can promote their classroom achievement by praising them frequently for the things they do well. At the same time, we must keep in mind that some students (especially at the secondary level) may be more concerned about gaining the approval of *peers* and that those peers may disapprove of high academic achievement (Juvonen & Weiner, 1993; L. Steinberg, 1996; Wigfield et al., 1996). If being a high achiever is not the socially acceptable thing to do, many students will prefer that their ac-

Passing notes in class is one way that some students regularly address their need for affiliation.

Have students work together on some learning tasks.

A high school history teacher incorporates classroom debates, small-group discussions, and cooperative learning tasks into every month's activities.

Continually communicate the message that you like and respect your students.

A middle school teacher tells one of his students that he saw her dancing troupe's performance at the local mall over the weekend. "I had no idea you were so talented," he says. "How many years have you been studying dance?"

Create a classroom culture in which respect for *everyone's* needs and well-being is paramount.

When a fifth-grade teacher overhears two boys making fun of a fellow student who stutters, she discretely pulls them aside, explains that the classmate is extremely self-conscious about his disability and is working hard to overcome it, and reminds the boys that they, too, have imperfections as well as strengths.

Provide a means through which every student can feel part of a small, close-knit group.

During the first week of school, a ninth-grade math teacher establishes *base groups*—groups of three or four students who provide support and assistance for one another throughout the school year—in each of his classes. At the beginning or end of every class period, the teacher gives the groups five minutes to help one another with questions and concerns about daily lessons and homework assignments.

Give frequent praise to students who have a high need for approval.

Several students in a second-grade class have difficulty staying on task during independent assignments. Their teacher has found that they are more likely to stay on task when she commends them for doing so.

Praise students privately when being a high achiever is not sanctioned by their peer group.

While reading a stack of short stories that his students have written, a high school English teacher discovers that one of his students—a young woman who, he knows, is quite concerned about looking cool in front of her classmates—has written a particularly creative story. On the second page of her story (where the student's classmates won't be likely to see what he has written), he writes, "This is great work, Brigitta! I think it's good enough to enter into the state writing contest. I'd like to meet with you before or after school some day this week to talk more about the contest."

complishments be praised privately rather than publicly. Ultimately, how well our students are accomplishing instructional objectives is no one's business but theirs, their parents', and ours.

Relationships with peers and teachers are, for many students, a source of considerable pleasure and enjoyment. Conversely, difficulties in interpersonal interactions, which may impede students' ability to satisfy their need for relatedness, are often a source of sadness and anxiety. Pleasure, enjoyment, anxiety—all of these are examples of feelings, emotions, or what psychologists call *affect*. We turn to this topic now.

Affect and Its Effects

When we speak of motivation, we must also consider **affect**—the feelings and emotions that an individual brings to bear on a task. Motivation and affect are closely intertwined. For example, as just noted, students may feel happy or sad depending on whether their needs for affiliation and approval are being met at school. And in Chapter 12 we'll find that students respond differently to easy tasks—either with feelings of disappointment, on the one hand, or with relief, on the other—depending on the kinds of goals they set for their learning and performance in the classroom. We'll find, too, that students who master challenging tasks experience considerable pleasure, satisfaction, and pride in their accomplishments.

In this section we examine two aspects of affect that are particularly relevant to our work as teachers: hot cognition and anxiety.

Hot Cognition

EXPERIENCING FIRSTHAND *Flying High*

As you read each of the following statements, decide whether it evokes positive feelings (e.g., happiness, excitement), negative feelings (e.g., sadness, anger), or no feelings whatsoever. Check the appropriate blank in each case.

	Positive Feelings	Negative Feelings	No Feelings
1. The city of Denver opened DIA, its new international airport, in 1995.	____	____	____
2. In a recent commercial airline crash, ninety passengers and eight crew members lost their lives.	____	____	____
3. A dozen people survived that crash, including a 3-month-old infant found in the rear of the plane.	____	____	____
4. The area of an airplane in which food is prepared is called the *galley*.	____	____	____
5. Several major airlines are offering $69 round-trip fares to Acapulco, Mexico.	____	____	____
6. Those $69 fares apply only to those flights leaving at 5:30 in the morning.	____	____	____
7. Some flights between North America and Europe now include two full-course meals.	____	____	____

Might your knowledge of terrorist attacks involving commercial airlines have influenced your emotional reactions to the statements in this exercise? If so, how?

You probably had little if any emotional reaction to statements 1 (the opening of DIA) and 4 (the definition of *galley*). In contrast, you may have had pleasant feelings when you read statements 3 (the surviving infant) and 5 (the low fares to Acapulco), and unpleasant feelings when you read statements 2 (the high number of deaths) and 6 (the dreadful departure time for those Acapulco flights). Your response to statement 7 (the two full-course meals) may have been positive, negative, or neutral, depending on your previous experiences with airline cuisine.

The concept of *hot cognition* tells us that students are more likely to attend to and remember things that not only stimulate their thinking but also elicit emotional reactions.

Sometimes learning and cognitive processing are emotionally charged—a phenomenon known as **hot cognition** (e.g., Hoffman, 1991; P. H. Miller, 1993). For example, students might get excited when they read about advances in science that could lead to effective treatments of spinal cord injuries, cancer, AIDS, or mental illness. They may feel sad when they read about the living conditions in certain parts of the world. They will, we hope, get angry when they learn about the atrocities committed against African American slaves in the pre–Civil War days of the United States or against millions of Jewish people and members of other minority groups during World War II.

Affect is clearly intertwined with learning and cognition. Students are more likely to pay attention to things that evoke strong emotions, such as excitement, sadness, or anger (LaBar & Phelps, 1998; Reisberg & Heuer, 1992). When they are interested in a topic about which they are reading (perhaps finding it exciting or upsetting), they process information more effectively—for example by engaging in more meaningful learning and visual imagery (Hidi & Anderson, 1992; Tobias, 1994). In addition, students can usually retrieve information with high emotional content more easily than they can recall relatively nonemotional information (Barkley, 1996; LaBar & Phelps, 1998; Reisberg & Heuer, 1992). In general, then, students will learn and remember more when they become involved in classroom subject matter not only cognitively but emotionally as well.

Problem solving also is easier when students enjoy what they're doing, and successful problem solutions are often accompanied by feelings of excitement, pleasure, and pride (McLeod & Adams, 1989; M. U. Smith, 1991). In contrast, students are likely to feel frustrated and anxious when they fail at a learning or problem-solving activity, especially if it appears to be an easy one, and they are apt to develop a dislike for what they've been doing (Carver & Scheier, 1990; Stodolsky, Salk, & Glaessner, 1991). An exchange between one of my educational psychology students (Brian) and his 16-year-old sister Megan illustrates:

Brian: How do you know when you have learned something?

Megan: I know that I have learned something when I get really excited about that topic while I am talking to a person about it. When I haven't learned something I tend to say that I hate it, because I don't understand it. When I am excited and can have a discussion about something is when I know that I fully understand and have studied enough on that topic. (courtesy of Brian Zottoli)

Anxiety

Imagine that you are enrolled in Professor Josiah S. Carberry's course in advanced psychoceramics. Today is your day to give a half-hour presentation on the topic of psychoceramic califractions. You have read several books and numerous articles on your topic and undoubtedly know more about psychoceramic califractions than anyone else in the room. Furthermore, you have meticulously prepared a set of note cards to refer to during your presentation. As you sit in class waiting for your turn to speak, you should be feeling calm and confident. But instead you're a nervous wreck: Your heart is pounding wildly, your palms are sweaty, and your stomach is in a knot. When Professor Carberry calls you to the front of the classroom and you begin to speak, you have trouble remembering what you wanted to say, and you can't read your note cards because your hands are shaking so much.

It's not as if you *want* to be nervous about speaking in front of your psychoceramics class. Furthermore, you can't think of a single reason why you *should* be nervous. After all, you are an expert on your topic, you know your underwear isn't showing (you double-checked), and your classmates are not the type to giggle or throw rotten tomatoes if you make a mistake. So what's the big deal? What happened to the self-assured student who stood practicing in front of the mirror last night?

You are a victim of **anxiety**: You have a feeling of uneasiness and apprehension about an event because you're not sure what its outcome will be. This feeling is accompanied by a variety of physiological symptoms, including a rapid heartbeat, increased perspiration, and muscular tension (e.g., a "knot" or "butterflies" in the stomach). Anxiety is similar to fear, but different in one important respect: Although we are usually *afraid* of something in particular (a roaring lion, a lightning storm, or the bogeymen under the bed), we usually don't know exactly why we're *anxious*. And it's difficult to deal with anxiety when we can't pinpoint its cause. In Figure 11.3, 11-year-old Laurel describes what she thinks anxiety, or "nervousness," is.

State Anxiety Versus Trait Anxiety

Almost everyone is anxious at one time or another. Many students become anxious just before a test they know is going to be difficult, and most get nervous when they have to give a prepared speech in front of their classmates. Such temporary feelings of anxiety are instances of **state anxiety**. Yet some students are anxious a good part of the time, even when the situation is not particularly dangerous or threatening. For example, some students may get excessively nervous even before very easy exams, and others may be so anxious about mathematics that they can't concentrate on the simplest math assignment. When an individual shows a pattern of responding with anxiety even in nonthreatening situations, we have a case of **trait anxiety**. It is our trait-anxious students whose performance is most hampered by anxiety and for whom we may have to go the extra mile to convince them that they can succeed at classroom tasks.

How Anxiety Affects Classroom Performance

Imagine, for a moment, that you are not at all anxious—not even the teeniest bit—about your grade in Professor Carberry's psychoceramics class. Without any anxiety at all, will you study for Carberry's tests? Will you turn in the assigned research papers? If you have no anxiety

NERVOUSNESS:

Nervousness has very little patience, and absolutely no Confidence. Nervousness and Fear often go together. One senses Nervousness' presence right before you do something you've never done before or when you're afraid about what will happen next. I felt nervous when I was on my way to camp.

FIGURE 11.3 Laurel (age 11) tries to put her finger on what "nervousness" (anxiety) feels like.

whatsoever, you might not even buy the textbook or go to class. And you probably won't get a very good grade in your psychoceramics class.

A small amount of anxiety often improves performance: It is **facilitating anxiety**. A little anxiety spurs people into action; for instance, it makes them go to class, read the textbook, do assignments, and study for exams (see Figure 11.4). It also makes them approach their class-work carefully and reflect before making their responses (Shipman & Shipman, 1985). Yet too much anxiety often interferes with effective performance: It is **debilitating anxiety**. Excessive anxiety distracts people and interferes with their attention to the task at hand.

At what point does anxiety stop facilitating and begin debilitating performance? In general, very easy tasks—things that students can do almost without thinking (e.g., running)—are facilitated by high levels of anxiety. But more difficult tasks—those that require considerable thought and effort—are best performed with only a small or moderate level of anxiety (Kirkland, 1971; Yerkes & Dodson, 1908). An excessive level of anxiety in difficult situations can interfere with several processes critical for successful learning and performance:

Did you previously believe that *any* amount of anxiety is detrimental? If so, have you now revised your thinking about anxiety's effects?

- Paying attention to what needs to be learned
- Processing information effectively (e.g., engaging in meaningful learning, organization, or elaboration)
- Remembering information and demonstrating skills that have already been learned

(Covington, 1992; Eysenck, 1992; Hagtvet & Johnsen, 1992; I. G. Sarason, 1980)

Anxiety is especially likely to interfere with such processes when a task places heavy demands on working memory or long-term memory—for instance, when a task involves creativity or problem solving (Eysenck, 1992; McLeod & Adams, 1989; Mueller, 1980; Tobias, 1985).

As you might expect, highly anxious students tend to achieve at levels below their potential; in other words, they are underachievers (K. T. Hill, 1984; Tobias, 1980; Zeidner, 1998). Highly anxious students are often so preoccupied about doing poorly that they simply can't get their minds on what they need to accomplish (Eccles & Wigfield, 1985; Wine, 1980).

A Stressful Situation

Once I had a science test that the teacher told us about two days ahead of time. Of course I hadn't thought to read the chapter yet so I had to read it and study. I got nervous and started throwing a fit. I was saying that I couldn't do it over and over again. Finally I took a deep breath and study as much as I could. The next day I took the test and I got, something like, a 96. I was so surprised, and relieved.

FIGURE 11.4 In this writing sample, Loretta, a ninth grader, describes a time when anxiety improved her classroom performance.

Sources of Anxiety

Under what circumstances are our students likely to experience debilitating anxiety? Students sometimes develop feelings of anxiety about particular stimuli through the process of classical conditioning (see Chapter 9). Students are also more likely to experience debilitating anxiety when they face a **threat**—a situation in which they believe that they have little or no chance of succeeding—than when they face a **challenge**—a situation in which they believe they can probably achieve success with a significant yet reasonable amount of effort (Combs, Richards, & Richards, 1976; Csikszentmihalyi & Nakamura, 1989; Deci & Ryan, 1992). Furthermore, many school-age children and adolescents experience a certain amount of anxiety about the following:

- *Physical appearance.* For example, students may be concerned about being too fat or thin or about reaching puberty either earlier or later than their classmates.
- *A new situation.* For example, students may experience uncertainty when moving to a new community.
- *Judgment or evaluation by others.* For example, students may be worried about being liked and accepted by classmates or about receiving a low grade from a teacher.
- *Classroom tests.* For example, students may panic at the mere thought of having to take an exam.
- *Excessive classroom demands.* For example, students are likely to feel anxious when teachers expect them to learn a great deal of material in a very short amount of time.
- *The future.* For example, adolescents may worry about how they will make a living after they graduate from high school.
- *Any situation in which self-esteem is threatened.* For example, students may feel anxious when they perform a task awkwardly or incorrectly in front of others. (Covington, 1992; Harter,

1992; Hembree, 1988; N. J. King & Ollendick, 1989; Phelan et al., 1994; I. G. Sarason, 1980; S. B. Sarason, 1972; Stipek, 1993; Stodolsky et al., 1991; Wigfield & Meece, 1988)

Several of these factors come into play when students make the transition from elementary to secondary school, as we shall see now.

Making the transition from elementary to secondary school. Elementary school classrooms are often very warm, nurturing ones in which teachers get to know twenty or thirty students very well. As students make the transition to secondary school, they simultaneously encounter many changes in the nature of their schooling:

- The school is larger and has more students.
- Students have several teachers at a time, and each teacher has many students. Teacher-student relationships are therefore more superficial and less personal than they were in elementary school.
- There is more whole-class instruction, with less individualized instruction that takes into account each student's particular needs.
- Competition among students (e.g., for popular classes and spots on an athletic team) is more common.
- Students have more independence and responsibility for their own learning; for instance, they sometimes have relatively unstructured assignments to be accomplished over a two- or three-week period, and they must take the initiative to seek help when they are struggling.
- Standards for assigning grades are more rigorous, so students' grades often decrease from what they were in elementary school. Grades are often assigned on a comparative and competitive basis, with only the highest-achieving students getting As and Bs. (Eccles & Midgley, 1989; Harter, 1996; Roderick & Camburn, 1999; Wentzel & Wigfield, 1998; Wigfield et al., 1996)

Students entering the secondary grades face new challenges—more stringent evaluation criteria, less individualized instruction, greater competition in classes and sports— while also undergoing the unsettling physiological changes of puberty.

Furthermore, previously formed friendships can be disrupted as students move to new (and sometimes different) schools (Pellegrini & Bartini, 2000; Wentzel, 1999). And, of course, students are also dealing with the physiological changes that accompany puberty and adolescence.

For many students, all these changes lead to decreased confidence, lower self-esteem, and considerable anxiety. Students develop less positive attitudes about school and academic subjects and show less intrinsic motivation to learn. Focus on social relationships increases, academic achievement drops, and some students become emotionally disengaged from the school environment—a disengagement that may eventually result in dropping out of school (Eccles & Midgley, 1989; Urdan & Maehr, 1995; Wigfield et al., 1996). Students in lower-income, inner-city school districts (especially males and minorities) are particularly at risk for making a rough transition from elementary to secondary school. For instance, in one recent study, 42 percent of students in the Chicago public schools had failed at least one major course in the first semester of ninth grade. By tenth grade, 50 percent had failed at least one course (Roderick & Camburn, 1999).

The concept of *middle school* was developed to ease the transition to secondary school (e.g., Kohut, 1988; Lounsbury, 1984). In principle, middle schools are designed to accommodate the unique needs of preadolescents and early adolescents, including their anxieties about more demanding academic expectations, the changing nature of their social relationships, and their own rapidly maturing bodies. Ideally, middle schools give attention to students' personal, emotional, and social development as well as to academic achievement and are attuned to students' individual differences and unique academic needs. They teach learning and study skills that help students move toward increasing independence as learners. At many middle schools, teams of four or five teachers work with a subset of the student population (perhaps 75 to 125 students per team), coordinating activities and exchanging information about how particular students are progressing. Such strategies often ease the transition to a secondary school setting; even so, many young adolescents have considerable difficulty adjusting to middle school (Eccles et al., 1998; Roderick & Camburn, 1999).

Keeping Students' Anxiety at a Facilitative Level

As teachers, we probably can't eliminate all sources of anxiety for our students; things such as physical appearance, acceptance by peers, and students' future circumstances are often beyond our control. Nevertheless, we can take several steps to keep students' anxiety about classroom tasks and activities at a productive and facilitative level. For one thing, we can reduce the uncertainty of the classroom environment by communicating our expectations for students' performance clearly and concretely. Highly anxious students, in particular, are likely to perform better in a well-structured classroom in which expectations for academic achievement and social behavior are explicitly laid out (Hembree, 1988; Stipek, 1993; Tobias, 1977).

In addition, we must make sure our students have a good chance of achieving classroom success and give them reasons to believe they can succeed with effort; in other words, we must make sure they have high self-efficacy about classroom tasks. Therefore, we are more likely to keep students' anxiety at a facilitative level when we

- Set realistic expectations for performance, taking such factors as students' ability and prior performance level into account
- Match the level of instruction to students' cognitive levels and capabilities—for example, by using concrete materials to teach mathematics to students not yet capable of abstract thought
- Provide supplementary sources of support for learning subject matter (e.g., additional practice, individual tutoring, a structure for taking notes) until mastery is attained
- Teach strategies (e.g., effective study skills) that enhance learning and performance
- Assess students' performance independently of how well their peers are doing, and encourage students to assess their own performance in a similar manner
- Provide feedback about specific behaviors, rather than global evaluations of students' performance

---

INTO THE CLASSROOM: *Keeping Students' Anxiety at a Facilitative Level*

Be aware of situations in which students are especially likely to be anxious, and take steps to reduce their anxiety on those occasions.

The day before students are scheduled to take a standardized college aptitude test, their teacher tells them, "The best way to prepare for the test is to get a good night's sleep and eat a good breakfast in the morning. As you take the test tomorrow, you certainly want to do the very best that you can do. But keep in mind that you aren't expected to know the answers to *all* of the questions. If you find a question you cannot answer, just skip it and go on to the next one. Return to it later if you have time."

Develop classroom routines that help create a comfortable and somewhat predictable work environment.

An elementary teacher has a list of classroom chores—getting a lunch count, feeding the fish, handing out paper, and so on—that are assigned to individual students on a rotating basis.

Communicate expectations for student performance clearly and concretely.

A high school history teacher begins a unit on World War II this way: "We will focus on the major battles that contributed to the Allied forces' victory. As you read your textbook, look for reasons why certain battles played a role in the war's final outcome. I will *not* expect you to memorize all the details—dates, generals, numbers of troops, and so on—of every single battle."

Make sure students have a reasonable chance of success and give them reasons to believe that they can succeed with effort.

A science teacher describes an upcoming quiz: "On the quizzes you've taken so far this year, you've had to describe only the basic principles of chemistry we've studied. But on the next quiz I'm going to ask you to apply what you know about chemistry to new situations and problems. I'll give you several practice questions this week so you'll know what to expect. I'll also give you two chances to take the quiz. If you don't do well the first time, we'll work together on your trouble spots, and then you can take the quiz again."

- Allow students to correct errors, so that no single mistake is ever a "fatal" one (Brophy, 1986; K. T. Hill & Wigfield, 1984; McCoy, 1990; I. G. Sarason, 1980; Stipek, 1993; Tryon, 1980; Zeidner, 1998)

As teachers, we must continually be on the lookout for how students' feelings of anxiety and other emotions are likely to affect their classroom learning and achievement. Sometimes students will actually tell us how they are feeling; for example, they may express their apprehensiveness about an upcoming exam. In other instances, we may see indications in their behavior; for example, we may observe that some students are clearly excited about an upcoming activity whereas others seem less enthusiastic. In still other cases, students' writing will uncover their feelings about classroom activities, as the following exercise illustrates.

INTERPRETING ARTIFACTS AND INTERACTIONS   *James Dean and Walt Disney*

Students in an eleventh-grade history class have been giving oral reports about prominent individuals and institutions in twentieth-century American culture. In the following reaction paper to the reports, 16-year-old Shelby expresses her feelings about several classmates' presentations and about her own presentation on Walt Disney. As you read the paper, look for examples of

- Facilitating or debilitating anxiety
- Hot cognition

The first oral that we listened to was Paula's talk about J. Edgar Hoover. Hoover was one of our presidents. He was racist and a very narrow-minded man. Allison gave her report on NASA. She had many facts and talked about different missions.

Another oral that the class listened to was Kevin's on James Dean. He was an actor and supposedly a heart throb of the 50's. He was in movies like "Rebel Without A Cause." I remember my mom saying awhile ago that she thought that he was pretty good looking. Kevin brought in some clips from "Rebel Without A Cause" and "East of Eden." They were interesting to watch. It seemed as though he was in many movies where he played a rebel or a slacker. I remember thinking that James Dean played characters that were good fighters and I remember people saying that he was a good fighter. After seeing these clips Mr. M. asked if any of the girls thought that James Dean was hot. Paula said that he was a hotty and Nicole and I were mumbling to each other that we thought he was pretty attractive, but we were too shy to say anything.

I think that it's amazing how people can be influenced so easily by movie stars. Back then people it seemed that people were influenced very easily by movie stars because they were so new and they seemed so cool and interesting. For example, many people started to smoke because James Dean smoked. I think that people also started to wear leather jackets because of James Dean.

Kevin said that he found out that James Dean might have been bisexual and he said that if this had gotten out back then his image might not have been so big. I agree with Kevin. I think that people back then weren't as open to homosexuals and bisexuals as they are now. I think that there is no way that he would have been such a heart throb back then if people knew. I also think that if the public knew there might have been a big decrease in smoking because people wouldn't want to be so much like him.

Before Kevin presented his oral I did mine on Walt Disney. I think that it went pretty well and I'm happy with the grade that I got. I was very nervous, although I don't know if you could tell. Nicole said that she couldn't. I think that it went well. I wish that I had had some more visuals and that I had some more information about him being racist and more about how he came up with the idea for the amusement parks. I also wish that I had more information about how and why Michael Eisner got the Disney company, because he's not related to Walt at all. I had a good time doing my oral though because it made me think of one of my favorite places and it also made me think of when I was younger.

One other oral that we heard this week was Kolo's on Malcolm X. I didn't really know anything about Malcolm X until Kolo's report. I learned that he did a lot with the Civil Rights Movement and many other things.

Shelby was anxious during her own presentation ("I was very nervous . . ."), but her anxiety appears to have been facilitative rather than debilitative (". . . I don't know if you could tell. Nicole said that she couldn't. I think that it went well"). She knows that she could have done some things more effectively, but all in all enjoyed her time in front of the class.

We see several signs that Shelby engaged in hot cognition as she listened to Kevin's presentation on James Dean. She thinks that Dean was attractive ("hot"). She is amazed (perhaps appalled) that many people began smoking because Dean was a smoker, and she wonders how Dean's image and popularity might have been different if his sexual orientation had been made public. Finally, notice how much Shelby focuses her paper on James Dean: She clearly remembers quite a bit of what Kevin had to say. In contrast, she seems to recall very little of the presentations on J. Edgar Hoover, NASA, and Malcolm X (in fact, she "recalls" that Hoover was president, thus confusing him with *Herbert* Hoover). We can reasonably guess that these presentations had little of the emotional impact that Kevin's report did.

Addressing Diversity in Motivation and Affect

In our discussion thus far, we've identified several sources of diversity in students' motivation and affect. For instance, we've learned that, although all students probably have the need to maintain their sense of self-worth, some students may paradoxically try to do so by engaging in self-handicapping and so undermine their own success. Furthermore, although all students probably have some need for relatedness, some have higher needs for affiliation or approval than others. And some students exhibit high trait anxiety, making them more vulnerable to debilitating anxiety on occasions when their classmates might successfully rise to a challenge.

Researchers have found that students' motivation often varies as a function of their ethnic background. For instance, although all students almost certainly have a need for relatedness, they may satisfy this need in somewhat different ways. In comparison to other groups, Asian students tend to spend less time socializing with their peers and to place greater importance on gaining their teachers' attention and approval (Dien, 1998; L. Steinberg, 1996). Furthermore, whereas Asian students are likely to have friends who encourage academic achievement, students from many other ethnic groups (boys especially) may be subject to considerable peer pressure *not* to achieve at high levels (e.g., recall our discussion of "acting White" in Chapter 3; B. B. Brown, 1993; Graham, 1997; L. Steinberg, 1996). An additional factor in students' need for relatedness is their family ties: Students from many ethnic groups (e.g., those from many Native American, Hispanic, and Asian communities) have especially strong loyalties to their family and may have been raised to achieve for their community, rather than just for themselves as individuals (see Chapter 4). Motivating statements such as "Think how proud your family will be!" and "If you go to college and get a good education, you can really help your community!" are likely to be especially effective for such students (Abi-Nader, 1993; Dien, 1998; Suina & Smolkin, 1994).

Students from various ethnic backgrounds may also differ in their levels and sources of anxiety. For instance, students from some Asian American families may feel considerable family pressure to perform well in school, to the point where they experience debilitating test anxiety (Pang, 1995). And students who are recent immigrants are frequently anxious about a variety of things in their new country—how to behave, how to interpret others' behaviors, how to make friends and, more generally, how to make sense of the strange new culture in which they now find themselves (Dien, 1998; Igoa, 1995).

We are apt to see gender differences in motivation as well. For example, girls are more likely than boys to have a high need for affiliation; perhaps for this reason, they achieve at higher levels when their teachers encourage cooperation rather than competition (Block, 1983; Eccles, 1989; Inglehart et al.,

Ethnicity and gender can be important factors influencing students' motivation, yet all students have certain basic motives, such as the need for self-worth and relatedness.

1994). Girls are also more concerned about doing well in school: They work harder on assignments, earn higher grades, engage in less self-handicapping, and are more likely to graduate from high school (Halpern, 1992; McCall, 1994; Urdan & Midgley, 2001). We will typically find more boys than girls achieving at levels far below their potential (Eccles et al.,

1998; McCall, 1994). Despite such differences, boys tend to have greater confidence in their academic ability and greater expectations for their future success (Cole et al., 1999; Deaux, 1984; Eccles et al., 1998).

As we consider how students from different groups are likely to be different, we must remember that those who are *least* likely to be motivated to do well in school—and those who are at greatest risk for failing and dropping out of school—are students from low socioeconomic backgrounds (see Chapter 4). It is for these students especially that we must make a concerted effort to make school a source of pleasure, companionship, emotional support, and success. Many of the motivational strategies that we identify in Chapter 12 will have particular relevance to students from low-income families.

Accommodating Students with Special Needs

Our students with special educational needs will typically be among those who show the greatest diversity in motivation. For example, students with learning disabilities may be

TABLE 11.2   STUDENTS IN INCLUSIVE SETTINGS

Enhancing Motivation in Students with Special Educational Needs

CATEGORY	CHARACTERISTICS YOU MIGHT OBSERVE	SUGGESTED CLASSROOM STRATEGIES
Students with specific cognitive or academic difficulties	• Less intrinsic motivation to succeed at academic tasks • High test anxiety • Reluctance to ask questions or seek assistance, especially at the secondary level	• Use extrinsic reinforcers to encourage students' classroom effort and achievement; gradually phase them out as students show signs of intrinsic motivation. • Minimize anxiety-arousing statements and procedures during testing situations (see Table 15.4 for ideas). • Offer assistance when you think that students may really need it, but refrain from offering help when you know that students are capable of succeeding on their own.
Students with social or behavioral problems	• Desire to succeed in the classroom, despite behaviors that may indicate a lack of motivation • Stronger desire for power over classmates than for affiliation with them (for some students with emotional and behavioral disorders) • Need for predictability; debilitating anxiety in new or unpredictable situations (for students with autism) • Excessive anxiety and uneasiness (for students with *anxiety disorders*)	• Provide the guidance and support that students need to succeed at classroom tasks. • Help students discover the benefits of equitable and prosocial (rather than domineering) interactions with classmates. • Create a structured and predictable classroom environment, especially for students with autism.
Students with general delays in cognitive and social functioning	• Less intrinsic motivation than age-mates; responsiveness to extrinsic motivators • Tendency to give up easily in the face of difficulty	• Use extrinsic reinforcers to encourage productive behaviors; gradually phase them out as students show signs of intrinsic motivation. • Reinforce persistence as well as success.
Students with physical or sensory challenges	• Fewer opportunities to satisfy affiliation needs	• Assign "buddies" who can help students with assigned tasks or provide companionship at lunch and on the playground. • Collaborate with parents to promote interaction with classmates outside of school.
Students with advanced cognitive development	• High intrinsic motivation (e.g., curiosity about how things work) • Strong commitment to specific (especially self-chosen) tasks • Persistence in the face of failure (although some may give up easily if they aren't accustomed to failure) • Social isolation (for some students who are exceptionally gifted) • Possible self-handicapping if there is a strong desire to affiliate with low-achieving peers	• Provide opportunities for students to pursue complex tasks and activities over an extended time. • Give assignments that students find stimulating and challenging. • Form special-interest groups for students who might otherwise be socially isolated. • Keep students' exceptional achievements confidential if their friends don't value high achievement.

Sources: Beirne-Smith et al., 2002; B. Clark, 1997; Covington, 1992; Friedel, 1993; Good & Brophy, 1994; A. W. Gottfried et al., 1994; Heward, 2000; Mercer, 1997; Morgan & Jenson, 1988; Patrick, 1997; Patton et al., 1996; B. N. Phillips, Pitcher, Worsham, & Miller, 1980; Piirto, 1999; S. Powell & Nelson, 1997; Renzulli, 1978; Sanborn, 1979; G. F. Schultz & Switzky, 1990; Turnbull et al., 1999; Winner, 1997, 2000b.

easily discouraged by challenging tasks, yet students who are gifted may become bored if classroom activities *don't* challenge their abilities (Mercer, 1997; Winner, 2000b). Furthermore, although some students with special needs are quite adept at social relationships, others will have greater-than-average difficulty satisfying their need for relatedness, perhaps as a result of few opportunities to interact with age-mates (true for many students with physical disabilities), poor social skills (true for many students with emotional and behavioral disorders), or interests and ability levels that are significantly different from those of classmates (true for some students who are highly gifted). Table 11.2 (presented on the preceding page) identifies additional ways in which students with exceptionalities are likely to show different motivational characteristics and behaviors than their peers; it also offers suggestions for addressing these students' unique needs.

The Big Picture

In our discussions of development and learning in earlier chapters, we've focused primarily on the question "What can our students do and learn?" Now that we've turned to the topic of motivation, we've begun to focus on a very different question: "How *likely* are they to do what they're capable of doing and to learn what they're capable of learning?" Even when our students have the capabilities and prior experiences necessary to do something, their *motivation* will determine whether they actually do it.

Occasionally I hear teachers and administrators talking about "unmotivated" students. In reality, all students (and in fact, all human beings) have needs and desires and are motivated to fulfill them. For instance, virtually all students want to feel safe and secure in their environment, want to believe that they are competent human beings, and want to "connect" with other people in some way. Some students may perceive school to be a place in which they can satisfy such needs, but others may find that one or more of their needs—perhaps their need for safety, self-worth, or relatedness—is actually thwarted in the classroom.

As teachers, we are more likely to motivate children and adolescents if our instructional strategies take their existing motives into account. Ideally, of course, we would like for them to find school subject matter intrinsically fascinating, enjoyable, and satisfying. If they do not initially have such intrinsic motivation, we can promote it in a variety of ways—for example, by relating classroom topics to their personal interests, showing them how academic skills will help them achieve their long-term goals, giving them choices about how to meet instructional objectives, and so on (more about such strategies in Chapter 12). On occasion, we may need to rely on extrinsic motivation, perhaps by praising or in some other way reinforcing them for learning the skills that will be essential for their long-term success in and outside of the classroom.

Our students' emotions (affect) will play a role as well. If they repeatedly discover that classroom topics are exciting and offer answers to some of life's puzzling mysteries, they will be eager to pursue those topics further. But if they instead find that assigned tasks more often lead to frustration and anxiety than to pleasure, they will avoid those tasks as often as possible.

Guiding Principles

If I could offer you only one piece of advice for motivating students, it would be this: Think not about how you can coerce students but instead how you can *entice* them into learning and achieving in the classroom. Following are three additional guiding principles to keep in mind (M. E. Ford, 1992):

■ *Remember that different students will respond to different motivational strategies.* When it comes to motivation, diversity may be more typical than uniformity: Although our students may share certain basic needs, they are likely to have widely varying abilities, interests, goals, and expectations, and such things will inevitably affect the approaches that are likely to be effective in enticing them to engage in classroom activities.

■ *Show students that they can be successful.* Throughout the book we have repeatedly talked about the importance of success for students' learning and achievement, but ultimately success experiences are most important in that they promote motivation. As we have seen in this chapter, successes are critical for maintaining a sense of self-worth. As we shall discover in Chapter 12, successes are also important for fostering "motivating" cognitions; they help students acquire self-efficacy for, find value in, and set and achieve goals related to mastering school subject matter.

■ *Above all, communicate respect for all students.* As teachers, we must always remember that each and every student is a human being with legitimate thoughts, beliefs, perspectives, strengths, needs, and goals. When we focus on their strong points rather than their weaknesses (and every student has many strengths), we are more likely to give them the confidence they need to do their best and also more likely to identify ways to *help* them do their best.

Mrs. Gaskill's second graders are just beginning to learn how to write the letters of the alphabet in cursive. Every day Mrs. Gaskill introduces a new cursive letter and shows her students how to write it correctly. She also shows them some common errors in writing the letter—for instance, claiming that she's going to make the "perfect *f*" and then making it much too short and crossing the lines in the wrong place—and the children delight in finding her mistakes. After the class explores each letter's shape, Mrs. Gaskill asks her students to practice it, first by writing it in the air using large arm movements and then by writing it numerous times on lined paper.

Meanwhile, Mrs. Gaskill has decided to compare the effects of two different kinds of feedback on the children's performance. She has placed a small sticker on each child's desk, with one color indicating membership in the control group and another indicating membership in the treatment group. When children in the control group write a letter with good form, she gives them a "happy face" token, says "Great" or "Perfect!" and either smiles at them or gives them a pat on the back. When children in the treatment group write a letter with good form at least once, she gives them a happy face token and says something along the lines of "You sure are working hard," "You can write beautifully in cursive," or "You are a natural at this." When children in either group fail to meet her standards for cursive writing, she gives them whatever corrective feedback they need.

Thus, the only way in which Mrs. Gaskill treats the two groups differently is in what she says to them when they do well, either giving them fairly cryptic feedback (for the control group) or telling them that they are trying hard or have high ability (for the treatment group). Despite such a seemingly minor difference, Mrs. Gaskill finds that the children in the treatment group say they enjoy cursive writing more, and they use it more frequently in their spelling tests and other writing tasks. Curiously, too, the children in the control group often seem disappointed when they receive their "positive" feedback. For instance, on one occasion a girl who writes beautifully but has the misfortune of being in the control group asks, "Am *I* a natural at this?" Although the girl consistently gets a grade of "+" for her cursive writing, she never writes in cursive voluntarily throughout the three-week period in which Mrs. Gaskill conducts her experiment. (Gaskill, 2001)

- Why might feedback such as "You sure are working hard" or "You can write beautifully in cursive" be more effective than feedback such as "Great" or "Perfect"? Use what you have learned about motivation to speculate.
- Might the control group's feedback be more effective if Mrs. Gaskill used it for *all*, rather than just some, of her students? Explain your reasoning. (For help in answering this question, return to the section "Factors Influencing the Development of Self-Views" in Chapter 3.)

Once you have answered these questions, compare your responses with those presented in Appendix B.

PRAXIS Turn to Appendix C, "Matching Book and Ancillary Content to the PRAXIS™ Principles of Learning and Teaching Tests," to discover sections of this chapter that may be especially applicable to the PRAXIS™ tests.

Now go to our Companion Website at http://www.prenhall.com/ormrod to assess your understanding of chapter content with "Multiple-Choice Questions," apply comprehension in "Essay Questions," broaden your knowledge of educational psychology with related "Web Links," gain greater insight about classroom learning in "Learning in the Content Areas," and analyze and assess classroom work in the "Student Artifact Library."

Key Concepts

motivation (p. 368)
situated motivation (p. 368)
extrinsic motivation (p. 369)
intrinsic motivation (p. 369)
trait theory of motivation (p. 370)
achievement motivation (p. 370)
drive (p. 372)

self-worth (p. 374)
self-handicapping (p. 374)
need for relatedness (p. 374)
need for affiliation (p. 375)
need for approval (p. 376)
affect (p. 377)
hot cognition (p. 378)

anxiety (p. 379)
state anxiety (p. 379)
trait anxiety (p. 379)
facilitating anxiety (p. 380)
debilitating anxiety (p. 380)
threat (p. 380)
challenge (p. 380)

12

Cognitive Factors in Motivation

*T*hink about the college courses you've taken in recent years. In which courses were you more interested in the grade you received than in anything you might learn in class? In which courses did you truly want to learn the subject matter, and why? Did you perceive some topics to be relevant to your own needs and goals? Were other topics so fascinating that you simply had to find out more about them? Did your instructors do anything in particular that made certain topics intriguing, thought-provoking, or just plain fun?

In this chapter we will look at how students' perceptions, beliefs, expectations, values, interests, goals, and attributions influence their motivation; in other words, we will focus on "cognitions that motivate." We will also examine the effects that *teacher* cognition—especially teachers' attributions and expectations regarding students' behaviors and accomplishments—have on students' performance and achievement. As we explore these issues, we will address questions such as these:

- How do students' beliefs about themselves affect their motivation to learn and succeed in the classroom?
- Under what conditions are students most likely to find school subject matter valuable, interesting, or in some other way desirable to learn?
- What kinds of goals do children and adolescents set for themselves and their achievement, and how do these goals affect their learning?
- How do students' explanations for success and failure (their *attributions*) influence their thoughts and behaviors?
- How are teachers' beliefs—especially their attributions and expectations for students' performance—likely to affect their behaviors toward students and thereby indirectly affect students' classroom achievement? As teachers, what precautions can we take to make sure that our beliefs bolster rather than impede students' progress?

CASE STUDY: *Passing Algebra*

Fourteen-year-old Michael has been getting failing grades in his eighth-grade algebra class, and so his family asks graduate student Valerie Tucker to tutor him. In their initial tutoring session, Michael tells Ms. Tucker that he has no hope of passing algebra because he has little aptitude for math and his teacher doesn't teach the subject matter very well. In his mind, he is powerless to change either his own ability or his teacher's instructional strategies, and so continuing failure is inevitable.

As Ms. Tucker works with Michael over the next several weeks, she encourages him to think more about what *he* can do to master algebra and less about what his teacher may or may not be doing to help him. She points out that he has done well in math in earlier grades and so he clearly does have the ability to learn algebra if he puts his mind to it. She also teaches him a variety of strategies for understanding and applying algebraic principles. Michael takes a first giant step forward when he finally realizes that his own efforts play a role in his classroom success:

> [M]aybe I can try a little harder. . . . The teacher is still bad, but maybe some of this other stuff can work. (Tucker & Anderman, 1999, p. 5)

As Michael sees gradual improvement on his algebra assignments and quizzes, he becomes increasingly aware that the specific *strategies* he uses are just as important as his effort:

> I learned that I need to understand information before I can hold it in my mind. . . . Now I do things in math step by step and listen to each step. I realize now that even if I don't like the teacher or don't think he is a good teacher, it is my responsibility to listen. I listen better now and ask questions more. . . . (Tucker & Anderman, 1999, p. 5)

As Michael's performance in algebra continues to improve in the weeks ahead, he gains greater confidence that he *can* master algebra after all, and he comes to realize that his classroom success is ultimately up to him:

> [T]he teacher does most of his part, but it's no use to me unless I do my part. . . . [N]ow I try and comprehend, ask questions and figure out how he got the answer. . . . I used to just listen and not even take notes. I always told myself I would remember but I always seemed to forget. Now I take notes and I study at home every day except Friday, even if I don't have homework. Now I study so that I know that I have it. I don't just hope I'll remember. (Tucker & Anderman, 1999, p. 6)

- On what factors does Michael initially blame his failure? What effects do his early beliefs appear to have on his classroom behavior and study habits?
- To what factors does Michael later attribute his success? How have his changing beliefs affected his learning strategies?

The Interplay of Cognition and Motivation

Initially Michael believes he is failing algebra because of two things he cannot control—his own low ability and his teacher's poor instruction—and so he doesn't listen very attentively or take notes in class. With Ms. Tucker's guidance, however, Michael acquires a better understanding of algebra and learns how to use it to solve mathematical problems. He also discovers that increased effort and better strategies (taking notes, asking questions when he doesn't understand, studying regularly, etc.) *do* affect his classroom performance. Suddenly Michael himself—not his teacher, and not some predetermined inability that lurks within him—is in control of the situation, and his confidence skyrockets.

Michael's dramatic turnaround illustrates a point we made in Chapter 11: *Motivation affects cognitive processing.* Like Michael, motivated students are more likely to pay attention, engage in meaningful learning, and seek help when they don't understand. Yet the case illustrates the reverse as well: *Cognitive processes affect motivation.* Michael's initial beliefs about his own ability (his self-efficacy) and his explanations for poor performance (low ability and poor instruction) contribute to a lackadaisical attitude: He simply *hopes* that he'll remember (but usually forgets) his teacher's explanations. Later, when Michael's appraisal of the situation changes (when his self-efficacy increases and he attributes success to effort and better strategies), he is a much more engaged and proactive learner.

As we explore the cognitive aspects of motivation (perceptions, expectancies, values, interests, goals, and attributions) in the pages that follow, we will frequently see how cognition and motivation interact in their effects on learning and behavior. We begin by looking at two self-perceptions that play key roles in intrinsic motivation: self-efficacy and self-determination.

Self-Perceptions and Intrinsic Motivation

EXPERIENCING FIRSTHAND   *Enjoyable Activities*

1. Make a list of five different things you like to do. You might list hobbies, favorite sports, or other activities in which you are intrinsically motivated to engage.

2. Using the following scale, rate each of the activities you've just listed in terms of *how successfully you usually perform it:*

I am rarely successful.		I am somewhat successful.		I am highly successful.
1	2	3	4	5

3. Using the following scale, rate each of your activities in terms of *how much choice you have regarding whether or not you engage in the activity:*

I have almost no choice about whether I perform the activity.		I have some degree of choice about whether I perform the activity.		I have a great deal of choice about whether I perform the activity.
1	2	3	4	5

Take a close look at the numerical ratings you've just assigned to your favorite activities. Chances are, your ratings were almost exclusively 3 or higher on both of the scales. A number of theorists have proposed that people are most likely to be intrinsically motivated to do something (to perform a particular task or engage in a particular activity) when two conditions exist:

1. They have high **self-efficacy:** They believe that they are capable of successfully accomplishing the task or activity.
2. They have a sense of **self-determination:** They believe that they are in control of their own destinies and can make choices regarding the directions that their lives will take. (Boggiano & Pittman, 1992; Corno & Rohrkemper, 1985; Deci & Ryan, 1985, 1992; R. M. Ryan & Deci, 2000; Spaulding, 1992)

Self-Efficacy

Our students are more likely to be intrinsically motivated to engage in classroom activities when they have high self-efficacy—what some motivation theorists call a *sense of competence*—about their ability to perform those activities successfully. Most 4- to 6-year-olds are quite confident about their ability to perform various tasks; in fact, they often overestimate what they are capable of doing (R. Butler, 1990; Eccles et al., 1998; Nicholls, 1979). As they move through the elementary grades, however, they can better recall their past successes and failures, and they become increasingly aware of how their performance compares with that of their classmates (Eccles et al., 1998; Feld, Ruhland, & Gold, 1979). Presumably as a result of these changes, they become less confident, though usually more realistic, about what they can and cannot do. In some situations, however, students significantly *under*estimate their capabilities. For instance, in the opening case, Michael's self-efficacy for passing his algebra class is initially rock-bottom: In his mind, he doesn't have the ability to succeed, and his teacher does little to help the situation.

In our discussion of social cognitive theory in Chapter 10, we identified several factors that affect the development of self-efficacy and, in the process, derived several strategies for enhancing it in the classroom:

- Make sure students master basic skills.
- Help them make noticeable progress on difficult tasks.
- Communicate confidence in students' abilities through both words and actions.
- Expose students to successful peers.

Motivation theorists have offered additional recommendations for enhancing students' self-efficacy and, indirectly, increasing intrinsic motivation:

■ *Provide competence-promoting feedback.* As we noted in Chapters 9 and 11, positive feedback is often an effective reinforcer for students. Positive feedback may also promote intrinsic motivation, especially if it conveys the message that students have the ability to perform the task successfully and thereby enhances their self-efficacy. In fact, even negative feedback can promote high self-efficacy if it tells students how they can improve their performance and communicates confidence that improvement is likely (Deci & Ryan, 1985; Pintrich & Schunk, 2002). Here are some examples of negative feedback that might positively influence student motivation:

- "I can see from the past few homework assignments that you're having trouble with long division. I think I know what the problem is. Here, let me show you what you need to do differently."
- "In the first draft of your research paper, many of your paragraphs don't lead logically to the ones that follow. A few headings and transitional sentences would make a world of difference. Let's find a time to discuss how you might use these techniques to improve the flow of your paper."
- "Your time in the 100-meter dash was not as fast as it could be. It's early in the season, though, and if you work on your endurance, I know you'll improve. Also, I think you might get a faster start if you keep low when you come out of the starting blocks."

■ *Promote mastery on challenging tasks.* As noted in Chapter 11, a challenge is a situation in which success isn't guaranteed but can probably be achieved with reasonable effort. A challenge encourages people to stretch themselves to their limits—perhaps to think in new ways or experiment with new strategies. In Chapter 2 we found that challenging activities promote cognitive development. In addition, mastery of challenges enhances self-efficacy and, as a result, promotes intrinsic motivation. Students who master challenging tasks experience considerable pleasure, satisfaction, and pride in their accomplishments (Csikszentmihalyi & Nakamura, 1989; Deci & Ryan, 1992; Shernoff, Knauth, & Makris, 2000; A. G. Thompson & Thompson, 1989; J. C. Turner, 1995).

Once students are intrinsically motivated, they frequently pursue further challenges of their own accord. They also exhibit considerable persistence in the face of difficulty, and they continue to remain interested in an activity even when they make frequent errors (Covington, 1992; Deci, 1992; Harter, 1992). As you can see, then, challenges and intrinsic motivation mutually enhance one another, leading to a "vicious" cycle of the most desirable sort.

As teachers, we are more likely to encourage students to tackle challenging tasks when, through the feedback we give and the criteria we use for evaluation, we create an environment in which our students feel free to take risks and make mistakes (Clifford, 1990). We can also provide greater rewards for succeeding at challenging tasks than for achieving easy successes; for example, we might give students a choice between doing an easy task or a more difficult one but give them more points for accomplishing the difficult one (Clifford, 1990; Lan, Repman, Bradley, & Weller, 1994).

At the same time, however, we must tailor the level of challenge to students' current self-efficacy levels: Students who (like Michael) have little or no confidence in their ability to perform a particular activity may initially respond more favorably when we give them tasks at which they will likely do well (Stipek, 1996). Furthermore, the school day shouldn't necessarily be one challenge after another. Such a state of affairs would be absolutely exhausting, and probably quite discouraging as well. Instead, we should probably strike a balance between easy tasks—those that will boost students' self-confidence over the short run—and the challenging tasks so critical for a long-term sense of competence and self-efficacy (Spaulding, 1992; Stipek, 1993, 1996).

■ *Promote self-comparison rather than comparison with others.* If we define success in terms of task accomplishment, skill improvement, or academic progress, then virtually all of our students can be successful. If we instead define success in terms of how well students perform in comparison with their peers, many will fare poorly. Such competition may motivate a few students who believe they can rise to meet the challenge; however, it will undermine the intrinsic motivation of the majority of their classmates, who will see failure as the most likely outcome (Deci & Ryan, 1992; Shih & Alexander, 2000; Stipek, 1996). Furthermore, some students (e.g., those from some Native American communities) may resist competing if they believe that their own successes will contribute to their classmates' failures (Grant & Gomez, 2001).

As noted earlier, over time students become increasingly aware of how their performance compares with that of classmates. Inevitably, then, some students begin to believe that they

As students master difficult tasks, their self-efficacy increases, and they may become eager to take on additional challenges.

simply don't measure up to their peers. As teachers, we shouldn't compound the problem. Most of our students will achieve at higher levels if we encourage them to define success in terms of their own improvement, rather than in terms of how they stack up against others (Covington, 1992; Graham & Golen, 1991).

We can do at least two things to encourage students to make self-comparisons rather than comparisons with others. First, we can minimize their awareness of their classmates' performance levels. For example, we can use absolute rather than comparative criteria to assess their work (awarding high grades to all students who meet those criteria rather than grading on a curve), keep performance on assignments confidential, and give feedback in private. Second, we can provide opportunities for students to assess their own performance and monitor their improvement over time. We must remember that children and adolescents are often impatient, expecting success overnight when in fact the development of knowledge and skills may take several days, months, or even years. We can help them focus on their successes rather than their imperfections by providing them with concrete mechanisms that highlight improvement—for example, by giving them progress charts that they can fill in themselves (e.g., see Figure 12.1) and providing frequent verbal or written feedback about the "little things" they are doing well. Veteran teacher Frances Hawkins recalls an incident in which she had been helping 7-year-old Dorothy and her classmates learn to weave on small, circular looms. Dorothy was distressed about all the mistakes she had made at the beginning of the project, but Hawkins helped her put those mistakes in perspective:

> [S]he was in tears, holding her now-finished small round weaving. Sorrow poured out: "Look," she said, tears falling, pointing to the pink and blue and yellow weaving, "it's so bad where I began. I didn't know how. Can I take it out and do it right like the last part?"
>
> In spite of early mistakes, the weaving was quite lovely. These circular looms absorb mistakes. . . . I had an idea: "Look, Dorothy, this is the history, your own history, of learning to weave. You can look at this and say, 'Why, I can see how I began, here I didn't know how very well, I went over two instead of one; but I learned, and then—it is perfect all the way to the end!' Now turn it over and do another." Dorothy thought about this. The tears stopped, and slowly she walked back to her group of weavers, still properly intent on her first weaving. The next visit she brought me an elegant and flawless circle in different shades of pink, with novelty yarns— some nubby, some plain—all done without consulting me! (F. P. L. Hawkins, 1997, p. 332)

■ *Be sure errors occur within an overall context of success.* At one time, many educators proposed that students should never be allowed to fail. But whether we like it or not, occasional failures are a normal, inevitable, and often beneficial part of the learning process, and students need to learn to take them in stride. When students never make mistakes, we can reasonably assume they are not being challenged by the tasks we are assigning. Furthermore, students unaccustomed to failure in their school curriculum have difficulty coping with failure when they eventually do encounter it (Dweck, 1986).

Yet when students encounter failure *too* frequently, they (like Michael) develop low self-efficacy, believing that nothing they do will produce positive results. Ideally, then, students should experience occasional failure within the context of overall success. This way, they learn that they *can* succeed if they try, while also developing a realistic attitude about failure—that it at worst is a temporary setback and at best can give them useful information about how to improve their performance.

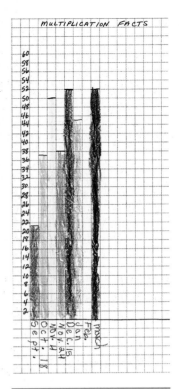

FIGURE 12.1 Nine-year-old Sophie charts her monthly progress in remembering multiplication facts. Although she has minor setbacks, her general progress is upward. (She was absent for February's assessment.)

Self-Determination

EXPERIENCING FIRSTHAND *Painting Between the Lines*

Imagine that I give you a set of watercolor paints, a paintbrush, a small and a large sheet of paper, and some paper towels. I ask you to paint a picture of your house, apartment building, or dormitory and then give you the following instructions:

> Before you begin, I want to tell you some things that you will have to do. They are rules that I have about painting. You have to keep the paints clean. You can paint only on this small sheet of paper, so don't spill any paint on the big sheet. And you must wash out your brush and wipe it with a paper towel before you switch to a new color of paint, so that you don't get the colors all mixed up. In general, I want you to be a good

art student and not make a mess with the paints. (based on Koestner, Ryan, Bernieri, & Holt, 1984, p. 239)

How much fun do you think your task would be? After reading my rules about painting, how eager are you to begin painting?

My rules about painting are somewhat restrictive, aren't they? In fact, they are quite *controlling:* They make it clear that I am in charge of the situation and that you, as the artist, have little choice about how to go about your task. Chances are, you have little intrinsic motivation to paint the picture I've asked you to paint (Deci, 1992; Koestner et al., 1984). Furthermore, you would probably be less creative in your painting than if I had not been so controlling (Amabile & Hennessey, 1992).

Students are more likely to be intrinsically motivated when they have a sense of self-determination—in other words, when they have some feeling of *autonomy* regarding the things they do and the directions their lives take (Boggiano & Pittman, 1992; deCharms, 1972; Deci, 1992; Deci & Ryan, 1992; Spaulding, 1992; J. C. Turner, 1995). A sense of self-determination increases the likelihood that students will become actively engaged in in-class and extracurricular activities and that they will stay in school rather than drop out before graduation (Hardre & Reeve, 2001; E. J. Langer, 1997; J. Reeve, Bolt, & Cai, 1999; Shernoff et al., 2000). Even kindergartners seem to value classroom activities of their own choosing, and students' perceptions of autonomy versus control are often seen in their notions of "play" and "work" (E. J. Langer, 1997; Paley, 1984). Kindergarten teacher Vivian Gussin Paley recounts a conversation she once had with some of the girls in her class:

Mary Ann:	The boys don't like to work.
Ms. Paley:	They're making a huge train setup right now.
Mary Ann:	That's not work. It's just playing.
Ms. Paley:	When do girls play?
Charlotte:	In the doll corner.
Ms. Paley:	How about at the painting table?
Mary Ann:	That's work. You could call it play sometimes, but it's really schoolwork.
Ms. Paley:	When is it work and when is it play?
Clarice:	If you paint a real picture, it's work, but if you splatter or pour into an egg carton, then it's play.
Charlotte:	It's mostly work, because that's where the teacher tells you how to do stuff. (Paley, 1984, pp. 30–31)

The boys in Ms. Paley's class had a similar perspective:

Ms. Paley:	The girls think the block area is for play and not for work. Is that what you think?
Jonathan:	It *is* for play. But you could be a work person.
Ms. Paley:	If you're a work person, then what do you do in the blocks?
Andrew:	Build very neatly and don't knock it down and don't play.
Ms. Paley:	How can you tell if you're working or playing?
Andrew:	No Star Wars or superheroes. None of that stuff.
Paul:	No shooting. And no robbers.
Jonathan:	And no running.
Ms. Paley:	What else is work in this room?
Andrew:	If you color or put your name on a thing. On a paper.
Paul:	It has to be work if *you* tell us to do something. (Paley, 1984, p. 31)

Students are more likely to be intrinsically motivated when they have a sense of self-determination about classroom activities.

Naturally, we can't always give students total freedom about what they will and will not do in the classroom. Nor can we always convince them that classroom activities are really play rather than work. Nevertheless, we *can* do several things to enhance students' sense of self-determination about school-related tasks and assignments:

- *Present rules and instructions in an informational rather than controlling manner.* Virtually any classroom needs a few rules and procedures to ensure that students act appropriately and that class activities run smoothly. Furthermore, for a variety of reasons, we must often impose guidelines and restrictions related to how students carry out their assignments. The challenge is to present these rules, procedures, guidelines, and restrictions without communicating a message of *control* (like that in the "Painting Between the Lines" exercise). Instead, we can present them as *information*—for instance, as conditions that can help students accomplish classroom objectives (Deci, 1992; Koestner et al., 1984). Here are three examples of rules or instructions presented in an informational rather than controlling manner:

- "We can make sure everyone has an equal chance to speak and be heard if we listen without interrupting and if we raise our hands when we want to contribute to the discussion."
- "I'm giving you a particular format to follow when you do your math homework. If you use this format, it will be easier for me to find your answers and to figure out how I can help you improve."
- "Let's remember that other students will be using the same paints and brushes later today, so as we work, we need to make sure everything we use now is still in tip-top shape when we're done. It's important, then, that we rinse our brushes in water and wipe them on a paper towel before we switch to a new color. We should also clean our brushes thoroughly when we're done painting."

You can find additional examples in Figure 14.2 of Chapter 14.

- *Provide opportunities for students to make choices.* Sometimes there is only one way to accomplish a particular instructional objective. But, more often, a variety of routes will lead to the same destination. In such cases, why not let students choose how they want to get there? For example, we might allow them to make decisions, either individually or as a group, about some or all of the following:

- Rules and procedures to make the class run more smoothly
- Ways of achieving mastery of a classroom objective (e.g., which of several possible procedures to use, whether to work individually or in small groups)
- Specific topics for research or writing projects
- Specific works of literature to be read
- Due dates for some assignments
- The order in which specific tasks are accomplished during the school day
- Ways of demonstrating that an objective has been mastered (e.g., see Figure 12.2)
- Criteria by which some assignments will be evaluated
  (Kohn, 1993; Meece, 1994; Stipek, 1993)

When students can make choices such as these, they are more likely to be interested in what they are doing, to work diligently, to complete assignments quickly and efficiently, and to take pride in their work (Deci & Ryan, 1992; Lepper & Hodell, 1989; J. A. Ross, 1988; J. C. Turner, 1995). Furthermore, students who are given choices—even students with serious behavior problems—are less likely to misbehave in class (Dunlap et al., 1994; S. Powell & Nelson, 1997; B. J. Vaughn & Horner, 1997).

In some situations, students' choices can be almost limitless; for example, in a unit on expository writing, a wide variety of student-selected research topics might be equally appropriate. In other situations, we may need to impose certain limits on the choices students make; for example, if we allow a class to set its own due dates for certain assignments, we might insist that the final schedule provide enough time for us to grade each assignment. In still other situations, we may want to provide a handful of options from which students can choose; for instance, we might allow them to choose from among several works of literature, specialize in one of several art media (e.g., watercolors, pastels, clay), or select a piece of equipment (e.g., parallel bars, rings, floor mats) on which to develop gymnastic skills.

- *Give students considerable autonomy within their organized extracurricular activities.* Ideally, students' extracurricular activities (clubs, theater groups, community service projects, etc.) can provide both the challenges that enhance students' self-efficacy and the autonomy that enhances their sense of self-determination (Larson, 2000). When we supervise such activities, then, we can foster intrinsic motivation—not to mention the development of initiative and skills in planning and negotiation—by giving students considerable freedom

FIGURE 12.2 We can enhance students' sense of self-determination by giving them choices about how to accomplish instructional objectives. Here a sixth-grade language arts teacher gives her students several options for demonstrating their understanding of a science fiction book.

Choose One!

SCIENCE FICTION BOOK PROJECTS

_____ Write a "Dear Abby" letter from one of the main characters, in which he or she asks for advice on solving his or her main problem. Then answer the letter.

_____ Draw a time line of the main events of the book.

_____ Create a comic book or a comic strip page that features a major scene from the book in each box.

_____ Make a collage of objects and printed words from newspapers and magazines that give the viewer a feeling for the mood of the book.

_____ Your book probably takes place in an unusual or exotic setting, so illustrate and write a travel brochure describing that location.

_____ Imagine yourself as a scientist who has been asked to explain the unusual events in the book. Write up a report in scientific style.

_____ With other students who have read the same book, plan a bulletin board display. Write a plot summary; character and setting descriptions; discussions of special passages. Each group member must contribute one artistic piece—for example, new book cover, bookmark, poster, banner, some of the ideas listed above. Arrange the writing and artwork under a colorful heading announcing the book.

and responsibility in determining the direction the activities take (Larson, 2000). At the same time, we will often need to provide the guidance students may need to tackle challenges, for instance by helping them think through the likely outcomes of various courses of action (Larson, 2000).

■ *Evaluate students' performance in a noncontrolling fashion.* As teachers, we will inevitably need to evaluate students' accomplishments. But we must keep in mind that external evaluations may undermine students' intrinsic motivation, especially if communicated in a controlling manner (Deci & Ryan, 1992; Harter, Whitesell, & Kowalski, 1992). Ideally, we should present our evaluations of students' work, not as "judgments" to remind students of how they *should* perform, but as information that can help them improve their knowledge and skills (Stipek, 1996). Furthermore, we can give students criteria by which they can evaluate *themselves* in the self-comparative manner described earlier.

■ *Minimize reliance on extrinsic reinforcers, but use them when necessary.* The discussion of behaviorism in Chapter 9 emphasized the importance of relying on intrinsic reinforcers—for example, on students' own feelings of pride and satisfaction about their accomplishments—as often as possible. A problem with using extrinsic reinforcers—praise, stickers, favorite activities, and so on—is that they may undermine intrinsic motivation, especially when students perceive them as controlling behavior and limiting choices (Deci, 1992; A. E. Gottfried, Fleming & Gottfried, 1994; Lepper & Hodell, 1989). Extrinsic reinforcers may also communicate the message that classroom tasks are unpleasant "chores" (why else would a reinforcer be necessary?), rather than activities to be carried out and enjoyed for their own sake (Hennessey, 1995; Stipek, 1993).

Intrinsic motivation and extrinsic motivation are not necessarily incompatible; oftentimes students are simultaneously motivated by both the extrinsic reinforcers and the intrinsic feelings of pleasure that their actions bring (Cameron & Pierce, 1994; Deci, 1998). Furthermore, students may sometimes need occasional extrinsic reinforcers to carry them through the more tedious and boring topics and skills they must learn in order to master a complex task or content domain (Covington, 2000; Deci, Koestner, & Ryan, 1999; Hidi & Harackiewicz, 2000). So how can we use extrinsic reinforcers without diminishing students' sense of self-determination? For one thing, we can use reinforcers such as praise to communicate information rather than to control behavior (Deci, 1992; R. M. Ryan, Mims, & Koestner, 1983); consider these statements as examples:

- "Your description of the main character in your short story makes her come alive."
- "I think you have finally mastered the rolling R sound in Spanish."
- "This poster clearly states the hypothesis, method, results, and conclusions of your science project. Your use of a bar graph makes the differences between your treatment and control groups easy to see and interpret."

Furthermore, as noted in the discussion of self-regulation in Chapter 10, we may want to encourage *self*-reinforcement—a practice that clearly keeps control in the hands of students.

■ *Help students keep externally imposed constraints in proper perspective.* Our students will often encounter circumstances that cast a "controlling" light on school activities: Competitions, extrinsic rewards, and external evaluation are frequent events in most schools. For example, students often compete in athletic contests, spelling bees, and science fairs. They may make the Honor Roll, win a first-place ribbon at an art exhibit, or receive a free pizza coupon for reading a certain number of books each month. And they will almost inevitably receive grades, in one form or another, that reflect their teachers' evaluations of their achievement.

To help our students keep such external constraints in perspective as they engage in a learning task, we should remind them that although competition, extrinsic rewards, or evaluation may be present, the most important thing is for them to focus on the inherent value of the task itself (Amabile & Hennessey, 1992; Hennessey, 1995). For example, we might encourage them to tell themselves something along this line:

> I like to get good grades, and when I bring home a good report card, my parents always give me money. But that's not what's really important. I like to learn a lot. There are a lot of things that interest me, and I want to learn about them, so I work hard because I enjoy it. (Amabile & Hennessey, 1992, p. 68)

Self-efficacy and self-determination are not necessarily the only factors involved in intrinsic motivation. Students' expectations and values are also important, as we shall see now.

Expectancies and Values

Some theorists (e.g., Eccles [Parsons], 1983; Feather, 1982; Weiner, 2000; Wigfield, 1994; Wigfield & Eccles, 2000) have proposed that motivation for performing a particular task depends on two variables, both of which are fairly subjective. First of all, students must have a high expectation, or **expectancy**, that they will be successful. Certainly students' self-efficacy about their ability to perform a task has a strong influence on their expectation for success. But other factors affect expectancy level as well, including the perceived difficulty of the task, the availability of environment resources and support, the quality of instruction (remember Michael's concerns about his algebra teacher), and the amount of effort that may be necessary (Dweck & Elliott, 1983; Wigfield & Eccles, 1992; Zimmerman et al., 1992). From factors such as these, students come to a conclusion—perhaps correct, perhaps not—about their chances of success.

Equally important is **value**: Students must believe that there are direct or indirect benefits in performing a task. Theorists have suggested several possible reasons why value might be high or low (Eccles [Parsons], 1983; Eccles & Wigfield, 1985). Some activities are valued because they are associated with certain personal qualities; for example, a boy who wants to be smart and thinks that smart people do well in school will place a premium on academic success. Other activities have high value because they are seen as means to a desired goal; for example, much as she found mathematics confusing and frustrating, my daughter Tina struggled through four years of high school math classes because many colleges require that much math. Still other activities are valued simply because they bring pleasure and enjoyment; for example, you may recall Anya's passion for art in the preceding chapter's opening case study.

We can also anticipate the circumstances in which students will probably *not* value an activity very much (Eccles & Wigfield, 1985; Eccles [Parsons], 1983). Some activities may require a lot more effort than they are worth; for example, you could probably become an expert on some little-known topic (e.g., the nature of rats' dreams, animal-eating plants of Borneo), but I'm guessing that you have more important things to which to devote your time and energy

These girls may be motivated in their math class because they *expect* to be successful in it and because they find *value* in the problem-solving skills they are learning.

right now. Other activities may be associated with too many bad feelings; for example, if students become frustrated often enough in their efforts to understand mathematics, they may eventually begin to steer clear of the subject whenever possible. And of course anything likely to threaten a student's sense of self-worth is a "must" to avoid.

In the early elementary years, students often pursue activities they find interesting and enjoyable, regardless of their expectancies for success (Wigfield, 1994). As they get older, however, they attach greater value to activities for which they have high expectancy for success and to activities that they think will help them meet their long-term goals (Wigfield, 1994). Sadly, the value students find in many school subjects (e.g., math, English, music, and sports) declines markedly over the school years (Eccles et al., 1998; Wigfield et al., 1991). As one 16-year-old put it, "School's fun because you can hang out with your friends, but I know I won't use much of this stuff when I leave here" (Valente, 2001).

Internalizing the Values of Others

As they get older, most students begin to adopt some of the values of the people around them. Such **internalized motivation** typically develops gradually over time, perhaps in the following sequence (Deci & Ryan, 1995):

1. *External regulation.* Students are motivated to behave (or not behave) in certain ways based primarily on the external consequences that will follow behaviors; in other words, they are extrinsically motivated. For instance, students may do schoolwork mostly to avoid being punished for poor grades, and they are likely to need a lot of prodding to get their work done.
2. *Introjection.* Students behave in particular ways to gain the approval of others; for example, they may willingly complete an easy, boring assignment as a means of gaining their teacher's praise. At this point, students feel some internal pressure to adopt certain behaviors; for instance, they may feel guilty when they violate certain standards or rules. However, they do not fully understand the rationale behind such standards and rules; instead, their primary motives appear to be avoiding a negative self-evaluation and protecting their sense of self-worth.
3. *Identification.* Students now see behaviors as being personally important or valuable. For instance, they may value learning and academic success in and of themselves, perceive assigned classroom tasks as being essential for helping them learn, and so need little prodding to get their work done.
4. *Integration.* Students have fully accepted the desirability of certain behaviors and integrated them into an overall system of motives and values. For example, a student might have acquired a keen interest in science as a career goal; if so, we are likely to see that interest reflected in many things the student does regularly.

As you can see, then, extrinsic and intrinsic motivation are not necessarily either/or phenomena; in some situations, extrinsic motivation gradually evolves into internalized values.

Theorists have suggested that three conditions promote the development of internalized motivation (R. M. Ryan et al., 1992). First, growing children need a *warm, responsive, and supportive environment* in which they gain a feeling of relatedness to important individuals (e.g., their parents and teachers) in their lives. Second, they need *some degree of autonomy,* so that they have a sense of self-determination as they make choices and decisions. Finally, they need *appropriate guidance and structure,* including information about expected behaviors and why they're important, as well as clear consequences for inappropriate behaviors. Fostering the development of internalized motivation, then, involves a delicate balancing act between giving students enough opportunities to experience self-determination and providing some guidance about appropriate behavior. In a sense, we need to "scaffold" desired behaviors at first, gradually reducing such scaffolding as our students exhibit those behaviors more easily and frequently.

Fostering Expectancies and Values in the Classroom

As teachers, we must certainly give students reasons why they should expect to succeed at classroom tasks—for instance, by providing the necessary resources, support, and strategies that will enable them to do so (recall how Ms. Tucker taught Michael strategies for mastering algebra). We must also help them find value in school activities. Let's consider how one teacher tries to foster value for classroom subject matter.

INTERPRETING ARTIFACTS AND INTERACTIONS   *Why We Study History*

After a fifth-grade class discusses the importance of studying history, the teacher asks her students to write an essay summarizing and reacting to the discussion. As you read 10-year-old Renata's essay,

- Identify the primary reason Renata gives for studying history
- Speculate about the likelihood that Renata will actually pursue history with the enthusiasm she describes

> *Why We Study History*
>
> One reason we study history is to provent us from making mistakes that were made in the past. As an old saying goes; if you do not know your history then you are dumed to repet it. Just thinking about that saying makes me want to jump up grab a 1,000 paged history book and read the whole thing because I would hate to make the same mistakes that were made in the past. You are supost to learn from the past, not repet it.
>
> But the there are somethings you do want to repet such as the kindness of Teodore Roosevelt and Abraham Lincon, the determenation of Benjaman Franclin, and the courage of Harriet Tubman.

Renata focuses on the same reason for studying history that I heard as a student many years ago (perhaps you heard it as well): History allows us to avoid making the same mistakes as our predecessors. I suspect that such a reason is too abstract and vague to cultivate a genuine desire to learn about historical events. Although Renata initially shows considerable enthusiasm—she wants to jump up and read a 1,000-page history book—we can reasonably guess that she never follows up by actually reading such a book. *Showing* that you value something is a lot more convincing than merely *saying* you do.

Theorists and practitioners have offered several suggestions for fostering value for academic subject matter. For instance, we can show how we ourselves value academic activities—for example, by sharing our fascination with certain topics and describing how we apply the things we've learned in school (Brophy, 1987; Brophy & Alleman, 1991). We can embed the use of many basic skills within the context of meaningful, real-world (authentic) tasks (e.g., Newmann & Wehlage, 1993). And we should refrain from asking students to engage in activities with little long-term benefit—memorizing trivial facts for no good reason, reading material that is clearly beyond students' comprehension level, and so on (Brophy, 1987).

One common reason that we value something is that we find it interesting. Let's find out what theorists have to say about the role of interest in human motivation.

Interest

When we say that people have **interest** in a particular topic or activity, we mean that they find the topic or activity intriguing and enticing. Interest, then, is a form of intrinsic motivation. Positive affect accompanies interest; for example, people pursuing a task in which they are interested experience such feelings as pleasure, excitement, and liking (Hidi & Anderson, 1992).

Take a minute to consider your own interests in the following exercise.

EXPERIENCING FIRSTHAND   *The Doctor's Office*

You have just arrived at the doctor's office for your annual checkup. The receptionist tells you that the doctor is running late and you will probably have to wait an hour before you can be seen. As you sit down in the waiting room, you notice six magazines on the coffee table: *Better Homes and Gardens, National Geographic, Newsweek, People, Popular Mechanics,* and *Sports Illustrated.*

1. Rate each of these magazines in terms of how *interesting* you think its articles would be to you:

	Not at All Interesting	Somewhat Interesting	Very Interesting
Better Homes and Gardens	_____	_____	_____
National Geographic	_____	_____	_____
Newsweek	_____	_____	_____
People	_____	_____	_____
Popular Mechanics	_____	_____	_____
Sports Illustrated	_____	_____	_____

2. Even though you think some of the magazines will be more interesting than others, you decide to spend ten minutes reading each one. Estimate how much you think you might *remember* from what you read in each of the six magazines:

	Hardly Anything	A Moderate Amount	Quite a Bit
Better Homes and Gardens	_____	_____	_____
National Geographic	_____	_____	_____
Newsweek	_____	_____	_____
People	_____	_____	_____
Popular Mechanics	_____	_____	_____
Sports Illustrated	_____	_____	_____

Now compare your two sets of ratings. Chances are, the magazines that you rated highest in interest to you are also the magazines from which you will learn and remember the most.

Students who are interested in a particular topic show greater cognitive engagement in that topic (Pintrich et al., 1994; Wigfield, 1994). They are also more likely to learn in a meaningful and elaborative fashion—for example, by relating new material to things they already know, drawing inferences, forming visual images, generating their own examples, and identifying potential applications (Hidi & Anderson, 1992; Pintrich & Schrauben, 1992; Schiefele, 1991, 1992; Tobias, 1994). Thus, as you might guess, students who are interested in what they are studying are more likely to remember it over the long run and use it as a foundation for future learning (Garner et al., 1991; Renninger, Hidi, & Krapp, 1992; Scholes & Kardash, 1996; Wigfield, 1994).

Situational Versus Personal Interest

Theorists distinguish between two general types of interest (Hidi & Harackiewicz, 2000; Renninger et al., 1992; Schraw & Lehman, 2001). **Situational interest** is evoked by something in the immediate environment. Things that are new, different, unexpected, or especially vivid often generate situational interest, as do things with a high activity level or intense emotions (Hidi, 1990; Mitchell, 1993; Renninger et al., 1992; Schank, 1979). Furthermore, certain topics—for example, death, destruction, danger, money, romance, and sex—appear to be inherently interesting for human beings (Schank, 1979). Works of fiction (novels, short stories, movies, and so on) are more interesting and engaging when they include themes and characters with which people can personally identify (Hidi & Harackiewicz, 2000; Schank, 1979; Wade, 1992). Nonfiction is more interesting when it is easy to understand and relationships among ideas are clear (Schraw & Lehman, 2001; Wade, 1992). And challenging tasks are often more interesting than easy ones (Danner & Lonky, 1981; Harter, 1978).

Other interests lie within: Students tend to have personal preferences regarding the topics they pursue and the activities in which they engage. Because such **personal interests** are

Soccer, the Pride and Passion

The sharp light blinds all onlookers from the reflection off the newly polished cast iron gauntlets of the twenty-two men of steel. Helms lowered, bodies bent in preparation for the battle Royal. Weapons drawn, shields raised, minds focused, focused on their enemy, their foe, their fellow competitor. Small colored flags wave in the stands, color coded with their respective prides and passions. Noises rumble through the stadium as random as the droplets of sweat flowing down the warriors' faces; teeth gritted, fists clenched, hearts pounding, pounding in anticipation of the things to come, the ultimate challenge of wills, the will to win for your fans, for your teammates, for yourself.

Fussebol, calcio, football, soccer; hundreds of names, one sport. Soccer is the most popular and most played game in the world, but that is not why I play the "Beautiful Game." Twenty-two players on a 120 by 90-yard battlefield scraping, fighting over one ball; that is not why I play it. Millions of players striving to be on their country's roster to play in the world's tournament that occurs only once every four years; that is not why I play it. The dream of playing in front of thousands of roaring fans and scoring the game-winning goal; that is not why I play it. For the emotion and passion of being able to walk out of my door every day to play the game I love, to give my all to the game, while taking everything I can from it, and not just progressing as a player, but a person; that is why I play it. That is why I play the "world's game." That is why I play soccer. . . .

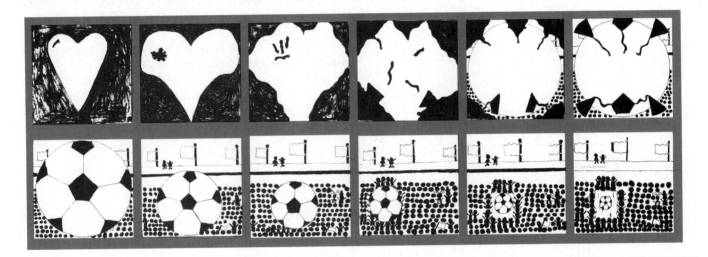

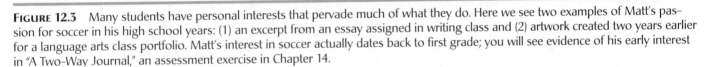

FIGURE 12.3 Many students have personal interests that pervade much of what they do. Here we see two examples of Matt's passion for soccer in his high school years: (1) an excerpt from an essay assigned in writing class and (2) artwork created two years earlier for a language arts class portfolio. Matt's interest in soccer actually dates back to first grade; you will see evidence of his early interest in "A Two-Way Journal," an assessment exercise in Chapter 14.

relatively stable over time, we see a consistent pattern in the choices students make (see Figure 12.3). For example, each of my children has shown unique individual interests from an early age. When Tina was growing up, she spent many hours talking either to or about boys, and as a college student she joined a coeducational "fraternity" house with a ratio of three males to every female. For many years, Alex had a thing for critters; he was fascinated with ants as a toddler, and he had an intense interest in various kinds of reptiles (lizards, snakes, dinosaurs) throughout the elementary and middle school years, to the point where he once subscribed to a herpetology magazine and read every issue from cover to cover. Jeff has always been a Lego man, putting all his allowance toward Lego building sets and spending many long hours in the basement designing architectural wonders.

The origins of personal interest have not been investigated as fully as sources of situational interest have. Many personal interests probably come from students' prior experiences with various activities and topics; for example, events and subject matter that initially invoke situational interest may provide the seeds from which personal interests will eventually grow (Hidi & Harackiewicz, 2000). Students may also find that acquiring more knowledge and skill in a particular area enhances their sense of self-efficacy, thereby enhancing their intrinsic motivation. Often, interest and knowledge seem to perpetuate each other: Personal interest in a topic fuels a quest to learn more about the topic, and the increased knowledge gained, in turn, promotes greater interest (Hidi & McLaren, 1990; Kintsch, 1980; Tobias, 1994).

In the early grades, interests are largely situational: Young children are readily attracted to novel, attention-getting events and stimuli. By the middle to upper elementary grades, however, students acquire specific interests—perhaps in reptiles, ballet, or outer space—that persist over time (Eccles et al., 1998). By and large, students form interests in activities that they can do well and that are stereotypically appropriate for their gender and social class (L. S. Gottfredson, 1981; Wigfield, 1994).

Promoting Interest in Classroom Subject Matter

Students' personal interests provide the force that will ultimately sustain their involvement in an activity over the long run (P. A. Alexander et al., 1994). As teachers, we can certainly capitalize on students' personal interests by allowing some flexibility in the topics about which students read, learn, write, and study (e.g., see Figure 12.4). Furthermore, we can tie traditional classroom subjects to things students are naturally curious about; for example, we might explain how we could use latitude and longitude to help locate the Titanic (Brophy, 1986). Students are often interested in topics related to people and culture (e.g., disease, violence, holidays), nature (e.g., dinosaurs, weather, the sea), and current events (e.g., television shows, popular music, substance abuse, gangs) (Zahorik, 1994).

On other occasions, we can temporarily pique students' interest, and in the process perhaps stimulate the beginnings of more enduring personal interests, by the activities we develop and the ways we present information. In particular, we can

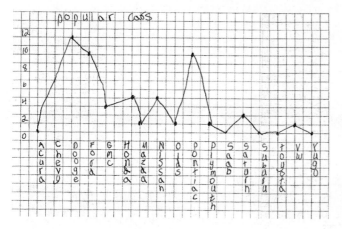

FIGURE 12.4 We can capitalize on students' personal interests by allowing flexibility in the topics that students explore as they work on basic skills. Here 12-year-old Connor practices basic research and graphing skills by surveying his fellow students about one of his favorite topics: cars.

- Include variety and novelty in classroom materials or procedures
- Present inconsistent or discrepant information
- Encourage occasional fantasy and make-believe
- Convey our own enthusiasm for a topic
- Provide opportunities for students to get actively involved with the subject matter
- Ask students to apply new knowledge and skills to events and concerns in their personal lives
- Ask students to teach what they learn to others
  (Anand & Ross, 1987; Brophy, 1987, 1999; Covington, 1992; Deci, 1992; Deci & Ryan, 1992; Hidi & Anderson, 1992; Hidi, Weiss, Berndorff, & Nolan, 1998; Lepper & Hodell, 1989; R. P. Perry, 1985; J. A. Ross, 1988; Wade, 1992; Zahorik, 1994)

To illustrate, here are some specific things we might do:

- In a unit on musical instruments, let students experiment with a variety of simple instruments.
- In a lesson about sedimentary, metamorphic, and igneous rocks, give cooperative groups a bag of rocks and have them categorize each one.
- In a lesson about alcoholic beverages, have students role-play being at a party and being tempted to have a beer or wine cooler.
- In a reading group, turn a short story into a play, with each student taking a part.
- In biology, have a classroom debate about the ethical implications of conducting medical research on animals.
- In spelling, occasionally depart from the standard word lists, instead asking students to learn how to spell the names of favorite television shows or classmates' surnames.
- In an aerobics workout in physical education, incorporate steps from swing, hip-hop, or country line dancing.
- In an art class, have students make a mosaic from items they've found on a scavenger hunt around the school building and its grounds.
- In a unit on aerodynamics, have each student make several paper airplanes and then fly them to see which design travels farthest.
- In arithmetic, have students play computer games to improve their automaticity for number facts.
- In history, have students read children's perspectives of historical events (e.g., Anne Frank's diary during World War II, Zlata Filipovic's diary during the Bosnian War).
- In geography, present household objects not found locally and ask students to guess where in the world they might be from.

Yet another strategy for generating interest is to relate classroom subject matter to students' short-term and long-term goals (Brophy, 1987; Parsons et al., 1982). Let's look at the kinds of goals our students are likely to have.

Goals

As you discovered in Chapter 10, social cognitive theorists propose that much of human behavior is goal-directed. Many motivation theorists echo this idea: People set goals for themselves and choose courses of action that they think will help them achieve those goals (e.g., Dweck & Elliott, 1983; M. E. Ford, 1996; Kaplan, 1998; Locke & Latham, 1994). Some goals (e.g., "I want to finish reading my dinosaur book") are short-term and transitory; others (e.g., "I want to be a paleontologist") are long-term and relatively enduring. Students' goals influence the extent to which they actively engage themselves in academic tasks and the kinds of learning strategies they use as they read and study (Anderman & Maehr, 1994; Nolen, 1996; Winne & Marx, 1989). Goal setting is also an important component of self-regulated learning: Self-regulated learners know what they want to accomplish when they read or study, direct their thoughts and learning strategies accordingly, and continually monitor their progress toward their goals (Carver & Scheier, 1990; Schunk & Zimmerman, 1994). Furthermore, by achieving their goals in a particular domain, students enhance their self-efficacy for tasks and activities within that domain (Bandura & Schunk, 1981). To produce these benefits, however, goals must be accomplishable; if they are unrealistically high, consistent failure to achieve them may result in anxiety or depression (Bandura, 1986).

Children and adolescents typically have a wide variety of goals: Being happy and healthy, doing well in school, being popular with classmates, gaining recognition for accomplishments, defeating others in competitive events, earning money, and finding a long-term mate are just a few of the many possibilities (M. E. Ford, 1996; Schutz, 1994). Yet among their many goals are certain **core goals** that drive much of what they do (Schutz, 1994). For instance, students who attain high levels of academic achievement typically make classroom learning a high priority; students who achieve at lower levels are often more concerned with social relationships (Wentzel & Wigfield et al., 1996).

Here we look at research findings related to several kinds of goals: mastery and performance goals, work-avoidance goals, social goals, and career goals. We then identify ways to capitalize on students' goals in order to enhance their motivation to learn and achieve in the classroom.

Mastery and Performance Goals

Mr. Wesolowski, the physical education teacher, is teaching a unit on basketball. He asks Tim, Travis, and Tony to get on the court and try dribbling, passing, and shooting baskets. Consider what the three boys are thinking as they begin to practice:

Tim: This is my chance to show all the guys what a great basketball player I am. If I stay near the basket, Travis and Tony will keep passing to me, and I'll score a lot of points. I can really impress Wesolowski and my friends.

Travis: Boy, I hope I don't screw this up. If I shoot at the basket and miss, I'll look like a real jerk. Maybe I should just stay outside the three-point line and keep passing to Tim and Tony.

Tony: I'd really like to become a better basketball player. I can't figure out why I don't get more of my shots into the basket. I'll ask Wesolowski to give me feedback about how I can improve my game. Maybe some of my friends will have suggestions, too.

All three boys want to play basketball well, but for different reasons. Tim is concerned mostly about his performance—about looking good in front of his teacher and classmates—and so he wants to maximize opportunities to demonstrate his skill on the court. Travis is also concerned about the impression he'll make, but he just wants to make sure he does *not* look *bad*. Unlike Tim and Travis, Tony isn't thinking about how his performance will appear to others. Instead, he is interested mainly in developing his skill in the game and doesn't expect immediate success. For Tony, making mistakes is an inevitable part of learning a new skill, not a source of embarrassment or humiliation.

Tony's approach to basketball illustrates a **mastery goal** (also known as a *learning goal*), a desire to acquire additional knowledge or master new skills. Tim and Travis are each setting a

performance goal, a desire to present oneself as competent in the eyes of others. More specifically, Tim has a **performance-approach goal:** He wants to look good and receive favorable judgments from others. In contrast, Travis has a **performance-avoidance goal:** He wants to *avoid* looking bad and receiving unfavorable judgments. In some instances, performance goals also have an element of social comparison, in that students are concerned about how their accomplishments compare to those of their peers (Elliot & McGregor, 2000; Elliot & Thrash, 2001; Midgley et al., 1998).

Mastery goals, performance-approach goals, and performance-avoidance goals are not necessarily mutually exclusive; students may simultaneously have two kinds, or even all three (Covington & Müeller, 2001; Hidi & Harackiewicz, 2000; Meece & Holt, 1993). For example, returning to our basketball example, we could imagine another boy, Trey, who wants to improve his basketball skills *and* look good in front of his classmates *and* not come across as a klutz.

In which of these goal(s) do you see intrinsic motivation? In which do you see extrinsic motivation?

Effects of Mastery and Performance Goals

A considerable body of research indicates that mastery goals are the optimal situation. As Table 12.1 illustrates, students with mastery goals tend to engage in the very activities that

TABLE 12.1   COMPARE/CONTRAST

Students with Mastery Versus Performance Goals

STUDENTS WITH MASTERY GOALS	STUDENTS WITH PERFORMANCE GOALS (ESPECIALLY THOSE WITH PERFORMANCE-AVOIDANCE GOALS)
Believe that competence develops over time through practice and effort	Believe that competence is a stable characteristic—that people either have talent or they don't
Choose tasks that maximize opportunities for learning	Choose tasks that maximize opportunities for demonstrating competence; avoid tasks and actions (e.g., asking for help) that make them look incompetent
React to easy tasks with feelings of boredom or disappointment	React to easy tasks with feelings of pride or relief
View effort as something necessary to improve competence	View effort as a sign of low competence; think that competent people shouldn't have to try very hard
Are more likely to be intrinsically motivated to learn course material	Are more likely to be extrinsically motivated—that is, by expectations of external reinforcement and punishment—and are more likely to cheat to obtain good grades
Exhibit more self-regulated learning and behavior	Exhibit less self-regulation
Use learning strategies that promote true comprehension of course material (e.g., meaningful learning, elaboration, comprehension monitoring)	Use learning strategies that promote only rote learning (e.g., repetition, copying, word-for-word memorization)
Willingly collaborate with peers when doing so is likely to enhance learning	Are willing to collaborate with peers primarily when such collaboration offers opportunities to look competent or enhance social status
Evaluate their own performance in terms of the progress they make	Evaluate their own performance in terms of how they compare with others
Interpret failure as a sign that they need to exert more effort	Interpret failure as a sign of low ability and therefore predictive of future failures
View errors as a normal and useful part of the learning process; use errors to help improve performance	View errors as a sign of failure and incompetence; engage in self-handicapping to provide apparent justification for errors and failures
Are satisfied with their performance if they try hard, even if their efforts result in failure	Are satisfied with their performance only if they succeed
View their teacher as a resource and guide to help them learn	View their teacher as a judge and as a rewarder or punisher

Sources: Ablard & Lipschultz, 1998; C. Ames & Archer, 1988; E. H. Anderman, Griesinger, & Westerfield, 1998; E. M. Anderman & Maehr, 1994; Dweck, 1986; Dweck & Elliott, 1983; Jagacinski & Nicholls, 1984, 1987; Kaplan & Midgley, 1999; Meece, 1994; P. K. Murphy, 2000; Newman & Schwager, 1995; Nolen, 1996; Rawsthorne & Elliot, 1999; A. M. Ryan et al., 2001; Urdan & Midgley, 2001; Urdan, Midgley, & Anderman, 1998.

will help them learn: They pay attention in class, process information in ways that promote effective long-term memory storage, and learn from their mistakes. Furthermore, students with mastery goals have a healthy perspective about learning, effort, and failure: They realize that learning is a process of trying hard and continuing to persevere even in the face of temporary setbacks. Consequently, it is usually these students who benefit the most from their classroom experiences.

In what areas do you have mastery goals? In what areas are you interested only in how you appear to others? How is your learning affected by the particular goals you have?

In contrast, students with performance goals—especially those with performance-*avoidance* goals—may stay away from some of the very tasks that, because of their challenging nature, would do the most to help them master new skills. Furthermore, these students often experience debilitating anxiety about tests and other classroom tasks (Middleton & Midgley, 1997; Skaalvik, 1997; J. C. Turner, Thorpe, & Meyer, 1998). Performance-*approach* goals are a mixed bag: They sometimes have very positive effects, spurring students on to achieve at high levels, especially in the secondary grades and especially in combination with mastery goals (Hidi & Harackiewicz, 2000; McNeil & Alibali, 2000; Pintrich, 2000; Rawsthorne & Elliott, 1999; Urdan, 1997). Yet by themselves, performance-approach goals may be less beneficial than mastery goals: To achieve them, students may use relatively superficial learning strategies (e.g., rote memorization), exert only the minimal effort necessary to achieve desired outcomes, engage in self-handicapping, and perhaps even cheat (E. M. Anderman et al., 1998; Brophy, 1987; Midgley, Kaplan, & Middleton, 2001). Performance-approach goals appear to be most detrimental when students have low self-efficacy for classroom tasks (Hidi & Harackiewicz, 2000).

Origins of Performance Goals

Unfortunately, performance goals seem to be far more prevalent than mastery goals among today's students, at least those in the secondary grades (Blumenfeld, 1992; W. Doyle, 1986b; Elliot & McGregor, 2000; Harter, 1992). Most students, if they are motivated to succeed in their schoolwork, are primarily concerned about getting good grades, and they prefer short, easy tasks to lengthier, more challenging ones. Performance goals are also common in team sports, where the focus is often more on winning and gaining public recognition than on developing new skills and seeing improvement over time (Roberts, Treasure, & Kavussanu, 1997).

Students with mastery goals recognize that competence comes only from effort and practice.

In some instances, students adopt performance goals as a means of protecting their sense of self-worth or gaining status with peers (L. H. Anderman & Anderman, 1999; Covington, 1992). In other cases, they may adopt performance goals because they believe that ability is something that they either have or don't have (rather than something they can increase with hard work) and so try to assess their "natural" ability by continually comparing their own performance with that of others (Dweck, 1999). Yet many common teaching and coaching practices also contribute to the development of performance goals. Scoring tests on a curve, reminding students that they need to get good grades if they want to go to college, displaying grades for everyone to see, focusing on surpassing other schools and teams—all of these strategies, though undoubtedly well intended, encourage students to focus their attention more on looking good than on learning.

Fostering Mastery Goals

Performance goals are probably inevitable in today's schools and in society at large (R. Butler, 1989; Elliot & McGregor, 2000). Children and adolescents will invariably look to their peers' performance as one means of evaluating their own performance, and many aspects of the adult world (gaining admission to college, seeking employment, working in private industry, playing professional sports, etc.) are inherently competitive in nature. Yet we do our students a disservice when we focus their attention primarily on how they appear to others and how often they do or do not surpass their classmates. When we instead point out how school subject matter will be useful in the future, encourage students to engage in meaningful learning rather than rote memorization, show students that they are making progress, and acknowledge that effective learning requires exerting effort and making mistakes, we are emphasizing goals that will help students better understand and more thoroughly master subject matter (C. Ames, 1992; E. M. Anderman & Maehr, 1994; Bong, 2001; Graham & Weiner, 1996; Meece, 1994).

Focusing learners' attention on mastery goals, especially when those goals relate to learners' own lives, may especially benefit students from diverse ethnic backgrounds and students at risk for academic failure (Alderman, 1990; Garcia, 1992; Wlodkowski & Ginsberg, 1995).

Work–Avoidance Goals

As we have just seen, students sometimes want to avoid looking bad as they perform classroom tasks. On other occasions, they may want to avoid having to do classroom tasks *at all*, or at least they will try to put as little effort as possible into those tasks. In other words, they may have a **work-avoidance goal** (Dowson & McInerney, 2001; Gallini, 2000; Nicholls, Cobb, Yackel, Wood, & Wheatley, 1990).

To date, research on work-avoidance goals has focused on the middle school grades, where such goals seem to be far too common (Dowson & McInerney, 2001; Gallini, 2000). Students with work-avoidance goals use a variety of strategies to minimize their workload; for instance, they may engage in off-task behavior, solicit help on easy tasks and problems, pretend they don't understand something even when they do, complain loudly about challenging assignments, and select the least taxing alternatives whenever choices are given (Dowson & McInerney, 2001). They rarely use effective learning strategies or pull their weight in small-group activities (Dowson & McInerney, 2001; Gallini, 2000).

Given the current paucity of research findings on work-avoidance goals, we can only speculate about how these goals originate. But we can reasonably guess that students are most likely to adopt them when they find little value or interest in classroom academic subject matter, have low self-efficacy for learning it, and see no long-term payoffs for mastering it. In other words, students are most likely to have work-avoidance goals when they have neither intrinsic nor extrinsic motivation to achieve instructional objectives. Students with work-avoidance goals may thus be our biggest challenges, and we will have to use a wide variety of motivational strategies—probably including extrinsic reinforcement—to get them truly engaged in, and eventually committed to mastering, academic subject matter.

Social Goals

In Chapter 11 we noted that most students make social relationships a high priority, and in fact all students probably have some need for relatedness. Students are apt to have a variety of social goals, perhaps including the following:

- Forming and maintaining friendly or intimate relationships with others
- Becoming part of a cohesive, mutually supportive group
- Gaining other people's approval
- Achieving status and prestige among peers
- Meeting social obligations and keeping interpersonal commitments
- Assisting and supporting others, and ensuring their welfare
  (Dowson & McInerney, 2001; M. E. Ford, 1996; Hicks, 1997; Schutz, 1994)

The nature of students' social goals will undoubtedly affect their classroom behavior and academic performance. If students want to gain their teacher's attention and approval, they are apt to strive for good grades and in other ways shoot for performance goals (Hinkley, McInerney, & Marsh, 2001). If they want to gain the approval of low-achieving peers, they may exert little effort in their studies (see Chapter 3) and possibly even adopt work-avoidance goals. If they are seeking friendly relationships with classmates or are concerned about others' welfare, they may eagerly and actively engage in such activities as cooperative learning and peer tutoring (Dowson & McInerney, 2001). As teachers, we must continually consider how we can help students achieve their social goals at the same time that they work toward more academically oriented ones—for example, by making ample use of group work, enlisting students' assistance in schoolwide and community service projects, and providing opportunities for all students to "shine" in some way and thereby gain the admiration of their peers.

Career Goals

Many students include career goals among their long-term goals. Young children set such goals with little thought and change them frequently; for instance, a 6-year-old may want to be a firefighter one week and a professional baseball player the next. By late adolescence, some (though by no means all) have reached some tentative and relatively stable decisions about the career paths they want to pursue (Marcia, 1980).

In general, boys set higher aspirations for themselves than girls do, especially in domains that are stereotypically masculine (Deaux, 1984; Durkin, 1995; Lueptow, 1984). Many girls, especially those raised in fairly traditional cultures, tend to limit themselves to stereotypically female occupations (Durkin, 1995; Olneck, 1995; S. M. Taylor, 1994). In addition, many girls, but few boys, further limit themselves to careers that they believe will be compatible with their future roles as spouses and parents (Eccles [Parsons], 1984).

Certainly gender stereotypes and future family roles are not the only things affecting students' career goals; their self-efficacy, expectations for success, and values are also involved. As teachers, we best serve our students when we open their eyes to the many rewarding careers they might consider, expose them to adults of both genders and numerous ethnic groups successfully pursuing those careers, and help them achieve the successes they need to convince them that they, too, have what it takes to do well in a variety of professions.

needes

Surgeon
I want to be a surgeon because I can help people if the get sick and can treat the so they will feel better. And can save ther lives. I will study hard for lots of years.

Many children begin thinking about careers in the preschool and early elementary years. Here 7-year-old Ashton explains why he wants to be a surgeon.

Capitalizing on Students' Goals

As we've explored some of the goals that students are likely to have, we've also considered the implications of these goals for instructional practice. We now look at a few more general ways in which we can use students' goals to foster their academic achievement:

■ *Plan activities that enable students to meet several goals at once.* Most students have numerous goals at any one time and use a variety of strategies to juggle them. Sometimes students find activities that allow them to achieve two or more goals simultaneously; for instance, they may satisfy both academic and social goals by forming a study group to prepare for a test. But in other situations they may believe they have to abandon one goal to satisfy another (McCaslin & Good, 1996; Phelan, Yu, & Davidson, 1994). For example, as we have seen, students who want to do well in school may choose *not* to perform at their best so that they can maintain relationships with peers who don't value academic achievement. And students with mastery goals in particular subject areas may find that the multiple demands of school coerce them into focusing on performance goals (e.g., getting good grades) rather than studying the subject matter as thoroughly as they'd like. Brian, a junior high school student, expresses his concern about having to leave his mastery goals in the dust as he strives for performance goals:

I sit here and I say, "Hey, I did this assignment in five minutes and I still got an A+ on it." I still have a feeling that I could do better, and it was kind of cheap that I didn't do my best and I still got this A. . . . I think probably it might lower my standards eventually, which I'm not looking forward to at all. . . . I'll always know, though, that I have it in me. It's just that I won't express it that much. (S. Thomas & Oldfather, 1997, p. 119)

Our students will, of course, be most successful when their multiple goals all lead them in the same direction (M. E. Ford, 1992; Wentzel, 1999). For example, students might work toward mastery goals by learning and practicing new skills within the context of group projects (thus meeting their social goals) and with evaluation criteria that allow for risk taking and mistakes (thus also meeting their performance goals). Students are *unlikely* to strive for mastery goals when our assignments ask little of them (consider Brian's concern about low standards), when we insist that they compete with one another for resources or high test scores (thereby interfering with their social goals), and when any single failure has a significant impact on their final grades (thereby thwarting their progress toward performance goals).

■ *Relate classroom subject matter to students' present lives and future goals.* Some classroom activities will be naturally fun, interesting, or otherwise intrinsically motivating for students. But others—perhaps the drill and practice so essential for developing automaticity of basic skills, or perhaps the complex topics and procedures with which students must initially struggle—may sometimes be less than exciting. Our students will be more apt to engage themselves in unenticing classroom subject matter, and more likely to use effective cognitive processes as they learn it, when they see how it relates to their personal lives and professional aspirations (C. Ames, 1992; Brophy & Alleman, 1991; Pintrich et al., 1993). In other words, students learn classroom material more effectively when they have a self-perceived *need to know* that material. Thus, we might illustrate how mathematics plays a role in shopping and budgeting an allowance, how science helps us solve everyday problems, and how physical fitness helps us look and feel better. We might show our students how oral and written language skills are critical for making a favorable impression on future employers. We might point out how knowledge of current events and social studies will help them make informed decisions in the voting booth.

■ *Encourage students to set specific, short-term goals for their learning and achievement.* Oftentimes students respond more favorably to goals they set for themselves rather than those that others set for them (Wentzel, 1999), possibly because self-chosen goals help them maintain a sense of self-determination. Although we should certainly encourage students to develop long-term goals (e.g., going to college, becoming an environmental scientist), such goals are often too general and abstract to guide students' immediate behavior (Bandura, 1997; Husman & Freeman, 1999). Many students (younger ones especially) initially respond more favorably to short-term, concrete goals—perhaps learning a list of spelling words or solving a certain number of mathematics problems (Bandura & Schunk, 1981; Good & Brophy, 1994; Schunk & Rice, 1989). By setting and working for a series of short-term goals, students get regular feedback about the progress they are making, develop a greater sense of self-efficacy that they can master school subject matter, and achieve at higher levels (Bandura, 1981; Kluger & DeNisi, 1998; Page-Voth & Graham, 1999; Schunk, 1996).

For such reasons, goal setting is an important part of self-regulated learning (see Chapter 10).

INTERPRETING ARTIFACTS AND INTERACTIONS   *Goals for the Quarter*

At his teacher's request, 12-year-old Kelvin reflects on goals he has previously set for himself and identifies a new set of goals. As you read Kelvin's self-evaluation, think about

- How useful Kelvin's previous goals have been in helping him evaluate his academic progress over the last few weeks
- How useful his new goals are likely to be in directing his future efforts

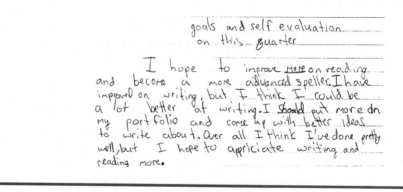

> goals and self evaluation on this quarter
>
> I hope to improve more on reading and become a more advanced speller. I have improved on writing, but I think I could be a lot better at writing. I should put more on my portfolio and come up with better ideas to write about. Over all I think I've done pretty well, but I hope to appriciate writing and reading more.

Kelvin's goals, old ones and new ones alike, are so vague and general that they are essentially useless in helping him direct his efforts and monitor his progress. For example, how will he know when he is a "more advanced speller" or "a lot better at writing"? We cannot necessarily blame Kelvin for his imprecision; as a 12-year-old, he probably hasn't had much practice with either goal setting or self-monitoring. When we ask students to set goals for their learning, we should give them examples of concrete criteria toward which they might strive. For instance, rather than become "better at writing," Kelvin might work toward "greater variety in sentence structure." And rather than "more advanced speller," he might shoot for "a maximum of two misspellings per page." We can often incorporate such suggestions into the feedback we give students about their work.

The topics we've explored so far have suggested numerous ideas about how we can enhance students' intrinsic motivation to learn academic subject matter. The feature "Promoting Intrinsic Motivation" identifies and illustrates just a few of them. We turn now to

INTO THE CLASSROOM: *Promoting Intrinsic Motivation*

Define success as eventual, rather than immediate, mastery of class material, and acknowledge that occasional mistakes are to be expected.

When a middle school student is disappointed in her mediocre performance on a difficult assignment, her teacher consoles her by saying, "You're a very talented student, and you're probably used to having your schoolwork come easily. But remember, as you move into the upper grades, your assignments will become more challenging. They *have* to challenge you, or else you wouldn't grow. With a little more study and practice, I know you'll improve quite a bit."

Encourage self-comparison, rather than comparison with other students.

In January an elementary school teacher asks his students to write a short story. After reading students' stories and writing feedback in the margins, he returns the stories to the authors; he also returns stories that the students wrote in early September. "Do you see how much your writing has improved over the past four months?" he asks. "The stories that you wrote this week are longer and better developed, and you made fewer spelling and grammatical errors."

Enhance students' sense of self-determination regarding classroom assignments and activities.

A high school science teacher tells her students, "I know you can't always complete your lab reports the same day that you did a lab in class. Let's see whether we can set some reasonable due dates for your reports so that *you* have time to write them and *I* have time to read them and give you feedback before the next lab activity."

Model your own interest in, and enthusiasm for, the subject matter.

A junior high school history teacher introduces the next reading assignment this way: "The chapter I've assigned for tonight is an exciting one. As the chapter un-folds, you'll see how the American colonists become increasingly discontented with British rule. You'll also learn how the colonists eventually managed to break free and form the United States of America. It's a story I never get tired of reading!"

Communicate the belief that students *want* to learn.

Early in the school year, a social studies teacher explains that her class will help students become "social scientists." She frequently refers back to this idea—for example, by saying, "Since you are social scientists, you will recognize that the description of this area as a tropical rain forest has implications about what kinds of crops will grow there," or "Thinking as social scientists, what conclusions might we draw from this information?" (Brophy, 1986, p. 46)

Relate classroom material to students' personal interests.

An elementary school teacher asks students to bring in objects they use to celebrate holidays at home. He incorporates these objects into a lesson on how holiday traditions differ not only from religion to religion but also from family to family.

Grab students' attention and pique their interest by occasionally introducing variety and novelty into classroom activities.

After clearing her strategy with the school principal, a high school psychology teacher brings Taffy, her mild-mannered cocker spaniel, to class for the day. She uses Taffy to demonstrate the various ways in which reinforcement (in this case, dog biscuits) can influence behavior.

Encourage students to set mastery goals.

A high school Spanish teacher often reminds his students, "The important thing in this class is to learn how to speak Spanish comfortably and with correct pronunciation. We'll all work together until we can communicate easily with one another in Spanish."

yet another cognitive factor affecting motivation: students' attributions for their successes and failures.

Attributions: Perceived Causes of Success and Failure

EXPERIENCING FIRSTHAND *Carberry and Seville #1*

1. Professor Josiah S. Carberry has just returned the first set of exams, scored and graded, in your advanced psychoceramics class. You discover that you've gotten one of the few high test scores in the class: an A−. Why did you do so well when most of your classmates did poorly? On a sheet of paper, jot down several possible explanations as to why you might have received a high grade in Carberry's class.

2. An hour later, you get the results of the first test in Professor Barbara F. Seville's socio-cosmetology class, and you learn that you *failed* it! Why did you do so poorly? Jot down several possible reasons for your F on Seville's test.
3. You will be taking second exams in both psychoceramics and sociocosmetology in about three weeks' time. How much will you study for each exam?

Here are some possible explanations for your A− in Carberry's class:

- You studied hard.
- You're smart.
- Psychoceramics just comes naturally to you.
- You were lucky. Carberry asked the right questions; if he'd asked different questions, you might not have done so well.
- Carberry likes you, so he gave you a good grade even though you didn't know what you were talking about.
- All those hours you spent in Carberry's office, asking questions about psychoceramics and requesting copies of the articles he's written (which you never actually read), really paid off.

In contrast, here are some possible reasons you failed the exam in Seville's class:

- You didn't study enough.
- You didn't study the right things.
- You didn't feel well when you took the test.
- The student next to you was sick, and the constant coughing and wheezing distracted you.
- You were unlucky. Seville asked the wrong questions; if she'd asked different questions, you would have done better.
- You're stupid.
- You've never been very good at sociocosmetology.
- It was a bad test: The questions were ambiguous and tested knowledge of trivial facts.
- Seville hates you and gave you a poor grade out of spite.

The amount of time you spend studying for your upcoming exams will, to some extent, depend on how you've interpreted your earlier performances (i.e., your success on Carberry's exam and your failure on Seville's exam). Let's first consider your A− on Professor Carberry's exam. If you think you did well because you studied hard, you will probably spend a lot of time studying for the second test as well. If you think you did well because you're smart or because you're a whiz at psychoceramics, you may not study quite as much. If you believe that your success was a matter of luck, you may not study much at all, but you might wear your lucky sweater when you take the next exam. And if you think the A− reflects how much Carberry likes you, you may decide that time spent flattering him is more important than time spent studying.

Now let's consider your failing grade on Professor Seville's exam. Once again, the reasons you identify for your failure will influence the ways in which you prepare for her second exam—if, in fact, you prepare at all. If you believe that you didn't study enough or didn't study the right things, you may spend more time studying the next time. If you think that your poor grade was due to a temporary situation—you were ill, the student sitting next to you distracted you, or Seville asked the wrong questions—then you may study in much the same way as you did before, hoping and praying that you'll do better on the second try. And if you believe that your failure was due to your stupidity, your ineptitude in sociocosmetology, Seville's dislike of you, or the fact that she writes lousy tests, then you may study even less than you did the first time. After all, what good will it do to study when your poor test performance is beyond your control?

The various causal explanations for success and failure just described are **attributions.** The attributions people assign to the things that happen to them—their beliefs about *what causes what*—do indeed guide their future behavior. The theoretical examination of these attributions and their influence on behavior is known as **attribution theory** (e.g., Dweck, 1986; Weiner, 1984, 1986, 1994, 2000).

Attributions are an example of knowledge construction in action. Students combine new information (in this case, a consequence they've just experienced) with their knowledge and beliefs about themselves and the world. They then construct what is, to them, a reasonable interpretation of what happened and why.

These middle schoolers are excited about their soccer team's victory over the middle school across town. Their attributions for the victory—whether they think it was due to hard work and practice, raw talent, a lucky break, and so on—will influence what and how much they do to achieve future victories.

Dimensions Underlying Students' Attributions

Our students may form a variety of attributions about the causes of classroom events; they will have beliefs about why they do well or poorly on tests and assignments, why they are popular with their classmates or have trouble making friends, why they are skilled athletes or total klutzes, and so on. They may attribute their school successes and failures to such factors as aptitude or ability (how smart or proficient they are), effort (how hard they tried), other people (how well the teacher taught or how much their classmates like them), task difficulty (how easy or hard something is), luck, mood, illness, fatigue, or physical appearance. These various attributions differ from one another in three primary ways: locus, stability, and controllability (Weiner, 1986, 2000).

1. *Locus ("place"): Internal versus external.* Students sometimes attribute the causes of events to *internal* things—to factors within themselves. Thinking that a good grade is due to your own hard work and believing that a poor grade is due to your lack of ability are examples of internal attributions. At other times, students attribute events to *external* things—to factors outside themselves. Concluding that you received a scholarship because you "lucked out" and interpreting a classmate's scowl as a sign of her bad mood (rather than the result of anything you might have done) are examples of external attributions.[1]

2. *Stability: Stable versus unstable.* Sometimes students believe that events are due to *stable* factors—to things that probably won't change much in the near future. For example, if you believe that you do well in science because of your innate intelligence or that you have trouble making friends because you're overweight, then you are attributing events to stable, relatively long-term causes. But sometimes students instead believe that events result from *unstable* factors—things that can change from one time to the next. Thinking that winning a tennis game was just a matter of luck and believing that you got a bad test grade because you were tired when you took the test are examples of attributions involving unstable factors.[2]

3. *Controllability: Controllable versus uncontrollable.* On some occasions, students attribute events to *controllable* factors—to things they can influence and change. For example, if you believe that a classmate invited you to his birthday party because you always smile and say nice things to him, and if you think that you probably failed a test simply because you didn't study the right things, then you are attributing these events to controllable factors. On other occasions, students attribute events to *uncontrollable* factors—to things over which they themselves have no influence. For example, if you think that you were chosen for the lead in the school play only because the drama teacher thinks you look "right" for the part or that you played a lousy game of basketball because you were sick, then you are attributing these events to uncontrollable factors.

With these three factors in mind, let's return to Michael in the opening case study. Notice how Michael initially attributes his failure in algebra to two stable and uncontrollable factors: low aptitude (an internal attribution) and poor instruction (an external attribution). As his tutor helps him understand algebraic principles and procedures, however, Michael begins to attribute his performance to two factors that are internal, unstable, and controllable: effort and better strategies. As his attributions change, his expectations for success change as well.

In general, students tend to attribute their successes to internal causes (e.g., high ability, hard work) and their failures to external causes (e.g., luck, behaviors of others) (H. W. Marsh, 1990a; Whitley & Frieze, 1985). By patting themselves on the back for the things they do well and putting the blame elsewhere for poor performance, they are able to maintain their sense of self-worth (Clifford, 1990; Paris & Byrnes, 1989). Attributions don't always reflect the true state of affairs, however; for example, a student may blame a low test grade on a "tricky" test or an "unfair" teacher when the cause is really the student's own lack of effort or poor study skills (e.g., Horgan, 1990).

---

[1]This dimension is sometimes referred to as *locus of control*; however, Weiner (1986, 2000) has pointed out that *locus* and *control* are probably two somewhat different dimensions.

[2]People occasionally think of *effort* and *luck* as being relatively stable, long-term characteristics (Weiner, 1986). To be consistent with much of the literature in attribution theory, however, we will use both terms to refer to a temporary state of affairs.

How Attributions Influence Affect, Cognition, and Behavior

I have already alluded to some of the effects that attributions may have. In the following paragraphs, we look more closely at such effects.

Emotional reactions to success and failure. Naturally, students will be happy when they succeed. But they will also have feelings of pride and satisfaction when they attribute their successes to internal causes—that is, to something they themselves have done. When they instead credit their successes to the actions of another person or to some other external force, they are apt to feel grateful rather than proud (Weiner, Russell, & Lerman, 1978, 1979). Along a similar vein, students will usually feel a certain amount of sadness after a failure. They will also feel guilty or ashamed when they blame their failures on internal causes, such as their own lack of ability or effort. But when they blame their failures on external causes—to events and people outside of themselves—they are likely to be angry (Weiner et al., 1978, 1979).

Expectations for future success or failure. When students attribute their successes and failures to stable factors, they expect their future performance to be similar to their current performance. In other words, successful students anticipate that they will continue to succeed, and failing students believe that they will always be failures. In contrast, when students attribute their successes and failures to *unstable* factors such as effort or luck, then their current success rate will have less influence on their expectation for future success, and a few failures won't put much of a dent in their self-efficacy (Dweck, 1978; Schunk, 1990; Weiner, 1986). The most optimistic students—those with the highest expectations for future success—are the ones who attribute their successes to stable factors such as innate ability and their failures to unstable factors such as lack of effort or inappropriate strategies (Fennema, 1987; Schunk, 1990; Weiner, 1984).

Expenditure of effort. When students believe that their failures result from their own lack of effort, they are likely to try harder in future situations and to persist in the face of difficulty (Dweck, 1975; Feather, 1982; Weiner, 1984). But when students instead attribute failure to a lack of innate ability (they couldn't do it even if they tried), they give up easily and sometimes can't even perform tasks they have previously accomplished successfully (Dweck, 1978; Eccles [Parsons], 1983).

Help-seeking behavior. Students who believe that success is a result of their own doing—those who attribute success to internal and controllable causes—are more inclined to seek the support that will facilitate their future learning. For instance, they may ask for their teacher's assistance if they don't understand course material, or they may voluntarily attend the extra help sessions that are offered (R. Ames, 1983). In contrast, students who believe that their learning successes and failures are beyond their control are unlikely to seek outside support even when it's readily available.

Classroom performance. We find consistent correlations between students' attributions and their academic achievement. For example, students who expect to succeed get better grades than students of equal ability who expect to fail (Eccles [Parsons], 1983). Students who expect to succeed are apt to approach problem-solving tasks in a logical, systematic manner; students who expect to fail are apt to solve problems through random trial and error or to memorize problem-solving procedures in a rote, meaningless fashion (Tyler, 1958).

Future choices. As you might expect, students whose attributions lead them to expect success in a particular subject area are more likely to pursue that area—for example, by enrolling in more courses in the same discipline (Eccles [Parsons], 1984; Stipek & Gralinski, 1990; Weiner, 1986). Students who believe that their chances for future success in an activity are slim will avoid that activity whenever they can. And naturally, when students don't continue to pursue an activity, they can't possibly get better at it.

Developmental Trends in Attributions

Students become increasingly able to distinguish among various attributions as they get older. In the preschool years, children don't have a clear understanding of the differences among the possible causes—effort, ability, luck, task difficulty, and so on—of their successes and failures (Eccles et al., 1998; Nicholls, 1990). Especially troublesome is the distinction between effort

Students are usually happy when they succeed at classroom tasks. But whether they also feel proud and satisfied, on the one hand, or relieved and grateful, on the other, depends on whether they attribute their success to internal or external causes. (Self-portrait by Corey, age 9)

and ability, which they gradually get a better handle on over time (Nicholls, 1990). At about age 6, they begin to recognize that effort and ability are separate qualities but see them as positively correlated: People who try hardest have the greatest ability, and effort is the primary determiner of success. Sometime around age 9, they begin to understand that effort and ability often compensate for one another and that people with less ability may have to exert greater effort to achieve the same outcome as their more able peers. By age 13 or so, they make a clear distinction between effort and ability: They realize that people differ both in their inherent ability to perform a task and in the amount of effort they exert on a task. They also know that ability and effort can compensate for each other but that a lack of ability sometimes precludes success no matter *how* much effort a person puts forth.

A related trend is an increasing tendency to attribute success and failure to ability rather than to effort (Covington, 1992; Dweck & Elliott, 1983; Nicholls, 1990). In the early elementary grades, students tend to attribute their successes to hard work and practice; therefore, they are usually relatively optimistic about their chances for success and so may try harder when they fail. As students get older, many of them begin to attribute their successes and failures to an inherited ability—for instance, to "intelligence"—that they perceive to be fairly stable and beyond their control. If these students are usually successful at school tasks, then they will have high self-efficacy about such tasks; if failures are frequent, their self-efficacy may plummet (Dweck, 1986; Eccles [Parsons], 1983; Schunk, 1990).

Whether intelligence is actually a stable or unstable characteristic is a matter of considerable controversy (see Chapter 4), and even school-age children and adolescents have differing opinions on this matter. Students with an **entity view** believe that intelligence is a "thing" that is fairly permanent and unchangeable. Students with an **incremental view** believe that intelligence can and does improve with effort and practice (Dweck & Leggett, 1988; Weiner, 1994). As you might guess, students who have an incremental view of intelligence and other abilities are more likely to attribute their failures to a temporary and unstable, rather than permanent, state of affairs.

Factors Influencing the Development of Attributions

Why does one student see a certain failure as a temporary setback due to her own insufficient effort, whereas another thinks it reveals a lack of ability and so signals more failures to come, and still another blames the failure on a teacher's capricious and unpredictable actions? Researchers have identified several factors that influence students' attributions: past successes and failures, reinforcement and punishment, messages from adults, and image management.

Past successes and failures.   Students' attributions are partly the result of their previous success and failure experiences (Covington, 1987; Hong, Chiu, & Dweck, 1995; Klein, 1990). Students who usually succeed when they give a task their best shot are likely to credit success to internal factors such as effort or high ability. Those who frequently fail despite their best efforts are likely to attribute success to something beyond their control—perhaps to an ability they don't possess or to such external factors as luck or a teacher's arbitrary judgment. Here we find yet another reason to promote student success on a regular basis: In doing so, we also promote more internal, and thus more productive, attributions.

When we know that our students have high self-efficacy about the subject matter in question, we may occasionally want to give them a series of tasks that they can perform successfully only if they exert considerable time and mental effort. In doing so, we can promote **learned industriousness**: Students will begin to realize that they can succeed at some tasks only with effort, persistence, and well-chosen strategies (Eisenberger, 1992; Winne, 1995).

How might learned industriousness be related to students' epistemological beliefs (see Chapter 8)?

Reinforcement and punishment.   In general, children are more likely to attribute events to internal, controllable causes when adults reinforce their successes but don't punish their failures. Conversely, they are more likely to make external attributions when adults punish failures and ignore successes (Katkovsky, Crandall, & Good, 1967). It appears that our students will be more apt to accept responsibility for their failures if, as teachers, we don't make a big deal out of them.

As noted in Chapter 9, however, mild punishment is sometimes necessary to discourage behaviors that seriously interfere with classroom learning. On such occasions, we must make response-consequence contingencies clear—for example, by describing unacceptable behaviors in advance and by using punishment in a consistent, predictable fashion. In the process, we help students learn that their *own behaviors* lead to desirable and undesirable consequences and that they can therefore influence the events that occur by changing how they behave. Hence, we help them develop internal attributions regarding the consequences they experience and a greater sense of control over classroom events.

Messages from adults. Adults communicate their beliefs about students' strengths and weaknesses in a variety of subtle, and sometimes not so subtle, ways (more about these ways in the upcoming section on "Teacher Expectations and Attributions"). When adults communicate their belief that students are incapable of mastering a task, students are likely to attribute their failures to low ability and may therefore conclude that they will gain little by trying harder (Butler, 1994; Weiner, 2000; D. K. Yee & Eccles, 1988). In some instances, adults may directly offer attributions for students' successes and failures (Parsons et al., 1982; Schunk, 1982). As an example, let's return to the case study "When 'Perfect' Isn't Good Enough" at the end of Chapter 11. For students in the treatment group, Mrs. Gaskill attributes good writing to either ability ("You are a natural at this") or effort ("You sure are working hard"). Curiously, the students in Mrs. Gaskill's control group appear to be frustrated that they're aren't getting such information ("Am *I* a natural at this?"). Children don't always jump to quick conclusions about why they are or are not doing well; in some cases, they eagerly seek out information to help them explain their successes and failures (Weiner, 2000).

Image management. As students get older, they discover that different kinds of attributions elicit different kinds of reactions from other people, and so they begin to modify their attributions for the particular audience at hand. One attribution theorist calls this phenomenon *face-saving* (Juvonen, 2000); I think the term *image management* is more descriptive. For example, teachers are often sympathetic and forgiving when students fail because of something beyond their control (illness, lack of ability, etc.) but frequently get angry when students fail because they didn't try very hard. By the time students reach fourth grade, most of them are aware of this fact and so may verbalize attributions that are likely to elicit a favorable reaction (Juvonen, 2000). To illustrate, a student who knows very well that she did poorly on an assignment because she didn't put forth her best effort may distort the truth, telling her teacher that she "doesn't understand this stuff" or "wasn't feeling well."

Students become equally adept at tailoring their attributions for the ears of their classmates. Generally speaking, fourth graders believe that their peers value diligence and hard work, and so they are likely to tell their classmates that they did well on an assignment because they worked hard. By eighth grade, however, many students believe that their peers will disapprove of those who exert much effort on academic tasks, and so they often prefer to convey the impression that they *aren't* working very hard. For instance, they might tell peers that they "didn't study very much" for an important exam (Juvonen, 2000).

For reasons we've just identified, different students may interpret the same events in very different ways. As they grow older, students gradually develop predictable patterns of attributions and expectations for their future performance, as we shall see now.

Mastery Orientation Versus Learned Helplessness

Consider these two students, keeping in mind that *their actual academic ability is the same:*

> Jared is an enthusiastic, energetic learner. He seems to enjoy working hard at school activities and takes obvious pleasure in doing well. He likes challenges and especially likes to solve the "brain teaser" problems that his teacher assigns as extra credit work each day. He can't always solve the problems, but he takes failure in stride and is eager for more problems the following day.

> Jerry is an anxious, fidgety student. He doesn't seem to have much confidence in his ability to accomplish school tasks successfully. In fact, he is always underestimating what he can do: Even when he has succeeded, he doubts that he can do it again. He seems to prefer filling out drill-and-practice worksheets that help him practice skills he's already mastered, rather than attempting new tasks and problems. As for those daily brain teasers, he sometimes takes a stab at them, but he gives up quickly if the answer isn't obvious.

Over time, some students, like Jared, develop a general sense of optimism that they can master new tasks and succeed in a variety of endeavors. They attribute their accomplishments to their own ability and effort and have an *I can do it* attitude known as a **mastery orientation.** Other students, like Jerry, who are either unsure of their chances for success or else convinced that they can*not* succeed, display a growing sense of futility about their chances for future success. They have an *I can't do it* attitude known as **learned helplessness.**

Even though students with a mastery orientation and those with learned helplessness may have equal ability initially, those with a mastery orientation behave in ways that lead to higher achievement over the long run: They set ambitious goals, seek challenging situations, and persist in the face of failure. Students with learned helplessness behave very differently: Because they underestimate their own ability, they set goals they can easily accomplish, avoid the challenges likely to maximize their learning and growth, and respond to failure in counterproductive ways (e.g., giving up quickly) that almost guarantee future failure (Dweck, 1986; Graham, 1989; C. Peterson, 1990; Seligman, 1991).

Even preschoolers can develop learned helplessness about a particular task if they consistently encounter failure when attempting it (Burhans & Dweck, 1995). As a general rule, however, children younger than 8 rarely exhibit learned helplessness, perhaps because they still believe that success is due largely to their own efforts (Eccles et al., 1998; Paris & Cunningham, 1996). By early adolescence, feelings of helplessness are more common: Some middle schoolers believe they cannot control what happens to them and are at a loss for strategies about how to avert future failures (Paris & Cunningham, 1996; C. Peterson, Maier, & Seligman, 1993).

Many of the strategies we've identified for enhancing self-efficacy—giving competence-promoting feedback, promoting mastery on challenging tasks, encouraging self-comparison rather than comparison with others, and so on—should promote a mastery orientation as well. Nevertheless, even when students are highly motivated to learn, they cannot always do so on their own. They should have a variety of resources to which they can turn in times of difficulty. These include their teacher, of course, and possibly such additional resources as supplementary readings, extra practice sheets, self-instructional computer programs, or outside tutoring (perhaps by classmates, older students, or community volunteers). Our students must have sufficient academic support to believe that *I can do this if I really want to.*

As mentioned earlier, the messages that teachers and other adults give students can have a significant influence on the attributions that students form. We now look more closely at the effects that teachers' expectations and attributions are likely to have. As we do so, we'll identify additional strategies for promoting productive attributions.

Teacher Expectations and Attributions

Teachers typically draw conclusions about their students relatively early in the school year, forming opinions about each one's strengths, weaknesses, and potential for academic success. In many instances, teachers size up their students fairly accurately: They know which ones need help with reading skills, which ones have short attention spans, which ones have trouble working together in the same cooperative group, and so on, and they can adapt their instruction and assistance accordingly (Goldenberg, 1992; Good & Brophy, 1994; Good & Nichols, 2001).

Yet even the best teachers inevitably make errors in their judgments. For example, teachers often underestimate the abilities of students who

- Are physically unattractive
- Misbehave frequently in class
- Speak in dialects other than Standard English
- Are members of ethnic minority groups
- Are recent immigrants
- Come from low-income backgrounds
  (Banks & Banks, 1995; Bennett, Gottesman, Rock, & Cerullo, 1993; Knapp & Woolverton, 1995; McLoyd, 1998; Oakes & Guiton, 1995; Ritts, Patterson, & Tubbs, 1992)

All too often, teachers perceive students' ability levels to be relatively fixed and stable; in other words, they have an *entity* view of intelligence (Oakes & Guiton, 1995; Reyna, 2000). Their beliefs about these "stable" abilities affect their expectations for students' performance, which in turn lead them to behave differently toward different students. For example, when teachers have high expectations for students, they create a warmer classroom climate, interact with students more frequently, provide more opportunities for students to respond, and

Think of the distinction between a mastery orientation and learned helplessness as a continuum of individual differences rather than a complete dichotomy. You might also look at it as a difference between *optimists* and *pessimists* (C. Peterson, 1990; Seligman, 1991).

Minority students with a history of academic failure are especially likely to be the recipients of teacher behaviors that signal low ability (Graham, 1990).

Teachers who hold high expectations for their students are more likely to give specific feedback about the strengths and weaknesses of students' responses.

give more positive feedback; they also present more course material and more challenging topics. In contrast, when teachers have low expectations for certain students, they offer fewer opportunities for speaking in class, ask easier questions, give less feedback about students' responses, and present few if any challenging assignments (Babad, 1993; Good & Brophy, 1994; Graham, 1990; R. Rosenthal, 1994).

Teachers' beliefs about students' abilities also affect their attributions for students' successes and failures (Weiner, 2000). Consider the following interpretations of a student's success:

- "You did it! You're so smart!"
- "That's wonderful. Your hard work has really paid off, hasn't it?"
- "You've done very well. It's clear that you really know how to study."
- "Terrific! This is certainly your lucky day!"

And now consider these interpretations of a student's failure:

- "Hmmm, maybe this just isn't something you're good at. Perhaps we should try a different activity."
- "Why don't you practice a little more and then try again?"
- "Let's see whether we can come up with some study strategies that might work better for you."
- "Maybe you're just having a bad day."

All of these comments are presumably intended to make a student feel good. But notice the different attributions they imply. The student's success or failure is attributed in some cases to uncontrollable abilities (being smart or not "good at" something); in other cases to controllable—and therefore changeable—student behaviors (hard work, lack of practice, effective or ineffective study strategies); and in still other cases to external, uncontrollable causes (a lucky break, a bad day).

Teachers communicate their attributions for students' successes and failures in more subtle ways as well—for instance, through the emotions they convey (Reyna, 2000; Reyna & Weiner, 2001; Weiner, 2000). As an example, let's return to the opening case study of Michael, who is initially doing very poorly in his eighth-grade algebra class. Imagine that you are Michael's teacher. Imagine, too, that you believe Michael has low mathematical ability: He just doesn't have a "gift" for math. When you see him get Ds and Fs consistently on his assignments and quizzes, you might reasonably conclude that such poor performance is beyond his control, and so you frequently communicate pity and sympathy. But now imagine, instead, that you believe Michael has *high* math ability: He definitely has what it takes to do well in your class. When you see his poor marks on assignments and quizzes, you naturally assume he isn't trying very hard. In your eyes, Michael has complete control over the amount of effort he exerts, and so you might express anger or annoyance when he doesn't do well. Some teachers might even punish him for his poor performance (Reyna & Weiner, 2001).

How Expectations and Attributions Affect Classroom Performance

Most children and adolescents are well aware of their teachers' differential treatment of individual students and use such treatment to draw logical inferences about their own and others' abilities (Butler, 1994; Good & Nichols, 2001; R. S. Weinstein, 1993). When their teachers repeatedly give them low-ability messages, they may begin to see themselves as their teachers see them. Furthermore, their behavior may mirror their self-perceptions; for example, they may exert little effort on academic tasks, or they may frequently misbehave in class (Marachi, Friedel, & Midgley, 2001; Murdock, 1999). In some cases, then, teachers' expectations and attributions may lead to a **self-fulfilling prophecy**: What teachers expect students to achieve becomes what students actually *do* achieve.

Certainly teacher expectations don't always lead to self-fulfilling prophecies. In some cases, teachers follow up on low expectations by offering the kinds of instruction and assistance that students need to improve, and so students *do* improve (Goldenberg, 1992). In other cases, students may develop an "I'll show *you*" attitude that spurs them on to greater effort and achievement than a teacher anticipated (Good & Nichols, 2001). In still other cases, assertive parents may step in and offer evidence that their children are more capable than a teacher initially thought (Good & Nichols, 2001).

So how prevalent are self-fulfilling prophecies? In other words, to what extent do teacher expectations affect students' classroom performance and overall academic growth? Research on this topic yields mixed results (Eccles et al., 1998; Goldenberg, 1992; R. Rosenthal, 1994). Some research indicates that girls, students from low-income families, and students from ethnic minority groups are more susceptible to teacher expectations than boys from European American backgrounds (Graham, 1990; Jussim, Eccles, & Madon, 1996). Teacher expectations also appear to have a greater influence in the early elementary school years (grades 1 and 2), in the first year of secondary school, and, more generally, within the first few weeks of school—in other words, at times when students are entering new and unfamiliar school environments (Jussim et al., 1996; Raudenbush, 1984; R. S. Weinstein, Madison, & Kuklinski, 1995).

Forming Productive Expectations and Attributions for Student Performance

Sometimes teacher expectations are based on completely erroneous information. More often, however, teachers' initial impressions of students are reasonably accurate. In the latter case, a problem emerges when teachers don't *change* their expectations in the light of new data (Cooper & Good, 1983; Good & Brophy, 1994). The constructive nature of learning and memory often gets in the way here: People's prior beliefs and expectations influence how they interpret new information (see Chapter 7). For example, if you have already read Chapter 4, then you may recall the opening case study involving 6-year-old Lupita, the daughter of migrant workers who has been raised in Mexico by her grandmother (Carrasco, 1981). Lupita's kindergarten teacher, Ms. Padilla, quickly jumps to the conclusion that Lupita has few academic skills and probably needs a second year of kindergarten. She is quite surprised to see a very different, and very competent, side of Lupita captured by a researcher's video camera. Ms. Padilla readily admits that her early expectations have colored her assessment of Lupita: "I had written her off . . . her and three others. They had met my expectations and I just wasn't looking for anything else." Just as Ms. Padilla does, teachers often look for evidence that confirms and perpetuates their own previously formed beliefs and expectations, and they may turn a blind eye and a deaf ear to any evidence to the contrary.

Unfortunately, teachers' beliefs about students' ability, as well as their attributions for students' performance, are sometimes affected by gender and ethnic stereotypes (Deaux, 1984; C. B. Murray & Jackson, 1982/1983; Reyna, 2000). For instance, a high school math teacher who believes that "girls aren't good in math" is likely to express pity and offer considerable help with classroom tasks. A fourth-grade teacher who believes that a particular ethnic group is "lazy" and "doesn't care about education" is apt to blame members of that group for their own failures and so give them little emotional support or assistance. Even the most fair-minded of us can be influenced by deep-seated biases and stereotypes of which we are consciously unaware (Dovidio, Kawakami, & Gaertner, 2000). For instance, Michael, in the chapter's opening case study, is African American. Had I given you this information at the beginning of the chapter, do you think it would have influenced your own explanations (attributions) for Michael's initially poor math achievement?

As teachers, we are most likely to facilitate our students' learning and to motivate them to achieve at high levels if we have optimistic expectations for their performance (within realistic limits, of course) and if we attribute their successes and failures to things over which either they or we have control (*their* effort, *our* instructional methods, etc.). Several strategies are helpful here:

■ *Remember that teachers can definitely make a difference.* We are more likely to have high expectations for our students when we are confident in our ability to help them achieve academic and social success (Ashton, 1985; R. S. Weinstein et al., 1995). We must keep in mind

The opening case study in Chapter 4, "Hidden Treasure," is on pp. 103–104.

All students have their strengths; for instance, some are good readers, others are inquisitive scientists, and still others are creative storytellers. As teachers, we are more likely to have high expectations for students when we look for things they do *well* rather than focus entirely on their weaknesses.

an important point that Chapter 4 makes about intelligence and creativity: Ability can and does change over time, especially when environmental conditions are conducive to such change. For this reason, we should take an *incremental view* of our students' intelligence and other abilities (Pintrich & Schunk, 2002). Accordingly, we must continually reassess our expectations and attributions for individual students, modifying them as new evidence presents itself.

■ *Look for strengths in every student.* Sometimes students' weaknesses are all too evident. It is essential that we also look for the many unique qualities and strengths that our students will inevitably have. For example, many African American students show considerable creativity when they converse; they joke, tease, and tell lively stories (Hale-Benson, 1986). We can certainly take advantage of such playfulness in students' speech—perhaps by having students create songs, jokes, or short stories that relate to classroom subject matter.

■ *Communicate optimistic and controllable attributions.* As teachers, we must be careful about the attributions we make about student performance. Probably the optimal course of action is to attribute success partly to a relatively stable ability (thus promoting optimism about future success) and partly to such controllable factors as effort and learning strategies (thereby emphasizing that continued success will come only with hard work). When considering possible causes for failure, however, we should focus primarily on factors that are internal, unstable, and controllable; thus, attributions for failures should focus on effort and learning strategies, rather than on low ability (which students are likely to believe is stable and uncontrollable) or external factors (Pressley, Borkowski, & Schneider, 1987; Schunk, 1983a; C. E. Weinstein, Hagen, & Meyer, 1991).

We can communicate optimistic attributions and expectations for student performance through statements such as these:

- "You've done very well. Obviously you're good at this, and you've been trying very hard to get better."
- "Your project shows a lot of talent and a lot of hard work."
- "The more you practice, the better you will get."
- "Perhaps you need to study a little bit more next time. And let me give you some suggestions on how you might study a little differently, too."

Studies have shown that when students' failures are consistently attributed to ineffective learning strategies or a lack of effort, rather than to low ability or uncontrollable external factors, and when new strategies or increased effort *do* produce success, then students work harder, persist longer in the face of failure, and seek help when they need it (Dweck & Elliott, 1983; Eccles & Wigfield, 1985; Graham, 1991; Paris & Paris, 2001).

We must be careful when we attribute either success or failure to effort, however. There are at least two occasions when such attributions can backfire. To see what I mean, try the next exercise.

EXPERIENCING FIRSTHAND   *Carberry and Seville #2*

1. Imagine that Professor Carberry wants you to learn to spell the word *psychoceramics* correctly. He gives you ten minutes of intensive training in the spelling of the word. He then praises you profusely when you are able to spell it correctly. In which of the following ways would you be most likely to respond?
    a. You are delighted that he approves of your performance.
    b. You proudly show him that you've also learned how to spell *sociocosmetology*.
    c. You wonder, "Hey, is this all he thinks I can do?"
2. Now imagine that you drop by Professor Seville's office to find out why you did so poorly on her sociocosmetology exam. Professor Seville is warm and supportive, suggesting that you simply try harder next time. But the fact is, you tried as hard as you could the *first* time. Which one of the following conclusions would you be most likely to draw?
    a. You need to try even harder next time.
    b. You need to exert the same amount of effort the next time and just keep your fingers crossed that you'll make some lucky guesses.
    c. Perhaps you just weren't meant to be a sociocosmetologist.

Research results tell us that you probably answered *c* to both questions. Let's first consider the situation in which Carberry spent ten minutes teaching you how to spell *psychoceramics*. When students succeed at a very easy task and are then praised for their effort, they may get the unintended message that their teacher doesn't have much confidence in their ability (Graham, 1991; Stipek, 1996). Attributing students' successes to effort is likely to be beneficial only when students have, in fact, exerted a great deal of effort.

Now consider the second scenario, the one in which Seville encouraged you to try harder even though you had already studied as hard as you could for the first exam. When students fail at a task at which they've expended a great deal of effort and are then told that they didn't try hard enough, they are likely to conclude that they simply don't have the ability to perform the task successfully (Curtis & Graham, 1991; Robertson, 2000; Stipek, 1996). Attributing students' failures to a lack of effort is likely to be helpful only when they really haven't given classroom tasks their best shot.

When students have worked hard but still failed, we should probably attribute their failure to a lack of effective strategies (Curtis & Graham, 1991; Pressley et al., 1987). As we discovered in our discussion of metacognition in Chapter 8, students can and do acquire more effective learning and study strategies over time, especially when they are specifically trained to use these strategies. By teaching effective strategies, not only do we promote our students' academic success, but we also promote their beliefs that they can control that success (C. E. Weinstein et al., 1991).

■ *Learn more about students' backgrounds and home environments.* Teachers are most likely to have low expectations for students' performance when they have formed rigid stereotypes about students from certain ethnic or socioeconomic groups (McLoyd, 1998; R. E. Snow et al., 1996). Such stereotypes often stem from ignorance about students' cultures and home environments (K. L. Alexander, Entwisle, & Thompson, 1987). So education is the key here: We must learn as much as we can about our students' backgrounds and local communities. When we have a clear picture of their activities, habits, values, and families, we are far more likely to think of them as individuals than as stereotypical members of any particular group.

INTO THE CLASSROOM: *Promoting Productive Attributions*

Communicate high expectations for student performance.

> In September a high school teacher tells his class, "Next spring, I will ask you to write a fifteen-page research paper. Fifteen pages may seem like a lot now, but in the next few months we will work on the various skills you will need to research and write your paper. By April, fifteen pages won't seem like a big deal at all!"

Attribute students' successes to a combination of high ability and such controllable factors as effort and learning strategies.

> In a unit on basketball, a physical education teacher tells his class, "From what I've seen so far, you all have the capability to play a good game of basketball. And it appears that many of you have been practicing after school."

Attribute students' successes to effort only when they have actually exerted that effort.

> A teacher observes that his students complete a particular assignment more quickly and easily than he expected. He briefly acknowledges their success and then moves on to a more challenging task.

Attribute students' failures to factors that are controllable and easily changed.

> A high school student seeks his teacher's advice as to how he might do better in her class. "I know you can do better than you have been, Frank," she replies. "I'm wondering if part of the problem might be that, with your part-time job and all your extracurricular activities, you just don't have enough time to study. Let's sit down before school tomorrow and look at what and how much you're doing to prepare for class."

When students fail despite obvious effort, attribute their failures to a lack of effective strategies and then help them acquire such strategies.

> A student in an advanced science class is having difficulty on the teacher's challenging weekly quizzes. The student works diligently on her science every night and attends the after-school help sessions her teacher offers on Thursdays, yet to no avail. Her teacher observes that the student is trying to learn the material by rote—an ineffective strategy for answering the higher-level questions the quizzes typically ask—and helps the student develop strategies that promote more meaningful learning.

■ *Assess students' progress regularly and objectively.* Because our expectations for students' performance are likely to color our informal evaluations of what they actually accomplish, we need to identify more objective ways of assessing learning and achievement. Furthermore, we should assess students' progress frequently, so that we have ongoing and reasonably accurate information with which to make instructional decisions (Goldenberg, 1992). Chapter 16 identifies several strategies for enhancing our ability to assess students' work objectively.

Considering Diversity in the Cognitive Aspects of Motivation

We've seen numerous instances of student diversity in our discussion of cognitive factors in motivation. For instance, we've learned that students have widely varying personal interests and will find greater or lesser value in particular subject areas. Furthermore, the degree to which students have high self-efficacy, mastery goals, productive attributions, and a mastery orientation will influence whether they prefer challenges, persist at difficult tasks, and take failure in stride. Let's look at some of the specific ways in which the cognitive aspects of motivation are likely to vary because of ethnicity, gender, socioeconomic background, and special educational needs.

Ethnic Differences

Children and adolescents from most ethnic groups place high value on getting a good education, but those from some minority groups have lower expectancies for academic and professional success, perhaps as a result of the discriminative practices they often encounter in society (Eccles et al., 1998; Fordham & Ogbu, 1986). Furthermore, students from different groups may define academic success differently and so set different goals for themselves. For instance, Asian students, on average, shoot for higher grades than students in other ethnic groups, in part because, they report, their parents would be angry if they got grades lower than A− (Steinberg, 1996). Students raised in cultures that value group achievement over individual achievement (e.g., many Native American, Mexican American, Southeast Asian, and Pacific Islander cultures; see Chapter 4) may focus their goals not on how much they alone can improve, but instead on how much they and their classmates can improve (Kaplan, 1998).

Students' ethnic backgrounds influence their attributions as well. For instance, students from Asian backgrounds are more likely to attribute classroom success and failure to unstable factors—effort in the case of academic achievement, and temporary situational factors in the case of appropriate or inappropriate behaviors—than students brought up in mainstream Western culture (R. D. Hess, Chih-Mei, & McDevitt, 1987; Lillard, 1997; L. Steinberg, 1996). Also, some studies indicate a greater tendency for African American students to develop a sense of learned helplessness about their ability to achieve academic success (Graham, 1989; Holliday, 1985). To some extent, racial prejudice may contribute to their learned helplessness: Some students may begin to believe that, because of the color of their skin, they have little chance of success no matter what they do (Sue & Chin, 1983; van Laar, 2000).

Gender Differences

Boys and girls may find greater or lesser value in various academic domains depending on whether they view these domains as being stereotypically appropriate for boys or girls. Many (but by no means all) students perceive some domains (e.g., writing, instrumental music) to be for girls and others (e.g., math, science) to be for boys (Eccles et al., 1998; Kahle, 1983; Pajares & Valiante, 1999), and such perceptions invariably influence their effort and course selection.

A gender difference appears in students' long-term goals as well. As we have seen, girls tend to have lower long-term aspirations for themselves; this is true despite the fact that they have higher average school achievement than boys (see Chapter 4). Two research findings may help explain this seeming paradox. First, girls sometimes report lower self-efficacy for academic tasks than boys do, especially in stereotypically male domains. When gender differences in self-efficacy are seen, they may reflect a tendency for girls to *under*estimate their competence and for boys to *over*estimate it (D. A. Cole et al., 1999; Eccles et al., 1998; Middleton, 1999).

Second, girls are more likely to be discouraged by their failures than boys are (Dweck, 1986), a difference we can explain, at least in part, by looking at gender differences in attributions. Some research studies indicate that boys have a tendency to attribute their successes to a fairly stable ability and their failures to lack of effort, thus having the attitude that *I know I can do this*. Girls show the reverse pattern: They attribute their successes to effort and their failures to lack of ability, believing that *I don't know whether I can keep on doing it, because I'm not very good at this type of thing*. Such differences, which can appear even when boys' and girls' previous levels of achievement are equivalent, are more frequently observed in stereotypically male domains such as mathematics and sports (Eccles & Jacobs, 1986; Fennema, 1987; Stipek, 1984; Vermeer et al., 2000).

Have you observed this difference in the males and females you know? Can you think of individuals who are exceptions to the pattern?

As we work to encourage high levels of motivation in all of our students, we may want to focus our efforts in somewhat different directions for males and females. For boys, we may need to stress the relationship of high classroom achievement to their own long-term goals. For girls, we may need to encourage openmindedness about a wide variety of career options (including traditionally "masculine" ones) and demonstrate quite clearly that these options are, with effort and appropriate strategies, well within their grasp.

Socioeconomic Differences

When working with students from lower socioeconomic backgrounds, we should remember that two conditions—self-efficacy and self-determination—are probably essential for intrinsic motivation. We are most likely to enhance students' self-efficacy if we have high (yet realistic) expectations for their performance and if we provide the academic support through which they can meet those expectations (Brophy & Evertson, 1976). And when we give them a sense of self-determination and control over their lives—for instance, when we involve them in classroom decision making and teach them effective ways of bringing about change in their local communities—they will attend school more regularly and achieve at higher levels (deCharms, 1972; NCSS Task Force on Ethnic Studies Curriculum Guidelines, 1992).

In addition, we can increase the perceived value of school activities by making those activities relevant to students' own lives and experiences (P. A. Alexander et al., 1994; Knapp et al., 1990; Tobias, 1994; Wlodkowski & Ginsberg, 1995). As we present new topics, we should draw on the knowledge that the students are apt to have, thereby increasing the likelihood of meaningful learning; for instance, we might keep in mind that these students are more likely to have encountered dogs and cats than elephants and zebras, more likely to have seen a grocery store or city park than a dairy farm or airport. We should also relate classroom tasks and activities to the specific, day-to-day needs and interests of our students; for example, we should teach academic subject matter within the context of authentic activities as often as we can. And we can occasionally solicit students' ideas about issues and questions that they'd like to study in class.

Accommodating Students with Special Needs

Students with specific or general academic difficulties (e.g., those with learning disabilities, those with mental retardation) may show signs of learned helplessness with regard to classroom tasks, especially if their past efforts have repeatedly met with failure (Deshler & Schumaker, 1988; Jacobsen, Lowery, & DuCette, 1986; Seligman, 1975). Students who have difficulty getting along with their classmates (e.g., those with emotional and behavioral disorders) may inappropriately attribute their social failures to factors beyond their control (e.g., see the discussion of *hostile attributional bias* in Chapter 3). Table 12.2 presents a summary of these and other motivational patterns in students with special needs.

Students are more likely to be intrinsically motivated when they have a sense of self-determination (e.g., when they can choose some of their activities) and when they have high self-efficacy (e.g., when they are successful in those activities). Experiences that promote self-determination and self-efficacy can be especially important for students with disabilities.

In recent years, special educators have become especially concerned about the need for students with disabilities to develop a sense of self-determination—to believe that they have some control over the direction that their lives take (Sands & Wehmeyer, 1996). Many of these students, especially those with physical or sensory challenges, may live in sheltered environments in which other people are calling most of the shots (Wehmeyer, 1996). We can do many simple things to enhance the self-determination that these students feel; for instance, we can let them make choices and set some of their own goals, help them develop skills that enable them to gain increasing independence, and teach the many self-regulation strategies that we identified in Chapter 10 (Abery & Zajac, 1996; L. E. Powers et al., 1996).

TABLE 12.2   STUDENTS IN INCLUSIVE SETTINGS

Promoting "Cognitions That Motivate" in Students with Special Educational Needs

CATEGORY	CHARACTERISTICS YOU MIGHT OBSERVE	SUGGESTED CLASSROOM STRATEGIES
Students with specific cognitive or academic difficulties	• Low self-efficacy for many classroom tasks • Tendency to attribute poor achievement to low ability rather than to more controllable factors; tendency to attribute successes to external causes (e.g., luck) • Tendency to give up easily; learned helplessness regarding performance on some classroom tasks	• Establish challenging yet realistic goals for achievement. • Teach effective learning strategies and encourage students to attribute their successes to such strategies. • Encourage students to develop more productive attributions regarding their achievement difficulties (e.g., attributing failures to insufficient effort or ineffective strategies).
Students with social or behavioral problems	• Tendency to interpret praise as an attempt to control them (when students exhibit defiance or oppositional behavior) • Perception of classroom tasks as having little relevance to personal needs and goals • Tendency to attribute negative consequences to uncontrollable factors (things just "happen")	• When students are concerned about control issues, use subtle reinforcers (e.g., leave notes describing productive behaviors) rather than more obvious and seemingly controlling ones. • Provide choices about academic activities as a way of increasing a sense of self-determination. • Relate the curriculum to specific needs and interests that students may have. • Teach behaviors that lead to desired consequences; stress cause-effect relationships between actions and outcomes.
Students with general delays in cognitive and social functioning	• Limited (if any) ability to conceptualize long-term goals • Tendency to attribute poor achievement to low ability or to external sources rather than to more controllable factors; in some situations, a sense of learned helplessness	• Set specific, short-term goals for performance. • Help students see the relationship between their own actions and the consequences that result.
Students with physical or sensory challenges	• Low sense of self-determination regarding the course that their lives are taking	• Give students some choices within the curriculum. • Teach self-regulating behaviors and independence skills.
Students with advanced cognitive development	• High self-efficacy • Boredom when classroom tasks don't challenge their abilities • May seek out challenges on their own • Variety of interests, sometimes pursued with a passion • Higher than average goal-directedness	• Encourage students to set high goals, but without expecting perfection. • Promote learned industriousness by assigning a series of tasks that require considerable effort and persistence.

Sources: Beirne-Smith et al., 2002; M. Carr & Borkowski, 1989; B. Clark, 1997; Duchardt, Deshler, & Schumaker, 1995; Dunlap et al., 1994; Foster-Johnson, Ferro, & Dunlap, 1994; A. E. Gottfried et al., 1994; Heward, 2000; Hoge & Renzulli, 1993; Jacobsen et al., 1986; Knowlton, 1995; D. P. Morgan & Jenson, 1988; Piirto, 1999; S. Powell & Nelson, 1997; Sands & Wehmeyer, 1996; Turnbull et al., 1999; U.S. Department of Education, 1992; Winner, 1997, 2000a, 2000b; Wong, 1991b.

The Big Picture

In Chapters 11 and 12, we've found that motivation can facilitate learning and achievement in a variety of ways; for example, appropriately motivated students pay attention, process information meaningfully, persist in the face of failure, use their errors to help improve skills, and seek out ever more challenging tasks. We have also seen how learning and achievement can foster the development of productive motivational patterns: When students discover that they can usually accomplish academic tasks successfully, they bring a sense of self-confidence and a desire to learn when they come to class. So motivation and learning go hand in hand, with each playing a crucial role in the development of the other.

The best-case scenario is that students are *intrinsically* motivated to learn and master classroom subject matter. They are most likely to be intrinsically motivated when they believe that

- They have the ability to succeed, especially if they apply reasonable effort and appropriate strategies
- Sufficient resources and support in the classroom are available to *help* them succeed
- They find the subject matter interesting and relevant to their goals
- They are voluntarily choosing to pursue the activity in question

In some situations, however, students may not be intrinsically motivated to learn important building blocks for more complex and interesting material. In such situations, we can foster extrinsic motivation, and possibly some degree of intrinsic motivation, in a variety of ways. For instance, we can have students set short-term goals with which they can monitor their progress, embed skills practice within enjoyable small-group activities, and reinforce students' achievements.

As teachers, we will invariably find that each student has unique strengths and weaknesses. Yet we must remember that our own behaviors toward students—how challenging our assignments are, how often we call on students in class, how we interpret their successes and failures, and so on—provide regular messages about how we have sized up each student's potential for learning and classroom success. Our early assessments of students' abilities should guide us in our choice of instructional strategies; they should *not* give students reason to question their ability and thereby undermine students' confidence about mastering classroom subject matter.

General Principles of Motivation

We've considered many strategies for motivating students to learn and achieve in the classroom. Table 12.3 presents highlights of our discussion of motivation, listing several general principles and their implications for classroom practice. These principles are not intended as an exhaustive list; however, if you look at them closely, you will find that they reflect many of the concepts we've addressed in both Chapter 11 and 12, including self-efficacy, expectancy, self-determination, need for relatedness, value, interest, goals, hot cognition, anxiety, and attributions.

Revisiting the Four Theoretical Perspectives

As we've discussed motivation, we've drawn ideas from each of the theoretical perspectives identified in Chapter 11; we've also drawn from what we've learned about learning in earlier chapters. Following are some examples of how the trait, behaviorist, social cognitive, and cognitive perspectives have each entered into our discussion:

Trait Perspective

- Students differ in their *need for affiliation* with others and in their *need for approval* from others.
- Students' *personal interests* tend to be relatively stable over time.

TABLE 12.3 PRINCIPLES/ASSUMPTIONS

General Principles of Motivation

PRINCIPLE	EDUCATIONAL IMPLICATION	EXAMPLE
Students are more likely to be intrinsically motivated when they expect to succeed and when they believe that they have some choice and control about their course of action.	Give students many opportunities to achieve the successes they need for high self-efficacy, and let them make choices regarding certain aspects of classroom tasks and activities.	Allow students to choose among several ways of accomplishing the same instructional objective, being sure that each choice provides sufficient scaffolding to make success likely.
Students need to feel connected with other people; for many, interpersonal relationships are a high priority.	Include interactive activities in each week's class schedule.	Have students work in small groups to tackle a challenging issue or problem for which there is no single "right" answer.
Students are more likely to pursue an activity when they see its relevance to their own interests and goals.	Make frequent connections between academic subject matter and students' lives outside of the classroom.	Ask students to conduct a scientific investigation about an issue that concerns them.
Students who truly want to master a domain are more likely to learn effectively than students who are primarily concerned about how they appear to or compare with others.	Acknowledge that test scores and class grades are important, but focus students' attention more on the intrinsic value of acquiring new knowledge and skills.	Model enthusiasm for classroom material, showing how it has helped you better understand the world.
Students who are emotionally involved in a topic or activity tend to learn and remember it more effectively, although very high levels of affect (e.g., high anxiety) can be detrimental.	Get students excited about the subject matter, but try to keep any anxiety about their performance at a facilitating (low to moderate) level.	Hold realistic expectations for student performance and communicate those expectations clearly and concretely.
Students are most likely to put forth effort in the classroom when they attribute their successes and failures to factors over which they have control.	Foster the belief that classroom success is a function of sufficient effort and appropriate strategies.	When students struggle with classroom material, teach them study strategies that will help them remember the material more effectively.

Behaviorist Perspective

- Motivation determines what particular things are *reinforcing* to different students.
- Students are more likely to attribute success to internal factors when they are *reinforced* (e.g., praised) for success.

Social Cognitive Perspective

- Students are more likely to be intrinsically motivated to engage in and persist at classroom tasks when they have high *self-efficacy* about performing those tasks.
- We can foster intrinsic motivation to learn classroom subject matter when we *model* our own interest and enthusiasm about school subject matter.
- Students' *expectations* (expectancies) for future success and failure—expectations derived from their beliefs about their ability, their perceptions of classroom support for their efforts, and their attributions for previous successes and failures—influence their choices and actions.

Cognitive Perspective

- Students who have mastery goals rather than performance goals are more likely to engage in *meaningful learning* and *elaboration*.
- Students' attributions regarding events—their *constructed interpretations* of the causes of successes and failures—influence how they respond to those events.
- Students are more optimistic about future success when they attribute failure to ineffective *study strategies* rather than to a general and relatively permanent lack of ability.

The principles and theories of learning and motivation that we have examined in Chapters 6 through 12 have yielded innumerable strategies for helping our students learn and achieve more successfully in the classroom. In the chapters to come, we translate the same principles and theories more directly into classroom practice as we consider instruction, classroom management, and assessment.

PRAXIS Turn to Appendix C, "Matching Book and Ancillary Content to the PRAXIS™ Principles of Learning and Teaching Tests," to discover sections of this chapter that may be especially applicable to the PRAXIS™ tests.

Now go to our Companion Website at http://www.prenhall.com/ormrod to assess your understanding of chapter content with "Multiple-Choice Questions," apply comprehension in "Essay Questions," broaden your knowledge of educational psychology with related "Web Links," gain greater insight about classroom learning in "Learning in the Content Areas," and analyze and assess classroom work in the "Student Artifact Library."

CASE STUDY: *Writer's Block*

On the first day of school, Mr. Grunwald tells students in his English composition class, "I expect you all to be proficient writers by the end of the school year. In fact, you won't get a passing grade from me unless you can write a decent essay by May."

Mr. Grunwald's statement raises anxious thoughts in many of his students. After all, a passing grade in English composition is a requirement for high school graduation. Furthermore, the colleges and universities to which some students are applying prefer As and Bs in composition. A few students are beginning to worry that their straight A averages will be destroyed.

Mr. Grunwald is far less concerned than his students; he firmly believes that all students should be able to develop writing proficiency before the year is out. He gives his students a new writing assignment every Monday, making each one more challenging than those preceding it. When he finds poorly written work among the papers he grades at the end of the week, he tries to motivate his students to do better with such comments as, "Below average work this time—you can do better," or, "Try harder next week."

The writing skills of some students improve as the year progresses. But those of other students seem almost to be deteriorating. He questions Janis, one of his low-achieving students, about the problem and is startled to hear her response.

"No matter what I do, I seem to get poor grades in your class," she laments. "I've pretty much given up trying. I guess I just wasn't meant to be a writer."

- How is Mr. Grunwald defining success in his English composition class? How are his students defining success? Are they focusing their attention on mastery goals or performance goals?
- To what does Janis attribute her writing failure? What effect has her attribution had on her behavior?
- What strategies might Mr. Grunwald use to help his students become more intrinsically motivated to develop proficient writing skills?

Once you have answered these questions, compare your responses with those presented in Appendix B.

Key Concepts

self-efficacy (p. 391)
self-determination (p. 391)
expectancy (p. 397)
value (p. 397)
internalized motivation (p. 398)
interest (p. 399)
situational interest (p. 400)
personal interest (p. 400)

core goal (p. 403)
mastery goal (p. 403)
performance goal (p. 404)
performance-approach goal (p. 404)
performance-avoidance goal (p. 404)
work-avoidance goal (p. 406)
attribution (p. 410)
attribution theory (p. 410)

entity view of intelligence (p. 413)
incremental view of intelligence (p. 413)
learned industriousness (p. 413)
mastery orientation (p. 415)
learned helplessness (p. 415)
self-fulfilling prophecy (p. 416)

13

Instructional Strategies

$\mathcal{U}$nder what conditions do you best learn and achieve in your college classes? Do you learn more when your instructors have carefully identified what they want you to learn and have planned their lessons accordingly? What kinds of instructional methods—lectures, hands-on activities, class discussions, cooperative learning groups, and so on—effectively help you understand and remember classroom material? Does the general "climate" in the classroom—for instance, whether the instructor is aloof or friendly, whether the atmosphere is businesslike or very laid-back—make a difference for you? And how do your instructors' assessment practices (tests, papers, group projects, etc.) influence what you study and learn?

Such issues are the focus of Part 3 of the book, "Understanding Instructional Processes." In these final four chapters, we will consider how planning and carrying out instruction (Chapter 13), creating a productive classroom environment (Chapter 14), and assessing student learning (Chapters 15 and 16) are all essential aspects of effective teaching and have an impact on what students ultimately learn and achieve. Yet as we make decisions related to each of these areas, we must also keep in mind what we know about our *students*. As we proceed through this and the next three chapters, we will repeatedly see examples of how planning, instruction, the classroom environment, and assessment practices affect one another and how, in addition, they both influence and are influenced by student behaviors and characteristics (see Figure 13.1).

Throughout Part 3 we will revisit principles and concepts introduced in previous chapters. For instance, as we consider planning and carrying out instruction, we will draw from cognitive, behaviorist, and social cognitive views of learning. As we discuss ways of creating a productive classroom environment, we will make use of such "old friends" as *scaffolding, socialization, cueing,* and *self-determination*. And as we explore various strategies for assessing student learning, we will discover that our assessment practices are likely to influence students' long-term memory storage processes, motivation, and self-regulation.

In this chapter we will apply what we have learned in Parts 1 and 2 as we examine a variety of instructional strategies. Our focus will be on questions such as these:

- How can we plan effectively for instruction, both on a daily basis and over the course of the school year?
- How can we effectively teach new material through *expository instruction*—that is, by directly presenting the information we want our students to know, understand, and apply?
- How can we also help students acquire new knowledge and skills through more *hands-on* approaches?
- What strategies can maximize students' ability to learn *from one another* as well as from us?
- How can we best accommodate students' diverse backgrounds, characteristics, and needs when we plan and implement classroom instruction?
- What guiding principles can help us identify the most appropriate instructional strategies for different situations?

CASE STUDY: *Oregon Trail*

Fifth-grade teacher Michele Minichiello has recently begun a unit about American settlers traveling west on the Oregon Trail during the 1840s. Today's lesson focuses on how families prepared for the long, arduous trip.[1]

---

[1] I observed Michele's lesson when I was supervising her teaching internship at the end of her master's program, and I'm delighted that she gave me permission to describe it here. The students' names are pseudonyms.

"The covered wagons were about 4 feet by 10 feet," Ms. Minichiello tells her class. She has her students move their desks to clear the middle of the classroom and then instructs two students to mark a 4-by-10-foot rectangle on the carpet with masking tape. "These are the dimensions of a typical covered wagon. How much room would that give you for your family and supplies?" The students agree that the wagon is smaller than they had realized and that it would not provide much room for an entire family.

"So they would have to be pretty choosy about what they brought on their trip," Ms. Minichiello observes. "Let's brainstorm some of the things that the settlers might have packed." The students volunteer many possibilities—food, spare wagon parts, pots and pans, blankets, extra clothes, rifles, bullets, barrels of water, medicine—and Ms. Minichiello writes them on the chalkboard at the front of the room. She has the class get more specific about the list (e.g., what kinds of food? how much of each kind?) and then passes out reading materials that describe the supplies that a typical family would actually pack for the journey. As the students read the materials in their cooperative groups, Ms. Minichiello circulates among them to show photographs of how the inside of a covered wagon looked when occupied by a family and its possessions.

Once the students have finished their reading, Ms. Minichiello directs their attention to their own supply list on the chalkboard, and the following discussion ensues with the students and Ms. Berry, a special education teacher who is in the room at the time.

Ms. M:	Do you think our list was accurate? Is there anything you want to change?
Lacy:	We need much more flour.
Janie:	(referring to an item listed in the reading materials) I don't think they should bring 100 pounds of coffee.
Curt:	(also referring to the reading materials) I don't think they need 50 pounds of lard.
Ms. M:	Does anyone know what lard is?
Tom:	It's a kind of animal fat.
Ms. B:	They used it for cooking, but they used it for lots of other things, too.
Ms. M:	Do you think they used it for water-proofing?
Ms. B:	Maybe so.
Ms. M:	What were some of the things that pioneers had to be prepared for? (Here she is asking students to recall information they have just learned from the reading materials.)
Mark:	Mountain travel.
René:	Crossing rivers.
Ms. B:	How about if you were going across the desert?
Lacy:	You'd need a lot of water.
Tom:	Food for the oxen.
Ms. M:	If *you* were taking such a trip now—if you were moving far away from where you live now—what things would you bring with you?
Misha:	Computer.
Lou:	Cell phone.
Dana:	Refrigerator.
Cerise:	My dog.
Ms. M:	Where would pioneers go now?
Curt:	North or south pole.
Tom:	Space.
Ms. M:	Imagine that your family isn't doing well, and so you decide to travel to a distant planet. It's very expensive to travel there. You can only take *one* item, so pick the one item you would bring. Assume there will be food and a place to sleep. Take five minutes to pick one item, and explain why you would take it.

Ms. Minichiello distributes index cards on which the students can write their responses. She gives them a few minutes to do so and then asks, "Who found that it was hard to pick just one item?" Almost all of the students raise their hands. "What I wanted you to realize is that if you were a child back then, it would be really hard to leave most of your things behind."

- Are the students engaged in the lesson? What evidence do you see to indicate that they are learning?
- What specific instructional strategies is Ms. Minichiello using to engage and motivate her students? What strategies is she using to help them understand the nature of travel in the mid-1800s?

Overview of Instructional Strategies

The students in Ms. Minichiello's class are clearly engaged in the lesson (e.g., they are actively responding to her questions), and they have definitely learned some things (e.g., they notice differences between the supply list in their reading and the list they've generated themselves, and they can recall some of the difficulties that the settlers faced). To engage and motivate her students, Ms. Minichiello uses several strategies that we identified in Chapters 11 and 12: She gets the students physically active (they move their desks and make a "wagon" on the floor), presents discrepant information (the list in the reading materials doesn't completely match the one the class has generated), poses a challenging task ("You can only take *one* item. . . ."), and makes the lesson a very social, interactive one. Furthermore, Ms. Minichiello promotes learning and understanding by encouraging visual imagery, meaningful learning, organization, and elaboration—for instance, by making the subject matter concrete and vivid (through the masking-tape wagon and the photographs), having the class consider cause-effect relationships that justify the supply list ("What were some of the things that pioneers had to be prepared for?"), and asking students to relate the settlers' situation to one that they themselves might face.

In this chapter we'll explore a wide variety of instructional strategies. The first step any teacher must take, of course, is to plan a course of action—to decide in advance both what needs to be accomplished and how best to accomplish it—and so we'll begin our discussion by looking at strategies that can help us plan appropriately. We will then examine many of the instructional techniques we can use to help our students learn effectively. I have organized these techniques into three major categories: *expository approaches* (directly presenting the information to be learned), *hands-on approaches* (involving students physically in the subject matter and having them discover a phenomenon for themselves, practice a new procedure, or apply a concept to a new situation), and *interactive and collaborative approaches* (having students discuss topics and in other ways help one another learn). This organizational scheme is depicted in Figure 13.2.

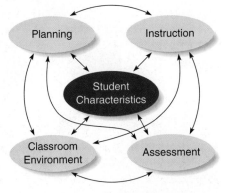

FIGURE 13.1 Planning, instruction, the classroom environment, assessment, and student characteristics are not independent; each one influences the others.

FIGURE 13.2 An organizational scheme for our discussion of instructional strategies

---

PLANNING INSTRUCTION

- Identifying the goals of instruction
- Conducting a task analysis
- Developing a lesson plan

↓

DELIVERING INSTRUCTION

Expository Approaches

- Lectures and textbooks
- Mastery learning
- Direct instruction
- Computer-based instruction
- Online research

Hands-on Approaches

- Discovery learning
- In-class activities
- Computer simulations and applications
- Homework
- Authentic activities

Interactive and Collaborative Approaches

- Teacher questions
- Class discussions
- Reciprocal teaching
- Technology-based discussions
- Cooperative learning
- Peer tutoring

Please note that the categories I've just identified are not as cut-and-dried as Figure 13.2 makes them out to be. For instance, planning does not take place *only* before instruction begins; as teachers, we will continue to revise our plans (mentally, if not on paper) as a lesson or instructional unit proceeds (recall Figure 13.1). Expository approaches sometimes have a hands-on element (the Experiencing Firsthand exercises in this textbook are an example), often involve some teacher-student interaction, and may involve student-student interaction as well. And some hands-on activities are very collaborative in nature; for instance, students may work on challenging problems or authentic activities in small, cooperative groups. Furthermore, as teachers, we will frequently find that the best way to accomplish our instructional goals is to combine two or more strategies. For example, in the opening case study, Ms. Minichiello employs expository instruction (e.g., the reading materials) as well as hands-on instruction (e.g., the masking-tape wagon) and interactive instruction (e.g., the discussion of needed supplies).

We can subdivide instructional strategies in another way as well: teacher-directed or student-directed.[2] In **teacher-directed instruction**, the teacher calls most of the shots, choosing what topics will be addressed, directing the course of the lesson, and so on; most forms of expository instruction fall into this category. In **student-directed instruction**, students have considerable say in the issues they address and how to address them; most hands-on, interactive, and collaborative approaches fall into this category. Increasingly, educators are recognizing the value of student-directed activities not only for fostering classroom learning and achievement but also for promoting the metacognitive and self-regulatory skills essential for lifelong success (e.g., De Lisi & Golbeck, 1999; Vye et al., 1998). But ultimately, we will choose teacher-directed or student-directed strategies based on our goals for instruction and on the knowledge and skills that our students bring to the situation.

When students are actively involved in designing and carrying out classroom projects, they can develop important self-regulatory skills.

As you read the chapter, then, don't think about selecting a single "best" approach or two. Instead, think about how different strategies may be more or less suitable in different situations. Think, too, about how you might effectively use many or all of them over the course of the school year.

Planning for Instruction

Effective teaching begins long before students enter the classroom. Good teachers engage in considerable advance planning: They identify the knowledge and skills they want their students to acquire, determine an appropriate sequence in which to foster such knowledge and skills, and develop classroom activities that will promote maximal learning and keep students continually motivated and on task. Here we consider three aspects of instructional planning: identifying the goals of instruction, conducting a task analysis, and developing lesson plans.

Identifying the Goals of Instruction

An essential part of planning is identifying the specific things we want our students to learn during a lesson or unit, as well as the things we want them to accomplish over the course of the semester or school year. Educators use a variety of terms for such goals (e.g., *outcomes, proficiencies, targets, benchmarks*), but the term **instructional objectives** is probably the most common.

When we identify our objectives before we begin teaching, we are in a better position to choose an effective method of instruction; we can also develop an appropriate means of evaluating our students' achievement. For example, if our objective for a unit on addition is *knowledge* of number facts, then we may want to use drill and practice (perhaps flash cards, perhaps

---

[2]Some educators instead use the terms *teacher-centered* and *student-centered*. In my mind, these terms misrepresent the distinction. Virtually all instructional strategies focus (center) on the *student's* learning; the essential difference lies in who has control of the instructional activity.

gamelike computer software) to enhance students' automaticity for these facts, and we may want to use a timed test to measure students' ability to recall them quickly and easily. But if our objective is *application* of number facts, then we may want to focus our instruction and assessment methods on word problems, or perhaps on activities involving real objects, hands-on measurements, and so on.

Students, too, benefit from knowing the objectives for a lesson or unit. When they know what their teacher hopes they will accomplish, they can make more informed decisions about how to focus their efforts and allocate their study time, and they can more effectively monitor their comprehension as they read and study (Gronlund, 2000; McAshan, 1979). For example, if we tell our students that we expect them to "apply mathematics procedures to everyday situations," they will probably think about and study mathematics very differently than if we were to tell them to "know all the definitions by heart."

Have you ever been in a situation where you couldn't figure out what a teacher expected you to learn? Do you remember feeling confused, frustrated, or otherwise "lost" in that situation?

Choosing Appropriate Objectives

School districts typically identify numerous objectives for students at different grade levels. Yet as teachers, we will undoubtedly add our own objectives to any list that the school district provides. As we do so, we may want to consult national or international standards in the discipline, as well as classifications (*taxonomies*) of knowledge and skills that have been developed by educators.

National and international standards. Many discipline-specific professional groups have established **standards** for their discipline—general descriptions of the knowledge and skills that students should achieve and the characteristics that students' accomplishments should reflect. These standards vary considerably in specificity and in their focus on knowledge versus skills, as the following two examples illustrate:

Example from the *National Science Education Standards* (1996):

As a result of their activities in grades 5–8, all students should develop understanding of

- Structure and function in living systems
- Reproduction and heredity
- Regulation and behavior
- Populations and ecosystems
- Diversity and adaptations of organisms (p. 155)

Example from *Geography for Life: National Geography Standards* (National Geographic Education Project, 1994):

By the end of the twelfth grade, the student should know and understand how to . . . systematically locate and gather geographic information from a variety of primary and secondary sources, as exemplified by being able to

- Gather data in the field by multiple processes—observing, identifying, naming, describing, organizing, sketching, interviewing, recording, measuring
- Gather data in the classroom and library from maps, photographs, videos, and other media (e.g., CD-ROM), charts, aerial photographs, and other nonbook sources, and then use the data to identify, name, describe, organize, sketch, measure, and evaluate items of geographic interest
- Gather data by spatial sampling in both secondary sources and the field . . .
- Use quantitative measures (e.g., means, medians, and modes) to describe data (p. 53)

Currently, no data exist to indicate that the use of such standards actually improves student achievement (Wolf, 1998) or that meeting the standards enhances students' later performance in the workforce (Levin, 1998). Nevertheless, standards typically reflect the combined thinking of many experts in a discipline and so almost certainly reflect the best of what the discipline has to offer. Figure 13.3 presents Web sites at which you can find standards for a variety of academic subject areas.

Taxonomies of knowledge and skills. We don't necessarily want to limit our objectives just to the acquisition and use of information—in other words, to the **cognitive domain**. Other important objectives might involve body movements and actions (the **psychomotor domain**), and still others might involve students' feelings, attitudes, and values about what they learn (the **affective domain**). Educators have developed taxonomies in each of these domains that describe a variety of possible educational objectives; Table 13.1 presents three classic

Why is the third domain called *affective*?

FIGURE 13.3 Web sites for standards in various academic disciplines

Content Domain	Organization	Internet Address	Once you get there . . .[a]
Civics and government	Center for Civic Education	http://www.civiced.org	Go to *Curricular Materials.*
English and language arts	National Council of Teachers of English	http://www.ncte.org/standards	Click on *The Standards.*
Foreign language	American Council on the Teaching of Foreign Language	http://www.actfl.org	Go to *Publications.*
Geography	National Council for Geographic Education	http://www.ncge.org	Scroll down the *Jump to page* menu and select *Standards.*
Health, physical education, and dance	American Alliance for Health, Physical Education, Recreation and Dance	http://www.aahperd.org	Type "Standards" in the search box.
History	National Center for History in the Schools	http://www.sscnet.ucla.edu/nchs	Click on *History Standards.*
Mathematics	National Council of Teachers of Mathematics	http://www.nctm.org	Click on *NCTM Standards.*
Music	National Association for Music Education	http://www.menc.org	Select *Music Standards* from the *Resources* menu.
Science	National Academy of Sciences	http://www.nap.edu/readingroom/books/nses/html	—
Visual arts	National Art Education Association	www.getty.edu/artsednet/resources/Scope/Standards/national.html[b]	—

Note. For an example of a school district's local standards in many content domains, go to the site of the Madison, Wisconsin, Metropolitan School District at http://www.madison.k12.wi.us. When you get there, click on *Curricular Standards.*

[a]These steps worked for me when I completed this chapter in November, 2001. Given the dynamic nature of many Web sites, you may find that you have to do something different when you get to the site in question.

[b]The NAEA site does not list the standards; however, you can find them here.

ones. Although certainly not exhaustive lists, such taxonomies can nevertheless give us an idea of the kinds of objectives we may want to consider (Krathwohl, 1994).

Despite such standards and taxonomies, teachers, parents, taxpayers, and even experts cannot always agree on the instructional objectives that students of various age levels should achieve. For example, some constituencies ask us to increase students' factual knowledge—a perspective sometimes referred to as "back to the basics" or "cultural literacy" (e.g., Hirsch, 1996). Yet others encourage us to foster higher-level thinking skills such as problem solving and critical thinking and to help students develop the "habits of mind" (e.g., scientific reasoning, drawing inferences from historical documents) central to various academic disciplines (P. A. Alexander, 1997; Berliner, 1997; L. S. Shulman & Quinlan, 1996). As teachers, we must remember that, at least at the present, there is no definitive list of objectives for any age-group. We will ultimately have to tailor our instructional objectives to the particular characteristics of our students and to the particular expectations of the schools, communities, and cultures in which we teach.

Developing Useful Objectives

EXPERIENCING FIRSTHAND *Being a Good Citizen*

Consider this instructional objective:

Students will learn and practice principles of good citizenship.

Write down at least three implications of this objective for your own classroom practice.

TABLE 13.1

COMPARE/CONTRAST

Writing Objectives at Different Levels and in Different Domains

LEVEL AND DEFINITION	EXAMPLES
The Cognitive Domain (Bloom's Taxonomy) (adapted from Bloom, Engelhart, Furst, Hill, & Krathwohl, 1956)	
1. *Knowledge*: Rote memorizing of information in a basically word-for-word fashion	• Reciting definitions of terms • Remembering lists of items
2. *Comprehension*: Translating information into one's own words	• Rewording a definition • Paraphrasing a rule
3. *Application*: Using information in a new situation	• Applying mathematical principles to the solution of word problems • Applying psychological theories of learning to educational practice
4. *Analysis*: Breaking information down into its constituent parts	• Discovering the assumptions underlying a philosophical essay • Identifying fallacies in a logical argument
5. *Synthesis*: Constructing something new by integrating several pieces of information	• Developing a theory • Presenting a logical defense of a particular viewpoint within a debate
6. *Evaluation*: Placing a value judgment on data	• Critiquing a theory • Examining the internal and external validity of an experiment
The Psychomotor Domain (adapted from Harrow, 1972)	
1. *Reflex movements*: Responding to a stimulus involuntarily, without conscious thought	• Ducking to avoid being hit by an oncoming object • Shifting weight to help maintain one's balance
2. *Basic-fundamental movements*: Making basic voluntary movements directed toward a particular purpose	• Walking • Holding a pencil
3. *Perceptual abilities*: Responding appropriately to information received through the senses	• Following a moving object with one's eyes • Maintaining eye-hand coordination
4. *Physical abilities*: Developing general abilities in the areas of endurance, strength, flexibility, and agility	• Running a long distance • Exercising with weights • Changing direction quickly
5. *Skilled movements*: Performing a complex action with some proficiency or mastery	• Swimming • Throwing a football • Sawing a piece of wood
6. *Nondiscursive communication*: Communicating feelings and emotions through bodily actions	• Doing pantomime • Dancing to communicate the mood of a musical piece
The Affective Domain (adapted from Krathwohl, Bloom, & Masia, 1964)	
1. *Receiving*: Being aware of, or paying attention to, something	• Recognizing that there may be two sides to a story • Knowing that there are differences among people of different cultural backgrounds
2. *Responding*: Making an active and willing response to something	• Obeying playground rules • Reading books for pleasure
3. *Valuing*: Consistently demonstrating interest in a particular activity so that ongoing involvement or commitment in the activity is reflected	• Writing a letter to a newspaper regarding an issue one feels strongly about • Consistently eating a balanced diet
4. *Organization*: Integrating a new value into one's existing set of values and building a value system	• Forming judgments about the directions in which society should move • Setting priorities for one's life
5. *Characterization by a value or value complex*: Consistently behaving in accordance with an organized value system and integrating that system into a total philosophy of life	• Perceiving situations objectively, realistically, and with tolerance • Relying increasingly on scientific methods to answer questions about the world and society

Certainly good citizenship is a goal toward which all students should strive. But did you find yourself having trouble translating the objective into specific things you might do in the classroom? Did you also find yourself struggling with what the term *good citizenship* means (honesty? empathy? involvement in school activities? all of the above?)? The "good citizenship" objective is nothing more than *word magic*: It looks great at first glance but really doesn't give us specific information about what we want students to achieve (Dyer, 1967).

Ideally, we should develop instructional objectives that can guide us as we plan instructional activities and assessment procedures. Following are several strategies for developing useful objectives:

■ *Include objectives at varying degrees of complexity and sophistication.* The taxonomies presented in Table 13.1 include activities that range from very simple to fairly complex. For instance, the taxonomy for the cognitive domain (often called **Bloom's taxonomy**) includes both lower-level skills (knowledge, comprehension) and higher-level skills (application, analysis, synthesis, evaluation). We will undoubtedly want to include *both* kinds of skills in our objectives. As an illustration, consider these objectives for a lesson on the physics of light:

- Students will describe laws related to the reflection and refraction of light.
- Students will identify examples of reflection and refraction in their own lives (e.g., mirrors, eyeglasses).
- Students will use the law of reflection and laws of geometry to determine the actual location of objects viewed in a mirror.
- Students will use the law of refraction to explain how microscopes and telescopes make objects appear larger.

We will usually want to include higher-level skills, such as application and analysis, in our instructional objectives.

Although all four objectives lie within the cognitive domain, they reflect different levels of that domain. The first objective focuses exclusively on knowledge of separate facts that students might conceivably learn by rote, in isolation from anything else they know. But the other three objectives, which involve application and analysis, should encourage students to engage in meaningful learning and can therefore promote effective concept learning, transfer, and problem solving.

■ *Focus on what students should do, not on what teachers should do.* Consider these goals for a unit on soccer:

- Describe the rules of the game.
- Show students how to kick, dribble, and pass the ball.
- Teach the playing positions (e.g., center forward, goalkeeper) and the responsibilities of players in each position.

The problem with these goals is that they tell us only what the teacher will do during instruction; they tell us nothing about what students should be able to do as a result of that instruction. Useful objectives focus on what students will do rather than on what the teacher will do (Gronlund, 2000). With this point in mind, let's consider some alternative objectives for our soccer unit:

- Students will describe the basic rules of the game and identify the procedures to be followed in various situations (e.g., when a player touches the ball with an arm or hand, when the ball goes out of bounds).
- Students will demonstrate appropriate ways of kicking, dribbling, and passing the ball.
- Students will identify the eleven playing positions and describe the roles of players in each position.

Here we have refocused our objectives on student accomplishments; in other words, we have described the knowledge and skills we want our students to acquire during their unit on soccer.

■ *Describe the expected outcomes of instruction.* Consider these objectives for a French class:

- Students will study the meanings of French words.

- Students will practice pronouncing French words.
- Students will learn how to conjugate French verbs.

These objectives describe what students will do during French class; in other words, they describe learning *processes*. Yet objectives are usually more helpful when they tell us what students should be able to do at the end of instruction—in other words, when they describe *outcomes* (Gronlund, 2000). With this point in mind, we might revise our French class objectives as follows:

- Students will give the English meanings of French words.
- Students will pronounce French words correctly.
- Students will correctly conjugate common French verbs in the present and past tenses.

In past years many behaviorists recommended that we describe desired objectives using specific, observable behaviors (e.g., *recite, define, perform*); essentially, they were suggesting that we apply the concept of *terminal behavior* (see Chapter 9) when we develop our objectives. Such objectives can often be quite helpful for a single unit or lesson; for instance, the objectives for a soccer unit presented earlier are fairly specific and might help us keep our focus. But particularly when we look at what we want to accomplish over a lengthy period of time—perhaps a month, a semester, or the school year—too much emphasis on specific behaviors can lead to very long lists of relatively trivial outcomes (R. L. Linn & Gronlund, 2000; Newmann, 1997; Popham, 1995).

Ultimately, we must adjust our level of specificity to the time frame in question. If we are developing general objectives to guide us over the long run, we may want to omit any reference to specific knowledge or skills. One workable approach is to describe a few general and relatively abstract objectives (perhaps three to ten items) and then list examples of behaviors that reflect each one (Gronlund, 2000). The following objectives illustrate this approach:

Demonstrates thinking skills in reading.

- Distinguishes between main ideas and supporting details.
- Distinguishes between facts and opinions.
- Distinguishes between facts and inferences.
- Identifies cause-effect relations.
- Identifies errors in reasoning.
- Distinguishes between valid and invalid conclusions.
- Identifies assumptions underlying conclusions. . . .

Prepares a plan for an experiment.

- Identifies the problem to be solved.
- Formulates questions relevant to the problem.
- Formulates hypotheses in appropriate verbal or mathematical forms.
- Describes controls for variables.
- Formulates experimental procedures.
- Formulates observation and measurement procedures.
- Describes the methods of data analysis.
- Describes how the results will be presented. (objectives from Gronlund, 2000, p. 52)

Obviously, not all facets of thinking skills in reading or planning for experiments are identified, but the examples listed give both us and our students a good idea of the kinds of behaviors that reflect achievement of each objective.

■ *Identify both short-term and long-term goals.* Ideally, our instructional goals should include both **short-term objectives**—those that can be accomplished within a limited period of time (perhaps within a single lesson or unit, and certainly within a single school year)—and **long-term objectives**—those that require years of instruction and practice before they are achieved (Brophy & Alleman, 1991; N. S. Cole, 1990; Gronlund, 2000). When we want our students to use effective learning strategies as they study, read critically rather than take everything at face value, and apply scientific methods as they try to understand and explain the world around them, we are setting long-term objectives.

Some short-term objectives are "minimum essentials": Students *must* accomplish them before proceeding to the next unit, course, or grade level (Gronlund, 2000). For example, elementary school students must know how to add before they move to multiplication, and high school students must know the symbols for the chemical elements before they learn how to symbolize chemical reactions. In contrast, many long-term objectives can be thought of as "developmental" in nature: They include skills and abilities that continue to evolve and improve throughout the school years, and perhaps into adulthood as well (Gronlund, 2000). Yet even when long-term objectives cannot be completely accomplished within the course of students' formal education, they are often among the most important ones for us to set for our students and must therefore have a prominent place in our list of objectives.

■ *Incorporate opportunities for self-regulation and self-determination.* On some occasions, it is both appropriate and desirable for our students to identify their *own* objectives. For example, different students might choose different authors to read, different athletic skills to master, or different art media to use. By allowing students to establish some of their own objectives, we are encouraging the *goal setting* that, from the perspective of social cognitive theory, is an important aspect of self-regulation. We are also fostering the sense of *self-determination* that many theorists believe is so critical for intrinsic motivation.

How do we break down a large instructional task—for example, a course in government, a unit on basketball, or a driver education class—into specific objectives? Several procedures known collectively as *task analysis* can help us analyze the components of a complex topic or skill.

Conducting a Task Analysis

Consider these five teachers:

Ms. Begay plans to teach her third graders how to solve arithmetic word problems. She also wants to help her students learn more effectively from the things they read.

Mr. Marzano, a middle school physical education teacher, is beginning a unit on basketball. He wants his students to develop enough proficiency in the sport to feel comfortable playing both on organized school basketball teams and in less formal games with friends and neighbors.

Ms. Flores, an eighth-grade social studies teacher, is going to introduce the intricacies of the federal judicial system to her classes.

Mr. Wu, a junior high school music teacher, needs to teach his new trumpet students how to play a recognizable version of *Seventy-Six Trombones* in time for the New Year's Day parade.

Mr. McKenzie must teach the students in his high school driver education class how to drive a car safely through the city streets.

These teachers have something in common: They want to teach complex topics or skills. All five should probably conduct a **task analysis:** They should identify the specific knowledge and behaviors necessary to master the subject matter in question. Such a task analysis can then guide them as they select the most appropriate methods and sequence in which to teach that subject matter.

Figure 13.4 illustrates three general approaches to task analysis (Jonassen, Hannum, & Tessmer, 1989):

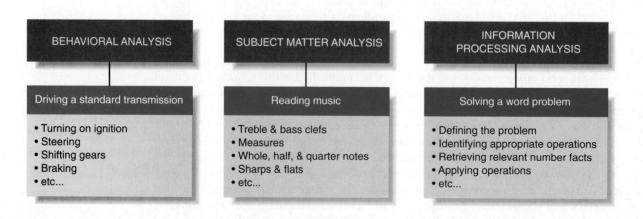

FIGURE 13.4 Three ways of analyzing a task

- *Behavioral analysis.* One way of analyzing a complex task is to identify the specific behaviors required to perform it (much as a behaviorist might do). For example, Mr. Marzano can identify the specific physical movements involved in dribbling, passing, and shooting a basketball. Mr. McKenzie can identify the actions required in driving an automobile with a standard transmission—turning on the ignition, steering, accelerating, stepping on the clutch, shifting gears, releasing the clutch, and braking. And Mr. Wu can identify the behaviors that students must master to play a trumpet successfully—holding the instrument with the fingers placed appropriately on the valves, blowing correctly into the mouthpiece, and so on.

- *Subject matter analysis.* Another approach is to break down the subject matter into the specific topics, concepts, and principles that it includes. To illustrate, Ms. Flores can identify various aspects of the judicial system (concepts such as "innocent until proven guilty" and "reasonable doubt," the roles that judges and juries play, etc.) and their interrelationships. Mr. Wu, who needs to teach his new trumpet students how to read music as well as how to play the instrument, can identify the basic elements of written music that students must know to interpret written music: the difference between the treble and bass clefs, the number of beats associated with different kinds of notes, and so on.

  Subject matter analysis is especially important when the subject matter being taught includes many interrelated ideas and concepts. From the perspective of cognitive psychology, we can help students learn class material more meaningfully, organize it better in their long-term memories, and remember it more effectively if we teach them the interconnections among various ideas and concepts along with the ideas and concepts themselves.

- *Information processing analysis.* A third approach, using a cognitive perspective once again, is to specify the cognitive processes involved in a task. To illustrate, Ms. Begay can identify the mental processes involved in successfully solving an arithmetic word problem, such as correct classification (encoding) of the problem (determining what operations—addition, subtraction, and so on—to perform) and rapid retrieval of basic number facts. Similarly, she can identify some specific cognitive strategies useful in reading comprehension, such as finding main ideas, learning meaningfully, elaborating, and summarizing.

EXPERIENCING FIRSTHAND   *Making a Peanut Butter Sandwich*

Conduct a task analysis for the process of making a peanut butter sandwich:

1. Decide whether your approach should be a behavioral analysis, a subject matter analysis, or an information processing analysis.
2. Now, using the approach you've selected, break the sandwich-making task into a number of small, "teachable" steps.

Conducting task analyses for complex skills and topics has at least two advantages (Desberg & Taylor, 1986; Jonassen et al., 1989). First, when we identify a task's specific components—whether those components be behaviors, concepts and ideas, or cognitive processes—we have a better sense of what things our students need to learn and the order in which they can most effectively learn them. For example, Mr. McKenzie must teach his driver education students how to control the clutch before he can teach them how to shift gears, and Mr. Wu must teach his trumpet students how to blow into the mouthpiece before he can teach them how to play different notes. At the same time, we may find that certain skills or topics we thought were important are actually *not* important. For example, a science teacher may realize that learning the history of science, though possibly having value in its own right, has little to do with how well students can apply scientific principles.

A second advantage in conducting a task analysis is that it helps us choose appropriate instructional strategies. Different tasks—and perhaps even different components of a single task—may require different approaches to instruction. For example, if one necessary component of solving arithmetic word problems is the rapid retrieval of math facts from memory, then repeated practice of these facts may be critical for developing automaticity. If another component of solving these problems is identifying the appropriate operation to apply in various situations, then promoting a true understanding of mathematical concepts and principles (perhaps by using concrete manipulatives or authentic activities) is essential.

Sometimes a task analysis will lead us to conclude that we can most effectively teach a complex task by teaching some or all of its components separately from one another. For instance, Mr. Wu may ask his beginning trumpet students to practice blowing into the mouthpiece correctly without worrying about the specific notes they produce. Yet on other occasions, it may be more appropriate to teach the desired knowledge and behaviors entirely within the context of the overall task; by doing so, we make the subject matter more meaningful for our students. For instance, Ms. Begay should almost certainly teach her students the processes involved in learning effectively from reading materials—elaborating, summarizing, and so on—primarily within the context of authentic reading tasks.

A task analysis of a topic or skill can help us identify the specific things we should teach and appropriate strategies for teaching them.

Developing a Lesson Plan

Once they have identified their goals for instruction, and perhaps conducted a task analysis as well, effective teachers develop a lesson plan to guide them during instruction. A lesson plan typically includes the following:

- The objective(s) of instruction
- The instructional strategies used, and in what sequence
- Instructional materials (e.g., textbooks, handouts) and equipment required
- The assessment method(s) planned

Any lesson plan should, of course, take into account the students who will be learning—their developmental levels, prior knowledge, cultural backgrounds, and so on.

As a beginning teacher, you will probably want to develop a fairly detailed lesson plan that describes how you are going to help your students learn the subject matter in question (Calderhead, 1996; Sternberg & Horvath, 1995). For instance, when I taught middle school geography, I spent many hours each week writing down the information, examples, questions, and student activities I wanted to use during the following week (one of my early lessons appears in the *Study Guide and Reader* that accompanies this book). But as you gain experience teaching certain topics, you will learn which strategies work effectively and which do not, and you may use some of the effective ones frequently enough that you can retrieve them quickly and easily from long-term memory. As time goes on, you will find that planning lessons becomes far less time-consuming and that you can do a lot of your planning in your head rather than on paper (Calderhead, 1996).

We should think of lesson plans more as guides than as recipes—in other words, as a general plan of attack that we can and should adjust as the situation warrants (Calderhead, 1996). For instance, during the course of a lesson, we may find that our students have less prior knowledge than we realized, and so we may have to "back up" and teach material we thought they had already mastered. Or, if our students express curiosity or have intriguing insights about a particular topic, we may want to spend more time exploring that topic than we had originally intended.

As we proceed through the school year, our long-range plans will also change somewhat. For instance, we may find that our task analyses of desired knowledge and skills were overly simplistic. Or we may discover that the expectations we have for students' achievement, as reflected in the instructional objectives we've developed, are either unrealistically high or unnecessarily low. We must continually revise our plans as instruction proceeds and as classroom assessments reveal how well our students are learning and achieving.

In planning our lessons, we must, of course, choose instructional strategies that are suitable for our objectives. As we examine various strategies in the pages that follow, we will identify the circumstances in which each one might be most appropriate and effective.

Expository Approaches

Without a doubt, the most widely used approach to teaching is **expository instruction**: Information is presented (*exposed*) in essentially the same form that students are expected to learn it. Ms. Minichiello's lesson on the Oregon Trail has elements of expository instruction: She gives her students reading materials about how the settlers packed for the long trip west, and she shows photographs depicting the inside of a typical covered wagon. Some forms of expository instruction are largely "one-way" in nature, in that information goes primarily from teacher to student; textbooks are the best example of such one-way communication. Other forms are more interactive, in that they incorporate an exchange of information between teacher (or perhaps a "virtual" teacher, such as a computer) and student. In this section we consider several instructional formats and methods that are primarily expository: lectures and textbooks, mastery learning, direct instruction, computer-based instruction, and online research.[3]

Educational videos and field trips are two additional forms of expository instruction. What particular benefits might these forms of instruction have?

Lectures and Textbooks

Some theorists have criticized lectures and textbooks for putting students in a passive role. For instance, from a behaviorist perspective, students learn only when they are actively making responses (and perhaps getting reinforced for those responses), and students make very few observable responses when they sit quietly listening to a lecture or reading a textbook (Skinner, 1968). However, many cognitivists argue that students are often *mentally* active during such seemingly passive activities (Ausubel et al., 1978; Pressley, 1995; Weinert & Helmke, 1995). From the perspective of cognitive psychology, the degree to which students learn from expository instruction depends on how they process information—that is, on the particular cognitive responses they make. The more students pay attention, and the more they engage in meaningful learning, organization, elaboration, and so on, the more they are likely to benefit from the lectures they hear and the textbooks they read.

Unfortunately, lectures and textbooks don't always present information in ways that facilitate learning. For instance, you can undoubtedly think of high school or college instructors you've had whose lectures were dry, disorganized, confusing, or in some other way *non*motivating and *non*informative. And analyses of school textbooks in such diverse disciplines as history, geography, and science have found that the focus of most texts is on teaching specific facts, with little attention to helping students learn these facts in a meaningful way (Bochenhauer, 1990; Calfee & Chambliss, 1988; Chambliss, Calfee, & Wong, 1990; McKeown & Beck, 1990).

What specific techniques can we use to help our students learn from our classroom lectures and from the textbook readings we assign? The following exercise might give you a few ideas about techniques that work for *you* as a student.

EXPERIENCING FIRSTHAND   *Finding Pedagogy in the Book*

1. Look back at two or three of the chapters you've already read in this book. Find several places where specific things that I've done have helped you learn and remember the material more effectively. What specific techniques did I use to facilitate your cognitive processing?
2. In those same chapters, can you find places where you had difficulty processing the material presented? What might I have done differently in such instances?

I'm hoping that the Experiencing Firsthand exercises and some of the questions in the margins have helped you relate new topics to your own knowledge and experiences. Perhaps some of the graphics, tables, and summaries have helped you organize concepts and principles. Perhaps the Interpreting Artifacts and Interactions features have encouraged you to elaborate on and apply what you were reading. If you've found certain parts of the books particularly troublesome, I'm hoping you'll let me know.[4]

Researchers have identified several factors that facilitate students' learning from lectures, textbooks, and other forms of expository instruction. Table 13.2 describes and illustrates these factors as general principles that can help us whenever we need to present information in a

---

[3]Many theorists use the term *expository instruction* primarily in reference to lectures and textbooks. I am using the term more broadly to refer to any approach that centers around the *transmission* of information from expert (e.g., classroom teacher, textbook writer, computer software designer) to student.

[4]I'm always eager to hear my readers' suggestions for improving the book (e-mail address: jormrod@ttlc.net).

TABLE 13.2   PRINCIPLES/ASSUMPTIONS

Principles of Expository Instruction

PRINCIPLE	EDUCATIONAL IMPLICATION	EXAMPLE
An **advance organizer**—a verbal or graphic introduction that lays out the general organizational framework of the material—helps students organize and interrelate the things they learn.	Introduce a new unit by describing the major ideas and concepts to be discussed and showing how they are interrelated.	Introduce a unit on vertebrates by saying something like this: "Vertebrates all have backbones. We will be talking about five phyla of vertebrates—mammals, birds, reptiles, amphibians, and fish—which differ from one another in several ways, including whether their members are warm-blooded or cold-blooded; whether they have hair, scales, or feathers; and whether they lay eggs or bear live young."
Connections to prior knowledge help students learn classroom material more meaningfully, provided that their prior "knowledge" is accurate. (See the section "When Knowledge Construction Goes Awry" in Chapter 7.)	Remind students of something they already know and point out how a new idea is similar. This strategy is known as **prior knowledge activation.**	Draw an analogy between *peristalsis* (muscular contractions that push food through the digestive tract) and the process of squeezing ketchup from a packet: "You squeeze the packet near one corner and run your fingers along the length of the packet toward an opening at the other corner. When you do this, you push the ketchup through the packet, in one direction, ahead of your fingers, until it comes out of the opening" (Newby, Ertmer, & Stepich, 1994, p. 4).
An **organized presentation** of material helps students make appropriate interconnections among ideas.	Help students organize material in a particular way by presenting the information using that same organizational structure.	Use a *concept map* to depict the main concepts and ideas of a topic and their interrelationships (see the section "Organizing" in Chapter 8).
Various **signals** built into a presentation (e.g., italicized print, interspersed questions) can draw students' attention to important points.	Stress important points—for instance, by writing them on the chalkboard, asking questions about them, or simply telling students what things are most important to learn.	When assigning a textbook chapter for homework, identify several questions that students should try to answer as they read the chapter.
Visual aids help students encode material visually as well as verbally.	Illustrate new material through pictures, photographs, diagrams, maps, physical models, and demonstrations.	When describing major battles of the American Civil War, present a map illustrating where each battle took place and point out that some battles were fought in especially strategic locations.
Appropriate **pacing** gives students adequate time to process information.	Pace a presentation slowly enough that students can engage in meaningful learning, elaboration, and other effective storage processes.	Intersperse lengthy explanations with demonstrations or hands-on activities that illustrate some of the principles you are describing.
Summaries help students review and organize material and identify main ideas.	After a lecture or reading assignment, summarize the key points of the lesson.	At the end of a unit on Emily Dickinson, summarize her work by describing the characteristics that made her poetry so unique and influential.

Sources: Ausubel et al., 1978; Bulgren, Deshler, Schumaker, & Lenz, 2000; Corkill, 1992; Dansereau, 1995; Donnelly & McDaniel, 1993; E. L. Ferguson & Hegarty, 1995; Hall & O'Donnell, 1994; Hansen & Pearson, 1983; Hartley & Trueman, 1982; Krajcik, 1991; J. R. Levin & Mayer, 1993; M. C. Linn et al., 1996; R. F. Lorch, Lorch, & Inman, 1993; Mayer, 1989; Mayer & Gallini, 1990; McDaniel & Einstein, 1989; Newby et al., 1994; Pittman & Beth-Halachmy, 1997; R. E. Reynolds & Shirey, 1988; Sadoski & Paivio, 2001; Scevak, Moore, & Kirby, 1993; M. Y. Small, Lovett, & Scher, 1993; Tennyson & Cocchiarella, 1986; Wade, 1992; P. T. Wilson & Anderson, 1986; Winn, 1991; Zook, 1991; Zook & Di Vesta, 1991.

largely "one-way" fashion. Once you have examined the table, apply what you have learned in the following exercise.

INTERPRETING ARTIFACTS AND INTERACTIONS   *Apartheid*

A middle school social studies class has been studying the repressive Apartheid policy in South Africa during the last few decades of the twentieth century. At one point, the teacher asks students to compare the progression of Apartheid to the American civil rights movement during the same time period. He has his students create two parallel time lines depicting significant events in South Africa and the United States; one student's work appears at the top of the next page. As you look at the artifact, think about

- What cognitive process(es) the activity may facilitate
- What cognitive process(es) the activity does *not* necessarily facilitate

The activity clearly helps students organize events in the two countries in chronological order; it may also promote visual imagery by making verbal information more graphic. The activity does little more than these things, however. To promote maximal understanding of Apartheid in South Africa, the civil rights movement in the United States, and their possible parallels—for instance, to promote meaningful learning and elaboration about the events, as well as greater organization and visual imagery—the teacher might supplement the activity with verbal explanations of why certain events were critical, old magazine articles and newspaper editorials about injustices in the two countries, videotapes depicting Nelson Mandela or Martin Luther King, Jr., and so on.

Lectures, textbooks, and other one-way forms of instruction have a distinct advantage: They allow teachers to present information quickly and efficiently. A major *disadvantage* is that, in and of themselves, they do not allow us to assess students' progress in learning the subject matter. When we need to make sure that students master information and skills that are prerequisites for later lessons, mastery learning may be a better approach.

Mastery Learning

Imagine that a class of 27 students is beginning a unit on fractions. The class progresses through several lessons as follows:

Lesson 1

The class studies the basic idea that a fraction represents parts of a whole: The denominator indicates the number of pieces into which the whole has been divided, and the numerator indicates how many of those pieces are present. By the end of the lesson, 23 children understand what a fraction is. But Sarah, LaShaun, Jason K., and Jason M. are either partly or totally confused.

Lesson 2

The class studies the process of reducing fractions to their lowest terms. For example, ¾ can be reduced to ½, and ¹²⁄₂₀ can be reduced to ⅗. By the end of the lesson, 20 children understand the process of reducing fractions. But Alison, Reggie, and Jason S. haven't mastered the idea that they need to divide both the numerator and denominator by the same number. And of course, Sarah, LaShaun, and the other two Jasons still don't understand what fractions *are* and so have trouble with this lesson as well.

Lesson 3

The class studies the process of adding two fractions together. At this point, the students look only at situations in which the denominators are the same. For example, $\frac{2}{5} + \frac{2}{5} = \frac{4}{5}$ and $\frac{1}{20} + \frac{11}{20} = \frac{12}{20}$. By the end of the lesson, 19 children can add fractions with the same denominator. Matt, Charlie, Maria F., and Maria W. keep adding the denominators together as well as the numerators (thus figuring that $\frac{2}{5} + \frac{2}{5} = \frac{4}{10}$). And Sarah, LaShaun, Jason K., and Jason M. still don't know what fractions actually are.

Lesson 4

The class combines the processes of adding fractions and reducing fractions to their lowest terms. They must first add two fractions together and then, if necessary, reduce the sum to its lowest terms. For example, after adding $\frac{1}{20} + \frac{11}{20}$, they must reduce the sum of $\frac{12}{20}$ to $\frac{3}{5}$. Here we lose Muhammed, Aretha, and Karen because they keep forgetting to reduce the sum to lowest terms. And of course, we've already lost Sarah, LaShaun, Alison, Reggie, Matt, Charlie, the two Marias, and the three Jasons on prerequisite skills. We now have 13 of our original 27 students understanding what they are doing—less than half the class! (See Figure 13.5.)

When we move through lessons without making sure that all students master the content of each one, we lose more and more students as we go along, particularly if early lessons provide the foundation for later ones. **Mastery learning**, in which students demonstrate mastery of one topic before proceeding to the next, minimizes the likelihood that we leave students in the dust

Can you recall a time when you were unable to master something critical for your later classroom success? How did you feel in that situation?

FIGURE 13.5 Sequential nature of mastery learning

Students	Lesson 1: Concept of Fraction	Lesson 2: Reducing to Lowest Terms (Builds on Lesson 1)	Lesson 3: Adding Fractions with Same Denominator (Builds on Lesson 1)	Lesson 4: Adding Fractions with Different Denominators (Builds on Lessons 2 & 3)
Sarah	−	−	−	−
LaShaun	−	−	−	−
Jason K.	−	−	−	−
Jason M.	−	−	−	−
Alison	+	−	+	−
Reggie	+	−	+	−
Jason S.	+	−	+	−
Matt	+	+	−	−
Charlie	+	+	−	−
Maria F.	+	+	−	−
Maria W.	+	+	−	−
Muhammed	+	+	+	−
Aretha	+	+	+	−
Karen	+	+	+	−
Kevin	+	+	+	+
Nori	+	+	+	+
Marcy	+	+	+	+
Janelle	+	+	+	+
Joyce	+	+	+	+
Ming Tang	+	+	+	+
Georgette	+	+	+	+
LaVeda	+	+	+	+
Mark	+	+	+	+
Seth	+	+	+	+
Joanne	+	+	+	+
Rita	+	+	+	+
Shauna	+	+	+	+

Students become "lost" when they fail to master important building blocks on which later material depends. For these students, mastery is indicated by a solid line and nonmastery is indicated by a dotted line. Notice how we have lost 14 of the 27 students by the end of Lesson 4.

as we move to increasingly challenging material (e.g., Bloom, 1981; Guskey, 1985; Hunter, 1982; J. F. Lee & Pruitt, 1984). This approach is based on three underlying assumptions:

- Almost every student can learn a particular topic to mastery.
- Some students need more time to master a topic than others.
- Some students need more assistance than others.

As you can see, mastery learning represents a very optimistic approach to instruction: It assumes that most children *can* learn school subject matter if they are given sufficient time and instruction to do so.

Mastery learning usually includes the following components:

1. *Small, discrete units.* The subject matter is broken up into a number of separate units or lessons, with each one covering a limited amount of material and aimed at accomplishing a small number (perhaps one to three) of instructional objectives.
2. *A logical sequence.* Units are sequenced such that basic, foundational concepts and procedures are learned first and more complex concepts and procedures are learned later. For example, a unit in which students learn what a fraction is would obviously come before a unit in which they learn how to add two fractions.
3. *Demonstration of mastery at the completion of each unit.* Before moving from one unit to the next, students must show that they have mastered the current unit, often by taking a test on the content of that unit. (Here is an example of how instruction and assessment often work hand in hand.)
4. *A concrete, observable criterion for mastery of each unit.* Mastery of a topic is defined in specific and concrete terms. For example, to "pass" a unit on adding fractions with the same denominator, students might have to answer at least 90 percent of test items correctly.
5. *Additional "remedial" activities for students needing extra help or practice to attain mastery.* Students do not always demonstrate mastery on the first try. Additional support and resources (perhaps alternative approaches to instruction, different materials, workbooks, study groups, and individual tutoring) are provided for students who need them.

Students engaged in mastery learning often proceed through the various units at their own speed; hence, different students may be studying different units at any given time. But it is also possible for an entire class to proceed through a sequence at the same time: Students who master a unit earlier than their classmates can pursue various enrichment activities, or they can serve as tutors for those still working on the unit (Block, 1980; Guskey, 1985).

We find justification for mastery learning in several theoretical perspectives. Operant conditioning theorists tell us that complex behaviors are often more easily learned through *shaping,* whereby a simple response is reinforced until it occurs frequently (i.e., until it is mastered), then a slightly more difficult response is reinforced, and so on. Cognitive psychologists point out that information and skills that need to be retrieved rapidly or used in complex problem-solving situations must be practiced and learned thoroughly so that *automaticity* is attained. Finally, as social cognitive theorists have noted, the ability to perform a particular task successfully and easily is likely to enhance students' sense of self-efficacy for performing similar tasks.

Research indicates that mastery learning has several advantages over nonmastery approaches. In particular, students tend to

Considering the subject matter you will be teaching, what important information and skills would you want your students to master?

- Learn more and perform better on classroom assessments
- Maintain better study habits, studying regularly rather than procrastinating and cramming
- Enjoy their classes and teachers more
- Have greater interest in the subject
- Have more self-confidence about their ability to learn the subject
  (Block & Burns, 1976; Born & Davis, 1974; C. C. Kulik, Kulik, & Bangert-Drowns, 1990; J. A. Kulik, Kulik, & Cohen, 1979; Shuell, 1996)

Mastery learning is most appropriate when the subject matter is hierarchical in nature—that is, certain concepts and skills provide the foundation for future learning. When instructional objectives deal with such basics as word recognition, rules of grammar, addition and subtraction, or key scientific concepts, instruction designed to promote mastery learning may be in order. Nevertheless, the very notion of mastery may be *inappropriate* for some of our long-term objectives. As noted earlier, skills such as critical reading, scientific reasoning, and creative writing may continue to improve over the years without ever really being mastered.

Direct Instruction

An approach incorporating elements of both expository instruction and mastery learning is **direct instruction**, which uses a variety of techniques designed to keep students continually and actively engaged in learning and applying classroom subject matter (Englemann & Carnine, 1982; R. M. Gagné, 1985; Rosenshine & Stevens, 1986; Tarver, 1992; Weinert & Helmke, 1995). To some extent, direct instruction is based on behaviorist principles of learning; for instance, it requires learners to make frequent overt responses and provides immediate reinforcement of correct responses through teacher feedback. But it also considers principles from cognitive psychology, including the importance of attention and long-term memory storage processes in learning, the limited capacity of working memory, and the value of learning basic skills to automaticity (Rosenshine & Stevens, 1986).

Different theorists describe and implement direct instruction somewhat differently. But in general, this approach involves small and carefully sequenced steps, fast pacing, and a great deal of teacher-student interaction. Each lesson typically involves most or all of the following components (Rosenshine & Stevens, 1986):

1. *Review of previously learned material.* The teacher reviews relevant content from previous lessons, checks homework assignments involving that content and, if necessary, reteaches any information or skills that students have apparently not yet mastered.
2. *Statement of the goals of the lesson.* The teacher describes one or more objectives that students should accomplish during the new lesson.
3. *Presentation of new material in small, carefully sequenced steps.* The teacher presents a small amount of information or a specific skill using an expository approach—perhaps through a verbal explanation, modeling, and one or more examples. The teacher may also provide an advance organizer, ask questions, or in other ways scaffold students' efforts to process and remember the material.
4. *Guided student practice and assessment after each step.* Students have frequent opportunities to practice what they are learning, perhaps by answering questions, solving problems, or performing modeled procedures. The teacher gives hints during students' early responses, provides immediate feedback about their performance, makes suggestions about how to improve, and provides remedial instruction as needed.
5. *Assessment of student progress.* After students have completed guided practice, the teacher checks to be sure they have mastered the information or skill in question, perhaps by having them answer a series of follow-up questions or summarize what they've learned.
6. *Independent practice.* Once students have acquired some mastery (e.g., by answering 80 percent of questions correctly), they engage in further practice either independently or in small, cooperative groups. By doing so, they work toward achieving automaticity for the material in question.
7. *Frequent follow-up reviews.* The teacher provides many opportunities for students to review previously learned material over the course of the school year—perhaps through homework assignments, writing assignments, or paper-pencil quizzes.

The teacher proceeds back and forth among these steps as necessary to ensure that all students are truly mastering the subject matter.

Direct instruction typically involves many opportunities to practice new skills, often with considerable teacher guidance in the early stages.

Like mastery learning, direct instruction is most suitable for teaching information and skills that are well-defined and should be taught in a step-by-step sequence (Rosenshine & Stevens, 1986). Because of the high degree of teacher-student interaction, it is often more easily implemented with small groups of students rather than with an entire classroom. Under such circumstances, research indicates that it can be a highly effective instructional technique, leading to substantial gains in achievement of both basic skills and higher-level thinking processes, high student interest and self-efficacy for the subject matter in question, and low rates of student misbehavior (Rosenshine & Stevens, 1986; Tarver, 1992; Weinert & Helmke, 1995).

One advantage of both mastery learning and direct instruction approaches is that because students must demonstrate mastery at the completion of each unit, they receive frequent feedback about the progress they are making. Yet another approach—computer-based instruction—may provide even *more* frequent feedback, as we shall see now.

Computer-Based Instruction

As we have seen, behaviorists argue that students learn effectively only when they are actively and physically involved in a learning activity. In behaviorism's heyday in the middle decades of the twentieth century, B. F. Skinner (1954, 1968) suggested an approach known as **programmed instruction**, which incorporates three principles of operant conditioning as it presents new material:

1. *Active responding.* The learner is continually making responses—for instance, by answering questions or filling in blanks in incomplete statements.
2. *Shaping.* Instruction begins with information the learner already knows, then it breaks new information into tiny pieces and presents them one at a time over the course of a lesson. As the learner acquires more information and answers questions of increasing difficulty, the desired terminal behavior (mastery of the subject matter) is gradually shaped.
3. *Immediate reinforcement.* Because instruction involves such a gradual progression through the material, mastery of each piece is almost guaranteed. Thus, the learner has a high probability of responding correctly to the questions asked and is reinforced immediately by getting feedback that the answers are correct.

You can find an example of paper-pencil programmed instruction in "A Shocking Lesson" in the *Study Guide and Reader*.

In the 1950s and 1960s, programmed instruction was typically presented through books and other printed materials. But with the increasing availability and affordability of computers in the 1970s and 1980s, most programmed instruction was presented by means of computers and so became known as **computer-assisted instruction (CAI)**.

Contemporary educational computer programs often incorporate cognitivist principles as well as those of behaviorism. For example, effective programs often take steps to capture and hold students' *attention,* elicit students' *prior knowledge* about a topic, and encourage long-term retention and transfer (R. M. Gagné, Briggs, & Wager, 1992; P. F. Merrill et al., 1996). Some programs provide drill and practice of basic knowledge and skills (e.g., math facts, typing, fundamentals of music), helping students develop automaticity in these areas (P. F. Merrill et al., 1996). Yet others serve as "intelligent tutors" that skillfully guide students through complex subject matter and can anticipate and address a wide variety of learning difficulties (Lajoie & Derry, 1993). The term **computer-based instruction (CBI)** encompasses recent innovations in computer-delivered instruction as well as the more traditional CAI.

Although some computer-based instructional programs provide a fairly lockstep sequence of instruction, others do not. Perhaps, as a student, you have had experience with computer programs that allowed you to jump around from one topic to other, related topics, thereby enabling you to decide what things to study and in what order to study them. If so, then you have had experience with either hypertext or hypermedia (e.g., Jonassen, 1996; P. F. Merrill et al., 1996). **Hypertext** is a collection of computer-based verbal material that allows students to read about one topic and then proceed to related topics of their own choosing; for example, you might read a short, introductory passage about airplanes and then decide whether to proceed to more specific information about aerodynamics, the history of air travel, or military aircraft. **Hypermedia** include such other media as pictures, sound, animations, and videos as well as text; for example, some computer-based encyclopedias enable students to bounce from text to a voice message and then to a video about a particular topic. The use of hypertext and hypermedia for instructional purposes is based on the assumption that students benefit from imposing their own organization on a subject area and selecting those topics that are most personally relevant (Jonassen, 1996; R. V. Small & Grabowski, 1992). Keep in mind, however, that not all students are capable of making wise choices about what to study and in what sequence to study it. For example, they may be overwhelmed by the large number of choices the computer offers, have trouble identifying important information, or lack sufficient comprehension-monitoring skills to determine when they have mastered the material (Garhart & Hannafin, 1986; Lanza & Roselli, 1991; E. R. Steinberg, 1989).

The *Simulations in Educational Psychology and Research* CD that accompanies this book is an example of hypermedia.

Numerous research studies have documented the effectiveness of CBI: Students often have higher academic achievement and better attitudes toward their schoolwork than is true for students taught with more traditional methods (J. A. Kulik, Kulik, & Cohen, 1980; Lepper & Gurtner, 1989; P. F. Merrill et al., 1996; Roblyer, Castine, & King, 1988; Tudor, 1995;

Wise & Olson, 1998). Furthermore, students studying academic subject matter on a computer may gain an increased sense that they can control their own learning, thereby developing more intrinsic motivation to learn (Swan, Mitrani, Guerrero, Cheung, & Schoener, 1990).

Computers offer several advantages for instruction that we often cannot achieve through any other medium. For one thing, instructional programs can include animations, video clips, and spoken messages—components that are, of course, not possible with traditional printed materials. Second, a computer can record and maintain ongoing data for each of our students, including such information as how far they have progressed in the program, how often they are right and wrong, how quickly they respond, and so on. With such data, we can monitor each student's progress through the program and identify students who are having particular difficulty with the material. And, finally, a computer can be used to provide instruction when flesh-and-blood teachers are not available; for example, CBI is often used in **distance learning**—a situation in which learners receive technology-based instruction at a location physically separate from that of their instructor.

In later sections of the chapter, we will explore additional uses of computer technology. Yet keep in mind that using a computer is not, *in and of itself,* necessarily the key to better instruction (R. E. Clark, 1983). A computer can help our students achieve at higher levels only when it provides instruction that we cannot offer as easily or effectively by other means. There is little to be gained when a student is merely reading information on a computer screen instead of reading it in a textbook.

Online Research

Which uses of computer technology just described are largely *teacher-directed?* Which are more *student-directed?*

Students' access to new information through computer technology is not necessarily limited to the computer programs in our own schools and classrooms. Through telephone and cable lines, students at many schools now have access to the Internet and particularly to the *World Wide Web,* a network of computers and computer databases that can be accessed from any microcomputer with the appropriate hardware and software. For instance, my middle school geography students and I once used the U.S. Geological Survey Web site (http://www.usgs.gov) to track the path of a hurricane as it made its way through the Caribbean and up the Atlantic coast. Many government Web sites offer a wealth of information and resources for students and teachers alike (e.g., check out the U.S. Census Bureau at http://www.census.gov or the National Aeronautic and Space Administration at http://www.nasa.gov). Other public institutions, private associations, and even individual educators provide information, lesson plans, and links to other relevant Web sites; following are a few examples you might want to explore:

National Museum of Natural History
    http://www.mnh.si.edu/edu_resources.html
Educational Resources Information Center (ERIC)
    http://www.eric.edu.gov
The Knowledge Loom
    http://knowledgeloom.org/index.shtml
Kathy Schrock's Guide for Educators
    http://school.discovery.com/schrockguide

In addition, Internet *search engines,* such as Yahoo (http://www.yahoo.com) and Altavista (http://www.altavista.com), allow students and teachers to find Web sites on virtually any topic.

Educators are just beginning to explore the vast potential of the Internet for students' learning, and we still await systematic research on its potential benefits and liabilities. Considerable anecdotal evidence indicates that students often use it for beneficial purposes (e.g., finding information for research papers and oral presentations) but may sometimes venture into unproductive domains (e.g., stumbling upon Web sites that preach racist attitudes or offer pornographic images). Clearly, then, the Internet offers a mixed bag of resources, and we must carefully monitor its use in the classroom.

Hands-On Approaches

In the opening case study, Ms. Minichiello doesn't just describe the dimensions of a covered wagon; she has the students measure those dimensions for themselves and thereby get a firsthand view of a family's living space. More generally, when we talk about *hands-on* approaches, we are talking about having students actually *do* something rather than just hear or read about it. Here we look at several hands-on approaches: discovery learning, in-class activities, computer simulations and applications, homework, and authentic activities.

Discovery Learning

Think about something you've learned through your own research or experimentation. How thoroughly did you learn that information or skill? Do you think you learned it more thoroughly and understood it better than you would have if you had simply read about it in a book or heard about it from another person?

Unlike expository instruction, where information is presented in its final form, **discovery learning** is a process through which students interact with their physical or social environment—for example, by exploring and manipulating objects, performing experiments, or wrestling with questions and controversies—and derive information for themselves. Common examples of discovery learning are laboratory experiments, library research projects, and opportunities for students to learn by trial and error (e.g., as they "fiddle" with computer software, a soccer ball, or watercolor paints). Discovery learning can sometimes be incorporated into other forms of instruction; for example, the Experiencing Firsthand exercises in this very "expository" book have, I hope, helped you discover a number of important principles on your own.

Research studies indicate that people often remember and transfer information more effectively when they construct it for themselves rather than when they simply read it in expository material (de Jong & van Joolingen, 1998; McDaniel & Schlager, 1990; D. S. McNamara & Healy, 1995). We can easily explain this finding using principles of cognitive psychology (Bruner, 1961, 1966; McDaniel, Waddill, & Einstein, 1988; B. Y. White & Frederiksen, 1998). When learners discover something on their own, they typically give more thought to (process) that information or skill than they might otherwise, and so they are more likely to engage in meaningful learning. In addition, learners often learn classroom subject matter in a more complete and integrated way (i.e., they achieve greater *conceptual understanding*) when they have opportunities to explore and manipulate their environment firsthand (see Chapter 7). Furthermore, when learners *see* something as well as hear or read about it, they can encode it in long-term memory visually as well as verbally. And from a developmental perspective, many students, especially those in the elementary grades, understand concrete experiences more easily than abstract ideas (see Chapter 2).

Students may better understand scientific principles when they actually observe those principles in action.

How effective is discovery learning in a classroom context? Unfortunately, research does not give us a clear answer. Ideally, to determine whether discovery learning works better than other approaches, we would need to compare two groups of students who differ on only *one* variable: the extent to which discovery learning is a part of their instructional experience. Yet few research studies have made this crucial comparison, and the studies that have been conducted give us contradictory results. Nevertheless, some general conclusions about discovery learning can be gleaned from research findings:

- When we consider *overall academic achievement,* discovery learning is not necessarily better or worse than "traditional" (e.g., more expository) approaches to instruction; research yields mixed findings on this issue.
- When we consider *higher-level thinking skills,* discovery learning is often preferable for fostering transfer, problem solving, creativity, and self-regulated learning.
- When we consider *affective objectives,* discovery learning often promotes a more positive attitude toward teachers and schoolwork than does traditional instruction; in other words, students like school better. (E. L. Ferguson & Hegarty, 1995; Giaconia & Hedges, 1982; Marshall, 1981; Mayer, 1974, 1987; P. L. Peterson, 1979; Roughead & Scandura, 1968; Shymansky, Hedges, & Woodworth, 1990; B. Y. White & Frederiksen, 1998)

At the same time, we should note two potential problems with discovery learning (Hammer, 1997; Schauble, 1990). First, students may sometimes construct incorrect understandings from their discovery activities; for instance, they may distort or in some other way misinterpret the evidence they collect in a laboratory experiment. Second, discovery learning activities often take considerably more time than expository instruction, and teachers may feel torn between providing discovery experiences and "covering" all the school district's objectives for the year. In my own experience I've found that my students typically remember what they've learned in hands-on discovery activities so much more effectively than what they've learned through expository instruction that the extra time I've devoted to those activities has been time well spent (another instance of the *less is more* principle).

Psychologists and educators have offered numerous suggestions for making discovery learning effective (e.g., see the Into the Classroom feature "Promoting Discovery Learning"). Two general guidelines are probably most critical:

■ *Make sure students have the knowledge they need to interpret their findings appropriately.* Students are most likely to benefit from a discovery learning activity when they can draw on prior knowledge to interpret their observations (Bruner, 1966; de Jong & van Joolingen, 1998; N. Frederiksen, 1984a). For example, having students conduct experiments to determine the influence of gravity on the velocity of a falling object will typically be more beneficial if students are already familiar with the concepts *gravity* and *velocity*. As cognitive psychologists tell us, meaningful learning can occur only when students have appropriate knowledge to which they can relate new experiences. And from Vygotsky's perspective, students must ultimately tie their discoveries to the ways in which their culture interprets the world. The central concepts and principles of various academic disciplines are, indeed, a very important part of that culture.

■ *Provide some structure to guide students' discovery activities.* Young children often learn from random exploration of their environment—for example, by experimenting with, and thereby discovering the properties of, dry sand, wet sand, and water (Hutt, Tyler, Hutt, & Christopherson, 1989). At the elementary and secondary school levels, however, students are more likely to benefit from carefully planned and structured activities that help them construct appropriate interpretations (Hickey, 1997; Minstrell & Stimpson, 1996; B. Y. White & Frederiksen, 1998). In science, for example, such structure (*scaffolding*) might take the form of questions that guide students' thinking; here are three examples:

- In what ways has the culture in this petri dish changed since yesterday?
- How can we measure an object's rate of acceleration in an objective way?
- When we add these two chemicals together and then heat them, how can we be sure the *heat,* rather than some other variable, is bringing about the change that we see?

Refer back to the discussion of *cognitive apprenticeship* in Chapter 2. How might such an apprenticeship incorporate discovery learning?

The degree to which a discovery session needs to be structured depends somewhat on the reasoning and problem-solving skills of the students (de Jong & van Joolingen, 1998; B. Y. White & Frederiksen, 1998). For example, some students may have difficulty tackling vague, ill-defined problems (see Chapter 8). And many other students—perhaps those who have not yet acquired formal operational thinking capabilities—may have trouble formulating and testing hypotheses, or separating and controlling variables (see Chapter 2). Such students will probably work more effectively when they are given problems and questions that are concrete and well-defined and when they are given specific suggestions about how to proceed.

With what you have learned about discovery learning in mind, try the following exercise.

INTERPRETING ARTIFACTS AND INTERACTIONS   *Pig Lungs*

A fifth-grade class works in small groups to dissect the lungs of a pig. Afterward the students write individual lab reports describing what they have observed and learned. As you read 10-year-old Berlinda's report, consider

- What Berlinda has learned from the activity
- What Berlinda may *not* have learned from the activity

Pig Lungs Dissection

It was 10:40 a.m. on Friday November 1, 1996. We were going to dissect a set of lungs which had belonged to a pig. I could read just about everyones minds. Ew. Grose. Its bloody. This thing stinks!

Our table was given an esophogus which felt wet and smooth. The main blood vessel which felt hard, almost as though someone had stuck a toothpick inside of it. The tracea which felt felt, wet and slitely textured. The heart which, well you couldn't tell. Two lungs which felt a little pit like silly pudy. As 11:30 rolled around most of us had changed our thoughts. It was now cool, neat, and still bloody.

Berlinda has clearly learned what some of a pig's internal organs look and feel like. She has responded to the activity emotionally as well as cognitively (e.g., "grose" [gross], "cool, neat"), and this *hot cognition* will undoubtedly help her remember what she has experienced (see Chapter 11). However, there is no evidence that Berlinda has related her observations to her previous knowledge and beliefs about anatomy or tied them to an understanding of respiration in mammals. To help the students make such connections, the teacher might have asked the students to respond to questions that would guide their exploration and writing (e.g., "Do the lungs look and feel the way you thought they would?" "How do the lungs help the pig get oxygen into its body?").

In-Class Activities

Students are typically asked to accomplish a wide variety of tasks and assignments in class during the school year. For example, they might be asked to complete worksheets, solve problems, write short stories, draw pictures, practice basketball skills, play musical instruments, or perhaps (as in the opening case study) imagine trying to pack for a trip to a distant planet. Naturally, students can do only so many things in any single school year. How do we decide which activities are likely to be most beneficial to their long-term learning and achievement?

How might Ms. Minichiello's "distant planet" activity in the opening case study help students learn?

As teachers, we should, first and foremost, assign in-class activities that will help students accomplish our instructional objectives (Brophy & Alleman, 1992; W. Doyle, 1983). In some cases, these objectives may be at a "knowledge" level; for instance, we may want students to conjugate the French verb *être* ("to be"), know members of different biological classes and orders, and be familiar with current events around the globe. But in other cases, we may have higher-level objectives; for instance, we may want our students to write a persuasive essay, use scientific principles to interpret physical phenomena, or use arithmetic operations to solve real-world problems. Particularly when such higher-level objectives are involved, we will want to assign activities that help students learn classroom material in a meaningful, integrated way.

In addition to matching our in-class activities to our objectives, we are more likely to facilitate students' learning and achievement when we assign activities that

- Accommodate student diversity in abilities and interests
- Clearly define each task and its purpose
- Generate students' interest in accomplishing the task
- Begin at an appropriate difficulty level for students—ideally, presenting a task that challenges students to "stretch" their knowledge and skills (a task within students' zone of proximal development)
- Provide sufficient scaffolding to promote success
- Progress in difficulty and complexity as students become more proficient
- Provide opportunities for frequent teacher monitoring and feedback on students' progress
- Encourage students to reflect on and evaluate the work they've completed (Brophy & Alleman, 1991, 1992; Brophy & Good, 1986)

The ways in which we assess students' performance will also have an impact on what our in-class activities actually accomplish (W. Doyle, 1983). For example, if we give full credit for completing an assignment without regard to the *quality* of responses, our students may focus more on "getting the work done" than on developing a conceptual understanding of what they are studying. Yet if our criteria for acceptable performance are overly strict, we may discourage students from taking risks and making errors—risks and errors that are inevitable when students are seeking out and pursuing the challenges that will promote their cognitive growth.

Computer Simulations and Applications

Earlier we talked about computer-based instruction as a means of introducing new material. Yet we can also use computer technology to give students some valuable hands-on experiences with a variety of academic topics and skills—for instance, by using simulations and such computer tools as word processing programs, databases, and spreadsheets.

Simulations

How helpful have the simulated activities on the *Simulations in Educational Psychology and Research* CD been for your own learning?

Some computer programs promote higher-level thinking skills (e.g., problem solving) within the context of gamelike or authentic tasks. One popular software program, Where in the World Is Carmen Sandiego?, teaches geography while the student acts as a detective. Other programs provide simulations of such events as running a lemonade stand, dissecting a frog, growing plants under varying environmental conditions, or exploring the effects of various business practices. Still others present authentic problem-solving tasks; as an example, see the description of the Adventures of Jasper Woodbury series in the section "Cognitive Factors Affecting Problem Solving" in Chapter 8. Computer simulations are often both motivating and challenging (thereby keeping students on task for extended periods) and can significantly enhance students' problem-solving and scientific reasoning skills (Cognition and Technology Group at Vanderbilt, 1996; de Jong & van Joolingen, 1998; Vye et al., 1998; B. Y. White & Frederiksen, 1998).

Computer Tool Applications

What computer applications might be especially relevant to the subject matter you will be teaching?

Computer skills are essential to students in today's society. For example, many professions may require expertise in such *computer tools* as word processing, desktop publishing, databases, and spreadsheets. Hence, our instructional objectives may sometimes include computer skills in addition to skills in more traditional academic areas.

As we teach students to use computer tools, we can simultaneously help them accomplish objectives in more traditional academic areas. Word processing programs can often facilitate better writing (Sitko, 1998). Database programs can help students organize information about

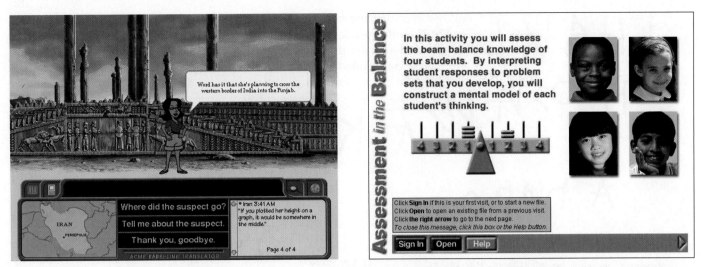

"Where in the World Is Carmen Sandiego?" is a popular software program that promotes higher-level thinking skills in children and young adolescents. Similarly, the simulated activities on your *Simulations in Educational Psychology and Research* CD can enhance your ability to apply what you're learning in your educational psychology class.

trees or planets. Spreadsheets enable students to predict changes in weather patterns or trends in the populations of endangered species. Tools known as *music editors* let students create musical compositions and experiment with different notes, keys, instrumental sounds, and time signatures (P. F. Merrill et al., 1996). And hypermedia programs (e.g., HyperCard) can help students develop engaging multimedia presentations on topics they have studied (Lehrer, 1993).

Homework

Our students can accomplish only so much during class time, and homework provides a means through which we can, in essence, extend the school day. On some occasions, we may want to use homework to give students extra practice with familiar information and procedures (perhaps as a way of promoting review and automaticity) or to introduce them to new yet simple material (Cooper, 1989). In other situations, we can give homework assignments that ask students to apply classroom material to their outside lives (Alleman & Brophy, 1998). For example, in a unit on lifestyle patterns, we might ask second graders to

- Compare their own home with houses of different time periods (e.g., caves, stone huts, log cabins)
- Look through their closets and identify clothes that they use for different functions (e.g., household chores, formal occasions)
- Tour their homes (perhaps with a parent) and identify the modern conveniences that make their lives easier and more comfortable (e.g., sinks, electrical outlets, thermostats)
- Ask their parents to explain why they made the choices they did about where they live (e.g., considering the tradeoffs of renting versus purchasing a residence) (Alleman & Brophy, 1998)

On still other occasions, we might encourage students to bring items and ideas from home (e.g., tadpoles from the local pond, events that occurred over the weekend) and use them as the basis for in-class activities (Corno, 1996; C. Hill, 1994). When we ask students to make connections between classroom material and the outside world through our homework assignments, we are, of course, promoting transfer.

Homework appears to be more beneficial for older students than for younger ones. Research tells us that doing homework has a small effect on the achievement of middle school and high school students but little if any effect on achievement at the elementary level (Cooper, 1989; Cooper, Lindsay, Nye, & Greathouse, 1998; Cooper & Valentine, 2001). Furthermore, students report that their motivation to do their homework is largely extrinsic; for instance, they are more likely to do their homework because they want to please their teacher and stay out of trouble than because they enjoy a subject and want to master it (J. M. T. Walker, 2001). I should point

When I was young it was almost impossible to read. One of my teachers told me I could learn to read if I worked hard. Learning to read was like climbing Mount Rushmore. It took a very long time but I finally got it. My Mom said she was vary proud. Reading was hard for me. It took five years for me to learn to read. Every day I would go to the learning center to learn my 400 site words. It was hard for me to learn these words but I did it. Reading is one of the most important things I have learned so far in my life.

Daniel, a fifth grader who struggles with reading and writing, wrote this very cohesive paragraph with the help of a word processing program. A spell checker enabled him to spell most, but not all, of the words correctly (he meant to use *very* and *sight*, not *vary* and *site*).

i HAVL HOMWRK

A hdrew

Dear Parents:

Tomorrow we will be working on the letter T . Could you please help your child find an object that begins with the letter T for show and tell tomorrow. Thank you!

T +

Young children connect home with school when asked to bring in household items that relate to classroom topics. Six-year-old Andrew and his teacher jointly constructed the homework reminder shown here.

out, however, that research studies have typically not examined the *quality* of homework assignments (e.g., the extent to which they encourage meaningful learning and elaboration rather than rote memorization), which must obviously make a difference in the long-term effects that such assignments have. Furthermore, homework in the elementary grades, even if it does not enhance achievement very much, may help students begin to develop some of the study strategies and self-regulatory skills they will need in later years (Cooper & Valentine, 2001; Zimmerman, 1998).

When we assign homework, we must keep in mind that students will differ considerably in the time and resources (reference books, computers, etc.) they will have available to them and in the amount and kind of assistance they can get from parents and other family members (Cooper, 1989; Hoover-Dempsey et al., 2001). Furthermore, we should assign tasks that will truly help them achieve important educational objectives; we should *never* assign homework simply because we think students should have it every night or, worse still, because we want to punish them for misbehavior.

We can maximize the benefits of homework by following a few simple guidelines (Cooper, 1989):

- Use assignments primarily for instructional and diagnostic purposes; minimize the degree to which homework is used to assess learning and determine final class grades.
- Provide the information and structure that students need to complete assignments without assistance from others.
- Give a mixture of required and voluntary assignments (voluntary ones should help to give students a sense of self-determination and control, hence enhancing intrinsic motivation).

Let's consider how one teacher's homework assignment measures up in terms of the preceding discussion.

INTERPRETING ARTIFACTS AND INTERACTIONS *Book Report*

A first-grade teacher asks her students to write short reports at home about books they've been reading in school. Here we look at one of 6-year-old Katie's book reports. Katie's mother (an elementary school teacher) explains how she has helped Katie with each of her reports: "She would dictate, I'd write, and then she copied. Or, she wrote, and I helped her fix spelling." As you read Katie's report, consider

- Possible advantages of the teacher's assignment
- Possible disadvantages of the assignment

Book Report

Name Katie

Title of Book: Me Too Iguana
Author : Jacquelyn Reinach
Main Characters : Iguana and her friends

Write 3 or more sentences telling about the book.

Iguana had lovely things but she wasn't satisfied. She wanted to look like every one else. When she dressed like her friends they got worried. They had an iguana party to show her that being herself was better.

Draw and color a picture about your book.

Clearly, Katie's mother can scaffold Katie's efforts at what, for most first graders, would be a fairly challenging task. Furthermore, with her mother's assistance, Katie might develop her writing and spelling skills. At the same time, not all of Katie's classmates will have the expert guidance that Katie does. Some well-meaning parents may provide the wrong kind of help, perhaps using confusing instructional methods, focusing on rote-level drill and practice, or providing so much direction that their children lose any sense of autonomy about the task (Cooper & Valentine, 2001; Gallimore & Goldenberg, 2001). Some parents may not have the basic skills they need to assist their children, particularly as the children get older and encounter more challenging schoolwork (J. L. Epstein & Van Voorhis, 2001). And, of course, some parents may be so overwhelmed with other issues and responsibilities that they simply do not have the time or energy to help.

Why might some autonomy in homework be important? For answers, see the discussions of self-regulation (Chapter 10) and self-determination (Chapter 12).

Authentic Activities

In our discussion of knowledge construction in Chapter 7, and again in our discussion of transfer and situated cognition in Chapter 8, we noted the value of activities similar to those that students are likely to encounter in the outside world. When we assign such *authentic activities,* we are more likely to promote meaningful connections between classroom subject matter and real-world contexts and, as a result, more likely to find students applying what they learn in school to their own personal and professional lives. Figure 13.6 presents examples of authentic activities in different academic disciplines.

It may occasionally be possible to assign authentic activities as homework; for example, we might ask students to write an editorial, design an electrical circuit, or plan a family budget

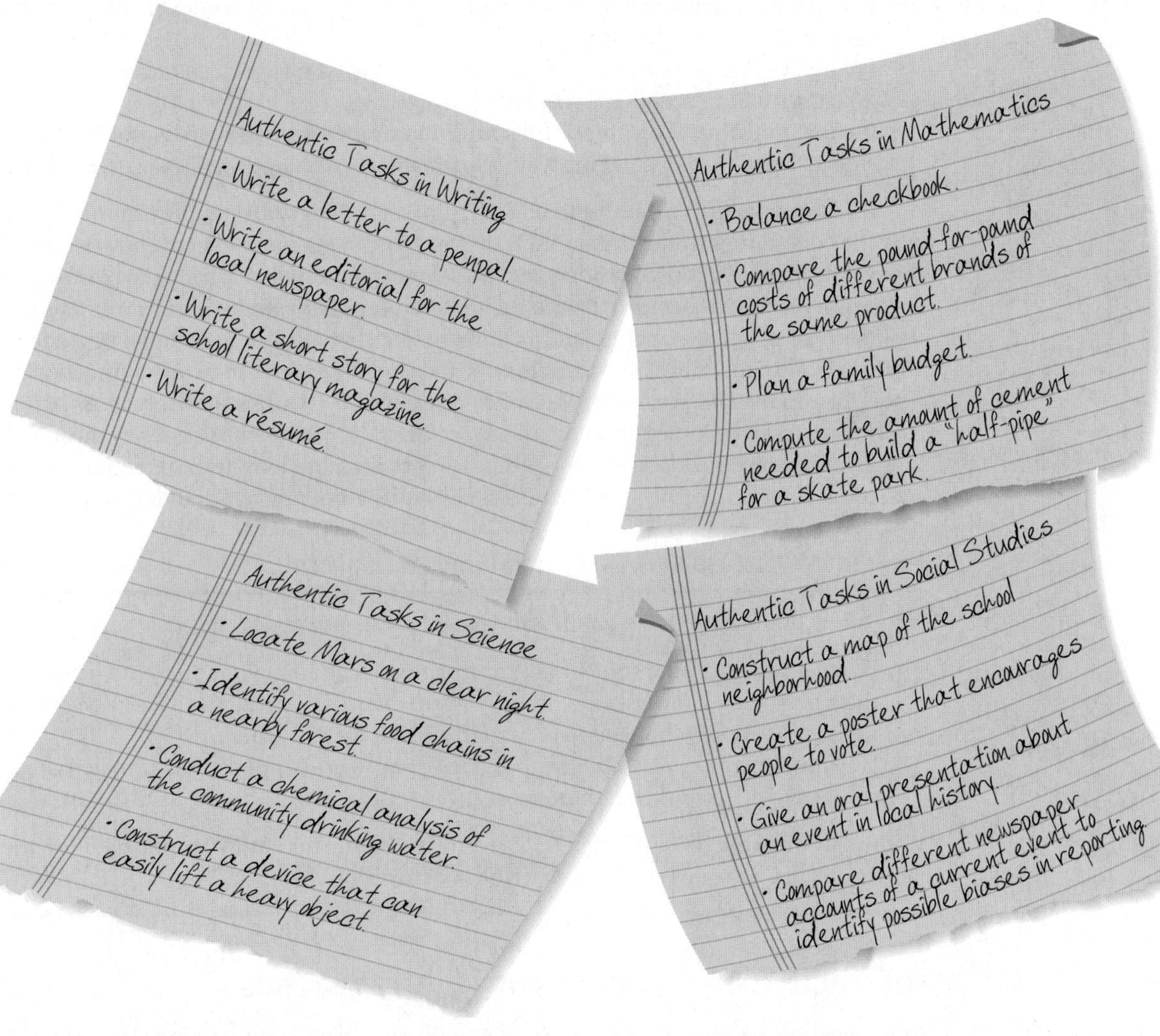

Authentic Tasks in Writing
- Write a letter to a penpal.
- Write an editorial for the local newspaper.
- Write a short story for the school literary magazine.
- Write a résumé.

Authentic Tasks in Mathematics
- Balance a checkbook.
- Compare the pound-for-pound costs of different brands of the same product.
- Plan a family budget.
- Compute the amount of cement needed to build a "half-pipe" for a skate park.

Authentic Tasks in Science
- Locate Mars on a clear night.
- Identify various food chains in a nearby forest.
- Conduct a chemical analysis of the community drinking water.
- Construct a device that can easily lift a heavy object.

Authentic Tasks in Social Studies
- Construct a map of the school neighborhood.
- Create a poster that encourages people to vote.
- Give an oral presentation about an event in local history.
- Compare different newspaper accounts of a current event to identify possible biases in reporting.

FIGURE 13.6 Examples of authentic tasks in different disciplines

while working at home in the evening (if we do so, we should keep in mind the earlier guidelines about assigning homework). But many authentic activities may require considerable interaction, with students asking questions of one another, sharing their ideas, and offering explanations of their thinking (Hickey, 1997; Newmann & Wehlage, 1993; Paris & Turner, 1994). Furthermore, because authentic activities are typically less structured and more complex than traditional classroom tasks, they may require considerable teacher scaffolding (Brophy, 1992a). For such reasons, many authentic activities can be accomplished more effectively in class than at home, or perhaps through a combination of group work during class and independent work after school hours.

Researchers have only begun to study the effects of authentic activities on students' learning and achievement, but preliminary results are encouraging (Cognition and Technology Group at Vanderbilt, 1993; Gregg & Leinhardt, 1994; E. H. Hiebert & Fisher, 1992). For example, students' writing skills may show greater improvement in both quality and quantity when students write stories, essays, and letters to real people, rather than when they complete short, artificial writing exercises (E. H. Hiebert & Fisher, 1992). Likewise, students gain a more complete understanding of how to use and interpret maps effectively when they construct their own maps than when they engage in workbook exercises involving map interpretation (Gregg & Leinhardt, 1994).

Theorists have suggested that an authentic activity is most likely to be effective when it has characteristics such as these:

- It requires a fair amount of background knowledge about a particular topic; in other words, students must know the subject matter thoroughly and have learned it in a meaningful fashion.
- It promotes higher-level thinking skills; for example, it may involve synthesizing information, forming and testing hypotheses, solving problems, and drawing conclusions.
- It requires students to seek out information in a variety of contexts and perhaps from a variety of academic disciplines.
- It conveys high expectations for students' performance, yet also encourages students to take risks and experiment with new strategies.
- Its final outcome is complex and somewhat unpredictable; there is not necessarily a single "right" response or answer. (Newmann & Wehlage, 1993; Paris & Turner, 1994)

It is not necessarily desirable to fill the entire school day with complex, authentic tasks, however. For one thing, students can often master basic skills more effectively when they practice them in relative isolation from other activities; for example, when learning to play the violin, they need to master their fingering before they join an orchestra, and when learning to play soccer, they need to practice dribbling and passing before they play in a game (J. R. Anderson et al., 1996). Second, some authentic tasks may be too expensive and time-consuming to warrant their regular use in the classroom (M. M. Griffin & Griffin, 1994). It is probably most important that classroom tasks encourage students to engage in such cognitive processes as meaningful learning, organization, and elaboration—processes that promote long-term retention and transfer of classroom subject matter—than that tasks always be authentic (J. R. Anderson et al., 1996).

EXPERIENCING FIRSTHAND   *Thinking Authentically*

Take a few minutes to think about and answer these questions:

- In what ways will the subject matter that you teach help your students be successful in their personal or professional lives? In other words, how would you like your students to use and apply school subject matter outside the classroom?
- How might you translate those long-term, real-world applications into activities your students can do in the classroom?

With your answers in mind, develop several authentic activities appropriate for the subject matter and age range of students that you will be teaching.

Interactive and Collaborative Approaches

In the opening case study, we see a lesson with considerable interaction. Ms. Minichiello asks several questions that get her students thinking about and then discussing westward migration in the 1840s. In Chapter 7 we identified numerous advantages of social interaction in the classroom; for instance, when students talk about and exchange ideas, they must organize and elaborate on their own thoughts, may discover gaps and inconsistencies in their understandings, and may encounter explanations that are more accurate and useful than their own. Clearly, then, our students have a great deal to gain from interacting with one another, as well as with us, on a regular basis.

Before you read further, you may want to refer back to the section "Knowledge Construction as a Social Process" in Chapter 7.

In this section we examine six interactive and collaborative strategies: teacher questions, class discussions, reciprocal teaching, technology-based discussions, cooperative learning, and peer tutoring. Of these, the last five are largely student-directed. Only the first—teacher questions—is teacher-directed, and it often provides the impetus for student-directed class discussions.

Teacher Questions

Teacher questioning is a widely used teaching strategy (e.g., Mehan, 1979). Many teacher questions are **lower-level questions** that ask students to retrieve information they've presumably already learned. Such questions have several benefits (Airasian, 1994; F. W. Connolly & Eisenberg, 1990; P. W. Fox & LeCount, 1991; Wixson, 1984). First, they enable us to determine what students' prior knowledge and misconceptions about a topic are likely to be (see Chapter 7). Second, they tend to keep students' attention on the lesson in progress (see Chapter 6). Third, they help us assess whether students are learning class material successfully or are confused about particular points; even very experienced teachers sometimes overestimate what students are actually learning during expository instruction. Fourth, they give students the opportunity to monitor their *own* comprehension—to determine whether they understand the information being presented or whether they should ask for help or clarification. Finally, when questions ask students about material they've studied earlier, they encourage review of that material, which should promote greater recall later on. Following is an example of how one eighth-grade teacher (we'll call her Teacher A) promoted review of a lesson on ancient Egypt by asking questions:

In Chapter 16 we will consider possible strategies for using questions to assess students' learning.

Teacher:	The Egyptians believed the body had to be preserved. What did they do to preserve the body in the earliest times?
Student:	They dried them and stuffed them.
Teacher:	I am talking about from the earliest times. What did they do? Carey.
Carey:	They buried them in the hot sands.
Teacher:	Right. They buried them in the hot sands. The sand was very dry, and the body was naturally preserved for many years. It would deteriorate more slowly, at least compared with here. What did they do later on after this time?
Student:	They started taking out the vital organs.
Teacher:	Right. What did they call the vital organs then?
Norm:	Everything but the heart and brain.
Teacher:	Right, the organs in the visceral cavity. The intestines, liver, and so on which were the easiest parts to get at.
Teacher:	Question?
Student:	How far away from the Nile River was the burial of most kings? (Aulls, 1998, p. 62)

At the end of the dialogue, a *student* asks a question—one that requests information not previously presented. The student is apparently trying to elaborate on the material; perhaps he or she is thinking that only land that was a considerable distance from the Nile would be dry enough to preserve bodies for a lengthy period. We can encourage such elaboration, and therefore also encourage new knowledge construction, by asking **higher-level questions**—those that require students to go beyond the information they have learned (Meece, 1994; Minstrell & Stimpson, 1996). For instance, a higher-level question might ask students to think of their own examples of a concept, use a new principle to solve a problem, or speculate about possible explanations for a cause-effect relationship. As an illustration, consider these questions from a lesson on the telegraph:

Was the need for a rapid communications system [in North America] greater during the first part of the nineteenth century than it had been during the latter part of the eighteenth century? Why do you think so? (Torrance & Myers, 1970, p. 214)

To answer these questions, students must recall what they know about the eighteenth and nineteenth centuries (including the increasing movement of settlers to distant western territories) and pull that knowledge together in a way they have perhaps never done before.

When we ask questions during a group lesson or provide follow-up questions to a reading assignment that students have completed on their own, we will often enhance students' achievement (Allington & Weber, 1993; Liu, 1990; Redfield & Rousseau, 1981). This is especially likely when we ask higher-level questions that call for inferences, applications, justifications, or solutions to problems. Yet we must give students adequate time to respond to the questions we ask. Just as students need time to process the information they are hearing or reading, they also need time to consider questions and retrieve information relevant to possible answers. As we discovered in our discussion of *wait time* in Chapter 6, when teachers allow at least three seconds to elapse after asking questions in class, a greater number of students volunteer answers, and their responses tend to be longer, more complex, and more accurate. Furthermore, even when students can retrieve an answer almost immediately, those from some ethnic backgrounds may allow several seconds to elapse before responding as a way of showing courtesy and respect (see Chapter 4).

Given what you now know about teacher questioning, as well as about effective learning processes, try the following exercise.

INTERPRETING ARTIFACTS AND INTERACTIONS   *Round Robin*

An eighth-grade social studies teacher (we'll call him Teacher B) is conducting a review session for a unit on ancient Egypt. He is using a technique that he calls a "round robin." Each row of students comprises a team, and the teams compete to see which one remembers the most about ancient Egyptian society. He presents a definition of a concept or a description of a certain location and then calls on a particular student to give the term or place to which he is referring. A student who fails to respond correctly must stand up beside his or her desk, indicating a "strike" for the team. After three strikes, the team is out of the competition. The following dialogue exemplifies his approach. As you read it, be aware that the class has two students named Scott, and consider

- What objectives the teacher appears to have for his students
- How his lesson compares to Teacher A's review session (presented earlier) on the same topic

Teacher:	. . . Scott, "a society at an advanced stage of culture."
Scott:	Pass. [Strike one]
Teacher:	Stand up, please. . . . Robert?
Robert:	*Civilization.*
Teacher:	. . . "Shortage of food," Helen.
Helen:	That is a *drought.*
Teacher:	Marcy, "a substance used for making paper."
Marcy:	*Parchment.*
Teacher:	Fred, "a water-raising device."
Fred:	(No response) [Strike two]
Teacher:	Stand up, please. . . . Remember the definitions you were given. . . . Scott Parker.
Scott:	*Shadoof.*
Teacher:	Rula, "a city along the rapids."
Rula:	Not sure. [Strike three]
Teacher:	The right side row has three strikes. OK, next row. . . . (Aulls, 1998, p. 61; punctuation and italics added)

Teacher B apparently wants his students to learn basic information about ancient Egypt (especially terminology and place names), perhaps to a level of automaticity (note his lack of wait time). His focus, then, is on lower-level skills. Unfortunately, the activity promotes rote learning (memorization of word-for-word definitions) and discourages meaningful learning. Teacher A's question-and-answer session (about Egyptian burials) also focuses on lower-level skills, but it is more likely to facilitate learning and achievement for at least three reasons:

(1) It fosters meaningful learning and integration of ideas rather than verbatim recall of isolated facts, (2) it gives students the opportunity to ask questions, and (3) it focuses less on evaluating students and so is more likely to promote intrinsic motivation.

Teacher questions, especially higher-level questions, often get the ball rolling in class discussions. By asking thought-provoking questions, we can encourage students to think about what they have already learned and begin to elaborate on it with their peers (Aulls, 1998; Pogrow & Londer, 1994). We now look at additional strategies for conducting effective discussions.

Class Discussions

What knowledge and skills have you learned primarily through discussions with your peers? Does a fellow student sometimes explain confusing course material more clearly than an instructor has? Do you sometimes understand course material better after *you* have explained it to someone else? Do classroom debates about controversial issues help you clarify your own thinking about those issues?

As you know from reading Chapter 7, social constructivists propose that learners often work together to construct meaningful interpretations of their world. Class discussions in which students feel that they can speak freely, asking questions and presenting their ideas and opinions in either a whole-class or small-group context, obviously provide an important mechanism for promoting such socially constructed understandings (Haseman, 1999; G. J. Kelly & Chen, 1998; Marshall, 1992).

Class discussions lend themselves readily to a variety of academic disciplines. For example, students may discuss various interpretations of classic works of literature, addressing questions that have no easy or "right" answers; when they do so, they are more likely to relate what they are reading to their personal lives and understand it better as a result (Eeds & Wells, 1989; E. H. Hiebert & Raphael, 1996; L. M. McGee, 1992). In history classes, students may study and discuss various documents related to a single historical event and so begin to recognize that history is not necessarily as cut-and-dried as traditional history textbooks portray it (Leinhardt, 1994). In science classes, discussions of various and conflicting explanations of observed phenomena may enhance scientific reasoning skills, promote conceptual change, and help students begin to understand that science is not "fact" as much as it is a dynamic and continually evolving understanding of the world (Bereiter, 1994; K. Hogan et al., 2000; Schwarz et al., 2000). And in mathematics, class discussions that focus on alternative approaches to solving the same problem can promote a more meaningful understanding of mathematical principles and lead to better transfer of those principles to new situations and problems (Cobb et al., 1991; J. Hiebert & Wearne, 1996; Lampert, 1990).

Although students typically do most of the talking in classroom discussions, teachers nevertheless play a critical role. Theorists have offered several guidelines for how we can promote effective classroom discussions:

■ *Focus on topics that lend themselves to multiple perspectives, explanations, or approaches* (L. M. Anderson, 1993; E. H. Hiebert & Raphael, 1996; Lampert, 1990; Onosko, 1996). Controversial topics appear to have several benefits: Students are more likely to express their views to their classmates, seek out new information that resolves seemingly contradictory data, reevaluate their own positions on the issues under discussion, and develop a meaningful and well-integrated understanding of the subject matter (E. G. Cohen, 1994; D. W. Johnson & Johnson, 1985; Kuhn, Shaw, & Felton, 1997; K. Smith, Johnson, & Johnson, 1981).

■ *Make sure students have enough prior knowledge about a topic to discuss it intelligently.* Such knowledge may come either from previous class sessions or from students' personal experiences (Bruning, Schraw, & Ronning, 1995). In many cases, it is likely to come from studying a particular topic in depth (Onosko, 1996).

■ *Create a classroom atmosphere conducive to open debate and the constructive evaluation of ideas.* Students are more likely to share their ideas and opinions if their teacher is supportive of multiple viewpoints and if disagreeing with classmates is socially acceptable (Cobb & Yackel, 1996; Eeds & Wells, 1989; Lampert et al., 1996; Onosko, 1996). To promote such an atmosphere in the classroom, we might

- Communicate the message that understanding a topic at the end of a discussion is more important than having the "correct" answer at the beginning of the discussion (Hatano & Inagaki, 1993).
- Communicate the beliefs that asking questions reflects curiosity, that differing perspectives on a controversial topic are both inevitable and healthy, and that changing one's opinion on a topic is a sign of thoughtful reflection (Onosko, 1996).
- Encourage students to explain their reasoning and to try to understand one another's explanations (Cobb & Yackel, 1996; Cobb, Gravemeijer, Yackel, McClain, & Whitenack, 1997).
- Encourage students to be open in their agreement or disagreement with their classmates (to "agree to disagree") and to view a challenge to their own reasoning as a contribution to the group's understanding rather than as a personal attack (Cobb & Yackel, 1996; Herrenkohl & Guerra, 1998; Lampert et al., 1996).
- Depersonalize challenges to a student's line of reasoning by framing questions in a third-person voice—for example, by saying, "What if someone were to respond to your claim by saying . . . ?" (Onosko, 1996).
- Occasionally ask students to defend a position that is in direct opposition to what they actually believe (Onosko, 1996; Reiter, 1994).
- Require students to develop compromise solutions that take opposing perspectives into account (Onosko, 1996).

■ *Use small-group discussions as a way of encouraging all students to participate.* Students are more likely to speak openly when their audience is a handful of classmates rather than the class as a whole; the difference is especially noticeable for girls (Théberge, 1994). On some occasions, then, we may want to have our students discuss an issue in small groups first, thereby giving them the chance to test and possibly gain support for their ideas in a relatively private context; we can then bring them together for a whole-class discussion (Minstrell & Stimpson, 1996; Onosko, 1996).

Many students feel more comfortable discussing issues in a small group than in front of the entire class.

■ *Provide a structure to guide the discussion.* Our class discussions are likely to be more effective when we structure them in some way. For example, as noted earlier, we might ask one or more thought-provoking (higher-level) questions to get the discussion underway. We might ask the class to examine a textbook or other source of information with a particular goal in mind (Calfee, Dunlap, & Wat, 1994). Before conducting an experiment, we might ask students to make predictions about what will happen and to explain and defend their predictions; later, after students have observed the outcome of the experiment, we might ask them to explain what happened and why (Hatano & Inagaki, 1991; B. Y. White & Frederiksen, 1998). Another strategy, useful when the topic under discussion is especially controversial, is to follow a sequence such as this one:

1. The class is divided into groups of four students apiece. Each group of four subdivides into two pairs.
2. Within a group, each pair of students studies a particular position on the issue and presents its position to the other two students.
3. The group of four has an open discussion of the issue, giving each student an opportunity to argue persuasively for his or her own position.
4. Each pair presents the perspective of the *opposing* side as sincerely and persuasively as possible.
5. The group strives for consensus on a position that incorporates all the evidence presented. (Deutsch, 1993)

By following such a procedure, and in particular by asking students to argue both sides of an issue, we encourage them to think critically about various viewpoints and to begin to recognize that opposing perspectives may *both* have some validity (Reiter, 1994).

At the same time, we must recognize that the most effective group discussions are often the ones in which students have some control over the direction of discourse—perhaps by asking their own questions, initiating new issues related to the topic, or going out on a risky but creative "limb" (Aulls, 1998; Hogan et al., 2000; Onosko, 1996). Student-directed discussions (rather than teacher-directed ones) are also more likely to encourage effective group interaction skills (R. C. Anderson et al., 2001). For instance, when fourth graders meet in small, self-directed groups to discuss children's literature, they may develop and model such skills as expressing agreement ("I agree with Kordell because . . ."), disagreeing tactfully ("Yeah, but they could see the fox sneak in"), justifying an opinion ("I think it shouldn't be allowed, because if he got to be king, who knows what he would do to the kingdom"), and seeking everyone's participation ("Ssshhh! Be quiet! Let Zeke talk!") (R. C. Anderson et al., 2001, pp. 16, 25). Ultimately, the amount of structure we impose must depend on how much scaffolding students need to have a productive discussion; for instance, we may want to be more directive with a small discussion group that seems to be unfocused and floundering than with one that is effectively articulating, critiquing, and building on one another's ideas (K. Hogan et al., 2000).

■ *Give students guidance about how to behave.* Our students are likely to have more productive discussions when we describe appropriate behaviors for discussion sessions. We must take steps to ensure that our students' reactions to one another's ideas are not disparaging or mean-spirited (Onosko, 1996). And we may find it helpful to provide guidelines such as these for small-group discussions:

- Encourage everyone to participate, and listen to everyone's ideas.
- Restate what someone else has said if you don't understand.
- Be critical of ideas rather than people.
- Try to pull ideas from both sides together in a way that makes sense.
- Focus not on winning, but on resolving the issue in the best possible way.
- Change your mind if the arguments and evidence presented indicate that you should do so (based on Deutsch, 1993).

■ *Provide closure at the end of the discussion.* Although students may sometimes come to consensus about a topic at the end of a class discussion, this will certainly not always be the case. Nevertheless, a class discussion should have some form of closure that helps students tie various ideas together. For instance, when I conduct discussions about controversial topics in my own classes, I spend a few minutes at the end of class identifying and summarizing the key issues that students have raised during the class period. Another strategy is to have students explain how a particular discussion has helped them understand a topic more fully (Onosko, 1996).

Whole-class and small-group discussions are not necessarily stand-alone instructional strategies; for instance, we may often want to incorporate them into expository instruction or discovery learning sessions. Student dialogues not only encourage students to think about and process classroom subject matter more completely; they can also promote more effective learning strategies during reading and listening activities (A. L. Brown & Reeve, 1987; Cross & Paris, 1988; Palincsar & Brown, 1989; Paris & Winograd, 1990). One particular form of discussion, *reciprocal teaching,* is especially effective for this purpose.

Reciprocal Teaching

As you may recall from our discussion of metacognition in Chapter 8, students typically know very little about how they can best learn information. As illustrations, here are three high school students' descriptions of how they study a textbook (A. L. Brown & Palincsar, 1987, p. 83):

". . . I stare real hard at the page, blink my eyes and then open them—and cross my fingers that it will be right here." (Student points at head).

"It's easy, if [the teacher] says study, I read it twice. If she says read, it's just once through."

"I just read the first line in each paragraph—it's usually all there."

None of these students mentions any attempt to understand the information, relate it to prior knowledge, or otherwise think about it in any way, so we might guess that they are *not* engaging in meaningful learning, organization, or elaboration. In other words, they are not using cognitive processes that should help them store and retain information in long-term memory.

One obvious objective of our educational system is that students learn to read. But an equally important objective is that students *read to learn*—in other words, that they acquire new information from the things they read. When we examine the cognitive processes that good readers (successful learners) often use, especially when reading challenging material, we find strategies such as these (A. L. Brown & Palincsar, 1987):

How often do *you* engage in these processes when you read? Can you explain the value of each one by relating it to effective memory storage processes?

- *Summarizing.* Good readers identify the main ideas—the gist—of what they read.
- *Questioning.* Good readers ask themselves questions to make sure they understand what they are reading; in other words, they monitor their comprehension as they proceed through reading material.
- *Clarifying.* When good readers discover that they don't comprehend something—for example, when a sentence is confusing or ambiguous—they take steps to clarify what they are reading, perhaps by rereading it or making logical inferences.
- *Predicting.* Good readers anticipate what they are likely to read next; they make predictions about the ideas that are likely to follow the ones they are currently reading.

In contrast, poor readers (those who learn little from textbooks and other reading materials) rarely summarize, question, clarify, or predict. For example, many students cannot adequately summarize a typical *fifth*-grade textbook until high school or even junior college (A. L. Brown & Palincsar, 1987; Palincsar & Brown, 1984). Clearly, many students do not easily acquire the ability to read for learning.

Reciprocal teaching (A. L. Brown & Palincsar, 1987; Palincsar & Brown, 1984, 1989; Palincsar & Herrenkohl, 1999) is an approach to teaching reading through which students learn effective reading-to-learn strategies by observing and imitating what their teacher and fellow students do. The teacher and several students meet in a group to read a piece of text, occasionally stopping to discuss and process the text aloud. Initially, the teacher leads the discussion, asking questions about the text to promote summarizing, questioning, clarifying, and predicting. But gradually, he or she turns the role of "teacher" over to different students, who then take charge of the discussion and ask one another the same kinds of questions that their teacher has modeled. Eventually, the students can read and discuss a text almost independently of the teacher: They work together to construct meaning and check one another for comprehension and possible misunderstandings, and they become increasingly flexible in how they apply the strategies they've learned.

Why is this approach called *reciprocal* teaching?

As an illustration, the following is a reciprocal teaching session for a group of six first graders reading a passage about snowshoe rabbits. In this particular case, the classroom teacher reads the text in small segments (at higher grade levels, the students themselves take turns reading). After each segment, the teacher pauses while students discuss and process the segment. As you read the dialogue, look for examples of summarizing, questioning, clarifying, and predicting (there is at least one instance of each).

The children were reading about the snowshoe rabbit, and it was the sixteenth day of dialogue. The teacher had just read a segment of text describing the season in which baby rabbits are born and the ways in which the mother rabbit cares for her babies. A student named Kam is the dialogue leader.

Kam:	When was the babies born?
Teacher:	That's a good question to ask. Call on someone to answer that question.
Kam:	Robby? Milly?
Milly:	Summer.
Teacher:	What would happen if the babies were born in the winter? Let's think.

Several children make a number of responses, including: "The baby would be very cold." "They would need food." "They don't have no fur when they are just born."

Kam:	I have another question. How does she get the babies safe?
Kris:	She hides them.
Kam:	That's right but something else. . . .
Teacher:	There is something very unusual about how she hides them that surprised me. I didn't know this.
Travis:	They are all in a different place.

Teacher:	Why do you think she does this?
Milly:	Probably because I heard another story, and when they're babies they usually eat each other or fight with each other.
Teacher:	That could be! And what about when that lynx comes?

Several children comment that that would be the end of all the babies.

Travis:	If I was the mother, I would hide mine, I would keep them all together.
Kris:	If the babies are hidden and the mom wants to go and look at them, how can she remember where they are?
Teacher:	Good question. Because she does have to find them again. Why? What does she bring them?
Milly:	She needs to bring food. She probably leaves a twig or something.
Teacher:	Do you think she puts out a twig like we mark a trail?

Several children disagree and suggest that she uses her sense of smell. One child, recalling that the snowshoe rabbit is not all white in the winter, suggests that the mother might be able to tell her babies apart by their coloring.

Teacher:	So we agree that the mother rabbit uses her senses to find her babies after she hides them. Kam, can you summarize for us now?
Kam:	The babies are born in the summer. . . .
Teacher:	The mother . . .
Kam:	The mother hides the babies in different places.
Teacher:	And she visits them . . .
Kam:	To bring them food.
Travis:	She keeps them safe.
Teacher:	Any predictions?
Milly:	What she teaches her babies . . . like how to hop.
Kris:	They know how to hop already.
Teacher:	Well, let's read and see. (dialogue courtesy of A. Palincsar)

Reciprocal teaching provides a mechanism through which both the teacher and students can model effective reading and learning strategies; hence, this approach has an element of social cognitive theory. But when we consider that we are encouraging effective cognitive processes by first having students practice them aloud in group sessions, then we realize that Vygotsky's theory of cognitive development is also at work here: Students should eventually *internalize* the processes that they first use in their discussions with others. Furthermore, the structured nature of a reciprocal teaching session scaffolds students' efforts to make sense of the things they read and hear. For example, in the preceding dialogue, the teacher models elaborative questions and connections to prior knowledge ("What would happen if the babies were born in the winter?" "Do you think she puts out a twig like we mark a trail?") and provides general guidance and occasional hints about how students should process the passage about snowshoe rabbits ("Kam, can you summarize for us now?" "And she visits them . . ."). Also notice in the dialogue how students support one another in their efforts to process what they are reading; consider this exchange:

Kam:	I have another question. How does she get the babies safe?
Kris:	She hides them.
Kam:	That's right but something else. . . .

Reciprocal teaching has been used successfully with a wide variety of students, ranging from first graders to college students, to teach effective reading and listening comprehension skills (Alfassi, 1998; E. R. Hart & Speece, 1998; Johnson-Glenberg, 2000; K. D. McGee, Knight, & Boudah, 2001; Palincsar & Brown, 1989; Rosenshine & Meister, 1994). For example, in an early study of reciprocal teaching (Palincsar & Brown, 1984), six seventh-grade students with a history of poor reading comprehension participated in twenty reciprocal teaching sessions, each lasting about thirty minutes. Despite this relatively short intervention, students showed remarkable improvement in their reading comprehension skills. They became increasingly able to

Can you find at least one example each of summarizing, questioning, clarifying, and predicting in this dialogue? What strategies does the teacher use to elicit desired student responses?

In what way does reciprocal teaching reflect a *cognitive apprenticeship* (see Chapter 2)?

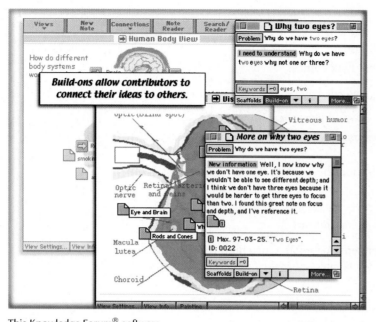

Build-ons allow contributors to connect their ideas to others.

This Knowledge Forum® software allows students to exchange and interconnect ideas not only with their classmates but also with peers and adults at other institutions.
Knowledge Forum® <www.KnowledgeForum.com> was designed by Marlene Scardamalia, Carl Bereiter, and the CSILE/Knowledge-Building Team at the Ontario Institute of Studies in Education at the University of Toronto (OISE-UT) and is published by Learning in Motion, Inc.

Judging from the students' summary, what can we say about their *epistemological beliefs* (Chapter 8) related to anthropology?

process reading material in an effective manner and to do so independently of their classroom teacher. Furthermore, they generalized their new reading strategies to other classes, sometimes even surpassing the achievement of their classmates (A. L. Brown & Palincsar, 1987; Palincsar & Brown, 1984).

Reciprocal teaching can be employed with an entire classroom of students almost as easily as in a small group. Although teachers are often very skeptical of such a radically different approach to teaching and learning, their enthusiasm grows once they've tried it themselves (A. L. Brown & Palincsar, 1987; Palincsar & Brown, 1989).

Technology-Based Discussions

Effective student discussions don't necessarily have to be face to face. Through such mechanisms as electronic mail (e-mail), Web-based chat rooms, and electronic bulletin boards, computer technology enables students to communicate with their peers (either in their own classroom or elsewhere), exchange perspectives, and build on one another's ideas (Fabos & Young, 1999; Hewitt & Scardamalia, 1996; J. Schacter, 2000).

Researchers do not yet have a good handle on the particular benefits that cross-school and cross-cultural discussions may have (Fabos & Young, 1999), but at least one form of within-class electronic "discussion" shows considerable promise. Researchers at the University of Toronto have developed software that allows students to communicate regularly using a class-wide database (Hewitt & Scardamalia, 1996; Lamon, Chan, Scardamalia, Burtis, & Brett, 1993).[5] Students use the database to share their questions, ideas, notes, writing products, and graphic constructions. Their classmates (and sometimes a subject matter expert as well) respond regularly, perhaps by giving feedback, building on ideas, offering alternative perspectives, or summarizing what has been learned. As an example, in an anthropology unit on "Prehistory of the New World" in a fifth- and sixth-grade classroom, students worked in groups of three or four to study particular topics and then shared their findings through their computer database (Hewitt, Brett, Scardamalia, Frecker, & Webb, 1995). One group, which studied various theories about how human beings first migrated from Asia to the Americas, reported the following:

> **What We Have Learned:** We know that we have learned lots on this project, but the more that we learn the more we get confused about which is fact and which is fiction. The problem within this problem is that there isn't any real proof to say when they came or how. The theory that is most believed is the Bering Strait theory in which people from Asia walked over a land bridge. Another theory is they kayaked the distance between the two continents. We have also unfortunately found racist theories done by people who hate people unlike their own saying that the people of the New World are these people because of human sacrifices and only this race of people would do that.

> We have made are [our] own theories using information we found and trying to make sense of it. We have heard some people say they come from outer space but this theory is pretty much out of the question. I don't think the Native peoples or the Inuit would like to hear that theory either. How they came isn't easily answered for some of the theories but it does make since [sense] with the Bering Strait theory. (Hewitt et al., 1995, p. 7)

Early observations of the interactive software's effects have been encouraging: Students are concerned about truly understanding classroom subject matter rather than simply "getting things done" (i.e., they adopt mastery goals rather than performance goals), actively try to relate new material to what they already know (i.e., they engage in meaningful learning), and show an

---

[5]An early version of this software was known as Computer Supported Intentional Learning Environment, or SCILE (pronounced like the name Cecil). A second generation of CSILE, called Knowledge Forum® (available commercially from Learning in Motion, Inc.) allows collaboration across schools and other institutions. You can visit CSILE and Knowledge Forum Websites at http://csile.oise.utoronto.ca, and http://www.KnowledgeForum.com.

increased ability to remember and apply classroom subject matter (e.g., Lamon et al., 1993). As you can see, too, the software enables the classroom to become a *community of learners* in which students regularly cooperate with one another and contribute to one another's learning and achievement. We now look at other approaches for promoting cooperative learning.

You can find another example of a technology-based discussion in the section "Creating a Community of Learners" in Chapter 7.

Cooperative Learning

EXPERIENCING FIRSTHAND   *Purple Satin*

Imagine yourself as a student in each of the three classrooms described here. Imagine how you would behave in each situation.

1. Mr. Alexander tells your class, "Let's find out which students can learn the most in this week's unit on the human digestive system. The three students getting the highest scores on Friday's unit test will get free tickets to the Purple Satin concert." Purple Satin is a popular musical group; you would give your eyeteeth to hear them perform, but the concert has been sold out for months.
2. Ms. Bernstein introduces her lesson this way: "Let's see whether each of you can learn all about the digestive system this week. If you can get a score of at least 90 percent on this Friday's test, then you will get a free ticket to the Purple Satin concert."
3. Mr. Camacho begins the same lesson like this: "Today we begin studying the human digestive system. Let's see how many students can get scores of 90 percent or better on Friday's test. I want you to work in groups of three to help one another learn the material. If all three members of a group score at least 90 percent on the test, then that group will get free tickets to the Purple Satin concert."

In which class(es) are you likely to work hard to get free tickets to Purple Satin? How might you work *differently* in the different situations?

The first classroom (Mr. Alexander's) is obviously a very competitive one: Only the three best students are getting tickets to the concert. Will you try to earn one of those tickets? It all depends on what you think your chances are of being a top scorer on Friday's test. If you have been doing well on tests all year, then you will undoubtedly study harder than ever for this week's unit. If, instead, you have been doing poorly in class despite your best efforts, then you probably won't work for something you are unlikely to get. But in either case, will you help your fellow students learn about the digestive system? Not if you want to go to the concert yourself!

In Ms. Bernstein's classroom there's no competition for concert tickets. As long as you get a score of 90 percent or higher on the test, you get a ticket. Even if you think half the students in class are smarter than you are, you know that you have a good chance of going to the concert, and so you will probably study diligently for Friday's test. But will you help your classmates understand what the pancreas does or learn the difference between the large and small intestines? Maybe . . . *if* you have the time and are in a good mood.

Now consider Mr. Camacho's classroom. Whether or not you get a concert ticket depends on how well you *and two other students* score on Friday's test. Are you going to help those two students learn about salivation and digestive enzymes? And can you expect them, in turn, to help you understand where the liver fits into the whole system? Absolutely!

Cooperative learning is an approach to instruction in which students work in small groups to help one another learn. Unlike an individualistic classroom such as Ms. Bernstein's (where one student's success is unrelated to classmates' achievement) or a competitive classroom such as Mr. Alexander's (where one student's success actually depends on the failure of others), students in a cooperative learning environment such as Mr. Camacho's work together to achieve common successes. In other words, they *sink or swim together* (D. W. Johnson & Johnson, 1991).

We find justification for cooperative learning in several theoretical frameworks. From the perspective of cognitive psychology, cooperative learning yields the same benefits that emerge from class discussions: greater comprehension and integration of the subject matter, recognition of inadequacies or misconceptions in understanding, and increased perspective taking. Furthermore, when students help one another learn, they create scaffolding for one another's efforts, and they may jointly construct more sophisticated ideas and strategies than any single group member might be able to construct alone (Good et al., 1992; Hatano & Inagaki, 1991; O'Donnell & O'Kelly, 1994; N. M. Webb & Palincsar, 1996). From a behaviorist point of view, reinforcing group success is consistent with the operant conditioning notion of a *group contingency*. From a social cognitive perspective, students are likely to have higher self-efficacy for performing a task when they know that they will have the help of other group members; furthermore, students can model effective learning and problem-solving strategies for one another (A. L. Brown & Palincsar, 1989; Good et al., 1992). And theorists of various theoretical persuasions point out that cooperative ventures are important elements of scientific inquiry and adult work environments (Greeno, 1997; D. W. Johnson & Johnson, 1991).

How often do adults need to collaborate in the workplace? Do you think they might have benefited from cooperative experiences during their school years?

Numerous research studies indicate that cooperative learning activities, when designed and structured appropriately, are effective in many ways. For one thing, students of all ability levels show higher academic achievement; females, members of minority groups, and students at risk for academic failure are especially likely to show increased achievement (Lou et al., 1996; Nichols, 1996; Pérez, 1998; Qin, Johnson, & Johnson, 1995; Shachar & Sharan, 1994; R. J. Stevens & Slavin, 1995). Cooperative learning activities may also promote higher-level thinking skills: Students essentially "think aloud," modeling various learning and problem-solving strategies for one another and developing greater metacognitive awareness as a result (Good et al., 1992; A. King, 1999; Paris & Winograd, 1990).

The benefits of cooperative learning activities are not limited to gains in learning and achievement. Students have greater confidence about the likelihood of success (i.e., higher self-efficacy), express more intrinsic motivation to learn school subject matter, and participate more actively in classroom activities. They better understand the perspectives of others and more frequently engage in prosocial behavior—making decisions about how to divide a task fairly and equitably, resolving interpersonal conflicts, and encouraging and supporting one another's learning. In classrooms that emphasize cooperative learning, students are more likely to believe they are liked and accepted by their classmates, and friendships across racial and ethnic groups and between students with and without disabilities are more apt to form (Lou et al., 1996; H. W. Marsh & Craven, 1997; J. D. Nichols, 1996; Slavin, 1990; R. J. Stevens & Slavin, 1995; N. M. Webb & Palincsar, 1996).

However, there are also some potential pitfalls in cooperative learning. Some students may be less interested in mastering the material than they are in meeting social and performance goals (e.g., making friends, creating a good impression, getting the right answer), and their willingness to assist one another or ask for help may be compromised as a result (Levy, Kaplan, & Patrick, 2000; M. C. Linn et al., 1996; Moje & Shepardson, 1998). The students who do most of the work and most of the talking are likely to learn more than other group members (Blumenfeld, 1992; Gayford, 1992; N. M. Webb, 1989). Students may occasionally agree to use an incorrect strategy or method that a particular group member has suggested, or they may share misconceptions about the topic they are studying (Good et al., 1992; Stacey, 1992). In some cases, students may simply not have the skills to help one another learn (D. M. Hogan & Tudge, 1999; O'Donnell & O'Kelly, 1994). Clearly, then, we must keep a close eye on the discussions that cooperative groups have and the products that they create, providing additional structure and guidance when necessary to promote maximal learning and achievement.

Cooperative learning has personal and social benefits as well as academic ones. For instance, it often promotes self-efficacy, intrinsic motivation, social skills, and cross-cultural friendships.

As you can see, cooperative learning is not simply a process of putting students in groups and setting them loose to work on an assignment together. Oftentimes, our students will be more accustomed to competitive and individualistic classroom situations than they are to working cooperatively with their classmates. For a cooperative learning activity to be successful, we must structure the activity in such a way that cooperation is not only helpful for academic success but in fact even necessary for it (D. W. Johnson & Johnson, 1991). Following are several strategies that enhance the effectiveness of cooperative groups:

■ *Form groups based on which students are likely to work effectively with one another.* Cooperative groups are typically comprised of two to six members; groups of three to four students are especially effective (Hatano & Inagaki, 1991; Lou et al., 1996). In most cases, *we* should form the groups, identifying combinations of students that are likely to be productive (D. W. Johnson & Johnson, 1991).

Many advocates of cooperative learning suggest that each group be relatively heterogeneous—that each group include high achievers and low achievers, boys and girls, and children of various ethnic backgrounds (D. W. Johnson & Johnson, 1991; Shachar & Sharan, 1994; R. J. Stevens & Slavin, 1995; N. M. Webb, Nemer, Chizhik, & Sugrue, 1998). In recent years, however, some theorists have begun to question the practice of combining students of widely differing achievement levels, arguing that such a practice makes ability differences among students more obvious than they would be otherwise. High-achieving students may dominate discussions and discourage low-achieving students from fully participating; low-achieving students may be reluctant to ask for help in understanding the material being studied, or they may simply sit back and let other group members do most or all of the work (E. G. Cohen & Lotan, 1995; Moje & Shepardson, 1998; O'Donnell & O'Kelly, 1994; S. E. Peterson, 1993; N. M. Webb & Palincsar, 1996).

Research regarding the effects of heterogeneous ability groupings has yielded mixed results. Some studies indicate that heterogeneous groups benefit both high-achieving students, who can sharpen their understanding of class material by explaining it to their classmates, and low-achieving students, who benefit from hearing such explanations (Lou et al., 1996; R. J. Stevens & Slavin, 1995; N. M. Webb et al., 1998; N. M. Webb & Palincsar, 1996). Yet other studies indicate that high-achieving students do not always gain from working with their low-achieving peers; in fact, these students occasionally even lose ground (D. M. Hogan & Tudge, 1999; Lou et al., 1996). Furthermore, students of similar ability levels may sometimes be able to work more collaboratively than students of widely differing abilities (L. S. Fuchs, Fuchs, Hamlett, & Karns, 1998). Given such mixed messages from research, our best bet is probably to experiment with varying degrees of heterogeneity in our cooperative groups and to determine which approach works best in our own circumstances.

■ *Give group members one or more common goals toward which to work.* At the beginning of a cooperative group activity, we should specify clearly and concretely what each group should accomplish (Crook, 1995; D. W. Johnson & Johnson, 1991). For instance, when my daughter Tina was enrolled in high school Spanish, the goal of one cooperative activity was to write and videotape an episode of a television soap opera spoken entirely in Spanish. The students knew that these *telenovelas* would eventually be shown at an "Academy Awards" banquet for the students and parents, and "Oscars" would be presented for best picture, best screenplay, best leading and supporting actors and actresses, and so on. Another example, this one used in an eighth-grade social studies class, is presented in Figure 13.7.

■ *Provide clear guidelines about how to behave.* Without instruction about appropriate group behaviors, students may act in a decidedly uncooperative manner; for example, they may try to dominate discussions, ridicule one another's ideas, or exert pressure to complete the task in a particular way (Blumenfeld, Marx, Soloway, & Krajcik, 1996; N. M. Webb & Palincsar, 1996). Instruction on such group skills as these seems to increase cooperative and productive group behaviors:

- Listening to others politely and attentively
- Giving encouragement to others
- Making sure everyone has an equal chance to participate
- Refraining from insulting or yelling at others
- Offering assistance to those who need it
- Asking clear, precise questions when one doesn't understand
  (E. G. Cohen, 1994; Deutsch, 1993; Gillies & Ashman, 1998; Lou et al., 1996; O'Donnell & O'Kelly, 1994; N. M. Webb & Farivar, 1999)

■ *Structure tasks so that group members are dependent on one another for their success.* We should structure cooperative learning activities in such a way that each student's success depends on the help and participation of other group members; furthermore, each student must believe it is to his or her advantage that *other* group members do well (Deutsch, 1993; Karau & Williams, 1995; Lou et al., 1996). For instance, tasks that involve creative problem solving and have more than one right answer are likely to encourage students to work cooperatively with one another, presumably because students recognize that several heads will be better than one in solving them (Blumenfeld et al., 1996). In some situations, each student might have a unique and essential function within the group, perhaps serving as group leader, critic, bookkeeper, summarizer, and

FIGURE 13.7 To be effective, cooperative groups should work toward common goals. In these project guidelines, eighth-grade history teacher Mark Nichols identifies several things that students need to accomplish as they prepare their group presentations about colonial America.

<u>Colonial Economies</u>

Textbook Chapters:
  Planting Colonies - Chapter 4

   - Spain Builds a Large Empire (Mr. Nichols)
   - French and Dutch Colonies (Group 1)
   - English Settlers in Virginia (Group 2)
   - The Pilgrims at Plymouth (Group 3)

  English Colonies Take Root - Chapter 5

   - New England Colonies (Group 4)
   - Middle Colonies (Group 5)
   - Southern Colonies (Group 6)
   - Governing the Colonies (Group 7)

Group Responsibilities:

  Groups will be established with 3-4 students.

  Each group will be responsible for reading and thoroughly understanding their assigned sub-chapter.

  Each group will prepare an outline of the chapter which will be typed in final draft format. Copies will be made for each student in class.

  Each group will create an artistic example of their material and a board game to be played at the end of the presentations.

  The day before your group presentation you are to instruct the class to read your sub-chapter and prepare a homework assignment for the class.

  A presentation of the material will be made to the class, which will include going over the homework assignment, the outline, and explanation of your creative display of the sub-chapter information. Class members are required to question the presenting group on their material.

  An open note test will be given at the end of this unit in order to ensure understanding of the material.

so on (A. L. Brown & Palincsar, 1989; D. W. Johnson & Johnson, 1991). In other situations, the **jigsaw technique** is useful: New information is divided equally among all group members, and each student must teach his or her portion to the other group members (Aronson & Patnoe, 1997). Still another approach is to assign projects that require such a wide range of talents and skills that every group member is likely to have something truly unique and useful to contribute to the group's overall success (E. G. Cohen, 1994; Schofield, 1995).

When students are novices at cooperative learning, it is often helpful to give them a set of steps (a "script" to follow) that guides their interaction (A. King, 1999; Meloth & Deering, 1994; N. M. Webb & Palincsar, 1996). In one approach, known as **scripted cooperation**, students work together in pairs to read and study expository text. One member of the pair might act as "recaller," summarizing the contents of a textbook passage. The other student acts as "listener," correcting any errors and recalling additional important information. For the next passage, the two students switch roles. Such an approach can help students improve such learning strategies as elaboration, summarizing, and comprehension monitoring (Dansereau, 1988; O'Donnell, 1999).

■ *Serve more as a resource and monitor than as a "director."* During any cooperative learning activity, we should continually monitor each group to be sure that interactions are productive and socially appropriate (D. W. Johnson & Johnson, 1991; Meloth & Deering, 1999). For instance, we might consider issues such as these:

• Are students working toward a common goal?
• Are they all actively participating?
• Are they listening to one another's perspectives?

- Are they asking one another questions when they don't understand?
- Are they criticizing ideas rather than people?

We might also offer assistance in situations where group members are unable to provide information or insights that are critical for accomplishing the group's goal. Too much intervention may be counterproductive, however: Students tend to talk less with one another when their teacher joins the group (E. G. Cohen, 1994).

■ *Make students individually accountable for their achievement, but also reinforce them for group success.* Students are more likely to learn assigned classroom subject matter during cooperative learning activities when they know that they will have to demonstrate individual mastery or accomplishment of the group's goal—for example, by taking a quiz or answering questions in class. Such an approach minimizes the likelihood that some students will do most or all of the work while others get a "free ride" (Karau & Williams, 1995; Slavin, 1990; N. M. Webb & Palincsar, 1996).

In addition to holding students accountable for their own learning and achievement, we should also reinforce group members for the success of the group as a whole—a group contingency in action (Lou et al., 1996; Slavin, 1990; Stipek, 1996). Such group rewards often promote higher achievement overall, perhaps because students have a vested interest in helping one another learn and so make a concerted effort to help fellow group members understand the material that the group is studying (Slavin, 1983; R. J. Stevens & Slavin, 1995). One commonly used approach is to give students a quiz over material they have studied in their cooperative groups and then award bonus points when all group members perform at or above a certain level.

■ *At the end of an activity, have the groups evaluate their effectiveness.* After cooperative groups have accomplished their goals, we should have them look analytically and critically (perhaps with our assistance) at the ways in which they have functioned effectively and the ways in which they need to improve (E. G. Cohen, 1994; Deutsch, 1993; D. W. Johnson & Johnson, 1991). We might ask them to consider some of the same issues we kept in mind as we monitored the activity—for instance, whether everyone participated equally, whether group members asked one another questions when they didn't understand, and whether everyone criticized ideas rather than people.

■ *Consider forming long-term cooperative groups.* Many groups are formed on a short-term basis to accomplish specific tasks—perhaps to study new material, solve a problem, or complete an assigned project. Yet on other occasions, it may be beneficial to form groups that work toward long-term classroom goals. For instance, **base groups** are cooperative groups that work together the entire semester or school year; they provide a means through which students can clarify assignments for one another, help one another with class notes, and give one another a general sense of support and belonging in the classroom (D. W. Johnson & Johnson, 1991).

One of the reasons that cooperative learning is so often effective is that students tutor one another in the subject matter they are studying. Such peer tutoring is our next topic of discussion.

Peer Tutoring

As noted in our earlier discussion of mastery learning, some students may need more time to master a topic than others; hence, they may need more instructional time, and perhaps more individualized instruction, than their classmates. As teachers, we can't always devote much time to one-on-one instruction. **Peer tutoring**—students who have mastered a topic teaching those who have not—can provide an effective alternative for teaching fundamental knowledge and skills. In some cases, we can have students within a single class tutor one another. In other situations, we might have older students teaching younger ones; for instance, fourth or fifth graders might tutor students in kindergarten or first grade (A. L. Brown & Campione, 1994; Inglis & Biemiller, 1997; Kermani & Moallem, 1997).

Like mastery learning, direct instruction, and computer-based instruction, peer tutoring sessions give students many opportunities to make the active responses that, from a behaviorist perspective, are so essential to learning. From a more cognitive framework, tutoring encourages students to organize and elaborate on what they have already learned in order to make the material clear to someone else. And cross-age tutoring is consistent with Vygotsky's

INTO THE CLASSROOM: *Promoting Cooperative Learning*

Form groups of students who are likely to work together productively.

An elementary school teacher divides her class into cooperative groups of four or five students each. He makes sure that each group includes boys and girls, students of various ethnic backgrounds, and students who will be able to contribute different skills to the task at hand.

Provide clear goals toward which groups should work.

In a unit on Shakespeare, an English teacher asks cooperative groups to identify the attitudes toward Jewish people expressed in *The Merchant of Venice,* as reflected in the actions and statements of Shylock and other characters.

Give each group member a different role or task within the group.

A biology teacher asks cooperative groups to prepare for an upcoming classroom debate on the pros and cons of preserving tropical rain forests. She gives each student a unique function. One student acts as *reader* of information about rain forests, another acts as *recorder* of group members' arguments, a third acts as *checker* to determine whether all group members agree with each argument, and so on.

Monitor group interactions.

A social studies teacher asks cooperative groups to identify an effective way of helping the homeless find suitable housing. When he hears one student insulting another because of a difference of opinion, he reminds the group that students should criticize ideas rather than people.

Provide critical information and insights when (but only when) a group is unlikely or unable to provide such information and insights for itself.

The same social studies teacher tells a group, "The solution you have developed assumes that most taxpayers would be willing to pay much higher taxes than they do now. Is that realistic?"

Make students individually accountable for their achievement.

A mathematics teacher has incorporated cooperative learning into a unit on calculating the area of squares, rectangles, and triangles. Later, she gives all students a quiz to assess their individual mastery of the subject.

Reinforce group success.

The same math teacher awards bonus points to students whose entire group performs at or above a certain test score.

Ask students to evaluate their effectiveness in working as a group.

After cooperative groups have completed their assigned tasks, a teacher asks the groups to answer questions such as these: "Did all group members actively participate?" "Did they ask questions when they didn't understand one another?" "Did they criticize ideas rather than people?"

---

belief that older and more competent individuals are invaluable in promoting the cognitive development of younger children.

In some cases, peer tutoring leads to greater academic gains than either mastery learning or more traditional whole-class instruction (D. Fuchs, Fuchs, Mathes, & Simmons, 1997; Greenwood, Carta, & Hall, 1988). One possible reason for its effectiveness is that it provides a context in which struggling students may be more comfortable asking questions when they don't understand something. In one study (Graesser & Person, 1994), students asked 240 times as many questions during peer tutoring as they did during whole-class instruction!

Peer tutoring typically benefits tutors as well as those being tutored (D. Fuchs et al., 1997; Inglis & Biemiller, 1997; Semb et al., 1993; N. M. Webb & Palincsar, 1996). When students study material with the expectation that they will be teaching it to someone else, they are more intrinsically motivated to learn it, find it more interesting, process it in a more meaningful way, and remember it longer (Benware & Deci, 1984; Semb et al., 1993). Furthermore, when students who are relatively weak in a particular domain (compared to their age-mates) guide younger students in that domain, they develop greater ability to guide *themselves* (i.e., they develop greater self-regulation) in that domain (Biemiller et al., 1998). Peer tutoring has nonacademic benefits as well. Cooperation and other social skills improve, classroom behavior problems diminish, and friendships develop among students of different ethnic groups and between students with and without disabilities (DuPaul et al., 1998; Greenwood et al., 1988).

Like other interactive approaches to instruction, peer tutoring is most effective when teachers follow certain guidelines in its use. Following are several suggestions for using peer tutoring effectively:

Why might teaching younger students a particular skill enhance tutors' self-regulation related to that skill? Explain this finding using Vygotsky's concept of internalization (Chapter 2).

■ *Make sure tutors have mastered the material they are teaching and use effective instructional techniques.* Good tutors have a meaningful understanding of the subject matter they are teaching and provide explanations that focus on such understanding; poor tutors are more likely to describe procedures without explaining why the procedures are useful (L. S. Fuchs et al., 1996). Good tutors also use teaching strategies that are likely to promote learning: They ask questions, give hints, scaffold responses when necessary, provide feedback, and so on (Lepper, Aspinwall, Mumme, & Chabey, 1990).

Students don't always have the knowledge and skills that will enable them to become effective tutors, especially at the elementary school level (Greenwood et al., 1988; Kermani & Moallem, 1997; D. Wood, Wood, Ainsworth, & O'Malley, 1995). It is essential, then, that tutoring sessions be limited to subject matter that the student tutors know well. Training in effective tutoring skills is also helpful; for example, we might show student tutors how to establish a good relationship with the students they are tutoring, how to break a task into simple steps, how and when to give feedback, and so on (Fueyo & Bushell, 1998; Inglis & Biemiller, 1997; Kermani & Moallem, 1997).

In many cases, when one student tutors another, the tutor learns as much from the experience as the student being tutored.

■ *Provide a structure for students' interactions.* Providing a structure for tutoring sessions can often help students tutor their classmates more effectively (Fantuzzo, King, & Heller, 1992; D. Fuchs et al., 1997; L. S. Fuchs et al., 1996; A. King, 1999). As an example, in one study (D. Fuchs et al., 1997), twenty second- through sixth-grade classes participated in a project called Peer-Assisted Learning Strategies (PALS), designed to foster more effective reading comprehension skills. In each classroom, students were ranked by reading ability, and the ranked list was divided in two. The first-ranked student in the top half of the list was paired with the first-ranked student in the bottom half of the list, the second student in the top half was paired with the second student in the bottom half, and so on down the line; through this procedure, students who were paired together had moderate but not extreme differences in their reading levels. Each pair read text at the level of the weaker reader and engaged in these activities:

- *Partner reading with retell.* The stronger reader read aloud for five minutes, then the weaker reader read the same passage of text. Reading something that had previously been read presumably enabled the weaker reader to read the material easily. After the double reading, the weaker reader described the material that the pair had just read.
- *Paragraph summary.* The students both read a passage one paragraph at a time. Then, with help from the stronger reader, the weaker reader tried to identify the subject and main idea of the paragraph.
- *Prediction relay.* Both students read a page of text, and then, with help from the stronger reader, the weaker reader would summarize the text and also make a prediction about what the next page would say. The students would read the following page, then the weaker reader would confirm or disconfirm the prediction, summarize the new page, make a new prediction, and so on.

Such a procedure enabled students in the PALS program to make significantly greater progress in reading than students who had more traditional reading instruction, even though the amount of class time devoted to reading instruction was similar for both groups. The researchers speculated that the PALS students performed better because they had more frequent opportunities to make verbal responses to the things they were reading, received more frequent feedback about their performance and, in general, were more frequently encouraged to use effective reading strategies.

At the secondary level, we can incorporate a tutoring component into paired study sessions by teaching students the kinds of questions they should ask one another as they jointly study science, social studies, and other academic disciplines. In one approach (A. King, 1997), students learn to ask their partners questions that promote meaningful learning, elaboration, and metacognition—for instance, questions such as these:

- Describe . . . in your own words.
- What is the difference between . . . and . . . ?
- What do you think would happen to . . . if . . . happened?
- How did you figure that out?

When we give students guidance about the kinds of questions that can help them promote one another's learning, highly effective tutoring sessions often result. Following is an example in which two seventh graders are following a prescribed questioning procedure as they study biology:

Jon: How does the muscular system work, Kyle?

Kyle: Well . . . it retracts and contracts when you move.

Jon: Can you tell me more?

Kyle: Um . . . well . . .

Jon: Um, why are muscles important, Kyle?

Kyle: They are important because if we didn't have them we couldn't move around.

Jon: But . . . how do muscles work? Explain it more.

Kyle: Um, muscles have tendons. Some muscles are called skeletal muscles. They are in the muscles that—like—in your arms—that have tendons that hold your muscles to your bones—to make them move and go back and forth. So you can walk and stuff.

Jon: Good. All right! How are the skeletal muscles and the cardiac muscles the same?

Kyle: Uhh—the cardiac and the smooth muscles?

Jon: The cardiac and the skeletal.

Kyle: Well, they're both a muscle. And they're both pretty strong. And they hold things. I don't really think they have much in common.

Jon: Okay. Why don't you think they have much in common?

Kyle: Because the smooth muscle is—I mean the skeletal muscle is voluntary and the cardiac muscle is involuntary. Okay, I'll ask now. What do you think would happen if we didn't have smooth muscles?

Jon: We would have to be chewing harder. And so it would take a long time to digest food. We would have to think about digesting because the smooth muscles—like the intestines and stomach—are *involuntary*.

Kyle: Have you really thought about it?

Jon: Yeah.

Kyle: Yeah, well—um—but, do you think it would *hurt* you if you didn't have smooth muscles?

Jon: Well, yeah—because you wouldn't have muscles to push the food along—in the stomach and intestines—you'd get plugged up! Maybe you'd hafta drink liquid—just liquid stuff. Yuk. (A. King, Staffieri, & Adelgais, 1998, p. 141)

Notice how Kyle asks questions that encourage Jon to go beyond the material he has specifically learned (e.g., "How are the skeletal muscles and the cardiac muscles the same?" "Do you think it would hurt you if you didn't have smooth muscles?"). Kyle also asks questions that encourage Jon to think about his thinking and thereby may promote metacognition (e.g., "Why don't you think they have much in common?" "Have you really thought about it?"). Through such structured interactions, even students at the same grade and ability levels can provide valuable scaffolding for one another's learning efforts (A. King, 1998).

■ *Be careful that your use of higher-achieving students to tutor lower-achieving students is not excessive or exploitive.* As we have seen, tutors often gain just as much from tutoring sessions as the students they are tutoring. Nevertheless, we must not assume that high-achieving students will always learn from a tutoring session; we should therefore monitor the effects of a peer tutoring program to make sure that all of our students are reaping its benefits.

■ *Use peer tutoring to help students with special educational needs.* Peer tutoring has been used effectively to help students with learning disabilities, physical disabilities, and other special educational needs (Cushing & Kennedy, 1997; DuPaul et al., 1998; D. Fuchs et al., 1997). For example, in one study (Cushing & Kennedy, 1997), low-achieving students were assigned as tutors for classmates who had moderate or severe intellectual or physical disabilities. The student tutors clearly benefited from their tutoring assignments: They became more attentive in class, completed classroom tasks more frequently, and participated in class more regularly. I suspect that the opportunity to tutor classmates less capable than themselves may have enhanced their own self-efficacy for learning classroom subject matter,

Have you ever tutored a student who had a disability? If so, what benefits did *you* gain from the experience?

which in turn would encourage them to engage in the kinds of behaviors that would ensure academic success.

■ *Make sure that all students have experience tutoring their classmates.* Ideally, we should make sure that *all* of our students have an opportunity to tutor their classmates at one time or another (Greenwood, 1991). This is often easier said than done, as a few of our students may show consistently lower achievement than most of their peers. One potentially effective strategy in such situations is to teach those students specific tasks or procedures that they can share with their higher-achieving, but in this case uninformed, classmates (E. G. Cohen, Lockheed, & Lohman, 1976; N. M. Webb & Palincsar, 1996).

In fact, how we can best accommodate student diversity must be a top consideration no matter which instructional strategy we use. We turn now to a more focused discussion of individual and group differences and their potential implications for various instructional strategies.

Taking Student Diversity into Account

The instructional strategies we choose will inevitably depend on the particular students we will be teaching. We must base our decisions, in part, on our students' ages and developmental levels. Strategies that involve teaching well-defined topics, require a great deal of active student responding, and provide frequent feedback (e.g., mastery learning, direct instruction, computer-based instruction) will often be more appropriate for younger students than for older ones (Rosenshine & Stevens, 1986). Lectures (which are often somewhat abstract) and homework assignments appear to be more effective with older students (Ausubel et al., 1978; Cooper & Valentine, 2001).

The knowledge and skills that our students bring to a topic should also be a consideration (Gustafsson & Undheim, 1996; Rosenshine & Stevens, 1986). Structured, teacher-directed approaches are probably most appropriate for students who know little or nothing about the subject matter. Students who have already mastered basic knowledge and skills, and particularly those who are self-regulated learners, should begin directing some of their own learning, perhaps in group discussions, authentic activities, or use of hypermedia and the Internet. In general, however, virtually *any* student should have experience with a wide variety of instructional methods. For instance, although some students may need to spend considerable time on basic skills, too much time spent in structured, teacher-directed activities may minimize opportunities to choose what and how to study and learn and, as a result, may prevent students from developing a sense of self-determination (Battistich et al., 1995). In addition, authentic activities, though often unstructured and complex, give students of all levels a greater appreciation for the relevance and meaningfulness of classroom subject matter than may be possible with more traditional classroom tasks.

Some instructional strategies adapt themselves readily to a wide variety of student abilities and needs. For example, mastery learning provides a means through which students can learn at their own pace. Computer-based instructional programs often tailor instruction to students' prior knowledge and skills. Homework assignments can be easily individualized for the amount and kinds of practice that different students need.

Considering Group Differences

Our students' ethnic and cultural backgrounds may sometimes guide our choice of instructional strategies. Recent immigrants from some Asian countries may be more accustomed to teacher-directed instruction than to student-directed classroom activities (Igoa, 1995). Yet students from cultures that place a high premium on interpersonal cooperation (e.g., as is true in many Hispanic and Native American communities) are likely to achieve at higher levels in classrooms with many interactive and collaborative activities (Garcia, 1994, 1995; McAlpine & Taylor, 1993; N. M. Webb & Palincsar, 1996). In situations where students have limited English skills, technology can often come to our assistance, perhaps in the form of English-language tutorials, computer programs that "read" electronic "books" to a student, and word processing programs with spell checkers and grammar checkers (P. F. Merrill et al., 1996).

Collaborative and cooperative approaches to instruction may also be helpful for our female students. Small-group discussions and activities encourage girls to participate more actively than they typically do during whole-class instruction (Théberge, 1994). We should note, however, that boys sometimes take control during small-group activities. If we regularly

Identifying Objectives and Instructional Strategies Especially Suitable for Students with Special Educational Needs

CATEGORY	CHARACTERISTICS YOU MIGHT OBSERVE	SUGGESTED CLASSROOM STRATEGIES
Students with specific cognitive or academic difficulties	• Uneven patterns of achievement • Difficulty with complex cognitive tasks in some content domains • Difficulty processing or remembering information presented in particular modalities • Poor listening and/or reading skills • Greater-than-average difficulty in completing homework	• Establish challenging yet realistic objectives; tailor objectives to individual students' strengths and weaknesses. • Use an information processing analysis to identify the specific cognitive skills involved in a complex task; consider teaching each skill separately. • Use mastery learning, direct instruction, computer-based instruction, cooperative learning, and peer tutoring to help students master basic knowledge and skills. • During expository instruction, provide information through multiple modalities (e.g., with videotapes, audiotapes, graphic materials), and provide advance organizers and study guides. • Have students use computer tools (e.g., grammar and spell checkers) to compensate for areas of weakness. • Assign homework that provides additional practice in basic skills; individualize assignments for students' unique abilities and needs; provide extra scaffolding (e.g., solicit parents' help, explicitly teach effective study habits). • Use reciprocal teaching to promote listening and reading comprehension.
Students with social or behavioral problems	• Frequent off-task behavior • Inability to work independently for extended periods • Poor social skills	• Provide small-group direct instruction and peer tutoring as ways of providing one-on-one attention. • Keep unsupervised seatwork assignments to a minimum. • Use cooperative learning to foster social skills and friendships. • Give explicit guidelines about how to behave during interactive learning sessions. (As appropriate, also use strategies above for students with specific cognitive or academic difficulties.)
Students with general delays in cognitive and social functioning	• Difficulty with complex tasks • Difficulty thinking abstractly • Need for a great deal of repetition and practice of basic information and skills • Difficulty transferring information and skills to new situations	• Establish realistic objectives in both the academic and social arenas. • Use task analysis to break complex behaviors into simpler responses that students can more easily learn. • Present information as concretely as possible (e.g., by engaging students in hands-on experiences). • Use direct instruction, computer-assisted instruction, and in-class activities to provide extended practice in basic skills. • Embed basic skills within authentic tasks to promote transfer to the outside world. • Use peer tutoring as a means of promoting friendships with nondisabled classmates; identify skills that students have mastered and can teach to their classmates or to younger students.
Students with physical or sensory challenges	• Average intelligence in most instances • Tendency to tire easily (for some) • Limited motor skills (for some) • Difficulty with speech (for some)	• Aim for instructional objectives similar to those for nondisabled students unless there is a compelling reason to do otherwise. • Allow frequent breaks from strenuous or intensive activities. • Use computer-based instruction (perhaps with specially adapted input mechanisms) to allow students to progress through material at their own pace and make active responses during instruction. • When students have difficulty speaking, provide another means of enabling them to participate actively in class discussions and cooperative learning groups (perhaps through technology).
Students with advanced cognitive development	• Greater frequency of responses at higher levels of Bloom's taxonomy (e.g., analysis, synthesis) • Rapid learning • Greater ability to think abstractly; appearance of abstract thinking at a younger age • Greater conceptual understanding of classroom material • Ability to learn independently	• Identify standards and objectives that challenge students and encourage them to develop to their full potential. • Provide opportunities to pursue topics in greater depth (e.g., through assigned readings, computer-based instruction, or homogeneous cooperative groups). • Teach strategies that enable students to learn on their own (e.g., library skills, scientific methods, use of hypermedia and the Internet). • Encourage students to communicate via the Internet with others who have similar interests and abilities. • Ask predominantly higher-level questions. • Use advanced students as peer tutors only if both tutors and learners will benefit.

Sources: T. Bryan, Burstein, & Bryan, 2001; Carnine, 1989; DuNann & Weber, 1976; DuPaul et al., 1998; Fiedler et al., 1993; Greenwood et al., 1988; Heward, 2000; C. C. Kulik et al., 1990; Mercer, 1997; P. F. Merrill et al., 1996; Morgan & Jenson, 1988; Piirto, 1999; A. Robinson, 1991; Ruef et al., 1998; Schiffman, Tobin, & Buchanan, 1984; Spicker, 1992; R. J. Stevens & Slavin, 1995; Tarver, 1992; Turnbull et al., 1999; J. W. Wood & Rosbe, 1985.

see such male dominance, we may occasionally want to form all-female groups; by doing so, we are likely to increase girls' participation in group activities and encourage them to take leadership roles (Fennema, 1987; MacLean et al., 1995).

Interactive strategies are especially valuable when our objectives include promoting social development as well as academic achievement. Peer tutoring encourages friendly relationships across ethnic and racial lines (Greenwood et al., 1988). Cooperative learning groups, especially when students work on tasks involving a number of different skills and abilities, can foster an appreciation for the various strengths that students with diverse backgrounds are likely to contribute (E. G. Cohen, 1994; E. G. Cohen & Lotan, 1995). And virtually any "cooperative" approach to instruction—cooperative learning, reciprocal teaching, peer tutoring—may help students begin to recognize that despite the obvious diversity among them, they are more similar to one another than they are different (Schofield, 1995).

Accommodating Students with Special Needs

We may sometimes want to tailor our instructional objectives to students' specific cognitive abilities or disabilities; for example, we may need to modify our expectations in some academic areas for students with learning disabilities, and we may find it beneficial to set more challenging goals for students who are gifted. In addition, different instructional strategies may be more or less useful for students with special educational needs. For instance, strictly expository instruction (e.g., a lecture) may provide a quick and efficient means of presenting new ideas to students who think abstractly and process information quickly yet be incomprehensible and overwhelming to students with low cognitive ability. Similarly, discovery learning is often effective in enhancing the academic achievement of students with high ability; however, it may actually be detrimental to the achievement of lower-ability students who have not yet mastered basic concepts and skills (Corno & Snow, 1986). And mastery learning and direct instruction have been shown to be effective with students who have learning difficulties, including many students with special educational needs, yet they may prevent rapid learners from progressing at a rate commensurate with their abilities (Arlin, 1984; DuPaul et al., 1998; Leinhardt & Pallay, 1982; Rosenshine & Stevens, 1986).

As teachers, we will often need to adapt instructional strategies to the unique strengths and weaknesses of particular students with special needs. For example, when students have difficulty with certain aspects of information processing (e.g., when they have certain learning disabilities), it may be especially important to provide a variety of supports (advance organizers, visual aids, study guides, etc.) during expository instruction (Mercer, 1997). When students have social or behavioral problems, we may find that we need to provide close supervision and frequent encouragement and feedback during independent in-class assignments. Table 13.3 provides a "memory refresher" for some of the characteristics of students with special needs that we have considered in previous chapters; it also presents some instructional strategies we can use to accommodate such characteristics.

The Big Picture

Historically, many theorists and practitioners have looked for—and in some cases decided that they've found—the single "best" way to teach children and adolescents. The result has been a series of movements in which educators advocate a particular instructional approach and then, a few years later, advocate a very different approach (K. R. Harris & Alexander, 1998; Sfard, 1998). I've often wondered why the field of education is characterized by such "pendulum swings," and I've developed several hypotheses. Perhaps some people are looking for a teaching *algorithm*—a specific procedure they can follow to guarantee high achievement. Perhaps they confuse theory with fact, thinking that the latest theoretical fad must inevitably be the "correct" explanation of how children learn or develop, and so conclude that the teaching im-

plications they derive from the theory must certainly be just as correct. Or maybe they just have an overly simplistic view of what the goals of our educational system should be.

When we consider which instructional strategies to use in our classrooms, we must remember that *there is no single best approach to classroom instruction*. Each of the strategies we've examined has its merits, and each is useful in different situations and for different students. In general, our choice of an instructional strategy must depend on at least three things: the objective of the lesson, the nature of the subject matter, and the characteristics and abilities of our students. Table 13.4 presents general conditions and specific examples in which each strategy might be most appropriate.

TABLE 13.4

COMPARE/CONTRAST

Choosing an Instructional Strategy

YOU MIGHT USE . . .	WHEN . . .	FOR EXAMPLE, YOU MIGHT . . .
Lectures and/or textbook readings	• The *objective* is to acquire knowledge within the cognitive domain. • The *lesson* involves information best learned within a specific organizational structure. • *Students* are capable of abstract thought, have knowledge to which they can relate new material, and have adequate reading skills and learning strategies for assigned readings.	• Enumerate the critical battles of World War I to advanced history students. • Demonstrate several defensive strategies to the varsity soccer team.
Mastery learning	• The *objective* is to learn knowledge or skills to mastery (perhaps to automaticity). • The *lesson* provides critical information or skills for later instructional units. • *Students* vary in the time they need to achieve mastery.	• Have each student in instrumental music practice the C major scale until he or she can do so perfectly. • Have students practice 100 single-digit addition facts until they can answer all the facts correctly within a five-minute period.
Direct instruction	• The *objective* is to learn a well-defined body of knowledge and skills. • The *lesson* provides critical information or skills for later instructional units. • *Students* are likely to need considerable guidance and practice in order to learn successfully.	• Explain how to add fractions with different denominators and give students practice in adding such fractions both in class and through homework. • Demonstrate how to use a jigsaw and watch carefully as students use the tool to cut irregularly shaped pieces of wood.
Computer-based instruction	• The *objective* is to acquire knowledge and skills within the cognitive domain. • The *lesson* involves information that students can learn from reading text or from watching and listening to multimedia presentations. • *Students* have some familiarity with computers and can work with only minimal guidance from their teacher.	• Use a typing-skills tutorial that helps students develop automaticity in keyboarding. • Assign a research project that requires the use of a computer-based, multimedia encyclopedia.
Online research	• The *objective* is to gain expertise in finding information available on the World Wide Web. • The *lesson* requires information not readily available in the classroom. • *Students* have some familiarity with Internet software (e.g., Web browsers) and search engines.	• Ask students to identify demographic differences among various regions of the United States using data from the U.S. Census Bureau. • Have students read about current events on the Web sites of national news bureaus and newsmagazines.
Discovery learning	• The *objective* is to develop firsthand knowledge of physical or social phenomena. • The *lesson* involves information that can be correctly deduced from hands-on experimentation with concrete objects or from direct social interaction with others. • *Students* have enough knowledge to interpret their findings correctly but sometimes have difficulty learning from strictly abstract material.	• Ask students to find out what happens when two primary colors of paint (red and yellow, red and blue, or yellow and blue) are mixed together. • Create a classroom situation in which students discover firsthand how it feels to experience "taxation without representation."
In-class activities	• The *objective* is to practice using new information or skills. • The *lesson* requires considerable teacher monitoring and scaffolding. • *Students* cannot yet work independently on the task.	• Have beginning tennis students practice their serves. • Have students work in pairs to draw portraits of their classmates.
Computer simulations and applications	• The *objective* is to gain experience in a domain that can be explored more easily in a "virtual" world *or* to gain experience with computer tools. • The *lesson* involves any task for which simulation software is available *or* that lends itself to a computer application. • *Students* have some familiarity with computers and can work with only minimal guidance from their teacher.	• Have students explore human anatomy through a computer simulation that gives an inside "look" at various anatomical structures. • Have students write a résumé using a word processing program.

TABLE 13.4

COMPARE/CONTRAST

Choosing an Instructional Strategy—Continued

YOU MIGHT USE . . .	WHEN . . .	FOR EXAMPLE, YOU MIGHT . . .
Homework	• The *objective* is to learn new yet simple material, obtain additional practice with familiar information and procedures, or relate classroom subject matter to the outside world. • The *lesson* is one that students can complete with little if any help from others. • *Students* exhibit enough self-regulation to perform the task independently.	• Have students read the next chapter in their health book. • In a unit on migration, have students find out what state, province, or country their parents and grandparents were born in.
Authentic activities	• The *objective* is to apply classroom material to real-world situations. • The *lesson* involves synthesizing and applying a variety of knowledge and skills. • *Students* have mastered the knowledge and skills necessary to perform the task.	• Have students grow sunflowers using varying amounts of water, plant food, and sunlight. • Have students construct maps of their local community, using appropriate symbols to convey direction, scale, physical features, and so on.
Teacher questions	• The *objective* is to understand and elaborate on a topic in greater depth. • The *lesson* involves complex material, such that frequent monitoring of students' learning is essential, mental elaboration of ideas is beneficial, or both. • *Students* are not likely to elaborate spontaneously or to monitor their own comprehension effectively.	• Ask questions that promote recall and review of the previous day's lesson. • Ask students for examples of how nonrenewable resources are recycled in their own community.
Class discussion	• The *objective* is to achieve greater conceptual understanding, acquire a multisided perspective of a topic, or both. • The *lesson* involves complex and possibly controversial issues. • *Students* have sufficient knowledge about the topic to voice informed ideas and opinions.	• Ask students to discuss the ethical implications of the United States' decision to drop an atomic bomb on Hiroshima. • Ask groups of four or five students to prepare arguments for an upcoming debate regarding the pros and cons of increasing the minimum wage.
Reciprocal teaching	• The *objective* is to develop reading comprehension and learning strategies. • The *lesson* requires students to cognitively process material in relatively complex ways. • *Students* have poor reading comprehension and learning strategies.	• Model four types of questions—summarizing, questioning, clarifying, and predicting—as students read aloud a passage from a textbook. • Ask students to take turns being "teacher" and ask similar questions of their classmates.
Technology-based discussion	• The *objective* is to construct new knowledge as a group and continue to revise it over time. • The *lesson* involves a topic that is sufficiently multifaceted that all students have something to contribute. • *Students* have adequate reading comprehension skills to learn independently or in small groups, and adequate computer literacy to exchange information electronically.	• In a community where students have easy access to computers and the Internet, set up an electronic bulletin board that allows students to share their questions and ideas about homework assignments. • On the classroom computer's desktop, create several "folders" in which students can save essays for one another to read and critique.
Cooperative learning	• The *objective* is to develop the ability to work cooperatively with others on academic tasks. • The *lesson* involves tasks that are too large or difficult for a single student to accomplish independently. • *Students'* cultural backgrounds emphasize cooperation rather than competition.	• Have groups of two or three students work together on mathematics "brain teasers." • Have students in a Spanish class work in small groups to write and videotape a soap opera spoken entirely in Spanish.
Peer tutoring	• The *objective* is to learn basic knowledge or skills. • The *lesson* contains material that can effectively be taught by students. • *Students* vary in their mastery of the material, yet even the most advanced can gain increased understanding by teaching it to someone else.	• Have students work in pairs to practice conjugating irregular French verbs. • Have some students help others work through simple mathematical word problems.

A successful classroom—one in which students are acquiring and using school subject matter in truly meaningful ways—is undoubtedly a classroom in which a variety of approaches to instruction can be found. As you gain experience as a classroom teacher, you will become increasingly adept at using many (perhaps all) of the strategies we've explored in this chapter. You will, I hope, experiment with different approaches to determine which ones work most effectively for your own objectives, academic discipline(s), and students. Furthermore, as noted in Chapter 1, you can continue to grow as a teacher if you keep yourself up to date both on the subject matter you are teaching and on theoretical and research perspectives on effective classroom instruction.

Yet knowing how to plan and implement instruction is not enough. Effective teachers also create a classroom environment conducive to student learning. Furthermore, they regularly monitor their students' progress toward achieving classroom objectives and adapt instruction when warranted. We will consider the classroom environment and assessment in the next three chapters.

PRAXIS Turn to Appendix C, "Matching Book and Ancillary Content to the PRAXIS™ Principles of Learning and Teaching Tests," to discover sections of this chapter that may be especially applicable to the PRAXIS™ tests.

Now go to our Companion Website at http://www.prenhall.com/ormrod to assess your understanding of chapter content with "Multiple-Choice Questions," apply comprehension in "Essay Questions," broaden your knowledge of educational psychology with related "Web Links," gain greater insight about classroom learning in "Learning in the Content Areas," and analyze and assess classroom work in the "Student Artifact Library."

CASE STUDY: *Uncooperative Students*

Ms. Mihara is beginning a unit entitled "Customs in Other Lands" in her fourth-grade class. Having heard about the benefits of cooperative learning, she asks students to form groups of four that will work together throughout the unit. On Monday she assigns each group a particular country: Australia, Colombia, Ireland, Israel, Greece, Japan, or South Africa. She then instructs the groups, "Today we will go to the school library, where you can find information on the customs of your country and check out materials you think will be useful. Over the next two weeks, you will have time every day to work as a group. You should learn all you can about the customs of your country. A week from Friday, each group will give an oral report to the rest of the class."

During the next few class sessions, Ms. Mihara runs into more problems than she ever imagined she would. For example, when the students form their groups, she notices that the high achievers have gotten together to form one group and that the socially oriented, "popular" students have flocked to three others. The remaining two groups are comprised of whichever students are left over. Some groups get immediately to work on their task, others spend their group time sharing gossip and planning upcoming social events, and still others are neither academically or socially productive.

As the unit progresses, Ms. Mihara hears more and more complaints from students about their task ("Janet and I are doing all the work; Karen and Mary Kay aren't helping at all." "Eugene thinks he can boss the rest of us around because we're studying Ireland and he's Irish." "We're spending all this time but just can't seem to get anywhere!"). And the group reports at the end of the unit differ markedly in quality: Some are carefully planned and informative, whereas others are disorganized and lack substantive information.

"So much for this cooperative learning stuff," Ms. Mihara mumbles to herself. "If I want students to learn something, I'll just have to teach it to them myself."

- Why have Ms. Mihara's cooperative learning groups not been as productive as she had hoped? Considering the features of cooperative learning that we examined in this chapter, what did Ms. Mihara do wrong?
- How might you orchestrate the cooperative learning unit differently than Ms. Mihara?

Once you have answered these questions, compare your responses with those presented in Appendix B.

Key Concepts

teacher-directed instruction (p. 430)
student-directed instruction (p. 430)
instructional objective (p. 430)
standards (p. 431)
cognitive domain (p. 431)
psychomotor domain (p. 431)
affective domain (p. 431
Bloom's taxonomy (p. 434)
short-term objective (p. 435)
long-term objective (p. 435)
task analysis (p. 436)

expository instruction (p. 438)
advance organizer (p. 440)
prior knowledge activation (p. 440)
signal (in a lecture or textbook) (p. 440)
mastery learning (p. 442)
direct instruction (p. 444)
programmed instruction (p. 445)
computer-assisted instruction (CAI) (p. 445)
computer-based instruction (CBI) (p. 445)
hypertext (p. 445)
hypermedia (p. 445)

distance learning (p. 446)
discovery learning (p. 447)
lower-level question (p. 455)
higher-level question (p. 455)
reciprocal teaching (p. 460)
cooperative learning (p. 463)
jigsaw technique (p. 466)
scripted cooperation (p. 466)
base group (p. 467)
peer tutoring (p. 467)

14

Creating and Maintaining a Productive Classroom Environment

*T*hink back to your elementary and secondary school years. In which teachers' classrooms were you more likely to work hard and stay on task? In which teachers' classrooms were you more likely to misbehave? What strategies did the more effective teachers use to help you be productive?

Effective teachers not only choose instructional strategies that promote effective learning and cognitive processing, but they also create an environment that keeps students busily engaged in classroom activities. In this chapter we will consider how we can plan and create a classroom environment conducive to students' learning and achievement. In particular, we will address the following questions:

■ How can we create a classroom environment that promotes student learning and minimizes off-task behavior?
■ How can we effectively deal with the misbehaviors that *do* occur?
■ What strategies are especially helpful when we have students from diverse backgrounds?
■ How can we coordinate our efforts with other teachers, community agencies, and students' parents?

CASE STUDY: *A Contagious Situation*

Ms. Cornell received her teaching certificate in May; soon after, she accepted a position as a fifth-grade teacher at Twin Pines Elementary School. She spent the summer planning her classroom curriculum: She identified the objectives she wanted her students to accomplish during the year and developed numerous activities to help them meet those objectives. She now feels well prepared for her first year in the classroom.

After the long, hot summer, most of Ms. Cornell's students seem happy to be back at school. So on the very first day of school, Ms. Cornell jumps headlong into the curriculum she has planned. But three problems quickly present themselves—problems in the form of Eli, Jake, and Vanessa.

These three students seem determined to disrupt the class at every possible opportunity. They move about the room without permission, making a point of annoying others as they walk to the pencil sharpener or wastebasket. They talk out of turn, sometimes being rude and disrespectful to their teacher and classmates and at other times belittling the classroom activities that Ms. Cornell has so carefully planned. They rarely complete their in-class assignments, preferring instead to engage in horseplay or practical jokes. They seem particularly prone to misbehavior at "down" times in the class schedule—for example, at the beginning and end of the school day, before and after recess and lunch, and on occasions when Ms. Cornell is preoccupied with other students.

Ms. Cornell continues to follow her daily lesson plans, ignoring her problem students and hoping they will begin to see the error of their ways. Yet, with the three of them egging one another on, the disruptive behavior continues. Furthermore, it begins to spread to other students. By the middle of October, Ms. Cornell's class is a three-ring circus, with general chaos reigning in the classroom and instructional objectives rarely being accomplished. The few students who still seem intent on learning something are having a difficult time doing so.

Creating an Environment Conducive to Learning

As a first-year teacher, Ms. Cornell is well prepared in some respects but not at all prepared in others. She has carefully identified her objectives and the activities through which she intends to accomplish those objectives. But she has neglected to think about how she might keep students on task or how she might adjust her lesson plans based on how students are progressing. And she has not considered how she might nip behavior problems in the bud, before such misbehaviors begin to interfere with students' learning. In the absence of such planning, no curriculum—not even one grounded firmly in principles of learning and development—is likely to promote student achievement.

Students learn more effectively in some classroom environments than in others. Consider these four classrooms as examples:

Mr. Aragon's class is calm and orderly. The students are working independently at their seats, and all of them appear to be concentrating on their assigned tasks. Occasionally, students approach Mr. Aragon to seek clarification of an assignment or to get feedback about a task they've completed, and he confers quietly with them.

Mr. Boitano's class is chaotic and noisy. A few students are doing their schoolwork, but most are engaged in very nonacademic activities. One girl is painting her nails behind a large dictionary propped up on her desk, a boy nearby is picking wads of gum off the underside of his desk, several students are exchanging the latest school gossip, and a group of boys is reenacting the Battle of Waterloo with rubber bands and paper clips.

Mr. Cavalini's classroom is as noisy as Boitano's. But rather than exchanging gossip or waging war, students are debating (often loudly and passionately) about the pros and cons of nuclear energy. After twenty minutes of heated discussion, Cavalini stops them, lists their various arguments on the board, and then explains in simple philosophical terms why there is no easy or "correct" resolution of the issue.

Mr. Durocher believes that students learn most effectively when rules for their behavior are clearly spelled out. So he has rules for almost every conceivable occasion—fifty-three rules in all. Following is a small sample:

- Be in your seat before the bell rings.
- Use a ballpoint pen with blue or black ink for all assignments.
- Use white lined paper with straight edges; do not use paper with loose-leaf holes or spiral notebook "fringe."
- Raise your hand if you wish to speak, and then speak only when called upon.
- Do not ask questions unrelated to the topic being studied.
- Never leave your seat without permission.

Durocher punishes each infraction severely enough that students follow the rules to the letter. So his students are a quiet and obedient (if somewhat anxious) bunch, but they never seem to learn as much as Durocher knows they are capable of learning.

Two of these classrooms are quiet and orderly; the other two are active and noisy. Yet as you can see, the activity and noise levels are not good indicators of how much students are learning. Students are learning both in Mr. Aragon's quiet classroom and in Mr. Cavalini's rambunctious one. At the same time, neither the students in Mr. Boitano's loud, chaotic battlefield nor those in Mr. Durocher's peaceful military dictatorship seem to be learning much at all.

Effective **classroom management**—creating and maintaining a classroom environment conducive to learning and achievement—has little to do with noise or activity level. A well-managed classroom is one in which students are consistently engaged in productive learning activities and in which students' behaviors rarely interfere with the achievement of instructional objectives (W. Doyle, 1990; Emmer & Evertson, 1981; Munn, Johnstone, & Chalmers, 1990).

Is it possible to *over*manage a classroom? If so, what might be the negative ramifications of doing so?

Creating and maintaining an environment in which students participate eagerly and actively in classroom activities can be a challenging task indeed. After all, we must tend to the unique needs of many different students, we must sometimes coordinate several activities at the same time, and we must often make quick decisions about how to respond to unanticipated events (W. Doyle, 1986a). Furthermore, we must vary our classroom management techniques considerably depending on the particular instructional strategies (expository, hands-on, or interactive) that we are using (Emmer & Stough, 2001). So it is not surprising that beginning teachers often mention classroom management as their number one concern (Veenman, 1984).

To create and maintain a productive learning environment, effective teachers typically

- Physically arrange the classroom in a way that facilitates teacher-student interactions and keeps distracting influences to a minimum
- Create a classroom climate in which students have a sense of belonging and an intrinsic motivation to learn
- Set reasonable limits for student behavior
- Plan classroom activities that encourage on-task behavior
- Continually monitor what all students are doing
- Modify instructional strategies when necessary

A well-managed classroom is one in which students are consistently engaged in learning. It is not necessarily one in which everyone is quiet.

In the pages that follow, we will consider specific ways to implement each of these strategies.

Arranging the Classroom

As we arrange the furniture in the classroom, decide where to put various instructional materials and pieces of equipment, and think about where each student might sit, we should consider the effects that various arrangements are likely to have on students' behaviors. Ultimately, we want a situation in which we can

- Minimize distractions
- Interact easily with any student
- Survey the entire class at any given time

Minimizing Distractions

Stuart is more likely to poke a classmate with his pencil if he has to brush past the classmate to get to the pencil sharpener. Marlene is more likely to fiddle with instructional materials at an inappropriate time if they are within easy reach of her desk. David is more likely to gossip with a friend if that friend is sitting right beside him. As teachers, we should arrange our classrooms in ways that minimize the probability that such off-task behaviors will occur (Emmer, Evertson, Clements, & Worsham, 1994; Sabers, Cushing, & Berliner, 1991). For example, we can establish traffic patterns that allow students to move around the classroom without disturbing one another, keep intriguing materials out of sight and reach until it is time to use them, and situate overly chatty friends on opposite sides of the room.

Facilitating Teacher-Student Interaction

Ideally, we should arrange desks, tables, and chairs so that we can easily interact and converse with our students (Davis & Thomas, 1989). Students seated near us are more likely to pay attention, interact with us, and become actively involved in classroom activities; hence, we may want to place chronically misbehaving or uninvolved students close at hand (W. Doyle, 1986a; Schwebel & Cherlin, 1972; C. S. Weinstein, 1979; Woolfolk & Brooks, 1985).

Surveying the Entire Class

As we proceed through various lessons and activities—even when we're working with a single individual or small group—we should ideally be able to see *all* of our students (Emmer et al., 1994). By occasionally surveying the classroom for possible signs of confusion, frustration, or boredom, we can more easily detect minor student difficulties and misbehaviors before they develop into serious problems.

Creating an Effective Classroom Climate

Think back on your many years as a student. Can you remember a class in which you were afraid of being ridiculed if you asked a "stupid" question? Can you remember one in which you and your fellow students spent more time goofing off than getting your work done because no one seemed to take the class seriously? Can you remember one in which you never knew what to expect because your instructor was continually changing expectations and giving last-minute assignments without warning?

In addition to the classroom's physical environment, we must also consider the psychological environment, or **classroom climate**, that we create. Ideally, we want a classroom in which students make their own learning a high priority and feel free to take the risks and make the mistakes so critical for long-term academic success. To create such a classroom climate, we should

- Communicate acceptance of, respect for, and caring about our students as human beings
- Establish a businesslike, yet nonthreatening, atmosphere
- Communicate appropriate messages about school subject matter
- Give students some control over classroom activities
- Create a sense of community among the students

Showing Acceptance, Respect, and Caring

As you should recall from Chapter 11, human beings may have a fundamental need to feel socially connected with others. This *need for relatedness* expresses itself somewhat differently in different students. Many students have a high need for affiliation: They actively seek out friendly relationships with others. Many also have a high need for approval: They want to gain the acceptance and high regard of those around them.

We can help our students meet such needs through our own actions, including the many little things we do daily. For example, we can give students a smile and warm greeting at the beginning of each class day. We can compliment them when they get a new haircut, excel in an extracurricular activity, or receive recognition in the local newspaper. We can ask them for information or advice about a topic of particular interest to them. We can offer our support when they struggle at challenging classroom tasks and let them know we're pleased when they eventually succeed at such tasks. We can be good listeners when they come to school angry or upset. And we can show them how we, too, are fallible human beings by sharing some of our own concerns, problems, and frustrations (Diamond, 1991; Spaulding, 1992).

Research is clear on this point: Effective teachers are warm, caring individuals who, through a variety of statements and actions, communicate a respect for students, an acceptance of them as they are, and a genuine concern about their well-being. When students believe that their teachers are genuinely caring and supportive, they have higher self-efficacy, find classroom subject matter more interesting and enjoyable, are more likely to ask for help when they need it, are less likely to cheat on classroom assignments, and achieve at higher levels (C. B. Hayes, Ryan, & Zseller, 1994; Kim, Solomon, & Roberts, 1995; Murdock, Hale, Weber, Tucker, & Briggs, 1999; Osterman, 2000; A. M. Ryan & Patrick, 2001; A. M. Ryan et al., 2001; Wentzel & Wigfield, 1998). In the following exercise you will look at a communication strategy that one teacher used.

Such teacher behaviors may be particularly beneficial for those students who have few caring relationships to draw on at home (Diamond, 1991).

Midway through the school year, a first-grade teacher has her students begin *dialogue journals* that will allow them to communicate individually with her every day. Following are several entries in 6-year-old Matt's journal. As you read the entries, consider

- What purpose(s) this activity might serve
- Whether Matt's writing skills are adequate to make the activity meaningful

I am a couch potato ara you?

Sometimes I am! I like to curl up under an afghan and read until way past my bedtime. What else do you like to do?

I love soccer. I am grait at goll.

I see you playing soccer all the time at recess. And I saw you at Woodridge fields last fall. You really are good! Do you play any other sports?

I play bas ball sam tim. Do you play int sprts?

I love to play basketball. I used to be on a team in high school. I am a good skier too. And I like to swim and dive.

I lok Skein SPshal don hilscein. Are you gd at sceih?

I am a very good skier. I like to go fast. Do you think you could keep

up with me? We used to have our own ski lift in our back yard!

I can go fastr than you.

I guess we will just have to have a race sometime! Where do you usually go skiing? Besides, you said you are a couch potato. I am sure that I can beat a couch potato! Cinchy!

The journal exchange serves both academic and social purposes: It allows the students to practice their reading and writing skills within an authentic task (actual communication with another person), and it provides a way for the teacher to express her unconditional regard and support for each student. Although Matt's writing skills are far from perfect—he leaves out some capital letters and periods and misspells many words (e.g., *especially downhill skiing* is "spshal don hilscein")—they are certainly adequate to communicate his thoughts. Notice how the teacher does *not* correct Matt's misspellings. Her primary purposes are to encourage him to write and to open the lines of communication, and negative feedback about spelling might interfere with both of these ends. Instead, the teacher simply models correct spelling in her own entries.

How might the teacher adapt the journal assignment for students who cannot yet read and write?

Establishing a Businesslike, Nonthreatening Atmosphere

As we have just seen, an important element of effective classroom management is developing positive relationships with our students. At the same time, we must recognize that we and our students alike are in school to get certain things accomplished. Accordingly, we should maintain a relatively businesslike atmosphere in the classroom most of the time (Davis & Thomas, 1989). This is not to say that our classroom activities must be boring and tedious; on the contrary, they can often be exciting and engaging. But excitement and entertainment should not be thought of as goals in and of themselves. Rather, they are means to a more important goal: achieving instructional objectives.

Yet it is important that this businesslike atmosphere is not uncomfortable or threatening. As noted in Chapter 11, students who are excessively anxious about their class performance are unlikely to give us their best. How can we be businesslike without being threatening? Among other things, we can hold our students accountable for achieving instructional objectives yet not place them under continual surveillance. We can point out their mistakes yet not make them feel like failures (C. R. Rogers, 1983). And we can admonish them for misbehavior yet not hold grudges against them from one day to the next (Spaulding, 1992).

Communicating Messages About School Subject Matter

In earlier chapters we've stressed the importance of making school subject matter relevant to students' lives. All too often, however, students view school activities and assignments more as things to "get done" than as things that will help them be successful over the long run (L. M. Anderson, Brubaker, Alleman-Brooks, & Duffy, 1985; Brophy & Alleman, 1991; Stodolsky et al., 1991).

As teachers, we give students messages about the value of school subject matter not only in what we say but also in what we do (W. Doyle, 1983). If we ask students to spend hours each day engaged in what seems like meaningless busy work, and if we assess learning primarily through tests that encourage rote memorization, we are indirectly telling students that classroom tasks are merely things that need to be "done." Furthermore, if we continually focus their attention on performance goals—what their test grades are, how their work compares to that of their classmates, and so on—we increase their anxiety about school subject matter and indirectly increase the frequency of disruptive behavior (Marachi et al., 2001; A. M. Ryan & Patrick, 2001). If, instead, we continually demonstrate how classroom topics relate to the outside world, if we assess learning in ways that require meaningful learning and elaboration, and if we focus on how well each student is improving over time, we show students that the subject matter isn't just something to be learned for its own sake—that it can enhance the quality of their lives—and create a climate more conducive to learning and productivity.

Giving Students a Sense of Control

To make sure our students accomplish instructional goals, we must control the direction of classroom events to some extent. Nevertheless, we can give our students a sense that they, too, control some aspects of classroom life. For example, we can use strategies such as these (Spaulding, 1992):

- Give students advance notice of upcoming activities and assignments (enabling them to plan ahead).
- Create regular routines for accomplishing assignments (enabling students to complete the assignments successfully with minimal guidance from us).
- Allow students to set some of their own deadlines for completing assignments (enabling them to establish a reasonable timeframe for themselves).
- Provide opportunities for students to make choices about how to complete assignments or spend some of their class time (enabling them to set some of their own priorities).

In what sense do Eli, Jake, and Vanessa have control in Ms. Cornell's class? What might Ms. Cornell do to help them control their classroom lives in more productive ways?

By giving students opportunities to work independently and choose some of their own means of achieving classroom objectives, we promote the sense of self-determination so important for intrinsic motivation (see Chapter 12). We also promote the self-regulated learning so essential for students' long-term academic success (see Chapter 10).

Creating a Sense of Community

In the preceding chapter I described an activity in which cooperative groups in my daughter's high school Spanish class wrote and videotaped Spanish soap operas. Later the teacher awarded a variety of "Oscars" for these *telenovelas,* being sure that every student received an Oscar for some aspect of his or her performance. Occasionally, competition among *groups* of students can be productive *if* all groups have an equal chance of winning—for instance, if every group has diverse abilities and talents represented—and *if* the final outcome is determined more by student effort than by intelligence or other seemingly uncontrollable factors (Stipek, 1996).

In general, however, a competitive classroom environment is often counterproductive when we consider principles of motivation presented in Chapter 12. For one thing, competitive situations focus students' attention on performance goals rather than mastery goals (Nicholls, 1984; Spaulding, 1992); hence, students are more likely to worry about how competent they appear to their teacher and classmates than about how well they understand classroom material. Second, competition creates a situation in which most students become losers rather than winners; their self-efficacy decreases as a result, and their intrinsic motivation to learn is undermined (Deci & Ryan, 1985, 1992). Finally, when students consistently see others performing more successfully than themselves, they are more likely to attribute their own failures to a lack of ability: They conclude that they simply don't have what it takes to succeed at classroom tasks (C. Ames, 1984).

Ideally our students will be more productive if they cooperate, rather than compete, with one another (C. Ames, 1984; Deci & Ryan, 1985). Not only can they support one another in their efforts to master classroom topics, but they can also nurture the peer relationships that, for many, are so important for their social development and psychological well-being. Students have higher academic self-efficacy, are more motivated to learn and achieve, and are more consistently on task when they can collaborate with their classmates on assignments, believe that their peers accept and respect them, and have little fear that others will ridicule them if they make errors or ask for help (Osterman, 2000; A. M. Ryan & Patrick, 2001; A. M. Ryan et al., 2001).

In Chapter 7 we considered the concept of a *community of learners,* a classroom in which teacher and students consistently work together to help one another learn. Ultimately, we want to create a **sense of community** in the classroom—a sense that we and our students have shared goals, are mutually respectful and supportive of one another's efforts, and believe that everyone makes an important contribution to classroom learning (Hom & Battistich, 1995; Kim et al., 1995; Lickona, 1991; Osterman, 2000). Theorists have identified several strategies that can help create a sense of classroom community:

- Make frequent use of interactive and collaborative teaching strategies (class discussions, cooperative learning activities, etc.).
- Solicit students' ideas and opinions, and incorporate them into classroom discussions and activities.
- Create mechanisms through which students can help make the classroom run smoothly and efficiently (e.g., assigning various "helper" roles to students on a rotating basis).
- Emphasize such prosocial values as sharing and cooperation.
- Provide opportunities for students to help one another (e.g., by asking, "Who has a problem that someone else might be able to help you solve?").
- Institute a "no exclusion" policy in group activities (e.g., by insisting that any student who wants to be involved in a play activity *can* be involved).
- Encourage students to be on the lookout for classmates on the periphery of ongoing activities (perhaps students with disabilities) and encourage them to join in.
- Work on social skills with those students whose interpersonal behaviors may alienate others.
- Provide public recognition of students' contributions to the overall success of the classroom.
- Convey the general message that *all* students deserve the respect of their classmates and are important members of the classroom community. (Emmer et al., 1994; Kim et al., 1995; Lickona, 1991; Osterman, 2000; Sapon-Shevin, Dobbelaere, Corrigan, Goodman, & Mastin, 1998; A. M. Ryan & Patrick, 2001; Turnbull et al., 2000)

Students achieve at higher levels in the classroom when they have a *sense of community*—that is, when they have shared goals and are respectful and supportive of one another's efforts.

When students share a sense of community, they are more likely to exhibit prosocial behavior, stay on task, express enthusiasm about classroom activities, and achieve at high levels. Furthermore, a sense of classroom community is associated with lower rates of emotional distress, disruptive classroom behavior, truancy, violence, drug use, and dropping out (D. C. Gottfredson, 2001; Hom & Battistich, 1995; Kim et al., 1995; Osterman, 2000; M. D. Resnick et al., 1997).

Setting Limits

In the opening case study, Ms. Cornell failed to provide guidelines for how students should behave—something she should have done in the first week. A class without guidelines for appropriate behavior is apt to be chaotic and unproductive. And students must learn that certain behaviors—especially those that cause injury, damage school property, or interfere with classmates' learning and performance—will definitely not be tolerated. Setting reasonable limits on classroom behavior not only promotes a more productive learning environment but also contributes to students' socialization by encouraging them to develop behaviors essential for successful participation in the adult world.

Recall our discussion of *socialization* in Chapter 3.

FIGURE 14.1 Beginning the school year with a few rules

Effective teachers typically begin the school year with a few rules that will help classroom activities run smoothly. Here are several examples of rules you might want to include in your list (adapted from Emmer et al., 1994):

Bring all needed materials to class. (Students should have books, homework assignments, permission slips, and any needed supplies for planned activities.)

Be in your seat and ready to work when the bell rings. (Students should be at their desks, have paper out and pencils sharpened, and be physically and mentally ready to work.)

Respect and be polite to all people. (Students should listen attentively when someone else is speaking, behave appropriately for a substitute teacher, and refrain from insults, fighting, and other disrespectful or hostile behavior.)

Respect other people's property. (Students should keep the classroom clean and neat, refrain from defacing school property, ask for permission to borrow another's possessions, and return those possessions in a timely fashion.)

Obey all school rules. (Students must obey the rules of the school building as well as the rules of the classroom.)

Experienced educators have offered several suggestions for setting reasonable limits on students' classroom behavior. More specifically, they suggest that we

- Establish a few rules and procedures at the beginning of the year
- Present rules and procedures in an informational rather than controlling manner
- Periodically review the usefulness of existing rules and procedures
- Acknowledge students' feelings about classroom requirements

As we consider these suggestions, we will also consider how we can preserve students' sense of control and self-determination.

Establishing Initial Rules and Procedures

The first few days and weeks of the school year are critical ones for establishing classroom procedures and setting expectations for student behavior. Effective classroom managers establish and communicate certain rules and procedures right from the start (Borko & Putnam, 1996; Davis & Thomas, 1989; W. Doyle, 1986a, 1990). They identify acceptable and unacceptable behaviors (e.g., see Figure 14.1). They develop consistent procedures and routines for such things as completing seatwork, asking for help, and turning in assignments. And they have procedures in place for nonroutine events such as school assemblies, field trips, and fire drills.

Ideally, our students should understand that rules and procedures are not merely the result of our personal whims but are designed to help the classroom run smoothly and efficiently. One way of promoting such understanding is to include students in decision making about the rules and procedures by which the class will operate (Davis & Thomas, 1989; Fuller, 2001; Lickona, 1991). For example, we might solicit students' suggestions for making sure that unnecessary distractions are kept to a minimum and that everyone has a chance to speak during class discussions. By incorporating students' ideas and concerns regarding the limits we set, we help students understand the reasons for—and thereby help them adhere to—those limits (Emmer et al., 1994).

Once rules and procedures have been formulated, we should communicate them clearly and explicitly, describe the consequences of noncompliance, and enforce them consistently. Taking time to clarify and enforce rules and procedures seems to be especially important in the early elementary grades, when students may not be as familiar with "how things are done" at school (Evertson & Emmer, 1982; Gettinger, 1988).

Keep in mind that rules and procedures are easier to remember and therefore easier to follow if they are relatively simple and few in number (Davis & Thomas, 1989). Effective classroom managers tend to stress only the most important rules and procedures at the beginning of the school year; they introduce other rules and procedures later on as needed (W. Doyle, 1986a). Also keep in mind that, although some order and predictability are essential for student productivity, *too much* order may make our classroom a rather boring, routine place—

Figure 14.2 Presenting classroom rules and procedures as information

Our students are more likely to be intrinsically motivated to follow classroom rules and procedures if we present them as items of information rather than as forms of control.

We might say this (information):	**. . . rather than this (control):**
"You'll get your independent assignments done more quickly if you get right to work."	"Please be quiet and do your own work."
"As we practice for our fire drill, it is important that we line up quickly and be quiet so that we can hear the instructions we are given and will know what to do."	"When the fire alarm sounds, line up quickly and quietly and then wait for further instructions."
"This assignment is designed to help you develop the writing skills you will need after you graduate. It is unfair to other authors to copy their work word for word, so we will practice putting ideas into our own words and giving credit to authors whose ideas we borrow. Passing off another's writing and ideas as your own can lead to suspension in college or a lawsuit in the business world."	"Cheating and plagiarism are not acceptable in this classroom."
"It's important that I can clearly read your writing. If your words are illegible and your cross-outs are confusing, I may not be able to give you as high a grade as you deserve on an assignment."	"Use good penmanship on all assignments and erase any errors carefully and completely. Points will be deducted for sloppy writing."

one without an element of fun and spontaneity. We don't necessarily need rules and procedures for everything!

Presenting Rules and Procedures as Information

As we learned in Chapter 12, we are more likely to maintain students' sense of self-determination if we present rules and procedures as items of information instead of as forms of control. Figure 14.2 lists several examples of rules and procedures presented in an informational manner; each of these statements includes the reasons for imposing certain guidelines. The following scenario provides a simple illustration of how giving a reason can make all the difference in the world:

> Gerard is a boy with a low tolerance for frustration. Whenever he asks Ms. Donnelly for assistance, he wants it *now*. If she is unable to help him immediately, he screams, "You're no good!" or "You don't care!" and shoves other students' desks as he walks angrily back to his seat.
>
> At one point during the school year, the class has a unit on interpersonal skills. One lesson in the unit addresses *timing*—the most appropriate and effective time to ask for another person's assistance with a problem.
>
> A week later, Gerard approaches Ms. Donnelly for help with a math problem. She is working with another student, but she turns briefly to Gerard and says, "Timing."
>
> Ms. Donnelly waits expectantly for Gerard's usual screaming. Instead, he responds, "Hey, Ms. D., I get it! I can ask you at another time!" He returns to his seat with a smile on his face. (based on Sullivan-DeCarlo, DeFalco, & Roberts, 1998, p. 81)

For additional benefits of providing reasons, see the discussion of *induction* in Chapter 3.

Reviewing Existing Rules and Procedures

As the school year progresses, we may occasionally want to revise the rules and procedures we established earlier. For instance, we may find that rules about when students can and cannot move around the room are overly restrictive or that procedures for turning in homework don't adequately accommodate students who must sometimes leave class early to attend athletic events.

Regularly scheduled class meetings provide one mechanism through which we and our students can periodically review classroom rules and procedures (D. E. Campbell, 1996; Glasser, 1969). Consider this scenario as an example:

> Every Friday at 2:00, Ms. Ayotte's students move their chairs into one large circle, and the weekly class meeting begins. First on the agenda is a review of the past week's successes, including both academic achievements and socially productive events. Next, the group identifies problems that have emerged during the week and brainstorms possible ways to

avert such problems in the future. Finally, the students consider whether existing classroom rules and procedures are serving their purpose. They may decide to modify some existing rules and procedures or may establish new ones.

During the first few class meetings, Ms. Ayotte leads the group discussions. But once students have gotten the hang of things, she begins to relinquish control of the meetings to one or another of her students on a rotating basis.

Do you see parallels between *authoritative parenting* (Chapter 3) and the guidelines for setting limits described in this chapter?

By providing such opportunities for students to revise classroom policies frequently, we find one more way of giving them a sense of ownership in such policies. Furthermore, perhaps because of the authoritative atmosphere and the conversations about moral dilemmas that student decision making may entail, more advanced levels of moral reasoning (described in Chapter 3) may result (Power et al., 1989; Power & Power, 1992).

Acknowledging Students' Feelings

There will undoubtedly be times when we must ask our students to do something they would prefer not to do. Rather than pretend that such feelings don't exist, we are better advised to acknowledge them (Deci & Ryan, 1985). For example, we might tell students that we know how difficult it can be to sit quietly during an unexpectedly lengthy school assembly or to spend an entire evening on a particular homework assignment. At the same time, we can explain that the behaviors we request of them, though not always intrinsically enjoyable, do, in fact, contribute to the long-term goals they have set for themselves. By acknowledging students' feelings about tasks they would rather not do yet also pointing out the benefits of performing those tasks, we increase the likelihood that the students will accept the limitations imposed on their behavior (Deci & Ryan, 1985).

Planning Activities That Keep Students on Task

As noted in Chapter 13, effective teachers plan their lessons ahead of time. Furthermore, they plan activities that not only facilitate students' learning and cognitive processing but also motivate students to *want* to learn. For instance, they think about how to make subject matter interesting and incorporate variety into lessons, perhaps by employing colorful audiovisual aids, using novel activities (e.g., small-group discussions, class debates), or moving to a different location (e.g., the media center or school yard) (Davis & Thomas, 1989; Munn et al., 1990).

As we plan our upcoming classroom activities, then, we should simultaneously plan specific ways of keeping our students on task. In addition to using the motivational strategies described in Chapters 11 and 12, we should

- Be sure students will always be busy and engaged
- Choose tasks at an appropriate academic level
- Provide a reasonable amount of structure for activities and assignments
- Make special plans for transition times in the school day

Keeping Students Busy and Engaged
EXPERIENCING FIRSTHAND   *Take Five*

For the next five minutes, you are going to be a student who has nothing to do. *Remain exactly where you are,* put your book aside, and *do nothing.* Time yourself so that you spend exactly five minutes on this "task." Let's see what happens.

What kinds of responses did you make during your five-minute break? Did you fidget a bit, perhaps wiggling tired body parts, scratching newly detected itches, or picking at your nails? Did you "interact" in some way with something or someone else, perhaps tapping loudly on a table, turning on a radio, or talking to someone else in the room? Did you get out of your seat altogether—something I specifically asked you *not* to do?

The exercise I just gave you was a somewhat artificial one, to be sure, and the things I am defining as "misbehaviors" in this instance (wiggling your toes, tapping the table, getting out of your seat, etc.) won't necessarily qualify as misbehaviors in your classroom. Yet the exercise has, I hope, shown you that it is very difficult to do *nothing at all* for any length of time.

Like us, our students will be most likely to misbehave when they have a lot of free time on their hands.

Effective classroom managers make sure that there is little "empty" time in which nothing is going on. As teachers, we can use numerous strategies to keep our students busy and engaged; as examples, we can

- Have something specific for students to do each day, even on the first day of class
- Have materials organized and equipment set up before class
- Have activities that ensure *all* students' involvement and participation
- Maintain a brisk pace throughout each lesson (although not so fast that students can't keep up)
- Ensure that student comments are relevant and helpful but not excessively long-winded (perhaps by taking any chronic time-monopolizers aside for a private discussion about letting others have a chance to express their thoughts)
- Spend only short periods of time dealing with individual students during class unless other students are capable of working independently and productively in the meantime
- Have a system in place that ensures that students who finish an assigned task quickly have something else to do (perhaps writing in a class journal or reading a book)

(Davis & Thomas, 1989; W. Doyle, 1986a; Emmer et al., 1994; Evertson & Harris, 1992; Gettinger, 1988; Munn et al., 1990)

Students who are busily engaged in classroom activities rarely exhibit problem behaviors.

Choosing Tasks at an Appropriate Level

Our students are more likely to get involved in their classwork, rather than in off-task behavior, when they have academic tasks and assignments appropriate for their current ability levels (W. Doyle, 1986a; Emmer et al., 1994). They are apt to misbehave when they are asked to do things that are probably too difficult for them—in other words, when they are incapable of completing assigned tasks successfully. Thus, classroom misbehaviors are more often observed in students who have a history of struggling in their coursework (W. Doyle, 1986a).

This is not to suggest that we should plan activities so easy that our students are not challenged and learn nothing new in doing them. One workable strategy is to *begin* the school year with relatively easy tasks that students can readily complete. Such early tasks enable students to practice normal classroom routines and procedures; they also give students a sense that they can enjoy and be successful in classroom activities. Once a supportive classroom climate has been established and students are comfortable with classroom procedures, we can gradually introduce more difficult and challenging assignments (W. Doyle, 1990; Emmer et al., 1994; Evertson & Emmer, 1982). We might take a similar approach when introducing new instructional strategies; for instance, when we first ask students to engage in cooperative activities, we might have them work with relatively familiar content so that they can focus on mastering effective group interaction skills (asking for help, giving explanations, etc.) without being distracted by difficult subject matter (N. M. Webb & Farivar, 1999).

With this point in mind, how might Ms. Cornell (in the opening case study) have gotten the year off to a better start?

Providing Structure

EXPERIENCING FIRSTHAND   *Take Five More*

Grab a blank sheet of paper and a pen or pencil, and complete these two tasks:

Task A: Using short phrases, list six characteristics of an effective teacher.

Task B: Describe *schooling*.

Don't continue reading until you've spent a total of at least *five minutes* on these tasks.

Once you have completed the two tasks, answer either "Task A" or "Task B" to each of the following questions:

1. For which task did you have a better understanding of what you were being asked to do?
2. During which task did your mind more frequently wander to irrelevant topics?
3. During which task did you engage in more off-task behaviors (e.g., looking around the room, doodling on the paper, getting out of your seat)?

I am guessing that you found the first task to be relatively straightforward, whereas the second wasn't at all clear-cut. Did Task B's ambiguity lead to more irrelevant thoughts and off-task behaviors for you?

Just as may have been the case for you in the preceding exercise, off-task behavior in the classroom occurs more frequently when activities are so loosely structured that students don't have a clear sense of what they are supposed to do. Effective teachers tend to give assignments with some degree of structure. They also give clear directions about how to proceed with a task and a great deal of feedback about appropriate responses, especially during the first few weeks of class (W. Doyle, 1990; Evertson & Emmer, 1982; Munn et al., 1990; Weinert & Helmke, 1995).

Yet we need to strike a happy medium here. We don't want to structure classroom tasks to the point where students never make their own decisions about how to proceed or to the point where only lower-level thinking skills are required. Ultimately, we want our students to develop and use higher-level processes—for example, to think analytically, critically, and creatively—and we must have classroom assignments and activities that promote such processes (W. Doyle, 1986a; Weinert & Helmke, 1995).

The concept of *scaffolding* (first described in Chapter 2) is helpful in this context: We can provide a great deal of structure for tasks early in the school year, gradually removing that structure as students become better able to structure tasks for themselves. For example, when introducing students to cooperative learning, we might structure initial group meetings by breaking down each group task into several subtasks, giving clear directions as to how each subtask should be carried out, and assigning every group member a particular role to serve in the group. As the school year progresses and students become more adept at learning cooperatively with their classmates, we gradually can become less directive about how group tasks are accomplished.

Planning for Transitions

In the opening case study, Eli, Jake, and Vanessa often misbehaved at the beginning and end of the school day, as well as before and after recess and lunch. Transition times—as students end one activity and begin a second, or as they move from one classroom to another—are times when misbehaviors are especially likely to occur. Effective classroom managers take steps to ensure that such transitions proceed quickly and without a loss of momentum (Arlin, 1979; W. Doyle, 1984; Emmer et al., 1994). For example, they establish procedures for moving from one activity to the next. They ensure that there is little slack time in which students have nothing to do. And especially at the secondary level, where students change classes every hour or so, effective classroom managers typically have a task for students to perform as soon as class begins.

Can you relate this strategy to *behavioral momentum* (Chapter 9)?

How might we plan for the various transitions that occur throughout the school day? Here are some examples:

- A physical education teacher has students begin each class session with five minutes of stretching exercises.
- An elementary school teacher has students follow the same procedure each day as lunchtime approaches. Students must (1) place completed assignments in a basket on the teacher's desk, (2) put away classroom supplies (e.g., pencils, paint, scissors) they have been using, (3) get their lunch boxes from the coatroom, and (4) line up quietly by the classroom door.
- A middle school mathematics teacher has students copy the new homework assignment as soon as they come to class.
- A junior high school history teacher has formed long-term cooperative learning groups (*base groups*) of three or four students each. The groups are given a few minutes at the end of each class to compare notes on material presented that day and get a head start on the evening's reading assignment.
- A high school English composition teacher writes a topic or question (e.g., "My biggest pet peeve," "Whatever happened to hula hoops?") on the chalkboard at the beginning of each class period. Students know that when they come to class, they should immediately take out pencil and paper and begin to write on the topic or question of the day.

All of these strategies, though very different in nature, share the common goal of keeping students focused on their schoolwork.

Monitoring What Students Are Doing

Effective teachers communicate something called **withitness:** They know (and their students *know* that they know) what students are doing at all times in the classroom. In a sense, "with-it" teachers act as if they have eyes in the back of their heads. They make it clear that they are aware of what everyone is doing. They regularly scan the classroom and make frequent eye contact with individual students. They know what misbehaviors are occurring *when* those misbehaviors occur, and they know who the perpetrators are (Davis & Thomas, 1989; Emmer et al., 1994; Kounin, 1970). Consider the following scenario as an example:

Effective teachers communicate *withitness:* They know what each of their students is doing at all times.

> An hour and a half of each morning in Mr. Rennaker's elementary school classroom is devoted to reading. Students know that, for part of this time, they will meet with Mr. Rennaker in their small reading groups. They spend the remainder of the time working on independent assignments tailored to their individual reading skills. As Mr. Rennaker works with each reading group in one corner of the classroom, he situates himself with his back to the wall so that he can simultaneously keep one eye on students working independently at their seats. He sends a quick and subtle signal—perhaps a stern expression, a finger to the lips, or a call of a student's name—to any student who begins to be disruptive.

When we demonstrate such withitness, especially at the beginning of the school year, our students are more likely to stay on task and display appropriate classroom behavior (W. Doyle, 1986a; Woolfolk & Brooks, 1985). Not surprisingly, they are also more likely to achieve at high levels (W. Doyle, 1986a).

Modifying Instructional Strategies

As we have repeatedly seen, principles of effective classroom management go hand in hand with principles of learning and motivation. When our students are learning and achieving successfully and when they clearly want to pursue the curriculum that the classroom offers, they are likely to be busily engaged in productive classroom activities for most of the school day (W. Doyle, 1990). In contrast, when they have difficulty understanding classroom subject matter or when they have little interest in learning it, they are likely to exhibit the nonproductive or even counterproductive classroom behaviors that result from frustration or boredom.

Research tell us that when students misbehave, beginning teachers often think about what the students are doing wrong. In contrast, experienced, "expert" teachers are more apt to think about what *they themselves* can do differently to keep students on task, and they modify their plans accordingly (Emmer & Stough, 2001; Sabers et al., 1991; H. L. Swanson, O'Connor, & Cooney, 1990). So when behavior problems crop up, we should start thinking as the experts do, by considering questions such as the following:

- How can I alter instructional strategies to capture students' interest and excitement?
- Are instructional materials so difficult that students are becoming frustrated? Or are they so easy that students are bored?
- What are students really concerned about? For example, are they more concerned about interacting with their classmates than in gaining new knowledge and skills?
- How can I address students' motives and goals (e.g., their desire to affiliate with classmates) while simultaneously helping them achieve classroom objectives?

Answering such questions helps us focus our efforts on our ultimate goal: to help students *learn.*

Occasionally, current events on the international, national, or local scene (e.g., a terrorist attack, a president's impeachment trial, or a tragic car accident involving fellow students) may take priority. When students' minds are justifiably preoccupied with something other than the topic of instruction, they will have difficulty paying attention to that preplanned topic and are

From your own perspective, what are the key ingredients of a successfully managed classroom?

Physically arrange the classroom in a way that facilitates teacher-student interactions and keeps distracting influences to a minimum.

An elementary school teacher has arranged the twenty-eight student desks in his classroom into seven clusters of four desks each. The students who sit together in clusters form base groups for many of the classroom's cooperative learning activities. The teacher occasionally asks students to move their chairs into a large circle for whole-class discussions.

Show students that you care about and respect them as human beings, and give them some say about what happens in the classroom.

A high school teacher realizes that she is continually admonishing one particular student for his off-task behavior. To establish a more positive relationship with the student, she makes a point to greet him warmly in the hallway before school every day. At the end of one day in which his behavior has been especially disruptive, she catches him briefly to express her concern, and the two agree to meet the following morning to discuss ways of helping him stay on task more regularly.

Set reasonable limits for student behavior.

After describing the objectives of an instrumental music class on the first day of school, a junior high school teacher tells his students, "There is one rule for this class to which I will hold firm. You must not engage in any behavior that will interfere with your own learning or with that of your classmates."

Plan classroom activities that encourage on-task behavior.

Before each class, a creative writing teacher writes the day's topic on the chalkboard. Her students know that when they arrive at class, they are to take out a pencil and paper and begin an essay addressing that topic.

Show students that you are continually aware of what they are doing.

While meeting with each reading group in one corner of the classroom, an elementary school teacher sits with his back to the wall so that he can keep an eye on those students who are working together in centers or independently at their desks.

Modify your plans for instruction when necessary.

A teacher discovers that students quickly complete the activity she thought would take them an entire class period. She wraps up the activity after fifteen minutes and then begins the lesson she had originally planned for the following day.

likely to learn little about it. In such extenuating circumstances, we may want to abandon our lesson plans altogether.

Despite our best efforts, students may sometimes behave in ways that disrupt classroom activities and interfere with student learning. Effective teachers not only plan and structure a classroom that minimizes potential behavior problems but they also deal with the misbehaviors that do occur (W. Doyle, 1990). What strategies are most effective in dealing with student misbehaviors? We turn to this topic now.

Dealing with Misbehaviors

For purposes of our discussion, we will define a **misbehavior** as any action that can potentially disrupt classroom learning and planned classroom activities (W. Doyle, 1990). Some classroom misbehaviors are relatively minor ones that have little long-term impact on students' achievement. Such behaviors as talking out of turn, writing notes to classmates during a lecture, and submitting homework assignments after their due date—particularly if such behaviors occur infrequently—generally fall in this category. Other misbehaviors are far more serious, in that they definitely interfere with the learning and achievement of one or more students. For example, when students scream at their teachers, hit their classmates, or habitually refuse to participate in classroom activities, then classroom learning—certainly the learning of the "guilty party," and often the learning of other students as well—may be adversely affected. Furthermore, such behaviors may, in some cases, threaten the physical safety or psychological well-being of others in the classroom.

As teachers, we need to plan ahead about how to respond to the variety of misbehaviors we may see in the classroom. As we do so, we must keep in mind that different strategies may be appropriate under different circumstances. In the following pages we will consider six general strategies and the situations in which each is likely to be appropriate:

TABLE 14.1   PRINCIPLES/ASSUMPTIONS

Six Strategies for Dealing with Student Misbehavior

STRATEGY	SITUATIONS IN WHICH IT'S APPROPRIATE	POSSIBLE EXAMPLES
Ignoring the behavior	• The misbehavior is unlikely to be repeated. • The misbehavior is unlikely to spread to other students. • Unusual circumstances elicit the misbehavior temporarily. • The misbehavior does not seriously interfere with learning.	• One student surreptitiously passes a note to another student just before the end of class. • A student accidentally drops her books, startling other students and temporarily distracting them from their work. • An entire class is hyperactive on the last afternoon before spring break.
Cueing the student	• The misbehavior is a minor infraction yet interferes with students' learning. • The behavior is likely to change with a subtle reminder.	• A student forgets to close his notebook at the beginning of a test. • A cooperative learning group is talking unnecessarily loudly. • Several students are exchanging jokes during an independent seatwork assignment.
Discussing the problem privately with the student	• Cueing has been ineffective in changing the behavior. • The reasons for the misbehavior, if made clear, might suggest possible strategies for reducing it.	• A student is frequently late to class. • A student refuses to do certain kinds of assignments. • A student shows a sudden drop in motivation for no apparent reason.
Promoting self-regulation	• The student has a strong desire to improve his or her behavior.	• A student doesn't realize how frequently she interrupts her classmates. • A student seeks help in learning to control his anger. • A student wants to develop more regular study habits.
Using behaviorist techniques	• The misbehavior has continued over a period of time and significantly interferes with student learning. • The student seems unwilling or unable to use self-regulation techniques.	• A student has unusual difficulty sitting still for reasonable periods of time. • A student's obscene remarks continue even though her teacher has spoken with her about the behavior on several occasions. • A member of the football team displays unsportsmanlike conduct that is potentially dangerous to other players.
Conferring with parents	• The source of the problem may lie outside school walls. • Parents are likely to work collaboratively with school personnel to bring about a behavior change.	• A student does well in class but rarely turns in required homework assignments. • A student is caught stealing, vandalizing school property, or engaging in other unethical or illegal behavior. • A student falls asleep in class almost every day.

- Ignoring the behavior
- Cueing the student
- Discussing the problem privately with the student
- Promoting self-regulation
- Using behaviorist approaches
- Conferring with parents

These six strategies are summarized in Table 14.1.

Ignoring the Behavior

Consider these situations:

> Dimitra rarely breaks classroom rules. But on one occasion, after you have just instructed your students to work quietly and independently at their seats, you see her whisper briefly to the student beside her. None of the other students seems to notice that Dimitra has disobeyed your instructions.

Herb is careless in chemistry lab and accidentally knocks over a small container of liquid (a harmless one, fortunately). He quickly apologizes and cleans up the mess with paper towels.

Are these misbehaviors likely to interfere with Dimitra's or Herb's academic achievement? Are they contagious behaviors likely to spread to other students, as the horseplay did in Ms. Cornell's class? The answer to both these questions is, "Probably not."

On some occasions our best course of action is *no* action, at least nothing of a disciplinary nature (Davis & Thomas, 1989; Silberman & Wheelan, 1980). Whenever we stop an instructional activity to deal with a misbehavior, even for a few seconds, we run the danger of disrupting the momentum of the activity and possibly drawing students' attention to their misbehaving classmates (W. Doyle, 1986a). If we respond every time a student gets a little bit out of line, our own actions may be more distracting than the student actions we are trying to curtail. Furthermore, by drawing class attention to a particular student's behavior, we may actually be reinforcing that behavior rather than discouraging it.

Dimitra's misbehavior—whispering briefly to a classmate during independent seatwork— is unlikely to spread to her classmates (they didn't notice her behavior) and is probably not an instance of cheating (it occurred before she began working on the assignment). Herb's misbehavior—knocking over a container of liquid in chemistry lab—has, in and of itself, resulted in an unpleasant consequence for Herb; the natural consequence is that he has to clean up the mess. In both situations, *ignoring* the misbehavior is probably the best thing we can do. The following are some general circumstances in which ignoring misbehavior may be the wisest course of action:

Can you relate *ignoring* to a specific concept in operant conditioning?

- When the behavior is a rare occurrence and probably won't be repeated
- When the behavior is unlikely to "spread"—that is, to be imitated by other students
- When unusual circumstances (e.g., the last day of school before a holiday, or an unsettling event in a student's personal life) elicit inappropriate behavior only temporarily
- When the behavior is typical for a particular age-group (e.g., when kindergartners become restless after sitting for an extended time, when fifth-grade boys and girls resist holding one another's hands during dance instruction)
- When the behavior's result (its natural consequence) is unpleasant enough to deter a student from repeating the behavior
- When the behavior is not seriously affecting students' classroom learning (Davis & Thomas, 1989; W. Doyle, 1986a; Dreikurs & Cassel, 1972; Munn et al., 1990; Silberman & Wheelan, 1980; Wynne, 1990)

Why is ignoring *not* an effective strategy in Ms. Cornell's classroom?

Cueing the Student

Consider these misbehaviors:

As you are explaining a difficult concept to your class, Marjorie is busily writing. At first, you think she is taking notes, but then you see her pass the paper across the aisle to Kang. A few minutes later, you see the same sheet of paper being passed back to Marjorie. Obviously, the two students are spending class time writing notes to each other and probably not hearing a word you are saying.

You have separated your class into small groups for a cooperative learning exercise. One group seems to be more interested in discussing weekend plans than in accomplishing assigned work. The group is not making the progress that other groups are making and probably won't complete the assignment if its members don't get down to business soon.

In some situations, student misbehaviors, though not serious in nature, *do* interfere with classroom learning and must therefore be discouraged. Effective classroom managers handle such minor behavior problems as unobtrusively as possible: They don't stop the lesson, distract other students, or call unnecessary attention to the behavior they are trying to stop (W. Doyle, 1990; Emmer, 1987). In many cases, they use **cueing:** They let the students know, through a signal of one kind or another, that they are aware of the misbehavior and would like it to stop.

You may wish to refer back to the sections "Cueing" and "Cueing Inappropriate Behaviors" in Chapter 9.

We can cue students about unacceptable behaviors in a variety of ways. One strategy is to use body language—perhaps frowning, making eye contact, or raising a finger to the lips to indicate "be quiet." A second is to use a signal of some kind—perhaps ringing a small bell or flicking the light switch on and off to get students' attention. We might also want to move closer to misbehaving students; such physical proximity communicates our withitness about what they are doing.

When such subtle cues are unlikely to work, we will have to use explicit verbal cues. In these situations, we should try to focus students' attention on what *should* be done, rather than on what *isn't* being done (Emmer et al., 1994; Good & Brophy, 1994). Here are some examples of simple yet potentially effective verbal cues:

- "Students who are quietest go to lunch first."
- "By now, all groups should have completed the first part of the assignment and should be working on the second part."
- "I see some art supplies that still need to be put back on the shelves before we can be dismissed."

Discussing the Problem Privately with the Student

Consider these misbehaviors:

> Alonzo is almost always several minutes late to your third-period algebra class. When he finally arrives, he takes an additional two or three minutes pulling his textbook and other class materials out of his backpack. You have often reminded Alonzo about the importance of coming to class on time, yet the tardiness continues.

> Trudy rarely completes classroom assignments; in fact, she often doesn't even *begin* them. On many occasions, you have tried unsuccessfully to get her on task with explicit verbal cues (e.g., "Your book should be open to page 27," "Your cooperative group is brainstorming possible solutions to a difficult problem, and they could really use your ideas"). A few times, when you have looked Trudy in the eye and asked her point-blank to get to work, she has defiantly responded, "I'm not going to do it. You can't make me!"

Sometimes in-class signals are insufficient to change a student's misbehavior. In such situations, talking with the student about the behavior is the next logical step. The discussion should be a *private* one for several reasons. First, as noted earlier, calling classmates' attention to a problem behavior may actually reinforce that behavior rather than discourage it. Or instead, the attention of classmates may cause a student to feel excessively embarrassed or humiliated—feelings that may make the student overly anxious about being in the classroom in the future. Finally, when we spend too much class time dealing with a single misbehaving student, other students are likely to get off task as well (Scott & Bushell, 1974).

If cueing a misbehaving student is ineffective, a private conversation might be the best next step. From a motivational standpoint, how might private discussions with students be helpful?

Conversations with individual students give us, as teachers, a chance to explain why certain behaviors are unacceptable and must stop. (As noted earlier, students are more likely to obey rules when they understand the reasons behind the rules.) Furthermore, teacher-student conversations give students a chance to offer reasons for their misbehaviors. To illustrate, when talking with Alonzo, we may discover that he is chronically tardy because, as a diabetic, he must check his blood sugar level between his second- and third-period classes. He can perform the procedure himself, but it takes a few minutes; besides, he would prefer to do it in the privacy of the nurse's office at the other end of the building. When speaking with Trudy about her refusal to do assigned work, she may express her frustration about not being able to read or understand the subject matter as well as her classmates do.

Students' explanations can sometimes provide clues about how best to deal with their behavior over the long run. For example, given Alonzo's diabetes, we may not be able to change his ongoing tardiness to class; instead, we might reassign him to a seat by the door so that he can join class unobtrusively each day, and we might ask the student next to him to fill him in quietly on what we have done before his arrival. Trudy's frustrations with her schoolwork suggest that she needs additional scaffolding to help her succeed; they also hint at a possible undiagnosed learning disability that may warrant a referral to the school psychologist. In some cases, our conversations with students may reveal maladaptive interpretations of social situations. For instance, a chronically aggressive student may express her belief that her classmates "are always trying to pick a fight" when we ourselves know that this perception is not accurate (recall our discussion of *hostile attributional bias* in Chapter 3). In such instances, we might consult with the school counselor about how to help the student interpret social interactions in a more productive manner.

You can learn more about how some students misperceive social situations in the section "Social Cognition" in Chapter 3.

Yet our students won't always provide explanations that lead to such logical solutions. For example, it may be that Alonzo is late to class simply because he wants to spend a few extra minutes hanging out with his friends in the hall. Or perhaps Trudy tells you she doesn't want to do her assignments because she's sick and tired of other people telling her what to do all the time. In such circumstances, it is essential that we not get in a power struggle—a situation where one person "wins" by dominating over the other in some way (Diamond, 1991; Emmer et al., 1994). Several strategies can minimize the likelihood of a power struggle:

- Listen empathically to what the student has to say, being openly accepting of the student's feelings and opinions (e.g., "I get the impression that you don't enjoy classroom activities very much; I'd really like to hear what your concerns are").
- Summarize what you believe the student has told you and seek clarification if necessary (e.g., "It sounds as if you'd rather not let your friends know how much trouble you're having with your schoolwork. Is that the problem, or is it something else?").
- Describe the effects of the problem behavior, including your own reactions to it (e.g., "When you come to class late every day, I worry that you are getting further and further behind, and sometimes I even feel a little hurt that you don't seem to value your time in my classroom").
- Give the student a choice of some sort (e.g., "Would you rather try to work quietly at your group's table, or would it be easier if you sat somewhere by yourself to complete your work?"). (derived from suggestions by Emmer et al., 1994)

Ultimately, we must communicate our interest in the student's long-term school achievement, our concern that the misbehavior is interfering with that achievement, and our commitment to working cooperatively with the student to alleviate the problem.

Promoting Self-Regulation

Sometimes, in addition to exploring reasons for a student's misbehavior and its unacceptability in the classroom, we may also want to develop a long-term plan for changing the student's behavior. Consider these situations as examples:

Brian doesn't seem to be making much progress toward instructional objectives; for instance, his performance on assignments and tests is usually rather low. As Brian's teacher, you are certain he is capable of better work, because he occasionally turns in an assignment or test paper of exceptionally high quality. The root of Brian's problem seems to be that he is off task most of the time. When he should be paying attention to a lesson or doing an assignment, he is instead sketching pictures of sports cars and airplanes, fiddling with whatever objects he has found on the floor, or daydreaming. Brian would really like to improve his academic performance but doesn't seem to know how to go about doing so.

Georgia frequently speaks out in class without permission. She blurts out answers to your questions, preventing anyone else from answering them first. She rudely interrupts other students' comments with her own point of view. And she initiates conversations with one or another of her classmates at the most inopportune times. You have talked with Georgia several times; she readily agrees that there *is* a problem and vows to restrain herself in the future. After each conversation with you, her behavior improves for a short time, but within a few days her mouth is off and running once again.

Brian's off-task behavior interferes with his own academic achievement, and Georgia's excessive chattiness interferes with the learning of her classmates. Cueing and private discussions haven't led to any improvement. But both Brian and Georgia have something going for them: They *want* to change their behavior. When students genuinely want to improve their own behavior, why not teach them ways to bring about desired changes *themselves*?

Here we revisit the topic of self-regulation, which we previously addressed within the context of social cognitive theory (Chapter 10). Social cognitive theorists offer several strategies for helping students begin to regulate and control their own behavior. *Self-monitoring* is especially valuable when students need a "reality check" about the severity of the problem behavior. Some students may underestimate the frequency with which they exhibit certain misbehaviors or the impact that those behaviors have on classroom learning. Georgia, for example, seems to blurt things out without even realizing that her actions interfere with her classmates' attempts to participate in classroom discussions. Other students may not be aware of how *infrequently* they exhibit appropriate behaviors. Brian, for instance, may think he is on task in the classroom far more often than he really is. To draw students' attention to the extent of their problem, we can ask them simply to record the frequency with which certain behaviors appear. For example, we might ask Georgia to make a check mark on a piece of paper every time she talks without permission. Or we might equip Brian with a timer set to "beep" every five minutes and ask him to write down, at the sound of each beep, whether he has been paying attention to his schoolwork. Research studies tell us that some behaviors improve significantly when we do nothing more than ask students to record their own behavior. In fact, both Georgia's and Brian's problems have been successfully dealt with in just this way (Broden, Hall, & Mitts, 1971; K. R. Harris, 1986; Mace et al., 1989; Mace & Kratochwill, 1988).

Self-instructions and *self-regulated problem-solving strategies* provide students with methods of reminding themselves about appropriate actions. For instance, we might provide Georgia with a simple list of instructions that she can give herself whenever she wants to contribute to a classroom discussion:

1. "Button" my lips (by holding them tightly together)
2. Raise my hand
3. Wait until I'm called on

Likewise, as noted in Chapter 10, we might help overly aggressive students handle interpersonal conflicts more constructively by following a prescribed sequence of steps: defining the problem, identifying several possible solutions, predicting the likely outcome of each approach, choosing and carrying out the best solution, and evaluating the results.

Self-evaluation and *self-imposed contingencies* provide a means through which we can encourage students to evaluate their progress and reinforce themselves for appropriate behavior. For example, we might ask Brian to give himself one point for each five-minute period that he's been on task. We might instruct Georgia to give herself a check mark for every fifteen-minute period in which she has spoken only when called on. By accumulating a certain number of points or check marks, students could earn the opportunity to engage in a favorite activity.

Self-regulatory strategies have several advantages. They enable us to avoid power struggles with students about who's "in charge." They are likely to increase students' sense of self-determination, hence also increasing students' intrinsic motivation to learn and achieve in the classroom. Furthermore, self-regulation techniques benefit students over the long run, promoting productive behaviors that are likely to continue long after students have moved on from a particular classroom or school. And of course, when we teach our students to monitor and modify their own behavior, rather than to depend on us to do it for them, we become free to do other things—for example, to *teach*!

At this point, let's look at how the teachers at one school try to encourage good behavior through self-regulation.

For more information, revisit the section "Self-Regulated Problem Solving" in Chapter 10.

INTERPRETING ARTIFACTS AND INTERACTIONS   *What Did I Do?*

Teachers at an elementary school use the following form to encourage productive behaviors and minimize unproductive ones. As you examine the form, think about

- Its potential strength(s)
- Its potential drawback(s)

Scoring: 2 = great effort 1 = OK effort 0 = effort needs improvement	9:00–10:30	11:00–12:30	1:30–3:00
Did I listen when the teacher or adult was speaking?			
Did I try my hardest and have a positive attitude?			
Did I stay in my seat during listening and work time?			
Total			

In theory, at least, the form should encourage students to self-monitor a variety of on-task behaviors. However, it has several drawbacks that are likely to limit its effectiveness. First, trying "my hardest" and having "a positive attitude" are virtually impossible to evaluate objectively. Even *listening* (in the first question) may be difficult to judge accurately: Young children in particular are apt to think of listening as sitting quietly and not interrupting, rather than as actually paying attention to and understanding what is being said (see Chapter 2). A second drawback is the time interval involved: Ninety minutes is sufficiently long that students may have trouble recalling how they behaved for the entire time. A third weakness is that the form attempts to be a one-size-fits-all rating sheet, when such is probably not possible. If we want students to monitor their own behavior, we should tailor the forms they use to the particular responses that are of concern for each student (e.g., see Figure 10.4 on page 351).

Using Behaviorist Approaches

There may occasionally be times when our students are either unwilling or unable to change their own behavior. Consider these situations:

> Tucker is out of his chair so often that, at times, you have to wonder whether he even knows where his chair *is*. He finds many reasons to roam about the room—he "has to" sharpen a pencil, he "has to" get his homework out of his backpack, he "has to" get a drink of water, and so on. Naturally, Tucker gets very little of his work done. Furthermore, his classmates are continually being distracted by his perpetual motion.

> Janet's verbal abusiveness is getting out of hand. She often insults her classmates by using sexually explicit language, and she frequently likens you to a female dog or a certain body part. You have tried praising her on occasions when she is pleasant with others, and she seems to appreciate your doing so, yet her abusive remarks continue unabated.

Imagine that both Tucker and Janet are in your class. You have already spoken with each of them about their inappropriate behaviors, yet you've seen no improvement. You have suggested methods of self-regulation, but the two students don't seem interested in changing for the better. So what do you do now?

When a particular misbehavior occurs so frequently that it is clearly interfering with a student's learning and achievement (and possibly with the learning and achievement of classmates as well) and when such other strategies as cueing and self-regulating techniques do not seem to decrease that misbehavior, then a more intensive intervention is in order. Behaviorist approaches described in Chapter 9 may be especially useful here: *applied behavior analysis* (which is based on principles related to response-consequence contingencies, shaping, etc.) and *functional analysis* and *positive behavioral support* (which also address the purposes that misbehaviors may serve for students). Behaviorist approaches may be especially effective when used in combination with other techniques, such as addressing perspective-taking ability and other aspects of social cognition, teaching effective social skills, and providing self-regulatory strategies (e.g., D. C. Gottfredson, 2001; T. R. Robinson, Smith, Miller, & Brownell, 1999).

How might we use behaviorist techniques to improve Tucker's classroom behavior? Applying principles of operant conditioning, we might identify one or more effective reinforcers (given Tucker's constant fidgeting, opportunities for physical activity might be reinforcing) and then make those reinforcers contingent on Tucker's staying in his seat for a specified length of time. As Tucker improves, we would gradually reinforce longer and longer periods of sedentary behavior. Since some out-of-seat responses (e.g., getting a reference book from the bookshelf, delivering a completed assignment to the teacher's "In" basket) are quite appropriate, we might also give Tucker a reasonable "allotment" of out-of-seats he can use during the day. Any out-of-seats that exceed this allotment should probably result in a mild yet punishing consequence—perhaps the logical consequence of spending time after school to make up uncompleted work.

It may be, however, that out-of-seat behavior serves a particular purpose for Tucker. Perhaps the behavior allows him to avoid tasks he has difficulty performing successfully. Or perhaps it enables him to release the energy that his body seems to overproduce. To identify the

You may want to revisit the section "Addressing Especially Difficult Classroom Behaviors" in Chapter 9.

Sometimes misbehaviors help students satisfy certain needs or achieve certain goals. In such situations, we may want to identify and encourage alternative behaviors that will enable students to accomplish the same ends.

possible function of Tucker's misbehavior, we would determine the kinds of situations in which Tucker is most likely to misbehave and then form and test hypotheses as to *why* he is occasionally hyperactive. If we discover that Tucker acts out only when he expects challenging assignments (as was true for Samantha in Chapter 9), then we should provide the instruction and support he needs to accomplish those assignments successfully. If, instead, we find that Tucker's hyperactivity appears regularly regardless of the situation, we may instead suspect a physiological cause and so give him numerous opportunities to release pent-up energy throughout the school day.

A behaviorist approach may be helpful with Janet as well. In this case, we might suspect that Janet has learned few social skills with which she can interact effectively with others; we might therefore need to begin by teaching her such skills through modeling, role playing, and so on (see "Fostering Social Skills" in Chapter 3). Once we know that Janet possesses effective interpersonal skills, we can begin to reinforce her for using those skills (perhaps with praise, as she has responded positively to such feedback in the past). Meanwhile, we should also punish (perhaps with a time-out) any relapses into old, abusive behavior patterns.

In our use of both reinforcement and punishment, we must keep in mind two guidelines that we identified in our discussion of behaviorism in Chapter 9. For one thing, we should be very explicit about response-consequence contingencies: We must let our students know ahead of time, in concrete terms, what behaviors will be followed by what consequences (e.g., we might use *contingency contracts*, described in Chapter 9). Furthermore, we should follow through with those consequences when the specified behaviors occur; effective classroom managers deal with inappropriate student behaviors quickly and consistently (W. Doyle, 1986a; Evertson & Emmer, 1982). Failing to follow through communicates the message that we were not really serious about the contingencies we described.

> What behaviorist techniques might Ms. Cornell use to help Eli, Jake, and Vanessa become more productive members of her classroom?

> Social cognitive theorists also advocate following through with the consequences students are expecting. Do you recall their rationale?

Conferring with Parents

Consider these problem behaviors:

> You assign short homework assignments almost every night; over the past three months, Carolyn has turned in only about a third of them. You're pretty sure that Carolyn is capable of doing the work, and you know from previous teacher conferences that her parents give her the time and support she might need at home to get her assignments done. You have spoken with Carolyn about the situation on several occasions, but she shrugs you off as if she doesn't really care whether she does well in your class or not.

> Students have frequently found things missing from their tote trays or desks when Roger has been in the vicinity. A few students have told you that they've seen Roger taking things that belong to others. Many of the missing objects have later turned up in Roger's possession. When you confront him about your suspicion that he's been stealing from his classmates, Roger adamantly denies it. He says he has no idea how Cami's gloves or Marvin's baseball trading cards ended up in his desk.

As we deal with classroom misbehaviors, we may sometimes need to involve students' parents, especially when the misbehaviors show a pattern over time and have serious implications for students' long-term success. In some instances, a simple telephone call may be sufficient (Emmer et al., 1994); for example, Carolyn's parents may be unaware that she hasn't been doing her homework (she's been telling them that she doesn't have any) and may be able to take the steps necessary to ensure that it is done from now on. In other cases, a school conference may be more productive; for example, you may want to discuss Roger's stealing habits with both Roger and his parent(s) together—something you can do more effectively when you all sit face-to-face in the same room. A little later in the chapter, we'll identify strategies for discussing problem behavior with students' parents.

Taking Student Diversity into Account

As we plan for a productive classroom environment, we must always take the diverse characteristics and needs of our students into account. For instance, we should make an extra effort to establish a supportive classroom climate, especially for students of ethnic minority groups and for students from lower-income neighborhoods. We may also need to define and respond to misbehaviors in somewhat different ways, depending on the particular ethnic and socioeconomic groups in our classrooms. Finally, we may often have to make special accommodations for students with special educational needs. Let's briefly consider each of these issues.

Creating a Supportive Climate

Earlier in the chapter we noted the value of creating a warm, supportive classroom atmosphere. Such an atmosphere may be especially important for students from ethnic minority groups (García, 1995; Ladson-Billings, 1994a). For example, African American students in one eighth-grade social studies class were asked why they liked their teacher so much. Their responses were very revealing:

"She listens to us!"

"She respects us!"

"She lets us express our opinions!"

"She looks us in the eye when she talks to us!"

"She smiles at us!"

"She speaks to us when she sees us in the hall or in the cafeteria!" (Ladson-Billings, 1994a, p. 68)

A warm, supportive classroom climate may be especially important for students from diverse ethnic backgrounds.

Simple gestures such as these go a long way toward establishing the kinds of teacher-student relationships that lead to a productive learning environment. It's essential, too, that we create a sense of community in the classroom—a sense that we and our students share common goals and are mutually supportive of everyone's reaching those goals. This sense of community is consistent with the cooperative spirit evident in many Hispanic, Native American, and African American groups (Cazden, 1988; Ladson-Billings, 1994a).

When working with students from lower-socioeconomic, inner-city backgrounds, we should also take special pains to create a classroom that feels safe and orderly (D. U. Levine & Lezotte, 1995; Roderick & Camburn, 1999). Many students from inner-city neighborhoods may be exposed to crime and violence almost daily; their outside world may be one in which they can rarely control the course of events. A classroom that is dependable and predictable can provide a sense of self-determination that students may not be able to find anywhere else; hence, it can be a place to which they look forward to coming each day.

Defining and Responding to Misbehaviors

As we determine which behaviors to define as *misbehaviors* in our classrooms, we must remember that some behaviors considered unacceptable in one culture may be quite acceptable in another culture. Let's consider some examples based on the cultural differences described in Chapter 4:

A student is frequently late for school, sometimes arriving more than an hour after the school bell has rung. A student who is chronically tardy may live in a community that does not observe strict schedules and timelines, a pattern common in some Hispanic and Native American communities.

Two students are sharing answers as they take a classroom test. Although this behavior represents cheating to many people, it may reflect the cooperative spirit and emphasis on group achievement evident in the cultures of many Native American and Mexican American students.

Several students are shouting at one another, hurling insults that become increasingly more derogatory and obscene. Such an interaction might seem to spell trouble, but it may instead be an instance of sounding, a friendly verbal interchange common in some African American communities.

Some of these behaviors are likely to have little if any adverse effect on students' learning. When some of them *do* have an effect, we must be patient and understanding as we help students acquire behaviors that are more conducive to academic productivity.

Accommodating Students with Special Needs

As we create a classroom environment that promotes student learning, we must take into account any special educational needs of our students. In general, an orderly classroom—one in which procedures for performing certain tasks are specified, expectations for student behavior are clear, and misbehaviors are treated consistently—makes it easier for students with special needs to adapt comfortably to a general education setting (Pfiffner & Barkley, 1998; M. C. Reynolds & Birch, 1988; Scruggs & Mastropieri, 1994).

When students have a history of behavior problems (e.g., as those with emotional and behavioral disorders often do), we may need to provide a great deal of guidance and support to help them develop productive classroom behavior. Furthermore, many students with special needs may need explicit feedback about their classroom performance. When praising desirable behavior, rather than saying "well done" or "nice work," we should describe exactly what responses we are praising. For example, we might say, "You did a good job following my instructions on your math assignment today," or "Thank you for remembering to sign yourself out when you went down the hall to use the drinking fountain just now." Similarly, when students display inappropriate behavior, we should tell them exactly what they have done wrong. For example, when speaking with a student with chronic behavior problems, we might say, "You borrowed Austin's book without asking him first. You know that taking other students' possessions without their permission is against the class rules we all agreed on at the beginning of the year." Additional suggestions for accommodating students with special needs are presented in Table 14.2.

Coordinating Efforts with Others

As we work to promote students' learning and development, we will be far more effective when we coordinate our efforts with the other people in students' lives. In particular, we must work cooperatively with other teachers, with the community at large and, most importantly, with parents.

Working with Other Teachers

Although teachers spend much of the school day working in individual classrooms, they are far more effective when they

- Communicate and collaborate regularly with one another
- Have common objectives regarding what students should learn and achieve
- Work together to identify obstacles to students' learning and to develop strategies for overcoming those obstacles
- Are committed, as a group, to promoting equality and multicultural sensitivity throughout the school community
  (Battistich, Solomon, Watson, & Schaps, 1997; Gottfredson, 2001; J. A. Langer, 2000; Levine & Lezotte, 1995)

Ideally, we should not only create a sense of community within our individual classrooms but also create an overall **sense of school community** (Battistich et al., 1995; Battistich, Solomon, Watson, & Schaps, 1997). Our students should get the same message from every teacher—that we are working together to help them become informed, successful, and productive citizens, and that they can and should *help one another* as well.

When teachers and other school personnel communicate an overall sense of school community, students have more positive attitudes toward school, are more motivated to achieve at high levels, and exhibit more prosocial behavior, and students from diverse backgrounds are more likely to interact with one another. Furthermore, teachers have higher expectations for students' achievement and a greater sense of self-efficacy about their own teaching effectiveness (Battistich et al., 1995, 1997; J. A. Langer, 2000). In fact, when teachers work together, they may have higher **collective self-efficacy**—a belief that, working as a group, they can definitely have an impact on students' learning and achievement—and this collective self-confidence is indeed related to students' performance (Bandura, 2000; Goddard et al., 2000). Such a "team spirit" has an additional advantage for beginning teachers: It provides the support structure (the scaffolding) they may need, especially when working with students who are at risk for school failure.

TABLE 14.2

STUDENTS IN INCLUSIVE SETTINGS

Planning for Students with Special Educational Needs

CATEGORY	CHARACTERISTICS YOU MIGHT OBSERVE	SUGGESTED CLASSROOM STRATEGIES
Students with specific cognitive or academic difficulties	• Difficulty staying on task • Misbehaviors such as hyperactivity, impulsiveness, disruptiveness, inattentiveness (in some students) • Poor time management skills and/or a disorganized approach to accomplishing tasks (in some students)	• Closely monitor students during independent assignments. • Make sure students understand their assignments; if appropriate, give them extra time to complete the assignments. • Make expectations for behavior clear, and enforce classroom rules consistently. • Cue students regarding appropriate behavior. • Reinforce (e.g., praise) desired behaviors immediately. • For hyperactive students, plan short activities that help them settle down after periods of physical activity (e.g., after recess, lunch, or physical education). • For impulsive students, teach self-instructions (see Chapter 10). • Teach students strategies for organizing their time and work (e.g., tape a schedule of daily activities to their desks, provide folders they can use to carry assignments between school and home).
Students with social or behavioral problems	• Frequent overt misbehaviors, such as acting out, aggression, noncompliance, destructiveness, or stealing (in some students) • Difficulty inhibiting impulses • Misbehaviors triggered by changes in the environment or daily routine or by sensory overstimulation (for students with autism) • Difficulty interacting effectively with classmates • Difficulty staying on task • Tendency to engage in power struggles with the teacher (for some students)	• Specify in precise terms what behaviors are acceptable and unacceptable in the classroom; establish and enforce rules for behavior. • Maintain a predictable schedule; warn students ahead of time about changes in the routine. • Use self-regulation techniques and behaviorist approaches to promote productive classroom behaviors. • Teach social skills (see Chapter 3). • Closely monitor students during independent assignments. • Give students a sense of self-determination about some aspects of classroom life; minimize the use of coercive techniques. • Make an extra effort to show students that you care about them as human beings.
Students with general delays in cognitive and social functioning	• Occasionally disruptive classroom behavior • Dependence on others for guidance about how to behave • More appropriate classroom behavior when expectations are clear	• Establish clear, concrete rules for classroom behavior. • Cue students regarding appropriate behavior; keep directions simple. • Use self-regulation techniques and behaviorist approaches to promote desired behaviors. • Give explicit feedback about what students are and are not doing appropriately.
Students with physical or sensory challenges	• Social isolation from classmates (for some students) • Difficulty accomplishing tasks as quickly as other students • Difficulty interpreting spoken messages (if students have hearing loss)	• Establish a strong sense of community within the classroom. • When appropriate, give extra time to complete assignments. • Keep unnecessary classroom noise to a minimum if one or more students have hearing loss.
Students with advanced cognitive development	• Off-task behavior in some students, often due to boredom during easy assignments and activities	• Assign tasks appropriate to students' cognitive abilities.

Sources: Achenbach & Edelbrock, 1981; Barkley, 1998; Beirne-Smith et al., 2002; Buchoff, 1990; B. Clark, 1997; Dempster & Corkill, 1999; Diamond, 1991; Friedel, 1993; Granger, Whalen, Henker, & Cantwell, 1996; Heward, 2000; Koegel et al., 1996; Landau & McAninch, 1993; Mercer, 1997; D. P. Morgan & Jenson, 1988; Ogden & Germinario, 1988; Patton et al., 1996; Pellegrini & Horvat, 1995; Piirto, 1999; M. C. Reynolds & Birch, 1988; Turnbull et al., 1999; Winner, 1997.

New teachers report greater confidence in their own ability to help their students learn and achieve when they collaborate regularly with their colleagues (Chester & Beaudin, 1996).

Working with the Community at Large

Students almost always have regular contact with other institutions besides school—possibly with youth groups, community organizations, social services, churches, hospitals, mental health clinics, or local judicial systems. And some of them are probably growing up in cultural environments unfamiliar to many teachers.

Not all students come from traditional two-parent families, such as this one drawn by 5-year-old Haley. Many children have single parents, grandparents, aunts and uncles, foster parents, or other individuals as their primary caretakers.

As teachers, we will be most effective if we understand the environments within which our students live and if we think of ourselves as part of a larger team that promotes their long-term development. For example, we must educate ourselves about students' cultural backgrounds, perhaps by taking coursework or getting involved in local community events after school hours (Hadaway, Florez, Larke, & Wiseman, 1993; Ladson-Billings, 1994a). We must also keep in contact with other people and institutions who play major roles in students' lives, coordinating our efforts whenever possible (J. L. Epstein, 1996).

Working with Parents

Above all, we must work cooperatively with students' parents or other primary caretakers. We can best think of our relationship with parents as a *partnership* in which we collaborate to promote students' long-term development and learning (Hidalgo et al., 1995). Such a relationship may be especially important when working with students from diverse cultural backgrounds (Hidalgo et al., 1995; Salend & Taylor, 1993). And as we discovered in Chapter 5, it is *essential* when working with students who have special educational needs.

It is important to recognize that families come in a variety of forms and that students' primary caretakers are not always their parents. For example, in some ethnic minority communities, grandmothers take the primary responsibility for raising children (Stack & Burton, 1993; M. Wilson, 1989). For simplicity, I use the term *parents* in upcoming discussions, but I am in fact referring to all primary caretakers.

Communicating with Parents

At the very minimum, we must stay in regular contact with parents about the progress students are making. We must inform them of their children's accomplishments and alert them to any behaviors that are consistently interfering with learning and achievement. Regular communication also provides a means through which parents can give *us* information. Such information might suggest ideas about how we can best assist or motivate their children; at the least, it will help us understand why our students sometimes behave as they do. Finally, we can coordinate our classroom strategies with those that parents use at home; our efforts to help students succeed will almost certainly yield greater returns if expectations for academic performance and social behavior are similar both in and out of school. The following paragraphs describe several ways in which we can communicate regularly with parents.

Parent-teacher conferences. In most school districts, formal parent-teacher conferences are scheduled one or more times a year. Oftentimes we will want to include students in these conferences, and in some instances we might even ask students to *lead* them (Popham, 1995; Stiggins, 2001). When students play an active role in a parent conference, we increase the likelihood that parents will come to the conference, we encourage students to reflect on their own academic progress, and we give them practice in communication and leadership skills. Furthermore, teachers, students, and parents alike are apt to leave such meetings with a shared understanding of the progress that has been made and the steps to be taken next. Several suggestions for conducting effective conferences are presented in Figure 14.3.

FIGURE 14.3 Conducting effective parent–teacher conferences

Suggestions for any conference:

- Schedule each conference at a time that accommodates parents' work schedules and other obligations.
- Prepare for the conference ahead of time; for example, organize your notes, review information you have about the student, plan an agenda for your meeting, and have examples of the student's work at hand.
- Create a warm, nonjudgmental atmosphere. For example, express your appreciation that the parents have come, actively encourage them to express their thoughts and perspectives, and give them sufficient time to do so. Remember that your objective is to work cooperatively and constructively together to create the best educational program possible for the student.
- Express your thoughts clearly, concisely, and honestly.
- Avoid educational jargon with which parents may be unfamiliar; describe the student's performance in ways a noneducator can understand.
- End the conference on a positive note—for instance, with a review of a student's many strengths and the progress he or she has made.
- After the conference, follow through with anything you have said you will do.

Additional suggestions for a student-led conference:

- Meet with the student ahead of time to agree on appropriate work samples to share.
- Model and role-play effective conferences in class, and give students time to practice with their classmates.
- Schedule a backup "audience" (e.g., one of the student's former teachers, a trusted friend) who can sit in if the parents don't show up.
- Offer additional time in which you can meet without the student present if the parents so desire.
- Talk with the student afterward about what went well and how, together, you might improve the next conference.

Sources: R. L. Linn & Gronlund, 2000; Polloway & Patton, 1993; Salend & Taylor, 1993; Stiggins, 2001.

Written communication.   Written communication can take a variety of forms. It can be a regularly scheduled, teacher-constructed checklist or grade sheet that documents a student's academic progress. It can be a quick, informal note acknowledging a significant accomplishment. Or it can be a general newsletter describing noteworthy classroom activities. All of these have something in common: They let parents know what is happening at school while also conveying our intention to stay in touch on an ongoing basis. The following exercise provides an illustration.

INTERPRETING ARTIFACTS AND INTERACTIONS   *A Letter Home*

Second-grade teacher Ann Reilly writes regular letters home to her students' parents. She wrote the following one on September 14, 2001, just three days after the terrorist attack on the World Trade Center and during a week when her students were taking a districtwide standardized test. As you read her letter, think about

- The various ideas she is trying to communicate
- The strategies she uses to increase parents' involvement in their children's education

9/14/01

Dear Parents,

I have been lucky so far and have not had to go back for jury duty. I have two more weeks to go [in terms of possibly being summoned for duty] and hope I will continue to be in the classroom.

We have been trying to keep the routine pretty regular, despite one or two testing sessions per day. The children have been pretty focused, although it is difficult when they are unfamiliar with the format and look to us for help. I don't like telling them that they are on their own! We are done, thank goodness. I believe you will receive results in the mail.

Homework and spelling will resume next week. I could also use my regular volunteers to help get through the spelling assessments. The times you have been coming are still fine. Call or e-mail me if you need the available times for helping.

We finished our unit on germs and sanitation, although we did not get into any discussions about Anthrax. It seems that you are keeping the children protected at home from details of the scary news, as we are at school. We kept our discussions to common illnesses that they are aware of and how they can avoid them with proper sanitation.

When would it be inappropriate to suggest that parents use e-mail to communicate?

A few classrooms are doing activities to raise money for many of the children involved in the tragedy. Sarah [the teacher intern] and I decided not to work with our children on a fundraiser because we don't want to get into anxiety-producing discussions. It is hard to help young children understand that they are safe where they are and that it is unlikely that they will be involved in such things.

Next week, we will be starting a Nutrition Unit and beginning to read some Halloween stories. We will continue working to become automatic with math facts, along with our regular routine of phonics lessons, DOL [daily oral language], reading, writing, spelling, etc.

We are running out of Kleenex and could use some donations. We would also like some boxes of baby wipes to use in cleaning hands and desks when there is not time for the entire class to wash. Someone mentioned to me that there is a homemade recipe for baby wipes out there somewhere. Is there a parent who knows and would be willing to share?

Have a great weekend.

Ann

To what concept is the teacher referring when she talks about becoming "automatic" with math facts?

With this letter, Ms. Reilly communicates a great deal of information: what topics the class is studying, how parents will get results of the standardized testing, and why the class is not addressing issues related to the World Trade Center attack. She communicates attitudes as well; for instance, she is eager to keep the lines of communication with parents open, is approachable (she signs the letter "Ann"), and cares about how well the students are doing (e.g., "I don't like telling them that they are on their own" during the classroom assessments). She also suggests several simple ways in which parents might contribute to the class: volunteering to help with spelling assessment, donating tissues or baby wipes, and providing instructions for making baby wipes.

Telephone conversations.   Telephone calls are useful when issues require immediate attention. We might call a parent to express our concern when a student's behavior deteriorates unexpectedly and without apparent provocation. But we might also call to express our excitement about an important step forward that a student has made. Parents, too, should feel free to call us. Keep in mind that many parents are at work during the school day; hence, it is often helpful to accept and encourage calls at home during the early evening hours.

Parent discussion groups.   In some instances, we may want to assemble a group of parents to discuss issues of mutual concern. For example, we might use such a group as a sounding board when we can pick and choose among topics to include in our classroom curriculum, or perhaps when we are thinking about assigning controversial yet potentially valuable works of literature (e.g., Rudman, 1993). Alternatively, we might want to use a discussion group as a mechanism through which we can all share ideas about how best to promote students' academic, personal, and social development (e.g., J. L. Epstein, 1996).

None of the communication strategies just described will, in and of themselves, guarantee a successful working relationship with parents. Parent-teacher conferences and parent discussion groups typically occur infrequently. Written communication is ineffective with parents who have limited literacy skills. And, of course, not everyone has a telephone. Ideally, we want not only to communicate with parents but to get them actively involved in school activities as well.

Getting Parents Involved in School Activities

Effective teachers get parents and other important family members (e.g., grandparents, older siblings) actively involved in school life and in their children's learning (Davis & Thomas, 1989; J. L. Epstein, 1996; D. U. Levine & Lezotte, 1995). Students whose parents are involved in school activities have better attendance records, higher achievement, and more positive attitudes toward school (J. L. Epstein, 1996).

Most parents become involved in school activities only when they have a specific invitation to do so and when they know that school personnel genuinely *want* them to be involved (A. A. Carr, 1997; Hoover-Dempsey & Sandler, 1997). For example, we might invite parents to an open house or choir performance in the evening, or we might request their help with a fund-raiser on a Saturday afternoon. We might seek volunteers to help with field trips, special projects, or individual tutoring during the school day. And we should certainly use our parents and other community members as resources to give us a multicultural perspective of the community in which we work (McCarty & Watahomigie, 1998; Minami & Ovando, 1995; H. L. Smith, 1998).

Yet some parents, especially those from some minority groups, may not take our invitations seriously. Consider one African American parent's explanation of why she rarely attends school events:

> If we are talking about slavery times . . . the slaves were all around, plantation owner came to the plantation [and said] "Oh, we're having a party over next door, come on over!" He would say, "Come on over," there was an invitation without any qualification as to who was to come. The African Americans, the slaves would not come because they knew the invitation was not for them. . . . They were not expected to participate. . . . (A. A. Carr, 1997, p. 2)

In such cases, a personal invitation can often make the difference, as this parent's statement demonstrates:

> The thing of it is, had someone not walked up to me and asked me specifically, I would not hold out my hand and say, "I'll do it." . . . You get parents here all the time, black parents that are willing, but maybe a little on the shy side and wouldn't say I really want to serve on this subject. You may send me the form, I may never fill the form out. Or I'll think about it and not send it back. But you know if that principal, that teacher, my son's math teacher called and asked if I would. . . . (A. A. Carr, 1997, p. 2)

Encouraging "Reluctant" Parents

Despite our best efforts, a few parents will remain uninvolved in their children's education; for example, some parents may rarely if ever attend scheduled parent-teacher conferences. Before we jump too quickly to the conclusion that these parents are also *uninterested* in their children's education, we must recognize several possible reasons why parents might be reluctant to make contact with us. Some may have an exhausting work schedule or lack adequate child care. Others may have difficulty communicating in English or finding their way through the school system to the people they most need to talk with (H.-Z. Ho, Hinckley, Fox, Brown, & Dixon, 2001; Salend & Taylor, 1993). Still others may believe that it's inappropriate to bother teachers with questions about their children's progress or to offer information and suggestions (Hidalgo et al., 1995; Olneck, 1995; Pérez, 1998). And a few may simply have had bad experiences with school when they themselves were children (Salend & Taylor, 1993).

Educators have offered numerous suggestions for getting reluctant parents more involved in their children's schooling:

- Make an extra effort to establish parents' trust and confidence—for instance, by demonstrating that we value their input and would never make them appear foolish.
- Encourage parents to be assertive when they have questions or concerns.
- Invite other important family members (e.g., grandparents, aunts, uncles) to participate in school activities, especially if a student's cultural background is one that places high value on the extended family.
- Give parents suggestions about learning activities they can easily do with their children at home.
- Find out what various parents do exceptionally well (e.g., carpentry, cooking) and ask them to share their talents with the class.
- Provide opportunities for parents to volunteer for jobs that don't require them to leave home (e.g., to be someone whom students can call when they're not sure of homework assignments).
- Identify specific individuals (e.g., bilingual parents) who can translate for those who speak little or no English.
- Conduct parent-teacher conferences or parent discussions at times and locations more convenient for families; make use of home visits *if* such visits are welcomed.
- Offer resources for parents at the school building (e.g., contacts with social and health services; classes in English, literacy, home repairs, arts and crafts). (J. L. Epstein, 1996; Finders & Lewis, 1994; Hidalgo et al., 1995; H.-Z. Ho et al., 2001; Howe, 1994; G. R. López, 2001; Salend & Taylor, 1993; M. G. Sanders, 1996)

Another potentially effective strategy is to reinforce *parents* as well as students when the students do well at school. One administrator at a school with a large population of immigrant students put it this way:

> One of the things we do . . . is that we identify those students that had perfect attendance, those students that passed all areas of the [statewide achievement tests] and were successful. We

don't honor the student, we honor the parents. We give parents a certificate. Because, we tell them, "through your efforts, and through your hard work, your child was able to accomplish this." (G. R. López, 2001, p. 273)

Discussing Problem Behaviors with Parents

As noted earlier, we may sometimes need to speak with parents about a chronic behavior problem at school. Put yourself in a parent's shoes in the following exercise.

EXPERIENCING FIRSTHAND   *Putting Yourself in a Parent's Shoes*

Imagine that you are the parent of a seventh grader named Tommy. As you and your son are eating dinner one evening, the telephone rings. You get up to answer the phone.

You:	Hello?
Ms. J.:	Hi. This is Ms. Johnson, Tommy's teacher. May I talk with you for a few minutes?
You:	Of course. What can I do for you?
Ms. J.:	Well, I'm afraid I've been having some trouble with your son, and I thought you ought to know about it.
You:	Oh, really? What seems to be the problem?
Ms. J.:	For one thing, Tommy hardly ever gets to class on time. When he does arrive, he spends most of his time talking and laughing with his friends, rather than paying attention to what I'm saying. It seems as if I have to speak to him three or four times every day about his behavior.
You:	How long has all this been going on?
Ms. J.:	For several weeks now. And the problem is getting worse rather than better. I'd really appreciate it if you'd talk with Tommy about the situation.
You:	I'll do it right now. And thank you for letting me know about this.
Ms. J.:	You're most welcome. Good night.
You:	Good night, Ms. Johnson.

Take a few minutes to jot down some of the things that, as a parent, you might be thinking after this telephone conversation.

You may have had a variety of reactions to your conversation with Ms. Johnson. Here are some of the possibilities:

- Why isn't Tommy taking his schoolwork more seriously?
- Isn't Tommy doing anything *right*?
- Has Ms. Johnson tried anything else besides reprimanding Tommy for his behavior? Or is she laying all of this on *my* shoulders?

Notice how Ms. Johnson focused strictly on the "negatives" of Tommy's classroom performance. As a result, you (as Tommy's parent) may possibly have felt anger at your son or guilt about your ineffective parenting skills. Alternatively, you may have maintained your confidence in your son's scholastic abilities and in your own ability to be a parent; if so, you may have begun to wonder about Ms. Johnson's ability to teach and motivate seventh graders.

How might a chronically abusive parent react to the conversation with Ms. Johnson?

We will be more effective when working with parents if we set a positive, upbeat tone in any communication. For one thing, we will always want to couch any negative aspects of a student's classroom performance within the context of the many things that the student does *well*. (For example, rather than starting out by complaining about Tommy's behavior, Ms. Johnson might have begun by saying that Tommy is a bright and capable young man with many friends and a good sense of humor.) And we must be clear about our commitment to working *together* with parents to help a student succeed in the classroom.

Following are some additional suggestions for enhancing your chances for a successful outcome when you must speak with a parent about a problem behavior:

- *Don't place blame; instead, acknowledge that raising children is rarely easy.* Parents are more apt to respond constructively to your concerns if you don't blame them for their child's misbehavior.

INTO THE CLASSROOM: *Working Effectively with Parents*

Confer with parents if a collaborative effort might bring about a behavior change.

At a parent-teacher conference, a high school math teacher expresses his concern that a student is not turning in her homework assignments. Her parents are surprised to hear this, saying that, "Carolyn usually tells us that she doesn't *have* any homework." Together they work out a strategy for communicating about what assignments have been given and when they are due.

Use a variety of formats to communicate with parents.

A middle school language arts teacher works with her students to produce a monthly newsletter for parents. Two versions of the newsletter are created, one in English and one in Spanish.

Encourage parents and other family members to get involved in school activities.

Several elementary school teachers and their students decide to coordinate their efforts to help flood victims in a nearby town. They ask parents to contribute old clothing and household items and, if possible, to assist with collecting, organizing, or distributing the items.

Tell parents about children's many strengths, even when communicating information about their shortcomings.

A teacher talks on the phone with the father of one of her students. She describes several areas in which the student has made considerable progress and then asks for advice about strategies for helping him stay on task and be more careful in his work.

Acknowledge the strengths of families' varying backgrounds.

When planning a lesson on the history of farming in Colorado, a middle school social studies teacher asks a student's mother if she would be willing to talk about her own childhood experiences as a member of an immigrant family that harvested crops every summer.

Be sensitive to parents' concerns about the limits of their influence.

A high school teacher talks with worried parents of a 16-year-old girl who has begun smoking and possibly experimenting with illegal drugs. Thinking about the girl's keen interest in photography, the teacher seeks an opening in an after-school photography club, with hopes that the companionship of more academically oriented peers might get her back on the right track.

- *Express your desire for whatever support they can give you.* Parents are more likely to be cooperative if you present the problem as one that can be effectively addressed if everyone works together to understand and solve it.
- *Ask for information and be a good listener.* If you show that you truly want to hear their perspective, parents are more likely to share their ideas regarding possible causes of the problem and possible ways of addressing it.
- *Agree on a strategy.* You are more likely to bring about an improvement in behavior if both you and a student's parents have similar expectations for behavior and similar consequences when those expectations are not met. Some parents, if making decisions on their own, may administer excessive or ineffective forms of punishment; agreement during your discussion as to what consequences are appropriate may avert such a situation. (derived from suggestions by Emmer et al., 1994)

When a student's parents speak a language other than English, we will, of course, want to include in the conversation someone who can converse fluently with the parents in their native tongue (and ideally, someone whom the parents trust). We must be aware, too, that people from different cultural groups sometimes have radically different ideas about how children should be disciplined. For example, many parents from Asian cultures believe that Western schools are too lenient in the ways they try to correct inappropriate behavior (Dien, 1998; Hidalgo et al., 1995). In some Native American and Asian cultures, a child's misbehaviors may be seen as bringing shame on the family or community; thus, a common disciplinary strategy is to ignore or ostracize the child for an extended period of time (Pang, 1995; Salend & Taylor, 1993). As we confer with parents from cultures and backgrounds different from our own, we must listen with an open mind to the opinions they express and try to find common ground on which to develop strategies for helping their children become more productive students (Good & Nichols, 2001; Salend & Taylor, 1993).

Most parents ultimately want what's best for their children and recognize the value of a good education (Gallimore & Goldenberg, 2001; Hidalgo et al., 1995; Okagaki, 2001). It's essential, then, that we not leave them out of the loop when we're concerned about how their children are performing in school.

When it comes to classroom management, an ounce of prevention is worth a pound of cure. We will be far more effective classroom managers if we are proactive in our thinking—that is, if we consider in advance how we can best keep our students engaged and on task throughout the activities we are planning. In this chapter we have identified a variety of strategies for keeping our students engaged and learning: arranging the classroom to facilitate interaction, creating a climate in which students feel safe and respected, setting reasonable limits for behavior, planning activities that keep students on task, continually monitoring what students are doing, and modifying instructional strategies when necessary.

Yet despite our best efforts, students will sometimes exhibit behaviors that interfere with either their own or their classmates' learning. Regardless of the roots of these misbehaviors—whether they result from students' temperaments, family circumstances, peer influences, prior schooling, cognitive or emotional disabilities, or events in our own classrooms—we can nevertheless do many things to bring about positive changes in students' conduct. In other words, we *can make a difference* in students' behavioral development as well as in their cognitive and social development. Different approaches will be effective with different students, of course; some will respond favorably to subtle cues or brief conversations, while others may need planned, long-term interventions. Yet all students ultimately want to succeed at school, and virtually all of them respond favorably to teachers who clearly care for and respect them and have their best interests at heart.

As teachers, we will be most effective in helping children and adolescents if we realize that we are just one part (albeit a very important part) of a team of teachers, parents, and other community members who are helping children and adolescents acquire behaviors that will serve them well in the adult world. It is especially important that we keep in regular contact with students' parents, sharing information in both directions about the progress that students are making and coordinating efforts at school with those on the home front.

CASE STUDY: *Old Friends*

Mr. Schulak has wanted to be a teacher for as long as he can remember. In his many volunteer activities over the years—coaching a girls' basketball team, assisting in a Boy Scout troop, teaching Sunday school—he has discovered how much he enjoys working with children. The children obviously enjoy working with him as well: Many of them occasionally call or stop by his home to shoot baskets, talk over old times, or just say hello. Some of them even call him by his first name.

Now that he has completed his college degree and obtained his teaching certificate, Mr. Schulak is a first-year teacher at his hometown's junior high school. He is delighted to find that he already knows many of his students—he has coached them, taught them, or gone to school with their older brothers and sisters—and so he spends the first few days of class renewing his friendships with them. But by the end of the week, he realizes that he and his students have accomplished little of an academic nature.

The following Monday, Mr. Schulak vows to get down to business. He begins each of his six classes that day by describing the objectives for the weeks to come; he then begins the first lesson. He is surprised to discover that many of his students—students with whom he has such a good rapport—are resistant to settling down and getting to work. They want to move from one seat to another, talk with their friends, toss wadded-up paper "baseballs" across the room, and, in fact, do anything *except* the academic tasks that Mr. Schulak has in mind. In his second week as a new teacher, Mr. Schulak has already lost total control of his classroom.

- Why is Mr. Schulak having so much difficulty bringing his classroom to order? What critical things has Mr. Schulak not done in his first week of teaching?
- Given that Mr. Schulak has gotten the school year off on the wrong foot, what might he do now to remedy the situation?

Once you have answered these questions, compare your responses with those presented in Appendix B.

PRAXIS Turn to Appendix C, "Matching Book and Ancillary Content to the PRAXIS™ Principles of Learning and Teaching Tests," to discover sections of this chapter that may be especially applicable to the PRAXIS™ tests.

 Now go to our Companion Website at http://www.prenhall.com/ormrod to assess your understanding of chapter content with "Multiple-Choice Questions," apply comprehension in "Essay Questions," broaden your knowledge of educational psychology with related "Web Links," gain greater insight about classroom learning in "Learning in the Content Areas," and analyze and assess classroom work in the "Student Artifact Library."

Key Concepts

classroom management (p. 481)
classroom climate (p. 482)
sense of community (p. 485)

withitness (p. 491)
misbehavior (p. 492)
cueing (p. 494)

sense of school community (p. 501)
collective self-efficacy (p. 501)

15

Basic Concepts and Issues in Assessment

*W*ith what knowledge and skills should we begin instruction? Which instructional objectives have students accomplished? Why are some students having greater difficulty mastering classroom material than their classmates? To answer such questions, we will inevitably need to assess our students' abilities and achievements in one way or another.

As teachers, it is essential that we know what educational assessment tools—tests, assignments, observations, and so on—can and cannot do for us. In this chapter we begin our exploration of educational assessment strategies by addressing the following questions:

- What do we mean by *assessment*, and what different forms can it take in classroom settings?
- For what reasons might we need to assess students' achievement and abilities? In what ways do classroom assessments affect students' learning?
- What qualities characterize useful educational assessment instruments?
- What kinds of tests are available from test publishers, and what information can they give us?
- How do we interpret various types of test scores?
- What are the ramifications of using tests to hold students and teachers accountable for classroom learning?
- Who should know the results of students' test performance, and how can we communicate those results in an understandable manner?
- What issues must we consider as we assess students with diverse backgrounds and needs?

In Chapter 16 we look more specifically at strategies for assessing students' ongoing progress in the classroom, as well as at ways of summarizing their final achievements.

CASE STUDY: *The Math Test*

Ms. Ford is teaching mathematics to a class of middle school students with low mathematical ability. She has just returned a set of test papers she has scored. The following discussion with her students ensues:

Ms. Ford:	When I corrected these papers, I was really, really shocked at some of the scores. And I think you will be too. I thought there were some that were so-so, and there were some that were devastating, in my opinion.
Student:	[Noise increasing.] Can we take them over?
Ms. Ford:	I am going to give them back to you. This is what I would like you to do: Every single math problem that you got wrong, for homework tonight and tomorrow, it is your responsibility to correct these problems and turn them in. In fact, I will say this, I want this sheet back to me by Wednesday at least. All our math problems that we got wrong I want returned to me with the correct answer.
Student:	Did anybody get 100?
Ms. Ford:	No.
Student:	Nobody got 100? [Groans]
Ms. Ford:	OK, boys and girls, shhh. I would say, on this test in particular, boys and girls, if you received a grade below 75 you definitely have to work on it. I do expect

this quiz to be returned with Mom or Dad's signature on it. I want Mom and Dad to be aware of how we're doing.

Student: No!

Student: Do we have to show our parents? Is it a requirement to pass the class?

Ms. Ford: If you do not return it with a signature, I will call home. (dialogue from J. C. Turner, Meyer, et al., 1998, pp. 740–741)

- What information have the test results actually given to Ms. Ford? What inferences does Ms. Ford make based on this information?
- What effects might this class discussion have on students' future motivation in class?

Assessments as Tools

The one thing Ms. Ford knows for sure is that her students have performed poorly on their recent math test. From this fact she assumes that they have not mastered the knowledge and skills that the test was designed to assess. Ms. Ford appears to be angry rather than sympathetic about the test results; if we consider our discussion of teacher attributions in Chapter 12, we might reasonably conclude that she is attributing the poor performance to a lack of effort or some other factor that students can control.

If Ms. Ford motivates her students to work harder on their math at all, she is certainly not promoting *intrinsic* motivation to master it. By focusing on students' test scores, she is fostering performance goals rather than mastery goals. Furthermore, notice how controlling, even threatening, some of her statements are: "it is your responsibility to correct these problems and turn them in. . . . All our math problems that we got wrong I want returned to me with the correct answer. . . . If you do not return it with a signature, I will call home." Such comments will almost certainly undermine students' sense of self-determination, and they are hardly going to endear students to the subject of mathematics.

Some tests involve paper and pencil, but others do not. In this industrial arts class, the students have designed and constructed rockets, and their teacher is assessing how well each rocket performs.

Our assessment practices influence virtually every other aspect of the classroom (recall Figure 13.1 on p. 429). They affect our future planning and instruction (e.g., what we teach and how we teach it), the classroom environment (e.g., whether it feels threatening or psychologically "safe"), and students' motivation and affect (e.g., whether students develop mastery or performance goals, whether they feel confident or anxious). Only when we consider the very integral role that assessment plays in the classroom can we truly harness its benefits to help our students achieve important instructional objectives.

Paper-pencil tests, such as the one that Ms. Ford has given, provide one means through which we can assess student achievement. Yet not all classroom assessment involves paper and pencil. The statements students make in class, the ways they respond to questions, the questions *they* ask—all of these tell us something about what they have learned. Nonverbal behaviors give us information as well: We can observe how well students use a pair of scissors, how carefully they set up laboratory equipment, or how they perform on physical fitness tasks. Some forms of assessment take only a few seconds, whereas others may take several hours or even several days. Some are planned and developed in advance; others occur spontaneously during the course of a lesson or classroom activities.

So what exactly do we mean by *assessment*? The following definition sums up its major features:

Assessment is a process of observing a sample of students' behavior and drawing inferences about their knowledge and abilities.

Several parts of the definition are important to note. First, we are looking at students' *behavior*. As behaviorists have pointed out, it's impossible to look inside students' heads and see what knowledge lurks there; we can see only how students actually respond in the classroom. Second, we typically use just a *sample* of students' classroom behavior; we certainly cannot observe and keep track of every single thing that every single student does during the school day.

Finally, we must draw *inferences* from the specific behaviors we do observe to make judgments about students' overall classroom achievement—a tricky business at best. As we proceed through this chapter and the next, we will discover how to select behaviors that can give us a reasonably accurate estimate of what our students know and can do.

Notice that our definition of assessment doesn't include anything about decision making. Assessment instruments do not, in and of themselves, dictate the decisions that should be made. Instead, *people*—teachers, administrators, government officials, parents, and sometimes even students themselves—interpret assessment results and make judgments based on them. When people use classroom assessments for the wrong purpose, or when they interpret assessment results as those results were never meant to be interpreted, then it is people, rather than the assessment instruments, who are to blame.

Assessments are *tools* that can help us to make informed decisions about how best to help our students learn and achieve. The usefulness of these tools depends on how well matched they are to the circumstances in which we are using them. In the upcoming pages we will explore the many forms that assessment might take and the situations in which each might be helpful.

Can you think of classroom tests you've taken that were probably *not* good samples of what they were supposed to measure?

The Various Forms of Educational Assessment

Figure 15.1 summarizes four distinctions that educators often make regarding classroom assessment instruments. Let's look more closely at each one.

Informal versus formal assessment. Spontaneous, day-to-day observations of how students perform in class constitute **informal assessment**. When we conduct an informal assessment, we rarely have a specific agenda in mind, and we are likely to learn different things about different students. For instance, we may discover that Tony has a misconception about gravity when he asks, "How come people in Australia don't fall into space?" We may wonder if Jaffa needs an appointment with the eye doctor when we see her continually squinting at the chalkboard. And we may conclude that Marty has a high need for approval when he is constantly seeking our attention and praise.

In contrast, **formal assessment** is typically planned in advance and used for a specific purpose—perhaps to determine what students have learned from a geography unit, whether they can solve word problems requiring addition and subtraction, or how their strength and agility compare with those of students nationwide. It is "formal" in the sense that a particular time is set aside for it, students can prepare for it ahead of time, and it is intended to yield information about particular instructional objectives.

Informal assessment:
Results from teachers' spontaneous, day-to-day observations of students' performance in class.
vs.
Formal assessment:
Is planned in advance and used to assess a predetermined content domain.

Paper-pencil assessment:
Asks students to respond in writing to questions, topics, or problems.
vs.
Performance assessment:
Asks students to demonstrate knowledge or skills in a nonwritten fashion.

ASSESSMENT

Traditional assessment:
Assesses basic knowledge and skills in relative isolation from typical real-world tasks.
vs.
Authentic assessment:
Assesses students' ability to use what they've learned in tasks similar to those in the outside world.

Standardized test:
Is developed by test construction experts and published for use in many schools.
vs.
Teacher-developed assessment:
Is developed by a teacher for use in his or her own classroom.

FIGURE 15.1 The various forms that classroom assessment can take

Paper-pencil versus performance assessment. As teachers, we may sometimes choose **paper-pencil assessment**, in which we present questions to answer, topics to address, or problems to solve, and our students must write their responses on paper. Yet we may also find it helpful to use **performance assessment**, in which students demonstrate (*perform*) their abilities—for example, by giving an oral presentation, using a computer spreadsheet, jumping hurdles, or identifying acids and bases in a chemistry lab.

Traditional versus authentic assessment. Historically, educational assessment instruments have focused on measuring basic knowledge and skills in relative isolation from tasks typically found in the outside world. Spelling quizzes, mathematics word problems, and physical fitness tests are examples of such **traditional assessment.** Yet ultimately, our students must be able to apply their knowledge and skills to complex tasks outside the classroom. The notion of **authentic assessment**—measuring the actual knowledge and skills we want students to demonstrate in an "authentic," real-life context—is gaining increasing popularity among educators (Darling-Hammond, 1991; Lester, Lambdin, & Preston, 1997; Paris & Paris, 2001; Valencia, Hiebert, & Afflerbach, 1994).

This distinction represents a *continuum* rather than an either-or situation: Assessment tasks can resemble real-world situations to varying degrees.

In some situations, authentic assessment involves paper and pencil. For example, we might ask students to write a letter to a friend or develop a school newspaper. But in many cases, it is based on nonwritten performance and closely integrated with instruction. For example, we might assess students' ability to present a persuasive argument, bake a cake, converse in a foreign language, design and build a bookshelf, or successfully maneuver a car into a parallel parking space. As teachers, we must consider what our students should be able to do when they join the adult world, and our assessment practices must, to some extent, reflect those real-life tasks.[1]

Standardized tests versus teacher-developed assessments. Sometimes classroom assessments involve tests developed by test construction experts and published for use in many different schools and classrooms. Such instruments, commonly called **standardized tests,** can be quite helpful in measuring general scholastic abilities and tracking students' general progress in various content domains, so they are often used by school psychologists, counselors, and other specialists to identify special educational needs. We will look more closely at standardized tests a bit later in the chapter.

Unfortunately, standardized tests typically assess such broad abilities that they yield little information about what students specifically have and have not learned. When we want to assess students' learning and achievement related to specific instructional objectives—for example, whether students can do long division or whether they can apply what they've just learned in a social studies lesson—we will usually want to construct our own **teacher-developed assessment instruments.** We will consider numerous strategies for constructing teacher-developed assessments in Chapter 16.

Using Assessment for Different Purposes

On some occasions, we will engage in **formative evaluation:** We will assess what students know and can do *before or during instruction.* Ongoing formative evaluation can help us determine how well our students understand the topic at hand, what misconceptions they have, whether they need further practice on a particular skill, and so on. We can then develop or revise our lesson plans accordingly.

At other times, we will engage in **summative evaluation:** We will conduct an assessment *after instruction* to make final decisions about what students have achieved. Summative evaluations are used to determine whether students have mastered the content of a lesson or unit, what final grades to assign, which students are eligible for more advanced classes, and the like.

With these two basic kinds of evaluation in mind, let's consider how teachers and other school personnel might use educational assessments for the following purposes:

---

[1]Educators are not in complete agreement in their use of the terms *performance assessment* and *authentic assessment,* and many treat them more or less as synonyms. I find it useful to consider separately whether an assessment involves *performance* (rather than paper and pencil) and whether it involves a complex, real-world (*authentic*) task. In the discussion here, then, I do *not* use the two terms interchangeably.

- To promote learning
- To guide instructional decision making
- To diagnose learning and performance problems
- To promote self-regulation
- To determine what students have learned

See "Assessment in the Balance" in *Simulations in Educational Psychology and Research.*

Promoting Learning

When we use formative evaluation to develop or modify our lesson plans, we are obviously using assessment to facilitate students' learning. Yet summative evaluation can influence learning as well. More specifically, summative assessments can motivate students to study and learn, provide an opportunity to review previously learned material, influence how students cognitively process information, offer new ways to use and apply classroom subject matter, and provide feedback to help students enhance their knowledge and skills. Let's look more closely at each of these effects.

Assessments as motivators.   Imagine that you are a student in two classes, one taught by Professor Carberry and the other taught by Professor Seville. Carberry tells you that you won't be tested on course material—that you should study it simply because it will help you in your later personal and professional life. Seville says that she will give a test over her course material every three weeks. In which class are you apt to study more?

Other things being equal, you will probably study more in Professor Seville's class. Most students study class material more and learn it better when they are told they will be tested on it or in some other way held accountable for it, rather than when they are simply told to learn it (Blumenfeld, Hamilton, Bossert, Wessels, & Meece, 1983; N. Frederiksen, 1984b; Halpin & Halpin, 1982). Assessments are especially effective as motivators when students see them as good measures of course objectives and feel challenged to do their very best (Natriello & Dornbusch, 1984; Paris, Lawton, Turner, & Roth, 1991). When an assessment task is too easy, students may not exert much effort (e.g., they may not study very much), and we may mistakenly conclude that they have learned something they haven't really learned at all. When an assessment task is exceptionally difficult, students may become discouraged and believe that they are incapable of mastering the subject matter.

Although our classroom assessment instruments can be highly motivating, we must remember that, in and of themselves, they are *extrinsic* motivators; thus, they may direct students' attention to performance goals and undermine any intrinsic motivation to learn (Grolnick & Ryan, 1987; Paris & Turner, 1994). They are especially likely to have this adverse effect when students perceive them as being primarily an evaluation of their performance rather than as a mechanism for helping them learn (Spaulding, 1992).

Assessments as mechanisms for review.   As we discovered in Chapter 6, long-term memory is not necessarily "forever": for a variety of reasons, people tend to forget things as time goes on. Students have a better chance of remembering classroom subject matter over the long run when they review it at a later time. Studying for formal assessments provides one way of reviewing material related to important instructional objectives (Dempster, 1991; Kiewra, 1989).

Assessments as influences on cognitive processing.   What and how students learn depend partly on how they expect their learning to be assessed. For example, students will typically spend more time studying the things they think will be on a test than the things they think the test won't cover (Corbett & Wilson, 1988; J. R. Frederiksen & Collins, 1989; N. Frederiksen, 1984b). Their expectations about the kinds of tasks they will need to perform and the questions they will need to answer also will influence whether they memorize isolated facts, on the one hand, or strive to learn a meaningful, integrated body of information, on the other (L. A. Shepard, 2000). Unfortunately, many students believe (incorrectly) that trying to learn information meaningfully—that is, trying to understand and make sense of what they study—interferes with their ability to do well on classroom tests that emphasize knowledge of isolated facts (Crooks, 1988).

What and how students study is, in part, a function of how they expect their learning will be assessed.

Assessments as learning experiences.   You can probably recall classroom assessments that actually taught you something. Perhaps an essay question asked you to compare two things

Give a formal or informal pretest to determine where to begin instruction.

When beginning a new unit on cultural geography, a teacher gives a pretest designed to identify misconceptions that students may have about various cultural groups—misconceptions he can then address during instruction.

Choose or develop an assessment instrument that reflects the actual knowledge and skills you want students to achieve.

When planning how to assess his students' achievement, a teacher initially decides to use questions from the test bank that accompanies his textbook. When he looks more closely at the test bank, however, he discovers that the items measure only knowledge of isolated facts. Instead, he develops several authentic assessment tasks that better reflect his primary instructional objective: Students should be able to apply what they've learned to real-world problems.

Construct assessment instruments that reflect how you want students to process information when they study.

A teacher tells her students, "As you study for next week's vocabulary test, remember that the test questions will ask you to put definitions in your own words and give your own examples to show what each word means."

Use an assessment task as a learning experience in and of itself.

A high school science teacher has students collect samples of the local drinking water and test them for bacterial content. She is assessing her students' ability to use procedures she has taught them, but she also hopes they will learn something about their community's natural resources.

Use an assessment to give students specific feedback about what they have and have not mastered.

As he grades students' persuasive essays, a teacher writes numerous notes in the margins of students' papers to indicate places where they have analyzed a situation correctly or incorrectly, identified a relevant or irrelevant example, proposed an appropriate or inappropriate solution, and so on.

Provide criteria that students can use to evaluate their *own* performance.

The teacher of a "foods and nutrition" class gives her students a checklist of qualities to look for in the pies they have baked.

you hadn't compared before and so helped you discover similarities you hadn't noticed earlier. Or perhaps a test problem asked you to apply a scientific principle to a situation you hadn't realized was related to that principle. Such assessment tasks not only measured what you learned, they also *helped* you learn.

In general, the very process of completing an assessment on class material helps students learn the material better, particularly if the assessment tasks ask students to elaborate on it in some way (Fall, Webb, & Chudowsky, 2000; Foos & Fisher, 1988; N. Frederiksen, 1984b). But two qualifications are important to note here. First, an assessment helps students learn only the material it specifically addresses (N. Frederiksen, 1984b). Second, when we present *incorrect* information on an assessment (as we often do in true-false and multiple-choice questions), students may eventually remember that misinformation as being true rather than false (A. S. Brown, Schilling, & Hockensmith, 1999; Voss, 1974).

Assessments as feedback. Regular classroom assessments can provide valuable feedback to students about which things have and have not been mastered. But simply knowing one's final assessment score (e.g., knowing the percentage of items answered correctly) is not terribly helpful. To facilitate student learning, assessment results must include concrete information about where students have succeeded and where they've had difficulty (Baron, 1987; Krampen, 1987).

Guiding Instructional Decision Making

Is the emphasis on formative evaluation or summative evaluation here?

In some cases, we might actually want to assess students' knowledge and understanding *before* we teach a topic; for instance, a quick pretest can help us determine a suitable point at which to begin instruction. We will also want to monitor students' learning throughout a lesson or unit (through either formal assessments or more informal means) to get ongoing information about the appropriateness of our instructional objectives and the effectiveness of our instructional strategies. For example, if we find that almost all of our students are completing assignments quickly and easily, we might set our instructional goals a bit higher. If we discover that many students are struggling with material we have presented in class lectures, we might consider trying a different instructional approach—perhaps a more concrete, hands-on one.

Diagnosing Learning and Performance Problems

Why is Louis having trouble learning to read? Why is Gretel misbehaving in class? Why does Martin seem excessively anxious during exams? We ask such questions when we suspect that certain students might learn differently from their classmates and may possibly require special educational services. Many standardized tests have been designed specifically to identify the special academic, social, and emotional needs that some students may have. Most of these tests require explicit training in their use and so are often administered and interpreted by specialists (school psychologists, counselors, speech and language pathologists, etc.).

Yet teacher-developed assessment instruments can provide considerable diagnostic information as well, especially when they suggest where students are going wrong and why. In other words, they can, and ideally they *should,* give us information we can use to help students improve (Baek, 1994; Baxter, Elder, & Glaser, 1996; Covington, 1992). In addition, when we pass such diagnostic information on to students, it can promote greater self-regulation—our next topic of discussion.

Promoting Self-Regulation

In our discussion of self-regulation in Chapter 10, we noted the importance of *self-monitoring* (students must be aware of how well they are doing as they study and learn) and *self-evaluation* (students must be able to assess their final performance accurately). An important function of our classroom assessment practices should be to help students engage in such self-regulating processes (Covington, 1992; Paris & Ayres, 1994; Vye et al., 1998). We will look at ways for promoting self-regulation in our discussion of classroom assessment strategies in Chapter 16.

Determining What Students Have Learned

We will almost certainly use one or more formal assessments to determine whether students have achieved instructional objectives. Such information will be essential if we are using a mastery-learning approach to instruction; it will also be important as we assign final grades. School counselors and administrators, too, may use assessment results for making placement decisions, such as deciding which students are most likely to do well in advanced classes, which might need additional coursework in basic skills, and so on.

In some cases, assessments of students' achievement are used to make major decisions about students, teachers, and schools. For instance, some school districts use one or more assessments to determine which students graduate, which teachers get raises, and which schools get extra funds and other resources. As you might guess, such *high-stakes* assessments are a source of considerable controversy, and so we will look at them more closely later in the chapter.

Let's now apply what we have learned to a critique of an actual classroom assessment instrument.

INTERPRETING ARTIFACTS AND INTERACTIONS   *Geology Test*

A sixth-grade science teacher gives a test on a unit on rocks. As you examine the test, think about

- What purpose the teacher had in mind for the test
- What effects the test is apt to have on students' future learning efforts
- What the answer to the last question on the test might be

> A. Write whether each of the rocks shown at the front of the room is a sedimentary, igneous, or metamorphic rock.
>   1. _____
>   2. _____
>   3. _____

B. The following are various stages of the rock cycle. Number them from 1 to 9 to indicate the order in which they occur.

_____ Heat and pressure
_____ Crystallization and cooling
_____ Igneous rock forms
_____ Magma
_____ Weathering and erosion into sediments
_____ Melting
_____ Sedimentary rock forms
_____ Pressure and cementing
_____ Metamorphic rock forms

C. Write the letter for the correct definition of each rock group.

1. _____ Igneous   a. Formed when particles of eroded rock are deposited together and become cemented.

2. _____ Sedimentary   b. Produced by extreme pressures or high temperatures below the earth's surface.

3. _____ Metamorphic   c. Formed by the cooling of molten rock material from within the earth.

D. Fill in the blanks in each sentence.

1. The process of breaking down rock by the action of water, ice, plants, animals, and chemical changes is called _____.

2. All rocks are made of _____.

3. The hardness of rocks can be determined by a _____.

4. Continued weathering of rock will eventually produce _____.

5. Every rock has a _____.

[The test continues with several additional fill-in-the-blank and short-answer items.]

The teacher used the test for summative evaluation: to assess students' final knowledge and understanding of basic principles of rock formation before moving to a different topic. Part A (identifying rocks shown at the front of the room) may be assessing either basic knowledge or transfer, depending on whether the students have seen those particular rocks before. The rest of the test clearly focuses on memorized facts—stages of the rock cycle, definitions of terms, and so on—and is likely to encourage students to engage in rote learning when they study for future tests. For instance, consider the last item, "Every rock has a _____." Students can answer this item correctly *only* if they have learned the material verbatim: The missing word here is "story."

Especially when we use classroom assessments to make final decisions about individual students—decisions related to class grades, graduation, and so on—we must be sure the assessments accurately reflect what students have achieved. How do we know when our assessment instruments and procedures are giving us accurate information? We'll answer this question as we consider four characteristics of good assessment.

Important Qualities of Good Assessments

As a student, have you ever been assessed in a way you thought was unfair? If so, *why* was it unfair? For example:

1. Did the teacher evaluate students' responses inconsistently?
2. Were some students assessed under more favorable conditions than others?
3. Was it a poor measure of what you had learned?
4. Was the assessment so time-consuming that, after a while, you no longer cared how well you performed?

In light of your experiences, what characteristics do *you* think are essential for a good classroom assessment instrument?

The four numbered questions just posed reflect, respectively, four "RSVP" characteristics of good classroom assessment:

A quick review: What do we call a memory aid such as *RSVP*? (You can find the answer in Chapter 6.)

- Reliability
- Standardization
- Validity
- Practicality

The RSVP Characteristics of Good Assessment

CHARACTERISTIC	DEFINITION	RELEVANT QUESTIONS TO CONSIDER
Reliability	The extent to which the assessment instrument yields consistent results for each student	• How much are students' scores affected by temporary conditions unrelated to the characteristic being measured (*test-retest reliability*)? • Do different people score students' performance similarly (*scorer reliability*, also known as *interrater reliability*)? • Do different parts of a single assessment instrument lead to similar conclusions about a student's achievement (*internal consistency reliability*)?
Standardization	The extent to which assessment procedures are similar for all students	• Are all students assessed on identical or similar content? • Do all students have the same types of tasks to perform? • Are instructions the same for everyone? • Do all students have similar time constraints? • Is everyone's performance evaluated using the same criteria?
Validity	The extent to which an assessment instrument measures what it is supposed to measure	• Does the assessment tap into a representative sample of the content domain being assessed (*content validity*)? • Do students' scores predict their success at a later task (*predictive validity*)? • Does the instrument measure a particular psychological or educational characteristic (*construct validity*)?
Practicality	The extent to which an assessment is easy and inexpensive to use	• How much class time does the assessment take? • How quickly and easily can students' responses be scored? • Is special training required to administer or score the assessment? • Does the assessment require specialized materials that must be purchased?

These RSVP characteristics are summarized in Table 15.1. Let's look more closely at each one.

Reliability

EXPERIENCING FIRSTHAND   *Fowl Play*

Consider the following sequence of events:

- *Monday.* After a unit on the bone structures of both birds and dinosaurs, Ms. Fowler asks her students to write an essay explaining why many scientists believe that birds are descended from dinosaurs. After school, she tosses the pile of essays in the back seat of her cluttered '57 Chevy.
- *Tuesday.* Ms. Fowler looks high and low for the essays both at home and in her classroom, but she can't find them anywhere.
- *Wednesday.* Because Ms. Fowler wants to use the essay to determine what her students have learned, she asks the class to write the same essay a second time.
- *Thursday.* Ms. Fowler discovers Monday's essays in the back seat of her Chevy.
- *Friday.* Ms. Fowler grades both sets of essays. She is surprised to find little consistency between them: Students who wrote the best essays on Monday did not necessarily do well on Wednesday, and some of Monday's poorest performers did quite well on Wednesday.

Which results should Ms. Fowler use—Monday's or Wednesday's?

The **reliability** of an assessment technique is the extent to which it yields consistent information about the knowledge, skills, or abilities we are trying to measure. When we assess students' learning and achievement, we must be confident that our conclusions will be essentially the same regardless of whether we give the assessment Monday or Wednesday, whether the weather is sunny or rainy, and whether we evaluate students' responses while in a good mood or a foul frame of mind. Ms. Fowler's assessment technique has poor reliability: The

Informal observations of student performance can give us valuable information, but ultimately we should draw firm conclusions about students' achievement only when we know that our assessment methods are *reliable,* yielding consistent results about individual students time after time.

results are completely different from one day to another. So which day's results should she use? I've asked you a trick question. We have no way of knowing which set is more accurate.

The same assessment instrument will rarely give us *exactly* the same results for the same student on two different occasions, even if the knowledge or ability we are assessing (e.g., the extent to which a student knows basic addition facts, can execute a swan dive, or can compare the bone structures of birds and dinosaurs) remains the same. Many temporary conditions unrelated to what we are trying to measure—distractions in the classroom, variability in instructions and time limits, inconsistencies in rating students' responses, and so on—are likely to affect students' performance. Factors such as these almost invariably lead to some fluctuation in assessment results.

What temporary conditions might have differentially affected students' performance on Ms. Fowler's essay on Monday and Wednesday? Following are a few possibilities:

- *Day-to-day changes in students*—for example, changes in health, motivation, mood, and energy level

    The 24-hour Netherlands Flu was making the rounds in Ms. Fowler's classroom that week.
- *Variations in the physical environment*—for example, variations in room temperature, noise level, and outside distractions

    On Monday, students who sat by the window in Ms. Fowler's classroom enjoyed peace and quiet; on Wednesday, those who sat by the window worked while noisy construction machinery tore up the pavement outside.
- *Variations in administration of the assessment*—for example, variations in instructions, timing, and the teacher's responses to students' questions

    On Monday, a few students had to write the essay after school because of play rehearsal during class time; Ms. Fowler explained the task more clearly than she had during class that day and gave students as much time as they needed to finish. On Wednesday, a different group of students had to write the essay after school because of a band concert during class time; Ms. Fowler explained the task very hurriedly and collected students' essays before they had finished.
- *Characteristics of the assessment instrument*—for example, the length of the task, and ambiguous or excessively difficult tasks (longer tasks tend to be more reliable, because small errors have less of an impact on overall results; ambiguous and very difficult tasks increase students' tendency to guess randomly)

    The essay topic "Explain why many scientists believe that birds are descended from dinosaurs" was a vague one that students interpreted differently from one day to the next.
- *Subjectivity in scoring*—for example, tasks for which the teacher must make judgments about "rightness" or "wrongness" and situations in which students' responses are scored on the basis of vague, imprecise criteria

    Ms. Fowler graded both sets of essays while she watched "Chainsaw Murders at Central High" on television Friday night; she gave higher scores during kissing scenes, lower scores during stalking scenes.

Whenever we draw conclusions about students' learning and achievement, we must be confident that the information on which we've based our conclusions is not overly distorted by temporary factors irrelevant to what we are trying to assess. How do we determine the reliability of an assessment instrument? We begin by getting two scores on the same instrument for the same group of students. We can derive these two scores in different ways, and each approach gives us a somewhat different angle on the instrument's reliability. If we assess students using the same instrument on two different occasions, we get information about *test-retest reliability,* the degree to which the instrument yields similar information over a short time interval. If we ask two or more people to judge students' performance (to grade the same set of essay papers, rate the same performance of gymnastic skills, etc.), we get information about *scorer reliability,* the degree to which different experts are likely to agree in their assessment of complex behaviors. If we compute two or more subscores for different items on the same instrument and look at how similar those subscores are, we get information about *internal consistency reliability,* the extent to which different parts of the instrument are all measuring the same characteristic.

Once we have two sets of scores for a group of students, we can determine how similar they are by computing a statistic known as a *correlation coefficient* (described in Appendix A); in this case, it is more frequently called a **reliability coefficient**. The coefficient will typically range from 0 to +1.[2] A number close to +1 indicates high reliability: The two sets of test scores are very similar. Although a perfect reliability coefficient of 1.00 is rare, many published achievement and intelligence tests have reliabilities of .90 or above, reflecting a high degree of consistency in the scores they yield. As reliability coefficients decrease, they indicate more error in our assessment results—error due to temporary, and in most cases irrelevant, factors. Publishers of regional and national achievement and ability tests typically calculate and report reliability coefficients for the various scores and subscores that the tests yield.

Estimating Error in Assessment Results

A reliability coefficient tells us, in general, the extent to which temporary errors contribute to fluctuations in students' assessment results. But how much error is apt to be present in a *single* score? In other words, how close is a particular student's score to what it actually should be? The **standard error of measurement (SEM)** gives us an estimate of how close or far off we might be. (The standard error of measurement is calculated from the reliability coefficient; see Anastasi & Urbina [1997] or R. M. Thorndike [1997] for details.)

Imagine that Susan takes an academic achievement test known as the Basic Skills Test; we'll call it the BST. Imagine, too, that given how well Susan can read, she *should* get a score of 40 on the BST's reading subtest. Susan's ideal score of 40 is her **true score**: This is what she would theoretically get if we could measure her reading achievement with *complete accuracy*. But Susan misinterprets a few test items, answering them incorrectly when in fact she knows the correct answers, so she actually gets a score of only 37. We cannot see inside Susan's head, so we have no way of determining what her true score is; we know only that she's gotten a 37 on the test. To estimate the amount of error in her score, we consult the BST test manual to find the standard error of measurement for the reading subtest: 5 points. We can then guess that Susan's true score in reading probably lies somewhere within a range that is one SEM to either side of her test score: 37±5, or 32–42.

Because almost any assessment score includes a certain amount of error, assessment results are sometimes reported not as a specific score, but as a range or **confidence interval** extending one SEM to either side of the actual test score.[3] Figure 15.2 shows how we might report Susan's scores on different subtests of the BST. Notice that the confidence intervals for the different subtests are different lengths, because each subtest has a different standard error of measurement.

Enhancing the Reliability of Classroom Assessments

As classroom teachers, we will probably not have the time (and some may not have the expertise) to mathematically determine the reliability of every classroom assessment instrument we use. Even so, we must take precautions to maximize the extent to which any single instrument gives us reliable results. For instance, we should

- Include several tasks in each instrument and look for consistency in students' performance from one task to another
- Define each task clearly enough that students know exactly what they are being asked to do
- Identify specific, concrete criteria with which to evaluate students' performance
- Try not to let expectations for students' performance influence judgments

---

[2]Theoretically, reliability coefficients can range from +1 to −1. A negative coefficient would be obtained only when an inverse relationship between the two sets of scores exists—that is, when students who get the highest scores one time get the lowest scores the other time, and vice versa. Such an outcome is highly unlikely.

[3]When we use a single standard error of measurement (SEM) to determine the confidence interval, there is a 68 percent chance that the student's true score lies within that interval. If we instead use two SEMs to determine the interval (for Susan's reading score, identifying an interval of 27 to 47), we can be 95 percent confident that the true score lies within it. If you have some familiarity with descriptive statistics, it may help you to know that the SEM is the standard deviation for the hypothetical distribution of all possible scores that a student with a particular true score might get.

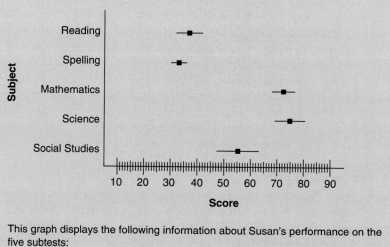

This graph displays the following information about Susan's performance on the five subtests:

Subtest	Score	SEM	Confidence Interval
Reading	37	5	32–42
Spelling	33	3	30–36
Mathematics	72	4	68–76
Science	75	6	69–81
Social Studies	55	8	47–63

- Avoid assessing students' learning when they are obviously ill, tired, or out of sorts
- Administer the assessment in similar ways and under similar conditions for all students

My last recommendation suggests that our assessment procedures be *standardized*—a characteristic we turn to now.

Standardization

A second important characteristic of good assessment is **standardization**: An assessment instrument involves similar content and format and is administered and scored in the same way for everyone. In most situations, all students should be given the same instructions, perform identical or similar tasks, have the same time limits, and work under the same constraints (making appropriate adjustments for students with special needs). Furthermore, students' responses should be scored as consistently as possible; for example, we shouldn't use tougher standards for one student than for another.

As noted earlier, many tests constructed and published by testing experts are called *standardized* tests; this label indicates that such tests have explicit procedures for administration and scoring that are consistently applied whenever the tests are used. Yet standardization is important in our own classroom assessments as well: It reduces the error in our assessment results, especially error due to variation in test administration or subjectivity in scoring. The more an assessment is standardized for all students, then, the higher its reliability. Equity is an additional consideration: Except in unusual situations, it is only fair to ask all students to be evaluated under similar conditions.

Validity

EXPERIENCING FIRSTHAND *FTOI*

A few minutes ago, you read about *reliability*. Let's see whether you can apply (transfer) your understanding of that concept to this situation:

I have developed a new test called the FTOI: the Fathead Test of Intelligence. It consists of only a tape measure and a table of norms describing how others have performed on the test. Administration of the FTOI is quick and easy: You measure a student's head circumference just above the eyebrows (firmly but not too tightly) and compare your measure against the table of norms. Large heads (comparatively speaking) receive high IQ scores. Smaller heads receive low scores.

Does the FTOI have high reliability? Answer the question before you read further.

No matter how often you measure a person's head circumference, you are going to get a similar score: Fatheads will continue to be fatheads, and pinheads will always be pinheads. So the answer to my question is yes: The FTOI has high reliability because it yields consistent results. If you answered no, you were probably thinking that the FTOI isn't a very good measure of intelligence—but that's a problem with the instrument's *validity*, not with its reliability.

The **validity** of an assessment instrument is the extent to which it measures what it is supposed to measure. Does the FTOI measure intelligence? Are scores on a standardized, multiple-choice achievement test a good indication of how much students have learned during the school year? Does students' performance at a school concert reflect what they have achieved in their instrumental music class? When our assessments don't do these things well—when they are poor measures of students' knowledge and abilities—then we have a validity problem.

As noted earlier, numerous irrelevant factors are likely to influence how well our students perform in assessment situations. Some of these—students' health, distractions in the classroom, errors in scoring, and so on—are temporary conditions that lead to fluctuation in our assessment results and thereby lower reliability. But other irrelevant factors—perhaps reading ability, self-efficacy, trait anxiety—are more stable, and so their effects on our assessment results will be relatively constant. For example, if Joe has poor reading skills, he may get consistently low scores on paper-pencil, multiple-choice achievement tests regardless of how much he has actually achieved in science, mathematics, or social studies. If Jane suffers debilitating anxiety whenever she performs in front of an audience, her performance at a public concert may not be a good reflection of how well she can play the cello. When our assessment results continue to be affected by the same irrelevant variables, then we must question the validity of our instruments.

Psychologists distinguish among different kinds of validity, each of which is important in different situations. Three kinds of particular interest to educators and other practitioners are content validity, predictive validity, and construct validity.

Content validity. As classroom teachers, we will usually be most concerned with **content validity**, the extent to which the tasks we ask students to perform are a representative sample of the knowledge and skills we are trying to assess. In an assessment instrument with high content validity, test items and performance tasks reflect all parts of the content domain in appropriate proportions and require the particular behaviors and skills identified in instructional objectives. High content validity is *essential* whenever we are using a classroom assessment instrument for summative evaluation purposes—that is, to determine what students have ultimately learned in our classes.

How can we ensure that an assessment instrument is truly a representative sample of the content domain? The most widely recommended strategy is to construct a *blueprint* that identifies the specific things we want to measure and the proportion of the instrument that addresses each one. This blueprint frequently takes the form of a **table of specifications**: a two-way grid that indicates both the topics to be covered and the behaviors associated with them (i.e., the things that students should be able to *do* with each topic). In each cell of the grid, we indicate the relative importance of each topic-behavior combination, perhaps as a particular number or percentage of tasks or test items to be included in the overall assessment. Figure 15.3 shows two examples, one for a paper-pencil test on addition and a second for a combined paper-pencil and performance assessment on simple machines. Once we have developed a table of specifications, we can develop paper-pencil items or performance tasks that reflect both the topics and the behaviors we want to assess and have some confidence that our assessment instrument has content validity for the domain it is designed to represent.

Content validity is important not only for teacher-developed assessments but also for any published achievement tests that we use in our school districts. Because these tests have already been constructed, we can follow the steps for ensuring content validity in reverse order. By looking at the items on the test, we can identify the topics covered and the behaviors (e.g., recalling information, applying procedures, solving problems) required. Once again we can

Sometimes the behaviors listed in a table of specifications are those in Bloom's taxonomy, such as "knowledge," "comprehension," and "application" (see Chapter 13).

FIGURE 15.3 Two examples
of a table of specifications

Behaviors

Topic	Computation using number line	Rapid recall of sum	Regrouping ("carrying")	Estimation	Application to word problems
Single digits	2	6			4
Multiples of 10 and 100		2			2
Two-digit numbers			2	2	3
Three-digit numbers			2	2	3

This table provides specifications for a thirty-item paper-pencil test on addition. It assigns different weights (different numbers of items) to different topic-behavior combinations, with some combinations not being measured at all.

Behaviors

Topic	Make simple drawing of machine	Describe work that machine performs	Recognize examples among common objects	Solve problems by using machine
Inclined plane	5%	5%	5%	5%
Wedge	5%	5%	5%	5%
Lever	5%	5%	5%	5%
Wheel and axle	5%	5%	5%	5%
Pulley	5%	5%	5%	5%

This table provides specifications for a combination paper-pencil and performance assessment on simple machines. It assigns equal importance (the same percentage of points) to each topic-behavior combination.

construct a table of specifications, indicating the number of test items that fall in each cell.[4] We can then decide whether the table of specifications matches our curriculum closely enough that the test has content validity for our particular situation—that is, whether the test represents what we actually do in our classrooms.

Predictive validity. Shantel is thinking about a career in mathematics. But even though she is doing well in her junior high school math class, she worries that she will eventually have trouble with advanced courses in trigonometry and calculus. To get an idea of her chances for future math success, Shantel takes the Mathematics Aptitude Test (we'll call it the MAT). She does quite well on the MAT, renewing her confidence that she will succeed in a mathematics career. But does the MAT actually measure a student's potential for future success in mathematics? This is a question of **predictive validity**, the extent to which an assessment instrument predicts future performance in some arena.

Publishers of widely used ability tests often determine the accuracy with which test scores predict later success in certain domains. To do so, they first give a test to a group of people; at a later time, they measure the same group's success or competence in the behavior being predicted (the criterion behavior). They then calculate the correlation coefficient between the test scores and the criterion behavior. As is true for a reliability coefficient, this **validity coefficient** is typically a number between 0 and +1, with higher numbers indicating greater predictive validity. Tests with relatively high predictive validity for a particular behavior (validity coefficients in the .60s or .70s are usually considered high) predict that behavior fairly well. Those with lower predictive validity (e.g., coefficients in the .30s or .40s) are less accurate and will lead to more mistakes in our predictions.

Keep in mind that a test has no *single* predictive validity. Its validity in a given situation depends on the specific behavior being predicted, the age-group being tested (tests often have greater predictive validity for older students than for younger ones), and the amount of time that has elapsed since the test was taken.

---

[4]Sometimes you can find a table of specifications in the test manual. In other instances, you can obtain one by contacting the test publisher.

Construct validity. Psychologists use the term *construct* to refer to a hypothesized internal trait that cannot be directly observed but must instead be inferred from the consistencies we see in people's behavior. *Motivation, self-esteem, intelligence,* and *visual-spatial ability* are all constructs; we can't actually *see* any of them but must instead draw conclusions about them from the things that students do and don't do. For example, we might use our observations of students' on-task and off-task behavior in class to make inferences about their motivation to learn academic subject matter. Similarly, we might use tasks that ask them to reason abstractly to make inferences about their intelligence.

By **construct validity**, then, we mean the extent to which an assessment instrument actually measures a general, abstract characteristic. Construct validity is of most concern when we are trying to draw general conclusions about students' traits and abilities so that we can better adapt instructional methods and materials to meet their individual needs.

How do we determine whether a test or other assessment instrument measures something we cannot see? Assessment experts have developed a variety of strategies for doing so. For instance, they might determine how well test scores correlate with other tests designed to measure the same trait (e.g., do scores on one intelligence test correlate with the scores on other IQ tests?). They might find out whether older students perform better than younger students on instruments measuring traits that presumably increase with age (e.g., do 12-year-olds correctly answer more items on an intelligence test than 6-year-olds?). They might compare the performance of two groups who are known to be different with respect to the trait in question (e.g., do nondisabled 12-year-olds perform better on an intelligence test than 12-year-olds identified as having mental retardation?). When data from a variety of sources are consistent with what we would expect if the instrument were a measure of the characteristic in question, we conclude that it probably *does* have construct validity.

This teacher may be making inferences about her student's motivation to master basic writing skills. When we want to draw conclusions about underlying traits such as motivation, we must consider the *construct validity* of our assessment methods.

One principle that applies to all three forms of validity is this: *An assessment tool may be more valid for some purposes than for others.* A mathematics achievement test may be a valid measure of how well students can add and subtract but a terrible measure of how well they can use addition and subtraction in real-life situations. A paper-pencil test on the rules of tennis may accurately assess students' knowledge of how many games are in a set, what *deuce* means, and so on, but it probably won't tell us much about how well students can actually play the game.

We should note, too, that *reliability is a necessary condition for validity:* Assessments can yield valid results only when they also yield reliable results—results that are only minimally affected by variations in administration, subjectivity in scoring, and so on. Reliability does not guarantee validity, however, as the FTOI exercise you did earlier illustrates.

Practicality

The last of the four RSVP characteristics is **practicality**, the extent to which assessment instruments and procedures are relatively easy to use.[5] Practicality includes concerns such as these:

- How much time will it take to develop the instrument?
- How easily can the assessment be administered to a large group of students?
- Are expensive materials involved?
- How much time will the assessment take away from instructional activities?
- How quickly and easily can students' performance be evaluated?

There is often a trade-off between practicality and such other characteristics as validity and reliability. For example, a true-false test on tennis will be easier to construct and administer, but a performance assessment in which students actually demonstrate their tennis skills—even though it takes more time and energy—is undoubtedly a more valid measure of how well students have mastered the game.

Of our four RSVP characteristics, validity is the most important: We *must* have an assessment technique that measures what we want it to measure. Reliability ensures the dependability of our assessment results (in doing so, it indirectly affects their validity), and standardization can enhance the reliability of those results. Practicality should be a consideration only when validity, reliability, and standardization are not seriously jeopardized.

Without looking back at Table 15.1, test yourself by describing the four characteristics of good assessment.

---

[5]Many psychologists use the term *usability*, but I think *practicality* better communicates the idea here.

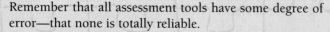

Remember that all assessment tools have some degree of error—that none is totally reliable.

A teacher uses several test scores plus numerous other assessments of classroom performance to determine students' final grades.

Include confidence intervals when reporting standardized test results to students and their parents.

At a parent-teacher conference, a teacher gives a student and her parents a computer-printed report. The teacher tells them, "Here are Mary's scores on the achievement test she took in November. Please remember that these scores are only approximate indicators of Mary's achievement. The bars on this graph indicate the likely margin of error for each score."

When holding some or all students to the same standards for achievement, be sure that assessments of their accomplishments are identical or equivalent in content, format, administration, and scoring criteria (making appropriate exceptions for students with disabilities).

When three students are absent on the day of an important quiz, their teacher constructs an alternative quiz for them based on the same table of specifications he used in constructing the first one.

Follow the prescribed directions for administering and scoring a standardized test.

As a teacher administers a nationwide achievement test, she reads the instructions in the test manual word for word. She also uses a stopwatch to make sure she gives students the prescribed amount of time to take the test.

Construct classroom assessment instruments that reflect both the topics you want to assess and the things you expect students to do with those topics.

A teacher follows the table of specifications he has developed when writing a paper-pencil test, making sure that the items assess both lower-level and higher-level skills.

When using test scores to judge students' capabilities, consider recent assessment results only.

When talking with a colleague, a high school teacher expresses her concern that one student, Mark, is having trouble grasping essential mathematics concepts. The colleague volunteers, "I had Mark four or five years ago when I was teaching middle school. As I recall, his standardized test scores showed a poor aptitude for quantitative ability. Maybe he's just not cut out for math." Mark's current teacher decides to ignore this information. Instead, she consults with the school psychologist about possible strategies for determining where Mark's problem may lie.

Make a classroom assessment instrument as practical as you can without sacrificing reliability, standardization, and validity.

When trying to decide whether to use a paper-pencil test or several performance tasks to assess students' achievement in a particular unit, a teacher realizes that performance tasks are the only valid way to assess whether students have met the instrumental objectives. He identifies three performance tasks that can be administered to the class as a whole and will adequately represent the domain he wants to assess.

Now that we have examined the characteristics of good assessments, let's apply what we have learned as we examine the nature of standardized tests.

Standardized Tests

Standardized tests are *standardized* in several ways: All students are given the same instructions and time limits, respond to the same (or very similar) questions or tasks, and have their responses evaluated in accordance with the same criteria. Standardized tests come with test manuals that describe the instructions to give students, the time limits to impose, and explicit scoring criteria. Usually, these manuals also provide information about test reliability for various populations and age-groups, as well as information from which we can draw inferences about test validity for our own purpose and situation.

Occasionally, standardized tests are designed to yield **criterion-referenced scores**, which indicate specifically what a student can and cannot do in relation to certain standards or criteria. More often, however, they are designed to yield **norm-referenced scores**, which are derived by comparing a student's performance with that of other students on the same task(s). Hence, most standardized tests are accompanied by data regarding the typical performance (**norms**) of different groups of students, and these norms are used in calculating overall test scores. We will learn more about both criterion-referenced and norm-referenced scores later in the chapter.

TABLE 15.2   COMPARE/CONTRAST

Comparing Standardized Tests of Achievement, General Scholastic Aptitude, and Specific Aptitude

KIND OF TEST	PURPOSE	RELIABILITY AND VALIDITY	SPECIAL CONSIDERATIONS
Achievement tests	To assess how much students have learned from what they have specifically been taught	• *Reliability* coefficients are often .90 or higher; they are typically higher for secondary students than for elementary students. Coefficients may be somewhat lower for subtest scores. • *Content validity* must be determined for each situation.	• These tests are usually more appropriate for measuring broad areas of achievement than specific knowledge or skills.
Scholastic aptitude tests	To assess students' general capability to learn; to predict their general academic success over the short run	• *Reliability* coefficients are often .90 or higher; they are typically higher for secondary students than for elementary students. • *Predictive validity* for academic success ranges from .40 to .70, depending on the situation and student population.	• Test scores should not be construed as an indication of learning potential over the long run. • Individually administered tests (in which the tester works one-on-one with a particular student) are preferable when students' verbal skills are limited or when significant exceptionality is suspected.
Specific aptitude tests	To predict how well students are likely to perform in a specific content domain	• *Reliability* coefficients are often .90 or higher. • *Predictive validity* for academic success often falls below .50.	• Test scores should not be construed as an indication of learning potential over the long run.

Let's look at the general nature of standardized achievement and ability tests and at recent technological innovations in standardized testing. We will then consider several guidelines for choosing and using standardized tests.

Types of Standardized Tests

A wide variety of standardized tests is currently available on the market.[6] The three kinds school districts use most frequently are tests of achievement, scholastic aptitude, and specific aptitude. Critical aspects of these tests are summarized in Table 15.2.

Achievement Tests

Standardized achievement tests are designed to assess how much students have learned from the things they have specifically been taught. Test items are, at least in theory, written to reflect the curriculum common to most schools; for example, a history test will focus on national or world history rather than the history of a particular state, province, or community. The overall test scores usually reflect achievement in a very broad sense: They tell us how much a student has learned about mathematics or language mechanics (relative to a norm group) but not necessarily whether the student knows how to multiply fractions or use commas appropriately.

Standardized achievement tests are useful in at least two ways (Ansley, 1997). First, they enable us to determine how well our students' performance compares with that of students elsewhere; this information may indirectly tell us something about the effectiveness of our instructional programs. Second, they provide a means of tracking students' general progress over time and raising red flags about potential trouble spots. For example, if Lucas has been getting average test scores over the years, then suddenly performs well below average in eighth grade (even though the test and norm group are the same as in previous years), we have a signal that Lucas may possibly not be learning and performing at a level commensurate with his ability. At this point, we would want to ascertain whether the low performance was a fluke (perhaps due to illness on the test day or to some other temporary condition) or whether the relative decline in performance is due to other, longer-term factors that need our attention.

---

[6]You can find descriptions of several widely used standardized tests at http://www.ctb.com (for CTB and McGraw-Hill), http://www.riverpub.com (for Riverside Publishing), and http://www.hbem.com (for Harcourt Brace).

Content validity is our main concern when we assess achievement, and we need to determine each test's validity for our own situation. We can determine the content validity of a standardized achievement test by comparing a table of specifications (either one that the test manual provides or one that we construct ourselves) to our own curriculum. We should also scrutinize the actual test items to see whether they address lower- or higher-level thinking skills; some commonly used achievement tests focus predominantly on lower-level skills (Alleman & Brophy, 1997; Marzano & Costa, 1988). A test has high content validity for our situation only if both the topics and thinking skills emphasized in test items match our own objectives.

Scholastic Aptitude Tests

What tests (if any) did you take when applying to college? Would you characterize these tests as achievement tests or scholastic aptitude tests?

Achievement tests are designed to assess what students have specifically learned from the school curriculum. In contrast, **scholastic aptitude tests** are designed to assess a general *capacity* to learn. Traditionally, many of these tests have been called *intelligence tests* (recall our discussion of such tests in Chapter 4). However, some experts are beginning to shy away from the latter terminology because of the confusion about what "intelligence" is and the widespread misconception that IQ scores reflect inherited ability almost exclusively (R. L. Linn & Gronlund, 2000). Other commonly used terms are *general aptitude test, school ability test,* and *cognitive ability test.*

Regardless of what we call them, tests that fall in this category are used mainly for prediction—that is, to estimate how well students are likely to learn and perform in a future academic situation. One way to predict how well students can learn in the future is to assess what they have learned already, and in fact achievement tests can be quite useful as predictors of later academic performance (Jencks & Crouse, 1982; Sax, 1989; J. J. Stevens & Clauser, 1996). But rather than focus on what students have specifically been taught in school, scholastic aptitude tests typically assess how much students have learned and deduced from their general, everyday experiences. For example, many of these tests include vocabulary items designed to assess students' understanding of words they have presumably encountered over the years. They sometimes include analogies, intended to assess how well students can recognize similarities among well-known relationships. They may also ask students to analyze pictures or manipulate concrete objects. Most of them include measures of general knowledge as well as tasks requiring deductive reasoning and problem solving.

Some standardized tests are administered one-on-one. Such tests enable the examiner to observe a student's attention span, motivation, and other factors that may affect academic performance. For this reason, individualized tests are typically used when identifying special needs.

Specific Aptitude Tests

General scholastic aptitude tests are useful when we want to predict overall academic performance. But when we are interested in how well students are apt to perform in a particular area—perhaps in art, music, or auto mechanics—then **specific aptitude tests** are more appropriate. Some aptitude tests are designed to predict future performance in just one content domain; others, called *multiple aptitude batteries,* yield subscores for a variety of domains simultaneously.

Aptitude tests are sometimes used by school personnel to select students for specific instructional programs—for example, to identify those students most likely to succeed in a particular course. They may also be used for counseling students about future educational plans and career choices. Aptitude tests are based on the notion that one's ability to learn in a specific area is fairly stable. In recent years, however, many educators have begun to argue that we should focus more on developing abilities in *all* students than on identifying the specific aptitudes that may be present in *some* students (Boykin, 1994; P. D. Nichols & Mittelholtz, 1997). Accordingly, specific aptitude tests now appear less frequently in wide-scale school testing programs than they once did.

Technology and Assessment

The past few years have seen a rapid rise in the use of technology to administer and score standardized tests, and this trend will almost certainly continue. Computer technology and other technological advances provide several options that are either impractical or impossible with paper-pencil tests:

- They allow **adaptive testing**, which adjusts the difficulty level of items as students proceed through a test and can thereby zero in on students' specific strengths and weaknesses fairly quickly.
- They can include animations, simulations, videos, and audiotaped messages that greatly expand the kinds of knowledge and skills that can be assessed.

- They enable easy assessment of how students approach specific problems and how quickly they accomplish specific tasks.
- They allow the possibility of assessing students' abilities under varying levels of support (e.g., by providing one or more hints as needed to guide students' reasoning).
- They can provide on-the-spot, objective scoring and analyses of students' performance. (Anastasi & Urbina, 1997; R. L. Linn & Gronlund, 2000; Sattler, 2001)

Although computer-based assessment is still in its infancy, preliminary results indicate that it yields reliability and validity coefficients similar to those of traditional paper-pencil tests, often with less time and fewer items (Anastasi & Urbina, 1997). Its use should, of course, be limited to students who have adequate keyboarding skills and familiarity and comfort with computers.

Guidelines for Choosing and Using Standardized Tests

As teachers, we will sometimes have input into the selection of standardized tests for our districts, and we will often be involved in administering them. Following are some guidelines for choosing and using standardized tests appropriately:

■ *Choose a test that has high validity for your particular purpose and high reliability for students similar to your own.* So far, we have talked about achievement, general scholastic aptitude, and specific aptitude tests as if they are all distinctly different entities, but in fact the differences among the three are not always so clear-cut. To some extent, all three assess what a student has already learned, and all three can be used to predict future performance. Our best bet is to choose the test that has the best validity for our particular purpose, regardless of what the test might be called. Of course, we also want a test that has been shown to be highly reliable with students like ours.

■ *Make sure that the test's norm group is relevant to your own population.* Scrutinize the test manual's description of the norm group used for the test, with questions like this in mind:

- Is the norm group a representative sample of the population at large or in some other way appropriate for any comparisons you plan to make?
- Does it include students of the same age, educational level, and cultural background as your own students?
- Does it include students of both genders?
- Is it a large enough sample that the average scores reported are probably an accurate depiction of the population it represents?
- Have the normative data been collected recently enough that they reflect how students typically perform at the present time?

When we determine norm-referenced test scores by comparing students with an inappropriate norm group, those scores are meaningless. For example, I recall a situation in which teacher education students at a major state university were required to take basic skills tests in language and mathematics. The tests had been normed on a high school population, and so the university students' performance was compared to norms for high school seniors—a practice that made no sense whatsoever.

■ *When administering the test, follow the directions closely, and report any unusual circumstances.* We will usually want to prepare students ahead of time for any standardized test they will be taking. For example, we can encourage them to get a good night's sleep, eat a good breakfast, and try their best yet not be overly anxious (more about test anxiety shortly). Once the testing session begins, we should follow the test administration procedures to the letter, distributing test booklets as directed, asking students to complete any practice items provided, keeping time faithfully, responding to questions in the manner prescribed, and so on. Remember, the test's norm group has taken the test under certain standardized conditions, and we must replicate those conditions as closely as possible. At the same time, some events (a noisy construction project nearby, an unexpected power failure, etc.) may be beyond our control. When such events significantly alter the conditions under which our students are taking the test, they limit our ability to compare their performance with the norm group and so must be reported. We should also make note of any individual students who are behaving in ways unlikely to lead to maximum performance—students who appear exceptionally nervous, stare out the window for long periods, seem to be marking answers haphazardly, and so on (R. L. Linn & Gronlund, 2000).

Once we have given a standardized test, we need to make good use of its results. We look now at various types of test scores and at strategies for interpreting them appropriately.

Types of Test Scores

Not all assessment instruments yield quantitative information; for instance, as we will see in the next chapter, one method of summarizing students' achievement—portfolios—is more useful for the *qualitative* information it yields. Many teacher-developed assessments do lend themselves to quantitative analysis, however, and virtually all standardized tests do. Oftentimes, students' performance on a particular assessment is summarized by one or more *test scores*. These scores typically take one of three forms: raw scores, criterion-referenced scores, and norm-referenced scores (Table 15.3).

Raw Scores

Sometimes a test score is simply the number or percentage of items to which a student has responded correctly. At other times it is the sum of the points a student has earned—2 points for one item, 5 for another, and so on. A score based solely on the number or point value of correct responses is a **raw score**.

Raw scores are easy to calculate, and they appear to be easy to understand. But in fact, we sometimes have trouble knowing what raw scores really mean. Is 75 percent a good score or a bad one? Without knowing what kinds of tasks an assessment instrument includes or how other students have performed on the same assessment, we have no way to determine how good or bad a score of 75 percent really is. For this reason, raw scores are not always as useful as criterion-referenced or norm-referenced scores.

TABLE 15.3   COMPARE/CONTRAST

Interpreting Different Kinds of Test Scores

SCORE	HOW SCORE IS DETERMINED	USES	POTENTIAL DRAWBACKS
Raw score	By counting the number (or calculating a percentage) of correct responses or points earned	Often used in teacher-developed assessment instruments	Scores may be difficult to interpret without knowledge of how performance relates to either a specific criterion or a norm group.
Criterion-referenced score	By comparing performance to one or more criteria or standards for success	Useful when determining whether specific instructional objectives have been achieved	Criteria for assessing mastery of complex skills may be difficult to identify.
Age or grade equivalent (norm-referenced)	By equating a student's performance to the average performance of students at a particular age or grade level	Useful when explaining norm-referenced test performance to people unfamiliar with standard scores	Scores are frequently misinterpreted, especially by parents. Scores may be inappropriately used as a standard that all students must meet. Scores are often inapplicable when achievement at the secondary level or higher is being assessed.
Percentile rank (norm-referenced)	By determining the percentage of students at the same age or grade level who obtained lower scores	Useful when explaining norm-referenced test performance to people unfamiliar with standard scores	Scores overestimate differences near the mean and underestimate differences at the extremes.
Standard score (norm-referenced)	By determining how far the performance is from the mean (for the age or grade level) with respect to standard deviation units	Useful when describing a student's standing within the norm group	Scores are not easily understood by people without some knowledge of statistics.

**Springside Parks and Recreation Department
Beginner Swimmer Class**

Students must demonstrate proficiency in each of
the following:

☐ Jump into chest-deep water
☐ Hold breath under water for 8 seconds
☐ Float in prone position for 10 seconds
☐ Glide in prone position with flutter kick
☐ Float on back for 10 seconds
☐ Glide on back with flutter kick
☐ Demonstrate crawl stroke and rhythmic
   breathing while standing in chest-deep water
☐ Show knowledge of basic water safety rules

Criterion-Referenced Scores

A *criterion-referenced score* tells us what students have achieved in relation to specific instructional objectives. Many criterion-referenced scores are "either-or" scores: They indicate that a student has passed or failed a unit, mastered or not mastered a skill, or met or not met an objective. Others indicate various levels of competence or achievement. For example, a criterion-referenced score on a fifth-grade test of written composition might reflect four levels of writing ability, three of which reflect mastery of essential writing skills, as follows:

In progress: Is an underdeveloped and/or unfocused message.

Essential: Is a series of related ideas. The pattern of organization and the descriptive or supporting details are adequate and appropriate.

Proficient: Meets Essential Level criteria and contains a logical progression of ideas. The pattern of organization and the transition of ideas flow. Word choice enhances the writing.

Advanced: Meets Proficient Level criteria and contains examples of one or more of the following: insight, creativity, fluency, critical thinking, or style. (adapted from "District 6 Writing Assessment, Narrative and Persuasive Modes, Scoring Criteria, Intermediate Level" [Working Copy] by School District 6 [Greeley/Evans, CO], 1993; adapted by permission)

If a particular assessment instrument is designed to assess only one instructional objective, then it may yield a single score. If it is designed to assess several objectives simultaneously, a student's performance may be reported as a list of the various objectives passed and not passed. As an example, a student's performance in a swimming class is often reported in a multiple-objective, criterion-referenced fashion (see Figure 15.4).

We will often want to use a criterion-referenced approach to summarize what our students have learned, particularly when we are assessing basic skills that are essential prerequisites for later learning. Only through criterion-referenced assessment can we determine what specific objectives students have attained, what particular skills they have mastered, and where their individual weaknesses lie.

Norm-Referenced Scores

A *norm-referenced score* is derived by comparing a student's performance with the performance of other students, perhaps that of classmates or that of a nationwide norm group. Rather than tell us specifically what a student has or has not learned, such a score tells us how well the student stacks up against others at the same age or grade level.

Most scores on published standardized tests are norm-referenced scores. In some cases, the scores are derived by comparing a student's performance with the performance of students at a variety of grade or age levels; such comparisons give us grade- or age-equivalents. In other cases, the scores are based on comparisons only with students of the *same* age or grade; these comparisons give us either percentile scores or standard scores.

Grade-Equivalents and Age-Equivalents

Imagine that Shawn takes the Reading Achievement Test (RAT) and gets 46 of the 60 test items correct (46 is his raw score). We turn to the norms reported in the test manual and find the average raw scores for students at different grade and age levels:

Normative Data for the RAT

Norms for Grade Levels		*Norms for Age Levels*	
Grade	Average Raw Score	Age	Average Raw Score
5	19	10	18
6	25	11	24
7	30	12	28
8	34	13	33
9	39	14	37
10	43	15	41
11	46	16	44
12	50	17	48

Shawn's raw score of 46 is the same as the average score of eleventh graders in the norm group, so he has a **grade-equivalent** score of 11. His score is halfway between the average score of 16-year-old and 17-year-old students, so he has an **age-equivalent** score of about 16½. Shawn himself is 13 years old and in eighth grade, so he has obviously done well on the RAT.

More generally, grade- and age-equivalents are determined by matching a student's raw score to a particular grade or age level in the norm group. A student who performs as well as the average second grader on a reading test will get a grade-equivalent of 2, regardless of what grade level the student is actually in. A student who gets the same raw score as the average 10-year-old on a physical fitness test will get an age-equivalent of 10, regardless of whether that student is 5, 10, or 15 years old.

Grade- and age-equivalents are frequently used because they seem so simple and straightforward. But they have a serious drawback: They give us no idea of the typical *range* of performance for students at a particular age or grade level. For example, a raw score of 34 on the RAT gives us a grade-equivalent of 8, but obviously not all eighth graders will get raw scores of exactly 34. It is possible, and in fact quite likely, that many eighth graders will get raw scores several points above or below 34, thus getting grade-equivalents of 9 or 7 (perhaps even 10 or higher, or 6 or lower). Yet grade-equivalents are often used inappropriately as a standard for performance: Parents, school personnel, government officials, and the public at large may believe that *all* students should perform at grade level on an achievement test. Given the normal variability within most classrooms, this goal is probably impossible to meet.

Percentile Ranks

A different approach is to compare students only with others at the same age or grade level. One way of making such a peer-based comparison is using a **percentile rank:** the percentage of people getting a raw score less than or equal to the student's raw score. (Such a score is sometimes known simply as a **percentile**.) To illustrate, let's once again consider Shawn's performance on the RAT. Because Shawn is in eighth grade, we turn to the eighth-grade norms and discover that his raw score of 46 is at the 98th percentile. This means that Shawn has done as well as or better than 98 percent of eighth graders in the norm group on the Reading Achievement Test. Similarly, a student getting a percentile rank of 25 has performed better than 25 percent of the norm group, and a student getting a score at the 60th percentile has done better than 60 percent. It is important to note that percentile ranks refer to a percentage of *people,* not to the percentage of correct items—a common misconception among teacher education students (Lennon et al., 1990).

Because percentile ranks are relatively simple to understand, they are used frequently in reporting test results. But they have a major weakness: They distort actual differences among students. To illustrate, consider the percentile ranks of these four boys on the RAT:

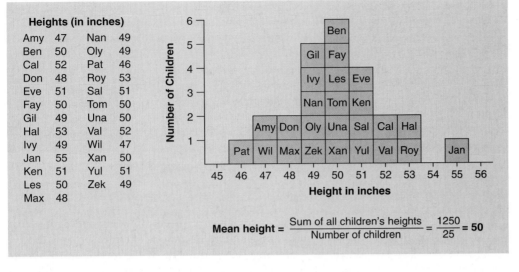

Heights (in inches)			
Amy	47	Nan	49
Ben	50	Oly	49
Cal	52	Pat	46
Don	48	Roy	53
Eve	51	Sal	51
Fay	50	Tom	50
Gil	49	Una	50
Hal	53	Val	52
Ivy	49	Wil	47
Jan	55	Xan	50
Ken	51	Yul	51
Les	50	Zek	49
Max	48		

$$\text{Mean height} = \frac{\text{Sum of all children's heights}}{\text{Number of children}} = \frac{1250}{25} = 50$$

FIGURE 15.5 Heights of children in Ms. Oppenheimer's third-grade class

Student	Percentile Rank
Ernest	45
Frank	55
Giorgio	89
Nick	99

In *actual achievement* (as measured by the RAT), Ernest and Frank are probably very similar to one another even though their percentile ranks are 10 points apart. Yet a 10-point difference at the upper end of the scale probably reflects a substantial difference in achievement: Giorgio's percentile rank of 89 tells us that he knows quite a bit, but Nick's percentile rank of 99 tells us that he knows an exceptional amount. In general, percentiles tend to *over*estimate differences in the middle range of the characteristic being measured: Scores a few points apart reflect similar achievement or ability. Meanwhile, they *under*estimate differences at the lower and upper extremes: Scores only a few points apart often reflect significant differences in achievement or ability. We avoid this problem when we use standard scores.

Standard Scores

The school nurse measures the heights of all 25 students in Ms. Oppenheimer's third-grade class. The students' heights are presented on the left side of Figure 15.5. The nurse then makes a bar graph of the children's heights, as you can see on the right side of Figure 15.5.

Notice that the bar graph is high in the middle and low on both ends. This shape tells us that most of Ms. Oppenheimer's students are more or less average in height, with only a handful of very short students (e.g., Pat, Amy, and Wil) and just a few very tall ones (e.g., Hal, Roy, and Jan).

Many psychologists believe that educational and psychological characteristics (achievement and aptitude included) typically follow the same pattern we see for height: Most people are close to average, with fewer and fewer people as we move farther from this average. This theoretical pattern of educational and psychological characteristics is called the **normal distribution** (or **normal curve**) and looks like this:

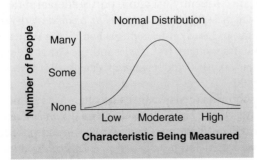

Standard scores are test scores that reflect this normal distribution: Many students get scores in the middle range, and only a few get very high or very low scores.

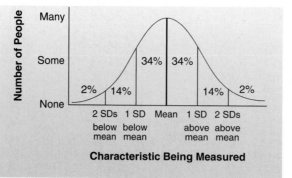

Before we examine standard scores in more detail, we need to understand two numbers we use to derive these scores—the mean and standard deviation. The **mean (M)** is the average of a set of scores: We add all the scores together and divide by the total number of scores (or people). For example, if we add the heights of all 25 students in Ms. Oppenheimer's class and then divide by 25, we get a mean height of 50 inches (see the calculation at the bottom of Figure 15.5).

The **standard deviation (SD)** indicates the *variability* of a set of scores. A small number tells us that, generally speaking, the scores are close together, and a large number tells us that they are spread far apart. For example, third graders tend to be more similar in height than eighth graders (some eighth graders are less than five feet tall, whereas other eighth graders may be almost six feet tall). The standard deviation for the heights of third graders is therefore smaller than the standard deviation for the heights of eighth graders. The procedure for computing a standard deviation is more complex than that for computing a mean. If you are curious, you can find the details in one of the supplementary readings in the *Study Guide and Reader* that accompanies this book.

The mean and standard deviation can be used to divide the normal distribution into several parts, as shown in Figure 15.6. The vertical line at the middle of the curve shows the mean; for a normal distribution, it is at the midpoint and highest point of the curve. The thinner lines to either side reflect the standard deviation: We count out a standard deviation's worth higher and lower than the mean and mark those spots with two lines, and then count another standard deviation to either side and draw two more lines. When we divide the normal distribution in this way, the percentages of students getting scores in each part are always the same. Approximately two-thirds (68%) get scores within one standard deviation of the mean (34% in each direction). As we go farther away from the mean, we find fewer and fewer students, with 28 percent lying between one and two standard deviations away (14% on each side) and only 4 percent being more than two standard deviations away (2% at each end).

Now that we better understand the normal distribution and two statistics that describe it, let's return to standard scores. A standard score reflects a student's position in the normal distribution: It tells us how far the student's performance is from the mean with respect to standard deviation units. Unfortunately, not all standard scores use the same scale: Different scores have different means and standard deviations. Four commonly used standard scores, depicted graphically in Figure 15.7, are these:

- **IQ scores.** IQ scores are frequently used to report students' performance on intelligence tests. They have a *mean of 100* and, for most tests, a *standard deviation of 15*.
- **ETS scores.** ETS scores are used on tests published by the Educational Testing Service, such as the Scholastic Assessment Test (SAT) and the Graduate Record Examination (GRE). They have a *mean of 500* and a *standard deviation of 100*; however, no scores fall below 200 or above 800.
- **Stanines.** Stanines (short for *standard nines*) are often used to report standardized achievement test results. They have a *mean of 5* and a *standard deviation of 2*. Because they are always reported as whole numbers, each score reflects a *range* of test performance (reflected by the shaded and nonshaded portions of the upper right-hand curve in Figure 15.7).
- **z-scores.** Standard scores known as z-scores are often used by statisticians. They have a *mean of 0* and a *standard deviation of 1*.

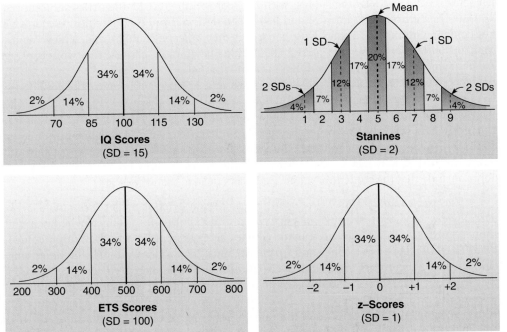

FIGURE 15.7 Distributions of four types of standard scores

Norm- Versus Criterion-Referenced Scores in the Classroom

For teacher-developed assessments, norm-referenced scores may occasionally be appropriate. For example, such comparative scores may be necessary when designating "first chair" in an instrumental music class or choosing the best entries for a regional science fair. We may also need to resort to a norm-referenced approach when assessing complex skills that are difficult to describe as "mastered." Some complex tasks—for example, writing poetry, demonstrating advanced athletic skills, or critically analyzing works of literature—can sometimes be evaluated more easily by comparing students with one another than by specifying an absolute level of accomplishment. When we assign norm-referenced scores on our own assessments, the norm group is likely to be all the students in our class: We give high scores to students who exhibit the best performance and low scores to students who, comparatively speaking, perform poorly. To use common lingo, we are "grading on the curve."

We should probably *not* use norm-referenced scores on a regular basis, however. For one thing, they create a competitive situation: Students do well only if their performance surpasses that of their classmates. As we discovered in Chapter 12, competitive situations create many more losers than winners and so are likely to undermine students' self-efficacy and intrinsic motivation to learn classroom material. Furthermore, norm-referenced scores are inconsistent with the *sense of community* discussed in Chapter 14.

In most instances, criterion-referenced scores communicate what teachers and students alike most need to know: whether instructional objectives have been accomplished. In doing so, they focus attention on mastery goals rather than performance goals and, by showing improvement over time, should enhance students' self-efficacy for learning academic subject matter.

Most experts urge us to use criterion-referenced scores more frequently than norm-referenced scores when evaluating students' work. Why are criterion-referenced scores usually a better choice?

Some educators believe that classroom assessment scores should *always* be criterion-referenced. What do you think?

Interpreting Test Scores Appropriately

In and of themselves, test scores tell us only so much; ideally, they should be accompanied by specific, concrete feedback about the strengths and weaknesses of students' responses, as well as by suggestions that can help students improve over the long run. Furthermore, we must be careful that we don't place too much stock in the specific scores that tests yield. Following are several guidelines to keep in mind:

■ *Compare two norm-referenced test scores only when those scores are derived from the same or equivalent norm group(s).* Because different standardized tests almost always have different norm groups, we cannot really compare students' performance on one test with their performance on another. For example, if Susan takes the Basic Skills Test (BST), we can compare her score on the BST Reading subtest with her score on the BST Mathematics subtest because both scores are from the same test and have been derived from the same norms. But we cannot compare Susan's BST scores with her scores on a *different* standardized achievement test, such as the Reading Achievement Test (RAT) that Shawn took, because the two sets of scores are likely to be based on entirely different norm groups.

When two or more scores are from the same test, however, we can use the confidence intervals for the scores to make meaningful comparisons. In the discussion of reliability earlier in the chapter, Figure 15.2 depicted confidence intervals for Susan's scores on the BST. Test publishers often report confidence intervals for norm-referenced scores (e.g., percentile ranks, standard scores). Overlapping confidence intervals for any two subtests indicate that the student has performed equally well in the two areas. If the intervals show no overlap, we can reasonably conclude that the student has done better in one area than the other.

■ *Have a clear and justifiable rationale for establishing cutoff scores for "acceptable" performance.* If we want to use test results to make either-or decisions—for instance, whether a student should move to a more advanced math course, be exempt from a basic writing course, be awarded certification as a teacher, and so on—we must have a clear rationale for identifying the cutoff score. This process can be relatively easy for criterion-referenced scores, provided that they truly reflect mastery and nonmastery of the subject matter. It is far more difficult for norm-referenced scores: At what point does a student's performance become "acceptable"? At the 20th percentile? the 50th percentile? a stanine of 3? a stanine of 6? Without more information about what knowledge and skills such scores represent, there is no way of knowing.

■ *Never use a single test score to make important decisions.* As we have seen, no test, no matter how carefully constructed and widely used, has perfect reliability and validity. Every test is fallible, and students may do poorly on them for a variety of reasons. Thus, we should never—and I do mean *never*—use a single assessment instrument or single test score to make important decisions about individual students. Nor should we use single test scores to make important decisions about large groups of students or about the teachers who teach them. We will look more closely at these issues in the following section on high-stakes testing and accountability. Before we do so, however, let's take a look at how one student's standardized test scores have been reported.

INTERPRETING ARTIFACTS AND INTERACTIONS   *A Computer Printout*

Twelve-year-old Ingrid takes a standardized achievement test. At an after-school conference several weeks later, her teacher shares the results with Ingrid and her parents. As you look at the following computer printout, think about

■ What the stanine and percentile scores tell us about Ingrid's achievement
■ What the "national percentile bands" refer to
■ Which content areas are relative strengths and weaknesses for Ingrid
■ Why the numbers for the scale on the right are unevenly spaced

	STANINE	PERCENTILE	NATIONAL PERCENTILE BANDS						
			WELL BELOW AVERAGE	BELOW AVERAGE	AVERAGE	ABOVE AVERAGE	WELL ABOVE AVERAGE		
			1 5 10 20	30 40	50 60	70 80	90 95 99		
READING COMPREHENSION	8	92					XXXXXXXXXXXXX		
SPELLING	4	39		XXXXXXXXXXXX					
MATH COMPUTATION	4	37		XXXXXXXXXX					
MATH CONCEPTS	5	57			XXXXXXXXXXXX				
SCIENCE	8	90					XXXXXXXXXXXXX		
SOCIAL STUDIES	7	84				XXXXXXXX			
			1 5 10 20	30 40	50 60	70 80	90 95 99		

On the basis of her stanine scores and percentile ranks, Ingrid appears to have achieved at average or slightly below-average levels in spelling and math but well above average in reading comprehension, science, and social studies. The "national percentile bands" are confidence intervals for Ingrid's percentile scores; the percentiles and stanines have both been computed by comparing Ingrid's raw scores with those of a national norm group. Ingrid's confidence intervals for spelling and math overlap, so even though she has gotten somewhat higher scores in math concepts than in spelling or math computation, the scores are not different *enough* to say that she is better at math concepts than in the other two areas. The confidence intervals for reading comprehension, science, and social studies overlap as well, so she performed similarly in these three areas. The confidence intervals for her three highest scores do *not* overlap with those for her lowest three scores. We can say, then, that Ingrid's relative strengths are in reading comprehension, science, and social studies; she has achieved at lower levels in spelling and math.

Why are the numbers used to depict the percentile confidence intervals unevenly spaced on the computer printout? Remember, percentile ranks tend to overestimate differences near the mean and underestimate differences at the extremes. The uneven spacing is the test publisher's way of showing this fact: It squishes the middle percentile scores close together and spreads high and low percentile scores farther apart. In this way, it tries to give students and parents an idea about where students' performance falls on a normal curve.

High-Stakes Testing and Accountability

Within the past two or three decades, many politicians, business leaders, and other public figures have lamented what appear to be low achievement levels among our students and have called for major overhauls of our educational system.[7] Many of these reform-minded individuals equate high achievement with high scores on standardized tests and, conversely, low achievement with low test scores. They have been putting considerable pressure on teachers and educational administrators to get the test scores up, and some threaten serious consequences (reduced funding, restrictions on salary, etc.) for those schools and school employees who do *not* get the scores up. Here we are talking about both **high-stakes testing**—making major decisions on the basis of single assessments—and **accountability**—holding teachers, administrators, and other school personnel responsible for students' performance on those assessments.

Sometimes students too are held accountable for their performance on schoolwide assessments. Some school districts have used students' performance on tests or other assessments as a basis for promotion to the next grade level or for awarding high school diplomas (e.g., Boschee & Baron, 1993; Guskey, 1994).[8] Typically, school personnel begin by identifying certain *standards* or *competencies* that students' final achievement should reflect. They then assess students' performance levels (sometimes known as *outcomes*) at the end of instruction, and only those students whose performance meets the predetermined standards and competencies move forward. Such an approach was particularly prevalent in the late 1970s and early 1980s, but difficulties in constructing and administering highly valid and reliable assessment instruments, combined with a growing dissatisfaction with the emphasis on minimum rather than maximum levels of performance, have led to its decline in recent years (R. L. Linn & Gronlund, 2000; D. P. Resnick, 1980).

Certainly our schools are not perfect. We still have a great deal to learn about how best to help students of all ages and backgrounds acquire the basic knowledge and skills they need to succeed in an increasingly complex world and, better still, to achieve at the highest possible levels. But the current emphasis on boosting students' test scores is fraught with difficulties, and solutions to these difficulties are only beginning to emerge. Let's consider both the problems and the potential solutions.

Problems with High-Stakes Testing

Experts have identified several problems with the heavy reliance on high-stakes tests to make decisions about students, educators, and school programs:

---

[7] In the United States a report entitled *A Nation at Risk,* published by the National Commission on Excellence in Education in 1983, has been particularly influential.

[8] Such approaches go by a variety of names; *outcomes-based education* and *minimum competency testing* are two common ones.

- *The tests don't necessarily reflect important instructional objectives.* Standardized achievement tests don't always have validity for the situations in which they're used. For one thing, they may reflect only a small portion of a particular school's instructional objectives (Stiggins, 2001). Furthermore, the preponderance of multiple-choice and other objectively scorable items on standardized tests may limit the ability of the tests to assess higher-level thinking skills and performance on authentic, real-life tasks (Darling-Hammond, 1991; E. H. Hiebert & Raphael, 1996; L. A. Shepard, 2000).

- *Teachers spend a great deal of time teaching to the tests.* When teachers are being held accountable for their students' performance on a particular test, many of them will understandably devote many class hours to the knowledge and skills that the test assesses, and students may focus their studying efforts on that same material (Darling-Hammond, 1991; R. L. Linn, 2000; L. B. Resnick & Resnick, 1992). The result is often that students perform at higher levels on a high-stakes test *without* improving their achievement and abilities more generally (Amrein & Berliner, 2002). If a test truly measures the things that are most important for students to learn—including such higher-level skills as transfer, problem solving, and critical thinking—then focusing on those things is quite appropriate. If the test primarily assesses rote knowledge and lower-level skills, however, then such emphasis may undermine the improvements we *really* want to see in students' achievement.

- *School personnel have disincentives to include the test results of students with special educational needs and other low achievers.* If a teacher or school administrator wanted to maximize the average test performance of a particular classroom or school, he or she might conclude that *dishonesty* is the best policy and find reasons why students with a pattern of low achievement should *not* take the test. Such a practice is not only dishonest, it is also a disservice to the students who are left out of the assessment process. We are in a better position to help students achieve at high levels when we know what their current levels are.

- *Different criteria lead to different conclusions about which students and schools are performing at high levels.* When we base school funding, salary increases, and other incentives on students' test performance, exactly what criteria do we use? A predetermined, absolute level of achievement? Improvement over time? Superior performance relative to other school districts? There is no easy answer to this question; for instance, students from lower-income neighborhoods achieve at lower levels than those from higher-income levels (on average), often through no fault of their teachers (R. L. Linn, 2000; McLoyd, 1998). Yet depending on which criteria we use, we will reach different conclusions as to which students and schools are and are not performing well (R. L. Linn, 2000).

- *Too much emphasis is placed on punishing low-performing students and schools; not enough is placed on helping those students and schools improve.* Sadly, too many advocates of school reform think that a quick and easy "fix" to the low achievement levels of many students is simply to reward those schools and students that do well and to punish those that do not (L. A. Shepard, 2000). This strategy is unlikely to be effective, particularly if some of the factors affecting students' academic performance (health, nutrition, family support, peer group norms, etc.) are beyond teachers' and administrators' control. In fact, at the present time there is no convincing evidence that holding school personnel accountable for students' performance on high-stakes assessments has a significant and positive influence on learning and achievement (Amrein & Berliner, 2002; R. L. Linn, 2000; D. B. Swanson, Norman, & Linn, 1995).

Potential Solutions to the Problems

Public concerns about students' achievement levels are not going away any time soon, nor should they. Many of our students *are* achieving at low levels, particularly those in low-income school districts, those with diverse cultural backgrounds, and those with special educational needs (see Chapters 4 and 5). So I offer several potential solutions—I say *potential* solutions because none of them is either easy or perfect—which, in combination, may alleviate some of the problems just identified:

- *We must identify and assess those things that are most important for students to know and do.* If we are going to base important decisions about students, teachers, and schools on assessment results, we must make sure that we are assessing achievements most critical for students' long-term success both in school and in the adult world.

■ *We must educate the public about what standardized tests can and cannot do for us.* What I've seen and heard in the media leads me to think that many politicians and other policy makers overestimate how much standardized achievement tests can tell us: They assume that such instruments are highly accurate and comprehensive measures of students' overall academic achievement. True, these tests are developed by experts with considerable training in test construction, but no test is completely reliable, and its validity will vary considerably depending on the circumstances in which it is being used. It behooves all of us—teachers, school administrators, parents, and so on—to learn for ourselves what the limitations of standardized tests are likely to be and to educate our fellow citizens accordingly.

■ *We must look at alternatives to traditional objective tests.* Especially when a test is going to be administered to large numbers of students at a time, it is apt to be objective and machine-scorable in format, and multiple-choice items are often used. As we shall discover in Chapter 16, well-constructed multiple-choice tests can certainly assess higher-level thinking skills. Nevertheless, paper-pencil tasks that ask students to choose from among four or five alternatives will inevitably limit how effectively we can assess important information and skills; for instance, they will tell us little about students' ability to write well (Traub, 1993). Thus, some experts argue that we begin to use performance assessments either instead of or in addition to more traditional paper-pencil tests (e.g., L. B. Resnick & Resnick, 1992; L. A. Shepard, 2000). We should be aware, however, that those states and school districts that have begun to use performance measures for large-scale assessments of students' achievement have encountered difficulties with reliability and validity (more on this point in Chapter 16), and so we must tread cautiously as we move in this direction (Khattri & Sweet, 1996).

■ *We must advocate for the use of multiple measures in any high-stakes decisions.* No matter what kind of assessment instruments we use, any one instrument is unlikely to give us a complete picture of what students have learned and achieved. Even if an instrument could give us such a picture, perfect reliability is an elusive goal: Students' test results will inevitably be subject to temporary swings in motivation, attention, mood, health, and other factors. To base life-altering decisions on a single test score, then, is unconscionable.

Confidentiality and Communication About Assessment Results

How would you feel if your instructor

- Returned test papers in the order of people's test scores, so that those with highest scores were handed out first, and you received yours *last*?
- Told your other instructors how poorly you had done on the test, so that they could be on the lookout for other stupid things you might do?
- Looked through your school records and discovered that you got an IQ score of 92 on an intelligence test you took last year, and furthermore that your personality test results indicate some unusual sexual fantasies?

You would probably be outraged that your instructor would do any of these things. Your test results should be considered somewhat confidential. But exactly *how* confidential? When should people know the results of students' assessments, and who should know them?

In the United States we get legal guidance on these questions from the **Family Educational Rights and Privacy Act (FERPA)**, passed by the U.S. Congress in 1974. This legislation limits school testing practices primarily to the assessment of achievement and scholastic aptitude, two things that are clearly within the school's domain. Furthermore, it restricts knowledge of students' test results to the few individuals who really need to know them: students themselves, their parents, and school personnel directly involved with students' education and well-being. School test results can be shared with other individuals (e.g., a family doctor or private psychologist) *only* when parents or students (if at least 18 years old) give written permission.

This legislative mandate for confidentiality has several implications for our assessment practices in the classroom. For example, we *cannot*

- Ask students to reveal their political affiliation, sexual behavior or attitudes, illegal or antisocial behavior, potentially embarrassing mental or psychological problems, or family income. (An exception: Questions about income are appropriate when used to determine eligibility for financial assistance.)

- Ask students to score one another's test papers.
- Post test scores in ways that allow students to learn one another's scores. For example, we cannot post scores according to birthdays, social security numbers, or code numbers that reflect the alphabetical order of students in the class.
- Distribute papers in any way that allows students to observe one another's scores. For example, we cannot let students search through a stack of scored papers to find their own.

How often have your own teachers used practices prohibited by the Family Educational Rights and Privacy Act? How did such practices make you feel?

Keeping students' test scores confidential makes educational as well as legal sense. Students getting low test scores may feel embarrassed or ashamed if classmates know their scores, and they may become more anxious about their future test performance than they would be otherwise. Students with high test scores may also suffer from having their scores made public: In many classrooms it isn't cool to be smart, and high achievers may perform at lower levels to avoid risking the rejection of peers.

An additional provision of FERPA is that parents and students (if at least 18 years old) have the right to review test scores and other school records. Furthermore, school personnel must present and interpret this information in a way that parents and students can understand. Let's look at some strategies for doing so.

Communicating Classroom Assessment Results

Let's return to the opening case study, in which Ms. Ford returns disappointing math papers to her students. Notice the approach she takes in communicating the test scores to the students' parents:

Ms. Ford: OK, boys and girls, shhh. I would say, on this test in particular, boys and girls, if you received a grade below 75 you definitely have to work on it. I do expect this quiz to be returned with Mom or Dad's signature on it. I want Mom and Dad to be aware of how we're doing.

Student: No!

Student: Do we have to show our parents? Is it a requirement to pass the class?

Ms. Ford: If you do not return it with a signature, I will call home. (dialogue from J. C. Turner, Meyer, et al., 1998, p. 741)

Is Ms. Ford's strategy for communicating the test results with parents likely to be effective? Why or why not?

Ms. Ford obviously wants her students' parents to know that their children are not doing well in her math class. However, there are three drawbacks to her approach. First, many students may find it easier to forge an adultlike signature than to deliver bad news to their parents. Second, parents who do see their children's test papers won't have much information to help them interpret the results (are the low scores due to low effort? to poor study strategies? to an undiagnosed learning disability? to insufficient instruction?). Finally, Ms. Ford focuses entirely on the problem—low achievement—without offering any suggestions for *solving* the problem.

Whenever we assess our students' achievement and abilities, we must remember that our primary purpose is to *help students learn and achieve more effectively* (Stiggins, 2001). When students perform well on our assessment instruments, we have cause for celebration, and we know that our instructional strategies are working as they should. But when students perform poorly, our primary concern, and that of students and parents as well, should be how to improve the situation.

Ultimately, we must think of ourselves as working in cooperation with students and parents for something that all of us want—students' classroom success. Our primary goal in communicating classroom assessment results is to share information that will help us achieve that end. The section "Working with Parents" in Chapter 14 includes several strategies for creating partner-

Whenever we assess students' achievement and abilities, we must remember that our primary purpose is to help students learn and achieve more effectively.

ships with parents to facilitate students' success at school. In Chapter 16 we will consider strategies for getting students actively involved in their own assessment; such strategies will indirectly promote their learning and achievement as well.

Explaining Standardized Test Results

When we need to report the results of standardized tests, we have a somewhat different challenge. How do we describe tests and test results to students and parents who, in all likelihood, have never read a chapter on assessment in an educational psychology textbook? Following are some general guidelines that experts offered many years ago yet still have relevance today (Durost, 1961; Ricks, 1959):

■ *Make sure you understand the results yourself.* As teachers, we need to know something about a test's reliability and validity for the situation in which we have used it. We also need to know how the test scores have been derived. For example, we should know whether the scores are criterion-referenced or norm-referenced. If they're norm-referenced, we should also know something about the norm group that was used.

■ *Remember that, in many cases, it is sufficient to describe the test and students' test performance in broad, general terms.* To illustrate, we might describe an achievement test as a general measure of how much a student has learned in mathematics compared to other students around the country, or we might describe a scholastic aptitude test as something that gives a rough idea about how well a student is likely to do in a particular instructional program. It's sometimes possible to describe a student's test performance without mentioning test scores at all. For example, we might say, "Your daughter scores like students who do well in college mathematics courses" or "Your son had more than average difficulty on the spelling portion of the achievement test; this is an area in which he may need extra help in the next few years." However, if parents want to know their child's specific test scores, in the United States the Family Educational Rights and Privacy Act requires that we reveal those scores and help parents understand what they mean.

■ *When reporting specific test scores, use percentile ranks and stanines rather than grade equivalents or IQs.* Many parents mistakenly believe that a child's grade-equivalent score reflects the grade that the child should actually be in, so they may argue for advanced placement of their high-achieving children or feel distressed that their low-achieving children are in over their heads. And many parents interpret IQ scores as reflecting a permanent, unchangeable ability rather than as just an estimate of a child's present cognitive functioning. By reporting test scores as percentile ranks or stanines instead, we are less likely to have parents jumping to such erroneous conclusions. Many parents are familiar with percentile ranks, and most others can easily grasp the notion of a percentile if it is explained to them. But because percentile ranks misrepresent actual differences between students (overestimating differences in the middle range and underestimating differences at the extremes), we may also want to provide stanine scores. Although most parents are unfamiliar with standard scores in general, we can often present stanines in a graphic and concrete fashion, such as I have done in Figure 15.8.

■ *If you know the standard error of measurement, give parents the confidence interval for a test score.* By reporting confidence intervals along with specific test scores, you communicate an important point about the tests you give: Any test score has some error associated with it.

Taking Student Diversity into Account

As we identify and implement ways to assess learning and achievement, we must remember that students often differ from one another in ways that affect their performance in assessment situations. When two students have *learned equally* yet *perform differently* on our assessments, then the information we obtain from those assessments has questionable validity. In this section we will look at the effects of student diversity from several angles:

- Developmental differences
- Test anxiety
- Cultural bias
- Language differences
- Testwiseness

FIGURE 15.8 A graphic technique for explaining stanines to parents (modeled after Durost, 1951)

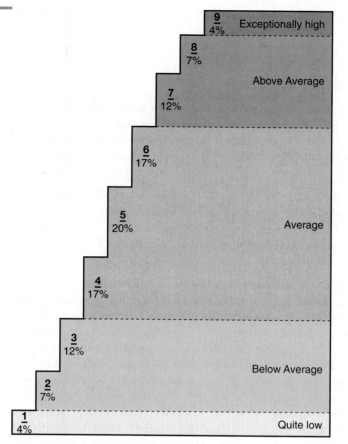

We will then consider how we might adapt our classroom assessment procedures to accommodate students with special needs.

Developmental Differences

As we have seen, a variety of irrelevant factors—motivation, mood, energy level, and so on—affect students' performance on tests and other assessments. When factors such as these are relatively stable characteristics, they affect the validity of an assessment instrument. When factors are temporary and variable from day or day (perhaps even hour to hour), they affect an instrument's reliability and so indirectly affect its validity as well. Such sources of error in students' test scores and other assessment results are especially common in young children, who may have limited language skills, short attention spans, little motivation to do their best, and low tolerance for frustration (Bracken & Walker, 1997; Messick, 1983). Furthermore, young children's erratic behaviors may make it difficult to maintain standardized testing conditions (Wodtke, Harper, & Schommer, 1989).

Some test publishers have developed standardized tests that can be quite helpful if we are looking for significant developmental delays that will require our immediate attention (Bracken & Walker, 1997; Lidz, 1991). But for children without such delays, standardized test results (e.g., those from school "readiness" tests) tend to be poor predictors of success in kindergarten and the early elementary grades (Lidz, 1991; C. E. Sanders, 1997).

Test Anxiety

How anxious do you get when you know you will be taking a test in class? Do you worry the night before, wondering if you've read all the assigned readings? Do you become nervous while the test is being handed out, thinking that maybe you don't know everything as well as you should? Do you have a lot of trouble remembering things you knew perfectly well when you studied them? Do you get in such a panic that you can barely read the test questions at all? If your answer to any of these questions is yes, then you, like most students, experience **test anxiety**. In Figure 15.9, 8-year-old Connie describes her anxiety about tests with strict time limits.

Students are typically not anxious about learning new knowledge and skills. But as we discovered in Chapter 11, many of them *are* anxious at the thought that they will be evaluated and judged and perhaps found to be "stupid" or in some other way inadequate. A little bit of test anxiety may actually be a good thing: Students are more likely to prepare for an assessment and to respond to questions and tasks carefully if they are concerned about how well they are going to perform (Shipman & Shipman, 1985). But their performance is apt to be impaired when they are *very* test anxious, particularly when assigned tasks require them to use what they have learned in a flexible and creative manner (Hagtvet & Johnsen, 1992; Kirkland, 1971). In cases of extreme test anxiety, students may have difficulty retrieving things from long-term memory and may not even be able to understand what we are asking them to do.

We will see debilitating test anxiety more frequently in older students, students from some minority groups, and students from lower socioeconomic backgrounds (K. T. Hill, 1984; Kirkland, 1971; Pang, 1995; B. N. Phillips et al., 1980). Often, students with the highest test anxiety are those who have performed poorly in school in the past (Kirkland, 1971; Tryon, 1980). An important strategy for helping students overcome excessive test anxiety, then, is to help those students master course material in the first place (Tryon, 1980).

We don't necessarily want to eliminate test anxiety altogether; we just want to keep it at a beneficial level. When students are going to be taking a standardized test, we can encourage them to do their best without describing the test as a life-or-death matter (Sax, 1989). We can also give them practice with the item types and format of a test—for example, by showing them how to answer multiple-choice questions and how to fill in computer-scored answer sheets (Kirkland, 1971; Sax, 1989). But we must keep in mind that, while attempting to minimize students' anxiety, we must nevertheless administer any standardized test in accordance with the instructions in the test manual.

Fortunately, we have more control over how we administer the assessment instruments we develop ourselves. For example, we can eliminate time limits when we aren't trying to measure how *quickly* students can do something (K. T. Hill & Wigfield, 1984). We can describe our assessments more as opportunities to increase knowledge and improve skills than as occasions for evaluation (Spaulding, 1992). And by making statements such as "We're here to learn, and you can't do that without making mistakes" (Brophy, 1986, p. 47), we can help students keep a healthy perspective on their imperfections. Table 15.4 distinguishes between classroom practices that are likely to lead to facilitating anxiety and those that may produce debilitating anxiety.

FIGURE 15.9 Eight-year-old Connie describes how over-whelming test anxiety can be.

Cultural Bias

EXPERIENCING FIRSTHAND   *Predicting the Future*

Imagine you are taking a test designed to predict your success in future situations. Following are the first three questions on the test:

1. When you enter a hogan, in which direction should you move around the fire?
2. Why is turquoise often attached to a baby's cradleboard?
3. If you need black wool for weaving a rug, how can you can obtain the blackest color? Choose one of the following:

   a. Dye the wool by using a mixture of sumac, ochre, and piñon gum.

   b. Dye the wool by using a mixture of indigo, lichen, and mesquite.

   c. Use the undyed wool of specially bred black sheep.

Try to answer these questions before you read further.

Did you have trouble answering some or all of the questions? If so, your difficulty was probably due to the fact that the questions are written from the perspective of a particular culture—that of the Navajos. Unless you have had considerable exposure to Navajo culture, you would probably perform poorly on the test. By the way, the three answers are (1) clockwise; (2) to ward off evil; and (3) dye the wool by using a mixture of sumac, ochre, and piñon gum (Gilpin, 1968).

TABLE 15.4

COMPARE/CONTRAST

Keeping Students' Test Anxiety at a Facilitative Level

WHAT TO DO	WHAT *NOT* TO DO
Point out the value of the assessment as a feedback mechanism to improve learning.	Stress the fact that students' competence is being evaluated.
Administer a practice assessment or pretest that gives students an idea of what the final assessment instrument will be like.	Keep the nature of the assessment a secret until the day it is administered.
Encourage students to do their best.	Remind students that failing will have dire consequences.
Provide or allow the use of memory aids (e.g., a list of formulas or a single note card containing key facts) when instructional objectives do not require students to commit information to memory.	Insist that students commit even trivial facts to memory.
Eliminate time limits unless speed is an important part of the skill being measured.	Give more questions or tasks than students can possibly respond to in the time allotted.
Be available to answer students' questions during the assessment.	Hover over students, watching them closely as they respond.
Use unannounced ("pop") quizzes only for formative evaluation (e.g., to determine an appropriate starting point for instruction).	Give occasional pop quizzes to motivate students to study regularly and to punish those who do not.
Use the results of several assessments to make decisions (e.g., to assign grades).	Evaluate students on the basis of a single assessment.

Sources: Brophy, 1986; Gaudry & Bradshaw, 1971; K. T. Hill, 1984; K. T. Hill & Wigfield, 1984; Popham, 1990; Sax, 1989; Sieber, Kameya, & Paulson, 1970.

Is the test culturally biased? That depends. If the test is designed to assess your ability to succeed in a Navajo community, then the questions may be very appropriate. But if it's designed to assess your ability to succeed in a school system in which knowledge of Navajo culture is totally irrelevant, then such questions are culturally biased.

Note that the term *cultural bias* includes biases related to gender and socioeconomic status as well as to culture and ethnicity.

An assessment instrument has **cultural bias** if any of its items either offend or unfairly penalize some students on the basis of their ethnicity, gender, or socioeconomic status (e.g., Popham, 1995). For example, imagine a test question that implies that boys are more competent than girls, and imagine another that has a picture in which members of a particular ethnic group are engaging in criminal behavior. Such questions have cultural bias because some groups of students (girls in the first situation, and members of the depicted ethnic group in the second) may be offended by the questions and thus distracted from doing their best on the test. And consider these two assessment tasks:

Task 1

Would you rather swim in the ocean, a lake, or a swimming pool? Write a two-page essay defending your choice.

Task 2

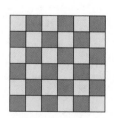

Mary is making a patchwork quilt from 36 separate squares of fabric, as shown on the left. Each square of fabric has a perimeter of 20 inches. Mary sews the squares together, using a ½-inch seam allowance. She then sews the assembled set of squares to a large piece of cotton that will serve as the flip side of the quilt, again using a ½-inch seam allowance. How long is the perimeter of the finished quilt?

Task 1 will obviously be difficult for students who haven't been swimming in all three environments, and even more difficult for those who have never swum at all; students from low-income, inner-city families might easily fall into one of these two categories. Task 2 assumes a fair amount of knowledge about sewing (e.g., what a seam allowance is); this is knowledge that some students (especially girls) are more likely to have than others. Such tasks have cultural bias because some students will perform better than others because of differences in their background experiences, *not* because of differences in what they have learned in the classroom.

An assessment instrument isn't necessarily biased just because one group gets higher test scores than another group. It is biased only if the groups' scores are different when the characteristic we're trying to measure *isn't* different, or if the instrument has higher predictive validity for one group than for another. Yes, we may sometimes see group differences in students' performance on assessment instruments, but these differences often reflect inequities in students' previous experiences that will affect their future educational performance. For example, if high school girls earn lower scores on mathematics achievement tests than high school boys (on average), the difference may be partly due to the fact that the girls have had fewer "mathematical" toys and experiences than the boys (P. A. Campbell, 1986; Eccles & Jacobs, 1986; Kahle & Lakes, 1983). Similarly, if students from low-income families have had few opportunities to venture beyond their immediate neighborhoods (fewer museum trips, less travel, etc.), their more limited exposure to diverse environments is likely to impact both their test performance *and* their classroom achievement.

In fact, most companies that publish large-scale standardized tests now employ individuals who represent numerous minority groups, and they actively screen their test items for possible sources of bias (R. L. Linn & Gronlund, 2000). Furthermore, most scholastic aptitude tests show similar predictive validity for various ethnic and cultural groups, provided that the members of those groups are native English speakers (R. T. Brown, Reynolds, & Whitaker, 1999; Sattler, 2001). Nevertheless, before using any standardized test, school personnel should scrutinize it carefully for any items that either gender or any cultural group may find offensive, as well as for items that might be more difficult for one group than another for reasons unrelated to the characteristic to be measured. And classroom teachers should be continually on the lookout for any unintentional cultural bias in the assessment instruments that they themselves construct.

Look again at the treehouse problem in Figure 8.4 (p. 279). Is this problem culturally biased? Why or why not?

Is this discussion of cultural bias consistent with your previous beliefs about the topic? If not, can you reconcile the inconsistencies?

Language Differences

In the preceding section on cultural bias, I said that most scholastic aptitude tests show similar predictive validity for various groups *provided that the members of those groups are native English speakers*. Without question, students' facility with the English language will affect their performance on English-based classroom assessments. Poor reading and writing skills are likely to interfere with success on paper-pencil tasks; poor speaking skills will adversely influence students' ability to accomplish performance tasks such as classroom debates or oral reports. If we are trying to assess students' achievement in areas unrelated to the language arts—perhaps achievement in mathematics, music, or physical education—then we may in some cases want to minimize our dependence on language to assess those areas.

In the United States, the Individuals with Disabilities Education Act (IDEA) mandates that any tests and other assessments used to identify students with special needs be administered in the students' primary language (see the section "Public Law 94–142" in Chapter 5). Although this practice may be critical for an accurate appraisal of students' achievement and abilities, we will typically have little or no reliability and validity data for the instruments in their translated forms, nor will we have appropriate norm groups to which we can compare our own students' performance (E. C. Lopez, 1997; Sattler, 2001). We must therefore be especially cautious in interpreting and using the results of assessment instruments that have been translated for students with diverse language backgrounds.

Testwiseness

EXPERIENCING FIRSTHAND   *Califractions*

Imagine you are enrolled in a course called Califractions. One day, your instructor gives you a surprise quiz before you've had a chance to do the assigned readings. Three quiz questions follow; see whether you can figure out the correct answers even though you *haven't* studied any califractions. Choose the single best answer for each item.

1. Because they are furstier than other califractions, califors are most often used to
   a. Reassignment of matherugs
   b. Disbobble a fwing
   c. Mangelation
   d. In the burfews
2. Calendation is a process of
   a. Combining two califors
   b. Adding two califors together
   c. Joining two califors
   d. Taking two califors apart
3. The furstiest califraction is the
   a. Califor
   b. Calderost
   c. Calinga
   d. Calidater

You may have found that you were able to answer the questions even though you knew nothing whatsoever about califractions. Because the first quiz item says ". . . califors are most often used to . . . ," the answer must begin with a verb. Alternatives *a* and *c* apparently begin with nouns ("reassign*ment*" and "mangela*tion*"), and *d* begins with a preposition ("in"), so *b* is the only possible correct answer. Item 2 presents three alternatives (*a*, *b*, and *c*) that all say the same thing, so, because there can be only one right answer, the correct choice must be *d*. And the answer to item 3 (the "furstiest califraction") must be *a* (a califor) because item 1 has already stated that califors are furstier than other califractions.

If you did well on the califractions quiz, then you have some degree of **testwiseness**; that is, you use test-taking strategies that enhance your test performance. Testwiseness includes strategies such as these:

- *Using time efficiently*—for example, allocating enough time for each task and saving difficult items for last
- *Avoiding sloppy errors*—for example, checking answers a second time and erasing any stray pencil marks on a computer-scored answer sheet
- *Deductive reasoning*—for example, eliminating two alternatives that say the same thing and using information from one question to answer another
- *Guessing*—for example, eliminating obviously wrong alternatives and then guessing one of the others, and guessing randomly if time runs out and there is no penalty for guessing

(Millman, Bishop, & Ebel, 1965; Petersen, Sudweeks, & Baird, 1990)

Even when we find no culturally biased content in our assessment instruments, we must remember that some students may not be familiar with certain types of assessment tasks; for example, students whose prior schooling has occurred within a different culture may be inexperienced in answering true-false, multiple-choice, or essay questions. In some instances, we may be able to make our assessment tasks similar to those with which students have had previous experience. In other situations—perhaps when the school district requests that we give a standardized, multiple-choice achievement test—we should be sure to explain the general nature of the tasks involved (Popham, 1990). For example, we might mention that we don't expect students to know all the answers and point out that many students will not have enough time to answer every question. We should also give students ample practice with the forms of any test items or performance tasks we use (Popham, 1990).

The sources of diversity just described point to the need for considerable flexibility in our approaches to classroom assessment; they also underscore the importance of assessing students' achievement in a variety of ways rather than depending too much on a single instrument (Baek, 1994; Drake, 1993; C. Hill & Larsen, 1992). Ultimately, our assessment practices must be fair and equitable for students of all ages, backgrounds, and group memberships.

Accommodating Students with Special Needs

We may often have to modify assessment instruments and procedures to accommodate students with special educational needs. In the United States, the Individuals with Disabilities Education Act (IDEA) mandates appropriate accommodations for students' disabilities: presenting questions orally to students with delayed reading skills, giving extra time to students whose cognitive or physical disabilities require it, and so on. The *Standards for Educational and Psychological Testing* (American Educational Research Association, American Psychological Association, & National Council on Measurement in Education, 1999) ask us to consider six types of accommodations for students who have been identified as having special educational needs:

- Modifying the presentation format of the assessment (e.g., using Braille or American Sign Language to present test items and other assessment tasks)
- Modifying the response format (e.g., dictating answers, using a word processor)
- Modifying the timing (e.g., giving extra time or frequent breaks)
- Modifying the assessment setting (e.g., having a student take a standardized paper-pencil test alone in a quiet room)
- Administering part but not all of an instrument
- Using instruments different from those given nondisabled classmates, to be more compatible with students' ability levels and needs

We can often use students' individualized education programs (IEPs; see Chapter 5) for guidance about appropriate accommodations for each student.

Table 15.5 provides examples of specific accommodations to consider when administering standardized tests. In Chapter 16 we will identify accommodations that have more relevance to teacher-developed assessments.

Whenever we modify educational assessment instruments for students with special needs, we must recognize that there is a trade-off between two of our RSVP characteristics. On the one hand, we are violating the idea that an assessment instrument should be standardized with respect to content, administration, and scoring criteria. On the other hand, if we fail to accommodate the particular disabilities that some of our students may have, we will inevitably get results that have little validity regarding the knowledge and skills that students have acquired. There is no magic formula for determining the right balance between standardization and validity for students with special needs; as teachers, we must use our best professional judgment (and perhaps seek the advice of specialists as well) in each situation.

We must keep in mind, too, that modifying assessment instruments or procedures for a standardized test may render the test's norms irrelevant, and hence any norm-referenced scores we derive may be uninterpretable. Standardized testing procedures and norm-referenced scores are sometimes appropriate for students with special needs when our purpose is to identify existing learning and performance difficulties. But when we are later concerned about how to modify instructional methods and materials to *address* those difficulties, criterion-referenced scores and a close inspection of students' responses to particular tasks and items may be more helpful.

TABLE 15.5

STUDENTS IN INCLUSIVE SETTINGS

Using Standardized Tests with Students with Special Educational Needs

CATEGORY	CHARACTERISTICS YOU MIGHT OBSERVE	SUGGESTED CLASSROOM STRATEGIES
Students with specific cognitive or academic difficulties	• Poor listening, reading, and/or writing skills (for some students) • Tendency for test scores to underestimate overall achievement levels (if students have poor reading skills) • Inconsistent performance due to off-task behaviors (e.g., hyperactivity, inattentiveness), affecting reliability and validity of scores (for some students with learning disabilities or ADHD) • Higher than average test anxiety	• Modify test administration procedures to accommodate disabilities identified in students' IEPs (e.g., when administering a standardized essay test, allow students with writing disabilities to use a word processor and spell checker). • Have students take tests in a room with minimal distractions. • Make sure students understand what they are being asked to do. • Be sure students are motivated to do their best but are not overly anxious. • Use classroom assessments (both formal and informal) to either confirm or disconfirm results of standardized test results. • Record and report all modifications made.
Students with social or behavioral problems	• Inconsistent performance due to off-task behaviors or lack of motivation, affecting reliability and validity of scores (for some students)	• Modify test administration procedures to accommodate disabilities identified in students' IEPs (e.g., when students are easily distracted, administer tests individually in a quiet room). • Use classroom assessments (both formal and informal) to either confirm or disconfirm results of standardized test results. • Record and report all modifications made.
Students with general delays in cognitive and social functioning	• Slow learning and cognitive processing • Limited if any reading skills • Poor listening skills	• Choose instruments appropriate for students' cognitive abilities and reading and writing skills. • Minimize use of instruments that are administered to an entire class at once; rely more on instruments that are administered to one student at a time. • Make sure students understand what they are being asked to do.
Students with physical or sensory challenges	• Mobility problems (for some students with physical challenges) • Tendency to tire easily (for some students with physical challenges) • Less developed language skills, affecting reading and writing ability (for some students with hearing loss)	• Obtain modified test materials for students with visual impairments (e.g., large-print or Braille test booklets). • Modify test administration procedures to accommodate students' unique needs (e.g., have a sign language interpreter give directions to students with hearing loss, have students with limited muscle control dictate their answers). • If reading and writing skills are impaired, read test items to students. • Break lengthy assessments into segments that can be administered on separate occasions. • Schedule tests at times when students feel rested and alert. • Record and report all modifications made. • Don't compare a student's performance to the norm group if significant modifications have been made.
Students with advanced cognitive development	• Greater interest and engagement in challenging tests • Tendency in some students to hide giftedness to avoid possible ridicule by peers (e.g., some minority students may want to avoid "acting White") • In some instances, ability levels beyond the scope of typical tests for the grade level	• Keep assessment results confidential. • When students consistently earn perfect or near-perfect scores (e.g., percentile ranks of 99), request individualized testing that can more accurately assess actual ability levels.

Sources: Barkley, 1998; Beirne-Smith et al. 2002; D. Y. Ford & Harris, 1992; A. W. Gottfried et al., 1994; Mastropieri & Scruggs, 2000; Mercer, 1997; Meyer, 2000; B. N. Phillips et al., 1980; Piirto, 1999; Pitoniak & Royer, 2001; Turnbull et al., 1999; Venn, 2000.

As we have seen, assessment is a process of observing a sample of students' behavior and drawing inferences about their knowledge and abilities. On some occasions, we will use assessment instruments primarily for formative evaluation—perhaps to make instructional decisions and facilitate students' future learning. On other occasions, we will use them more for summative purposes—perhaps to determine whether students have sufficiently mastered instructional objectives to move to the next unit. But regardless of our reasons for assessing students' knowledge and abilities, the following general principles can guide us in our efforts:

■ *All assessment instruments and practices should be evaluated with respect to the RSVP characteristics.* Ideally, good assessments have four characteristics. First, they are *reliable*, yielding consistent results that are only minimally affected by students' moods, environmental conditions, and other temporary, irrelevant factors. Second, they should be *standardized* in content, administration, and scoring criteria, especially if students are to be compared with one another. Third, they should be *valid* for their intended purpose, accurately reflecting the knowledge or skills being assessed or accurately predicting a future behavior of concern. Finally, they should be *practical,* staying within reasonable costs and time constraints.

■ *Most assessment instruments focus on cognitive factors affecting learning and achievement; they give short shrift to other factors that may be equally influential in students' classroom performance.* Most standardized tests and teacher-developed assessments are designed to assess competence or aptitude in particular domains. They may also require language skills (e.g., reading and writing ability), logical thinking skills, testwiseness, and other cognitive abilities. Occasionally, noncognitive factors (e.g., test anxiety) enter into the equation, but by and large, the assessment instruments we use will *not* reflect motivational and affective variables—goals, dispositions, interests, attitudes, and so on—that are important factors in students' learning and achievement. No matter how valid and reliable our assessments may be, they are unlikely to give us a complete description of how well our students are doing and why.

■ *Considerable information is lost when students' performance is summarized by a single test score.* For practical and logistical reasons, we will often find it helpful to summarize students' performance in terms of a number—perhaps a raw score, criterion-referenced score, grade-equivalent, percentile rank, or standard score. Yet by boiling down students' performance on an assessment instrument into a single score, we lose valuable information about their specific strengths and weaknesses, their likes and dislikes, their inclinations and disinclinations, and so on—information that may ultimately be more useful as we plan how best to tailor instruction to meet students' unique needs.

■ *Classroom assessment practices have a significant influence on what and how students learn.* Regardless of our primary purpose in assessing students' learning and achievement, we must remember that the nature of our assessment instruments—what topics they include, whether they focus on lower-level or higher-level skills, and so on—will communicate messages about what is most important for students to learn and about how students should study classroom subject matter. Assessing the knowledge and skills we truly want students to master is essential in any educational assessment, and particularly so for high-stakes assessments that may have a major impact on students' lives, administrative decisions, and educational policy.

■ *Educational assessments are useful yet imperfect tools.* Standardized tests and teacher-developed assessments can tell us a great deal about what students know and can do and what students still need to learn and master. The usefulness of any assessment instrument depends on how well matched it is to the situation in which we want to use it and how reliable and valid it is for that situation. No assessment instrument ever has perfect reliability or validity, however, and so we must not take the results of any single assessment too seriously. As a general rule, we should think of any educational assessment instrument as a tool that, in combination with the other tools at our disposal, can help us improve classroom instruction and maximize students' learning and achievement.

Our ongoing assessments of students' progress and achievement will guide many of our decisions in the classroom. In the following chapter we will consider strategies for conducting informal and formal assessments that yield the information we will need to make the best decisions possible.

CASE STUDY: *Can Johnny Read?*

Ms. Beaudry is serving on a committee to study reading curricula in her school district. As part of her work with the committee, she plans to administer a standardized reading achievement test to determine whether her sixth graders have mastered the reading skills she has been trying to teach them this year. She's been given the opportunity to select the test from three instruments approved for purchase in her district. She scrutinizes the test manuals carefully and eliminates one test when she sees that its test-retest reliability coefficients fall below .85. She analyzes the tables of specifications for the other two tests, comparing each one to her own sixth-grade curriculum. She eventually settles on the Colorado Reading Test (CRT) as being the most reliable and valid measure.

Ms. Beaudry gives the test to her class, following the prescribed administration procedures closely. Because the test consists entirely of multiple-choice items, she is able to score the results quickly and easily that night. She computes each student's raw score and then turns to the norms in the test manual to obtain stanine scores. Her students' stanines range from 3 to 8.

"Hmmm, what now?" she asks herself. "After all this, I still don't know if my students have learned what I've been trying to teach them."

- Ms. Beaudry has chosen the wrong test for her purpose. What specifically did she do wrong?
- Was Ms. Beaudry's approach to determining test validity appropriate in this situation? Why or why not?
- Ms. Beaudry eliminated one test on the basis of reliability coefficients below .85. Was this a good decision? Why or why not?

Once you have answered these questions, compare your responses with those presented in Appendix B.

PRAXIS Turn to Appendix C, "Matching Book and Ancillary Content to the PRAXIS™ Principles of Learning and Teaching Tests," to discover sections of this chapter that may be especially applicable to the PRAXIS™ tests.

Now go to our Companion Website at http://www.prenhall.com/ormrod to assess your understanding of chapter content with "Multiple-Choice Questions," apply comprehension in "Essay Questions," broaden your knowledge of educational psychology with related "Web Links," gain greater insight about classroom learning in "Learning in the Content Areas," and analyze and assess classroom work in the "Student Artifact Library."

Key Concepts

16

Classroom Assessment Strategies

$\mathcal{I}$n your many years as a student, in what various ways have your teachers assessed your achievement? In general, has your performance on classroom assessments accurately reflected what you learned in class? Can you recall a situation in which a test or other classroom assessment seemed to have little or no relationship to important instructional objectives?

As teachers, we will often need to assess students' learning and achievement so that we can make informed decisions in the classroom. For instance, when we begin a new topic, we will want to identify existing knowledge and skills so that we can gear instruction to an appropriate level. We will also want to monitor students' progress as we go along so that we can address any difficulties students are having. And ultimately, we must determine what each student has accomplished during the school year. According to one estimate, we may spend one-third of our time, possibly even more, in assessment-related activities (Stiggins & Conklin, 1992).

It is essential that we use assessment techniques that accurately reflect what our students know and can do; it is equally essential that such techniques promote students' learning and achievement over the long run. In this chapter we will examine a variety of potentially effective assessment strategies and identify the situations in which each one is appropriate. As we do so, we will address these questions:

- In what situations is informal assessment most appropriate and useful?
- What steps should we take as we plan a test, assignment, or other formal assessment of students' learning?
- What guidelines can help us design valid paper-pencil measures of student learning?
- When is performance assessment better than a paper-pencil task, and how can we use such assessment effectively?
- How can we get students actively involved in the assessment process? How can we encourage them to take risks even when their performance is being evaluated?
- How do we evaluate an assessment instrument's effectiveness after we have used it?
- What approaches can we take to summarize students' achievement?

CASE STUDY: *Studying Europe*

Ellen and Roslyn are taking geography this year. Although they have different teachers, they both have the same textbook and often study together. In fact, they are each taking a test on Chapter 6 in their respective classes tomorrow. Here is a snippet of their conversation as they study the night before:

Ellen: Let's see . . . what's the capital of Sweden?

Roz: Stockholm, I think. Why?

Ellen: Because I need to memorize all the capitals of the countries in Europe. I know most of them, I guess. I'd better move on and study the rivers.

Roz: Geez, are you expected to know all those things?

Ellen: Oh, yeah. For our test, Ms. Peterson will give us a map of Europe and ask us to label all the countries, their capitals, and the rivers that run through them.

Roz: Wow! That's not what we're doing in Ms. Montgomery's class at all. We're supposed to learn the topography, climate, and culture of all the European countries. Ms. Montgomery says she'll ask us to use what we know about these things to explain why each country imports and exports the products that it does.

Assessment, Cognition, and Metacognition

Ellen's teacher wants students to learn where European countries are located, what their capitals are, and what rivers run through them. In other words, she wants them to learn facts—an objective that involves lower-level skills. In contrast, Roz's teacher asks students to use what they've learned about topography, climate, and culture to explain each country's imports and exports—an objective that requires such higher-level skills as application (transfer), analysis, and synthesis. If both girls want to do well on their tests, they are wise to study differently, with Ellen focusing on isolated facts and Roz focusing on cause-effect relationships. Ellen may very well accomplish her goal simply by memorizing European place names, but Roz will have to engage in meaningful learning and elaboration to understand why various countries have certain imports and exports. Most probably, then, Roz will remember what she has learned more effectively than Ellen.

Our students will draw inferences about our instructional objectives from the ways we assess their learning, and different assessment tasks may lead them to study and learn differently (J. R. Frederiksen & Collins, 1989; Lundeberg & Fox, 1991; Newmann, 1997; Poole, 1994). Our assessment practices will not only influence students' cognitive processes, but it will influence their metacognition as well. Many students make deliberate choices about what and how they can most effectively study, and over time they learn that certain learning strategies pay off (e.g., by yielding higher test scores) and others do not. It will serve them better in the long run to discover that they can succeed on classroom assessments only if they construct an integrated understanding of a topic (a task that requires meaningful learning, organization, and elaboration) than if they find that learning discrete facts is sufficient.

How we assess students' learning is also likely to affect their views about the nature of various academic disciplines—that is, their *epistemological beliefs*. When Ms. Peterson asks students to label countries, cities, and rivers on a blank map, they may very well conclude that, as a discipline, geography is little more than knowledge about the locations of various natural and manmade features. When Ms. Montgomery asks students to explain why countries import and export certain products, she is communicating a very different message: Geography involves understanding relationships between people and their environments.

In the upcoming pages we will explore both informal and formal approaches to classroom assessment. As we go along, we will consider the instructional objectives for which different assessment strategies might be most appropriate and the RSVP characteristics (reliability, standardization, validity, and practicality) of each type of assessment.

You can refresh your memory about epistemological beliefs by rereading the section "Factors Affecting Strategy Use" in Chapter 8.

Informal Assessment

From our daily observations of students' verbal and nonverbal behaviors, we can often draw conclusions about what students have and have not learned and make reasonable decisions about how future instruction should proceed. Such informal assessment takes many forms, including the following:

Assessment of verbal behaviors:

- Asking questions
- Listening to whole-class and small-group discussions
- Having students write daily or weekly entries in personal journals
- Holding brief conferences with individual students

Assessment of nonverbal behaviors:

- Observing how well students perform physical skills
- Looking at the relative frequency of on-task and off-task behaviors
- Identifying the activities in which students engage voluntarily
- Watching the "body language" that may reflect students' feelings about classroom tasks

Informal assessment has several advantages (Airasian, 1994; Stiggins, 2001). First and foremost, it provides continuing feedback about the effectiveness of the day's instructional tasks and activities. Second, it is easily adjusted at a moment's notice; for example, when students express misconceptions about a particular topic, we can ask follow-up questions that probe their beliefs and reasoning processes. Third, it provides information that may either support or call into question the data we obtain from more formal assessments such as paper-pencil tests. Finally, informal procedures provide clues about social, emotional, and motivational factors affecting students' classroom performance and may often be the only practical means through which we can assess such objectives as "shows courtesy" or "enjoys reading."

Why do you think affective outcomes are usually assessed informally rather than formally?

RSVP Characteristics of Informal Assessment

When we get information about students' characteristics and achievements through informal means, we must be aware of the strengths and limitations of this approach with respect to reliability, standardization, validity, and practicality.

Reliability

Most informal assessments are quite short; for example, we may notice that Naomi is off task during an activity, hear Manuel's answer to a question we've asked, or have a brief conversation with Jacquie after school. But such snippets of students' behavior can be unreliable indicators of their overall accomplishments and dispositions. Perhaps we happen to look at Naomi during the *only* time she is off task. Perhaps we ask Manuel one of the few questions to which he *doesn't* know the answer. Perhaps we misinterpret what Jacquie is trying to say during our conversation with her. When we use informal assessment to draw conclusions about what students know and can do, we should base our conclusions on many observations over a long period (Airasian, 1994).

Furthermore, we should keep in mind a principle from cognitive psychology: Long-term memory is not a totally accurate or dependable record of previous experience (see Chapter 6). We will remember some student behaviors but not recall others. If we depend heavily on our in-class observations of students, we should keep ongoing, written records of the things we see and hear (R. L. Linn & Gronlund, 2000; Stiggins, 2001).

Standardization

Our informal assessments will rarely, if ever, be standardized; for example, we will ask different questions of different students, and we will probably observe each student's behavior in different contexts. Hence, such assessments will definitely *not* give us the same information for each student. We will rarely be able to make legitimate comparisons among our students on the basis of casual observations alone.

Validity

Even if we see consistency in students' behavior over time, we will not always get accurate data about what they have learned (Airasian, 1994; Stiggins, 2001). For instance, Tom may intentionally answer questions incorrectly so that he doesn't look "smart" in front of his friends. Margot may be reluctant to say anything at all because she is embarrassed by a speech impediment.

Group Participation and Work Habits

Date:

☺ **Demonstrates attentiveness as a listener through body language or facial expressions-** Meghan is still developing this skill. Sometimes it is difficult for her to listen when she is sitting near her friends.

☺ **Follows directions.**

☺ **Enters ongoing discussion on the subject.** -Sometimes needs to be encouraged to share her ideas.

☺ **Makes relevant contributions to ongoing activities.**

☺ **Completes assigned activities.** -Meghan is very responsible about her assignments.

☺ **Shows courtesy in conversations and discussions by waiting for turn to speak.**

Meghan enjoys lunch with her friends.

Some skills can probably be assessed only through informal means. In this page from a kindergarten portfolio, a teacher describes Meghan's progress in social skills and work habits.

INTO THE CLASSROOM: *Using Teacher Questions to Assess Learning and Achievement*

Direct questions to the entire class, not just to a few who seem eager to respond.

The girls in a high school science class rarely volunteer when their teacher asks questions. Although the teacher often calls on students who raise their hands, he occasionally calls on those who do not, and he makes sure that he calls on *every* student at least once a week.

Have students "vote" when a question has only a few possible answers.

When beginning a lesson on dividing one fraction by another, a middle school math teacher writes this problem on the chalkboard:

$$\frac{3}{4} \div \frac{1}{2} = ?$$

She asks, "Before we talk about how we solve this problem, how many of you think the answer will be less than 1? How many think it will be greater than 1? How many think it will be *exactly* 1?" She tallies the number of hands that go up after each question and then says, "Hmmm, most of you think the answer will be less than 1. Let's look at how we solve a problem like this. Then each of you will know whether you were right or wrong."

Ask follow-up questions to probe students' reasoning.

In a geography lesson on Canada, a fourth-grade teacher points out the St. Lawrence River on a map. "Which way does the water flow—toward the ocean or away from it?" One student shouts out, "Away from it." "Why do you think so?" the teacher asks. The student's explanation reveals a common misconception: that rivers can flow only from north to south, never vice versa.

In general, when we use in-class questions to assess students' learning, we must be aware that some students (especially females and students from certain ethnic minority groups) will be less eager to respond than others (B. Kerr, 1991; Sadker & Sadker, 1994; Villegas, 1991).

Principles from our discussion of knowledge construction (Chapter 7) are also relevant to the validity of informal assessment: We impose meanings on the things we see and hear, and those meanings are influenced by the things we already know or believe to be true. Our own biases and expectations will affect our interpretations of students' behaviors, inevitably affecting the accuracy of our conclusions (Farwell & Weiner, 1996; Ritts et al., 1992; Stiggins, 2001). We may expect academic or social competence from a student we like or admire and so are likely to perceive that student's actions in a positive light—a phenomenon known as the **halo effect**. In much the same way, we might expect inappropriate behavior from a student with a history of misbehavior, and our observations may be biased accordingly (we could call this the "horns effect").

As we discovered in Chapter 12, teachers' expectations for their students are often influenced by students' ethnicity, gender, and socioeconomic status, and such expectations may unfairly bias teachers' judgments of student performance. An experiment by Darley and Gross (1983) provides an example. Undergraduate students were told that they were participating in a study on teacher evaluation methods and were asked to view a videotape of a fourth-grade girl named Hannah. Two versions of the videotape gave differing impressions about Hannah's socioeconomic status: Hannah's clothing, the kind of playground on which she played, and information about her parents' occupations indirectly conveyed to some students that she was from a high socioeconomic background and to others that she was from a low socioeconomic background. All students watched Hannah taking an oral achievement test (one on which she performed at grade level) and were asked to rate Hannah on several characteristics. Students who had been led to believe that Hannah came from wealthy surroundings rated her ability well above grade level, whereas students believing that she came from a poor family evaluated her as being below grade level. The two groups of students also rated Hannah's work habits, motivation, social skills, and general maturity differently.

Practicality

The greatest strength of informal assessment is its practicality. It involves little if any of our time either beforehand or after the fact (except when we keep written records of our observations). Furthermore, it is flexible: We can adapt our assessment procedures on the spur of the moment, altering them as events in the classroom change.

Despite the practicality of informal assessment, we have noted serious problems regarding its reliability, standardization, and validity. Hence, we should treat any conclusions we draw only as *hypotheses* that we must either confirm or disconfirm through other means. In the end, we must rely more heavily on formal assessment techniques to determine whether our students have achieved our instructional objectives.

Planning a Formal Assessment

Formal assessments are most likely to be valid and reliable when they have been carefully planned ahead of time. Such planning involves addressing two key questions:

- What types of tasks will best measure students' achievement?
- How can we get a representative sample of the domain?

Selecting Appropriate Tasks

We maximize content validity when the tasks we ask students to perform are as similar as possible to the things we ultimately want them to be able to do—in other words, when our assessment tasks reflect our instructional objectives. In some situations, such as when the desired outcome is simple recall of facts, asking students to respond to multiple-choice or short-answer questions on a paper-pencil test may be both valid and practical. In other situations—for instance, when our objective is for students to critique a literary work or to explain everyday phenomena by using scientific principles—essay questions that require students to follow a logical line of reasoning may be appropriate. *If* we can truly assess knowledge of a domain by having students respond to questions on paper, then a paper-pencil assessment is the most practical choice.

Yet many skills—cooking a hard-boiled egg, executing a front dismount from the parallel bars, identifying specific microorganisms through a microscope—are difficult (perhaps impossible) to assess with paper and pencil. In such situations, only performance assessment can give us reasonable content validity. Performance assessment can also be especially useful when we are concerned about students' ability to apply classroom subject matter to real-world situations. In the end, we may find that the most valid yet practical approach is a combination of both paper-pencil and performance tasks (Messick, 1994; Stiggins, 2001; D. B. Swanson et al., 1995).

What kinds of performance tasks might be appropriate in the subject area you will be teaching?

Obtaining a Representative Sample

EXPERIENCING FIRSTHAND   *Ants and Spiders*

Consider this situation:

> The students in Mr. Tyburczy's biology class are complaining about the quiz they just took. The class spent two weeks studying insects and only one day studying arachnids, yet the quiz was entirely on arachnids. Students who forgot what arachnids were failed the quiz, even though some of them knew quite a bit about insects.

Why is Mr. Tyburczy's assessment strategy a poor one? Which aspect of Mr. Tyburczy's quiz are his students complaining about: reliability, standardization, validity, or practicality?

Most classroom assessment activities, even paper-pencil ones, can give us only a small sample of what students know and can do. It would be terribly impractical, and in most cases virtually impossible, to assess *everything* that a student has acquired from a unit on insects and arachnids, a chapter in a social studies textbook, or a semester of physical education. Instead, we must typically present a few questions or tasks to elicit behaviors that will reflect students' overall knowledge and skills.

Mr. Tyburczy's quiz does reflect a sample of what students have studied in his unit on insects and arachnids. The problem is that his questions are not representative of the unit as a whole: They focus exclusively on arachnids. The quiz, then, has poor *content validity*. Ideally, Mr. Tyburczy's quiz questions should reflect the various parts of the unit in appropriate proportions. His questions should also ask students to do the kinds of things that his instructional objectives describe—perhaps comparing arachnids to insects, identifying examples of each class, and so on.

Sometimes a paper-pencil instrument is an adequate measure of what students have learned. At other times, however, one or more performance tasks are more valid indicators of achievement.

The most widely recommended strategy for ensuring the content validity of a teacher-developed assessment is to construct and follow a *table of specifications* that identifies both the topics to be covered and the things that students should be able to do with those topics. For more information about constructing such a table, return to the section "Validity" in Chapter 15.

Once we have decided on the general nature of our assessment instrument, we should turn our attention to specific questions and tasks, administration procedures, and scoring criteria. We'll address these issues separately for paper-pencil and performance assessment.

Paper-Pencil Assessment

Let's return to the opening case study in which Ellen and Roz are studying for their geography tests. Ellen's test focuses exclusively on knowledge of discrete facts, even though her teacher, Ms. Peterson, almost certainly has higher-level as well as lower-level objectives in mind for her students. Sadly, many teacher-developed paper-pencil tests focus primarily on lower-level skills, perhaps because such tests are the easiest to write (J. R. Frederiksen & Collins, 1989; Nickerson, 1989; Poole, 1994; Silver & Kenney, 1995).

Questions that require brief responses, such as short-answer, matching, true-false, and multiple-choice, are often suitable for assessing students' knowledge of single, isolated facts. Paper-pencil tasks that require extended responses—essays, for instance—lend themselves more easily to assessing such higher-level skills as problem solving, critical thinking, and synthesis of ideas (J. R. Frederiksen & Collins, 1989; Popham, 1995; Stiggins, 2001). Yet item type alone does not tell us whether we are assessing lower-level or higher-level skills. Although many classroom teachers use multiple-choice items primarily to assess knowledge of basic facts, we can also construct multiple-choice items that assess higher-level skills, as the following example illustrates:

> An inventor has just designed a new device for cutting paper. Without knowing anything else about his invention, we can predict that it is probably which type of machine?
>
> a. A lever
>
> b. A movable pulley
>
> c. An inclined plane
>
> d. A wedge
>
> (The correct answer is *d*.)

With a little ingenuity, we can even develop relatively "authentic" paper-pencil tasks that assess students' ability to apply classroom subject matter to real-world tasks (Gronlund, 1993; D. B. Swanson et al., 1995). Here is an example:

> You are to play the role of an advisor to President Nixon after his election to office in 1968. As his advisor, you are to make a recommendation about the United States' involvement in Vietnam.
>
> Your paper is to be organized around three main parts: An introduction that shows an understanding of the Vietnam War up to this point by explaining who is involved in the war and what their objectives are; also in the Introduction, you are to state a recommendation in one or two sentences to make the advice clear.
>
> The body of the paper should be written to convince the President to follow your advice by discussing: (a) the pros of the advice, including statistics, dates, examples, and general information . . . ; (b) the cons of the advice, letting the President know that the advisor is aware of how others might disagree. Anticipate one or two recommendations that others might give, and explain why they are not the best advice.
>
> The conclusion makes a final appeal for the recommendation and sells the President on the advice. (Newmann, 1997, p. 368)

An additional consideration is whether recognition or recall tasks better match our instructional objectives. **Recognition tasks** ask students to identify correct answers within the context of incorrect statements or irrelevant information; examples include multiple-choice, true-false, and matching questions. **Recall tasks** require students to generate the correct an-

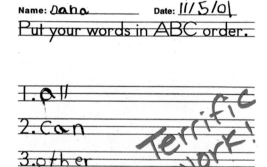

Even in the early grades, we can often use paper-pencil tasks to assess students' ability to apply what they've learned. Here 6-year-old Dana has shown that she can put several new spelling words in alphabetical order.

swers themselves; examples include short-answer questions, essays, and word problems. As noted in Chapter 6, recognition tasks are typically easier than recall tasks because they provide more retrieval cues to aid recall of relevant information from long-term memory.

Recognition and recall tasks each have advantages and disadvantages. Students can often answer many recognition questions in a short time; hence, such questions allow us to sample a wide range of knowledge and skills. In addition, we can score students' responses quickly and consistently, thus addressing our needs for practicality and reliability. However, recognition tasks tend to overestimate achievement: Students can often guess correctly when they don't know the material. In addition, students who see incorrect statements in true-false and multiple-choice items may recall them later as *true* statements (A. S. Brown et al., 1999).

When we want to assess students' ability to remember knowledge and skills without the benefit of having the correct answer in front of them, then recall tasks obviously have greater validity for assessing our instructional objectives. Furthermore, recall tasks are better suited to assessing students' ability to organize information, follow a line of reasoning, design an experiment, or justify their position on a controversial topic. Yet because students may require considerable time to respond to each item, we will be able to ask fewer items in a single assessment session (affecting reliability) and tap a more limited sample of the content domain (affecting content validity). In addition, we will typically take longer to score such items (a practicality issue) and make more errors in scoring them (an additional reliability issue).

We must weigh such advantages and disadvantages when deciding whether to use recognition items, recall items, or a combination of the two. We must also keep in mind that in some content domains—for example, when assessing writing skills—recognition tasks may simply not yield the same kind of information that recall tasks do (Traub, 1993).

Students tend to study more for essay tests than for multiple-choice tests (D'Ydewalle, Swerts, & De Corte, 1983; G. Warren, 1979). Why might this be so?

Constructing the Assessment Instrument

Writing good paper-pencil assessment items, especially those that assess higher-level thinking skills, takes considerable time and practice. In the following pages we will look at several formats:

Recognition Tasks

- Alternative-response items
- Matching items
- Multiple-choice items

Recall Tasks

- Short-answer items
- Completion items
- Problems
- Interpretive exercises
- Essays[1]

We will then identify several general guidelines for constructing a paper-pencil assessment instrument.

Alternative-Response Items

An *alternative-response item* is one for which there are only two or three possible answers, perhaps *true* versus *false*, or *fact* versus *opinion*. Such items are typically used to assess knowledge of discrete facts, although they can also be used for assessing such higher-level skills as discriminating between facts and opinions or identifying cause-effect relationships (Linn & Gronlund, 2000). The following items illustrate the use of an alternative-response format for assessing students' ability to identify cause and effect in science:

> In each of the following statements, both parts of the statement are true. You are to decide whether the second part explains why the first part is true. If it does, circle Yes. If it does not, circle No.

---

[1]Essays are sometimes classified as *performance assessments* because often they are more authentic than such item types as alternative-response, matching, and multiple-choice. Although some theorists use the terms *performance assessment* and *authentic assessment* interchangeably, I have been using them as terms with somewhat different meanings (see the section "The Various Forms of Educational Assessment" in Chapter 15).

Yes	(No)	1. Leaves are essential	*because*	they shade the tree trunk.
Yes	(No)	2. Whales are mammals	*because*	they are large.
(Yes)	No	3. Some plants do not need sunlight	*because*	they get their food from other plants.

(R. L. Linn & Gronlund, 2000, p. 180)

If the subject matter lends itself easily to assessment in an either-or fashion, alternative-response items allow us to ask a large number of questions in a short time and so may enhance our ability to sample the domain in question. Yet many subject areas cannot be assessed with this format, and students can get about half of the items correct simply by guessing. Furthermore, writing *good* alternative-response items is more difficult than you might think; following are a few guidelines:

■ *Rephrase ideas presented in class or the textbook.* When students know that assessment items will be taken word for word from class material, they may try to learn that material verbatim. When they instead know that we will check for understanding by using different words and phrases to express the same idea, they will be more likely to engage in meaningful learning.

■ *Write statements that clearly reflect one alternative or the other (e.g., statements that are clearly true or false).* A knowledgeable student should be able to respond to each item with certainty. When items are "sort of" true or "possibly" false, or they contain words with imprecise meanings (e.g., *sometimes, often*), then even our best students must resort to guessing what we had in mind when we wrote the items. Such guessing leads to a higher error factor in students' overall performance and so leads to lower test reliability.

■ *Avoid excessive use of negatives, especially for false statements.* Consider these true-false items:

The south poles of two magnets don't repel each other.

In the history of human civilization, the beginning of animal domestication was unrelated to human settlement patterns.

Were these questions difficult to answer? Did the negatives (the *don't* in the first item and the *un-* in the second one) confuse you? Negative words and prefixes in true-false items (e.g., *no, not, never, un-, mis-*) often lead to confusion, especially when the statements themselves are false. By the way, both of the items are false.

Matching Items

A matching item presents two columns of words, phrases, or data; students must match each item in the first column with an appropriate item in the second. Matching items lend themselves most readily to ideas that can be easily paired—words and their meanings, countries and their capitals, parts of the body and their functions, and so on. When our instructional objectives truly involve such factual knowledge, matching items provide an efficient way of assessing it. Following are two guidelines to keep in mind when constructing these items:

■ *Keep the items in each column homogeneous.* Consider this matching question from a world history test:

Match each item on the left with its description on the right:

a. German battleship that sank numerous British ships	1. George Patton
b. Year in which the Japanese attacked Pearl Harbor	2. The *Graf Spee*
c. Country invaded by Germany in 1939	3. Poland
d. General who led American troops into Italy	4. 1941

Even if you know nothing about World War II, you should be able to match the items easily. After all, the first item in the right-hand column is a person, and there is only one description of a person on the left. Similarly, there is only one country, one year, and one "name of something" (in italics), so the question gives itself away. Instead, the items in each column should all be members of the same category (perhaps dates, generals, capital cities, or word definitions) so as to give students few clues to the correct response.

■ *Have more items in one column than in the other.* Consider this matching item about the human digestive system:

Match each function with the component of the digestive system where that function occurs. Items on the right can be used only once.

1. Production of enzyme secreted to the mouth
2. Mixing of food with digestive enzymes
3. Production of bile
4. Production of insulin

a. Pancreas
b. Liver
c. Stomach
d. Salivary glands

Developing paper-pencil items that reflect important instructional objectives often takes considerable planning and creativity.

Even if you don't know much about human digestion, you can probably identify some of the correct answers here. If you can figure out three of the four items correctly, you know the last one by a simple process of elimination. But consider an alternative version of the same question:

Match each function with the component of the digestive system where that function occurs. Items on the right can be used more than once.

1. Production of enzyme secreted to the mouth
2. Mixing of food with digestive enzymes
3. Production of bile
4. Production of insulin
5. Storage place for food

a. Colon
b. Gall bladder
c. Stomach
d. Salivary glands
e. Liver
f. Large intestine
g. Pancreas

Here the process of elimination doesn't work. Items on the right can be used more than once ("stomach" is the correct choice for both 2 and 5), and three terms on the right aren't correct responses at all.

Multiple-Choice Items

A multiple-choice item consists of a question or incomplete statement (the *stem*) followed by a series of alternatives. In most cases, only one alternative correctly answers the question or completes the statement; the other (incorrect) alternatives are *distractors*.

Of the various recognition items we might use, most assessment experts recommend multiple-choice items for two reasons. First, the number of items that students get correct simply by guessing is relatively low, especially in comparison with true-false and other alternative-response items (e.g., when items have four possible answers, students can get only about 25% of them correct through guessing alone). Second, of all the recognition item types, the multiple-choice format lends itself most readily to measuring higher-level thinking skills. These items cannot assess *everything*, of course; for instance, they can't assess students' ability to organize and express ideas coherently, nor can they assess what students would actually do in a real-life situation.

If a multiple-choice format is appropriate for the knowledge or skills you wish to assess, following are several guidelines to keep in mind:

■ *Present distractors that are clearly wrong to students who know the material but plausible to students who haven't mastered it.* Distractors should not be obviously incorrect. Instead, they should reflect common errors and misunderstandings, as the following question illustrates:

John takes an achievement test and gets a percentile rank of 65. This score means that John has

a. Mastered course objectives
b. Failed to master course objectives
c. Performed better than 65 percent of the norm group
d. Answered 65 percent of the questions correctly

The correct answer is *c*: John's score indicates that he has performed better than 65 percent of the people who have taken the test. Buried in the three distractors are two misconceptions that many students have: A percentile rank reflects the number of items correctly answered, and norm-referenced test scores can give us information about mastery and nonmastery.

■ *Avoid putting negatives in both the stem and the alternatives.* Having negatives such as *not* and *don't* in two places at once amounts to a double negative that students have trouble understanding. Consider the following question, modeled after one actually found in the publisher's suggested test items, or **test bank**, for an educational psychology textbook:

> Which one of the following is *not* a characteristic of most gifted children (in comparison with their classmates)?
>
> a. They are not as old.
> b. They are physically uncoordinated.
> c. They do not feel uncomfortable in social situations.
> d. They do not perform poorly on standardized achievement tests.

Confused? It's difficult to sort through all the *nots* and *uns* in order to determine which statement is true and which three are false. The answer in this case is *b*: Contrary to a popular stereotype, students who are gifted are just as coordinated as their nongifted peers.

■ *Use "all of the above" or "none of the above" seldom if at all.* Listing three correct answers and then adding "all of the above" as the fourth choice is certainly an easy way to write a multiple-choice question. Yet my own experiences as a test-taker have taught me that "all of the above" is the correct choice more often than not, and many of my students tell me that they have learned likewise. Furthermore, when we tell students to choose the "best" or "most accurate" answer and then give them "all of the above" or "none of the above" as an alternative, they may understandably become confused about their task.

■ *Avoid giving logical clues about the correct answer.* Recall the califractions quiz that you took in one of the Experiencing Firsthand exercises in Chapter 15. You could answer one question correctly simply by picking the only alternative that grammatically fit the stem, and you could answer another by eliminating three alternatives with the same meaning. Following are several ways to avoid giving logical clues about the correct alternative:

- Make all alternatives grammatically consistent with the stem, so that each one, when combined with the stem, forms a complete sentence.
- Make all alternatives different in meaning (don't present two or more alternatives that say essentially the same thing).
- Make all alternatives equally long and precise. (Novice test writers tend to make the correct alternative longer and more specific than the distractors.)

Short-Answer and Completion Items

A short-answer item poses a question to be answered with a single word or number, a phrase, or a couple of sentences. A completion item presents a sentence with a blank for students to fill in. Both formats require recall (rather than recognition) of information, but they lend themselves most readily to measuring lower-level skills, and scoring students' responses becomes more subjective, thereby decreasing reliability. Following are two guidelines to keep in mind when writing short-answer and completion items:

■ *Indicate the type of response required.* Consider this item from a middle school science test:

> Explain why it is colder in winter than in summer.

A student could conceivably write several paragraphs on this topic. Fortunately, the teacher who wrote the item gave students some guidance about how to respond to it and the other short-answer items on her test:

> Provide a short answer (1–2 sentences) for each of the following questions. You must use complete and clearly stated sentences. Please use part of the question to introduce your response.

■ *For completion items, include only one or two blanks per item.* Too many blanks make an item difficult, perhaps impossible, to interpret. To see what I mean, try filling in the blanks in this statement concerning material presented in Chapter 15:

> Constructing an assessment instrument with high _____ _____ for one's instructional objectives can be accomplished by developing a _____ that describes both the _____ and the _____ .

FIGURE 16.1   Example of an interpretive exercise

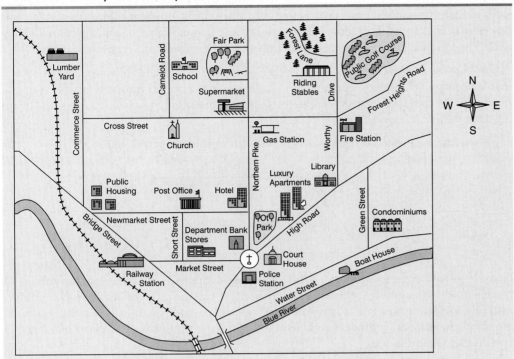

Here is a map of a small city named Riverdale. Apply principles of geography to answer the following questions. In each case, explain your reasoning.

1. Where in the city would you be most likely to find a steel mill?
2. Where would you be most likely to find upper-income, single-family homes?
3. Which area of the city appears to be undergoing urban renewal?
4. Where in the city would you expect traffic to be heaviest?

Answer Key: (1) between the river and the railroad tracks, where both water and transportation are easily accessible; (2) near the riding stables and golf course, as horseback riding and golf are popular but expensive forms of recreation; (3) the southeastern part of the city, as evidenced by the luxury apartments and condominiums; (4) in the south central area, which appears to be the central business district.

Note. Map adapted from "Reconceptualizing Map Learning" by J. E. Ormrod, R. K. Ormrod, E. D. Wagner, & R. C. McCallin, 1988, *American Journal of Psychology, 101,* p. 428. Adapted with permission of the University of Illinois Press.

Are you having trouble filling in the blanks? If so, I'm not surprised. There are so many blanks that it's hard to know what information is being called for. (The answers I had in mind are "content validity," "table of specifications," "topic to be covered," and "student behaviors related to each topic," or words to that effect.)

Problems and Interpretive Exercises

In a *problem,* students must manipulate or synthesize data and develop a solution to a new problem situation. We most often see this item type as word problems in mathematics, but we can use it in other subject areas as well; following is an example for science:

> You have a four-liter container of hot water (60°C) and a one-liter container of cold water (10°C). If you mix the water in the two containers together, what temperature will the water be?

In an *interpretive exercise,* students are given new material (e.g., a table, graphs, map, or paragraph of text) and asked to analyze and draw conclusions from it (R. L. Linn & Gronlund, 2000).[2] The item in Figure 16.1 provides an illustration.

---

[2]R. L. Linn and Gronlund (2000) suggest using true-false or multiple-choice questions in interpretive exercises, making them recognition rather than recall tasks. In fact, the questions we ask in both problems and interpretive exercises could be *either* recognition or recall in format.

Problems and interpretive exercises are especially suitable for assessing students' ability to transfer what they have learned to new situations; they may also involve such higher-level skills as analysis, synthesis, and critical thinking. They can be time-consuming to develop, but this time is well spent if we gain greater validity in assessing important instructional objectives. The following two guidelines apply to both problems and interpretive exercises:

■ *Use new examples and situations.* When you present problems or interpretive material that students have already encountered, students may respond correctly simply because they've memorized the answers. We can truly assess transfer only when we ask students to apply what they've learned to a novel context.

■ *Include irrelevant information.* What is the area of this parallelogram?

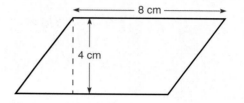

Even if you have completely forgotten how to compute the area of a parallelogram, you might be able to solve the problem correctly simply because you are given only two pieces of information. Calculating area typically involves multiplication, and you only have two numbers to multiply, so *voila!* you get the correct answer of 32 square centimeters. But now imagine that you instead see this figure:

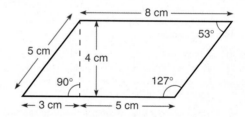

If you couldn't remember how to calculate the area of a parallelogram, you might be led astray by some of the information the figure provides.

Our purpose in adding extraneous information isn't necessarily to make the problem or exercise more difficult; rather, it is to make the assessment activity as similar as possible to real-life situations. In fact, the outside world typically presents a great deal of information that has little or nothing to do with the task at hand, and students must ultimately be able to determine what is relevant.

Essay Tasks

An essay task requires a student to write a lengthy verbal response—at least a paragraph, and perhaps as much as several pages. Essays are especially useful when we want students to show their writing ability or to demonstrate higher-level thinking skills (e.g., to analyze a piece of literature, compare and contrast two points of view, or apply scientific principles to explain various phenomena) in a written format. Essay items have two serious limitations, however. First, students can respond to only a small number of questions in a single assessment, thereby limiting sampling of the content domain (and hence limiting content validity). Second, scoring is time-consuming and subjective (so somewhat unreliable), especially when the questions require lengthy, relatively unstructured responses. The guidelines that follow are designed to maximize the information we can get from students' essays while simultaneously ensuring reasonable validity and reliability:

■ *Have several essays requiring shorter responses rather than one essay requiring a lengthy response.* The more items an assessment instrument includes, the more widely it can sample from the content domain it is meant to represent and the more reliable it is likely to be. In most situations, an assessment consisting of only one or two essay questions cannot cover the breadth of knowledge and skills that we expect students to have acquired, and errors in our scoring can seriously impact overall test scores. Unless we are confident that one or two essay questions *do* provide a representative sample of the domain being tested and, furthermore, that each question yields responses that can be scored consistently, we probably want to use one of two alternatives: (a) having several shorter essay questions or (b) combining one or two lengthy essays with other item types that can be answered quickly and easily.

■ *Give students a structure for responding.* You may remember essay tests you've taken that provided little information or structure about how to respond; for example, perhaps you had to respond to an item such as this one:

> List the causes of the American Civil War.

You may remember other tests that provided clear guidance about the nature of the responses required, such as this item does:

> Identify three policies or events between 1850 and 1860 that contributed to the outbreak of the American Civil War. For each of the three things you identify, explain in three to five sentences how it increased tension between the North and the South.

When we ask a totally unstructured question, students' responses may go in so many different directions that we will have difficulty scoring them consistently and reliably. Especially in situations where a great deal of material is potentially relevant, we should give students some guidance about the length and completeness of the desired response and about the things they should specifically address. My second essay question concerning the Civil War illustrates how we might guide students toward responding in particular ways without necessarily giving the answer away.

■ *Ask questions that can clearly be scored as correct or incorrect.* Consider this essay question:

> How can the dilemma of the world's diminishing rain forests best be solved?

The question asks for students' opinions, which will be difficult to score as right or wrong. We do not necessarily have to limit our essay questions to those with only one correct answer, however. Consider this revision of the "rain forest" question:

> Develop and explain a possible solution to the problem of the world's diminishing rain forests. Show how your solution addresses at least two of the economic, social, or political factors contributing to rain forest devastation.

Students' responses can be judged on how well their proposed solutions address factors that contribute to deforestation—factors that were presumably discussed in class or presented in the textbook.

General Guidelines for Constructing Paper-Pencil Assessments

EXPERIENCING FIRSTHAND   *Assessing Assessment*

Your educational psychology instructor gives you a test that includes these questions:

1. List four qualities of a good classroom assessment instrument.
2. Summarize the purposes of classroom assessment.

Take a few minutes to think about how you might answer each question. Jot down your thoughts about what you would include in your responses.

Was your answer to question 1 as simple as "reliability, standardization, validity, and practicality"? Did you think you would need to explain each of the RSVP characteristics? Did you identify legitimate qualities of "goodness" other than the four RSVP characteristics? And what about question 2? What purposes did you focus on, and how long do you think your actual summary might be? Words such as *list, qualities,* and *summarize* are difficult to interpret and may even be misleading to students.

Regardless of the kinds of items we use, we should follow several guidelines as we construct and administer a paper-pencil assessment instrument:

■ *Define tasks clearly and unambiguously.* Contrary to what some teachers believe, little is to be gained from assigning ambiguous tasks to assess students' learning and achievement (Sax, 1989). Whether or not students know how to respond to assessment tasks, they should at least understand what we are asking them to do.

■ *Decide whether students should have access to reference materials.* In some cases, we may want our students to have only one resource—their long-term memory—as they carry out an assessment activity. But in others, it may be appropriate to let them use reference materials (perhaps a dictionary, an atlas, or a magazine article) as they work. An assessment task in which reference materials are allowed is especially appropriate when our objective is for students to locate and use information rather than memorize it.

Having students use reference materials during a formal assessment is quite appropriate when instructional objectives focus on the ability to find and apply, rather than recall, information.

■ *Specify scoring criteria in advance.* We will typically want to identify correct responses at the same time that we develop our assessment items. In situations where there will be more than one correct answer (as may be true for an essay), we should identify the components of a good response. In many situations, we will want to share our scoring criteria with students; doing so gives them guidance about how they can best prepare and maximize their performance. Furthermore, we should develop policies to guide our scoring when students give partially correct answers, respond correctly but include additional incorrect information, or write responses with numerous grammatical and spelling errors.

■ *Place easier and shorter items at the beginning of the instrument; place more challenging ones near the end.* Some students approach tests very strategically, answering quick and easy items first regardless of the order in which the items are sequenced. But other students answer items in the order they appear, sometimes spending so much time on one item (perhaps a lengthy essay) that they leave little time to tackle other, shorter ones. By beginning an assessment with short, relatively easy items, we put students at ease (thereby keeping test anxiety at a facilitative level) and ensure that they show us some of what they know before they get bogged down in an especially challenging task. Other things being equal, students perform better on paper-pencil assessments when items are arranged in order from easy to difficult (Gronlund, 1993; Sax & Cromack, 1966).

■ *Set parameters for students' responses.* Students cannot always read our minds about how we expect them to respond to items on a paper-pencil assessment. So in addition to constructing the items themselves, we should develop directions that specify the following:

• *Time limits*—for example, how long students should spend on each item, and whether they have a limited time to complete the overall assessment
• *Nature of desired responses*—for example, whether they should choose a single best answer on each multiple-choice question or instead mark all correct alternatives
• *Method of recording responses*—for example, whether students should indicate their answers on the instrument itself or on a separate answer sheet
• *Acceptability of guessing*—for example, whether students should guess if they're not sure, or whether points will be subtracted for wrong answers (many assessment experts recommend that we encourage guessing rather than penalize for it)

Administering the Assessment

Our concern about maximizing the validity of a paper-pencil assessment cannot end once we've constructed the assessment instrument. We must also consider validity as we administer the instrument and score students' responses. For instance, we are more likely to get valid indicators of what students know and can do if their anxiety remains at a facilitative level (see Table 15.4 on p. 544). Following are three additional strategies that are likely to increase the validity of our results:

- *Provide a quiet and comfortable environment.* Students are more likely to perform at their best when they complete an assessment in a comfortable environment with acceptable room temperature, adequate lighting, reasonable workspace, and minimal distractions. This comfort factor may be especially important for students who are easily distracted, unaccustomed to formal assessments, or unmotivated to perform well on them; for example, it may be especially important for students at risk (Popham, 1990).

- *Encourage students to ask questions when tasks are not clear.* As noted earlier, students need to know what we are asking them to do. Yet despite our best intentions, we may present a task or question that is unclear, ambiguous, or even misleading. (Even after more than twenty-five years' experience developing assignments and exams, I still have students occasionally interpreting them in ways I didn't anticipate.) To increase the likelihood that our students will respond appropriately, we should encourage them to ask for clarification whenever they are uncertain about a task. Such encouragement is especially important for students from ethnic minority groups, many of whom may be reluctant to ask questions during a formal assessment situation (L. R. Cheng, 1987).

- *Take steps to discourage cheating.* Cheating on an assessment invalidates the results of that assessment; the only thing we have learned is that a student was not intrinsically motivated to complete it. The prevalence of cheating increases as students get older, and at the secondary level, more than 40 percent of students are likely to cheat at one time or another (Evans & Craig, 1990; Paris et al., 1991). Students cheat for a variety of reasons. For instance, they may be more interested in doing well on an assessment than in actually learning the subject matter; that is, performance goals predominate over mastery goals (Anderman et al., 1998). Students may believe that their teachers' expectations for their performance are so high as to be unattainable and that success is out of their control unless they *do* cheat (Evans & Craig, 1990). They may perceive certain assessments, tests especially, to be poorly constructed, arbitrarily graded, or in some other way a poor reflection of what they have learned (Paris et al., 1991). Furthermore, peer group norms may tell them that cheating is quite acceptable (Evans & Craig, 1990).

The best approach is prevention—making sure students don't cheat in the first place. For instance, we can

- Make success without cheating a realistic possibility
- Construct assessment instruments with obvious validity for important instructional objectives
- Explain exactly what cheating is and why it is unacceptable
- Have assigned seats during assessments that require individual (rather than group) work, and seat students as far away from one another as possible
- Use two or more assessment instruments that are equivalent in form and content but have different answers

If, despite reasonable precautions, an incident of cheating does occur, we should administer a consequence severe enough to discourage a student from cheating again, yet not so severe that the student's motivation and chances for academic success are affected over the long run. Our final grades should ultimately reflect what a student has and has not learned, however. For this reason, one expert recommends that the consequence for cheating *not* be a low (or failing) grade for a course in which the student has, in other graded assignments, demonstrated mastery of the subject matter (Stiggins, 2001).

Do you agree with Stiggins? Why or why not?

Scoring Students' Responses

INTERPRETING ARTIFACTS AND INTERACTIONS   *The Magic Baseball Bat*

Imagine you are a fourth-grade teacher. You have asked your class to write short stories. On the following page is 9-year-old Seth's story. As you read it, consider

- What letter grade (A, B, C, D, or F) you might give it
- What criteria you would use to make your decision

The Magic Baseball Bat

One April 3 I sined up for baseball. A week later we started baseball. On the first pratice we lernd how to hit the ball. When I was up I hit a homer and I haven't even hit a ball in my life. I was surprised that I hit it. All the other pratices until the game I hit the ball. When we had the first game I used anther bat and struk out so I dicitid to use that one bat. At the next game I use that one bat and hit a homer it was ausum. The kid after me used the bat and he hit a homer to then are wholl team used the the bat. Other teams wanted to trade bat but we didn't want to. Are team was the best, top, hiesd. I couldnt believe it and no one had playd befor. One of the team we played chedid. They put a magni it in the ball and bat. But we fond out because when one of their players was up the bat broke. At the end of the secon we were the top team. It trnd out ore bat was magic. After the last game we had a treat at Burgr King it was fun and cool. Next secon the wholl team is going to sine up. and I hope were togeth er agin. Tonight are team is going to have a party at are coaches house it will be fun. Tomora my fanly and I are going to play baseball for fun

THE
H N
END

How did you grade the story about the magic baseball bat? What criteria did you use when you made your decision? How important was the student's development of plot? the student's creativity? the grammar, spelling, and punctuation? Different teachers might weigh each of these criteria differently, and their grades for the same story would differ as a result. In fact, in another month, you might grade the story differently than you did today.

The more variable and complex students' responses on a paper-pencil assessment instrument are, the greater difficulty we will have scoring those responses objectively and reliably, and the more our expectations for students' performance may bias our judgments. As an example, imagine that we have one student, Mary, who consistently performs well in her classwork, and another, Susan, who more typically turns in sloppy, incomplete assignments. Let's say that both girls turn in an essay of marginal quality. We are likely to *over*rate Mary's performance and *under*rate Susan's—another example of the *halo effect* mentioned earlier.

Several strategies can help us score students' responses in an objective, reliable, and standardized manner:

■ *Specify scoring criteria in concrete terms.* Whenever an assessment task involves subjective evaluation of a complex performance—for instance, when it involves scoring lengthy essay responses—we should list the components that a correct response must include or the characteristics we will consider as we judge it. Such a list is sometimes known as a **rubric**. Figure 16.2 shows a rubric that a fourth-grade teacher uses for judging students' performance on mathematics word problems; notice how she provides spaces for both herself and the student to evaluate the performance (more about students' self-assessments later).

■ *Unless specifically assessing writing skills, score grammar and spelling separately from the content of students' responses to the extent possible.* This recommendation is especially important when assessing students with limited English proficiency (Hamp-Lyons, 1992; Scarcella, 1990).

■ *Skim a sample of students' responses ahead of time, looking for unanticipated responses and revising the criteria if necessary.* If we need to change our scoring criteria for unexpected reasons, we are more likely to score student responses consistently, fairly, and reliably if we change those criteria *before* we begin scoring rather than midway through a stack of papers.

FIGURE 16.2 Example of a rubric for evaluating performance on mathematics word problems

Elements	Possible Points	Points Earned Self	Points Earned Teacher
1. You highlighted the question(s) to solve.	2	——	——
2. You picked an appropriate strategy.	2	——	——
3. Work is neat and organized.	2	——	——
4. Calculations are accurate.	2	——	——
5. Question(s) answered.	2	——	——
6. You have explained in words how you solved the problem.	5	——	——
TOTAL ——		——	——

■ *Score item by item rather than test by test.* When students' responses involve some subjectivity in scoring, we can score them more reliably when we score them item by item—for example, scoring all students' responses to the first question, then all their responses to the second question, and so on.

■ *Try not to let prior expectations for students' performance influence judgments of their actual performance.* Strategies such as shuffling papers after grading one question and using small self-stick notes to cover up students' names can help us keep our expectations from inappropriately influencing our judgments.

■ *Accompany any overall scores with detailed feedback.* As we score students' responses, we should remember that our assessments should promote students' future learning as well as determine current achievement levels. Accordingly, we should give students detailed comments about their responses that tell them what they did well, where their weaknesses lie, and how they can improve (Bangert-Drowns et al., 1991; Deci & Ryan, 1985; Krampen, 1987).

RSVP Characteristics of Paper–Pencil Assessment

How do paper-pencil assessments measure up in terms of the RSVP characteristics? Let's consider each characteristic in turn.

Reliability

When we have tasks and questions with definite right and wrong answers—that is, when we have objectively scorable responses—we can evaluate students' responses with a high degree of consistency and reliability. To the extent that we must make subjective judgments about the relative rightness or wrongness of students' responses, reliability will inevitably decrease.

Standardization

As a general rule, paper-pencil instruments are easily standardized. We can present similar tasks and instructions to all students, provide similar time limits and environmental conditions, and score everyone's responses in more or less the same way. Nevertheless, we probably don't want to go overboard in this respect. For example, we might sometimes allow students to choose a writing topic, perhaps as a way of increasing their sense of self-determination (see Chapter 12). We may also need to tailor assessment tasks to the particular abilities and disabilities of our students with special needs.

Validity

When we ask questions that require only short, simple responses (e.g., true-false, multiple-choice, and matching questions), we can sample students' knowledge about many topics within a relatively short period of time. In this sense, then, such questions can give us greater content validity. Yet in some situations, such items may not accurately reflect our instructional objectives. To assess our students' ability to apply what they've learned to new situations, or to find out how well students can solve problems (especially the ill-defined ones so common in the adult world), we may need to be satisfied with a few tasks requiring lengthy responses.

Practicality

Paper-pencil assessment is typically more practical than performance assessment; for instance, we will require no "equipment" other than paper and writing implements, and we can easily assess the knowledge and skills of all of our students at the same time. Some paper-pencil assessments have the additional advantage of being relatively quick and easy to score.

Because paper-pencil assessment is so practical, it should generally be our method of choice *if* it can also yield a valid measure of what students know and can do. But in situations where paper-pencil tasks are clearly not a good reflection of what students have learned, we may need to sacrifice such practicality to gain the greater validity that a performance assessment provides.

INTERPRETING ARTIFACTS AND INTERACTIONS   *Life Functions*

Following is a three-part test given in a high school biology class. As you look at the test, consider the extent to which it satisfies the four RSVP characteristics: reliability, standardization, validity, and practicality.

Test on Life Functions

1. Column A lists terms. Column B lists definitions. Print the letter from column B that *best matches* each term in column A.

    _____ Enzymes   a. Passage of simple substances into the internal parts of plants and animals

    _____ Locomotion   b. Matter that was never alive

    _____ Self-repair   c. Changing digested food into new living material

    .   .

    .   .

    .   .

    [20 terms and 20 definitions are listed]

2. A paramecium is a single-celled organism. Name three more single-celled organisms.

    _____ _____ _____

3. List any five life functions and describe how the paramecium performs each one.

The biology test is certainly practical: It can be easily administered and scored. It should also be easy to administer in a consistent, standardized fashion for everyone. Items 1 and 2 can be scored consistently and reliably, in that answers are definitely right or wrong. Item 3 can probably be scored reliably as well: A paramecium is a simple enough organism that descriptions of basic life functions (how it reproduces, how it moves, how it excretes waste products, etc.) are fairly simple and straightforward. The big problem with this test is its validity: Items 1 and 2 require nothing more than rote memorization. Whether item 3 assesses rote learning or more effective learning processes (e.g., meaningful learning, elaboration) depends on whether the class has specifically studied how a paramecium exhibits various life functions. We can reasonably assume that the instructional objectives of a high school science class would *not* be limited to lower-level skills, yet the test focuses almost exclusively on them.

Performance Assessment

A wide variety of performance tasks can be used to assess students' mastery of instructional objectives. Here are just a few of the many possibilities:

In which category do most performance tasks fall—*recognition* or *recall* tasks?

- Playing a musical instrument
- Conversing in a foreign language
- Identifying an unknown chemical substance
- Engaging in a debate about social issues
- Taking dictation in shorthand
- Fixing a malfunctioning machine
- Role-playing a job interview
- Performing a workplace routine
- Creating a computer simulation of a real-world task
    (Gronlund, 1993; C. Hill & Larsen, 1992; D. B. Swanson et al., 1995)

Performance assessment lends itself particularly well to the assessment of complex achievements, such as those that involve coordinating a number of skills simultaneously. It may also be quite helpful in assessing such higher-level cognitive skills as problem solving, critical thinking, and creativity. Furthermore, performance tasks are often more meaningful and thought-provoking, and so often more motivating, than paper-pencil tasks (Khattri & Sweet, 1996; Paris & Paris, 2001; D. P. Resnick & Resnick, 1996). The following problem, which has been used to assess fourth graders' math and literacy skills, is an example of an assessment task that students find highly motivating:

> In a letter from the principal, it is announced that the fourth-grade classroom will be getting a 30-gallon aquarium. The students in that classroom have the responsibility of buying fish for the tank. The class will receive $25 to spend on fish and a *Choosing Fish for Your Aquarium* brochure. The brochure provides the necessary information about the size of each type of fish, how much each costs, and the special needs of each fish. The students are instructed to choose as many different kinds of fish as possible and then to write a letter explaining which fish were chosen. In the letter, the students must indicate how many of each kind of fish were selected and the reasons why they were chosen, demonstrate that the fish will not be overcrowded in the aquarium, and provide that the purchases maintain the limited budget of $25. (D. P. Resnick & Resnick, 1996, pp. 30–31)

Of course, we can also assess complex skills in ways that don't entail the expense and long-term commitment that maintaining a classroom aquarium would. In the upcoming pages we will examine various kinds of performance tasks we might use to assess students' learning and achievement. We will then identify strategies for developing, administering, and scoring performance assessments and consider how well these assessments reflect the RSVP characteristics.

Choosing Appropriate Performance Tasks

As we select tasks for a performance assessment, we must have a clear purpose in mind: We must identify the specific conclusions we wish to draw from our observations of students' performance. We must also consider whether particular tasks will enable us to make reasonable generalizations about what our students know and can do in the content domain in question (Popham, 1995; Wiggins, 1992). Let's look at four distinctions that can help us zero in on the tasks most appropriate for our purposes: products versus processes, individual versus group performance, restricted versus extended performance, and static versus dynamic assessment.

Some skills, such as the ability to converse with others in a foreign language, can be assessed only with performance tasks.

Products Versus Processes

In performance assessment we can focus on products, processes, or both (E. H. Hiebert, Valencia, & Afflerbach, 1994; Messick, 1994; Paris & Paris, 2001). In some situations, we can look at tangible *products* that students have created—perhaps a pen-and-ink drawing, a scientific invention, or a poster display. In situations with no tangible product, we must instead look at the specific *processes and behaviors* that students exhibit—perhaps giving an oral presentation, demonstrating a forward roll, or playing an instrumental solo. In the latter case, we can sometimes ascertain students' *thinking processes* as well.

Performance tasks that allow us to examine students' thinking processes can be especially useful for formative evaluation. For instance, if we want to determine whether students have developed some of the concrete operational or formal operational abilities that Piaget described (conservation, multiple classification, separation and control of variables, etc.), we might present tasks similar to those that Piaget used and ask students to explain their reasoning (De Corte et al., 1996). And we can often learn a great deal about how students conceptualize and reason about scientific phenomena when we ask them to manipulate physical objects (e.g., chemicals in a chemistry lab, electrical circuit boards in a physics class), make predictions about what will happen under varying circumstances, and then explain their results (Magnusson, Boyle, & Templin, 1994; Quellmalz & Hoskyn, 1997).

Individual Versus Group Performance

Many performance tasks require *individual* students to complete them with little or no assistance from others. Other tasks are sufficiently complex that they are best accomplished by a *group* of students. For instance, we might assess high school students' mastery of a unit on urban geography using a field-based cooperative group project such as this one:

> First, select one of the neighborhoods marked on the city map. Second, identify its current features by doing an inventory of its buildings, businesses, housing, and public facilities. Also, identify current transportation patterns and traffic flow. From the information made available, identify any special problems this neighborhood has, such as dilapidated housing, traffic congestion, or a high crime rate. Third, as a group, consider various plans for changing and improving your neighborhood. (Newmann, 1997, p. 369)

Such a task requires students to collect data systematically, use the data to draw conclusions and make predictions and, more generally, think as an urban planner would think (Newmann, 1997).

One challenge in using group tasks for assessment purposes is determining how to evaluate each student's contribution. Often, teachers consider individual students' behaviors and achievements (what and how much a student contributes to the group effort, how much the student has learned by the end of the project, etc.) in addition to, or perhaps instead of, the entire group's accomplishments (Lester et al., 1997; Stiggins, 2001).

Restricted Versus Extended Performance

Some of our performance tasks are apt to be quite short; that is, they involve *restricted performance*. For instance, in a beginning instrumental music class, we might ask each student to play the C major scale to make sure that everyone has mastered the scale on his or her respective instrument. In a chemistry class we might ask students to demonstrate mastery of basic safety procedures before beginning their lab experiments.

We assess *extended performance* when we want to determine what students are capable of doing over several days or weeks (Alleman & Brophy, 1997; De Corte et al., 1996; Lester et al., 1997). Extended performance tasks might provide opportunities for students to collect data, engage in collaborative problem solving, and edit and revise their work. Many extended performance tasks embody authentic assessment: They closely resemble the situations and problems that students may eventually encounter in the outside world.

Static Versus Dynamic Assessment

Most assessments, whether they be paper-pencil or performance tasks, focus on identifying students' existing abilities and achievements. When used in isolation from other assessments, they do not specifically address how students learn and change over time; thus, you might think of them as *static* indicators. Static assessment is consistent with Vygotsky's concept of a child's *actual developmental level*, reflecting the tasks that the child can easily do on his or her own (see Chapter 2).

In recent years some theorists have suggested an approach that focuses not on assessing existing abilities but on assessing students' ability to learn in new situations, perhaps with the assistance of a teacher or other more competent individual (Calfee & Masuda, 1997; Feuerstein, Feuerstein, & Gross, 1997; L. A. Shepard, 2000). Such an approach, sometimes called **dynamic assessment**, reflects Vygotsky's *zone of proximal development* and can give us an idea of what our students are likely to be able to accomplish with appropriate structure and guidance. Hence, it is most appropriate for formative (rather than summative) evaluation.

The use of dynamic assessment in educational settings is still in its infancy, and educators are only beginning to explore its potential. It appears to be especially helpful in assessing students' cognitive processes and deficiencies, as well as in gathering information about students' dispositions and motivation (Feuerstein et al., 1997; Hamers & Ruijssenaars, 1997; Tzuriel, 2000). Furthermore, it often yields more optimistic evaluations of students' cognitive abilities than traditional assessment tasks do and may be particularly useful in assessing the abilities of students from diverse cultural backgrounds and lower-income families (Feuerstein, 1979; Tzuriel, 2000).

Planning and Administering the Assessment

Several of the guidelines presented in the section on paper-pencil assessment are equally relevant for performance assessment; in particular, we should

- Define tasks clearly and unambiguously
- Specify scoring criteria in advance (more about this point shortly)
- Standardize administration procedures as much as possible
- Encourage students to ask questions when tasks are not clear

Three additional guidelines pertain specifically to conducting performance assessments:

■ *Consider incorporating the assessment into normal instructional activities.* Some theorists and practitioners recommend that we incorporate performance assessments into everyday instructional activities (Baxter et al., 1996; Boschee & Baron, 1993; Kennedy, 1992; Stiggins, 2001). We make more efficient use of our limited time with students if we can combine instruction and assessment into one activity. In addition, we may reduce the "evaluative" climate in our classroom; as you may recall from Chapter 12, external evaluation lowers students' sense of self-determination and can discourage risk taking.

We must recognize, however, that by instructing and assessing students in one fell swoop, we may not be able to standardize the conditions under which students are being assessed, and we will not necessarily see students' best work. Furthermore, although it is quite appropriate to give students assistance or feedback during instruction, it may often be *in*appropriate to do so during a summative evaluation of what they have achieved (L. M. Carey, 1994). In some situations, then, we may want to conduct an assessment separately from instructional activities, announce it in advance, and give students some guidance as to how they can maximize their performance (Stiggins, 2001).

■ *Provide an appropriate amount of structure.* We will probably want to structure performance tasks to some degree; for example, we can provide detailed directions about what we want students to accomplish, what materials and equipment they should use, and how we will evaluate their performance (Gronlund, 1993; E. H. Hiebert et al., 1994; Stiggins, 2001). Such structure helps to standardize the assessment and so enables us to evaluate students' performance more reliably. Yet too much structure will reduce the authenticity of a task if performance conditions are less like those in the outside world. Thus, we must consider both reliability and validity as we determine the appropriate amount of structure to impose in any performance assessment.

In some situations, we can incorporate assessment into everyday instructional activities.

■ *Plan classroom management strategies for the assessment activity.* As we conduct a performance assessment, we should put into practice two important principles of classroom management presented in Chapter 14: Effective teachers are continually aware of what their students are doing (the notion of *withitness*), and they make sure all students are busy and engaged. Particularly in situations when we must assess only a few students (or perhaps only one) at a time, we must make sure other students are actively involved in a learning activity (L. M. Carey, 1994). For example, in an English class, when one student is giving an oral presentation, we might have the other students jot down notes about the topic being presented, including facts they find interesting, ideas they disagree with, and questions they wonder about. In a unit on soccer, when a few students are demonstrating their ability to dribble and pass the ball as they run down the field, we might have other students work in pairs to practice their footwork.

Scoring Students' Responses

Occasionally, responses to performance assessment tasks are objectively scorable; for example, we can easily count the errors on a typing test or time students' performance in a 100-meter dash. But more often than not, we will find ourselves making somewhat subjective decisions when we assess performance. There are no clear-cut right or wrong responses when students give oral reports, create clay sculptures, or engage in heated debates on controversial issues. If we aren't careful, our judgments may be unduly influenced by our expectations for each student (L. M. Carey, 1994; Stiggins, 2001).

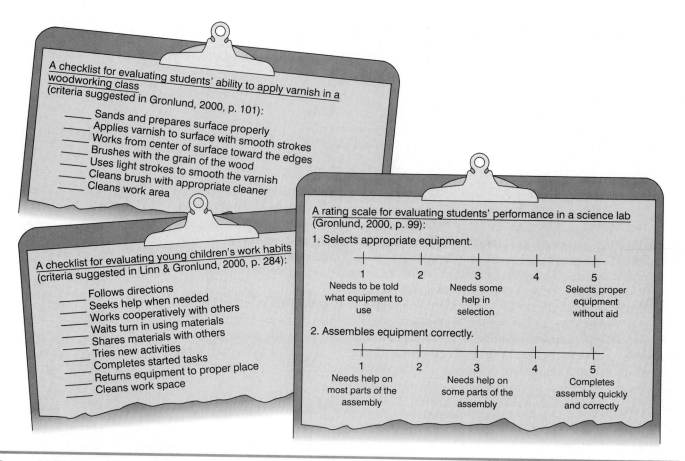

FIGURE 16.3 Examples of checklists and rating scales

Especially for summative evaluations, we should carefully consider the criteria to use as we judge students' responses and develop a rubric that identifies these criteria. A rubric can guide us during the evaluation process, and later on, it can serve as a written record of what we have observed. The following strategies can help us design and use scoring rubrics effectively when we conduct performance assessments:

■ *Consider using checklists, rating scales, or both in your rubric.* Some tasks lend themselves well to **checklists,** with which we evaluate student performance by indicating whether specific behaviors or qualities are present or absent. Other tasks are more appropriately evaluated with **rating scales,** with which we evaluate student performance by rating aspects of the performance on one or more continua (see Figure 16.3). Both approaches enhance the reliability of scoring and have instructional benefits as well: They identify any specific areas of difficulty for a student and so give feedback about how performance can be improved.

Which approach do raters use at the Olympics: analytic or holistic?

■ *Decide whether analytic or holistic scoring better serves your purpose(s) in conducting the assessment.* When we need detailed information about students' performance, we may want to use **analytic scoring,** in which we evaluate various aspects of the performance separately, perhaps with a checklist or several rating scales. In contrast, when we need to summarize students' performance in a single score, we should probably use **holistic scoring,** in which we consider all relevant criteria when making a single judgment; for instance, we might have a single 1-to-5 rating scale that describes the various performance characteristics that would be rated at different points along the scale. Analytic scoring is typically more useful in conducting formative evaluations and promoting students' learning, whereas holistic scoring is often used in summative evaluation.

Use the concept of *working memory* (Chapter 6) to explain the value of having only a few criteria.

■ *Limit the criteria to the most important aspects of the desired response.* Our criteria should focus on aspects of the performance that are critical for a "good" response and most relevant to our instructional objectives (Stiggins, 2001; Wiggins, 1992). They should also be relatively few in number (perhaps five or six at the most) so that we can keep track of them as we observe each student's performance (Airasian, 1994; Gronlund, 1993; Popham, 1995).

Colonial Economies Rubric

The following rubric will help the student to understand the expectations for each component of the group project. The number value represents the level of mastery. Higher numbers reflect greater mastery.

Outline: The outline is organized and concise while summarizing important information.

    Organization: The outline is formatted according to the style discussed in class and aligned with the book.

        5   4   3   2   1

    Clarity: The text of the outline is organized in a manner which helps students to fully understand the material.

        5   4   3   2   1

    Information: The outline information is to the point and does not exceed 1 sheet of paper (both sides).

        5   4   3   2   1

Artistic Interpretation: The creative project displays some of the important information within the subchapter.

    Creativity: The product reflects prior thought, effort, and artistry.

        5   4   3   2   1

    Interpretation: The product properly represents the material within the subchapter.

        5   4   3   2   1

    Attraction: The final product reflects organization and engages the audience through color, size, and a high level of quality.

        5   4   3   2   1

Board Game: The board game is designed to entertain and teach 3–4 students at one time for approximately 10 minutes about the information in the subchapter.

    Information: The game provides a means to test the players' knowledge about the assigned subchapter.

        5   4   3   2   1

    Creativity: The game reflects prior thought, artistry, and imagination.

        5   4   3   2   1

    Application: The game effectively helps students to apply their knowledge of the subchapter through the rules and organization of play.

        5   4   3   2   1

Homework: The homework is assigned to the class the day prior to the presentation. Students are instructed to read the text and complete an assignment.

    Organization: The assignment holds each student in class responsible for understanding key information.

        5   4   3   2   1

    Originality: The assignment shows imagination and effort along with innovative ways to help students learn.

        5   4   3   2   1

    Information: The homework assignment is clearly stated and focuses on important information which will help students to understand the material.

        5   4   3   2   1

Presentations:

    Preparedness: The group members are each prepared for the presentation with thorough knowledge of the material. They show preparedness through a sense of confidence in their presentation.

        5   4   3   2   1

    Clarity: The information presented is well organized and clearly stated. Members of the group make eye contact with the class and engage each student with understanding of the material.

        5   4   3   2   1

    Organization: The members of the group successfully organize the presentation so that there is an order and a pace which will enable students to gain a clear understanding of the material.

        5   4   3   2   1

■ *Describe the criteria as explicitly and concretely as possible.* Criteria such as "excellent" and "needs improvement" don't tell us very much, nor do they offer much feedback for students. We can score students' performance more objectively and reliably, and provide more constructive feedback, when our criteria focus on specific, observable qualities of students' products or behaviors (R. L. Linn & Gronlund, 2000; Stiggins, 2001; Wiggins, 1992). For example, Chapter 13 describes a cooperative group activity that an eighth-grade history teacher uses in a unit on colonial America (see Figure 13.7 on p. 466). Figure 16.4 presents the rubric that the same teacher uses to evaluate students' performance in this activity.

- *Make note of any other significant aspects of a student's performance that the rubric doesn't address.* Rubrics are rarely perfect. Whenever we break down students' performance on a complex task into discrete behaviors, we can lose valuable information in the process (Delandshere & Petrosky, 1998). When we use rubrics to assist us in scoring performance, then, we may occasionally want to jot down other noteworthy characteristics of students' performance. This aspect of our scoring process will be neither standardized nor reliable, of course, but it can sometimes be useful in identifying students' unique strengths and needs and can therefore assist us in our future instructional planning.

RSVP Characteristics of Performance Assessment

Compared with traditional paper-pencil assessment, performance assessment techniques are relative newcomers on the educational scene; hence, psychologists and educators are only beginning to address concerns related to reliability, standardization, validity, and practicality. Let's look at the data that researchers report, as well as at strategies for enhancing each of the four RSVP characteristics.

Reliability

Researchers have reported varying degrees of reliability in performance assessments; in many cases, results are inconsistent over time, and different teachers may rate the same performance differently (S. Burger & Burger, 1994; R. L. Linn, 1994; Shavelson, Baxter, & Pine, 1992; D. B. Swanson et al., 1995). There are probably several reasons why performance assessments often yield low reliability (L. M. Carey, 1994; Wiley & Haertel, 1996). First, students don't always behave consistently; even in a task as simple as shooting a basketball, a student is likely to make a basket on some occasions but not others. Second, we sometimes need to evaluate various aspects of complex behaviors relatively quickly; things may happen so fast that we miss important parts of a student's performance. If we have no tangible product, we cannot reevaluate the performance. Finally, one form of reliability, *internal consistency* (see Chapter 15), is simply inappropriate for complex, multifaceted behaviors.

Given these limitations, a single performance assessment may very well *not* be a reliable indicator of what our students have achieved. Accordingly, we should ask students to demonstrate behaviors related to important instructional objectives on more than one occasion (Airasian, 1994; L. M. Carey, 1994). And whenever possible, we should have more than one rater evaluate each student's performance (Stiggins, 2001; R. M. Thorndike, 1997).

Standardization

Some performance assessments are easily standardized, but others are not. If we want to assess typing ability, we can easily make the instructions, time limits, and material the same for everyone. In contrast, if we want to assess artistic creativity, we may want to give students free rein regarding the materials they use and the particular products they create. In such nonstandardized situations, it is especially important to use multiple assessments and look for consistency in students' performance across several occasions.

Validity

As previously noted, performance assessment tasks may sometimes provide more valid indicators of what our students have accomplished relative to instructional objectives. Researchers are finding, however, that students' responses to a *single* performance assessment task are frequently *not* a good indication of their overall achievement (Koretz, Stecher, Klein, & McCaffrey, 1994; R. L. Linn, 1994; Shavelson et al., 1992; D. B. Swanson et al., 1995). Content validity is at stake here: If we have time for students to perform only one or two complex tasks, we may not get a sufficiently representative sample of what they have learned and can do. In addition, any biases that affect our judgments (e.g., any beliefs that we have about particular students' abilities) may distort the conclusions we draw from their performance, further reducing the validity of our assessments (Airasian, 1994; L. M. Carey, 1994).

As a general rule, then, we will typically want to administer several *different* performance assessments, or perhaps administer the same task under different conditions, to ensure that our conclusions are reasonably valid (R. L. Linn, 1994; Messick, 1994; Stiggins, 2001;

D. B. Swanson et al., 1995). For efficiency, we may want to incorporate some of these assessment activities into everyday instructional activities (Shavelson & Baxter, 1992).

Practicality

Unfortunately, performance assessments are often less practical than more traditional paper-pencil assessments (L. M. Carey, 1994; Hambleton, 1996; Popham, 1995). Administering an assessment can be quite time-consuming, especially when we observe students one at a time or when they perform relatively complex (perhaps authentic) tasks. In addition, we may need considerable equipment to conduct the assessment, perhaps enough that every student has his or her own set. Furthermore, performance assessments used in large-scale, high-stakes testing are much more expensive than traditional paper-pencil tests (Hardy, 1996). Clearly, then, we must carefully consider whether the benefits of a performance assessment outweigh its impracticality (Messick, 1994; Tzuriel, 2000; Worthen & Leopold, 1992).

As we have just seen, performance assessments can be unreliable and impractical; furthermore, they may tap an insufficient sample of what students have learned. Yet in many situations, they may more closely resemble the long-term objectives we have for our students, and in this sense they may be more valid indicators of students' achievement. As educators gain experience in the use of performance assessment in the years to come, increasingly valid, reliable, and practical measures of student performance will undoubtedly emerge. In the meantime, the most reliable, valid, and practical assessment strategy overall may be to use *both* paper-pencil and performance assessments when drawing conclusions about what our students have achieved (Gronlund, 1993; R. L. Linn, 1994).

At this point, you should be in a fairly good position to distinguish useful and dependable assessments from less valid and reliable ones. In the following exercise you can apply what you have learned to an actual assessment instrument.

See "Assessment in the Balance" in *Simulations in Educational Psychology and Research.*

INTERPRETING ARTIFACTS AND INTERACTIONS   *Golden Boot Island*

A seventh-grade social studies class is learning techniques and conventions for depicting elevation and topography. Following are a take-home assignment for the unit and 12-year-old Francisco's responses to it (an aerial view of "Golden Boot Island" and two side views of the same island). As you look at the artifacts, evaluate the assigned task's reliability, standardization, validity, and practicality.

Island Map Assignment

1. Using a contour interval of 15 feet and a scale of one inch to one mile, construct a contour map of an island that

   a. Is 6 miles from east to west and 4 miles from north to south

   b. Has a maximum elevation of 124 feet, but rises to at least 105 feet

   c. Is steepest on the east side

   d. Has a stream running into the ocean on the west shore, with its source at an elevation of 90 feet

2. Draw two profile maps of your island, one showing the island from west to east and the other showing it from north to south.

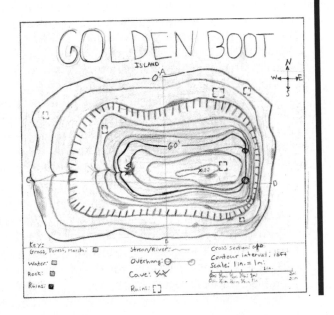

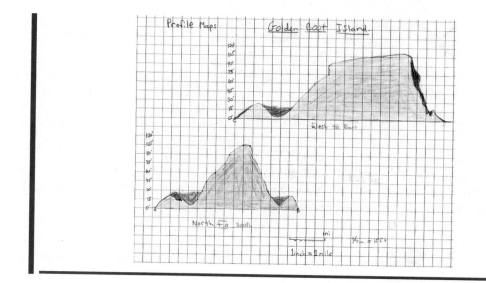

Students' maps must conform to certain measurements, and the teacher can probably ascertain whether they do with some objectivity and reliability. Predetermined scoring criteria can nevertheless enhance scorer reliability, given the variation and creativity the task allows (e.g., Francisco goes beyond the minimal specifications for the task and includes a moat-shaped body of water on his island). The task is standardized in some but not all respects: Students all have the same assignment and directions but are completing it at home, where some of them have greater access to resources (including helpful family members) than others. Content validity is probably a strong point: Although we don't know the teacher's instructional objectives, we can reasonably assume that they include not only knowledge of mapping techniques but also the ability to apply those techniques to realistic situations. The task is certainly practical, in that it involves minimal materials, very little in-class time (the task is completed at home), and probably would not take very much time to score.

Table 16.1 presents a summary of our RSVP analyses of informal assessment, formal paper-pencil assessment, and formal performance assessment. We now turn our attention to strategies for including students in the assessment process.

Including Students in the Assessment Process

In Chapter 15 we noted that classroom assessments are extrinsic motivators: They provide an externally imposed reason for learning school subject matter and achieving instructional objectives. Ideally, however, we want students to be *intrinsically* motivated to learn and achieve in the classroom, and they are more likely to be so if they have some sense of self-determination about classroom activities (see Chapter 12). Furthermore, if students are to become successful self-regulated learners, they must acquire skills in self-monitoring and self-evaluation (see Chapter 10). For such reasons, students should be regular and active participants in the assessment of their learning and performance. As teachers, we should think of assessment as something we do *with* students rather than *to* them.

Students become increasingly skillful in self-assessment as they grow older (van Kraayenoord & Paris, 1997), but even students in the elementary grades have some ability to evaluate their own performance if they have the tools to do so (e.g., see Figure 16.5). Following are several strategies for including students in the assessment process and helping them develop important self-monitoring and self-evaluation skills:

- Make evaluation criteria explicit and easily observable (e.g., the criteria in Figure 16.4 were given to students at the beginning of the "Colonial Economies" activity).
- Provide examples of "good" and "poor" products and ask students to compare them on the basis of several criteria.
- Solicit students' ideas about evaluation criteria and rubric design.
- Have students compare self-ratings with teacher ratings (e.g., refer back to the word problem rubric in Figure 16.2).
- Have students keep ongoing records of their performance and chart their progress over time.

TABLE 16.1   C O M P A R E / C O N T R A S T

Evaluating the RSVP Characteristics of Different Types of Assessment

ASSESSMENT TYPE	RELIABILITY	STANDARDIZATION	VALIDITY	PRACTICALITY
Informal assessment	A single, brief assessment is not a reliable indicator of achievement. We must look for consistency in a student's performance across time and in different contexts.	Informal observations are rarely, if ever, standardized. Thus, we should not compare one student to another on the basis of informal assessment alone.	Students' "public" behavior in the classroom is not always a valid indicator of their achievement (e.g., some may try to hide high achievement from peers).	Informal assessment is definitely practical: It is flexible and can occur spontaneously during instruction.
Formal paper-pencil assessment	Objectively scorable items are highly reliable. We can enhance the reliability of subjectively scorable items by specifying scoring criteria in concrete terms.	In most instances, paper-pencil instruments are easily standardized for all students. Giving students choices (e.g., about topics to write about or questions to answer), although advantageous from a motivational standpoint, reduces standardization.	Using numerous questions that require short, simple responses can make an assessment a more representative sample of the content domain. But tasks requiring lengthier responses may sometimes more closely match objectives.	Paper-pencil assessment is usually practical: All students can be assessed at once, and no special materials are required.
Formal performance assessment	It is often difficult to score performance assessment tasks reliably. We can enhance reliability by specifying scoring criteria in concrete terms.	Some performance assessment tasks are easily standardized, whereas others are not.	Performance tasks may sometimes be more consistent with instructional objectives than paper-pencil tasks. A single performance task may not provide a representative sample of the content domain; several tasks may be necessary to ensure content validity.	Performance assessment is typically less practical than other approaches: It may involve special materials, and it can take a fair amount of classroom time, especially if students must be assessed one at a time.

- Have students reflect on their work in daily or weekly journal entries, where they can keep track of objectives they have and have not achieved, as well as learning strategies that have and have not been effective.
- Ask students to write practice questions similar to those they expect to see on upcoming quizzes and tests.
- Ask students to lead parent conferences (see Chapter 14, especially Figure 14.3). (A. L. Brown & Campione, 1996; R. L. Linn & Gronlund, 2000; Paris & Ayres, 1994; L. A. Shepard, 2000; Stiggins, 2001; Valencia et al., 1994)

An additional strategy is having students compile portfolios of their work; we will look at portfolios more closely later in the chapter.

Encouraging Risk Taking

Not only should students be actively involved in assessing their own learning and performance, but they should also feel comfortable enough about the assessment process that they feel free to take risks and make mistakes: Only under these circumstances will students tackle the challenging tasks that are likely to maximize their learning and cognitive development (Clifford, 1990). We encourage risk taking—and lower anxiety levels as well—when our assessment strategies give students some leeway to be wrong without penalty (Clifford, 1990). And certainly no single assessment should ever be "sudden death" for those who earn low scores.

Over the years, educators have developed a variety of strategies for encouraging risk taking and ensuring a reasonable comfort level about classroom assessments. Three important ones are frequent assessments, allowing retakes, and providing opportunities to correct errors.

June Self-Progress Report

READING   I am able to Read mote Books, Read longer Books. i have fun Reading.

WRITING   I can spell mote Word s. Write mote and Write neater.

MATH   Better at times, and reading clock's and grafts.

SCIENCE/SOCIAL STUDIES   I like eletricity because I like to use it.

WORK HABITS   I can work faster and better.

SOCIAL BEHAVIOR   I talk at Work times.

Comments about my year in third grade.   I went on feld trips of and have mote friends.

FIGURE 16.5 At the end of his third-grade year, 9-year-old Philip reviewed his work over the course of the year and identified his strengths and weaknesses.

To encourage risk taking and reduce anxiety about classroom assessments, assess frequently and provide opportunities for students to correct errors. Here a teacher uses a student's errors on a paper-pencil assessment to guide her future studying efforts.

Frequent assessments. Frequent assessment of students' learning and achievement is important for several reasons. First, it provides ongoing information to both students and ourselves about the progress that students are making and about areas of weakness that need attention. Second, students are less likely to experience debilitating anxiety when they have a number of assessments that each contribute only a small amount to their final grades (e.g., Sax, 1989). Third, frequent assessment motivates students, especially those with lower ability, to study regularly (Sax, 1989). Fourth, with the pressure off to perform well on every single test and assignment, students are less likely to cheat to obtain good grades (E. D. Evans & Craig, 1990). The bottom line is that students who are assessed frequently learn and achieve at higher levels than students who are assessed infrequently (Crooks, 1988; Gaynor & Millham, 1976; Glover, 1989).

Retakes. As noted in the discussion of mastery learning in Chapter 13, some students will invariably need more time to master a topic than others and may therefore need to be assessed on the same material more than once. Furthermore, students are less likely to have debilitating test anxiety when they know they will have a second try at an assessment task if they need one. Yet allowing retakes has disadvantages as well. When students know they can eventually retake an assessment if they get a low score the first time, they may prepare less well than they would otherwise. Furthermore, students who are allowed to retake the *same* instrument may study the specific things that the instrument covers without studying equally important but nonassessed material (remember, most assessment tasks can be only small samples of the domain being assessed).

If we truly want students to master course material but also to take risks in their learning and classroom performance, then we may want to make retakes a regular practice. To encourage students to take the original test seriously and to discourage them from studying only test content for the retake, we can construct two assessment instruments for the same content domain, using one as the initial assessment and the other for retakes. If this strategy will be too time-consuming to be practical, we can allow students to redo the same assessment a second time but then average the two scores earned.

Opportunities to correct errors. Particularly when an assessment includes most or all of the content domain in question, students may learn as much—possibly even more—by correcting the errors they've made on an assessment task. One high school mathematics teacher, Dan Wagner, uses what he calls a *mastery reform* as a way of allowing students to make mistakes and then learn from them. When it is clear from classroom assessments that students haven't demonstrated mastery of a mathematical procedure, Dan has them complete an assignment that includes the following:

1. *Identification of the error.* Students describe in a short paragraph exactly what it is that they do not yet know how to do.
2. *Statement of the process.* Students explain the steps involved in the procedure they are trying to master; in doing so, they must demonstrate their understanding by using words rather than mathematical symbols.
3. *Practice.* Students show their mastery of the procedure with three new problems similar to the problem(s) they previously solved incorrectly.
4. *Statement of mastery.* Students state in a sentence or two that they have now mastered the procedure.

By completing the four prescribed steps, students can replace a grade on a previous assessment with the higher one that they earn by attaining mastery. Such assignments can have long-term benefits as well: Dan tells me that many of his students eventually incorporate the four steps into their regular, more internalized learning strategies.

Throughout much of our discussion so far, we have considered what we can learn about our students when we give an assessment. Yet we should also learn something about our assessment practices, as we shall see now.

Evaluating an Assessment Through Item Analysis

In the process of scoring students' performance on an assessment instrument, we may discover that some items or tasks simply don't provide the information we had hoped they would. For example, it may become obvious that one item is not measuring the knowledge or skill we had in mind (a validity problem) and that another is hard to score consistently (a reliability problem that indirectly affects validity as well). We can't always predict ahead of time which items and tasks are going to be good ones and which are not. For this reason, assessment experts frequently recommend an **item analysis** after an assessment has been administered and scored. Such an analysis typically involves an examination of both the difficulty level and discriminative power of each item on the assessment instrument.

Item difficulty. We can determine the difficulty of each item simply by finding out how many students responded to it correctly. The **item difficulty** (p) of an item is the proportion of students responding correctly relative to the total number of students who took the assessment:

$$p = \frac{\text{Number of students getting the item correct}}{\text{Number of students taking the assessment}}$$

This formula yields a number between 0.0 and 1.0. A high p value indicates that the item was a relatively easy one for students; for example, a p of .85 means that 85 percent of the students answered it correctly. A low p value indicates that the item was difficult; for example, a p of .10 means that only 10 percent gave a correct response.

On norm-referenced tests (such as many standardized tests), p values tell us which items have a difficulty level that is best for comparing the performance of individual students. In this situation, ideal p values are somewhere between .30 and .70, indicating that the items are difficult enough that some, but not all, students get them wrong. In contrast, when almost all students answer an item in the same way—either correctly (a very high p) or incorrectly (a very low p)—we get little if any information about how the students differ from one another.

In contrast, on criterion-referenced tests (such as many teacher-developed assessments), there is no "best" item difficulty value. In this case, p values help us determine how effectively we are accomplishing our instructional objectives. If most students have responded to an item correctly, and if we can rule out other factors (e.g., guessing or implausible distractors) that may have contributed to the high success rate, we can conclude that our students have mastered the knowledge or skill the item represents. A low p value tells us either that our students haven't learned what we are assessing or that the item doesn't accurately reflect what students *did* learn.

Item discrimination. Imagine that you have just given your class a thirty-item multiple-choice test and are scoring your students' test papers. You notice that your best students, although they have done well on most of the test, answered question 12 incorrectly. You also notice several students who got very low test scores got question 12 *correct*. This doesn't make sense: You would expect the students who do well on any one item to be the same ones who perform well on the test overall. When the "wrong" students are getting an item correct—when the item "discriminates" among informed and uninformed students inaccurately—we have a problem with **item discrimination.**

Item discrimination (D) is determined using the approach I have just described. More specifically, we identify two groups of students, those who have gotten the highest overall scores and those who have gotten the lowest scores, putting about 20 to 30 percent of the total number of students in each group. We then compare the proportions of students in the two groups getting each item correct, like this:

$$D = \frac{\text{Number of high-scoring students getting item correct}}{\text{Total number of high-scoring students}} - \frac{\text{Number of low-scoring students getting item correct}}{\text{Total number of low-scoring students}}$$

The D formula yields a number ranging from -1.0 to $+1.0$. Positive D values tell us that a greater proportion of high-scoring students have done well on an item than low-scoring students; in other words, the item discriminates between knowledgeable and unknowledgeable students, which is exactly the situation we want. In contrast, negative D values reflect a situation like that of question 12 on the multiple-choice test described earlier: Low-scoring students are answering the item correctly, but high-scoring students are not. A negative D is often a sign that something is wrong with the item; perhaps it misleads knowledgeable students to choose what was intended to be an incorrect response, or perhaps we have marked an incorrect answer on the answer key.

But let's return to an assumption we made earlier: Students who do well on any single item should be the same ones who perform well overall. Here we are talking about *internal consistency reliability*, the extent to which different parts of an assessment instrument are all measuring more or less the same thing. When the items or tasks on an assessment instrument are all designed to measure very *different* things (as is often true for performance assessment), then *D* values are less helpful in evaluating an item's effectiveness.

Many teachers save their good assessment items in an item file for use on future occasions. For example, they might paste each item on an index card, with scoring criteria and item analysis data listed on the reverse side, or they might save their good items in a specially marked folder on their computer. As they continue to add items to their files over the years, they eventually have a large enough collection that they don't have to use any one item very often.

Summarizing Students' Achievement

Many of our assessments will provide a considerable amount of information regarding students' strengths and weaknesses, and we must eventually boil it down into more general indicators of what our students have accomplished. Two widely used approaches are *final class grades* and *portfolios*.

Determining Final Class Grades

Over the years, teachers' grading practices have been a source of considerable controversy. Fueling the fire are several problems inherent in our attempts to assign final grades to students' achievement. First, because our individual assessment instruments have less than perfect validity and reliability, grades based on these measures may also be somewhat inaccurate. Second, different teachers use different criteria to assign grades; for instance, some are more lenient than others, and some stress rote memorization whereas others stress higher-level skills (recall the opening case study). Third, in heterogeneous classes (e.g., those that include students from diverse backgrounds and students with special educational needs), different students may be working to accomplish different instructional objectives. Fourth, typical grading practices promote performance goals rather than mastery goals (see Chapter 12) and may encourage students to go for the "easy A" rather than take risks (Stipek, 1993; S. Thomas & Oldfather, 1997). Finally, students under pressure to achieve high grades may resort to undesirable behaviors (e.g., cheating, plagiarism) to attain those grades.

Despite such problems, final grades continue to be the most common method of summarizing students' overall classroom achievement. As teachers, we can take several steps to ensure that the grades we assign are as accurate a reflection of what each student has accomplished as we can possibly make them:

- *Take the job of grading seriously.* Consider these scenarios:

  A high school mathematics teacher who uses a formula to determine final grades makes numerous errors in his calculations. As a result, some students get lower grades than they've earned.

  A middle school Spanish teacher asks her teenage son to calculate her students' final grades. Some of the columns in her grade book are for test scores that students have earned when they've taken a test a second time to improve their record; students who did well on exams the first time have blanks in these columns. Not understanding the teacher's system, her son treats all blank spaces as a "zero." The highest achievers—those students who have many blank spots in the teacher's grade book—are quite surprised to discover that they've earned Ds and Fs for the semester.

A mathematics teacher who makes mathematical errors? A Spanish teacher who relies on a teenager to determine final grades? Preposterous? No, both cases are true stories. Here we have teachers who assign grades that are totally meaningless. Students' final class grades are often the *only* data that appear in their school records. We must take the time and make the effort to ensure that those grades are accurate.

Many computer software packages are now available to assist with record keeping and grading. In addition to helping us keep track of a sizable body of assessment information, such software makes it easier for us to share our records with students regularly (e.g., see Figure 16.6).

What are students likely to conclude about these two teachers?

We cannot use grading software mindlessly, however. For example, if we make errors when entering information or don't take the time to learn the proper use of our record-keeping system, we might as well have the Spanish teacher's son calculate our grades for us!

■ *Base grades on hard data.* Subjective teacher judgments typically correlate with actual student achievement, but they are imperfect assessments at best, and some teachers are better judges than others (Gaines & Davis, 1990; Hoge & Coladarci, 1989). Furthermore, although teachers can generally judge the achievement of high-ability students with some accuracy, they are less accurate when they subjectively assess the achievement of low-ability students (Hoge & Coladarci, 1989). Teachers are especially likely to underestimate the achievement of students from minority groups and those from low socioeconomic backgrounds (Gaines & Davis, 1990). For these reasons and for the sake of our students (who learn more and achieve at higher levels when we tell them what we expect in concrete terms), we should base grades on objective and observable information derived from formal assessment instruments, *not* from our subjective impressions of how well students have done in our classes.

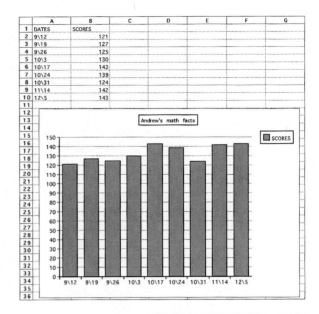

FIGURE 16.6 Computer software can often help us keep track of students' performance on classroom assessments. Here we see 10-year-old Andrew's performance on regular quizzes of math facts. Each quiz is worth 150 points.

■ *Be selective about the assessments used to determine grades.* Using multiple assessments to determine final grades can help us compensate for the imperfect reliability and validity of any single assessment instrument. At the same time, we probably don't want to consider everything our students do. As already noted, we must create an atmosphere in which students feel free to take risks and make mistakes. Thus, we may not want to include students' early efforts at new tasks, which are likely to involve some trial and error on their part (Canady & Hotchkiss, 1989). And many assessments may be more appropriately used for formative evaluation purposes—to help students learn—than for summative evaluation (Frisbie & Waltman, 1992).

■ *Identify a reasonable grading system and stick to it.* Consider this situation:

Ms. Giroux tells her middle school students that class grades will be based solely on quiz and test scores throughout the semester. After a couple of months, she realizes that most students are struggling with her exams and will probably get Ds or Fs as a result. So near the end of the semester, she asks students to turn in all their homework assignments; completed assignments will contribute 20 percent to students' final grades. Believing that she is being quite generous, she is surprised when her students protest loudly and angrily. Many of them, thinking that there was no reason to keep previous homework assignments, have already discarded their previous work.

If most students are getting Ds and Fs, something is definitely wrong. Perhaps Ms. Giroux didn't take students' prior knowledge into account when she chose a starting point for instruction. Perhaps she's moving too quickly through the curriculum and so students never achieve mastery of a topic. Perhaps her instructional methods aren't as effective as other approaches might be. Perhaps her quizzes and tests are extremely difficult and reflect unrealistic expectations about what her students can do.

As teachers, we can't always anticipate how best to teach a new topic or how well our students will perform on our classroom assessment instruments. Nevertheless, if we want to give our students a sense that they have some control over their grades (recall the discussion of attribution theory in Chapter 12), we must tell them early in the semester or school year what our grading criteria will be. If we find that our criteria are overly stringent, we may need to "lighten up" in some way, perhaps by adjusting cutoffs or by allowing retakes of critical assessments. But we must never change our criteria midstream in a way that unfairly penalizes some students or imposes additional, unanticipated requirements.

Considering Improvement, Effort, and Extra Credit

Our discussion so far has been based on the assumption that class grades should reflect students' achievement of instructional objectives. Yet some educators suggest that students be graded on the basis of how much they improve, how hard they try, or how much extra work they do (e.g., Kane, 1983). Let's consider the implications of incorporating each of these factors into our final class grades.

Grading improvement.   There are two good arguments against basing final grades solely on students' improvement over the course of a semester or school year. Some students may come to the first day of class already possessing some of the knowledge and skills in the curriculum we've planned, and so there is little room for improvement. In addition, when we use improvement as a criterion, students trying to "beat the system" may quickly learn that they can achieve high grades simply by performing as poorly as possible at the beginning of the year (Airasian, 1994; Sax, 1989).

Yet in our discussion of promoting self-efficacy and intrinsic motivation in Chapter 12, we noted the importance of focusing students' attention on their own improvement, rather than on how their performance compares with that of their peers. One reasonable compromise here is to assign greater weight to assessments conducted at the end of the semester or school year, after *all* students have had a reasonable opportunity to achieve instructional objectives (Lester et al., 1997). Two other strategies are ones mentioned previously: administering retakes (perhaps using items or tasks different from those presented the first time) and giving students a chance to correct their errors and, in the process, demonstrate their mastery of the subject matter.

Grading effort.   Most assessment experts recommend that we *not* base final grades on the amount of effort that students exert in the classroom. For one thing, students who begin the year already performing at a high level are penalized because they may not have to work as hard as their less knowledgeable classmates. Furthermore, "effort" is something that we can evaluate only subjectively and imprecisely at best (R. L. Linn & Gronlund, 2000; Sax, 1989; Stiggins, 2001).

Obviously, we enhance students' motivation when we acknowledge their effort, and so we may often want to communicate our informal assessment of it to our students and their parents (Pintrich & Schunk, 2002). Some school systems have multidimensional grading systems that allow teachers to assign separate grades to the various aspects of students' classroom performance. Such mechanisms as letters to parents, parent-teacher conferences, and letters of recommendation provide an additional means by which we can describe the multifaceted nature of students' classroom performance.

Giving extra credit.   Over the years I have occasionally had students appear at my office door, asking, sometimes begging, for an opportunity to improve their grades by completing extra-credit projects. Usually these students are failing one of my courses and are desperately trying to save their grade point average at the last minute. My response is invariably no, and for a very good reason: My course grades are based on the extent to which students achieve my instructional objectives, as determined by their performance on tests and assignments that are the same or equivalent (therefore standardized and fair) for all students. Extra-credit projects assigned to only one or two students (typically those achieving at the lowest levels) are insufficient to demonstrate mastery of the subject matter, and they are not standardized for the entire class.

Certainly, we can consider some extra-credit work as we assign grades, provided that the work relates to classroom objectives and all students are given the same opportunity to complete it. But incorporating extra credit into final evaluations is not the most appropriate way to help a failing student—one who has not met course objectives—achieve a passing grade.

Would a student who does little work all semester but pulls off a passing grade by doing an extra-credit project "learn a lesson" and develop more regular study habits? Why or why not?

Choosing Criterion- or Norm-Referenced Grades

Many experts recommend that, as a general rule, final grades should reflect mastery of classroom subject matter and instructional objectives; in other words, our grades should be criterion-referenced (e.g., Stiggins, 2001; Terwilliger, 1989). Criterion-referenced grades are especially appropriate during the elementary years: Much of the elementary curriculum consists of basic skills that are either mastered or not mastered, and there is little need to use grades as a basis for comparing students to one another.

The issue becomes more complicated at the secondary level: Students' grades are sometimes used to choose college applicants, award scholarships, and so on. My personal recommendation is that high school grades be criterion-referenced to the extent that such is possible. The most critical decisions for which grades are used—decisions about promotion and graduation—should be based on students' mastery or nonmastery of the school curriculum, not on their standing relative to others. Furthermore, different classes of students often differ in ability level; if grading were strictly norm-referenced, then a student's performance in one class (e.g., honors math) might be graded as C, whereas the same performance in another class (e.g., general math) might warrant an A. (Under such circumstances, a student striving for a high grade point average would be a fool to enroll in the honors section.) Finally, only a very few students (the highest achievers) find a norm-referenced grading system motivating; most students quickly resign themselves to achieving at an average level at best (e.g., Wlodkowski, 1978).

When we set up a criterion-referenced grading system, we must determine as concretely as possible what we want each grade to communicate about students' achievement. For example, if we are using traditional letter grades, we might use criteria such as the following:

Grade	Criteria
A	The student has a firm command of both basic and advanced knowledge and skills in the content domain. He or she is well prepared for future learning tasks.
B	The student has mastered all basic knowledge and skills; mastery at a more advanced level is evident in some, but not all, areas. In most respects, he or she is ready for future learning tasks.
C	The student has mastered basic knowledge and skills but has difficulty with more advanced aspects of the subject matter. He or she lacks a few of the prerequisites critical for future learning tasks.
D	The student has mastered some but not all of the basics in the content domain. He or she lacks many prerequisites for future learning tasks.
F	The student shows little if any mastery of instructional objectives and cannot demonstrate the most elementary knowledge and skills. He or she lacks most of the prerequisites essential for success in future learning tasks. (based on criteria described by Frisbie & Waltman, 1992)

Summarizing students' many achievements with a single class grade can be quite challenging, and we inevitably lose a great deal of information in the process (Delandshere & Petrosky, 1998). Hence, some educators suggest that we communicate what students have achieved through other techniques that reflect the multifaceted nature of students' accomplishments. One strategy now gaining wide acceptance is portfolios.

INTO THE CLASSROOM: *Summarizing Students' Achievement*

Base final grades on objective and observable data.

Carolyn always sits passively at the back of the classroom and never contributes to class discussions. Her teacher is surprised when she earns high scores on his first two classroom tests. He eventually realizes that, despite her lack of class participation, Carolyn is definitely achieving his instructional objectives and so grades her accordingly.

Use as many sources of data as is reasonably possible to determine grades.

When determining semester grades, a high school teacher considers her students' performance on five paper-pencil tests, three formal performance assessments, a research paper, and numerous smaller assignments.

Don't count everything.

A teacher frequently assigns homework as a way of encouraging students to practice new skills. He gives students feedback on their work but does not consider these assignments when determining course grades.

Evaluate actual achievement separately from such other factors as effort, improvement, and extra-credit projects.

At a parent-teacher conference, a teacher describes Stan's performance this way: "Stan has gotten all Bs and Cs this term—grades that indicate adequate but not exceptional achievement. I have noticed a great deal of inconsistency in his classroom performance. When he puts forth the effort, he learns class material quite well; otherwise, he does poorly."

Assign criterion-referenced grades unless there is a compelling reason to do otherwise.

A teacher assigns criterion-referenced grades for Algebra I, knowing that those grades will be used by school counselors to determine an appropriate math class for each student next year.

Use portfolios to summarize students' accomplishment of complex, multifaceted tasks.

A teacher has students develop portfolios of their fiction and nonfiction writing. These portfolios, which document students' mastery of some writing skills and progress on others, are shared with parents at the end of the school year.

Using Portfolios

A **portfolio** is a systematic collection of a student's work over a lengthy period. It need not be limited to paper-pencil products that students have developed; it might also include photographs, audiotapes, videotapes, or objects that a student has created (e.g., see Figure 16.7). Some portfolios are "developmental" in nature: Various products are included to show how a student has improved over a period of time. Others may include only the student's best work as a reflection of his or her final achievement (Spandel, 1997; Winograd & Jones, 1992).

Portfolios have several advantages (C. Hill & Larsen, 1992; F. L. Paulson, Paulson, & Meyer, 1991; Popham, 1995; Spandel, 1997; Paris & Paris, 2001). First, they capture the complex nature of students' achievement, often over a prolonged period, in ways that single letter grades can't possibly do. Second, they provide a mechanism through which we can easily intertwine assessment with instruction: Students typically include products that we may have assigned primarily for instructional purposes. Third, the process of constructing a portfolio encourages students to reflect on and evaluate their accomplishments. And fourth, portfolios sometimes influence the very nature of the instruction that takes place; because the focus is on complex skills, teachers may be more likely to *teach* those skills (Koretz et al., 1994).

RSVP characteristics are often a source of concern for portfolios, however, particularly if they are being used to evaluate, rather than simply communicate, students' learning and achievement. When portfolios must be scored in some way, such scoring is often unreliable: There may be little agreement among teachers about how any particular portfolio should be rated (Koretz et al., 1994; Popham, 1995). In addition, we have an obvious standardization problem: Because each portfolio will include a unique set of products, we will be evaluating each student on the basis of different information. Validity may or may not be a problem: A portfolio must include a sufficient number of work samples to provide a representative sample of what students have accomplished relative to instructional objectives (Arter & Spandel, 1992; Koretz et al., 1994). Last but not least, we must realize that portfolios, if used properly, are likely to take a great deal of our time, both during class and after hours (Airasian, 1994; Koretz et al., 1994; Popham, 1995); in this sense at least, they are less practical than other methods of summarizing achievement. All this is not to say that we should shy away from using portfolios. But we should make sure the potential benefits outweigh the disadvantages when we ask students to compile them, and we must use them cautiously when they serve as summative evaluations of what students have accomplished.

Advocates of portfolios have offered several suggestions for using portfolios effectively:

■ *Consider the specific purpose for which a portfolio will be used.* Different kinds of portfolios are useful for different purposes. Developmental portfolios, which include products from the entire school year or perhaps from an even longer period, are most useful when we want to see whether our students are making reasonable progress toward long-term instructional objectives. Such portfolios are also invaluable for showing students *themselves* how much they've improved. In contrast, "best work" portfolios are more useful for summarizing students' final achievement, perhaps as a way of communicating students' accomplishments to parents, students' future teachers, or college admissions officers (Spandel, 1997).

■ *Involve students in the selection of a portfolio's contents.* In most cases, students should decide for themselves which products to include in their portfolios (F. L. Paulson et al., 1991; Popham, 1995; Spandel, 1997). Such practice gives students a sense of "ownership" of their portfolios and can enhance their sense of self-determination and intrinsic motivation to learn. We can help students make appropriate choices by scheduling periodic one-on-one conferences in which we jointly discuss the products that best reflect their achievements (Popham, 1995). We might also show them examples of portfolios that other students have

Meghan makes arrangements of six in math.

Meghan displays her collection of 100.

FIGURE 16.7 In a kindergarten portfolio, Meghan and her teacher included these two digital photographs that illustrate Meghan's developing math skills.

Students have more ownership of a portfolio when they have played a role in selecting its contents.

created; however, we should do so only if those students and their parents have given permission or if a portfolio's creator can remain confidential (F. L. Paulson et al., 1991; Stiggins, 2001).

■ *Identify the criteria by which products should be selected and evaluated.* Students are more likely to make wise selections when they have guidelines for making their selections and (if applicable) when they know the criteria by which their portfolio will eventually be evaluated (Popham, 1995; Spandel, 1997; Stiggins, 2001). (If we are using portfolios for final evaluations, we will also want to develop a rubric for scoring it.) In some instances, we may want to include students themselves in the process of identifying the criteria to be used (Popham, 1995). Such a strategy further enhances their sense of self-determination; it can also enhance their ability to self-evaluate in future projects and assignments.

■ *Ask students to reflect on the products they include.* In addition to examples of students' work, many portfolios include documentation that describes each product and the reason it was included. For instance, consider how a student in an eighth-grade language arts class describes and evaluates the writing samples he has included in his class portfolio (he has included two or more drafts of each piece of writing):

Self-Evaluation

The three pieces of writing in my portfolio that best represent who I am are: 1) "Author Ben Hoff," which is a story in the language of Ben Hoff; 2) "Quotes from The Tao of Pooh"; and 3) "Discrimination."

What "Author Ben Hoff" shows about me as a learner or a writer is that I am able to analyze and absorb the types and styles of an author and then transfer what I learn onto paper in a good final understandable piece of writing. This piece has good description, a good plot line, gets the point across, has a basic setting, and is understandable. I did not change too much of this piece from one draft to the next except punctuation, grammar and spelling. I did, however, add a quote from The Tao of Pooh.

"Quotes from The Tao of Pooh" shows that I am able to pull out good and significant quotes from a book, understand them, and put them into my own words. Then I can make them understandable to other people. This piece gets the point across well and is easy to understand. I really only corrected spelling and punctuation from one draft to the next.

"Discrimination" shows me that I am learning more about discrimination and how it might feel (even though I have never experienced really bad discrimination). I found I can get my ideas across through realistic writing. This piece has good description and was well written for the assignment. Besides correcting some punctuation and spelling, I changed some wording to make the story a little more clear.

For all three pieces, the mechanics of my writing tend to be fairly poor on my first draft, but that is because I am writing as thoughts come into my mind rather than focusing on details of grammar. Then my final drafts get better as I get comments and can turn my attention to details of writing.

The four most important things that I'm able to do as a writer are to: 1) get thoughts pulled into a story; 2) have that story understandable and the reader get something from it; 3) have the reader remember it was a good piece of writing; and 4) like the piece myself.

Such documentation encourages students to reflect on and judge their own work in ways that teachers typically do (Airasian, 1994; Arter & Spandel, 1992; Popham, 1995). Thus, it is likely to promote the self-monitoring and self-evaluation skills so essential for self-regulated learning.

Portfolios can be especially useful in capturing and communicating the strengths that students with diverse backgrounds and needs are likely to have. We now look more generally at the implications of student diversity for our classroom assessment practices.

Taking Student Diversity into Account

As we have seen, standardization of assessment instruments and procedures is important for fairness, reliability, and (indirectly) validity in our assessment results. Yet standardization has a down side: It limits our ability to accommodate students' diverse backgrounds and needs, capitalize on their individual strengths, and help them compensate for any areas of weakness.

Standardization in classroom assessment practices is essential if we want to make comparisons among our students, and especially if we also intend to use our assessment results to make decisions that may significantly impact students' future lives. In other situations—for example, when we are trying to ascertain appropriate starting points for instruction or specific weaknesses that each student needs to address—standardization is less critical. In some instances,

Using Classroom Assessments with Students with Special Educational Needs

CATEGORY	CHARACTERISTICS YOU MIGHT OBSERVE	SUGGESTED CLASSROOM STRATEGIES
Students with specific cognitive or academic difficulties	• Poor listening, reading, and/or writing skills • Inconsistent performance due to off-task behaviors (for some students with learning disabilities or ADHD) • Difficulty processing specific kinds of information • Higher than average test anxiety	• Make paper-pencil instruments easy to respond to; for instance, type (rather than hand-write) tests, space items far apart, and have students respond directly on their test papers rather than on separate answer sheets. • Minimize reliance on reading and writing skills if appropriate. • Let students take tests in a quiet place (e.g., the school's resource room). • Give explicit directions. • Be sure students are motivated to do their best but not overly anxious. • Provide extra time to complete assessments. • Score responses separately for content and quality of writing. • Look at students' errors for clues about processing difficulties. • Use informal assessments to either confirm or disconfirm results of formal assessments.
Students with social or behavioral problems	• Inconsistent performance on classroom assessments due to off-task behaviors or lack of motivation (for some students)	• Make modifications in assessment procedures as necessary (see strategies presented above for students with specific cognitive or academic difficulties). • Use informal assessments to either confirm or disconfirm results of formal classroom assessments.
Students with general delays in cognitive and social functioning	• Slow learning and cognitive processing • Limited if any reading skills • Poor listening skills	• Be explicit about what you are asking students to do. • Make sure any reading materials are appropriate for students' reading level. • Use performance assessments that require little reading or writing. • Allow sufficient time for students to complete assigned tasks.
Students with physical or sensory challenges	• Mobility problems (for some students with physical challenges) • Tendency to tire easily (for some students with physical challenges) • Less developed language abilities (for some students with hearing loss)	• Use written rather than oral assessments (for students with hearing loss). • Minimize reliance on visual materials (for students with visual impairments). • Use appropriate technology to facilitate students' performance. • Provide extra time to complete assessments. • Limit assessments to short time periods, and give frequent breaks. • Use simple language if students have language difficulties.
Students with advanced cognitive development	• Greater ability to perform exceptionally complex tasks • Unusual, sometimes creative, responses to classroom assessment instruments • Tendency in some students to hide giftedness to avoid possible ridicule by peers	• Use performance assessments to assess complex activities. • Establish scoring criteria that allow unusual and creative responses. • Provide opportunities for students to demonstrate their achievements privately. • Keep assessment results confidential.

Sources: Barkley, 1998; Beirne-Smith et al., 2002; D. Y. Ford & Harris, 1992; Mercer, 1997; D. P. Morgan & Jenson, 1988; Piirto, 1999; Turnbull et al., 1999.

in fact, we may find that the best way of assessing one student's learning is a relatively *ineffec-tive* way of assessing another's. Let's remind ourselves of a few sources of diversity that we iden-tified in Chapter 4 (remember that these are *average* differences):

- Boys tend to talk more in class than girls.
- Girls tend to work harder on classroom assignments than boys.
- Some students have grown up speaking a language other than English.
- Mainstream Western culture values individual achievement, but students from some cultural backgrounds are more accustomed to working as a group than to working alone.
- Many students raised in mainstream Western culture are quite accustomed to showing others what they know and can do, but students from some cultural backgrounds are accustomed to practicing skills in private until they have achieved mastery.

- Students from very poor families may lack adequate nutrition and health care to perform at their best in the classroom.
- Students at risk for academic failure may find little relevance in academic subject matter for their own lives.

Such factors will, of course, affect students' ability to learn and achieve in the classroom. But they may also affect how students perform on our informal and formal assessments *independently* of their learning and achievement. Here we see still another reason why we should consider multiple measures—as well as several different kinds of measures—whenever we are using our classroom assessment results to assign grades and make other important decisions.

Accommodating Students with Special Needs

In Chapter 15 we noted the importance of making appropriate accommodations for students with special needs: We are unlikely to get valid results unless we *do* make such accommodations. The specific modifications to our assessment instruments and procedures must, of course, be tailored to students' particular disabilities. For example, we may need to read paper-pencil test questions to students with limited reading skills (e.g., to some students with learning disabilities). We may need to break a lengthy assessment task into several shorter tasks for students with a limited attention span (e.g., for some students with ADHD or emotional and behavioral disorders). And we may have to construct individualized assessment instruments when instructional objectives differ for some of our students (e.g., as may often be the case for students with mental retardation). Additional accommodations for students with special needs are presented in Table 16.2.

We should also keep students' unique needs and disabilities in mind when we summarize and communicate their final achievements. For instance, if the instructional objectives for a student are different from those for the rest of the class, our grading criteria should be altered accordingly, perhaps to be in line with the student's IEP (Mastropieri & Scruggs, 2000; Venn, 2000). Yet letter grades alone communicate very little definitive information about what students have learned and achieved; if we change the criteria for a particular student, the grades communicate even *less* information. Portfolios (perhaps including teacher checklists, photographs, audiotapes, and videotapes, as well as students' written work) can be particularly helpful for conveying the progress and achievements of students with a variety of disabilities and special needs (Mastropieri & Scruggs, 2000; Venn, 2000).

The Big Picture

Assessment is one of the most important aspects of our jobs as teachers, and it is certainly not a task we can take lightly. On the contrary, we must give considerable thought to how we can best determine what our students are learning and devote considerable time and effort to designing our assessment instruments. Let's briefly remind ourselves of the many ways in which our assessment practices are likely to affect students' learning and motivation. We will then identify several general strategies that can guide our classroom assessment practices.

Learning, Motivation, and Assessment

Our assessment practices will, without doubt, be closely intertwined with our planning, instruction, and efforts to create a productive classroom environment. For instance, they should reflect our instructional objectives, and the information they yield will guide our future planning and instruction. Furthermore, they will impact the overall classroom atmosphere that students

experience—for instance, whether students feel free to take on challenges and make mistakes or whether they become so anxious about test scores that their learning, performance, and psychological well-being suffer.

Our assessments will indirectly affect students' learning and achievement through their influences on planning, instruction, and the classroom environment. But as we have seen, they will also have several more direct effects on *learning*:

- They will communicate messages about how students should study and what things are most important to learn.
- They will provide opportunities for students to review, practice, and apply what they've learned.
- They will give feedback about students' strengths and weaknesses.
- They will, if students themselves play an active role in the assessment process, promote such skills as self-monitoring and self-evaluation and so set the stage for increasing self-regulation.

Our classroom assessment practices are apt to have an impact on *motivation* as well:

- They may foster either extrinsic motivation and a focus on performance goals (if any single assessment has major consequences) or intrinsic motivation and mastery goals (if assessments are treated as mechanisms for helping students learn and if students have input into the assessment criteria).
- They may encourage students either to strive for increasingly complex knowledge and skills (if they are challenging yet take students' existing abilities into account) or to lose interest in classroom subject matter (if they are too easy or exceptionally difficult).

As we develop our classroom assessment instruments, then, and as we consider how best to summarize students' achievement at the end of the semester or school year, we should continually ask ourselves questions such as these:

- Do our assessment tasks reflect knowledge and skills essential for students' long-term academic and personal success?
- Are our scoring criteria stringent enough to ensure that important instructional objectives are achieved yet not so stringent that success is impossible?
- Do our assessment practices allow students to take risks and make mistakes as they study and learn?
- Are we involving students in assessing their own performance often enough that they are acquiring the skills they will ultimately need to be self-regulated learners?

Even when we are conducting summative evaluations of what students have learned, our ultimate goal should be to *help students learn better.*

General Guidelines for Classroom Assessment

This chapter has presented a wide variety of strategies for assessing students' learning and numerous guidelines for using them. Following are several general suggestions that should apply across the board:

■ *Match assessment instruments and practices to important instructional objectives.* If there is one single guideline that bears repeating in the final pages of the chapter, this is it. Our classroom assessments are worthless if they don't tell us what we really need to know. If fact, they can be counterproductive if they encourage students to adopt ineffective learning strategies (e.g., verbatim memorization of isolated facts) rather than strategies and processes that are likely to serve them well over the long run (e.g., meaningful learning, elaboration, and critical thinking).

■ *Consider the RSVP characteristics of every assessment.* The three general approaches to assessment we have considered—informal assessment, paper-pencil assessment, and performance assessment—have different strengths and weaknesses. Informal assessments are practical, in that they take little time and effort, but they are rarely standardized, and the little snippets we observe may not be dependable (reliable) or accurate (valid) reflections of more general characteristics and achievements.

When properly constructed, paper-pencil assessment instruments with recognition items (e.g., multiple-choice, alternative-response) are easily standardized and can be both reliable and practical; however, many teachers focus primarily on knowledge of basic facts when writing such items, limiting their validity for assessing higher-level skills. Other, more open-ended types of paper-pencil tasks lend themselves more readily to measuring higher-level skills, especially when they involve extended responses (as some essay questions do), but often at the expense of reliability and practicality. Performance assessments are typically less reliable and practical than paper-pencil assessments, yet they may be the only valid means of measuring some types of knowledge and skills. Clearly, then, we will have difficulty maximizing all four RSVP characteristics at once. Of the four, our ultimate concern must be *content validity:* Our assessment tasks should provide a representative sample of what students have accomplished relative to our instructional objectives.

■ *Specify scoring criteria as explicitly as possible.* Teachers and students alike benefit when scoring criteria are explicit. Teachers can evaluate students' responses more consistently, reliably, and (often) quickly, and they can more easily determine whether students are achieving instructional goals. Meanwhile, students have clear targets to shoot for as they study and practice.

■ *Look at students' errors for clues about where their difficulties lie.* In the section on learning disabilities in Chapter 5, I suggested that we analyze students' errors for clues about their processing difficulties. In fact, we should take such an approach with *every* student. Knowing where students are having difficulty is often more useful than knowing what they do well, provided that we use their errors as a guide for helping them improve.

■ *Don't summarize students' achievement any more than necessary.* The more we summarize, the more information we lose. As we plan our future lessons, the nitty-gritty details of students' performance on assessment tasks—the specific things they do and do not know, the mistakes they make, the misconceptions they reveal—are apt to be more useful than overall test scores and class grades.

■ *Evaluate assessment instruments after their use to be sure they have yielded the needed information, and look for ways to improve them in the future.* After almost thirty years of teaching experience, I still don't construct "perfect" tests and assignments. I'm getting better, to be sure, but I occasionally write test items that students misinterpret, and their misinterpretations show up as low p values in an item analysis. And although I clearly specify my scoring criteria when I assign performance tasks, I sometimes find that those criteria don't adequately capture the knowledge and skills I'm trying to assess. I do what I can to correct the situation for the time being (e.g., I throw out bad test items, and I make do with my inadequate criteria), but I learn from my mistakes and am careful not to make the same ones in future classes.

Learning how to construct good classroom assessment instruments may be one of your most challenging tasks as a teacher, and you, too, will make mistakes as you go along. The ending case study indicates just how much one teacher still has to learn.

Knowing that frequent review of class material leads to higher achievement and that a paper-pencil test is one way of providing such review, Mr. Bloskas tells his middle school science students that they will have a quiz every Friday. As a first-year teacher, he has had little experience developing test questions, so he decides to use the questions in the test bank that accompanies the class textbook. The night before the first quiz, Mr. Bloskas types thirty multiple-choice and true-false items from the test bank, making sure they cover the specific topics that he has covered in class.

His students complain that the questions are "picky." As he looks carefully at his quiz, he realizes that his students are right: The quiz measures nothing more than memorization of trivial details. So when he prepares the second quiz, Mr. Bloskas casts the test bank aside and writes two essay questions asking students to apply scientific principles they have studied to real-life situations. He's proud of his efforts: His quiz clearly measures higher-level thinking skills.

The following Friday, his students complain even more loudly about the second quiz than they had about the first ("This is too hard!" "We never studied this stuff!" "I liked the first quiz better!"). As Mr. Bloskas scores the essays, he is appalled to discover how poorly his students have performed. "Back to the test bank," he tells himself.

- What mistakes does Mr. Bloskas make in developing the first quiz? What mistakes does he make in developing the second quiz? Are the quizzes likely to have content validity? Why or why not?
- Why do the students react as negatively as they do to the second quiz?

Once you have answered these questions, compare your responses with those presented in Appendix B.

PRAXIS Turn to Appendix C, "Matching Book and Ancillary Content to the PRAXIS™ Principles of Learning and Teaching Tests," to discover sections of this chapter that may be especially applicable to the PRAXIS™ tests.

 Now go to our Companion Website at http://www.prenhall.com/ormrod to assess your understanding of chapter content with "Multiple-Choice Questions," apply comprehension in "Essay Questions," broaden your knowledge of educational psychology with related "Web Links," gain greater insight about classroom learning in "Learning in the Content Areas," and analyze and assess classroom work in the "Student Artifact Library."

Key Concepts

halo effect (p. 556)
recognition task (p. 558)
recall task (p. 558)
test bank (p. 562)
rubric (p. 568)

dynamic assessment (p. 572)
checklist (p. 574)
rating scale (p. 574)
analytic scoring (p. 574)
holistic scoring (p. 574)

item analysis (p. 581)
item difficulty (p. 581)
item discrimination (p. 581)
portfolio (p. 586)

APPENDIX A
Describing Relationships with Correlation Coefficients

- Do students with high self-esteem perform better in school than students with low self-esteem?
- Which students are more likely to answer questions correctly—those who answer questions quickly or those who are slow to respond?
- Do two different intelligence tests taken at the same time typically yield similar scores for the same student?
- Are intellectually gifted students more emotionally well-adjusted than their classmates of average intelligence?

Each of these questions asks about a relationship between two variables—whether it be the relationship between self-esteem and school achievement, between speed and accuracy in answering questions, between two sets of intelligence test scores, or between giftedness and emotional adjustment. The nature of such relationships is sometimes summarized by a statistic known as a **correlation coefficient**.

A correlation coefficient is a number between -1 and $+1$; most correlation coefficients are decimals (either positive or negative) somewhere between these two extremes. A correlation coefficient for two variables tells us about both the direction and strength of the relationship between those variables.

Direction. The direction of the relationship is indicated by the *sign* of the correlation coefficient—in other words, by whether the number is a positive or negative one. A positive number indicates a *positive correlation*: As one variable increases, the other variable also increases. For example, there is a positive correlation between self-esteem and school achievement: Students with higher self-esteem achieve at higher levels (e.g., Marsh, 1990a). In contrast, a negative number indicates a *negative correlation*: As one variable increases, the other variable decreases instead. For example, there is a negative correlation between speed and accuracy in answering questions: Students who take longer to answer questions tend to make fewer errors in answering them (e.g., Shipman & Shipman, 1985). Figure A.1 graphically depicts each of these relationships.

Strength. The strength of the relationship is indicated by the *size* of the correlation coefficient. A number close to either $+1$ or -1 (e.g., $+.89$ or $-.76$) indicates a *strong* correlation: The two variables are closely related, so knowing the level of one variable allows us to predict the level of the other variable with some accuracy. For example, we often find a strong relationship between two intelligence tests taken at the same time: Students tend to get similar scores on both tests, especially if both tests cover similar kinds of content (e.g., McGrew, Flanagan, Zeith, & Vanderwood, 1997). In contrast, a number close to 0 (e.g., $+.15$ or $-.22$) indicates a *weak* correlation: Knowing the level of one variable allows us to predict the level of the other variable, but we cannot predict with much accuracy. For example, there is a weak relationship between intellectual giftedness and emotional adjustment: In general, students with higher IQ scores show greater emotional maturity than students with lower scores (e.g.,

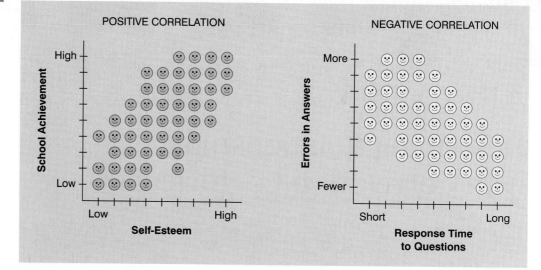

Each face in these two graphs represents one student in a group of fifty students. The location of the face tells the extent to which the student is high or low on the two characteristics indicated. There is a *positive correlation* between self-esteem and school achievement: Students with higher self-esteem tend to achieve at higher levels. There is a *negative correlation* between the length of time it takes for students to respond to questions and the number of errors in their answers: Students who take longer to answer questions tend to have fewer errors in their responses.

Janos & Robinson, 1985), but there are many students who are exceptions to this rule. Correlations in the middle range (e.g., those in the .40s and .50s—whether positive or negative) indicate a *moderate* correlation.

As teachers, we will often find correlation coefficients in research articles in our professional books and journals. For example, we might read that students' visual-spatial thinking ability is positively correlated with their success in a mathematics class or that there is a negative correlation between class size and students' achievement test scores. Whenever we see such evidence of correlation, we must remember one very important point: *Correlation does not necessarily indicate causation.* For example, we cannot say that visual-spatial thinking ability specifically *leads to* greater mathematical ability, nor can we say that class size specifically *interferes with* classroom achievement; both of these italicized phrases imply a causal relationship between one variable and another that does not necessarily exist. As Chapter 1 indicates, only carefully designed experimental studies enable us to draw conclusions about the extent to which one thing causes or influences another.

Many calculators are now programmed to compute correlation coefficients. Computing a correlation coefficient by hand is somewhat complicated but certainly not impossible. If you are curious, you can find the formula in most introductory statistics textbooks.

APPENDIX B
Analyses of the Ending Case Studies

Chapter 1: More Harm Than Good? (p. 16)

■ *Is the computer software somehow making mathematics more difficult for students? Or is there another possible explanation for students' lower scores?*

We cannot say that the software is the cause of students' difficulty because we haven't eliminated other possible explanations for the differences between computer users and non-computer users. A number of factors probably influenced students' decisions to use or not use the computer lab—their involvement in other after-school activities, their access to transportation home in the later afternoon, and so on—and so the two groups of students are probably different in a variety of ways. One likely explanation for the computer users' lower scores is that students who used the software were having considerable trouble understanding class material, whereas many who did *not* use it were finding it easy to master the material on their own.

■ *Which kind of study has Mr. Gualtieri conducted—descriptive, correlational, or experimental?*

He has looked at the relationship between two things, computer use and class performance, as they occur naturally in the environment. Therefore, he has conducted a correlational study, which does not allow inferences about cause and effect.

■ *Did Mr. Gualtieri make a good or a bad decision in advising his students to use the computer software? Is there any way to answer this question from the information he has obtained?*

There is insufficient information to determine the effectiveness of the software on students' understanding of class material. To answer this question, Mr. Gualtieri would have to have insisted that some students use the software and that other students definitely not use it; the two groups would have to have been essentially the same in ability, motivation, and so on. By randomly assigning students to groups, he could assume that the two groups were similar (on average) to begin with; therefore, any achievement differences that emerged later would have been due to software use. Note, however, that conducting a study of this nature—one in which some students are denied access to potentially helpful software—would not be appropriate from a pedagogical or ethical standpoint. As a general rule, a teacher should provide as much instructional support as possible to *all* students.

Chapter 2: In the Eye of the Beholder (pp. 58–59)

■ *What went wrong? Can you explain the students' inability to learn within the context of Piaget's theory of cognitive development? Can you explain it using some of Vygotsky's ideas? Can you explain it from an information processing perspective?*

From Piaget's perspective, students may have assimilated the new information into their existing knowledge of how we see (i.e., we look *at* something) and so misinterpreted what Ms. Kontos actually said. From Vygotsky's perspective, the learning task may have been beyond students' zone of proximal development, or Ms. Kontos may have provided insufficient scaffolding to enable them to grasp the ideas she was presenting. From an information processing perspective, students may not have adequately processed what Ms. Kontos said; for instance, perhaps they weren't paying attention during the lesson, or perhaps they elaborated on the material inaccurately. Recall, too, that the students nodded when Ms. Kontos asked them if they understood her explanation; students of all ages often have difficulty assessing their own knowledge accurately (reflecting a weakness in metacognition).

■ *In what ways might students' language capabilities have been insufficient to enable them to understand?*

Ms. Kontos may have used vocabulary with which students were unfamiliar or complex sentence structures that the students had difficulty interpreting.

■ *What things might Ms. Kontos have done differently?*

When Ms. Kontos asked her students, "Do you all understand how our eyes work?" the students nodded that they did. Although they may have *thought* they understood, many obviously did not. At a minimum, Ms. Kontos should have checked for comprehension by asking questions or presenting tasks that students could respond to correctly only if they had a true understanding of how light is involved in human sight.

Chapter 3: A Discussion of Runaway Slaves (p. 100)

■ *Are you as surprised as Mr. Dawson is? What stages of moral reasoning are evident in the opinions of these four students? Are these stages typical or atypical for eighth graders?*

From Kohlberg's perspective, all four students are reasoning at either a preconventional or conventional level. Mark is reasoning at Stage 3, the "good boy/good girl" stage: His primary concern is the plantation owners' opinion of him. Lacy appears to be at Stage 1, the "punishment avoidance" stage: She is concerned only with the punishment she might receive for harboring runaways. Kevin may be in Stage 2, the "exchange of favors" stage: He is willing to help the slaves, but only if he himself doesn't suffer in the process. Pam, too, is in Stage 2: She will help a slave if he, in turn, will help her. Such moral reasoning is hardly surprising in eighth graders. Data collected by Kohlberg and others indicates that postconventional thinking is rare before the college years. Junior high school students typically reason at either a preconventional or conventional level (see Table 3.2).

Chapter 4: The Active and the Passive (p. 141)

■ *What are some possible reasons why the girls and minority students are not participating in classroom activities? What strategies might Ms. Stewart use to increase their participation?*

Here are several possible reasons based on Chapter 4's discussion of ethnic and gender differences (you may have identified other reasons as well):

- Because some of the boys are responding to Ms. Stewart's questions almost immediately, there is little, if any, wait time that might allow the girls and minority students to speak up.
- Some of the minority students may find question-answer sessions inconsistent with their culture's preference for private conversations.
- The teacher's question-answer sessions may create a competitive atmosphere in which some girls and students from minority cultures feel uncomfortable.
- The girls may be concerned that their public displays of science knowledge will be frowned on by their classmates.
- When boys and girls work together on classroom tasks, it is typically the boys who take the more active role.
- By the secondary grade level, girls are less confident about their ability to succeed in stereotypically male domains such as science and mathematics.

Possible strategies to remedy the situation include these:

- Ignoring the hands that go up immediately and allowing sufficient time for other students to respond
- Incorporating cooperative learning activities into the weekly schedule
- Giving students opportunities to respond to questions in a more private manner (e.g., on paper)

- Forming all-male and all-female groups for laboratory activities
- Providing genuine success experiences that can help females and minorities gain self-confidence about their ability to succeed in science

Chapter 5: Quiet Amy (p. 184)

■ *Mr. Mahoney suspects that Amy may qualify for special educational services. If she does, in what category of special needs might she fall? Can you develop at least three different hypotheses as to where her difficulties may lie?*

Here are four possible hypotheses:

- A learning disability (see Figure 5.2 for specific possibilities)
- A communication disorder
- An emotional or behavioral disorder
- Hearing loss

We can probably rule out ADHD and mental retardation, because Amy can apparently attend to arts and crafts projects for significant periods of time and performs at an appropriate age level on those projects. Before identifying Amy as belonging to *any* category of special needs, the interdisciplinary team should rule out the possibility that Amy's behaviors are simply the result of an environment that has encouraged and reinforced such behaviors.

■ *Amy's evaluation will undoubtedly take several weeks to complete. In the meantime, what strategies might Mr. Mahoney try to improve Amy's classroom performance?*

Here are just a few possibilities (you might have identified others as well):

- Teach basic academic skills (e.g., letter recognition, basic number concepts) within the context of arts and crafts activities.
- Have Amy work one-on-one with an adult (e.g., a teacher aide or parent volunteer) on basic spoken language skills.
- To promote interaction with classmates, design one or more activities in which students work in pairs; match Amy with a student with strong social skills.

Chapter 6: How Time Flies (p. 224)

■ *Why might Ms. Llewellyn's students be having difficulty learning and remembering the things that she teaches them? Can you think of possible reasons related to the class curriculum? to Ms. Llewellyn's style of teaching? to Ms. Llewellyn's reading assignments?*

The *curriculum* includes too much material for a single school year. It necessitates such a fast pace and such superficial coverage that students probably don't have enough time to learn the material meaningfully or elaborate on it effectively. The *teaching style* is almost exclusively lecture. Ms. Llewellyn presents so much information that students may have difficulty determining which things are important and which things are not. Furthermore, students may be experiencing information overload, to the point where they simply cannot store everything in working memory, let alone in long-term memory. And because Ms. Llewellyn seems to be doing most, if not all, of the talking, it is difficult to know how well students are paying attention. As for the *reading assignments*, the history textbook is probably suitable if it is truly written at the students' reading level. However, many high school students don't have the needed background knowledge, and possibly don't have the reading skills either, to gain much from reading articles in professional journals.

■ *From the perspective of cognitive psychology, what would you do differently than Ms. Llewellyn?*

Here are some possible strategies:

- Plan more variety in teaching methods, including some that involve active student participation (discussions, debates, etc.). Also, incorporate many visual aids (maps, old newsreels, etc.) to complement verbal presentations.
- Make numerous connections between historical events and students' prior knowledge (e.g., relate emotions during the Civil War to emotions students might feel when embroiled in an argument over acceptable behavior).

- Cut down the amount of information presented. If the district curriculum requires coverage of the entire time span Ms. Llewellyn is covering, then identify key events to focus on and downplay other, perhaps less important, aspects of history. Also, eliminate details that contribute little to students' overall understanding and so are needless sources of distraction.
- Eliminate the professional journals. Instead, assign readings that are likely to capture students' interest, such as newspaper clippings from various eras, excerpts from diaries (e.g., *The Diary of Anne Frank, The Oregon Trail*), or novels set during particular time periods (e.g., *The Red Badge of Courage, From Here to Eternity*).

Chapter 7: Earth-Shaking Summaries (pp. 255–256)

■ *Why is Ms. Jewell not convinced that Frank and Mitchell have mastered the material? What critical aspects of the lesson did each boy omit in his response?*

Frank omits the idea that the earth's crust consists of separate pieces (plates). Both boys omit the idea that earthquakes result when two plates rub against each other as they move.

■ *What pieces of information from the lesson did Adrienne, Toni, and Jonathan apparently use when answering Ms. Jewell's question? Can you explain their responses using the concept of knowledge construction?*

Adrienne apparently interprets *tectonics* as being related to technology (e.g., computers) and therefore infers that computers are involved in the scientific study of earthquakes. Toni interprets *plates* as eating utensils and deduces that such plates move during an earthquake. Jonathan hears the word *fault* and interprets it as a *person's* fault, deducing logically that earthquakes aren't caused by people's actions. All three of these ideas may be accurate, but none of them were presented in Ms. Jewell's lesson.

■ *What instructional strategies might Ms. Jewell have used to help her students gain a better understanding of plate tectonics?*

There are numerous possible strategies that Ms. Jewell might use (see the section "Promoting Effective Knowledge Construction"). Following are two examples:

- She could have students experiment with a similar phenomenon on a small scale; perhaps she might give the students two sheets of cardboard with a small amount of sand or sugar placed on them and then have the students observe what happens when the edges of the two sheets are pressed against each other and shifted in opposite directions.
- She might ask her students to explain their interpretations of earthquakes to one another—a process through which they are likely to clarify their thinking and possibly find flaws in their own or their classmates' logic.

Chapter 8: Checks and Balances (pp. 296–297)

■ *How thoroughly have these students learned the material that Mr. Chen was trying to teach them? Why are they apparently unable to identify new examples of checks and balances?*

Debra misunderstands "checks and balances." Mark has a vague idea about the system of checks and balances but can't describe it precisely or identify concrete examples. Neither Seth nor Karen has any notion of the material they have presumably studied. None of the four students, then, have really mastered the unit and so cannot effectively transfer what they've learned to a new situation (in this case, by generating a new example).

■ *What evidence do you see that Mr. Chen's students have poor study skills? If you were teaching Mr. Chen's class, what might you do to help the students study and learn more effectively?*

Two obvious pieces of evidence indicating that the students have poor study skills are Seth's omission of important information from his class notes and Karen's illusion of knowing the material. It appears that the students have a great deal to learn about note taking, meaningful learning, elaboration, and comprehension monitoring.

Chapter 9: Hostile Helen (p. 330)

■ *In behaviorist terminology, what is Mr. Washington trying to do when he ignores Helen's inappropriate behavior? What are some possible reasons this approach isn't working?*

Mr. Washington is trying to avoid reinforcing the behavior, hoping that *extinction* will occur. From an operant conditioning perspective, this approach may not be working for any one of several possible reasons:

- Perhaps other students (e.g., Helen's friends) are reinforcing the behavior.
- Perhaps Helen has been reinforced only intermittently for the behavior in the past; therefore, the behavior has become highly resistant to extinction.
- Perhaps Mr. Washington's attention has never been a reinforcer; instead, Helen simply has a very high baseline for such behavior.
- Perhaps Helen experiences some sort of intrinsic reinforcement for her behavior (e.g., physical aggression releases pent-up energy and so "feels good").

■ *In behaviorist terminology, what is Mr. Washington trying to do when he praises Helen's appropriate behavior? What are some possible reasons this approach isn't working either?*

Mr. Washington is trying to *reinforce an incompatible behavior.* Several reasons may explain why this strategy isn't working:

- Perhaps Mr. Washington's praise is not a reinforcer for Helen.
- Perhaps Mr. Washington's praise would be effective if given in private, but it is not effective when given in front of Helen's peers.
- Perhaps Mr. Washington's praise is somewhat reinforcing, but the reinforcers Helen receives for behaving aggressively are more powerful.
- Reinforcement seldom occurs (Mr. Washington praises her only on "rare occasions").
- Reinforcement may be occurring inconsistently, because Mr. Washington can reinforce Helen only when he actually notices her behaving appropriately.

■ *How might you use behaviorist learning principles to bring about a behavior change in Helen?*

Here are several suggestions:

- Specify the terminal behavior in precise, concrete terms.
- Identify a reinforcer that is clearly reinforcing for Helen (e.g., a favorite activity).
- Find a desired behavior that, although possibly not optimal, occurs frequently enough that you can reinforce it regularly.
- Use *shaping*, reinforcing small improvements over a period of time, rather than expect overnight success.
- Monitor the effects of your reinforcer on Helen's behavior; choose a different one if you are seeing little or no change over a reasonable period of time.

Chapter 10: Teacher's Lament (p. 364)

■ *Why were the students who had been doing their homework regularly so upset? Can you explain their reaction using social cognitive theory?*

Mr. Adams is right that some students have home environments that are not terribly conducive to doing homework; for this and other reasons, homework should not be a major factor in assigning final grades (see Chapter 13). However, Mr. Adams has already told his students that homework will contribute 20 percent to final class grades. Students who have been doing their homework regularly are upset because the reinforcement they expected to receive for doing their homework did not occur.

■ *From a social cognitive perspective, Mr. Adams inadvertently punished some students and reinforced others. Which students in the class were reinforced, and how? Which students were punished, and how?*

Students who had not been doing their homework were reinforced: They did not receive the unpleasant consequences they had expected. Students who had been doing their homework were punished: They did not receive the reinforcement they had expected.

■ *What might Mr. Adams do to encourage and help all students to complete homework assignments?*

Research indicates that homework improves student achievement, at least at the middle school and secondary school grades (see Chapter 13), and so Mr. Adams should ideally find some way of enabling all his students to complete it. Following are several possible strategies (you might have thought of others as well):

- If his students live within walking distance of school, he might offer after-school homework sessions in his classroom.
- If some students live far enough away that they take the bus to and from school, he might confer with their parents or guardians and see if, by working together on the problem, they can identify a quiet time and place for doing a small amount of homework every night.
- He and his fellow teachers could agree that some study hall periods would be specifically used for doing homework for certain classes.
- If Mr. Adams discovers too late that some students have not been doing their homework for reasons beyond their control, he should identify assignments that these students can reasonably complete to make up for the work that they have missed.

Chapter 11: When "Perfect" Isn't Good Enough (p. 387)

■ *Why might feedback such as "You sure are working hard" or "You can write beautifully in cursive" be more effective than feedback such as "Great" or "Perfect"? Use what you have learned about motivation to speculate.*

The students in the experimental group appear to have more *intrinsic* motivation to write in cursive: They enjoy cursive writing more than those in the control group, and they use it more frequently in writing assignments. Feedback such as "You sure are working hard" and "You can write beautifully in cursive" probably enhances students' sense of competence and self-worth to a greater degree than "Great!" or "Perfect!", in that it specifically communicates the recognition that the students themselves are responsible for their successes. Making a connection between students' effort and abilities, on the one hand, and their success in cursive writing, on the other, is an example of an *attribution* (Chapter 12).

■ *Might the control group's feedback be more effective if Mrs. Gaskill used it for all, rather than just some, of her students? Explain your reasoning. (For help in answering this question, return to the section "Factors Influencing the Development of Self-Views" in Chapter 3.)*

As noted in Chapter 3, how students evaluate their own performance partly depends on how it compares to that of their peers. In this situation, students in the control group are hearing some of their classmates get what appears to be more favorable feedback than they themselves are getting. If everyone were getting the same cryptic feedback they were, praise such as "Great!" and "Perfect!" would be interpreted quite positively.

Chapter 12: Writer's Block (p. 424)

■ *How is Mr. Grunwald defining success in his English composition class? How are his students defining success? Are they focusing their attention on mastery goals or performance goals?*

Mr. Grunwald is probably defining success as acquiring proficient writing skills—a mastery goal. His students are defining it as earning an A or B—a performance goal.

■ *To what does Janis attribute her writing failure? What effect has her attribution had on her behavior?*

She is attributing her failure to a general inability to write, which in her mind is an internal, stable, and uncontrollable characteristic. By believing that she has no control over her successes and failures in class, she is exhibiting learned helplessness. Learning to write is, in her view, a lost cause.

■ *What strategies might Mr. Grunwald use to help his students become more intrinsically motivated to develop proficient writing skills?*

Here are three strategies he might use:

- Downplay the importance of grades rather than threatening students with failing grades.
- Describe what he means by a "decent essay" in specific, concrete terms so that students have a clear goal toward which they can direct their efforts. For example, he might distribute copies of a scoring guide (rubric) he will use to evaluate students' papers. (See Chapter 16 for more about the nature of rubrics.)

- Give more specific feedback about what students are doing well and how they can improve.

Additional possibilities are presented in the Into the Classroom feature "Promoting Intrinsic Motivation" on page 409.

Chapter 13: Uncooperative Students (p. 476)

■ *Why have Ms. Mihara's cooperative learning groups not been as productive as she had hoped? Considering the features of cooperative learning that we examined in this chapter, what did Ms. Mihara do wrong?*

If we consider recommended procedures for conducting a cooperative learning activity, we can identify at least three things Ms. Mihara has done wrong:

- She let students form their own groups, so the groups were not necessarily ones that would be able to work effectively together.
- The objective of the activity was ambiguous. Students were told only to find information and give an oral report.
- She did nothing to ensure that all students would participate actively in the activity.

■ *How might you orchestrate the cooperative learning unit differently than Ms. Mihara?* You might

- Form the groups yourself, making sure that each one is heterogeneous in membership.
- Present a clear goal toward which each group should strive (e.g., to identify religious affiliations, national and religious holidays, typical diets, and so on).
- Create one or more unique roles for each group member (e.g., researcher, secretary, presenter, coordinator, and the like), so that each student's involvement is essential for overall group success.
- Assess what each student has learned (ensuring individual accountability).

Chapter 14: Old Friends (p. 509)

■ *Why is Mr. Schulak having so much difficulty bringing his classroom to order? What critical things has Mr. Schulak not done in his first week of teaching?*

Mr. Schulak has not established a businesslike atmosphere; he has instead established one that seems to be all fun and games. Furthermore, he has not set any limits for behavior—something he should have done in the first few days of class.

■ *Given that Mr. Schulak has gotten the school year off on the wrong foot, what might he do now to remedy the situation?*

He needs to emphasize that there are instructional objectives his students must achieve this year and that it is time to get down to business. He might involve his classes in a discussion of some reasonable rules and procedures for accomplishing those objectives; this strategy should be motivating for students in that it will enhance their sense of self-determination and give them ownership of the rules and procedures by which the class will operate. After his rocky start, Mr. Schulak should not expect overnight success; it may take a while for his students to become focused on their schoolwork, and he will have to be consistent about enforcing the new rules and procedures.

Chapter 15: Can Johnny Read? (p. 550)

■ *Ms. Beaudry has chosen the wrong test for her purpose. What specifically did she do wrong?*

Ms. Beaudry has apparently chosen a test that yields only stanines, norm-referenced scores that allow her to compare each student's performance to that of a national norm group of the same age or grade level. The test does not tell her specifically whether her students have acquired certain reading skills. To get such information, she should ideally use a test that yields criterion-referenced scores.

■ *Was Ms. Beaudry's approach to determining test validity appropriate in this situation? Why or why not?*

Yes, Ms. Beaudry's approach was appropriate. When measuring achievement in a particular content domain (such as reading), one should be most concerned with a test's *content* validity. The best way to determine content validity is to look at the match between the test and the curriculum, perhaps by using a table of specifications.

■ *Ms. Beaudry eliminated one test on the basis of reliability coefficients below .85. Was this a good decision? Why or why not?*

Yes, it was a good decision. Many published achievement tests have reliability coefficients of .90 or above, so there is no reason to settle for anything less.

Chapter 16: Pick and Choose (p. 591)

■ *What mistakes does Mr. Bloskas make in developing the first quiz? What mistakes does he make in developing the second quiz? Are the quizzes likely to have content validity? Why or why not?*

In constructing the first quiz, Mr. Bloskas does not match his questions to his objectives, which presumably go beyond rote memorization of trivial details. He would be wise to construct a table of specifications first and then either find or construct quiz items that assess both the key ideas of the unit and the specific behaviors he wants students to demonstrate in relation to those ideas. In constructing the second quiz, Mr. Bloskas gives only two essay questions, which may not provide an adequate sample of the content domain. Both quizzes, then, may have questionable content validity—the first because it does not focus on desired behaviors, and the second because it is too restricted in the topics that it covers.

■ *Why do the students react as negatively as they do to the second quiz?*

Mr. Bloskas has neglected to consider the effects that classroom assessment practices have on students' future studying and learning. Expecting the second quiz to be similar to the first, his students probably studied for the quiz by memorizing trivial details rather than thinking about ways to apply what they had learned. Students should know what to expect on a classroom assessment instrument so that they can prepare accordingly. Any radical changes in the nature of assessment from one time to the next should be clearly described ahead of time; for example, a teacher might show students a few questions similar to those that will be on an upcoming quiz.

APPENDIX C
Matching Book and Ancillary Content to the PRAXIS™ Principles of Learning and Teaching Tests

In the United States, state teacher licensing requirements in approximately thirty-five states include passing PRAXIS tests published by Educational Testing Service (ETS). Among the PRAXIS tests are three Principles of Learning and Teaching (PLT) tests, one each for teachers seeking licensure for grades K–6, 5–9, and 7–12. *Educational Psychology: Developing Learners* addresses most of the topics covered in the PLT tests. In the left column of Table C.1, I present the topics covered on the tests, as identified in the *Principles of Learning and Teaching Study Guide* (Educational Testing Service, 2001). In the middle column of the table, I indicate chapters and sections in *Educational Psychology: Developing Learners* that are relevant to these topics. In the right column, I suggest appropriate exercises and readings in the *Study Guide and Reader* that accompanies the textbook, as well as activities on the *Simulations in Educational Psychology and Research* CD packaged with the book.

The PRAXIS tests involve reading and analyzing case studies. For this reason, the case studies presented in *Educational Psychology: Developing Learners* may be especially helpful as you prepare for these tests. The opening case in each chapter is addressed in several places throughout the chapter. The ending case poses questions that encourage you to apply chapter content; I urge you to develop your own answers to these questions before looking at how I answer them in Appendix B. You will find additional cases in the Interpreting Artifacts and Interactions features in the textbook, in the Application Exercises in the *Study Guide and Reader,* and in each of the five activities on the *Simulations in Educational Psychology and Research* CD.

You may also want to obtain a copy of the *Principles of Learning and Teaching Study Guide* that ETS publishes to assist students as they prepare for the PRAXIS tests. This guide provides practice case studies and offers suggestions for analyzing them and for responding to test questions. You can purchase a copy online at http://www.ets.org/store.html. Once there, select *Teaching and Learning* and, on the next screen, *Praxis Products.* On the following screen, scroll down until you find *A Guide to the Principles of Learning and Teaching Tests.*

TABLE C.1

Matching Book and Ancillary Content to the PRAXIS™ Principles of Learning and Teaching Tests

TOPICS IN THE PRAXIS™ PRINCIPLES OF LEARNING AND TEACHING TESTS	WHERE TOPICS APPEAR IN ORMROD'S *EDUCATIONAL PSYCHOLOGY* (4TH ED.)	WHERE TOPICS AND PRACTICE OPPORTUNITIES APPEAR IN STUDENT SUPPLEMENTS
I. Students as Learners (approximately 35% of total score)		
A. Student Development and the Learning Process		
1. Theoretical foundations about how learning occurs: how students construct knowledge, acquire skills, and develop habits of mind	**Chapters 6–10:** Entire chapters **Chapter 2:** "An Information Processing View of Cognitive Development" (pp. 42–48)	**Study Guide and Reader:** Application Exercises 9–18 (pp. 88–93, 103–106, 119–122, 137–141, 153–158); Supplementary Reading 8, "Learning in the Content Areas" (pp. 307–358) **Simulations CD:** "Bartlett's Ghosts"; "Intuitive Physics"; "Assessment in the Balance"
Examples of important theorists: • Albert Bandura	**Chapter 10:** Entire chapter; especially see "Basic Assumptions of Social Cognitive Theory" (pp. 334–335)	**Study Guide and Reader:** Application Exercises 17, 18 (pp. 153–158)
• Jerome Bruner		
• John Dewey		
• Jean Piaget	**Chapter 2:** "Piaget's Theory of Cognitive Development" (pp. 23–36) **Chapter 6:** Figure 6.1 (p. 190); "Meaningful Learning" (pp. 203–206)	**Study Guide and Reader:** Application Exercises 3, 4 (pp. 30–35)
• Lev Vygotsky	**Chapter 2:** "Vygotsky's Theory of Cognitive Development" (pp. 36–42); "General Themes in Cognitive and Linguistic Development" (pp. 57–58) **Chapter 6:** Figure 6.1 (p. 190); "How Procedural Knowledge Is Learned" (pp. 210–211) **Chapter 10:** "Self-Instructions" (p. 352) **Chapter 13:** "Reciprocal Teaching" (pp. 459–462); "Peer Tutoring" (pp. 467–471)	**Study Guide and Reader:** Application Exercise 2 (pp. 28–29)
• Howard Gardner	**Chapter 4:** "Gardner's Theory of Multiple Intelligences" (pp. 108–111); Table 4.2 (p. 109)	
• Abraham Maslow	**Chapter 11:** "What Basic Needs Do People Have?" (pp. 373–377)	**Study Guide and Reader:** Application Exercises 19, 20 (pp. 168–171); Supplementary Reading 4, "Maslow's Hierarchy of Needs" (pp. 291–294)
• B. F. Skinner	**Chapter 9: "Case Study: The Attention Getter" (p. 299);** "Operant Conditioning" (pp. 305–314); "Shaping New Behaviors" (pp. 314–315); "Effects of Antecedent Stimuli and Responses" (pp. 315–318); "Using Intermittent Reinforcement" (p. 325)	**Study Guide and Reader:** Application Exercises 15, 16 (pp. 137–141); Supplementary Reading 6, "A Shocking Lesson" (pp. 299–302)
Important terms that relate to learning theory • Constructivism	**Chapter 2:** "Piaget's Basic Assumptions" (pp. 23–25) **Chapter 3:** "General Themes in Personal, Social, and Moral Development" (pp. 99–100) **Chapter 6:** "Basic Assumptions of Cognitive Psychology" (pp. 191–94); "Visual Imagery" (pp. 209–210); "Reconstruction Error" (pp. 218–219) **Chapter 7: "Case Study: Pulling It All Together" (pp. 227–228);** "Constructive Processes in Learning and Memory" (pp. 228–231); "Knowledge Construction as a Social Process" (pp. 231–232); "When Knowledge Construction Goes Awry: Origins and Effects of Misconceptions" (pp. 241–242); "Considering Diversity in Constructive Processes" (pp. 253–255); **"Case Study: Earth-Shaking Summaries" (pp. 255–256)** **Chapter 13:** "Class Discussions" (pp. 457–459)	**Study Guide and Reader:** Application Exercises 11, 12 (pp. 103–106); Supplementary Reading 8, "Learning in the Content Areas" (pp. 307–358) **Simulations CD:** "Bartlett's Ghosts"; "Assessment in the Balance"
• Metacognition	**Chapter 2:** "Metacognition" (pp. 46–48) **Chapter 8: "Case Study: A Question of Speed" (pp. 259–260);** "Metacognition and Study Strategies" (pp. 261–273); **"Case Study: Checks and Balances" (pp. 296–297)** **Chapter 13:** "Reciprocal Teaching" (pp. 459–462); "Cooperative Learning" (pp. 463–467) **Chapter 16:** "Assessment, Cognition, and Metacognition" (p. 554)	**Study Guide and Reader:** Application Exercise 13 (pp. 119–120); Supplementary Reading 8, "Learning in the Content Areas" (pp. 307–358)

TABLE C.1—continued

Matching Book and Ancillary Content to the PRAXIS™ Principles of Learning and Teaching Tests

TOPICS IN THE PRAXIS™ PRINCIPLES OF LEARNING AND TEACHING TESTS	WHERE TOPICS APPEAR IN ORMROD'S *EDUCATIONAL PSYCHOLOGY* (4TH ED.)	WHERE TOPICS AND PRACTICE OPPORTUNITIES APPEAR IN STUDENT SUPPLEMENTS
I. Students as Learners (approximately 35% of total score)—continued		
A. Student Development and the Learning Process—continued		
• Readiness	**Chapter 2:** "Role of the Brain in Cognitive Development" (p. 22); "Piaget's Basic Assumptions" (pp. 23–25)	
• Schemata	**Chapter 2:** "Piaget's Basic Assumptions" (pp. 23–25) **Chapter 7:** "Schemas and Scripts" (pp. 238–239)	**Study Guide and Reader:** Application Exercise 11 (pp. 103–104) **Simulations CD:** "Bartlett's Ghosts"
• Transfer	**Chapter 8:** "Transfer" (pp. 273–279)	**Study Guide and Reader:** Application Exercise 14 (pp. 121–122) **Simulations CD:** "Intuitive Physics"
• Scaffolding	**Chapter 2:** "Current Perspectives on Vygotsky's Theory" (pp. 38–42) **Chapter 5:** "Mental Retardation" (pp. 166–169) **Chapter 8:** "Identifying Important Information" (pp. 262–263); "Retrieving Relevant Prior Knowledge" (pp. 265–267); "Teaching Problem-Solving Strategies" (pp. 282–283); "Accommodating Students with Special Needs" (p. 295) **Chapter 13:** "Discovery Learning" (pp. 447–449); "Authentic Activities" (pp. 453–454); "Cooperative Learning" (pp. 463–490) **Chapter 14:** "Providing Structure" (pp. 489–490)	**Study Guide and Reader:** Supplementary Reading 8, "Learning in the Content Areas" (pp. 307–358)
• Bloom's taxonomy	**Chapter 13:** "Developing Useful Objectives" (pp. 432–436); Table 13.1 (p. 433)	
• Zone of proximal development	**Chapter 2:** "Vygotsky's Basic Assumptions" (pp. 36–38) **Chapter 5:** "Giftedness" (pp. 177–180)	**Study Guide and Reader:** Application Exercise 2 (pp. 28–29)
• Intrinsic and extrinsic motivation	**Chapter 9:** "Operant Conditioning" (pp. 305–314); "Strengths and Potential Limitations of Behavioral Approaches" (pp. 328–330) **Chapter 10:** "How Self-Efficacy Affects Behavior" (p. 346) **Chapter 11: "Case Study: Quick Draw" (pp. 367–368);** "Intrinsic Versus Extrinsic Motivation" (pp. 369–370) **Chapter 12:** "Self-Perceptions and Intrinsic Motivation" (pp. 390–397); "Expectancies and Values" (pp. 397–399); "Interest" (pp. 399–403); "Goals" (pp. 403–409); "The Big Picture" (pp. 422–424) **Chapter 15:** "Assessments as Tools" (pp. 512–513)	**Study Guide and Reader:** Application Exercises 19, 20 (pp. 168–171)
2. Human development in the physical, social, emotional, moral, and cognitive domains	**Chapters 2–3:** Entire chapters **Chapter 10:** "Factors in the Development of Self-Efficacy" (pp. 346–349) **Chapter 12:** "Developmental Trends in Attributions" (pp. 412–413); "Factors Influencing the Development of Attributions" (pp. 413–414) **Chapter 15:** "Developmental Differences" (p. 542)	**Study Guide and Reader:** Application Exercises 2–6 (pp. 28–36, 47–52); Supplementary Reading 2, "Physical Development Across Childhood and Adolescence" (pp. 277–285); Supplementary Reading 3, "Parenting Styles and Children's Behavior" (pp. 287–290); Supplementary Reading 8, "Learning in the Content Areas" (pp. 307–358) **Simulations CD:** "Pendulum Experiment"; "Assessing Moral Reasoning"; "Assessment in the Balance"
• The theoretical contributions of important theorists such as Erik Erikson, Lawrence Kohlberg, Carol Gilligan, Jean Piaget, Abraham Maslow, Albert Bandura, and Lev Vygotsky	**Chapter 2:** "Piaget's Theory of Cognitive Development" (pp. 23–36); "Vygotsky's Theory of Cognitive Development" (pp. 36–42); "An Information Processing View of Cognitive Development" (pp. 42–48); "Theoretical Perspectives on Language Development" (pp. 48–49) **Chapter 3:** "Erikson's Eight Stages of Psychosocial Development" (Figure 3.3, p. 68); "Development of Moral Reasoning: Kohlberg's Theory" (pp. 87–91); "Possible Gender Differences in Moral Reasoning: Gilligan's Theory" (p. 91) **Chapter 10:** Entire chapter; especially see "Modeling" (pp. 338–345) and "Self-Efficacy" (pp. 345–349) **Chapter 11:** "What Basic Needs Do People Have?" (pp. 373–377)	**Study Guide and Reader:** Application Exercises 2–5, 17–20 (pp. 28–35, 47–50, 153–158, 168–171); Supplementary Reading 4, "Maslow's Hierarchy of Needs" (pp. 291–294) **Simulations CD:** "Pendulum Experiment"; "Assessing Moral Reasoning"

continued

TABLE C.1—continued

Matching Book and Ancillary Content to the PRAXIS™ Principles of Learning and Teaching Tests

TOPICS IN THE PRAXIS™ PRINCIPLES OF LEARNING AND TEACHING TESTS	WHERE TOPICS APPEAR IN ORMROD'S *EDUCATIONAL PSYCHOLOGY* (4TH ED.)	WHERE TOPICS AND PRACTICE OPPORTUNITIES APPEAR IN STUDENT SUPPLEMENTS
I. Students as Learners (approximately 35% of total score)—continued		
A. Student Development and the Learning Process—continued		
• The major progressions in each developmental domain and the ranges of individual variation within each domain	**Chapter 2:** "Piaget's Stages of Cognitive Development" (pp. 25–32); "Current Perspectives on Piaget's Theory" (pp. 32–36); "An Information Processing View of Cognitive Development" (pp. 42–48); "Trends in Language Development" (pp. 49–53) **Chapter 3:** "Developmental Changes in Students' Self-Views" (pp. 67–73); "Peer Relationships" (pp. 73–78); "Perspective Taking" (pp. 79–81); "Development of Moral Reasoning: Kohlberg's Theory" (pp. 87–91); "Emotional Components of Moral Development" (p. 92); **"Case Study: A Discussion of Runaway Slaves" (p. 100)**	**Study Guide and Reader:** Application Exercises 3, 5 (pp. 30–33, 47–50); Supplementary Reading 2, "Physical Development Across Childhood and Adolescence" (pp. 277–285) **Simulations CD:** "Pendulum Experiment"; "Assessing Moral Reasoning"; "Assessment in the Balance"
• The impact of students' physical, social, emotional, moral, and cognitive development on their learning and how to address these factors when making instructional decisions	**Chapter 2:** "Piaget's Stages of Cognitive Development" (pp. 25–32); "Current Perspectives on Piaget's Theory" (pp. 32–36); "An Information Processing View of Cognitive Development" (pp. 42–48); "Trends in Language Development" (pp. 49–53) **Chapter 3:** "Development of a Sense of Self" (pp. 64–73); "Social Development" (pp. 73–86); "Moral and Prosocial Development" (pp. 86–95) **Chapter 5:** "Emotional and Behavioral Disorders" (pp. 160–163); "Mental Retardation" (pp. 166–169) **Chapter 14:** "Creating an Effective Classroom Climate" (pp. 482–485)	**Study Guide and Reader:** Application Exercises 4, 6, 20, 30 (pp. 34–35, 51–52, 170–171, 241–243); Supplementary Reading 8, "Learning in the Content Areas" (pp. 307–358) **Simulations CD:** "Pendulum Experiment"; "Assessing Moral Reasoning"
• How development in one domain, such as physical, may affect performance in another domain, such as social	**Chapter 2:** "Role of the Brain in Cognitive Development" (p. 22) **Chapter 3:** "Early Adolescence" (pp. 69–70); "Factors Affecting Progression Through Kohlberg's Stages" (pp. 89–90) **Chapter 4:** "Factors Interfering with School Success" (pp. 132–133) **Chapter 6:** "Learning and the Brain" (pp. 190–191)	**Study Guide and Reader:** Supplementary Reading 2, "Physical Development Across Childhood and Adolescence" (pp. 277–285)
B. Students as Diverse Learners		
1. Differences in the ways students learn and perform	**Chapter 4:** Entire chapter **Chapters 2–16:** "Diversity" sections (pp. 55–56, 96–98, 138–139, 180–181, 223, 253–255, 293–295, 328–330, 361–363, 384–386, 420–422, 471–473, 499–501, 587–589) **Chapter 2:** "Learning a Second Language" (pp. 53–55) **Chapter 3:** "Temperamental Differences" (p. 62); "Effects of Culture" (pp. 63–64)	**Study Guide and Reader:** Application Exercise 7 (pp. 63–64); Supplementary Reading 8, "Learning in the Content Areas" (pp. 307–358)
• Learning styles	**Chapter 2:** "Learning Strategies" (pp. 43–45) **Chapter 6:** "Accommodating Diversity in Cognitive Processes" (p. 223)	
• Multiple intelligences	**Chapter 4:** "Gardner's Theory of Multiple Intelligences" (pp. 108–111); Table 4.2 (p. 109)	
• Performance modes – Concrete operational thinkers – Visual and aural learners	**Chapter 1:** "An Example: Research on Visual-Spatial Thinking" (p. 6) **Chapter 2:** "Concrete Operations Stage" (pp. 28–29); Tables 2.1, 2.2 (pp. 27, 29) **Chapter 5:** "Learning Disabilities" (pp. 153–156) **Chapter 6:** "The Various Forms of Knowledge" (pp. 201–202); "Visual Imagery" (pp. 209–210)	**Simulations CD:** "Pendulum Experiment"
• Gender differences	**Chapter 3:** "Possible Gender Differences in Moral Reasoning: Gilligan's Theory" (p. 91) **Chapter 4:** "Gender Differences" (pp. 128–131); Table 4.3 (p. 129); **"Case Study: The Active and the Passive" (p. 141)** **Chapter 10:** "Characteristics of Effective Models" (pp. 340–342) **Chapter 11:** "Addressing Diversity in Motivation and Affect" (pp. 384–386) **Chapter 12:** "Gender Differences" (pp. 420–421) **Chapter 13:** "Considering Group Differences" (pp. 471–473) **Chapter 15:** "Cultural Bias" (pp. 543–545)	**Study Guide and Reader:** Application Exercise 7 (pp. 63–64)

TABLE C.1—continued

Matching Book and Ancillary Content to the PRAXIS™ Principles of Learning and Teaching Tests

TOPICS IN THE PRAXIS™ PRINCIPLES OF LEARNING AND TEACHING TESTS	WHERE TOPICS APPEAR IN ORMROD'S *EDUCATIONAL PSYCHOLOGY* (4TH ED.)	WHERE TOPICS AND PRACTICE OPPORTUNITIES APPEAR IN STUDENT SUPPLEMENTS
I. Students as Learners (approximately 35% of total score)—continued		
B. Students as Diverse Learners—continued		
• Cultural expectations and styles	**Chapter 1: "Case Study: More Than Meets the Eye" (pp. 1–2)** Chapter 3: "Effects of Culture" (pp. 63–64) **Chapter 4: "Case Study: Hidden Treasure" (pp. 103–104);** "Cultural and Ethnic Differences" (pp. 118–128); **"Case Study: The Active and the Passive" (p. 141)** Chapter 12: "Ethnic Differences" (p. 420) Chapter 13: "Considering Group Differences" (pp. 471–473) Chapter 14: "Defining and Responding to Misbehaviors" (p. 500)	**Study Guide and Reader:** Application Exercise 7 (pp. 63–64)
2. Areas of exceptionality in students' learning	**Chapter 5:** Entire chapter; especially see **"Case Study: Four Students" (pp. 143–144) and "Case Study: Quiet Amy" (p. 184)** **Chapters 1–16:** Students in Inclusive Settings tables (pp. 13, 56, 97, 139, 152, 222, 254, 294, 329, 362, 385, 422, 472, 502, 548, 588) **Chapters 2–4, 6–16:** "Students with Special Needs" sections (pp. 55–56, 96–98, 138–139, 223, 254–255, 295, 328–330, 362–363, 385–386, 421–422, 473, 501, 547–548, 589) **Chapter 10:** "Factors in the Development of Self-Efficacy" (pp. 346–349)	**Study Guide and Reader:** Application Exercise 8 (pp. 75–76)
• Visual and perceptual difficulties	**Chapter 5:** Figure 5.2 (p. 153)	
• Special physical or sensory challenges	**Chapter 5:** "Students with Physical and Sensory Challenges" (pp. 169–177)	
• Learning disabilities	**Chapter 5:** "Learning Disabilities" (pp. 153–156) **Chapter 10:** "Factors in the Development of Self-Efficacy" (pp. 346–349)	**Study Guide and Reader:** Supplementary Reading 8, "Learning in the Content Areas" (pp. 307–358)
• Attention Deficit Disorder (ADD): Attention Deficit-Hyperactivity Disorder (ADHD)	**Chapter 5:** "Attention-Deficit Hyperactivity Disorder (ADHD)" (pp. 156–158)	**Study Guide and Reader:** Supplementary Reading 8, "Learning in the Content Areas" (pp. 307–358)
• Functional mental retardation	**Chapter 5:** "Mental Retardation" (pp. 166–169)	
3. Legislation and institutional responsibilities relating to exceptional students		
• Americans with Disabilities Act (ADA)		
• Individuals with Disabilities Education Act (IDEA)	**Chapter 5:** "Public Law 94-142: The Individuals with Disabilities Education Act (IDEA)" (pp. 145–147)	
• Inclusion, Mainstreaming, and "Least Restrictive Environment"	**Chapter 5:** "Educating Students with Special Needs in General Education Classrooms" (pp. 144–149) **Chapters 1–16:** Students in Inclusive Settings tables (pp. 13, 56, 97, 139, 152, 222, 254, 294, 329, 362, 385, 422, 472, 502, 548, 588)	
• IEP (Individual Education Plan), including what, by law, must be included in each IEP	**Chapter 5:** "Individualized Education Program (IEP)" (p. 147); Figure 5.1 (p. 148) **Chapter 16:** "Accommodating Students with Special Needs" (p. 589)	
4. Process of second language acquisition and strategies to support the learning of students for whom English is not a first language	**Chapter 2:** "Learning a Second Language" (pp. 53–55) **Chapter 15:** "Language Differences" (p. 545)	
5. Understanding of influences of individual experiences, talents, and prior learning, as well as language, culture, family and community values on students' learning	**Chapter 1: "Case Study: More Than Meets the Eye" (pp. 1–2)** **Chapter 3: "Case Study: The Bad Apple" (p. 61)** **Chapter 5:** "Considering Diversity When Identifying and Addressing Special Needs" (pp. 180–181) **Chapter 6: "Case Study: Darren's Day at School" (pp. 187–188)**	**Study Guide and Reader:** Supplementary Reading 3, "Parenting Styles and Children's Behavior" (pp. 287–290)

continued

TABLE C.1—continued

Matching Book and Ancillary Content to the PRAXIS™ Principles of Learning and Teaching Tests

TOPICS IN THE PRAXIS™ PRINCIPLES OF LEARNING AND TEACHING TESTS	WHERE TOPICS APPEAR IN ORMROD'S *EDUCATIONAL PSYCHOLOGY* (4TH ED.)	WHERE TOPICS AND PRACTICE OPPORTUNITIES APPEAR IN STUDENT SUPPLEMENTS
I. Students as Learners (approximately 35% of total score)—continued		
B. Students as Diverse Learners—continued		
• Multicultural backgrounds	**Chapter 3:** "Effects of Culture" (pp. 63–64); "Promoting Social Interaction Among Diverse Groups" (pp. 84–86) **Chapter 4:** "Cultural and Ethnic Differences" (pp. 118–128) **Chapter 6:** "Accommodating Diversity in Cognitive Processes" (p. 223) **Chapter 7:** "Considering Diversity in Constructive Processes" (pp. 253–255) **Chapter 15:** "Cultural Bias" (pp. 543–545); "Testwiseness" (pp. 545–547)	**Study Guide and Reader:** Application Exercises 7, 30 (pp. 63–64, 241–243)
• Age-appropriate knowledge and behavior	**Chapter 2: "Case Study: Economic Activities" (pp. 19–20);** "Piaget's Stages of Cognitive Development" (pp. 25–32); "An Information Processing View of Cognitive Development" (pp. 42–48); "Trends in Language Development" (pp. 49–53)	
• The student culture at school	**Chapter 3:** "Peer Relationships" (pp. 73–78); "Promoting Social Interaction Among Diverse Groups" (pp. 84–86) **Chapter 4:** "Navigating Different Cultures at Home and at School" (pp. 119–120)	
• Family backgrounds	**Chapter 3:** "Effects of Parenting" (pp. 62–63) **Chapter 4:** "Socioeconomic Differences" (pp. 131–134)	**Study Guide and Reader:** Supplementary Reading 3, "Parenting Styles and Children's Behavior" (pp. 287–290)
• Linguistic patterns and differences	**Chapter 2:** "Linguistic Development" (pp. 48–55) **Chapter 5:** "Speech and Communication Disorders" (pp. 158–159) **Chapter 15:** "Language Differences" (p. 545)	**Study Guide and Reader:** Application Exercise 7 (pp. 63–64)
• Cognitive patterns and differences	**Chapter 6:** "Accommodating Diversity in Cognitive Processes" (p. 223) **Chapter 7:** "Considering Diversity in Constructive Processes" (pp. 253–255)	**Simulations CD:** "Assessment in the Balance"
• Social and emotional issues	**Chapter 3:** "Emotional Components of Moral Development" (p. 92) **Chapter 5:** "Emotional and Behavioral Disorders" (pp. 160–163) **Chapter 11:** "Anxiety" (pp. 379–384) **Chapter 15:** "Test Anxiety" (pp. 542–543)	**Study Guide and Reader:** Application Exercises 20, 30 (pp. 170–171, 241–243)
6. Approaches for accommodating various learning styles, intelligences, or exceptionalities	**Chapter 4:** "Gardner's Theory of Multiple Intelligences" (pp. 108–111) **Chapter 5:** Entire chapter **Chapter 6:** "Accommodating Diversity in Cognitive Processes" (p. 223) **Chapters 2–16:** Students in Inclusive Settings tables (pp. 56, 97, 139, 152, 222, 254, 294, 329, 362, 385, 422, 472, 502, 548, 588)	
• Differentiated instruction	**Chapters 2–16:** "Diversity" sections (pp. 55–56, 96–98, 138–139, 180–181, 223, 253–255, 293–295, 328–330, 361–363, 384–386, 420–422, 471–473, 499–501, 587–589) **Chapters 2–16:** Students in Inclusive Settings tables (pp. 56, 97, 139, 152, 222, 254, 294, 329, 362, 385, 422, 472, 502, 548, 588)	
• Alternative assessments	**Chapter 5:** "Giftedness" (pp. 177–180) **Chapter 16:** "Informal Assessment" (pp. 554–557); "Performance Assessment" (pp. 570–578); "Taking Student Diversity into Account" (pp. 587–589)	
• Testing modifications	**Chapter 15:** "Accommodating Students with Special Needs" (pp. 547–548) **Chapter 16:** "Accommodating Students with Special Needs" (p. 589)	
C. Student Motivation and the Learning Environment		
1. Theoretical foundations about human motivation and behavior	**Chapters 11–12:** Entire chapters	**Study Guide and Reader:** Application Exercises 19–23 (pp. 168–171, 182–187)

TABLE C.1—continued

Matching Book and Ancillary Content to the PRAXIS™ Principles of Learning and Teaching Tests

TOPICS IN THE PRAXIS™ PRINCIPLES OF LEARNING AND TEACHING TESTS	WHERE TOPICS APPEAR IN ORMROD'S *EDUCATIONAL PSYCHOLOGY* (4TH ED.)	WHERE TOPICS AND PRACTICE OPPORTUNITIES APPEAR IN STUDENT SUPPLEMENTS
I. Students as Learners (approximately 35% of total score)—continued		
C. Student Motivation and the Learning Environment—continued		
• Abraham Maslow	**Chapter 11:** "What Basic Needs Do People Have?" (pp. 373–377)	**Study Guide and Reader:** Application Exercises 19, 20 (pp. 168–171); Supplementary Reading 4, "Maslow's Hierarchy of Needs" (pp. 291–294)
• Albert Bandura	**Chapter 10:** Entire chapter; especially see "The Social Cognitive View of Reinforcement and Punishment" (pp. 335–338); "Self-Efficacy" (pp. 345–349)	**Study Guide and Reader:** Application Exercises 17, 18, 21 (pp. 153–158, 182–183)
• B. F. Skinner	**Chapter 9:** "Operant Conditioning" (pp. 305–314)	**Study Guide and Reader:** Application Exercises 15, 16 (pp. 137–141); Supplementary Reading 6, "A Shocking Lesson" (pp. 299–302)
Important terms that relate to motivation and behavior • Hierarchy of needs	**Chapter 11:** "What Basic Needs Do People Have?" (pp. 373–377)	**Study Guide and Reader:** Supplementary Reading 4, "Maslow's Hierarchy of Needs" (pp. 291–294)
• Correlational and causal relationships	**Chapter 12: "Case Study: Passing Algebra" (pp. 389–390);** "Attributions: Perceived Causes of Success and Failure" (pp. 409–415)	**Study Guide and Reader:** Application Exercise 1 (pp. 13–15)
• Intrinsic motivation	**Chapter 8:** "The Role of Dispositions in Higher-Level Thinking" (pp. 292–293) **Chapter 9:** "Positive Reinforcement" (pp. 308–309); "Promoting Intrinsic Reinforcement" (pp. 324–325); "Strengths and Potential Limitations of Behavioral Approaches" (pp. 328–330) **Chapter 10:** "How Self-Efficacy Affects Behavior" (p. 346) **Chapter 11: "Case Study: Quick Draw" (pp. 367–368);** "Intrinsic Versus Extrinsic Motivation" (pp. 369–370) **Chapter 12:** "Self-Perceptions and Intrinsic Motivation" (pp. 390–397); "Expectancies and Values" (pp. 397–399); "Interest" (pp. 399–403); "Goals" (pp. 403–409); "The Big Picture" (pp. 422–424) **Chapter 15:** "Assessments as Tools" (pp. 512–513)	**Study Guide and Reader:** Application Exercises 19–21 (pp. 168–171, 182–183)
• Extrinsic motivation	**Chapter 9:** "Operant Conditioning" (pp. 305–314) **Chapter 11:** "Intrinsic Versus Extrinsic Motivation" (pp. 369–370) **Chapter 12:** "Goals" (pp. 403–409)	**Study Guide and Reader:** Application Exercises 16, 19–21 (pp. 139–141, 168–171, 182–183)
• Learned helplessness	**Chapter 12:** "Mastery Orientation Versus Learned Helplessness" (pp. 414–415); **"Case Study: Writer's Block" (p. 424)**	
• Self-efficacy	**Chapter 3:** "Development of a Sense of Self" (pp. 64–73) **Chapter 10: "Case Study: Parlez-vous français?" (p. 333);** "Self-Efficacy" (pp. 345–349); "Using Diverse Models to Promote Success and Self-Efficacy" (pp. 361–362) **Chapter 12:** "Self-Efficacy" (pp. 391–393)	**Study Guide and Reader:** Application Exercises 17, 18, 21 (pp. 153–158, 182–183)
• Operant conditioning	**Chapter 9:** "Operant Conditioning" (pp. 305–314)	**Study Guide and Reader:** Application Exercise 15 (pp. 137–138)
• Reinforcement	**Chapter 9: "Case Study: The Attention Getter" (p. 299);** "Reinforcement in the Classroom" (pp. 306–311); "Using Reinforcement Effectively" (pp. 311–314); "Reinforcing Incompatible Behaviors" (pp. 319–320) **Chapter 10:** "Vicarious Experiences" (pp. 336–337) **Chapter 14:** "Using Behaviorist Approaches" (pp. 498–499)	**Study Guide and Reader:** Application Exercise 15 (pp. 137–138)
• Positive reinforcement	**Chapter 9:** "Positive Versus Negative Reinforcement" (pp. 308–310)	**Study Guide and Reader:** Application Exercise 15 (pp. 137–138)

continued

TABLE C.1—continued

Matching Book and Ancillary Content to the PRAXIS™ Principles of Learning and Teaching Tests

TOPICS IN THE PRAXIS™ PRINCIPLES OF LEARNING AND TEACHING TESTS	WHERE TOPICS APPEAR IN ORMROD'S *EDUCATIONAL PSYCHOLOGY* (4TH ED.)	WHERE TOPICS AND PRACTICE OPPORTUNITIES APPEAR IN STUDENT SUPPLEMENTS
I. Students as Learners (approximately 35% of total score)—continued		
C. Student Motivation and the Learning Environment—continued		
• Negative reinforcement	**Chapter 9:** "Positive Versus Negative Reinforcement" (pp. 308–310)	**Study Guide and Reader:** Application Exercise 15 (pp. 137–138)
• Shaping successive approximations	**Chapter 9:** "Shaping New Behaviors" (pp. 314–315)	**Study Guide and Reader:** Supplementary Reading 6, "A Shocking Lesson" (pp. 299–302)
• Prevention	**Chapter 14:** "Creating an Environment Conducive to Learning" (pp. 480–492)	
• Extinction	**Chapter 9:** "Reducing and Eliminating Undesirable Behaviors" (pp. 318–324); **"Case Study: Hostile Helen" (p. 330)** **Chapter 14:** "Ignoring the Behavior" (pp. 593–594)	
• Punishment	**Chapter 9:** "Punishment" (pp. 320–324) **Chapter 10:** "Vicarious Experiences" (pp. 336–337)	
• Continuous reinforcement	**Chapter 9:** "Using Reinforcement Effectively" (pp. 311–314)	**Study Guide and Reader:** Application Exercise 16 (pp. 139–141)
• Intermittent reinforcement	**Chapter 9:** "Using Intermittent Reinforcement" (p. 325)	**Study Guide and Reader:** Application Exercise 16 (pp. 139–141)
2. How knowledge of human motivation and behavior should influence strategies for organizing and supporting individual and group work in the classroom	**Chapter 8:** "The Role of Dispositions in Higher-Level Thinking" (pp. 292–293) **Chapter 11:** Entire chapter; especially see "How Motivation Affects Learning and Behavior" (pp. 368–369); "Guiding Principles" (p. 386) **Chapter 12:** Entire chapter; especially see Table 12.3 (p. 423)	**Study Guide and Reader:** Application Exercises 16, 20, 21, 23 (pp. 139–141, 170–171, 182–183, 186–187)
3. Factors and situations that are likely to promote or diminish students' motivation to learn, and how to help students to become self-motivated	**Chapters 11–12:** Entire chapters **Chapter 8:** "The Role of Dispositions in Higher-Level Thinking" (pp. 292–293) **Chapter 10:** "Self-Regulation" (pp. 349–359) **Chapter 14:** "Promoting Self-Regulation" (pp. 496–498)	**Study Guide and Reader:** Application Exercises 18–21, 23 (pp. 156–158, 168–171, 182–183, 186–187)
4. Principles of effective classroom management and strategies to promote positive relationships, cooperation, and purposeful learning	**Chapter 14:** Entire chapter **Chapter 3:** "Fostering Social Skills" (pp. 82–84)	**Study Guide and Reader:** Application Exercise 26 (pp. 216–218)
• Establishing daily procedures and routines	**Chapter 14:** "Giving Students a Sense of Control" (p. 484); **"Case Study: Old Friends" (p. 509)**	
• Establishing classroom rules, punishments, and rewards	**Chapter 10:** "Expectations" (p. 336); "Nonoccurrence of Expected Consequences" (p. 338) **Chapter 14:** "Setting Limits" (pp. 485–488)	**Simulations CD:** "Assessing Moral Reasoning"
• Giving timely feedback	**Chapter 9:** "Positive Versus Negative Reinforcement" (pp. 308–310); "Importance of Timing" (p. 310) **Chapter 11: "Case Study: When 'Perfect' Isn't Good Enough" (p. 387)** **Chapter 14:** "Cueing the Student" (pp. 494–496); "Discussing the Problem Privately with the Student" (pp. 495–496) **Chapter 16:** "Scoring Students' Responses" (pp. 567–585)	
• Maintaining accurate records	**Chapter 16:** "Informal Assessment" (pp. 554–557); "Determining Final Class Grades" (pp. 582–585)	
• Communicating with parents and caregivers	**Chapter 5:** "Strategies for Helping All Students with Special Needs" (pp. 182–184) **Chapter 14:** "Conferring with Parents" (p. 499); "Working with Parents" (pp. 503–508) **Chapter 15:** "Communicating Classroom Assessment Results" (pp. 540–541)	

TABLE C.1—continued

Matching Book and Ancillary Content to the PRAXIS™ Principles of Learning and Teaching Tests

TOPICS IN THE PRAXIS™ PRINCIPLES OF LEARNING AND TEACHING TESTS	WHERE TOPICS APPEAR IN ORMROD'S *EDUCATIONAL PSYCHOLOGY* (4TH ED.)	WHERE TOPICS AND PRACTICE OPPORTUNITIES APPEAR IN STUDENT SUPPLEMENTS
I. Students as Learners (approximately 35% of total score)—continued		
C. Student Motivation and the Learning Environment—continued		
• Using objective behavior descriptions	**Chapter 3:** "Fostering Social Skills" (pp. 82–84) **Chapter 5:** "General Recommendations for Students with Social or Behavioral Problems" (pp. 164–166) **Chapter 9:** "Positive Versus Negative Reinforcement" (pp. 308–310); "Addressing Especially Difficult Classroom Behaviors" (pp. 325–328) **Chapter 14:** "Using Behaviorist Approaches" (pp. 498–499); "Accommodating Students with Special Needs" (p. 501)	
• Responding to student misbehavior	**Chapter 9:** "Addressing Especially Difficult Classroom Behaviors" (pp. 325–328) **Chapter 14:** "Dealing with Misbehaviors" (pp. 492–499)	**Study Guide and Reader:** Application Exercise 27 (pp. 219–222)
• Arranging of classroom space	**Chapter 14:** "Arranging the Classroom" (pp. 481–482)	
• Pacing and structuring the lesson	**Chapter 5:** "Mental Retardation" (pp. 166–169) **Chapter 6: "Case Study: How Time Flies" (p. 224)** **Chapter 13:** Table 13.2 (p. 440) **Chapter 14:** "Planning Activities That Keep Students on Task" (pp. 488–490)	
II. Instruction and Assessment (approximately 35% of total score)		
A. Instructional Strategies		
1. Major cognitive processes associated with student learning	**Chapters 6–8:** Entire chapters **Chapter 13: "Case Study: Oregon Trail" (pp. 427–429)**	**Study Guide and Reader:** Application Exercises 9–14 (pp. 88–93, 103–106, 119–122); Supplementary Reading 8, "Learning in the Content Areas" (pp. 307–358)
• Critical thinking	**Chapter 8:** "Critical Thinking" (pp. 290–292)	
• Creative thinking	**Chapter 4:** "Creativity" (pp. 114–118)	
• Higher-order thinking	**Chapter 8:** Entire chapter; especially see "The Nature of Higher-Level Thinking" (pp. 260–261); "The Role of Dispositions in Higher-Level Thinking" (pp. 292–293)	
• Inductive and deductive thinking	**Chapter 2:** "Piaget's Stages of Cognitive Development" (pp. 25–32) **Chapter 8:** "Critical Thinking" (pp. 290–292)	**Study Guide and Reader:** Supplementary Reading 8, "Learning in the Content Areas" (pp. 307–358)
• Problem-structuring and problem-solving	**Chapter 8:** "Problem Solving" (pp. 279–290)	**Study Guide and Reader:** Application Exercise 14 (pp. 121–122); Supplementary Reading 8, "Learning in the Content Areas" (pp. 307–358) **Simulations CD:** "Assessment in the Balance"
• Invention	**Chapter 4:** "Creativity" (pp. 114–118)	
• Memorization and recall	**Chapter 6:** Entire chapter	**Study Guide and Reader:** Application Exercises 9–12 (pp. 88–93, 103–106)
2. Major categories, advantages, and appropriate uses of instructional strategies	**Chapter 13:** Entire chapter **Chapter 15:** "Promoting Learning" (pp. 515–516)	**Study Guide and Reader:** Application Exercise 25 (pp. 201–205)
• Cooperative learning	**Chapter 7:** "Benefits of Group Meaning-Making in the Classroom" (pp. 231–232) **Chapter 13:** "Cooperative Learning" (pp. 463–467); **"Case Study: Uncooperative Students" (p. 476)**	
• Direct instruction	**Chapter 13:** "Direct Instruction" (pp. 444–445)	
• Discovery learning	**Chapter 13:** "Discovery Learning" (pp. 447–449)	

continued

TABLE C.1—continued

Matching Book and Ancillary Content to the PRAXIS™ Principles of Learning and Teaching Tests

TOPICS IN THE PRAXIS™ PRINCIPLES OF LEARNING AND TEACHING TESTS	WHERE TOPICS APPEAR IN ORMROD'S *EDUCATIONAL PSYCHOLOGY* (4TH ED.)	WHERE TOPICS AND PRACTICE OPPORTUNITIES APPEAR IN STUDENT SUPPLEMENTS
II. Instruction and Assessment (approximately 35% of total score)—continued		
A. Instructional Strategies—continued		
• Whole-group discussion	**Chapter 7:** "Benefits of Group Meaning-Making in the Classroom" (pp. 231–232); "Promoting Dialogue" (pp. 246–247) **Chapter 13:** "Class Discussions" (pp. 457–459)	**Study Guide and Reader:** Supplementary Reading 8, "Learning in the Content Areas" (pp. 307–358)
• Independent study	**Chapter 5:** "Giftedness" (pp. 177–180) **Chapter 13:** "Computer-Based Instruction" (pp. 445–446)	**Study Guide and Reader:** Supplementary Reading 6, "A Shocking Lesson" (pp. 299–302)
• Interdisciplinary instruction	**Chapter 6:** "Making Multiple Connections with Existing Knowledge" (pp. 215–216) **Chapter 8:** "Factors Affecting Transfer" (pp. 275–278); "Depth and Integration of Knowledge Relevant to the Problem" (pp. 286–287)	
• Concept mapping	**Chapter 8:** "Organizing" (pp. 265–267) **Chapter 13:** Table 13.2 (p. 440)	
• Inquiry method	**Chapter 7:** "Providing Opportunities for Experimentation" (p. 243)	**Study Guide and Reader:** Supplementary Reading 8, "Learning in the Content Areas" (pp. 307–358)
• Questioning	**Chapter 4:** "Fostering Creativity in the Classroom" (pp. 115–118) **Chapter 8:** "The Nature of Higher-Level Thinking" (pp. 260–261) **Chapter 13:** "Teacher Questions" (pp. 455–457)	**Simulations CD:** "Pendulum Experiment"; "Assessing Moral Reasoning"; "Bartlett's Ghosts"
3. Methods for enhancing student learning through the use of a variety of resources and materials		
• Computers, Internet resources, Web pages, e-mail	**Chapter 5:** "General Recommendations for Students with Physical and Sensory Challenges" (pp. 174–177) **Chapter 7:** "Creating a Community of Learners" (pp. 248–249) **Chapter 13:** "Computer-Based Instruction" (pp. 445–446); "Online Research" (p. 446); "Computer Simulations and Applications" (pp. 450–451); "Technology-Based Discussions" (pp. 462–463)	**Study Guide and Reader:** Application Exercise 25 (pp. 201–205); Supplementary Reading 6, "A Shocking Lesson" (pp. 299–302)
• Audio-visual technologies such as videos and compact discs	**Chapter 5:** "General Recommendations for Students with Physical and Sensory Challenges" (pp. 174–177) **Chapter 8:** "Using Computer Technology to Promote Effective Problem Solving" (pp. 288–290) **Chapter 10:** "Using Diverse Models to Promote Success and Self-Efficacy" (pp. 361–362)	
• Local experts	**Chapter 5:** "Giftedness" (pp. 177–180)	
• Primary documents and artifacts		**Study Guide and Reader:** Supplementary Reading 8, "Learning in the Content Areas" (pp. 307–358)
• Field trips	**Chapter 5:** "Students with Physical and Sensory Challenges" (pp. 169–177)	**Study Guide and Reader:** Chapter 13 (see "Answers to Selected Margin Notes," pp. 206–207)
• Libraries		
• Service learning	**Chapter 3:** "Promoting Moral Development in the Classroom" (pp. 93–95)	
4. Principles, techniques, and methods associated with major instructional strategies, especially direct instruction and student-centered models	**Chapter 13:** Entire chapter	**Study Guide and Reader:** Application Exercises 10, 25 (pp. 90–93, 201–205)
<u>Direct Instruction</u> • Madeline Hunter's "Effective Teaching Model"		

TABLE C.1—continued

Matching Book and Ancillary Content to the PRAXIS™ Principles of Learning and Teaching Tests

TOPICS IN THE PRAXIS™ PRINCIPLES OF LEARNING AND TEACHING TESTS	WHERE TOPICS APPEAR IN ORMROD'S *EDUCATIONAL PSYCHOLOGY* (4TH ED.)	WHERE TOPICS AND PRACTICE OPPORTUNITIES APPEAR IN STUDENT SUPPLEMENTS
II. Instruction and Assessment (approximately 35% of total score)—continued		
A. Instructional Strategies—continued		
• David Ausubel's "Advance Organizers"	**Chapter 8:** Table 8.2 (p. 272)	**Study Guide and Reader:** Application Exercise 25 (pp. 201–205)
• Mastery learning	**Chapter 13:** "Mastery Learning" (pp. 441–444)	
• Demonstrations	**Chapter 10:** "Modeling" (pp. 338–345); "Successes and Failures of Others" (p. 348)	**Study Guide and Reader:** Application Exercises 17, 18 (pp. 153–158) **Simulations CD:** "Bartlett's Ghosts"
• Mnemonics	**Chapter 5:** "Learning Disabilities" (pp. 153–156) **Chapter 6:** "Using Mnemonics in the Absence of Relevant Prior Knowledge" (pp. 212–214)	
• Note-taking	**Chapter 8:** "Taking Notes" (pp. 263–265)	
• Outlining	**Chapter 8:** "Organizing" (pp. 265–267)	
• Use of visual aids	**Chapter 5:** "Visual Impairments" (pp. 171–172) **Chapter 6:** "Visual Imagery" (pp. 209–210) **Chapter 13:** Table 13.2 (p. 440)	
Student-Centered Models • Inquiry model	**Chapter 7:** "Providing Opportunities for Experimentation" (p. 243)	
• Discovery learning	**Chapter 13:** "Discovery Learning" (pp. 447–449)	
• Cooperative learning (pair-share, jigsaw, STAD, teams, games, tournaments)	**Chapter 13:** "Cooperative Learning" (pp. 463–467)	
• Collaborative learning	**Chapter 13:** "Cooperative Learning" (pp. 463–467); "Peer Tutoring" (pp. 467–471)	
• Concept models (concept development, concept attainment, concept mapping)	**Chapter 7:** "Concepts" (pp. 233–238) **Chapter 8:** "Organizing" (pp. 265–267) **Chapter 13:** Table 13.2 (p. 440)	**Study Guide and Reader:** Application Exercises 11, 12 (pp. 103–106) **Simulations CD:** "Intuitive Physics"; "Assessment in the Balance"
• Discussion models	**Chapter 7:** "Creating a Community of Learners" (pp. 248–249) **Chapter 13:** "Class Discussions" (pp. 457–459); "Technology-Based Discussions" (pp. 462–463)	
• Laboratories		**Study Guide and Reader:** Supplementary Reading 8, "Learning in the Content Areas" (pp. 307–358); see **"Case Study: All Charged Up," pp. 357–358)**
• Project-based learning	**Chapter 7:** "Using Authentic Activities" (pp. 245–246) **Chapter 13:** "Authentic Activities" (pp. 453–454)	
• Simulations	**Chapter 13:** "Computer Simulations and Applications" (pp. 450–451)	**Simulations CD** (all activities)
B. Planning Instruction		
1. Techniques for planning instruction to meet curriculum goals, including the incorporation of learning theory, subject matter, curriculum development, and student development	**Chapter 13:** "Planning for Instruction" (pp. 430–438) **Chapter 14: "Case Study: A Contagious Situation" (pp. 479–480)**	
• National and state learning standards	**Chapter 13:** "National and International Standards" (p. 431); Figure 13.3 (p. 432)	
• State and local curriculum frameworks	**Chapter 13:** Figure 13.3 (p. 432; see Madison, WI, Web site address)	

continued

TABLE C.1—continued

Matching Book and Ancillary Content to the PRAXIS™ Principles of Learning and Teaching Tests

TOPICS IN THE PRAXIS™ PRINCIPLES OF LEARNING AND TEACHING TESTS	WHERE TOPICS APPEAR IN ORMROD'S *EDUCATIONAL PSYCHOLOGY* (4TH ED.)	WHERE TOPICS AND PRACTICE OPPORTUNITIES APPEAR IN STUDENT SUPPLEMENTS
II. Instruction and Assessment (approximately 35% of total score)—continued		
B. Planning Instruction—continued		
• State and local curriculum guides		
• Scope and sequence in specific disciplines	**Chapter 13:** "Taxonomies of Knowledge and Skills" (pp. 431–432); "Conducting a Task Analysis" (pp. 436–438)	
• Units and lessons	**Chapter 13:** "Developing a Lesson Plan" (p. 438)	**Study Guide and Reader:** Supplementary Reading 5, "Example of a Lesson Plan" (pp. 295–298)
• Behavioral objectives: affective, cognitive, psychomotor	**Chapter 13:** Table 13.1 (p. 433)	
• Learner objectives and outcomes	**Chapter 13:** "Identifying the Goals of Instruction" (pp. 430–436) **Chapter 16: "Case Study: Studying Europe" (pp. 553–554);** "Planning a Formal Assessment" (pp. 557–558); "General Guidelines for Classroom Assessment" (p. 590)	**Study Guide and Reader:** Application Exercises 24, 25 (pp. 199–205)
2. Techniques for creating effective bridges between curriculum goals and students' experiences		
• Modeling	**Chapter 10:** "Modeling" (pp. 338–345); "Using Diverse Models to Promote Success and Self-Efficacy" (pp. 361–362)	**Study Guide and Reader:** Application Exercises 17, 18 (pp. 153–158) **Simulations CD:** "Assessing Moral Reasoning"
• Guided practice	**Chapter 2:** "Guided Participation" (p. 39); "Scaffolding" (p. 39); "Apprenticeships" (pp. 40–41)	
• Independent practice, including homework	**Chapter 10:** "Self-Regulated Learning" (pp. 355–357) **Chapter 13:** "Homework" (pp. 451–453) **Chapter 14:** "Promoting Self-Regulation" (pp. 496–498)	**Study Guide and Reader:** Application Exercise 25 (pp. 201–205)
• Transitions	**Chapter 14:** "Planning for Transitions" (p. 490)	
• Activating students' prior knowledge	**Chapter 6:** "Moving Information to Long-Term Memory: Connecting New Information with Prior Knowledge" (p. 199); "Prior Knowledge and Working Memory in Long-Term Memory Storage" (pp. 211–212) **Chapter 8:** "Retrieving Relevant Prior Knowledge" (pp. 265–267) **Chapter 13:** Table 13.2 (p. 440)	**Study Guide and Reader:** Application Exercises 10, 25 (pp. 90–93, 201–205)
• Anticipating preconceptions	**Chapter 2: "Case Study: In the Eye of the Beholder" (pp. 58–59)** **Chapter 7:** "When Knowledge Construction Goes Awry: Origins and Effects of Misconceptions" (pp. 241–242); "Promoting Conceptual Change" (pp. 249–253)	**Study Guide and Reader:** Application Exercise 12 (pp. 105–106) **Simulations CD:** "Intuitive Physics"
• Encouraging exploration and problem-solving	**Chapter 2:** "Piaget's Basic Assumptions" (pp. 23–25) **Chapter 7:** "Providing Opportunities for Experimentation" (p. 243) **Chapter 8:** "Problem Solving" (pp. 279–290) **Chapter 10:** "Self-Regulated Problem Solving" (pp. 357–359) **Chapter 13:** "Discovery Learning" (pp. 447–449)	**Simulations CD:** "Pendulum Experiment"
• Building new skills on those previously acquired	**Chapter 4:** "Building on Students' Strengths" (p. 134) **Chapter 6:** "How Procedural Knowledge Is Learned" (pp. 210–211) **Chapter 9:** "Shaping New Behaviors" (pp. 314–315) **Chapter 12:** "Socioeconomic Differences" (p. 421) **Chapter 13:** "Mastery Learning" (pp. 441–444)	

TABLE C.1—continued

Matching Book and Ancillary Content to the PRAXIS™ Principles of Learning and Teaching Tests

TOPICS IN THE PRAXIS™ PRINCIPLES OF LEARNING AND TEACHING TESTS	WHERE TOPICS APPEAR IN ORMROD'S *EDUCATIONAL PSYCHOLOGY* (4TH ED.)	WHERE TOPICS AND PRACTICE OPPORTUNITIES APPEAR IN STUDENT SUPPLEMENTS
II. Instruction and Assessment (approximately 35% of total score)—continued		
C. Assessment Strategies		
1. Types of assessments	**Chapter 15:** "The Various Forms of Educational Assessment" (pp. 513–514) **Chapter 16:** "Informal Assessment" (pp. 554–557); "Paper-Pencil Assessment" (pp. 558–570); "Performance Assessment" (pp. 570–578) **Chapters 1–16:** Interpreting Artifacts and Interactions exercises (throughout chapters)	**Simulations CD:** "Assessment in the Balance"
• Standardized tests, norm-referenced or criterion-referenced	**Chapter 15:** "Standardization" (p. 522); "Standardized Tests" (pp. 526–530)	
• Achievement tests	**Chapter 15:** "Achievement Tests" (pp. 527–530); **"Case Study: Can Johnny Read?" (p. 550)**	
• Aptitude tests	**Chapter 15:** "Scholastic Aptitude Tests" (p. 528); "Specific Aptitude Tests" (p. 528)	
• Structured observations		**Simulations CD:** "Assessment in the Balance"
• Anecdotal notes	**Chapter 16:** "Informal Assessment" (pp. 554–557)	
• Assessments of prior knowledge	**Chapter 15:** "Guiding Instructional Decision Making" (pp. 516–517)	
• Student responses during a lesson	**Chapter 16:** "Informal Assessment" (pp. 554–557)	**Simulations CD:** "Pendulum Experiment"; "Assessing Moral Reasoning"
• Portfolios	**Chapter 16:** "Using Portfolios" (pp. 586–587)	**Study Guide and Reader:** Application Exercise 31 (pp. 254–258)
• Essays written to prompts	**Chapter 16:** "Essay Tasks" (pp. 564–565)	**Simulations CD:** "Assessment in the Balance"
• Journals	**Chapter 14:** "Showing Acceptance, Respect, and Caring" (pp. 482–483) **Chapter 16:** "Informal Assessment" (pp. 554–557)	
• Self-evaluations	**Chapter 10:** "Self-Regulation" (pp. 349–359) **Chapter 16:** "Including Students in the Assessment Process" (pp. 578–579); "Using Portfolios" (pp. 586–587)	
• Performance assessments	**Chapter 16:** "Performance Assessment" (pp. 586–587)	**Study Guide and Reader:** Application Exercise 31 (pp. 254–258)
2. Characteristics of assessments	**Chapter 16: "Case Study: Studying Europe" (pp. 553–554); "Case Study: Pick and Choose" (p. 591)**	
• Validity	**Chapter 15:** "Validity" (pp. 522–525) **Chapter 16:** "RSVP Characteristics of Informal Assessment" (pp. 555–557); "RSVP Characteristics of Paper-Pencil Assessment" (pp. 569–570); "RSVP Characteristics of Performance Assessment" (pp. 576–578)	**Study Guide and Reader:** Application Exercise 28 (pp. 237–238)
• Reliability	**Chapter 15:** "Reliability" (pp. 519–522) **Chapter 16:** "RSVP Characteristics of Informal Assessment" (pp. 555–557); "RSVP Characteristics of Paper-Pencil Assessment" (pp. 569–570); "RSVP Characteristics of Performance Assessment" (pp. 576–578)	**Study Guide and Reader:** Application Exercise 28 (pp. 237–238)
• Norm-referenced	**Chapter 15:** "Norm-Referenced Scores" (pp. 531–534); "Norm- Versus Criterion-Referenced Scores in the Classroom" (p. 535) **Chapter 16:** "Evaluating an Assessment Through Item Analysis" (pp. 580–582); "Choosing Criterion- or Norm-Referenced Grades" (pp. 584–585)	

continued

TABLE C.1—continued

Matching Book and Ancillary Content to the PRAXIS™ Principles of Learning and Teaching Tests

TOPICS IN THE PRAXIS™ PRINCIPLES OF LEARNING AND TEACHING TESTS	WHERE TOPICS APPEAR IN ORMROD'S *EDUCATIONAL PSYCHOLOGY* (4TH ED.)	WHERE TOPICS AND PRACTICE OPPORTUNITIES APPEAR IN STUDENT SUPPLEMENTS
II. Instruction and Assessment (approximately 35% of total score)—continued		
C. Assessment Strategies—continued		
• Criterion-referenced	**Chapter 15:** "Criterion-Referenced Scores" (p. 531); "Norm- Versus Criterion-Referenced Scores in the Classroom" (p. 535) **Chapter 16:** "Evaluating an Assessment Through Item Analysis" (pp. 580–582); "Choosing Criterion- or Norm-Referenced Grades" (pp. 584–585)	
• Mean, median, mode	**Chapter 15:** "Standard Scores" (pp. 533–534)	
• Sampling strategy	**Chapter 15:** "Content validity" (pp. 523–524) **Chapter 16:** "Obtaining a Representative Sample" (pp. 557–558)	
3. Scoring assessments	**Chapter 15:** "Reliability" (pp. 519–522) **Chapter 16:** "RSVP Characteristics of Informal Assessment" (pp. 555–557); "Paper-Pencil Assessment" (pp. 558–570); "Performance Assessment" (pp. 570–578); "General Guidelines for Classroom Assessment" (p. 590)	
• Analytical scoring	**Chapter 16:** "Performance Assessment" (pp. 570–578), especially the section "Scoring Students' Responses" (pp. 573–576)	
• Holistic scoring	**Chapter 16:** "Performance Assessment" (pp. 570–578), especially the section "Scoring Students' Responses" (pp. 573–576)	
• Rubrics	**Chapter 16:** "Paper-Pencil Assessment" (pp. 558–570), especially the section "Scoring Students' Responses" (pp. 567–569); Figures 16.2, 16.4 (pp. 569, 575)	
• Reporting assessment results – Percentile rank – Stanines – Mastery levels – Raw score – Scaled score – Grade equivalent score – Standard deviation – Standard error of measurement	**Chapter 15:** "Estimating Error in Assessment Results" (p. 521); "Types of Test Scores" (pp. 530–537); "Explaining Standardized Test Results" (p. 541)	**Study Guide and Reader:** Application Exercises 29, 30 (pp. 239–243); Supplementary Reading 7, "Calculating Standard Deviations" (pp. 303–306)
4. Uses of assessments	**Chapter 15:** "Using Assessment for Different Purposes" (pp. 514–518) **Chapters 1–16:** Interpreting Artifacts and Interactions exercises (throughout chapters)	**Simulations CD:** "Assessment in the Balance"
• Formative evaluation	**Chapter 15:** "Promoting Learning" (pp. 514–518); "Guiding Instructional Decision Making" (pp. 516–517)	
• Summative evaluation	**Chapter 15:** "Determining What Students Have Learned" (pp. 517–518)	
• Diagnostic evaluation	**Chapter 15:** "Diagnosing Learning and Performance Problems" (p. 517)	
5. Understanding of measurement theory and assessment-related issues	**Chapter 15:** "Important Qualities of Good Assessments" (pp. 518–526); "High-Stakes Testing and Accountability" (pp. 537–539); "Developmental Differences" (p. 542); "Test Anxiety" (pp. 542–543); "Cultural Bias" (pp. 543–545); "Language Differences" (p. 545); "Testwiseness" (pp. 545–547)	**Study Guide and Reader:** Application Exercise 31 (pp. 254–258)
III. Communication Techniques (approximately 15% of total score)		
A. Basic, effective verbal and nonverbal communication techniques		
	Chapter 4: "Helping Students at Risk Stay in School" (pp. 136–138) **Chapter 5:** "Using People-First Language" (p. 151) **Chapter 11:** "Case Study: When 'Perfect' Isn't Good Enough" (p. 387)	

TABLE C.1—continued

Matching Book and Ancillary Content to the PRAXIS™ Principles of Learning and Teaching Tests

TOPICS IN THE PRAXIS™ PRINCIPLES OF LEARNING AND TEACHING TESTS	WHERE TOPICS APPEAR IN ORMROD'S *EDUCATIONAL PSYCHOLOGY* (4TH ED.)	WHERE TOPICS AND PRACTICE OPPORTUNITIES APPEAR IN STUDENT SUPPLEMENTS
III. Communication Techniques (approximately 15% of total score)—continued		
B. Effect of cultural and gender differences on communications in the classroom		
	Chapter 12: "Self-Determination" (pp. 393–397); "Forming Productive Expectations and Attributions for Student Performance" (pp. 417–420) **Chapter 14:** "Creating an Effective Classroom Climate" (pp. 482–485); "Presenting Rules and Procedures as Information" (p. 487); "Discussing the Problem Privately with the Student" (pp. 495–496); "Working with Parents" (pp. 503–508) **Chapter 15: "Case Study: The Math Test" (pp. 511–512);** "Confidentiality and Communication About Assessment Results" (pp. 539–541) **Chapter 4:** "Sociolinguistic conventions" (pp. 121–122); "Eye contact" (p. 123)	
C. Types of questions that can stimulate discussion in different ways for particular purposes		
	Chapter 13: "Teacher Questions" (pp. 455–457)	
• Probing for learner understanding	**Chapter 5:** "Hearing Loss" (pp. 172–173) **Chapter 6:** "Attention in the Classroom" (p. 197)	**Simulations CD:** "Assessment in the Balance"
• Helping students articulate their ideas and thinking processes	**Chapter 6:** "Giving Students Time to Process: Effects of Increasing Wait Time" (pp. 220–221) **Chapter 7:** "Promoting Conceptual Change" (pp. 249–253)	**Simulations CD:** "Assessing Moral Reasoning"
• Promoting risk-taking and problem-solving	**Chapter 4:** "Creativity" (pp. 114–118) **Chapter 8:** "Problem Solving" (pp. 279–290)	**Simulations CD:** "Pendulum Experiment"
• Facilitating factual recall	**Chapter 6:** "Factors Affecting Retrieval" (pp. 215–218); "Giving Students Time to Process: Effects of Increasing Wait Time" (pp. 220–221)	
• Encouraging convergent and divergent thinking	**Chapter 4:** "Creativity" (pp. 114–118) **Chapter 6:** "Elaboration" (pp. 208–209)	
• Stimulating curiosity	**Chapter 13:** "Discovery Learning" (pp. 447–449)	
• Helping students to question	**Chapter 8:** "Elaborating" (pp. 267–268); "Monitoring Comprehension" (pp. 268–269); "Critical Thinking" (pp. 290–292)	
IV. Profession and Community (approximately 15% of total score)		
A. The Reflective Practitioner		
1. Types of resources available for professional development and learning		
• Professional literature	**Chapter 1:** "Developing as a Teacher" (pp. 10–11)	
• Colleagues	**Chapter 14:** "Working with Other Teachers" (pp. 501–502)	
• Professional associations	**Chapter 5:** "General Categories of Students with Special Needs" (pp. 150–152)	
• Professional development activities	**Chapter 1:** "Developing as a Teacher" (pp. 10–11)	
2. Ability to read and understand articles and books about current views, ideas, and debates regarding best teaching practices	**Chapter 1:** "Drawing Conclusions from Psychological and Educational Research" (pp. 4–7); **"Case Study: More Harm Than Good?" (p. 16)**	**Study Guide and Reader:** Application Exercise 1 (pp. 13–15)
3. Why personal reflection on teaching practices is critical, and approaches that can be used to do so	**Chapter 1:** "Drawing Conclusions from Psychological and Educational Research" (pp. 4–7); "Developing as a Teacher" (pp. 10–11)	

continued

TABLE C.1—continued

Matching Book and Ancillary Content to the PRAXIS™ Principles of Learning and Teaching Tests

TOPICS IN THE PRAXIS™ PRINCIPLES OF LEARNING AND TEACHING TESTS	WHERE TOPICS APPEAR IN ORMROD'S *EDUCATIONAL PSYCHOLOGY* (4TH ED.)	WHERE TOPICS AND PRACTICE OPPORTUNITIES APPEAR IN STUDENT SUPPLEMENTS
IV. Profession and Community (approximately 15% of total score)—continued		
B. The Larger Community		
1. Role of the school as a resource to the larger community		
2. Factors in the students' environment outside of school (family circumstances, community environments, health and economic conditions) that may influence students' life and learning	**Chapter 4:** "Heredity, Environment, and Group Differences" (p. 113); "Navigating Different Cultures at Home and at School" (pp. 119–120); "Family Relationships and Expectations" (p. 124); "Socioeconomic Differences" (pp. 131–134); "Students at Risk" (pp. 134–138) **Chapter 14:** "Defining and Responding to Misbehaviors" (p. 500)	**Study Guide and Reader:** Application Exercise 7 (pp. 63–64); Supplementary Reading 3, "Parenting Styles and Children's Behavior" (pp. 287–290)
3. Basic strategies for involving parents/guardians and leaders in the community in the educational process	**Chapter 5:** "Giftedness" (pp. 177–180); "Strategies for Helping All Students with Special Needs" (pp. 182–184) **Chapter 14:** "Working with the Community at Large" (pp. 502–503); "Working with Parents" (pp. 503–508)	
4. Major laws related to students' rights and teacher responsibilities		
• Equal education		
• Appropriate education for handicapped students	**Chapter 5:** "Public Law 94-142: The Individuals with Disabilities Education Act (IDEA)" (pp. 145–147) **Chapter 15:** "Language Differences" (p. 545); "Accommodating Students with Special Needs" (pp. 547–548)	**Study Guide and Reader:** Application 31 (pp. 254–258)
• Confidentiality and privacy	**Chapter 15:** "Confidentiality and Communication About Assessment Results" (pp. 539–541)	**Study Guide and Reader:** Application Exercise 30 (pp. 241–243)
• Appropriate treatment of students		
• Reporting in situations related to possible child abuse	**Chapter 5:** "Emotional and Behavioral Disorders" (pp. 160–163)	**Study Guide and Reader:** Supplementary Reading 3, "Parenting Styles and Children's Behavior" (pp. 287–290)

Glossary

Accommodation. In Piaget's theory, dealing with a new event by either modifying an existing scheme or forming a new one.

Accountability. Holding teachers and other school personnel responsible for students' performance on high-stakes assessments.

Achievement motivation. The need for excellence for its own sake, without regard for any external rewards that one's accomplishments might bring.

Action research. Research conducted by teachers and other school personnel to address issues and problems in their own schools or classrooms.

Activation. The degree to which a particular piece of information in memory is currently being attended to and mentally processed.

Activity reinforcer. An opportunity to engage in a favorite activity.

Actual developmental level. In Vygotsky's theory, the extent to which one can successfully perform a task independently.

Adaptive behavior. Behavior related to daily living skills and appropriate conduct in social situations; a deficit in adaptive behavior is used as a criterion for identifying students with mental retardation.

Adaptive testing. Computer-based assessment in which students' performance on early items determines which items are presented subsequently; allows more rapid measurement of a characteristic or ability than is possible in traditional paper-pencil testing.

Advance organizer. An introduction to a lesson that provides an overall organizational scheme for the lesson.

Affect. The feelings and emotions that an individual brings to bear on a task.

Affective domain. The domain of learning tasks that includes attitudes and values about the things one learns.

African American dialect. A dialect of some African American communities that includes some pronunciations, grammatical constructions, and idioms different from those of Standard English.

Age-equivalent score. A test score that indicates the age level of students to whom a student's test performance is most similar.

Aggressive behavior. Action intentionally taken to hurt another, either physically or psychologically.

Algorithm. A prescribed sequence of steps guaranteeing a correct problem solution.

Analytic scoring. Scoring students' performance on an assessment by evaluating various aspects of their performance separately.

Antecedent response. A response that increases the likelihood that another, particular response will follow.

Antecedent stimulus. A stimulus that increases the likelihood that a particular response will follow.

Anxiety. A feeling of uneasiness and apprehension concerning a situation with an uncertain outcome.

Applied behavior analysis (ABA). The systematic application of behaviorist principles in educational and therapeutic settings; sometimes known as *behavior modification*.

Apprenticeship. A situation in which a learner works intensively with an expert to learn how to accomplish complex tasks.

Assessment. The process of observing a sample of students' behavior and drawing inferences about their knowledge and abilities.

Assimilation. In Piaget's theory, dealing with a new event in a way that is consistent with an existing scheme.

Attachment. A strong, affectionate bond formed between a child and another individual (e.g., a parent); usually formed early in the child's life.

Attention. The focusing of mental processes on particular environmental stimuli.

Attention-deficit hyperactivity disorder (ADHD). A category of special needs marked either by inattention or by both hyperactivity and impulsive behavior (or by all three of these); such characteristics probably have a biological origin.

Attribution. An internally constructed causal explanation for one's success or failure.

Attribution theory. A theoretical perspective that focuses on people's attributions concerning the causes of events that befall them, as well as on the behaviors that result from such attributions.

Authentic activity. A classroom activity similar to one students are likely to encounter in the outside world.

Authentic assessment. Assessment of students' knowledge and skills in an authentic, "real-life" context; in many cases, an integral part of instruction rather than a separate activity.

Authoritative parenting. A parenting style characterized by emotional warmth, high expectations and standards for behavior, consistent enforcement of rules, explanations of the reasons behind these rules, and the inclusion of children in decision making.

Autism. A category of special needs characterized by impaired social interaction and communication, repetitive behaviors, restricted interests, and a strong need for a predictable environment; underlying the condition may be either an undersensitivity or an oversensitivity to sensory stimulation.

Automaticity. The ability to respond quickly and efficiently while mentally processing or physically performing a task.

Backup reinforcer. A reinforcer that a student can "purchase" with one or more tokens earned in a token economy.

Base group. A cooperative learning group that works together for an entire semester or school year and provides a means through which students can be mutually supportive of one another's academic efforts and activities.

Baseline. The frequency of a response before operant conditioning takes place.

Behavioral momentum. An increased tendency for an individual to make a particular response immediately after making similar responses.

Behaviorism. A theoretical perspective in which learning and behavior are described and explained in terms of stimulus-response relationships. Adherents to this perspective are called **behaviorists**.

Behavior modification. See *applied behavior analysis*.

Bilingual education. An approach to second-language instruction in which students are instructed in academic subject areas in their native language while simultaneously being taught to speak and write in the second language. The amount of instruction delivered in the native language decreases as students become more proficient in the second language.

Bloom's taxonomy. A taxonomy in which six learning tasks, varying in degrees of complexity, are identified for the cognitive domain: knowledge, comprehension, application, analysis, synthesis, and evaluation.

Challenge. A situation in which a person believes that he or she can probably succeed with sufficient effort.

Checklist. An assessment tool with which a teacher evaluates student performance by indicating whether specific behaviors or qualities are present or absent.

Classical conditioning. A form of learning whereby a new, involuntary response is acquired as a result of two stimuli being presented at the same time.

Classroom climate. The psychological atmosphere of the classroom.

Classroom management. Establishing and maintaining a classroom environment conducive to learning and achievement.

Clique. Moderately stable friendship group of perhaps three to ten members.

Cognitive apprenticeship. A mentorship in which a teacher and a student work together to accomplish a challenging task or solve a difficult problem; in the process, the teacher provides guidance about how to think about the task or problem.

Cognitive domain. The domain of learning tasks that includes knowledge of information, as well as ways of thinking about and using that information.

Cognitive processes. The ways in which one thinks about (processes) information.

Cognitive psychology. A theoretical perspective that focuses on the mental processes underlying human learning and behavior. Adherents to this perspective are sometimes called **cognitivists.**

Collective self-efficacy. People's beliefs about their ability to be successful when they work together on a task.

Community of learners. A classroom in which teacher and students actively and collaboratively work to help one another learn.

Comprehension monitoring. The process of checking oneself to make sure one understands the things being read or heard.

Computer-assisted instruction (CAI). Programmed instruction presented by means of a computer; it is one form of computer-based instruction.

Computer-based instruction (CBI). Instruction provided via computer technology.

Concept. A mental grouping of objects or events that have something in common.

Concept map. A diagram of concepts within an instructional unit and the interrelationships among them.

Conceptual change. Revising one's knowledge and understanding of a topic in response to new information about that topic.

Conceptual understanding. Knowledge acquired in an integrated and meaningful fashion.

Concrete operations stage. Piaget's third stage of cognitive development, in which adultlike logic appears but is limited to concrete reality.

Concrete reinforcer. A reinforcer that can be touched.

Conditioned response (CR). A response that, through classical conditioning, begins to be elicited by a particular stimulus.

Conditioned stimulus (CS). A stimulus that, through classical conditioning, begins to elicit a particular response.

Conditioning. Another word for learning; commonly used by behaviorists.

Confidence interval. A range around an assessment score reflecting the amount of error likely to be affecting the score's accuracy.

Conservation. The realization that if nothing is added or taken away, amount (e.g., number, mass) stays the same regardless of any alterations in shape or arrangement.

Construction. A mental process in which a learner takes many separate pieces of information and uses them to build an overall understanding or interpretation of an event.

Constructivism. A theoretical perspective that proposes that learners construct a body of knowledge from their experiences—knowledge that may or may not be an accurate representation of external reality. Adherents to this perspective are called **constructivists.**

Construct validity. The extent to which an assessment accurately measures an unobservable educational or psychological characteristic.

Content validity. The extent to which an assessment includes a representative sample of tasks within the content domain being assessed.

Contiguity. The occurrence of two or more events at the same time. **Contiguous** is the adjective used to refer to events having contiguity.

Contingency. A situation in which one event happens only after another event has already occurred. One event is **contingent** on another's prior occurrence.

Contingency contract. A formal agreement between a teacher and a student that identifies behaviors the student will exhibit and the reinforcers that will follow those behaviors.

Continuous reinforcement. Reinforcing a response every time it occurs.

Control group. A group of people in a research study who are given either no treatment or a presumably ineffective (placebo) treatment. The subsequent performance of this group is compared to the performance of one or more treatment groups.

Conventional morality. Acceptance of society's conventions regarding right and wrong; behaving to please others or to live up to society's expectations for appropriate behavior.

Convergent thinking. Pulling several pieces of information together to draw a conclusion or solve a problem.

Cooperative learning. An approach to instruction whereby students work with their classmates to achieve group goals and help one another learn.

Cooperative teaching. A general education teacher and special education teacher collaborating to teach all students in a class, including students both with and without special educational needs, throughout the school day.

Core goal. A long-term goal that drives much of what a person does.

Correlation. The extent to which two variables are related to each other, such that when one variable increases, the other either increases or decreases in a somewhat predictable way.

Correlational feature. In concept learning, a characteristic present in many positive instances of a concept but not essential for concept membership.

Correlational study. A research study that explores relationships among variables. Such a study enables researchers to predict one variable on the basis of their knowledge of another but not to draw a conclusion about a cause-effect relationship.

Correlation coefficient. A statistic that indicates the nature of the relationship between two variables.

Cortex. The upper part of the brain; site of conscious and higher-level thinking processes.

Creativity. New and original behavior that yields an appropriate and productive result.

Criterion-referenced score. A test score that specifically indicates what students know and can do.

Critical thinking. Evaluating the accuracy and worth of information or arguments.

Cueing. A teacher's use of signals to indicate that a particular behavior is desired or that a particular behavior should stop.

Cultural bias. The extent to which the items or tasks of an assessment instrument either offend or unfairly penalize some students because of their ethnicity, gender, or socio-economic status.

Cultural mismatch. A situation in which a child's home culture and the school culture hold conflicting expectations for the child's behavior.

Culture. Behaviors and belief systems of a particular social group.

Culture shock. A sense of confusion that occurs when a student encounters a culture with very different expectations for behavior than the expectations with which the student has been raised.

Debilitating anxiety. Anxiety that interferes with performance. A high level of anxiety is likely to be debilitating.

Decay. A hypothesized weakening over time of information stored in long-term memory, especially if the information is used infrequently or not at all.

Declarative knowledge. Knowledge related to "what is," to the nature of how things are, were, or will be (as opposed to *procedural knowledge,* which relates to how to do something).

Deductive reasoning. Drawing a logical inference about something that must be true, given other information that has already been presented as true.

Defining feature. In concept learning, a characteristic that must be present in all positive instances of a concept.

Delay of gratification. The ability to forego small, immediate reinforcers in order to obtain larger ones later on.

Descriptive study. A research study that describes situations. Such a study enables researchers to draw conclusions about the current state of affairs but not about correlational or cause-effect relationships.

Developmental milestone. The appearance of a new, developmentally more advanced behavior.

Dialect. A form of English (or other language) characteristic of a particular region or ethnic group.

Direct instruction. An approach to instruction that uses a variety of techniques (brief explanations, teacher questioning, rapid pacing, guided and independent practice) to promote learning of basic skills.

Discovery learning. An approach to instruction whereby students develop an understanding of a topic through firsthand interaction with the physical or social environment.

Discrimination. A phenomenon in operant conditioning whereby an individual learns that a response is reinforced in the presence of one stimulus but not in the presence of another, similar stimulus.

Disequilibrium. In Piaget's theory, an inability to explain new events by using existing schemes.

Disposition. A general inclination to approach and think about a task in a particular way.

Distance learning. A situation in which learners receive technology-based instruction at a location physically separate from their instructor.

Distributed cognition. A process whereby people think about an issue or problem together, sharing ideas and working collaboratively to draw conclusions or develop solutions.

Distributed intelligence. The idea that people are more likely to act "intelligently" when they have physical and/or social support systems to assist them.

Divergent thinking. Taking a single idea in many different directions.

Drive. A motivational state in which something necessary for optimal functioning (food, water, etc.) is missing.

Dynamic assessment. Examining how a student's knowledge or reasoning may change over the course of performing a specific task.

Educational psychology. A discipline encompassing psychological principles and theories related to learning, motivation, child and adolescent development, individual and group differences, and psychological assessment, especially as these topics relate to classroom practice.

Egocentric speech. Speaking without taking the perspective and knowledge of the listener into account.

Elaboration. A cognitive process in which learners expand on new information based on what they already know.

Elaborative interrogation. A study strategy in which students develop and answer knowledge-expanding (elaborative) questions about the material they are trying to learn.

Emotional and behavioral disorders. A category of special needs characterized by behaviors or emotional states that are present over a substantial period of time and significantly disrupt students' academic learning and performance.

Empathy. Experiencing the same feelings as someone in unfortunate circumstances.

Encoding. Changing the format of new information as it is being stored in memory.

Entity view of intelligence. A belief that intelligence is a "thing" that is relatively permanent and unchangeable.

Epistemological beliefs. One's beliefs about the nature of knowledge and knowledge acquisition.

Equilibration. In Piaget's theory, the movement from equilibrium to disequilibrium and back to equilibrium—a process that promotes the development of more complex forms of thought and knowledge.

Equilibrium. In Piaget's theory, a state of being able to explain new events by using existing schemes.

Equity (in instruction). Instruction without favoritism or bias toward particular individuals or groups of students.

Ethnic group. A group of people with a common set of values, beliefs, and behaviors. The group's roots either precede the creation of, or are external to, the country in which the group resides.

Ethnic identity. Awareness of one's membership in a particular ethnic or cultural group, and willingness to adopt certain behaviors characteristic of that group.

ETS score. A standard score with a mean of 500 and a standard deviation of 100.

Exemplar. A specific example that is an important part of a learner's general knowledge and understanding of a concept. Several exemplars taken together give the learner a sense of the variability that exists within any category of objects or events.

Expectancy. In motivation theory, the belief that one will be successful in accomplishing a task or achieving a goal.

Experimental study (experiment). A research study that involves the manipulation of one variable to determine its possible effect on another variable. It enables researchers to draw conclusions about cause-effect relationships.

Expository instruction. An approach to instruction whereby information is presented in more or less the same form in which students are expected to learn it.

Expressive language. The ability to communicate effectively through speaking and writing.

Externalizing behavior. A symptom of an emotional or behavioral disorder that has direct or indirect effects on other people (e.g., aggression, disobedience, stealing).

Extinction. In classical conditioning, the eventual disappearance of a conditioned response as a result of the conditioned stimulus being repeatedly presented alone (i.e., in the absence of the unconditioned stimulus). In operant conditioning, the eventual disappearance of a response that is no longer being reinforced.

Extrinsic motivation. Motivation promoted by factors external to the individual and unrelated to the task being performed.

Extrinsic reinforcer. A reinforcer that comes from the outside environment, rather than from within the individual.

Facilitating anxiety. Anxiety that enhances performance. Relatively low levels of anxiety are usually facilitating.

Failure to store. One's failure to mentally process information in ways that promote its storage in long-term memory.

Family Educational Rights and Privacy Act (FERPA). U.S. legislation passed in 1974 mandating that teachers and other school personnel (a) restrict access to students' test results and school records only to students, their parents, and school employees directly involved in the students' education; (b) upon request, make test scores and other information in students' records available for inspection by students and parents; and (c) help students and parents appropriately interpret this information.

Formal assessment. A systematic attempt to ascertain what students have learned. It is typically planned in advance and used for a specific purpose.

Formal discipline. A view of transfer that postulates that the study of rigorous subjects enhances one's ability to learn other, unrelated things.

Formal operational egocentrism. The inability of individuals in Piaget's formal operations stage to separate their own abstract logic from the perspectives of others and from practical considerations.

Formal operations stage. Piaget's fourth and final stage of cognitive development, in which logical reasoning processes are applied to abstract ideas as well as to concrete objects.

Formative evaluation. An evaluation conducted during instruction to facilitate students' learning.

Functional analysis. Examining a student's inappropriate behavior, as well as its antecedents and consequences, to determine the function(s) that the behavior might serve for the student.

g. The theoretical notion that intelligence includes a *general factor* that influences people's ability to learn in a wide variety of content domains.

Gang. A cohesive social group characterized by initiation rites, distinctive colors and symbols, territorial orientation, and feuds with rival groups.

Generalization. A phenomenon in both classical conditioning and operant conditioning whereby an individual learns a response to a particular stimulus and then makes the same response in the presence of similar stimuli.

General transfer. An instance of transfer in which the original learning task and the transfer task do not overlap in content.

Giftedness. A category of special needs characterized by unusually high ability in one or more areas, to the point where students require special educational services to help them meet their full potential.

Grade-equivalent score. A test score that indicates the grade level of students to whom a student's test performance is most similar.

Group contingency. A situation in which everyone in a group must make a particular response before reinforcement occurs.

Group differences. Consistently observed differences, on average, among certain groups of individuals.

Guided participation. Giving a child the necessary guidance and support to perform an activity in the adult world.

Guilt. The feeling of discomfort that individuals experience when they know that they have caused someone else pain or distress.

Halo effect. A phenomenon whereby people are more likely to perceive positive behaviors in a person they like or admire.

Hearing loss. A category of special needs characterized by malfunctions of the ear or associated nerves that interfere with the perception of sounds within the frequency range of normal human speech.

Heuristic. A general problem-solving strategy that may or may not yield a problem solution.

Higher-level question. A question that requires students to do something new with information they have learned—for example, to apply, analyze, synthesize, or evaluate it.

Higher-level thinking. Thought that involves going beyond information specifically learned (e.g., application, analysis, synthesis, evaluation).

High-stakes testing. Using students' performance on a single assessment instrument to make major decisions about students or school personnel.

Holistic scoring. Summarizing students' performance on an assessment with a single score.

Hostile attributional bias. A tendency to interpret others' behaviors (especially ambiguous ones) as reflecting hostile or aggressive intentions.

Hot cognition. Learning or cognitive processing that is emotionally charged.

Hypermedia. A collection of computer-based instructional material, including both verbal text and such other media as pictures, sound, and animations. The material is interconnected in such a way that students can learn about one topic and then proceed to related topics of their own choosing.

Hypertext. A collection of computer-based verbal material that allows students to read about one topic and then proceed to related topics of their own choosing.

Identity. A self-constructed definition of who a person thinks he or she is and what things are important in life.

Ill-defined problem. A problem in which the desired goal is unclear, information needed to solve the problem is missing, and/or several possible solutions to the problem exist.

Illusion of knowing. Thinking one knows something that one actually does not know.

Imaginary audience. The belief that one is the center of attention in any social situation.

Immersion. An approach to second-language instruction in which students hear and speak that language almost exclusively within the classroom.

Inability to retrieve. Failing to locate information that currently exists in long-term memory.

Incentive. A hoped-for, but not certain, consequence of behavior.

Inclusion. The practice of educating all students, including those with severe and multiple disabilities, in neighborhood schools and general education classrooms.

Incompatible behaviors. Two or more behaviors that cannot be performed simultaneously.

Incremental view of intelligence. The belief that intelligence can and does improve with effort and practice.

Individual constructivism. A theoretical perspective that focuses on how people, as individuals, construct meaning from the events around them.

Individual differences. The ways in which people of the same age are different from one another.

Individualized education program (IEP). A written description of an appropriate instructional program for a student with special needs. In the United States, an IEP is mandated by the Individuals with Disabilities Education Act (IDEA) for all students with disabilities.

Individuals with Disabilities Education Act (IDEA). U.S. legislation granting educational rights to people with cognitive, emotional, or physical disabilities from birth until age 21; it guarantees a free and appropriate education, fair and nondiscriminatory evaluation, education in the least restrictive environment, an individualized education program, and due process.

Induction. A method for encouraging moral development in which one explains why a certain behavior is unacceptable, often with a focus on the pain or distress that someone has caused another.

Informal assessment. Assessment that results from teachers' spontaneous, day-to-day observations of how students behave and perform in class.

Information processing theory. A theoretical perspective that focuses on the specific ways in which individuals mentally think about and "process" the information they receive.

Inner speech. "Talking" to oneself mentally rather than aloud.

In-school suspension. A form of punishment in which a student is placed in a quiet, boring room within the school building. It often lasts one or more school days and involves close adult supervision.

Instructional objective. A statement describing a final goal or outcome of instruction.

Intelligence. The ability to modify and adjust one's behaviors in order to accomplish new tasks successfully. It involves many different mental processes, and its nature may vary, depending on the culture in which one lives.

Intelligence test. A general measure of current cognitive functioning, used primarily to predict academic achievement over the short run.

Interest. A feeling that a topic is intriguing or enticing.

Interference. A phenomenon whereby something stored in long-term memory inhibits one's ability to remember something else correctly.

Intermittent reinforcement. Reinforcing a response only occasionally, with some occurrences of the response going unreinforced.

Internalization. In Vygotsky's theory, the process through which social activities evolve into mental activities.

Internalized motivation. The adoption of behaviors that others value, without regard for the external consequences of such behaviors.

Internalizing behavior. A symptom of an emotional or behavioral disorder that primarily affects the student with the disorder, with little or no effect on others (e.g., anxiety, depression).

Intrinsic motivation. The internal desire to perform a particular task.

Intrinsic reinforcer. A reinforcer provided by oneself or inherent in the task being performed.

IQ score. A score on an intelligence test. It is determined by comparing one's performance on the test with the performance of others in the same age-group; for most tests, it is a standard score with a mean of 100 and a standard deviation of 15.

Irreversibility. An inability to recognize that certain processes can be undone, or reversed.

Item analysis. An analysis of students' responses to the individual items of an assessment instrument; used to identify possibly flawed items.

Item difficulty (p). The proportion of students getting a particular assessment item correct. A high p value indicates an easy item; a low p value indicates a difficult item.

Item discrimination (D). The relative proportion of high-scoring and low-scoring students getting a particular assessment item correct. A positive D indicates that an item appears to discriminate between knowledgeable and unknowledgeable students; a negative D indicates that the item may be providing misinformation about what students know and can do.

Jigsaw technique. An instructional technique in which instructional materials are divided among members of a cooperative learning group, with individual students being responsible for learning different material and then teaching that material to other group members.

Keyword method. A mnemonic technique in which an association is made between two ideas by forming a visual image of one or more concrete objects (**keywords**) that either sound similar to, or symbolically represent, those ideas.

Knowledge base. One's knowledge about specific topics and the world in general.

Learned helplessness. A general belief that one is incapable of accomplishing tasks and has little or no control of the environment.

Learned industriousness. The recognition that one can succeed at some tasks only with effort, persistence, and well-chosen strategies.

Learning. A relatively permanent change, due to experience, in either behavior or mental associations.

Learning disabilities. A category of special needs characterized by lower academic achievement than would be predicted from students' IQ scores and a deficiency in one or more specific cognitive processes.

Learning strategy. One or more cognitive processes used intentionally for a particular learning task.

Least restrictive environment. The most typical and standard educational environment that can reasonably meet a student's needs.

Level of potential development. In Vygotsky's theory, the extent to which one can successfully execute a task with the assistance of a more competent individual.

Limited English proficiency (LEP). A limited ability to understand and communicate in oral or written English, usually because English is not one's native language.

Live model. An individual whose behavior is observed "in the flesh."

Logical consequence. A consequence that follows logically from a student's misbehavior; in other words, the punishment fits the crime.

Long-term memory. The component of memory that holds knowledge and skills for a relatively long period of time.

Long-term objective. An objective that requires months or years of instruction and practice to be accomplished.

Lower-level question. A question that requires students to express what they have learned in essentially the same way they learned it—for example, by reciting a textbook's definition of a concept or describing an application their teacher presented in class.

Mainstreaming. The practice of having students with special needs join general education classrooms primarily when their abilities enable them to participate in normally scheduled activities as successfully as other students.

Maintenance rehearsal. See *rehearsal*.

Mastery goal. A desire to acquire additional knowledge or master new skills.

Mastery learning. An approach to instruction whereby students learn one topic thoroughly before moving to a more difficult one.

Mastery orientation. A general belief that one is capable of accomplishing challenging tasks.

Maturation. The unfolding of genetically controlled changes as a child develops.

Mean (M). The arithmetic average of a set of scores. It is calculated by adding all the scores and then dividing by the total number of people who have obtained those scores.

Meaningful learning. A cognitive process in which learners relate new information to the things they already know.

Meaningful learning set. An attitude that one can make sense of the information one is studying.

Mediation training. Training that involves teaching students how to mediate conflicts among classmates by asking opposing sides to express their differing viewpoints and then work together to devise a reasonable resolution.

Memory. A learner's ability to save something (mentally) that he or she has previously learned, *or* the mental "location" where such information is saved.

Mental retardation. A category of special needs characterized by significantly below-average general intelligence and deficits in adaptive behavior.

Mental set. Encoding a problem in a way that excludes potential problem solutions.

Metacognition. One's knowledge and beliefs about one's own cognitive processes, and one's resulting attempts to regulate those cognitive processes to maximize learning and memory.

Metacognitive scaffolding. A support structure that guides students in their use of metacognitive strategies.

Metalinguistic awareness. The extent to which one is able to think about the nature of language.

Misbehavior. An action that has the potential to disrupt students' learning and planned classroom activities.

Misconception. Previously learned but incorrect information.

Mnemonic. A special memory aid or trick designed to help students learn and remember a specific piece of information.

Moral dilemma. A situation in which there is no clear-cut answer regarding the morally correct thing to do.

Motivation. A state that energizes, directs, and sustains behavior.

Multicultural education. Education that integrates the perspectives and experiences of numerous cultural groups throughout the curriculum.

Multiple classification. The recognition that objects may belong to several categories simultaneously.

Need for affiliation. The tendency to seek out friendly relationships with others.

Need for approval. A desire to gain the approval and acceptance of others.

Need for relatedness. The need to feel socially connected to others, as well as to secure their love and respect.

Negative instance. A nonexample of a concept.

Negative reinforcement. A consequence that brings about the increase of a behavior through the removal (rather than the presentation) of a stimulus.

Negative transfer. A phenomenon whereby something learned at one time interferes with learning or performance at a later time.

Negative wait time. The tendency to interrupt someone who has not yet finished speaking.

Neglected students. Students whom peers rarely select as people they would either really like or really *not* like to do something with.

Neuron. A cell in the brain or another part of the nervous system that transmits information to other cells.

Neutral stimulus. A stimulus that does not elicit any particular response.

Normal distribution (normal curve). A theoretical pattern of educational and psychological characteristics in which most individuals lie somewhere in the middle range and only a few lie at either extreme.

Norm-referenced score. A score that indicates how a student's performance on an assessment compares with the average performance of other students (i.e., with the performance of a norm group).

Norms. As related to socialization, society's rules for acceptable and unacceptable behavior. As related to testing practice, data regarding the typical performance of various groups of students on a standardized test or other norm-referenced assessment.

Object permanence. The realization that objects continue to exist even after they are removed from view.

Observational learning effect. Occurs when an observer acquires a new behavior after watching someone else demonstrate it.

Operant conditioning. A form of learning whereby a response increases in frequency as a result of its being followed by reinforcement.

Operations. In Piaget's theory, organized and integrated systems of thought processes.

Organization. A cognitive process in which learners find connections (e.g., by forming categories, identifying hierarchies, determining cause-effect relationships) among the various pieces of information they need to learn.

Overgeneralization. An overly broad meaning for a word that includes some situations where the word is not appropriate; an overly broad view of what objects or events a concept includes.

Overregularization. Applying syntactical rules in situations where those rules don't apply.

Paper-pencil assessment. Assessment in which students provide written responses to written items.

Pedagogical content knowledge. Knowledge about effective methods of teaching a specific content area.

Peer pressure. A phenomenon whereby a student's peers strongly encourage some behaviors and discourage others.

Peer tutoring. An approach to instruction whereby students who have mastered a topic teach those who have not.

People-first language. Language in which a student's disability is identified *after* the student (e.g., "student with a learning disability" rather than "learning disabled student").

Percentile rank (percentile). A test score that indicates the percentage of people in the norm group getting a raw score less than or equal to a particular student's raw score.

Performance-approach goal. A desire to look good and receive favorable judgments from others.

Performance assessment. Assessment in which students demonstrate their knowledge and skills in a nonwritten fashion.

Performance-avoidance goal. A desire not to look bad and receive unfavorable judgments from others.

Performance goal. A desire either to look good and receive favorable judgments from others, or else *not* to look bad and receive unfavorable judgments.

Personal fable. The belief that one is completely unlike anyone else and so cannot be understood by other individuals.

Personal interest. A long-term, relatively stable interest in a particular topic or activity.

Personal theory. A self-constructed explanation for one's observations about a particular aspect of the world; it may or may not be consistent with generally accepted explanations of scientific phenomena.

Perspective taking. The ability to look at a situation from someone's else viewpoint.

Physical and health impairments. A category of special needs characterized by general physical or medical conditions (usually long-term) that interfere with students' school performance to such an extent that special instruction, curricular materials, equipment, or facilities are necessary.

Popular students. Students whom many peers like and perceive to be kind and trustworthy.

Portfolio. A systematic collection of a student's work over a lengthy period of time.

Positive behavioral support. A modification of traditional applied behavior analysis that includes identifying the purpose that an undesirable behavior serves for a student and providing an alternative way for the student to achieve the same purpose.

Positive feedback. A message that an answer is correct or a task has been well done.

Positive instance. A specific example of a concept.

Positive reinforcement. A consequence that brings about the increase of a behavior through the presentation (rather than removal) of a stimulus.

Positive transfer. A phenomenon whereby something learned at one time facilitates learning or performance at a later time.

Postconventional morality. Behaving in accordance with one's own, self-developed, abstract principles regarding right and wrong.

Practicality. The extent to which an assessment instrument or procedure is inexpensive and easy to use and takes only a small amount of time to administer and score.

Pragmatics. Knowledge about the culture-specific social conventions guiding verbal interactions.

Preconventional morality. A lack of internalized standards about right and wrong; making decisions based on what is best for oneself, without regard for others' needs and feelings.

Predictive validity. The extent to which the results of an assessment predict future performance.

Premack principle. A phenomenon whereby individuals do less-preferred activities in order to engage in more-preferred activities.

Preoperational egocentrism. In Piaget's theory, the inability of children in the preoperational stage to view situations from another person's perspective.

Preoperational stage. Piaget's second stage of cognitive development, in which children can think about objects beyond their immediate view but do not yet reason in logical, adultlike ways.

Presentation punishment. A form of punishment involving the presentation of a new stimulus, presumably one that an individual finds unpleasant.

Primary reinforcer. A stimulus that satisfies a basic physiological need.

Principle. A description of how one variable influences another variable. It evolves when similar research studies yield similar results time after time.

Prior knowledge activation. Reminding students of information they have already learned relative to a new topic.

Private speech. See *self-talk.*

Proactive aggression. Deliberate aggression against another as a means of obtaining a desired goal.

Procedural knowledge. Knowledge concerning how to do something (as opposed to *declarative knowledge,* which relates to how things are).

Programmed instruction. An approach to instruction whereby students independently study a topic that has been broken into small, carefully sequenced segments.

Proportional reasoning. The ability to understand proportions (e.g., fractions, decimals, ratios) and use them effectively in mathematical problem solving.

Prosocial behavior. Behavior directed toward promoting the well-being of someone else.

Prototype. A mental representation of a "typical" positive instance of a concept.

Psychological punishment. Any consequence that seriously threatens a student's self-concept and self-esteem.

Psychomotor domain. The domain of learning tasks that includes simple and complex physical movements and actions.

Punishment. A consequence that decreases the frequency of the response it follows.

Rating scale. An assessment tool with which a teacher evaluates student performance by rating aspects of the performance on one or more continua.

Raw score. A test score based solely on the number or point value of correctly answered items.

Reactive aggression. An aggressive response to frustration or provocation.

Recall task. A memory task in which one must retrieve information in its entirety from long-term memory.

Receptive language. The ability to understand the language that one hears or reads.

Reciprocal causation. The interdependence of environment, behavior, and personal variables as these three factors influence learning.

Reciprocal teaching. An approach to teaching reading and listening comprehension whereby students take turns asking teacher-like questions of their classmates.

Recognition task. A memory task in which one must identify correct information among irrelevant information or incorrect statements.

Reconstruction error. Constructing a logical but incorrect "memory" by using information retrieved from long-term memory plus one's general knowledge and beliefs about the world.

Rehearsal. A cognitive process in which information is repeated over and over as a possible way of learning and remembering it. When it is used to maintain information in working memory, it is called *maintenance rehearsal.*

Reinforcement. The act of following a particular response with a reinforcer and thereby increasing the frequency of that response.

Reinforcer. A consequence (stimulus) of a response that leads to an increased frequency of that response.

Rejected students. Students whom many peers identify as being undesirable social partners.

Reliability. The extent to which an assessment instrument yields consistent information about the knowledge, skills, or abilities one is trying to measure.

Reliability coefficient. A numerical index of an assessment tool's reliability; ranges from 0 to 1, with higher numbers indicating higher reliability.

Removal punishment. A form of punishment involving the removal of an existing stimulus, presumably one that an individual views as desirable and doesn't want to lose.

Resilient self-efficacy. The belief that one can perform a task successfully even after experiencing setbacks; includes the belief that effort and perseverance are essential for success.

Resilient students. Students who succeed in school despite exceptional hardships in their home lives.

Response (R). A specific behavior that an individual exhibits.

Response cost. The loss either of a previously earned reinforcer or of an opportunity to obtain reinforcement.

Response disinhibition effect. Occurs when an observer displays a previously forbidden or punished behavior more frequently after seeing someone else exhibit that behavior without adverse consequences.

Response facilitation effect. Occurs when an observer displays a previously learned behavior more frequently after seeing someone else being reinforced for that behavior.

Response inhibition effect. Occurs when an observer displays a previously learned behavior less frequently after seeing someone else being punished for that behavior.

Retrieval. The process of "finding" information previously stored in memory.

Retrieval cue. A hint about where to "look" for a piece of information in long-term memory.

Reversibility. The ability to recognize that certain processes can be undone, or reversed.

Roles. Patterns of behavior acceptable for individuals having different functions within a society.

Rote learning. Learning information primarily through verbatim repetition, without attaching any meaning to it.

Rubric. A list of components that performance on an assessment task should ideally include; used to guide the scoring of students' responses.

Salience (of features). In concept learning, the degree to which a particular feature or characteristic is obvious and easily noticeable.

Savant syndrome. A syndrome characterized by an extraordinary ability to perform a specific task despite difficulty in other aspects of mental functioning; occasionally observed in students with autism.

Scaffolding. A support mechanism, provided by a more competent individual, that helps a learner successfully perform a task within his or her zone of proximal development.

Schema. In contemporary cognitive psychology, an organized body of knowledge about a specific topic.

Scheme. In Piaget's theory, an organized group of similar actions or thoughts.

Scholastic aptitude test. A test designed to assess one's general capacity to learn; typically used to predict students' success in future learning situations.

Script. A schema that involves a predictable sequence of events related to a common activity.

Scripted cooperation. In cooperative learning, a technique in which cooperative groups follow a set of steps or "script" that guides members' verbal interactions.

Secondary reinforcer. A stimulus that becomes reinforcing over time through its association with another reinforcer; it is sometimes called a **conditioned reinforcer.**

Self-concept. One's perceptions of, and beliefs about, oneself.

Self-contained class. A class in which students with special needs are educated as a group apart from other students.

Self-determination. A sense that one has some choice and control regarding the future course of one's life.

Self-efficacy. The belief that one is capable of executing certain behaviors or reaching certain goals.

Self-esteem. Judgments and beliefs about one's own general value and worth.

Self-evaluation. The process of evaluating one's own performance or behavior.

Self-fulfilling prophecy. A situation in which one's expectations for an outcome either directly or indirectly lead to the expected result.

Self-handicapping. Undermining one's own success, often as a way of protecting one's sense of self-worth when being asked to perform difficult tasks.

Self-imposed contingencies. Contingencies that students provide for themselves; the self-reinforcements and self-punishments that follow various behaviors.

Self-instructions. Instructions that students give themselves as they perform a complex behavior.

Self-monitoring. The process of observing and recording one's own behavior.

Self-questioning. The process of asking oneself questions as a way of checking one's understanding of a topic.

Self-regulated behavior. Engaging in self-chosen behaviors that lead to the accomplishment of personally chosen standards and goals.

Self-regulated learning. Regulating one's own cognitive processes to learn successfully; includes goal setting, planning, attention control, use of effective learning strategies, self-monitoring, and self-evaluation.

Self-regulated problem-solving strategy. A strategy that helps students solve their own interpersonal problems.

Self-regulation. The process of setting standards and goals for oneself and engaging in cognitive processes and behaviors that lead to the accomplishment of those standards and goals.

Self-talk. Talking to oneself as a way of guiding oneself through a task; also known as *private speech*.

Self-worth. Beliefs about one's own general ability to deal effectively with the environment.

Semantics. The meanings of words and word combinations.

Sense of community. In the classroom, a widely shared feeling that teacher and students have common goals, are mutually respectful and supportive of one another's efforts, and believe that everyone makes an important contribution to classroom learning.

Sense of school community. The sense that all faculty and students within a school are working together to help every student learn and succeed.

Sensitive period. An age range during which a certain aspect of a child's development is especially susceptible to environmental conditions.

Sensorimotor stage. Piaget's first stage of cognitive development, in which schemes are based on behaviors and perceptions.

Sensory register. A component of memory that holds incoming information in an unanalyzed form for a very brief period of time (probably less than a second for visual input and two or three seconds for auditory input).

Separation and control of variables. The ability to test one variable at a time while holding all other variables constant.

Setting event. In behaviorism, a complex environmental condition in which a particular behavior is most likely to occur.

Severe and multiple disabilities. A category of special needs in which students have two or more disabilities, the combination of which requires significant adaptations and highly specialized services in students' educational programs.

Shame. A feeling of embarrassment or humiliation that children feel after failing to meet the standards for moral behavior that adults have set.

Shaping. A process of reinforcing successively closer and closer approximations of a desired terminal behavior.

Short-term memory. See *working memory*.

Short-term objective. An objective that can typically be accomplished within the course of a single lesson or unit.

Signal. In expository instruction, a cue that lets students know that something is important to learn.

Single classification. The ability to classify objects in only one way at any given point in time.

Situated cognition. Knowledge and thinking skills that are acquired and used primarily within certain contexts, with limited if any transfer to other contexts.

Situated motivation. A phenomenon whereby aspects of one's immediate environment enhance one's motivation to learn particular things or behave in particular ways.

Situational interest. Interest evoked temporarily by something in the environment.

Social cognition. Considering how other people are likely to think, act, and react.

Social cognitive theory. A theoretical perspective in which learning by observing others is the focus of study.

Social constructivism. A theoretical perspective that focuses on people's collective efforts to impose meaning on the world.

Socialization. The process of molding a child's behavior to fit the norms and roles of the child's society.

Social reinforcer. A gesture or sign that one person gives another to communicate positive regard.

Social skills. Behaviors that enable a person to interact effectively with others.

Sociocultural perspective. A theoretical perspective that emphasizes the importance of society and culture for promoting cognitive development.

Socioeconomic status (SES). One's general social and economic standing in society, encompassing such variables as family income, occupation, and level of education.

Sociolinguistic conventions. Specific language-related behaviors that appear in some cultures or ethnic groups but not in others.

Specific aptitude test. A test designed to predict students' ability to learn in a particular content domain.

Specific transfer. An instance of transfer in which the original learning task and the transfer task overlap in content.

Speech and communication disorders. A category of special needs characterized by impairments in spoken language or language comprehension that significantly interfere with students' classroom performance.

Stage theory. A theory that depicts development as a series of relatively discrete periods (or **stages**), with relatively slow growth within each stage and more rapid growth during the transition from one stage to another.

Standard deviation (SD). A statistic that reflects how close together or far apart a set of scores are and thereby indicates the variability of the scores.

Standard English. The form of English generally considered acceptable at school, as reflected in textbooks, grammar instruction, and so on.

Standard error of measurement (SEM). A statistic estimating the amount of error likely to be present in a particular score on a test or other assessment instrument.

Standardization. The extent to which assessment instruments and procedures involve similar content and format and are administered and scored in the same way for everyone.

Standardized test. A test developed by test construction experts and published for use in many different schools and classrooms.

Standards. General statements regarding the knowledge and skills that students should achieve and the characteristics that their accomplishments should reflect.

Standard score. A test score that indicates how far a student's performance is from the mean with respect to standard deviation units.

Stanine. A standard score with a mean of 5 and a standard deviation of 2; it is always reported as a whole number.

State anxiety. A temporary feeling of anxiety elicited by a threatening situation.

Stereotype. A rigid, simplistic, and erroneous caricature of a particular group of people.

Stimulus (S) (pl. stimuli). A specific object or event that influences an individual's learning or behavior.

Storage. The process of "putting" new information into memory.

Student-directed instruction. An approach to instruction in which students have considerable say in the issues they address and how to address them.

Students at risk. Students who have a high probability of failing to acquire the minimal academic skills necessary for success in the adult world.

Students with special needs. Students who are different enough from their peers that they require specially adapted instructional materials and practices.

Subculture. A group that resists the ways of the dominant culture and adopts its own norms for behavior.

Summative evaluation. An evaluation conducted after instruction is completed and used to assess students' final achievement.

Superimposed meaningful structure. A familiar shape, word, sentence, poem, or story imposed on information to make it easier to recall; used as a *mnemonic*.

Symbolic model. A real or fictional character portrayed in the media (television, books, etc.) that influences an observer's behavior.

Symbolic thinking. The ability to represent and think about external objects and events in one's head.

Sympathy. A feeling of sorrow or concern for another person's problems or distress.

Synapse. A junction between two neurons that allows messages to be transmitted from one to the other.

Syntax. The set of rules that one uses (often unconsciously) to put words together into sentences.

Table of specifications. A two-way grid that indicates both the topics to be covered in an assessment and the things that students should be able to do with each topic.

Task analysis. A process of identifying the specific knowledge and/or behaviors necessary to master a particular subject area or skill.

Teacher-developed assessment instrument. An assessment tool developed by an individual teacher for use in his or her own classroom.

Teacher-directed instruction. An approach to instruction in which the teacher is largely in control of the course of the lesson.

Temperament. A genetic predisposition to respond in particular ways to one's physical and social environments.

Terminal behavior. The form and frequency of a desired response that a teacher or other practitioner is shaping through operant conditioning.

Test anxiety. Excessive anxiety about a particular test or about assessment in general.

Test bank. A collection of test items for a particular content domain; sometimes provided by publishers of classroom textbooks.

Testwiseness. Test-taking know-how that enhances test performance.

Theory. An organized body of concepts and principles developed to explain certain phenomena; a description of possible underlying mechanisms to explain why certain principles are true.

Threat. A situation in which people believe that they have little or no chance of success.

Time-out. A procedure whereby a misbehaving student is placed in a dull, boring situation with no opportunity to interact with others and no opportunity to obtain reinforcement.

Token economy. A technique whereby desired behaviors are reinforced by tokens, reinforcers that students can use to "purchase" a variety of other reinforcers.

Traditional assessment. Assessment that focuses on measuring basic knowledge and skills in relative isolation from tasks more typical of the outside world.

Trait anxiety. A pattern of responding with anxiety even in nonthreatening situations.

Trait theory (of motivation). A theoretical perspective portraying motivation as involving enduring personality characteristics that people have to a greater or lesser extent.

Transductive reasoning. Making a mental leap from one specific thing to another, such as identifying one event as the cause of another simply because the two events occur close together in time.

Transfer. A phenomenon whereby something that an individual has learned at one time affects how the individual learns or performs in a later situation.

Treatment group. A group of people in a research study who are given a particular experimental treatment (e.g., a particular method of instruction).

True score. The score a student would obtain if an assessment instrument could measure a characteristic with complete accuracy.

Unconditioned response (UCR). A response that, without prior learning, is elicited by a particular stimulus.

Unconditioned stimulus (UCS). A stimulus that, without prior learning, elicits a particular response.

Undergeneralization. An overly restricted meaning for a word that excludes some situations to which the word does, in fact, apply; an overly narrow view of what objects or events a concept includes.

Universals (in development). The similar patterns we see in how children change over time regardless of the specific environment in which they are raised.

Validity. The extent to which an assessment instrument actually measures what it is intended to measure.

Validity coefficient. A numerical index of an assessment tool's predictive validity; ranges from 0 to 1, with higher numbers indicating more accurate predictions.

Value. The belief that an activity has direct or indirect benefits.

Verbal mediator. A word or phrase that forms a logical connection or "bridge" between two pieces of information; used as a *mnemonic*.

Verbal reprimand. A scolding for inappropriate behavior.

Vicarious punishment. A phenomenon whereby a response decreases in frequency when another (observed) person is punished for that response.

Vicarious reinforcement. A phenomenon whereby a response increases in frequency when another (observed) person is reinforced for that response.

Visual imagery. The process of forming mental pictures of objects or ideas.

Visual impairments. A category of special needs characterized by malfunctions of the eyes or optic nerves that prevent students from seeing normally even with corrective lenses.

Visual-spatial thinking. The ability to imagine and mentally manipulate two- and three-dimensional figures.

Wait time. The length of time a teacher pauses, either after asking a question or hearing a student's comment, before saying something else.

Well-defined problem. A problem in which the goal is clearly stated, all information needed to solve the problem is present, and only one correct answer exists.

Withitness. The appearance that a teacher knows what all students are doing at all times.

Work-avoidance goal. A desire to avoid having to perform classroom tasks or to complete them with only minimal effort.

Working memory. A component of memory that holds and processes a limited amount of information; also known as *short-term memory*. The duration of information stored in working memory is probably about five to twenty seconds.

Zone of proximal development (ZPD). In Vygotsky's theory, the range of tasks between one's actual developmental level and one's level of potential development—that is, the range of tasks that one cannot yet perform independently but can perform with the help and guidance of others.

z-score. A standard score with a mean of 0 and a standard deviation of 1.

References

Abdul-Jabbar, K., & Knobles, P. (1983). *Giant steps: The autobiography of Kareem Abdul-Jabbar.* New York: Bantam Books.

Abery, B., & Zajac, R. (1996). Self-determination as a goal of early childhood and elementary education. In D. J. Sands & M. L. Wehmeyer (Eds.), *Self-determination across the life span: Independence and choice for people with disabilities.* Baltimore: Brookes.

Abi-Nader, J. (1993). Meeting the needs of multicultural classrooms: Family values and the motivation of minority students. In M. J. O'Hair & S. J. Odell (Eds.), *Diversity and teaching: Teacher education yearbook I.* Fort Worth, TX: Harcourt Brace Jovanovich.

Ablard, K. E., & Lipschultz, R. E. (1998). Self-regulated learning in high-achieving students: Relations to advanced reasoning, achievement goals, and gender. *Journal of Educational Psychology, 90,* 94–101.

Achenbach, T. M., & Edelbrock, C. S. (1981). Behavioral problems and competencies reported by parents of normal and disturbed children aged four through sixteen. *Monographs of the Society for Research in Child Development, 46*(1, Serial No. 188).

Adalbjarnardottir, S., & Selman, R. L. (1997). "I feel I have received a new vision": An analysis of teachers' professional development as they work with students on interpersonal issues. *Teaching and Teacher Education, 13,* 409–428.

Adams, G. R., Gullotta, T. P., & Markstrom-Adams, C. (1994). *Adolescent life experiences* (3rd ed.). Pacific Grove, CA: Brooks/Cole.

Adams, P. A., & Adams, J. K. (1960). Confidence in the recognition and reproduction of words difficult to spell. *American Journal of Psychology, 73,* 544–552.

Adelman, H. S. (1996). Appreciating the classification dilemma. In W. Stainback & S. Stainback (Eds.), *Controversial issues confronting special education: Diverse perspectives.* Boston: Allyn & Bacon.

Aiello, B. (1988). The Kids on the Block and attitude change: A 10-year perspective. In H. E. Yuker (Ed.), *Attitudes toward persons with disabilities.* New York: Springer.

Airasian, P. W. (1994). *Classroom assessment* (2nd ed.). New York: McGraw-Hill.

Alapack, R. (1991). The adolescent first kiss. *Humanistic Psychologist, 19,* 48–67.

Alderman, M. K. (1990). Motivation for at-risk students. *Educational Leadership, 48*(1), 27–30.

Alexander, K. L., Entwisle, D. R., & Thompson, M. (1987). School performance, status relations, and the structure of sentiment: Bringing the teacher back in. *American Sociological Review, 52,* 665–682.

Alexander, P. A. (1997). Mapping the multidimensional nature of domain learning: The interplay of cognitive, motivational, and strategic forces. In P. R. Pintrich & M. L. Maehr (Eds.), *Advances in motivation and achievement* (Vol. 10). Greenwich, CT: JAI Press.

Alexander, P. A., Graham, S., & Harris, K. R. (1998). A perspective on strategy research: Progress and prospects. *Educational Psychology Review, 10,* 129–154.

Alexander, P. A., & Jetton, T. L. (1996). The role of importance and interest in the processing of text. *Educational Psychology Review, 8,* 89–121.

Alexander, P. A., & Judy, J. E. (1988). The interaction of domain-specific and strategic knowledge in academic performance. *Review of Educational Research, 58,* 375–404.

Alexander, P. A., Kulikowich, J. M., & Schulze, S. K. (1994). How subject-matter knowledge affects recall and interest. *American Educational Research Journal, 31,* 313–337.

Alfassi, M. (1998). Reading for meaning: The efficacy of reciprocal teaching in fostering reading comprehension in high school students in remedial reading classes. *American Educational Research Journal, 35,* 309–332.

Alleman, J., & Brophy, J. (1997). Elementary social studies: Instruments, activities, and standards. In G. D. Phye (Ed.), *Handbook of classroom assessment: Learning, achievement, and adjustment.* San Diego, CA: Academic Press.

Alleman, J., & Brophy, J. (1998, April). *Strategic learning opportunities during out-of-school hours.* Paper presented at the annual meeting of the American Educational Research Association, San Diego, CA.

Allen, K. D. (1998). The use of an enhanced simplified habit-reversal procedure to reduce disruptive outbursts during athletic performance. *Journal of Applied Behavior Analysis, 31,* 489–492.

Alley, G., & Deshler, D. (1979). *Teaching the learning disabled adolescent: Strategies and methods.* Denver, CO: Love.

Allington, R. L., & Weber, R. (1993). Questioning questions in teaching and learning from texts. In B. K. Britton, A. Woodward, & M. Binkley (Eds.), *Learning from textbooks: Theory and practice.* Hillsdale, NJ: Erlbaum.

Altermatt, E. R., Jovanovic, J., & Perry, M. (1998). Bias or responsivity? Sex and achievement-level effects on teachers' classroom questioning practices. *Journal of Educational Psychology, 90,* 516–527.

Amabile, T. M., & Hennessey, B. A. (1992). The motivation for creativity in children. In A. K. Boggiano & T. S. Pittman (Eds.), *Achievement and motivation: A social-developmental perspective.* Cambridge, England: Cambridge University Press.

Ambrose, D., Allen, J., & Huntley, S. B. (1994). Mentorship of the highly creative. *Roeper Review, 17,* 131–133.

American Association on Mental Retardation. (1992). *Mental retardation: Definition, classification, and systems of supports* (9th ed.). Washington, DC: Author.

American Educational Research Association, American Psychological Association, & National Council on Measurement in Education. (1999). *Standards for Educational and Psychological Testing* (2nd ed.). Washington, DC: American Educational Research Association.

American Psychiatric Association. (1994). *Diagnostic and statistical manual of mental disorders* (4th ed.). Washington, DC: Author.

Ames, C. (1984). Competitive, cooperative, and individualistic goal structures: A cognitive-motivational analysis. In R. Ames & C. Ames (Eds.), *Research on motivation in education: Vol. 1. Student motivation.* San Diego, CA: Academic Press.

Ames, C. (1992). Classrooms: Goals, structures, and student motivation. *Journal of Educational Psychology, 84,* 261–271.

Ames, C., & Archer, J. (1988). Achievement goals in the classroom: Students' learning strategies and motivation processes. *Journal of Educational Psychology, 80,* 260–267.

Ames, R. (1983). Help-seeking and achievement orientation: Perspectives from attribution theory. In A. Nadler, J. Fisher, & B. DePaulo (Eds.), *New directions in helping* (Vol. 2). New York: Academic Press.

Amrein, A. L., & Berliner, D. C. (2002, March 28). High-stakes testing, uncertainty, and student learning. *Educational Policy Analysis Archives, 10*(18). Retrieved April 9, 2002, from http://epaa.asu.edu/epaa/v10n18/.

Anand, P., & Ross, S. (1987). A computer-based strategy for personalizing verbal problems in teaching mathematics. *Educational Communication and Technology Journal, 35,* 151–162.

Anastasi, A., & Urbina, S. (1997). *Psychological testing.* Upper Saddle River, NJ: Prentice Hall.

Anderman, E. M., Griesinger, T., & Westerfield, G. (1998). Motivation and cheating during early adolescence. *Journal of Educational Psychology, 90,* 84–93.

Anderman, E. M., & Maehr, M. L. (1994). Motivation and schooling in the middle grades. *Review of Educational Research, 64,* 287–309.

Anderman, L. H., & Anderman, E. M. (1999). Social predictors of changes in students' achievement goal orientation. *Contemporary Educational Psychology, 25,* 21–37.

Anderson, J. R. (1983). *The architecture of cognition.* Cambridge, MA: Harvard University Press.

Anderson, J. R. (1987). Skill acquisition: Compilation of weak-method problem solutions. *Psychological Review, 94*, 192–210.

Anderson, J. R. (1990). *Cognitive psychology and its implications* (3rd ed.). New York: Freeman.

Anderson, J. R. (1995). *Learning and memory: An integrated approach.* New York: Wiley.

Anderson, J. R., Greeno, J. G., Reder, L. M., & Simon, H. A. (2000). Perspectives on learning, thinking, and activity. *Educational Researcher, 29*(4), 11–13.

Anderson, J. R., Reder, L. M., & Simon, H. A. (1996). Situated learning and education. *Educational Researcher, 25*(4), 5–11.

Anderson, J. R., Reder, L. M., & Simon, H. A. (1997). Situative versus cognitive perspectives: Form versus substance. *Educational Researcher, 26*(1), 18–21.

Anderson, L. H. (1999). *Speak.* New York: Puffin Books.

Anderson, L. M. (1993). Auxiliary materials that accompany textbooks: Can they promote "higher-order" learning? In B. K. Britton, A. Woodward, & M. Binkley (Eds.), *Learning from textbooks: Theory and practice.* Hillsdale, NJ: Erlbaum.

Anderson, L. M., Brubaker, N. L., Alleman-Brooks, J., & Duffy, G. (1985). A qualitative study of seatwork in first-grade classrooms. *Elementary School Journal, 86*, 123–140.

Anderson, L. W., & Pellicer, L. O. (1998). Toward an understanding of unusually successful programs for economically disadvantaged students. *Journal of Education for Students Placed at Risk, 3*, 237–263.

Anderson, N. S. (1987). Cognition, learning, and memory. In M. A. Baker (Ed.), *Sex differences in human performance.* Chichester, England: Wiley.

Anderson, R. C., Nguyen-Jahiel, K., McNurlen, B., Archodidou, A., Kim, S.-Y., Reznitskaya, A., Tillmanns, M., & Gilbert, L. (2001). The snowball phenomenon: Spread of ways of talking and ways of thinking across groups of children. *Cognition and Instruction, 19*, 1–46.

Anderson, R. C., Reynolds, R. E., Schallert, D. L., & Goetz, E. T. (1977). Frameworks for comprehending discourse. *American Educational Research Journal, 14*, 367–381.

Anderson, V., & Hidi, S. (1988/1989). Teaching students to summarize. *Educational Leadership, 46*(4), 26–28.

Andre, T. (1986). Problem solving and education. In G. D. Phye & T. Andre (Eds.), *Cognitive classroom learning: Understanding, thinking, and problem solving.* San Diego, CA: Academic Press.

Anglin, J. M. (1977). *Word, object, and conceptual development.* New York: Norton.

Ansley, T. (1997). The role of standardized achievement tests in grades K–12. In G. D. Phye (Ed.), *Handbook of classroom assessment: Learning, achievement, and adjustment.* San Diego, CA: Academic Press.

Anzai, Y. (1991). Learning and use of representations for physics expertise. In K. A. Ericsson & J. Smith (Eds.), *Toward a general theory of expertise: Prospects and limits.* Cambridge, England: Cambridge University Press.

Archer, S. L. (1982). The lower age boundaries of identity development. *Child Development, 53*, 1551–1556.

Ardoin, S. P., Martens, B. K., & Wolfe, L. A. (1999). Using high-probability instructional sequences with fading to increase student compliance during transitions. *Journal of Applied Behavior Analysis, 32*, 339–351.

Arlin, M. (1979). Teacher transitions can disrupt time flow in classrooms. *American Educational Research Journal, 16*, 42–56.

Arlin, M. (1984). Time, equality, and mastery learning. *Review of Educational Research, 54*, 65–86.

Armstrong, T. (1994). *Multiple intelligences in the classroom.* Alexandria, VA: Association for Supervision and Curriculum Development.

Arnett, J. (1995). The young and the reckless: Adolescent reckless behavior. *Current Directions in Psychological Science, 4*, 67–71.

Arnett, J. J. (1999). Adolescent storm and stress, reconsidered. *American Psychologist, 54*, 317–326.

Arnold, M. L. (2000). Stage, sequence, and sequels: Changing conceptions of morality, post-Kohlberg. *Educational Psychology Review, 12*, 365–383.

Aronson, E., & Patnoe, S. (1997). *The jigsaw classroom: Building cooperation in the classroom* (2nd ed.). New York: Longman.

Arter, J. A., & Spandel, V. (1992). Using portfolios of student work in instruction and assessment. *Educational Measurement: Issues and Practice, 11*(1), 36–44.

Asher, S. R., & Parker, J. G. (1989). Significance of peer relationship problems in childhood. In B. H. Schneider, G. Attili, J. Nadel, & R. P. Weissberg (Eds.), *Social competence in developmental perspective.* Dordrecht, Netherlands: Kluwer.

Asher, S. R., & Renshaw, P. D. (1981). Children without friends: Social knowledge and social skill training. In S. R. Asher & J. M. Gottman (Eds.), *The development of children's friendships.* New York: Cambridge University Press.

Ashton, P. (1985). Motivation and the teacher's sense of efficacy. In C. Ames & R. Ames (Eds.), *Research on motivation in education: Vol. 2. The classroom milieu.* San Diego, CA: Academic Press.

Assor, A., & Connell, J. P. (1992). The validity of students' self-reports as measures of performance affecting self-appraisals. In D. H. Schunk & J. L. Meece (Eds.), *Student perceptions in the classroom.* Hillsdale, NJ: Erlbaum.

Astington, J. W. (1991). Intention in the child's theory of mind. In D. Frye & C. Moore (Eds.), *Child's theories of mind.* Hillsdale, NJ: Erlbaum.

Astor, R. A. (1994). Children's moral reasoning about family and peer violence: The role of provocation and retribution. *Child Development, 65*, 1054–1067.

Astor, R. A., Meyer, H. A., & Behre, W. J. (1999). Unowned places and times: Maps and interviews about violence in high schools. *American Educational Research Journal, 36*, 3–42.

Atkinson, J. W., & Feather, N. T. (Eds.) (1966). *A theory of achievement motivation.* New York: Wiley.

Atkinson, R. C., & Shiffrin, R. M. (1968). Human memory: A proposed system and its control processes. In K. W. Spence & J. T. Spence (Eds.), *The psychology of learning and motivation: Advances in research and theory* (Vol. 2). San Diego, CA: Academic Press.

Atkinson, R. K., Derry, S. J., Renkl, A., & Wortham, D. (2000). Learning from examples: Instructional principles from the worked examples research. *Review of Educational Research, 70*, 181–214.

Atkinson, R. K., Levin, J. R., Kiewra, K. A., Meyers, T., Kim, S., Atkinson, L. A., Renandya, W. A., & Hwang, Y. (1999). Matrix and mnemonic text-processing adjuncts: Comparing and combining their components. *Journal of Educational Psychology, 91*, 342–357.

Au, K. H. (1980). Participation structures in a reading lesson with Hawaiian children: Analysis of a culturally appropriate instructional event. *Anthropology and Education Quarterly, 11*, 91–115.

Aulls, M. W. (1998). Contributions of classroom discourse to what content students learn during curriculum enactment. *Journal of Educational Psychology, 90*, 56–69.

Ausubel, D. P. (1968). *Educational psychology: A cognitive view.* New York: Holt, Rinehart & Winston.

Ausubel, D. P., Novak, J. D., & Hanesian, H. (1978). *Educational psychology: A cognitive view* (2nd ed.). New York: Holt, Rinehart & Winston.

Babad, E. (1993). Teachers' differential behavior. *Educational Psychology Review, 5*, 347–376.

Baddeley, A. D. (1986). *Working memory.* New York: Oxford University Press.

Baek, S. (1994). Implications of cognitive psychology for educational testing. *Educational Psychology Review, 6*, 373–389.

Bahrick, H. P., Bahrick, L. E., Bahrick, A. S., & Bahrick, P. E. (1993). Maintenance of foreign language vocabulary and the spacing effect. *Psychological Science, 4*, 316–321.

Baillargeon, R. (1987). Object permanence in 3½- and 4½-month-old infants. *Developmental Psychology, 23*, 655–664.

Baillargeon, R. (1993). The object concept revisited: New directions in the investigation of infants' physical knowledge. In C. E. Granrud (Ed.), *Visual perception and cognition in infancy.* Hillsdale, NJ: Erlbaum.

Baker, L. (1989). Metacognition, comprehension monitoring, and the adult reader. *Educational Psychology Review, 1*, 3–38.

Baker, L., & Brown, A. L. (1984). Metacognitive skills of reading. In D. Pearson (Ed.), *Handbook of reading research.* White Plains, NY: Longman.

Balla, D. A., & Zigler, E. (1979). Personality development in retarded persons. In N. R. Ellis (Ed.), *Handbook of mental deficiency: Psychological theory and research* (2nd ed.). Hillsdale, NJ: Erlbaum.

Bandura, A. (1977). *Social learning theory.* Upper Saddle River, NJ: Prentice Hall.

Bandura, A. (1981). Self-referent thought: A developmental analysis of self-efficacy. In J. Flavell & L. Ross (Eds.), *Social cognitive development: Frontiers and possible futures.* Cambridge, England: Cambridge University Press.

Bandura, A. (1982). Self-efficacy mechanism in human agency. *American Psychologist, 37*, 122–147.

Bandura, A. (1986). *Social foundations of thought and action: A social cognitive theory.* Upper Saddle River, NJ: Prentice Hall.

Bandura, A. (1989). Human agency in social cognitive theory. *American Psychologist, 44*, 1175–1184.

Bandura, A. (1997). *Self-efficacy: The exercise of control.* New York: Freeman.

Bandura, A. (2000). Exercise of human agency through collective efficacy. *Current Directions in Psychological Science, 9*, 75–78.

Bandura, A., Ross, D., & Ross, S. A. (1961) Transmission of aggression through imitation of aggressive models. *Journal of Abnormal and Social Psychology, 63*, 575–582.

Bandura, A., Ross, D., & Ross, S. A. (1963). Imitation of film-mediated aggressive models. *Journal of Abnormal and Social Psychology, 66*, 3–11.

Bandura, A., & Schunk, D. H. (1981). Cultivating competence, self-efficacy, and intrinsic interest through proximal self-motivation. *Journal of Personality and Social Psychology, 41*, 586–598.

Bangert-Drowns, R. L., Kulik, C. C., Kulik, J. A., & Morgan, M. (1991). The instructional effect of feedback in test-like events. *Review of Educational Research, 61*, 213–238.

Banks, J. A. (1991). Multicultural literacy and curriculum reform. *Educational Horizons, 69*(3), 135–140.

Banks, J. A. (1994). *An introduction to multicultural education.* Needham Heights, MA: Allyn & Bacon.

Banks, J. A. (1995). Multicultural education: Historical development, dimensions, and practice. In J. A. Banks & C. A. M. Banks (Eds.), *Handbook of research on multicultural education.* New York: Macmillan.

Banks, J. A., & Banks, C. A. M. (Eds.). (1995). *Handbook of research on multicultural education.* New York: Macmillan.

Barbetta, P. M. (1990). GOALS: A group-oriented adapted levels system for children with behavior disorders. *Academic Therapy, 25,* 645–656.

Barbetta, P. M., Heward, W. L., Bradley, D. M., & Miller, A. D. (1994). Effects of immediate and delayed error correction on the acquisition and maintenance of sight words by students with developmental disabilities. *Journal of Applied Behavior Analysis, 27,* 177–178.

Barenboim, C. (1981). The development of person perception in childhood and adolescence: From behavioral comparisons to psychological constructs to psychological comparisons. *Child Development, 52,* 129–144.

Barga, N. K. (1996). Students with learning disabilities in education: Managing a disability. *Journal of Learning Disabilities, 29,* 413–421.

Barkley, R. A. (1996). Linkages between attention and executive functions. In G. R. Lyon & N. A. Krasnegor (Eds.), *Attention, memory, and executive function.* Baltimore: Brookes.

Barkley, R. A. (1998). *Attention-deficit hyperactivity disorder: A handbook for diagnosis and treatment* (2nd ed.). New York: Guilford Press.

Barnes, D. (1976). *From communication to curriculum.* London: Penguin.

Barnett, J. E. (2001, April). *Study strategies and preparing for exams: A survey of middle and high school students.* Paper presented at the annual meeting of the American Educational Research Association, Seattle, WA.

Barnett, J. E., Di Vesta, F. J., & Rogozinski, J. T. (1981). What is learned in note taking? *Journal of Educational Psychology, 73,* 181–192.

Baron, J. B. (1987). Evaluating thinking skills in the classroom. In J. B. Baron & R. J. Sternberg (Eds.), *Teaching thinking skills: Theory and practice.* New York: Freeman.

Baroody, A. J. (1999). Children's relational knowledge of addition and subtraction. *Cognition and Instruction, 17,* 137–175.

Barrish, H. H., Saunders, M., & Wolf, M. M. (1969). Good behavior game: Effects of individual contingencies for group consequences on disruptive behavior in a classroom. *Journal of Applied Behavior Analysis, 2,* 119–124.

Barron, B. (2000). Problem solving in video-based microworlds: Collaborative and individual outcomes of high-achieving sixth-grade students. *Journal of Educational Psychology, 92,* 391–398.

Bartlett, F. C. (1932). *Remembering: A study in experimental and social psychology.* Cambridge, England: Cambridge University Press.

Basinger, K. S., Gibbs, J. C., & Fuller, D. (1995). Context and the measurement of moral judgment. *International Journal of Behavioral Development, 18,* 537–556.

Bassett, D. S., Jackson, L., Ferrell, K. A., Luckner, J., Hagerty, P. J., Bunsen, T. D., & MacIsaac, D. (1996). Multiple perspectives on inclusive education: Reflections of a university faculty. *Teacher Education and Special Education, 19,* 355–386.

Bassok, M. (1990). Transfer of domain-specific problem-solving procedures. *Journal of Experimental Psychology: Learning, Memory, and Cognition, 16,* 522–533.

Bassok, M. (1996). Using content to interpret structure: Effects on analogical transfer. *Current Directions in Psychological Science, 5,* 54–58.

Bates, E., & MacWhinney, B. (1987). Competition, variation, and language learning. In B. MacWhinney (Ed.), *Mechanisms of language acquisition.* Hillsdale, NJ: Erlbaum.

Bates, J. A. (1979). Extrinsic reward and intrinsic motivation: A review with implications for the classroom. *Review of Educational Research, 49,* 557–576.

Batshaw, M. L., & Shapiro, B. K. (1997). Mental retardation. In M. L. Batshaw (Ed.), *Children with disabilities* (4th ed.). Baltimore: Brookes.

Batson, C. D., & Thompson, E. R. (2001). Why don't moral people act morally? Motivational considerations. *Current Directions in Psychological Science, 10,* 54–57.

Battin-Pearson, S., Newcomb, M. D., Abbott, R. D., Hill, K. G., Catalano, R. F., & Hawkins, J. D. (2000). Predictors of early high school dropout: A test of five theories. *Journal of Educational Psychology, 92,* 568–582.

Battistich, V., Solomon, D., Kim, D., Watson, M., & Schaps, E. (1995). Schools as communities, poverty levels of student populations, and students' attitudes, motives, and performance: A multilevel analysis. *American Educational Research Journal, 32,* 627–658.

Battistich, V., Solomon, D., Watson, M., & Schaps, E. (1997). Caring school communities. *Educational Psychologist, 32,* 137–151.

Baumeister, A. A. (1989). Mental retardation. In C. G. Lask & M. Hersen (Eds.), *Handbook of child psychiatric diagnosis.* New York: Wiley.

Baumeister, R. F., Smart, L., & Boden, J. M. (1996). Relation of threatened egotism to violence and aggression: The dark side of high self-esteem. *Psychological Review, 103,* 5–33.

Baumrind, D. (1971). Current patterns of parental authority. *Developmental Psychology Monograph, 4* (1, Pt. 2).

Baumrind, D. (1989). Rearing competent children. In W. Damon (Ed.), *Child development today and tomorrow.* San Francisco: Jossey-Bass.

Baxter, G. P., Elder, A. D., & Glaser, R. (1996). Knowledge-based cognition and performance assessment in the science classroom. *Educational Psychologist, 31,* 133–140.

Bay-Hinitz, A. K., Peterson, R. F., & Quilitch, H. R. (1994). Cooperative games: A way to modify aggressive and cooperative behaviors in young children. *Journal of Applied Behavior Analysis, 27,* 435–446.

Bear, G. G., & Richards, H. C. (1981). Moral reasoning and conduct problems in the classroom. *Journal of Educational Psychology, 73,* 644–670.

Becker, B. J. (1986). Influence again: An examination of reviews and studies of gender differences in social influence. In J. S. Hyde & M. C. Linn (Eds.), *The psychology of gender differences: Advances through meta-analysis.* Baltimore: Johns Hopkins University Press.

Bédard, J., & Chi, M. T. H. (1992). Expertise. *Current Directions in Psychological Science, 1,* 135–139.

Begg, I., Anas, A., & Farinacci, S. (1992). Dissociation of processes in belief: Source recollection, statement familiarity, and the illusion of truth. *Journal of Experimental Psychology: General, 121,* 446–458.

Behrmann, M. (2000). The mind's eye mapped onto the brain's matter. *Current Directions in Psychological Science, 9,* 50–54.

Beirne-Smith, M., Ittenbach, R. F., & Patton, J. R. (2002). *Mental retardation* (6th ed.). Upper Saddle River, NJ: Merrill/Prentice Hall.

Belfiore, P. J., & Hornyak, R. S. (1998). Operant theory and application to self-monitoring in adolescents. In D. H. Schunk and B. J. Zimmerman (Eds.), *Self-regulated learning: From teaching to self-reflective practice.* New York: Guilford Press.

Belfiore, P. J., Lee, D. L., Vargas, A. U., & Skinner, C. H. (1997). Effects of high-preference single-digit mathematics problem completion on multiple-digit mathematics problem performance. *Journal of Applied Behavior Analysis, 30,* 327–330.

Bellezza, F. S. (1986). Mental cues and verbal reports in learning. In G. H. Bower (Ed.), *The psychology of learning and motivation: Advances in research and theory* (Vol. 20). San Diego, CA: Academic Press.

Bender, T. A. (1997). Assessment of subjective well-being during childhood and adolescence. In G. D. Phye (Ed.), *Handbook of classroom assessment: Learning, achievement, and adjustment.* San Diego, CA: Academic Press.

Bennett, G. K., Seashore, H. G., & Wesman, A. G. (1982). *Differential Aptitude Tests.* San Antonio, TX: Psychological Corporation.

Bennett, R. E., Gottesman, R. L., Rock, D. A., & Cerullo, F. (1993). Influence of behavior perceptions and gender on teachers' judgments of students' academic skill. *Journal of Educational Psychology, 85,* 347–356.

Benware, C., & Deci, E. L. (1984). Quality of learning with an active versus passive motivational set. *American Educational Research Journal, 21,* 755–765.

Bereiter, C. (1994). Implications of postmodernism for science, or, science as progressive discourse. *Educational Psychologist, 29*(1), 3–12.

Bereiter, C. (1995). A dispositional view of transfer. In A. McKeough, J. Lupart, & A. Marini (Eds.), *Teaching for transfer: Fostering generalization in learning.* Mahwah, NJ: Erlbaum.

Bereiter, C. (1997). Situated cognition and how to overcome it. In D. Kirshner & J. A. Whitson (Eds.), *Situated cognition: Social, semiotic, and psychological perspectives.* Mahwah, NJ: Erlbaum.

Bereiter, C., & Scardamalia, M. (1987). *The psychology of written composition.* Hillsdale, NJ: Erlbaum.

Berk, L. E. (1994). Why children talk to themselves. *Scientific American, 271,* 78–83.

Berk, L. E. (2000). *Child development* (5th ed.). Boston: Allyn & Bacon.

Berkowitz, M. W., Guerra, N., & Nucci, L. (1991). Sociomoral development and drug and alcohol abuse. In W. M. Kurtines & J. L. Gewirtz (Eds.), *Moral behavior and development: Vol. 3. Application.* Hillsdale, NJ: Erlbaum.

Berliner, D. C. (1988, February). *The development of expertise in pedagogy.* Paper presented at the American Association of Colleges for Teacher Education, New Orleans, LA.

Berliner, D. C. (1997, March). Discussant's comments. In H. Borko (Chair), *Educational psychology and teacher education: Perennial issues.* Symposium conducted at the annual meeting of the American Educational Research Association, Chicago.

Berlyne, D. E. (1960). *Conflict, arousal, and curiosity.* New York: McGraw-Hill.

Berndt, T. J. (1992). Friendship and friends' influence in adolescence. *Current Directions in Psychological Science, 1,* 156–159.

Berndt, T. J., Hawkins, J. A., & Jiao, Z. (1999). Influences of friends and friendships on adjustment to junior high school. *Merrill Palmer Quarterly, 45,* 13–41.

Berndt, T. J., & Keefe, K. (1996). Friends' influence on school adjustment: A motivational analysis. In J. Juvonen & K. R. Wentzel (Eds.), *Social motivation: Understanding children's school adjustment* (pp. 248–278). Cambridge, England: Cambridge University Press.

Berndt, T. J., Laychak, A. E., & Park, K. (1990). Friends' influence on adolescents' academic achievement motivation: An experimental study. *Journal of Educational Psychology, 82,* 664–670.

Berzonsky, M. D. (1988). Self-theorists, identity status, and social cognition. In D. K. Lapsley & F. C. Power (Eds.), *Self, ego, and identity: Integrative approaches* (pp. 243–261). New York: Springer-Verlag.

Beyer, B. K. (1985). Critical thinking: What is it? *Social Education, 49,* 270–276.

Bialystok, E. (1994a). Representation and ways of knowing: Three issues in second language acquisition. In N. C. Ellis (Ed.), *Implicit and explicit learning of languages.* London: Academic Press.

Bialystok, E. (1994b). Towards an explanation of second language acquisition. In G. Brown, K. Malmkjær, A. Pollitt, & J. Williams (Eds.), *Language and understanding.* Oxford, England: Oxford University Press.

Bialystok, E. (2001). *Bilingualism in development: Language, literacy, and cognition.* Cambridge, England: Cambridge University Press.

Bidell, T. R., & Fischer, K. W. (1997). Between nature and nurture: The role of human agency in the epigenesis of intelligence. In R. J. Sternberg & E. L. Grigorenko (Eds.), *Intelligence, heredity, and environment* (pp. 193–242). Cambridge, England: Cambridge University Press.

Biemiller, A., Shany, M., Inglis, A., & Meichenbaum, D. (1998). Factors influencing children's acquisition and demonstration of self-regulation on academic tasks. In D. H. Schunk & B. J. Zimmerman (Eds.), *Self-regulated learning: From teaching to self-reflective practice* (pp. 203–224). New York: Guilford Press.

Bierman, K. L., Miller, C. L., & Stabb, S. D. (1987). Improving the social behavior and peer acceptance of rejected boys: Effect of social skill training with instructions and prohibitions. *Journal of Consulting and Clinical Psychology, 55,* 194–200.

Binder, L. M., Dixon, M. R., & Ghezzi, P. M. (2000). A procedure to teach self-control to children with attention deficit hyperactivity disorder. *Journal of Applied Behavior Analysis, 33,* 233–237.

Binns, K., Steinberg, A., Amorosi, S., & Cuevas, A. M. (1997). *The Metropolitan Life survey of the American teacher 1997: Examining gender issues in public schools.* New York: Louis Harris and Associates.

Bjorklund, D. F. (1987). How age changes in knowledge base contribute to the development of children's memory: An interpretive review. *Developmental Review, 7,* 93–130.

Bjorklund, D. F., & Coyle, T. R. (1995). Utilization deficiencies in the development of memory strategies. In F. E. Weinert & W. Schneider (Eds.), *Research on memory development: State of the art and future directions.* Hillsdale, NJ: Erlbaum.

Bjorklund, D. F., & Green, B. L. (1992). The adaptive nature of cognitive immaturity. *American Psychologist, 47,* 46–54.

Bjorklund, D. F., Muir-Broaddus, J. E., & Schneider, W. (1990). The role of knowledge in the development of strategies. In D. F. Bjorklund (Ed.), *Children's strategies: Contemporary views of cognitive development.* Hillsdale, NJ: Erlbaum.

Bjorklund, D. F., Schneider, W., Cassel, W. S., & Ashley, E. (1994). Training and extension of a memory strategy: Evidence for utilization deficiencies in high- and low-IQ children. *Child Development, 65,* 951–965.

Blake, S. B., & Clark, R. E. (1990, April). *The effects of metacognitive selection on far transfer in analogical problem solving tasks.* Paper presented at the annual meeting of the American Educational Research Association, Boston.

Blasi, A. (1980). Bridging moral cognition and moral action: A critical review of the literature. *Psychological Bulletin, 88,* 593–637.

Blasi, A. (1995). Moral understanding and the moral personality: The process of moral integration. In W. M. Kurtines & J. L. Gewirtz (Eds.), *Moral development: An introduction.* Boston: Allyn & Bacon.

Block, J. H. (1980). Promoting excellence through mastery learning. *Theory into Practice, 19*(1), 66–74.

Block, J. H. (1983). Differential premises arising from differential socialization of the sexes: Some conjectures. *Child Development, 54,* 1335–1354.

Block, J. H., & Burns, R. B. (1976). Mastery learning. In L. Shulman (Ed.), *Review of research in education* (Vol. 4). Itasca, IL: Peacock.

Bloom, B. S. (1981). *All our children learning.* New York: McGraw-Hill.

Bloom, B. S., Englehart, M. D., Furst, E. J., Hill, W. H., & Krathwohl, D. R. (1956). *Taxonomy of educational objectives. The classification of educational goals: Handbook I. Cognitive domain.* New York: David McKay.

Blumenfeld, P. C. (1992). The task and the teacher: Enhancing student thoughtfulness in science. In J. Brophy (Ed.), *Advances in research on teaching: Vol. 3. Planning and managing learning tasks and activities.* Greenwich, CT: JAI Press.

Blumenfeld, P., Hamilton, V. L., Bossert, S., Wessels, K., & Meece, C. (1983). Teacher talk and student thought: Socialization into the student role. In J. Levine & U. Wang (Eds.), *Teacher and student perceptions: Implications for learning.* Hillsdale, NJ: Erlbaum.

Blumenfeld, P. C., Marx, R. W., Soloway, E., & Krajcik, J. (1996). Learning with peers: From small group cooperation to collaborative communities. *Educational Researcher, 25*(8), 37–40.

Bochenhauer, M. H. (1990, April.) *Connections: Geographic education and the National Geographic Society.* Paper presented at the annual meeting of the American Educational Research Association, Boston.

Boggiano, A. K., & Pittman, T. S. (Eds.). (1992). *Achievement and motivation: A social-developmental perspective.* Cambridge, England: Cambridge University Press.

Boldizar, J. P., Perry, D. G., & Perry, L. C. (1989). Outcome values and aggression. *Child Development, 60,* 571–579.

Bolles, R. C. (1975). *Theory of motivation* (2nd ed.). New York: Harper & Row.

Bong, M. (2001). Between- and within-domain relations of academic motivation among middle and high school students: Self-efficacy, task-value, and achievement goals. *Journal of Educational Psychology, 93,* 23–34.

Borko, H., & Putnam, R. T. (1996). Learning to teach. In D. C. Berliner & R. C. Calfee (Eds.), *Handbook of educational psychology.* New York: Macmillan.

Borkowski, J. G., Carr, M., Rellinger, E., & Pressley, M. (1990). Self-regulated cognition: Interdependence of metacognition, attributions, and self-esteem. In B. F. Jones & L. Idol (Eds.), *Dimensions of thinking and cognitive instruction.* Hillsdale, NJ: Erlbaum.

Born, D. G., & Davis, M. L. (1974). Amount and distribution of study in a personalized instruction course and in a lecture course. *Journal of Applied Behavior Analysis, 7,* 365–375.

Bornholt, L. J., Goodnow, J. J., & Cooney, G. H. (1994). Influences of gender stereotypes on adolescents' perceptions of their own achievement. *American Educational Research Journal, 31,* 675–692.

Bosacki, S. L. (2000). Theory of mind and self-concept in preadolescents: Links with gender and language. *Journal of Educational Psychology, 92,* 709–717.

Boschee, F., & Baron, M. A. (1993). *Outcome-based education: Developing programs through strategic planning.* Lancaster, PA: Technomic.

Bouchard, T. J., Jr. (1997). IQ similarity in twins reared apart: Findings and responses to critics. In R. J. Sternberg & E. L. Grigorenko (Eds.), *Intelligence, heredity, and environment* (pp. 126–160). Cambridge, England: Cambridge University Press.

Bouchard, T. J., Jr., Lykken, D. T., McGue, M., Segal, N. L., & Tellegen, A. (1990, October 12). Sources of human psychological differences: The Minnesota study of twins reared apart. *Science, 250,* 223–228.

Bousfield, W. A. (1953). The occurrence of clustering in the recall of randomly arranged associates. *Journal of General Psychology, 49,* 229–240.

Boutte, G. S., & McCormick, C. B. (1992). Authentic multicultural activities: Avoiding pseudomulticulturalism. *Childhood Education, 68*(3), 140–144.

Bower, G. H., Black, J. B., & Turner, T. J. (1979). Scripts in memory for text. *Cognitive Psychology, 11,* 177–220.

Bower, G. H., & Clark, M. C. (1969). Narrative stories as mediators for serial learning. *Psychonomic Science, 14,* 181–182.

Bower, G. H., Clark, M. C., Lesgold, A. M., & Winzenz, D. (1969). Hierarchical retrieval schemes in recall of categorized word lists. *Journal of Verbal Learning and Verbal Behavior, 8,* 323–343.

Bower, G. H., Karlin, M. B., & Dueck, A. (1975). Comprehension and memory for pictures. *Memory and Cognition, 3,* 216–220.

Bowey, J. (1986). Syntactic awareness and verbal performance from preschool to fifth grade. *Journal of Psycholinguistic Research, 15,* 285–308.

Bowman, B. T. (1989). Educating language-minority children: Challenges and opportunities. *Phi Delta Kappan, 71,* 118–120.

Bowman, L. G., Piazza, C. C., Fisher, W. W., Hagopian, L. P., & Kogan, J. S. (1997). Assessment of preference for varied versus constant reinforcers. *Journal of Applied Behavior Analysis, 30,* 451–458.

Boyatzis, R. E. (1973). Affiliation motivation. In D. C. McClelland & R. S. Steele (Eds.), *Human motivation: A book of readings.* Morristown, NJ: General Learning Press.

Boykin, A. W. (1994). Harvesting talent and culture: African-American children and educational reform. In R. J. Rossi (Ed.), *Schools and students at risk: Context and framework for positive change.* New York: Teachers College Press.

Bracken, B. A., McCallum, R. S., & Shaughnessy, M. F. (1999). An interview with Bruce A. Bracken and R. Steve McCallum, authors of the Universal Nonverbal Intelligence Test (UNIT). *North American Journal of Psychology, 1,* 277–288.

Bracken, B. A., & Walker, K. C. (1997). The utility of intelligence tests for preschool children. In D. P. Flanagan, J. L. Genshaft, & P. L. Harrison (Eds.), *Contemporary intellectual assessment: Theories, tests, and issues* (pp. 484–502). New York: Guilford Press.

Braden, J. P. (1992). Intellectual assessment of deaf and hard-of-hearing people: A quantitative and qualitative research synthesis. *School Psychology Review, 21,* 82–94.

Bradley, L., & Bryant, P. E. (1991). Phonological skills before and after learning to read. In S. A. Brady & D. P. Shankweiler (Eds.), *Phonological processes in literacy.* Hillsdale, NJ: Erlbaum.

Bradley, R. H., & Caldwell, B. M. (1984). The relation of infants' home environments to achievement test performance in first grade: A follow-up study. *Child Development, 55,* 803–809.

Brainerd, C. J., Reyna, V. F., Howe, M. L., & Kingma, J. (1990). The development of forgetting and reminiscence. *Monographs of the Society for Research in Child Development, 55* (Serial No. 222).

Bransford, J. D., & Franks, J. J. (1971). The abstraction of linguistic ideas. *Cognitive Psychology, 2,* 331–350.

Bransford, J. D., Franks, J. J., Vye, N. J., & Sherwood, R. D. (1989). New approaches to instruction: Because wisdom can't be told. In S. Vosniadou & A. Ortony (Eds.), *Similarity and analogical reasoning.* Cambridge, England: Cambridge University Press.

Bransford, J. D., & Johnson, M. K. (1972). Contextual prerequisites for understanding: Some investigations of comprehension and recall. *Journal of Verbal Learning and Verbal Behavior, 11,* 717–726.

Brantlinger, E. (1997). Using ideology: Cases of nonrecognition of the politics of research and practice in special education. *Review of Educational Research, 67,* 425–459.

Braukmann, C. J., Kirigin, K. A., & Wolf, M. M. (1981). Behavioral treatment of juvenile delinquency. In S. W. Bijou & R. Ruiz (Eds.), *Behavior modification: Contributions to education.* Hillsdale, NJ: Erlbaum.

Braun, L. J. (1998). *The cat who saw stars.* New York: G. P. Putnam's Sons.

Brenner, M. E., Mayer, R. E., Moseley, B., Brar, T., Durán, R., Reed, B. S., & Webb, D. (1997). Learning by understanding: The role of multiple representations in learning algebra. *American Educational Research Journal, 34,* 663–689.

Brigham, F. J., & Scruggs, T. E. (1995). Elaborative maps for enhanced learning of historical information: Uniting spatial, verbal, and imaginal information. *Journal of Special Education, 28,* 440.

Britton, B. K., Stimson, M., Stennett, B., & Gülgöz, S. (1998). Learning from instructional text: Test of an individual differences model. *Journal of Educational Psychology, 90,* 476–491.

Broden, M., Hall, R. V., & Mitts, B. (1971). The effect of self-recording on the classroom behavior of two eighth grade students. *Journal of Applied Behavior Analysis, 4,* 191–199.

Brody, G. H., & Shaffer, D. R. (1982). Contributions of parents and peers to children's moral socialization. *Developmental Review, 2,* 31–75.

Brody, N. (1992). *Intelligence* (2nd ed.). San Diego, CA: Academic Press.

Brody, N. (1997). Intelligence, schooling, and society. *American Psychologist, 52,* 1046–1050.

Bronson, M. B. (2000). *Self-regulation in early childhood: Nature and nurture.* New York: Guilford Press.

Brooke, R. R., & Ruthren, A. J. (1984). The effects of contingency contracting on student performance in a PSI class. *Teaching of Psychology, 11,* 87–89.

Brooks, L. W., & Dansereau, D. F. (1987). Transfer of information: An instructional perspective. In S. M. Cormier & J. D. Hagman (Eds.), *Transfer of learning: Contemporary research and applications.* San Diego, CA: Academic Press.

Brooks-Gunn, J., Klebanov, P. K., & Duncan, G. J. (1996). Ethnic differences in children's intelligence test scores: Role of economic deprivation, home environment, and maternal characteristics. *Child Development, 67,* 396–408.

Brooks-Gunn, J., & Paikoff, R. L. (1993). "Sex is a gamble, kissing is a game": Adolescent sexuality and health promotion. In S. G. Millstein, A. C. Petersen, & E. O. Nightingale (Eds.), *Promoting the health of adolescents: New directions for the twenty-first century* (pp. 180–208). New York: Oxford University Press.

Brophy, J. E. (1986). *On motivating students* (Occasional Paper No. 101). East Lansing: Michigan State University, Institute for Research on Teaching.

Brophy, J. E. (1987). Synthesis of research on strategies for motivating students to learn. *Educational Leadership, 45*(2), 40–48.

Brophy, J. E. (Ed.). (1991). *Advances in research on teaching: Vol. 2. Teachers' knowledge of subject matter as it relates to their teaching practice.* Greenwich, CT: JAI Press.

Brophy, J. E. (1992a). Conclusions: Comments on an emerging field. In J. Brophy (Ed.), *Advances in research on teaching: Vol. 3. Planning and managing learning tasks and activities.* Greenwich, CT: JAI Press.

Brophy, J. E. (1992b). Probing the subtleties of subject-matter teaching. *Educational Leadership, 49*(7), 4–8.

Brophy, J. (1999). Toward a model of the value aspects of motivation in education: Developing appreciation for particular learning domains and activities. *Educational Psychologist, 34,* 75–85.

Brophy, J. E., & Alleman, J. (1991). Activities as instructional tools: A framework for analysis and evaluation. *Educational Researcher, 20*(4), 9–23.

Brophy, J. E., & Alleman, J. (1992). Planning and managing learning activities: Basic principles. In J. Brophy (Ed.), *Advances in research on teaching: Vol. 3. Planning and managing learning tasks and activities.* Greenwich, CT: JAI Press.

Brophy, J. E., & Alleman, J. (1996). *Powerful social studies for elementary students.* Fort Worth, TX: Harcourt Brace.

Brophy, J. E., & Evertson, C. (1976). *Learning from teaching: A developmental perspective.* Needham Heights, MA: Allyn & Bacon.

Brophy, J. E., & Good, T. L. (1986). Teacher effects. In M. C. Wittrock (Ed.), *Handbook of research on teaching* (3rd ed.). New York: Macmillan.

Brophy, J. E., & VanSledright, B. (1997). *Teaching and learning history in elementary schools.* New York: Teachers College Press.

Brown, A. L., Ash, D., Rutherford, M., Nakagawa, K., Gordon, A., & Campione, J. C. (1993). Distributed expertise in the classroom. In G. Salomon (Ed.), *Distributed cognitions: Psychological and educational considerations.* Cambridge, England: Cambridge University Press.

Brown, A. L., & Campione, J. C. (1994). Guided discovery in a community of learners. In K. McGilly (Ed.), *Classroom lessons: Integrating cognitive theory and classroom practice.* Cambridge, MA: MIT Press.

Brown, A. L., & Campione, J. C. (1996). Psychological theory and the design of innovative learning environments: On procedures, principles, and systems. In L. Schauble & R. Glaser (Eds.), *Innovations in learning: New environments for education.* Mahwah, NJ: Erlbaum.

Brown, A. L., Campione, J., & Day, J. (1981). Learning to learn: On training students to learn from texts. *Educational Researcher, 10*(2), 14–21.

Brown, A. L., & Palincsar, A. S. (1987). Reciprocal teaching of comprehension strategies: A natural history of one program for enhancing learning. In J. Borkowski & J. D. Day (Eds.), *Cognition in special education: Comparative approaches to retardation, learning disabilities, and giftedness.* Norwood, NJ: Ablex.

Brown, A. L., & Palincsar, A. S. (1989). Guided, cooperative learning and individual knowledge acquisition. In L. B. Resnick (Ed.), *Knowing, learning, and instruction: Essays in honor of Robert Glaser.* Hillsdale, NJ: Erlbaum.

Brown, A. L., & Reeve, R. A. (1987). Bandwidths of competence: The role of supportive contexts in learning and development. In L. S. Liben (Ed.), *Development and learning: Conflict or congruence?* Hillsdale, NJ: Erlbaum.

Brown, A. L., Smiley, S. S., Day, J. D., Townsend, M. A. R., & Lawton, S. C. (1977). Intrusion of a thematic idea in children's comprehension and retention of stories. *Child Development, 48,* 1454–1466.

Brown, A. S., Schilling, H. E. H., & Hockensmith, M. L. (1999). The negative suggestion effect: Pondering incorrect alternatives may be hazardous to your knowledge. *Journal of Educational Psychology, 91,* 756–764.

Brown, B. B. (1990). Peer groups. In S. Feldman & G. Elliott (Eds.), *At the threshold: The developing adolescent* (pp. 171–196). Cambridge, MA: Harvard University Press.

Brown, B. B. (1993). School culture, social politics, and the academic motivation of U.S. students. In T. M. Tomlinson (Ed.), *Motivating students to learn: Overcoming barriers to high achievement.* Berkeley, CA: McCutchan.

Brown, B. B. (1999). "You're going out with *who?*" Peer group influences on adolescent romantic relationships. In W. Furman, B. B. Brown, & C. Feiring (Eds.), *The development of romantic relationships in adolescence* (pp. 291–329). Cambridge, England: Cambridge University Press.

Brown, B. B., Eicher, S. A., & Petrie, S. (1986). The importance of peer group ("crowd") affiiation in adolescence. *Journal of Adolescence, 9,* 73–96.

Brown, B. B., Feiring, C., & Furman, W. (1999). Missing the love boat: Why researchers have shied away from adolescent romance. In W. Furman, B. B. Brown, & C. Feiring (Eds.), *The development of romantic relationships in adolescence* (pp. 1–16). Cambridge, England: Cambridge University Press.

Brown, F. G. (1981). *Measuring classroom achievement.* New York: Holt, Rinehart & Winston.

Brown, J. S., Collins, A., & Duguid, P. (1989). Situated cognition and the culture of learning. *Educational Researcher, 18*(1), 32–42.

Brown, L. M., Tappan, M. B., & Gilligan, C. (1995). Listening to different voices. In W. M. Kurtines & J. L. Gewirtz (Eds.), *Moral development: An introduction.* Boston: Allyn & Bacon.

Brown, R., & McNeill, D. (1966). The "tip of the tongue" phenomenon. *Journal of Verbal Learning and Verbal Behavior, 5,* 325–337.

Brown, R. D., & Bjorklund, D. F. (1998). The biologizing of cognition, development, and education: Approach with cautious enthusiasm. *Educational Psychology Review, 10,* 355–373.

Brown, R. T. (1989). Creativity: What are we to measure? In J. A. Glover, R. R. Ronning, & C. R. Reynolds (Eds.), *Handbook of creativity.* New York: Plenum Press.

Brown, R. T., Reynolds, C. R., & Whitaker, J. S. (1999). Bias in mental testing since *Bias in Mental Testing. School Psychology Quarterly, 14,* 208–238.

Brown, W. H., Fox, J. J., & Brady, M. P. (1987). Effects of spatial density on 3- and 4-year-old children's socially directed behavior during freeplay: An investigation of a setting factor. *Education and Treatment of Children, 10,* 247–258.

Brownell, M. T., Mellard, D. F., & Deshler, D. D. (1993). Differences in the learning and transfer performance between students with learning disabilities and other low-achieving students on problem-solving tasks. *Learning Disabilities Quarterly, 16,* 138–156.

Brown-Mizuno, C. (1990). Success strategies for learners who are learning disabled as well as gifted. *Teaching Exceptional Children, 23*(1), 10–12.

Bruer, J. T. (1997). Education and the brain: A bridge too far. *Educational Researcher, 26*(8), 4–16.

Bruer, J. T. (1999). *The myth of the first three years: A new understanding of early brain development and lifelong learning*. New York: Free Press.

Bruner, J. S. (1961). The act of discovery. *Harvard Educational Review, 31,* 21–32.

Bruner, J. S. (1966). *Toward a theory of instruction.* Cambridge, MA: Harvard University Press.

Bruner, J. S., Goodnow, J., & Austin, G. (1956). *A study of thinking.* New York: Wiley.

Bruning, R. H., Schraw, G. J., & Ronning, R. R. (1995). *Cognitive psychology and instruction* (2nd ed.). Upper Saddle River, NJ: Merrill/Prentice Hall.

Bryan, J. H. (1975). Children's cooperation and helping behaviors. In E. M. Hetherington (Ed.), *Review of child development research* (Vol. 5). Chicago: University of Chicago Press.

Bryan, T. (1991). Social problems and learning disabilities. In B. Y. L. Wong (Ed.), *Learning about learning disabilities*. San Diego, CA: Academic Press.

Bryan, T., Burstein, K., & Bryan, J. (2001). Students with learning disabilities: Homework problems and promising practices. *Educational Psychologist, 36,* 167–180.

Bryant, P., Nunes, T., & Aidinis, A. (1999). Different morphemes, same spelling problems: Cross-linguistic developmental studies. In M. Harris & G. Hatano (Eds.), *Learning to read and write: A cross-linguistic perspective.* Cambridge, England: Cambridge University Press.

Buchoff, T. (1990). Attention deficit disorder: Help for the classroom teacher. *Childhood Education, 67*(2), 86–90.

Budwig, N. (1995). *A developmental-functionalist approach to child language.* Mahwah, NJ: Erlbaum.

Bugelski, B. R., & Alampay, D. A. (1961). The role of frequency in developing perceptual sets. *Canadian Journal of Psychology, 15,* 205–211.

Buhrmester, D. (1992). The developmental courses of sibling and peer relationships. In F. Boer and J. Dunn (Eds.), *Children's sibling relationships: Developmental and clinical issues.* Hillsdale, NJ: Erlbaum.

Bulgren, J. A., Deshler, D. D., Schumaker, J. B., & Lenz, B. K. (2000). The use and effectiveness of analogical instruction in diverse secondary content classrooms. *Journal of Educational Psychology, 92,* 426–441.

Bulgren, J. A., Schumaker, J. B., & Deshler, D. D. (1994). The effects of a recall enhancement routine on the test performance of secondary students with and without learning disabilities. *Learning Disabilities Research and Practice, 9,* 2–11.

Burger, H. G. (1973). Cultural pluralism and the schools. In C. S. Brembeck & W. H. Hill (Eds.), *Cultural challenges to education: The influence of cultural factors in school learning.* Lexington, MA: Heath.

Burger, S., & Burger, D. (1994). Determining the validity of performance-based assessment. *Educational Measurement: Issues and Practices, 13*(1), 9–15.

Burhans, K. K., & Dweck, C. S. (1995). Helplessness in early childhood: The role of contingent worth. *Child Development, 66,* 1719–1738.

Bushman, B. J., & Anderson, C. A. (2001). Media violence and the American public: Scientific facts versus media misinformation. *American Psychologist, 56,* 477–489.

Butler, D. L., & Winne, P. H. (1995). Feedback and self-regulated learning: A theoretical synthesis. *Review of Educational Research, 65,* 245–281.

Butler, R. (1989). Mastery versus ability appraisal: A developmental study of children's observations of peers' work. *Child Development, 60,* 1350–1361.

Butler, R. (1990). The effects of mastery and competitive conditions on self-assessment at different ages. *Child Development, 61,* 201–210.

Butler, R. (1994). Teacher communication and student interpretations: Effects of teacher responses to failing students on attributional inferences in two age groups. *British Journal of Educational Psychology, 64,* 277–294.

Butler, R. (1998a). Age trends in the use of social and temporal comparison for self-evaluation: Examination of a novel developmental hypothesis. *Child Development, 69,* 1054–1073.

Butler, R. (1998b). Determinants of help seeking: Relations between perceived reasons for classroom help-avoidance and help-seeking behaviors in an experimental context. *Journal of Educational Psychology, 90,* 630–644.

Butterfield, E. C., & Ferretti, R. P. (1987). Toward a theoretical integration of cognitive hypotheses about intellectual differences among children. In J. G. Borkowski & J. D. Day (Eds.), *Cognition in special children: Approaches to retardation, learning disabilities, and giftedness.* Norwood, NJ: Ablex.

Byrnes, J. P. (1988). Formal operations: A systematic reformulation. *Developmental Review, 8,* 66–87.

Byrnes, J. P. (1996). *Cognitive development and learning in instructional contexts.* Boston: Allyn & Bacon.

Byrnes, J. P., & Fox, N. A. (1998). The educational relevance of research in cognitive neuroscience. *Educational Psychology Review, 10,* 297–342.

Cairns, H. S. (1996). *The acquisition of language* (2nd ed.). Austin, TX: Pro-Ed.

Calderhead, J. (1996). Teachers: Beliefs and knowledge. In D. C. Berliner & R. C. Calfee (Eds.), *Handbook of educational psychology.* New York: Macmillan.

Calfee, R. (1981). Cognitive psychology and educational practice. In D. C. Berliner (Ed.), *Review of research in education* (Vol. 9). Washington, DC: American Educational Research Association.

Calfee, R., & Chambliss, M. J. (1988, April). *The structure of social studies textbooks: Where is the design?* Paper presented at the annual meeting of the American Educational Research Association, New Orleans, LA.

Calfee, R., Dunlap, K., & Wat, A. (1994). Authentic discussion of texts in middle grade schooling: An analytic-narrative approach. *Journal of Reading, 37,* 546–556.

Calfee, R. C., & Masuda, W. V. (1997). Classroom assessment as inquiry. In G. D. Phye (Ed.), *Handbook of classroom assessment: Learning, achievement, and adjustment.* San Diego, CA: Academic Press.

Cameron, J., & Pierce, W. D. (1994). Reinforcement, reward, and intrinsic motivation: A meta-analysis. *Review of Educational Research, 64,* 363–423.

Campbell, A. (1984). *The girls in the gang: A report from New York City.* New York: Blackwell.

Campbell, D. E. (1996). *Choosing democracy: A practical guide to multicultural education.* Upper Saddle River, NJ: Merrill/Prentice Hall.

Campbell, F. A., & Ramey, C. T. (1994). Effects of early intervention on intellectual and academic achievement: A follow-up study of children from low-income families. *Child Development, 65,* 684–698.

Campbell, F. A., & Ramey, C. T. (1995). Cognitive and school outcomes for high-risk African-American students at middle adolescence: Positive effects of early intervention. *American Educational Research Journal, 32,* 742–772.

Campbell, L., Campbell, B., & Dickinson, D. (1998). *Teaching and learning through multiple intelligences* (2nd ed.). Boston: Allyn & Bacon.

Campbell, P. A. (1986). What's a nice girl like you doing in a math class? *Phi Delta Kappan, 67,* 516–520.

Campione, J. C., Brown, A. L., & Bryant, N. R. (1985). Individual differences in learning and memory. In R. J. Sternberg (Ed.), *Human abilities: An information-processing approach.* New York: Freeman.

Campione, J. C., Shapiro, A. M., & Brown, A. L. (1995). Forms of transfer in a community of learners: Flexible learning and understanding. In A. McKeough, J. Lupart, & A. Marini (Eds.), *Teaching for transfer: Fostering generalization in learning.* Mahwah, NJ: Erlbaum.

Canady, R. L., & Hotchkiss, P. R. (1989). It's a good score! Just a bad grade. *Phi Delta Kappan, 71,* 68–71.

Candler-Lotven, A., Tallent-Runnels, M. K., Olivárez, A., & Hildreth, B. (1994, April). *A comparison of learning and study strategies of gifted, average-ability, and learning-disabled ninth grade students.* Paper presented at the annual meeting of the American Educational Research Association, New Orleans, LA.

Caprara, G. V., Barbaranelli, C., Pastorelli, C., Bandura, A., & Zimbardo, P. G. (2000). Prosocial foundations of children's academic achievement. *Psychological Science, 11,* 302–306.

Capron, C., & Duyme, M. (1989). Assessment of effects of socio-economic status on IQ in a full cross-fostering study. *Nature, 340,* 552–554.

Carey, L. M. (1994). *Measuring and evaluating school learning* (2nd ed.). Needham Heights, MA: Allyn & Bacon.

Carey, S. (1978). The child as word learner. In M. Halle, J. Bresnan, & G. A. Miller (Eds.), *Linguistic theory and psychological reality.* Cambridge, MA: MIT Press.

Carey, S. (1985). *Conceptual change in childhood.* Cambridge, MA: MIT Press.

Carey, S. (1986). Cognitive science and science education. *American Psychologist, 41,* 1123–1130.

Carnine, D. (1989). Teaching complex content to learning disabled students: The role of technology. *Exceptional Children, 55,* 524–533.

Carpenter, P. A., & Just, M. A. (1986). Cognitive processes in reading. In J. Orasanu (Ed.), *Reading comprehension: From research to practice.* Hillsdale, NJ: Erlbaum.

Carr, A. A. (1997, March). *The participation "race": Kentucky's site based decision teams.* Paper presented at the annual meeting of the American Educational Research Association, Chicago.

Carr, E. G., Levin, L., McConnachie, G., Carlson, J. I., Kemp, D. C., & Smith, C. E. (1994). *Communication-based intervention for problem behavior: A user's guide for producing positive change.* Baltimore: Brookes.

Carr, M., & Biddlecomb, B. (1998). Metacognition in mathematics from a constructivist perspective. In D. J. Hacker, J. Dunlosky, & A. C. Graesser (Eds.), *Metacognition in educational theory and practice* (pp. 69–91). Mahwah, NJ: Erlbaum.

Carr, M., & Borkowski, J. G. (1989). Attributional training and the generalization of reading strategies with underachieving children. *Learning and Individual Differences, 1,* 327–341.

Carr, M., Kurtz, B. E., Schneider, W., Turner, L. A., & Borkowski, J. G. (1989). Strategy acquisition and transfer among American and German children: Environmental influences on metacognitive development. *Developmental Psychology, 25,* 765–771.

Carraher, T. N., Carraher, D. W., & Schliemann, A. D. (1985). Mathematics in the streets and in the schools. *British Journal of Developmental Psychology, 3,* 21–29.

Carrasco, R. L. (1981). Expanded awareness of student performance: A case study in applied ethnographic monitoring in a bilingual classroom. In H. T. Trueba, G. P. Guthrie, & K. H. Au (Eds.), *Culture and the bilingual classroom: Studies in classroom ethnography.* Rowley, MA: Newbury House.

Carter, K. R. (1991). Evaluation of gifted programs. In N. Buchanan & J. Feldhusen (Eds.), *Conducting research and evaluation in gifted education: A handbook of methods and applications.* New York: Teachers College Press.

Carter, K. R., & Ormrod, J. E. (1982). Acquisition of formal operations by intellectually gifted children. *Gifted Child Quarterly, 26,* 110–115.

Cartledge, G., & Milburn, J. F. (1995). *Teaching social skills to children and youth: Innovative approaches* (3rd ed.). Needham Heights, MA: Allyn & Bacon.

Carver, C. S., & Scheier, M. F. (1990). Origins and functions of positive and negative affect: A control-process view. *Psychological Review, 97,* 19–35.

Casanova, U. (1987). Ethnic and cultural differences. In V. Richardson-Koehler (Ed.), *Educator's handbook: A research perspective.* White Plains, NY: Longman.

Case, R., & Okamoto, Y., in collaboration with Griffin, S., McKeough, A., Bleiker, C., Henderson, B., & Stephenson, K. M. (1996). The role of central conceptual structures in the development of children's thought. *Monographs of the Society for Research in Child Development, 61*(1, Serial No. 246).

Caseau, D., Luckasson, R., & Kroth, R. L. (1994). Special education services for girls with serious emotional disturbance: A case of gender bias? *Behavioral Disorders, 20*(1), 51–60.

Casey, W. M., & Burton, R. V. (1982). Training children to be consistently honest through verbal self-instructions. *Child Development, 53,* 911–919.

Caspi, A., Taylor, A., Moffitt, T. E., & Plomin, R. (2000). Neighborhood deprivation affects children's mental health: Environmental risks identified in a genetic design. *Psychological Science, 11,* 338–342.

Casserly, P. L. (1980). Factors affecting female participation in Advanced Placement programs in mathematics, chemistry, and physics. In L. H. Fox, L. Brody, & D. Tobin (Eds.), *Women and the mathematical mystique.* Baltimore: Johns Hopkins University Press.

Cazden, C. B. (1968). The acquisition of noun and verb inflections. *Child Development, 39,* 433–448.

Cazden, C. B. (1976). Play with language and metalinguistic awareness: One dimension of language experience. In J. Bruner, A. Jolly, & K. Sylva (Eds.), *Play: Its role in development and evolution.* New York: Basic Books.

Cazden, C. B. (1988). *Classroom discourse: The language of teaching and learning.* Portsmouth, NJ: Heinemann.

Cazden, C. B., & Leggett, E. L. (1981). Culturally responsive education: Recommendations for achieving *Lau* Remedies II. In H. T. Trueba, G. P. Guthrie, & K. H. Au (Eds.), *Culture and the bilingual classroom: Studies in classroom ethnography.* Rowley, MA: Newbury House.

Ceci, S. J., & Williams, W. M. (1997). Schooling, intelligence, and income. *American Psychologist, 52,* 1051–1058.

Chalfant, J. C. (1989). Learning disabilities: Policy issues and promising approaches. *American Psychologist, 44,* 392–398.

Chall, J. S. (1996). *Stages of reading development* (2nd ed.). Fort Worth, TX: Harcourt Brace.

Chalmers, J., & Townsend, M. (1990). The effects of training in social perspective taking on socially maladjusted girls. *Child Development, 61,* 178–190.

Chambliss, M. J. (1994). Why do readers fail to change their beliefs after reading persuasive text? In R. Garner & P. A. Alexander (Eds.), *Beliefs about text and instruction with text.* Hillsdale, NJ: Erlbaum.

Chambliss, M. J., Calfee, R. C., & Wong, I. (1990, April). *Structure and content in science textbooks: Where is the design?* Paper presented at the annual meeting of the American Educational Research Association, Boston.

Chan, C., Burtis, J., & Bereiter, C. (1997). Knowledge building as a mediator of conflict in conceptual change. *Cognition and Instruction, 15,* 1–40.

Chandler, M., & Moran, T. (1990). Psychopathy and moral development: A comparative study of delinquent and nondelinquent youth. *Development and Psychopathology, 2,* 227–246.

Chao, R. K. (1994). Beyond parental control and authoritarian parenting style: Understanding Chinese parenting through the cultural notion of training. *Child Development, 65,* 1111–1119.

Chapman, J. W. (1988). Learning disabled children's self-concepts. *Review of Educational Research, 58,* 347–371.

Chapman, J. W., Tunmer, W. E., & Prochnow, J. E. (2000). Early reading-related skills and performance, reading self-concept, and the development of academic self-concept: A longitudinal study. *Journal of Educational Psychology, 92,* 703–708.

Cheatham, S. K., Smith, J. D., Rucker, H. N., Polloway, E. A., & Lewis, G. W. (1995, September). Savant syndrome: Case studies, hypotheses, and implications for special education. *Education and Training in Mental Retardation,* 243–253.

Chen, X., Rubin, K. H., & Sun, Y. (1992). Social reputation and peer relationships in Chinese and Canadian children: A cross-cultural study. *Child Development, 63,* 1336–1343.

Chen, Z. (1999). Schema induction in children's analogical problem solving. *Journal of Educational Psychology, 91,* 703–715.

Cheng, L. R. (1987). *Assessing Asian language performance.* Rockville, MD: Aspen.

Cheng, P. W. (1985). Restructuring versus automaticity: Alternative accounts of skill acquisition. *Psychological Review, 92,* 414–423.

Cherry, E. C. (1953). Some experiments on the recognition of speech, with one and with two ears. *Journal of the Acoustical Society of America, 25,* 975–979.

Chester, M. D., & Beaudin, B. Q. (1996). Efficacy beliefs of newly hired teachers in urban schools. *American Educational Research Journal, 33,* 233–257.

Cheyne, J. A., & Walters, R. H. (1970). Punishment and prohibition: Some origins of self-control. In T. M. Newcomb (Ed.), *New directions in psychology.* New York: Holt, Rinehart & Winston.

Chi, M. T. H. (1978). Knowledge structures and memory development. In R. S. Siegler (Ed.), *Children's thinking: What develops?* Hillsdale, NJ: Erlbaum.

Chi, M. T. H., Feltovich, P., & Glaser, R. (1981). Categorization and representation of physics problems by experts and novices. *Cognitive Science, 5,* 121–152.

Chinn, C. A., & Brewer, W. F. (1993). The role of anomalous data in knowledge acquisition: A theoretical framework and implications for science instruction. *Review of Educational Research, 63,* 1–49.

Chomsky, C. S. (1969). *The acquisition of syntax in children from 5 to 10.* Cambridge, MA: MIT Press.

Chomsky, N. (1965). *Aspects of the theory of syntax.* Cambridge, MA: MIT Press.

Chomsky, N. (1972). *Language and mind* (enlarged ed.). San Diego, CA: Harcourt Brace Jovanovich.

Christie, J. F., & Johnsen, E. P. (1983). The role of play in social-intellectual development. *Review of Educational Research, 53,* 93–115.

Clark, B. (1997). *Growing up gifted* (5th ed.). Upper Saddle River, NJ: Merrill/Prentice Hall.

Clark, C. C. (1992). Deviant adolescent subcultures: Assessment strategies and clinical interventions. *Adolescence, 27*(106), 283–293.

Clark, C. M., & Peterson, P. L. (1986). Teachers' thought processes. In M. C. Wittrock (Ed.), *Handbook on research on teaching* (3rd ed.). New York: Macmillan.

Clark, E. V. (1971). On the acquisition of the meaning of "before" and "after." *Journal of Verbal Learning and Verbal Behavior, 10,* 266–275.

Clark, J. M., & Paivio, A. (1991). Dual coding theory and education. *Educational Psychology Review, 3,* 149–210.

Clark, R. E. (1983). Reconsidering research on learning from media. *Review of Educational Research, 53,* 445–459.

Clarke, S., Dunlap, G., Foster-Johnson, L., Childs, K. E., Wilson, D., White, R., & Vera, A. (1995). Improving the conduct of students with behavioral disorders by incorporating student interests into curricular areas. *Behavioral Disorders, 20,* 221–237.

Clarke-Stewart, K. A. (1988). Parents' effects on children's development: A decade of progress? *Journal of Applied Developmental Psychology, 9,* 41–84.

Claude, D., & Firestone, P. (1995). The development of ADHD boys: A 12-year follow-up. *Canadian Journal of Behavioural Science, 27,* 226–249.

Clawson, D. L., & Fisher, J. S. (1998). *World regional geography: A development approach* (6th ed.). Upper Saddle River, NJ: Prentice Hall.

Clifford, M. M. (1990). Students need challenge, not easy success. *Educational Leadership, 48*(1), 22–26.

Cobb, P., Gravemeijer, K., Yackel, E., McClain, K., & Whitenack, J. (1997). Mathematizing and symbolizing: The emergence of chains of significance in one first-grade classroom. In D. Kirshner & J. A. Whitson (Eds.), *Situated cognition: Social, semiotic, and psychological perspectives.* Mahwah, NJ: Erlbaum.

Cobb, P., Wood, T., Yackel, E., Nicholls, J., Wheatley, G., Trigatti, B., & Perlwitz, M. (1991). Assessment of a problem centered second-grade mathematics project. *Journal for Research in Mathematics Education, 22,* 3–29.

Cobb, P., & Yackel, E. (1996). Constructivist, emergent, and sociocultural perspectives in the context of developmental research. *Educational Psychologist, 31,* 175–190.

Cochran, K. F., & Jones, L. L. (1998). The subject matter knowledge of preservice science teachers. In B. J. Fraser & K. G. Tobin (Eds.), *International Handbook of Science Education. Part II.* Dordrecht, The Netherlands: Kluwer.

Cochran-Smith, M., & Lytle, S. (1993). *Inside out: Teacher research and knowledge.* New York: Teachers College Press.

Coe, J., Salamon, L., & Molnar, J. (1991). *Homeless children and youth.* New Brunswick, NJ: Transaction.

Cognition and Technology Group at Vanderbilt. (1990). Anchored instruction and its relationship to situated cognition. *Educational Researcher, 19*(6), 2–10.

Cognition and Technology Group at Vanderbilt. (1993). Anchored instruction and situated cognition revisited. *Educational Technology, 33*(3), 52–70.

Cognition and Technology Group at Vanderbilt. (1996). Looking at technology in context: A framework for understanding technology and education research. In D. C. Berliner & R. C. Calfee (Eds.), *Handbook of educational psychology* (pp. 807–840). New York: Macmillan.

Cohen, E. G. (1994). Restructuring the classroom: Conditions for productive small groups. *Review of Educational Research, 64,* 1–35.

Cohen, E. G., Lockheed, M. E., & Lohman, M. R. (1976). The center for interracial cooperation: A field experiment. *Sociology of Education, 59,* 47–58.

Cohen, E. G., & Lotan, R. A. (1995). Producing equal-status interaction in the heterogeneous classroom. *American Educational Research Journal, 32,* 99–120.

Cohen, R. L. (1989). Memory for action events: The power of enactment. *Educational Psychology Review, 1,* 57–80.

Coie, J. D., & Cillessen, A. H. N. (1993). Peer rejection: Origins and effects on children's development. *Current Directions in Psychological Science, 2,* 89–92.

Coie, J. D., & Dodge, K. A. (1998). Aggression and antisocial behavior. In W. Damon (Editor-in-Chief) & N. Eisenberg (Vol. Ed.), *Handbook of child psychology: Vol. 3. Social, emotional, and personality development* (5th ed., pp. 779–862). New York: Wiley.

Colby, A., & Kohlberg, L. (1984). Invariant sequence and internal consistency in moral judgment stages. In W. M. Kurtines & J. L. Gewirtz (Eds.), *Morality, moral behavior, and moral development.* New York: Wiley.

Colby, A., & Kohlberg, L. (1987). *The measurement of moral judgment: Theoretical foundations and research validation* (Vol. 1). Cambridge, England: Cambridge University Press.

Colby, A., Kohlberg, L., Gibbs, J., & Lieberman, M. (1983). A longitudinal study of moral judgment. *Monographs of the Society for Research in Child Development, 48*(1–2, Serial No. 200).

Cole, D. A., Martin, J. M., Peeke, L. A., Seroczynski, A. D., & Fier, J. (1999). Children's over- and underestimation of academic competence: A longitudinal study of gender differences, depression, and anxiety. *Child Development, 70,* 459–473.

Cole, N. S. (1990). Conceptions of educational achievement. *Educational Researcher, 19*(3), 2–7.

Collaer, M. L., & Hines, M. (1995). Human behavioral sex differences: A role for gonadal hormones during early development? *Psychological Bulletin, 118,* 55–107.

Collier, V. P. (1992). The Canadian bilingual immersion debate: A synthesis of research findings. *Studies in Second Language Acquisition, 14,* 87–97.

Collins, A., Brown, J. S., & Newman, S. E. (1989). Cognitive apprenticeship: Teaching the crafts of reading, writing, and mathematics. In L. B. Resnick (Ed.), *Knowing, learning, and instruction: Essays in honor of Robert Glaser.* Hillsdale, NJ: Erlbaum.

Collins, W. A., Maccoby, E. E., Steinberg, L., Hetherington, E. M., & Bornstein, M. H. (2000). Contemporary research on parenting: The case for nature and nurture. *American Psychologist, 55,* pp. 218–232.

Collins, W. A., & Sroufe, L. A. (1999). Capacity for intimate relationships: A developmental construction. In W. Furman, B. B. Brown, & C. Feiring (Eds.), *The development of romantic relationships in adolescence* (pp. 125–147). Cambridge, England: Cambridge University Press.

Combs, A. W., Richards, A. C., & Richards, F. (1976). *Perceptual psychology: A humanistic approach to the study of persons.* New York: Harper & Row.

Cone, T. E., Wilson, L. R., Bradley, C. M., & Reese, J. H. (1985). Characteristics of LD students in Iowa: An empirical investigation. *Learning Disability Quarterly, 8,* 211–220.

Conlon, C. J. (1992). New threats to development: Alcohol, cocaine, and AIDS. In M. L. Batshaw & Y. M. Perret (Eds.), *Children with disabilities: A medical primer* (3rd ed.). Baltimore: Brookes.

Connell, J. P. (1990). Context, self, and action: A motivational analysis of self-system processes across the life span. In D. Cicchetti & M. Beeghly (Eds.), *The self in transition: Infancy to childhood.* Chicago: University of Chicago Press.

Connell, J. P., & Wellborn, J. G. (1991). Competence, autonomy, and relatedness: A motivational analysis of self-system processes. In M. R. Gunnar & L. A. Sroufe (Eds.), *Self processes and development: The Minnesota Symposia on Child Psychology* (Vol. 23). Hillsdale, NJ: Erlbaum.

Connolly, F. W., & Eisenberg, T. E. (1990). The feedback classroom: Teaching's silent friend. *T.H.E. Journal, 17*(5), 75–77.

Connolly, J., & Goldberg, A. (1999). Romantic relationships in adolescence: The role of friends and peers in their emergence and development. In W. Furman, B. B. Brown, & C. Feiring (Eds.), *The development of romantic relationships in adolescence* (pp. 266–290). Cambridge, England: Cambridge University Press.

Conte, R. (1991). Attention disorders. In B. Y. L. Wong (Ed.), *Learning about learning disabilities.* San Diego, CA: Academic Press.

Cook, B., & Semmel, M. (1999). Peer acceptance of included students with disabilities as a function of severity of disability and classroom composition. *Journal of Special Education, 33*(10), 50–62.

Cooney, C. (1997). *Wanted.* New York: Scholastic.

Cooney, J. B. (1991). Reflections on the origin of mathematical intuition and some implications for instruction. *Learning and Individual Differences, 3,* 83–107.

Cooper, H. (1989). Synthesis of research on homework. *Educational Leadership, 47*(3), 85–91.

Cooper, H. M., & Good, T. (1983). *Pygmalion grows up: Studies in the expectation communication process.* White Plains, NY: Longman.

Cooper, H., Lindsay, J. J., Nye, B., & Greathouse, S. (1998). Relationships among attitudes about homework, amount of homework assigned and completed, and student achievement. *Journal of Educational Psychology, 90,* 70–83.

Cooper, H., & Valentine, J. C. (2001). Using research to answer practical questions about homework. *Educational Psychologist, 36,* 143–153.

Corbett, H. D., & Wilson, B. (1988). Raising the stakes in statewide mandatory minimum competency testing. *Politics of Education Association Yearbook,* 27–39.

Corkill, A. J. (1992). Advance organizers: Facilitators of recall. *Educational Psychology Review, 4,* 33–67.

Cormier, S. M. (1987). The structural processes underlying transfer of training. In S. M. Cormier & J. D. Hagman (Eds.), *Transfer of learning: Contemporary research and applications.* San Diego, CA: Academic Press.

Cornell, D. G., Pelton, G. M., Bassin, L. E., Landrum, M., Ramsay, S. G., Cooley, M. R., Lynch, K. A., & Hamrick, E. (1990). Self-concept and peer status among gifted program youth. *Journal of Educational Psychology, 82,* 456–463.

Corno, L. (1993). The best-laid plans: Modern conceptions of volition and educational research. *Educational Researcher, 22,* 14–22.

Corno, L. (1996). Homework is a complicated thing. *Educational Researcher, 25*(8), 27–30.

Corno, L., & Rohrkemper, M. M. (1985). The intrinsic motivation to learn in classrooms. In C.

Ames & R. Ames (Eds.), *Research on motivation in education: Vol. 2. The classroom milieu.* San Diego, CA: Academic Press.

Corno, L., & Snow, R. E. (1986). Adapting teaching to individual differences among learners. In M. C. Wittrock (Ed.), *Handbook of research on teaching* (3rd ed.). New York: Macmillan.

Cothern, N. B., Konopak, B. C., & Willis, E. L. (1990). Using readers' imagery of literary characters to study text meaning construction. *Reading Research and Instruction, 30,* 15–29.

Cottrol, R. J. (1990). America the multicultural. *American Educator, 14*(4), 18–21.

Council for Exceptional Children. (1995). *Toward a common agenda: Linking gifted education and school reform.* Reston, VA: Author.

Courchesne, E., Townsend, J., Akshoomoff, N. A., Saitoh, O., Yeung-Courchesne, R., Lincoln, A. J., James, H. E., Haas, R. H. Schreibman, L., & Lau, L. (1994). Impairment of shifting attention in autistic and cerebellar patients. *Behavioral Neuroscience, 108,* 848–865.

Covington, M. V. (1987). Achievement motivation, self-attributions, and the exceptional learner. In J. D. Day & J. G. Borkowski (Eds.), *Intelligence and exceptionality.* Norwood, NJ: Ablex.

Covington, M. V. (1992). *Making the grade: A self-worth perspective on motivation and school reform.* Cambridge, England: Cambridge University Press.

Covington, M. (2000). Intrinsic versus extrinsic motivation in schools: A reconciliation. *Current Directions in Psychological Science, 9,* 22–25.

Covington, M. V., & Beery, R. M. (1976). *Self-worth and school learning.* New York: Holt, Rinehart & Winston.

Covington, M. V., & Müeller, K. J. (2001). Intrinsic versus extrinsic motivation: An approach/avoidance reformulation. *Educational Psychology Review, 13,* 157–176.

Cowan, N. (1995). *Attention and memory: An integrated framework.* New York: Oxford University Press.

Cox, B. D. (1997). The rediscovery of the active learner in adaptive contexts: A developmental-historical analysis of transfer of training. *Educational Psychologist, 32,* 41–55.

Craft, M. (1984). Education for diversity. In M. Craft (Ed.), *Educational and cultural pluralism.* London: Falmer Press.

Craft, M. A., Alberg, S. R., & Heward, W. L. (1998). Teaching elementary students with developmental disabilities to recruit teacher attention in a general education classroom: Effects on teacher praise and academic productivity. *Journal of Applied Behavior Analysis, 31,* 399–415.

Crago, M. B., Annahatak, B., & Ningiuruvik, L. (1993). Changing patterns of language socialization in Inuit homes. *Anthropology and Education Quarterly, 24,* 205–223.

Craik, F. I. M., & Watkins, M. J. (1973). The role of rehearsal in short-term memory. *Journal of Verbal Learning and Verbal Behavior, 12,* 598–607.

Crain, S. (1993). Language acquisition in the absence of experience. In P. Bloom (Ed.), *Language acquisition: Core readings.* Cambridge, MA: MIT Press.

Creasey, G. L., Jarvis, P. A., & Berk, L. E. (1998). Play and social competence. In O. N. Saracho & B. Spodek (Eds.), *Multiple perspectives on play in early childhood education.* Albany: State University of New York Press.

Crick, N. R., & Dodge, K. A. (1994). A review and reformulation of social information-processing mechanisms in children's social adjustment. *Psychological Bulletin, 115,* 74–101.

Crick, N. R., & Dodge, K. A. (1996). Social information-processing mechanisms in reactive and proactive aggression. *Child Development, 67,* 993–1002.

Crick, N. R., & Grotpeter, J. K. (1995). Relational aggression, gender, and social-psychological adjustment. *Child Development, 66,* 710–722.

Crockett, L., Losoff, M., & Peterson, A. C. (1984). Perceptions of the peer group and friendship in early adolescence. *Journal of Early Adolescence, 4,* 155–181.

Cromer, R. F. (1993). Language growth with experience without feedback. In P. Bloom (Ed.), *Language acquisition: Core readings.* Cambridge, MA: MIT Press.

Crook, C. (1995). On resourcing a concern for collaboration within peer interactions. *Cognition and Instruction, 13,* 541–547.

Crooks, T. J. (1988). The impact of classroom evaluation practices on students. *Review of Educational Research, 58,* 438–481.

Cross, D. R., & Paris, S. G. (1988). Developmental and instructional analyses of children's metacognitive and reading comprehension. *Journal of Educational Psychology, 80,* 131–142.

Crowder, R. (1993). Short-term memory: Where do we stand? *Memory and Cognition, 21,* 142–145.

Crowley, K., & Siegler, R. S. (1999). Explanation and generalization in young children's strategy learning. *Child Development, 70,* 304–316.

Crowne, D. P., & Marlowe, D. (1964). *The approval motive: Studies in evaluative dependence.* New York: Wiley.

Csikszentmihalyi, M. (1990). *Flow: The psychology of optimal experience.* New York: HarperPerennial.

Csikszentmihalyi, M. (1996). *Creativity: Flow and the psychology of discovery and invention.* New York: HarperCollins.

Csikszentmihalyi, M., & Nakamura, J. (1989). The dynamics of intrinsic motivation: A study of adolescents. In C. Ames & R. Ames (Eds.), *Research on motivation in education: Vol. 3. Goals and cognitions.* San Diego, CA: Academic Press.

Cunningham, C. E., & Cunningham, L. J. (1998). Student-mediated conflict resolution programs. In R. A. Barkley, *Attention-deficit hyperactivity disorder: A handbook for diagnosis and treatment* (2nd ed., pp. 491–509). New York: Guilford Press.

Cunningham, T. H., & Graham, C. R. (2000). Increasing native English vocabulary recognition through Spanish immersion: Cognate transfer from foreign to first language. *Journal of Educational Psychology, 92,* 37–49.

Curtis, K. A., & Graham, S. (1991, April). *Altering beliefs about the importance of strategy: An attributional intervention.* Paper presented at the annual meeting of the American Educational Research Association, Chicago.

Cushing, L. S., & Kennedy, C. H. (1997). Academic effects of providing peer support in general education classrooms on students without disabilities. *Journal of Applied Behavior Analysis, 30,* 139–151.

Dalrymple, N. J. (1995). Environmental supports to develop flexibility and independence. In K. A. Quill (Ed.), *Teaching children with autism: Strategies to enhance communication and socialization.* New York: Delmar.

D'Amato, R. C., Chitooran, M. M., & Whitten, J. D. (1992). Neuropsychological consequences of malnutrition. In D. I. Templer, L. C. Hartlage, & W. G. Cannon (Eds.), *Preventable brain damage: Brain vulnerability and brain health.* New York: Springer.

Damon, W. (1988). *The moral child: Nurturing children's natural moral growth.* New York: Free Press.

Damon, W. (1991). Putting substance into self-esteem: A focus on academic and moral values. *Educational Horizons, 70*(1), 12–18.

Damon, W., & Hart, D. (1988). *Self understanding from childhood and adolescence.* New York: Cambridge University Press.

Danner, F. W., & Day, M. C. (1977). Eliciting formal operations. *Child Development, 48,* 1600–1606.

Danner, F. W., & Lonky, E. (1981). A cognitive-developmental approach to the effects of rewards on intrinsic motivation. *Child Development, 52,* 1043–1052.

Dansereau, D. F. (1988). Cooperative learning strategies. In C. E. Weinstein, E. T. Goetz, & P. A. Alexander (Eds.), *Learning and study strategies: Issues in assessment, instruction, and evaluation.* San Diego, CA: Academic Press.

Dansereau, D. F. (1995). Derived structural schemas and the transfer of knowledge. In A. McKeough, J. Lupart, & A. Marini (Eds.), *Teaching for transfer: Fostering generalization in learning.* Mahwah, NJ: Erlbaum.

Darley, J. M., & Gross, P. H. (1983). A hypothesis-confirming bias in labeling effects. *Journal of Personality and Social Psychology, 44,* 20–33.

Darling-Hammond, L. (1991). The implications of testing policy for quality and equality. *Phi Delta Kappan, 73,* 220–225.

Darling-Hammond, L. (1995). Inequality and access to knowledge. In J. A. Banks & C. A. M. Banks (Eds.), *Handbook of research on multicultural education.* New York: Macmillan.

Davidson, J. E., & Sternberg, R. J. (1998). Smart problem solving: How metacognition helps. In D. J. Hacker, J. Dunlosky, & A. C. Graesser (Eds.), *Metacognition in educational theory and practice* (pp. 47–68). Mahwah, NJ: Erlbaum.

Davidson, P., Turiel, E., & Black, A. (1983). The effect of stimulus familiarity on the use of criteria and justifications in children's social reasoning. *British Journal of Developmental Psychology, 1,* 49–65.

Davis, G. A., & Rimm, S. B. (1998). *Education of the gifted and talented* (4th ed.). Boston: Allyn & Bacon.

Davis, G. A., & Thomas, M. A. (1989). *Effective schools and effective teachers.* Needham Heights, MA: Allyn & Bacon.

Deaux, K. (1984). From individual differences to social categories: Analysis of a decade's research on gender. *American Psychologist, 39,* 105–116.

deCharms, R. (1972). Personal causation training in the schools. *Journal of Applied Social Psychology, 2,* 95–113.

Deci, E. L. (1992). The relation of interest to the motivation of behavior: A self-determination theory perspective. In K. A. Renninger, S. Hidi, & A. Krapp (Eds.), *The role of interest in learning and development.* Hillsdale, NJ: Erlbaum.

Deci, E. L. (1998). The relation of interest to motivation and human needs: The self-determination theory viewpoint. In L. Hoffman, A. Krapp, K. Renninger, & J. Baumert (Eds.), *Interest and learning: Proceedings of the Seeon Conference on interest and gender* (pp. 146–163). Keil, Germany: IPN.

Deci, E. L., Koestner, R., & Ryan, R. M. (1999). A meta-analytic review of experiments examining the effects of extrinsic rewards on intrinsic motivation. *Psychological Bulletin, 125,* 627–688.

Deci, E. L., & Ryan, R. M. (1985). *Intrinsic motivation and self-determination in human behavior.* New York: Plenum Press.

Deci, E. L., & Ryan, R. M. (1992). The initiation and regulation of intrinsically motivated learning and achievement. In A. K. Boggiano & T. S. Pittman (Eds.), *Achievement and motivation: A social-developmental perspective.* Cambridge, England: Cambridge University Press.

Deci, E. L., & Ryan, R. M. (1995). Human autonomy: The basis for true self-esteem. In M. H. Kernis (Ed.), *Efficacy, agency, and self-esteem.* New York: Plenum Press.

De Corte, E., Greer, B., & Verschaffel, L. (1996). Mathematics teaching and learning. In D. C. Berliner & R. C. Calfee (Eds.), *Handbook of educational psychology.* New York: Macmillan.

Dee-Lucas, D., & Larkin, J. H. (1991). Equations in scientific proofs: Effects on comprehension. *American Educational Research Journal, 28,* 661–682.

DeGangi, G. A., Wietlisbach, S., Poisson, S., Stein, E., & Royeen, C. (1994). The impact of culture and socioeconomic status on family-professional collaboration: Challenges and solutions. *Topics in Early Childhood Special Education, 14,* 503–520.

DeGrandpre, R. J. (2000). A science of meaning: Can behaviorism bring meaning to psychological science? *American Psychologist, 55,* pp. 721–739.

de Jong, T., & van Joolingen, W. R. (1998). Scientific discovery learning with computer simulations of conceptual domains. *Review of Educational Research, 68,* 179–201.

DeLain, M. T., Pearson, P. D., & Anderson, R. C. (1985). Reading comprehension and creativity in black language use: You stand to gain by playing the sounding game! *American Educational Research Journal, 22,* 155–173.

Delandshere, G., & Petrosky, A. R. (1998). Assessment of complex performances: Limitations of key measurement assumptions. *Educational Researcher, 27,* 14–24.

Delgado-Gaitan, C. (1994). Socializing young children in Mexican-American families: An intergenerational perspective. In P. M. Greenfield & R. R. Cocking (Eds.), *Cross-cultural roots of minority child development.* Hillsdale, NJ: Erlbaum.

De Lisi, R., & Golbeck, S. L. (1999). Implications of Piagetian theory for peer learning. In A. M. O'Donnell & A. King (Eds.), *Cognitive perspectives on peer learning* (pp. 3–37). Mahwah, NJ: Erlbaum.

DeLisle, J. R. (1984). *Gifted children speak out.* New York: Walker.

DeLoache, J. S., & Todd, C. M. (1988). Young children's use of spatial categorization as a mnemonic strategy. *Journal of Experimental Child Psychology, 46,* 1–20.

DeMarie-Dreblow, D., & Miller, P. H. (1988). The development of children's strategies for selective attention: Evidence for a transitional period. *Child Development, 59,* 1504–1513.

Dempster, F. N. (1985). Proactive interference in sentence recall: Topic-similarity effects and individual differences. *Memory and Cognition, 13,* 81–89.

Dempster, F. N. (1991). Synthesis of research on reviews and tests. *Educational Leadership, 48*(7), 71–76.

Dempster, F. N., & Corkill, A. J. (1999). Interference and inhibition in cognition and behavior: Unifying themes for educational psychology. *Educational Psychology Review, 11,* 1–88.

Denkla, M. B. (1986). New diagnostic criteria for autism and related behavioral disorders: Guidelines for research protocols. *Journal of the American Academy of Child Psychiatry, 25,* 221–224.

DeRidder, L. M. (1993). Teenage pregnancy: Etiology and educational interventions. *Educational Psychology Review, 5,* 87–107.

Derry, S. J. (1996). Cognitive schema theory in the constructivist debate. *Educational Psychologist, 31,* 163–174.

Derry, S. J., Levin, J. R., Osana, H. P., & Jones, M. S. (1998). Developing middle school students' statistical reasoning abilities through simulation gaming. In S. P. Lajoie (Ed.), *Reflections on statistics: Learning, teaching, and assessment in grades K–12* (pp. 175–195). Mahwah, NJ: Erlbaum.

Desberg, P., & Taylor, J. H. (1986). *Essentials of task analysis.* Lanham, MD: University Press of America.

Deshler, D. D., & Schumaker, J. B. (1988). An instructional model for teaching students how to learn. In J. L. Graden, J. E. Zins, & M. J. Curtis (Eds.), *Alternative educational delivery systems: Enhancing instructional options for all students.* Washington, DC: National Association of School Psychologists.

Deutsch, M. (1993). Educating for a peaceful world. *American Psychologist, 48,* 510–517.

DeVault, G., Krug, C., & Fake, S. (1996, September). Why does Samantha act that way: Positive behavioral support leads to successful inclusion. *Exceptional Parent,* 43–47.

Devine, P. G. (1995). Prejudice and out-group perception. In A. Tesser (Ed.), *Advanced social psychology.* New York: McGraw-Hill.

DeVries, R. (1997). Piaget's social theory. *Educational Researcher, 26*(2), 4–17.

DeVries, R., & Zan, B. (1996). A constructivist perspective on the role of the sociomoral atmosphere in promoting children's development. In C. T. Fosnot (Ed.), *Constructivism: Theory, perspectives, and practice.* New York: Teachers College Press.

Dewhurst, S. A., & Conway, M. A. (1994). Pictures, images, and recollective experience. *Journal of Experimental Psychology: Learning, Memory, and Cognition, 20,* 1088–1098.

Diamond, S. C. (1991). What to do when you can't do anything: Working with disturbed adolescents. *Clearing House, 64,* 232–234.

Diaz, R. M. (1983). Thought and two languages: The impact of bilingualism on cognitive development. In E. W. Gordon (Ed.), *Review of research in education* (Vol. 10). Washington, DC: American Educational Research Association.

Diaz, R. M., & Berk, L. E. (1995) A Vygotskian critique of self-instructional training. *Development and Psychopathology, 7,* 369–392.

Diaz, R. M., & Klingler, C. (1991). Toward an explanatory model of the interaction between bilingualism and cognitive development. In E. Bialystok (Ed.), *Language processing in bilingual children.* Cambridge, England: Cambridge University Press.

Dien, T. (1998). Language and literacy in Vietnamese American communities. In B. Pérez (Ed.), *Sociocultural contexts of language and literacy.* Mahwah, NJ: Erlbaum.

Dirks, J. (1982). The effect of a commercial game on children's Block Design scores on the WISC-R test. *Intelligence, 6,* 109–123.

diSessa, A. A. (1982). Unlearning Aristotelian physics: A study of knowledge-based learning. *Cognitive Science, 6,* 37–75.

diSessa, A. A. (1996). What do "just plain folk" know about physics? In D. R. Olson & N. Torrance (Eds.), *The handbook of education and human development: New models of learning, teaching, and schooling.* Cambridge, MA: Blackwell.

Dishion, T. J., McCord, J., & Poulin, F. (1999). When interventions harm: Peer groups and problem behavior. *American Psychologist, 54,* pp. 755–764.

Dishion, T. J., Spracklen, K. M., Andrews, D. W., & Patterson, G. R. (1996). Deviancy training in male adolescents' friendships. *Behavior Therapy, 27,* 373–390.

Di Vesta, F. J., & Gray, S. G. (1972). Listening and notetaking. *Journal of Educational Psychology, 63,* 8–14.

Di Vesta, F. J., & Peverly, S. T. (1984). The effects of encoding variability, processing activity and rule example sequences on the transfer of conceptual rules. *Journal of Educational Psychology, 76,* 108–119.

Di Vesta, F. J., & Smith, D. A. (1979). The pausing principle: Increasing the efficiency of memory for ongoing events. *Contemporary Educational Psychology, 4,* 288–296.

Dodge, K. A. (1986). A social information processing model of social competence in children. In M. Perlmutter (Ed.), *Minnesota Symposia on Child Psychology: Vol. 18. Cognitive perspectives in children's social and behavioral development.* Hillsdale, NJ: Erlbaum.

Dodge, K. A., Lochman, J. E., Harnish, J. D., Bates, J. E., & Pettit, G. S. (1997). Reactive and proactive aggression in school children and psychiatrically impaired chronically assaultive youth. *Journal of Abnormal Psychology, 106,* 37–51.

Doescher, S. M., & Sugawara, A. I. (1989). Encouraging prosocial behavior in young children. *Childhood Education, 65,* 213–216.

Dole, J. A., Duffy, G. G., Roehler, L. R., & Pearson, P. D. (1991). Moving from the old to the new: Research on reading comprehension instruction. *Review of Educational Research, 61,* 239–264.

Dominowski, R. L. (1998). Verbalization and problem solving. In D. J. Hacker, J. Dunlosky, & A. C. Graesser (Eds.), *Metacognition in educational theory and practice* (pp. 25–45). Mahwah, NJ: Erlbaum.

Donaldson, M. (1978). *Children's minds.* New York: Norton.

Donnelly, C. M., & McDaniel, M. A. (1993). Use of analogy in learning scientific concepts. *Journal of Experimental Psychology: Learning, Memory, and Cognition, 19,* 975–987.

Dovidio, J. F., & Gaertner, S. L. (1999). Reducing prejudice: Combating intergroup biases. *Current Directions in Psychological Science, 8,* 101–105.

Dovidio, J. F., Kawakami, K., & Gaertner, S. L. (2000). Reducing contemporary prejudice: Combating explicit and implicit bias at the individual and intergroup level. In S. Oskamp (Ed.), *Reducing prejudice and discrimination* (pp. 137–163). Mahwah, NJ: Erlbaum.

Downey, G., Bonica, C., & Rincón, C. (1999). Rejection sensitivity and adolescent romantic relationships. In W. Furman, B. B. Brown, & C. Feiring (Eds.), *The development of romantic relationships in adolescence* (pp. 148–174). Cambridge, England: Cambridge University Press.

Dowson, M., & McInerney, D. M. (2001). Psychological parameters of students' social and work avoidance goals: A qualitative investigation. *Journal of Educational Psychology, 93,* 35–42.

Doyle, A. (1982). Friends, acquaintances, and strangers: The influence of familiarity and ethnolinguistic backgrounds on social interaction. In K. Rubin & H. Ross (Eds.), *Peer relationships and social skills in childhood.* New York: Springer-Verlag.

Doyle, W. (1983). Academic work. *Review of Educational Research, 53,* 159–199.

Doyle, W. (1984). How order is achieved in classrooms: An interim report. *Journal of Curriculum Studies, 16,* 259–277.

Doyle, W. (1986a). Classroom organization and management. In M. C. Wittrock (Ed.), *Handbook of research on teaching* (3rd ed.). New York: Macmillan.

Doyle, W. (1986b). Content representation in teachers' definitions of academic work. *Journal of Curriculum Studies, 18,* 365–379.

Doyle, W. (1990). Classroom management techniques. In O. C. Moles (Ed.), *Student discipline strategies: Research and practice.* Albany: State University of New York Press.

Drake, D. D. (1993). Student diversity: Implications for classroom teachers. *The Clearing House, 66,* 264–266.

Dreikurs, R. (1998). *Maintaining sanity in the classroom: Classroom management techniques* (2nd ed.). Bristol, PA: Hemisphere.

Dreikurs, R., & Cassel, P. (1972). *Discipline without tears* (2nd ed.). New York: Dutton.

Drevno, G. E., Kimball, J. W., Possi, M. K., Heward, W. L., Gardner, R., III, & Barbetta, P. M. (1994). Effects of active student responding during error correction on the acquisition, maintenance, and generalization of science vocabulary by elementary students: A systematic replication. *Journal of Applied Behavior Analysis, 27,* 179–180.

Driver, B. L. (1996). Where do we go from here? Sustaining and maintaining co-teaching relationships. *Learning Disabilities Forum, 21*(2), 29–32.

Driver, R. (1995). Constructivist approaches to science teaching. In L. P. Steffe & J. Gale (Eds.), *Constructivism in education.* Hillsdale, NJ: Erlbaum.

Driver, R., Asoko, H., Leach, J., Mortimer, E., & Scott, P. (1994). Constructing scientific knowledge in the classroom. *Educational Researcher, 23*(7), 5–12.

DuBois, N. F., Kiewra, K. A., & Fraley, J. (1988, April). *Differential effects of a learning strategy course.* Paper presented at the annual meeting of the American Educational Research Association, New Orleans, LA.

Duchardt, B. A., Deshler, D. D., & Schumaker, J. B. (1995). A strategy intervention for enabling students with learning disabilities to identify and change their ineffective beliefs. *Learning Disability Quarterly, 18,* 186–201.

Duit, R. (1991). Students' conceptual frameworks: Consequences for learning science. In S. M. Glynn, R. H. Yeany, & B. K. Britton (Eds.), *The psychology of learning science.* Hillsdale, NJ: Erlbaum.

Duke, N. K. (2000). For the rich it's richer: Print experiences and environments offered to children in very low- and very high-socioeconomic status first-grade classrooms. *American Educational Research Journal, 37,* 441–478.

DuNann, D. G., & Weber, S. J. (1976). Short- and long-term effects of contingency managed instruction on low, medium, and high GPA students. *Journal of Applied Behavior Analysis, 9,* 375–376.

Duncker, K. (1945). On problem solving. *Psychological Monographs, 58* (Whole No. 270).

Dunlap, G., dePerczel, M., Clarke, S., Wilson, D., Wright, S., White, R., & Gomez, A. (1994). Choice making to promote adaptive behavior for students with emotional and behavioral challenges. *Journal of Applied Behavior Analysis, 27,* 505–518.

Dunn, J., Bretherton, I., & Munn, P. (1987). Conversations about feeling states between mothers and their young children. *Developmental Psychology, 23,* 132–139.

DuPaul, G. J., Barkley, R. A., & Connor, D. F. (1998). Stimulants. In R. A. Barkley, *Attention-deficit hyperactivity disorder: A handbook for diagnosis and treatment* (2nd ed., pp. 510–551). New York: Guilford Press.

DuPaul, G. J., & Eckert, T. L. (1994). The effects of social skills curricula: Now you see them, now you don't. *School Psychology Quarterly, 9,* 113–132.

DuPaul, G. J., Ervin, R. A., Hook, C. L., & McGoey, K. E. (1998). Peer tutoring for children with attention deficit hyperactivity disorder: Effects on classroom behavior and academic performance. *Journal of Applied Behavior Analysis, 31,* 579–592.

Duran, B. J., & Weffer, R. E. (1992). Immigrants' aspirations, high school process, and academic outcomes. *American Educational Research Journal, 29,* 163–181.

Durkin, K. (1987). Social cognition and social context in the construction of sex differences. In M. A. Baker (Ed.), *Sex differences in human performance.* Chichester, England: Wiley.

Durkin, K. (1995). *Developmental social psychology: From infancy to old age.* Cambridge, MA: Blackwell.

Durost, W. N. (1961). How to tell parents about standardized test results. *Test Service Notebook* (No. 26). New York: Harcourt, Brace, & World.

Dweck, C. S. (1975). The role of expectations and attributions in the alleviation of learned helplessness. *Journal of Personality and Social Psychology, 31,* 674–685.

Dweck, C. S. (1978). Achievement. In M. E. Lamb (Ed.), *Social and personality development.* New York: Holt, Rinehart & Winston.

Dweck, C. S. (1986). Motivational processes affecting learning. *American Psychologist, 41,* 1040–1048.

Dweck, C. S. (1999). *Self-theories: Their role in motivation, personality, and development.* Philadelphia: Taylor & Francis.

Dweck, C. S., & Elliott, E. S. (1983). Achievement motivation. In E. M. Hetherington (Ed.), *Handbook of child psychology: Vol. 4. Socialization, personality, and social development* (4th ed.). New York: Wiley.

Dweck, C. S., & Leggett, E. L. (1988). A social-cognitive approach to motivation and personality. *Psychological Review, 95,* 256–273.

D'Ydewalle, G., Swerts, A., & De Corte, E. (1983). Study time and test performance as a function of test expectations. *Contemporary Educational Psychology, 8*(1), 55–67.

Dyer, H. S. (1967). The discovery and development of educational goals. *Proceedings of the 1966 Invitational Conference on Testing Problems.* Princeton, NJ: Educational Testing Service.

Eacott, M. J. (1999). Memory for the events of early childhood. *Current Directions in Psychological Science, 8,* 46–49.

Eaton, J. F., Anderson, C. W., & Smith, E. L. (1984). Students' misconceptions interfere with science learning: Case studies of fifth-grade students. *Elementary School Journal, 84,* 365–379.

Eaton, W. O., & Enns, L. R. (1986). Sex differences in human motor activity level. *Psychological Bulletin, 100,* 19–28.

Eccles, J. S. (1989). Bringing young women to math and science. In M. Crawford & M. Gentry (Eds.), *Gender and thought: Psychological perspectives.* New York: Springer-Verlag.

Eccles, J. S., & Jacobs, J. E. (1986). Social forces shape math attitudes and performance. *Signs: Journal of Women in Culture and Society, 11,* 367–380.

Eccles, J. S., Jacobs, J., Harold-Goldsmith, R., Jayaratne, T., & Yee, D. (1989, April). *The relations between parents' category-based and target-based beliefs: Gender roles and biological influences.* Paper presented at the Society for Research in Child Development, Kansas City, MO.

Eccles, J. S., & Midgley, C. (1989). Stage-environment fit: Developmentally appropriate classrooms for young adolescents. In C. Ames & R. Ames (Eds.), *Research on motivation in education: Vol. 3. Goals and cognition.* San Diego, CA: Academic Press.

Eccles, J. S., & Wigfield, A. (1985). Teacher expectations and student motivation. In J. B. Dusek (Ed.), *Teacher expectancies.* Hillsdale, NJ: Erlbaum.

Eccles, J., Wigfield, A., Flanagan, C., Miller, C., Reuman, D., & Yee, D. (1989). Self-concepts, domain values, and self-esteem: Relations and changes at early adolescence. *Journal of Personality, 57,* 283–310.

Eccles, J. S., Wigfield, A., & Schiefele, U. (1998). Motivation to succeed. In W. Damon (Editor-in-Chief) & N. Eisenberg (Vol. Ed.), *Handbook of child psychology: Vol. 3. Social, emotional, and personality development* (5th ed.). New York: Wiley.

Eccles (Parsons), J. S. (1983). Expectancies, values, and academic behaviors. In J. T. Spence (Ed.), *Achievement and achievement motivation.* San Francisco: Freeman.

Eccles (Parsons), J. S. (1984). Sex differences in mathematics participation. In M. Steinkamp & M. Maehr (Eds.), *Women in science.* Greenwich, CT: JAI Press.

Eckert, P. (1989). *Jocks and burnouts: Social categories and identity in the high school.* New York: Teachers College Press.

Eden, G. F., Stein, J. F., & Wood, F. B. (1995). Verbal and visual problems in reading disability. *Journal of Learning Disabilities, 28,* 272–290.

Edens, K. M., & Potter, E. F. (2001). Promoting conceptual understanding through pictorial representation. *Studies in Art Education, 42,* 214–233.

Educational Testing Service. (2001). *Principles of Learning and Teaching study guide.* Princeton, NJ: Author.

Eeds, M., & Wells, D. (1989). Grand conversations: An explanation of meaning construction in literature study groups. *Research in the Teaching of English, 23,* 4–29.

Eisenberg, N. (1982). The development of reasoning regarding prosocial behavior. In N. Eisenberg (Ed.), *The development of prosocial behavior.* San Diego, CA: Academic Press.

Eisenberg, N. (1987). The relation of altruism and other moral behaviors to moral cognition: Methodological and conceptual issues. In N. Eisenberg (Ed.), *Contemporary topics in developmental psychology* (pp. 165–189). New York: Wiley.

Eisenberg, N., Carlo, G., Murphy, B., & Van Court, N. (1995). Prosocial development in late adolescence: A longitudinal study. *Child Development, 66,* 1179–1197.

Eisenberg, N., & Fabes, R. A. (1991). Prosocial behavior: A multimethod developmental perspective. In M. S. Clark (Ed.), *Review of personality and social psychology* (Vol. 2, pp. 34–61). Newbury Park, CA: Sage.

Eisenberg, N., Lennon, R., & Pasternack, J. F. (1986). Altruistic values and moral judgment. In N. Eisenberg (Ed.), *Altruistic emotion, cognition, and behavior.* Hillsdale, NJ: Erlbaum.

Eisenberg, N., Lennon, R., & Roth, K. (1983). Prosocial development: A longitudinal study. *Developmental Psychology, 19,* 846–855.

Eisenberg, N., Martin, C. L., & Fabes, R. A. (1996). Gender development and gender effects. In D. C. Berliner & R. C. Calfee (Eds.), *Handbook of educational psychology.* New York: Macmillan.

Eisenberg, N., Miller, P. A., Shell, R., McNalley, S., & Shea, C. (1991). Prosocial development in adolescence: A longitudinal study. *Developmental Psychology, 27,* 849–857.

Eisenberger, R. (1992). Learned industriousness. *Psychological Review, 99,* 248–267.

Elia, J. P. (1994). Homophobia in the high school: A problem in need of a resolution. *Journal of Homosexuality, 77*(1), 177–185.

Elkind, D. (1981). *Children and adolescents: Interpretive essays on Jean Piaget* (3rd ed.). New York: Oxford University Press.

Elkind, D. (1984). *All grown up and no place to go.* Reading, MA: Addison-Wesley.

Ellenwood, S., & Ryan, K. (1991). Literature and morality: An experimental curriculum. In W. M. Kurtines & J. L. Gewirtz (Eds.), *Moral behavior and development: Vol. 3. Application.* Hillsdale, NJ: Erlbaum.

Elliot, A. J., & McGregor, H. A. (2000, April). Approach and avoidance goals and autonomous-controlled regulation: Empirical and conceptual relations. In A. Assor (Chair), *Self-determination theory and achievement goal theory: Convergences, divergences, and educational implications.* Symposium conducted at the annual meeting of the American Educational Research Association, New Orleans, LA.

Elliot, A. J., & Thrash, T. M. (2001). Achievement goals and the hierarchical model of achievement motivation. *Educational Psychology Review, 13,* 139–156.

Elliott, D. J. (1995). *Music matters: A new philosophy of music education.* New York: Oxford University Press.

Elliott, R., & Vasta, R. (1970). The modeling of sharing: Effects associated with vicarious reinforcement, symbolization, age, and generalization. *Journal of Experimental Child Psychology, 10,* 8–15.

Elliott, S. N., & Busse, R. T. (1991). Social skills assessment and intervention with children and adolescents. *School Psychology International, 12,* 63–83.

Ellis, E. S., & Friend, P. (1991). Adolescents with learning disabilities. In B. Y. L. Wong (Ed.), *Learning about learning disabilities.* San Diego, CA: Academic Press.

Ellis, H. C., & Hunt, R. R. (1983). *Fundamentals of human memory and cognition* (3rd ed.). Dubuque, IA: Wm. C. Brown.

Ellis, N. C. (Ed.). (1994). *Implicit and explicit learning of languages.* London: Academic Press.

Ellis, N. R. (Ed.). (1979). *Handbook of mental deficiency: Psychological theory and research.* Hillsdale, NJ: Erlbaum.

Elrich, M. (1994). The stereotype within. *Educational Leadership, 51*(8), 12–15.

Emmer, E. T. (1987). Classroom management and discipline. In V. Richardson-Koehler (Ed.), *Educators' handbook: A research perspective.* White Plains, NY: Longman.

Emmer, E. T. (1994, April). *Teacher emotions and classroom management.* Paper presented at the annual meeting of the American Educational Research Association, New Orleans, LA.

Emmer, E. T., & Evertson, C. M. (1981). Synthesis of research on classroom management. *Educational Leadership, 38,* 342–347.

Emmer, E. T., Evertson, C. M., Clements, B. S., & Worsham, M. E. (1994). *Classroom management for secondary teachers* (3rd ed.). Needham Heights, MA: Allyn & Bacon.

Emmer, E. T., & Stough, L. M. (2001). Classroom management: A critical part of educational psychology, with implications for teacher education. *Educational Psychologist, 36,* 103–112.

Empson, S. B. (1999). Equal sharing and shared meaning: The development of fraction concepts in a first-grade classroom. *Cognition and Instruction, 17,* 283–342.

Englemann, S., & Carnine, D. (1982). *Theory of instruction: Principles and applications.* New York: Irvington.

Epstein, H. (1978). Growth spurts during brain development: Implications for educational policy and practice. In J. Chall & A. Mirsky (Eds.), *Education and the brain: The 77th yearbook of the National Society for the Study of*

Education, Part II. Chicago: University of Chicago Press.

Epstein, J. L. (1983). Longitudinal effects of family-school-person interactions on student outcomes. *Research in Sociology of Education and Socialization, 4,* 101–127.

Epstein, J. L. (1986). Friendship selection: Developmental and environmental influences. In E. Mueller & C. Cooper (Eds.), *Process and outcome in peer relationships* (pp. 129–160). New York: Academic Press.

Epstein, J. L. (1996). Perspectives and previews on research and policy for school, family, and community partnerships. In A. Booth & J. F. Dunn (Eds.), *Family-school links: How do they affect educational outcomes?* Mahwah, NJ: Erlbaum.

Epstein, J. L., & Van Voorhis, F. L. (2001). More than minutes: Teachers' roles in designing homework. *Educational Psychologist, 36,* 181–193.

Epstein, J. S. (1998). Introduction: Generation X, youth culture, and identity. In J. S. Epstein (Ed.), *Youth culture: Identity in a postmodern world.* Malden, MA: Blackwell.

Epstein, T. (2000). Adolescents' perspectives on racial diversity in U.S. history: Case studies from an urban classroom. *American Educational Research Journal, 37,* 185–214.

Erdley, C. A. (1996). Motivational approaches to aggression within the context of peer relationships. In J. Juvonen & K. R. Wentzel (Eds.), *Social motivation: Understanding children's school adjustment* (pp. 98–125). Cambridge, England: Cambridge University Press.

Erdley, C. A., & Asher, S. R. (1996). Children's social goals and self-efficacy perceptions as influences on their responses to ambiguous provocation. *Child Development, 67,* 1329–1344.

Ericsson, K. A., & Chalmers, N. (1994). Expert performance: Its structure and acquisition. *American Psychologist, 49,* 725–747.

Eriks-Brophy, A., & Crago, M. B. (1994). Transforming classroom discourse: An Inuit example. *Language and Education, 8*(3), 105–122.

Erikson, E. H. (1963). *Childhood and society* (2nd ed.). New York: Norton.

Erikson, E. H. (1972). Eight ages of man. In C. S. Lavatelli & F. Stendler (Eds.), *Readings in child behavior and child development.* San Diego, CA: Harcourt Brace Jovanovich.

Eron, L. D. (1980). Prescription for reduction of aggression. *American Psychologist, 35,* 244–252.

Erwin, P. (1993). *Friendship and peer relations in children.* Chichester, England: Wiley.

Esquivel, G. B. (1995). Teacher behaviors that foster creativity. *Educational Psychology Review, 7,* 185–202.

Etaugh, C. (1983). Introduction: The influence of environmental factors on sex differences in children's play. In M. B. Liss (Ed.), *Social and cognitive skills: Sex roles and children's play.* San Diego, CA: Academic Press.

Evans, E. D., & Craig, D. (1990). Teacher and student perceptions of academic cheating in middle and senior high schools. *Journal of Educational Research, 84*(1), 44–52.

Evans, G. W., & Oswalt, G. L. (1968). Acceleration of academic progress through the manipulation of peer influence. *Behaviour Research and Therapy, 6,* 189–195.

Evertson, C. M., & Emmer, E. T. (1982). Effective management at the beginning of the year in junior high classes. *Journal of Educational Psychology, 74,* 485–498.

Evertson, C. M., & Harris, A. H. (1992). What we know about managing classrooms. *Educational Leadership, 49*(7), 74–78.

Eysenck, M. W. (1992). *Anxiety: The cognitive perspective.* Hove, England: Erlbaum.

Eysenck, M. W., & Keane, M. T. (1990). *Cognitive psychology: A student's handbook.* Hove, England: Erlbaum.

Fabes, R. A., Eisenberg, N., Jones, S., Smith, M., Guthrie, I., Poulin, R., Shepard, S., & Friedman, J. (1999). Regulation, emotionality, and preschoolers' socially competent peer interactions. *Child Development, 70,* 432–442.

Fabos, B., & Young, M. D. (1999). Telecommunication in the classroom: Rhetoric versus reality. *Review of Educational Research, 69,* 217–259.

Fagot, B. I., Hagan, R., Leinbach, M. D., & Kronsberg, S. (1985). Differential reactions to assertive and communicative acts of toddler boys and girls. *Child Development, 56,* 1499–1505.

Fagot, B. I., & Leinbach, M. D. (1983). Play styles in early childhood: Social consequences for boys and girls. In M. B. Liss (Ed.), *Social and cognitive skills: Sex roles and children's play.* San Diego, CA: Academic Press.

Fairchild, H. H., & Edwards-Evans, S. (1990). African American dialects and schooling: A review. In A. M. Padilla, H. H. Fairchild, & C. M. Valadez (Eds.), *Bilingual education: Issues and strategies.* Newbury Park, CA: Sage.

Fall, R., Webb, N. M., & Chudowsky, N. (2000). Group discussion and large-scale language arts assessment: Effects on students' comprehension. *American Educational Research Journal, 37,* 911–941.

Fantuzzo, J. W., King, J., & Heller, L. R. (1992). Effects of reciprocal peer tutoring on mathematics and school adjustment: A component analysis. *Journal of Educational Psychology, 84,* 331–339.

Faraone, S. V., Biederman, J., Chen, W. J., Milberger, S., Warburton, R., & Tsuang, M. T. (1995). Genetic heterogeneity in attention-deficit hyperactivity disorder (ADHD): Gender, psychiatric comorbidity, and maternal ADHD. *Journal of Abnormal Psychology, 104,* 334–345.

Farrell, E. (1990). *Hanging in and dropping out: Voices of at-risk high school students.* New York: Teachers College Press.

Farwell, L., & Weiner, B. (1996). Self-perception of fairness in individual and group contexts. *Personality and Social Psychology Bulletin, 22,* 867–881.

Feather, N. T. (1982). *Expectations and actions: Expectancy-value models in psychology.* Hillsdale, NJ: Erlbaum.

Feld, S., Ruhland, D., & Gold, M. (1979). Developmental changes in achievement motivation. *Merrill-Palmer Quarterly, 25,* 43–60.

Feldhusen, J. F. (1989). Synthesis of research on gifted youth. *Educational Leadership, 26*(1), 6–11.

Feldhusen, J. F., & Treffinger, D. J. (1980). *Creative thinking and problem solving in gifted education.* Dubuque, IA: Kendall/Hunt.

Feldhusen, J. F., Treffinger, D. J., & Bahlke, S. J. (1970). Developing creative thinking: The Purdue Creativity Program. *Journal of Creative Behavior, 4,* 85–90.

Feldhusen, J. F., Van Winkle, L., & Ehle, D. A. (1996). Is it acceleration or simply appropriate instruction for precocious youth? *Teaching Exceptional Children, 28*(3), 48–51.

Feltz, D. L., Chaase, M. A., Moritz, S. E., & Sullivan, P. J. (1999). A conceptual model of coaching efficacy: Preliminary investigation and instrument development. *Journal of Educational Psychology, 91,* 765–776.

Fennema, E. (1987). Sex-related differences in education: Myths, realities, and interventions. In V. Richardson-Koehler (Ed.), *Educators'*

handbook: A research perspective. White Plains, NY: Longman.

Ferguson, E. L., & Hegarty, M. (1995). Learning with real machines or diagrams: Application of knowledge to real-world problems. *Cognition and Instruction, 13,* 129–160.

Ferguson, R. (1998). Can schools narrow the Black-White test score gap? In C. Jencks & M. Phillips (Eds.), *The Black-White test score gap* (pp. 318–374). Washington, DC: Brookings Institute.

Fessler, M. A., Rosenberg, M. S., & Rosenberg, L. A. (1991). Concomitant learning disabilities and learning problems among students with behavioral/emotional disorders. *Behavioral Disorders, 16,* 97–106.

Feuerstein, R. (1979). *The dynamic assessment of retarded performers: The Learning Potential Assessment Device, theory, instruments, and techniques.* Baltimore: University Park Press.

Feuerstein, R., Feuerstein, R., & Gross, S. (1997). The Learning Potential Assessment Device. In D. P. Flanagan, J. L. Genshaft, & P. L. Harrison (Eds.), *Contemporary intellectual assessment: Theories, tests, and issues* (pp. 297–313). New York: Guilford Press.

Feuerstein, R., Klein, P. R., & Tannenbaum, A. (Eds.). (1991). *Mediated learning experience: Theoretical, psychosocial, and learning implications.* London: Freund.

Fey, M. E., Catts, H., & Larrivee, L. (1995). Preparing preschoolers for the academic and social challenges of school. In M. E. Fey, J. Windsor, & S. F. Warren (Eds.), *Language intervention: Preschool through elementary years.* Baltimore: Brookes.

Fiedler, E. D., Lange, R. E., & Winebrenner, S. (1993). In search of reality: Unraveling the myths about tracking, ability grouping and the gifted. *Roeper Review, 16*(1), 4–7.

Field, D. (1987). A review of preschool conservation training: An analysis of analyses. *Developmental Review, 7,* 210–251.

Finders, M., & Lewis, C. (1994). Why some parents don't come to school. *Educational Leadership, 51*(8), 50–54.

Finkelhor, D., & Ormrod, R. (2000, December). *Juvenile victims of property crimes.* Washington, DC: U.S. Department of Justice, Office of Justice Programs, Office of Juvenile Justice and Delinquency Prevention.

Finn, J. D. (1989). Withdrawing from school. *Review of Educational Research, 59,* 117–142.

Finn, J. D. (1991). How to make the dropout problem go away. *Educational Researcher, 20*(1), 28–30.

Fischer, K. W., & Bidell, T. (1991). Constraining nativist inferences about cognitive capacities. In S. Carey & R. Gelman (Eds.), *The epigenesis of mind: Essays on biology and cognition.* Hillsdale, NJ: Erlbaum.

Fischer, K. W., & Rose, S. P. (1996). Dynamic growth cycles of brain and cognitive development. In R. Thatcher, G. R. Lyon, J. Rumsey, & N. Krasnegor (Eds.), *Developmental neuroimaging: Mapping the development of brain and behavior.* New York: Academic Press.

Fisher, W. W., & Mazur, J. E. (1997). Basic and applied research on choice responding. *Journal of Applied Behavior Analysis, 30,* 387–410.

Fivush, R., Haden, C., & Adam, S. (1995). Structure and coherence of preschoolers' personal narratives over time: Implications for childhood amnesia. *Journal of Experimental Child Psychology, 60,* 32–56.

Flavell, J. H. (1985). *Cognitive development* (2nd ed.). Upper Saddle River, NJ: Prentice Hall.

Flavell, J. H. (1994). Cognitive development: Past, present, and future. In R. D. Parke, P. A.

Ornstein, J. J. Rieser, & C. Zahn-Waxler (Eds.), *A century of developmental psychology.* Washington, DC: American Psychological Association.

Flavell, J. H. (1996). Piaget's legacy. *Psychological Science, 7,* 200–203.

Flavell, J. H., Friedrichs, A. G., & Hoyt, J. D. (1970). Developmental changes in memorization processes. *Cognitive Psychology, 1,* 324–340.

Flavell, J. H., Miller, P. H., & Miller, S. A. (1993). *Cognitive development* (3rd ed.). Upper Saddle River, NJ: Prentice Hall.

Fletcher, K. L., & Bray, N. W. (1995). External and verbal strategies in children with and without mild mental retardation. *American Journal on Mental Retardation, 99,* 363–475.

Flynn, J. R. (1987). Massive IQ gains in 14 nations: What IQ tests really measure. *Psychological Bulletin, 101,* 171–191.

Foos, P. W., & Fisher, R. P. (1988). Using tests as learning opportunities. *Journal of Educational Psychology, 80,* 179–183.

Ford, D. Y. (1996). *Reversing underachievement among gifted black students.* New York: Teachers College Press.

Ford, D. Y., & Harris, J. J. (1992). The American achievement ideology and achievement differentials among preadolescent gifted and nongifted African American males and females. *Journal of Negro Education, 61*(1), 45–64.

Ford, M. E. (1992). *Motivating humans: Goals, emotions, and personal agency beliefs.* Newbury Park, CA: Sage.

Ford, M. E. (1996). Motivational opportunities and obstacles associated with social responsibility and caring behavior in school contexts. In J. Juvonen & K. R. Wentzel (Eds.), *Social motivation: Understanding children's school adjustment* (pp. 126–153). Cambridge, England: Cambridge University Press.

Fordham, S., & Ogbu, J. U. (1986). Black students' school success: Coping with "the burden of 'acting white.' " *The Urban Review, 18,* 176–206.

Forsyth, J. P., & Eifert, G. H. (1998). Phobic anxiety and panic: An integrative behavioral account of their origin and treatment. In J. J. Plaud & G. H. Eifert (Eds.), *From behavior theory to behavior therapy* (pp. 38–67). Needham Heights, MA: Allyn & Bacon.

Fosnot, C. T. (1996). Constructivism: A psychological theory of learning. In C. T. Fosnot (Ed.), *Constructivism: Theory, perspectives, and practice.* New York: Teachers College Press.

Foster-Johnson, L., Ferro, J., & Dunlap, G. (1994). Preferred curriculum activities and reduced problem behaviors in students with intellectual disabilities. *Journal of Applied Behavior Analysis, 27,* 493–504.

Fowler, S. A., & Baer, D. M. (1981). "Do I have to be good all day?" The timing of delayed reinforcement as a factor in generalization. *Journal of Applied Behavior Analysis, 14,* 13–24.

Fox, L. H. (1979). Programs for the gifted and talented: An overview. In A. H. Passow (Ed.), *The gifted and the talented: Their education and development. The seventy-eighth yearbook of the National Society for the Study of Education.* Chicago: University of Chicago Press.

Fox, L. H. (1981). *The problem of women and mathematics.* New York: Ford Foundation.

Fox, P. W., & LeCount, J. (1991, April). *When more is less: Faculty misestimation of student learning.* Paper presented at the annual meeting of the American Educational Research Association, Chicago.

Frasier, M. M. (1989). Identification of gifted black students: Developing new perspectives. In C. J. Maker & S. W. Schiever (Eds.), *Critical issues in gifted education: Vol. 2. Defensible programs for cultural and ethnic minorities.* Austin, TX: Pro-Ed.

Frederiksen, J. R., & Collins, A. (1989). A systems approach to educational testing. *Educational Researcher, 18*(9), 27–32.

Frederiksen, N. (1984a). Implications of cognitive theory for instruction in problem-solving. *Review of Educational Research, 54,* 363–407.

Frederiksen, N. (1984b). The real test bias: Influences of testing on teaching and learning. *American Psychologist, 39,* 193–202.

Freedman, K. (1996). The social reconstruction of art education: Teaching visual culture. In C. A. Grant & M. L. Gomez, *Making schooling multicultural: Campus and classroom.* Upper Saddle River, NJ: Merrill/Prentice Hall.

Freedman, S. G. (1990). *Small victories: The real world of a teacher, her students, and their high school.* New York: Harper & Row.

Freeland, J. T., & Noell, G. H. (1999). Maintaining accurate math responses in elementary school students: The effects of delayed intermittent reinforcement and programming common stimuli. *Journal of Applied Behavior Analysis, 32,* 211–215.

Freiberg, H. J. (1987). Teacher self-evaluation and principal supervision. *NASSP Bulletin* (National Association of Secondary School Principals), *71,* 85–92.

French, E. G. (1956). Motivation as a variable in work partner selection. *Journal of Abnormal and Social Psychology, 53,* 96–99.

Friedel, M. (1993). *Characteristics of gifted/creative children.* Warwick, RI: National Foundation for Gifted and Creative Children.

Friedman, L. (1995). The space factor in mathematics: Gender differences. *Review of Educational Research, 65,* 22–50.

Friedrich, L. K., & Stein, A. H. (1973). Aggressive and pro-social television programs and the natural behavior of preschool children. *Society for Research in Child Development Monographs, 38* (Whole No. 151).

Frisbie, D. A., & Waltman, K. K. (1992). Developing a personal grading plan. *Educational Measurement: Issues and Practices, 11,* 35–42. Reprinted in K. M. Cauley, F. Linder, & J. H. McMillan (Eds.), (1994), *Educational psychology 94/95.* Guilford, CT: Dushkin.

Frost, J. L., Shin, D., & Jacobs, P. J. (1998). Physical environments and children's play. In O. N. Saracho & B. Spodek (Eds.), *Multiple perspectives on play in early childhood education.* Albany: State University of New York Press.

Fuchs, D., Fuchs, L. S., Mathes, P. G., & Simmons, D. C. (1997). Peer-assisted learning strategies: Making classrooms more responsive to diversity. *American Educational Research Journal, 34,* 174–206.

Fuchs, L. S., Fuchs, D., Hamlett, C. L., & Karns, K. (1998). High-achieving students' interactions and performance on complex mathematical tasks as a function of homogeneous and heterogeneous pairings. *American Educational Research Journal, 35,* 227–267.

Fuchs, L. S., Fuchs, D., Karns, K., Hamlett, C. L., Dutka, S., & Katzaroff, M. (1996). The relation between student ability and the quality and effectiveness of explanations. *American Educational Research Journal, 33,* 631–664.

Fueyo, V., & Bushell, D., Jr. (1998). Using number line procedures and peer tutoring to improve the mathematics computation of low-performing first graders. *Journal of Applied Behavior Analysis, 31,* 417–430.

Fuligni, A. J. (1998). The adjustment of children from immigrant families. *Current Directions in Psychological Science, 7,* 99–103.

Fuller, M. L. (2001). Multicultural concerns and classroom management. In C. A. Grant & M. L. Gomez, *Campus and classroom: Making schooling multicultural* (2nd ed., pp. 109–134). Upper Saddle River, NJ: Merrill/Prentice Hall.

Funder, D. C. (1991). Global traits: A neo-Allportian approach to personality. *Psychological Science, 2,* 31–39.

Furman, W., & Simon, V. A. (1999). Cognitive representations of adolescent romantic relationships. In W. Furman, B. B. Brown, & C. Feiring (Eds.), *The development of romantic relationships in adolescence* (pp. 75–98). Cambridge, England: Cambridge University Press.

Gage, N. L. (1991). The obviousness of social and educational research results. *Educational Researcher, 20*(1), 10–16.

Gagné, E. D. (1985). *The cognitive psychology of school learning.* Boston: Little, Brown.

Gagné, R. M. (1985). *The conditions of learning and theory of instruction* (4th ed.). New York: Holt, Rinehart & Winston.

Gagné, R. M., Briggs, L. J., & Wager, W. W. (1992). *Principles of instructional design* (4th ed.). Fort Worth, TX: Harcourt Brace Jovanovich.

Gaines, M. L., & Davis, M. (1990, April). *Accuracy of teacher prediction of elementary student achievement.* Paper presented at the annual meeting of the American Educational Research Association, Boston.

Gallagher, J. J. (1991). Personal patterns of underachievement. *Journal for the Education of the Gifted, 14,* 221–233.

Gallimore, R., & Goldenberg, C. (2001). Analyzing cultural models and settings to connect minority achievement and school improvement research. *Educational Psychologist, 36,* 45–56.

Gallimore, R., & Tharp, R. (1990). Teaching mind in society: Teaching, schooling, and literate discourse. In L. C. Moll (Ed.), *Vygotsky and education: Instructional implications and applications of sociohistorical psychology.* Cambridge, England: Cambridge University Press.

Gallini, J. (2000, April). *An investigation of self-regulation developments in early adolescence: A comparison between non at-risk and at-risk students.* Paper presented at the annual meeting of the American Educational Research Association, New Orleans, LA.

Garcia, E. E. (1992). "Hispanic" children: Theoretical, empirical, and related policy issues. *Educational Psychology Review, 4,* 69–93.

Garcia, E. E. (1994). *Understanding and meeting the challenge of student cultural diversity.* Boston: Houghton Mifflin.

García, E. E. (1995). Educating Mexican American students: Past treatment and recent developments in theory, research, policy, and practice. In J. A. Banks & C. A. M. Banks (Eds.), *Handbook of research on multicultural education.* New York: Macmillan.

Gardner, H. (1983). *Frames of mind: The theory of multiple intelligences.* New York: Basic Books.

Gardner, H. (1995). Reflections on multiple intelligences: Myths and messages. *Phi Delta Kappan, 77,* 200–209.

Gardner, H. (1998, April). *Where to draw the line: The perils of new paradigms.* Paper presented at the annual meeting of the American Educational Research Association, San Diego, CA.

Gardner, H. (1999). *Intelligence reframed: Multiple intelligences for the 21st century.* New York: Basic Books.

Gardner, H. (2000). *The disciplined mind: Beyond facts and standardized tests, the K–12 education that every child deserves.* New York: Penguin Books.

Gardner, H., & Hatch, T. (1990). Multiple intelligences go to school: Educational implications of the theory of multiple intelligences. *Educational Researcher, 18*(8), 4–10.

Garhart, C., & Hannafin, M. J. (1986). The accuracy of cognitive monitoring during computer-based instruction. *Journal of Computer-Based Instruction, 13,* 88–93.

Garibaldi, A. M. (1992). Educating and motivating African American males to succeed. *The Journal of Negro Education, 61*(1), 4–11.

Garibaldi, A. M. (1993). Creating prescriptions for success in urban schools: Turning the corner on pathological explanations for academic failure. In T. M. Tomlinson (Ed.), *Motivating students to learn: Overcoming barriers to high achievement.* Berkeley, CA: McCutchan.

Garner, R., Alexander, P. A., Gillingham, M. G., Kulikowich, J. M., & Brown, R. (1991). Interest and learning from text. *American Educational Research Journal, 28,* 643–659.

Garner, R., Brown, R., Sanders, S., & Menke, D. J. (1992). "Seductive details" and learning from text. In K. A. Renninger, S. Hidi, & A. Krapp (Eds.), *The role of interest in learning and development.* Hillsdale, NJ: Erlbaum.

Garnier, H. E., Stein, J. A., & Jacobs, J. K. (1997). The process of dropping out of high school: A 19-year perspective. *American Educational Research Journal, 34,* 395–419.

Garrison, L. (1989). Programming for the gifted American Indian student. In C. J. Maker & S. W. Schiever (Eds.), *Critical issues in gifted education: Vol. 2: Defensible programs for cultural and ethnic minorities.* Austin, TX: Pro-Ed.

Garvey, C., & Horgan, R. (1973). Social speech and social interaction: Egocentrism revisited. *Child Development, 44,* 562–568.

Gaskill, P. J. (2001, April). *Differential effects of reinforcement feedback and attributional feedback on second-graders' self-efficacy.* Paper presented at the annual meeting of the American Educational Research Association, Seattle, WA.

Gathercole, S. E., & Hitch, G. J. (1993). Developmental changes in short-term memory: A revised working memory perspective. In A. F. Collins, S. E. Gathercole, M. A. Conway, & P. E. Morris (Eds.), *Theories of memory.* Hove, England: Erlbaum.

Gaudry, E., & Bradshaw, G. D. (1971). The differential effect of anxiety on performance in progressive and terminal school examinations. In E. Gaudry & C. D. Spielberger (Eds.), *Anxiety and educational achievement.* Sydney, Australia: Wiley.

Gauntt, H. L. (1991, April). *The roles of prior knowledge of text structure and prior knowledge of content in the comprehension and recall of expository text.* Paper presented at the annual meeting of the American Educational Research Association, Chicago.

Gavin, L. A., & Fuhrman, W. (1989). Age differences in adolescents' perceptions of their peer groups. *Developmental Psychology, 25,* 827–834.

Gay, J., & Cole, M. (1967). *The new mathematics and an old culture.* New York: Holt, Rinehart & Winston.

Gayford, C. (1992). Patterns of group behavior in open-ended problem solving in science classes of 15-year-old students in England. *International Journal of Science Education, 14,* 41–49.

Gaynor, J., & Millham, J. (1976). Student performance and evaluation under variant teaching and testing methods in a large college course. *Journal of Educational Psychology, 68,* 312–317.

Gearheart, B. R., Weishahn, M. W., & Gearheart, C. J. (1992). *The exceptional child in the regular classroom* (5th ed.). Upper Saddle River, NJ: Merrill/Prentice Hall.

Geary, D. C. (1998). What is the function of mind and brain? *Educational Psychology Review, 10,* 377–387.

Gelman, R., & Baillargeon, R. (1983). A review of some Piagetian concepts. In J. H. Flavell & E. M. Markman (Eds.), *Handbook of child psychology: Vol. 3. Cognitive development.* New York: Wiley.

Genova, W. J., & Walberg, H. J. (1984). Enhancing integration in urban high schools. In D. E. Bartz & M. L. Maehr (Eds.), *Advances in motivation and achievement: Vol 1. The effects of school desegregation on motivation and achievement.* Greenwich, CT: JAI Press.

Gerst, M. S. (1971). Symbolic coding processes in observational learning. *Journal of Personality and Social Psychology, 19,* 7–17.

Gettinger, M. (1988). Methods of proactive classroom management. *School Psychology Review, 17,* 227–242.

Giaconia, R. M. (1988). Teacher questioning and wait-time (Doctoral dissertation, Stanford University, 1988). *Dissertation Abstracts International, 49,* 462A.

Giaconia, R. M., & Hedges, L. V. (1982). Identifying features of effective open education. *Review of Educational Research, 52,* 579–602.

Giangreco, M. F. (1997). Responses to Nietupski et al. *Journal of Special Education, 31,* 56–57.

Gick, M. L., & Holyoak, K. J. (1987). The cognitive basis of knowledge transfer. In S. M. Cormier & J. D. Hagman (Eds.), *Transfer of learning: Contemporary research and applications.* San Diego, CA: Academic Press.

Giedd, J. N., Blumenthal, J., Jeffries, N. O., Castellanos, F. X., Liu, H., Zijdenbos, A., Paus, T., Evans, A. C., & Rapoport, J. L. (1999a). Brain development during childhood and adolescence: A longitudinal MRI study. *Nature Neuroscience, 2,* 861–863.

Giedd, J. N., Blumenthal, J., Jeffries, N. O., Rajapakse, J. C., Vaituzis, A. C., Liu, H., Berry, Y. C., Tobin, M., Nelson, J., & Castellanos, F. X. (1999b). Development of the human corpus callosum during childhood and adolescence: A longitudinal MRI study. *Progress in Neuro-Psychopharmacology and Biological Psychiatry, 23,* 571–588.

Gillberg, I. C., & Coleman, M. (1996). Autism and medical disorders: A review of the literature. *Developmental Medicine and Child Neurology, 38,* 191–202.

Gillies, R. M., & Ashman, A. D. (1998). Behavior and interactions of children in cooperative groups in lower and middle elementary grades. *Journal of Educational Psychology, 90,* 746–757.

Gilligan, C. F. (1982). *In a different voice.* Cambridge, MA: Harvard University Press.

Gilligan, C. F. (1985, March). Keynote address. Conference on Women and Moral Theory, Stony Brook, NY.

Gilligan, C. F. (1987). Moral orientation and moral development. In E. F. Kittay & D. T. Meyers (Eds.), *Women and moral theory.* Totowa, NJ: Rowman & Littlefield.

Gilligan, C., & Attanucci, J. (1988). Two moral orientations: Gender differences and similarities. *Merrill-Palmer Quarterly, 34,* 223–237.

Gilliland, H. (1988). Discovering and emphasizing the positive aspects of the culture. In H. Gilliland & J. Reyhner (Eds.), *Teaching the Native American.* Dubuque, IA: Kendall/Hunt.

Gilpin, L. (1968). *The enduring Navaho.* Austin: University of Texas Press.

Ginsberg, D., Gottman, J. M., & Parker, J. G. (1986). The importance of friendship. In J. M. Gottman & J. G. Parker (Eds.), *Conversations of friends: Speculations on affective development* (pp. 3–48). Cambridge, England: Cambridge University Press.

Girotto, V., & Light, P. (1993). The pragmatic bases of children's reasoning. In P. Light & G. Butter-

worth (Eds.), *Context and cognition: Ways of learning and knowing.* Hillsdale, NJ: Erlbaum.

Glanzer, M., & Nolan, S. D. (1986). Memory mechanisms in text comprehension. In G. H. Bower (Ed.), *The psychology of learning and motivation: Advances in research and theory* (Vol. 20). San Diego, CA: Academic Press.

Glass, A. L., & Holyoak, K. J. (1975). Alternative conceptions of semantic memory. *Cognition, 3,* 313–339.

Glass, A. L., Holyoak, K. J., & Santa, J. L. (1979). *Cognition.* Reading, MA: Addison-Wesley.

Glasser, W. (1969). *Schools without failure.* New York: Harper & Row.

Glover, J. A. (1989). The "testing" phenomenon: Not gone but nearly forgotten. *Journal of Educational Psychology, 81,* 392–399.

Glover, J. A., Ronning, R. R., & Reynolds, C. R. (Eds.). (1989). *Handbook of creativity.* New York: Plenum Press.

Glucksberg, S., & Krauss, R. M. (1967). What do people say after they have learned to talk? Studies of the development of referential communication. *Merrill-Palmer Quarterly, 13,* 309–316.

Glynn, S. M., Yeany, R. H., & Britton, B. K. (1991). A constructive view of learning science. In S. M. Glynn, R. H. Yeany, & B. K. Britton (Eds.), *The psychology of learning science.* Hillsdale, NJ: Erlbaum.

Goddard, R. D. (2001). Collective efficacy: A neglected construct in the study of schools and student achievement. *Journal of Educational Psychology, 93,* 467–476.

Goddard, R. D., Hoy, W. K., & Woolfolk Hoy, A. (2000). Collective teacher efficacy: Its meaning, measure, and impact on student achievement. *American Educational Research Journal, 37,* 479–507.

Goldenberg, C. (1992). The limits of expectations: A case for case knowledge about teacher expectancy effects. *American Educational Research Journal, 29,* 517–544.

Gollnick, D. M., & Chinn, P. C. (1994). *Multicultural education in a pluralistic society* (4th ed.). Upper Saddle River, NJ: Merrill/Prentice Hall.

Good, T. L., & Brophy, J. E. (1994). *Looking in classrooms* (6th ed.). New York: HarperCollins.

Good, T. L., McCaslin, M. M., & Reys, B. J. (1992). Investigating work groups to promote problem solving in mathematics. In J. Brophy (Ed.), *Advances in research on teaching: Vol. 3. Planning and managing learning tasks and activities.* Greenwich, CT: JAI Press.

Good, T. L., & Nichols. S. L. (2001). Expectancy effects in the classroom: A special focus on improving the reading performance of minority students in first-grade classrooms. *Educational Psychologist, 36,* 113–126.

Goodenow, C. (1993). Classroom belonging among early adolescent students: Relationships to motivation and achievement. *Journal of Early Adolescence, 13,* 21–43.

Goodnow, J. J. (1992). *Parental belief systems: The psychological consequences for children.* Hillsdale, NJ: Erlbaum.

Gootman, M. E. (1998). Effective in-house suspension. *Educational Leadership, 56*(1), 39–41.

Gopnik, M. (Ed.). (1997). *The inheritance and innateness of grammars.* New York: Oxford University Press.

Gorski, J. D., & Pilotto, L. (1993). Interpersonal violence among youth: A challenge for school personnel. *Educational Psychology Review, 5,* 35–61.

Gottfredson, D. C. (2001). *Schools and delinquency.* Cambridge, England: Cambridge University Press.

Gottfredson, D. C., Fink, C. M., & Graham, N. (1994). Grade retention and problem behavior. *American Educational Research Journal, 31,* 761–784.

Gottfredson, G. D., & Gottfredson, D. C. (1985). *Victimization in schools.* New York: Plenum Press.

Gottfredson, L. S. (1981). Circumscription and compromise: A developmental theory of occupational aspirations. *Journal of Counseling Psychology Monograph, 28,* 545–579.

Gottfried, A. E. (1990). Academic intrinsic motivation in young elementary school children. *Journal of Educational Psychology, 82,* 525–538.

Gottfried, A. E., Fleming, J. S., & Gottfried, A. W. (1994). Role of parental motivational practices in children's academic intrinsic motivation and achievement. *Journal of Educational Psychology, 86,* 104–113.

Gottfried, A. E., Fleming, J. S., & Gottfried, A. W. (2001). Continuity of academic intrinsic motivation from childhood through late adolescence: A longitudinal study. *Journal of Educational Psychology, 93,* 3–13.

Gottfried, A. W., Gottfried, A. E., Bathurst, K., & Guerin, D. W. (1994). *Gifted IQ: Early developmental aspects.* New York: Plenum Press.

Gottlieb, G. (2000). Environmental and behavioral influences on gene activity. *Current Directions in Psychological Science, 9,* 93–97.

Gottman, J. M. (1986). The world of coordinated play: Same- and cross-sex friendship in young children. In J. M. Gottman & J. G. Parker (Eds.), *Conversations of friends: Speculations on affective development* (pp. 139–191). Cambridge, England: Cambridge University Press.

Gottman, J. M., & Mettetal, G. (1986). Speculations about social and affective development: Friendship and acquaintanceship through adolescence. In J. M. Gottman & J. G. Parker (Eds.), *Conversations of friends: Speculations on affective development* (pp. 192–237). Cambridge, England: Cambridge University Press.

Grabe, M. (1986). Attentional processes in education. In G. D. Phye & T. Andre (Eds.), *Cognitive classroom learning: Understanding, thinking, and problem solving.* San Diego, CA: Academic Press.

Graesser, A., & Person, N. K. (1994). Question asking during tutoring. *American Educational Research Journal, 31,* 104–137.

Graham, S. (1989). Motivation in Afro-Americans. In G. L. Berry & J. K. Asamen (Eds.), *Black students: Psychosocial issues and academic achievement.* Newbury Park, CA: Sage.

Graham, S. (1990). Communicating low ability in the classroom: Bad things good teachers sometimes do. In S. Graham & V. S. Folkes (Eds.), *Attribution theory: Applications to achievement, mental health, and interpersonal conflict.* Hillsdale, NJ: Erlbaum.

Graham, S. (1991). A review of attribution theory in achievement contexts. *Educational Psychology Review, 3,* 5–39.

Graham, S. (1994). Motivation in African Americans. *Review of Educational Research, 64,* 55–117.

Graham, S. (1997). Using attribution theory to understand social and academic motivation in African American youth. *Educational Psychologist, 32,* 21–34.

Graham, S., & Golen, S. (1991). Motivational influences on cognition: Task involvement, ego involvement, and depth of information processing. *Journal of Educational Psychology, 83,* 187–194.

Graham, S., Harris, K. R., & Fink, B. (2000). Is handwriting causally related to learning to write? Treatment of handwriting problems in beginning writers. *Journal of Educational Psychology, 92,* 620–633.

Graham, S., & Hudley, C. (1994). Attributions of aggressive and nonaggressive African-American male early adolescents: A study of construct accessibility. *Developmental Psychology, 30,* 365–373.

Graham, S., & Weiner, B. (1996). Theories and principles of motivation. In D. C. Berliner & R. C. Calfee (Eds.), *Handbook of educational psychology.* New York: Macmillan.

Grandin, T. (1995). *Thinking in pictures and other reports of my life with autism.* New York: Random House.

Granger, D. A., Whalen, C. K., Henker, B., & Cantwell, C. (1996). ADHD boys' behavior during structured classroom social activities: Effects of social demands, teacher proximity, and methylphenidate. *Journal of Attention Disorders, 1*(1), 16–30.

Grant, C. A., & Gomez, M. L. (2001). *Campus and classroom: Making schooling multicultural* (2nd ed.). Upper Saddle River, NJ: Merrill/Prentice Hall.

Gray, C., & Garaud, J. D. (1993). Social stories: Improving responses of students with autism with accurate social information. *Focus on Autistic Behavior, 8,* 1–10.

Gray, W. D., & Orasanu, J. M. (1987). Transfer of cognitive skills. In S. M. Cormier & J. D. Hagman (Eds.), *Transfer of learning: Contemporary research and applications.* San Diego, CA: Academic Press.

Green, L., Fry, A. F., & Myerson, J. (1994). Discounting of delayed rewards: A life-span comparison. *Psychological Science, 5,* 33–36.

Greene, B. A. (1994, April). *Instruction to enhance comprehension of unfamiliar text: Should it focus on domain-specific or strategy knowledge?* Paper presented at the annual meeting of the American Educational Research Association, New Orleans, LA.

Greenfield, P. M. (1994). Independence and interdependence as developmental scripts: Implications for theory, research, and practice. In P. M. Greenfield & R. R. Cocking (Eds.), *Cross-cultural roots of minority child development.* Hillsdale, NJ: Erlbaum.

Greeno, J. G. (1997). On claims that answer the wrong questions. *Educational Researcher, 26*(1), 5–17.

Greenough, W. T., Black, J. E., & Wallace, C. S. (1987). Experience and brain development. *Child Development, 58,* 539–559.

Greenspan, S., & Granfield, J. M. (1992). Reconsidering the construct of mental retardation: Implications of a model of social competence. *American Journal of Mental Retardation, 96,* 442–453.

Greenwood, C. R. (1991). Classwide peer tutoring: Longitudinal effects on the reading, language, and mathematics achievement of at-risk students. *Journal of Reading, Writing, and Learning Disabilities International, 7*(2), 105–123.

Greenwood, C. R., Carta, J. J., & Hall, R. V. (1988). The use of peer tutoring strategies in classroom management and educational instruction. *School Psychology Review, 17,* 258–275.

Gregg, M., & Leinhardt, G. (1994, April). *Constructing geography.* Paper presented at the annual meeting of the American Educational Research Association, New Orleans, LA.

Gresham, F. M., & MacMillan, D. L. (1997). Social competence and affective characteristics of students with mild disabilities. *Review of Educational Research, 67,* 377–415.

Griffin, M. M., & Griffin, B. W. (1994, April). *Some can get there from here: Situated learning, cognitive style, and map skills.* Paper presented at the annual meeting of the American Educational Research Association, New Orleans, LA.

Griffin, S. A., Case, R., & Capodilupo, A. (1995). Teaching for understanding: The importance of the central conceptual structures in the elementary mathematics curriculum. In A. McKeough, J. Lupart, & A. Marini (Eds.), *Teaching for transfer: Fostering generalization in learning.* Mahwah, NJ: Erlbaum.

Griffore, R. J. (1981). *Child development: An educational perspective.* Springfield, IL: Charles C Thomas.

Grinberg, D., & McLean-Heywood, D. (1999). *Perceptions of behavioural competence in depressed and non-depressed children with behavioural difficulties.* Paper presented at the annual meeting of the American Educational Research Association, Montreal, Canada.

Grissmer, D. W., Williamson, S., Kirby, S. N., & Berends, M. (1998). Exploring the rapid rise in Black achievement scores in the United States (1970–1990). In U. Neisser (Ed.), *The rising curve: Long-term gains in IQ and related measures* (pp. 251–285). Washington, DC: American Psychological Association.

Griswold, K. S., & Pessar, L. F. (2000). Management of bipolar disorder. *American Family Physician, 62,* 1343–1356.

Grodzinsky, G. M., & Diamond, R. (1992). Frontal lobe functioning in boys with attention-deficit hyperactivity disorder. *Developmental Neuropsychology, 8,* 427–445.

Grolnick, W. S., & Ryan, R. M. (1987). Autonomy in children's learning: An experimental and individual difference investigation. *Journal of Personality and Social Psychology, 52,* 890–898.

Gronlund, N. E. (1993). *How to make achievement tests and assessments* (5th ed.). Needham Heights, MA: Allyn & Bacon.

Gronlund, N. E. (2000). *How to write and use instructional objectives* (6th ed.). Upper Saddle River, NJ: Merrill/Prentice Hall.

Grossman, H. L. (1994). *Classroom behavior management in a diverse society.* Mountain View, CA: Mayfield.

Grusec, J. E., & Redler, E. (1980). Attribution, reinforcement, and altruism. *Developmental Psychology, 16,* 525–534.

Guay, F., Boivin, M., & Hodges, E. V. E. (1999). Social comparison processes and academic achievement: The dependence of the development of self-evaluations on friends' performance. *Journal of Educational Psychology, 91,* 564–568.

Guerra, N. G., & Slaby, R. G. (1990). Cognitive mediators of aggression in adolescent offenders: 2. Intervention. *Developmental Psychology, 26,* 269–277.

Guess, D., Roberts, S., Siegel-Causey, E., & Rues, J. (1995). Replication and extended analysis of behavior state, environmental events, and related variables among individuals with profound disabilities. *American Journal on Mental Retardation, 100,* 36–51.

Gunstone, R. F. (1994). The importance of specific science content in the enhancement of metacognition. In P. J. Fensham, R. F. Gunstone, & R. T. White (Eds.), *The content of science: A constructivist approach to its teaching and learning.* London: Falmer Press.

Gunstone, R. F., & White, R. T. (1981). Understanding of gravity. *Science Education, 65,* 291–299.

Guskey, T. R. (1985). *Implementing mastery learning.* Belmont, CA: Wadsworth.

Guskey, T. R. (1994, April). *Outcome-based education and mastery learning: Clarifying the differences.* Paper presented at the annual meeting of the American Educational Research Association, New Orleans, LA.

Gustafsson, J., & Undheim, J. O. (1996). Individual differences in cognitive functions. In D. C. Berliner & R. C. Calfee (Eds.), *Handbook of educational psychology*. New York: Macmillan.

Hacker, D. J. (1998a). Definitions and empirical foundations. In D. J. Hacker, J. Dunlosky, & A. C. Graesser (Eds.), *Metacognition in educational theory and practice* (pp. 1–23). Mahwah, NJ: Erlbaum.

Hacker, D. J. (1998b). Self-regulated comprehension during normal reading. In D. J. Hacker, J. Dunlosky, & A. C. Graesser (Eds.), *Metacognition in educational theory and practice* (pp. 165–191). Mahwah, NJ: Erlbaum.

Hacker, D. J., Bol, L., Horgan, D. D., & Rakow, E. A. (2000). Test prediction and performance in a classroom context. *Journal of Educational Psychology, 92,* 160–170.

Hadaway, N. L., Florez, V., Larke, P. J., & Wiseman, D. (1993). Teaching in the midst of diversity: How do we prepare? In M. J. O'Hair & S. J. Odell (Eds.), *Diversity and teaching: Teacher education yearbook I.* Fort Worth, TX: Harcourt Brace Jovanovich.

Haenan, J. (1996). Piotr Gal'perin's criticism and extension of Lev Vygotsky's work. *Journal of Russian and East European Psychology, 34*(2), 54–60.

Hagen, J. W., & Stanovich, K. G. (1977). Memory: Strategies of acquisition. In R. V. Kail, Jr., & J. W. Hagen (Eds.), *Perspectives on the development of memory and cognition.* Hillsdale, NJ: Erlbaum.

Hagtvet, K. A., & Johnsen, T. B. (Eds.). (1992). *Advances in test anxiety research* (Vol. 7). Amsterdam: Swets & Zeitlinger.

Hahn, H. (1989). The politics of special education. In D. K. Lipsky & A. Gartner (Eds.), *Beyond separate education: Quality education for all.* Baltimore: Brookes.

Hakuta, K., & McLaughlin, B. (1996). Bilingualism and second language learning: Seven tensions that define the research. In D. C. Berliner & R. C. Calfee (Eds.), *Handbook of educational psychology*. New York: Macmillan.

Hale, G. A. (1983). Students' predictions of prose forgetting and the effects of study strategies. *Journal of Educational Psychology, 75,* 708–715.

Hale-Benson, J. E. (1986). *Black children: Their roots, culture, and learning styles.* Baltimore: Johns Hopkins University Press.

Halford, G. S. (1989). Cognitive processing capacity and learning ability: An integration of two areas. *Learning and Individual Differences, 1,* 125–153.

Hall, R. H., & O'Donnell, A. (1994, April). *Alternative materials for learning: Cognitive and affective outcomes of learning from knowledge maps.* Paper presented at the annual meeting of the American Educational Research Association, New Orleans, LA.

Hallenbeck, M. J. (1996). The cognitive strategy in writing: Welcome relief for adolescents with learning disabilities. *Learning Disabilities Research and Practice, 11,* 107–119.

Haller, E. P., Child, D. A., & Walberg, H. J. (1988). Can comprehension be taught? A quantitative synthesis of "metacognitive" studies. *Educational Researcher, 17*(9), 5–8.

Hallinan, M. T., & Teixeria, R. A. (1987). Opportunities and constraints: Black-white differences in the formation of interracial friendships. *Child Development, 58,* 1358–1371.

Hallowell, E. (1996). *When you worry about the child you love.* New York: Simon and Schuster.

Halpern, D. F. (1992). *Sex differences in cognitive abilities* (2nd ed.). Hillsdale, NJ: Erlbaum.

Halpern, D. F. (1997a). *Critical thinking across the curriculum: A brief edition of thought and knowledge.* Mahwah, NJ: Erlbaum.

Halpern, D. F. (1997b). Sex differences in intelligence: Implications for education. *American Psychologist, 52,* 1091–1102.

Halpern, D. F. (1998). Teaching critical thinking for transfer across domains. *American Psychologist, 53,* 449–455.

Halpern, D. F., & LaMay, M. L. (2000). The smarter sex: A critical review of sex differences in intelligence. *Educational Psychology Review, 12,* 229–246.

Halpin, G., & Halpin, G. (1982). Experimental investigations of the effects of study and testing on student learning, retention, and ratings of instruction. *Journal of Educational Psychology, 74,* 32–38.

Halvorsen, A. T., & Sailor, W. (1990). Integration of students with severe and profound disabilities: A review of research. In R. Gaylord-Ross (Ed.), *Issues and research in special education* (Vol. 1, pp. 110–172). New York: Teachers College Press.

Hambleton, R. K. (1996). Advances in assessment models, methods, and practices. In D. C. Berliner & R. C. Calfee (Eds.), *Handbook of educational psychology*. New York: Macmillan.

Hamers, J. H. M., & Ruijssenaars, A. J. J. M. (1997). Assessing classroom learning potential. In G. D. Phye (Ed.), *Handbook of academic learning: Construction of knowledge.* San Diego, CA: Academic Press.

Hamman, D., Berthelot, J., Saia, J., & Crowley, E. (2000). Teachers' coaching of learning and its relation to students' strategic learning. *Journal of Educational Psychology, 92,* 342–348.

Hamman, D., Shell, D. F., Droesch, D., Husman, J., Handwerk, M., Park, Y., & Oppenheim, N. (1995, April). *Middle school readers' on-line cognitive processes: Influence of subject-matter knowledge and interest during reading.* Paper presented at the annual meeting of the American Educational Research Association, San Francisco.

Hammer, D. (1997). Discovery learning and discovery teaching. *Cognition and Instruction, 15,* 485–529.

Hamp-Lyons, L. (1992). Holistic writing assessment for L.E.P. students. In *Focus on evaluation and measurement* (Vol. 2). Washington, DC: U.S. Department of Education.

Hampton, J. A. (1981). An investigation of the nature of abstract concepts. *Memory and Cognition, 9,* 149–156.

Hansen, J., & Pearson, P. D. (1983). An instructional study: Improving the inferential comprehension of good and poor fourth-grade readers. *Journal of Educational Psychology, 75,* 821–829.

Hardre, P. L., & Reeve, J. (2001, April). *A motivational model of rural high school students' dropout intentions.* Paper presented at the annual meeting of the American Educational Research Association, Seattle, WA.

Hardy, R. (1996). Performance assessment: Examining the costs. In M. B. Kane & R. Mitchell (Eds.), *Implementing performance assessment: Promises, problems, and challenges* (pp. 107–117). Mahwah, NJ: Erlbaum.

Harlow, H. F., & Zimmerman, R. R. (1959). Affectional responses in the infant monkey. *Science, 130,* 421–432.

Harnishfeger, K. K. (1995). The development of cognitive inhibition: Theories, definitions, and research evidence. In F. N. Dempster & C. J. Brainerd (Eds.), *Interference and inhibition in cognition.* San Diego, CA: Academic Press.

Harp, S. F., & Mayer, R. E. (1998). How seductive details do their damage: A theory of cognitive interest in science learning. *Journal of Educational Psychology, 90,* 414–434.

Harris, A. C. (1986). *Child development.* St. Paul, MN: West.

Harris, C. R. (1991). Identifying and serving the gifted new immigrant. *Teaching Exceptional Children, 23*(4), 26–30.

Harris, J. R. (1995). Where is the child's environment? A group socialization theory of development. *Psychological Review, 102,* 458–489.

Harris, J. R. (1998). *The nurture assumption: Why children turn out the way they do.* New York: Free Press.

Harris, K. R. (1982). Cognitive-behavior modification: Application with exceptional students. *Focus on Exceptional Children, 15,* 1–16.

Harris, K. R. (1986). Self-monitoring of attentional behavior versus self-monitoring of productivity: Effects of on-task behavior and academic response rate among learning disabled children. *Journal of Applied Behavior Analysis, 19,* 417–423.

Harris, K. R., & Alexander, P. A. (1998). Integrated, constructivist education: Challenge and reality. *Educational Psychology Review, 10,* 115–127.

Harris, M. (1992). *Language experience and early language development: From input to uptake.* Hove, England: Erlbaum.

Harris, M. B. (1997). Preface: Images of the invisible minority. In M. B. Harries (Ed.), *School experiences of gay and lesbian youth: The invisible minority* (pp. xiv–xxii). Binghamton, NY: Harrington Park Press.

Harris, M. J., & Rosenthal, R. (1985). Mediation of interpersonal expectancy effects: 31 meta-analyses. *Psychological Bulletin, 97,* 363–386.

Harris, R. J. (1977). Comprehension of pragmatic implications in advertising. *Journal of Applied Psychology, 62,* 603–608.

Harrow, A. J. (1972). *A taxonomy of the psychomotor domain: A guide for developing behavioral objectives.* New York: David McKay.

Harry, B., Allen, N., & McLaughlin, M. (1995). Communication versus compliance: African-American parents' involvement in special education. *Exceptional Children, 61,* 364–377.

Hart, C. H., Ladd, G. W., & Burleson, B. (1990). Children's expectations of the outcomes of social strategies: Relations with sociometric status and maternal disciplinary styles. *Child Development, 61,* 127–137.

Hart, D. (1988). The adolescent self-concept in social context. In D. K. Lapsley & F. C. Power (Eds.), *Self, ego, and identity: Integrative approaches* (pp. 71–90). New York: Springer-Verlag.

Hart, D., & Fegley, S. (1995). Prosocial behavior and caring in adolescence: Relations to self-understanding and social judgment. *Child Development, 66,* 1346–1359.

Hart, E. L., Lahey, B. B., Loeber, R., Applegate, B., & Frick, P. J. (1995). Developmental changes in attention-deficit hyperactivity disorder in boys: A four-year longitudinal study. *Journal of Abnormal Child Psychology, 23,* 729–750.

Hart, E. R., & Speece, D. L. (1998). Reciprocal teaching goes to college: Effects for postsecondary students at risk for academic failure. *Journal of Educational Psychology, 90,* 670–681.

Harter, S. (1975). Mastery motivation and the need for approval in older children and their relationship to social desirability response tendencies. *Developmental Psychology, 11,* 186–196.

Harter, S. (1978). Pleasure derived from challenge and the effects of receiving grades on children's difficulty level choices. *Child Development, 49,* 788–799.

Harter, S. (1982). The perceived competence scale for children. *Child Development, 53,* 87–97.

Harter, S. (1983a). Children's understanding of multiple emotions: A cognitive-developmental approach. In W. F. Overton (Ed.), *The relation-*

ship between social and cognitive development. Hillsdale, NJ: Erlbaum.

Harter, S. (1983b). Developmental perspectives on the self-system. In E. M. Hetherington (Ed.), *Handbook of child psychology: Vol. 4. Socialization, personality, and social development* (4th ed.). New York: Wiley.

Harter, S. (1988). The construction and conservation of the self: James and Cooley revisited. In D. K. Lapsley & F. C. Power (Eds.), *Self, ego, and identity: Integrative approaches* (pp. 43–69). New York: Springer-Verlag.

Harter, S. (1990). Causes, correlates, and the functional role of global self-worth: A life-span perspective. In R. J. Sternberg & J. Kolligian, Jr. (Eds.), *Competence considered*. New Haven, CT: Yale University Press.

Harter, S. (1992). The relationship between perceived competence, affect, and motivational orientation within the classroom: Processes and patterns of change. In A. K. Boggiano & T. S. Pittman (Eds.), *Achievement and motivation: A social-developmental perspective*. Cambridge, England: Cambridge University Press.

Harter, S. (1996). Teacher and classmate influences on scholastic motivation, self-esteem, and level of voice in adolescents. In J. Juvonen & K. Wentzel (Eds.), *Social motivation: Understanding children's school adjustment*. New York: Cambridge University Press.

Harter, S., Whitesell, N. R., & Junkin, L. J. (1998). Similarities and differences in domain-specific and global self-evaluations of learning-disabled, behaviorally disordered, and normally achieving adolescents. *American Educational Research Journal, 35,* 653–680.

Harter, S., Whitesell, N. R., & Kowalski, P. (1992). Individual differences in the effects of educational transitions on young adolescents' perceptions of competence and motivational orientation. *American Educational Research Journal, 29,* 777–807.

Hartley, J., & Trueman, M. (1982). The effects of summaries on the recall of information from prose: Five experimental studies. *Human Learning, 1,* 63–82.

Hartup, W. W. (1983). Peer relations. In P. H. Mussen (Ed.), *Handbook of child psychology: Vol. IV. Socialization* (4th ed., pp. 103–196). New York: Wiley.

Hartup, W. W. (1989). Social relationships and their developmental significance. *American Psychologist, 44,* 120–126.

Hartup, W. W. (1992). Friendships and their developmental significance. In H. McGurk (Ed.), *Contemporary issues in childhood social development*. London: Routledge.

Harway, M., & Moss, L. T. (1983). Sex differences: The evidence from biology. In M. B. Liss (Ed.), *Social and cognitive skills: Sex roles and children's play*. San Diego, CA: Academic Press.

Harwood, R. L., Miller, J. G., & Irizarry, N. L. (1995). *Culture and attachment: Perceptions of the child in context.* New York: Guilford Press.

Haseman, A. L. (1999, April). *Cross talk: How students' epistemological beliefs impact the learning process in a constructivist course.* Paper presented at the annual meeting of the American Educational Research Association, Montreal, Canada.

Hatano, G., & Inagaki, K. (1991). Sharing cognition through collective comprehension activity. In L. B. Resnick, J. M. Levine, & S. D. Teasley (Eds.), *Perspectives on socially shared cognition*. Washington, DC: American Psychological Association.

Hatano, G., & Inagaki, K. (1993). Desituating cognition through the construction of concep-

tual knowledge. In P. Light & G. Butterworth (Eds.), *Context and cognition: Ways of learning and knowing*. Hillsdale, NJ: Erlbaum.

Hattie, J., Biggs, J., & Purdie, N. (1996). Effects of learning skills interventions on student learning: A meta-analysis. *Review of Educational Research, 66,* 99–136.

Hawkins, F. P. L. (1997). *Journey with children: The autobiography of a teacher.* Niwot: University Press of Colorado.

Hawkins, R. D., & Bower, G. H. (Eds.). (1989). *Computational models of learning in simple neural systems*. San Diego, CA: Academic Press.

Hayes, C. B., Ryan, A. W., & Zseller, E. B. (1994, April). *African-American students' perceptions of caring teacher behaviors.* Paper presented at the annual meeting of the American Educational Research Association, New Orleans, LA.

Hayes, S. C., Rosenfarb, I., Wulfert, E., Munt, E. D., Korn, Z., & Zettle, R. D. (1985). Self-reinforcement effects: An artifact of social standard setting? *Journal of Applied Behavior Analysis, 18,* 201–214.

Hayes-Roth, B., & Thorndyke, P. W. (1979). Integration of knowledge from text. *Journal of Verbal Learning and Verbal Behavior, 18,* 91–108.

Hayslip, B., Jr. (1994). Stability of intelligence. In R. J. Sternberg (Ed.), *Encyclopedia of human intelligence* (Vol. 2). New York: Macmillan.

Hearold, S. (1986). A synthesis of 1,043 effects of television on social behavior. In G. Comstock (Ed.), *Public communication and behavior* (Vol. 1). New York: Academic Press.

Heath, S. B. (1980). Questioning at home and at school: A comparative study. In G. Spindler (Ed.), *The ethnography of schooling: Educational anthropology in action*. New York: Holt, Rinehart & Winston.

Heath, S. B. (1989). Oral and literate traditions among black Americans living in poverty. *American Psychologist, 44,* 367–373.

Hedges, L. V., & Nowell, A. (1995). Sex differences in mental test scores, variability, and numbers of high-scoring individuals. *Science, 269,* 41–45.

Hegarty, M., & Kozhevnikov, M. (1999). Types of visual-spatial representations and mathematical problem solving. *Journal of Educational Psychology, 91,* 684–689.

Hegland, S., & Andre, T. (1992). Helping learners construct knowledge. *Educational Psychology Review, 4,* 223–240.

Heindel, P., & Kose, G. (1990). The effects of motoric action and organization on children's memory. *Journal of Experimental Child Psychology, 50,* 416–428.

Heller, J. I., & Hungate, H. N. (1985). Implications for mathematics instruction of research on scientific problem solving. In E. A. Silver (Ed.), *Teaching and learning mathematical problem solving: Multiple research perspectives*. Hillsdale, NJ: Erlbaum.

Helton, G. B., & Oakland, T. D. (1977). Teachers' attitudinal responses to differing characteristics of elementary school students. *Journal of Educational Psychology, 69,* 261–266.

Hembree, R. (1988). Correlates, causes, effects, and treatment of test anxiety. *Review of Educational Research, 58,* 47–77.

Hennessey, B. A. (1995). Social, environmental, and developmental issues and creativity. *Educational Psychology Review, 7,* 163–183.

Hennessey, B. A., & Amabile, T. M. (1987). *Creativity and learning*. Washington, DC: National Education Association.

Herrenkohl, L. R., & Guerra, M. R. (1998). Participant structures, scientific discourse, and student engagement in fourth grade. *Cognition and Instruction, 16,* 431–473.

Herrnstein, R. J., & Murray, C. (1994). *The bell curve: Intelligence and class structure in American life.* New York: Free Press.

Hess, G. A., Jr., Lyons, A., & Corsino, L. (1990, April). *Against the odds: The early identification of dropouts.* Paper presented at the annual meeting of the American Educational Research Association, Boston.

Hess, R. D., Chih-Mei, C., & McDevitt, T. M. (1987). Cultural variations in family beliefs about children's performance in mathematics: Comparisons among People's Republic of China, Chinese-American, and Caucasian-American families. *Journal of Educational Psychology, 79,* 179–188.

Hess, R. D., & Holloway, S. D. (1984). Family and school as educational institutions. In R. D. Parke, R. N. Emde, H. P. McAdoo, & G. P. Sackett (Eds.), *Review of child development research* (Vol. 7). Chicago: University of Chicago Press.

Hettinger, H. R., & Knapp, N. F. (2001). Potential, performance, and paradox: A case study of J.P., a verbally gifted, struggling reader. *Journal for the Education of the Gifted, 24,* 248–289.

Heward, W. L. (2000). *Exceptional children: An introduction to special education* (6th ed.). Upper Saddle River, NJ: Merrill/Prentice Hall.

Hewitt, J., Brett, C., Scardamalia, M., Frecker, K., & Webb, J. (1995, April). *Schools for thought: Transforming classrooms into learning communities.* Paper presented at the annual meeting of the American Educational Research Association, San Francisco.

Hewitt, J., & Scardamalia, M. (1996, April). *Design principles for the support of distributed processes.* Paper presented at the annual meeting of the American Educational Research Association, New York.

Hewitt, J., & Scardamalia, M. (1998). Design principles for distributed knowledge building processes. *Educational Psychology Review, 10,* 75–96.

Heymann, S. J., & Earle, A. (2000). Low-income parents: How do working conditions affect their opportunity to help school-age children at risk? *American Educational Research Journal, 37,* 833–848.

Hickey, D. T. (1997). Motivation and contemporary socio-constructivist instructional perspectives. *Educational Psychologist, 32,* 175–193.

Hicks, L. (1997). Academic motivation and peer relationships—how do they mix in an adolescent world? *Middle School Journal, 28,* 18–22.

Hidalgo, N. M., Siu, S., Bright, J. A., Swap, S. M., & Epstein, J. L. (1995). Research on families, schools, and communities: A multicultural perspective. In J. A. Banks & C. A. M. Banks (Eds.), *Handbook of research on multicultural education*. New York: Macmillan.

Hidi, S. (1990). Interest and its contribution as a mental resource for learning. *Review of Educational Research, 60,* 549–571.

Hidi, S., & Anderson, V. (1986). Producing written summaries: Task demands, cognitive operations, and implications for instruction. *Review of Educational Research, 86,* 473–493.

Hidi, S., & Anderson, V. (1992). Situational interest and its impact on reading and expository writing. In K. A. Renninger, S. Hidi, & A. Krapp (Eds.), *The role of interest in learning and development*. Hillsdale, NJ: Erlbaum.

Hidi, S., & Harackiewicz, J. M. (2000). Motivating the academically unmotivated: A critical issue for the 21st century. *Review of Educational Research, 70,* 151–179.

Hidi, S., & McLaren, J. (1990). The effect of topic and theme interestingness on the production of school expositions. In H. Mandl, E. De Corte, N. Bennett, & H. F. Friedrich (Eds.), *Learning and* instruction in an international context. Oxford, England: Pergamon Press.

Hidi, S., Weiss, J., Berndorff, D., & Nolan, J. (1998). The role of gender, instruction, and a cooperative learning technique in science education across formal and informal settings. In L. Hoffman, A. Krapp, K. Renninger, & J. Baumert (Eds.), Interest and learning: Proceedings of the Seeon Conference on interest and gender (pp. 215–227). Kiel, Germany: IPN.

Hiebert, E. H., & Fisher, C. W. (1992). The tasks of school literacy: Trends and issues. In J. Brophy (Ed.), Advances in research on teaching: Vol. 3. Planning and managing learning tasks and activities. Greenwich, CT: JAI Press.

Hiebert, E. H., & Raphael, T. E. (1996). Psychological perspectives on literacy and extensions to educational practice. In D. C. Berliner & R. C. Calfee (Eds.), Handbook of educational psychology. New York: Macmillan.

Hiebert, E. H., Valencia, S. W., & Afflerbach, P. P. (1994). Definitions and perspectives. In S. W. Valencia, E. H. Hiebert, & P. P. Afflerbach (Eds.), Authentic reading assessment: Practices and possibilities. Newark, DE: International Reading Association.

Hiebert, J., Carpenter, T. P., Fennema, E., Fuson, K. C., Wearne, D., Murray, H., Olivier, A., & Human, P. (1997). Making sense: Teaching and learning mathematics with understanding. Portsmouth, NH: Heinemann.

Hiebert, J., & Lefevre, P. (1986). Conceptual and procedural knowledge in mathematics: An introductory analysis. In J. Hiebert (Ed.), Conceptual and procedural knowledge: The case of mathematics. Hillsdale, NJ: Erlbaum.

Hiebert, J., & Wearne, D. (1996). Instruction, understanding, and skill in multidigit addition and subtraction. Cognition and Instruction, 14, 251–283.

Higgins, A. (1995). Educating for justice and community: Lawrence Kohlberg's vision of moral education. In W. M. Kurtines & J. L. Gewirtz (Eds.), Moral development: An introduction. Boston: Allyn & Bacon.

Higgins, A. T., & Turnure, J. E. (1984). Distractibility and concentration of attention in children's development. Child Development, 55, 1799–1810.

Hill, C. (1994). Testing and assessment: An applied linguistic perspective. Educational Assessment, 2(3), 179–212.

Hill, C., & Larsen, E. (1992). Testing and assessment in secondary education: A critical review of emerging practices. Berkeley: University of California, National Center for Research in Vocational Education.

Hill, K. T. (1984). Debilitating motivation and testing: A major educational problem, possible solutions, and policy applications. In R. Ames & C. Ames (Eds.), Research on motivation in education: Vol. 1. Student motivation. San Diego, CA: Academic Press.

Hill, K. T., & Wigfield, A. (1984). Test anxiety: A major educational problem and what can be done about it. Elementary School Journal, 85, 105–126.

Hilliard, A., & Vaughn-Scott, M. (1982). The quest for the minority child. In S. G. Moore & C. R. Cooper (Eds.), The young child: Reviews of research (Vol. 3). Washington, DC: National Association for the Education of Young Children.

Hinkley, J. W., McInerney, D. M., & Marsh, H. W. (2001, April). The multi-faceted structure of school achievement motivation: A case for social goals. Paper presented at the annual meeting of the American Educational Research Association, Seattle, WA.

Hirsch, E. D., Jr. (1996). The schools we need and why we don't have them. New York: Doubleday.

Hirschfeld, L. A., & Gelman, S. A. (Eds.). (1994). Mapping the mind: Domain specificity in cognition and culture. Cambridge, England: Cambridge University Press.

Ho, D. Y. F. (1986). Chinese pattern of socialization: A critical review. In M. H. Bond (Ed.), The psychology of Chinese people. Oxford: Oxford University Press.

Ho, D. Y. F. (1994). Cognitive socialization in Confucian heritage cultures. In P. M. Greenfield & R. R. Cocking (Eds.), Cross-cultural roots of minority child development. Hillsdale, NJ: Erlbaum.

Ho, H.-Z., Hinckley, H. S., Fox, K. R., Brown, J. H., & Dixon, C. N. (2001, April). Family literacy: Promoting parent support strategies for student success. Paper presented at the annual meeting of the American Educational Research Association, Seattle, WA.

Hobbs, N. (1980). An ecologically oriented service-based system for the classification of handicapped children. In E. Salzinger, J. Antrobus, & J. Glick (Eds.), The ecosystem of the "risk" child. New York: Academic Press.

Hocevar, D., & Bachelor, P. (1989). A taxonomy and critique of measurements used in the study of creativity. In J. A. Glover, R. R. Ronning, & C. R. Reynolds (Eds.), Handbook of creativity. New York: Plenum Press.

Hodges, E., Malone, J., & Perry, D. (1997). Individual risk and social risk as interacting determinants of victimization in the peer group. Developmental Psychology, 32, 1033–1039.

Hofer, B. K. (2001). Personal epistemology research: Implications for learning and teaching. Educational Psychology Review, 13, 353–383.

Hofer, B. K., & Pintrich, P. R. (1997). The development of epistemological theories: Beliefs about knowledge and knowing and their relation to learning. Review of Educational Research, 67, 88–140.

Hofferth, S. L. (1990). Trends in adolescent sexual activity, contraception, and pregnancy in the United States. In J. Bancroft & J. M. Reinisch (Eds.), Adolescence and puberty (pp. 217–233). New York: Oxford University Press.

Hoffman, M. L. (1970). Moral development. In P. H. Mussen (Ed.), Carmichael's manual of child psychology (Vol. 2). New York: Wiley.

Hoffman, M. L. (1975). Altruistic behavior and the parent-child relationship. Journal of Personality and Social Psychology, 31, 937–943.

Hoffman, M. L. (1991). Empathy, social cognition, and moral action. In W. M. Kurtines & J. L. Gewirtz (Eds.), Moral behavior and development: Vol. 1. Theory (pp. 275–301). Hillsdale, NJ: Erlbaum.

Hogan, D. M., & Tudge, J. R. H. (1999). Implications of Vygotsky's theory for peer learning. In A. M. O'Donnell & A. King (Eds.), Cognitive perspectives on peer learning (pp. 39–65). Mahwah, NJ: Erlbaum.

Hogan, K., Nastasi, B. K., & Pressley, M. (2000). Discourse patterns and collaborative scientific reasoning in peer and teacher-guided discussions. Cognition and Instruction, 17, 379–432.

Hogdon, L. A. (1995). Visual strategies for improving communication: Vol. 1. Practical supports for school and home. Troy, MI: Quirk Roberts.

Hoge, R. D., & Coladarci, T. (1989). Teacher-based judgments of academic achievement: A review of literature. Review of Educational Research, 59, 297–313.

Hoge, R. D., & Renzulli, J. S. (1993). Exploring the link betwen giftedness and self-concept. Review of Educational Research, 63, 449–465.

Holley, C. D., & Dansereau, D. F. (1984). Spatial learning strategies: Techniques, applications, and related issues. San Diego, CA: Academic Press.

Holliday, B. G. (1985). Towards a model of teacher-child transactional processes affecting black children's academic achievement. In M. B. Spencer, G. K. Brookins, & W. R. Allen (Eds.), Beginnings: The social and affective development of black children. Hillsdale, NJ: Erlbaum.

Hollins, E. R. (1996). Culture in school learning: Revealing the deep meaning. Mahwah, NJ: Erlbaum.

Hollon, R. E., Roth, K. J., & Anderson, C. W. (1991). Science teachers' conceptions of teaching and learning. In J. Brophy (Ed.), Advances in research on teaching: Vol. 2. Teachers' knowledge of subject matter as it relates to their teaching practice. Greenwich, CT: JAI Press.

Holt-Reynolds, D. (1992). Personal history-based beliefs as relevant prior knowledge in course work. American Educational Research Journal, 29, 325–349.

Hom, A., & Battistich, V. (1995, April). Students' sense of school community as a factor in reducing drug use and delinquency. Paper presented at the annual meeting of the American Educational Research Association, San Francisco.

Homme, L. E., deBaca, P. C., Devine, J. V., Steinhorst, R., & Rickert, E. J. (1963). Use of the Premack principle in controlling the behavior of nursery school children. Journal of the Experimental Analysis of Behavior, 6, 544.

Hong, Y., Chiu, C., & Dweck, C. S. (1995). Implicit theories of intelligence: Reconsidering the role of confidence in achievement motivation. In M. H. Kernis (Ed.), Efficacy, agency, and self-esteem. New York: Plenum Press.

Hong, Y., Morris, M. W., Chiu, C., & Benet-Martínez, V. (2000). Multicultural minds: A dynamic constructivist approach to culture and cognition. American Psychologist, 55, 709–720.

Hoover-Dempsey, K. V., Battiato, A. C., Walker, J. M. T., Reed, R. P., DeJong, J. M., & Jones, K. P. (2001). Parental involvement in homework. Educational Psychologist, 36, 195–209.

Hoover-Dempsey, K. V., & Sandler, H. M. (1997). Why do parents become involved in their children's education? Review of Educational Research, 67, 3–42.

Horgan, D. (1990, April). Students' predictions of test grades: Calibration and metacognition. Paper presented at the annual meeting of the American Educational Research Association, Boston.

Horgan, D. D. (1995). Achieving gender equity: Strategies for the classroom. Needham Heights, MA: Allyn & Bacon.

Hosmer, E. (1987, June). Paradise lost: The ravaged rainforest. Multinational Monitor, 8(6), 6–8

Hossler, D., & Stage, F. K. (1992). Family and high school experience influences on the postsecondary educational plans of ninth-grade students. American Educational Research Journal, 29, 425–451.

Houtz, J. C. (1990). Environments that support creative thinking. In C. Hedley, J. Houtz, & A. Baratta (Eds.), Cognition, curriculum, and literacy. Norwood, NJ: Ablex.

Howe, C. K. (1994). Improving the achievement of Hispanic students. Educational Leadership, 51(8), 42–44.

Hudley, C., & Graham, S. (1993). An attributional intervention to reduce peer-directed aggression among African American boys. Child Development, 64, 124–138.

Huff, J. A. (1988). Personalized behavior modification: An in-school suspension program that teaches students how to change. School Counselor, 35, 210–214.

Hughes, F. P. (1998). Play in special populations. In O. N. Saracho & B. Spodek (Eds.), *Multiple perspectives on play in early childhood education* (pp. 171–193). Albany: State University of New York Press.

Hughes, J. N. (1988). *Cognitive behavior therapy with children in schools.* New York: Pergamon Press.

Humphreys, L. G. (1992). What both critics and users of ability tests need to know. *Psychological Science, 3,* 271–274.

Hunt, E. (1997). Nature vs. nurture: The feeling of *vujà dé.* In R. J. Sternberg & E. L. Grigorenko (Eds.), *Intelligence, heredity, and environment* (pp. 531–551). Cambridge, England: Cambridge University Press.

Hunt, P., & Goetz, L. (1997). Research on inclusive educational programs, practices, and outcomes for students with severe disabilities. *Journal of Special Education, 31,* 3–29.

Hunter, M. (1982). *Mastery teaching.* El Segundo, CA: TIP.

Husman, J., & Freeman, B. (1999, April). *The effect of perceptions of instrumentality on intrinsic motivation.* Paper presented at the annual meeting of the American Educational Research Association, Montreal, Canada.

Huston, A. C. (1983). Sex-typing. In E. M. Hetherington (Ed.), *Handbook of child psychology: Vol. 4. Socialization, personality, and social development* (4th ed.). New York: Wiley.

Huston, A. C., Donnerstein, E., Fairchild, H., Feshbach, N. D., Katz, P. A., Murray, J. P., Rubenstein, E. A., Wilcox, B. L., & Zuckerman, D. (1992). *Big world, small screen: The role of television in American society.* Lincoln: University of Nebraska Press.

Hutt, S. J., Tyler, S., Hutt, C., & Christopherson, H. (1989). *Play, exploration, and learning: A natural history of the pre-school.* London: Routledge.

Hyde, J. S., Fennema, E., & Lamon, S. J. (1990). Gender differences in mathematics performance: A meta-analysis. *Psychological Bulletin, 107,* 139–155.

Hyde, J. S., & Linn, M. C. (1988). Gender differences in verbal ability: A meta-analysis. *Psychological Bulletin, 104,* 53–69.

Hymel, S. (1986). Interpretations of peer behavior: Affective bias in childhood and adolescence. *Child Development, 57,* 431–445.

Hymel, S., Comfort, C., Schonert-Reichl, K., & McDougall, P. (1996). Academic failure and school dropout: The influence of peers. In J. Juvonen & K. R. Wentzel (Eds.), *Social motivation: Understanding children's school adjustment* (pp. 313–345). Cambridge, England: Cambridge University Press.

Hynd, C. (1998a). Conceptual change in a high school physics class. In B. Guzzetti & C. Hynd (Eds.), *Perspectives on conceptual change: Multiple ways to understand knowing and learning in a complex world* (pp. 27–36). Mahwah, NJ: Erlbaum.

Hynd, C. (1998b). Observing learning from different perspectives: What does it mean for Barry and his understanding of gravity? In B. Guzzetti & C. Hynd (Eds.), *Perspectives on conceptual change: Multiple ways to understand knowing and learning in a complex world* (pp. 235–244). Mahwah, NJ: Erlbaum.

Igoa, C. (1995). *The inner world of the immigrant child.* Mahwah, NJ: Erlbaum.

Igoe, A. R., & Sullivan, H. (1991, April). *Gender and grade-level differences in student attributes related to school learning and motivation.* Paper presented at the annual meeting of the American Educational Research Association, Chicago.

Inglehart, M., Brown, D. R., & Vida, M. (1994). Competition, achievement, and gender: A stress

theoretical analysis. In P. R. Pintrich, D. R. Brown, & C. E. Weinstein (Eds.), *Student motivation, cognition, and learning: Essays in honor of Wilbert J. McKeachie.* Hillsdale, NJ: Erlbaum.

Inglis, A., & Biemiller, A. (1997, March). *Fostering self-direction in mathematics: A cross-age tutoring program that enhances math problem solving.* Paper presented at the annual meeting of the American Educational Research Association, Chicago.

Inhelder, B., & Piaget, J. (1958). *The growth of logical thinking from childhood to adolescence* (A. Parsons & S. Milgram, Trans.). New York: Basic Books.

Irujo, S. (1988). An introduction to intercultural differences and similarities in nonverbal communication. In J. S. Wurzel (Ed.), *Toward multiculturalism: A reader in multicultural education.* Yarmouth, ME: Intercultural Press.

Irvine, J. J., & York, D. E. (1995). Learning styles and culturally diverse students: A literature review. In J. A. Banks & C. A. M. Banks (Eds.), *Handbook of research on multicultural education.* New York: Macmillan.

Iwata, B. A., & Bailey, J. S. (1974). Reward versus cost token systems: An analysis of the effects on students and teacher. *Journal of Applied Behavior Analysis, 7,* 567–576.

Izard, C., Fine, S., Schultz, D., Mostow, A., Ackerman, B., & Youngstrom, E. (2001). Emotion knowledge as a predictor of social behavior and academic competence in children at risk. *Psychological Science, 12,* 18–23.

Jacklin, C. N. (1989). Female and male: Issues of gender. *American Psychologist, 44,* 127–133.

Jackson, D. L., & Ormrod, J. E. (1998). *Case studies: Applying educational psychology.* Upper Saddle River, NJ: Merrill/Prentice Hall.

Jacobsen, B., Lowery, B., & DuCette, J. (1986). Attributions of learning disabled children. *Journal of Educational Psychology, 78,* 59–64.

Jacobson, J. L., & Wille, D. E. (1986). The influence of attachment pattern on developmental changes in peer interaction from the toddler to the preschool period. *Child Development, 57,* 338–347.

Jacoby, R., & Glauberman, N. (Eds.). (1995). *The bell curve debate: History, documents, opinions.* New York: Random House.

Jagacinski, C. M., & Nicholls, J. G. (1984). Conceptions of ability and related affects in task involvement and ego involvement. *Journal of Educational Psychology, 76,* 909–919.

Jagacinski, C. M., & Nicholls, J. G. (1987). Competence and affect in task involvement and ego involvement: The impact of social comparison information. *Journal of Educational Psychology, 79,* 107–114.

James, W. (1890). *Principles of psychology.* New York: Holt.

Janos, P. M., & Robinson, N. M. (1985). Psychosocial development in intellectually gifted children. In F. D. Horowitz & M. O'Brien (Eds.), *The gifted and talented: Developmental perspectives.* Washington, DC: American Psychological Association.

Janosz, M., Le Blanc, M., Boulerice, B., & Tremblay, R. E. (2000). Predicting different types of school dropouts: A typological approach with two longitudinal samples. *Journal of Educational Psychology, 92,* 171–190.

Jencks, C., & Crouse, J. (1982). Should we relabel the SAT . . . or replace it? In W. Shrader (Ed.), *New directions for testing and measurement: Measurement, guidance, and program improvement* (No. 13). San Francisco: Jossey-Bass.

Jenlink, C. L. (1994, April). *Music: A lifeline for the self-esteem of at-risk students.* Paper presented at

the annual meeting of the American Educational Research Association, New Orleans, LA.

Jimerson, S., Egeland, B., & Teo, A. (1999). A longitudinal study of achievement trajectories: Factors associated with change. *Journal of Educational Psychology, 91,* 116–126.

Johanning, D. I., D'Agostino, J. V., Steele, D. F., & Shumow, L. (1999, April). *Student writing, post-writing group collaboration, and learning in pre-algebra.* Paper presented at the annual meeting of the American Educational Research Association, Montreal, Canada.

Johnson, D. W., & Johnson, R. T. (1985). Classroom conflict: Controversy versus debate in learning groups. *American Educational Research Journal, 22,* 237–256.

Johnson, D. W., & Johnson, R. T. (1988). Critical thinking through structured controversy. *Educational Leadership, 45(8),* 58–64.

Johnson, D. W., & Johnson, R. T. (1991). *Learning together and alone: Cooperative, competitive, and individualistic learning* (3rd ed.). Upper Saddle River, NJ: Prentice Hall.

Johnson, D. W., & Johnson, R. T. (1996). Conflict resolution and peer mediation programs in elementary and secondary schools: A review of the research. *Review of Educational Research, 66,* 459–506.

Johnson, D. W., & Johnson, R. T. (2001, April). *Teaching students to be peacemakers: A meta-analysis.* Paper presented at the annual meeting of the American Educational Research Association, Seattle, WA.

Johnson, D. W., Johnson, R., Dudley, B., Ward, M., & Magnuson, D. (1995). The impact of peer mediation training on the management of school and home conflicts. *American Educational Research Journal, 32,* 829–844.

Johnson, H. C., & Friesen, B. (1993). Etiologies of mental and emotional disorders in children. In H. Johnson (Ed.), *Child mental health in the 1990s: Curricula for graduate and undergraduate.* Washington, DC: U.S. Department of Health and Human Services.

Johnson, J. S., & Newport, E. L. (1989). Critical period effects in second language learning. *Cognitive Psychology, 21,* 60–99.

Johnson-Glenberg, M. C. (2000). Training reading comprehension in adequate decodes/poor comprehenders: Verbal versus visual strategies. *Journal of Educational Psychology, 92,* 772–782.

John-Steiner, V. (1997). *Notebooks of the mind: Explorations of thinking* (Rev. ed.). New York: Oxford University Press.

John-Steiner, V., & Mahn, H. (1996). Sociocultural approaches to learning and development: A Vygotskian framework. *Educational Psychologist, 31,* 191–206.

Johnstone, A. H., & El-Banna, H. (1986). Capacities, demands and processes—a predictive model for science education. *Education in Chemistry, 23,* 80–84.

Jonassen, D. H. (1996). *Computers in the classroom: Mindtools for critical thinking.* Upper Saddle River, NJ: Merrill/Prentice Hall.

Jonassen, D. H., Hannum, W. H., & Tessmer, M. (1989). *Handbook of task analysis procedures.* New York: Praeger.

Jones, D., & Christensen, C. A. (1999). Relationship between automaticity in handwriting and students' ability to generate written text. *Journal of Educational Psychology, 91,* 44–49.

Jones, E. E., & Berglas, S. (1978). Control of attributions about the self through self-handicapping strategies: The appeal of alcohol and the role of underachievement. *Personality and Social Psychology Bulletin, 4,* 200–206.

Jones, G. P., & Dembo, M. H. (1989). Age and sex role differences in intimate friendships during childhood and adolescence. *Merrill-Palmer Quarterly, 35,* 445–462.

Jones, K. M., Drew, H. A., & Weber, N. L. (2000). Noncontingent peer attention as treatment for disruptive classroom behavior. *Journal of Applied Behavior Analysis, 33,* 343–346.

Jones, M. C. (1924). The elimination of children's fears. *Journal of Experimental Psychology, 7,* 382–390.

Jones, M. S., Levin, M. E., Levin, J. R., & Beitzel, B. D. (2000). Can vocabulary-learning strategies and pair-learning formats be profitably combined? *Journal of Educational Psychology, 92,* 256–262.

Joshi, M. S., & MacLean, M. (1994). Indian and English children's understanding of the distinction between real and apparent emotion. *Child Development, 65,* 1372–1384.

Josselson, R. (1988). The embedded self: I and Thou revisited. In D. K. Lapsley & F. C. Power (Eds.), *Self, ego, and identity: Integrative approaches* (pp. 91–106). New York: Springer-Verlag.

Jovanovic, J., & King, S. S. (1998). Boys and girls in the performance-based science classroom: Who's doing the performing? *American Educational Research Journal, 35,* 477–496.

Jozefowicz, D. M., Arbreton, A. J., Eccles, J. S., Barber, B. L., & Colarossi, L. (1994, April). *Seventh grade student, parent, and teacher factors associated with later school dropout or movement into alternative educational settings.* Paper presented at the annual meeting of the American Educational Research Association, New Orleans, LA.

Judd, C. H. (1932). Autobiography. In C. Murchison (Ed.), *History of psychology in autobiography* (Vol. 2). Worcester, MA: Clark University Press.

Jussim, L., Eccles, J., & Madon, S. (1996). Social perception, social stereotypes, and teacher expectations: Accuracy and the quest for the powerful self-fulfilling prophecy. In L. Berkowitz (Ed.), *Advances in experimental social psychology.* New York: Academic Press.

Juvonen, J. (1991). Deviance, perceived responsibility, and negative peer reactions. *Developmental Psychology, 27,* 672–681.

Juvonen, J. (2000). The social functions of attributional face-saving tactics among early adolescents. *Educational Psychology Review, 12,* 15–32.

Juvonen, J., & Hiner, M. (1991, April). *Perceived responsibility and annoyance as mediators of negative peer reactions.* Paper presented at the annual meeting of the American Educational Research Association, Chicago.

Juvonen, J., Nishina, A., & Graham, S. (2000). Peer harassment, psychological adjustment, and school functioning in early adolescence. *Journal of Educational Psychology, 92,* 349–359.

Juvonen, J., & Weiner, B. (1993). An attributional analysis of students' interactions: The social consequences of perceived responsibility. *Educational Psychology Review, 5,* 325–345.

Kagan, J. (1998). Biology and the child. In W. Damon (Editor-in-Chief) & N. Eisenberg (Vol. Ed.), *Handbook of child psychology: Vol. 3. Social, emotional, and personality development* (5th ed., pp. 177–235). New York: Wiley.

Kagan, J., Snidman, N., & Arcus, D. M. (1992). Initial reactions to unfamiliarity. *Current Directions in Psychological Science, 1,* 171–174.

Kahl, B., & Woloshyn, V. E. (1994). Using elaborative interrogation to facilitate acquisition of factual information in cooperative learning settings: One good strategy deserves another. *Applied Cognitive Psychology, 8,* 465–478.

Kahle, J. B. (1983). *The disadvantaged majority: Science education for women.* Burlington, NC: Carolina Biological Supply Co.

Kahle, J. B., & Lakes, M. K. (1983). The myth of equality in science classrooms. *Journal of Research in Science Teaching, 20,* 131–140.

Kail, R. (1990). *The development of memory in children* (3rd ed.). New York: Freeman.

Kail, R. V. (1998). *Children and their development.* Upper Saddle River, NJ: Prentice Hall.

Kane, R. J. (1983). In defense of grade inflation. *Today's Education, 67*(4), 41.

Kaplan, A. (1998, April). *Task goal orientation and adaptive social interaction among students of diverse cultural backgrounds.* Paper presented at the annual meeting of the American Educational Research Association, San Diego, CA.

Kaplan, A., & Midgley, C. (1999). The relationship between perceptions of the classroom goal structure and early adolescents' affect in school: The mediating role of coping strategies. *Learning and Individual Differences, 11,* 187–212.

Karau, S. J., & Williams, K. D. (1995). Social loafing: Research findings, implications, and future directions. *Current Directions in Psychological Science, 4,* 134–140.

Kardash, C. A. M., & Amlund, J. T. (1991). Self-reported learning strategies and learning from expository text. *Contemporary Educational Psychology, 16,* 117–138.

Kardash, C. A. M., & Scholes, R. J. (1996). Effects of preexisting beliefs, epistemological beliefs, and need for cognition on interpretation of controversial issues. *Journal of Educational Psychology, 88,* 260–271.

Karmiloff-Smith, A. (1979). Language development after five. In P. Fletcher & M. Garman (Eds.), *Language acquisition: Studies in first language development.* Cambridge, England: Cambridge University Press.

Karmiloff-Smith, A. (1993). Innate constraints and developmental change. In P. Bloom (Ed.), *Language acquisition: Core readings.* Cambridge, MA: MIT Press.

Karplus, R., Pulos, S., & Stage, E. K. (1983). Proportional reasoning of early adolescents. In R. Lesh & M. Landau (Eds.), *Acquisition of mathematics concepts and processes.* San Diego, CA: Academic Press.

Karpov, Y. V., & Haywood, H. C. (1998). Two ways to elaborate Vygotsky's concept of mediation: Implications for instruction. *American Psychologist, 53,* 27–36.

Katchadourian, H. (1990). Sexuality. In S. S. Feldman & G. R. Elliott (Eds.), *At the threshold: The developing adolescent* (pp. 330–351). Cambridge, MA: Harvard University Press.

Katkovsky, W., Crandall, V. C., & Good, S. (1967). Parental antecedents of children's beliefs in internal-external control of reinforcements in intellectual achievement situations. *Child Development, 38,* 765–776.

Katz, E. W., & Brent, S. B. (1968). Understanding connectives. *Journal of Verbal Learning and Verbal Behavior, 7,* 501–509.

Katz, L. (1993). All about me: Are we developing our children's self-esteem or their narcissism? *American Educator, 17*(2), 18–23.

Kearins, J. M. (1981). Visual spatial memory in Australian aboriginal children of desert regions. *Cognitive Psychology, 13,* 434–460.

Kehle, T. J., Clark, E., & Jenson, W. R. (1996). Interventions for students with traumatic brain injury: Managing behavioral disturbances. *Journal of Learning Disabilities, 29,* 633–642.

Kehle, T. J., Clark, E., Jenson, W. R., & Wampold, B. (1986). Effectiveness of the self-modeling procedure with behaviorally disturbed elementary age children. *School Psychology Review, 15,* 289–295.

Keil, F. C. (1986). The acquisition of natural kind and artifact terms. In W. Demopolous & A. Marras (Eds.), *Language learning and concept acquisition.* Norwood, NJ: Ablex.

Keil, F. C. (1987). Conceptual development and category structure. In U. Neisser (Ed.), *Concepts and conceptual development: Ecological and intellectual factors in categorization.* Cambridge, England: Cambridge University Press.

Keil, F. C. (1989). *Concepts, kinds, and cognitive development.* Cambridge, MA: MIT Press.

Keil, F. C. (1991). Theories, concepts, and the acquisition of word meaning. In S. A. Gelman & J. P. Byrnes (Eds.), *Perspectives on language and thought: Interrelations in development.* Cambridge, England: Cambridge University Press.

Keil, F. C. (1994). The birth and nurturance of concepts by domains: The origins of concepts of living things. In L. A. Hirschfeld & S. A. Gelman (Eds.), *Mapping the mind: Domain specificity in cognition and culture.* New York: Cambridge University Press.

Keil, F. C., & Silberstein, C. S. (1996). Schooling and the acquisition of theoretical knowledge. In D. R. Olson & N. Torrance (Eds.), *The handbook of education and human development: New models of learning, teaching, and schooling.* Cambridge, MA: Blackwell.

Kelemen, D. (1999). Why are rocks pointy? Children's preference for teleological explanations of the natural world. *Developmental Psychology, 35,* 1440–1452.

Kelley, M. L., & Carper, L. B. (1988). Home-based reinforcement procedures. In J. C. Witt, S. N. Elliott, & F. M. Gresham (Eds.), *Handbook of behavior therapy in education.* New York: Plenum Press.

Kelly, A., & Smail, B. (1986). Sex stereotypes and attitudes to science among eleven-year-old children. *British Journal of Educational Psychology, 56,* 158–168.

Kelly, G. J., & Chen, C. (1998, April). *The sound of music: Experiment, discourse, and writing of science as sociocultural practices.* Paper presented at the annual meeting of the American Educational Research Association, San Diego, CA.

Kennedy, R. (1992). What is performance assessment? *New Directions for Education Reform, 1*(2), 21–27.

Keogh, B. A., & Becker, L. D. (1973). Early detection of learning problems: Questions, cautions, and guidelines. *Exceptional Children, 39,* 5–11.

Keogh, B. K., & MacMillan, D. L. (1996). Exceptionality. In D. C. Berliner & R. C. Calfee (Eds.), *Handbook of educational psychology.* New York: Macmillan.

Kermani, H., & Moallem, M. (1997, March). *Cross-age tutoring: Exploring features and processes of peer-mediated learning.* Paper presented at the annual meeting of the American Educational Research Association, Chicago.

Kern, L., Dunlap, G., Childs, K. E., & Clark, S. (1994). Use of a classwide self-management program to improve the behavior of students with emotional and behavioral disorders. *Education and Treatment of Children, 17,* 445–458.

Kerns, L. L., & Lieberman, A. B. (1993). *Helping your depressed child.* Rocklin, CA: Prima.

Kerr, B. (1991). Educating gifted girls. In N. Coangelo & G. A. Davis (Eds.), *Handbook of gifted education.* Needham Heights, MA: Allyn & Bacon.

Kerr, M. M., & Nelson, C. M. (1989). *Strategies for managing behavior problems in the classroom* (2nd ed.). Upper Saddle River, NJ: Merrill/Prentice Hall.

Khattri, N., & Sweet, D. (1996). Assessment reform: Promises and challenges. In M. B. Kane & R. Mitchell (Eds.), *Implementing performance assessment: Promises, problems, and challenges* (pp. 1–21). Mahwah, NJ: Erlbaum.

Kiewra, K. A. (1985). Investigating notetaking and review: A depth of processing alternative. *Educational Psychologist, 20,* 23–32.

Kiewra, K. A. (1989). A review of note-taking: The encoding-storage paradigm and beyond. *Educational Psychology Review, 1,* 147–172.

Kim, D., Solomon, D., & Roberts, W. (1995, April). *Classroom practices that enhance students' sense of community.* Paper presented at the annual meeting of the American Educational Research Association, San Francisco.

Kimberg, D. Y., D'Esposito, M., & Farah, M. J. (1997). Cognitive functions in the prefrontal cortex-working memory and executive control. *Current Directions in Psychological Science, 6,* 185–192.

Kimble, G. A. (2000). Behaviorism and unity in psychology. *Current Directions in Psychological Science, 9,* 208–212.

Kindermann, T. A., McCollam, T., & Gibson, E. (1996). Peer networks and students' classroom engagement during childhood and adolescence. In J. Juvonen & K. Wentzel (Eds.), *Social motivation: Understanding children's school adjustment.* Cambridge, England: Cambridge University Press.

King, A. (1992). Comparison of self-questioning, summarizing, and notetaking-review as strategies for learning from lectures. *American Educational Research Journal, 29,* 303–323.

King, A. (1994). Guiding knowledge construction in the classroom: Effects of teaching children how to question and how to explain. *American Educational Research Journal, 31,* 338–368.

King, A. (1997). ASK to THINK - TEL WHY®©: A model of transactive peer tutoring for scaffolding higher level complex learning. *Educational Psychologist, 32,* 221–235.

King, A. (1998). Transactive peer tutoring: Distributing cognition and metacognition. *Educational Psychology Review, 10,* 57–74

King, A. (1999). Discourse patterns for mediating peer learning. In A. M. O'Donnell & A. King (Eds.), *Cognitive perspectives on peer learning* (pp. 87–115). Mahwah, NJ: Erlbaum.

King, A., Staffieri, A., & Adelgais, A. (1998). Mutual peer tutoring: Effects of structuring tutorial interaction to scaffold peer learning. *Journal of Educational Psychology, 90,* 134–152.

King, N. J., & Ollendick, T. H. (1989). Children's anxiety and phobic disorders in school settings: Classification, assessment, and intervention issues. *Review of Educational Research, 59,* 431–470.

Kintsch, W. (1980). Learning from text, levels of comprehension, or: Why anyone would read a story anyway. *Poetics, 9,* 87–98.

Kirkland, M. C. (1971). The effect of tests on students and schools. *Review of Educational Research, 41,* 303–350.

Kirschenbaum, R. J. (1989). Identification of the gifted and talented American Indian student. In C. J. Maker & S. W. Schiever (Eds.), *Critical issues in gifted education: Vol. 2. Defensible programs for cultural and ethnic minorities.* Austin, TX: Pro-Ed.

Kitsantis, A., Zimmerman, B. J., & Cleary, T. (2000). The role of observation and emulation in the development of athletic self-regulation. *Journal of Educational Psychology, 92,* 811–817.

Klein, J. D. (1990, April). *The effect of interest, task performance, and reward contingencies on self-efficacy.* Paper presented at the annual meeting of the American Educational Research Association, Boston.

Kletzien, S. B. (1988, April). *Achieving and non-achieving high school readers' use of comprehension strategies for reading expository text.* Paper presented at the annual meeting of the American Educational Research Association, New Orleans, LA.

Kluger, A. N., & DeNisi, A. (1998). Feedback interventions: Toward the understanding of a double-edged sword. *Current Directions in Psychological Science, 7,* 67–72.

Knapp, M. S., Turnbull, B. J., & Shields, P. M. (1990). New directions for educating the children of poverty. *Educational Leadership, 48*(1), 4–9.

Knapp, M. S., & Woolverton, S. (1995). Social class and schooling. In J. A. Banks & C. A. M. Banks (Eds.), *Handbook of research on multicultural education.* New York: Macmillan.

Knowlton, D. (1995). Managing children with oppositional behavior. *Beyond Behavior, 6*(3), 5–10.

Koegel, L. K. (1995). Communication and language intervention. In R. L. Koegel & L. K. Koegel (Eds.), *Strategies for initiating positive interactions and improving learning opportunities.* Baltimore: Brookes.

Koegel, L. K., Koegel, R. L., & Dunlap, G. (Eds.). (1996). *Positive behavioral support: Including people with difficult behavior in the community.* Baltimore: Brookes.

Koeppel, J., & Mulrooney, M. (1992). The Sister Schools Program: A way for children to learn about cultural diversity—when there isn't any in their school. *Young Children, 48*(1), 44–47.

Koestner, R., Ryan, R. M., Bernieri, F., & Holt, K. (1984). Setting limits in children's behavior: The differential effects of controlling versus informational styles on intrinsic motivation and creativity. *Journal of Personality, 52,* 233–248.

Kogan, N. (1983). Stylistic variation in childhood and adolescence: Creativity, metaphor, and cognitive style. In J. H. Flavell & E. M. Markman (Eds.), *Handbook of child psychology: Vol. 3. Cognitive development.* New York: Wiley.

Kohlberg, L. (1975). The cognitive-developmental approach to moral education. *Phi Delta Kappan, 57,* 670–677.

Kohlberg, L. (1976). Moral stages and moralization: The cognitive-developmental approach. In T. Lickona (Ed.), *Moral development and behavior: Theory, research, and social issues.* New York: Holt, Rinehart & Winston.

Kohlberg, L. (1981). *The philosophy of moral development: Moral stages and the idea of justice.* San Francisco: Harper & Row.

Kohlberg, L. (1984). *The psychology of moral development: The nature and validity of moral stages.* San Francisco: Harper & Row.

Kohlberg, L. (1986). A current statement on some theoretical issues. In S. Modgil & C. Modgil (Eds.), *Lawrence Kohlberg: Consensus and controversy.* Philadelphia: Falmer Press.

Kohlberg, L., & Candee, D. (1984). The relationship of moral judgment to moral action. In W. M. Kurtines & J. L. Gewirtz (Eds.), *Morality, moral behavior, and moral development.* New York: Wiley.

Kohn, A. (1993). Choices for children: Why and how to let students decide. *Phi Delta Kappan, 75*(1), 8–20.

Kohut, S., Jr. (1988). *The middle school: A bridge between elementary and high schools* (2nd ed.). Washington, DC: National Education Association.

Kolodner, J. (1985). Memory for experience. In G. H. Bower (Ed.), *The psychology of learning and motivation: Advances in research and theory* (Vol. 19). San Diego, CA: Academic Press.

Koretz, D., Stecher, B., Klein, S., & McCaffrey, D. (1994). The Vermont portfolio assessment program: Findings and implications. *Educational Measurement: Issues and Practices, 13*(3), 5–16.

Kosslyn, S. M. (1985). Mental imagery ability. In R. J. Sternberg (Ed.), *Human abilities: An information-processing approach.* New York: Freeman.

Kounin, J. S. (1970). *Discipline and group management in classrooms.* New York: Holt, Rinehart & Winston.

Kovacs, D. M., Parker, J. G., & Hoffman, L. W. (1996). Behavioral, affective, and social correlates of involvement in cross-sex friendship in elementary school. *Child Development, 67,* 2269–2286.

Koyanagi, C., & Gaines, S. (1993). *All systems failure: An examination of the results of neglecting the needs of children with serious emotional disturbance.* Alexandria, VA: National Mental Health Association.

Krajcik, J. S. (1991). Developing students' understanding of chemical concepts. In S. M. Glynn, R. H. Yeany, & B. K. Britton (Eds.), *The psychology of learning science.* Hillsdale, NJ: Erlbaum.

Krampen, G. (1987). Differential effects of teacher comments. *Journal of Educational Psychology, 79,* 137–146.

Krashen, S. D. (1996). *Under attack: The case against bilingual education.* Culver City, CA: Language Education Associates.

Krathwohl, D. R. (1994). Reflections on the taxonomy: Its past, present, and future. In L. W. Anderson & L. A. Sosniak (Eds.), *Bloom's taxonomy: A forty-year perspective. Ninety-third yearbook of the National Society for the Study of Education, Part II.* Chicago: National Society for the Study of Education.

Krathwohl, D. R., Bloom, B. S., & Masia, B. B. (1964). *Taxonomy of educational objectives: Handbook II. Affective domain.* New York: David McKay.

Krumboltz, J. D., & Krumboltz, H. B. (1972). *Changing children's behavior.* Upper Saddle River, NJ: Prentice Hall.

Kucan, L., & Beck, I. L. (1997). Thinking aloud and reading comprehension research: Inquiry, instruction, and social interaction. *Review of Educational Research, 67,* 271–299.

Kuhl, J. (1985). Volitional mediators of cognition-behavior consistency: Self-regulatory processes and actions versus state orientation. In J. Kuhl & J. Beckmann (Eds.), *Action control: From cognition to behavior.* Berlin, Germany: Springer-Verlag.

Kuhl, J. (1987). Action control: The maintenance of motivational states. In F. Halisch & J. Kuhl (Eds.), *Motivation, intention, and volition.* Berlin, Germany: Springer-Verlag.

Kuhn, D. (2001). How do people know? *Psychological Science, 12,* 1–8.

Kuhn, D., Amsel, E., & O'Loughlin, M. (1988). *The development of scientific thinking skills.* San Diego, CA: Academic Press.

Kuhn, D., Garcia-Mila, M., Zohar, A., & Andersen, C. (1995). Strategies of knowledge acquisition. *Monographs of the Society for Research in Child Development, 60* (Whole No. 245).

Kuhn, D., Shaw, V., & Felton, M. (1997). Effects of dyadic interaction on argumentative reasoning. *Cognition and Instruction, 15,* 287–315.

Kulhavy, R. W., Lee, J. B., & Caterino, L. C. (1985). Conjoint retention of maps and related discourse. *Contemporary Educational Psychology, 10,* 28–37.

Kulik, C. C., Kulik, J. A., & Bangert-Drowns, R. L. (1990). Effectiveness of mastery learning programs: A meta-analysis. *Review of Educational Research, 60,* 265–299.

Kulik, J. A., & Kulik, C. C. (1988). Timing of feedback and verbal learning. *Review of Educational Research, 58,* 79–97.

Kulik, J. A., & Kulik, C. C. (1997). Ability grouping. In N. Colangelo & G. Davis (Eds.), *Handbook of gifted education* (2nd ed., pp. 230–242). Boston: Allyn & Bacon.

Kulik, J. A., Kulik, C. C., & Cohen, P. A. (1979). A meta-analysis of outcome studies of Keller's Personalized System of Instruction. *American Psychologist, 34,* 307–318.

Kulik, J. A., Kulik, C. C., & Cohen, P. A. (1980). Effectiveness of computer-based college teaching: A meta-analysis of findings. *Review of Educational Research, 50,* 525–544.

Kunc, N. (1984). Integration: Being realistic isn't realistic. *Canadian Journal for Exceptional Children, 1*(1), 4–8.

Kupersmidt, J. B., Buchele, K. S., Voegler, M. E., & Sedikides, C. (1996). Social self-discrepancy: A theory relating peer relations problems and school maladjustment. In J. Juvonen & K. R. Wentzel (Eds.), *Social motivation: Understanding children's school adjustment* (pp. 66–97). Cambridge, England: Cambridge University Press.

Kupersmidt, J. B., & Coie, J. D. (1990). Preadolescent peer status, aggression, and school adjustment as predictors of externalizing problems in adolescence. *Child Development, 61,* 1350–1362.

Kurtines, W. M., Berman, S. L., Ittel, A., & Williamson, S. (1995). Moral development: A co-constructivist perspective. In W. M. Kurtines & J. L. Gewirtz (Eds.), *Moral development: An introduction.* Boston: Allyn & Bacon.

Kyle, W. C., & Shymansky, J. A. (1989, April). Enhancing learning through conceptual change teaching. *NARST News, 31,* 7–8.

LaBar, K. S., & Phelps, E. A. (1998). Arousal-mediated memory consolidation: Role of the medial temporal lobe in humans. *Psychological Science, 9,* 490–493.

LaBlance, G. R., Steckol, K. F., & Smith, V. L. (1994). Stuttering: The role of the classroom teacher. *Teaching Exceptional Children, 26*(2), 10–12.

Laboratory of Human Cognition. (1982). Culture and intelligence. In R. J. Sternberg (Ed.), *Handbook of human intelligence.* Cambridge, England: Cambridge University Press.

Labov, W. (1973). The boundaries of words and their meanings. In C. J. N. Bailey & R. W. Shuy (Eds.), *New ways of analyzing variations in English.* Washington, DC: Georgetown University Press.

Ladd, G. W. (1990). Having friends, keeping friends, making friends, and being liked by peers in the classroom: Predictors of children's early school adjustment? *Child Development, 61,* 1081–1100.

Ladson-Billings, G. (1994a). *The dreamkeepers: Successful teachers of African American children.* San Francisco: Jossey-Bass.

Ladson-Billings, G. (1994b). What we can learn from multicultural education research. *Educational Leadership, 51*(8), 22–26.

Ladson-Billings, G. (1995). Toward a theory of culturally relevant pedagogy. *American Educational Research Journal, 32,* 465–491.

LaFromboise, T., Coleman, H. L. K., & Gerton, J. (1993). Psychological impact of biculturalism: Evidence and theory. *Psychological Bulletin, 114,* 395–412.

Lahey, B. B., & Carlson, C. L. (1991). Validity of the diagnostic category of attention deficit disorder without hyperactivity: A review of the literature. *Journal of Learning Disabilities, 24,* 110–120.

Lajoie, S. P., & Derry, S. J. (Eds.). (1993). *Computers as cognitive tools.* Hillsdale, NJ: Erlbaum.

Lamborn, S. D., Mounts, N. S., Steinberg, L., & Dornbusch, S. M. (1991). Patterns of competence and adjustment among adolescents from authoritative, authoritarian, indulgent, and neglectful families. *Child Development, 62,* 1049–1065.

Lamon, M., Chan, C., Scardamalia, M., Burtis, P. J., & Brett, C. (1993, April). *Beliefs about learning and constructive processes in reading: Effects of a computer supported intentional learning environment (CSILE).* Paper presented at the annual meeting of the American Educational Research Association, Atlanta, GA.

Lampert, M. (1990). When the problem is not the question and the solution is not the answer: Mathematical knowing and teaching. *American Educational Research Journal, 27,* 29–63.

Lampert, M., Rittenhouse, P., & Crumbaugh, C. (1996). Agreeing to disagree: Developing sociable mathematical discourse. In D. R. Olson & N. Torrance (Eds.), *The handbook of education and human development: New models of learning, teaching, and schooling.* Cambridge, MA: Blackwell.

Lan, W. Y., Repman, J., Bradley, L., & Weller, H. (1994, April). *Immediate and lasting effects of criterion and payoff on academic risk taking.* Paper presented at the annual meeting of the American Educational Research Association, New Orleans, LA.

Landau, S., & McAninch, C. (1993). Young children with attention deficits. *Young Children, 48*(4), 49–58.

Landauer, T. K. (1962). Rate of implicit speech. *Perceptual and Motor Skills, 15,* 646.

Landesman, S., & Ramey, C. (1989). Developmental psychology and mental retardation: Integrating scientific principles with treatment practices. *American Psychologist, 44,* 409–415.

Lane, D. M., & Pearson, D. A. (1982). The development of selective attention. *Merrill-Palmer Quarterly, 28,* 317–337.

Langer, E. J. (1997). *The power of mindful learning.* Reading, MA: Addison-Wesley.

Langer, E. J. (2000). Mindful learning. *Current Directions in Psychological Science, 9,* 220–223.

Langer, J. A. (2000). Excellence in English in middle and high school: How teachers' professional lives support student achievement. *American Educational Research Journal, 37,* 397–439.

Lanthier, R. P., & Bates, J. E. (1997, March). *Does infant temperament predict adjustment in adolescence?* Paper presented at the annual meeting of the American Educational Research Association, Chicago.

Lanza, A., & Roselli, T. (1991). Effect of the hypertextual approach versus the structured approach on students' achievement. *Journal of Computer-Based Instruction, 18*(2), 48–50.

Laosa, L. M. (1982). School, occupation, culture, and family: The impact of parental schooling on the parent-child relationship. *Journal of Educational Psychology, 74,* 791–827.

Lapsley, D. K. (1993). Toward an integrated theory of adolescent ego development: The "new look" at adolescent egocentrism. *American Journal of Orthopsychiatry, 63,* 562–571.

Larkin, R. W. (1979). *Suburban youth in cultural crisis.* New York: Oxford University Press.

Larson, R. W. (2000). Toward a psychology of positive youth development. *American Psychologist, 55,* pp. 170–183.

Larson, R. W., Clore, G. L., & Wood, G. A. (1999). The emotions of romantic relationships: Do they wreak havoc on adolescents? In W. Furman, B. B. Brown, & C. Feiring (Eds.), *The development of romantic relationships in adolescence*

(pp. 19–49). Cambridge, England: Cambridge University Press.

Laupa, M., & Turiel, E. (1995). Social domain theory. In W. M. Kurtines & J. L. Gewirtz (Eds.), *Moral development: An introduction.* Boston: Allyn & Bacon.

Lave, J. (1993). Word problems: A microcosm of theories of learning. In P. Light & G. Butterworth (Eds.), *Context and cognition: Ways of learning and knowing.* Hillsdale, NJ: Erlbaum.

Lave, J., & Wenger, E. (1991). *Situated learning: Legitimate peripheral participation.* Cambridge, England: Cambridge University Press.

Law, D. J., Pellegrino, J. W., & Hunt, E. B. (1993). Comparing the tortoise and the hare: Gender differences and experience in dynamic spatial reasoning tasks. *Psychological Science, 4,* 35–40.

Learning Technology Center, Vanderbilt University. (1996). *Jasper in the Classroom* (videodisc). Mahwah, NH: Erlbaum.

Leary, M. R. (1999). Making sense of self-esteem. *Current Directions in Psychological Science, 8,* 32–35.

Leary, M. R., & Hill, D. A. (1996). Moving on: Autism and movement disturbance. *Mental Retardation, 34,* 39–53.

Lee, C. D., & Slaughter-Defoe, D. T. (1995). Historical and sociocultural influences on African and American education. In J. A. Banks & C. A. M. Banks (Eds.), *Handbook of research on multicultural education.* New York: Macmillan.

Lee, J. F., Jr., & Pruitt, K. W. (1984). *Providing for individual differences in student learning: A mastery learning approach.* Springfield, IL: Charles C Thomas.

Lee, O. (1999). Science knowledge, world views, and information sources in social and cultural contexts: Making sense after a natural disaster. *American Educational Research Journal, 36,* 187–219.

Lee, O., & Anderson, C. W. (1993). Task engagement and conceptual change in middle school science classrooms. *American Educational Research Journal, 30,* 585–610.

Lee, S. (1985). Children's acquisition of conditional logic structure: Teachable? *Contemporary Educational Psychology, 10,* 14–27.

Lee-Pearce, M. L., Plowman, T. S., & Touchstone, D. (1998). Starbase-Atlantis, a school without walls: A comparative study of an innovative science program for at-risk urban elementary students. *Journal of Education for Students Placed at Risk, 3,* 223–235.

Leffert, J. S., Siperstein, G. N., & Millikan, E. (1999). *Social perception and strategy generation: Two key social cognitive processes in children with mental retardation.* Paper presented at the biennial meeting of the Society for Research in Child Development, Albuquerque, NM.

Lehrer, R. (1993). Authors of knowledge: Patterns of hypermedia design. In S. P. Lajoie & S. J. Derry (Eds.), *Computers as cognitive tools* (pp. 197–227). Hillsdale, NJ: Erlbaum.

Leichtman, M. D., & Ceci, S. J. (1995). The effects of stereotypes and suggestions on preschoolers' reports. *Developmental Psychology, 31,* 568–578.

Leinhardt, G. (1994). History: A time to be mindful. In G. Leinhardt, I. L. Beck, & C. Stainton (Eds.), *Teaching and learning in history.* Hillsdale, NJ: Erlbaum.

Leinhardt, G., & Pallay, A. (1982). Restrictive educational settings: Exile or haven? *Review of Educational Research, 52,* 557–578.

Leiter, J., & Johnsen, M. C. (1997). Child maltreatment and school performance declines: An event-history analysis. *American Educational Research Journal, 34,* 563–589.

Lejuez, C. W., Schaal, D. W., & O'Donnell, J. (1998). Behavioral pharmacology and the treatment of substance abuse. In J. J. Plaud & G. H. Eifert (Eds.), *From behavior theory to behavior therapy* (pp. 116–135). Needham Heights, MA: Allyn & Bacon.

Lenneberg, E. H. (1967). *Biological foundations of language.* New York: Wiley.

Lennon, R., Eisenberg, N., & Carroll, J. L. (1983). The assessment of empathy in early childhood. *Journal of Applied Developmental Psychology, 4,* 295–302.

Lennon, R., Ormrod, J. E., Burger, S. F., & Warren, E. (1990, October). *Belief systems of teacher education majors and their possible influences on future classroom performance.* Paper presented at the Northern Rocky Mountain Educational Research Association, Greeley, CO.

Lentz, F. E. (1988). Reductive procedures. In J. C. Witt, S. N. Elliott, & F. M. Gresham (Eds.), *Handbook of behavior therapy in education.* New York: Plenum Press.

Lepper, M. R. (1981). Intrinsic and extrinsic motivation in children: Detrimental effects of superfluous social controls. In W. A. Collins (Ed.), *Minnesota Symposia on Child Psychology* (Vol. 14). Hillsdale, NJ: Erlbaum.

Lepper, M. R., Aspinwall, L. G., Mumme, D. L., & Chabay, R. W. (1990). Self-perception and social perception processes in tutoring: Subtle social control strategies of expert tutors. In J. M. Olson & M. P. Zanna (Eds.), *Self-inference processes: The Ontario Symposium.* Hillsdale, NJ: Erlbaum.

Lepper, M. R., & Greene, D. (Eds.). (1978). *The hidden costs of reward.* Hillsdale, NJ: Erlbaum.

Lepper, M. R., & Gurtner, J. (1989). Children and computers: Approaching the twenty-first century. *American Psychologist, 44,* 170–178.

Lepper, M. R., & Hodell, M. (1989). Intrinsic motivation in the classroom. In C. Ames & R. Ames (Eds.), *Research on motivation in education: Vol. 3. Goals and cognitions.* San Diego, CA: Academic Press.

Lerman, D. C., & Iwata, B. A. (1995). Prevalence of the extinction burst and its attenuation during treatment. *Journal of Applied Behavior Analysis, 28,* 93–94.

Lerner, J. W. (1985). *Learning disabilities: Theories, diagnosis, and teaching strategies* (4th ed.). Boston: Houghton Mifflin.

Leslie, A. M. (1991). The theory of mind impairment in autism: Evidence for a modular mechanism of development? In A. Whiten (Ed.), *Natural theories of mind: Evolution, development and simulation of everyday mindreading.* Oxford, England: Blackwell.

Lester, F. K., Jr., Lambdin, D. V., & Preston, R. V. (1997). A new vision of the nature and purposes of assessment in the mathematics classroom. In G. D. Phye (Ed.), *Handbook of classroom assessment: Learning, achievement, and adjustment.* San Diego, CA: Academic Press.

Levin, G. R. (1983). *Child psychology.* Monterey, CA: Brooks/Cole.

Levin, H. M. (1998). Educational performance standards and the economy. *Educational Researcher, 27*(4), 4–10.

Levin, J. R., & Mayer, R. E. (1993). Understanding illustrations in text. In B. K. Britton, A. Woodward, & M. Binkley (Eds.), *Learning from textbooks: Theory and practice.* Hillsdale, NJ: Erlbaum.

Levine, D. U., & Lezotte, L. W. (1995). Effective schools research. In J. A. Banks & C. A. M. Banks (Eds.), *Handbook of research on multicultural education.* New York: Macmillan.

Levine, M. (1966). Hypothesis behavior by humans during discrimination learning. *Journal of Experimental Psychology, 71,* 331–338.

Levitt, M. J., Guacci-Franco, N., & Levitt, J. L. (1993). Convoys of social support in childhood and early adolescence: Structure and function. *Developmental Psychology, 29,* 811–818.

Levitt, M. J., Levitt, J. L., Bustos, G. L., Crooks, N. A., Santos, J. D., Telan, P., & Silver, M. E. (1999, April). *The social ecology of achievement in pre-adolescents: Social support and school attitudes.* Paper presented at the annual meeting of the American Educational Research Association, Montreal, Canada.

Levy, I., Kaplan, A., & Patrick, H. (2000, April). *Early adolescents' achievement goals, intergroup processes, and attitudes towards collaboration.* Paper presented at the annual meeting of the American Educational Research Association, New Orleans, LA.

Lewis, R. B., & Doorlag, D. H. (1991). *Teaching special students in the mainstream* (3rd ed.). Upper Saddle River, NJ: Merrill/Prentice Hall.

Lickona, T. (1991). Moral development in the elementary school classroom. In W. M. Kurtines & J. L. Gewirtz (Eds.), *Moral behavior and development: Vol. 3. Application.* Hillsdale, NJ: Erlbaum.

Lidz, C. S. (1991). Issues in the assessment of preschool children. In B. A. Bracken (Ed.), *The psychoeducational assessment of preschool children* (2nd ed., pp. 18–31). Boston: Allyn & Bacon.

Lieberman, L. M. (1992). Preserving special education . . . for those who need it. In W. Stainback & S. Stainback (Eds.), *Controversial issues confronting special education: Divergent perspectives.* Boston: Allyn & Bacon.

Light, J. G., & Defries, J. C. (1995). Comorbidity of reading and mathematics disabilities: Genetic and environmental etiologies. *Journal of Learning Disabilities, 28,* 96–106.

Light, P., & Butterworth, G. (Eds.). (1993). *Context and cognition: Ways of learning and knowing.* Hillsdale, NJ: Erlbaum.

Lillard, A. S. (1997). Other folks' theories of mind and behavior. *Psychological Science, 8,* 268–274.

Lind, G. (1994, April). *Why do juvenile delinquents gain little from moral discussion programs?* Paper presented at the annual meeting of the American Educational Research Association, New Orleans, LA.

Lindberg, M. (1991). A taxonomy of suggestibility and eyewitness memory: Age, memory process, and focus of analysis. In J. L. Doris (Ed.), *The suggestibility of children's recollections.* Washington, DC: American Psychological Association.

Linderholm, T., Gustafson, M., van den Broek, P., & Lorch, R. F., Jr. (1997, March). *Effects of reading goals on inference generation.* Paper presented at the annual meeting of the American Educational Research Association, Chicago.

Linn, M. C., Clement, C., Pulos, S., & Sullivan, P. (1989). Scientific reasoning during adolescence: The influence of instruction in science knowledge and reasoning strategies. *Journal of Research in Science Teaching, 26,* 171–187.

Linn, M. C., & Hyde, J. S. (1989). Gender, mathematics, and science. *Educational Researcher, 18*(8), 17–19, 22–27.

Linn, M. C., & Petersen, A. C. (1985). Emergence and characterization of sex differences in spatial ability: A meta-analysis. *Child Development, 56,* 1479–1498.

Linn, M. C., Songer, N. B., & Eylon, B. (1996). Shifts and convergences in science learning and instruction. In D. C. Berliner & R. C. Calfee (Eds.), *Handbook of educational psychology.* New York: Macmillan.

Linn, R. L. (1994). Performance assessment: Policy promises and technical measurement standards. *Educational Researcher, 23*(9), 4–14.

Linn, R. L. (2000). Assessments and accountability. *Educational Researcher, 29*(2), 4–16.

Linn, R. L., & Gronlund, N. E. (2000). *Measurement and assessment in teaching* (8th ed.). Upper Saddle River, NJ: Merrill/Prentice Hall.

Lipson, M. Y. (1982). Learning new information from text: The role of prior knowledge and reading ability. *Journal of Reading Behavior, 14,* 243–261.

Lipson, M. Y. (1983). The influence of religious affiliation on children's memory for text information. *Reading Research Quarterly, 18,* 448–457.

Liss, M. B. (1983). Learning gender-related skills through play. In M. B. Liss (Ed.), *Social and cognitive skills: Sex roles and children's play.* San Diego, CA: Academic Press.

Little, L. (2002). Middle class mothers' perceptions of peer and sibling victimization among children with Asperger's syndrome and nonverbal learning disorders. *Comprehensive Pediatric Nursing, 25,* 43–57.

Little, T. D., Oettingen, G., Stetsenko, A., & Baltes, P. B. (1995). Children's action-control beliefs about school performance: How do American children compare with German and Russian children? *Journal of Personality and Social Psychology, 69,* 686–700.

Littlewood, W. T. (1984). *Foreign and second language learning: Language-acquisition research and its implications for the classroom.* Cambridge, England: Cambridge University Press.

Liu, L. G. (1990, April). *The use of causal questioning to promote narrative comprehension and memory.* Paper presented at the annual meeting of the American Educational Research Association, Boston.

Livesley, W. J., & Bromley, D. B. (1973). *Person perception in childhood and adolescence.* New York: Wiley.

Lloyd, D. N. (1978). Prediction of school failure from third-grade data. *Educational and Psychological Measurement, 38,* 1193–1200.

Lochman, J. E., & Dodge, K. A. (1994). Social–cognitive processes of severely violent, moderately aggressive, and nonaggressive boys. *Journal of Consulting and Clinical Psychology, 62,* 366–374.

Lochman, J. E., Wayland, K. K., & White, K. J. (1993). Social goals: Relationship to adolescent adjustment and to social problem solving. *Journal of Abnormal Child Psychology, 21,* 1993.

Locke, E. A., & Latham, G. P. (1990). *A theory of goal setting and task performance.* Upper Saddle River, NJ: Prentice Hall.

Locke, E. A., & Latham, G. P. (1994). Goal setting theory. In H. F. O'Neil, Jr., & M. Drillings (Eds.), *Motivation: Theory and research.* Hillsdale, NJ: Erlbaum.

Lodico, M. G., Ghatala, E. S., Levin, J. R., Pressley, M., & Bell, J. A. (1983). The effects of strategy monitoring training on children's selection of effective memory strategies. *Journal of Experimental Child Psychology, 35,* 273–277.

Loeber, R., & Stouthamer-Loeber, M. (1998). Development of juvenile aggression and violence. *American Psychologist, 53,* 242–259.

Loftus, E. F. (1991). Made in memory: Distortions in recollection after misleading information. In G. H. Bower (Ed.), *The psychology of learning and motivation: Advances in research and theory* (Vol. 27). San Diego, CA: Academic Press.

Loftus, E. F., & Loftus, G. R. (1980). On the permanence of stored information in the human brain. *American Psychologist, 35,* 409–420.

Logan, K. R., Alberto, P. A., Kana, T. G., & Waylor-Bowen, T. (1994). Curriculum development and instructional design for students with profound disabilities. In L. Sternberg (Ed.), *Individuals with profound disabilities: Instructional and assistive strategies* (3rd ed.). Austin, TX: Pro-Ed.

Lomawaima, K. T. (1995). Educating Native Americans. In J. A. Banks & C. A. M. Banks (Eds.), *Handbook of research on multicultural education*. New York: Macmillan.

Long, M. (1995). The role of the linguistic environment in second language acquisition. In W. C. Ritchie & T. K. Bhatia (Eds.), *Handbook of language acquisition: Vol. 2. Second language acquisition*. San Diego, CA: Academic Press.

Lopez, E. C. (1997). The cognitive assessment of limited English proficient and bilingual children. In D. P. Flanagan, J. L. Genshaft, & P. L. Harrison (Eds.), *Contemporary intellectual assessment: Theories, tests, and issues* (pp. 503–516). New York: Guilford Press.

López, G. R. (2001). Redefining parental involvement: Lessons from high-performing migrant-impacted schools. *American Educational Research Journal, 38*, 253–288.

Loranger, A. L. (1994). The study strategies of successful and unsuccessful high school students. *Journal of Reading Behavior, 26,* 347–360.

Lorch, E. P., Diener, M. B., Sanchez, R. P., Milich, R., Welsh, R., & van den Broek, P. (1999). The effects of story structure on the recall of stories in children with attention deficit hyperactivity disorder. *Journal of Educational Psychology, 91,* 251–260.

Lorch, R. F., Jr., Lorch, E. P., & Inman, W. E. (1993). Effects of signaling topic structure on text recall. *Journal of Educational Psychology, 85,* 281–290.

Losey, K. M. (1995). Mexican American students and classroom interaction: An overview and critique. *Review of Educational Research, 65,* 283–318.

Lou, Y., Abrami, P. C., Spence, J. C., Poulsen, C., Chambers, B., & d'Apollonia, S. (1996). Within-class grouping: A meta-analysis. *Review of Educational Research, 66,* 423–458.

Lounsbury, J. H. (Ed.). (1984). *Perspectives: Middle school education 1964–1984*. Columbus, OH: National Middle School Association.

Lovell, K. (1979). Intellectual growth and the school curriculum. In F. B. Murray (Ed.), *The impact of Piagetian theory: On education, philosophy, psychiatry, and psychology*. Baltimore: University Park Press.

Lovett, S. B., & Flavell, J. H. (1990). Understanding and remembering: Children's knowledge about the differential effects of strategy and task variables on comprehension and memorization. *Child Development, 61,* 1842–1858.

Lovitt, T. C., Guppy, T. E., & Blattner, J. E. (1969). The use of free-time contingency with fourth graders to increase spelling accuracy. *Behaviour Research and Therapy, 7,* 151–156.

Lowry, R., Sleet, D., Duncan, C., Powell, K., & Kolbe, L. (1995). Adolescents at risk for violence. *Educational Psychology Review, 7,* 7–39.

Lubart, T. I. (1994). Creativity. In R. J. Sternberg (Ed.), *Thinking and problem solving*. San Diego, CA: Academic Press.

Luchins, A. S. (1942). Mechanization in problem solving: The effect of Einstellung. *Psychological Monographs, 54* (Whole No. 248).

Luchins, A. S., & Luchins, E. H. (1950). New experimental attempts at preventing mechanization in problem solving. *Journal of General Psychology, 42,* 279–297.

Lueptow, L. B. (1984). *Adolescent sex roles and social change*. New York: Columbia University Press.

Lundeberg, M. A., & Fox, P. W. (1991). Do laboratory findings on test expectancy generalize to classroom outcomes? *Review of Educational Research, 61,* 94–106.

Lupart, J. L. (1995). Exceptional learners and teaching for transfer. In A. McKeough, J. Lupart, & A. Marini (Eds.), *Teaching for transfer: Fostering generalization in learning*. Mahwah, NJ: Erlbaum.

Lyon, M. A. (1984). Positive reinforcement and logical consequences in the treatment of classroom encopresis. *School Psychology Review, 13,* 238–243.

Ma, X., & Kishor, N. (1997). Attitude toward self, social factors, and achievement in mathematics: A meta-analytic review. *Educational Psychology Review, 9,* 89–120.

Maccoby, E. E., & Hagen, J. W. (1965). Effects of distraction upon central versus incidental recall: Developmental trends. *Journal of Experimental Child Psychology, 2,* 280–289.

Maccoby, E. E., & Martin, J. A. (1983). Socialization in the context of the family: Parent-child interaction. In E. M. Hetherington (Ed.), *Handbook of child psychology: Vol. 4. Socialization, personality, and social development* (4th ed.). New York: Wiley.

Mace, F. C., Belfiore, P. J., & Shea, M. C. (1989). Operant theory and research on self-regulation. In B. J. Zimmerman & D. H. Schunk (Eds.), *Self-regulated learning and academic achievement: Theory, research, and practice*. New York: Springer-Verlag.

Mace, F. C., Hock, M. L., Lalli, J. S., West, B. J., Belfiore, P., Pinter, E., & Brown, D. K. (1988). Behavioral momentum in the treatment of noncompliance. *Journal of Applied Behavior Analysis, 21,* 123–141.

Mace, F. C., & Kratochwill, T. R. (1988). Self-monitoring. In J. C. Witt, S. N. Elliott, & F. M. Gresham (Eds.), *Handbook of behavior therapy in education*. New York: Plenum Press.

Machiels-Bongaerts, M., Schmidt, H. G., & Boshuizen, H. P. A. (1991, April). *The effects of prior knowledge activation on free recall and study time allocation*. Paper presented at the annual meeting of the American Educational Research Association, Chicago.

MacLean, D. J., Sasse, D. K., Keating, D. P., Stewart, B. E., & Miller, F. K. (1995, April). *All-girls' mathematics and science instruction in early adolescence: Longitudinal effects*. Paper presented at the annual meeting of the American Educational Research Association, San Francisco.

MacMillan, D. L., & Meyers, C. E. (1979). Educational labeling of handicapped learners. In D. C. Berliner (Ed.), *Review of research in education* (No. 7). Washington, DC: American Educational Research Association.

Madden, N. A., & Slavin, R. E. (1983). Mainstreaming students with mild handicaps: Academic and social outcomes. *Review of Educational Research, 53,* 519–569.

Maehr, M. L. (1984). Meaning and motivation: Toward a theory of personal investment. In R. Ames & C. Ames (Eds.), *Research on motivation in education: Vol. 1. Student motivation*. San Diego, CA: Academic Press.

Maehr, M. L., & Meyer, H. A. (1997). Understanding motivation and schooling: Where we've been, where we are, and where we need to go. *Educational Psychology Review, 9,* 371–409.

Magnusson, S. J., Boyle, R. A., & Templin, M. (1994, April). *Conceptual development: Re-examining knowledge construction in science*. Paper presented at the annual meeting of the American Educational Research Association, New Orleans, LA.

Maker, C. J. (1993). Creativity, intelligence, and problem solving: A definition and design for cross-cultural research and measurement related to giftedness. *Gifted Education International, 9*(2), 68–77.

Maker, C. J., & Schiever, S. W. (Eds.). (1989). *Critical issues in gifted education: Vol. 2. Defensible programs for cultural and ethnic minorities*. Austin, TX: Pro-Ed.

Mandler, G., & Pearlstone, Z. (1966). Free and constrained concept learning and subsequent recall. *Journal of Verbal Learning and Verbal Behavior, 5,* 126–131.

Manis, F. R. (1996). Current trends in dyslexia research. In B. J. Cratty & R. L. Goldman (Eds.), *Learning disabilities: Contemporary viewpoints*. Amsterdam: Harwood Academic.

Manset, G., & Semmel, M. I. (1997). Are inclusive programs for students with mild disabilities effective? A comparative review of model programs. *Journal of Special Education, 31,* 155–180.

Marachi, R., Friedel, J., & Midgley, C. (2001, April). *"I sometimes annoy my teacher during math": Relations between student perceptions of the teacher and disruptive behavior in the classroom*. Paper presented at the annual meeting of the American Educational Research Association, Seattle, WA.

Maratsos, M. (1998). Some problems in grammatical acquisition. In W. Damon (Series Ed.), D. Kuhn, & R. S. Siegler (Vol. Eds.), *Handbook of child psychology: Vol. 2. Cognition, perception, and language* (5th ed.). New York: Wiley.

Marcia, J. E. (1980). Identity in adolescence. In J. Adelson (Ed.), *Handbook of adolescent psychology*. New York: Wiley.

Marcia, J. E. (1988). Common processes underlying ego identity, cognitive/moral development, and individuation. In D. K. Lapsley & F. C. Power (Eds.), *Self, ego, and identity: Integrative approaches* (pp. 211–225). New York: Springer-Verlag.

Marcus, G. F. (1996). Why do children say "breaked"? *Current Directions in Psychological Science, 5,* 81–85.

Marcus, R. F. (1980). Empathy and popularity of preschool children. *Child Study Journal, 10,* 133–145.

Maria, K. (1998). Self–confidence and the process of conceptual change. In B. Guzzetti & C. Hynd (Eds.), *Perspectives on conceptual change: Multiple ways to understand knowing and learning in a complex world* (pp. 7–16). Mahwah, NJ: Erlbaum.

Markman, E. M. (1977). Realizing that you don't understand: A preliminary investigation. *Child Development, 48,* 986–992.

Markman, E. M. (1979). Realizing that you don't understand: Elementary school children's awareness of inconsistencies. *Child Development, 50,* 643–655.

Marks, H. M. (2000). Student engagement in instructional activity: Patterns in the elementary, middle, and high school years. *American Educational Research Journal, 37,* 153–184.

Marks, J. (1995). *Human biodiversity: Genes, race, and history*. New York: Aldine de Gruyter.

Markus, H. R., & Kitayama, S. (1991). Culture and the self: Implications for cognition, emotion, and motivation. *Psychological Review, 98,* 224–253.

Marsh, H. W. (1990a). Causal ordering of academic self-concept and academic achievement: A multiwave, longitudinal panel analysis. *Journal of Educational Psychology, 82,* 646–656.

Marsh, H. W. (1990b). A multidimensional, hierarchical model of self-concept: Theoretical and empirical justification. *Educational Psychology Review, 2,* 77–172.

Marsh, H. W., Chessor, D., Craven, R., & Roche, L. (1995). The effects of gifted and talented programs on academic self-concept: The big fish strikes again. *American Educational Research Journal, 32*, 285–319.

Marsh, H. W., & Craven, R. (1997). Academic self-concept: Beyond the dustbowl. In G. D. Phye (Ed.), *Handbook of classroom assessment: Learning, achievement, and adjustment.* San Diego, CA: Academic Press.

Marsh, H. W., Parada, R. H., Yeung, A. S., & Healey, J. (2001). Aggressive school troublemakers and victims: A longitudinal model examining the pivotal role of self-concept. *Journal of Educational Psychology, 93*, 411–419.

Marsh, H. W., & Yeung, A. S. (1997). Coursework selection: Relations to academic self-concept and achievement. *American Educational Research Journal, 34*, 691–720.

Marsh, H. W., & Yeung, A. S. (1998). Longitudinal structural equation models of academic self-concept and achievement: Gender differences in the development of math and English constructs. *American Educational Research Journal, 35*, 705–738.

Marsh, R. W. (1985). Phrenobylsis: Real or chimera? *Child Development, 56*, 1059–1061.

Marshall, H. H. (1981). Open classrooms: Has the term outlived its usefulness? *Review of Educational Research, 51*, 181–192.

Marshall, H. H. (1992). *Redefining student learning: Roots of educational change.* Norwood, NJ: Ablex.

Martin, S. S., Brady, M. P., & Williams, R. E. (1991). Effects of toys on the social behavior of preschool children in integrated and nonintegrated groups: Investigation of a setting event. *Journal of Early Intervention, 15*, 153–161.

Marzano, R. J., & Costa, A. L. (1988). Question: Do standardized tests measure general cognitive skills? Answer: No. *Educational Leadership, 45* (8), 66–71.

Maslow, A. H. (1973). Theory of human motivation. In R. J. Lowry (Ed.), *Dominance, self-esteem, self-actualization: Germinal papers of A. H. Maslow.* Monterey, CA: Brooks/Cole.

Maslow, A. H. (1987). *Motivation and personality* (3rd ed.). New York: Harper & Row.

Massialas, B. G., & Zevin, J. (1983). *Teaching creatively: Learning through discovery.* Malabar, FL: Krieger.

Masten, A. S. (2001). Ordinary magic: Resilience processes in development. *American Psychologist, 56*, pp. 227–238.

Masten, A. S., & Coatsworth, J. D. (1998). The development of competence in favorable and unfavorable environments. *American Psychologist, 53*, 205–220.

Mastropieri, M. A., & Scruggs, T. E. (1992). Science for students with disabilities. *Review of Educational Research, 62*, 377–411.

Mastropieri, M. A., & Scruggs, T. E. (2000). *The inclusive classroom: Strategies for effective instruction.* Upper Saddle River, NJ: Merrill/Prentice Hall.

Mastropieri, M. A., Scruggs, T. E., & Butcher, K. (1997). How effective is inquiry learning for students with mild disabilities? *Journal of Special Education, 31*, 199–211.

Masur, E. F., McIntyre, C. W., & Flavell, J. H. (1973). Developmental changes in apportionment of study time among items in a multitrial free recall task. *Journal of Experimental Child Psychology, 15*, 237–246.

Maxmell, D., Jarrett, O. S., & Dickerson, C. (1998, April). *Are we forgetting the children's needs? Recess through the children's eyes.* Paper presented at the annual meeting of the American Educational Research Association, San Diego, CA.

Mayer, R. E. (1974). Acquisition processes and resilience under varying testing conditions for structurally different problem solving procedures. *Journal of Educational Psychology, 66*, 644–656.

Mayer, R. E. (1984). Aids to text comprehension. *Educational Psychologist, 19*, 30–42.

Mayer, R. E. (1985). Implications of cognitive psychology for instruction in mathematical problem solving. In E. A. Silver (Ed.), *Teaching and learning mathematical problem solving: Multiple research perspectives.* Hillsdale, NJ: Erlbaum.

Mayer, R. E. (1986). Mathematics. In R. F. Dillon & R. J. Sternberg (Eds.), *Cognition and instruction.* San Diego, CA: Academic Press.

Mayer, R. E. (1987). *Educational psychology: A cognitive approach.* Boston: Little, Brown.

Mayer, R. E. (1989). Models for understanding. *Review of Educational Research, 59*, 43–64.

Mayer, R. E. (1992). *Thinking, problem solving, cognition* (2nd ed.). New York: Freeman.

Mayer, R. E. (1996). Learning strategies for making sense out of expository text: The SOI model for guiding three cognitive processes in knowledge construction. *Educational Psychology Review, 8*, 357–371.

Mayer, R. E. (1998). Does the brain have a place in educational psychology? *Educational Psychology Review, 10*, 389–396.

Mayer, R. E., & Gallini, J. (1990). When is an illustration worth ten thousand words? *Journal of Educational Psychology, 82*, 715–726.

Mayer, R. E., & Wittrock, M. C. (1996). Problem-solving transfer. In D. C. Berliner & R. C. Calfee (Eds.), *Handbook of educational psychology.* New York: Macmillan.

McAdoo, H. P. (1985). Racial attitude and self-concept of young Black children over time. In H. P. McAdoo & J. L. McAdoo (Eds.), *Black children: Social, educational, and parental environments.* Newbury Park, CA: Sage.

McAlpine, L. (1992). Language, literacy and education: Case studies of Cree, Inuit and Mohawk communities. *Canadian Children, 17*(1), 17–30.

McAlpine, L., & Taylor, D. M. (1993). Instructional preferences of Cree, Inuit, and Mohawk teachers. *Journal of American Indian Education, 33*(1), 1–20.

McAshan, H. H. (1979). *Competency-based education and behavioral objectives.* Englewood Cliffs, NJ: Educational Technology.

McCall, R. B. (1993). Developmental functions for general mental performance. In D. K. Detterman (Ed.), *Current topics in human intelligence* (Vol. 3). Norwood, NJ: Ablex.

McCall, R. B. (1994). Academic underachievers. *Current Directions in Psychological Science, 3*, 15–19.

McCallum, R. S., & Bracken, B. A. (1993). Interpersonal relations between school children and their peers, parents, and teachers. *Educational Psychology Review, 5*, 155–176.

McCarty, T. L., & Watahomigie, L. J. (1998). Language and literacy in American Indian and Alaska Native communities. In B. Pérez (Ed.), *Sociocultural contexts of language and literacy.* Mahwah, NJ: Erlbaum.

McCaslin, M., & Good, T. L. (1996). The informal curriculum. In D. C. Berliner & R. C. Calfee (Eds.), *Handbook of educational psychology.* New York: Macmillan.

McClelland, D. C., Atkinson, J. W., Clark, R. A., & Lowell, E. L. (1953). *The achievement motive.* New York: Appleton-Century-Crofts.

McCloskey, M. E., & Glucksberg, S. (1978). Natural categories: Well-defined or fuzzy sets? *Memory and Cognition, 6*, 462–472.

McCoy, K. (1994). *Understanding your teenager's depression.* New York: Perigee.

McCoy, L. P. (1990, April). *Correlates of mathematics anxiety.* Paper presented at the annual meeting of the American Educational Research Association, Boston.

McCutchen, D. (1996). A capacity theory of writing: Working memory in composition. *Educational Psychology Review, 8*, 299–325.

McDaniel, L. (1997). *For better, for worse, forever.* New York: Bantam Books.

McDaniel, M. A., & Einstein, G. O. (1989). Material-appropriate processing: A contextualist approach to reading and studying strategies. *Educational Psychology Review, 1*, 113–145.

McDaniel, M. A., & Masson, M. E. J. (1985). Altering memory representations through retrieval. *Journal of Experimental Psychology: Learning, Memory, and Cognition, 11*, 371–385.

McDaniel, M. A., & Schlager, M. S. (1990). Discovery learning and transfer of problem-solving skills. *Cognition and Instruction, 7*, 129–159.

McDaniel, M. A., Waddill, P. J., & Einstein, G. O. (1988). A contextual account of the generation effect: A three-factor theory. *Journal of Memory and Language, 27*, 521–536.

McDevitt, T. M. (1990). Encouraging young children's listening skills. *Academic Therapy, 25*, 569–577.

McDevitt, T. M., & Ford, M. E. (1987). Processes in young children's communicative functioning and development. In M. E. Ford & D. H. Ford (Eds.), *Humans as self-constructing living systems: Putting the framework to work.* Hillsdale, NJ: Erlbaum.

McDevitt, T. M., Spivey, N., Sheehan, E. P., Lennon, R., & Story, R. (1990). Children's beliefs about listening: Is it enough to be still and quiet? *Child Development, 61*, 713–721.

McGee, K. D., Knight, S. L., & Boudah, D. J. (2001, April). *Using reciprocal teaching in secondary inclusive English classroom instruction.* Paper presented at the annual meeting of the American Educational Research Association, Seattle, WA.

McGee, L. M. (1992). An exploration of meaning construction in first graders' grand conversations. In C. K. Kinzer & D. J. Leu (Eds.), *Literacy research, theory, and practice: Views from many perspectives.* Chicago: National Reading Conference.

McGill, P. (1999). Establishing operations: Implications for the assessment, treatment, and prevention of problem behavior. *Journal of Applied Behavior Analysis, 32*, 393–418.

McGinn, P. V., Viernstein, M. C., & Hogan, R. (1980). Fostering the intellectual development of verbally gifted adolescents. *Journal of Educational Psychology, 72*, 494–498.

McGlynn, S. M. (1998). Impaired awareness of deficits in a psychiatric context: Implications for rehabilitation. In D. J. Hacker, J. Dunlosky, & A. C. Graesser (Eds.), *Metacognition in educational theory and practice* (pp. 221–248). Mahwah, NJ: Erlbaum.

McGowan, R. J., & Johnson, D. L. (1984). The mother-child relationship and other antecedents of childhood intelligence: A causal analysis. *Child Development, 55*, 810–820.

McGrew, K. S., Flanagan, D. P., Zeith, T. Z., & Vanderwood, M. (1997). Beyond g: The impact of Gf–Gc specific cognitive abilities research on the future use and interpretation of intelligence tests in the schools. *School Psychology Review, 26*, 189–210.

McGue, M., Bouchard, T. J., Jr., Iacono, W. G., & Lykken, D. T. (1993). Behavioral genetics of cognitive ability: A life-span perspective. In R. Plomin & G. E. McClearn (Eds.), *Nature, nurture, and psychology.* Washington, DC: American Psychological Association.

McKeachie, W. J., Lin, Y., Milholland, J., & Isaacson, R. (1966). Student affiliation motives, teacher warmth, and academic achievement. *Journal of Personality and Social Psychology, 4,* 457–461.

McKeon, D. (1994). When meeting "common" standards is uncommonly difficult. *Educational Leadership, 51*(8), 45–49.

McKeown, M. G., & Beck, I. L. (1990). The assessment and characterization of young learners' knowledge of a topic in history. *American Educational Research Journal, 27,* 688–726.

McLeod, D. B., & Adams, V. M. (Eds.). (1989). *Affect and mathematical problem solving: A new perspective.* New York: Springer-Verlag.

McLoyd, V. C. (1998). Socioeconomic disadvantage and child development. *American Psychologist, 53,* 185–204.

McMillan, J. H., & Reed, D. F. (1994). At-risk students and resiliency: Factors contributing to academic success. *Clearing House, 67*(3), 137–140.

McMillan, J. H., Singh, J., & Simonetta, L. G. (1994). The tyranny of self-oriented self-esteem. *Educational Horizons, 72,* 141–145.

McNamara, D. S., & Healy, A. F. (1995). A generation advantage for multiplication skill training and nonword vocabulary acquisition. In A. F. Healy & L. E. Bourne, Jr. (Eds.), *Learning and memory of knowledge and skills: Durability and specificity.* Thousand Oaks, CA: Sage.

McNamara, E. (1987). Behavioural approaches in the secondary school. In K. Wheldall (Ed.), *The behaviourist in the classroom.* London: Allen & Unwin.

McNeil, N. M., & Alibali, M. W. (2000). Learning mathematics from procedural instruction: Externally imposed goals influence what is learned. *Journal of Educational Psychology, 92,* 734–744.

McRobbie, C., & Tobin, K. (1995). Restraints to reform: The congruence of teacher and student actions in a chemistry classroom. *Journal of Research in Science Teaching, 32,* 373–385.

McWhiter, C. C., & Bloom, L. A. (1994). The effects of a student-operated business curriculum on the on-task behavior of students with behavioral disorders. *Behavioral Disorders, 19*(2), 136–141.

Meece, J. L. (1994). The role of motivation in self-regulated learning. In D. H. Schunk & B. J. Zimmerman (Eds.), *Self-regulation of learning and performance: Issues and educational applications.* Hillsdale, NJ: Erlbaum.

Meece, J. L., & Holt, K. (1993). A pattern analysis of students' achievement goals. *Journal of Educational Psychology, 85,* 582–590.

Mehan, H. (1979). *Social organization in the classroom.* Cambridge, MA: Harvard University Press.

Meichenbaum, D. (1977). *Cognitive-behavior modification: An integrative approach.* New York: Plenum Press.

Meichenbaum, D. (1985). Teaching thinking: A cognitive-behavioral perspective. In S. F. Chipman, J. W. Segal, & R. Glaser (Eds.), *Thinking and learning skills: Vol. 2. Research and open questions.* Hillsdale, NJ: Erlbaum.

Meichenbaum, D., & Goodman, J. (1971). Training impulsive children to talk to themselves: A means of developing self-control. *Journal of Abnormal Psychology, 77,* 115–126.

Meloth, M. S., & Deering, P. D. (1994). Task talk and task awareness under different cooperative learning conditions. *American Educational Research Journal, 31,* 138–165.

Meloth, M. S., & Deering, P. D. (1999). The role of the teacher in promoting cognitive processing during collaborative learning. In A. M.

O'Donnell & A. King (Eds.), *Cognitive perspectives on peer learning* (pp. 235–255). Mahwah, NJ: Erlbaum.

Menyuk, P., & Menyuk, D. (1988). Communicative competence: A historical and cultural perspective. In J. S. Wurzel (Ed.), *Toward multiculturalism: A reader in multicultural education.* Yarmouth, ME: Intercultural Press.

Mercer, C. D. (1997). *Students with learning disabilities* (5th ed.). Upper Saddle River, NJ: Merrill/Prentice Hall.

Mercer, C. D., Jordan, L., Allsopp, D. H., & Mercer, A. R. (1996). Learning disabilities definitions and criteria used by state education departments. *Learning Disabilities Quarterly, 19,* 217–231.

Merrill, M. D., & Tennyson, R. D. (1977). *Concept teaching: An instructional design guide.* Englewood Cliffs, NJ: Educational Technology.

Merrill, M. D., & Tennyson, R. D. (1978). Concept classification and classification errors as a function of relationships between examples and non-examples. *Improving Human Performance, 7,* 351–364.

Merrill, P. F., Hammons, K., Vincent, B. R., Reynolds, P. L., Christensen, L., & Tolman, M. N. (1996). *Computers in education* (3rd ed.). Needham Heights, MA: Allyn & Bacon.

Mervis, C. B. (1987). Child-basic object categories and early lexical development. In U. Neisser (Ed.), *Concepts and conceptual development: Ecological and intellectual factors in categorization.* Cambridge, England: Cambridge University Press.

Messick, S. (1983). Assessment of children. In W. Kessen (Ed.), *Handbook of child psychology* (Vol. 1). New York: Wiley.

Messick, S. (1994). The interplay of evidence and consequences in the validation of performance assessments. *Educational Researcher, 23*(2), 13–23.

Metz, K. E. (1995). Reassessment of developmental constraints on children's science instruction. *Review of Educational Research, 65,* 93–127.

Meyer, B. J. F., Brandt, D. H., & Bluth, G. J. (1980). Use of top-level structure in text: Key for reading comprehension of ninth-grade students. *Reading Research Quarterly, 16,* 72–103.

Meyer, K. A. (1999). Functional analysis and treatment of problem behavior exhibited by elementary school children. *Journal of Applied Behavior Analysis, 32,* 229–232.

Meyer, M. S. (2000). The ability-achievement discrepancy: Does it contribute to an understanding of learning disabilities? *Educational Psychology Review, 12,* 315–337.

Meyers, D. T. (1987). The socialized individual and individual autonomy: An intersection between philosophy and psychology. In E. F. Kittay and D. T. Meyers (Eds.), *Women and moral theory.* Totowa, NJ: Rowman & Littlefield.

Michael, J. (2000). Implications and refinements of the establishing operation concept. *Journal of Applied Behavior Analysis, 33,* 401–410.

Middleton, M. J. (1999, April). *Classroom effects on the gender gap in middle school students' math self-efficacy.* Paper presented at the annual meeting of the American Educational Research Association, Montreal, Canada.

Middleton, M. J., & Midgley, C. (1997). Avoiding the demonstration of lack of ability: An under-explored aspect of goal theory. *Journal of Educational Psychology, 89,* 710–718.

Midgley, C., Kaplan, A., & Middleton, M. (2001). Performance-approach goals: Good for what, for whom, under what circumstances, and at what cost? *Journal of Educational Psychology, 93,* 77–86.

Midgley, C., Kaplan, A., Middleton, M., Maehr, M., Urdan, T., Anderman, L., Anderman, E., &

Roeser, R. (1998). The development and validation of scales assessing students' achievement goal orientations. *Contemporary Educational Psychology, 23,* 113–131.

Mikaelsen, B. (1996). *Countdown.* New York: Hyperion Books.

Milch-Reich, S., Campbell, S. B., Pelham, W. E., Jr., Connelly, L. M., & Geva, D. (1999). Developmental and individual differences in children's on-line representations of dynamic social events. *Child Development, 70,* 413–431.

Miller, B. C., & Benson, B. (1999). Romantic and sexual relationship development during adolescence. In W. Furman, B. B. Brown, & C. Feiring (Eds.), *The development of romantic relationships in adolescence* (pp. 99–121). Cambridge, England: Cambridge University Press.

Miller, D. L., & Kelley, M. L. (1994). The use of goal setting and contingency contracting for improving children's homework performance. *Journal of Applied Behavior Analysis, 27,* 73–84.

Miller, G. A. (1956). The magical number seven, plus or minus two: Some limits on our capacity for processing information. *Psychological Review, 63,* 81–97.

Miller, J. G., & Bersoff, D. M. (1992). Culture and moral judgment: How are conflicts between justice and interpersonal responsibilities resolved? *Journal of Personality and Social Psychology, 62,* 541–554.

Miller, L. S. (1995). *An American imperative: Accelerating minority educational advancement.* New Haven, CT: Yale University Press.

Miller, N. E., & Dollard, J. C. (1941). *Social learning and imitation.* New Haven, CT: Yale University Press.

Miller, P. H. (1993). Focus on the interface of cognition, social-emotional behavior and motivation. In P. H. Miller (Ed.), *Theories of developmental psychology* (3rd ed.). New York: Freeman.

Miller, R. R., & Barnet, R. C. (1993). The role of time in elementary associations. *Current Directions in Psychological Science, 2,* 106–111.

Millman, J., Bishop, C. H., & Ebel, R. (1965). An analysis of test-wiseness. *Educational and Psychological Measurement, 25,* 707–726.

Mills, G. E. (2000). *Action research: A guide for the teacher researcher.* Upper Saddle River, NJ: Merrill/Prentice Hall.

Minami, M., & Ovando, C. J. (1995). Language issues in multicultural contexts. In J. A. Banks & C. A. M. Banks (Eds.), *Handbook of research on multicultural education.* New York: Macmillan.

Minstrell, J., & Stimpson, V. (1996). A classroom environment for learning: Guiding students' reconstruction of understanding and reasoning. In L. Schauble & R. Glaser (Eds.), *Innovations in learning: New environments for education.* Mahwah, NJ: Erlbaum.

Mintzes, J. J., Trowbridge, J. E., Arnaudin, M. W., & Wandersee, J. H. (1991). Children's biology: Studies on conceptual development in the life sciences. In S. M. Glynn, R. H. Yeany, & B. K. Britton (Eds.), *The psychology of learning science.* Hillsdale, NJ: Erlbaum.

Mintzes, J. J., Wandersee, J. H., & Novak, J. D. (1997). Meaningful learning in science: The human constructivist perspective. In G. D. Phye (Ed.), *Handbook of academic learning: Construction of knowledge.* San Diego, CA: Academic Press.

Mitchell, M. (1993). Situational interest: Its multi-faceted structure in the secondary school mathematics classroom. *Journal of Educational Psychology, 85,* 424–436.

Mohatt, G., & Erickson, F. (1981). Cultural differences in teaching styles in an Odawa school: A sociolinguistic approach. In H. T. Trueba, G. P.

Guthrie, and K. H. Au (Eds.), *Culture and the bilingual classroom: Studies in classroom ethnography.* Rowley, MA: Newbury House.

Moje, E. B., & Shepardson, D. P. (1998). Social interactions and children's changing understanding of electric circuits: Exploring unequal power relations in "peer"-learning groups. In B. Guzzetti & C. Hynd (Eds.), *Perspectives on conceptual change: Multiple ways to understand knowing and learning in a complex world* (pp. 225–234). Mahwah, NJ: Erlbaum.

Moles, O. C. (Ed.). (1990). *Student discipline strategies: Research and practice.* Albany: State University of New York Press.

Moll, L. C., & Diaz, S. (1985). Ethnographic pedagogy: Promoting effective bilingual instruction. In E. E. Garcia & R. V. Padilla (Eds.), *Advances in bilingual education research.* Tucson: University of Arizona Press.

Montagu, A. (Ed.). (1999). *Race and IQ* (expanded ed.). New York: Oxford University Press.

Montgomery, D. (1989). Identification of giftedness among American Indian people. In C. J. Maker & S. W. Schiever (Eds.), *Critical issues in gifted education: Vol. 2. Defensible programs for cultural and ethnic minorities.* Austin, TX: Pro-Ed.

Moon, S. M., Feldhusen, J. F., & Dillon, D. R. (1994). Long-term effects of an enrichment program based on the Purdue Three-Stage Model. *Gifted Child Quarterly, 38,* 38–48.

Mooney, C. M. (1957). Age in the development of closure ability in children. *Canadian Journal of Psychology, 11,* 219–226.

Moore, D. S., & Erickson, P. I. (1985). Age, gender, and ethnic differences in sexual and contraceptive knowledge, attitudes, and behavior. *Family and Community Health, 8,* 38–51.

Moran, C. E., & Hakuta, K. (1995). Bilingual education: Broadening research perspectives. In J. A. Banks & C. A. M. Banks (Eds.), *Handbook of research on multicultural education.* New York: Macmillan.

Moran, S. (1991). Creative reading: Young adults and paperback books. *Horn Book Magazine, 67,* 437–441.

Morgan, D. P., & Jenson, W. R. (1988). *Teaching behaviorally disordered students: Preferred practices.* Upper Saddle River, NJ: Merrill/Prentice Hall.

Morrison, G., Furlong, M., & Smith, G. (1994). Factors associated with the experience of school violence among general education, leadership class, opportunity class, and special day class pupils. *Education and Treatment of Children, 17,* 356–369.

Morrow, S. L. (1997). Career development of lesbian and gay youth: Effects of sexual orientation, coming out, and homophobia. In M. B. Harris (Ed.), *School experiences of gay and lesbian youth: The invisible minority* (pp. 1–15). Binghamton, NY: Harrington Park Press.

Mueller, E. (1972). The maintenance of verbal exchanges between young children. *Child Development, 43,* 930–938.

Mueller, J. H. (1980). Test anxiety and the encoding and retrieval of information. In I. G. Sarason (Ed.), *Test anxiety: Theory, research, and applications.* Hillsdale, NJ: Erlbaum.

Munn, P., Johnstone, M., & Chalmers, V. (1990, April). *How do teachers talk about maintaining effective discipline in their classrooms?* Paper presented at the annual meeting of the American Educational Research Association, Boston.

Murdock, T. B. (1999). The social context of risk: Status and motivational predictors of alienation in middle school. *Journal of Educational Psychology, 91,* 62–75.

Murdock, T. B. (2000). Incorporating economic context into educational psychology: Methodological and conceptual challenges. *Educational Psychologist, 35,* 113–124.

Murdock, T. B., Hale, N., Weber, M. J., Tucker, V., & Briggs, W. (1999, April). *Relations of cheating to social and academic motivation among middle school students.* Paper presented at the annual meeting of the American Educational Research Association, Montreal, Canada.

Murphy, D. M. (1996). Implications of inclusion for general and special education. *Elementary School Journal, 96,* 469–492.

Murphy, P. K. (2000). A motivated exploration of motivation terminology. *Contemporary Educational Psychology, 25,* 3–53.

Murray, C. B., & Jackson, J. S. (1982/1983). The conditioned failure model of black educational underachievement. *Humboldt Journal of Social Relations, 10,* 276–300.

Murray, F. B. (1978). Teaching strategies and conservation training. In A. M. Lesgold, J. W. Pellegrino, S. D. Fokkema, & R. Glaser (Eds.), *Cognitive psychology and instruction.* New York: Plenum Press.

Nadel, L., & Jacobs, W. J. (1998). Traumatic memory is special. *Current Directions in Psychological Science, 7,* 154–157.

Narváez, D. (1998). The influence of moral schemas on the reconstruction of moral narratives in eighth graders and college students. *Journal of Educational Psychology, 90,* 13–24.

Narváez, D., & Rest, J. (1995). The four components of acting morally. In W. M. Kurtines & J. L. Gewirtz (Eds.), *Moral development: An introduction.* Boston: Allyn & Bacon.

National Assessment of Educational Progress. (1985). *The reading report card: Progress toward excellence in our schools; trends in reading over four national assessments, 1971–1984.* Princeton, NJ: NAEP.

National Association of Bilingual Education. (1993). Census reports sharp increase in number of non-English speaking Americans. *NABE News, 16*(6), 1, 25.

National Commission on Excellence in Education. (1983). *A nation at risk: The imperative for educational reform.* Washington, DC: U.S. Government Printing Office.

National Geographic Education Project. (1994). *Geography for life: National geography standards.* Washington, DC: National Geographic Research and Education, National Geographical Society.

National Joint Committee on Learning Disabilities. (1994). Learning disabilities: Issues on definition, a position paper of the National Joint Committee on Learning Disabilities. In *Collective perspectives on issues affecting learning disabilities: Position papers and statements.* Austin, TX: Pro-Ed.

National Science Education Standards. (1996). Washington, DC: National Academy Press.

Natriello, G., & Dornbusch, S. M. (1984). *Teacher evaluative standards and student effort.* White Plains, NY: Longman.

Navarro, R. A. (1985). The problems of language, education, and society: Who decides. In E. E. Garcia & R. V. Padilla (Eds.), *Advances in bilingual education research.* Tucson: University of Arizona Press.

NCSS Task Force on Ethnic Studies Curriculum Guidelines. (1992). Curriculum guidelines for multicultural education. *Social Education, 56,* 274–294.

Neel, R. S., Jenkins, Z. N., & Meadows, N. (1990). Social problem-solving behaviors and aggression in young children: A descriptive observational study. *Behavioral Disorders, 16*(1), 39–51.

Neisser, U. (1967). *Cognitive psychology.* New York: Appleton-Century-Crofts.

Neisser, U. (1998a). Introduction: Rising test scores and what they mean. In U. Neisser (Ed.), *The rising curve: Long-term gains in IQ and related measures* (pp. 3–22). Washington, DC: American Psychological Association.

Neisser, U. (Ed.). (1998b). *The rising curve: Long-term gains in IQ and related measures.* Washington, DC: American Psychological Association.

Neisser, U., Boodoo, G., Bouchard, T. J., Boykin, A. W., Brody, N., Ceci, S. J., Halpern, D. F., Loehlen, J. C., Perloff, R., Sternberg, R. J., & Urbina, S. (1996). Intelligence: Knowns and unknowns. *American Psychologist, 51,* 77–101.

Nelson, J. R., Smith, D. J., Young, R. K., & Dodd, J. M. (1991). A review of self-management outcome research conducted with students who exhibit behavioral disorders. *Behavioral Disorders, 16,* 169–179.

Nelson, T. O., & Dunlosky, J. (1991). When people's judgments of learning (JOLs) are extremely accurate at predicting subsequent recall: The "delayed-JOL effect." *Psychological Science, 2,* 267–270.

Nelson-Barber, S., & Estrin, E. (1995). Bringing Native American perspectives to mathematics and science teaching. *Theory into Practice, 34,* 174–185.

Nevin, J. A., Mandell, C., & Atak, J. R. (1983). The analysis of behavioral momentum. *Journal of the Experimental Analysis of Behavior, 39,* 49–59.

Newby, T. J., Ertmer, P. A., & Stepich, D. A. (1994, April). *Instructional analogies and the learning of concepts.* Paper presented at the annual meeting of the American Educational Research Association, New Orleans, LA.

Newcomb, A. F., & Bagwell, C. L. (1995). Children's friendship relations: A meta-analysis review. *Psychological Bulletin, 117,* 306–347.

Newcombe, N., & Huttenlocher, J. (1992). Children's early ability to solve perspective-taking problems. *Developmental Psychology, 28,* 635–643.

Newman, R. S., & Schwager, M. T. (1995). Students' help seeking during problem solving: Effects of grade, goal, and prior achievement. *American Educational Research Journal, 32,* 352–376.

Newmann, F. M. (1981). Reducing student alienation in high schools: Implications of theory. *Harvard Educational Review, 51,* 546–564.

Newmann, F. M. (1997). Authentic assessment in social studies: Standards and examples. In G. D. Phye (Ed.), *Handbook of classroom assessment: Learning, achievement, and adjustment.* San Diego, CA: Academic Press.

Newmann, F. M., & Wehlage, G. G. (1993). Five standards of authentic instruction. *Educational Leadership, 50*(7), 8–12.

Newport, E. L. (1993). Maturational constraints on language learning. In P. Bloom (Ed.), *Language acquisition: Core readings.* Cambridge, MA: MIT Press.

Nicholls, J. G. (1979). Development of perception of own attainment and causal attributions for success and failure in reading. *Journal of Educational Psychology, 71,* 94–99.

Nicholls, J. G. (1984). Conceptions of ability and achievement motivation. In R. Ames & C. Ames (Eds.), *Research on motivation in education: Vol 1. Student motivation.* San Diego, CA: Academic Press.

Nicholls, J. G. (1990). What is ability and why are we mindful of it? A developmental perspective. In R. J. Sternberg & J. Kolligian (Eds.), *Competence considered.* New Haven, CT: Yale University Press.

Nicholls, J. G., Cobb, P., Yackel, E., Wood, T., & Wheatley, G. (1990). Students' theories of mathematics and their mathematical knowledge: Multiple dimensions of assessment. In G. Kulm (Ed.), *Assessing higher order thinking in mathematics.* Washington, DC: American Association for the Advancement of Science.

Nichols, J. D. (1996). The effects of cooperative learning on student achievement and motivation in a high school geometry class. *Contemporary Educational Psychology, 21*, 467–476.

Nichols, J. D., Ludwin, W. G., & Iadicola, P. (1999). A darker shade of gray: A year-end analysis of discipline and suspension data. *Equity and Excellence in Education, 32*(1), 43–55.

Nichols, M. L., & Ganschow, L. (1992). Has there been a paradigm shift in gifted education? In N. Coangelo, S. G. Assouline, & D. L. Ambroson (Eds.), *Talent development: Proceedings from the 1991 Henry B. and Jocelyn Wallace National Research Symposium on Talent Development*. New York: Trillium.

Nichols, P. D., & Mittelholtz, D. J. (1997). Constructing the concept of aptitude: Implications for the assessment of analogical reasoning. In G. D. Phye (Ed.), *Handbook of academic learning: Construction of knowledge*. San Diego, CA: Academic Press.

Nickerson, R. S. (1989). New directions in educational assessment. *Educational Researcher, 18*(9), 3–7.

Nieto, S. (1995). A history of the education of Puerto Rican students in U.S. mainland schools: "Losers," "outsiders," or "leaders"? In J. A. Banks & C. A. M. Banks (Eds.), *Handbook of research on multicultural education*. New York: Macmillan.

Nippold, M. A. (1988). The literate lexicon. In M. A. Nippold (Ed.), *Later language development: Ages nine through nineteen*. Boston: Little, Brown.

Nist, S. L., Simpson, M. L., Olejnik, S., & Mealey, D. L. (1991). The relation between self-selected study processes and test performance. *American Educational Research Journal, 28*, 849–874.

Nix, R. L., Pinderhughes, E. E., Dodge, K. A., Bates, J. E., Pettit, G. S., & McFadyen-Ketchum, S. A. (1999). The relation between mothers' hostile attribution tendencies and children's externalizing behavior problems: The mediating role of mothers' harsh discipline practices. *Child Development, 70*, 896–909.

Noddings, N. (1985). Small groups as a setting for research on mathematical problem solving. In E. A. Silver (Ed.), *Teaching and learning mathematical problem solving: Multiple research perspectives*. Hillsdale, NJ: Erlbaum.

Nolen, S. B. (1996). Why study? How reasons for learning influence strategy selection. *Educational Psychology Review, 8*, 335–355.

Nolen-Hoeksema, S. (2001). Gender differences in depression. *Current Directions in Psychological Science, 10*, 173–176.

Norman, D. A. (1969). *Memory and attention: An introduction to human information processing*. New York: Wiley.

Northup, J., Broussard, C., Jones, K., George, T., Vollmer, T. R., & Herring, M. (1995). The differential effects of teachers and peer attention on the disruptive classroom behavior of three children with a diagnosis of attention deficit hyperactivity disorder. *Journal of Applied Behavior Analysis, 28*, 227–228.

Nottelmann, E. D. (1987). Competence and self-esteem during transition from childhood to adolescence. *Developmental Psychology, 23*, 441–450.

Novak, J. D. (1998). *Learning, creating, and using knowledge: Concept maps as facilitative tools in schools and corporations*. Mahwah, NJ: Erlbaum.

Novak, J. D., & Gowin, D. B. (1984). *Learning how to learn*. Cambridge, England: Cambridge University Press.

Novak, J. D., & Musonda, D. (1991). A twelve-year longitudinal study of science concept learning. *American Educational Research Journal, 28*, 117–153.

Nucci, L. P., & Nucci, M. S. (1982a). Children's responses to moral and social conventional transgressions in free-play settings. *Child Development, 53*, 1337–1342.

Nucci, L. P., & Nucci, M. S. (1982b). Children's social interactions in the context of moral and conventional transgressions. *Child Development, 53*, 403–412.

Nunner-Winkler, G. (1984). Two moralities? A critical discussion of an ethic of care and responsibility versus an ethic of rights and justice. In W. M. Kurtines & J. L. Gewirtz (Eds.), *Morality, moral behavior, and moral development*. New York: Wiley.

Nussbaum, J. (1985). The earth as a cosmic body. In R. Driver (Ed.), *Children's ideas of science*. Philadelphia: Open University Press.

Nussbaum, N., & Bigler, E. (1990). *Identification and treatment of attention deficit disorder*. Austin, TX: Pro-Ed.

Nuthall, G. (1996). Commentary: Of learning and language and understanding the complexity of the classroom. *Educational Psychologist, 31*, 207–214.

Oakes, J., & Guiton, G. (1995). Matchmaking: The dynamics of high school tracking decisions. *American Educational Research Journal, 32*, 3–33.

O'Boyle, M. W., & Gill, H. S. (1998). On the relevance of research findings in cognitive neuroscience to educational practice. *Educational Psychology Review, 10*, 397–409.

O'Donnell, A. M. (1999). Structuring dyadic interaction through scripted cooperation. In A. M. O'Donnell & A. King (Eds.), *Cognitive perspectives on peer learning* (pp. 179–196). Mahwah, NJ: Erlbaum.

O'Donnell, A. M., & O'Kelly, J. (1994). Learning from peers: Beyond the rhetoric of positive results. *Educational Psychology Review, 6*, 321–349.

Ogbu, J. U. (1992). Understanding cultural diversity and learning. *Educational Researcher, 21*(8), 5–14, 24.

Ogbu, J. U. (1994). From cultural differences to differences in cultural frame of reference. In P. M. Greenfield & R. R. Cocking (Eds.), *Cross-cultural roots of minority child development*. Hillsdale, NJ: Erlbaum.

Ogbu, J. U. (1999). Beyond language: Ebonics, proper English, and identity in a Black-American speech community. *American Educational Research Journal, 36*, 147–184.

Ogden, E. H., & Germinario, V. (1988). *The at-risk student: Answers for educators*. Lancaster, PA: Technomic.

O'Grady, W. (1997). *Syntactic development*. Chicago: University of Chicago.

Okagaki, L. (2001). Triarchic model of minority children's school achievement. *Educational Psychologist, 36*, 9–20.

O'Leary, K. D., Kaufman, K. F., Kass, R. E., & Drabman, R. S. (1970). The effects of loud and soft reprimands on the behavior of disruptive students. *Exceptional Children, 37*, 145–155.

O'Leary, K. D., & O'Leary, S. G. (Eds.). (1972). *Classroom management: The successful use of behavior modification*. New York: Pergamon Press.

Olneck, M. R. (1995). Immigrants and education. In J. A. Banks & C. A. M. Banks (Eds.), *Handbook of research on multicultural education*. New York: Macmillan.

Onosko, J. J. (1989). Comparing teachers' thinking about promoting students' thinking. *Theory and Research in Social Education, 17*, 174–195.

Onosko, J. J. (1996). Exploring issues with students despite the barriers. *Social Education, 60*(1), 22–27.

Onosko, J. J., & Newmann, F. M. (1994). Creating more thoughtful learning environments. In J. N. Mangieri & C. C. Block (Eds.), *Advanced educational psychology: Enhancing mindfulness*. Fort Worth, TX: Harcourt Brace Jovanovich.

Ormrod, J. E. (1999). *Human learning* (3rd ed.). Upper Saddle River, NJ: Merrill/Prentice Hall.

Ormrod, J. E., & Carter, K. R. (1985). Systematizing the Piagetian clinical interview for classroom use. *Teaching of Psychology, 12*, 216–219.

Ormrod, J. E., & Jenkins, L. (1989). Study strategies in spelling: Correlations with achievement and developmental changes. *Perceptual and Motor Skills, 68*, 643–650.

Ormrod, J. E., Ormrod, R. K., Wagner, E. D., & McCallin, R. C. (1988). Reconceptualizing map learning. *American Journal of Psychology, 101*, 425–433.

Ormrod, J. E., & Wagner, E. D. (1987, October). *Spelling conscience in undergraduate students: Ratings of spelling accuracy and dictionary use*. Paper presented at the annual meeting of the Northern Rocky Mountain Educational Research Association, Park City, UT.

Oskamp, S. (Ed.). (2000). *Reducing prejudice and discrimination*. Mahwah, NJ: Erlbaum.

Osterman, K. F. (2000). Students' need for belonging in the school community. *Review of Educational Research, 70*, 323–367.

O'Sullivan, J. T., & Joy, R. M. (1990, April). *Children's theories about reading difficulty: A developmental study*. Paper presented at the annual meeting of the American Educational Research Association, Boston.

Otero, J., & Kintsch, W. (1992). Failures to detect contradictions in a text: What readers believe versus what they read. *Psychological Science, 3*, 229–235.

Owens, R. E., Jr. (1995). *Language disorders: A functional approach to assessment and intervention* (2nd ed.). Boston: Allyn & Bacon.

Owens, R. E., Jr. (1996). *Language development* (4th ed.). Boston: Allyn & Bacon.

Packard, V. (1983). *Our endangered children: Growing up in a changing world*. Boston: Little, Brown.

Padilla, A. M. (1994). Bicultural development: A theoretical and empirical examination. In R. G. Malgady & O. Rodriguez (Eds.), *Theoretical and conceptual issues in Hispanic mental health* (pp. 20–51). Malabar, FL: Krieger.

Page-Voth, V., & Graham, S. (1999). Effects of goal setting and strategy use on the writing performance and self-efficacy of students with writing and learning problems. *Journal of Educational Psychology, 91*, 230–240.

Pajares, F., & Valiante, G. (1999). *Writing self-efficacy of middle school students: Relation to motivation constructs, achievement, gender, and gender orientation*. Paper presented at the annual meeting of the American Educational Research Association, Montreal, Canada.

Palardy, J. M., & Mudrey, J. E. (1973). Discipline: Four approaches. *Elementary School Journal, 73*, 297–305.

Paley, V. G. (1984). *Boys and girls: Superheroes in the doll corner*. Chicago: University of Chicago Press.

Palincsar, A. S., & Brown, A. L. (1984). Reciprocal teaching of comprehension-fostering and comprehension-monitoring activities. *Cognition and Instruction, 1*, 117–175.

Palincsar, A. S., & Brown, A. L. (1989). Classroom dialogues to promote self-regulated comprehension. In J. Brophy (Ed.), *Advances in research on teaching* (Vol. 1). Greenwich, CT: JAI Press.

Palincsar, A. S., & Herrenkohl, L. R. (1999). Designing collaborative contexts: Lessons from three research programs. In A. M. O'Donnell & A. King (Eds.), *Cognitive perspectives on peer learning* (pp. 151–177). Mahwah, NJ: Erlbaum.

Palmer, E. L. (1965). Accelerating the child's cognitive attainments through the inducement of cognitive conflict: An interpretation of the Piagetian position. *Journal of Research in Science Teaching, 3,* 324.

Pang, V. O. (1995). Asian Pacific American students: A diverse and complex population. In J. A. Banks & C. A. M. Banks (Eds.), *Handbook of research on multicultural education.* New York: Macmillan.

Paris, S. G. (1988). Models and metaphors of learning strategies. In C. E. Weinstein, E. T. Goetz, & P. A. Alexander (Eds.), *Learning and study strategies: Issues in assessment, instruction, and evaluation.* San Diego, CA: Academic Press.

Paris, S. G., & Ayres, L. R. (1994). *Becoming reflective students and teachers with portfolios and authentic assessment.* Washington, DC: American Psychological Association.

Paris, S. G., & Byrnes, J. P. (1989). The constructivist approach to self-regulation and learning in the classroom. In B. J. Zimmerman & D. H. Schunk (Eds.), *Self-regulated learning and academic achievement: Theory, research, and practice.* New York: Springer-Verlag.

Paris, S. G., & Cunningham, A. E. (1996). Children becoming students. In D. C. Berliner & R. C. Calfee (Eds.), *Handbook of educational psychology.* New York: Macmillan.

Paris, S. G., Lawton, T. A., Turner, J. C., & Roth, J. L. (1991). A developmental perspective on standardized achievement testing. *Educational Researcher, 20*(5), 12–20, 40.

Paris, S. G., & Paris, A. H. (2001). Classroom applications of research on self-regulated learning. *Educational Psychologist, 36,* 89–101.

Paris, S. G., & Turner, J. C. (1994). Situated motivation. In P. R. Pintrich, D. R. Brown, & C. E. Weinstein (Eds.), *Student motivation, cognition, and learning: Essays in honor of Wilbert J. McKeachie.* Hillsdale, NJ: Erlbaum.

Paris, S. G., & Winograd, P. (1990). How metacognition can promote academic learning and instruction. In B. F. Jones & L. Idol (Eds.), *Dimensions of thinking and cognitive instruction.* Hillsdale, NJ: Erlbaum.

Parke, R. D. (1974). Rules, roles, and resistance to deviation: Explorations in punishment, discipline, and self-control. In A. Pick (Ed.), *Minnesota Symposia on Child Psychology* (Vol. 8). Minneapolis: University of Minnesota Press.

Parker, W. D. (1997). An empirical typology of perfectionism in academically talented children. *American Educational Research Journal, 34,* 545–562.

Parkhurst, J. T., & Hopmeyer, A. (1998). Sociometric popularity and peer-perceived popularity: Two distinct dimensions of peer status. *Journal of Early Adolescence, 18,* 125–144.

Parks, C. P. (1995). Gang behavior in the schools: Reality or myth? *Educational Psychology Review, 7,* 41–68.

Parnes, S. J. (1967). *Creative behavior guidebook.* New York: Scribner's.

Parsons, J. E., Adler, T. F., & Kaczala, C. M. (1982). Socialization of achievement attitudes and beliefs: Parental influences. *Child Development, 53,* 310–321.

Parsons, J. E., Kaczala, C. M., & Meece, J. L. (1982). Socialization of achievement attitudes and beliefs: Classroom influences. *Child Development, 53,* 322–339.

Pascarella, E. T., & Terenzini, P. T. (1991). *How college affects students: Findings and insights from twenty years of research.* San Francisco: Jossey-Bass.

Patrick, H. (1997). Social self-regulation: Exploring the relations between children's social relationships, academic self-regulation, and school performance. *Educational Psychologist, 32,* 209–220.

Patterson, C. J. (1995). Sexual orientation and human development: An overview. *Developmental Psychology, 31,* 3–11.

Patterson, G. R., DeBaryshe, B. D., & Ramsey, E. (1989). A developmental perspective on antisocial behavior. *American Psychologist, 44,* 329–335.

Patterson, G. R., Littman, R., & Bricker, W. (1967). Assertive behavior in children: A step toward a theory of aggression. *Monographs of the Society for Research in Child Development, 32* (Serial No. 113).

Patton, J. R., Blackbourn, J. M., & Fad, K. S. (1996). *Exceptional individuals in focus* (6th ed.). Upper Saddle River, NJ: Merrill/Prentice Hall.

Paulson, F. L., Paulson, P. R., & Meyer, C. A. (1991). What makes a portfolio a portfolio? *Educational Leadership, 49*(5), 60–63.

Paulson, K., & Johnson, M. (1983). Sex-role attitudes and mathematical ability in 4th, 8th, and 11th grade students from a high socioeconomic area. *Developmental Psychology, 19,* 210–214.

Pavlov, I. P. (1927). *Conditioned reflexes* (G. V. Anrep, Trans.). London: Oxford University Press.

Pawlas, G. E. (1994). Homeless students at the school door. *Educational Leadership, 51*(8), 79–82.

Paxton, R. J. (1999). A deafening silence: History textbooks and the students who read them. *Review of Educational Research, 69,* 315–339.

Pea, R. D. (1993). Practices of distributed intelligence and designs for education. In G. Salomon (Ed.), *Distributed cognitions: Psychological and educational considerations.* Cambridge, England: Cambridge University Press.

Peck, C. A., Donaldson, J., & Pezzoli, M. (1990). Some benefits nonhandicapped adolescents perceive for themselves from their social relationships with peers who have severe handicaps. *Journal of the Association for Persons with Severe Handicaps, 15,* 241–249.

Pellegrini, A. D., & Bartini, M. (2000). A longitudinal study of bullying, victimization, and peer affiliation during the transition from primary school to middle school. *American Educational Research Journal, 37,* 699–725.

Pellegrini, A. D., Bartini, M., & Brooks, F. (1999). School bullies, victims, and aggressive victims: Factors relating to group affiliation and victimization in early adolescence. *Journal of Educational Psychology, 91,* 216–224.

Pellegrini, A. D., & Bjorklund, D. F. (1997). The role of recess in children's cognitive performance. *Educational Psychologist, 32,* 35–40.

Pellegrini, A. D., & Horvat, M. (1995). A developmental contextualist critique of attention deficit hyperactivity disorder. *Educational Researcher, 24*(1), 13–19.

Pellegrini, A. D., Huberty, P. D., & Jones, I. (1995). The effects of recess timing on children's playground and classroom behaviors. *American Educational Research Journal, 32,* 845–864.

Perera, K. (1986). Language acquisition and writing. In P. Fletcher & M. Garman (Eds.), *Language acquisition: Studies in first language development* (2nd ed.). Cambridge, England: Cambridge University Press.

Pérez, B. (1998). *Sociocultural contexts of language and literacy.* Mahwah, NJ: Erlbaum.

Perkins, D. N. (1990). The nature and nurture of creativity. In B. F. Jones & L. Idol (Eds.), *Dimensions of thinking and cognitive instruction.* Hillsdale, NJ: Erlbaum.

Perkins, D. N. (1992). *Smart schools: From training memories to educating minds.* New York: Free Press/Macmillan.

Perkins, D. N. (1995). *Outsmarting IQ: The emerging science of learnable intelligence.* New York: Free Press.

Perkins, D. N., & Salomon, G. (1987). Transfer and teaching thinking. In D. N. Perkins, J. Lochhead, & J. Bishop (Eds.), *Thinking: The second international conference.* Hillsdale, NJ: Erlbaum.

Perkins, D. N., & Salomon, G. (1989). Are cognitive skills context-bound? *Educational Researcher, 18*(1), 16–25.

Perkins, D. N., & Simmons, R. (1988). Patterns of misunderstanding: An integrative model for science, math, and programming. *Review of Educational Research, 58,* 303–326.

Perkins, D. N., Tishman, S., Ritchhart, R., Donis, K., & Andrade, A. (2000). Intelligence in the wild: A dispositional view of intellectual traits. *Educational Psychology Review, 12,* 269–293.

Perry, D. G., & Perry, L. C. (1983). Social learning, causal attribution, and moral internalization. In J. Bisanz, G. L. Bisanz, & R. Kail (Eds.), *Learning in children: Progress in cognitive development research.* New York: Springer-Verlag.

Perry, N. E. (1998). Young children's self-regulated learning and contexts that support it. *Journal of Educational Psychology, 90,* 715–729.

Perry, R. P. (1985). Instructor expressiveness: Implications for improving teaching. In J. G. Donald & A. M. Sullivan (Eds.), *Using research to improve teaching* (pp. 35–49). San Francisco: Jossey-Bass.

Petersen, G. A., Sudweeks, R. R., & Baird, J. H. (1990, April). *Test-wise responses of third-, fifth-, and sixth-grade students to clued and unclued multiple-choice science items.* Paper presented at the annual meeting of the American Educational Research Assocation, Boston.

Peterson, C. (1990). Explanatory style in the classroom and on the playing field. In S. Graham & V. S. Folkes (Eds.), *Attribution theory: Applications to achievement, mental health, and interpersonal conflict.* Hillsdale, NJ: Erlbaum.

Peterson, C., Maier, S., & Seligman, M. (1993). *Learned helplessness: A theory for the age of personal control.* New York: Oxford University Press.

Peterson, L. R., & Peterson, M. J. (1959). Short-term retention of individual items. *Journal of Experimental Psychology, 58,* 193–198.

Peterson, P. L. (1979). Direct instruction reconsidered. In P. L. Peterson & H. L. Walberg (Eds.), *Research on teaching: Concepts, findings and implications.* Berkeley, CA: McCutchan.

Peterson, P. L. (1988). Teachers' and students' cognitional knowledge for classroom teaching and learning. *Educational Researcher, 17*(5), 5–14.

Peterson, S. E. (1993). The effects of prior achievement and group outcome on attributions and affect in cooperative tasks. *Contemporary Educational Psychology, 18,* 479–485.

Petrill, S. A., & Wilkerson, B. (2000). Intelligence and achievement: A behavioral genetic perspective. *Educational Psychology Review, 12,* 185–199.

Pettigrew, T. F., & Pajonas, P. J. (1973). The social psychology of heterogeneous schools. In C. S. Brembeck & W. H. Hill, *Cultural challenges to education: The influence of cultural factors in school learning.* Lexington, MA: Heath.

Pettito, A. L. (1985). Division of labor: Procedural learning in teacher-led small groups. *Cognition and Instruction, 2,* 233–270.

Pettito, L. A. (1997). In the beginning: On the genetic and environmental factors that make early language acquisition possible. In M. Gopnik (Ed.), *The inheritance and innateness of grammars.* New York: Oxford University Press.

Pfiffner, L. J., & Barkley, R. A. (1998). Treatment of ADHD in school settings. In R. A. Barkley, *Attention-deficit hyperactivity disorder: A handbook for diagnosis and treatment* (2nd ed., pp. 458–490). New York: Guilford Press.

Pfiffner, L. J., & O'Leary, S. G. (1993). School-based psychological treatments. In J. L. Matson (Ed.), *Handbook of hyperactivity in children* (pp. 234–255). Boston: Allyn & Bacon.

Pfiffner, L. J., Rosen, L. A., & O'Leary, S. G. (1985). The efficacy of an all-positive approach to classroom management. *Journal of Applied Behavior Analysis, 18,* 257–261.

Phelan, P., Davidson, A. L., & Cao, H. T. (1991). Students' multiple worlds: Negotiating the boundaries of family, peer, and school cultures. *Anthropology and Education Quarterly, 22,* 224–250.

Phelan, P., Yu, H. C., & Davidson, A. L. (1994). Navigating the psychosocial pressures of adolescence: The voices and experiences of high school youth. *American Educational Research Journal, 31,* 415–447.

Phillip, R. A., Flores, A., Sowder, J. T., & Schappelle, B. P. (1994). Conceptions and practices of extraordinary mathematics teachers. *Journal of Mathematical Behavior, 13,* 155–180.

Phillips, B. N., Pitcher, G. D., Worsham, M. E., & Miller, S. C. (1980). Test anxiety and the school environment. In I. G. Sarason (Ed.), *Test anxiety: Theory, research, and applications.* Hillsdale, NJ: Erlbaum.

Phillips, D., & Zimmerman, M. (1990). The developmental course of perceived competence and incompetence among competent children. In R. Sternberg & J. Kolligian (Eds.), *Competence considered* (pp. 41–66). New Haven, CT: Yale University Press.

Phinney, J. (1989). Stages of ethnic identity development in minority group adolescents. *Journal of Early Adolescence, 9,* 34–39.

Phye, G. D. (1997). Classroom assessment: A multidimensional perspective. In G. D. Phye (Ed.), *Handbook of classroom assessment: Learning, achievement, and adjustment.* San Diego, CA: Academic Press.

Piaget, J. (1928). *Judgment and reasoning in the child* (M. Warden, Trans.). New York: Harcourt, Brace.

Piaget, J. (1929). *The child's conception of the world.* New York: Harcourt, Brace.

Piaget, J. (1952a). *The child's conception of number* (C. Gattegno & F. M. Hodgson, Trans.). London: Routledge & Kegan Paul.

Piaget, J. (1952b). *The origins of intelligence in children* (M. Cook, Trans.). New York: Norton.

Piaget, J. (1959). *The language and thought of the child* (3rd ed.; M. Gabain, Trans.). London: Routledge & Kegan Paul.

Piaget, J. (1970). Piaget's theory. In P. H. Mussen (Ed.), *Carmichael's manual of psychology.* New York: Wiley.

Piaget, J. (1980). *Adaptation and intelligence: Organic selection and phenocopy* (S. Eames, Trans.). Chicago: University of Chicago Press.

Piersel, W. C. (1987). Basic skills education. In C. A. Maher & S. G. Forman (Eds.), *A behavioral approach to education of children and youth.* Hillsdale, NJ: Erlbaum.

Pigott, H. E., Fantuzzo, J. W., & Clement, P. W. (1986). The effects of reciprocal peer tutoring and group contingencies on the academic performance of elementary school children. *Journal of Applied Behavior Analysis, 19,* 93–98.

Piirto, J. (1999). *Talented children and adults: Their development and education* (2nd ed.). Upper Saddle River, NJ: Merrill/Prentice Hall.

Pine, K. J., & Messer, D. J. (2000). The effect of explaining another's actions on children's implicit theories of balance. *Cognition and Instruction, 18,* 35–51.

Pinker, S. (1987). The bootstrapping problem in language acquisition. In B. MacWhinney (Ed.), *Mechanisms of language acquisition.* Hillsdale, NJ: Erlbaum.

Pintrich, P. R. (2000). Multiple goals, multiple pathways: The role of goal orientation in learning and achievement. *Journal of Educational Psychology, 92,* 544–555.

Pintrich, P. R., & De Groot, E. V. (1990). Motivational and self-regulated learning components of classroom academic performance. *Journal of Educational Psychology, 82,* 33–40.

Pintrich, P. R., & Garcia, T. (1994). Regulating motivation and cognition in the classroom: The role of self-schemas and self-regulatory strategies. In D. Schunk & B. Zimmerman (Eds.), *Self-regulation of learning and performance: Issues and educational applications.* Hillsdale, NJ: Erlbaum.

Pintrich, P. R., Garcia, T., & De Groot, E. (1994, April). *Positive and negative self-schemas and self-regulated learning.* Paper presented at the annual meeting of the American Educational Research Association, New Orleans, LA.

Pintrich, P. R., Marx, R. W., & Boyle, R. A. (1993). Beyond cold conceptual change: The role of motivational beliefs and classroom contextual factors in the process of conceptual change. *Review of Educational Research, 63,* 167–199.

Pintrich, P. R., & Schrauben, B. (1992). Students' motivational beliefs and their cognitive engagement in academic tasks. In D. Schunk & J. Meece (Eds.), *Students' perceptions in the classroom: Causes and consequences.* Hillsdale, NJ: Erlbaum.

Pintrich, P. R., & Schunk, D. H. (2002). *Motivation in education: Theory, research, and applications* (2nd ed.). Upper Saddle River, NJ: Merrill/Prentice Hall.

Piontkowski, D., & Calfee, R. (1979). Attention in the classroom. In G. A. Hale & M. Lewis (Eds.), *Attention and cognitive development.* New York: Plenum Press.

Pipher, M. (1994). *Reviving Ophelia: Saving the selves of adolescent girls.* New York: Putnam.

Pitoniak, M. J., & Royer, J. M. (2001). Testing accommodations for examinees with disabilities: A review of psychometric, legal, and social policy issues. *Review of Educational Research, 71,* 53–104.

Pittman, K., & Beth-Halachmy, S. (1997, March). *The role of prior knowledge in analogy use.* Paper presented at the annual meeting of the American Educational Research Association, Chicago.

Plomin, R. (1989). Environment and genes: Determinants of behavior. *American Psychologist, 44,* 105–111.

Plomin, R. (1994). *Genetics and experience: The interplay between nature and nurture.* Thousand Oaks, CA: Sage.

Plomin, R., Fulker, D. W., Corley, R., & DeFries, J. C. (1997). Nature, nurture, and cognitive development from 1 to 16 years: A parent-offspring adoption study. *Psychological Science, 8,* 442–447.

Plumert, J. M. (1994). Flexibility in children's use of spatial and categorical organizational strategies in recall. *Developmental Psychology, 30,* 738–747.

Poche, C., Yoder, P., & Miltenberger, R. (1988). Teaching self-protection to children using television techniques. *Journal of Applied Behavior Analysis, 21,* 253–261.

Pogrow, S., & Londer, G. (1994). The effects of an intensive general thinking program on the motivation and cognitive development of at-risk students: Findings from the HOTS program. In H. F. O'Neil, Jr., & M. Drillings (Eds.), *Motivation: Theory and research.* Hillsdale, NJ: Erlbaum.

Pollard, S. R., Kurtines, W. M., Carlo, G., Dancs, M., & Mayock, E. (1991). Moral education from the perspective of psychosocial theory. In W. M. Kurtines & J. L. Gewirtz (Eds.), *Moral behavior and development: Vol. 3. Application.* Hillsdale, NJ: Erlbaum.

Polloway, E. A., & Patton, J. R. (1993). *Strategies for teaching learners with special needs* (5th ed.). Upper Saddle River, NJ: Merrill/Prentice Hall.

Poole, D. (1994). Routine testing practices and the linguistic construction of knowledge. *Cognition and Instruction, 12,* 125–150.

Popham, W. J. (1990). *Modern educational measurement: A practitioner's perspective* (2nd ed.). Upper Saddle River, NJ: Prentice Hall.

Popham, W. J. (1995). *Classroom assessment: What teachers need to know.* Needham Heights, MA: Allyn & Bacon.

Porath, M. (1988, April). *Cognitive development of gifted children: A neo-Piagetian perspective.* Paper presented at the annual meeting of the American Educational Research Association, New Orleans, LA.

Porter, A. C. (1989). A curriculum out of balance: The case of elementary school mathematics. *Educational Researcher, 18*(5), 9–15.

Portes, P. R. (1996). Ethnicity and culture in educational psychology. In D. C. Berliner & R. C. Calfee (Eds.), *Handbook of educational psychology.* New York: Macmillan.

Posner, G. J., Strike, K. A., Hewson, P. W., & Gertzog, W. A. (1982). Accommodation of a scientific conception: Toward a theory of conceptual change. *Science Education, 66,* 211–227.

Postman, L., & Underwood, B. J. (1973). Critical issues in interference theory. *Memory and Cognition, 1,* 19–40.

Poulin, F., & Boivin, M. (1999). Proactive and reactive aggression and boys' friendship quality in mainstream classrooms. *Journal of Emotional and Behavioral Disorders, 7,* 168–177.

Powell, G. J. (1983). *The psychosocial development of minority children.* New York: Brunner/Mazel.

Powell, S., & Nelson, B. (1997). Effects of choosing academic assignments on a student with attention deficit hyperactivity disorder. *Journal of Applied Behavior Analysis, 30,* 181–183.

Power, F. C., Higgins, A., & Kohlberg, L. (1989). *Lawrence Kohlberg's approach to moral education.* New York: Columbia University Press.

Power, F. C., & Power, M. R. (1992). A raft of hope: Democratic education and the challenge of pluralism. *Journal of Moral Education, 21,* 193–205.

Powers, L. E., Sowers, J. A., & Stevens, T. (1995). An exploratory, randomized study of the impact of mentoring on the self-efficacy and community-based knowledge of adolescents with severe physical challenges. *Journal of Rehabilitation, 61*(1), 33–41.

Powers, L. E., Wilson, R., Matuszewski, J., Phillips, A., Rein, C., Schumacher, D., & Gensert, J. (1996). Facilitating adolescent self-determination. In D. J. Sands & M. L. Wehmeyer (Eds.), *Self-determination across the life span: Independence and choice for people with disabilities.* Baltimore: Brookes.

Powers, S. I., Hauser, S. T., & Kilner, L. A. (1989). Adolescent mental health. *American Psychologist, 44,* 200–208.

Prawat, R. S. (1989). Promoting access to knowledge, strategy, and disposition in students: A research synthesis. *Review of Educational Research, 59,* 1–41.

Prawat, R. S. (1992). From individual differences to learning communities: Our changing focus. *Educational Leadership, 49*(7), 9–13.

Prawat, R. S. (1993). The value of ideas: Problems versus possibilities in learning. *Educational Researcher, 22*(6), 5–16.

Premack, D. (1959). Toward empirical behavior laws: I. Positive reinforcement. *Psychological Review, 66,* 219–233.

Premack, D. (1963). Rate differential reinforcement in monkey manipulation. *Journal of Experimental Analysis of Behavior, 6,* 81–89.

Presseisen, B. Z., & Beyer, F. S. (1994, April). *Facing history and ourselves: An instructional tool for constructivist theory.* Paper presented at the annual meeting of the American Educational Research Association, New Orleans, LA.

Pressley, M. (1982). Elaboration and memory development. *Child Development, 53,* 296–309.

Pressley, M. (with McCormick, C. B.). (1995). *Advanced educational psychology for educators, researchers, and policymakers.* New York: Harper-Collins.

Pressley, M., Borkowski, J. G., & Schneider, W. (1987). Cognitive strategies: Good strategy users coordinate metacognition and knowledge. In R. Vasta (Ed.), *Annals of child development* (Vol. 4). Greenwich, CT: JAI Press.

Pressley, M., El-Dinary, P. B., Marks, M. B., Brown, R., & Stein, S. (1992). Good strategy instruction is motivating and interesting. In K. A. Renninger, S. Hidi, & A. Krapp (Eds.), *The role of interest in learning and development.* Hillsdale, NJ: Erlbaum.

Pressley, M., Harris, K. R., & Marks, M. B. (1992). But good strategy instructors are constructivists! *Educational Psychology Review, 4,* 3–31.

Pressley, M., Levin, J. R., & Delaney, H. D. (1982). The mnemonic keyword method. *Review of Educational Research, 52,* 61–91.

Pressley, M., Snyder, B. L., & Cariglia-Bull, T. (1987). How can good strategy use be taught to children? Evaluation of six alternative approaches. In S. M. Cormier & J. D. Hagman (Eds.), *Transfer of learning: Contemporary research and applications.* San Diego, CA: Academic Press.

Pressley, M., Woloshyn, V., Lysynchuk, L. M., Martin, V., Wood, E., & Willoughby, T. (1990). A primer of research on cognitive strategy instruction: The important issues and how to address them. *Educational Psychology Review, 2,* 1–58.

Pressley, M., Yokoi, L., van Meter, P., Van Etten, S., & Freebern, G. (1997). Some of the reasons why preparing for exams is so hard: What can be done to make it easier? *Educational Psychology Review, 9,* 1–38.

Price-Williams, D. R., Gordon, W., & Ramirez, M. (1969). Skill and conservation. *Developmental Psychology, 1,* 769.

Pritchard, R. (1990). The effects of cultural schemata on reading processing strategies. *Reading Research Quarterly, 25,* 273–295.

Proctor, R. W., & Dutta, A. (1995). *Skill acquisition and human performance.* Thousand Oaks, CA: Sage.

Pruitt, R. P. (1989). Fostering creativity: The innovative classroom environment. *Educational Horizons, 68*(1), 51–54.

Pulos, S., & Linn, M. C. (1981). Generality of the controlling variables scheme in early adolescence. *Journal of Early Adolescence, 1,* 26–37.

Purdie, N., & Hattie, J. (1996). Cultural differences in the use of strategies for self-regulated learning. *American Educational Research Journal, 33,* 845–871.

Purdie, N., Hattie, J., & Douglas, G. (1996). Student conceptions of learning and their use of self-regulated learning strategies: A cross-cultural comparison. *Journal of Educational Psychology, 88,* 87–100.

Putallaz, M., & Heflin, A. H. (1986). Toward a model of peer acceptance. In J. M. Gottman &

J. G. Parker (Eds.), *Conversations of friends: Speculations on affective development* (pp. 292–314). Cambridge, England: Cambridge University Press.

Putnam, R. T. (1992). Thinking and authority in elementary-school mathematics tasks. In J. Brophy (Ed.), *Advances in research on teaching: Vol. 3. Planning and managing learning tasks and activities.* Greenwich, CT: JAI Press.

Qin, Z., Johnson, D. W., & Johnson, R. T. (1995). Cooperative versus competitive efforts and problem solving. *Review of Educational Research, 65,* 129–143.

Quellmalz, E., & Hoskyn, J. (1997). Classroom assessment of reading strategies. In G. D. Phye (Ed.), *Handbook of classroom assessment: Learning, achievement, and adjustment.* San Diego, CA: Academic Press.

Quill, K. A. (1995). Visually cued instruction for children with autism and pervasive developmental disorders. *Focus on Autistic Behavior, 10*(3), 10–20.

Raber, S. M. (1990, April). *A school system's look at its dropouts: Why they left school and what has happened to them.* Paper presented at the annual meeting of the American Educational Research Association, Boston.

Rabinowitz, M., & Glaser, R. (1985). Cognitive structure and process in highly competent performance. In F. D. Horowitz & M. O'Brien (Eds.), *The gifted and the talented: Developmental perspectives.* Washington, DC: American Psychological Association.

Rachlin, H. (1991). *Introduction to modern behaviorism* (3rd ed.). New York: Freeman.

Radke-Yarrow, M., Zahn-Waxler, C., & Chapman, M. (1983). Children's prosocial dispositions and behavior. In E. M. Hetherington (Ed.), *Handbook of child psychology: Vol. 4. Socialization, personality, and social development.* New York: Wiley.

Radziszewska, B., & Rogoff, B. (1991). Children's guided participation in planning imaginary errands with skilled adult or peer partners. *Develomental Psychology, 27,* 381–389.

Raine, A., & Scerbo, A. (1991). Biological theories of violence. In J. S. Milner (Ed.), *Neuropsychology of aggression* (pp. 1–25). Boston: Kluwer.

Rakow, S. J. (1984). What's happening in elementary science: A national assessment. *Science and Children, 21*(4), 39–40.

Ramey, C. T. (1992). High-risk children and IQ: Altering intergenerational patterns. *Intelligence, 16,* 239–256.

Ramey, C. T., & Ramey, S. L. (1998). Early intervention and early experience. *American Psychologist, 53,* 109–120.

Ramsey, P. G. (1987). *Teaching and learning in a diverse world: Multicultural education for young children.* New York: Teachers College Press.

Ramsey, P. G. (1995). Growing up with the contradictions of race and class. *Young Children, 50,* 18–22.

Rapport, M. D., Murphy, H. A., & Bailey, J. S. (1982). Ritalin vs. response cost in the control of hyperactive children: A within-subject comparison. *Journal of Applied Behavior Analysis, 15,* 205–216.

Raudenbush, S. W. (1984). Magnitude of teacher expectancy effects on pupil IQ as a function of credibility induction: A synthesis of findings from 18 experiments. *Journal of Educational Psychology, 76,* 85–97.

Rawsthorne, L. J., & Elliot, A. J. (1999). Achievement goals and intrinsic motivation: A meta-analytic review. *Personality and Social Psychology Review, 3,* 326–344.

Redfield, D. L., & Rousseau, E. W. (1981). A meta-analysis of experimental research on teacher questioning behavior. *Review of Educational Research, 51,* 237–245.

Reeve, J., Bolt, E., & Cai, Y. (1999). Autonomy-supportive teachers: How they teach and motivate students. *Journal of Educational Psychology, 91,* 537–548.

Reeve, R. E. (1990). ADHD: Facts and fallacies. *Intervention in School and Clinic, 26*(2), 70–78.

Reich, P. A. (1986). *Language development.* Upper Saddle River, NJ: Prentice Hall.

Reid, N. (1989). Contemporary Polynesian conceptions of giftedness. *Gifted Education International, 6*(1), 30–38.

Reimann, P., & Schult, T. J. (1996). Turning examples into cases: Acquiring knowledge structures for analogical problem solving. *Educational Psychologist, 31,* 123–132.

Reimer, J., Paolitto, D. P., & Hersh, R. H. (1983). *Promoting moral growth: From Piaget to Kohlberg* (2nd ed.). White Plains, NY: Longman.

Reiner, M., Slotta, J. D., Chi, M. T. H., & Resnick, L. B. (2000). Naïve physics reasoning: A commitment to substance-based conceptions. *Cognition and Instruction, 18,* 1–34.

Reis, S. M. (1989). Reflections on policy affecting the education of gifted and talented students: Past and future perspectives. *American Psychologist, 44,* 399–408.

Reisberg, D. (1997). *Cognition: Exploring the science of the mind.* New York: Norton.

Reisberg, D., & Heuer, F. (1992). Remembering the details of emotional events. In E. Winograd & U. Neisser (Eds.), *Affect and accuracy in recall: Studies of "flashbulb" memories.* Cambridge, England: Cambridge University Press.

Reiter, S. N. (1994). Teaching dialogically: Its relationship to critical thinking in college students. In P. R. Pintrich, D. R. Brown, & C. E. Weinstein (Eds.), *Student motivation, cognition, and learning: Essays in honor of Wilbert J. McKeachie.* Hillsdale, NJ: Erlbaum.

Renkl, A., Mandl, H., & Gruber, H. (1996). Inert knowledge: Analyses and remedies. *Educational Psychologist, 31,* 115–121.

Renninger, K. A., Hidi, S., & Krapp, A. (Eds.). (1992). *The role of interest in learning and development.* Hillsdale, NJ: Erlbaum.

Renzulli, J. S. (1978). What makes giftedness? Reexamining a definition. *Phi Delta Kappan, 60,* 180–184.

Renzulli, J. S., & Reis, S. M. (1986). The enrichment triad/revolving door model: A schoolwide plan for the development of creative productivity. In J. Renzulli (Ed.), *Systems and models for developing programs for the gifted and talented.* Mansfield Center, CT: Creative Learning Press.

Rescorla, R. A. (1967). Pavlovian conditioning and its proper control procedures. *Psychological Review, 74,* 71–80.

Rescorla, R. A. (1988). Pavlovian conditioning: It's not what you think it is. *American Psychologist, 43,* 151–160.

Resnick, D. P. (1980). Minimum competency testing historically considered. *Review of Research in Education, 8,* 329.

Resnick, D. P., & Resnick, L. B. (1996). Performance assessment and the multiple functions of educational measurement. In M. B. Kane & R. Mitchell (Eds.), *Implementing performance assessment: Promises, problems, and challenges* (pp. 23–38). Mahwah, NJ: Erlbaum.

Resnick, L. B. (1983). Mathematics and science learning: A new conception. *Science, 220,* 477–478.

Resnick, L. B. (1988). Treating mathematics as an ill-structured discipline. In R. I. Charles & E. A.

Silver (Eds.), *The teaching and assessing of mathematical problem solving* (pp. 32–60). Hillsdale, NJ: Erlbaum.

Resnick, L. B. (1989). Developing mathematical knowledge. *American Psychologist, 44,* 162–169.

Resnick, L. B., & Resnick, D. P. (1992). Assessing the thinking curriculum: New tools for educational reform. In B. G. Gifford & M. C. O'Connor (Eds.), *Changing assessments: Alternative views of aptitude, achievement and instruction* (pp. 37–75). Boston: Kluwer.

Resnick, M. D., Bearman, P. S., Blum, R. W., Bauman, K. E., Harris, K. M., Jones, J., Tabor, J., Beuhring, T., Sieving, R. E., Shew, M., Ireland, M., Bearinger, L. H., & Udry, J. R. (1997). Protecting adolescents from harm: Findings from the National Longitudinal Study on Adolescent Health. *Journal of the American Medical Association, 278,* 823–832.

Rest, J., Narvaez, D., Bebeau, M., & Thoma, S. (1999). A neo-Kohlbergian approach: The DIT and schema theory. *Educational Psychology Review, 11,* 291–324.

Reusser, K. (1990, April). *Understanding word arithmetic problems: Linguistic and situational factors.* Paper presented at the annual meeting of the American Educational Research Association, Boston.

Reyna, C. (2000). Lazy, dumb, or industrious: When stereotypes convey attribution information in the classroom. *Educational Psychology Review, 12,* 85–110.

Reyna, C., & Weiner, B. (2001). Justice and utility in the classroom: An attributional analysis of the goals of teachers' punishment and intervention strategies. *Journal of Educational Psychology, 93,* 309–319.

Reynolds, M. C. (1984). Classification of students with handicaps. In E. W. Gordon (Ed.), *Review of research in education* (No. 11). Washington, DC: American Educational Research Association.

Reynolds, M. C., & Birch, J. W. (1988). *Adaptive mainstreaming: A primer for teachers and principals* (3rd ed.). White Plains, NY: Longman.

Reynolds, R. E., & Shirey, L. L. (1988). The role of attention in studying and learning. In C. E. Weinstein, E. T. Goetz, & P. A. Alexander (Eds.), *Learning and study strategies: Issues in assessment, instruction, and evaluation.* San Diego, CA: Academic Press.

Reynolds, R. E., Taylor, M. A., Steffensen, M. S., Shirey, L. L., & Anderson, R. C. (1982). Cultural schemata and reading comprehension. *Reading Research Quarterly, 17,* 353–366.

Ricciuti, H. N. (1993). Nutrition and mental development. *Current Directions in Psychological Science, 2,* 43–46.

Rice, M., Hadley, P. A., & Alexander, A. L. (1993). Social biases toward children with speech and language impairments: A correlative causal model of language limitations. *Applied Psycholinguistics, 14,* 445–471.

Richards, C. M., Symons, D. K., Greene, C. A., & Szuszkiewicz, T. A. (1995). The bidirectional relationship between achievement and externalizing behavior disorders. *Journal of Learning Disabilities, 28,* 8–17.

Ricks, J. H. (1959). On telling parents about test results. *Test Service Bulletin* (No. 59). New York: Psychological Corporation.

Riggs, J. M. (1992). Self-handicapping and achievement. In A. K. Boggiano & T. S. Pittman (Eds.), *Achievement and motivation: A social-developmental perspective.* Cambridge, England: Cambridge University Press.

Rimm, D. C., & Masters, J. C. (1974). *Behavior therapy: Techniques and empirical findings.* San Diego, CA: Academic Press.

Ripple, R. E. (1989). Ordinary creativity. *Contemporary Educational Psychology, 14,* 189–202.

Ritts, V., Patterson, M. L., & Tubbs, M. E. (1992). Expectations, impressions, and judgments of physically attractive students: A review. *Review of Educational Research, 62,* 413–426.

Ritvo, E. R., & Freeman, B. J. (1978). National Society for Autistic Children definition of the syndrome of autism. *Journal of Autism and Childhood Schizophrenia, 8,* 162–167.

Roberge, J. J. (1970). A study of children's abilities to reason with basic principles of deductive reasoning. *American Educational Research Journal, 7,* 583–596.

Roberts, G. C., Treasure, D. C., & Kavussanu, M. (1997). Motivation in physical activity contexts: An achievement goal perspective. *Advances in Motivation and Achievement, 10,* 413–447.

Robertson, J. S. (2000). Is attribution training a worthwhile classroom intervention for K–12 students with learning difficulties? *Educational Psychology Review, 12,* 111–134.

Robins, R. W., Gosling, S. D., & Craik, K. H. (1999). An empirical analysis of trends in psychology. *American Psychologist, 54,* pp. 117–128.

Robinson, A. (1991). Cooperation or exploitation? The argument against cooperative learning for talented students. *Journal for the Education of the Gifted, 14,* 9–27.

Robinson, T. R., Smith, S. W., Miller, M. D., & Brownell, M. T. (1999). Cognitive behavior modification of hyperactivity-impulsivity and aggression: A meta-analysis of school-based studies. *Journal of Educational Psychology, 91,* 195–203.

Roblyer, M. D., Castine, W. H., & King, F. J. (1988). *Assessing the impact of computer-based instruction: A review of recent research.* New York: Haworth.

Roderick, M. (1994). Grade retention and school dropout: Investigating the association. *American Educational Research Journal, 31,* 729–759.

Roderick, M., & Camburn, E. (1999). Risk and recovery from course failure in the early years of high school. *American Educational Research Journal, 36,* 303–343.

Roediger, H. L., III, & McDermott, K. B. (2000). Tricks of memory. *Current Directions in Psychological Science, 9,* 123–127.

Rogers, C. R. (1983). *Freedom to learn for the 80's.* Upper Saddle River, NJ: Merrill/Prentice Hall.

Rogers, T. B., Kuiper, N. A., & Kirker, W. S. (1977). Self-reference and the encoding of personal information. *Journal of Personality and Social Psychology, 35,* 677–688.

Rogoff, B. (1990). *Apprenticeship in thinking: Cognitive development in social context.* New York: Oxford University Press.

Rogoff, B. (1991). Social interaction as apprenticeship in thinking: Guidance and participation in spatial planning. In L. B. Resnick, J. M. Levine, & S. D. Teasley (Eds.), *Perspectives on socially shared cognition.* Washington, DC: American Psychological Association.

Rogoff, B. (1994, April). *Developing understanding of the idea of communities of learners.* Paper presented at the annual meeting of the American Educational Research Association, New Orleans, LA.

Rogoff, B., Matusov, E., & White, C. (1996). Models of teaching and learning: Participation in a community of learners. In D. R. Olson & N. Torrance (Eds.), *The handbook of education and human development: New models of learning, teaching, and schooling.* Cambridge, MA: Blackwell.

Rogoff, B., & Morelli, G. (1989). Perspectives on children's development from cultural psychology. *American Psychologist, 44,* 343–348.

Rogoff, B., & Waddell, K. J. (1982). Memory for information organized in a scene by children from two cultures. *Child Development, 53,* 1224–1228.

Rohner, R. P. (1998). Father love and child development: History and current evidence. *Current Directions in Psychological Science, 7,* 157–161.

Roopnarine, J. L., Lasker, J., Sacks, M., & Stores, M. (1998). The cultural contexts of children's play. In O. N. Saracho & B. Spodek (Eds.), *Multiple perspectives on play in early childhood education.* Albany: State University of New York Press.

Rortvedt, A. K., & Miltenberger, R. G. (1994). Analysis of a high-probability instructional sequence and time-out in the treatment of child noncompliance. *Journal of Applied Behavior Analysis, 27,* 327–330.

Rosch, E. H. (1973a). Natural categories. *Cognitive Psychology, 4,* 328–350.

Rosch, E. H. (1973b). On the internal structure of perceptual and semantic categories. In T. E. Moore (Ed.), *Cognitive development and the acquisition of language.* San Diego, CA: Academic Press.

Rosch, E. H. (1977). Human categorization. In N. Warren (Ed.), *Advances in cross-cultural psychology* (Vol. 1). San Diego, CA: Academic Press.

Rosch, E. H., Mervis, C. B., Gray, W. D., Johnson, D. M., & Boyes-Braem, P. (1976). Basic objects in natural categories. *Cognitive Psychology, 8,* 382–439.

Rose, A. J., & Asher, S. R. (1999). Children's goals and strategies in response to conflicts within a friendship. *Developmental Psychology, 35,* 69–79.

Rose, S. C., & Thornburg, K. R. (1984). Mastery motivation and need for approval in young children: Effects of age, sex, and reinforcement condition. *Educational Research Quarterly, 9*(1), 34–42.

Rosenberg, M. (1986). Self-concept from middle childhood through adolescence. In S. Suls & A. Greenwald (Eds.), *Psychological perspectives on the self* (Vol. 3, pp. 107–135). Hillsdale, NJ: Erlbaum.

Rosenshine, B., & Meister, C. (1992). The use of scaffolds for teaching higher-level cognitive strategies. *Educational Leadership, 49*(7), 26–33.

Rosenshine, B., & Meister, C. (1994). Reciprocal teaching: A review of the research. *Review of Educational Research, 64,* 479–530.

Rosenshine, B., Meister, C., & Chapman, S. (1996). Teaching students to generate questions: A review of the intervention studies. *Review of Educational Research, 66,* 181–221.

Rosenshine, B. V., & Stevens, R. (1986). Teaching functions. In M. C. Wittrock (Ed.), *Handbook of research on teaching* (3rd ed.). New York: Macmillan.

Rosenthal, R. (1994). Interpersonal expectancy effects: A 30-year perspective. *Current Directions in Psychological Science, 3,* 176–179.

Rosenthal, R., & Rubin, D. B. (1982). Further meta-analytic procedures for assessing cognitive gender differences. *Journal of Educational Psychology, 74,* 708–712.

Rosenthal, T. L., Alford, G. S., & Rasp, L. M. (1972). Concept attainment, generalization, and retention through observation and verbal coding. *Journal of Experimental Child Psychology, 13,* 183–194.

Rosenthal, T. L., & Bandura, A. (1978). Psychological modeling: Theory and practice. In S. L. Garfield & A. E. Begia (Eds.), *Handbook of psychotherapy and behavior change: An empirical analysis* (2nd ed.). New York: Wiley.

Rosenthal, T. L., & Zimmerman, B. J. (1978). *Social learning and cognition.* San Diego, CA: Academic Press.

Ross, B. H., & Spalding, T. L. (1994). Concepts and categories. In R. J. Sternberg (Ed.), *Handbook of perception and cognition* (Vol. 12). New York: Academic Press.

Ross, J. A. (1988). Controlling variables: A meta-analysis of training studies. *Review of Educational Research, 58,* 405–437.

Rosser, R. (1994). *Cognitive development: Psychological and biological perspectives.* Needham Heights, MA: Allyn & Bacon.

Rotenberg, K. J., & Mayer, E. V. (1990). Delay of gratification in Native and White children: A cross-cultural comparison. *International Journal of Behavioral Development, 13,* 23–30.

Roth, K. J. (1990). Developing meaningful conceptual understanding in science. In B. F. Jones & L. Idol (Eds.), *Dimensions of thinking and cognitive instruction.* Hillsdale, NJ: Erlbaum.

Roth, K. J., & Anderson, C. (1988). Promoting conceptual change learning from science textbooks. In P. Ramsden (Ed.), *Improving learning: New perspectives.* London: Kogan Page.

Roth, W., & Bowen, G. M. (1995). Knowing and interacting: A study of culture, practices, and resources in a grade 8 open-inquiry science classroom guided by a cognitive apprenticeship metaphor. *Cognition and Instruction, 13,* 73–128.

Rothbart, M. K., & Bates, J. E. (1998). Temperament. In W. Damon (Editor-in-Chief) & N. Eisenberg (Vol. Ed.), *Handbook of child psychology: Vol. 3. Social, emotional, and personality development* (5th ed., pp. 105–176). New York: Wiley.

Rothbaum, F., Weisz, J., Pott, M., Miyake, K., & Morelli, G. (2000). Attachment and culture: Security in the United States and Japan. *American Psychologist, 55,* 1093–1104.

Roughead, W. G., & Scandura, J. M. (1968). What is learned in mathematical discovery. *Journal of Educational Psychology, 59,* 283–289.

Rowe, D. C., Almeida, D. M., & Jacobson, K. C. (1999). School context and genetic influences on aggression in adolescence. *Psychological Science, 10,* 277–280.

Rowe, E. (1999, April). *Gender differences in math self-concept development: The role of classroom interaction.* Paper presented at the annual meeting of the American Educational Research Association, Montreal, Canada.

Rowe, M. B. (1974). Wait-time and rewards as instructional variables, their influence on language, logic, and fate control: Part one—wait time. *Journal of Research in Science Teaching, 11,* 81–94.

Rowe, M. B. (1978). *Teaching science as continuous inquiry.* New York: McGraw-Hill.

Rowe, M. B. (1987). Wait-time: Slowing down may be a way of speeding up. *American Educator, 11,* 38–43, 47.

Rubin, K. H. (1982). Nonsocial play in preschoolers: Necessarily evil? *Child Development, 53,* 651–657.

Rubin, K. H., Bukowski, W., & Parker, J. G. (1998). Peer interactions, relationships, and groups. In W. Damon (Editor-in-Chief) & N. Eisenberg (Vol. Ed.), *Handbook of child psychology: Vol. 3. Social, emotional, and personality development* (5th ed.). New York: Wiley.

Rubin, K. H., & Krasnor, L. R. (1986). Social-cognitive and social behavioral perspectives on problem solving. In M. Perlmutter (Ed.), *Minnesota Symposia on Child Psychology: Vol. 19. Cognitive perspectives on children's social and behavioral development.* Hillsdale, NJ: Erlbaum.

Rubin, K. H., & Pepler, D. J. (1995). The relationship of child's play to social-cognitive growth and development. In H. C. Foot, A. J. Chapman, & J. R. Smith (Eds.), *Friendship and social relations in children* (pp. 209–233). New Brunswick, NJ: Transaction.

Ruble, D. N. (1988). Sex-role development. In M. H. Bornstein & M. E. Lamb (Eds.), *Developmental psychology: An advanced textbook* (2nd ed.). Hillsdale, NJ: Erlbaum.

Ruble, D. N., & Ruble, T. L. (1982). Sex stereotypes. In A. G. Miller (Ed.), *In the eye of the beholder.* New York: Praeger.

Rudman, M. K. (1993). Multicultural children's literature: The search for universals. In M. K. Rudman (Ed.), *Children's literature: Resource for the classroom* (2nd ed.). Norwood, MA: Christopher-Gordon.

Rueda, R., & Moll, L. C. (1994). A sociocultural perspective on motivation. In H. F. O'Neil, Jr., & M. Drillings (Eds.), *Motivation: Theory and research.* Hillsdale, NJ: Erlbaum.

Ruef, M. B., Higgins, C., Glaeser, B., & Patnode, M. (1998). Positive behavioral support: Strategies for teachers. *Intervention in School and Clinic, 34*(1), 21–32.

Rueger, D. B., & Liberman, R. P. (1984). Behavioral family therapy for delinquent substance-abusing adolescents. *Journal of Drug Abuse, 14,* 403–418.

Ruff, H. A., & Lawson, K. R. (1990). Development of sustained, focused attention in young children during free play. *Developmental Psychology, 26,* 85–93.

Rumberger, R. W. (1995). Dropping out of middle school: A multilevel analysis of students and schools. *American Educational Research Journal, 32,* 583–625.

Rumelhart, D. E., & Ortony, A. (1977). The representation of knowledge in memory. In R. C. Anderson, R. J. Spiro, & W. E. Montague (Eds.), *Schooling and the acquisition of knowledge.* Hillsdale, NJ: Erlbaum.

Runco, M. A., & Chand, I. (1995). Cognition and creativity. *Educational Psychology Review, 7,* 243–267.

Rushton, J. P. (1980). *Altruism, socialization, and society.* Upper Saddle River, NJ: Prentice Hall.

Russ, S. W. (1993). *Affect and creativity: The role of affect and play in the creative process.* Hillsdale, NJ: Erlbaum.

Ryan, A. M. (2000). Peer groups as a context for the socialization of adolescents' motivation, engagement, and achievement in school. *Educational Psychologist, 35,* 101–111.

Ryan, A. M., & Patrick, H. (2001). The classroom social environment and changes in adolescents' motivation and engagement during middle school. *American Educational Research Journal, 38,* 437–460.

Ryan, A. M., Pintrich, P. R., & Midgley, C. (2001). Avoiding seeking help in the classroom: Who and why? *Educational Psychology Review, 13,* 93–114.

Ryan, R. M., Connell, J. P., & Grolnick, W. S. (1992). When achievement is *not* intrinsically motivated: A theory of internalization and self-regulation in school. In A. K. Boggiano & T. S. Pittman (Eds.), *Achievement and motivation: A social-developmental perspective.* Cambridge, England: Cambridge University Press.

Ryan, R. M., & Deci, E. L. (2000). Self-determination theory and the facilitation of intrinsic motivation, social development, and well-being. *American Psychologist, 55,* pp. 68–78.

Ryan, R. M., & Kuczkowski, R. (1994). The imaginary audience, self-consciousness, and public individuation in adolescence. *Journal of Personality, 62,* 219–237.

Ryan, R. M., & Lynch, J. H. (1989). Emotional autonomy versus detachment: Revisiting the vicissitudes of adolescence and young adulthood. *Child Development, 60,* 340–356.

Ryan, R. M., Mims, V., & Koestner, R. (1983). Relation of reward contingency and interpersonal context to intrinsic motivation: A review and test using cognitive evaluation theory. *Journal of Personality and Social Psychology, 45,* 736–750.

Ryan, R. M., Stiller, J. D., & Lynch, J. H. (1994). Representations of relationships to teachers, parents, and friends as predictors of academic motivation and self-esteem. *Journal of Early Adolescence, 14,* 226–249.

Sabers, D. S., Cushing, K. S., & Berliner, D. C. (1991). Differences among teachers in a task characterized by simultaneity, multidimensionality, and immediacy. *American Educational Research Journal, 28,* 63–88.

Sadker, M. P., & Miller, D. (1982). *Sex equity handbook for schools.* White Plains, NY: Longman.

Sadker, M. P., & Sadker, D. (1985). Sexism in the schoolroom of the '80s. *Psychology Today, 19,* 54–57.

Sadker, M. P., & Sadker, D. (1994). *Failing at fairness: How our schools cheat girls.* New York: Touchstone.

Sadker, M. P., Sadker, D., & Klein, S. (1991). The issue of gender in elementary and secondary education. In G. Grant (Ed.), *Review of research in education.* Washington, DC: American Educational Research Association.

Sadoski, M., Goetz, E. T., & Fritz, J. B. (1993). Impact of concreteness on comprehensibility, interest, and memory for text: Implications for dual coding theory and text design. *Journal of Educational Psychology, 85,* 291–304.

Sadoski, M., & Paivio, A. (2001). *Imagery and text: A dual coding theory of reading and writing.* Mahwah, NJ: Erlbaum.

Salend, S. J., & Taylor, L. (1993). Working with families: A cross-cultural perspective. *Remedial and Special Education, 14*(5), 25–32, 39.

Salisbury, C. L., Evans, I. M., & Palombaro, M. M. (1997). Collaborative problem solving to promote the inclusion of young children with significant disabilities in primary grades. *Exceptional Children, 63,* 195–210.

Saljo, R., & Wyndhamn, J. (1992). Solving everyday problems in the formal setting: An empirical study of the school as context for thought. In S. Chaiklin & J. Lave (Eds.), *Understanding practice.* New York: Cambridge University Press.

Salomon, G. (Ed.). (1993a). *Distributed cognitions: Psychological and educational considerations.* Cambridge, England: Cambridge University Press.

Salomon, G. (1993b). No distribution without individuals' cognition: A dynamic interactional view. In G. Salomon (Ed.), *Distributed cognitions: Psychological and educational considerations* (pp. 111–138). Cambridge, England: Cambridge University Press.

Saltz, E. (1971). *The cognitive bases of human learning.* Homewood, IL: Dorsey.

Sanborn, M. P. (1979). Counseling and guidance needs of the gifted and talented. In A. H. Passow (Ed.), *The gifted and the talented: Their education and development. The seventy-eighth yearbook of the National Society for the Study of Education.* Chicago: University of Chicago Press.

Sanchez, F., & Anderson, M. L. (1990). Gang mediation: A process that works. *Principal, 69*(4), 54–56.

Sanders, C. E. (1997). Assessment during the preschool years. In G. D. Phye (Ed.), *Handbook of classroom assessment: Learning, achievement, and adjustment.* San Diego, CA: Academic Press.

Sanders, M. G. (1996). Action teams in action: Interviews and observations in three schools in the Baltimore School–Family–Community Partnership Program. *Journal of Education for Students Placed at Risk, 1,* 249–262.

Sanders, S. (1987). Cultural conflicts: An important factor in academic failures of American Indian students. *Journal of Multicultural Counseling and Development, 15*(2), 81–90.

Sands, D. J., & Wehmeyer, M. L. (Eds.). (1996). *Self-determination across the life span: Independence and choice for people with disabilities.* Baltimore: Brookes.

Sansone, C., Weir, C., Harpster, L., & Morgan, C. (1992). Once a boring task always a boring task?

Interest as a self-regulatory mechanism. *Journal of Personality and Social Psychology, 63,* 379–390.

Santiago, I. S. (1986). The education of Hispanics in the United States: Inadequacies of the American melting-pot theory. In D. Rothermund & J. Simon (Eds.), *Education and the integration of ethnic minorities.* New York: St. Martin's Press.

Sapon-Shevin, M., Dobbelaere, A., Corrigan, C., Goodman, K, & Mastin, M. (1998). Everyone here can play. *Educational Leadership, 56*(1), 42–45.

Sarason, I. G. (Ed.). (1980). *Test anxiety: Theory, research, and applications.* Hillsdale, NJ: Erlbaum.

Sarason, S. B. (1972). What research says about test anxiety in elementary school children. In A. R. Binter & S. H. Frey (Eds.), *The psychology of the elementary school child.* Chicago: Rand McNally.

Sattler, J. M. (2001). *Assessment of children: Cognitive applications* (4th ed.). San Diego, CA: Author.

Sax, G. (1989). *Principles of educational and psychological measurement and evaluation* (3rd ed.). Belmont, CA: Wadsworth.

Sax, G., & Cromack, T. R. (1966). The effects of various forms of item arrangements on test performance. *Journal of Educational Measurement, 3,* 309–311.

Scarcella, R. (1990). *Teaching language-minority students in the multicultural classroom.* Upper Saddle River, NJ: Prentice Hall.

Scardamalia, M., & Bereiter, C. (1985). Fostering the development of self-regulation in children's knowledge processing. In S. F. Chipman, J. W. Segal, & R. Glaser (Eds.), *Thinking and learning skills: Vol. 2. Research and open questions.* Hillsdale, NJ: Erlbaum.

Scarr, S., & Weinberg, R. A. (1976). IQ test performance of black children adopted by white families. *American Psychologist, 31,* 726–739.

Scevak, J. J., Moore, P. J., & Kirby, J. R. (1993). Training students to use maps to increase text recall. *Contemporary Educational Psychology, 18,* 401–413.

Schacter, D. L. (1999). The seven sins of memory: Insights from psychology and neuroscience. *American Psychologist, 54,* pp. 182–203.

Schacter, J. (2000). Does individual tutoring produce optimal learning? *American Educational Research Journal, 37,* 801–829.

Schank, R. C. (1979). Interestingness: Controlling inferences. *Artificial Intelligence, 12,* 273–297.

Schank, R. C., & Abelson, R. P. (1995). Knowledge and memory: The real story. In R. S. Wyer, Jr. (Ed.), *Advances in social cognition: Vol. 8. Knowledge and memory: The real story.* Hillsdale, NJ: Erlbaum.

Schauble, L. (1990). Belief revision in children: The role of prior knowledge and strategies for generating evidence. *Journal of Experimental Child Psychology, 49,* 31–57.

Schell, T. L., Klein, S. B., & Babey, S. H. (1996). Testing a hierarchical model of self-knowledge. *Psychological Science, 7,* 170–173.

Schepis, M. M., Reid, D. H., & Fitzgerald, J. R. (1987). Group instruction with profoundly retarded persons: Acquisition, generalization, and maintenance of a remunerative work skill. *Journal of Applied Behavior Analysis, 20,* 97–105.

Schiefele, U. (1991). Interest, learning, and motivation. *Educational Psychologist, 26,* 299–323.

Schiefele, U. (1992). Topic interest and levels of text comprehension. In K. A. Renninger, S. Hidi, & A. Krapp (Eds.), *The role of interest in learning and development.* Hillsdale, NJ: Erlbaum.

Schiefele, U., Krapp, A., & Winteler, A. (1992). Interest as a predictor of academic achievement: A meta-analysis of research. In K. A. Renninger, S. Hidi, & A. Krapp (Eds.), *The role of interest in learning and development.* Hillsdale, NJ: Erlbaum.

Schiefele, U., & Wild, K. (1994, April). *Motivational predictors of strategy use and course grades.* Paper presented at the annual meeting of the American Educational Research Association, New Orleans, LA.

Schiffman, G., Tobin, D., & Buchanan, B. (1984). Microcomputer instruction for the learning disabled. *Annual Review of Learning Disabilities, 2,* 134–136.

Schimmoeller, M. A. (1998, April). *Influence of private speech on the writing behaviors of young children: Four case studies.* Paper presented at the annual meeting of the American Educational Research Association, San Diego, CA.

Schirmer, B. R. (1994). *Language and literacy development in children who are deaf.* Needham Heights, MA: Allyn & Bacon.

Schlaefli, A., Rest, J. R., & Thoma, S. J. (1985). Does moral education improve moral judgment? A meta-analysis of intervention studies using the defining issues test. *Review of Educational Research, 55,* 319–352.

Schliemann, A. D., & Carraher, D. W. (1993). Proportional reasoning in and out of school. In P. Light & G. Butterworth (Eds.), *Context and cognition: Ways of learning and knowing.* Hillsdale, NJ: Erlbaum.

Schloss, P. J., & Smith, M. A. (1994). *Applied behavior analysis in the classroom.* Needham Heights, MA: Allyn & Bacon.

Schmidt, R. A., & Bjork, R. A. (1992). New conceptualizations of practice: Common principles in three paradigms suggest new concepts for training. *Psychological Science, 3,* 207–217.

Schneider, W. (1993). Domain-specific knowledge and memory performance in children. *Educational Psychology Review, 5,* 257–273.

Schneider, W., & Pressley, M. (1989). *Memory development between 2 and 20.* New York: Springer-Verlag.

Schneider, W., & Shiffrin, R. M. (1977). Controlled and automatic human information processing: I. Detection, search, and attention. *Psychological Review, 84,* 1–66.

Schoenfeld, A. H. (1985). Metacognitive and epistemological issues in mathematical understanding. In E. A. Silver (Ed.), *Teaching and learning mathematical problem solving: Multiple research perspectives.* Hillsdale, NJ: Erlbaum.

Schoenfeld, A. H., & Hermann, D. J. (1982). Problem perception and knowledge structure in expert and novice mathematical problem solvers. *Journal of Experimental Psychology: Learning, Memory, and Cognition, 8,* 484–494.

Schofield, J. W. (1995). Improving intergroup relations among students. In J. A. Banks & C. A. M. Banks (Eds.), *Handbook of research on multicultural education.* New York: Macmillan.

Scholes, R. J., & Kardash, C. M. (1996, April). *The effect of topic interest on the relationship between text-based interest and importance in text comprehension.* Paper presented at the annual meeting of the American Educational Research Association, New York.

Schommer, M. (1994a). An emerging conceptualization of epistemological beliefs and their role in learning. In R. Garner & P. A. Alexander (Eds.), *Beliefs about text and instruction with text.* Hillsdale, NJ: Erlbaum.

Schommer, M. (1994b). Synthesizing epistemological belief research: Tentative understandings and provocative confusions. *Educational Psychology Review, 6,* 293–319.

Schommer, M. (1997). The development of epistemological beliefs among secondary students: A longitudinal study. *Journal of Educational Psychology, 89,* 37–40.

Schommer-Aikins, M. (2001). An evolving theoretical framework for an epistemological belief system. In B. K. Hofer & P. R. Pintrich (Eds.), *Personal epistemology: The psychology of beliefs about knowledge and knowing.* Hillsdale, NJ: Erlbaum.

Schonert-Reichl, K. A. (1993). Empathy and social relationships in adolescents with behavioral disorders. *Behavioral Disorders, 18,* 189–204.

Schraw, G., & Lehman, S. (2001). Situational interest: A review of the literature and directions for future research. *Educational Psychology Review, 13,* 23–52.

Schraw, G., & Moshman, D. (1995). Metacognitive theories. *Educational Psychology Review, 7,* 351–371.

Schraw, G., & Wade, S. (1991, April). *Selective learning strategies for relevant and important text information.* Paper presented at the annual meeting of the American Educational Research Association, Chicago.

Schreibman, L. (1988). *Autism.* Newbury Park, CA: Sage.

Schubert, J. G. (1986). Gender equity in computer learning. *Theory into Practice, 25,* 267–275.

Schultz, G. F., & Switzky, H. N. (1990). The development of intrinsic motivation in students with learning problems: Suggestions for more effective instructional practice. *Preventing School Failure, 34*(2), 14–20.

Schultz, K., Buck, P., & Niesz, T. (2000). Democratizing conversations: Racialized talk in a post-desegregated middle school. *American Educational Research Journal, 37,* 33–65.

Schultz, K., & Lochhead, J. (1991). A view from physics. In M. U. Smith (Ed.), *Toward a unified theory of problem solving: Views from the content domains.* Hillsdale, NJ: Erlbaum.

Schumaker, J. B., & Hazel, J. S. (1984). Social skill assessment and training for the learning disabled: Who's on first and what's on second? (Part 1). *Journal of Learning Disabilities, 17,* 422–431.

Schunk, D. H. (1981). Modeling and attributional effects on children's achievement: A self-efficacy analysis. *Journal of Educational Psychology, 73,* 93–105.

Schunk, D. H. (1982). Effects of effort attributional feedback on children's perceived self-efficacy and achievement. *Journal of Educational Psychology, 74,* 548–556.

Schunk, D. H. (1983a). Ability versus effort attributional feedback: Differential effects on self-efficacy and achievement. *Journal of Educational Psychology, 75,* 848–856.

Schunk, D. H. (1983b). Developing children's self-efficacy and skills: The roles of social comparative information and goal setting. *Contemporary Educational Psychology, 8,* 76–86.

Schunk, D. H. (1989a). Self-efficacy and achievement behaviors. *Educational Psychology Review, 1,* 173–208.

Schunk, D. H. (1989b). Self-efficacy and cognitive skill learning. In C. Ames & R. Ames (Eds.), *Research on motivation in education: Vol. 3. Goals and cognitions.* San Diego, CA: Academic Press.

Schunk, D. H. (1989c). Social cognitive theory and self-regulated learning. In B. J. Zimmerman & D. H. Schunk (Eds.), *Self-regulated learning and academic achievement: Theory, research, and practice.* New York: Springer-Verlag.

Schunk, D. H. (1990, April). *Socialization and the development of self-regulated learning: The role of attributions.* Paper presented at the annual meeting of the American Educational Research Association, Boston.

Schunk, D. H. (1991). *Learning theories: An educational perspective.* Upper Saddle River, NJ: Merrill/Prentice Hall.

Schunk, D. H. (1996). Goal and self-evaluative influences during children's cognitive skill learning. *American Educational Research Journal, 33,* 359–382.

Schunk, D. H. (1998). Teaching elementary students to self-regulate practice of mathematical skills with modeling. In D. H. Schunk & B. J. Zimmerman (Eds.), *Self-regulated learning: From teaching to self-reflective practice* (pp. 137–159). New York: Guilford Press.

Schunk, D. H., & Hanson, A. R. (1985). Peer models: Influence on children's self-efficacy and achievement. *Journal of Educational Psychology, 77,* 313–322.

Schunk, D. H., Hanson, A. R., & Cox, P. D. (1987). Peer-model attributes and children's achievement behaviors. *Journal of Educational Psychology, 79,* 54–61.

Schunk, D. H., & Rice, J. (1989). Learning goals and children's reading comprehension. *Journal of Reading Behavior, 21,* 279–293.

Schunk, D. H., & Swartz, C. W. (1993). Goals and progress feedback: Effects on self-efficacy and writing achievement. *Contemporary Educational Psychology, 18,* 337–354.

Schunk, D. H., & Zimmerman, B. J. (Eds.). (1994). *Self-regulation of learning and performance: Issues and educational applications.* Hillsdale, NJ: Erlbaum.

Schunk, D. H., & Zimmerman, B. J. (1997). Social origins of self-regulatory competence. *Educational Psychologist, 32,* 195–208.

Schutz, P. A. (1994). Goals as the transactive point between motivation and cognition. In P. R. Pintrich, D. R. Brown, & C. E. Weinstein (Eds.), *Student motivation, cognition, and learning: Essays in honor of Wilbert J. McKeachie.* Hillsdale, NJ: Erlbaum.

Schutz, P. A., & Davis, H. A. (2000). Emotions and self-regulation during test taking. *Educational Psychologist, 35,* 243–256.

Schwartz, B., & Reisberg, D. (1991). *Learning and memory.* New York: Norton.

Schwartz, D., Dodge, K. A., Coie, J. D., Hubbard, J. A., Cillesen, A. H., Lemerise, E. A., & Bateman, H. (1998). Social-cognitive and behavioral correlates of aggression and victimization in boys' play groups. *Journal of Abnormal Child Psychology, 26,* 431–440.

Schwartz, D., Dodge, K. A., Pettit, G. S., & Bates, J. E. (1997). The early socialization of aggressive victims of bullying. *Child Development, 68,* 665–675.

Schwartz, D., McFadyen-Ketchum, S., Dodge, K. A., Pettit, G. S., & Bates, J. E. (1999). Early behavior problems as a predictor of later peer victimization: Moderators and mediators in the pathways of social risk. *Journal of Abnormal Child Psychology, 27,* 191–201.

Schwarz, B. B., Neuman, Y., & Biezuner, S. (2000). Two wrongs may make a right . . . if they argue together! *Cognition and Instruction, 18,* 461–494.

Schwebel, A. I., & Cherlin, D. L. (1972). Physical and social distancing in teacher-pupil relationships. *Journal of Educational Psychology, 63,* 543–550.

Scott, J., & Bushell, D. (1974). The length of teacher contacts and students' off-task behavior. *Journal of Applied Behavior Analysis, 7,* 39–44.

Scott-Jones, D. (1984). Family influences on cognitive development and school achievement. In E. W. Gordon (Ed.), *Review of research in education* (Vol. 11). Washington, DC: American Educational Research Association.

Scruggs, T. E., & Mastropieri, M. A. (1989). Mnemonic instruction of learning disabled students: A field-based evaluation. *Learning Disabilities Quarterly, 12,* 119–125.

Scruggs, T. E., & Mastropieri, M. A. (1992). Classroom applications of mnemonic instruction: Acquisition, maintenance, and generalization. *Exceptional Children, 58,* 219–229.

Scruggs, T. E., & Mastropieri, M. A. (1994). Successful mainstreaming in elementary science classes: A qualitative study of three reputational cases. *American Educational Research Journal, 31,* 785–811.

Seaton, E., Rodriguez, A., Jacobson, L., Taylor, R., Caintic, R., & Dale, P. (1999, April). *Influence of economic resources on family organization and achievement in economically disadvantaged African-American families.* Paper presented at the annual meeting of the American Educational Research Association, Montreal, Canada.

Seeley, K. (1989). Facilitators for the gifted. In J. Feldhusen, J. VanTassel-Baska, & K. Seeley, *Excellence in educating the gifted.* Denver, CO: Love.

Seligman, M. E. P. (1975). *Helplessness: On depression, development, and death.* San Francisco: Freeman.

Seligman, M. E. P. (1991). *Learned optimism.* New York: Knopf.

Selman, R. L. (1980). *The growth of interpersonal understanding.* San Diego, CA: Academic Press.

Selman, R. L., & Byrne, D. F. (1974). A structural-developmental analysis of levels of role taking in middle childhood. *Child Development, 45,* 803–806.

Selman, R. L., & Schultz, L. H. (1990). *Making a friend in youth.* Chicago: University of Chicago Press.

Semb, G. B., & Ellis, J. A. (1994). Knowledge taught in school: What is remembered? *Review of Educational Research, 64,* 253–286.

Semb, G. B., Ellis, J. A., & Araujo, J. (1993). Long-term memory for knowledge learned in school. *Journal of Educational Psychology, 85,* 305–316.

Semmel, M. I., Gottlieb, J., & Robinson, N. M. (1979). Mainstreaming: Perspectives on educating handicapped children in the public school. In D. C. Berliner (Ed.), *Review of research in education* (Vol. 7). Washington, DC: American Educational Research Association.

Sfard, A. (1998). On two metaphors for learning and the dangers of choosing just one. *Educational Researcher, 27*(2), 4–13.

Shachar, H., & Sharan, S. (1994). Talking, relating, and achieving: Effects of cooperative learning and whole-class instruction. *Cognition and Instruction, 12,* 313–353.

Shaffer, D. R. (1988). *Social and personality development* (2nd ed.). Pacific Grove, CA: Brooks/Cole.

Shatz, M., & Gelman, R. (1973). The development of communication skills: Modifications in the speech of young children as a function of the listener. *Monographs of the Society for Research in Child Development, 38*(5, Serial No. 152).

Shavelson, R. J., & Baxter, G. P. (1992). What we've learned about assessing hands-on science. *Educational Leadership, 49*(8), 20–25.

Shavelson, R. J., Baxter, G. P., & Pine, J. (1992). Performance assessments: Political rhetoric and measurement reality. *Educational Researcher, 21*(4), 22–27.

Sheffield, F. D., Wulff, J. J., & Backer, R. (1951). Reward value of copulation without sex drive reduction. *Journal of Comparative and Physiological Psychology, 44,* 3–8.

Sheldon, A. (1974). The role of parallel function in the acquisition of relative clauses in English. *Journal of Verbal Learning and Verbal Behavior, 13,* 272–281.

Shepard, L. A. (2000). The role of assessment in a learning culture. *Educational Researcher, 29*(7), 4–14.

Shepard, R. N., & Metzler, J. (1971). Mental rotation of three-dimensional objects. *Science, 171,* 701–703.

Sherif, M., Harvey, O. J., White, B. J., Hood, W. R., & Sherif, C. (1961). *Inter-group conflict and cooperation: The Robbers Cave experiment.* Norman: University of Oklahoma Press.

Shernoff, D. J., Knauth, S., & Makris, E. (2000). The quality of classroom experiences. In M. Csikszentmihalyi & B. Schneider, *Becoming adult: How teenagers prepare for the world of work.* New York: Basic Books.

Sherrill, D., Horowitz, B., Friedman, S. T., & Salisbury, J. L. (1970). Seating aggregation as an index of contagion. *Educational and Psychological Measurement, 30,* 663–668.

Shih, S. S., & Alexander, J. M. (2000). Interacting effects of goal setting and self- or other-referenced feedback on children's development of self-efficacy and cognitive skill within the Taiwanese classroom. *Journal of Educational Psychology, 92,* 536–543.

Shipman, S., & Shipman, V. C. (1985). Cognitive styles: Some conceptual, methodological, and applied issues. In E. W. Gordon (Ed.), *Review of research in education* (Vol. 12). Washington, DC: American Educational Research Association.

Shoda, Y., Mischel, W., & Peake, P. K. (1990). Predicting adolescent cognitive and self-regulatory competencies from preschool delay of gratification: Identifying diagnostic conditions. *Developmental Psychology, 26,* 978–986.

Short, E. J., Schatschneider, C. W., & Friebert, S. E. (1993). Relationship between memory and metamemory performance: A comparison of specific and general strategy knowledge. *Journal of Educational Psychology, 85,* 412–423.

Shrager, L., & Mayer, R. E. (1989). Note-taking fosters generative learning strategies in novices. *Journal of Educational Psychology, 81,* 263–264.

Shrigley, R. L. (1979). Strategies in classroom management. *NASSP Bulletin, 63*(428), 1–9.

Shrum, W., & Cheek, N. H. (1987). Social structure during the school years: Onset of the degrouping process. *American Sociological Review, 52,* 218–223.

Shuell, T. J. (1996). Teaching and learning in a classroom context. In D. C. Berliner & R. C. Calfee (Eds.), *Handbook of educational psychology.* New York: Macmillan.

Shulman, L. S. (1986). Those who understand: Knowledge growth in teaching. *Educational Researcher, 15,* 4–14.

Shulman, L. S., & Quinlan, K. M. (1996). The comparative psychology of school subjects. In D. C. Berliner & R. C. Calfee (Eds.), *Handbook of educational psychology.* New York: Macmillan.

Shulman, S., Elicker, J., & Sroufe, L. A. (1994). Stages of friendship growth in preadolescence as related to attachment history. *Journal of Social and Personal Relationships, 11,* 341–361.

Shure, M. B., & Spivack, G. (1980). Interpersonal problem-solving as a mediator of behavioral adjustment in preschool and kindergarten children. *Journal of Applied Developmental Psychology, 1,* 29–44.

Shweder, R. A., Mahapatra, M., & Miller, J. G. (1987). Culture and moral development. In J. Kagan & S. Lamb (Eds.), *The emergence of morality in young children* (pp. 1–83). Chicago: University of Chicago Press.

Shymansky, J. A., Hedges, L. V., & Woodworth, G. (1990). A reassessment of the effects of inquiry-based science curricula of the 60s on student performance. *Journal of Research in Science Teaching, 27,* 127–144.

Sieber, J. E., Kameya, L. I., & Paulson, F. L. (1970). Effect of memory support on the problem-solving ability of test-anxious children. *Journal of Educational Psychology, 61,* 159–168.

Siegel, L., & Hodkin, B. (1982). The garden path to the understanding of cognitive development: Has Piaget led us into the poison ivy? In S. Modgil & C. Modgil (Eds.), *Jean Piaget: Consensus and controversy.* New York: Praeger.

Siegler, R. S. (1998). *Children's thinking* (3rd ed.). Upper Saddle River, NJ: Prentice Hall.

Siegler, R. S., & Richards, D. D. (1982). The development of intelligence. In R. J. Sternberg (Ed.), *Handbook of human intelligence.* Cambridge, England: Cambridge University Press.

Sigman, M., & Whaley, S. E. (1998). The role of nutrition in the development of intelligence. In U. Neisser (Ed.), *The rising curve: Long-term gains in IQ and related measures* (pp. 155–182). Washington, DC: American Psychological Association.

Silberman, M. L., & Wheelan, S. A. (1980). *How to discipline without feeling guilty: Assertive relationships with children.* Champaign, IL: Research Press.

Silver, E. A., & Kenney, P. A. (1995). Sources of assessment information for instructional guidance in mathematics. In T. Romberg (Ed.), *Reform in school mathematics and authentic assessment.* Albany, NY: State University of New York Press.

Simon, H. A. (1974). How big is a chunk? *Science, 183,* 482–488.

Simons, R. L., Whitbeck, L. B., Conger, R. D., & Conger, K. J. (1991). Parenting factors, social skills, and value commitments as precursors to school failure, involvement with deviant peers, and delinquent behavior. *Journal of Youth and Adolescence, 20,* 645–664.

Simonton, D. K. (2000). Creativity: Cognitive, personal, developmental, and social aspects. *American Psychologist, 55,* pp. 151–158.

Simonton, D. K. (2001). Talent development as a multidimensional, multiplicative, and dynamic process. *Current Directions in Psychological Science, 10,* 39–42.

Singer, D. G., & Singer, J. L. (1994). *Barney & Friends as education and entertainment: Phase 3. A national study: Can preschoolers learn through exposure to Barney & Friends?* New Haven, CT: Yale University Family Television Research and Consultation Center.

Singley, M. K., & Anderson, J. R. (1989). *The transfer of cognitive skill.* Cambridge, MA: Harvard University Press.

Sisk, D. A. (1989). Identifying and nurturing talent among American Indians. In C. J. Maker & S. W. Schiever (Eds.), *Critical issues in gifted education: Vol. 2. Defensible programs for cultural and ethnic minorities.* Austin, TX: Pro-Ed.

Sitko, B. M. (1998). Knowing how to write: Metacognition and writing instruction. In D. J. Hacker, J. Dunlosky, & A. C. Graesser (Eds.), *Metacognition in educational theory and practice* (pp. 93–115). Mahwah, NJ: Erlbaum.

Sizer, T. R. (1992). *Horace's school: Redesigning the American high school.* Boston: Houghton Mifflin.

Skaalvik, E. (1997). Self-enhancing and self-defeating ego orientation: Relations with task avoidance orientation, achievement, self-perceptions, and anxiety. *Journal of Educational Psychology, 89,* 71–81.

Skiba, R., & Raison, J. (1990). Relationship between the use of time-out and academic achievement. *Exceptional Children, 57,* 36–46.

Skinner, B. F. (1953). *Science and human behavior.* New York: Macmillan.

Skinner, B. F. (1954). The science of learning and the art of teaching. *Harvard Educational Review, 24,* 86–97.

Skinner, B. F. (1968). *The technology of teaching.* New York: Appleton-Century-Crofts.

Slaughter-Defoe, D. T. (2001). A longitudinal case study of Head Start eligible children: Implications for urban education. *Educational Psychologist, 36,* 31–44.

Slavin, R. E. (1983). When does cooperative learning increase student achievement? *Psychological Bulletin, 94,* 429–445.

Slavin, R. E. (1987). Ability grouping and student achievement in elementary schools: A best-evidence synthesis. *Review of Educational Research, 57,* 293–336.

Slavin, R. E. (1989). Students at risk of school failure: The problem and its dimensions. In R. E. Slavin, N. L. Karweit, & N. A. Madden (Eds.), *Effective programs for students at risk.* Needham Heights, MA: Allyn & Bacon.

Slavin, R. E. (1990). *Cooperative learning: Theory, research, and practice.* Upper Saddle River, NJ: Prentice Hall.

Slavin, R. E., Karweit, N. L., & Madden, N. A. (Eds.). (1989). *Effective programs for students at risk.* Needham Heights, MA: Allyn & Bacon.

Slavin, R. E., Madden, N. A., & Karweit, N. L. (1989). Effective programs for students at risk: Conclusions for practice and policy. In R. E. Slavin, N. L. Karweit, & N. A. Madden (Eds.), *Effective programs for students at risk.* Boston: Allyn & Bacon.

Sleeter, C. E., & Grant, C. A. (1999). *Making choices for multicultural education: Five approaches to race, class, and gender* (3rd ed.). Upper Saddle River, NJ: Merrill/Prentice Hall.

Slife, B. R., Weiss, J., & Bell, T. (1985). Separability of metacognition and cognition: Problem solving in learning disabled and regular students. *Journal of Educational Psychology, 77,* 437–445.

Slusher, M. P., & Anderson, C. A. (1996). Using causal persuasive arguments to change beliefs and teach new information: The mediating role of explanation availability and evaluation bias in the acceptance of knowledge. *Journal of Educational Psychology, 88,* 110–122.

Small, M. Y., Lovett, S. B., & Scher, M. S. (1993). Pictures facilitate children's recall of unillustrated expository prose. *Journal of Educational Psychology, 85,* 520–528.

Small, R. V., & Grabowski, B. L. (1992). An exploratory study of information-seeking behaviors and learning with hypermedia information systems. *Journal of Educational Multimedia and Hypermedia, 1,* 445–464.

Smetana, J. G. (1981). Preschool children's conceptions of moral and social rules. *Child Development, 52,* 1333–1336.

Smetana, J. G. (1983). Social-cognitive development: Domain distinctions and coordinations. *Developmental Review, 3,* 131–147.

Smith, C. L., Maclin, D., Grosslight, L., & Davis, H. (1997). Teaching for understanding: A study of students' preinstruction theories of matter and a comparison of the effectiveness of two approaches to teaching about matter and density. *Cognition and Instruction, 15,* 317–393.

Smith, C. L., Maclin, D., Houghton, C., & Hennessey, M. G. (2000). Sixth-grade students' epistemologies of science: The impact of school science experiences on epistemological development. *Cognition and Instruction, 18,* 349–422.

Smith, D. C., & Neale, D. C. (1991). The construction of subject-matter knowledge in primary science teaching. In J. Brophy (Ed.), *Advances in research on teaching: Vol. 2. Teacher's knowledge of subject matter as it relates to their teaching practice.* Greenwich, CT: JAI Press.

Smith, D. J., Young, K. R., West, R. P., Morgan, R. P., & Rhode, G. (1988). Reducing the disruptive behavior of junior high school students: A classroom self-management procedure. *Behavioral Disorders, 13,* 231–239.

Smith, E. E. (2000). Neural bases of human working memory. *Current Directions in Psychological Science, 9,* 45–49.

Smith, H. L. (1998). Literacy and instruction in African American communities: Shall we overcome? In B. Pérez (Ed.), *Sociocultural contexts of language and literacy.* Mahwah, NJ: Erlbaum.

Smith, J., & Russell, G. (1984). Why do males and females differ? Children's beliefs about sex differences. *Sex Roles, 11,* 1111–1120.

Smith, K., Johnson, D. W., & Johnson, R. T. (1981). Can conflict be constructive? Controversy versus concurrence seeking in learning groups. *Journal of Educational Psychology, 73,* 651–663.

Smith, M. U. (1991). A view from biology. In M. U. Smith (Ed.), *Toward a unified theory of problem solving: Views from the content domains.* Hillsdale, NJ: Erlbaum.

Smith, P. B., & Bond, M. H. (1994). *Social psychology across cultures: Analysis and perspectives.* Needham Heights, MA: Allyn & Bacon.

Smith, R. E., & Smoll, F. L. (1997). Coaching the coaches: Youth sports as a scientific and applied behavioral setting. *Current Directions in Psychological Science, 6*(1), 16–21.

Smitherman, G. (1994). "The blacker the berry the sweeter the juice": African American student writers. In A. H. Dyson & C. Genishi (Eds.), *The need for story: Cultural diversity in classroom and community.* Urbana, IL: National Council of Teachers of English.

Snarey, J. (1995). In a communitarian voice: The sociological expansion of Kohlbergian theory, research, and practice. In W. M. Kurtines & J. L. Gewirtz (Eds.), *Moral development: An introduction.* Boston: Allyn & Bacon.

Sneider, C., & Pulos, S. (1983). Children's cosmographies: Understanding the earth's shape and gravity. *Science Education, 67,* 205–221.

Snow, C. E. (1990). Rationales for native language instruction: Evidence from research. In A. M. Padilla, H. H. Fairchild, & C. M. Valadez (Eds.), *Bilingual education: Issues and strategies.* Newbury Park, CA: Sage.

Snow, R. E., Corno, L., & Jackson, D., III. (1996). Individual differences in affective and conative functions. In D. C. Berliner & R. C. Calfee (Eds.), *Handbook of educational psychology.* New York: Macmillan.

Solnick, J. V., Rincover, A., & Peterson, C. R. (1977). Some determinants of the reinforcing and punishing effects of timeout. *Journal of Applied Behavior Analysis, 10,* 415–424.

Sosniak, L. A., & Stodolsky, S. S. (1994). Making connections: Social studies education in an urban fourth-grade classroom. In J. Brophy (Ed.), *Advances in research on teaching: Vol. 4. Case studies of teaching and learning in social studies.* Greenwich, CT: JAI Press.

Sowell, E. R., & Jernigan, T. L. (1998). Further MRI evidence of late brain maturation: Limbic volume increases and changing asymmetries during childhood and adolescence. *Developmental Neuropsychology, 14,* 599–617.

Sowell, E. R., Thompson, P. M., Holmes, C. J., Jernigan, T. L., & Toga, A. W. (1999). *In vivo* evidence for post-adolescent brain maturation in frontal and striatal regions. *Nature Neuroscience, 2,* 859–861.

Spandel, V. (1997). Reflections on portfolios. In G. D. Phye (Ed.), *Handbook of academic learning: Construction of knowledge.* San Diego, CA: Academic Press.

Spaulding, C. L. (1992). *Motivation in the classroom.* New York: McGraw-Hill.

Spear, L. P. (2000). Neurobehavioral changes in adolescence. *Current Directions in Psychological Science, 9,* 11–114.

Spearman, C. (1904). General intelligence, objectively determined and measured. *American Journal of Psychology, 15,* 201–293.

Spearman, C. (1927). *The abilities of man: Their nature and measurement.* New York: Macmillan.

Spencer, M. B., & Markstrom-Adams, C. (1990). Identity processes among racial and ethnic minority children in America. *Child Development, 61,* 290–310.

Sperling, G. (1967). Successive approximations to a model for short-term memory. *Acta Psychologia, 27,* 285–292.

Spicker, H. H. (1992). Identifying and enriching: Rural gifted children. *Educational Horizons, 70*(2), 60–65.

Spires, H. A. (1990, April). *Learning from a lecture: Effects of comprehension monitoring.* Paper presented at the annual meeting of the American Educational Research Association, Boston.

Spires, H. A., & Donley, J. (1998). Prior knowledge activation: Inducing engagement with informational texts. *Journal of Educational Psychology, 90,* 249–260.

Spires, H. A., Donley, J., & Penrose, A. M. (1990, April). *Prior knowledge activation: Inducing text engagement in reading to learn.* Paper presented at the annual meeting of the American Educational Research Association, Boston.

Spivey, N. N. (1997). *The constructivist metaphor: Reading, writing, and the making of meaning.* San Diego, CA: Academic Press.

Sprafkin, C., Serbin, L. A., Denier, C., & Connor, J. M. (1983). Sex-differentiated play: Cognitive consequences and early interventions. In M. B. Liss (Ed.), *Social and cognitive skills: Sex roles and children's play.* San Diego, CA: Academic Press.

Sroufe, L. A. (1983). Infant-caregiver attachment and patterns of adaptation in preschool: The roots of maladaptation. In M. Perlmutter (Ed.), *Minnesota Symposia on Child Psychology: Vol. 16. Development and policy concerning children with special needs.* Hillsdale, NJ: Erlbaum.

Sroufe, L. A., Carlson, E., & Shulman, S. (1993). Individuals in relationships: Development from infancy through adolescence. In D. C. Funder, R. D. Parke, C. Tomlinson-Keasey, & K. Widaman (Eds.), *Studying lives through time: Personality and development* (pp. 315–342). Washington, DC: American Psychological Association.

Stacey, K. (1992). Mathematical problem solving in groups: Are two heads better than one? *Journal of Mathematical Behavior, 11,* 261–275.

Stack, C. B., & Burton, L. M. (1993). Kinscripts. *Journal of Comparative Family Studies, 24,* 157–170.

Stainback, S., & Stainback, W. (Eds.). (1985). *Integrating students with severe handicaps into regular schools.* Reston, VA: Council for Exceptional Children.

Stainback, S., & Stainback, W. (1990). Inclusive schooling. In W. Stainback & S. Stainback (Eds.), *Support networks for inclusive schooling: Interdependent integrated education.* Baltimore: Brookes.

Stainback, S., & Stainback, W. (1992). Schools as inclusive communities. In W. Stainback & S. Stainback (Eds.), *Controversial issues confronting special education: Divergent perspectives.* Needham Heights, MA: Allyn & Bacon.

Stainback, W., & Stainback, S. (1992). *Controversial issues confronting special education: Divergent perspectives.* Boston: Allyn & Bacon.

Stanley, J. C. (1980). On educating the gifted. *Educational Researcher, 9*(3), 8–12.

Stanovich, K. E. (1998). Cognitive neuroscience and educational psychology: What season is it? *Educational Psychology Review, 10,* 419–426.

Stanovich, K. E. (2000). *Progress in understanding reading: Scientific foundations and new frontiers.* New York: Guilford Press.

Starr, E. J., & Lovett, S. B. (2000). The ability to distinguish between comprehension and memory: Failing to succeed. *Journal of Educational Psychology, 92,* 761–771.

Staub, D. (1998). *Delicate threads: Friendships between children with and without special needs in inclusive settings.* Bethesda, MD: Woodbine House.

Staub, E. (1995). The roots of prosocial and antisocial behavior in persons and groups: Environmental influence, personality, culture, and socialization. In W. M. Kurtines & J. L. Gewirtz (Eds.), *Moral development: An introduction.* Boston: Allyn & Bacon.

Steffensen, M. S., Joag-Dev, C., & Anderson, R. C. (1979). A cross-cultural perspective on reading comprehension. *Reading Research Quarterly, 15,* 10–29.

Steinberg, E. R. (1989). Cognition and learner control: A literature review, 1977–1988. *Journal of Computer-Based Instruction, 16*(4), 117–121.

Steinberg, L. (1996). *Beyond the classroom: Why school reform has failed and what parents need to do.* New York: Touchstone.

Steinberg, L., Blinde, P. L., & Chan, K. S. (1984). Dropping out among language minority youth. *Review of Educational Research, 54,* 113–132.

Steinberg, L., Elmen, J., & Mounts, N. (1989). Authoritative parenting, psychosocial maturity, and academic success among adolescents. *Child Development, 60,* 1424–1436.

Stepans, J. (1991). Developmental patterns in students' understanding of physics concepts. In S. M. Glynn, R. H. Yeany, & B. K. Britton (Eds.), *The psychology of learning science.* Hillsdale, NJ: Erlbaum.

Stephens, T. M., Blackhurst, A. E., & Magliocca, L. A. (1988). *Teaching mainstreamed students* (2nd ed.). Oxford, England: Pergamon Press.

Sternberg, R. J. (1984). Toward a triarchic theory of human intelligence. *Behavioral and Brain Sciences, 7,* 269–287.

Sternberg, R. J. (1985). *Beyond IQ: A triarchic theory of human intelligence.* Cambridge, England: Cambridge University Press.

Sternberg, R. J. (1996a). Educational psychology has fallen, but it can get up. *Educational Psychology Review, 8,* 175–185.

Sternberg, R. J. (1996b). Myths, countermyths, and truths about intelligence. *Educational Researcher, 25*(2), 11–16.

Sternberg, R. J. (1997). The concept of intelligence and its role in lifelong learning and success. *American Psychologist, 52,* 1030–1037.

Sternberg, R. J. (1998a). Abilities are forms of developing expertise. *Educational Researcher, 27*(3), 11–20.

Sternberg, R. J. (1998b). Teaching triarchically improves school achievement. *Journal of Educational Psychology, 90,* 374–384.

Sternberg, R. J., & Detterman, D. K. (Eds.). (1986). *What is intelligence? Contemporary views on its nature and definition.* Norwood, NJ: Ablex.

Sternberg, R. J., Forsythe, G. B., Hedlund, J., Horvath, J. A., Wagner, R. K., Williams, W. M., Snook, S. A., & Grigorenko, E. L. (2000). *Practical intelligence in everyday life.* Cambridge, England: Cambridge University Press.

Sternberg, R. J., & Frensch, P. A. (1993). Mechanisms of transfer. In D. K. Detterman & R. J. Sternberg (Eds.), *Transfer on trial: Intelligence, cognition, and instruction.* Norwood, NJ: Ablex.

Sternberg, R. J., & Horvath, J. A. (1995). A prototype view of expert teaching. *Educational Researcher, 24*(6), 9–17.

Sternberg, R. J., & Wagner, R. K. (Eds.). (1994). *Mind in context: Interactionist perspectives on human intelligence.* Cambridge, England: Cambridge University Press.

Sternberg, R. J., & Zhang, L. (1995). What do we mean by giftedness? A pentagonal implicit theory. *Gifted Child Quarterly, 39,* 88–94.

Steuer, F. B., Applefield, J. M., & Smith, R. (1971). Televised aggression and the interpersonal aggression of preschool children. *Journal of Experimental Child Psychology, 11,* 442–447.

Stevahn, L., Johnson, D. W., Johnson, R. T., & Real, D. (1996). The impact of a cooperative or individualistic context on the effectiveness of conflict resolution training. *American Educational Research Journal, 33,* 801–823.

Stevahn, L., Oberle, K., Johnson, D. W., & Johnson, R. T. (2001, April). *Effects of role reversal training and use of integrative negotiation for classroom management on conflict resolution in kindergarten.* Paper presented at the annual meeting of the American Educational Research Association, Seattle, WA.

Stevens, J. J., & Clauser, P. (1996, April). *Longitudinal examination of a writing portfolio and the ITBS.* Paper presented at the annual meeting of the American Educational Research Association, New York.

Stevens, R. J., & Slavin, R. E. (1995). The cooperative elementary school: Effects of students' achievement, attitudes, and social relations. *American Educational Research Journal, 32,* 321–351.

Stevenson, H. C., & Fantuzzo, J. W. (1986). The generality and social validity of a competency-based self-control training intervention for underachieving students. *Journal of Applied Behavior Analysis, 19,* 269–272.

Stevenson, H. W., Chen, C., & Uttal, D. H. (1990). Beliefs and achievement: A study of black, white, and Hispanic children. *Child Development, 61,* 508–523.

Stewart, L., & Pascual–Leone, J. (1992). Mental capacity constraints and the development of moral reasoning. *Journal of Experimental Child Psychology, 54,* 251–287.

Stice, E., & Barrera, M., Jr. (1995). A longitudinal examination of the reciprocal relations between perceived parenting and adolescents' substance use and externalizing behaviors. *Developmental Psychology, 31,* 322–334.

Stiggins, R. J. (2001). *Student-involved classroom assessment* (3rd ed.). Upper Saddle River, NJ: Merrill/Prentice Hall.

Stiggins, R. J., & Conklin, N. F. (1992). *In teachers' hands: Investigating the practices of classroom assessment.* Albany: State University of New York Press.

Stipek, D. J. (1981). Children's perceptions of their own and their classmates' ability. *Journal of Educational Psychology, 73,* 404–410.

Stipek, D. J. (1984). Sex differences in children's attributions for success and failure on math and spelling tests. *Sex Roles, 11,* 969–981.

Stipek, D. J. (1993). *Motivation to learn: From theory to practice* (2nd ed.). Needham Heights, MA: Allyn & Bacon.

Stipek, D. J. (1996). Motivation and instruction. In D. C. Berliner & R. C. Calfee (Eds.), *Handbook of educational psychology.* New York: Macmillan.

Stipek, D. J., & Gralinski, H. (1990, April). *Gender differences in children's achievement-related beliefs and emotional responses to success and failure in math.* Paper presented at the annual meeting of the American Educational Research Association, Boston.

Stodolsky, S. S., Salk, S., & Glaessner, B. (1991). Student views about learning math and social studies. *American Educational Research Journal, 28,* 89–116.

Stone, N. J. (2000). Exploring the relationship between calibration and self-regulated learning. *Educational Psychology Review, 12*, 437–475.

Strike, K. A., & Posner, G. J. (1992). A revisionist theory of conceptual change. In R. A. Duschl & R. J. Hamilton (Eds.), *Philosophy of science, cognitive psychology, and educational theory and practice*. New York: State University of New York Press.

Sue, S., & Chin, R. (1983). The mental health of Chinese-American children: Stressors and resources. In G. J. Powell (Ed.), *The psychosocial development of minority children*. New York: Brunner/Mazel.

Suina, J. H., & Smolkin, L. B. (1994). From natal culture to school culture to dominant society culture: Supporting transitions for Pueblo Indian students. In P. M. Greenfield & R. R. Cocking (Eds.), *Cross-cultural roots of minority child development*. Hillsdale, NJ: Erlbaum.

Sullivan, J. S. (1989). Planning, implementing, and maintaining an effective in-school suspension program. *Clearing House, 62*, 409–410.

Sullivan, R. C. (1994). Autism: Definitions past and present. *Journal of Vocational Rehabilitation, 4*, 4–9.

Sullivan-DeCarlo, C., DeFalco, K., & Roberts, V. (1998). Helping students avoid risky behavior. *Educational Leadership, 56*(1), 80–82.

Sund, R. B. (1976). *Piaget for educators*. Upper Saddle River, NJ: Merrill/Prentice Hall.

Suttles, G. D. (1970). Friendship as a social institution. In G. J. McCall, M. McCall, N. K. Denzin, G. D. Scuttles, & S. Kurth (Eds.), *Social relationships* (pp. 95–135). Chicago: Aldine de Gruyter.

Sutton-Smith, B. (Ed.). (1979). *Play and learning*. New York: Gardner Press.

Swan, K., Mitrani, M., Guerrero, F., Cheung, M., & Schoener, J. (1990, April). *Perceived locus of control and computer-based instruction*. Paper presented at the annual meeting of the American Educational Research Association, Boston.

Swanborn, M. S. L., & de Glopper, K. (1999). Incidental word learning while reading: A meta-analysis. *Review of Educational Research, 69*, 261–285.

Swanson, D. B., Norman, G. R., & Linn, R. L. (1995). Performance-based assessment: Lessons from the health professions. *Educational Researcher, 24*(5), 5–11, 35.

Swanson, H. L. (1993). An information processing analysis of learning disabled children's problem solving. *American Educational Research Journal, 30*, 861–893.

Swanson, H. L., Cooney, J. B., & O'Shaughnessy, T. E. (1998). Learning disabilities and memory. In B. Y. L. Wong (Ed.), *Learning about learning disabilities* (2nd ed.). San Diego, CA: Academic Press.

Swanson, H. L., O'Connor, J. E., & Cooney, J. B. (1990). An information processing analysis of expert and novice teachers' problem solving. *American Educational Research Journal, 27*, 533–556.

Tamburrini, J. (1982). Some educational implications of Piaget's theory. In S. Modgil & C. Modgil (Eds.), *Jean Piaget: Consensus and controversy*. New York: Praeger.

Tarver, S. G. (1992). Direct Instruction. In W. Stainback & S. Stainback (Eds.), *Controversial issues confronting special education*. Boston: Allyn & Bacon.

Tate, W. F. (1995). Returning to the root: A culturally relevant approach to mathematics pedagogy. *Theory into Practice, 34*, 166–173.

Taylor, B. A., & Levin, L. (1998). Teaching a student with autism to make verbal initiations:

Effects of a tactile prompt. *Journal of Applied Behavior Analysis, 31*, 651–654.

Taylor, B. M. (1982). Text structure and children's comprehension and memory for expository material. *Journal of Educational Psychology, 74*, 323–340.

Taylor, I. A. (1976). A retrospective view of creativity investigation. In I. A. Taylor & J. W. Getzels (Eds.), *Perspectives in creativity*. Chicago: Aldine de Gruyter.

Taylor, J. C., & Romanczyk, R. G. (1994). Generating hypotheses about the function of student problem behavior by observing teacher behavior. *Journal of Applied Behavior Analysis, 27*, 251–265.

Taylor, S. M. (1994, April). *Staying in school against the odds: Voices of minority adolescent girls*. Paper presented at the annual meeting of the American Educational Research Association, New Orleans, LA.

Tennyson, R. D., & Cocchiarella, M. J. (1986). An empirically based instructional design theory for teaching concepts. *Review of Educational Research, 56*, 40–71.

Terwilliger, J. S. (1989). Classroom standard setting and grading practices. *Educational Measurement: Issues and Practices, 8*(2), 15–19.

Tessler, M., & Nelson, K. (1994). Making memories: The influence of joint encoding on later recall by young children. *Consciousness and Cognition, 3*, 307–326.

Tharp, R. G. (1989). Psychocultural variables and constants: Effects on teaching and learning in schools. *American Psychologist, 44*, 349–359.

Tharp, R. G. (1994). Intergroup differences among Native Americans in socialization and child cognition: An ethnogenetic analysis. In P. M. Greenfield & R. R. Cocking (Eds.), *Cross-cultural roots of minority child development*. Hillsdale, NJ: Erlbaum.

Théberge, C. L. (1994, April). *Small-group vs. whole-class discussion: Gaining the floor in science lessons*. Paper presented at the annual meeting of the American Educational Research Association, New Orleans, LA.

Thomas, J. R., & French, K. E. (1985). Gender differences across age in motor performance: A meta-analysis. *Psychological Bulletin, 98*, 260–282.

Thomas, J. W. (1993a). Expectations and effort: Course demands, students' study practices, and academic achievement. In T. M. Tomlinson (Ed.), *Motivating students to learn: Overcoming barriers to high achievement*. Berkeley, CA: McCutchan.

Thomas, J. W. (1993b). Promoting independent learning in the middle grades: The role of instructional support practices. *Elementary School Journal, 93*, 575–591.

Thomas, S., & Oldfather, P. (1997). Intrinsic motivations, literacy, and assessment practices: "That's my grade. That's me." *Educational Psychologist, 32*, 107–123.

Thomas, S. P., Groër, M., & Droppleman, P. (1993). Physical health of today's school children. *Educational Psychology Review, 5*, 5–33.

Thomas, W. P., Collier, V. P., & Abbott, M. (1993). Academic achievement through Japanese, Spanish, or French: The first two years of partial immersion. *Modern Language Journal, 77*, 170–179.

Thompson, A. G., & Thompson, P. W. (1989). Affect and problem solving in an elementary school mathematics classroom. In D. B. McLeod & V. M. Adams (Eds.), *Affect and mathematical problem solving: A new perspective*. New York: Springer-Verlag.

Thompson, H., & Carr, M. (1995, April). *Brief metacognitive intervention and interest as predictors of memory for text*. Paper presented at the

annual meeting of the American Educational Research Association, San Francisco.

Thompson, R. A. (1998). Early sociopersonality development. In W. Damon (Ed.), *Handbook of child psychology* (5th ed.). New York: Wiley.

Thompson, R. A., & Nelson, C. A. (2001). Developmental science and the media: Early brain development. *American Psychologist, 56*, pp. 5–15.

Thompson, R. A., & Wyatt, J. M. (1999). Current research on child maltreatment: Implications for educators. *Educational Psychology Review, 11*, 173–201.

Thompson, R. F. (1985). *The brain: An introduction to neuroscience*. New York: Freeman.

Thorndike, E. L. (1924). Mental discipline in high school studies. *Journal of Educational Psychology, 15*, 1–22, 83–98.

Thorndike, R. M. (1997). *Measurement and evaluation in psychology and education* (6th ed.). Upper Saddle River, NJ: Merrill/Prentice Hall.

Thousand, J. S., Villa, R. A., & Nevin, A. I. (1994). *Creativity and collaborative learning: A practical guide for empowering students and teachers*. Baltimore: Brookes.

Threadgill-Sowder, J. (1985). Individual differences and mathematical problem solving. In E. A. Silver (Ed.), *Teaching and learning mathematical problem solving: Multiple research perspectives*. Hillsdale, NJ: Erlbaum.

Thurstone, L. L. (1938). *Primary mental abilities*. Chicago: University of Chicago Press.

Thurstone, L. L., & Jeffrey, T. E. (1956). *FLAGS: A test of space thinking*. Chicago: Industrial Relations Center.

Tirosh, D., & Graeber, A. O. (1990). Evoking cognitive conflict to explore preservice teachers' thinking about division. *Journal for Research in Mathematics Education, 21*, 98–108.

Tisak, M. (1993). Preschool children's judgments of moral and personal events involving physical harm and property damage. *Merrill-Palmer Quarterly, 39*, 375–390.

Tobias, S. (1977). A model for research on the effect of anxiety on instruction. In J. E. Sieber, H. F. O'Neil, Jr., & S. Tobias (Eds.), *Anxiety, learning, and instruction*. Hillsdale, NJ: Erlbaum.

Tobias, S. (1980). Anxiety and instruction. In I. G. Sarason (Ed.), *Test anxiety: Theory, research, and applications*. Hillsdale, NJ: Erlbaum.

Tobias, S. (1985). Test anxiety: Interference, defective skills, and cognitive capacity. *Educational Psychologist, 20*, 135–142.

Tobias, S. (1994). Interest, prior knowledge, and learning. *Review of Educational Research, 64*, 37–54.

Tobin, K. (1987). The role of wait time in higher cognitive level learning. *Review of Educational Research, 57*, 69–95.

Tomasello, M. (2000). Culture and cognitive development. *Current Directions in Psychological Science, 9*, 37–40.

Tompkins, G. E., & McGee, L. M. (1986). Visually impaired and sighted children's emerging concepts about written language. In D. B. Yaden, Jr., & S. Templeton (Eds.), *Metalinguistic awareness and beginning literacy: Conceptualizing what it means to read and write*. Portsmouth, NH: Heinemann.

Torrance, E. P. (1970). *Encouraging creativity in the classroom*. Dubuque, IA: Wm. C. Brown.

Torrance, E. P. (1976). Creativity research in education: Still alive. In I. A. Taylor & J. W. Getzels (Eds.), *Perspectives in creativity*. Chicago: Aldine de Gruyter.

Torrance, E. P. (1989). A reaction to "Gifted black students: Curriculum and teaching strategies." In C. J. Maker & S. W. Schiever (Eds.), *Critical issues in gifted education: Vol. 2. Defensible* programs for cultural and ethnic minorities. Austin, TX: Pro-Ed.

Torrance, E. P. (1995). Insights about creativity: Questioned, rejected, ridiculed, ignored. *Educational Psychology Review, 7,* 313–322.

Torrance, E. P., & Myers, R. E. (1970). *Creative learning and teaching.* New York: Dodd, Mead.

Torres-Guzmán, M. E. (1998). Language, culture, and literacy in Puerto Rican communities. In B. Pérez (Ed.), *Sociocultural contexts of language and literacy.* Mahwah, NJ: Erlbaum.

Tourniaire, F., & Pulos, S. (1985). Proportional reasoning: A review of the literature. *Educational Studies in Mathematics, 16,* 181–204.

Traub, R. E. (1993). On the equivalence of the traits assessed by multiple-choice and constructed-response tests. In R. E. Bennett & W. C. Ward (Eds.), *Construction versus choice in cognitive measurement: Issues in constructed response, performance testing, and portfolio assessment* (pp. 29–44). Hillsdale, NJ: Erlbaum.

Trawick-Smith, J. (2000). *Early childhood development: A multicultural perspective* (2nd ed.). Upper Saddle River, NJ: Merrill/Prentice Hall.

Triandis, H. C. (1995). *Individualism and collectivism.* Boulder, CO: Westview Press.

Trueba, H. T. (1988). Peer socialization among minority students: A high school dropout prevention program. In H. T. Trueba & C. Delgado-Gaitan (Eds.), *School and society: Learning content through culture.* New York: Praeger.

Tryon, G. S. (1980). The measurement and treatment of anxiety. *Review of Educational Research, 50,* 343–372.

Tschannen-Moran, M., Woolfolk Hoy, A., & Hoy, W. K. (1998). Teacher efficacy: Its meaning and measure. *Review of Educational Research, 68,* 202–248.

Tucker, V. G., & Anderman, L. H. (1999, April). *Cycles of learning: Demonstrating the interplay between motivation, self-regulation, and cognition.* Paper presented at the annual meeting of the American Educational Research Association, Montreal, Canada.

Tudor, R. M. (1995). Isolating the effects of active responding in computer-based instruction. *Journal of Applied Behavior Analysis, 28,* 343–344.

Tulving, E. (1962). Subjective organization in free recall of "unrelated" words. *Psychological Review, 69,* 344–354.

Tulving, E. (1983). *Elements of episodic memory.* Oxford, England: Oxford University Press.

Tulving, E., & Thomson, D. M. (1973). Encoding specificity and retrieval processes in episodic memory. *Psychological Review, 80,* 352–373.

Turiel, E. (1983). *The development of social knowledge: Morality and convention.* Cambridge, England: Cambridge University Press.

Turiel, E. (1998). The development of morality. In W. Damon (Editor-in-Chief) & N. Eisenberg (Vol. Ed.), *Handbook of child psychology: Vol. 3. Social, emotional, and personality development* (5th ed., pp. 863–932). New York: Wiley.

Turiel, E., Smetana, J. G., & Killen, M. (1991). Social contexts in social cognitive development. In W. M. Kurtines & J. L. Gewirtz (Eds.), *Moral behavior and development: Vol. 2. Research.* Hillsdale, NJ: Erlbaum.

Turkheimer, E. (2000). Three laws of behavior genetics and what they mean. *Current Directions in Psychological Science, 9,* 160–164.

Turnbull, A. P. (1974). Teaching retarded persons to rehearse through cumulative overt labeling. *American Journal of Mental Deficiency, 79,* 331–337.

Turnbull, A. P., Pereira, L., & Blue-Banning, M. (2000). Teachers as friendship facilitators. *Teaching Exceptional Children, 32*(5), 66–70.

Turnbull, A., Turnbull, R., Shank, M., & Leal, D. (1999). *Exceptional lives: Special education in today's schools* (2nd ed.). Upper Saddle River, NJ: Merrill/Prentice Hall.

Turner, A. M., & Greenough, W. T. (1985). Differential rearing effects on rate visual cortex synapses. *Brain Research, 329,* 195–203.

Turner, J. C. (1995). The influence of classroom contexts on young children's motivation for literacy. *Reading Research Quarterly, 30,* 410–441.

Turner, J. C., Meyer, D. K., Cox, K. E., Logan, C., DiCintio, M., & Thomas, C. T. (1998). Creating contexts for involvement in mathematics. *Journal of Educational Psychology, 90,* 730–745.

Turner, J. C., Thorpe, P. K., & Meyer, D. K. (1998). Students' reports of motivation and negative affect: A theoretical and empirical analysis. *Journal of Educational Psychology, 90,* 758–771.

Tuttle, D. W., & Tuttle, N. R. (1996). *Self-esteem and adjusting with blindness: The process of responding to life's demands* (2nd ed.). Springfield, IL: Charles C Thomas.

Tyler, B. (1958). Expectancy for eventual success as a factor in problem solving behavior. *Journal of Educational Psychology, 49,* 166–172.

Tzuriel, D. (2000). Dynamic assessment of young children: Educational and intervention perspectives. *Educational Psychology Review, 12,* 385–435.

Udall, A. J. (1989). Curriculum for gifted Hispanic students. In C. J. Maker & S. W. Schiever (Eds.), *Critical issues in gifted education: Vol. 2. Defensible programs for cultural and ethnic minorities.* Austin, TX: Pro-Ed.

Ulichny, P. (1994, April). *Cultures in conflict.* Paper presented at the annual meeting of the American Educational Research Association, New Orleans, LA.

Underwood, B. J. (1948). "Spontaneous recovery" of verbal associations. *Journal of Experimental Psychology, 38,* 429–439.

Underwood, B. J. (1954). Studies of distributed practice: XII. Retention following varying degrees of original learning. *Journal of Experimental Psychology, 47,* 294–300.

Underwood, B. J. (1957). Interference and forgetting. *Psychological Review, 64,* 49–60.

Urdan, T. C. (1997). Achievement goal theory: Past results, future directions. In M. L. Maehr & P. R. Pintrich (Eds.), *Advances in motivation and achievement* (Vol. 10, pp. 99–141). Greenwich, CT: JAI Press.

Urdan, T. C., & Maehr, M. L. (1995). Beyond a two-goal theory of motivation and achievement: A case for social goals. *Review of Educational Research, 65,* 213–243.

Urdan, T., & Midgley, C. (2001). Academic self-handicapping: What we know, what more there is to learn. *Educational Psychology Review, 13,* 115–138.

Urdan, T. C., Midgley, C., & Anderman, E. M. (1998). The role of classroom goal structure in students' use of self-handicapping strategies. *American Educational Research Journal, 35,* 101–122.

U.S. Bureau of the Census. (1994). *Statistical abstract of the United States: 1994* (114th ed.). Washington, DC: Author.

U.S. Department of Education. (1992). *To assure the free appropriate public education of all children with disabilities: Fourteenth annual report to Congress on the implementation of the Individuals with Disabilities Education Act.* Washington, DC: Author.

U.S. Department of Education. (1993). *National excellence: A case for developing America's talent.* Washington, DC: Office of Educational Research and Improvement.

U.S. Department of Education. (1995). *To assure the free appropriate public education of all children with disabilities: Seventeenth annual report to Congress on the implementation of the Individuals with Disabilities Education Act.* Washington, DC: Author.

U.S. Department of Education. (1996). *To assure the free appropriate public education of all children with disabilities: Eighteenth annual report to Congress on the implementation of the Individuals with Disabilities Education Act.* Washington, DC: Author.

U.S. Department of Education. (1997). *To assure the free appropriate public education of all children with disabilities: Nineteenth annual report to Congress on the implementation of the Individuals with Disabilities Education Act.* Washington, DC: Author.

U.S. Department of Education, Office of Civil Rights. (1993). *Annual report to Congress.* Washington, DC: Author.

Valencia, S. W., Hiebert, E. H., & Afflerbach, P. P. (1994). Realizing the possibilities of authentic assessment: Current trends and future issues. In S. W. Valencia, E. H. Hiebert, & P. P. Afflerbach (Eds.), *Authentic reading assessment: Practices and possibilities.* Newark, DE: International Reading Association.

Valente, N. (2001). "Who cares about school?" A student responds to learning. Unpublished paper, University of New Hampshire.

Vallerand, R. J., Fortier, M. S., & Guay, F. (1997). Self-determination and persistence in a real-life setting: Toward a motivational model of high school dropout. *Journal of Personality and Social Psychology, 72,* 1161–1176.

Van Camp, C. M., Lerman, D. C., Kelley, M. E., Roane, H. S., Contrucci, S. A., & Vorndran, C. M. (2000). Further analysis of idiosyncratic antecedent influences during the assessment and treatment of problem behavior. *Journal of Applied Behavior Analysis, 33,* 207–221.

Van Houten, R., Nau, P., MacKenzie-Keating, S., Sameoto, D., & Colavecchia, B. (1982). An analysis of some variables influencing the effectiveness of reprimands. *Journal of Applied Behavior Analysis, 15,* 65–83.

van Kraayenoord, C. E., & Paris, S. G. (1997). Australian students' self-appraisal of their work samples and academic progress. *Elementary School Journal, 97,* 523–537.

van Laar, C. (2000). The paradox of low academic achievement but high self-esteem in African American students: An attributional account. *Educational Psychology Review, 12,* 33–61.

Van Meter, P. (2001). Drawing construction as a strategy for learning from text. *Journal of Educational Psychology, 93,* 129–140.

Van Rossum, E. J., & Schenk, S. M. (1984). The relationship between learning conception, study strategy, and learning outcome. *British Journal of Educational Psychology, 54,* 73–83.

VanSledright, B., & Brophy, J. (1992). Storytelling, imagination, and fanciful elaboration in children's historical reconstructions. *American Educational Research Journal, 29,* 837–859.

Vasquez, J. A. (1988). Contexts of learning for minority students. *Educational Forum, 6,* 243–253.

Vasquez, J. A. (1990). Teaching to the distinctive traits of minority students. *Clearing House, 63,* 299–304.

Vaughn, B. J., & Horner, R. H. (1997). Identifying instructional tasks that occasion problem behaviors and assessing the effects of student versus teacher choice among these tasks. *Journal of Applied Behavior Analysis, 30,* 299–312.

Vaughn, S. (1991). Social skills enhancement in students with learning disabilities. In B. Y. L.

Wong (Ed.), *Learning about learning disabilities*. San Diego, CA: Academic Press.

Veenman, S. (1984). Perceived problems of beginning teachers. *Review of Educational Research, 54*, 143–178.

Venn, J. J. (2000). *Assessing students with special needs* (2nd ed.). Upper Saddle River, NJ: Merrill/Prentice Hall.

Verdi, M. P., Kulhavy, R. W., Stock, W. A., Rittschof, K. A., & Johnson, J. T. (1996). Text learning using scientific diagrams: Implications for classroom use. *Contemporary Educational Psychology, 21*, 487–499.

Vermeer, H. J., Boekaerts, M., & Seegers, G. (2000). Motivational and gender differences: Sixth-grade students' mathematical problem-solving behavior. *Journal of Educational Psychology, 92*, 308–315.

Vernon, P. A. (1993). Intelligence and neural efficiency. In D. K. Detterman (Ed.), *Current topics in human intelligence* (Vol. 3). Norwood, NJ: Ablex.

Veroff, J., McClelland, L., & Ruhland, D. (1975). Varieties of achievement motivation. In M. T. S. Mednick, S. S. Tangri, & L. W. Hoffman (Eds.), *Women and achievement: Social and motivational analyses*. New York: Halsted.

Villegas, A. (1991). *Culturally responsive pedagogy for the 1990s and beyond*. Princeton, NJ: Educational Testing Service.

Vitaro, F., Gendreau, P. L., Tremblay, R. E., & Oligny, P. (1998). Reactive and proactive aggression differentially predict later conduct problems. *Journal of Child Psychology and Psychiatry and Allied Disciplines, 39*, 377–385.

Vollmer, T. R., & Hackenberg, T. D. (2001). Reinforcement contingencies and social reinforcement: Some reciprocal relations between basic and applied research. *Journal of Applied Behavior Analysis, 34*, 241–253.

Vorrath, H. (1985). *Positive peer culture*. New York: Aldine de Gruyter.

Vosniadou, S. (1994). Universal and culture-specific properties of children's mental models of the earth. In L. A. Hirschfeld & S. A. Gelman (Eds.), *Mapping the mind: Domain specificity in cognition and culture*. Cambridge, England: Cambridge University Press.

Vosniadou, S., & Brewer, W. F. (1987). Theories of knowledge restructuring in development. *Review of Educational Research, 57*, 51–67.

Voss, J. F. (1974). Acquisition and nonspecific transfer effects in prose learning as a function of question form. *Journal of Educational Psychology, 66*, 736–740.

Voss, J. F. (1987). Learning and transfer in subject-matter learning: A problem-solving model. *International Journal of Educational Research, 11*, 607–622.

Voss, J. F., Greene, T. R., Post, T. A., & Penner, B. D. (1983). Problem-solving skill in the social sciences. In G. H. Bower (Ed.), *The psychology of learning and motivation* (Vol. 17). San Diego, CA: Academic Press.

Voss, J. F., & Schauble, L. (1992). Is interest educationally interesting? An interest-related model of learning. In K. A. Renninger, S. Hidi, & A. Krapp (Eds.), *The role of interest in learning and development*. Hillsdale, NJ: Erlbaum.

Vye, N. J., Schwartz, D. L., Bransford, J. D., Barron, B. J., Zech, L., & The Cognition and Technology Group at Vanderbilt (1998). SMART environments that support monitoring, reflection, and revision. In D. J. Hacker, J. Dunlosky, & A. C. Graesser (Eds.), *Metacognition in educational theory and practice* (pp. 305–346). Mahwah, NJ: Erlbaum.

Vygotsky, L. S. (1962). *Thought and language* (E. Haufmann & G. Vakar, Eds. and Trans.). Cambridge, MA: MIT Press.

Vygotsky, L. S. (1978). *Mind in society: The development of higher psychological processes*. Cambridge, MA: Harvard University Press.

Vygotsky, L. S. (1987). *The collected works of L. S. Vygotsky* (Vol. 3; R. W. Rieber & A. S. Carton, Eds.). New York: Plenum Press.

Vygotsky, L. S. (1997). *Educational psychology* (R. Silverman, Trans.). Boca Raton, FL: St. Lucie Press.

Wade, S. E. (1992). How interest affects learning from text. In K. A. Renninger, S. Hidi, & A. Krapp (Eds.), *The role of interest in learning and development*. Hillsdale, NJ: Erlbaum.

Wagner, A. R. (1981). SOP: A model of automatic memory processing in animal behavior. In N. E. Spear & R. R. Miller (Eds.), *Information processing in animals: Memory mechanisms*. Hillsdale, NJ: Erlbaum.

Wagner, M. (1995). *The contributions of poverty and ethnic background to the participation of secondary school students in special education*. Washington, DC: U.S. Department of Education.

Wahlsten, D., & Gottlieb, G. (1997). The invalid separation of effects of nature and nurture: Lessons from animal experimentation. In R. J. Sternberg & E. L. Grigorenko (Eds.), *Intelligence, heredity, and environment* (pp. 163–192). Cambridge, England: Cambridge University Press.

Walberg, H. J., & Uguroglu, M. (1980). Motivation and educational productivity: Theories, results, and implications. In L. J. Fyans, Jr. (Ed.), *Achievement motivation: Recent trends in theory and research*. New York: Plenum Press.

Walker, J. E., & Shea, T. M. (1995). *Behavior management: A practical approach for educators* (6th ed.). Englewood Cliffs, NJ: Merrill/Prentice Hall.

Walker, J. M. T. (2001, April). *A cross-sectional study of student motivation, strategy knowledge and strategy use during homework: Implications for research on self-regulated learning*. Paper presented at the annual meeting of the American Educational Research Association, Seattle, WA.

Walker, L. J. (1991). Sex differences in moral reasoning. In W. M. Kurtines & J. L. Gewirtz (Eds.), *Handbook of moral behavior and development: Vol. 2. Research* (pp. 333–364). Hillsdale, NJ: Erlbaum.

Walker, L. J. (1995). Sexism in Kohlberg's moral psychology? In W. M. Kurtines & J. L. Gewirtz (Eds.), *Moral development: An introduction*. Boston: Allyn & Bacon.

Walters, G. C., & Grusec, J. E. (1977). *Punishment*. San Francisco: Freeman.

Wang, P. P., & Baron,, M. A. (1997). Language and communication: Development and disorders. In M. L. Batshaw (Ed.), *Children with disabilities* (4th ed.). Baltimore: Brookes.

Warren, A. R., & McCloskey, L. A. (1993). Pragmatics: Language in social contexts. In J. Berko Gleason (Ed.), *The development of language* (3rd ed.). New York: Macmillan.

Warren, G. (1979). Essay versus multiple-choice tests. *Journal of Research in Science Teaching, 16*(6), 563–567.

Warren, R. L. (1988). Cooperation and conflict between parents and teachers: A comparative study of three elementary schools. In H. T. Trueba & C. Delgado-Gaitan (Eds.), *School and society: Learning content through culture*. New York: Praeger.

Wasik, B. A., Karweit, N., Burns, L., & Brodsky, E. (1998, April). *Once upon a time: The role of rereading and retelling in storybook reading*. Paper presented at the annual meeting of the American Educational Research Association, San Diego, CA.

Waters, H. S. (1982). Memory development in adolescence: Relationships between metamemory, strategy use, and performance. *Journal of Experimental Child Psychology, 33*, 183–195.

Way, N. (1998). *Everyday courage: The lives and stories of urban teenagers*. New York: New York University Press.

Weaver, C. A., III, & Kelemen, W. L. (1997). Judgments of learning at delays: Shifts in response patterns or increased metamemory accuracy? *Psychological Science, 8*, 318–321.

Webb, J. T., Meckstroth, E. A., & Tolan, S. S. (1982). *Guiding the gifted child: A practical source for parents and teachers*. Dayton, OH: Ohio Psychology Press.

Webb, N. M. (1989). Peer interaction and learning in small groups. *International Journal of Educational Research, 13*, 21–39.

Webb, N. M., & Farivar, S. (1994). Promoting helping behavior in cooperative small groups in middle school mathematics. *American Educational Research Journal, 31*, 369–395.

Webb, N. M., & Farivar, S. (1999). Developing productive group interaction in middle school mathematics. In A. M. O'Donnell & A. King (Eds.), *Cognitive perspectives on peer learning* (pp. 117–149). Mahwah, NJ: Erlbaum.

Webb, N. M., Nemer, K. M., Chizhik, A. W., & Sugrue, B. (1998). Equity issues in collaborative group assessment: Group composition and performance. *American Educational Research Journal, 35*, 607–651.

Webb, N. M., & Palincsar, A. S. (1996). Group processes in the classroom. In D. C. Berliner & R. C. Calfee (Eds.), *Handbook of educational psychology*. New York: Macmillan.

Webber, J., Scheuermann, B., McCall, C., & Coleman, M. (1993). Research on self-monitoring as a behavior management technique in special education classrooms: A descriptive review. *Remedial and Special Education, 14*(2), 38–56.

Wehmeyer, M. L. (1996). Self-determination as an educational outcome. In D. J. Sands & M. L. Wehmeyer (Eds.), *Self-determination across the life span: Independence and choice for people with disabilities*. Baltimore: Brookes.

Weiner, B. (1984). Principles for a theory of student motivation and their application within an attributional framework. In R. Ames & C. Ames (Eds.), *Research on motivation in education: Vol. 1. Student motivation*. San Diego, CA: Academic Press.

Weiner, B. (1986). *An attributional theory of motivation and emotion*. New York: Springer-Verlag.

Weiner, B. (1994). Ability versus effort revisited: The moral determinants of achievement evaluation and achievement as a moral system. *Educational Psychologist, 29*, 163–172.

Weiner, B. (2000). Intrapersonal and interpersonal theories of motivation from an attributional perspective. *Educational Psychology Review, 12*, 1–14.

Weiner, B., Russell, D., & Lerman, D. (1978). Affective consequences of causal ascriptions. In J. Harvey, W. Ickes, & R. Kidd (Eds.), *New directions in attribution research* (Vol. 2). Hillsdale, NJ: Erlbaum.

Weiner, B., Russell, D., & Lerman, D. (1979). The cognition-emotion process in achievement-related contexts. *Journal of Personality and Social Psychology, 37*, 1211–1220.

Weinert, F. E., & Helmke, A. (1995). Learning from wise Mother Nature or Big Brother Instructor: The wrong choice as seen from an educational perspective. *Educational Psychologist, 30*, 135–142.

Weinstein, C. E., Goetz, E. T., & Alexander, P. A. (Eds.). (1988). *Learning and study strategies: Issues in assessment, instruction, and evaluation*. San Diego, CA: Academic Press.

Weinstein, C. E., Hagen, A. S., & Meyer, D. K. (1991, April). *Work smart . . . not hard: The effects of combining instruction in using strategies, goal using, and executive control on attributions and academic performance.* Paper presented at the annual meeting of the American Educational Research Association, Chicago.

Weinstein, C. S. (1979). The physical environment of the school: A review of the research. *Review of Educational Research, 49,* 577–610.

Weinstein, R. S. (1993). Children's knowledge of differential treatment in school: Implications for motivation. In T. M. Tomlinson (Ed.), *Motivating students to learn: Overcoming barriers to high achievement.* Berkeley, CA: McCutchan.

Weinstein, R. S., Madison, S. M., & Kuklinski, M. R. (1995). Raising expectations in schooling: Obstacles and opportunities for change. *American Educational Research Journal, 32,* 121–159.

Weisberg, R. W. (1993). *Creativity: Beyond the myth of genius.* New York: Freeman.

Weiss, M. R., & Klint, K. A. (1987). "Show and tell" in the gymnasium: An investigation of developmental differences in modeling and verbal rehearsal of motor skills. *Research Quarterly for Exercise and Sport, 58,* 234–241.

Weissberg, R. P. (1985). Designing effective social problem-solving programs for the classroom. In B. H. Schneider, K. H. Rubin, & J. E. Ledingham (Eds.), *Children's peer relations: Issues in assessment and intervention.* New York: Springer-Verlag.

Welch, G. J. (1985). Contingency contracting with a delinquent and his family. *Journal of Behavior Therapy and Experimental Psychiatry, 16,* 253–259.

Wellman, H. M. (1985). The child's theory of mind: The development of conceptions of cognition. In S. R. Yussen (Ed.), *The growth of reflection in children.* San Diego, CA: Academic Press.

Wellman, H. M. (1988). The early development of memory strategies. In F. Weinert & M. Perlmutter (Eds.), *Memory development: Universal changes and individual differences.* Hillsdale, NJ: Erlbaum.

Wellman, H. M., & Gelman, S. A. (1998). Acquisition of knowledge. In W. Damon (Series Ed.), D. Kuhn, & R. S. Siegler (Vol. Eds.), *Handbook of child psychology: Vol. 2. Cognition, perception, and language* (5th ed.). New York: Wiley.

Wentzel, K. R. (1999). Social-motivational processes and interpersonal relationships: Implications for understanding motivation at school. *Journal of Educational Psychology, 91,* 76–97.

Wentzel, K. R., & Asher, S. R. (1995). The academic lives of neglected, rejected, popular, and controversial children. *Child Development, 66,* 754–763.

Wentzel, K. R., & Wigfield, A. (1998). Academic and social motivational influences on students' academic performance. *Educational Psychology Review, 10,* 155–175.

Werner, E. E. (1995). Resilience in development. *Current Directions in Psychological Science, 4,* 81–85.

Wertsch, J. V. (1984). The zone of proximal development: Some conceptual issues. *Children's learning in the zone of proximal development: New directions for child development* (No. 23). San Francisco: Jossey-Bass.

West, C. K., Farmer, J. A., & Wolff, P. M. (1991). *Instructional design: Implications from cognitive science.* Upper Saddle River, NJ: Prentice Hall.

White, A. G., & Bailey, J. S. (1990). Reducing disruptive behaviors of elementary physical education students with sit and watch. *Journal of Applied Behavior Analysis, 23,* 353–359.

White, B. Y., & Frederiksen, J. R. (1998). Inquiry, modeling, and metacognition: Making science

accessible to all students. *Cognition and Instruction, 16,* 3–118.

White, J. J., & Rumsey, S. (1994). Teaching for understanding in a third-grade geography lesson. In J. Brophy (Ed.), *Advances in research on teaching: Vol. 4. Case studies of teaching and learning in social studies.* Greenwich, CT: JAI Press.

White, R. (1959). Motivation reconsidered: The concept of competence. *Psychological Review, 66,* 297–333.

White, R., & Cunningham, A. M. (1991). *Ryan White: My own story.* New York: Signet.

Whiting, B. B., & Edwards, C. P. (1988). *Children of different worlds.* Cambridge, MA: Harvard University Press.

Whitley, B. E., Jr., & Frieze, I. H. (1985). Children's causal attributions for success and failure in achievement settings: A meta-analysis. *Journal of Educational Psychology, 77,* 68–616.

Wideen, M., Mayer-Smith, J., & Moon, B. (1998). A critical analysis of the research on learning to teach: Making the case for an ecological perspective on inquiry. *Review of Educational Research, 68,* 130–178.

Wigfield, A. (1994). Expectancy-value theory of achievement motivation: A developmental perspective. *Educational Psychology Review, 6,* 49–78.

Wigfield, A. (1997). Reading motivation: A domain-specific approach to motivation. *Educational Psychologist, 32,* 59–68.

Wigfield, A., & Eccles, J. (1992). The development of achievement task values: A theoretical analysis. *Developmental Review, 12,* 265–310.

Wigfield, A., & Eccles, J. S. (1994). Children's competence beliefs, achievement values, and general self-esteem: Change across elementary and middle school. *Journal of Early Adolescence, 14,* 107–138.

Wigfield, A., & Eccles, J. (2000). Expectancy-value theory of achievement motivation. *Contemporary Educational Psychology, 25,* 68–81.

Wigfield, A., Eccles, J. S., & Pintrich, P. R. (1996). Development between the ages of 11 and 25. In D. C. Berliner & R. C. Calfee (Eds.), *Handbook of educational psychology.* New York: Macmillan.

Wigfield, A., Eccles, J., Mac Iver, D., Reuman, D., & Midgley, C. (1991). Transitions at early adolescence: Changes in children's domain-specific self-perceptions and general self-esteem across the transition to junior high school. *Developmental Psychology, 27,* 552–565.

Wigfield, A., & Meece, J. L. (1988). Math anxiety in elementary and secondary school students. *Journal of Educational Psychology, 80,* 210–216.

Wiggins, G. (1992). Creating tests worth taking. *Educational Leadership, 49*(8), 26–33.

Wilder, A. A., & Williams, J. P. (2001). Students with severe learning disabilities can learn higher order comprehension skills. *Journal of Educational Psychology, 93,* 268–278.

Wiley, D. E., & Haertel, E. H. (1996). Extended assessment tasks: Purposes, definitions, scoring, and accuracy. In M. B. Kane & R. Mitchell (Eds.), *Implementing performance assessment: Promises, problems, and challenges* (pp. 61–89). Mahwah, NJ: Erlbaum.

Wilkinson, L. C., & Marrett, C. B. (Eds.). (1985). *Gender influences in classroom interaction.* San Diego, CA: Academic Press.

Wilkinson, L. D., & Frazer, L. H. (1990, April). *Fine-tuning dropout prediction through discriminant analysis: The ethnic factor.* Paper presented at the annual meeting of the American Educational Research Association, Boston.

Will, M. C. (1986). Educating children with learning problems: A shared responsibility. *Exceptional Children, 52,* 411–415.

Williams, B., & Newcombe, E. (1994). Building on the strengths of urban learners. *Educational Leadership, 51*(8), 75–78.

Williams, D. (1996). *Autism: An inside-outside approach.* London: Jessica Kingsley.

Williams, J. P. (1991, November). *Comprehension of learning disabled and nondisabled students: Identification of narrative themes and idiosyncratic text representation.* Paper presented at the annual meeting of the National Reading Conference, Austin, TX.

Willig, A. C. (1985). A meta-analysis of selected studies on the effectiveness of bilingual education. *Review of Educational Research, 55,* 269–317.

Wilson, C. C., Piazza, C. C., & Nagle, R. (1990). Investigations of the effects of consistent and inconsistent behavioral example upon children's donation behaviors. *Journal of Genetic Psychology, 151,* 361–376.

Wilson, J. E. (1988). Implications of learning strategy research and training: What it has to say to the practitioner. In C. E. Weinstein, E. T. Goetz, & P. A. Alexander (Eds.), *Learning and study strategies: Issues in assessment, instruction, and evaluation.* San Diego, CA: Academic Press.

Wilson, M. (1989). Child development in the context of the black extended family. *American Psychologist, 44,* 380–383.

Wilson, P. S. (1988, April). The relationship of students' definitions and example choices in geometry. In D. Tirosh (Chair), *The role of inconsistent ideas in learning mathematics.* Symposium conducted at the annual meeting of the American Educational Research Association, New Orleans, LA.

Wilson, P. T., & Anderson, R. C. (1986). What they don't know will hurt them: The role of prior knowledge in comprehension. In J. Orasanu (Ed.), *Reading comprehension: From research to practice.* Hillsdale, NJ: Erlbaum.

Wine, J. D. (1980). Cognitive-attentional theory of test anxiety. In I. G. Sarason (Ed.), *Test anxiety: Theory, research, and applications.* Hillsdale, NJ: Erlbaum.

Winer, G. A., & Cottrell, J. E. (1996). Does anything leave the eye when we see? Extramission beliefs of children and adults. *Current Directions in Psychological Science, 5,* 137–142.

Wingfield, A., & Byrnes, D. L. (1981). *The psychology of human memory.* San Diego, CA: Academic Press.

Winn, W. (1991). Learning from maps and diagrams. *Educational Psychology Review, 3,* 211–247.

Winne, P. H. (1995). Inherent details in self-regulated learning. *Educational Psychologist, 30,* 173–187.

Winne, P. H., & Hadwin, A. F. (1998). Studying as self-regulated learning. In D. J. Hacker, J. Dunlosky, & A. C. Graesser (Eds.), *Metacognition in educational theory and practice* (pp. 277–304). Mahwah, NJ: Erlbaum.

Winne, P. H., & Marx, R. W. (1989). A cognitive-processing analysis of motivation with classroom tasks. In C. Ames & R. Ames (Eds.), *Research on motivation in education* (Vol. 3). San Diego, CA: Academic Press.

Winner, E. (1988). *The point of words.* Cambridge, MA: Harvard University Press.

Winner, E. (1997). Exceptionally high intelligence and schooling. *American Psychologist, 52,* 1070–1081.

Winner, E. (2000a). Giftedness: Current theory and research. *Current Directions in Psychological Science, 9,* 153–156.

Winner, E. (2000b). The origins and ends of giftedness. *American Psychologist, 55,* pp. 159–169.

Winograd, P., & Jones, D. L. (1992). The use of portfolios in performance assessment. *New Directions for Education Reform, 1*(2), 37–50.

Wise, B. W., & Olson, R. K. (1998). Studies of computer-aided remediation for reading disabilities. In C. Hulme & R. M. Joshi (Eds.), *Reading and spelling: Development and disorders*. Mahwah, NJ: Erlbaum.

Wittmer, D. S., & Honig, A. S. (1994). Encouraging positive social development in young children. *Young Children, 49*(5), 4–12.

Wittrock, M. C. (1994). Generative science teaching. In P. J. Fensham, R. F. Gunstone, & R. T. White (Eds.), *The content of science: A constructivist approach to its teaching and learning*. London: Falmer Press.

Wixson, K. K. (1984). Level of importance of postquestions and children's learning from text. *American Educational Research Journal, 21,* 419–433.

Wlodkowski, R. J. (1978). *Motivation and teaching: A practical guide*. Washington, DC: National Education Association.

Wlodkowski, R. J., & Ginsberg, M. B. (1995). *Diversity and motivation: Culturally responsive teaching*. San Francisco: Jossey-Bass.

Wodtke, K. H., Harper, F., & Schommer, M. (1989). How standardized is school testing? An exploratory observational study of standardized group testing in kindergarten. *Educational Evaluation and Policy Analysis, 11,* 223–235.

Wolf, R. M. (1998). National standards: Do we need them? *Educational Researcher, 27*(4), 22–24.

Wolpe, J. (1969). *The practice of behavior therapy*. Oxford: Pergamon Press.

Wolters, C. A. (1998). Self-regulated learning and college students' regulation of motivation. *Journal of Educational Psychology, 90,* 224–235.

Wong, B. Y. L. (1985). Self-questioning instructional research: A review. *Review of Educational Research, 55,* 227–268.

Wong, B. Y. L. (Ed.) (1991a). *Learning about learning disabilities*. San Diego, CA: Academic Press.

Wong, B. Y. L. (1991b). The relevance of metacognition to learning disabilities. In B. Y. L. Wong (Ed.), *Learning about learning disabilities*. San Diego, CA: Academic Press.

Wood, D., Bruner, J. S., & Ross, G. (1976). The role of tutoring in problem-solving. *Journal of Child Psychology and Psychiatry, 17,* 89–100.

Wood, D., Wood, H., Ainsworth, S., & O'Malley, C. (1995). On becoming a tutor: Toward an ontogenetic model. *Cognition and Instruction, 13,* 565–581.

Wood, E., Motz, M., & Willoughby, T. (1997, April). *Examining students' retrospective memories of strategy development*. Paper presented at the annual meeting of the American Educational Research Association, Chicago.

Wood, E., Willoughby, T., McDermott, C., Motz, M., Kaspar, V., & Ducharme, M. J. (1999). Developmental differences in study behavior. *Journal of Educational Psychology, 91,* 527–536.

Wood, E., Willoughby, T., Reilley, S., Elliott, S., & DuCharme, M. (1994, April). *Evaluating students' acquisition of factual material when studying independently or with a partner*. Paper presented at the annual meeting of the American Educational Research Association, New Orleans, LA.

Wood, J. W. (1998). *Adapting instruction to accommodate students in inclusive settings* (3rd ed.). Upper Saddle River, NJ: Merrill/Prentice Hall.

Wood, J. W., & Rosbe, M. (1985). Adapting the classroom lecture for the mainstreamed student in the secondary schools. *Clearing House, 58,* 354–358.

Woolfolk, A. E., & Brooks, D. M. (1985). The influence of teachers' nonverbal behaviors on students' perceptions and performances. *Elementary School Journal, 85,* 513–528.

Worthen, B. R., & Leopold, G. D. (1992). Impediments to implementing alternative assessment: Some emerging issues. *New Directions for Education Reform, 1*(2), 1–20.

Wright, L. S. (1982). The use of logical consequences in counseling children. *School Counselor, 30,* 37–49.

Wright, R. (1994). *The moral animal: The new science of evolutionary psychology*. New York: Pantheon Books.

Wright, S. C., & Taylor, D. M. (1995). Identity and the language of the classroom: Investigating the impact of heritage versus second-language instruction on personal and collective self-esteem. *Journal of Educational Psychology, 87,* 241–252.

Wright, S. C., Taylor, D. M., & Macarthur, J. (2000). Subtractive bilingualism and the survival of the Inuit language: Heritage- versus second-language education. *Journal of Educational Psychology, 92,* 63–84.

Wynne, E. A. (1990). Improving pupil discipline and character. In O. C. Moles (Ed.), *Student discipline strategies: Research and practice*. Albany: State University of New York Press.

Yarmey, A. D. (1973). I recognize your face but I can't remember your name: Further evidence on the tip-of-the-tongue phenomenon. *Memory and Cognition, 1,* 287–290.

Yee, A. H. (1992). Asians as stereotypes and students: Misperceptions that persist. *Educational Psychology Review, 4,* 95–132.

Yee, D. K., & Eccles, J. S. (1988). Parent perceptions and attributions for children's math achievement. *Sex Roles, 19,* 317–333.

Yell, M. L., Robinson, T. R., & Drasgow, E. (2001). Cognitive behavior modification. In T. J. Zirpoli & K. J. Melloy, *Behavior management: Applications for teachers* (3rd ed., pp. 200–246). Upper Saddle River, NJ: Merrill/Prentice Hall.

Yerkes, R. M., & Dodson, J. D. (1908). The relation of strength of stimulus to rapidity of habit-formation. *Journal of Comparative Neurology of Psychology, 18,* 459–482.

Yokoi, L. (1997, March). *The developmental context of notetaking: A qualitative examination of notetaking at the secondary level*. Paper presented at the annual meeting of the American Educational Research Association, Chicago.

Youniss, J., & Volpe, J. (1978). A relational analysis of children's friendships. In W. Damon (Ed.), *New directions for child development: Vol. 1. Social cognition* (pp. 1–22). San Francisco: Jossey-Bass.

Youniss, J., & Yates, M. (1999). Youth service and moral-civic identity: A case for everyday morality. *Educational Psychology Review, 11,* 361–376.

Ysseldyke, J. E., & Algozzine, B. (1984). *Introduction to special education*. Boston: Houghton Mifflin.

Yu, S. L., Elder, A. D., & Urdan, T. C. (1995, April). *Motivation and cognitive strategies in students with a "good student" or "poor student" self-schema*. Paper presented at the annual meeting of the American Educational Research Association, San Francisco.

Yuker, H. E. (Ed.). (1988). *Attitudes toward persons with disabilities*. New York: Springer.

Zahorik, J. A. (1994, April). *Making things interesting*. Paper presented at the annual meeting of the American Educational Research Association, New Orleans, LA.

Zeaman, D., & House, B. J. (1979). A review of attention theory. In N. R. Ellis (Ed.), *Handbook of mental deficiency: Psychological theory and research* (2nd ed.). Hillsdale, NJ: Erlbaum.

Zeidner, M. (1998). *Test anxiety: The state of the art*. New York: Plenum Press.

Zeldin, A. L., & Pajares, F. (2000). Against the odds: Self-efficacy beliefs of women in mathematical, scientific, and technological careers. *American Educational Research Journal, 37,* 215–246.

Zelli, A., Dodge, K. A., Lochman, J. E., & Laird, R. D. (1999). The distinction between beliefs legitimizing aggression and deviant processing of social cues: Testing measurement validity and the hypothesis that biassed processing mediates the effects of beliefs on aggression. *Journal of Personality and Social Psychology, 77,* 150–166.

Ziegler, S. G. (1987). Effects of stimulus cueing on the acquisition of groundstrokes by beginning tennis players. *Journal of Applied Behavior Analysis, 20,* 405–411.

Zigler, E. F., & Finn-Stevenson, M. (1992). Applied developmental psychology. In M. H. Bornstein & M. E. Lamb (Eds.), *Developmental psychology: An advanced textbook*. Hillsdale, NJ: Erlbaum.

Zigler, E. F., & Seitz, V. (1982). Social policy and intelligence. In R. J. Sternberg (Ed.), *Handbook of human intelligence* (pp. 586–641). Cambridge, England: Cambridge University Press.

Zigmond, N., Jenkins, J., Fuchs, L. S., Deno, S., Fuchs, D., Baker, J. N., Jenkins, L., & Couthino, M. (1995, March). Special education in restructured schools: Findings from three multi-year studies. *Phi Delta Kappan,* 531–540.

Zimmerman, B. J. (1998). Developing self-fulfilling cycles of academic regulation: An analysis of exemplary instructional models. In D. H. Schunk & B. J. Zimmerman (Eds.), *Self-regulated learning: From teaching to self-reflective practice* (pp. 1–19). New York: Guilford Press.

Zimmerman, B. J., Bandura, A., & Martinez-Pons, M. (1992). Self-motivation for academic attainment: The role of self-efficacy beliefs and personal goal setting. *American Educational Research Journal, 29,* 663–676.

Zimmerman, B. J., & Risemberg, R. (1997). Self-regulatory dimensions of academic learning and motivation. In G. D. Phye (Ed.), *Handbook of academic learning: Construction of knowledge*. San Diego, CA: Academic Press.

Zirin, G. (1974). How to make a boring thing more boring. *Child Development, 45,* 232–236.

Zirpoli, T. J., & Melloy, K. J. (2001). *Behavior management: Applications for teachers*. Upper Saddle River, NJ: Merrill/Prentice Hall.

Zook, K. B. (1991). Effects of analogical processes on learning and misrepresentation. *Educational Psychology Review, 3,* 41–72.

Zook, K. B., & Di Vesta, F. J. (1991). Instructional analogies and conceptual misrepresentations. *Journal of Educational Psychology, 83,* 246–252.

Zuckerman, G. A. (1994). A pilot study of a ten-day course in cooperative learning for beginning Russian first graders. *Elementary School Journal, 94,* 405–420.

Name Index

Bishop, C. H., 546
Bjork, R. A., 275, 277
Bjorklund, D. F., 22, 43, 45, 46, 197, 206, 212
Black, A., 90
Black, J. B., 238
Black, J. E., 22
Blackbourn, J. M., 159
Blackhurst, A. E., 175
Blake, S. B., 277, 278
Blasi, A., 91, 92
Blattner, J. E., 312
Blinde, P. L., 134
Block, J. H., 129, 130, 384, 443
Bloom, B. S., 261, 433, 443
Bloom, L. A., 162
Blue-Banning, M., 86, 183
Blumenfeld, P., 515
Blumenfeld, P. C., 261, 405, 464, 465
Blumenthal, J., 22
Bluth, G. J., 207
Bochenhauer, M. H., 439
Boden, J. M., 67
Boekaerts, M., 129, 421
Boggiano, A. K., 391, 394
Boivin, M., 66, 81
Boldizar, J. P., 82
Bol, L., 46
Bolles, R. C., 372
Bolt, E., 394
Bond, M. H., 96
Bong, M., 405
Bonica, C., 76
Borko, H., 4, 10, 486
Borkowski, J. G., 43, 272, 418, 422
Born, D. G., 443
Bornholt, L. J., 128, 129
Bornstein, M. H., 22
Bosacki, S. L., 79, 129
Boschee, F., 537, 573
Boshuizen, H. P. A., 206
Bossert, S., 515
Bouchard, T. J., Jr., 62, 113
Boudah, D. J., 461
Boulerice, B., 135
Bousfield, W. A., 207
Boutte, G. S., 125, 126
Bowen, G. M., 40
Bower, G. H., 191, 204, 207, 213, 238
Bowey, J., 53
Bowman, B. T., 119
Bowman, L. G., 312
Boyatzis, R. E., 376
Boyes-Braem, P., 236
Boykin, A. W., 528
Boyle, R. A., 252, 400, 571
Bracken, B. A., 74, 109, 129, 542
Braden, J. P., 172
Bradley, C. M., 56
Bradley, D. M., 329
Bradley, L., 53, 392
Bradley, R. H., 114
Bradshaw, G. D., 544
Brady, M. P., 183, 316
Brainerd, C. J., 195
Brandt, D. H., 207
Bransford, J. D., 193, 204, 207, 286
Brantlinger, E., 147
Braukmann, C. J., 84
Braun, Lilian Jackson, 341
Bray, N. W., 168
Brenner, M. E., 286
Brent, S. B., 50
Bretherton, I., 79
Brett, C., 462
Brewer, W. F., 242, 249, 250, 251, 252
Bricker, W., 81
Briggs, L. J., 445
Briggs, W., 482
Brigham, F. J., 156
Bright, J. A., 122
Britton, B. K., 204, 241
Broden, M., 497

Brodsky, E., 246
Brody, G. H., 94
Brody, N., 107, 108, 109, 113
Bromley, D. B., 79
Bronson, M. B., 350, 356, 357, 370
Brooke, R. R., 313
Brooks, D. M., 319, 482, 491
Brooks, L. W., 275
Brooks-Gunn, J., 76, 113, 114
Brophy, J., 228, 230, 245, 451, 528, 572
Brophy, J. E., 10, 92, 197, 245, 275, 329, 376, 383, 385, 399, 402, 403, 405, 408, 409, 415, 416, 417, 421, 435, 450, 454, 484, 495, 543, 544
Brown, A. L., 45, 232, 248, 249, 264, 268, 272, 295, 459, 460, 461, 462, 464, 466, 467, 579
Brown, A. S., 516, 559
Brown, B. B., 73, 74, 76, 375, 384
Brown, D. R., 129
Brown, J. H., 506
Brown, J. S., 40, 246
Brown, L. M., 91
Brown, R., 199, 216, 263, 271
Brown, R. D., 22
Brown, R. T., 115, 545
Brown, W. H., 316
Brownell, M. T., 294, 498
Brown-Mizuno, C., 96, 178
Brubaker, N. L., 484
Bruer, J. T., 22, 49, 53, 191
Bruner, J. S., 39, 235, 447, 448
Bruning, R. H., 457
Bryan, J., 472
Bryan, J. H., 339
Bryan, T., 96, 184, 472
Bryant, N. R., 295
Bryant, P., 51
Bryant, P. E., 53
Buchanan, B., 472
Buchele, K. S., 375
Buchoff, T., 157, 158, 160, 329, 502
Buck, P., 126
Budwig, N., 49
Bugelski, B. R., 229
Buhrmester, D., 73
Bukowski, W., 75
Bulgren, J. A., 213, 222, 440
Burger, D., 576
Burger, H. G., 123
Burger, S., 576
Burger, S. F., 4
Burhans, K. K., 415
Burleson, B., 82
Burns, L., 246
Burns, R. B., 443
Burstein, K., 472
Burtis, J., 251
Burtis, P. J., 462
Burton, L. M., 503
Burton, R. V., 352
Bushell, D., 495
Bushell, D., Jr., 469
Bushman, B. J., 338
Busse, R. T., 82, 84, 326, 343, 358
Butcher, K., 56
Butler, D. L., 268, 272, 308, 356, 357
Butler, R., 347, 356, 391, 405, 414, 416
Butterfield, E. C., 56, 168, 222, 254
Butterworth, G., 275
Byrne, D. F., 79
Byrnes, D. L., 196
Byrnes, J. P., 22, 33, 241, 411

Cai, Y., 394
Cairns, H. S., 49
Calderhead, J., 438
Caldwell, B. M., 114
Calfee, R., 197, 198, 439, 458
Calfee, R. C., 439, 571, 572
Camburn, E., 119, 134, 381, 382, 500

Cameron, J., 396
Campbell, A., 75
Campbell, B., 110
Campbell, D. E., 487
Campbell, F. A., 114
Campbell, L., 110
Campbell, P. A., 130, 131, 545
Campbell, S. B., 98
Campione, J., 264
Campione, J. C., 248, 249, 294, 295, 467, 579
Canady, R. L., 583
Candee, D., 91
Candler-Lotven, A., 178, 179, 294, 295
Cantwell, C., 502
Cao, H. T., 376
Capodilupo, A., 132
Caprara, G. V., 77, 87
Capron, C., 113
Carey, L. M., 573, 576, 577
Carey, S., 32, 33, 49, 234, 242, 249
Cariglia-Bull, T., 275
Carlo, G., 87, 92
Carlson, C. L., 157
Carlson, E., 62
Carnine, D., 444
Carpenter, P. A., 212
Carper, L. B., 312
Carr, A. A., 505, 506
Carr, E. G., 163, 164
Carr, M., 43, 232, 265, 272, 288, 422
Carraher, D. W., 31, 33, 288, 294
Carraher, T. N., 294
Carrasco, R. L., 104, 417
Carroll, J. L., 32
Carta, J. J., 468
Carter, K. R., 30, 56, 177, 178, 179
Cartledge, G., 97
Carver, C. S., 356, 378, 403
Casanova, U., 119, 121, 125, 127
Case, R., 33, 132
Caseau, D., 138
Casey, W. M., 352
Caspi, A., 132
Cassel, P., 494
Cassel, W. S., 43
Casserly, P. L., 130
Castellanos, F. X., 22
Castine, W. H., 445
Caterino, L. C., 202
Catts, H., 158
Cazden, C. B., 51, 53, 122, 500
Ceci, S. J., 113, 231
Census, U.S. Bureau of, 120
Cerullo, F., 415
Chaase, M. A., 308
Chabay, R. W., 469
Chalfant, J. C., 154
Chall, J. S., 172
Chalmers, J., 94
Chalmers, N., 114, 211
Chalmers, V., 481
Chambliss, M. J., 249, 250, 439
Chan, C., 251, 462
Chan, K. S., 134
Chand, I., 114, 115
Chandler, M., 91
Chao, R. K., 63
Chapman, J. W., 68, 154
Chapman, M., 339
Chapman, S., 267
Cheatham, S. K., 164
Cheek, N. H., 76
Chen, C., 131, 457
Chen, X., 63, 68
Chen, Z., 286
Cheng, L. R., 567
Cheng, P. W., 215
Cherlin, D. L., 197, 482
Cherry, E. C., 197
Chessor, D., 66
Chester, M. D., 502
Cheung, M., 446

Cheyne, J. A., 323
Chi, M. T. H., 45, 241, 244, 286
Chih-Mei, C., 420
Child, D. A., 268
Childs, K. E., 162
Chin, R., 420
Chinn, C. A., 249, 252
Chinn, P. C., 133
Chitooran, M. M., 113
Chiu, C., 119, 413
Chizhik, A. W., 465
Chomsky, C. S., 51
Chomsky, N., 48, 49, 50
Christensen, C. A., 216
Christie, J. F., 52
Christopherson, H., 448
Chudowsky, N., 516
Cillessen, A. H. N., 77, 97
Clark, B., 178, 222, 223, 294, 385, 422, 502
Clark, C. C., 75
Clark, C. M., 1
Clark, E., 361, 362
Clark, E. V., 51, 236
Clark, J. M., 209
Clark, M. C., 207, 213
Clark, R. A., 370
Clark, R. E., 277, 278, 446
Clark, S., 162
Clarke, S., 162
Clarke-Stewart, K. A., 63
Claude, D., 157
Clauser, P., 528
Clawson, D. L., 20
Cleary, T., 343
Clement, C., 33
Clement, P. W., 312
Clements, B. S., 481
Clifford, M. M., 67, 329, 392, 411, 579
Clore, G. L., 76
Coatsworth, J. D., 63, 133, 134
Cobb, P., 406, 457, 458
Cocchiarella, M. J., 235, 236, 440
Cochran, K. F., 10
Cochran-Smith, M., 10
Coe, J., 133
Cognition and Technology Group at Vanderbilt, 289, 450, 454
Cohen, E. G., 457, 465, 466, 467, 471, 473
Cohen, P. A., 443, 445
Cohen, R. L., 211, 343
Coie, J. D., 77, 82, 97
Coladarci, T., 583
Colarossi, L., 135
Colavecchia, B., 320
Colby, A., 88, 89, 90
Cole, D. A., 129, 347, 385, 420
Cole, M., 294
Cole, N. S., 55, 261, 435
Coleman, H. L. K., 119
Coleman, M., 163, 351
Collaer, M. L., 128, 129
Collier, V. P., 54
Collins, A., 40, 246, 272, 278, 515, 554, 558
Collins, W. A., 22, 62, 74, 76
Combs, A. W., 380
Comfort, C., 135
Cone, T. E., 56
Conger, K. J., 75
Conger, R. D., 75
Conklin, N. F., 553
Conlon, C. J., 180
Connell, J. P., 65, 346, 369, 374, 398
Connelly, L. M., 98
Connolly, F. W., 455
Connolly, J., 76
Connor, D. F., 156
Connor, J. M., 6
Conte, R., 153, 157
Conway, M. A., 209
Cook, B., 183

Cooney, Caroline, 341
Cooney, G. H., 129
Cooney, J. B., 153, 205, 222, 491
Cooper, H., 322, 451, 452, 453, 471
Cooper, H. M., 417
Corbett, H. D., 515
Corkill, A. J., 42, 97, 108, 440, 502
Corley, R., 113
Cormier, S. M., 278
Cornell, D. G., 69, 178
Corno, L., 322, 355, 356, 370, 391,
    419, 451, 473
Corrigan, C., 485
Corsino, L., 135
Costa, A. L., 528
Cothern, N. B., 223
Cottrell, J. E., 250
Cottrol, R. J., 125, 127
Council for Exceptional Children,
    152, 177
Courchesne, E., 222, 223
Covington, M., 370, 396
Covington, M. V., 74, 96, 137, 178,
    325, 351, 370, 374, 380, 385,
    392, 393, 402, 404, 405, 413, 517
Cowan, N., 196, 201
Cox, B. D., 277
Cox, P. D., 347
Coyle, T. R., 43
Craft, M., 121, 127
Craft, M. A., 313
Crago, M. B., 122, 123
Craig, D., 567, 580
Craik, F. I. M., 203
Craik, K. H., 191
Crain, S., 49
Crandall, V. C., 413
Craven, R., 64, 66, 96, 97, 98, 464
Creasey, G. L., 83
Crick, N. R., 77, 81, 82, 129
Crockett, L., 75
Cromack, T. R., 566
Cromer, R. F., 49
Crook, C., 465
Crooks, T. J., 205, 515, 580
Cross, D. R., 459
Crouse, J., 528
Crowder, R., 201
Crowley, E., 262
Crowley, K., 283
Crowne, D. P., 376
Crumbaugh, C., 247
Csikszentmihalyi, M., 115, 368, 369,
    380, 392
Cuevas, A. M., 129
Cunningham, A. E., 68, 134, 246,
    374, 415
Cunningham, A. M., 170–171
Cunningham, C. E., 82, 362, 363
Cunningham, L. J., 82, 362, 363
Cunningham, T. H., 54
Curtis, K. A., 419
Cushing, K. S., 481
Cushing, L. S., 470

D'Agostino, J. V., 288
Dalrymple, N. J., 163, 164
D'Amato, R. C., 113, 132
Damon, W., 66, 74, 82, 83, 92, 93, 94
Dancs, M., 87
Danner, F. W., 33, 400
Dansereau, D. F., 266, 275, 440, 466
Darling, J. M., 556
Darling-Hammond, L., 10, 514, 538
Davidson, A. L., 77, 376, 407
Davidson, J. E., 288
Davidson, P., 90
Davis, G. A., 139, 178, 319, 322,
    481, 483, 486, 488, 489, 491,
    494, 505
Davis, H., 250
Davis, H. A., 355
Davis, M., 583

Davis, M. L., 443
Day, J., 264
Day, M. C., 33
Deaux, K., 129, 385, 407, 417
deBaca, P. C., 312
DeBaryshe, B. D., 161
deCharms, R., 394, 421
Deci, E. L., 380, 391, 392, 394, 395,
    396, 398, 402, 468, 484, 485,
    488, 569
De Corte, E., 41, 246, 559, 571, 572
Dee, Barbara, 341
Dee-Lucas, D., 262, 263
Deering, P. D., 272, 466
DeFalco, K., 487
Defries, J. C., 113, 153
DeGangi, G. A., 182
de Glopper, K., 50
DeGrandpre, R. J., 301
De Groot, E., 272
De Groot, E. V., 262
de Jong, T., 447, 448, 449, 450
DeLain, M. T., 118, 121
Delandshere, G., 576, 585
Delaney, H. D., 213
Delgado-Gaitan, C., 51, 294
De Lisi, R., 94, 430
DeLisle, J. R., 178
DeLoache, J. S., 43
DeMarie-Dreblow, D., 43
Dembo, M. H., 129
Dempster, F. N., 42, 97, 108, 216,
    219, 502, 515
Denier, C., 6
DeNisi, A., 372, 408
Denkla, M. B., 163
DeRidder, L. M., 70
Derry, S. J., 39, 250, 283, 292, 445
Desberg, P., 437
Deshler, D., 154
Deshler, D. D., 213, 294, 421, 422, 440
D'Esposito, M., 191
Detterman, D. K., 105
Deutsch, M., 82, 84, 358, 458, 459,
    465, 467
DeVault, G., 165, 327
Devine, J. V., 312
Devine, P. G., 85
DeVries, R., 75, 94
Dewhurst, S. A., 209
Diamond, R., 157, 294
Diamond, S. C., 162, 482, 496, 502
Diaz, R. M., 53, 56
Diaz, S., 54
Dickerson, C., 73
Dickinson, D., 110
Dien, T., 376, 384, 508
Dillon, D. R., 179
Dirks, J., 108
diSessa, A. A., 241, 278
Dishion, T. J., 74, 83, 161
Di Vesta, F. J., 197, 216, 263, 277, 440
Dixon, C. N., 506
Dixon, M. R., 310
Dobbelaere, A., 485
Dodd, J. M., 362
Dodge, K. A., 77, 81, 82, 98, 254
Dodson, J. D., 380
Doescher, S. M., 94
Dole, J. A., 230, 262, 267
Dollard, J. C., 189
Dominowski, R. L., 288
Donaldson, J., 85
Donaldson, M., 32, 52
Donis, K., 293
Donley, J., 206, 265
Donnelly, C. M., 440
Doorlag, D. H., 159, 160
Dornbusch, S. M., 62, 515
Douglas, G., 270
Dovidio, J. F., 126, 417
Downey, G., 76
Dowson, M., 73, 375, 406

Doyle, A., 54, 96
Doyle, W., 73, 322, 375, 405, 450,
    481, 482, 484, 486, 489, 490,
    491, 492, 494, 499
Drabman, R. S., 321
Drake, D. D., 547
Drasgow, E., 353
Dreikurs, R., 321, 494
Drevno, G. E., 306
Drew, H. A., 326
Driver, B. L., 182
Driver, R., 230, 243, 250
Droppleman, P., 70
DuBois, N. F., 207, 265
DuCette, J., 421
Duchardt, B. A., 422
DuCharme, M., 203
Dudley, B., 358
Dueck, A., 204
Duffy, G., 484
Duffy, G. G., 230
Duguid, P., 40
Duit, R., 241, 250
Duke, N. K., 132
DuNann, D. G., 472
Duncan, C., 70
Duncan, G. J., 113
Duncker, K., 285
Dunlap, G., 162, 164, 395, 422
Dunlap, K., 458
Dunlosky, J., 269
Dunn, J., 79
DuPaul, G. J., 156, 161, 168, 183,
    294, 468, 470, 472, 473
Duran, B. J., 124
Durkin, K., 71, 129, 130, 310,
    350, 407
Durost, W. N., 541, 542
Dutta, A., 211, 215, 216
Duyme, M., 113
Dweck, C. S., 371, 393, 397, 403,
    404, 405, 410, 412, 413, 415,
    418, 421
D'Ydewalle, G., 559
Dyer, H. S., 434

Eacott, M. J., 243
Earle, A., 133
Eaton, J. F., 249
Eaton, W. O., 129
Ebel, R., 546
Eccles, J., 346, 375, 397, 398, 417
Eccles, J. S., 67, 69, 70, 71, 129, 130,
    131, 132, 135, 347, 348, 350,
    369, 370, 380, 381, 382, 384,
    384–385, 385, 391, 397, 398,
    401, 412, 414, 415, 417, 418,
    420, 421, 545
Eccles (Parsons), J. S., 67, 129, 397,
    407, 412, 413
Eckert, P., 73, 75, 76
Eckert, T. L., 161, 168, 294
Edelbrock, C. S., 502
Eden, G. F., 153
Edens, K. M., 209
Education, U.S. Department of, 134,
    135, 138, 139, 144, 153, 158,
    163, 167, 169, 172, 177, 180, 422
Education, U.S. Department of, Civil
    Rights Office, 178, 180
Edwards, C. P., 37
Edwards-Evans, S., 121
Eeds, M., 457
Egeland, B., 131
Ehle, D. A., 179
Eicher, S. A., 76
Eifert, G. H., 301
Einstein, G. O., 208, 265, 440, 447
Eisenberg, N., 32, 75, 91, 92, 93,
    128, 129, 139
Eisenberg, T. E., 455
Eisenberger, R., 413
El-Banna, H., 283

Elder, A. D., 65, 517
El-Dinary, P. B., 271, 272
Elia, J. P., 77
Elicker, J., 62
Eliot, A. J., 404
Elkind, D., 32, 70, 73
Ellenwood, S., 94
Elliot, A. J., 404, 405
Elliott, D. J., 40
Elliott, E. S., 371, 397, 403, 404,
    413, 418
Elliott, R., 339
Elliott, S., 203
Elliott, S. N., 82, 84, 326, 343, 358
Ellis, E. S., 154, 159, 160, 295, 329,
    362, 363
Ellis, H. C., 235
Ellis, J. A., 215, 217
Ellis, N. C., 50
Ellis, N. R., 294
Elmen, J., 62
Elrich, M., 96
Emmer, E. T., 290, 319, 326, 481,
    482, 485, 486, 489, 490, 491,
    494, 495, 496, 499, 508
Empson, S. B., 31
Englehart, M. D., 261, 433
Englemann, S., 444
Enns, L. R., 129
Entwisle, D. R., 419
Epstein, H., 25
Epstein, J. L., 64, 75, 122, 453, 503,
    505, 506
Epstein, J. S., 75
Epstein, T., 124
Erdley, C. A., 82
Erickson, F., 122, 221
Erickson, P. I., 76
Ericsson, K. A., 114, 211
Eriks-Brophy, A., 122
Erikson, Erik, 67, 68–69, 71
Eron, L. D., 82, 338
Ervin, R. A., 183
Erwin, P., 73, 74
Esquivel, G. B., 115
Estrin, E., 124, 126
Etaugh, C., 130
Evans, E. D., 567, 580
Evans, G. W., 308
Evans, I. M., 174
Evertson, C., 421
Evertson, C. M., 326, 481, 486, 489,
    490, 499
Eylon, B., 250
Eysenck, M. W., 200, 201, 229,
    236, 380

Fabes, R. A., 75, 82, 92
Fabos, B., 462
Fad, K. S., 159
Fagot, B. I., 130
Fairchild, H. H., 121
Fake, S., 165
Fall, R., 516
Fantuzzo, J., 469
Fantuzzo, J. W., 312, 355
Farah, M. J., 191
Faraone, S. V., 156
Farinacci, S., 241
Farivar, S., 83, 489
Farmer, J. A., 212
Farrell, E., 136
Farwell, L., 556
Feather, N. T., 370, 397, 412
Fegley, S., 93
Feiring, C., 76
Feldhusen, J. F., 115, 116, 179, 183
Feld, S., 391
Felton, M., 457
Feltovich, P., 286
Feltz, D. L., 308, 312
Fennema, E., 129, 130, 412, 421, 473
Ferguson, E. L., 440, 447

Ferguson, R., 132
Ferretti, R. P., 56, 168, 222, 254
Ferro, J., 422
Fessler, M. A., 162
Feuerstein, R., 243–244, 572
Feuerstein, R., 572
Fey, M. E., 158
Fiedler, E. D., 179, 472
Field, D., 33
Fier, J., 129, 420
Finders, M., 133, 506
Fink, B., 215
Fink, C. M., 135
Finkelhor, D., 81, 96
Finn, J. D., 135, 136, 138, 139
Finn-Stevenson, M., 108
Firestone, P., 157
Fischer, K. W., 22, 33, 113
Fisher, C. W., 245, 454
Fisher, J. S., 20
Fisher, R. P., 516
Fisher, W. W., 312
Fitzgerald, J. R., 308
Fivush, R., 44
Flanagan, D. P., 108
Flavell, J. H., 26, 32, 33, 44, 45, 46, 52, 68, 97, 223, 236
Fleming, J. S., 369, 396
Fletcher, K. L., 168
Flores, A., 10
Florez, V., 503
Flynn, J. R., 113
Foos, P. W., 516
Ford, D. Y., 119, 548, 588
Ford, M. E., 52, 351, 374, 375, 386, 403, 406, 407
Fordham, S., 420
Forsyth, J. P., 301
Fortier, M. S., 369
Fosnot, C. T., 232, 243
Foster-Johnson, L., 422
Fowler, S. A., 310
Fox, J. J., 316
Fox, K. R., 506
Fox, L. H., 131, 180
Fox, N. A., 22
Fox, P. W., 455, 554
Fraley, J., 207
Franks, J. J., 193, 207, 286
Frasier, M. M., 181, 294
Frazer, L. H., 135
Frecker, K., 462
Frederiksen, J. R., 447, 448, 449, 450, 458, 515, 554, 558
Frederiksen, N., 283, 448, 515, 516
Freebern, G., 264
Freedman, K., 125
Freedman, S. G., 76
Freeland, J. T., 325
Freeman, B., 408
Freeman, B. J., 163
Freiberg, H. J., 261
French, E. G., 376
French, K. E., 128, 129, 130
Frensch, P. A., 279, 286
Frick, P. J., 157
Friebert, S. E., 46
Friedel, J., 416
Friedel, M., 385, 502
Friedman, L., 6
Friedman, S. T., 94
Friedrich, L. K., 339
Friedrichs, A. G., 46
Friend, P., 154, 159, 160, 295, 329, 362, 363
Friesen, B., 161
Frieze, I. H., 411
Frisbie, D. A., 583, 585
Fritz, J. B., 209
Frost, J. L., 130, 316
Fry, A. F., 310
Fuchs, D., 465, 468, 469, 470
Fuchs, L. S., 465, 468, 469

Fueyo, V., 469
Fuhrman, W., 76
Fuligni, A. J., 124
Fulker, D. W., 113
Fuller, D., 73
Fuller, M. L., 122, 130, 321, 328, 486
Funder, D. C., 154
Furlong, M., 183
Furman, W., 76
Furst, E. J., 261, 433

Gaertner, S. L., 126, 417
Gage, N. L., 4
Gagné, E. D., 198, 201
Gagné, R. M., 211, 235, 444, 445
Gaines, M. L., 583
Gaines, S., 161
Gallagher, J. J., 179
Gallimore, R., 39, 453, 508
Gallini, J., 406, 440
Ganschow, L., 138, 139
Garaud, J. D., 98, 163
García, E. E., 53, 119, 122, 125, 126, 134, 136, 254, 406, 471, 500
Garcia-Mila, M., 33
Garcia, T., 65, 272
Gardner, H., 22, 108, 108n, 109, 110, 114, 178
Garhart, C., 445
Garibaldi, A. M., 136, 137, 138, 139
Garner, R., 199, 263, 400
Garnier, H. E., 134, 135
Garrison, L., 121, 123
Garvey, C., 79n
Gaskill, P. J., 387
Gathercole, S. E., 43
Gaundry, E., 544
Gauntt, H. L., 207
Gavin, L. A., 76
Gay, J., 294
Gayford, C., 464
Gaynor, J., 580
Gearheart, B. R., 172, 173, 184, 329
Gearheart, C. J., 172
Geary, D. C., 22, 375
Gelman, R., 32, 52
Gelman, S. A., 240, 241, 275
Gendreau, P. L., 81
Genova, W. J., 85
Germinario, V., 96, 502
Gerst, M. S., 343
Gerton, J., 119
Gertzog, W. A., 251
Gettinger, M., 486, 489
Geva, D., 98
Ghatala, E. S., 270
Ghezzi, P. M., 310
Giaconia, R. M., 221, 447
Giangreco, M. F., 174
Gibbs, J., 88
Gibbs, J. C., 73
Gibson, E., 74
Gick, M. L., 257, 278, 279
Giedd, J. N., 22
Gill, H. S., 22, 128
Gillberg, I. C., 163
Gillies, R. M., 465
Gilligan, C., 91
Gilligan, Carol, 87, 91
Gilliland, H., 121, 122, 123
Gillingham, M. G., 199
Gilpin, L., 543
Ginsberg, M. B., 118, 406, 421
Ginsburg, D., 73
Girotto, V., 33
Glaeser, B., 323
Glaessner, B., 378
Glanzer, M., 207, 212
Glaser, R., 45, 178, 222, 283, 286, 517
Glass, A. L., 236
Glasser, W., 487
Glauberman, N., 113
Glover, J. A., 115, 580

Glucksberg, S., 52, 236
Glynn, S. M., 241
Goddard, R. D., 349, 501
Goetz, E. T., 209, 228, 272
Goetz, L., 148, 149
Golbeck, S. L., 94, 430
Gold, M., 391
Goldberg, A., 76
Goldenberg, C., 415, 417, 420, 453, 508
Golen, S., 393
Gollnick, D. M., 133
Gomez, M. L., 223, 392
Good, S., 413
Good, T., 417
Good, T. L., 39, 197, 205, 244, 357, 385, 407, 408, 415, 416, 417, 450, 464, 495, 508
Goodenow, C., 375
Goodman, J., 352
Goodman, K., 485
Goodnow, J., 235
Goodnow, J. J., 63, 129
Gootman, M. E., 322
Gopnik, M., 48
Gordon, W., 55
Gorski, J. D., 96
Gosling, S. D., 191
Gottesman, R. L., 415
Gottfredson, D. C., 74, 135, 323, 485, 498, 501
Gottfredson, G. D., 323
Gottfredson, L. S., 402
Gottfried, A. E., 56, 369, 396, 422
Gottfried, A. W., 56, 178, 369, 385, 396, 548
Gottlieb, G., 22, 113
Gottlieb, J., 183
Gottman, J. M., 73, 74, 75, 76, 83
Gowin, D. B., 265, 266
Grabe, M., 197
Grabowski, B. L., 445
Graeber, A. O., 278
Graesser, A., 468
Graham, C. R., 54
Graham, N., 135
Graham, S., 44, 81–82, 82, 83, 96, 215, 254, 372, 384, 393, 405, 408, 415, 416, 417, 418, 419, 420
Gralinski, H., 412
Grandin, T., 163
Granfield, J. M., 98
Granger, D. A., 502
Grant, C. A., 85, 126, 127, 223, 392
Gravemeijer, K., 458
Gray, C., 98, 163
Gray, S. G., 197, 263
Gray, W. D., 236, 274
Greathouse, S., 451
Green, B. L., 46
Green, L., 310
Greene, B. A., 270
Greene, C. A., 162
Greene, D., 330
Greene, T. R., 286
Greenfield, P. M., 96
Greeno, J. G., 275, 464
Greenough, W. T., 22, 191
Greenspan, S., 98
Greenwood, C. R., 468, 469, 471, 472, 473
Greer, B., 41, 246
Gregg, M., 245, 454
Gresham, F. M., 97, 154, 157, 168
Griesinger, T., 404
Griffin, B. W., 454
Griffin, M. M., 454
Griffin, S. A., 132
Griffore, R. J., 67
Grinberg, D., 97, 161
Grissmer, D. W., 132
Griswold, K. S., 161
Grodzinsky, G. M., 157, 294

Groër, M., 70
Grolnick, W. S., 369, 398, 515
Gronlund, N. E., 431, 434, 435, 436, 504, 528, 529, 530, 537, 545, 555, 558, 559, 560, 563, 563n, 566, 570, 573, 574, 575, 577, 579, 584
Gross, P. H., 556
Gross, S., 572
Grosslight, L., 250
Grossman, H. L., 96
Grotpeter, J. K., 129
Gruber, H., 275
Grusec, J. E., 84, 323–324
Guacci-Franco, N., 73
Guay, F., 66, 73, 77, 369
Guerin, D. W., 56
Guerra, M. R., 458
Guerra, N., 90
Guerra, N. G., 82, 83
Guerrero, F., 446
Guess, D., 174
Guiton, G., 415
Gülgöz, S., 204
Gullotta, T. P., 96
Gunstone, R. F., 250, 262
Gunther, John, 94
Guppy, T. E., 312
Gurtner, J., 445
Guskey, T. R., 443, 537
Gustafson, M., 355
Gustafsson, J., 107, 129, 471

Hackenberg, T. D., 307
Hacker, D. J., 43, 46, 246, 262, 268, 269, 272
Hadaway, N. L., 503
Haden, C., 44
Hadley, P. A., 158
Hadwin, A. F., 355, 356, 357
Haenan, J., 38
Haertel, E. H., 576
Hagan, R., 130
Hagen, A. S., 418
Hagen, J. W., 42, 43
Hagopian, L. P., 312
Hagtvet, K. A., 380, 543
Hahn, H., 145
Hakuta, K., 53
Hale, G. A., 263
Hale, N., 482
Hale-Benson, J. E., 63, 418
Halford, G. S., 45
Hall, R. H., 440
Hall, R. V., 468, 497
Hallenbeck, M. J., 159
Haller, E. P., 268
Hallinan, M. T., 75
Hallowell, E., 157, 161
Halpern, D. F., 6, 104, 128, 129, 138, 139, 278, 290, 291, 292, 293, 384
Halpin, G., 515
Halpin, G., 515
Halvorsen, A. T., 148
Hambleton, R. K., 577
Hamers, J. H. M., 572
Hamilton, V. L., 515
Hamlett, C. L., 465
Hamman, D., 212, 262
Hammer, D., 447
Hamp-Lyons, L., 568
Hampton, J. A., 236
Hannafin, M. J., 445
Hannum, W. H., 436
Hansen, J., 440
Hanson, A. R., 344, 347, 348
Harackiewicz, J. M., 370, 396, 400, 401, 404, 405
Hardre, P. L., 134, 135, 369, 394
Hardy, R., 577
Harlow, H. F., 307
Harnish, J. D., 82
Harnishfeger, K. K., 355

Harold-Goldsmith, R., 67
Harp, S. F., 263
Harper, F., 542
Harpster, L., 356
Harris, A. C., 21
Harris, A. H., 489
Harris, C. R., 119, 178, 179
Harris, J. J., 548, 588
Harris, J. R., 63, 73, 75
Harris, K. R., 27, 44, 215, 243, 272, 294, 351, 354, 358, 473, 497
Harris, M., 56, 171, 172n
Harris, M. B., 77
Harris, M. J., 67
Harris, R. J., 290
Harrow, A. J., 433
Harry, B., 182
Hart, C. H., 82
Hart, D., 65, 68, 69, 82, 93
Hart, E. L., 157
Hart, E. R., 461
Harter, S., 64, 65, 67, 68, 69, 97, 98, 370, 376, 380–381, 381, 392, 396, 400, 405
Hartley, J., 440
Hartup, W. W., 62, 67, 74
Harvey, O. J., 75
Harway, M., 128
Harwood, R. L., 68
Haseman, A. L., 457
Hatano, G., 232, 243, 245, 458, 464
Hatch, T., 108
Hattie, J., 270, 272, 295
Hauser, S. T., 71
Hawking, Stephen, 361
Hawkins, F. P. L., 241, 393
Hawkins, J. A., 74
Hawkins, R. D., 191
Hayes, C. B., 482
Hayes, S. C., 354
Hayes-Roth, B., 207
Hayslip, B., Jr., 107
Haywood, H. C., 249
Hazel, J. S., 97, 254, 362
Healey, J., 82
Healy, A. F., 447
Hearold, S., 94
Heath, S. B., 108, 123
Hedges, L. V., 129, 447
Heflin, A. H., 77
Hegarty, M., 6, 129, 440, 447
Hegland, S., 193
Heindel, P., 211
Heller, J. I., 283, 286
Heller, L. R., 469
Helmke, A., 439, 444, 490
Helton, G. B., 63
Hembree, R., 381, 382
Henker, B., 502
Hennessey, B. A., 115, 116, 394, 396, 397
Hennessey, M. G., 271
Hermann, D. J., 286
Herrenkohl, L. R., 458, 460
Herrnstein, R. J., 113
Hersh, R. H., 89
Hess, G. A., 135
Hess, R. D., 63, 64, 114, 132, 420
Hetherington, E. M., 22
Hettinger, H. R., 178
Heuer, F., 378
Heward, W. L., 97, 139, 154, 222, 223, 294, 313, 329, 385, 422, 472, 502
Hewitt, J., 232, 248, 249, 462
Hewson, P. W., 251
Heymann, S. J., 133
Hickey, D. T., 448, 454
Hicks, L., 406
Hidalgo, N. M., 122, 503, 506, 508
Hidi, S., 267, 370, 378, 396, 399, 400, 401, 402, 404, 405
Hiebert, E. H., 232, 245, 454, 457, 514, 538, 571, 573

Hiebert, J., 58, 244, 246, 247, 457
Higgins, A., 93, 94
Higgins, A. T., 42
Higgins, C., 323
Hildreth, B., 178
Hill, C., 451, 547, 570, 586
Hill, D. A., 163
Hill, K. T., 380, 383, 543, 544
Hill, W. H., 261, 433
Hilliard, A., 119
Hinckley, H. S., 506
Hiner, M., 84, 85, 183
Hines, M., 128, 129
Hinkley, J. W., 406
Hirsch, E. D., Jr., 243, 432
Hirschfeld, L. A., 275
Hitch, G. J., 43
Ho, D. Y. F., 63, 295
Ho, H.-Z., 506
Hobbs, N., 151
Hocevar, D., 115
Hockensmith, M. L., 516
Hodell, M., 329, 330, 395, 396, 402
Hodges, E., 81
Hodges, E. V. E., 66
Hodkin, B., 32
Hofer, B. K., 270, 271
Hofferth, S. L., 76
Hoffman, L. W., 74
Hoffman, M. L., 92, 94, 378
Hogan, D. M., 464, 465
Hogan, K., 232, 457, 459
Hogan, R., 179
Hogdon, L. A., 164
Hoge, R. D., 178, 422, 583
Holley, C. D., 266
Holliday, B. G., 420
Hollins, E. R., 125
Hollon, R. E., 244
Holloway, S. D., 63, 64, 114, 132
Holmes, C. J., 22
Holt, K., 394, 404
Holt-Reynolds, D., 4, 242
Holyoak, K. J., 236, 257, 278, 279
Hom, A., 485
Homme, L. E., 312
Hong, Y., 119, 231, 413
Honig, A. S., 84, 94
Hood, W. R., 75
Hook, C. L., 183
Hoover-Dempsey, K. V., 452, 505
Hopmeyer, A., 77
Horgan, D., 411
Horgan, D. D., 46, 130
Horgan, R., 79n
Horner, R. H., 395
Hornyak, R. S., 351, 357
Horowitz, B., 94
Horvat, M., 158, 502
Horvath, J. A., 438
Hoskyn, J., 571
Hosmer, E., 260
Hossler, D., 124
Hotchkiss, P. R., 583
Houghton, C., 271
House, B. J., 97
Houtz, J. C., 116
Howe, C. K., 506
Howe, M. L., 195
Hoyt, J. D., 46
Hoy, W. K., 11, 349
Huberty, P. D., 323
Hudley, C., 82, 83, 254
Huff, J. A., 322
Hughes, F. P., 84, 97, 168, 254
Hughes, J. N., 328, 362
Humphreys, L. G., 133
Hungate, H. N., 283, 286
Hunt, E., 38
Hunt, E. B., 6
Hunt, P., 148, 149
Hunt, R. R., 235
Hunter, M., 443

Huntley, S. B., 180
Hurston, Zora Neale, 131
Husman, J., 408
Huston, A. C., 128, 130
Hutt, C., 448
Hutt, S. J., 448
Huttenlocher, J., 32
Hyde, J. S., 129
Hymel, S., 84, 135, 183, 369, 375
Hynd, C., 242, 249, 250, 251

Iacono, W. G., 113
Iadicola, P., 129, 323
Igoa, C., 119, 120, 313, 384, 471
Igoe, A. R., 379
Inagaki, K., 232, 243, 245, 458, 464
Inglehart, M., 129, 384
Inglis, A., 4, 359, 467, 468, 469
Inhelder, B., 23
Inman, W. E., 440
Irizarry, N. L., 68
Irujo, S., 121, 123
Isaacson, R., 376
Ittel, A., 92–93
Ittenbach, R. F., 56
Iwata, B. A., 318, 321
Izard, C., 79

Jacklin, C. N., 129
Jackson, D., III, 370, 419
Jackson, Dinah, 237
Jackson, D. L., 127, 165, 167, 170
Jackson, J. S., 417
Jacobs, J., 67
Jacobs, J. E., 131, 421, 545
Jacobs, J. K., 134
Jacobs, P. J., 130
Jacobs, W. J., 191
Jacobsen, B., 421, 422
Jacobson, J. L., 62
Jacobson, K. C., 82
Jacoby, R., 113
Jagacinski, C. M., 404
James, W., 274
Janos, P. M., 178
Janosz, M., 135, 136
Jarrett, O. S., 73
Jarvis, P. A., 83
Jayaratne, T., 67
Jeffrey, T. E., 6
Jeffries, N. O., 22
Jenkins, L., 47
Jenlink, C. L., 137
Jenson, W. R., 56, 162, 164, 222, 329, 361, 362, 385, 422, 472, 502, 588
Jernigan, T. L., 22
Jetton, T. L., 263
Jiao, Z., 74
Jimerson, S., 131, 133
Joag-Dev, C., 238
Johanning, D. I., 288
Johnsen, E. P., 52
Johnsen, M. C., 161
Johnsen, T. B., 380, 543
Johnson, D. L., 114
Johnson, D. M., 236
Johnson, D. W., 84, 94, 358, 457, 463, 464, 465, 466, 467
Johnson, H. C., 161
Johnson, J. S., 53
Johnson, J. T., 209
Johnson, M., 129
Johnson, M. K., 204
Johnson, R., 358
Johnson, R. T., 84, 94, 358, 457, 463, 464, 465, 466, 467
Johnson-Glenberg, M. C., 209, 461
John-Steiner, V., 40, 244
Johnstone, A. H., 283
Johnstone, M., 481
Jonassen, D. H., 436, 437, 445
Jones, D., 216

Jones, D. L., 586
Jones, E. E., 374
Jones, G. P., 129
Jones, I., 323
Jones, K. M., 326
Jones, L. L., 10
Jones, M. C., 305
Jones, M. S., 213, 292
Jordan, L., 153
Joshi, M. S., 63
Josselson, R., 69
Jovanovic, J., 129, 130, 131
Joy, R. M., 262
Jozefowicz, D. M., 135
Judd, C. H., 276
Judy, J. E., 278, 286
Junkin, L. J., 65
Jussim, L., 417
Just, M. A., 212
Juvonen, J., 81–82, 84, 85, 97, 183, 375, 376, 414

Kaczala, C. M., 130, 347, 403, 414
Kagan, J., 21, 62
Kahl, B., 267, 272
Kahle, J. B., 130, 420, 545
Kail, R., 21, 43, 45, 168
Kail, R. V., 109
Kameya, L. I., 544
Kana, T. G., 174
Kane, R. J., 584
Kaplan, A., 403, 404, 405, 420, 464
Karau, S. J., 465, 467
Kardash, C. A. M., 269, 291
Kardash, C. M., 400
Karlin, M. B., 204
Karmiloff-Smith, A., 48, 49, 51
Karns, K., 465
Karplus, R., 33
Karpov, Y. V., 249
Karweit, N., 246
Karweit, N. L., 136, 137
Kass, R. E., 321
Katchadourian, H., 76, 77
Katkovsky, W., 413
Katz, E. W., 50
Katz, L., 66, 67, 308
Kaufman, K. F., 321
Kavussanu, M., 405
Kawakami, K., 417
Keane, M. T., 200, 201, 229, 236
Kearins, J. M., 55
Keating, D. P., 130
Keefe, K., 74
Kehle, T. J., 361, 362
Keil, F. C., 234, 240, 241, 250
Keleman, D., 241
Kelemen, W. L., 269
Keller, Helen, 341
Kelley, M. L., 312, 313
Kelly, A., 129
Kelly, G. J., 457
Kennedy, C. H., 470
Kennedy, R., 573
Kenney, P. A., 558
Keogh, B. A., 182
Keogh, B. K., 97, 147, 149, 166, 177
Kermani, H., 467, 469
Kern, L., 162
Kerns, L. L., 162
Kerr, B., 556
Kerr, M. M., 160
Khattri, N., 539, 571
Kiewra, K. A., 197, 207, 263, 264, 515
Kiklinski, M. R., 417
Killen, M., 90
Kilner, L. A., 71
Kim, D., 370, 482, 485
Kimberg, D. Y., 191, 195n
Kimble, G. A., 300
Kindermann, T. A., 74, 75
King, A., 232, 267, 272, 288, 357, 464, 466, 469, 470

King, F. J., 445
King, J., 469
King, Martin Luther, Jr., 88–89, 341
King, N. J., 381
King, S. S., 129, 130
Kingma, J., 195
Kintsch, W., 230, 401
Kirby, J. R., 440
Kirby, S. N., 132
Kirigin, K. A., 84
Kirker, W. S., 205
Kirkland, M. C., 380, 543
Kirschenbaum, R. J., 114, 119, 124
Kishor, N., 65
Kitayama, S., 96
Kitsantis, A., 343, 344, 348
Klebanov, P. K., 113
Klein, J. D., 413
Klein, P. R., 244
Klein, S., 130, 576
Klein, S. B., 65
Kletzien, S. B., 207
Klingler, C., 53
Klint, K. A., 211
Kluger, A. N., 372, 408
Knapp, M. S., 74, 75, 132, 136, 139,
    415, 421
Knapp, N. F., 178
Knauth, S., 392
Knight, S. L., 461
Knobles, P., 74
Knowlton, D., 162, 165, 422
Koegel, L. K., 163, 164, 326, 502
Koegel, R. L., 164
Koeppel, J., 127
Koestner, R., 394, 395, 396
Kogan, J. S., 312
Kogan, N., 115
Kohlberg, L., 88, 89, 90, 91, 94
Kohlberg, Lawrence, 87–91, 94, 232
Kohn, A., 395
Kohut, S., Jr., 381
Kolbe, L., 70
Kolodner, J., 219, 230
Konopak, B. C., 223
Koretz, D., 576, 586
Kose, G., 211
Kosslyn, S. M., 209
Kounin, J. S., 491
Kovacs, D. M., 74
Kowalski, P., 396
Koyanagi, C., 161
Kozhevnikov, M., 6, 129
Krajcik, J., 465
Krajcik, J. S., 440
Krampen, G., 516, 569
Krapp, A., 369, 400
Krashen, S. D., 54
Krasnor, L. R., 77
Krathwohl, D. R., 261, 432, 433
Kratochwill, T. R., 351, 497
Krauss, R. M., 52
Kronsberg, S., 130
Kroth, R. L., 138
Krug, C., 165
Krumboltz, H. B., 319, 320
Krumboltz, J. D., 319, 320
Kucakowski, R., 70
Kucan, L., 272
Kuhl, J., 355, 356
Kuhn, D., 33, 250, 270, 272, 291,
    293, 457
Kuiper, N. A., 205
Kulhavy, R. W., 202, 209
Kulik, C. C., 179, 308, 310, 443,
    445, 472
Kulik, J. A., 179, 308, 310, 443, 445
Kulikowich, J. M., 199, 211
Kunc, N., 145
Kupersmidt, J. B., 82, 375
Kurtines, W. M., 87, 92–93
Kurtz, B. E., 43
Kyle, W. C., 242, 245, 250

LaBar, K. S., 378
LaBlance, G. R., 158
Laboratory of Human Cognition, 105
Labov, W., 236
Ladd, G. W., 82, 375
Ladson-Billings, G., 121, 126, 127,
    136, 254, 500, 503
LaFromboise, T., 119
Lahey, B. B., 157
Laird, R. D., 82
Lajoie, S. P., 39, 445
Lakes, M. K., 130, 545
LaMay, M. L., 6, 104, 128, 129
Lambdin, D. V., 514
Lamborn, S. D., 62
Lamon, M., 462, 463
Lamon, S. J., 129
Lampert, M., 247, 457, 458
Lan, W. Y., 392
Landauer, T. K., 198
Landau, S., 153, 156, 157, 158, 164,
    222, 329, 502
Landesman, S., 166
Lane, D. M., 42
Lange, R. E., 179
Langer, E. J., 285, 286, 394
Langer, J. A., 11, 501
Lanthier, R. P., 62
Lanza, A., 445
Laosa, L. M., 132
Lapsley, D. K., 70
Larke, P. J., 503
Larkin, J. H., 262, 263
Larkin, R. W., 76
Larrivee, L., 158
Larsen, E., 547, 570, 586
Larson, R. W., 76, 369, 370, 395, 396
Lasker, J., 75
Latham, G. P., 350, 403
Laupa, M., 90
Lave, J., 40, 275, 288
Law, D. J., 6
Lawson, K. R., 42
Lawton, T. A., 515
Laychak, A. E., 74
Leach, J., 230
Leal, D., 56
Learning Technology Center,
    Vanderbilt University, 289
Leary, M. R., 66, 163
Le Blanc, M., 135
LeCount, J., 455
Lee, C. D., 119, 121, 126
Lee, D. L., 317
Lee, Harper, 94, 131
Lee, J. B., 202
Lee, J. F., Jr., 443
Lee, O., 124, 231, 252
Lee, S., 33
Lee-Pearce, M. L., 136
Lefevre, P., 244
Leffert, J. S., 98
Leggett, E. L., 122, 413
Lehman, S., 400
Lehrer, R., 58, 451
Leichtman, M. D., 231
Leinbach, M. D., 130
Leinhardt, G., 245, 454, 457, 473
Leiter, J., 161
Lejuez, C. W., 307
Lenneberg, E. H., 48
Lennon, R., 4, 32, 46, 92, 93, 242, 532
Lentz, F. E., 312, 321
Lenz, B. K., 440
Leopold, G. D., 577
Lepper, M. R., 325, 329, 330, 395,
    396, 402, 445, 469
Lerman, D., 412
Lerman, D. C., 318
Lerner, J. W., 153, 154, 155
Lesgold, A. M., 207
Leslie, A. M., 163
Lester, F. K., Jr., 514, 572, 584

Levin, G. R., 21, 431
Levin, J. R., 213, 270, 292, 440
Levin, L., 315
Levin, M. E., 213
Levine, D. U., 500, 501, 505
Levine, M., 235
Levitt, J. L., 73
Levitt, M. J., 73
Levy, I., 464
Lewis, C., 133, 506
Lewis, G. W., 164
Lewis, R. B., 159, 160
Lezotte, L. W., 500, 501, 505
Liberman, R. P., 313
Lickona, T., 83, 485, 486
Lidz, C. S., 542
Lieberman, A. B., 162
Lieberman, L. M., 148
Lieberman, M., 88
Light, J. G., 153
Light, P., 33, 275
Lillard, A. S., 420
Lin, Y., 376
Lindberg, M., 212
Linderholm, T., 355
Lind, G., 97, 98
Lindsay, J. J., 451
Linn, M. C., 33, 34, 129, 179, 250,
    294, 296, 440, 464
Linn, R. L., 435, 504, 528, 529, 530,
    537, 538, 545, 555, 559, 560, 563,
    563n, 575, 576, 577, 579, 584
Lipschultz, R. E., 404
Lipson, M. Y., 238, 241
Liss, M. B., 130
Little, L., 82, 163n
Little, T. D., 372
Littlewood, W. T., 274
Littman, R., 81
Liu, L. G., 456
Livesley, W. J., 79
Lloyd, D. N., 134
Lochhead, J., 285
Lochman, J. E., 82, 98, 254
Locke, E. A., 350, 403
Lockheed, M. E., 471
Lodico, M. G., 270
Loeber, R., 129, 157
Loftus, E. F., 200, 230
Loftus, G. R., 200
Logan, K. R., 174
Lohman, M. R., 471
Lomawaima, K. T., 122
Londer, G., 457
Long, M., 53
Lonky, E., 400
Lopez, E. C., 545
López, G. R., 506, 507
Loranger, A. L., 262, 270
Lorch, E. P., 157, 222, 223, 440
Lorch, R. F., Jr., 355, 440
Losey, K. M., 119, 122
Losoff, M., 75
Lotan, R. A., 465, 473
Lounsbury, J. H., 381
Lou, Y., 464, 465, 467
Lovell, K., 33
Lovett, S. B., 46, 272, 440
Lovitt, T. C., 312
Lowell, E. L., 370
Lowery, B., 421
Lowry, R., 70, 74, 96, 338
Lubart, T. I., 116
Luchins, A. S., 285
Luchins, E. H., 285
Luckasson, R., 138
Ludwig, W. G., 129, 323
Lueptow, L. B., 407
Lundeberg, M. A., 554
Lupart, J. L., 178, 179, 362
Lykken, D. T., 62, 113
Lynch, J. H., 67, 73, 74
Lyon, M. A., 321

Lyons, A., 135
Lytle, S., 10

Ma, X., 65
Macarthur, J., 54
Maccoby, E. E., 22, 42, 43, 62, 63, 94
Mace, F. C., 317, 343, 351, 497
Machiels-Bongaerts, M., 206
Mac Iver, D., 375, 398
MacKenzie-Keating, S., 320
MacLean, D. J., 130, 473
MacLean, M., 63
Maclin, D., 250, 271
MacMillan, D. L., 97, 147, 149, 150,
    154, 157, 166, 168, 177
MacWhinney, B., 49
Madden, N. A., 85, 136, 137, 145,
    149, 183, 184
Madison, S. M., 417
Madon, S., 417
Maehr, M. L., 74, 368, 369, 376,
    381, 403, 404, 405
Magliocca, L. A., 175
Magnuson, D., 358
Magnusson, S. J., 571
Mahapatra, M., 96
Mahn, H., 244
Maier, S., 415
Maker, C. J., 97, 139, 178, 181, 294
Makris, E., 392
Malone, J., 81
Mandell, C., 317
Mandl, H., 275
Mandler, G., 206
Manis, F. R., 153
Manset, G., 148
Marachi, R., 416, 484
Maratsos, M., 51
Marcia, J. E., 71, 72, 407
Marcus, G. F., 51
Marcus, R. F., 82
Maria, K., 242, 244
Markman, E. M., 46, 268
Marks, H. M., 129
Marks, J., 113
Marks, M. B., 271, 272
Markstrom-Adams, C., 71, 96, 126
Markus, H. R., 96
Marlowe, D., 376
Marrett, C. B., 131
Marsh, H. W., 64, 65, 66, 67, 69, 82,
    96, 97, 98, 406, 411, 464
Marshall, H. H., 193, 245, 246,
    447, 457
Marsh, R. W., 25
Martens, B. K., 317
Martin, C. L., 75
Martin, J. A., 62, 63, 94
Martin, J. M., 129, 420
Martin, S. S., 183, 316
Martinez-Pons, M., 346, 397
Marx, R. W., 252, 372, 400, 403, 465
Marzano, R. J., 528
Masia, B. B., 433
Maslow, Abraham, 373
Masson, M. E. J., 216
Masten, A. S., 63, 133, 134
Masters, J. C., 308
Mastin, M., 485
Mastropieri, M. A., 56, 148, 154,
    155, 156, 169, 182, 183, 213,
    294, 501, 548, 589
Masuda, W. V., 571, 572
Masur, E. F., 46
Mathes, P. G., 468
Matusov, E., 248
Maxmell, D., 73, 323
Mayer, E. V., 310
Mayer, R. E., 22, 33, 199, 204, 263,
    264, 272, 275, 283, 285, 440, 447
Mayer-Smith, J., 4
Mayock, E., 87
Mazur, J. E., 312

Pang, V. O., 77, 96, 126, 342, 384, 508, 543
Paolitto, D. P., 89
Parada, R. H., 82
Paris, A. H., 352, 357, 368, 418, 514, 571, 586
Paris, S. G., 68, 134, 246, 271, 272, 350, 352, 353, 357, 368, 374, 411, 415, 418, 454, 459, 464, 514, 515, 515, 517, 567, 571, 578, 579, 586
Park, K., 74
Parke, R. D., 323
Parker, J. G., 73, 74, 75
Parker, W. D., 178, 180
Parkhurst, J. T., 77
Parks, C. P., 75, 76, 96
Parnes, S. J., 115
Parsons, J. E., 130, 347, 403, 414
Pascarella, E. T., 33
Pascual-Leone, J., 90
Pasternack, J. F., 92
Pastorelli, C., 77
Patnode, M., 323
Patnoe, S., 466
Patrick, H., 375, 385, 464, 482, 484, 485
Patterson, C. J., 77
Patterson, G. R., 74, 81, 161
Patterson, M. L., 415
Patton, J. R., 56, 159, 168, 169, 171, 172, 173, 180, 184, 254, 329, 385, 502, 504
Paulson, F. L., 544, 586, 587
Paulson, K., 129
Paulson, P. R., 586
Pavlov, Ivan, 302–303
Pawlas, G. E., 133
Paxton, R. J., 244, 261, 266, 270, 292
Pea, R. D., 112
Peake, P. K., 310
Pearlstone, Z., 206
Pearson, D. A., 42
Pearson, P. D., 118, 230, 440
Peck, C. A., 85
Peeke, L. A., 129, 420
Pelham, W. E., Jr., 98
Pellegrini, A. D., 73, 77, 81, 82, 158, 197, 323, 381, 502
Pellegrino, J. W., 6
Pellicer, L. O., 136
Penner, B. D., 286
Penrose, A. M., 265
Pepler, D. I., 79n
Pereira, L., 86, 183
Perera, K., 51
Pérez, B., 54, 84, 464, 506
Perkins, D. N., 39, 108, 112, 114, 116, 262, 274, 275, 276, 277, 278, 279, 283, 293
Perry, D., 81
Perry, D. G., 82, 323
Perry, L. C., 82, 323
Perry, M., 131
Perry, N. E., 357
Perry, R. P., 402
Person, N. K., 468
Pessar, L. F., 161
Petersen, A. C., 129
Petersen, G. A., 546
Peterson, A. C., 75
Peterson, C., 415
Peterson, C. R., 322
Peterson, L. R., 198
Peterson, M. J., 198
Peterson, P. L., 1, 262, 447
Peterson, R. F., 83
Peterson, S. E., 465
Petrie, S., 76
Petrill, S. A., 113
Petrosky, A. R., 576, 585
Pettigrew, T. F., 127
Pettit, G. S., 81, 82

Pettito, L. A., 172n
Peverly, S. T., 277
Pezzoli, M., 85
Pfiffner, L. J., 62, 158, 165, 197, 310, 312, 320, 321, 322, 323, 329, 501
Phelan, P., 77, 85, 119, 376, 381, 407
Phelps, E. A., 378
Phillip, R. A., 10
Phillips, B. N., 385, 543, 548
Phillips, D., 347, 374
Phinney, J., 71, 96
Phye, G. D., 201, 571
Piaget, Jean, 8, 22–36, 37, 38, 44, 45, 48, 50, 55, 57, 58, 70, 79, 81, 89, 109, 190, 193, 231, 232, 236, 241, 243, 275, 372, 571
Piazza, C. C., 94, 312
Pierce, W. D., 396
Piersel, W. C., 308, 326
Pigott, H. E., 312
Piirto, J., 56, 97, 139, 180, 222, 254, 294, 329, 362, 385, 422, 472, 502, 548, 588
Pilotto, L., 96
Pine, J., 576
Pine, K. J., 251, 253
Pinker, S., 49
Pintrich, P. R., 65, 68, 71, 252, 262, 270, 271, 272, 346, 347, 356, 368, 369, 372, 374, 392, 400, 404, 405, 408, 418, 584
Piontkowski, D., 197
Pipher, M., 75, 122
Pitcher, G. D., 385
Pitoniak, M. J., 548
Pittman, K., 440
Pittman, T. S., 391, 394
Plomin, R., 62, 113, 132
Plowman, T. S., 136
Plumert, J. M., 43
Poche, C., 338
Pogrow, S., 457
Poisson, S., 182
Pollard, S. R., 87
Polloway, E. A., 164, 504
Poole, D., 554, 558
Popham, W. J., 435, 503, 544, 546, 558, 567, 571, 574, 577, 586, 587
Porath, M., 294, 296
Porter, A. C., 275, 286
Portes, P. R., 131, 132, 133, 134, 135
Posner, G. J., 250, 251, 271
Postman, L., 219
Post, T. A., 286
Pott, M., 63
Potter, E. F., 209
Poulin, F., 81, 83
Powell, G. J., 68
Powell, K., 70
Powell, S., 385, 395, 422
Power, F. C., 94, 488
Power, M. R., 488
Powers, L. E., 342, 363, 421
Powers, S. I., 71
Prawat, R. S., 245, 248, 251, 262, 285
Premack, D., 308
Presseisen, B. Z., 247
Pressley, M., 44, 56, 139, 208, 213, 222, 232, 254, 262, 264, 270, 271, 272, 275, 294, 329, 418, 419, 439
Preston, R. V., 514
Price-Williams, D. R., 55
Pritchard, R., 294
Prochnow, J. E., 68
Proctor, R. W., 211, 215, 216
Pruitt, K. W., 443
Pruitt, R. P., 116
Pulos, S., 31, 33, 34, 179, 242, 294, 296
Purdie, N., 270, 271, 272, 295
Putallaz, M., 77
Putnam, R. T., 4, 10, 250, 486

Qin, Z., 464
Quellmalz, E., 571
Quilitch, H. R., 83
Quill, K. A., 164
Quinlan, K. M., 432

Raber, S. M., 134, 135
Rabinowitz, M., 45, 178, 222, 283
Rachlin, H., 301, 302, 310, 372
Radke-Yarrow, M., 339
Radziszewska, B., 39
Raine, A., 82
Raison, J., 323
Rajapakse, J. C., 22
Rakow, E. A., 46
Rakow, S. J., 278
Ramey, C., 166
Ramey, C. T., 113, 114, 136
Ramey, S. L., 136
Ramirez, M., 55
Ramsey, E., 161
Ramsey, P. G., 119, 126
Raphael, T. E., 232, 457, 538
Rapport, M. D., 321
Rasp, L. M., 343
Raudenbush, S. W., 417
Rawsthorne, L. J., 404
Real, D., 84
Reder, L. M., 211, 275
Redfield, D. L., 456
Redler, E., 84
Reed, D. F., 133, 134
Reese, J. H., 56
Reeve, J., 134, 135, 369, 394
Reeve, R. A., 459
Reeve, R. E., 157
Reich, P. A., 50, 51, 53
Reid, D. H., 308
Reid, N., 124
Reilley, S., 203
Reimann, P., 277, 283
Reimer, J., 88, 89, 90, 91, 95
Reiner, M., 241
Reis, S. M., 177, 179
Reisberg, D., 197, 199, 219, 236, 301, 378
Reiter, S. N., 292, 458
Rellinger, E., 272
Renkl, A., 275, 278, 283
Renninger, K. A., 400
Renshaw, P. D., 77
Renzulli, J. S., 177, 178, 385, 422
Repman, J., 392
Rescorla, R. A., 301, 302
Resnick, D. P., 216, 537, 538, 539, 571
Resnick, L. B., 32, 206, 230, 241, 280, 283, 285, 286, 538, 539, 571
Resnick, M. D., 485
Rest, J., 90, 90n, 92
Rest, J. R., 94
Reuman, D., 375, 398
Reusser, K., 285
Reyna, C., 415, 416, 417
Reyna, V. F., 195
Reynolds, C. R., 115, 545
Reynolds, M. C., 150, 171, 172, 184, 501, 502
Reynolds, R. E., 118, 199, 223, 228, 238, 262, 263, 440
Reys, B. J., 39
Rhode, G., 353
Ricciuti, H. N., 113
Rice, J., 408
Rice, M., 158
Richards, A. C., 380
Richards, C. M., 162
Richards, D. D., 32
Richards, F., 380
Richards, H. C., 91
Rickert, E. J., 312
Ricks, J. H., 541
Riggs, J. M., 374
Rimm, D. C., 308

Rimm, S. B., 139, 178
Rincón, C., 76
Rincover, A., 322
Ripple, R. E., 114, 115
Risemberg, R., 355, 356, 357
Ritchhart, R., 293
Rittenhouse, P., 247
Ritts, V., 415, 556
Rittschof, K. A., 209
Ritvo, E. R., 163
Roberge, J. J., 33
Roberts, G. C., 405
Roberts, S., 174
Roberts, V., 487
Roberts, W., 482
Robertson, J. S., 419
Robins, R. W., 191
Robinson, A., 472
Robinson, N. M., 178, 183
Robinson, T. R., 353, 498
Roblyer, M. D., 445
Roche, L., 66
Rock, D. A., 415
Roderick, M., 119, 134, 135, 381, 382, 500
Roediger, H. L., III, 219, 231
Roehler, L. R., 230
Rogers, C. R., 483
Rogers, T. B., 205
Rogoff, B., 39, 40, 55, 123, 248, 249
Rogozinski, J. T., 263
Rohner, R. P., 62
Rohrkemper, M. M., 391
Romanczyk, R. G., 300
Ronning, R. R., 115, 457
Roopnarine, J. L., 75
Roosevelt, Franklin D., 361
Rortvedt, A. K., 322
Rosbe, M., 155, 156, 158, 472
Rosch, E. H., 235, 236
Rose, A. J., 82
Rose, S. C., 376
Rose, S. P., 22
Roselli, T., 445
Rosen, L. A., 310
Rosenberg, L. A., 162
Rosenberg, M., 69
Rosenberg, M. S., 162
Rosenshine, B., 39, 267, 269, 272, 461
Rosenshine, B. V., 444, 471, 473
Rosenthal, R., 67, 128, 416, 417
Rosenthal, T. L., 335, 339, 340, 343
Ross, B. H., 236
Ross, D., 338
Ross, G., 39
Ross, J. A., 277, 395, 402
Ross, S., 402
Ross, S. A., 338
Rosser, R., 25, 32, 34
Rotenberg, K. J., 310
Roth, J. L., 515
Roth, K., 93
Roth, K. J., 241, 244, 250, 251, 252, 253
Roth, W., 40
Rothbart, M. K., 21
Rothbaum, F., 63
Roughead, W. G., 447
Rousseau, E. W., 456
Rowe, D. C., 82
Rowe, E., 129
Rowe, M. B., 122, 172, 221
Royeen, C., 182
Royer, J. M., 548
Rubin, D. B., 128
Rubin, K. H., 63, 75, 77, 79n, 83
Ruble, D. N., 128, 130
Ruble, T. L., 130
Rucker, H. N., 164
Rudman, M. K., 505
Rueda, R., 368
Ruef, M. B., 323, 326, 472
Rueger, D. B., 313

Rues, J., 174
Ruff, H. A., 42
Ruhland, D., 310, 391
Ruijssenaars, A. J. J. M., 572
Rumberger, R. W., 134, 135
Rumelhart, D. E., 212, 230, 238
Rumsey, S., 244, 245
Runco, M. A., 114, 115
Rushton, J. P., 87, 92, 94, 339, 340
Russ, S. W., 115
Russell, D., 412
Russell, G., 129
Ruthren, A. J., 313
Ryan, A. M., 73, 356, 372, 375, 404, 482, 484, 485
Ryan, K., 94
Ryan, R. M., 67, 70, 73, 74, 369, 380, 391, 392, 394, 395, 396, 398, 402, 484, 485, 488, 515, 569

Sabers, D. S., 481, 491
Sacks, M., 75
Sadker, D., 69, 130, 131, 139, 556
Sadker, M. P., 69, 130, 131, 139, 556
Sadoski, M., 201, 202, 209, 236, 440
Saia, J., 262
Sailor, W., 148
Salamon, L., 133
Salend, S. J., 124, 133, 503, 504, 506, 508
Salisbury, C. L., 174
Salisbury, J. L., 94
Saljo, R., 288
Salk, S., 378
Salomon, G., 232, 274, 275, 276, 277, 279
Saltz, E., 49, 233
Sameoto, D., 320
Sanborn, M. P., 180, 385
Sanchez, F., 84, 359
Sanders, C. E., 107, 542
Sanders, M. G., 138, 308, 506
Sanders, S., 122, 263
Sandler, H. M., 505
Sands, D. J., 183, 362, 363, 421, 422
Sansone, C., 356
Santa, J. L., 236
Sapon-Shevin, M., 485
Sarason, I. G., 380, 381, 383
Sarason, S. B., 381
Sasse, D. K., 130
Sattler, J. M., 107, 109, 112, 529, 545
Saunders, M., 312
Sax, G., 528, 543, 544, 566, 580, 584
Scandura, J. M., 447
Scarcella, R., 568
Scardamalia, M., 41, 45, 232, 248, 249, 462
Scarr, S., 113
Scerbo, A., 82
Scevak, J. J., 440
Schaal, D. W., 307
Schacter, D. L., 200, 218, 219
Schacter, J., 462
Schallert, D. L., 228
Schank, R. C., 246, 400
Schappelle, B. P., 10
Schaps, E., 370, 501
Schatschneider, C. W., 46
Schauble, L., 33, 369, 447
Scheier, M. F., 356, 378, 403
Schell, T. L., 65
Schenk, S. M., 204, 266
Schepis, M. M., 308
Scher, M. S., 440
Scheuermann, B., 351
Schiefele, U., 129, 369, 400
Schiever, S. W., 97, 139, 178, 181
Schiffman, G., 472
Schilling, H. E. H., 516
Schimmoeller, M. A., 37
Schirmer, B. R., 172
Schlaefli, A., 94

Schlager, M. S., 447
Schliemann, A. D., 31, 33, 288, 294
Schloss, P. J., 321, 344
Schmidt, H. G., 206
Schmidt, R. A., 275, 277
Schneider, W., 43, 44, 212, 215, 270, 272, 283, 418
Schoener, J., 446
Schoenfeld, A. H., 205, 286
Schofield, J. W., 84, 85, 466, 473
Scholes, R. J., 291, 400
Schommer, M., 262, 270, 271, 542
Schommer-Aikins, M., 270, 291
Schonert-Reichl, K. A., 97, 135
Schrauben, B., 400
Schraw, G., 263, 356, 400
Schraw, G. J., 457
Schreibman, L., 163
Schubert, J. G., 130
Schulman, S., 62
Schult, T. J., 277, 283
Schultz, G. F., 385
Schultz, K., 126, 285
Schultz, L. H., 78, 79
Schulze, S. K., 211
Schumaker, J. B., 97, 213, 254, 362, 421, 422, 440
Schunk, Dale, 334
Schunk, D. H., 68, 211, 343, 344, 346, 347, 348, 351, 357, 359, 362, 363, 369, 372, 374, 392, 403, 408, 412, 413, 414, 418, 584
Schutz, P. A., 355, 403, 406
Schwager, M. T., 404
Schwartz, B., 236, 301
Schwartz, D., 81, 82
Schwarz, B. B., 457
Schwebel, A. I., 197, 482
Scott, J., 495
Scott, P., 230
Scott, Walter, 212
Scott-Jones, D., 132
Scruggs, T. E., 56, 148, 154, 155, 156, 169, 182, 183, 213, 294, 501, 548, 589
Seashore, H. G., 6
Seaton, E., 132
Sedikides, C., 375
Seegers, G., 129, 421
Seeley, K., 180
Segal, N. L., 62
Seligman, M., 415
Seligman, M. E. P., 415, 421
Selman, R. L., 78, 79, 81, 83
Semb, G. B., 215, 217, 468
Semmel, M., 183
Semmel, M. I., 148, 183
Serbin, L. A., 6
Seroczynski, A. D., 129, 420
Setiz, V., 113
Sfard, A., 473
Shachar, H., 464, 465
Shaffer, D. R., 94, 161
Shakespeare, William, 87
Shank, M., 56
Shany, M., 359
Shapiro, A. M., 248
Shapiro, B. K., 166
Sharan, S., 464, 465
Shatz, M., 52
Shaughnessy, M. F., 109
Shavelson, R. J., 576, 577
Shaw, V., 457
Shea, C., 92
Shea, M. C., 343
Shea, T. M., 322
Sheehan, E. P., 46
Sheffield, F. D., 372
Sheldon, A., 51
Shell, R., 92
Shepard, L. A., 215, 515, 538, 539, 572, 579
Shepard, R. N., 6

Shepardson, D. P., 464, 465
Sherif, C., 75
Sherif, M., 75
Shernoff, D. J., 392
Sherrill, D., 94
Sherwood, R. D., 286
Shields, P. M., 421
Shiffrin, R. M., 196, 202, 215, 283
Shih, S.-S., 392
Shin, D., 130
Shipman, S., 380, 543
Shipman, V. C., 380, 543
Shirey, L. L., 199, 223, 262, 263, 440
Shoda, Y., 310
Short, E. J., 46
Shrager, L., 264
Shrigley, R. L., 319
Shrum, W., 76
Shuell, T. J., 249, 443
Shulman, L. S., 10, 432
Shulman, S., 62
Shumow, L., 288
Shure, M. B., 82
Shweder, R. A., 96
Shymansky, J. A., 242, 245, 250, 447
Sieber, J. E., 544
Siegel, L., 32
Siegel-Causey, E., 174
Siegler, R. S., 26, 32, 34, 44, 112, 283
Sigman, M., 132
Silberman, M. L., 494
Silberstein, C. S., 250
Silver, E. A., 558
Simmons, D. C., 468
Simmons, R., 278
Simon, H. A., 198, 211, 275
Simon, V. A., 76
Simonetta, L. G., 66
Simons, R. L., 75
Simonton, D. K., 113, 115, 116, 177
Simpson, M. L., 272
Singer, D. G., 94
Singer, J. L., 94
Singh, J., 66
Singley, M. K., 275
Siperstein, G. N., 98
Sisk, D. A., 119
Sitko, B. M., 293, 450
Siu, S., 122
Sizer, T. R., 245
Skaalvik, E., 405
Skiba, R., 323
Skinner, B. F., 305, 310, 439, 445
Skinner, C. H., 317
Slaby, R. G., 82, 83
Slaughter-Defoe, D. T., 114, 119, 121, 126
Slavin, R. E., 85, 134, 136, 137, 145, 148, 149, 164, 183, 184, 464, 465, 467, 472
Sleet, D., 70
Sleeter, C. E., 85, 126, 127
Slife, B. R., 294
Slotta, J. D., 241
Slusher, M. P., 251, 252
Smail, B., 129
Small, M. Y., 440
Small, R. V., 445
Smart, L., 67
Smetana, J. G., 86, 90
Smith, C. L., 250, 271
Smith, D. A., 216
Smith, D. C., 10
Smith, D. J., 353, 362
Smith, E. E., 191, 198n
Smith, E. L., 249
Smith, G., 183
Smith, H. L., 10, 505
Smith, J., 129
Smith, J. D., 164
Smith, K., 457
Smith, M. A., 321, 344
Smith, M. U., 378

Smith, P. B., 96
Smith, R., 338
Smith, R. E., 324
Smith, S. W., 498
Smith, V. L., 158
Smitherman, G., 121
Smolkin, L. B., 122, 384
Smoll, F. L., 324
Snarey, J., 89, 90, 96
Sneider, C., 242
Snidman, N., 62
Snow, C. E., 54
Snow, R. E., 370, 419, 473
Snyder, B. L., 275
Solnick, J. V., 322
Solomon, D., 370, 482, 501
Soloway, E., 465
Songer, N. B., 250
Sosniak, L. A., 193, 246, 247
Sowder, J. T., 10
Sowell, E. R., 22
Sowers, J. A., 342
Spalding, T. L., 236
Spandel, V., 586, 587
Spaulding, C. L., 351, 369, 391, 392, 394, 482, 483, 484, 515, 543
Spear, L. P., 70
Spearman, C., 108, 108n
Speece, D. L., 461
Spencer, M. B., 71, 126
Sperling, G., 198
Spicker, H. H., 180, 472
Spires, H. A., 206, 265, 269
Spivack, G., 82
Spivey, N., 46
Spivey, N. N., 267
Spracklen, K. M., 74
Sprafkin, C., 6, 130
Sroufe, L. A., 62, 76
Stabb, S. D., 84
Stacey, K., 464
Stack, C. B., 503
Staffieri, A., 470
Stage, E. K., 33
Stage, F. K., 124
Stainback, S., 145, 147, 148–149
Stainback, W., 145, 147, 148–149
Stanley, J. C., 179, 180, 294, 296
Stanovich, K. E., 22, 50, 216
Stanovich, K. G., 43
Starr, E. J., 272
Staub, D., 149
Staub, E., 82
Stecher, B., 576
Steckol, K. F., 158
Steele, D. F., 288
Steffensen, M. S., 223, 238
Stein, A. H., 339
Stein, E., 182
Stein, J. A., 134
Stein, J. F., 153
Stein, S., 271
Steinberg, A., 129
Steinberg, E. R., 445
Steinberg, L., 22, 62, 134, 135, 153, 368, 376, 384, 420
Steinhorst, R., 312
Stennett, B., 204
Stephens, T. M., 175, 182
Sternberg, R. J., 10, 105, 108, 111, 112, 114, 116, 177, 279, 280, 286, 288, 438
Sternberg, Robert, 296
Stetsenko, A., 372
Steuer, F. B., 338
Stevahn, L., 84, 358
Stevens, J. J., 528
Stevens, R., 444, 471, 473
Stevens, R. J., 464, 465, 467, 472
Stevens, T., 342
Stevenson, H. C., 355
Stevenson, H. W., 131, 133, 180, 374
Stevenson, Robert Louis, 194–195

Stewart, B. E., 130
Stewart, L., 90
Stice, E., 63
Stiggins, R. J., 503, 504, 538, 540, 553, 555, 556, 557, 558, 567, 572, 573, 574, 575, 576, 579, 584, 587
Stiller, J. D., 73
Stimpson, V., 448, 455, 458
Stimson, M., 204
Stipek, D. J., 68, 129, 351, 371, 376, 381, 382, 383, 392, 395, 396, 412, 419, 421, 467, 484, 582
Stock, W. A., 209
Stodolsky, S. S., 193, 246, 247, 378, 381, 484
Stone, N. J., 268
Stores, M., 75
Story, R., 46
Stough, L. M., 481, 491
Stouthamer-Loeber, M., 129
Strike, K. A., 250, 251, 271
Sudweeks, R. R., 546
Sue, S., 420
Sugawara, A. I., 94
Sugrue, B., 465
Suina, J. H., 122, 384
Sullivan, H., 376
Sullivan, J. S., 322
Sullivan, P., 33
Sullivan, P. J., 308
Sullivan, R. C., 163
Sullivan-DeCarlo, C., 487
Sun, Y., 63
Sund, R. B., 28
Suttles, G. D., 75
Sutton-Smith, B., 73
Swan, K., 446
Swanborn, M. S. L., 50
Swanson, D. B., 538, 557, 558, 570, 576–577
Swanson, H. L., 153, 154, 222, 294, 295, 491
Swap, S. M., 122
Swartz, C. W., 343
Sweet, D., 539, 571
Swerts, A., 559
Switzky, H. N., 385
Symons, D. K., 162
Szuszkiewicz, T. A., 162

Tallent-Runnels, M. K., 178
Tamburrini, J., 33
Tannenbaum, A., 243–244
Tappan, M. B., 91
Tarver, S. G., 159, 444, 472
Tate, W. F., 136
Taylor, A., 132
Taylor, B. A., 315
Taylor, B. M., 264
Taylor, D. M., 54, 96, 122, 126, 471
Taylor, I. A., 114
Taylor, J. C., 300
Taylor, J. H., 437
Taylor, L., 124, 133, 503, 504, 506, 508
Taylor, M. A., 223
Taylor, S. M., 133, 407
Teixeria, R. A., 75
Tellegen, A., 62
Templin, M., 571
Tennyson, R. D., 235, 236, 440
Teo, A., 131
Terezini, P. T., 33
Terwilliger, J. S., 584
Tessler, M., 246
Tessmer, M., 436
Tharp, R., 39
Tharp, R. G., 122, 221
Théberge, C. L., 458, 471
Thoma, S., 90
Thoma, S. J., 94
Thomas, J. R., 128, 129, 130

Thomas, J. W., 47, 268, 272, 357
Thomas, M. A., 319, 322, 481, 483, 486, 488, 489, 491, 494, 505
Thomas, S., 407, 582
Thomas, S. P., 70, 96
Thomas, W. P., 54
Thompson, A. G., 392
Thompson, E. R., 92
Thompson, H., 265
Thompson, M., 419
Thompson, P. M., 22
Thompson, P. W., 392
Thompson, R. A., 22, 62, 63, 132
Thompson, R. F., 22
Thomson, D. M., 216
Thornburg, K. R., 376
Thorndike, E. L., 274
Thorndike, R. M., 521, 576
Thorndyke, P. W., 207
Thorpe, P. K., 405
Thousand, J. S., 149
Thrash, T. M., 404
Threadgill-Sowder, J., 6
Thurstone, L. L., 6, 108
Tirosh, D., 278
Tisak, M., 90
Tishman, S., 293
Tobias, S., 369, 378, 380, 382, 400, 401, 421
Tobin, D., 472
Tobin, K., 221, 244, 261
Todd, C. M., 43
Toga, A. W., 22
Tolan, S. S., 177
Tomasello, M., 231
Tompkins, G. E., 171
Torrance, E. P., 115, 116, 134, 139, 178, 181, 294, 455
Torres-Guzmán, M. E., 121, 123
Touchstone, D., 136
Tourniaire, F., 31
Townsend, M., 94
Traub, R. E., 539, 559
Trawick-Smith, J., 37, 51, 55, 63, 71, 96, 121
Treasure, D. C., 405
Treffinger, D. J., 115, 116
Tremblay, R. E., 81, 135
Triandis, H. C., 96
Trowbridge, J. E., 241
Trueba, H. T., 126
Trueman, M., 440
Tryon, G. S., 383, 543
Tschannen-Moran, M., 11, 349
Tubbs, M. E., 415
Tucker, V., 482
Tucker, V. G., 389, 390
Tudge, J. R. H., 464, 465
Tudor, R. M., 445
Tulving, E., 201, 206, 216
Tunmer, W. E., 68
Turiel, E., 86, 90, 91, 92, 93, 96
Turkheimer, E., 22
Turnbull, A., 56, 97, 139, 147, 148, 149, 153, 155, 156, 158, 159, 160, 162, 163, 164, 166, 168, 169, 171, 172, 173, 174, 175, 222, 223, 254, 294, 329, 362, 385, 422, 472, 502, 548, 588
Turnbull, A. P., 86, 168, 183, 485
Turnbull, B. J., 421
Turnbull, R., 56
Turner, A. M., 191
Turner, J. C., 286, 293, 368, 392, 394, 395, 405, 454, 512, 515, 540
Turner, L. A., 43
Turner, T. J., 238
Turnure, J. E., 42
Tuttle, D. W., 171
Tuttle, N. R., 171
Tyler, B., 412
Tyler, S., 448

Tzuriel, D., 572, 577

Udall, A. J., 179
Uguroglu, M., 369
Ulichny, P., 121, 126
Underwood, B. J., 215, 219
Undheim, J. O., 107, 129, 471
Urbina, S., 521, 529
Urdan, T., 374, 384, 404
Urdan, T. C., 65, 74, 376, 381, 404, 405
Uttal, D. H., 131

Valencia, S. W., 514, 571, 579
Valente, N., 398
Valentine, J. C., 451, 452, 453, 471
Valiante, G., 129, 420
Vallerand, R. J., 369
Van Camp, C. M., 326
Van Court, N., 92
van den Broek, P., 355
Vanderwood, M., 108
Van Etten, S., 264
Van Houten, R., 320
van Joolingen, W. R., 447, 448, 449, 450
Van Kraayenoord, C. E., 350, 578
Van Laar, C., 96, 420
Van Meter, P., 209, 264
Van Rossum, E. J., 204, 266
VanSledright, B., 92, 228, 230, 245
Van Voorhis, F. L., 453
Van Winkel, L., 179
Vargas, A. U., 317
Vasquez, J. A., 119, 122
Vasta, R., 339
Vaughn, B. J., 395
Vaughn, S., 84, 183
Vaughn-Scott, M., 119
Veenman, S., 481
Venn, J. J., 548, 589
Verdi, M. P., 209
Vermeer, H. J., 129, 421
Vernon, P. A., 108
Veroff, J., 310, 370
Verschaffel, L., 41, 246
Vida, M., 129
Viernstein, M. C., 179
Villa, R. A., 149
Villegas, A., 556
Vitaro, F., 81, 82
Voegler, M. E., 375
Vollmer, T. R., 307
Volpe, J., 73
Vorrath, H., 84
Vosniadou, S., 242, 250, 251
Voss, J. F., 275, 277, 286, 369, 516
Vye, N. J., 286, 289, 352, 430, 450, 517
Vygotsky, Lev, 36–42, 48, 55, 57, 58, 179, 190, 232, 243, 245, 272, 345, 352, 359, 448, 461, 467–468, 571, 572

Waddell, K. J., 55
Waddill, P. J., 447
Wade, S., 263
Wade, S. E., 265, 400, 402, 440
Wager, W. W., 445
Wagner, A. R., 301
Wagner, E. D., 46, 563
Wagner, M., 166
Wagner, R. K., 112
Wahlsten, D., 113
Walberg, H. J., 85, 268, 369
Walker, J. E., 322
Walker, J. M. T., 370, 451
Walker, K. C., 542
Walker, L. J., 91
Wallace, C. S., 22
Walters, G. C., 323–324
Walters, R. H., 323

Waltman, K. K., 583, 585
Wampold, B., 362
Wandersee, J. H., 241, 265
Wang, P. P., 158
Ward, M., 358
Warren, A. R., 121
Warren, E., 4
Warren, G., 559
Warren, R. L., 124
Wasik, B. A., 246
Wat, A., 458
Watahomigie, L. J., 10, 505
Waters, H. S., 47, 208
Watkins, M. J., 203
Watson, M., 370, 501
Way, N., 71
Wayland, K. K., 82
Waylor-Bowen, T., 174
Wearne, D., 457
Weaver, C. A., III, 269
Webb, J., 462
Webb, J. T., 177
Webb, N. M., 83, 232, 464, 465, 466, 467, 468, 471, 489, 516
Webber, J., 351
Weber, M. J., 482
Weber, N. L., 326
Weber, R., 456
Weber, S. J., 472
Weffer, R. E., 124
Wehlage, G. G., 399, 454
Wehmeyer, M. L., 183, 362, 363, 421, 422
Weinberg, R. A., 113
Weiner, B., 85, 97, 372, 376, 397, 405, 410, 411, 411n, 412, 413, 414, 416, 556
Weinert, F. E., 439, 444, 490
Weinstein, C. E., 272, 418, 419
Weinstein, C. S., 482
Weinstein, R. S., 416, 417
Weir, C., 356
Weisberg, R. W., 115
Weishahn, M. W., 172
Weiss, J., 294, 402
Weiss, M. R., 211
Weissburg, R. P., 358
Weisz, J., 63
Welch, G. J., 313
Wellborn, J. G., 374
Weller, H., 392
Wellman, H. M., 43, 46, 240, 241
Wells, D., 457
Wenger, E., 40, 275
Wentzel, K. R., 73, 77, 376, 381, 403, 407, 408, 482
Werner, E. E., 133, 134
Wertsch, J. V., 38
Wesman, A. G., 6
Wessels, K., 515
West, C. K., 212
West, R. P., 353
Westerfield, G., 404
Whalen, C. K., 502
Whaley, S. E., 132
Wheatley, G., 406
Wheelan, S. A., 494
Whitaker, J. S., 545
Whitbeck, L. B., 75
White, A. G., 322
White, B. J., 75
White, B. Y., 447, 448, 449, 450, 458
White, C., 248
White, J. J., 244, 245
White, K. J., 82
White, R., 170–171, 374
White, R. T., 250
Whitenack, J., 458
Whitesell, N. R., 65, 396
Whiting, B. B., 37
Whitley, B. E., Jr., 411
Whitten, J. D., 113

Subject Index

maintaining desirable behaviors and, 324–325
mastery learning and, 443
misbehaviors and, 498
principles of, 305–306
reducing/eliminating undesirable behaviors
and, 318–324
reinforcement and, 306–314, 335
shaping new behaviors and, 314–315, 443
Operations, 28
Oral communication skills, 52, 153, 159
Organization
cognitive psychology and, 191
computer tool applications and, 450–451
declarative knowledge and, 203, 206–207
expository instruction and, 440
hypertext and hypermedia, 445
information processing theory and, 43, 45, 46, 48
interaction and, 455
knowledge construction and, 45, 232–241, 255
students with specific cognitive or academic
difficulties and, 158
study strategies and, 265–267, 269
Ormrod's Own Psychological Survey (OOPS), 2–4
Outcomes-based education (OBE), 537n
Outlining, 265, 269
Out-of-school suspension, 322–323
Overgeneralization, 49, 233
Overregularization, 51

Pacing, and expository instruction, 440
PALS (Peer-Assisted Learning Strategies), 469
Paper-pencil assessment
administration of, 566–567
assessments as tools and, 512
construction of, 559–566
high-stakes testing and, 539
language differences and, 545
performance assessment compared to, 514
practicality and, 559, 570, 579
reliability and, 559, 569, 579
scoring of, 567–569
standardization, 569, 579
table of specifications and, 523, 524
tasks and, 558–559
validity and, 559, 566, 569, 570, 579
Parenting styles, 62–63
Parents
approval needs and, 376
assessment results and, 539, 540–541, 542
attributions and, 417
coordinating efforts with, 503–508
diversity and, 96, 124, 503, 508
environmental influences and, 61, 62
homework and, 452, 453
misbehaviors and, 493, 499, 503, 507–508
moral development and, 93
parent discussion groups, 505
parent involvement and, 133, 505–507
personal development and, 62–63, 67
reinforcement and, 312
social development and, 62–63, 73
socioeconomic status and, 132, 133
students with general delays in cognitive and
social functioning and, 166
students with social or behavioral problems
and, 161
students with special needs and, 144, 147, 182
Parent-teacher conferences, 63, 503, 504, 579
Pavlov, Ivan, and classical conditioning, 302–305
PBS (positive behavioral support), 165, 326–328, 498
Pedagogical content knowledge, 10
Peer-Assisted Learning Strategies (PALS), 469
Peer relationships. See also Interaction
academic achievement and, 74
approval needs and, 376
class discussions and, 457
classroom environment and, 485
environmental influences and, 62
gender differences and, 73, 129, 130
peer interaction, 39, 41–42
peer pressure, 73–74, 312, 376
relatedness needs and, 375
self-concept and, 66–67

social development and, 64, 67, 73–78
social skills and, 73, 82–84
socioeconomic differences and, 132
students with advanced cognitive development
and, 178
students with social or behavioral problems
and, 160, 161, 164
students with special needs and, 145
students with specific cognitive or academic
difficulties and, 157
Peer tutoring
choice of, 475
community of learners and, 249
diversity and, 473
effects of, 4
as instructional strategy, 467–471
People-first language, 151
Percentile ranks, 530, 532–533, 537, 541
Performance
anxiety and, 4, 379–380
attributions and, 412, 416–420
authentic activities and, 454
classroom environment and, 484
cooperative learning activities and, 464
expectations and, 556
motivation and, 393, 403–405
performance goals and, 403–405, 407, 512, 515
self-concept and, 66
students with advanced cognitive development
and, 178
Performance-approach goals, 404, 405
Performance assessment
administration of, 573
authentic assessment and, 559n
complex achievements and, 570–571
high-stakes testing and, 539
paper-pencil assessment compared to, 514
practicality and, 577–578, 579
reliability and, 576, 577, 579
scoring of, 573–576, 578
standardization and, 576, 579
table of specifications and, 523, 524
tasks and, 571–573
validity and, 576–577, 579
Performance-avoidance goals, 404, 405
Performance goals, 403–405, 407, 512, 515, 582
Persistence, 346
Personal development
case studies and, 61
classroom climate and, 71
developmental differences in, 67–73
diversity and, 96
environmental influences on, 61, 62–64
ethnic differences and, 63–64, 71
interaction and, 73, 100
parental influence on, 62–63, 67
self-concept and, 64–73
themes in, 99–100
Personal effect, and reciprocal causation, 359–361
Personal fables, 70
Personal interests, 400–402
Personal theories, 232, 240–241, 250
Perspective taking
cooperative learning and, 463, 464
Eisenberg's prosocial behavior development
compared to, 92
misbehaviors and, 498
moral development and, 87, 92, 94
personal development and, 72–73
Selman's theory of, 78, 79, 83
social development and, 75, 79–81, 82, 83
Physical and health impairments, 152, 169–171.
See also Students with physical or sensory
challenges
Physical appearance, 380, 382
Physical competence, 65
Physical proximity, 319
Physical punishment, 322
Physiological needs, 373
Piaget, Jean
application of theory, 35–36
basic assumptions of, 23–25
cognitive development theory of, 22, 23

cognitive psychology and, 190
as constructivist theorist, 24, 231
current perspectives on, 32–35
information processing compared to, 42
Kohlberg's moral reasoning theory and, 89
personal development and, 79
Selman's perspective taking theory and, 79
stages of, 8, 25–32, 236
Vygotsky's theory compared to, 36
Planning. See also Instructional planning
self-regulated learning and, 355
Popular students, 77
Portfolios, 530, 579, 586–587, 589
Positive behavioral support (PBS), 165, 326–328, 498
Positive feedback, 308, 309, 328, 391–392, 416
Positive instances, 233, 235
Positive reinforcement, 308–309, 321
Positive transfer, 274
Postconventional morality, 88–89
Potential development level, 37
Practical intelligence, 111, 166
Practicality
as assessment characteristic, 518, 519,
525–526, 549
informal assessments and, 556–557, 579
paper-pencil assessments and, 559, 570, 579
performance assessments and, 577–578, 579
Practice opportunities, 276, 277
Pragmatics, 52, 121
Preconventional morality, 88, 89
Prediction, 5, 460
Predictive validity, 524, 545
Premack principle, 308
Preoperational egocentrism, 26–27
Preoperational stage, 25, 26–28, 32, 34–35
Preschool children
attention and, 42
attributions and, 412–413
cognitive development and, 22, 24, 25, 32
learned helplessness and, 415
memory limitation and, 46
moral development of, 90
oral communication skills and, 52
personal development and, 68
social development of, 79
timing of reinforcement and, 310
Presentation punishment, 320, 321
Prestige/power, 341
Primary reinforcers, 307
Principles
teacher decision making and, 7
theories and, 8
transfer and, 276–277
Prior knowledge
authentic activities and, 454
class discussions and, 457
cognitive development and, 8, 33, 58
cognitive psychology and, 191, 192, 193–194
computer-based instruction and, 445, 471
discovery learning and, 448, 449
expository instruction and, 440
intelligence and, 105, 111–112
knowledge construction and, 229, 230
lesson plans and, 438
linguistic development and, 52, 58
logic and, 32
long-term memory and, 199
lower-level questions and, 261, 455
meaningful learning and, 193–194, 206, 265
note taking and, 264
oral communications skills and, 52
storage and, 211–212
study strategies and, 15, 269
Private discussion, and misbehaviors, 493, 495–496
Private speech, 37
Private versus public performance, 122
Proactive aggression, 81, 82
Probabilistic reasoning, 290–291
Problems, 559, 563–564
Problem solving
authentic activities and, 289, 454
cognitive factors affecting, 283–288
computer technology and, 288–290, 450

hierarchical nature of, 65
personal development and, 64–73
self-efficacy and, 65, 346
students with advanced cognitive development and, 178
students with social or behavioral problems and, 161
students with special needs and, 148
students with specific cognitive or academic difficulties and, 154
Self-contained classes, 144
Self-determination
assessment and, 512
classroom assessment strategies and, 578
classroom climate and, 484, 500
homework and, 452
instructional objectives and, 396, 436
instructional strategies and, 471
intrinsic motivation and, 372, 391, 393–397, 421
limit setting and, 487
misbehaviors and, 395, 497
paper-pencil assessments and, 569
performance assessments and, 573
portfolios and, 586
students with social or behavioral problems and, 162
students with special needs and, 183, 421
Self-efficacy
anxiety and, 382
attributions and, 412, 413
career goals and, 407
competition and, 484, 535
cooperative learning activities and, 464, 485
direct instruction and, 444
diversity and, 361–362
intrinsic motivation and, 8, 356, 372, 391–393, 401, 421
mastery learning and, 443
motivation and, 372, 390, 391–393, 403
peer tutoring and, 470
performance-approach goals and, 405
reciprocal causation and, 359, 361
self-concept and, 65, 346
self-regulated problem solving and, 359
social cognitive theory and, 8, 345–349, 391
students at risk and, 136
successes/failures and, 347, 391, 392, 393
teachers and, 392–393, 415, 482, 501
Self-esteem
adolescents and, 69
anxiety and, 380
development of, 64, 68
gender differences and, 129
peer relationships and, 75
personal development and, 64, 66
psychological punishment and, 322
students with physical and sensory challenges and, 169
students with special needs and, 96, 148, 150
Self-evaluation, 352–354, 356, 357, 497, 517
Self-fulfilling prophecies, 416–417
Self-handicapping, 374, 384, 405
Self-imposed contingencies, 354–355, 497
Self-instructions
self-regulated problem solving and, 357
self-regulation and, 352, 497
Vygotsky's cognitive development theory and, 39
Selfish and self-centered orientation, 93
Self-monitoring, 351, 356, 496–498, 517
Self-motivational strategies, 355–356
Self-observation, 351
Self-perception
attributions and, 416
intrinsic motivation and, 390–391
Self-questioning, 269
Self-regulated behavior, 350–355
Self-regulation
assessment and, 517
classroom environment and, 484
homework and, 452
instructional objectives and, 436
instructional strategies and, 471
misbehaviors and, 493, 496–498

peer tutoring and, 468
self-regulated learning, 355–357, 403
self-regulated problem solving, 357–359, 497
social cognitive theory and, 334, 335, 349–359, 436, 496
student-directed instruction and, 430
students with social or behavioral problems and, 162
students with special needs and, 183, 421
Self-reinforcement, 397
Self-talk, 37, 39, 48
Self-worth, 374, 384, 405
Selman, Robert, perspective taking theory of, 78, 79, 83
SEM (standard error of measurement), 521, 521n, 541
Semantics, 49
Sensation seekers, 370, 371
Sense of community, 249, 484–485, 500, 535
Sense of school community, 375, 501
Sensitive periods, 22, 49, 53
Sensorimotor stage, 25, 26, 32
Sensory register, 196
SES (socioeconomic status), 132–133
Setting events, 316
Severe and multiple disabilities, 152. See also Students with physical or sensory challenges
Shame, 68, 92
Shaping, 314–315, 443, 445
Short-answer items, 559, 562–563
Short-term memory. See Working memory
Short-term objectives, 435–436
Signals, and expository instruction, 440
Similarity, and transfer, 276, 277–278
Single classification, 27, 35, 236
Situated cognition
problem solving and, 288, 294
transfer and, 275
Situational interests, 400–402
Skinner, B. F., 305
Social cognition, 73, 78–82, 163
Social cognitive theory
attention and, 336–337
basic assumptions of, 334–335
behaviorism and, 334, 335, 363, 364
case studies and, 333, 364
classroom climate and, 339, 348, 358
cognitive processes and, 334, 335, 337, 342, 359
cognitive psychology and, 334, 363, 364
control and, 363
cooperative learning activities and, 464
diversity and, 361–362
expectations and, 335, 336
instructional objectives and, 436
interaction and, 357–359
learning processes and, 189, 191, 334, 335
mastery learning and, 443
modeling and, 189, 338–345
motivation and, 334, 335, 363, 372, 373, 424
observation and, 3, 334, 363
punishment and, 335–338
reciprocal causation and, 359–361
reciprocal teaching and, 461
reinforcement and, 334, 335–338, 340, 354–355
self-efficacy and, 8, 345–349, 391
self-regulation and, 334, 335, 349–359, 436, 496
students with special needs and, 362–363
Social competence, 64, 67, 111
Social constructivism, 231, 255, 457
Social contract stage, 89
Social conventions, 90
Social development
case studies and, 61
classroom climate and, 86
diversity and, 84–86, 96
environmental influences on, 61, 62–64
interaction and, 73–78, 83, 100
interactive and collaborative approaches and, 473
peer relationships and, 64, 67, 73–78
social cognition and, 73, 78–82
socialization and, 63
social skills and, 82–84
students with advanced cognitive development and, 178

themes in, 99–100
Social goals, 406, 407, 464
Social groups, 75–76
Social information processing, 81
Social intelligence, 166
Social isolation, 77–78
Socialization, 63, 73–74, 128, 130, 485
Social learning theory. See Social cognitive theory
Social needs, 374–377
Social reinforcers, 308
Social skills
misbehaviors and, 498, 499
peer relationships and, 73, 82–84
peer tutoring and, 468
sense of community and, 485
students with general delays in cognitive and social functioning and, 167, 168
students with physical and sensory challenges and, 172
students with social or behavioral problems and, 161, 163, 164, 386
students with special needs and, 145, 148, 183
students with specific cognitive or academic difficulties and, 153, 154, 157
Societal, symbolic perspective taking, 78
Sociocultural perspective, 36–38
Socioeconomic differences
academic achievement and, 385
assessment and, 538, 545, 583
classroom environment and, 499–500
dynamic assessment and, 572
ethnic differences and, 119
homeless students and, 133
informal assessment and, 556
intelligence tests and, 113
motivation and, 402, 421
resilient students and, 133–134
social development and, 77
students at risk and, 134
students with special needs and, 138, 180
successes/failures and, 132–133
teacher expectations and, 132–133, 415, 417, 419, 556, 583
test anxiety and, 543
variables of, 131
Socioeconomic status (SES), 132–133
Sociolinguistic conventions, 121–122
Spatial intelligence, 109
Spearman, Charles, intelligence theory and, 108
Species-based learning principles, 300, 301–302
Specific aptitude tests, 527, 528
Specific transfer, 274–275
Speech and communication disorders, 56, 152, 158–159. See also Students with specific cognitive or academic difficulties
Speechreading, 172, 173
Spreadsheets, 451
Stability, and attributions, 411
Stage theories, 21, 33
Standard deviation (SD), 534
Standard English, 120
Standard error of measurement (SEM), 521, 521n, 541
Standardization. See also Behavioral standards
as assessment characteristic, 518, 519, 522, 549
content-area learning and, 432
informal assessment and, 555, 557, 579
paper-pencil assessments and, 569, 579
performance assessments and, 576, 579
portfolios and, 586
Standardized tests, 107, 514, 517, 526–530, 531, 539, 541, 543
Standards
national and international standards, 431
web sites for, 432
Standard scores, 530, 533–534, 535
Standards for Educational and Psychological Testing, 547
Stanines, 534, 535, 541, 542
State anxiety, 379
Static versus dynamic assessment, 572
Stereotypes, 126, 130, 419, 420